柳百新，材料科学家、中国科学院院士

Selected Papers by Academician Liu Baixin

柳百新院士论文集

清华大学材料学院　编

科学出版社
北　京

内 容 简 介

本书是为庆祝材料科学家柳百新院士八十华诞而集结的文集。全书主要分为六篇：第一篇柳百新传略；第二篇柳百新研究组发表的500篇SCI论文目录（1982—2015年）；第三篇35篇代表性论文；第四篇培养的研究生名单；第五篇主要获奖项目；第六篇同学、同事和学生的回忆文章。

本书适合有关离子束与固体的作用及材料改性、计算材料科学、薄膜材料、核材料等领域的专家学者、学生，以及对此学科领域感兴趣的人阅读和参考。

图书在版编目(CIP)数据

柳百新院士论文集/清华大学材料学院编. —北京：科学出版社，2015.4

ISBN 978-7-03-044046-4

Ⅰ. ①柳… Ⅱ. ①清… Ⅲ. ①柳百新-纪念文集②材料科学-文集 Ⅳ. ①K826.16-53 ②TB3-53

中国版本图书馆CIP数据核字（2015）第069014号

责任编辑：钱 俊 周 涵／责任校对：钟 洋
责任印制：肖 兴／封面设计：耕者设计工作室

科学出版社 出版
北京东黄城根北街16号
邮政编码：100717
http://www.sciencep.com
北京通州皇家印刷厂印刷
科学出版社发行 各地新华书店经销
*
2015年4月第 一 版 开本：889×1194 1/16
2015年4月第一次印刷 印张：36 3/4 彩插：1
字数：890 000

定价：198.00元（含光盘）

（如有印装质量问题，我社负责调换）

序　言

天增岁月人增寿，福满乾坤喜盈门。我国著名材料科学家、中国科学院院士、清华大学教授柳百新先生即将迎来 80 岁生日，清华大学材料学院为此特编辑了这本论文集。2006 年由中国科学技术出版社出版的《中国科学技术专家传略 · 理学篇 · 物理学卷 3》中收录了柳先生的传略，本论文集的开篇就用该传略作为对柳先生生平的简单介绍。

改革开放以来，柳先生在科研、教学以及国际学术交流方面做了大量的工作。他的主要研究领域包括离子束与固体的作用及材料改性、计算材料科学、薄膜和核材料等。30 多年来，柳先生和他带领的研究组迄今发表了 500 篇 SCI 论文。本论文集收录了已发表的全部论文的目录，以及 35 篇代表性论文的全文。我们还编制了 500 篇论文完整的电子版光盘附在论文集的后面，供有兴趣的读者查阅参考。

柳先生的众多好友和弟子得知我们编辑本论文集的时候，纷纷寄来了他们撰写的与柳先生一起生活、学习和工作的回忆性文章约 40 篇。从柳先生几位发小的描述中，我们可以看到柳先生儿时成长的足迹和童年珍贵的友谊；在志同道合的科学界朋友的文字里，我们感受到的更多的是科研思维的碰撞与激发。柳先生不拘一格地培养研究生，许多弟子现在已经在国内外知名大学担任教授，有的成为国际大跨国公司的高级管理人员，也有的成为国家的公务人员。兹兹师恩，悠悠情深。在弟子们的回忆里，柳先生是博学多才的先生，是和蔼可亲的长者，是科学研究的领路人，是人生成长的导师，是严谨勤奋的合作伙伴，亦是值得信任的忘年之交。通过阅读这些生动的文字回忆，相信对我们认识柳先生从事科学研究的精神、理念以及指导研究生的独特方法等会有一定的裨益。

我们在编辑这本论文集的同时，也根据柳先生的回忆，把改革开放后 30 多年来，他在参加国际学术交流中的所见所闻，编写了一本《科海之旅——柳百新院士国际学术交流活动纪实》，将与本论文集同时由科学出版社出版，使读者可以从另一个角度了解柳先生的科研工作。

在编辑本论文集的过程中，与柳先生有关的文稿中的许多细节，我们都与他一起讨论和校对，我们深深地感受到，几近 80 岁的柳先生依然精神矍铄、思维敏捷、记忆力过人。借本论文集出版之际，我们衷心地祝福柳先生，祝他福如东海长流水、寿比南山不老松！

特别感谢本书成书过程中每一位撰稿者的努力付出和科学出版社的大力支持。

清华大学材料学院

2015 年 1 月 30 日

目　　录

第一篇　柳百新传略

柳　百　新[1]

柳百新(1935—　)，材料科学家，中国科学院院士。提出离子束混合在二元金属系统中形成非晶态合金的经验规则和热力学模型，并用第一性原理计算论证了亚稳合金相的稳定性。提出金属多层膜中非晶化反应的判据，并用分子动力学方法揭示其原子运动机制。阐明了离子注入形成金属氮化物的规律。发展出强流金属离子注入制备金属硅化物的新技术。

柳百新，1935 年 6 月 10 日出生于上海市，原籍江苏省武进县。出生时他的父亲柳荫(培庆)是一个造诣很高的雕刻师，在印刷行业中雕刻印制钞票、证券等用的铜版。母亲戎悦礼是一个普通和善良的妇女，亲自操持家务。柳百新有两个哥哥、一个姐姐和一个弟弟。他父母在年轻时由于经济条件所限，只受过初等教育，但他们从生活经验中深感学习文化和技术的重要性，因此下决心要把孩子们送到最好的学校去求学。每当遇到经济困难时，他们紧缩其他开支或借债也要为孩子们交上学费。柳百新 6 岁时被送到上海市中西女中第二附小上学，四年级开始时因病而休学了两年。这个小学从三年级就开始教英文，注意发挥学生的学习主动性，从不在学生的成绩单中排名次，时过半个世纪，柳百新还记得这个小学的学习气氛和“不排名次”的特点。1947 年，由于搬家而转入协进女中附小继续学习。从那时起，柳百新一直是班上的第一名，直到高中毕业。

柳百新少年时曾经历过日本帝国主义对中国的侵略和国家经济落后、人民生活贫困的年代。因此，他怀着国家能够强盛起来的愿望迎来 1949 年的解放。这一年，他小学毕业了，并下决心长大后为国家建设出力。家庭中，父亲对工作的精益求精和十分节俭的作风，母亲不遗余力地辅助父亲的事业、悉心养育子女的深厚亲情都对柳百新以后的为人有深刻的影响。在小弟弟尚未出生前，全家 6 口人只住石库门房子中的两间半正房。但他的父母却为孩子们购置了商务印书馆出版的 500 本“小学生文库”。从文库中，柳百新读到了“孔融让梨”等故事，他还特别爱读“三国演义”。每逢年终，他母亲还要带孩子们到书店去选购一批图书。因此，柳百新从小就养成了爱读书的习惯。大哥柳小培和大嫂陈淑卿解放前就参加革命，中华人民共和国成立后在北京外国语大学工作，他们全心全意为人民服务的精神为柳百新树立了榜样；姐姐柳百敏对少年时体弱的柳百新总是倍加照顾，她毕业于上海外语学院，但从事的是她爱好的体育、教练和体育科研工作；二哥柳百成比柳百新大两岁，他们从小一起生活并长大，上的是同一个小学、中学和大学，现在都是清华大学的教授，哥哥是中国工程院院士，弟弟是中国科学院院士。柳百新的伯父柳溥庆是一位知名的印刷技术专家，生前任中国人民银行总行的总工程师。他 20 世纪 20 年代去法国勤工俭学，1926 年入党。1939—1941 年间和柳百新的父亲等人在上海为新四军秘密印制解放区使用的钞票，印制中用的铜版是柳百新的父亲精心设计和雕刻的。柳百新的姑姑柳静和姑夫吴朗西于 20 世纪 30 年代在上海创办文化生活出版社，出版进步的作品和名著，如鲁迅的作品、巴金的《家》《春》《秋》等。父亲一辈人为了民族富强、国家兴旺而奋发图强的精神深深地印在

① 本文摘自：中国科学技术协会编. 中国科学技术专家传略 •理学编 •物理学卷 3. 北京:中国科学技术出版社, 2006: 473-491.

柳百新的思想深处。

1949—1955 年，柳百新就读于上海市圣芳济中学（后改名为时代中学）。6 年的中学生活使他在 3 个方面大受裨益。一是系统和高水平的英语教学，老师的纯正发音，要求学生朗读课文等，使柳百新在中学期间打下了扎实的英语基础；二是比较灵活的教学方法，有些老师有大学或国外留学的学历，教学中带有启发性；三是非常重视体育，每天课后，几乎所有的学生都参加体育锻练。50 年代中，这个中学的排球队曾战胜包括成人队在内的所有对手而获得上海市冠军，成为体育界的一段佳话。柳百新在中学期间，以刻苦认真的学习取得优异成绩，有一年考试共 11 门课，他得了 7 个 100 分。在校期间，他积极参加体育活动，曾以 1.55 米的成绩获得过跳高亚军。因此，中学的 6 年也使他的体魄强健起来，并锻炼了他的毅力和意志。后来，他在清华大学学习期间，曾是校羽毛球队的队员。

1955 年，柳百新考入清华大学，被分配在工程物理系学习。大学期间，他特别注意自学能力的培养。1957 年，在学习“分析力学”时，柳百新发现由于课程衔接中没有学过“一阶偏微分方程”的基础知识，因此听课时有较大困难。他到图书馆找到了一本数学书，自学了两个月才真正体会到“分析力学”在处理多粒子问题中的“美妙”之处。柳百新认为外语是一个重要的工具，需要刻苦学习、反复练习才能达到“熟能生巧”的境界。三年级学习“光学”时，他就直接看俄文参考书。后来，他认为上课时听老师的讲解，课后再看俄文参考书，学会新的物理内容。因此，他找了一本内容不熟悉的俄文科学论文，用了一个多月时间，通过俄文理解了物理内容。

1961 年毕业后，柳百新被留在工程物理系工作，第一项任务是开“固体物理”课。他备课认真，写出详细的教案，讲课效果很好。1963 年，柳百新和同学了 6 年的倪蕙苓组织了自己的家。倪蕙苓是天津市人，1955 年进入清华大学工程物理系（核物理专业）学习，毕业后在中国科学院原子能研究所（后改为高能物理研究所）工作。她主持研制的亮度监测器，为 1988 年正负电子对撞机上正负电子的首次对撞成功提供了第一时间的直接证据。在将近半个世纪的岁月里，他们始终相互帮助，相互照顾，共同前进。

“文化大革命”期间，柳百新于 1969 年被派到江西鲤鱼洲农场去接受“再教育”。同年底被调回清华大学从事核能研究。1978 年，柳百新回到工程物理系做教学和研究工作。1980 年初，他靠着扎实的材料科学和英语的基础通过了选拔出国进修的 3 门考试，于 1981 年初由国家教委公派去美国加州理工学院做访问研究。

1981—1982 年，柳百新在美国加州理工学院做了大量研究工作，发表了 9 篇第一作者和 8 篇合作作者的论文。80 年代初，在“离子束材料改性”领域中提出了一种新的离子束混合实验方法，柳百新的第一份工作就是用这种方法研究非晶态合金的形成。经过调研，他提出了科学上的假设，并用系统的实验作了论证，由此提出了“结构差异规则”。1982 年，应邀在法国举行的第三届“离子束材料改性”国际会议上作报告，受到与会者的高度重视，一位法国教授把他报告的每一张胶片都拍了照。此外，加州理工学院活跃的学术氛围和学者们对基础研究的热情和“乐在其中”的精神状态给柳百新留下了深刻的印象。

1982 年底柳百新按时回国，并积极准备开展研究工作。1986 年，他获得了第一份国家自然科学基金，使他能启动思考了一段时间的基础研究。后来，他连续获得过 2 项重点和 8 项面上基金。随着工作的发展，他还获得过 863 和 973 项目的科研经费、国际原子能机构的资助、与美国通用汽车公司和美国联合技术公司合作的科研经费。他的研究领域包括载能离子束与固体的作用及材料改性、计算材料科学、薄膜材料和核材料等。20 年来，发表学术论文 330 多篇，其中国际会议论文 48 篇；SCI 收录论文 290 篇。1991 年他名列 SCI 收录个人发表论文数全国第一名。发表的论文迄今已被引用 2000 多次。他曾访问过 14 个国家以及香港和台湾地区，在国际会议上报告 40 次，其中邀请报告 20 次，并应邀在著名的大学和研究所做学术报告 40 多场次。柳百新的研究成果受到国内外同行的高度重视。1984 年，他当选为玻姆物理学会(Bohmische Physical Society) (专业为粒子-固体相互作用)的科学委员；1988—1989 年应邀担任中国高等科学技术中心特别成员。1993 年起应聘担任国际期刊 *J. Nuclear Materials* 的顾问编委会委员；1998 年当选为美国物理学会(American Physical Society)理事(Fellow)；1999—2000 年应聘担任国家重点基础研究发展规划的项目咨询顾问组成员。1999 年以来，还应聘担任国家自然科学奖、科技进步奖和发明奖，以及国家自然科学基金委学科评审组的专家等。柳百新曾以第一完成人获 1986 年和 1990 年度教委科技进步奖一等奖，1993 年度国家自然科学奖二等奖，1997 年度北京市科技进步奖一等奖和 1999 年度国家自然科学奖三等奖。他个人还获得中国物理学会授予的叶企孙(凝聚态)物理奖。2001 年，柳百新当选为中国科学院院士。

“离子束材料改性”是一个多学科交叉的新兴领域。离子束是从加速器引出的，具有较高的能量($10^2 \sim 10^3$ 千电子伏)，因此被称为载能离子束。将载能的离子束作用于材料，可以对材料进行表面改性和制备出新材料，它是 20 世纪下半叶发展出来的一种非平衡材料制备新技术。离子束与材料(固体)相互作用的物理过程具有远离平衡态、合金元素的动力掺入和离子束参数可精确调控等特点。在过去的 20 年里，柳百新充分发挥离子束与固体作用的特点，选择了材料科学和相关学科中的前沿课题，做了大量研究工作，并着重于揭示材料微观结构的形成与演化规律，以及结构与性能的关系。研究的内容不断扩展和深化，从系统的实验研究，归纳出经验规律，上升到热力学模型，并进而提出原子尺度的模型，乃至固体电子结构层次的物理诠释。许多成果为离子束制备新型材料和表面改性提供理论基础。有些成果则提出新的原理或技术路线，有些成果还揭示了新的物质状态，具有重要的理论意义。

提出离子束混合制备二元非晶态合金的经验模型

非晶态合金(或金属玻璃)是 P. Duwez 于 1959 年用液态熔体淬火获得的。从而开拓出一大类新型材料，也揭示了一种新的物质状态——非晶态固体。40 年来，非晶态合金的研究与应用一直是材料科学领域中的一个重要方向。这里面一个重要的科学问题是要阐明其形成规律，并预言在什么系统中、在什么成分范围内有可能制备出非晶态合金。

多层膜离子束混合是 1980 年提出来的一种新的实验方法。实验中，先在基体上交替沉积两种元素，然后用载能离子束进行辐照，使两种元素混合而形成化合物或合金。最初，离子束混合被应用于研究金属硅化物的形成。1982 年，柳百新设计了系统的多层膜离子束混合实验来考察二元金属系统中组元的结构、尺寸和电负性对非晶态合金形成的影响。实验结果论证了结构是决定性的因素，由此提出了离子束混合形成非晶态合金的第一个判据——结构差异规则。该规则预言：在具有不同晶体结构的二元合金系统中，合金成分选在两相区中间，在适当的实验条件下(基体温升不能过高、离子束流调节合适等)，有可能获得非晶态合金。论文发表在《应用物理快讯》上，迄今已被引用 130 次。他又进一步用实验论证了离子束混合也能在中间化合物的成分附近获得非晶态合金。换句话说，离子束混合实验揭示了：有利于形成非晶态合金的成分可以覆盖平衡相图中两相区的总宽度。

稍后，J. A. Alonso 用 A. R. Miedema 理论计算的生成热(ΔH_f)来表征二元金属系统的特性，并提出生成热判据：ΔH_f>+10 kJ/mol 的系统中，离子束混合不能形成非晶态合金。柳百新带领几名学生又做了系统的离子束混合实验，首次论证了ΔH_f>+10 kJ/mol 的系统中获得非晶态合金的可能性，同时指出正的ΔH_f 会限制有利于非晶态合金形成的成分范围。综合分析之后，提出了用二元金属系统中两相区总宽度和生成热两个参数来预言非晶态合金的形成及其成分范围的经验模型，与实验结果符合得很好。1986 年，应邀在第五届“离子束材料改性” 国际会议上作邀请报告。会议主席、美国 Sandia 国家实验室的 T. S. Picraux 博士评价为“近年里中国学者在离子束材料改性领域中提出的最好的工作”。Alonso 后来发表的论文中基本上同意柳百新提出的观点。1990 年 P. M. Ossi 在提出用其他参数预言玻璃形成能力的论文中明确地写道：柳百新等人提出的经验模型是“最成功的”。这项成果曾参与获得 1986 年度国家教委科技进步奖一等奖。

首创用离子束方法研究固体薄膜中的分形生长现象

20 世纪 80 年代中期，分形的研究在国际学术界形成了高潮，如 1985 年向《物理评论快讯》投稿的 1/3 和分形有关，但大多数是理论研究结果。柳百新在离子束混合研究非晶态合金形成的基础上，用离子束辐照研究非晶态合金晶化过程，带领几名学生进行实验研究，首次在非晶态-晶态相变临界点附近观察到从非晶态基体中析出的亚稳晶相凝聚而成的分形图像，1987 年发表在《物理评论快讯》上。他们还首次在电镜下观察到非晶态固体中的线缺陷——旋错环(相当于晶体中的位错环)，在二维平面内，旋错环是一种自避免的和封闭的奇数环，并用规范场理论作了近似处理，阐明了它的运动特性，1991 年发表在英国物理期刊上，被英国学者 Prof. N. Rivier 称之为“magnificent results, picture and theory”；1994 年，Rivier 在提出玻璃中元激发概念时的一个重要基础是非晶态固体中的奇数环，并引用柳百新的论文作为直接的实验证据。柳百新等人还首次观察到在离子束辐照下，金属-化合物界面混合所诱导的分形生长、分形生长中分形维数与离子束剂量的指数关系、磁性粒子在薄膜表面凝聚的分形生长等。柳百新等人在对薄膜中观察到的分形进行表征的研究中，用多标度分形和子波变换进行了计算，并首次用电镜观察到原子层错构成的分形，通过光学成像的分析说明子波变换作为数学显微镜对分形进行表征的适用性，等等。

这项工作不仅推动了分形科学的研究，而且在国内外都是较早将分形概念应用到材料科学研究中的。知名物理学家冯端院士评价为：“开创了固体薄膜用离子束方法研究分形的新局面，在国际上领先”。1987 年发表在《物理评论快讯》上的论文，很快被 T. Vicsek 于 1989 年出版的分形专著中列为参考文献，同时也引起其他学者仿效用离子束方法来研究分形。这项成果曾获得 1990 年度国家教委科技进步奖一等奖。柳百新个人还获得 1993 年度中国物理学会叶企孙(凝聚态)物理奖。近年里，柳百新的研究组在研究离子注入合成金属硅化物时，用分形维数来表征其生长动力学过程，深入地揭示了薄膜生长的机理。

阐明离子注入下金属氮(碳)化物的形成规律

氮(碳)离子注入在金属表面层中有可能形成相应的氮化物(碳化物)而改善材料的摩擦学性能。柳百新带领几名学生对 20 多种金属作了系统的研究，获得多种新的合金相，揭示了新相与母相结构匹配的重要性，由此提出结构适应性原则，并用快速切变机制解释了实验中观察到的有关相变。研究结果综合阐明了金属氮化物(碳化物)形成中热力学和生长动力学诸因素各自的作用和主次关系。1989 年应邀为德国《固态物理》期刊撰写了综述性论文。这项工作也是 863 材料表面优化专题中的课题，结题时受到专家组的表彰。

以上关于非晶、分形和氮(碳)化物的 3 项研究成果一起获得 1993 年度国家自然科学奖二等奖，获奖项目名称为：载能离子束与金属作用下合金相的形成与分形生长现象的研究。

为快中子反应堆的设计提供结构材料的辐照肿胀数据

20 世纪 80 年代后期，863 能源领域立项建造我国第一个快中子反应堆，总体设计中需要选择结构材料，而候选的材料在辐照下的行为是十分重要的一个因素。柳百新小组用高能(1 MeV)电子辐照来模拟中子辐照肿胀，对国内研制的 8 种材料进行了研究，初选出 3 种抗肿胀的改进型 316 不锈钢，为设计中选定国产不锈钢作为结构材料及时地提供了依据。结题时得到专家组的好评。

提出离子束混合形成亚稳合金相的热力学模型

柳百新领导的研究组以 A. R. Miedema 模型为理论框架对亚稳合金相进行热力学计算。首次考虑了多层膜中曾被忽略的界面能的作用，并将界面能加在多层膜的初始能态上。计算结果表明：对于生成热$\Delta H_f>0$ 的系统，界面能随界面份额(定义为界面层中的原子数与多层膜中的总原子数之比)的增加而增加，因此使多层膜的初始能态升高而与非晶相呈凸形的自由能曲线相交割，从而把合金成分划分为 3 个区域：中央区域中非晶相的自由能仍高于多层膜，而另外两侧的成分区域中多层膜的初始能态都已超过了非晶相。进一步提高多层膜中的界面份额使初始能态提高，也有可能在非晶相自由能最高的等原子比附近获得非晶态合金。这些预言都用离子束混合实验在多个二元金属系统中得到证实，论证了对于$\Delta H_f>0$ 的系统，界面能是非晶态合金形成的热力学驱动力；而对于$\Delta H_f<0$ 的系统，界面能的影响是较小的，负的ΔH_f本身是非晶化相变的驱动力。由此建立了适用于$\Delta H_f<0$ 和$\Delta H_f>0$ (实验中研究的系统的最大生成热为+65 kJ/mol) 的二元金属系统中多层膜离子束混合形成非晶态合金的热力学模型。

离子束混合还获得众多的亚稳晶态合金。经常观察到的是 A_3B 和 AB_3 型亚稳晶相(A 和 B 代表 A-B 二元金属系统的两个组元金属)。柳百新领导的研究组提出了改进的热力学算法，计算出这两种亚稳晶相的自由能曲线，由此构造了更为完善的 Gibbs 自由能图。对于计算得到的自由能图，首次提出用稳态退火的实验来检验其合理性的思想。结果表明：退火中有关合金相随升温而出现的次序与自由能图所预言的相符，由此肯定了构造的自由能图(至少在框架上)是合理的。

对于上述两类亚稳晶相，提出 bcc-hcp-fcc（体心立方-密堆六角-面心立方）两步骤相变的生长动力学机制，揭示了从 bcc 为基的合金中先后生长出 hcp 和 fcc 相的原子运动模型，并推导出 hcp 和 fcc 相的点阵常数，与实验中用衍射分析测定的值符合得很好。近年里，柳百新指导的博士生从第一性原理计算肯定了二元金属系统中存在相应的两种亚稳物质状态，对应于实验中获得的上述两种亚稳晶相，从固态电子结构的层次阐明了 A_3B 和 AB_3 型亚稳晶相的稳定性。

这项研究成果使经验规律上升到热力学和生长动力学的理论模型，对亚稳合金相的形成及相变理论的发展作出了有意义的贡献。阐明了界面能是$\Delta H_f>0$ 的系统中合金化和非晶化的主要驱动力，由此可以通过多层膜的设计而制备出成分可调的新型亚稳合金。本领域奠基人之一、美国工程院院士 J. W. Mayer 给予很高的评价，称之为 "multilayer technique"。1998 年，由 Mayer 和其他 4 位美国学者联合提名，柳百新因为"对离子束混合形成非晶态合金的理解所作出的杰出贡献"而当选为美国物理学会理事 (Fellow)。

用强流金属离子注入合成过渡(稀土)金属硅化物

1985 年，美国学者 I. Brown 发明了金属蒸气真空弧离子源(简写为 MEVVA 离子源)，这种离子源可以提供几乎所有的金属离子，束流密度可以高达 150 μA/cm^2，为强流金属离子注入材料改性提供了技术基础。20 世纪 90 年代，国内也能制造类似的 MEVVA 注入机。1992 年，柳百新提出用 MEVVA 离子源，将金属离子注入到硅片中，直接在硅表面形成金属硅化物的想法。第一批实验成功地制备出性能优良的 Ti，Co，Fe，Zr 和难熔金属的硅化物。又研究了 Ni-Si 系统，经分析发现 $NiSi_2$ 和 Si 在 380℃时的结构错配度为零。根据离子注入有可能在较低基体温度下合成化合物的特点，利用 Ni 离子束本身将 Si 基体加热到 380℃，首次在错配度为零的条件下制备出优质的 $NiSi_2$，其电阻率是用固态反应必须在 750℃以上才能合成的 $NiSi_2$ 的一半。众所周知，用固态反应方法合成稀土金属硅化物有一个临界温度现象，低于临界温度时反应很慢，而高于临界温度时反应是"爆炸式"的，使制备过程无法控制。柳百新领导的研究组发挥离子注入的特点克服了临界温度的问题，在 Si 表面获得 10 多种连续的稀土金属硅化物薄膜。这项研究工作发展出一项合成金属硅化物的新技术，并已应用于固体器件的制备中。

关于亚稳合金相的热力学模型和金属硅化物的研究成果一起获得 1997 年度北京市科技进步奖一等奖，并获得 1999 年度国家自然科学奖三等奖，获奖项目名称为：离子束材料改性中若干基础性问题的研究。

首先提出从原子相互作用势计算金属玻璃形成能力

离子束混合的研究结果表明，二元金属系统中金属玻璃形成的成分范围可以从中央区域一直扩展到有利于形成固溶体的边界。柳百新首先提出从理论上预言二元金属系统中的玻璃形成能力，实际上就是要从理论上计算出系统的临界固溶度。因此，相应的科学问题就是要计算随成分变化时，固溶体与非晶相的相对稳定性。从物质结构的角度来分析，就是要比较两者的原子组态的相对稳定性；而原子组态的稳定性直接决定于该系统的原子间相互作用势。他带领几名研究生首先对 Ni-Mo，Ni-Nb，Ni-Ta，Ni-Ti 等系统建立了比较符合实际的原子相互作用多体势，再从多体势出发，用固溶体模型进行分子动力学模拟：在固溶体中逐步增加溶质原子，直到固溶体失稳而转变为非晶态，由此计算出两个组元金属的临界固溶度。两个临界固溶度之间的合金成分范围就是系统中有利于形成金属玻璃的成分范围。计算值与实验结果符合得很好。柳百新还指出，所确定的金属玻璃形成能力是由系统的内禀特性所决定的，与实际中应用的制备技术无关，因此计算得到的是二元金属系统的本征玻璃形成能力；而用一种特定技术对某一个系统测定的玻璃形成能力，应该称为表观玻璃形成能力，它是与这种特定技术有关的。2002 年，柳百新领导的研究组还对生成热为正的二元金属系统提出了建立多体势的新方法：先用第一性原理计算出几个非平衡合金相的物理性能，再根据这些性能拟合出该系统的多体势。例如，建立了符合实际的 Cu-Ta 多体势，并进一步计算出玻璃形成的成分范围，计算结果与实验相符。

提出固态反应非晶化的热力学和原子运动模型

1983 年以来，文献中一直认为多层膜中固态反应非晶化的必要条件是系统的生成热很负和原子尺寸差很大。柳百新领导的研究组首先用系统的实验论证了固态反应非晶化也可以在生成热为正的系统中发生，论证了多层膜中的界面能是非晶化相变的驱动力。关于 Cu-Ta 多层膜的实验结果发表于 1995 年底，而国外用 Cu-Ta 双层膜观察到同样相变的工作发表于 1999 年。柳百新等人又进一步定义了热力学和动力学因子，对研究过的 28 个系统作了定量的计算，由此提出固态反应非晶化的理论判据，与迄今发表的实验结果相符合。

对 Ni-Mo，Ni-Nb，Ni-Ta，Ni-Ti 等系统，应用已建立的原子相互作用多体势，通过分子动力学方法在原子运动的层次研究了固态反应的动力学：观察到穿越界面的原子迁移，揭示了非晶化受扩散或界面控制的规律，揭示了界面织构可能在非晶化中起形核或生长位垒的作用，并观察到两种金属晶体无序化的先后次序。根据模拟和实验结果，柳百新等人首次阐明了晶态-非晶态相变的物理本质是晶格中固溶原子超过临界固溶度时的塌陷。由此推理：当两组元金属的固溶度有差异时，在其他条件相同的情况下，非晶层向固溶度小的金属方向生长得应该较快，所作预言与实验观察结果相符。

勤奋治学　教书育人

改革开放以后，柳百新在材料科学领域从事基础研究以及部分与高科技应用有密切联系的应用基础研究，他非常珍惜这样的机会，并以献身科学的精神投身到他热爱的工作中去。他在加州理工学院访问期间，每天工作 10 多个小时。他用离子束混合制备出第一个非晶态合金的实验是在一个星期日做的，那天整个实验室里只有他一个人在工作。如今，他已经 67 岁了，但他的勤奋精神依然如前，并深深地感染着他的学生们。他的研究生常常发现，柳百新经常是在许多人还在沉睡的清晨，为他们修改了论文，又通过网络传回给他们。20 年来，他和他指导的研究生在国际期刊上发表了 200 多篇论文，许多论文都是他在清晨或是在计算机前面对面地教学生怎样修改后定稿的。当有的高年级本科生有意报考他的研究生，向他询问对学生的要求时，他的回答非常简单：一要爱国，二要爱科学，因为他认为只有当一个人具有了强烈的爱国之心，热爱并立志为科学而献身的时候，这个人才会在科研中保持天天向上的工作姿态。

柳百新迄今共培养了 7 名硕士和 14 名博士，曾获得 1997 年度北京市教学优秀成果奖一等奖，获奖项目的名称是："培养国际一流水平博士生的研究与实践"。每每提到他培养的学生，柳百新总是说："我为我的学生而感到十分的骄傲！"例如，1993 年毕业的一名博士，现在担任清华大学材料科学研究院的副院长和国家 863 计划材料领域功能材料专家组副组长。1995 年毕业的一名博士获得首届全国百篇优秀博士论文奖，在国外做了近 6 年博士后研究之后，2001 年回到了柳百新的研究组，2002 年获得了国家杰出青年基金。

在科研和研究生的培养工作中，柳百新认为要做到 4 点，即选择学科前沿作为研究方向、勤奋地学习和工作、严谨求实的科学作风和唯物辩证的科学方法。他认为在基础研究中选择国际科学前沿的课题，才有可能给研究生在实验和理论上有一定创新的空间。此外，中国目前还是发展中的国家，仪器设备与发达国家相比还有差距，不宜于在一个大学科领域内全方位地开展工作，而是要注意发挥人的因素，选择具有优势或者是有较好基础的方向和课题，扎实工作、步步深入，做出国际先进或领先水平的成果来。柳百新也十分强调用唯物辩证的思想去指导科研工作，他把撰写高水平学术论文提高到唯物辩证的科研方法的高度来认识，对研究生也提出相应的要求。20 年来，他的研究组的许多论文发表在高影响因子的期刊上。此外，柳百新也认为，当一项研究工作做得比较系统，而且在理论上也建立了相应的模型时，应该撰写有份量的综述性论文。例如，他于 1986 年发表的一篇综述性论文，迄今被引用了 120 多次，2000—2001 年，他带领几名助手分别在物理学和材料科学影响因子最高的期刊上发表了两篇综述性论文。20 世纪 90 年代中，加州理工学院的副校长来清华大学访问，他在讲演中提到："加州理工学院的教授们把精力集中在发表高水平的科学论文和综述性论文上。"这也正是柳百新在基础研究工作中的理念和实施的模式。一位在学博士生很有体会地说："柳先生把撰写和发表学术论文看成是对科研工作的牵引。撰写一篇学术论文，其实就是撰写一份相对完整的科学报告。及时地整理研究工作的结果，撰写一篇学术论文，可以从总体上对工作的完整性、系统性和深入程度做一个阶段性的小结，同时也有助于对下一步的工作提出新的想法。"

经过多年的积累，柳百新领导的研究组里已经建立起必要的实验制样设备、热力学计算、分子动力学模拟和第一性原理计算的条件。因此，他要求新入学的研究生要在研究组原有工作的基础上从高的起点上起步，而且要求他们把理论与实验研究尽量地结合起来，从而做出高水平的成果。柳百新还十分重视在研究组里营造良好的人文环境，他经常强调他与研究生有三重关系：一是师生关系，二是研究中的合作者，三是生活中的"忘年交"。柳百新对学生的要求是严格的，在修改他们的论文稿子时，甚至细致到每个词、每个标点和空格。在日常生活中，他也多方面地关心每一个学生。在工作之余，他也和研究生一起聊天，谈科研中的思想方法、谈体育比赛、谈文艺和音乐等，这使得研究组里的师生关系非常融洽。贯穿在柳百新科研和研究生培养工作中的指导思想总结起来可以用"三个一流"来概括："做国际一流水平的研究，写国际一流水平的论文，育国际一流水平的人才。"而他自己却始终认为："天外有天，山外有山，我只是在我所从事研究的领域里做了一点点事情。"

柳百新从事的是材料科学的基础研究，综观材料科学理论的发展，他感到尚有不尽如人意之处，因此，还有许多工作要做。就金属物理的理论而言，20 世纪 30—50 年代只有经验的规律，70 年代中才有半经验的热力学理论，可以做一些半定量的计算。近几十年来，由于物理、化学、数学理论的发展，加上计算科学和计算机的发展，有可能将材料物理的理论向定量化发展。在此基础上，才有可能真正达到材料科学家的最终目标：按性能的要求设计材料的微观结构，并用特定的制备方法制备出需要的微观结构。构建材料科学领域中部分分支学科的定量理论框架是柳百新今后研究工作的重要目标之一，近年里他的研究组正在踏踏实实地工作，并不断地有所突破。学无止境，科学研究也是无止境的，科学探索的工作要不断地努力向前。这不仅仅是柳百新在科学研究中的信念，也是他在科学研究道路上不断奋斗的根本动力。

简　　历

1935 年 6 月 10 日	出生于上海市。
1955—1961 年	在清华大学工程物理系学习，毕业后留校工作至今。
1961 年—	任清华大学副教授、教授。
1981—1982 年	美国加州理工学院访问学者。
1984 年—	当选为国际玻姆物理学会科学委员。
1988—1989 年	任中国高等科学技术中心特别成员。
1992—1995 年	任国家自然科学基金委学科评审组成员。
1993 年—	任国际期刊 *Nuclear Materials* 顾问编委会委员。
1994 年—	任清华大学校务委员会委员。
1998 年—	当选为美国物理学会理事(Fellow)。
1999 年—	任国家自然科学奖、科技进步奖和发明奖学科评审组成员。
2001 年	当选为中国科学院院士。
2002 年—	任北京市学位委员会“材料科学与工程”学科评审组成员。
2002 年—	任国家自然科学基金委学科评审组成员。

代表性论著

1. Bai-Xin Liu, W.L.Johnson, M-A.Nicolet and S.S.Lau, Structural difference rule for amorphous alloy formation by ion mixing, Applied Phsyics Letters, 1983, 42(1): 45-47.
2. B.X.Liu, E.Ma, J.Li and L.J.Huang, Different behaviors of amorphization induced by ion mixing, Invited Paper. 5th Intl. Conf. on Ion Beam Modification of Materials, Catania, Italy, 1986, Nucl. Instr. Meth. in Phys. Res. B, 1987, 19/20: 682-690.
3. B.X.Liu, L.J.Huang, K.Tao, C.H.Shang and H-D.Li, Observations of fractal patterns induced in thin solid films by ion irradiation, Physical Review Letters, 1987, 59(7): 745-747.
4. B.X.Liu, C.H.Shang and H-D.Li, Disclination loops observed in Ni-Mo amorphous alloy-films induced by ion irradiation, J. Physics: Condensed Matter, 1991, 3(31): 5769-5781.
5. B.X.Liu, X.Zhou and H-D.Li, Thermodynamics and growth kinetical consideration of metal-nitride formation by nitrogen implantation, Review Article, 1989, Physica Status Solidi (A), 113(1): 11-22.
6. B.X.Liu, S.L.Lai and J.G.Sun, Effects of alloying and treatment on void swelling of 316 stainless steels, J.Materials Research, 1991, 6(8): 1650-1654.
7. D.H.Zhu, K.Tao, F.Pan and B.X.Liu, C54-$TiSi_2$ formed by direct high-current Ti-ion implantation, Applied Physics Letters, 1993, 62(19): 2356-2358.
8. B.X.Liu and F.Pan, Magnetic properties of vapor-deposited iron/noble-metal multilayers, Physical Review B, 1993, 48(13): 10276-10283.
9. Z.J.Zhang, O.Jin and B.X.Liu, Anomalous alloying behavior induced by ion irradiation in a system with a large positive heat of mixing, Physical Review B, 1995, 51(13): 8076-8085.

10. Y.G.Chen and B.X.Liu, Amorphous films formed by solid-state reaction in an immiscible Y-Mo system and their structural relaxation, Applied Physics Letters, 1996, 68(22): 3096-3098.
11. Q.Zhang, W.S.Lai and B.X.Liu, Glass-forming ability determined by atomic interaction potential for the Ni-Mo system, Physical Review B, 1999, 59(21): 13521-13524.
12. G.W.Yang, W.S.Lai, C.Lin and B.X.Liu, Irradiaition-induced growth of nano-quasicrystals from amorphous matrix in the equilibrium immiscible Fe-Cu system, Applied Physics Letters, 1999, 74(22): 3305-3307.
13. B.X.Liu, K.Y.Gao and H.N.Zhu, Metal silicides synthesized by high current metal-ion implantation, Invited Paper, First Intl. Conf. on Microelectronics and Advanced Materials, San Jose, US, March 1999, J. Vacuum Science and Technology B, 1999, 17(5): 2277-2283.
14. C.Lin, G.W.Yang and B.X.Liu, Prediction of solid-state amorphization in binary metal systems, Physical Reviw B, 2000, 61(23): 15649-15652.
15. B.X.Liu, W.S.Lai and Q.Zhang, Irradiation induced amorphization in metallic mulyilayeres and calculation of glass-forming ability from atomistic potentials in the binary metal systems, Review Article. Materials Science and Engineering: Reports 2000, 29(1-2): 1-48.
16. J.B.Liu, C.Z.Li and B.X.Liu, Stability of a non-euilibrium phase in an immiscible Ag-Ni system studied by ab initio calculations and ion-beam-mixing experiments, Physical Review B, 2001, 63(13): art. no. 132204.
17. B.X.Liu, W.S.Lai and Z.J.Zhang, Solid-state crystal-to-amorphous transition in metal-metal multilayeres and its thermodyanmic and atomistic modelling, Review Article. Advances in Physics, 2001, 50(4): 367-429.
18. Z.C.Li, D.P.Yu and B.X.Liu, Manipulation of ordered layered structure by interface-assisted ion beam mixing in immiscible Ag-Co and Ag-Ni systems, Physical Review B, 2002, 65(24): art. no. 245403.
19. R.F.Zhang and B.X.Liu, Proposed model for calculating the standard formation enthalpy of binary transition-metal systems, Applied Physics Letters, 2002, 81(7): 1219-1221.
20. H.R.Gong, L.T.Kong, W.S.Lai and B.X.Liu, Atomistic modeling of solid-state amorphization in an immiscible Cu-Ta system, Physical Review B, 2002, 66(10): art. no. 104204.

第二篇　柳百新研究组发表的500篇SCI论文目录(1982—2015年)

1982—1985年(1—15, 共15篇)

1. Formation of Au-Ge Metastable Phases by Ion Mixing
   B.X. Liu and M-A. Nicolet
   Phys. Stat. Sol. (A) 70(2), p.671-676 (1982)
2. Surface Morphology of Erbium Silicide
   S.S. Lau, C.S. Pai, C.S. Wu, T.F. Kuech and ***B.X. Liu***
   Appl. Phys. Lett. 41(1), p.77-80 (1982)
3. Improvement of Thermally Formed Nickel Silicide by Ion Irradiation
   L. Wielunski, C.D. Lien, ***B.X. Liu*** and M-A. Nicolet
   J. Vac. Sci. Technol. 20(2), p.182-185 (1982)
4. Ion Mixing of Ni and Pt Layers on Si
   L. Wielunski, B.M. Paine, ***B.X. Liu***, C.D. Lian and M-A. Nicolet
   Phys. Stat. Sol. (A) 72(1), p.399-404 (1982)
5. Ti-Au Metallic Glasses Formed by Ion Mixing
   B.X. Liu, M-A. Nicolet and S.S. Lau
   Phys. Stat. Sol. (A) 73(1), p.183-188 (1983)
6. Structural Difference Rule for Amorphous Alloy Formation by Ion Mixing
   B.X. Liu, W.L. Johnson, M-A. Nicolet and S.S. Lau
   Appl. Phys. Lett. 42(1), p.45-47 (1983)
7. Amorphous Film Formation by Ion Mixing in the Binary Metal Systems
   B.X. Liu, W.L. Johnson, M-A. Nicolet and S.S. Lau
   Oral presentation at 3rd Intl. Conf. on Ion Beam Modification of Materials, France, 1982. Nucl. Instr. Meth. 209, p.229-234 (1983)
8. Ion Mixing to Produce Amorphous Mo-Ru Superconducting Films
   B.X. Liu, B.M. Clemens, R. Gaboriaud, W.L. Johnson and M-A. Nicolet
   Appl. Phys. Lett. 42(7), p.624-626 (1983)
9. Metastable Phases in the Au-Co System Formed by Ion Mixing
   B.X. Liu and M-A. Nicolet
   Thin Solid Films 101(3), p.201-206 (1983)
10. Ion Mixing and Phase Diagrams
    S.S. Lau, ***B.X. Liu*** and M-A. Nicolet
    Nucl. Instr. Meth. 209, p.97-105 (1983)
11. Chemical Effects in Ion Mixing of Transition Metals on SiO_2
    T. Banwell, ***B.X. Liu***, I. Golecki and M-A. Nicolet
    Nucl. Instr. Meth. 209, p.125-129 (1983)
12. A Metastable Electron Compound Formed by Ion Irradiation
    B.X. Liu
    Phys. Stat. Sol. (A) 75(1), p.K77-K81 (1983)
13. Study of Ni-Nb System by Ion Mixing
    K.T-Y. Kung, ***B.X. Liu*** and M-A. Nicolet
    Phys. Stat. Sol. (A) 77(1), p.355-359 (1983)
14. Surface Morphology and Electronic Properties of $ErSi_2$

C.S. Wu, S.S. Lau, T.F. Keuch and ***B.X. Liu***
Thin Solid Films 104(1-2), p.175-182 (1983)

15. Further Studies of Ion Mixing in Binary Metal Systems
B.X. Liu
Nucl. Instr. Meth. in Phys. Res. B 7, p.547-551 (1985)

1986—1989 年(16—64, 共 49 篇)

16. Ion-Bombarded-Assisted Intermetallic Compound Formation in Ti-Sn Bilayer
E. Ma, ***B.X. Liu*** and H.D. Li
Nucl. Instr. Meth. in Phys. Res. B 14, p.294-296 (1986)
17. Ion Mixing and Metallic Alloy Phase Formation
B.X. Liu
Review Article, Phys. Stat. Sol. (A) 94(1), p.11-34 (1986)
18. Ion Mixing to Form Amorphous Alloys in the Co-Gd System
Z.H. Yan, ***B.X. Liu*** and H.D. Li
Phys. Stat. Sol. (A) 94(2), p.483-488 (1986)
19. An Explanation of the Formation of Metastable Ag-Cr Alloy by Ion Mixing
L.J. Huang, E. Ma and ***B.X. Liu***
Chin. Phys. Lett. 3(5), p.197-200 (1986)
20. Different Behaviors of Amorphization Induced by Ion Mixing
B.X. Liu, E. Ma, J. Li and L.J. Huang
Invited paper at 5th Intl. Conf. on Ion Beam Modification of Materials, Italy, 1986. Nucl. Instr. Meth. in Phys. Res. B 19, p. 682-690 (1987)
21. Prediction of Metallic Glass Formation by Ion Mixing
B.X. Liu
Mater. Lett. 5(9), p.322-327 (1987)
22. Amorphous RE-TR Magnetic Alloys Formed by Ion Mixing
Z.H. Yan, ***B.X. Liu*** and H.D. Li
Nucl. Instr. Meth. in Phys. Res. B 19, p.700-703 (1987)
23. Ternary Amorphous Films of Gdcoas Formed by Ion Mixing
F.Z. Cui, W.J. Zhang, H.D. Li, ***B.X. Liu*** and Z.H. Yan
Nucl. Instr. Meth. in Phys. Res. B 23, p.509-512 (1987)
24. Structural Transformation in Metal Layers Implanted by Nitrogen Implantation in Thin Metal Films
E. Ma, ***B.X. Liu***, X. Chen and H.D. Li
Thin Solid Films 147(1), p.49-55 (1987)
25. Observations of Fractal Patterns Induced in Thin Solid Films by Ion Irradiation
B.X. Liu, L.J. Huang, K. Tao, C.H. Shang and H.D. Li
Phys. Rev. Lett. 59(7), p.745-747 (1987)
26. Observations of Dendritic Patterns in the Ion Irradiated Ni-Mo Films
B.X. Liu, L.J. Huang and C.H. Shang
Chin. Phys. Lett. 4(2), p.53-56 (1987)
27. The Microstructure Features of Ion Induced Metastable Fe-Cu Phases

L.J. Huang and ***B.X. Liu***

Nucl. Instr. Meth. in Phys. Res. B 18, p.256-260 (1987)

28. Amorphization in Fe-Cu System by Tracing Its Microscopic Features

L.J. Huang, ***B.X. Liu*** and H.D. Li

Appl. Phys. A 44(3), p.269-272 (1987)

29. Quasicrystalline Al-Fe Phase Formed by Ion Mixing

B.X. Liu, G.A. Cheng and C.H. Shang

Philos. Mag. Lett. 55(6), p.265-269 (1987)

30. Cems to Characterize the Ion Induced Fe-Mo Metastable Phase

J. Li and ***B.X. Liu***

Review Article, Phys. Stat. Sol. (A) 99(1), p.K31-K34 (1987)

31. Cems Study Irradiation Effects on the Chemical Bonding of SnO_2

J. Li, H.D. Li and ***B.X. Liu***

Nucl. Instr. Meth. in Phys. Res. B 28, p.251-254 (1987)

32. Amorphization and Associated Structural Phase Transformation Induced by Ion Beam Mixing

B.X. Liu

Supplement to Trans. of JIM 29, p.29-36 (1988)

33. Percolation Scale Effects upon Amorphous Structural Phase Transition in an Alloy Film

L.J. Huang, ***B.X. Liu*** and H.D. Li

J. Phys.: Solid State Phys. 21(3), p.L51-55 (1988)

34. Observations of Percolation Structure Induced in Thin Solid Films by Ion Irradiation

J.R. Ding, L.J. Huang and ***B.X. Liu***

Chin. Phys. Lett. 5(7), p.321-324(1988)

35. Growth of the Fractal Patterns in Ni-Zr Thin Films During Ion-Solid Interaction

L.J. Huang, J.R. Ding, H.D. Li and ***B.X. Liu***

J. Appl. Phys. 63(8), p.2879-2881 (1988)

36. Fractal Growth at Dendritic Tips in an Ion-Irradiated Thin Solid Film

L.J. Huang, ***B.X. Liu*** and H.D. Li

Il Nuovo Cimento D, 10(9), p.1117-1123 (1988)

37. Cems Study on Sn Ion Induced Reaction in a Tin-Iron Oxide Bilayer

J. Li and ***B.X. Liu***

Hyperfine Interactions 42(1-4), p.997-1000 (1988)

38. Ion-Induced Mixing at Nb/Fe_2O_3 Interface Studied by Cems Technique

J. Li and ***B.X. Liu,*** H.D. Li and X.F. Zhang

Nucl. Instr. Meth. in Phys. Res. B 31, p.407-411 (1988)

39. Formation of Silver Trinitride by Nitrogen Implantation

X. Zhou, H.D. Li and ***B.X. Liu***

J. Phys.: Solid State Phys. 21(19), p.L683-L687 (1988)

40. Reverse Sequence of Formation of Titanium Nitrides by Nitrogen Implantation

X. Zhou, H.K. Dong, H.D. Li and ***B.X. Liu***

J. Appl. Phys. 63(10), p.4942-4945 (1988)

41. Formation of an Icosahedral Phase in Ion Irradiated Fe/Cu Multilayers

L.J. Huang, Q.M. Chen, Y.D. Fan, H.D. Li and ***B.X. Liu***

J. Phys. F: Metal Phys. 18(5), p.L69-L73 (1988)

42. Ion Induced Adhesion between Metals and Oxides
G.A. Cheng, H.D. Li and ***B.X. Liu***
Chin. Phys. Lett. 5(5), p.197-200 (1988)
43. An Icosahedral Phase Formed during Annealing of Ion-Irradiated Fe-Mo Amorphous Films
C.H. Shang, J. Li, H.D. Li, ***B.X. Liu***
J. Phys. F: Metal Phys. 18(9), p.L169-L173(1988)
44. The Band Structure and the Anomalous Alloying Behavior of Noble Metal Based Systems
L.J. Huang, E. Ma and ***B.X. Liu***
Phys. Stat. Sol. (A) 110(2), p.443-448 (1988)
45. Enhanced Adhesion in Metal-Oxide Pairs by Ion Irradiation
G.A. Cheng, H.D. Li and ***B.X. Liu***
Phys. Stat. Sol. (A) 107(1), p.K29-K32 (1988)
46. Metastable Phase and Dendritic Pattern Formation in Thin Solid Films by Ion Mixing
C.H. Shang and ***B.X. Liu***
Nucl. Instr. Meth. in Phys. Res. B 37, p.420-423 (1989)
47. Irradiation Effect on Thermal Stability of an Amorphous Fe-Mo Alloy
C.H. Shang, J. Li, H.D. Li and ***B.X. Liu***
Nucl. Instr. Meth. in Phys. Res. B 39, p.607-610 (1989)
48. Ion-Metal Interactions: Amorphous, Icosahedral Phase and Fractal Pattern Formation
B.X. Liu
Nucl. Instr. Meth. in Phys. Res. B 40, p.603-607 (1989)
49. Some New Structural Transformation Induced by Ion Beam
B.X. Liu
Vacuum 39(2), p.169-171 (1989)
50. Structural Correlation in Tatalum Nitride Formation by Direct Nitrogen Implantation
X. Zhou, ***B.X. Liu,*** H.K. Dong and H.D. Li
Vacuum 39(2), p.307-308 (1989)
51. Formation of Noble-Metal Nitrides by Nitrogen Implantation
X. Zhou, H.D. Li and ***B.X. Liu***
Nucl. Instr. Meth. in Phys. Res. B 39, p.583-586 (1989)
52. Ion Induced Phase Precipitation and Growth in Thin Films: Fractals and Dendrites
L.J. Huang, J.R. Ding, ***B.X. Liu*** and H.D. Li
Nucl. Instr. Meth. in Phys. Res. B 39, p.144-147 (1989)
53. Multilfractal Characterization of Magnetic-Microsphere Aggregation in Thin Films
L.J. Huang, ***B.X. Liu*** and H.D. Li
Phys. Rev. B 40(1), p.858-861 (1989)
54. Discontinuosly Branching Tree Morphology Induced at NaCl/AgCo Interface by Ion Irradiation
C.H. Shang, H.D. Li and ***B.X. Liu***
Phys. Rev. B 40(4), p.2733-2736 (1989)
55. Fractal Aggregation of Magnetic-Particles in Ag-Co Thin Film Surface
J.R. Ding and ***B.X. Liu***
Phys. Rev. B 40(8), p.5834-5836 (1989)

56. Linear Correlation of Fractal Dimension versus Atomic Magnetron in Magnetic-Particle Aggregation
B.X. Liu and J.R. Ding
Phys. Rev. B 40(10), p.7432-7434 (1989)

57. Scaling Features for the Surface of Ion-Induced Fractals
J.R. Ding and ***B.X. Liu***
J. Phys. A: Math. and Gen. 22(7), p.L265-269 (1989)

58. Formation of Percolation Networks in Ion-Irradiated Ag-Co Solid Films
J.R. Ding and ***B.X. Liu***
J. Mater. Res. 4(6), p.1296-1298 (1989)

59. Percolation upon Amorphous Phase Transition in Thin Films
L.J. Huang, ***B.X. Liu***, J.R. Ding and H.D. Li
Sci. China A 32(4), p.434-442 (1989)

60. An Fe-Cu Icosahedral Phase Formed in High Temperature Solid-State Interdiffusion
C.H. Shang and ***B.X. Liu***
Mater. Lett. 8(6), p.224-227 (1989)

61. Thermodynamics and Growth Kinetical Consideration of Metal-Nitride Formation by Nitrogen Implantation
B.X. Liu, X. Zhou and H.D. Li
Review Article, Phys. Stat. Sol. (A) 113(1), p.11-22 (1989)

62. Ion-Induced Disconnected Branching Tree Morphology: Correlation of Fractal Dimension with Ion Fluence
C.H. Shang and ***B.X. Liu***
J. Phys.:Condens. Matter 1(50), p.10187-10192 (1989)

63. Metastable Phase and Dentritic Pattern Formation in Thin Solid Films by Ion Mixing
C.H. Shang and ***B.X. Liu***
Nucl. Instr. Meth. in Phys. Res. B 37, p.420-423 (1989)

64. Icosahedral Incommensurate Fe-Mo Phase Formed by Solid-State Transformation
L.J. Huang; Q.M. Chen, ***B.X. Liu***, Y.D. Fan and H.D. Li
Phys. Stat. Sol. (A) 116(1), p. K51-K56 (1989)

1990—1992年(65—100，共36篇)

65. Local Scaling Properties of Fractals Observed in Ni-Zr Alloy Films
J.R. Ding, F. Wang, ***B.X. Liu***
Modern Phys. Lett. B 4, p.1111-1118(1990)

66. Fractal Corrosion of Alloy Films by Acid
J.R. Ding and ***B.X. Liu***
J. Phys.:Condens. Matter 2(8), p.1971-1975 (1990)

67. Stability of an Icosahedral Incommensurate Phase Formed in Immiscible Alloy System
L.J. Huang, ***B.X. Liu*** and H.D. Li
Phys. Rev. B 41(13), p.9523-9526 (1990)

68. Amorphous NbO Films Prepared by Reactive Evaporation
J.R. Ding, X. Zhou, J.N. Bai and ***B.X. Liu***

J. Vac. Sci. and Technol. A 8(4), p.3349-3351 (1990)

69. Fe-Cu Icosahedral Phase and Its Thermal and Magnetic Properties
    B.X. Liu, C.H. Shang, L.J. Huang and H.D. Li
    J. Non-Cryst. Solid 117, p.785-788 (1990)
70. Spontaneous Vitrification in an Immiscible Fe-Cu System
    L.J. Huang and ***B.X. Liu***
    Appl. Phys. Lett. 57(14), p.1401-1403 (1990)
71. Void Swelling Induced by 1 MeV Electron Irradiation in Ti- and Nb-Modified 316 Stainless Steels
    B.X. Liu, S.L. Lai, J.G. Sun, C.H. Shang and D. Xu
    J. Nucl. Mater. 175(1), p.129-134 (1990)
72. Study of Alloy Phase Formation Using Ion Beams
    B.X. Liu
    Vacuum 42(1), p.75-79 (1991)
73. Two Dimensional Chain Structures Observed in Carbon Ion Implanted Ni Thin Films
    B.X. Liu, J. Wang and Z.Z. Fang
    J. Phys.: Condens. Matter 3(12), p. 1941-1945 (1991)
74. Grain Growth Induced in Noble-Metal Films by N Implantation
    B.X. Liu and X. Zhou
    Phys. Stat. Sol. (A) 124(2), p.K101-K106 (1991)
75. Ion-Mixing-Induced Fractal Growth in Thin Alloy Films
    B.X. Liu
    Invited paper at 7th Intl. Conf. on Ion Beam Modification of Materials, USA, 1990. Nucl. Instr. Meth. in Phys. Res. B 59, p.475-480 (1991)
76. Hexagonal Cobalt Formed by Carbon Ion Implantation
    B.X. Liu, J. Wang and Z.Z. Fang
    J. Appl. Phys. 69(10), p.7342-7344 (1991)
77. Self-Avoiding Magnetic Chains Formed in Annealed Fe-Cu Multilayers:Experiment and Simulation
    C.H. Shang, H.D. Li and ***B.X. Liu***
    J. Phys.: Condens. Matter 3(23), p.4165-4171 (1991)
78. Disclination Loops in Ni-Mo Amorphous Alloy Films Induced by Ion Irradiation
    B.X. Liu, C.H. Shang and H.D. Li
    J. Phys.: Condens. Matter 3(31), p.5769-5781 (1991)
79. Glass Forming Ability of the Al-Ti System under Ion Mixing
    B.X. Liu and G.A. Cheng
    Phys. Stat. Sol. (A) 125(2), p.K93-K96 (1991)
80. Effects of Alloying and Treatment on Void Swelling of Type 316 Stainless Steels
    B.X. Liu, S.L. Lai and J.G. Sun
    J. Mater. Res. 6(8), p.1650-1654 (1991)
81. Observations of Self-Avoiding Fractals in Fe-Cu and Ni-Mo Thin Films
    B.X. Liu, C.H. Shang and H.D. Li
    Phys. Rev. B 44(9), p.4365-4370 (1991)
82. Observations of Two-Dimensional Fractal Growth in Solids
    C.H. Shang, ***B.X. Liu,*** J.G. Sun and H.D. Li
    Phys. Rev. B 44(10), p.5035-5039 (1991)

83. Evolution of Yb-Particle Fractals Towards Equilibrium Morphology on Yb-Co Alloy Films
B.X. Liu and J.R. Ding
Solid State Comm. 80(6), p.447-450 (1991)

84. One-Dimensional Topological Defect Observed in Ni-Mo Amorphous Films
C.H. Shang, **B.X. Liu** and H.D. Li
Phys. Rev. B 44(14), p.7302-7305 (1991)

85. Self-Avoiding Magnetic Chains
C.H. Shang, ***B.X. Liu*** and H.D. Li
Physica A 178(2), p.207-214 (1991)

86. Fractal Growth during Crystallization of Ion Mixed Co-Yb Amorphous Alloys
B.X. Liu, J.R. Ding and H.B. Zhang
Phys. Stat. Sol. (A) 126(2), p.K93-K98 (1991)

87. Diffusion-Limited Aggregation-Like Structure Induced in Co Thin Films by Carbon Ion Implantation
B.X. Liu, J. Wang and Z.Z. Fang
J. Phys.: Condens. Matter 3(47), p.9551-9557 (1991)

88. Aggregation Process in Ion Irradiated Solid Films
J. Wang, J. Cai, X.F. WU, ***B.X. Liu*** and Z.Z. Fang
Chin. Phys. Lett. 8(8), p.408- 411 (1991)

89. Two Metastable Simple Structured Metal Carbides Formed by Carbon Ion Implantation
B.X. Liu, J. Wang, X.Y. Cheng and Z.Z. Fang
Phys. Stat. Sol. (A) 128(2), p.K71-K75 (1991)

90. Metastable Alloys Formed in Some Yb-Based Systems upon Ion Irradiation
B.X. Liu, J.R. Ding, H.B. Zhang and D.Z. Che
Phys. Stat. Sol. (A) 129(1), p.103-108 (1991)

91. Amorphization Induced in Some Y-Based Systems by Ion Mixing in Some Y-Based Binary Metal Systems
B.X. Liu, D.Z. Che, Z.J. Zhang, S.L. Lai and J.R. Ding
Phys. Stat. Sol. (A) 128(2), p.345-352 (1991)

92. Metastable Phase Formed in Fe-Cu-Si Multilayered Films by Ion Irradiation
B.X. Liu, C.H. Shang and C. H. Liu
J. Mater. Res. 7(1), p.85-88 (1992)

93. A Metastable Cr Carbide of NaCl Structure Formed by Carbon-Ion Implantation into Chromium Films
B.X. Liu and X.Y. Cheng
J. Phys.: Condens. Matter 4(16), p.L265-L268 (1992)

94. Phase Transition of Al-Yb Alloy Films upon Ion Irradiation and Thermal Annealing
J.R. Ding, D.Z. Che, H.B. Zhang, K. Tao and ***B.X. Liu***
Appl. Phys. Lett. 60(8), p.944-946 (1992)

95. Effects of Pre-Implanted Helium on Void Formation in Electron Irradiated Stainless Steels
S.L. Lai, Z.J. Zhang, J.G. Sun and ***B.X. Liu***
Phys. Stat. Sol. (A) 130(2), p.313-318 (1992)

96. Epitaxial Growth of B.C.C. Cu(F.C.C.Fe) on Polycrystalline Fe(Cu) by Vapor Deposition
F. Pan, K. Tao and ***B.X. Liu***
Phys. Stat. Sol. (A) 132(1), p.K35-K38 (1992)

97. Magnetic Properties of Fe/Ag Nano-Multilayers
F. Pan, T. Yang, K. Tao and ***B.X. Liu***
J. Phys.: Condens. Matter 4(40), p.L519-L524 (1992)

98. Correlation of 3d Transition Metal Carbide Phase Formation with 3d Electron by Carbon Ion Implantation
J. Wang, X.F. Wu, ***B.X. Liu*** and Z.Z. Fang
Acta Metall. Mater. 40(6), p.1417-1420 (1992)

99. New Fcc Phase Formed in Immiscible Fe-Cu System by Solid State Diffusion
B.X. Liu, F. Pan and K. Tao
Chin. Phys. Lett. 9(12), p.663-666 (1992)

100. Disclination Loops Observed in Ion Irradiated Ni-Mo Amorphous Films and Their Fractal Characteristics
B.X. Liu and C.H. Shang
J. Non-Cryst. Solids 150(1), p.332-336 (1992)

1993—1995 年(101—149，共 49 篇)

101. Metastable Phase Formation in the Fe-Cu System by Ion Irradiation and Solid State Interdiffusion
F. Pan, T. Yang, K. Tao and ***B.X. Liu***
Phys. Stat. Sol. (A) 135(1), p.199-206 (1993)

102. Construction of the Gibbs Free Energy Diagram and Interpretation of Phase Evolution in the Ni-Mo System
H.Y. Bai and ***B.X. Liu***
Phys. Stat. Sol. (A) 136(1), p.73-80 (1993)

103. Phase Evolution upon Ion Mixing and Solid State Reaction and Thermodynamic Interpretation in the Ni-Nb System
Z.J. Zhang, H.Y. Bai, Q.L. Qiu, K. Tao and ***B.X. Liu***
J. Appl. Phys. 73(4), p.1702-1710 (1993)

104. C54-$TiSi_2$ Formed by Direct High Current Ti-Ion Implantation
D.H. Zhu, K. Tao, F. Pan and ***B.X. Liu***
Appl. Phys. Lett. 62(19), p.2356-2358 (1993)

105. Microstructure and Magnetic Properties of the Fe/Cu Nano-Multilayers by Vapour Deposition
F. Pan, K. Tao, T. Yang and ***B.X. Liu***
Phys. Stat. Sol. (A) 135(2), p.573-580 (1993)

106. Polycrystalline AlN Films of Fine Crystallinity Prepared by Ion-Beam Assisted Deposition
J. Yang, C. Wang, X.S. Yan, K. Tao, ***B.X. Liu*** and Y.D. Fan
Appl. Phys. Lett. 62(22), p.2790-2791 (1993)

107. Thermally Induced Phase Transition from Metastable Ni-Nb Hexagonal Phase to Amorphous and Its Thermodynamic Interpretation
B.X. Liu, H.Y. Bai, Z.J. Zhang and Q.L. Qiu
J. Alloys Compd. 196, p.37-40 (1993)

108. Formation of a Metastable Cubic Phase in an Immiscible Fe-Ag System by Ion Mixing
F. Pan and ***B.X. Liu***

J. Phys.: Condens. Matter 5(23), p.L315-L318 (1993)

109. Irradiation Induced Texture of Ag and Fe Grains in Ag/Fe Multilayers

B.X. Liu, F. Pan, T. Yang and K. Tao

Nucl. Instr. Meth. in Phys. Res. B 82, p.435-441 (1993)

110. Enhancement of Magnetic Moment of Iron Atoms in the Fe/Au Nanomultilayers

F. Pan, K. Tao and ***B.X. Liu***

J. Appl. Phys. 74(3), p.1929-1932 (1993)

111. Formation of Metastable Carbide and Fractal Structures in Co Thin Films by Carbon Ion Implantation

B.X. Liu and K. Tao

Nucl. Instr. Meth. in Phys. Res. B 80, p.332-335 (1993)

112. Construction of Free Energy Diagram and Phase Formation by Ion Mixing in the Ni-Nb System

H.Y. Bai, Z.J. Zhang and ***B.X. Liu***

Nucl. Instr. Meth. in Phys. Res. B 80, p.421-423 (1993)

113. Irradiation Induced Amorphization and Free Energy Calculation in Immiscible Fe-Cu Multilayers

H.Y. Bai and ***B.X. Liu***

Chin. Phys. Lett. 10, p.531-534 (1993)

114. A Preliminary Study of the Formation of WSi_2 by High-Current W Ion Implantation

D.H. Zhu, H.B. Lu, K. Tao and ***B.X. Liu***

J. Phys.: Condens. Matter 5(31), p.5505-5512 (1993)

115. Free Energy Diagram and Spontaneous Vitrification of an Ion Mixed Metastable Hexagonal Phase in the Ni-Mo System

B.X. Liu, Z.J. Zhang and H.Y. Bai

J. Non-Cryst. Solids 156-158, p.603-607 (1993)

116. Magnetic Properties of Vapor-Deposited Iron-Noble-Metal Mulilayers

B.X. Liu and F. Pan

Phys. Rev. B 48(14), p.10276-10283 (1993)

117. Fe/Pd Nano-Multilayers Prepared by Vapor Deposition, and Their Magnetic Anomaly

F. Pan, T. Yang, J. Zhang and ***B.X. Liu***

J. Phys.: Condens. Matter 5(40), p.L507-L514 (1993)

118. Experimental Evidence of Fractal Evolution Towards Equilibrium Morphology in the Fe-Ag and Co-Yb Films

B.X. Liu, F. Pan and J.R. Ding

Phys. Stat. Sol. (A) 140(2), p.K75-K79 (1993)

119. Reverse Martensitic Phase Transition Induced in Nb-Co Multilayers by Ion Irradiation

B.X. Liu and Z.J. Zhang

J. Mater. Res. 9, p.357-361 (1994)

120. Non-Equilibrium Soldi Phases Formed in Zr-Nb System with Positive Heat of Formation

O. Jin and ***B.X. Liu***

J. Phys.: Condens. Matter 6, p.L39-L42 (1994)

121. Solid State Phase Transition Induced by Ion Irradiation in the Co-Nb System: Experiments and Thermodynamics

Z.J. Zhang and ***B.X. Liu***

J. Phys.: Condens. Matter 6(13), p.2647-2658 (1994)

122. Microstructure and Magnetic Properties of Co/Pd Multilayer Films
T. Yang, F. Pan and ***B.X. Liu***
Phys. Stat. Sol. (A) 142(2), p.443-450 (1994)

123. A Possible New Fe-Cu Alloy Phase with Two Dimensional Long-Range Order
F. Pan, K. Tao, T. Yang and ***B.X. Liu***
Phys. Stat. Sol. (A) 142(1), p.K33-K36 (1994)

124. Metastable Phases Synthesized by Ion Beams and Thermodynamic Interpretation in Binary Metal Systems
B.X. Liu and Z.J. Zhang
Mater. Sci. Eng. A 179, p.189-192 (1994)

125. Synthesis of β- and α-$FeSi_2$ Phases by Fe Ion Implantation into Si Using Metal Vapor Vacuum Arc Ion Source
B.X. Liu, D.H. Zhu, H.B. Lu, F. Pan and K. Tao
J. Appl. Phys. 75(8), p.3847-3854 (1994)

126. Thermodynamics and Crystallographic Mechanism of Metastable Phase Formation in the Nb-Fe, Nb-Co, and Nb-Ni Systems by Ion Mixing
Z.J. Zhang and ***B.X. Liu***
J. Appl. Phys. 75(10), p.4948-4952 (1994)

127. Formation of Non-Equilibrium Solid Phases by Ion Irradiation in the Ni-Ta System and Their Thermdoynamic and Growth-Kinetic Interpretation
B.X. Liu and Z.J. Zhang
Phys. Rev. B 49(18), p.12519-12527 (1994)

128. Solid-State Reaction to Synthesize Ni-Mo Metastable Alloys
Z.J. Zhang and ***B.X. Liu***
J. Appl. Phys. 76(6), p.3351-3356 (1994)

129. Non-Equilibrium Crystalline Phases Formed in the Co-Ta System by Ion Beam Mixing
Z.J. Zhang and ***B.X. Liu***
J. Phys.: Condens. Matter 6(43), p.9065-9074 (1994)

130. Polarization of Pd Atoms in Ni/Pd Magnetic Multilayers
T. Yang, ***B.X. Liu***, F. Pan, J. Lou and K. Tao
J. Phys.: Condens. Matter 7(6), p.1121-1128 (1995)

131. Microstructure Evolution in the Zr-Mo Multilayers Induced by Ion Irradiation
O. Jin and ***B.X. Liu***
J. Phys.: Condens. Matter 7(14), p.2667-2672 (1995)

132. Refractory Metal Silicides Synthesized by Metal Vapor Vacuum Arc Ion Source Implantation
D.H. Zhu and ***B.X. Liu***
J. Appl. Phys. 77(8), p.3690-3696 (1995)

133. Anomalous Alloying Behavior Induced by Ion Irradiation in a System with a Large Positive Heat of Mixing
Z.J. Zhang, O. Jin and ***B.X. Liu***
Phys. Rev. B 51(13), p.8076-8085 (1995)

134. Ion-Irradiation Induced Solid State Phase Transformation in Some Metal Systems
B.X. Liu and Z.J. Zhang

Nucl. Instr. Meth. in Phys. Res. B 99(1-4), p.787-789 (1995)

135. Linear Relationship of the Enhanced Magnetization of Fe Atoms versus the Radius Difference of the Constituent Metals in Fe/F.C.C. Metal Multilayers

F. Pan, T. Yang and ***B.X. Liu***

Phys. Stat. Sol. (A) 149(2), p.677-683 (1995)

136. Alloying Behavior Induced by Ion Mixing in a System with Positive Heat of Formation

O. Jin and ***B.X. Liu***

J. Appl. Phys. 78(1), p.149-154 (1995)

137. Formation of Ti Silicides by Metal-Vapor Vacuum Arc Ion Source Implantation

D.H. Zhu and ***B.X. Liu***

J. Appl. Phys. 77(12), p.6257-6262 (1995)

138. Role of Interface in Ion-Induced Alloy Phase Formation in an Immiscible Y-Ta System

Z.J. Zhang and ***B.X. Liu***

Phys. Rev. B 51(22), p.16475-16478 (1995)

139. Correlation of Electron/Atom Ratio with Structural Stability in Mo-Fe, Mo-Co and Mo-Ni Alloys

Z.J. Zhang and ***B.X. Liu***

J. Phys.: Condens. Matter 7(23), p.L293-L298 (1995)

140. Metastable Phase Formation by Ion Mixing in the Hf-Nb System with a Positive Heat of Formation

O. Jin, Y. Ye, and ***B.X. Liu***

J. Phys.: Condens. Matter 7(41), p.7959-7967 (1995)

141. Formation of a $CoSi_2$ Layer by Co Ion Implantation Using a Metal Vapor Vacuum Arc Ion Source

D.H. Zhu, Y.G. Chen and ***B.X. Liu***

Nucl. Instr. Meth. in Phys. Res. B 101(4), p.394-399 (1995)

142. Spontaneous Vitrification in the Au-Ta System with a Small Size Difference

F. Pan, Y.G. Chen and ***B.X. Liu***

Appl. Phys. Lett. 67(6), p.780-782 (1995)

143. Magnetic Properties of Fe/Al Multilayers with Double-Periodicity Modulated Structure

F. Pan, ***B.X. Liu*** and K. Tao

Phys. Stat. Sol. (A) 151(2), p.407-413 (1995)

144. Role of Interface in Ion Mixing Induced Amorphization in the Ag-Mo System with Very Large Positive Heat of Formation

O. Jin, Z.J. Zhang and ***B.X. Liu***

Appl. Phys. Lett. 67(11), p.1524-1526 (1995)

145. Metastable Phases Formed by Ion Mixing in the Hf-Nb System with a Positive Heat of Formation

O. Jin, Y. Ye and ***B.X. Liu***

J. Phys.: Condens. Matter 7(41), p.7959-7967 (1995)

146. Interface Reactions of an Ag/Cr/AlN Sandwich during Annealing between 250 and 650℃

F. Pan, K. Tao, Y. Du, ***B.X. Liu***

Thin Solid Film 269, p.47-50 (1995)

147. The Establishment of a Potential-pH Diagram for Phosphorous Implanted Iron in Aqueous Solutions

X.D. Bai, D.H. Zhu and ***B.X. Liu***

Nucl. Instr. Meth. in Phys. Res. B 103(4), p.440-445 (1995)

148. Metastable Alloys Synthesized by Ion Mixing and Thermodynamic and Kinetic Modelling
B.X. Liu, Z.J. Zhang, O. Jin and F. Pan
Nucl. Instr. Meth. in Phys. Res. B 106(1-4), p.17-22 (1995)

149. Metal Vapor Vacuum Arc Ion Implantation to Synthesize $FeSi_2$ Layers on Si(100) and Si(111)
D.H. Zhu, Y.G. Chen and ***B.X. Liu***
Phys. Stat. Sol. (a) 152(2), p.467-476 (1995)

1996 年(150—166, 共 17 篇)

150. A New Silicidation Technique Metal Vapor Vacuum Arc Ion Implantation
D.H. Zhu, Y. G. Chen and ***B.X. Liu***
Ion Beam Modification of Materials, p.1098-1101 (1996)

151. Ion-Mixing-Induced Amorphization in an Immiscible Au-Mo System with a Small Size Difference
F. Pan and ***B.X. Liu***
J. Phys.: Condens. Matter 8(4), p.383-388 (1996)

152. Size Effect on Glass-Forming Ability in the Au-Ta System upon Ion Mixing
F. Pan, Y.G. Chen, Z.J. Zhang and ***B.X. Liu***
J. Non-Cryst. Solids 194(3), p.305-311 (1996)

153. Interface Enhanced Glass Forming Ability under Ion Mixing/Solid-State Reaction in an Immiscible Hf-Ta System
B.X. Liu, O. Jin and Y. Ye
J. Phys.: Condens. Matter 8(6), p.L79-L82 (1996)

154. Interface-Generated Vitrification in the Y-Mo System with a Small Positive Heat of Mixing
B.X. Liu and Z.J. Zhang
J. Phys.: Condens. Matter 8(11), p.L165-L171 (1996)

155. Unusual Alloying Behavior Observed in the Immiscible Ag-Mo and Ag-Nb Systems under Ion Irradiation
O. Jin and ***B.X. Liu***
Nucl. Instr. Meth. in Phys. Res. B 114(1-2), p.56-63 (1996)

156. Anodic and Air Oxidation of Niobium Studied by Ion Beam Analysis with Implanted Xe Marker
X.D. Bai, D.H. Zhu, ***B.X. Liu***
Nucl. Instr. Meth. in Phys. Res. B 114(1-2), p.64-69 (1996)

157. Hexagonal-Closed-Packed Face-Centered-Cubic Ansformation in Irradiated Hafnium Thin Films
O. Jin and ***B.X. Liu***
Mater. Lett. 27(4-5), p.165-169 (1996)

158. The Effect of Fe Layer Thickness on the Magnetic Moment in Fe/Cr Multilayers Prepared by Vapor Deposition
F. Pan, Y.D. Fan, K. Tao and ***B.X. Liu***
Phys. Stat. Sol. (a) 153(2), p.481-485 (1996)

159.Amorphous Films Formed by Solid-State Reaction in an Immiscible Y-Mo System and Their Structural Relaxation
Y.G. Chen and ***B.X. Liu***
Appl. Phys. Lett. 68(22), p.3096-3098 (1996)

160. Synthesize and Characterization of Iron Carbonitride Ultrafine Particles

X.Q. Zhao, Y. Liang, Z.Q. Hu and ***B.X. Liu***

J. Appl. Phys. 79(10), p.7911-7915 (1996)

161. Free Energy Diagram and Spontaneous Vitrification of an Ion-Mixed Metastable Hexagonal Phase in the Ni-Mo System

H.Y. Bai and ***B.X. Liu***

J. Mater. Sci. Lett. 15(13), p.1189-1191 (1996)

162. Thermodynamic Interpretation of the Martensitic Transformation in Ultrafine γ-Fe(N) Particles

X.Q. Zhao, L.A. Yong, Z.Q.Hu and ***B.X. Liu***

Jpn. J Appl. Phys. 35(8), p.4468-4473 (1996)

163. The Oxidation Behavior and Magnetic Properties of Iron Carbonitride Ultrafine Particles

X.Q. Zhao, Y. Liang, Z.Q. Hu and ***B.X. Liu***

J. Mater. Res. 11(11), p.2689-2692 (1996)

164. Oxidation Characteristics and Magnetic Properties of Iron Carbide and Iron Ultrafine Particles

X.Q. Zhao, Y. Liang, Z.Q. Hu and ***B.X. Liu***

J. Appl. Phys. 80(10), p.5857-5860 (1996)

165. Formation of Amorphous Alloys by Ion Mixing or Solid-State Reaction and Its Thermodynamics in Binary Metal Systems

B.X. Liu and Y.G. Chen

Proceedings of International Conference on Microstructures and Functions of Materials September 9-11, 1996 Tokyo, Japan

166. Oxidation Behavior and Magnetic Properties of Metallic Ultrafine Particies

X.Q. Zhao, ***B.X. Liu,*** Y. Liang, Z.Q. Hu

J. Magn. Magn. Mater. 164(3), p.401-410 (1996)

1997年(167—190, 共24篇)

167. Formation of Amorphous Alloys through Multilayer Method in an Immiscible Y-Nb System

Y.G. Chen, ***B.X. Liu*** and Q. Zhang

J. Phys.: Condens. Matter 9(2), p.389-394 (1997)

168. Amorphous Films Formed through Multilayer Technique in an Immiscible Y-Mo System and Their Elastic Properties

Y.G. Chen and ***B.X. Liu***

J. Phys. D: Appl. Phys. 30(4), p.510-516 (1997)

169. Synthesize of Metallic Glasses in Immiscible Mo-Cu System by Ion Mixing of Multilayers

Y.G. Chen, ***B.X. Liu***

Chin. Phys. Lett. 14(3), p.194-197 (1997)

170. Chemical and Interface Effects on Glass Forming Ability under Ion Mixing in Zr-Ta System of Positive Heat of Formation

O. Jin, ***B.X. Liu***

J. Non-Cryst. Solid 211(1-2), p.180-186 (1997)

171. Visible Photoluminescence Induced in Si/SiO_2 Samples by Si Implantation

A.D. Lan, ***B.X. Liu*** and X.D. Bai

J. Phys.: Condens. Matter 9(23), p.4987-4993 (1997)

172. Interface-Driven Solid-State Alloying in an Immiscible Cu-W System

Y.G. Chen and ***B.X. Liu***

J. Phys. D: Appl. Phys. 30(12), p.1729-1733 (1997)

173. Irradiation-Induced Alloying in an Immiscible Ta-Ti System

Y.G. Chen, Q. Zhang, ***B.X. Liu***

Nucl. Instr. Meth. in Phys. Res. B 124(4), p.523-527 (1997)

174. Luminescence from Si/SiO_2 with Si Implantation

A.D. Lan, ***B.X. Liu*** and X.D. Bai

Chin. Phys. Lett. 14(7), p.549-552 (1997)

175. Visible Luminescence Induced by Si-Ion Implantation into Si-Single Crystals Covered with a Thin SiO_2 Layer

A.D. Lan, ***B.X. Liu*** and X.D. Bai

Jpn. J Appl. Phys. Part 2, Lett. 36(8A), p.L1018-L1021(1997)

176. Amorphous Alloys Formed by Ion Mixing or Solid-State Reaction in Immiscible Y-Refractory Metal Systems and Their Elastic Properties

Y.G. Chen and ***B.X. Liu***

Nucl. Instr. Meth. in Phys. Res. B 127-128, p.145-148 (1997)

177. Si-Ion Implantation-Induced Luminescence from Si Single Crystals with a SiO_2 Overlayer

A.D. Lan, X. D. Bai and ***B.X. Liu***

Nucl. Instr. Meth. in Phys. Res. B 127-128, p.503-506 (1997)

178. Formation of Amorphous Films by Solid-State Reaction in an Immiscible Y-W System

Y.G. Chen and ***B.X. Liu***

Appl. Phys. A 65(1), p.73-76 (1997)

179. Formation and Theoretical Modelling of Non-Equilibrium Alloy Phases by Ion Mixing

B.X. Liu and O. Jin

Review Article, Phys. Stat. Sol. (a) 161(1), p.3-33 (1997)

180. Observations of Ion-Induced Alloy Phase Formation in an Immiscible Y-Ta System

Y.G. Chen and ***B.X. Liu***

J. Non-Cryst. Solids 217(2-3), p.308-316 (1997)

181. Alloy Phases Formed in Immiscible Cu-Mo and Cu-W Systems by Multilayer-Technique

Y.G. Chen and ***B.X. Liu***

J. Alloys Compd. 261(1-2), p.217-224 (1997)

182. Evidence of Diffusion-Controlled Itrification in Ni/Zr Bilayer at Medium Temperatures by Molecular-Dynamics Simulation

W.S. Lai and ***B.X. Liu***

Europhys. Lett. 39(4), p.401-405 (1997)

183. Surface Hardening of Al by High Current Fe-Ion Implantation

K.Y. Gao and ***B.X. Liu***

J. Appl. Phys. 82(5), p.2209-2214 (1997)

184. Magnetic Properties of Fcc Iron in Fe-Pt Nano-Scale Multilayers

M. Zhang, F. Pan and ***B.X. Liu***

J. Phys.: Condens. Matter 9(36), p.7623-7630 (1997)

185. Molecular Dynamics Simulation of Amorphization Process in Ni-Zr Multilayers upon Annealing at Medium Temperatures

W.S. Lai and ***B.X. Liu***

J. Phys.: Condens. Matter 9(35), p.L483-490 (1997)

186. Irradiation-Induced Alloying in Immiscible Mo-Cu System Through Multilayer Technique

Y.G. Chen and ***B.X. Liu***

J. Appl. Phys. 82(8), p.3815-3820 (1997)

187. Structure and Magnetic Properties of the Oxide Layers on Iron Ultrafine Particles

X.Q. Zhao, ***B.X. Liu,*** Y. Liang and Z.Q.Hu

Appl. Phys. A 64(5), p.483-486 (1997)

188. Different Driving Force for Metallic Glass Formation in Nb-Ni and Nb-Y Systems by Ion Mixing and Solid-State Reaction

Y.G. Chen and ***B.X. Liu***

Mater. Lett. 33(3-4), p.167-173 (1997)

189. High Current Ni-Ion Implantation into Al Films

K.Y. Gao and ***B.X. Liu***

Nucl. Instr. Meth. in Phys. Res. B 132(1), p.68-72 (1997)

190. Annealing-Induced Blue Shift in Luminescence Band from Si-Implanted SiO_2 Layer

A.D. Lan, ***B.X. Liu*** and X.D. Bai

J. Appl. Phys. 82(10), p. 5144-5147 (1997)

1998年(191—212, 共22篇)

191. Magnetic Properties and Microstructure of Fe/Ti Nano-Scale Multilayers

M. Zhang, F. Pan and ***B.X. Liu***

J. Magn. Magn. Mater. 182(1-2), p.89-95(1998)

192. Metastable Alloys Synthesized by Ion Mixing in Immiscible Ti-Nb and Ti-Ta Systems

Y.G. Chen and ***B.X. Liu***

Mater. Sci. Eng. B 52(1), p.1-7 (1998)

193. Observations of Unusual Modulated Structure with Double-Periodicity in Fe-Al Multilayers

F. Pan, ***B.X. Liu***, J. Luo and K. Tao

Thin Solid Films 311(1-2), p.89-92 (1998)

194. Some New Nd-Rich Carbides Formed by Solid-State Reaction of $Nd_2Fe_{14}B$ and Carbon

F. Pan, M. Zhang, R.F. Zhao, ***B.X. Liu*** and M.Tokunaga

J. Phys. D 31(5), p.488-493 (1998)

195. High Current Ni- and Fe-Ion Implantation into Al Surface to Modify Mechanical Properties

B.X. Liu and K.Y. Gao

Mater. Chem. Phys. 54(1-3), p.309-312 (1998)

196. Luminescence Band Evolution in Si Implanted SiO_2 upon High Temperature Annealing

B.X. Liu, A.D. Lan and X.D. Bai

Mater. Chem. Phys. 54(1-3), p.356-359 (1998)

197. Diffusion-Limited and Asymmetric Growth of Amorphous Layer in Ni/Zr Bilayer upon Annealing

W.S. Lai and ***B.X. Liu***

J. Mater. Res. 13(6), p.1712-1716(1998)

198. Formation of Zr-Disilicide by High-Current Zr Ion Implantation into Si Using Metal Vapor Vacuum Arc Ion Source

K.Y. Gao, H.N. Zhu, ***B.X. Liu***

Nucl. Instr. and Meth. B 140(1-2), p.129-136 (1998)

199. A Comparative Study of Metastable Alloy Formation by Ion Mixing and Thermal Annealing of Multilayers in Immiscible Y-Zr System

B.X. Liu, Z.J. Zhang and O. Jin

J. Alloys Compd. 270(1-2), p.186-193 (1998)

200. Influence of Interfacial Texture and Asymmetric Growth in Diffusion-Limited Amorphization in Ni-Zr Multilayers upon Medium-Temperature Annealing

W.S. Lai and ***B.X. Liu***

Phys. Rev. B 58(10), p.6063-6073 (1998)

201. Construction of an N-Body Potential and Molecular Dynamics Study of Interfacial Reaction in the Ni/Mo Bilayer

Q. Zhang, W.S. Lai, ***B.X. Liu***

Europhys. Lett. 43(4), p.416-421 (1998)

202. Amorphous Co-Mo Alloy Films Obtained by Alternate-Deposition

C. Lin, Y.G. Chen and ***B.X. Liu***

Phys. State Sol. (a) 169(1), p.105-113 (1998)

203. Solid-State Amorphization in the Ni/Mo Multilayered Films Studied with Molecular-Dynamics Simulation

Q. Zhang, W.S. Lai and ***B.X. Liu***

Phys. Rev. B 58(20), p.14020-14030 (1998)

204. Low Temperature Ion Beam Synthesis of $NiSi_2$ Layers with Fine Electrical Property

K.Y. Gao, ***B.X. Liu***

Nucl. Instr. Meth. in Phys. Res. B 143(4), p.499-502 (1998)

205. Analysis of Surface and Interface Modifications of Thin Multilayered Films

M.G. Beghi, C.E. Bottani, P.M. Ossi, R. Pastorelli, M. Poli, B. K. Tanner and ***B.X. Liu***

Surf. Coat. Technol. 100-101(1-3), p.324-328 (1998)

206. Enhancement of Atomic Rearrangement in Top Surface Layers by Low Energy Ions

Z.Q. Ma and ***B.X. Liu***

Chin. Phys. Lett. 15(9), p.668-670 (1998)

207. Ion-Induced Surface and Bulk Displacement Threshold for Epitaxial Growth

Z.Q. Ma, Y.F. Zheng and ***B.X. Liu***

Phys. Stat. Sol. (a) 169(2), p.239-248 (1998)

208. Glass-Forming Ability of Binary Metal Systems

Y.G. Chen and ***B.X. Liu***

Prog. Nat. Sci. 8(2), p.129-133(1998)

209. Magnetic Properties of Fcc Iron in Fe/Fcc Metal Multilayers

F. Pan, M. Zhang and ***B.X. Liu***

Thin Solid Films 334(1-2), p.196-200 (1998)

210. Formation of Non-Equilibrium Solid Phases in the Fe-Nb System by Ion Mixing
C. Lin, J.B. Liu and ***B.X. Liu***
J. Phys.: Condens. Matter 10(48), p.10805-10813 (1998)

211. Synthesis of Metallic Glasses in an Immiscible Y-W System by Solid-Statereaction of Multilayered Films
B.X. Liu and Y.G. Chen
Thin Solid Films 334(1-2), p.201-205 (1998)

212. Is Homogeneous Nucleation of Martensitic Transformation in Iron-Base Alloys Possible?
X.Q. Zhao and ***B.X. Liu***
Scripta Mater. 38(7), p.1137-1142(1998)

1999年(213—237，共25篇)

213. Sketching of Preferred Energy Regime for Ion Beam Assisted Epitaxy
Z.Q. Ma, Y.F. Zheng and ***B.X. Liu***
Appl. Sur. Sci. 137(1-4), p.184-190 (1999)

214. Formation of Metastable Crystalline by Solid-State Reaction in the Ni-Nb Multilayerd Films
G.W. Yang, C. Lin, J.B. Liu and ***B.X. Liu***
J. Phys. D: Appl. Phys. 32(2), p.79-83 (1999)

215. Percolation Network of PdGe Phase Formed on Ge Surface by High Current Pd-Ion Implantation
K.Y. Gao and ***B.X. Liu***
J. Phys.: Condens. Matter 11(1), p.39-45 (1999)

216. Influence of Annealing on the Magnetic Properties of Alternate Deposited Co/Mo Thin Film
C. Lin, Y.G. Chen and ***B.X. Liu***
Thin Solid Films 338(1-2), p.314-319 (1999)

217. High Current Ni-Ion Implantation to Synthesis $NiSi_2$ Layers on Si with Very Low Resistivity
K.Y. Gao and ***B.X. Liu***
Nucl. Instr. Meth. in Phys. Res. B 148(1-4), p.615-620 (1999)

218. Sequential Disordering During Ion-Induced Amorphization in the Mo-Fe Multilayered Films
C. Lin, Y.G. Chen and ***B.X. Liu***
Nucl. Instr. Meth. in Phys. Res. B 148(1-4), p.946-950 (1999)

219. Formation of a Face-Centered-Cubic Phases in Fe-Nb System by Solid-State Reaction
C. Lin, J.B. Liu, K.W. Yang and ***B.X. Liu***
J. Alloys Compd. 283(1-2), p.225-230 (1999)

220. Interface-Driven Alloying and Metallic Glass Formation in Nano-Multilayers in an Immiscible Y-Nb System
Y.G. Chen and ***B.X. Liu***
Acta Mater. 47(4), p.1389-1397 (1999)

221. Formation of High-Conductivity $NiSi_2$ Layer on Si at Zero-Mismatch Temperature by High-Current Ni-Ion Implantation
K.Y. Gao and ***B.X. Liu***
Appl. Phys. A 68(3), p.333-337 (1999)

222. Glass Forming Ability Determined by the Atomic Interaction Potential for the Ni-Mo System

Q. Zhang, W.S. Lai and ***B.X. Liu***

Phys. Rev. B 59(19), p.13521-13524 (1999)

223. Ion Mixing to Synthesize Amorphous and Metastable Crystalline Alloys in the Fe-Ta System

C. Lin, G.W. Yang, J.B. Liu and ***B.X. Liu***

J. Phys. D: Appl. Phys. 32(9), p.953-956 (1999)

224. Phase Evolution in Ni-Nb Multilayers upon Solid-State Reaction

G.W. Yang, C. Lin and ***B.X. Liu***

J. Mater. Res. 14, p.3027-3036 (1999)

225. Irradiaition Induced Nano-Quasicrystals Embedded from Amorphous Matrix in the Equilibrium Immiscible Fe-Cu System

G.W. Yang, W.S. Lai, C. Lin and ***B.X. Liu***

Appl. Phys. Lett. 74(22), p.3305-3307 (1999)

226. Metastable Crystalline Phases Formed in the Fe-Ta System by Solid-State Reaction

C. Lin, G.W. Yang, J.B. Liu and ***B.X. Liu***

J. Alloys Compd. 288(1-2), p.159-163 (1999)

227. Structural Evolution and Metastable Phase Formation in Ni-W Multilayers upon Ion Irradiation

G.W. Yang, C. Lin and ***B.X. Liu***

Appl. Phys. A 69(4), p.403-408 (1999)

228. Metal Silicides Synthesized by High Current Metal-Ion Implantation

B.X. Liu, K.Y. Gao and H.N. Zhu

J. Vac. Sci. Technol. B 17(5), p.2277-2283 (1999)

229. Experimental and Theoretical Studies on Composition Limits of Metallic Glass Formation in the Ni-Mo System

Z.C. Li and ***B.X. Liu***

Chin. Phys. Lett. 16, p.667-669 (1999)

230. Sequential Disordering of Crystalline Lattices in the Ni-Nb Multilayers upon Solid-State Interfacial Reaction

G.W. Yang, C. Lin and ***B.X. Liu***

Mater. Sci. Eng. B 65(2), p.139-143 (1999)

231. Epitaxial $CoSi_2$ Layers Farbricated by a Single-Step Technique of High-Current Co-Ion Implantation

H.N. Zhu and ***B.X. Liu***

J. Phys. D: Appl. Phys. 32(23), p.L119-L123 (1999)

232. Non-Destructive Characterization of Ion-Implanted Diamond

Z.Q. Ma, ***B.X. Liu***, H. Naramoto, Y. Aoki, S. Yamamoto and H. Takeshita

Vacuum 55(3), p.207-217 (1999)

233. Solid-State Amorphization of Ni/Zr Bilayer through Diffusion-Limited-Reaction Observed by Molecular-Dynamics Simulation

W.S. Lai and ***B.X. Liu***

Comput. Mater. Sci. 14(1-4), p.163-168 (1999)

234. Solid-State Amorphization in the Y-Nb and Au-Ta Systems

Y.G. Chen and ***B.X. Liu***

Prog. Nat. Sci. 9(3), p.223-229 (1999)

235. Atomistic Mechanism of Solid-State Amorphization in the Ni-Zr System Revealed by Molecular

Dynamics Simulation
W. S. Lai and ***B.X. Liu***
Prog. Nat. Sci. 9(2), p.133-139 (1999)

236. Metastable Rhombohedral Fe Phase Formed in Fe/Sb Multilayers and Its Magnetic Properties
F. Pan, M. Zhang, M. Ding, ***B.X. Liu***, Y.M. Zhou and D.S. Wang
Phys. Rev. B 59(17), p.11458-11464 (1999)

237. Molecular Dynamics Study of Solid State Interfacial Reaction in the Ni-Mo System
Q. Zhang, W.S. Lai and ***B.X. Liu***
J. Comput. Aided Mater. Des. 6(2-3), p.103-116 (1999)

2000 年(238—266, 共 29 篇)

238. A Possible New Metastable State Observed in the Ni-Nb System by Ion Irradiation
G.W. Yang, C. Lin and ***B.X. Liu***
Nucl. Instr. Meth. in Phys. Res. B 160(1), p.54-58 (2000)

239. Formation of Non-Equilibrium Alloy Phases in Cr-Cu Multilayered Films by Ion Mixing
C. Lin, G.W. Yang, Z.F. Li, ***B.X. Liu***
Mater. Lett. 42(1-2), p.7-11 (2000)

240. Atmoic Structure and Physical Properties of Ni-Nb Amorphous Alloys Determined by an N-Body Potential
Q. Zhang, W.S. Lai and ***B.X. Liu***
J. Non-Cryst. Solid 261(1-3), p.137-145 (2000)

241. Formation of N-Type $CrSi_2$ Semiconductor Layers on Si by High Current Cr Ion Implantation
H.N. Zhu, K.Y. Gao and ***B.X. Liu***
J. Phys. D: Appl. Phys. 33(5), p.L49-L52 (2000)

242. Sequential Formation of Quasicrystalline and Amorphous Phases in the Fe-Nb and Fe-Ta Multilayers upon Ion Irradiation
C. Lin, G.W. Yang and ***B.X. Liu***
J. Appl. Phys. 87(6), p.2821-2824 (2000)

243. Formation of Nb_3Al by Nb Ion Implantation Using Metal Vapor Vacuum Arc Ion Source
W. Miao, K. Tao, ***B.X. Liu*** and B. Li
Nucl. Instr. Meth. in Phys. Res. B 160(3), p.343-348 (2000)

244. Nucleation Thermodynamics of Quantum-Dot in V-Groove Structure
G.W. Yang and ***B.X. Liu***
Phys. Rev. B 61(7), p.4500-4502 (2000)

245. Interfacial Reaction, Amorphization Transition, and Associated Elastic Instability Studied by Molecular Dynamics Simulation in the Ni-Ta System
Q. Zhang, W.S. Lai and ***B.X. Liu***
Phys. Rev. B 61(14), p.9345-9355 (2000)

246. Lattice Stability of Some Ni-Ti Alloy Phases versus Their Chemical Composition and Disordering
W.S. Lai and ***B.X. Liu***
J. Phys.: Condens. Matter 12(5), p.L53-L60 (2000)

247. Characterization of Polycrystalline Grandient Thin Film by X-Ray Diffraction Method

B. Li, K. Tao, X.T. Liu and ***B.X. Liu***

Chin. Phys. 9(4), p.284-289 (2000)

248. Glass-Forming Range of the Ni-Mo System Derived from Molecular Dynamics Simulation and Generalized Lindemann Criterion

Q. Zhang, Z.C. Li, C. Lin, ***B.X. Liu*** and En Ma

J. Appl. Phys. 87(9), p.4147-4152 (2000)

249. Metastable Phases Induced by Ion Irradiation in the Equilibrium Immiscible Fe-Cu System

W. Yang, W.S. Lai, C. Lin and ***B.X. Liu***

J. Appl. Phys. 87(10), p.7232-7241 (2000)

250. Different Alloying Behaviors in Co-Mo Multilayered Films upon Ion Irradiation Thermal Annealing

C. Lin, G.W. Yang and ***B.X. Liu***

Appl. Phys. A 70(4), p.469-473 (2000)

251. Origin of Asymmetric Growth During Solid-State Amorphization Studied with Molecular-Dynamics Simulation

Q. Zhang, W.S. Lai and ***B.X. Liu***

J. Appl. Phys. 87(11), p.7696-7701 (2000)

252. Kinetic Model for Diamond Nucleation upon Chemical Vapor Deposition

G.W. Yang and ***B.X. Liu***

Diamond Relat. Mater. 9(2), p.156-161 (2000)

253. Prediction of Solid-State Amorphization in Binary Metal Systems

C. Lin, G.W. Yang and ***B.X. Liu***

Phys. Rev. B 61(23), p.15649-15652 (2000)

254. $CrSi_2$ Films Synthesized by High Current Cr Ion Implantation and Their Physical Properties

H.N. Zhu and ***B.X. Liu***

Appl. Surf. Sci. 161(1-2), p.240-248 (2000)

255. Pattern Evolution of $NiSi_2$ Grown on a Si Surface upon High-Current Pulsed Ni-Ion Implantation

H.N. Zhu, K.Y. Gao and ***B.X. Liu***

Phys. Rev. B 62(3), p.1647-1650 (2000)

256. Irradiation Induced Amorphization in Metallic Multilayers and Calculation of Glass-Forming Ability from Interatomic Potentials in the Binary Metal Systems

B.X. Liu, W.S. Lai and Q. Zhang

Review Article, Mater. Sci. Eng. R. 29(1-2), p.1-48 (2000)

257. Solid-State Interfacial Reaction and Asymmetric Growth of Amorphous Interlayers in Ni/Nb Multilayers, Molecular-Dynamics Simulation Together with Experiments

Q. Zhang, W.S. Lai and ***B.X. Liu***

Eur. Phys. J. B 16(2), p.223-231 (2000)

258. Solid-Sate Amorphization in Ni/Nb Multilayers Studied by Molecular-Dynamics Simulation Together with Experiments

Q. Zhang, W.S. Lai, G.W. Yang and ***B.X. Liu***

J. Phys.: Condens. Matter 12(31), p.6991-7004 (2000)

259. Structural Stability and Amorphization Transition in the Ni-Ti System Studied by Molecular-Dynamics Simulation with an N-Body Potential

W.S. Lai, Q. Zhang, ***B.X. Liu***, Evan Ma

J. Phys. Soc. of Japan 9, p.2923-2937 (2000)

260. Possible Metastable State in the Ni-W System Predicted by *Ab initio* Calculation

J.B. Liu, G.W. Yang, ***B.X. Liu,*** G. Kress and J. Hafner

Phys. Rev. B 62(17), p.11277-11279 (2000)

261. Formation of DO_{23}-Al_3Zr by Zr Ion Implantation Using a Metal Vapour Vacuum Arc Ion Source

W. Miao, K. Tao, B. Li and ***B.X. Liu***

J. Phys. D: Appl. Phys. 33(18), p.2300-2303 (2000)

262. Damage in Diamond Produced by Analysis Beam

Z.Q. Ma, ***B.X. Liu*** and H.Naramoto

J. Vac. Sci. Technol. A 18(5), p.2267-2270 (2000)

263. Direct Synthesise of Continuous Sarmarium Disilicide Films by Sm-Ion Implantation Using a Metal Vapour Vacuum Arc Ion Source

X.Q. Cheng, H.N. Zhu, R.C. Wang and ***B.X. Liu***

J. Phys.: Condens. Matter 12(44), p.9195-9200 (2000)

264. Interface Assisted Formation of a Metastable Hcp Phase by Ion Mixing Inan Immiscible Ag-Ni System

Z.C. Li, J.B. Liu, Z.F. Li and ***B.X. Liu***

J. Phys.: Condens. Matter 12(44), p.9231-9235 (2000)

265. Proposed Interpretation for Possible Solid-State Amorphization in Some Cu-Based Binary Metal Systems

Z.F. Li, W.S. Lai and ***B.X. Liu***

Appl. Phys. Lett. 77(24), p.3920-3922 (2000)

266. High Current Metal-Ion Implantation to Fabricate Metal Silicides

H.N. Zhu and ***B.X. Liu***

Surf. Coat. Technol. 131(1-3), p.307-316 (2000)

2001 年(267—287, 共 21 篇)

267. Solubility Criterion for Sequential Disordering in Metal-Metal Multilayersupon Solid-State Reaction

W.S. Lai, Q. Zhang, ***B.X. Liu***

Philos. Mag. Lett. 81(1), p.45-53 (2001)

268. Glass-Forming Ability of the Ni-Zr and Ni-Ti Systems by Interatomic Potentials

W.S. Lai and ***B.X. Liu***

J. Mater. Res. 16(2) p.446-450 (2001)

269. Stability of a Noneuilibrium Phase in an Immiscible Ag-Ni System Studied by *Ab initio* Calculations and Ion-Beam-Mixing Experiment

J.B. Liu, C.Z. Li and ***B.X. Liu***

Phys. Rev. B 63(13), 132204 (2001)

270. Pattern Evolution During the Growth of $CrSi_2$ Layers on Si (111) upon High Current Pulsed Cr Ion Implantation

H.N. Zhu and ***B.X. Liu***

Thin Solid Films 384(1), p.53-57 (2001)

271. Irradiation-Induced Amorphization and Growth of Dodecahedral Phase in an Immiscible Co-Cu

System

Z.F. Li and ***B.X. Liu***

Nucl. Instr. Meth. in Phys. Res. B 178(1-4), p.224-228 (2001)

272. Strain-Induced Structural Phase Transition of a Ni Lattice through Dissolving Ta Solute Atoms

Q. Zhang, W.S. Lai and ***B.X. Liu***

Phys. Rev. B 63(21), 212102 (2001)

273. Interface-Mediated Structural Evolution of Immiscible Co-Cu Multilayers upon Solid-State Reaction

Z.F. Li, Q. Zhang, D. P. Yu, C. Lin and ***B.X. Liu***

Phys. Rev. B 64(1), 014102 (2001)

274. Irradiation and Interface Induced Formation of a Nonequilibrium Ag_3Co Phase Predicted by *Ab initio* Calculation

J.B. Liu, Z.F. Li, J.X. Zhang and ***B.X. Liu***

Phys. Rev. B 64(5), 054102 (2001)

275. A Dodecagonal Phase Formed in an Immiscible Co-Ag System by Ion Mixing of Multilayers

Z.C. Li, Z.F. Li and ***B.X. Liu***

J. Phys.: Condens. Matter 13(19), p.L367-L370 (2001)

276. Formation of a Dodecagonal Phase in an Equilibrium Immiscible Co-Cu System Induced by Ion Irradiation and Associated Evolution

Z.F. Li, ***B.X. Liu***

J. Phys.: Condens. Matter 13(25), p.L583-L587 (2001)

277. Metstable Phases Formed in the Immiscible Co-Ag System by Ion Mixing

Z.C. Li, X.Q. Cheng, ***B.X. Liu***

J. Alloys Compd. 327(1-2), p.L1-L3 (2001)

278. Formation of YSi_{2-x} Layers on Si by High-Current Y Ion Implantation

R.S. Wang, X.Q. Cheng, W.S. Lai and ***B.X. Liu***

J. Phys. D: Appl. Phys. 34 (16), p.2465-2468 (2001)

279. Growth of Two-Dimensional Patterns in the Fe-Cu Multilayers Driven Far from Equilibrium by Ion Irradiation

G.W. Yang, C. Lin, ***B.X. Liu***

Mater. Lett. , 51(30), p.231-235 (2001)

280. Critical Solid Solubility of the Ni-Ti System Determined by Moleculardynamics Simulation and Ion Mixing

W.S. Lai, Q. Li, C. Lin and ***B.X. Liu***

Phys. Stat. Sol. B 227(2), p.503-514 (2001)

281. Solid-State Crystal-to-Amorphous Transition in Metal-Metal Multilayeres and Its Thermodyanmic and Atomistic Modelling

B.X. Liu, W.S. Lai and Z.J. Zhang

Adv. Phys. 50(4), p.367-429 (2001)

282. Formation of Al_3Ta by Ta Ion Implantation into Aluminum Using a Metal Vapor Vacuum Arc Ion Source

M. Wei, T. Kun, X.T. Liu, ***B.X. Liu***

Mater. Res. Bull. 36(10), p.1759-1766 (2001)

283. Formation of Al_3Hf by Hf Ion Implantation into Aluminum Using a Metal Vapor Vacuum Arc Ion Source

W. Miao, K. Tao, X.T. Liu, ***B.X. Liu***

Surf. Coat. Technol. 140(2), p.136-140 (2001)

284. Structural Phase Evolution in the Equilibrium Immiscible Co-Cu System Studied by Solid-State Reaction/Ion Beam Mixing of Nano-Sized Multilayers

Z.F. Li and ***B.X. Liu***

J. Phys. Soc. Jpn. 70(12), p.3596-3605 (2001)

285. Observations of Mesk-Like Pattern in the Immiscible Fe-Cu Multilayers upon Rapid Thermal Annealing

G.W. Yang and ***B.X. Liu***

J. Mater. Sci. Lett. 20(23), p.2109-2112 (2001)

286. Modification of Oxidation Resistance of Copper Films by Shallow Implantation

X.Q. Zhao, Y. F. Han, ***B.X. Liu***

J. Appl. Phys. 90(3), p.1638-1641(2001)

287. Boron-Doped Diamond-Like Amorphous Carbon as Photovoltaic Films in Solar Cell

Z.Q. Ma and ***B.X. Liu***

Sol. Energy Mater. Sol. Cells 69(4), p.339-344 (2001)

2002年(288—307, 共20篇)

288. Confirmation of the Nonequilibrium States of AB3 Type in an Immiscible Y-Ta System by *Ab initio* Calculation

J.B. Liu and ***B.X. Liu***

Jpn. J. Appl. Phys. 41(1AB), p.62-63 (2002)

289. Nonequilibrium Hcp and Fcc Phases Formed by Ion Mixing in an Immiscible Ni-Ru System

X.Y. Li, Z.F. Li and ***B.X. Liu***

J. Alloys Compd. 334(1-2), p.167-172 (2002)

290. Formation of a Dodecagonal Phase in the Nano-Sized Ag-Pt Multilayered Films upon Solid-State Reaction

Z.C. Li, L.T. Kong and ***B.X. Liu***

J. Phys.: Condens. Matter 14(1), p.1-5 (2002)

291. *Ab initio* Calculation to Predict Possible Non-Equilibrium Solid Phases in an Immiscible Y-Nb System

L.T. Kong, J.B. Liu and ***B.X. Liu***

J. Phys. Soc. Jpn. 71(1), p.141-143 (2002)

292. Prediction of Possible Metastable Alloy Phases in an Equilibrium Immiscible Y-Mo System by *Ab initio* Calculation

L.T. Kong, J.B. Liu and ***B.X. Liu***

J. Mater. Res. 17(3), p.528-531 (2002)

293. A Proposed Damage Gradient Model for the Sequential Disordering Induced in Sc-Ni Multilayers by Ion Irradiation

L. Hu, Z.F. Li, W.S. Lai and ***B.X. Liu***

J. Phys.: Condens. Matter 14(4), p.731-737 (2002)

294. Metastable States in an Equilibrium Immiscible Ni-Ru System Studied by *Ab initio* Calculation and Ion Mixing Experiemnts

J.B. Liu, X.Y. Li and ***B.X. Liu***

Solid State Commun. 121(6-7), p.375-379 (2002)

295. Formation of $ErSi_2$ Phase and the Associated Fractal Pattern on Si Surface upon High Current Er-Ion Implantation

X.Q. Cheng and ***B.X. Liu***

J. Alloys Compd. 336(1-2), p.253-258 (2002)

296. Correlation of Lattice Constant versus Tunstan Concentration of the Ni-Based Solid Solution Examined by Molecular Dynamics Simulation

L.T. Kong, J.B. Liu, W.S. Lai and ***B.X. Liu***

J. Alloys Compd. 337, p.143-147 (2002)

297. Manipulation of Ordered Latered Structures by Interface-Assisted Ion-Beam Mixing in Immiscible Ag-Co and Ag-Ni Systems

Z.C. Li, D.P. Yu and ***B.X. Liu***

Phys. Rev. B 65(24), 245403 (2002)

298. Structural and Morphological Evolution Emerging in Si Surface Layers upon High-Current Tb-Ion Implantation

X.Q. Cheng and ***B.X. Liu***

Jpn. J. Appl. Phys. 41 (5A), p.2859-2863 (2002)

299. Growth of Fractal Patterns During Irradiation-Induced Amorphization in Nano-Sized Ni-W Multilayers

Z.F. Li and ***B.X. Liu***

Appl. Phys. A 75(3), p.445-448 (2002)

300. Interfacial Reaction of W/Cu Examined by an N-Body Potential Through Molecular Dynamics Simulations

L.T. Kong, X.Y. Li, W.S. Lai, J.B. Liu and ***B.X. Liu***

Jpn. J Appl. Phys. 41(7A), p.4503-4508 (2002)

301. Influence of Layer Thickness on Amorphization Behavior Induced in the Ni-W Multilayers by Ion Irradiation

Z.F. Li and ***B.X. Liu***

J. Phys. Soc. Jpn. 71(9), p.2290-2294 (2002)

302. Proposed Model for Calculating the Standard Formation Enthalpy of Binary Transition-Metal Systems

R.F. Zhang and ***B.X. Liu***

Appl. Phys. Lett. 81(7), p.1219-1221 (2002)

303. Atomistic Modeling of Solid-State Amorphization in an Immiscible Cu-Ta System

H.R. Gong, L.T. Kong, W.S. Lai and ***B.X. Liu***

Phys. Rev. B 66(10), 1040204 (2002)

304. Comparative Study of Nonequilibrium Phase of A_3B and AB_3 Types in the Ni-Mo System by First Principles and Thermodynamic Calculations

J.B. Liu, R.F. Zhang, ***B.X. Liu***

J. Mater. Res. 17(10), p.2720-2726 (2002)

305. Fabrication of $PrSi_2$ Layers and Associated Morphology on Si Surface by a Single-Step High Current Pr-Ion Implantation

X.Q. Cheng and ***B.X. Liu***

J. Alloys Compd. 345(1-2), p.252-256 (2002)

306. Formation of $NdSi_2$ Phase by High-Current Nd-Ion Implantation

X.Q. Cheng, R.S. Wang and ***B.X. Liu***

Jpn. J Appl. Phys. 41(10), p.6127-6131 (2002)

307. Metastable Phase Formation in the Immiscible Ru-Pd System Studied by *Ab initio* Calculation and Ion Mixing

H.B. Guo, X.Y. Li and ***B.X. Liu***

J. Phys. Soc. Jpn. 71(12), p.2933-2935 (2002)

2003年(308—326, 共19篇)

308. *Ab initio* Calculation to Predict the Possible Nonequilibrium A_3B and AB_3 States in the Co-Mo System

H.B. Guo, L.T. Kong, J.B. Liu, ***B.X. Liu***

Solid State Commun. 125(7-8), p.435-437 (2003)

309. Construction of an N-Body Cu-Ta Potential and Study of Interfacial Behavior between Immiscible Cu and Ta through Molecular Dynamics Simulation

L.T. Kong, H.R. Gong, W.S. Lai and ***B.X. Liu***

J. Phys. Soc. Jpn. 72(1), p.5-8 (2003)

310. Formation of an Ordered Structure by Ion Beam Manipulation and Associated Structural Evolution in the Nanosized Pd-Ru Multilayers

X.Y. Li, Z.C. Li and ***B.X. Liu***

J. Phys. Soc. Jpn. 72(1), p.9-12 (2003)

311. Highly Energetic Nonequilibrium Microstructure Fabricated by Ion Beam Manipulation in the Ag-Pd System

Z.C. Li, ***B.X. Liu***

J. Phys.: Condens. Matter 15(8), p.1217-1221 (2003)

312. Construction of an Embedded-Atom Potential for an Immiscible Cu-V System

Y.X. Shen, L.T. Kong, H.R. Gong, W.S. Lai and ***B.X. Liu***

J. Phys. Soc. Jpn. 72(3), p.464-467 (2003)

313. Growth of $DySi_2$ Layers on Si Surface by High-Current Dy-Ion Implantation

X.Q. Cheng, ***B.X. Liu***

Jpn. J. Appl. Phys. 42(7A), p.4469-4472 (2003)

314. Formation of $LaSi_{2-x}$ Layers on Si by High-Current La Ion Implantation

X.J. Tang, X.Q. Cheng, R.S. Wang and ***B.X. Liu***

Jpn. J. Appl. Phys. 42(5A), p.2834-2838 (2003)

315. Role of Interface in Forming Non-Equilibrium Hcp Phase by Ion Mixing in an Immiscible Au-Co System

H.F. Yan, Z.C. Li and ***B.X. Liu***

J. Phys. D: Appl. Phys. 36(6), p.615-619 (2003)

316. Metastable Phase Formation in an Immiscible Cu-Ta System Studied by Ion-Beam Mixing, *Ab initio* Calculation, and Molecular Dynamics Simulation

H.R. Gong, L.T. Kong, W.S. Lai, ***B.X. Liu***

Acta Mater. 51(13), p.3885-3893 (2003)

317. Physical Origin of Ion Mixing Induced Amorphization and Associated Symmetric Growth in the Binary Metal Systems

L.Hu, Z.F. Li, W.S. Lai, ***B.X. Liu***

Nucl. Instr. Meth. in Phys. Res. B, p.127-131 (2003)

318. Formation of $MoSi_2$ and Associated Fractal Growth on Si Surface upon High Current Pulsed Mo-Ion Implantation

X.Q. Cheng, R.S. Wang, X.J. Tang, ***B.X. Liu***

Nucl. Instr. Meth. in Phys. Res. B 207(3), p.301-307 (2003)

319. Amorphous Alloys Synthesized by Interface-Assisted Ion Beam Mixing in the Ag-W System with the Largest Positive Heat of Formation

R.F. Zhang, ***B.X. Liu***

J. Mater. Res. 18(7), p.1499-1501 (2003)

320. Structural Evolution Induced in the Equilibrium Immiscible Cu-V System by Ion Irradiation

L.Hu, ***B.X. Liu***

J. Phys.: Condens. Matter 15(32), p.5543-5549 (2003)

321. Glass-Forming Ability Determined by an N-Body Potential in a Highly Immiscible Cu-W System Through Molecular Dynamics Simulations

H.R. Gong, L.T. Kong, W.S. Lai, ***B.X. Liu***

Phys. Rev. B 68(14), 144201 (2003)

322. Prediction of Metastable Phase Formation in an Immiscible Cu-Cr System from Interatomic Potential and *Ab initio* Calculation

H.R. Gong, L.T. Kong, ***B.X. Liu***

J. Mater. Res. 18(10), p.2300-2303 (2003)

323. Magnetic Properties of Co and Co-Ag Alloys in Equilibrium/Nonequilibrium Structures Studied by ab Initio Calculations

L.T. Kong, R.F. Zhang, Z.C. Li and ***B.X. Liu***

Phys. Rev. B 68(13), 134446 (2003)

324. Interface Stability and Solid-State Amorphization in an Immiscible Cu-Ta System

H.R. Gong and ***B.X. Liu***

Appl. Phys. Lett. 83(22), p.4515-4517 (2003)

325. Metastable Phase Formed in Immiscible Cu-W Multilayers by Ion Mixing

R.F. Zhang, Z.C. Li, ***B.X. Liu***

Jpn. J. Appl. Phys. 42(11), p.7009-7012 (2003)

326. Metastable Alloy Formation in the Immiscible Cu-Ru System by Ion Beam Manipulation

X. He, X.Y. Li and ***B.X. Liu***

J. Phys. Soc. Jpn. 72(12), p.3032-3034 (2003)

2004年(327—350, 共24篇)

327. Effect of Chemical and Magnetic Interactions on Fractal Growth under Eposition-Diffusion-Aggregation in Some Binary Metal Systems

L. Hu and ***B.X. Liu***

Appl. Phys. A 78(3), p.397-400 (2004)

328. Formation of $TaSi_2$ and Associated Fractal Growth on Si Surface upon High Current Pulsed Ta-Ion Implantation

X.Q. Cheng, R.S. Wang, X.J. Tang and ***B.X. Liu***

J. Alloys Compd. 363(1-2), p.231-236 (2004)

329. Formation of $CeSi_2$ on the Si Surface upon High Current Pulsed Ce-Ion Implantation

X.Q. Cheng, X.J. Tang and ***B.X. Liu***

J. Alloys Compd. 365(1-2), p.240-245 (2004)

330. Metastability of an Immiscible Cu-Mo System Calculated from First-Principles and a Derived N-Body Potential

H.R. Gong, L. T. Kong and ***B.X. Liu***

Phys. Rev. B 69 (2), 024202 (2004)

331. Structural Stability and Magnetic Properties of Metastable Fe-Cu Alloys Studied by *Ab initio* Calculations and Molecular Dynamics Simulations

H.R. Gong, L.T. Kong and ***B.X. Liu***

Phys. Rev. B 69 (5), 054203 (2004)

332. Structural Phase Transitions in the Cu-Based Cu-V Solid Solutions Studied by Molecular Dynamics Simulation

Y.X. Shen, H.R. Gong, L.T. Kong and ***B.X. Liu***

J. Alloys Compd. 366 (1-2), p.205-212 (2004)

333. Correlation of Magnetic Moment versus Spacing Distance of Metastable Fcc Structured Iron

L.T. Kong and ***B.X. Liu***

Appl. Phys. Lett. 84(18), p.3627-3629 (2004)

334. Atomic Structures of Nonequilibrium Alloys in an Immiscible Co-Ag System

H.B. Guo and ***B.X. Liu***

J. Mater. Res. 19(5), p.1364-1368 (2004)

335. Proposed Calculation Method for Structural Formation Enthalpy Including Magnetic Energy for Transition Metal Alloys

R.F. Zhang and ***B.X. Liu***

J. Phys. Soc. Jpn. 73(5), p.1097-1100(2004)

336. Structural Stability of Metastable Solid Solution in the Equilibrium Immiscible Ag-Mo System Predicted by *Ab initio* Derived Potential

X.D. Dai, H.R. Gong and ***B.X. Liu***

J. Phys. Soc. Jpn. 73(5), p.1222-1227 (2004)

337. Microchemical Inhomogeneity of Multicomponent Systems and Its Evaluation from Interatomic Potentials

J.H. Li, H.B. Guo, W.S. Lai and ***B.X. Liu***

Phys. Rev. B 69(17), 172201 (2004)

338. Structural Stability and the Correlation of Lattice Constant versus Tantalum Concentration of the Ag-Based Solid Solutions Studied by Molecular Dtynamics Simulation

Y.X. Shen, L.T. Kong, H.R. Gong and ***B.X. Liu***

Jpn. J. Appl. Phys. 43(5A), p.2589-2593 (2004)

339. Study of Metastable Alloy Formation by Thermodynamic Calculation and Ion Beam Manipulation in an Equilibrium Immiscible Au-W System

R.F. Zhang and ***B.X. Liu***

J. Alloys Compd. 375(1-2), p.179-185 (2004)

340. Atomistic Modeling of Metastable Phase Selection of a Highly Immiscible Ag-W System

R.F. Zhang, Y.X. Shen, H.R. Gong, L.T. Kong and ***B.X. Liu***

J. Phys. Soc. Jpn. 73(7), p.2023-2027 (2004)

341. Comparative Study of Metastable Phase Formation in the Immiscible Cu-W System by *Ab initio* Calculation and N-Body Potential

R.F. Zhang, L.T. Kong, H.R. Gong and ***B.X. Liu***

J. Phys.: Condens. Matter 16(29), p.5251-5258 (2004)

342. Calculation of Phonon Spectra to Predict the High-Pressure Metastable Phase in an Equilibrium Immiscible Cu-Ta System

Y. Kong, H.R. Gong and ***B.X. Liu***

Appl. Phys. Lett. 85(9), p.1517-1519 (2004)

343. Unusual Alloying Behavior at the Equilibrium Immiscible Cu-Nb Interfaces

H.R. Gong and ***B.X. Liu***

J. Appl. Phys. 96(5), p.3020-3022 (2004)

344. Influence of Interfacial Texture on Solid-State Amorphization and Associated Asymmetric Growth in Immiscible Cu-Ta Multilayers

H.R. Gong and ***B.X. Liu***

Phys. Rev. B 70(13), 134202 (2004)

345. Glass-Forming Ability Determined from Inter-Atomic Potentials for Some Miscible/Immiscible Binary Metal Systems

B.X. Liu, H.R. Gong, H.B. Guo and L.T. Kong

J. Mater. Sci. 39(16-17), p.5067-5070 (2004)

346. Proposed Definition of Microchemical Inhomogeneity and Application to Characterize Some Selected Miscible/Immiscible Binary Metal Systems

J.H. Li, L.T. Kong and ***B.X. Liu***

J. Phys. Chem. B 108(41), p.16071-16076 (2004)

347. Atomistic Modeling and Thermodynamic Interpretation of the Bridging Phenomenon Observed in the Co-Au System

H.B. Guo, J.H. Li and ***B.X. Liu***

Phys. Rev. B 70(19), 195434 (2004)

348. Metastable Phase Selection of an Immiscible Au-W System Studied by *Ab initio* Calculation, Molecular Dynamics Simulation and Ion-Beam Mixing

R.F. Zhang, Y.X. Shen, L.T. Kong and ***B.X. Liu***

Jpn. J. Appl. Phys. 43(11A), p.7648-7653 (2004)

349. Structural Transition and Glass-Forming Ability of the Ni-Hf Systemstudied by Molecular Dynamics Simulation

J.H. Li, L.T. Kong and ***B.X. Liu***

J. Mater. Res. 19(12), p.3547-3555 (2004)

350. Correlation of Magnetic Moment Versus Spacing Distance of Metastable Fcc Structured Iron

L.T. Kong and ***B.X. Liu***

Appl. Phys. Lett. 84(18), p.3627-3629 (2004)

2005年(351—373, 共23篇)

351. Structural Stability and Homogeneity of the Nonequilibrium Co-Ag Alloys

H.B. Guo and ***B.X. Liu***

J. Phys. Soc. Jpn. 74(1), p.375-381 (2005)

352. Crystallographic and Lattice Point Correlations of a New Hcp-to-Fcc Martensitic Transformation Observed in the Ni-Hf System

J.H. Li, H.B. Guo and ***B.X. Liu***

Acta Mater. 53(3), p.743-748 (2005)

353. Metastable Isomorphous Phase Diagram of the Peritectic Ni-Ru System Predicted by *Ab initio* and Molecular Dynamics Calculations

J.H. Li, H.B. Guo, L.T. Kong and ***B.X. Liu***

Phys. Rev. B 71(1), 014107 (2005)

354. Atomistic Modeling of Crystal-to-Amorphous Transition and Associated Kinetics in the Ni-Nb System by Molecular Dynamics Simulations

X.D. Dai, J.H. Li and ***B.X. Liu***

J. Phys. Chem. B 109(10), p.4717-4725 (2005)

355. Formation of Amorphous Alloys by Ion Beam Mixing and Its Multiscale Theoretical Modeling in the Equilibrium Immiscible Sc-W System

R.F. Zhang, Y.X. Shen, H.F. Yan and ***B.X. Liu***

J. Phys. Chem. B 109(10), p.4391-4397 (2005)

356. Nonequilibrium Solid Phase Formation Studied by Lattice Dynamics Calculation and Ion Beam Mixing in an Immiscible Co-Ag System

Y. Kong, H.B. Guo, H.F. Yan and ***B.X. Liu***

J. Phys. Chem. B 109(19), p.9362-9367 (2005)

357. Thermodynamic and Atomistic Modeling of Irradiation-Induced Amorphization in Nanosized Metal-Metal Multilayers

B.X. Liu, Z.C. Li and H.R. Gong

Surf. Coat. Technol. 196(1-3), p.2-9 (2005)

358. Response to "Comment on 'Proposed Model for Calculating the Standard Formation Enthalpy of Binary Transition-Metal Systems'"

R.F. Zhang and ***B.X. Liu***

Appl. Phys. Lett. 86(21), 216104 (2005)

359. Orientation and Composition Dependences of the Surface Energy and Work Function Observed by First-Principles Calculation for the Mo-Hf System

L.T. Kong and ***B.X. Liu***

J. Phys. Soc. Jpn. 74(6), p.1766-1771 (2005)

360. Calculation of Ferromagnetic States in Metastable Bcc and Hcp Ni by Projector-Augmented Wave Method

X. He, L.T. Kong and ***B.X. Liu***

J. Appl. Phys. 97(10), 106107 (2005)

361. Construction of N-Body Potentials for Hcp-Bcc Metal Systems within the Framework of Embedded Atom Method

R.F. Zhang, Y. Kong and ***B.X. Liu***

Phys. Rev. B 71(21), 214102 (2005)

362. Comparative Study of Irradiation-Induced and Thermally Induced Structural Phase Transitions in Equilibrium Immiscible Fe-Ag Systems

X.Y. Li, H.F. Yan and ***B.X. Liu***

J. Phys. Soc. Jpn. 74(7), p.2007-2010 (2005)

363. Role of Spatial Valence Charge Density on the Metastability of an Immiscible Binary Metal System at Equilibrium

Y. Kong, J.H. Li, L.T. Kong and ***B.X. Liu***

Phys. Rev. B 72(2), 024209 (2005)

364. Enhanced Magnetic Moment of Fe in Fcc-Structured Fe-Ag and Fe-Au Alloys Synthesized by Ion-Beam Manipulation

X.Y. Li, L.T. Kong and ***B.X. Liu***

Phys. Rev. B 72(5), 054118 (2005)

365. Solid-State Amorphization Observed in the Equilibrium-Immiscible Cu-Re System by Molecular Dynamics Simulations

J.H. Li, S.H. Liang and ***B.X. Liu***

J. Phys. Chem. B 109, p.16463-16468 (2005)

366. Evidence of a High-Spin Ferromagnetic State in Fcc-Structured Fe-Ag (Au) Alloys Synthesized by Ion Beam Manipulation

X.Y. Li, L.T. Kong and ***B.X. Liu***

J. Phys.: Condens. Matter 17(29), p.4647-4651 (2005)

367. Thermodynamic Criterion for the Formation of Laves Phases in Binary Transition-Metal Systems

R.F. Zhang and ***B.X. Liu***

Philos. Mag. Lett. 85(6), p.283-287 (2005)

368. Structural Phase Transition Induced by Ion Irradiation in the Equilibrium Immiscible Ag-Co System

H.F. Yan and ***B.X. Liu***

Appl. Phys. A 81(7), p.1435-1439 (2005)

369. Stability of the Metastable Phases in the Co-Ta System Studied by *Ab initio* and Thermodynamic Calculations Together with Ion-Beam-Mixing Experiment

X. He, L.T. Kong and ***B.X. Liu***

J. Phys. Soc. Jpn. 74(9), p.2501-2505 (2005)

370. First-Principles Calculations of the Isosteric Bain Path of Cobalt

H.B. Guo, J.H. Li, L.T. Kong and ***B.X. Liu***

Phys. Rev. B 72(13), 132102 (2005)

371. Four-Parameter Equation of State of Solids

J.H. Li, S.H. Liang, H.B. Guo and ***B.X. Liu***

Appl. Phys. Lett. 87(19), 194111 (2005)

372. Dual-Phase Metallic Glass and Its Two-Dimensional Fractal Morphology

R.F. Zhang, J.H. Li and ***B.X. Liu***

J. Phys. Soc. Jpn. 74(11), p.2937-2940 (2005)

373. Structural Phase Transformation in Ni-Hf and Ni-Ti Systems Studied by Molecular Dynamics Simulation

J.H. Li and ***B.X. Liu***

J. Phys. Soc. Jpn. 74(10), p.2699-2702 (2005)

2006年(374—385, 共12篇)

374. Formation and Structural Anomaly of the Metastable Phases in an Immiscible Ag-Mo System Studied by Ion Beam Mixing and Molecular Dynamics Simulation

K.P. Tai, X.D. Dai, Y.X. Shen and ***B.X. Liu***

J. Phys. Chem. B 110(1), p.595-606 (2006)

375. Distinct Magnetic States of Metastable Fcc Structured Fe and Fe-Cu Alloys Studied by *Ab initio* Calculations

L.T. Kong, ***B.X. Liu***

J. Alloys Compd. 414(1-2), p. 36-41 (2006)

376. Spinodal Decomposition Induced in a Highly Immiscible Ag-Mo System by Ion Irradiation

K.P. Tai, X.D. Dai and ***B.X. Liu***

Appl. Phys. Lett. 88(18), 184103 (2006)

377. Extended Finnis-Sinclair Potential for Bcc and Fcc Metals and Alloys

X.D. Dai, Y. Kong, J.H. Li and ***B.X. Liu***

J. Phys.: Condens. Matter 18(19), p.4527-4542 (2006)

378. First-Principles Calculations of the Structural Stability and Magnetic Property of the Metastable Phases in the Equilibrium Immiscible Co-Au System

Y. Kong, L.T. Kong and ***B.X. Liu***

J. Phys.: Condens. Matter 18(17), p.4345-4353 (2006)

379. Structure Stability and Magnetic Properties of the Ni-Ru System Studied by *Ab initio* and Molecular Dynamics Calculations Together with Ion Beam Mixing

X. He, L.T. Kong, J.H. Li, X.Y. Li and ***B.X. Liu***

Acta Mater. 54(12), p.3375-3381 (2006)

380. Icositetrahedral and Icosahedral Atomic Configurations Observed in the Nb-Ag Metallic Glasses Synthesized by Ion Beam Mixing

K.P. Tai, N. Gao, X.D. Dai, J.H. Li, W.S. Lai and ***B.X. Liu***

Appl. Phys. Lett. 89(9), 094108 (2006)

381. Solid-State Amorphization Observed in Ni-Sc System by Molecular Dynamics Simulation

S.H. Liang, J.H. Li and ***B.X. Liu***

J. Phys. Soc. Jpn. 75(8), 084603 (2006)

382. Formation and Structural Transformation of the Nonequilibrium Phases in the Ru-Ta System Induced by Ion Beam Mixing

W.C. Wang, Y.X. Shen, J.H. Li, X.Y. Li and ***B.X. Liu***

J. Phys.: Condens. Matter 18(43), p.9911-9916 (2006)

383. Observations of Distinct Atomic Packings in Cu-Nb Metallic Glasses Synthesized by Ion Beam Mixing

K.P. Tai, T.L. Wang, J.H. Li and ***B.X. Liu***

J. Phys.: Condens. Matter 18(37), p.L459-L464 (2006)

384. Nonequilibrium Solid Phases Studied by Thermodynamic Calculation, Molecular Dynamics Simulation, *Ab initio* Calculation and Ion-Beam Manipulation in an Immiscible Au-Co System at Equilibrium

H.F. Yan, H.B. Guo, Y.X. Shen, J.H. Li, ***B.X. Liu***

Acta Mater. 54(19), p.5293-5304 (2006)

385. Observation of Magnetism in the Nanoscale Amorphous Ruthenium Clusters Prepared by Ion Beam Mixing

W.C. Wang, Y. Kong, X. He and ***B.X. Liu***

Appl. Phys. Lett. 89(26), 262511 (2006)

2007 年(386—407, 共 22 篇)

386. Metastable Phase Formation in the Immiscible Cu-Co System Studied by Thermodynamic, Molecular Dynamics and *Ab initio* Calculations Together with Ion Beam Mixing

H.F. Yan, Y.X. Shen, H.B. Guo and ***B.X. Liu***

J. Phys.: Condens. Matter 19(2), 026219 (2007)

387. Atomistic Mechanism of Interfacial Reaction and Asymmetric Growth Kinetics in an Immiscible Cu-Ru System at Equilibrium

X. He, S.H. Liang, J.H. Li and ***B.X. Liu***

Phys. Rev. B 75(4), 045431 (2007)

388. A Binomial Truncation Function Proposed for the Second-Moment Approximation of Tight-Binding Potential and Application in the Ternary Ni-Hf-Ti System

J.H. Li, X.D. Dai, T.L. Wang and ***B.X. Liu***

J. Phys.: Condens. Matter 19(8), 086228 (2007)

389. First-Principles Calculation of the Structural, Magnetic, and Electronic Properties of the Co_xCu_{1-x} Solid Solutions Using Special Quasirandom Structures

Y. Kong and ***B.X Liu***

J. Phys. Soc. Jpn. 76(2), 024605 (2007)

390. Structural Phase Transition in the Hf-Ni System Studied by *Ab initio* Calculation and Ion Beam Mixing

H.F. Yan, H.B. Guo and ***B.X. Liu***

J. Alloys Compd. 430(1-2), p.142-148 (2007)

391. Oscillating Behavior of High-Pressure Stability Observed in the Immiscible Co-Cu System by First-Principles Calculation

Y. Kong, J.H. Li and ***B.X. Liu***

J. Appl. Phys. 101(5), 056102 (2007)

392. Molecular Statics Calculation of the Formation Enthalpy for Ternary Metal Systems Based on the Long-Range Empirical Interatomic Potentials

X. D. Dai, J. H. Li and ***B.X. Liu***

Appl. Phys. Lett. 90(13), 131904 (2007)

393. Structural Stability and Characteristics of the Metastable Ag-W Phases Studied by *Ab initio* and Molecular Dynamics Calculations

X.D. Dai, J.H. Li, H.B. Guo and ***B.X. Liu***

J. Appl. Phys. 101(6), 063512 (2007)

394. Four-Parameter Equation of State and Determination of the Thermal and Mechanical Properties of Metals

J.H. Li, S.H. Liang, H.B. Guo and ***B.X. Liu***

J. Alloys Compd. 431(1-2), p.23-31 (2007)

395. A Thermodynamic Model Proposed for Calculating the Standard Formation Enthalpies of Ternary Alloy Systems

W.C. Wang, J.H. Li, H.F. Yan and ***B.X. Liu***

Scripta Mater. 56, p.975-978 (2007)

396. The Metallic Glass-Forming Region of a Ternary Metal System Predicted by Interatomic Potential through Molecular Dynamics Simulation

X.D. Dai, J.H. Li and ***B.X. Liu***

Scripta Mater. 57, p.161-164 (2007)

397. Formation of Amorphous Phases in an Immiscible Cu-Nb System Studied by Molecular Dynamics Simulation and Ion Beam Mixing

T.L. Wang, J.H. Li, K.P. Tai and ***B.X. Liu***

Scripta Mater. 57, p.157-160 (2007)

398. Positive Correlation Between the Magnetic Moment of Fe and Atomic Volume in the Binary Fe-(Cu, Ag, Au) Alloys Revealed by *Ab initio* Calculations

J.H. Li, Y. Kong, K.W. Geng and ***B.X. Liu***

Scripta Mater. 57, p.105-108 (2007)

399. Predicting the Formation Enthalpies of Binary Intermetallic Compounds

R.F. Zhang, S.H. Sheng and ***B.X. Liu***

Chem. Phys. Lett. 442(4), p.511-514 (2007)

400. Long-Range Empirical Potential for The Bcc Structured Transition Metals

X. D. Dai, J. H. Li and Y. Kong

Physical Review B 75, 052102 (2007)

401. Long-Range Empirical Potential Model: Application to Fcc Transition Metals and Alloys

X. D. Dai, Y. Kong and J. H. Li

Physical Review B 75, 104101 (2007)

402. Formation and Atomic Configuration of Binary Metallic Glasses Studied by Ion Beam Mixing and Molecular Dynamics Simulation

K.P. Tai, N. Gao, X.D. Dai, J. H. Li and ***B.X. Liu***

J. Appl. Phys. 101, 124905 (2007)

403. In Situ Formation of Dual Amorphous Morphology by Ion Beam Mixing in Phases with Nanoscale Fractal the Ternary Y-Nb-Co System

W.C. Wang, H.F. Yan, J.H. Li, F. Zeng and ***B.X. Liu***

Scripta Mater. 57(7), p.583-586 (2007)

404. Fractal Growth of Nanocrystals in Association with Amorphous Spinodal Decomposition Observed in an Immiscible Hf-Nb System

K.P. Tai, T.L. Wang and ***B.X. Liu***

Appl. Phys. Lett. 91, 044106 (2007)

405. Proposed Power-Function N-Body Potential for the Fcc Structured Metals Ag, Au, Cu, Ni, Pd, and Pt

J.H. Li, Y. Kong, H.B. Guo, S.H. Liang and ***B.X. Liu***

Phys. Rev. B 76, 104101 (2007)

406. High-Spin Ferromagnetic State Observed in the Fe-Nb Alloys Synthesized by Ion Beam Mixing

K.P. Tai, T.L. Wang and ***B.X. Liu***

Appl. Phys. Lett. 91, 204101 (2007)

407. Distinct Atomic Structures of the Ni-Nb Metallic Glasses Formed by Ion Beam Mixing

K.P. Tai, T.L. Wang and ***B.X. Liu***

J. Appl. Phys. 102(12), 124902 (2007)

2008 年(408—418, 共 11 篇)

408. Interatomic Potentials of the Binary Transition Metal Systems and Some Applications in Materials Physics

J.H. Li, X.D. Dai, S.H. Liang, K.P. Tai, Y. Kong and ***B.X. Liu***

Review Article, Phys. Rep. 455, p.1-134 (2008)

409. Ferromagnetic States in Fe-Ru Systems Studied by *Ab initio* Calculation and Ion-Beam Mixing

X. He, W.C. Wang and ***B.X. Liu***

Phys. Rev. B, 012401 (2008)

410. Solid-State Amorphization of an Immiscible Nb-Zr System Simulated by Molecular Dynamics

S.H. Liang, J.H. Li and ***B.X. Liu***

Comput. Mater. Sci. 42(4), p.550-557 (2008)

411. Abnormal Alloying Behaviour Observed in an Immiscible Zr-Nb System

T.L. Wang, S.H. Liang, J.H. Li and ***B.X. Liu***

J. Phys. D: Appl. Phys. 095310 (2008)

412. Amorphous Phase Formation, Spinodal Decomposition, and Fractal Growth of Nanocrystals in an Immiscible Hf-Nb System Studied by Ion Beam Mixing and Atomistic Modeling

K.P. Tai, X. He and ***B.X. Liu***

J. Appl. Phys., 084910 (2008)

413. Formation of Nonequilibrium Phases and Associated Structural Transitions in the Rh-Ta System Induced by Ion Beam Mixing

W.C. Wang, J.H. Li, Y. Dai and ***B.X. Liu***

Scripta Mater. 59(1), p.3-6 (2008)

414. Metastable Phase Formation and Magnetic Properties of the Fe-Nb System Studied by Atomistic Modeling and Ion Beam Mixing

K.P. Tai, Y. Dai and ***B.X. Liu***

J. Appl. Phys. 104, 014914 (2008)

415. Effects of Ni, Ti and Hf on the Glass Forming Ability of the Ni-Ti-Hf Ternary Alloys

X.D. Dai, J.H. Li and ***B.X. Liu***

J. Alloys Compd. 456(1-2), p.358-363 (2008)

416. Solid-State Amorphization Observed in the Cu-Zr System by Molecular Dynamics Simulation

S.H. Liang, J.H. Li and ***B.X. Liu***

J. Phys. Soc. Jpn. 77(10), 104301 (2008)

417. Glass Forming Ability in the Equilibrium Immiscible Ag-Ta System Studied by Molecular Dynamics Simulation and Ion Beam Mixing

M. Zhao, X.D. Dai, Y.X. Shen, ***B.X. Liu***

J. Phys. Soc. Jpn. 77(7), 074601 (2008)

418. Development of N-Body Potentials for Hcp-Bcc and Fcc-Bcc Binary Transition Metal Systems

J.H. Li, Y. Dai, X.D. Dai and ***B.X. Liu***

Comput. Mater. Sci. 43(4), p.1207-1215 (2008)

2009 年(419—433, 共 15 篇)

419. Long-Range Empirical Potential Model: Extension to Hexagonal Close-Packed Metals

Y. Dai, J.H. Li and ***B.X. Liu***

J. Phys.: Condens. Matter 21(38), 385402 (2009)

420. Structural Stability and Magnetism of Metastable Ni-Pt Intermetallic Compounds Studied by *Ab initio* Calculation

X.L. Che, J.H. Li, Y. Dai and ***B.X. Liu***

Sci. China, Ser. E-Tech. Sci. 52(9), p.2681-2687 (2009)

421. Glass Forming Ability of the Fe-Zr-Cu System Studied by Thermodynamic Calculation and Ion Beam Mixing

T.L. Wang and ***B.X. Liu***

J. Alloys Compd. 481(1-2), p.156-160 (2009)

422. *Ab initio* Study on Structural and Magnetic Properties of Ni-Pb and Ni-Pt Linear and Zigzag Nanowires

X.L. Che, J.H. Li, Y. Dai and ***B.X. Liu***

Commun. Theor. Phys. 52(1), p.123-127 (2009)

423. Glass-Forming Region of the Ni-Nb-Ta Ternary Metal System Determined Directly from N-Body Potential Through Molecular Dynamics Simulations

Y. Dai, J.H. Li, X.L.Che, ***B.X. Liu***

J. Mater. Res. 24(5), p.1815-1819 (2009)

424. Fractal Morphologies of Dual Amorphous Phases Observed in Y-Ti(Nb)-Co Ternary Systems upon Ion Beam Mixing

W.C. Wang, J.H. Li, F. Zeng, Y.L. Gu and ***B.X. Liu***

J. Alloys Compd. 478(1-2), p.L28-L32 (2009)

425. Size-Composition-Dependent Magnetic Properties of Metastable Fe-Pt Nanocrystal Prepared by Ion Beam Mixing

W.C. Wang, J.H. Li, X. He and ***B.X. Liu***

J. Alloys Compd. 476(1-2), p.L21-L24 (2009)

426. Structural Phase Transition in the Fe-Ta System Studied by Ion Beam Mixing

N. Ding, T.L. Wang, K.P. Tai, J.H. Li, X. He, Y. Dai and ***B.X. Liu***

J. Alloys Compd. 476(1-2), p.253-256 (2009)

427. Proposed Long-Range Empirical Potential to Study the Metallic Glasses in the Ni-Nb-Ta System

Y. Dai, J.H. Li, X.L. Che and ***B.X. Liu***

J. Phys. Chem. B 113(20), p.7282-7290 (2009)

428. Magnetic Properties of Some Metastable Co-Ru Alloys Studied by Ion Beam Mixing and *Ab initio* Calculation

W.C. Wang, Y. Dai, T.L. Wang, J.H. Li, X. He and ***B.X. Liu***

Appl. Phys. Lett. 94(13), 131903 (2009)

429. Proposed Thermodynamic Method to Predict the Glass Formation of the Ternary Transition Metal Systems

T.L. Wang, J.H. Li and ***B.X. Liu***

Phys. Chem. Chem. Phys. 11(14), p.2371-2373 (2009)

430. *Ab initio* Study on the Structural Stability and Magnetism of Metastable A_3B Phases in Ni-Au (Cu, Zn, Al) Binary Systems

X.L. Che, J.H. Li, Y. Dai and ***B.X. Liu***

J. Phys. Soc. Jpn. 78(3), 034720 (2009)

431. Structural Stability of High-Pressure Phase in the Immiscible Cu-Nb System Studied by Lattice Dynamics Calculation

Y. Dai, Y. Kong, J.H. Li and ***B.X. Liu***

J. Alloys Compd. 468(1-2), p.299-302 (2009)

432. Point Defect Properties in Hcp and Bcc Zr with Trace Solute Nb Revealed by *Ab initio* Calculations

X.K. Xin, W.S. Lai and ***B.X. Liu***

J. Nucl. Mater. 393(1), p.197-202 (2009)

433. Non-Equilibrium Alloy Formation in the Ag-Zr System by Ion Beam Mixing

Y.Y. Cui, T.L. Wang, K.P. Tai and ***B.X. Liu***

J. Alloys Compd. 488(1), p.223-226 (2009)

2010 年(434—444, 共 11 篇)

434. Interatomic Potential to Predict the Binary Metallic Glass Formation

B.X. Liu, J.H. Li and W.S. Lai

J. Mater. Res. 25(5), p.976-981 (2010)

435. Glass Formation of the Fe-Hf System Studied by Thermodynamic Calculation and Ion Beam Mixing

T.L. Wang, W.C. Wang, J.H. Li and ***B.X. Liu***

J. Alloys Compd. 493(1-2), p.154-157 (2010)

436. Glass Forming Ability of the Binary Cu-Hf System Studied by Thermodynamic Calculation and Ion Beam Mixing

Y.Y. Cui, T.L. Wang and ***B.X. Liu***

Mater. Lett. 64(6), p.715-717 (2010)

437. Ion Beam Mixing to Study the Metallic Glass Formation of the Cu-Zr System

T.L. Wang, W.T. Huang, W.C. Wang and ***B.X. Liu***

Mater. Lett. 64(1), p.96-98 (2010)

438. Nonequilibrium Alloy Formation in the Immiscible Cu-Mo System Studied by Thermodynamic Calculation and Ion Beam Mixing

X. Bai, T. L. Wang, N. Ding, J. H. Li and ***B.X. Liu***

J. Appl. Phys. 108(7), 073534 (2010)

439. Proposed Truncated Cu-Hf Tight-Binding Potential to Study the Crystal-to-Amorphous Phase Transition

Y.Y. Cui, J.H. Li, Y. Dai and ***B.X. Liu***

J. Appl. Phys. 108(6), 063510 (2010)

440. *Ab initio* Calculations to Determine the Formation Enthalpy of Cu_3Au Phases

W.G. Wang, J.H. Li, Y. Dai and ***B.X.Liu***

Philos. Mag. Lett. 90(11), p.801-807 (2010)

441. Local Structure of the Zr-Al Metallic Glasses Studied by Proposed N-Body Potential through Molecular Dynamics Simulation

S.Z. Zhao, J.H. Li and ***B.X. Liu***

J. Mater. Res. 25(9), p.1679-1688 (2010)

442. Glass Forming Region of Cu-Ti-Hf Ternary Metal System Derived from the N-Body Potential through Molecular Dynamics Simulation

S.H. Liang, Y. Dai, J.H. Li and ***B.X. Liu***

J. Phys. Chem. B 114(29), p.9540-9545 (2010)

443. Analytic Calculation of Formation Enthalpies Directly from Interatomic Potentials for Binary and Ternary Refractory Metal Systems

Y. Dai, J.H. Li, X.L. Che and ***B.X. Liu***

Sci. China Tech. Sci. 53(7), p.2015-2019 (2010)

444. Formation of the Ni-Zr-Al Ternary Metallic Glasses Investigated by Interatomic Potential through Molecular Dynamic Simulation

S.Z. Zhao, J.H. Li and ***B.X. Liu***

J. Phys. Soc. Jpn. 79(6), 064607 (2010)

2011 年(445—458, 共 14 篇)

445. Interatomic Potential to Calculate the Driving Force, Optimized Composition, and Atomic Structure of the Cu-Hf-Al Metallic Glasses

Y.Y. Cui, J.H. Li, Y. Dai and ***B.X. Liu***

Appl. Phys. Lett. 99(1), 011911 (2011)

446. Glass Forming Ability of the Mo-Pd System Studied by Thermodynamic Modeling and Ion Beam Mixing

N. Ding, J.H. Li and ***B X. Liu***

J. Appl. Phys. 110(1), 013516 (2011)

447. An Atomic-Level Mechanism of Annealing Twinning in Copper Observed by Molecular Dynamics Simulation

W.G. Wang, Y. Dai, J.H. Li and ***B.X. Liu***

Cryst. Growth Des. 11(7), p.2928-2934 (2011)

448. Non-Equilibrium Phases in the Fe-Rh System Studied by Ion Beam Mixing and *Ab initio* Calculation

N. Ding, Y. Dai, J.H. Li and ***B.X. Liu***

Mater. Lett. 65(12), p. 1805-1807 (2011)

449. Synthesis of Amorphous Alloys and Amorphous-Crystalline Composites in the Cu-Nb-Hf System by Ion Beam Mixing

S.Y. Luo, Y.Y. Cui, T.L. Wang, N. Ding, J.H. Li and ***B.X. Liu***

J. Appl. Phys. 109(12), 123530 (2011)

450. Formation and Structure of Al-Zr Metallic Glasses Studied by Monte Carlo Simulations

J.H. Li, S.Z. Zhao, Y. Dai, Y.Y. Cui and ***B.X. Liu***

J. Appl. Phys. 109(11), 113538 (2011)

451. Prediction of Favored and Optimized Compositions for Cu-Zr-Ni Metallic Glasses by Interatomic Potential

Y.Y. Cui, J.H. Li, Y. Dai and ***B.X. Liu***

J. Phys. Chem. B 115 (16), p.4703-4708 (2011)

452. Glass-Forming Ability and Atomic-Level Structure of the Ternary Ag-Ni-Zr Metallic Glasses Studied by Molecular Dynamics Simulations

Y. Dai, J. H.Li and ***B.X. Liu***

J. Appl. Phys. 109(5), 053505 (2011)

453. Formation of Non-Equilibrium Phases and Associated Structural Transition in the Pd-Ta System Induced by Ion Beam Mixing

M. Zhao, Y. Dai, J.H. Li and ***B.X. Liu***

Sci. China Tech. Sci. 54(3), p.676-681 (2011)

454. Fractal Patterns in Au-Ta Multilayer Films upon Ion Beam Mixing

M. Zhao and ***B.X. Liu***

Philos. Mag. Lett. 91(3), p.229-236 (2011)

455. Thermodynamic Calculation and Interatomic Potential to Predict the Favored Composition Region for the Cu-Zr-Al Metallic Glass Formation

Y.Y. Cui, T.L. Wang, J.H. Li, Y. Dai and ***B.X. Liu***

Phys. Chem. Chem. Phys. 13(9), p.4103-4108 (2011)

456. A Possible Metastable $MoPd_2$ Bcc Phase in the Mo-Pd System Obtained by Ion Beam Mixing

N. Ding, J.H. Li and ***B.X. Liu***

Mater. Lett. 65(19-20), p.3024-3026 (2011)

457. Favored Composition Region for Metallic Glass Formation and Atomic Configurations in the Ternary Ni-Zr-Ti System Derived from N-Body Potential through Molecular Dynamics Simulations

S.Z. Zhao, J.H. Li and ***B.X. Liu***

J. Mater. Res. 26(16), p.2050-2064 (2011)

458. Atomistic Theory for Predicting the Binary Metallic Glass Formation

J.H. Li, Y. Dai, Y.Y. Cui and ***B.X. Liu***

Review Article:Mater. Sci. Eng. R. 70(1-2), p.1-28 (2011)

2012 年(459—474，共 16 篇)

459. Monte Carlo Simulations to Study the Forming Ability and Atomic Configuration of the Cu-Al Amorphous Alloys

S.Y. Luo, J.H. Li, Y.Y. Cui, Y.Dai and ***B.X. Liu***

Intermetallics 25, p. 109-114(2012)

460. Atomistic Modeling of Solid-State Amorphization and Atomic Structure of the Cu-Hf System

Y.Y. Cui, X.H. Yang, J.H. Li, Y. Dai and ***B.X. Liu***

Mater. Lett. 76, p.77-80 (2012)

461. Formation and Structure of Cu-Zr-Al Ternary Metallic Glasses Investigated by Ion Beam Mixing and Calculation

X.Bai, J.H. Li, Y.Y. Cui, Y. Dai, N. Ding and ***B.X. Liu***

J. Alloys Compd. 522, p.35-38 (2012)

462. Synthesis of Metallic Glasses and Metallic Glass Based Composites in the Cu-Mo-Hf System by Ion Beam Mixing

X. Bai, T.L. Wang, Y.Y. Cui, N. Ding, J.H. Li and ***B.X. Liu***

Sci. China Tech. Sci. 55, p.1353-1358 (2012)

463. Thermodynamic Prediction of Metastable Phases of Ni-Ti System Formed by Ion Beam Mixing

S.Z. Zhao, J.H. Li and ***B.X. Liu***

Sci. China Tech. Sci. 55, p.921-926 (2012)

464. Structure, Formation Energies and Elastic Constants of Uranium Metal Investigated by First Principles Calculations

J.H. Li, Q.B. Ren, C.H. Lu, L. Lu, Y. Dai and ***B.X. Liu***

J. Alloys Compd. 516, p.139-143 (2012)

465. Non-Equilibrium Alloy Phase Formation and Transformation Driven by Ion Beam Mixing in the Fe-Hf-Nb Multilayers

N. Li, T.L. Wang, N. Ding, Y. Dai, X. Bai and ***B.X. Liu***

Sci. China Tech. Sci. 55, p.640-645 (2012)

466. Prediction of Glass-Forming Ability and Characterization of Atomic Structure of the Co-Ni-Zr Metallic Glasses by a Proposed Long Range Empirical Potential

Y. Dai, J.H. Li and ***B.X. Liu***

J. Appl. Phys. 111, 033521 (2012)

467. Microchemical Inhomogeneity to Characterize Atomic Configurations in the Heating and Quenching of a $CuHf_2$ Alloy

Y.Y. Cui, J.H. Li, Y. Dai and ***B.X. Liu***

Phys. Chem. Chem. Phys. 14, p.8290-8293 (2012)

468. Metallic Glass Formation in the Ternary Ni-Nb-Mo System by Ion Beam Mixing

Y. Li, T.L. Wang, N. Ding, J.B. Liu and ***B.X. Liu***

Sci. China Tech. Sci. 55, p.1-6 (2012)

469. A Long-Range U-Nb Potential for the Calculation of Some Chemical and Physical Properties of the U-Nb System

Y. Dai, C.H. Lu, Q.B. Ren, L. Lu, J.H. Li and ***B.X. Liu***

J. Nucl. Mater. 427, p.239-244 (2012)

470. First-Principles Molecular Dynamics Simulations to Study the Crystal-to-Amorphous Transition in the Mg-Zn System

Y. Dai, J.H. Li and ***B.X. Liu***

Intermetallics 29, p.75-79 (2012)

471. Structural and Elastic Properties of Pd-Zr Compounds Studied by *Ab initio* Calculation

X. Bai, J.H. Li, Y. Dai and ***B.X. Liu***

Intermetallics 31, p.79-87 (2012)

472. Ion Beam Mixing Study of the Favored Glass-Forming Region of the Ternary Fe-Zr-Nb System

N. Li, N. Ding, S.H. Liang, J.H. Li and ***B.X. Liu***

Nucl. Instr. Meth. in Phys. Res. B 287, p.91-93 (2012)

473. Interatomic Potential to Predict the Favored and Optimized Compositions for Ternary Cu-Zr-Hf Metallic Glasses

S.Y. Luo, Y.Y.Cui, Y. Dai, J.H. Li and ***B.X. Liu***

J. Appl. Phys. 112(10), 103518 (2012)

474. An Intermediate Fcc Zr State Observed in the Cu-Zr-Ni System upon Ion Beam Mixing

Q. Wang, N. Ding, Y.Y. Cui, Y. Dai and ***B.X. Liu***

Mater. Lett. 89, p.90-92 (2012)

2013 年(475—486, 共 12 篇)

475. Calculation of Driving Force and Local Order to Predict the Favored and Optimized Compositions for Mg-Cu-Ni Metallic Glass Formation

Q. Wang, J.H. Li, Y.Y. Cui, J.B. Liu and ***B.X. Liu***

J. Appl. Phys. 114(15), 153503 (2013)

476. Synthesis of Amorphous Alloys and Amorphous-Crystalline Composites in Ternary Ni-Nb-Zr System by Ion Beam Mixing

Y. Li, S.H. Liang, N. Li, J.H. Li and ***B.X. Liu***

Mater. Chem. Phys. 141(2-3), p.960-966 (2013)

477. Different Atomic Structures Observed from Ternary Ni-Nb-Ta Metallic Glasses Obtained by Ion Beam Mixing

Y.Y. Wang, J.B. Liu, Y. Dai and ***B.X. Liu***

Sci. China Tech. Sci. 56(8), p.1842-1846 (2013)

478. Metastable Phase Formation and Transformation Studied by Ion Mixing and Computation for the Cu-Zr-Ni System

Q. Wang, Y.Y. Cui, N. Ding, J.H. Li and ***B.X. Liu***

Nucl. Instr. Meth. in Phys. Res. B 307, p.111-114 (2013)

479. Formation and Structure of Pd-Zr Metallic Glasses Studied by Molecular Dynamics Simulations

X. Bai, J.H. Li, Y.Y. Cui, Y. Dai and ***B.X. Liu***

J. Phys. Soc. Jpn. 82(6), 064802 (2013)

480. Glass-Formation and Atomic Structures of $Cu_x(Zr_{0.22}Hf_{0.78})_{1-x}$ and $(Cu_{0.61}Hf_{0.39})_{1-x}Zr_x$ Alloys Investigated by Monte Carlo Simulation

S.Y. Luo, J.H. Li, Y.Y. Cui and ***B.X. Liu***

Mater. Lett. 100, p.130-132 (2013)

481. Chemical and Topological Short-Range Orders in the Ternary Ni-Zr-Al Metallic Glasses Studied by Monte Carlo Simulations

S.Z. Zhao, J.H. Li and ***B.X. Liu***

J. Phys.: Condens. Matter 25(9), 095005 (2013)

482. Interatomic Potential to Predict Favored Composition for Hf-Cu-Ni Metallic Glasses Formation

Y.Y. Cui, X. Bai, S.Y. Luo, Q. Wang, J.H. Li and ***B.X. Liu***

J. Alloys Compd. 552, p.55-59 (2013)

483. Composition Reign Favored for the Formation of Cu-Zr-Al Amorphous Phases Investigated by Ion Beam Mixing

X. Bai, J.H. Li, Y.Y. Cui and ***B.X. Liu***

Mater. Lett. 92, p.281-283 (2013)

484. Glass-Forming Region of Ni-Nb-Ag Systemand the Corresponding Atomic Configuration Studied by Monte Carlo Simulation

S.Y. Luo, J.H. Li and ***B.X. Liu***

J. Phys. Soc. Jpn. 82, 124603 (2013)

485. Prediction of Glass-Forming Ability and Atomic-Level Structure of the Al-Zr-Pd Metallic Glasses by Molecular Dynamics Simulations

X. Bai, J.H. Li, N. Li, S.Y. Luo and ***B.X. Liu***

J. Phys. Soc. Jpn. 82(12), 124006 (2013)

486. Linear Correlations of Formation Enthalpies/Bulk Modules and Atomic Volumes Observed in Pt-Zr Compounds by *Ab initio* Calculation

X. Bai, J.H. Li,Y. Dai and ***B.X. Liu***

T. Nonferr. Metal. Soc. 23(12), p.3704-3713 (2013)

2014 年(487—498, 共 12 篇)

487. Effect of Y on the Glass Forming Ability of the Fe-Nb System Studied by Ion Beam Mixing

N. Li, J.H. Li,Y.Y. Wang and ***B.X. Liu***

Intermetallics 44, p.73-76 (2014)

488. Irradiation Induced Non-Equilibrium Phase Formation and Structural Transformation in the Fe-Ti-Nb Multilayered Films

N. Li, J.H. Li and ***B.X. Liu***

RSC Adv. 4(18), p.9098-9102 (2014)

489. Formation and Magnetic Properties of Metastable Phases Observed in the $Fe_{50}(Hf_xTa_{1-x})_{50}$ Films by Ion Beam Mixing

N. Li, J.H. Li, J.B. Liu and ***B.X. Liu***

Appl. Surf. Sci. 290, p.495-498 (2014)

490. Interatomic Potential to Predict the Glass-Forming Ability of Ni-Nb-Mo Ternary Alloys

Y. Li, S.Y. Luo, J.H. Li, J.B. Liu and ***B.X. Liu***

J. Mater. Sci. 49(20), p.7263-7272 (2014)

491. Amorphous Phase Formation in the Ni-Ti-Ta System Studied by Thermodynamic Calculation and Ion Beam Mixing

Y.Y. Wang, J.H. Li, T.L. Wang and ***B.X. Liu***

Intermetallics 53, p.102-106 (2014)

492. Effects of Mo Addition on the Metallic Glass Formation of $(ZrNi)_{100-x}Mo_x$ Alloys

M.H. Yang, N. Li, J.H. Li and ***B.X. Liu***

J. Alloys Compd. 606, p.7-10 (2014)

493. Atomic Modeling to Design Favored Compositions for the Ternary Ni-Nb-Zr Metallic Glass Formation

S.Y. Luo, J.H. Li, J.B. Liu and ***B.X. Liu***

Acta Mater. 76, p.482-492 (2014)

494. Structural Skeleton of Preferentially Interpenetrated Clusters and Correlation with Shear Localization in Mg-Cu-Ni Ternary Metallic Glasses

Q. Wang, J.H. Li, J.B. Liu and ***B.X. Liu***

Phys. Chem. Chem. Phys. 16(36), p.19590-601 (2014)

495. Glass Forming Abilities of the Fe-Ta-(Zr, Ti) Alloys Studied by Thermodynamic Calculation and Ion Beam Mixing

N. Li, J.H. Li and ***B.X. Liu.***

Appl. Surf. Science 308, p.316-320 (2014)

496. Favored Composition Design and Atomic Structure Characterization for Ternary Al-Cu-Y Metallic Glasses via Proposed Interatomic Potential

Q. Wang, J.H. Li, J.B. Liu and ***B.X. Liu***

J. Phys. Chem. B 118(16), p.4442-4449 (2014)

497. Simplified Thermodynamic Method to Predict the Glass Formation of the Ternary Transition Metal Systems

N. Li, J.H. Li and ***B.X. Liu***

Rsc Adv. 4(40), p.20616-20619 (2014)

498. Predicting Composition Dependence of Glass Forming Ability in Ternary Al-Cu-Y System by Thermodynamic Calculation

Q. Wang, J.H. Li, J.B. Liu and ***B.X. Liu***

Metals 4, p.519-529 (2014)

2015年(499—500, 共2篇)

499. Phase Stability and Mechanical Properties of Sigma Phase in Co-Mo System by First Principles Calculations

S.N. Li, J.B. Liu and ***B.X. Liu***

Computational Materials Science 98, p.424-429 (2015)

500. Atomic Approach to the Optimized Compositions of Ni-Nb-Ti Glassy Alloys with Large Glass-Forming Ability

Y. Li, J.H. Li, J.B. Liu and ***B.X. Liu***

RSC Advances 5(4), p.3054-3062 (2015)

第三篇　35 篇代表性论文

Structural difference rule for amorphous alloy formation by ion mixing

Bai-Xin Liu,[a] W. L. Johnson, and M-A. Nicolet
California Institute of Technology, Pasadena, California 91125
S. S. Lau
University of California, San Diego, La Jolla, California 92093

(Received 10 August 1982; accepted for publication 22 October 1982)

We formulate a rule which establishes a sufficient condition that an amorphous binary alloy will be formed by ion mixing of multilayered samples when the two constituent metals are of different crystalline structure, regardless of their atomic sizes and electronegativities. The rule is supported by the experimental results we have obtained on six selected binary metal systems, as well as by the previous data reported in the literature. The amorphization mechanism is discussed in terms of the competition between two different structures resulting in frustration of the crystallization process.

PACS numbers: 81.20.Pe, 61.40.Df, 61.80. – x, 68.90. + g

It is now established that ion mixing (IM) is well suited to form metastable materials with either crystalline (MX phase) or noncrystalline (amorphous phase) structures. Typically, the experiment consists of first depositing very thin (~100 Å) layers of two different metals in alternating sequence on an inert substrate to a total thickness of about 1000 Å. The overall atomic composition ratio is fixed by the thicknesses of the individual layers. This multilayered sample is then irradiated at room temperature or below by inert ions of a range that is commensurate with the thickness of the layer (typically Xe of several 100 keV), and to doses ranging from 10^{15} to 10^{16} ion/cm^2. Results on IM of binary metal systems have so far been reported on eight combinations, all involving transition metals only. Summarizing the experimental observations, it is found that (i) mixing takes place in each system, (ii) MX phases form in almost every system and typically have the structure of one of the parent metal phases, and (iii) no amorphous phase has been observed in those systems where the two constituent metals have the same crystalline structure (e.g., Au-Ni,[1] Ag-Cu,[2] and Ag-Ni[3]), while amorphous alloys were formed in those systems where two metals have different structures (e.g., Au-V,[1] Cu-Ta,[4] and Au-Co[1]). This observation strongly suggests that a structural difference between the constituent metals plays an important role in ion-induced amorphization.

From a metallurgical point of view, in addition to the structure, atomic size and electronegativity of the constituent metals are the main factors which determine the character of an alloy phase. It is generally accepted that small differences in size and electronegativity favor solid solutions (Hume–Rothery rule), while large differences in these two parameters favor amorphous phases.[5] We have therefore undertaken to investigate in particular whether structural difference in the parent elements dominates over these other two factors in producing amorphous materials. As most of the metals form in one of the three main structures, bcc, fcc, and hcp, six systems were selected to cover all the three different combinations among these three structures. Additionally, some systems were chosen to have almost identical atomic size, Al-Nb, Mo-Ru, and Ti-Au, or identical electronegativity, Ni-Mo and Mo-Co (see Table I).

Once a system was selected, the appropriate composition for forming an amorphous phase by IM remained to be chosen. It has been established that if the entire composition of the multilayered sample is close to either side of the phase diagram, IM tends to form a supersaturated solid solution (MX phase).[1] It is also possible that an equilibrium com-

[a] Permanent address: Qinghua University, Beijing, The People's Republic of China.

Applied Physics Letters 42, p.45-47 (1983).

TABLE I. Amorphous alloys formed by room temperature, 300-keV Xe^+ ion mixing in the selected binary metal systems.

Binary system with different structures	fcc-bcc Ni-Mo	fcc-bcc Al-Nb	bcc-hcp Mo-Co	bcc-hcp Mo-Ru	hcp-fcc Ti-Au	hcp-fcc Ti-Ni
Atomic size r(Å) and	1.24 1.39	1.43 1.46	1.39 1.25	1.39 1.34	1.47 1.46	1.47 1.24
$\frac{\Delta r}{r^*}$,[a]	11%	2%	10%	4%	1%	16%
Electronegativity n and	1.8 1.8	1.5 1.6	1.8 1.8	1.8 2.2	1.5 2.4	1.5 1.8
$\frac{\Delta n}{n^*}$,[a]	0%	6%	0%	18%	38%	17%
Amorphous alloys formed by IM	$Ni_{65}Mo_{35}$	$Al_{55}Nb_{45}$	$Co_{65}Mo_{35}$	$Mo_{55}Ru_{45}$		$Ti_{50}Ni_{50}$
	$Ni_{50}Mo_{50}$		$Co_{35}Mo_{65}$		$Ti_{65}Au_{35}$	
	$Ni_{35}Mo_{65}$				$Ti_{40}Au_{60}$	

Note: the larger r and n are used for reference.

pound would be formed by IM if the overall composition is close to that of the compound. An appropriate choice of composition for amorphous alloy formation is therefore away from the pure metals and from equilibrium compound compositions. Accordingly, most of the compositions chosen in this study are those which lie within the two-phase regions of the phase diagrams.

The experimental procedure in this study is similar to that described above. Xenon ions of 300 keV were chosen for irradiation because of their high mass, hence high efficiency in inducing atomic mixing.[7] The samples were all irradiated at room temperature to doses ranging from 2×10^{14}–2×10^{16} Xe/cm^2. Some samples were preannealed, followed by irradiation, to check the effect of the presence of equilibrium compounds on amorphization. All the samples were analyzed by MeV $^4He^+$ backscattering spectrometry (BS), x-ray diffraction (Read camera), and four-point probe resistivity measurements.

Some ten amorphous alloys have been obtained by IM (see Table I). The amorphous structure was identified by a diffuse band (or halo) on the x-ray diffraction pattern. The resistivities of the mixed films are on the order of 130–320 $\mu\Omega$ cm, which is higher than those expected of crystalline binary alloys, hence lending support to the x-ray data that the films are amorphous.

The formation of the amorphous alloys in all of the above selected systems clearly demonstrates that the structural difference of the constituent metals plays the key role in ion-induced amorphization and that atomic size and electronegativity effects are minor. It therefore leads us to formulate a rule that an amorphous binary alloy will be formed by ion mixing of multilayered samples when the two constituent metals are of different crystalline structure. We propose to call this the "structural difference rule for amorphous alloy formation" by ion mixing. The experimental evidence presented here allows only the conclusion that the rule is a sufficient condition to assure the formation of an amorphous phase by ion mixing; in fact, cases are known where binaries of similar structure do form amorphous phases (e.g., Au-Pb, both fcc).

To check the effect of the presence of equilibrium compound on amorphization, one multilayered sample of $Ti_{65}Au_{35}$ (between neighboring equilibrium compounds Ti_3Au and TiAu) was preannealed at 600 °C for 1 h and Ti_3Au and TiAu were formed as revealed by x-ray diffraction pattern. The preannealed and as-deposited samples were then irradiated at room temperature to the same dose of 5×10^{15} Xe/cm^2. Amorphous alloys were formed in both cases. This indicates that the presence of equilibrium compounds does not prevent the amorphous alloy formation by IM in this system. However, it has been reported[8] that in the Fe-W system, if the Fe_7W_6 compound is formed first by preannealing, its presence will hinder the subsequent amorphous alloy formation by IM. The presence of an equilibrium compound therefore varies in its effect from system to system.

The experimental evidence offered thus far in support of the structural difference rule for the formation of amorphous alloys includes the metals with bcc, fcc, and hcp, crystal structures, and the process of IM. Available experimental evidence indicates that the rule is valid beyond these specific conditions. Multilayered samples combining Si (diamond-type fcc) with Au (fcc) up to 70 at % of Au[9,10], Mo (bcc) in $Mo_{50}Si_{50}$ composition,[11] and Ru (hcp) in $Ru_{45}Si_{55}$ composition[11] also produced amorphous layers upon Xe irradiation. $Ge_{80}Au_{20}$ and $Ge_{60}Au_{40}$ multilayers were also found to amorphize, although the layers recrystallize within a few days at room temperature.[12] It therefore appears that the rule extends at least in part to the diamond lattice structure as well. The case of Si-Ge is exceptional, however, in that these covalently bonded elements can be amorphized already in their elemental form, so that their combination is expected to form amorphous, not polycrystalline films. A recent study of the Fe-W system shows that rf sputtering is capable of producing amorphous layers over a more extended range of composition than IM does.[13] A study of the

Pt-Si system[14] indicates that vapor quenching of the two elements produces amorphous layers whose properties are altered little upon subsequent irradiation. We therefore believe that the structural difference rule may be useful as well as a guide to the synthesis of amorphous materials by processes other than IM.

We believe that the structural difference rule is closely related to the eutectic criteria for amorphous phase formation first introduced by Turnbull.[15,16] The simple eutectic phase diagram is formed between two metals (call them *A* and *B*) having a different structure and no intermediate equilibrium compounds. In the two-phase portion of such a phase diagram, any single phase crystalline form of the alloy has a higher free energy than the two-phase equilibrium alloy. Ion mixing of multilayers tends to produce mutual dissolution of the *A* and *B* layers with the composition of each layer gradually moving toward the average composition of the multilayer. Beyond the equilibrium solubility limit of *B* in *A* (for example), the *A* layer (with the structure of pure *A*) becomes metastable. As the *B* concentration further increases, the free energy of the metastable *A* solution rises above that of the equilibrium two-phase material. But the formation of the two equilibrium phases requires nucleation of the *B* phase in the *A* layer. Under conditions of restricted kinetics (ion mixing at suitably low temperatures), the diffusion of *B* atoms required cannot occur. In contrast, the transition to the amorphous state is polymorphic (involves no change in composition) and thus becomes kinetically favored. Viewed in this light, the structural difference rule then formulates conditions where free energy and kinetic considerations favor glass formation. These conditions may occur equally well between two adjacent crystalline phases of any structure in a binary phase diagram. We thus surmise that the structural difference rule will apply also between adjacent equilibrium phases with a phase diagram that are not necessarily the terminal elements. For example, formation of amorphous $Zr_{10}Co_{90}$ (Ref. 17) and $Zr_{75}Co_{25}$ (Ref 18) by liquid quenching can be explained in this fashion; Zr and Co are both hcp, but the equilibrium phase diagram is divided into many two-phase regions by several intermetallic compounds. Amorphous $Zr_{10}Co_{90}$ lies between Co and $ZrCo_4$ (complex fcc)[19] and $Zr_{75}Co_{25}$ lies between Zr and Zr_2Co (bc tetragonal).[20]

According to this view, it is basically the competition between two different structures that results in frustration of the crystallization process and an amorphous phase is obtained.

The authors thank R. Fernandez for assistance in the preparation of the samples, and U. Shreter and R. Gaboriaud for help in irradiation and measuring of some samples. This work was executed under the benevolent U.R. Fund of the Böhmische Physical Society (B. M. Ullrich). The irradiation part of the study was financially supported in part by the U.S. Department of Energy through an agreement with the National Aeronautics and Space Administration and monitored by the Jet Propulsion Laboratory, (D. B. Bicker) at the California Institute of Technology, Pasadena, California.

[1] B-Y. Tsaur, S. S. Lau, L. S. Hung, and J. W. Mayer, Nucl. Inst. Methods **182/183**, 67 (1981).

[2] B-Y. Tsaur, S. S. Lau, and J. W. Mayer, Appl. Phys. Lett. **36**, 823 (1980).

[3] B-Y. Tsaur and J. W. Mayer, Appl. Phys. Lett. **37**, 389 (1980).

[4] B-Y. Tsaur, Ph.D. thesis, California Institute of Technology, 1980.

[5] S. S. Takayama, J. Mater. Sci. **11**, 164 (1976).

[6] *Table of Periodic Properties of the Elements* (Sargent–Welch, Chicago, 1968).

[7] B-Y. Tsaur, in *Proceedings of the Symposium on Thin Film Interfaces and Interactions*, edited by J. E. E. Baglin and J. M. Poate (The Electrochemical Society, Princeton, New Jersey, 1980), Vol. 80-2, p. 205.

[8] G. Göltz, R. Fernandez, and M-A. Nicolet, in *Metastable Materials Formation by Ion Implantation*, edited by S. T. Picraux and W. J. Choyke (North-Holland, New York 1982), MRS Symposia Proceedings Vol. 7, p. 227.

[9] B. X. Liu, L. Wieluński, M. Mäenpää, M-A. Nicolet, and S. S. Lau, in *Metastable Materials Formation by Ion Implantation*, edited by S. T. Picraux and W. J. Choyke (North-Holland, New York, 1982), MRS Symposia Proceedings Vol. 7, p. 133.

[10] B-Y. Tsaur and J. W. Mayer, Philos. Mag. A **43**, 345 (1981).

[11] B. X. Liu (unpublished).

[12] B. X. Liu and M-A. Nicolet, Phys. Status Solidi A **70**, 671 (1982).

[13] I. Suni (unpublished).

[14] B-Y. Tsaur, J. Appl. Phys. **51**, 5334 (1980).

[15] D. Turnbull, Contemp. Phys. **10**, 473 (1969).

[16] F. Spaepen and D. Turnbull, in *Rapidly Quenched Metals. II*, edited by N. J. Grant and B. C. Giessen (MIT, Boston, 1976), p. 205.

[17] A. Inoue, K. Kobayachi, and T. Masumoto, in *Proceedings of the Conference on Metallic Glasses: Science and Technology, Budapest, June 30–July 4, 1980*, edited by C. Hargitai, Bakonyi, and T. Kemeny (2v Magy Tud Akad. Kazp Fiz Kut Intez or Kultura, Budapest, 1981).

[18] A. Inoue, C. Suryanarayana, J. Kinchina, and T. Masumoto, in *Proceedings of the 4th International Conference on Rapidly Quenched Metals*, edited by T. Masumoto and K. Suzuki (Japan Institute of Metals, Tokoyo, 1982), Vol. 1, p. 1655.

[19] F. A. Shunk, *Constitution of Binary Alloys, Supplement* 2 (McGraw-Hill, New York, 1969), p. 268.

[20] R. P. Elliot, *Constitution of Binary Alloys, Supplement* 1 (McGraw-Hill, New York, 1965), p. 344.

Review Article

phys. stat. sol. (a) 94, 11 (1986)

Subject classification: 61.80 and 64.75; 61.70; S1.1; S1.2; S1.3; S4

Tsinghua University, Beijing[1])

Ion Mixing and Metallic Alloy Phase Formation

By

B. X. Liu

Contents

1. Introduction

The earliest use of an ion beam from the low energy accelerator to modify materials properties was initiated in the early sixties, i.e. the doping of semiconductors by ion implantation instead of the traditional thermal method. About ten years later, the study of ion implantation began to deal with metals. In this scheme, an ion beam is used to introduce alloying elements into materials (the ion species is the same as the alloying element required). It is now well established that ion implantation can modify various surface properties of metals and alloys, such as wear and corrosion resistances,

[1]) Beijing, The People's Republic of China.

Review Article, Phys. Stat. Sol. (a) 94, p.11-34 (1986).

catalytic property, superconductivity, etc. Another interesting aspect is that a number of new solid phases have been formed by ion implantation, e.g. phases of interstitial or substitutional solid solutions, amorphous metal–metalloid phases, etc. A terminology of "ion implantation metallurgy" [1, 2] has been proposed to name this new subject. However, in terms of forming various metallic alloy phases, the maximum obtainable composition in ion implantation is limited by the sputtering effect of the ion beam while interacting with the metal surface. Moreover, it would be even impossible to study various metal systems, if the implanter available is not equipped with a versatile metal ion source. In this case, ion mixing, which was introduced in the early seventies as an alternative scheme, is suitable for this purpose. In contrast to direct implantation, the ion beam (typically an inert gas ion beam) is used here mainly to trigger atomic collisions for inducing inter-mixing between deposited material B and the matrix A, or both deposited A and B bilayer or multilayers on a substrate, and thus forming a uniform A–B alloy phase. Table 1 shows the comparison between ion mixing and direct ion implantation for forming a metallic alloy phase. Using multilayered films, ion mixing is capable of producing various alloy phases with neither limitation of the alloy composition, nor of the metal species required. Consequently, it offers a novel technique to manufacture new alloy thin films, as well as a valuable means for investigating one of the important topics of physical metallurgy, i.e. the theory of the alloy phase, and this was named "microalloying" [3]. It appears that the new terminology of "ion beam metallurgy" is perhaps the better one fitting this rapidly growing field of metallurgy studied by both ion mixing and direct implantation.

In the past five years, more than 30 binary metal systems have so far been studied by ion mixing of multilayers, and a great number of metastable alloys, including various amorphous alloys, have been obtained, in which many alloys have not been produced or are even not obtainable by the traditional means. To have an overview of the outcome of these studies, Table 2 lists these systems in alphabetical order of the chemical symbols of the constituent metals for convenience of searching. In the meantime, researchers in this field have also tried to promote the understanding of the phase formation mechanisms. As the alloy phase is formed by ion irradiation of the metal layers through atomic collisions, which are commonly considered as a non-equilibrium process, the question has been whether, when, and how the thermodynamics of solids, as well as those physical metallurgy factors as crystalline structure, size, and electronegativity of the constituent metals, play roles in ion-induced alloy phase formation. Since 1982, some progress has been achieved to answer the question.

Table **1**

Comparison between ion mixing and ion implantation for forming metallic alloy phases

method	major effect of irradiation	typical dose and obtainable alloy composition	equipment requirements
ion mixing	physical mixing	10^{15} to 10^{16} ions/cm^2, no limitation on composition	gas ion source and deposition system
ion implantation	introducing alloy element	10^{17} to 10^{18} ions/cm^2, sputtering effect limits the maximum composition to around 30 at%	versatile metal ion source

Table 2
Binary metal systems that have been studied by ion mixing of multilayers up to date

system	phase formed by IM		ref.
	crystal	amorphous	
Ag–Co	Yes	*	[11]
Ag–Cu	yes	*	[12]
Ag–Ni	yes		[13]
Al–Co		yes	[8]
Al–Au	yes	yes	[8]
		yes	[14]
Al–Fe	yes		[15]
Al–Nb		yes	[6]
Al–Ni	yes	yes	[7]
		yes	[15]
Al–Pd	yes	yes	[7]
Al–Pt	yes	yes	[7]
Au–Co	yes	yes	[3]
	yes		[16]
Au–Fe	yes	*	[3]
Au–Ni	yes		[3]
Au–Ti	yes	yes	[17, 9]
Au–V	yes	yes	[3]
Co–Cu	yes		[11]
Co–Mo	yes	yes	[6]
Co–Ti		yes	[8]
Cu–Pd	no data available		[18]
Cu–Ta		yes	[19]
Er–Ni		yes	[6]
Fe–Ti	yes	yes	[20]
Fe–W	yes	yes	[21]
Hf–Ni		yes	[22]
Mo–Nb	yes		[23]
Mo–Ni	yes	yes	[6]
		yes	[24]
Mo–Ru		yes	[25]
Nb–Ni	yes	yes	[26]
Ni–Ti		yes	[6]
		yes	[27]
		yes	[24]
		yes	[8]
Ru–Ti		yes *	[28]
Ru–Zr		yes	[28]
		yes	[9]
Ti–Zr	yes		[23]

Notes with * will be discussed in detail in Section 5.

For instance, Liu et al. [4] conducted a systematic study and formulated a so-called "structural difference rule" in 1982 for synthesizing amorphous alloys of the first class by ion mixing of metal layers. What is important in this finding is that those authors pointed out the predominant role of the crystalline structure of the constituent metals in determining the structural character of the ion-mixed phase. At IBMM'82,

Lau et al. [5] presented the idea that the equilibrium phase diagram is still of importance for predicting what kind of phase would likely be formed in ion mixing. Later, Liu et al. [6], Hung et al. [7, 8], and Liu [9] reported more experimental results, suggesting another criterion for obtaining amorphous alloys of the second class by ion mixing. Using the free energy diagram, Liu [9] proposed a simple phenomenological model, which can explain the formation of nearly all the alloy phases obtained so far by ion mixing. All these results lead to the present situation that one is now able to produce various amorphous alloys by ion mixing, by simply choosing the appropriate compositions, though the amorphization mechanisms on the atomic scale are not yet well understood. As a logical deduction, it is also predictable under what condition a crystalline phase is likely to be formed. Johnson et al. [10] have studied this issue, using also the free energy diagram and a proposed polymorphic phase diagram, and come up with some similar rules for alloy phase formation.

Some very good papers have been published to review the subject of ion mixing [29]. Nevertheless, more attention is still needed to make a summary on metallic alloy phase formation by ion mixing of metal layers. It is so because the experimental data offered thus far as well as the recent progress enable one to make a summary now, and that such a summary may be of interest for researchers in the field of physical metallurgy, and those who are interested in producing amorphous alloy thin films for various uses.

In this paper, the main idea is to correlate the structural character of the ion-induced phase to the essential properties of the constituent metals, and to show that the equilibrium phase diagram is indeed a good guidance for predicting the alloy phase formation. Before going to the main content, the experimentation of ion mixing of multilayers is first briefly described, as some experimental parameters do effect the phase formation considerably, and it might be helpful for readers who have not been in the field of ion beam. After that, the author attempts to summarize the alloy phase formation data, to interpret the formation mechanisms with the views of thermodynamic and kinetic considerations, and to discuss the validity of the proposed rules in predicting phase formation. Finally, some intrigue phenomena, i.e. some unusual phase transitions induced by ion irradiation are discussed.

2. Experimentation of Ion Mixing of Metal Layers

Fig. 1 shows schematically the concept and the arrangement of ion mixing using multilayered films. Some of the important parameters influencing the character of the ion-induced phase, are discussed as follows.

2.1 Sample design and preparation

To design the nlultilayered sample, the irradiating ions and their energy should be chosen first, because the total thickness of the sample should match the range of the irradiating ions. Inert gas ions, such as Xe, Kr, Ne, or Ar, are frequently chosen to be the irradiating ions. The advantages of employing inert gas ions are that no chemical impurity effect would be involved, and the gas ion source is always available for the common implanters. One can of course use metal ions, (the ion species is one of the constituent metals),to do ion mixing to eliminate impurity effects absolutely, if this metal ion is easy to handle. As heavy ions induce more efficient mixing than light ones when the other conditions are kept the same, Xe ions are therefore mostly used. The typical energy of the irradiating ions is several 100 keV. Recently, there has been an example reporting on a MeV ion mixing study [24].

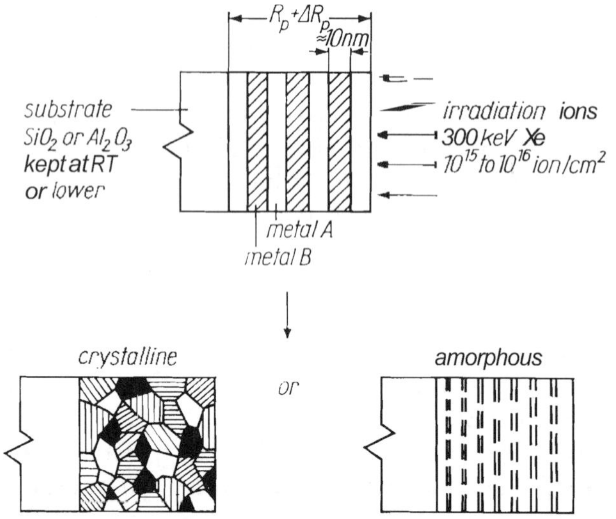

Fig. 1. Experimental arrangement of ion mixing using multilayered films

It was found that uniform mixing could be achieved well, if the total thickness of the multilayered film was designed to be the projected range R_p plus the projected range straggling ΔR_p of the irradiating ions. The R_p and ΔR_p for elemental metals can be calculated easily by the LSS theory [30]. For an alloy target of A_xB_{100-x}, where x refers to the atomic percentage of metal A, the projected range of the alloy can be calculated by the following equation [31]:

$$R_p(A_xB_{100-x}) = \frac{R_p(A)\ R_p(B)}{yR_p(B) + (100 - y)\ R_p(A)},$$

where y refers to the weight percentage of metal A in the alloy and is obtained from x easily. The calculation of the projected range straggling ΔR_p for the alloy is rather complicated. However, considering the errors involved in the calculation itself, as well as in controlling the thickness during deposition, the above equation is good enough for ΔR_p of the alloy, using it by simply replacing R_p by ΔR_p. The total thickness is then divided into the thicknesses of metals A and B, according to the desired atomic ratio of the alloy being studied. The individual layers of each metal are always designed to be around 10 nm to obtain good mixing efficiency. Clearly, ion mixing of multilayers designed in this way is capable of forming alloys with any required composition. The multilayered films are prepared in a vacuum system to deposit sequentially the metals A and B onto an inert substrate supporting the film, e.g. SiO_2 or Al_2O_3. The system is often an oil-free, multi-hearth e-gun evaporation system with the vacuum better than 6.6×10^{-5} Pa.

2.2 Irradiation parameters

It was found experimentally that the dose required to homogenize the discrete layered film is in the range of 10^{15} to 10^{16} ions/cm^2, and it varies from system to system. The ion beam current density is also an important parameter and should be controlled at low level, e.g. lower than 5 to 6 $\mu A/cm^2$, to avoid overheating of the multilayers during ion irradiation. In operating the implanter, the ion dose, which is measured by the electrical charge, is easy to adjust and control, ion mixing thus offers a unique method for investigating the phase formation or transition processes step by step. For example, by irradiating the same multilayered samples with various doses, it is possible to examine the intermediate states of the phase formation or transformation, which can hardly be studied by other methods.

Another important parameter in ion mixing is the temperature. As ion mixing often forms new solid phases, frequently new metastable alloys, ion irradiation is often performed at low temperature, e.g. at room temperature or down to liquid nitrogen temperature; a recent example reported on ion mixing performed at 4.2 K [14]. Nevertheless, the temperature mentioned for the experiments is often the apparent temperature measured at the sample holder, but not the effective temperature of the film being irradiated. The effective temperature is an important parameter in the processes induced by ion irradiation, and it should be compared with two characteristic temperatures of the materials. One is the critical temperature T,, below which the radiation-enhanced diffusion effect is negligible. The other one is the stable temperature of the newly formed phase, e.g., if one expects to form an amorphous alloy having a transition temperature T_{a-c} (from amorphous to crystalline), the effective temperature of the film during ion irradiation should of course be kept considerably lower than T_{a-c}.

2.3 *Analysis methods*

In most cases, the amount of mixing is analyzed by MeV He ion backscattering spectrometry. Fig. 2 shows an example of Ti–Au multilayers before and after ion mixing, in which two metals have quite different masses. Fig. 3 shows another example of Mo–Ru multilayers studied by ion mixing. As the mass numbers of Mo(96) and Ru(101) are very close, their signals in the BS spectra would be overlapping. However, by adjusting the tilt angle during analyses to overlap the signal of the first Mo layer with that of the second Ru layer and so on, one is still able to see the initial discrete layer structure of the film, and the mixing effect by ion irradiation. In other cases, SIMS and Auger spectrometry are used to analyze the composition depth profile of the mixed films.

The structure of the phases is identified mainly by X-ray diffraction (e.g. Read camera), and electron microscopy (TEM). Pour-point probe resistivity measurement is

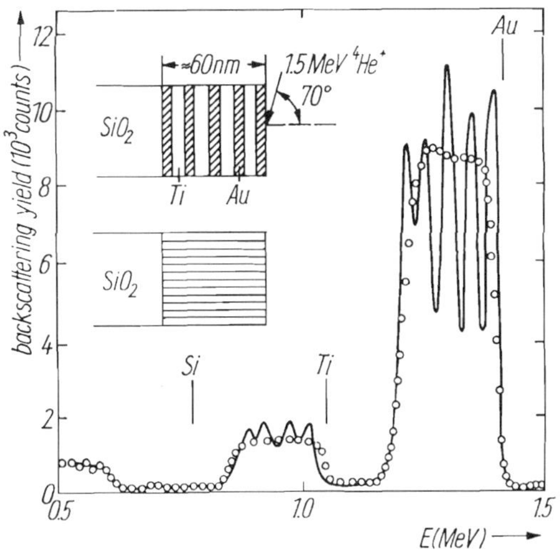

Fig. 2

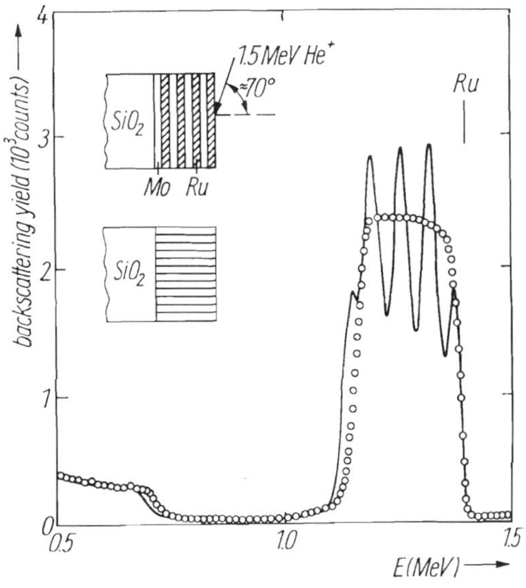

Fig. 3

Fig. 2. Backscattering spectra of Ti–Au multilayeredfilms before (solid line) and after ion mixing (5×10^{15} Xe/cm^2 at RT) (o)

Fig. 3. Backscattering spectra of Mo–Ru multilayered films before (solid line) and after ion mixing (7×10^{15} Xe/cm^2) (o) a supplemental method to give evidence of amorphous phase formation and transition to crystalline state, because the resistivity of the amorphous alloys is often greater than that of its orystalline counterpart.

3. Formation of Equilibrium or Metastable Crystalline Phases

3.1 Solid solutions

Solid solutions have been formed by ion mixing of multilayered films in eleven binary metal systems listed in Table 3. In all these systems, except Ti–Zr, Mo–Nb, and Co–Cu, multilayers with various atomic compositions from $A_{20}B_{80}$ to $A_{80}B_{20}$ have been studied under similar conditions, i.e., the metal layers were irradiated at temperatures from LN_2 to 250 °C by inert gas ions Xe, Kr, or Ne of several 100 keV. Generally, mixing took place in each system, though the amount of mixing varied from system to system. For instance, the dose required to induce uniform mixing of Fe–W multilayers was 1×10^{16} Xe/cm^2 or higher, whilc a dose of 2×10^{15} Xe/cm^2 was enough to homogenize

Table 3

Solid solutions formed by ion mixing of multilayers

system	structure	main feature of the phase diagram	ion mixed phase (structure)	ref.
Au–Ni	f.c.c.–f.c.c.	wide solid solution, miscibility gap	solid solution, f.c.c.	[3]
Ti–Zr	h.c.p.–h.c.p.	wide solid solution	sol. solution, h.c.p.	[23]
Mo–Nb	b.c.c.–b.c.c.	wide solid solution	sol. solution, b.c.c.	[23]
Au–Co	f.c.c.– f.c.c. / h.c.p.	eutectic	full range sol. solution, f.c.c.	[3]
Ag–Cu	f.c.c.–f.c.c.	eutectic	full range sol. solution, f.c.c.	[12]
Au–V	f.c.c.–b.c.c.	peritectic, compounds	two series of sol. solution, f.c.c. or b.c.c.	[3]
Au–Fe	f.c.c.– f.c.c. / b.c.c.	peritectic, compounds	two series of sol. solution, f.c.c. or b.c.c.	[3]
Fe–W	f.c.c. / b.c.c. –b.c.c.	peritectic, compounds	two series of sol. solution, Fe–b.c.c. or W–b.c.c.	[21]
Co–Cu	f.c.c. / h.c.p. –f.c.c.	peritectic	$Co_{50}Cu_{50}$ sol. solution, f.c.c., no other data	[11]
Ag–Ni	f.c.c.–f.c.c.	immiscible in solid and liquid states	two-phase mixture, Ag-rich and Ni-rich sol. solution, f.c.c. plus f.c.c.	[13]
Ag–Co	f.c.c.– f.c.c. / h.c.p.	immiscible in solid and liquid states	two-phase mixture, elemental Ag and Co separated, f.c.c. plus h.c.p.	[11]

In all systems listed above, except Ti–Zr and Mo–Nb, when the solid solubility of the ion mixed phases is beyond the equilibrium limit, these phases are metastable crystalline phases (MX), and they are supersaturated solid solutions.

the Ag–Cu multilayered films. As long as uniform mixing could be achieved, metallic alloy phases were observed by X-ray or electron diffraction analysis. The phase formation data in these systems are summarized in Table **3.** One sees that ion mixing is very powerful in producing new alloy phases:

(i) Single-phase solid solutions in the full composition range were formed in the Au–Ni system, which has a phase diagram of continuous solid solution type with miscibility gap in solid state. Ti–Zr and Mo–Nb systems have similar diagrams, but no miscibility gap exists. Single-phase solid solutions were also formed by ion mixing with some arbitrarily chosen compositions, e.g. $Ti_{70}Zr_{30}$.

(ii) Single-phase solid solutions in the full composition range were formed in simple eutectic systems Ag–Cu and Au–Co, indicating that ion mixing is able to extend the solubility substantially in this type of phase diagram.

(iii) Two series of solid solutions with extended solubilities from both terminal metals were formed in Au–V, Au–Fe, and Fe–W systems, in which intermetallic compounds divide the diagram into several sub-diagrams. That is the reason why solid solutions could not be formed throughout the full composition range.

(iv) In Ag–Ni and Ag–Co systems, in which two metals are immiscible even in the liquid state, and hence alloys could not be formed by traditional liquid melt techniques, ion niixing is capable of inducing mixing between the two nietals and forming alloys, though the micro-structure of the alloys is a two-phase mixture, each phase crystallizing in one of the structures of the metals.

All the above alloy phases were identified as solid solutions. Their lattice constants fitted those predicted by Vegard's law, and they are therefore substitutional solid solutions. Ti–Zr and Mo–Nb phases are equilibrium phases, while all other phases with solubilities beyond the equilibrium limits are metastable crystalline phases (abbreviated as MX hereafter). The MX phases are unstable upon thermal annealing, and a transition temperature T_T is introduced to define the metastability of the phase, i.e., the lowest temperature, at which half an hour annealing causes the MX phase to transit to another state of lower free energy. For most of the above MX phases, T_T is around **300** °C.

From a metallurgical point of view, one can find from the above observations that only simple crystalline structures, i.e. b.c.c., f.c.c., and h.c.p. have so far been formed by ion mixing, and that the structure of the ion-mixed phases is always the same as that of the major constituent metal of the alloy. For those systems having metal pairs of the same structure, e.g. Au–Ni, Ti–Zr, Mo–Nb, Ag–Cu, and Ag–Ni systems, the mixed phases have the same structure of both metals. While in the systems having metals of different structures, this structural correlation still holds, e.g., in the Au–V system the Au-rich phase has the same structure as f.c.c. Au, and the V-rich phase is of the same b.c.c. structure as V. In other words, it is the crystalline structure of the major constituent metal that predominantly determines the structure of the ion-mixed phase, i.e., the crystalline structure plays an important role in the ion mixing process.

3.2 Metastable electron compounds

Table 4 shows that a structurally similar MX phase of the h.c.p. structure has been formed by ion irradiation of multilayered films in five binary metal systems, i.e. Co–Au, Ti–Au, Co–Mo, Ni–Mo, and Ni–Nb systems (using A to refer to Co, Ti, and Ni, and B to **Au,** Mo, and Nb hereafter). These phases were formed in the A-rich multilayered films with overall compositions designed to be 65 to **80** at% of metal A but not otherwise. It is thus likely that these phases are enriched in metal A. The precise com-

Table 4
Structure data for the h.c.p. MX phase and its constituent metals

system	MX phase lattice constants (pm)	MX phase d_{cpp} (pm)	constituent metals*) lattice constants (pm)	constituent metals*) d_{cpp} (pm)	ref.
Co–Au	h.c.p.	$d_{002} = 260$	Co h.c.p.	$d_{002} = 202.3$	[16]
	$a = 324$		$a = 254$		
	$c = 521$		$c = 407$		
	$c/a = 1.61$		$c/a = 1.59$		
			Au f.c.c.	$d_{111} = 235.5$	
			$a = 4.08$		
Ti–Au	h.c.p.	$d_{002} = 263$	Ti h.c.p.	$d_{002} = 234$	[17]
	$a = 327$		$a = 259$		
	$c = 526$		$c = 469$		
	$c/a = 1.61$		$c/a = 1.59$		
			Au f.c.c.	$d_{111} = 235.5$	
			$a = 408$		
Co–Mo	h.c.p.	$d_{002} = 261$	Co h.c.p.	$d_{002} = 202.3$	[33]
	$a = 327$		$a = 254$		
	$c = 522$		$c = 407$		
	$c/a = 1.60$		$c/a = 1.59$		
			Mo b.c.c.	$d_{110} = 222.5$	
			$a = 314.7$		
Ni–Mo	h.c.p.	$d_{002} = 261$	Ni f.c.c.	$d_{111} = 203.4$	[6]
	$a = 325$		$a = 352$		
	$c = 521$				
	$c/a = 1.60$		Mo b.c.c.	$d_{110} = 222.5$	
			$a = 314.7$		
Ni–Nb	h.c.p.	$d_{002} = 261$	Ni f.c.c.	$d_{111} = 203.4$	[26]
	$a = 328$		$a = 325$		
	$c = 522$				
	$c/a = 1.59$		Nb b.c.c.	$d_{111} = 233$	
			$a = 330.7$		

*) All data were taken from [43].

position of the phases is not known, as they were always mixed with other phases, e.g. in the Ni–Mo case, this MX phase was mixed with an amorphous phase.

The structure of these phases are all h.c.p. and their lattice sizes are quite similar. Table 4 lists the crystal lattice parameters of these phases and of the constituent metals, as well as the spacings of the close-packed planes (d_{cpp}) in all mentioned structures. The parameter d_{cpp} was suggested to be a pertinent one in comparing the lattice size of different structures [16]. According to the data given in Table 4, the lattice sizes of these MX phases are all considerably larger than those of metals A and B, any combinations (applying Vegard's law) of the d_{cpp} values of metal A and metal B cannot give the d_{cpp} value of the MX phase, indicating that these phases are not substitutional solid solutions. The Co–Au MX phase was thought to be an interstitial solid solution, when it was first observed. But it is unlikely that this phase could be an interstitial phase, as the difference in atomic sizes is too small for Au atoms to sit in the interstitial sites of the lattice of Co, and the same reason also applies to the other four MX phases. The formation of these phases has later been attributed to the valence electron effect. For a close-packed hexagonal structure, the maximum number of electron states per atom, n, in the Jones' zone (including doubling for spin) can be calculated by the following equation [32]:

$$n = 2 - \frac{3}{4}\left(\frac{a}{c}\right)^2\left[1 - \frac{1}{4}\left(\frac{a}{c}\right)^2\right],$$

where a and c are the lattice constants of the h.c.p. structure. According to this calculation, the n values of these five phases are almost identical, i.e. n = 1.73 to 1.74, which is very close to the value of 7/4 = 1.75, corresponding to the well-defined Hume-Rothery 7/4 electron compound. These phases can therefore be considered as a metastable electron compounds [33].

It is of interest to notice the structural correlation in forming these MX phases. Obviously, the structures of the first three MX phases are the same as those of the nrajor constituent metals Co, Ti, and Co, respectively. For the last two-Ni-containing phases, the MX phases are h.c.p., while the major constituent metal Ni is of f.c.c. structure. However, from a crystallographical point of view, h.c.p. and f.c.c. are similar structures, both are built up by stacking of close-packed atomic planes differing only in stacking order. Therefore, it can be stated that the structure of the ion-induced phase (both solid solution and electron compound) is always the same as, or similar to, the nrajor constituent metal of the alloy. Besides, in forming this electron compound, the main feature of the MX phase is still controlled by the crystalline structure of the major metal, while the valence electron also plays a role, e.g., in determining the alloy composition.

4. Formation of Amorphous Alloys

It is well known that amorphous materials have in many respects unique properties, such as high strength, excellent corrosion resistance, good barrier properties against diffusion, etc. Great effort has been made in the last two decades to develop new manufacturing techniques to produce amorphous materials, as well as to promote an understanding of the amorphization mechanism. Ion mixing of multilayered film has recently been established to be a method for forming metallic glasses, and shown to be a valuable means for investigating the amorphization mechanism as well. Up to the present, a great number of amorphous alloys have been obtained by this technique, and especially two sufficient conditions have been formulated from the experimental data for producing amorphous alloys by ion mixing. Accordingly, amorphous alloys so obtained can be divided into two classes.

4.1 Alloy compositions in two-phase regions of the equilibrium phase diagram

The experimental results reported in the early studies of ion mixing in binary metal systems, i.e. Au–V, Cu–Ta, and Co–Au (see Table 5) suggested that a difference in structure of the component metals seemed to favour the formation of an amorphous phase. In 1982, Liu et al. [6] conducted a systematic study, by choosing several binary systems covering all the possible combinations among three simple structures, b.c.c., f.c.c., and h.c.p., and the extreme values of two more important metallurgical factors, i.e., atomic size and electronegativity of the metals. It was found that with a difference in structure, amorphous alloys could be formed by ion mixing, regardless of the other two factors. These results led to the so-called structural difference rule,

Table **5**

Amorphous alloys formed by ion mixing with average compositions in the two-phase region of the phase diagram

system	structure	$\Delta r/r$ (%)	$\Delta n/n$ (%)	amorphous alloy	T_{a-c} (°C)	ref.
Al–Nb	f.c.c.–b.c.c.	2	6	$Al_{55}Nb_{45}$	350 to 400	[6]
Au–V		8	38	$Au_{40}V_{60}$	350	[3]
				$Cu_{50}Ta_{50}$		
Cu–Ta		13	21	$Cu_{25}Ta_{75}$		[19]
Ni–Mo		11	0	$Ni_{65}Mo_{35}$	480 to 500	[6]
				$Ni_{35}Mo_{65}$	580 to 600	
				$Ni_{35}Nb_{65}$	550 to 600	[26]
Ni–Nb		15	11	$Ni_{55}Nb_{45}$	600 to 650	
				$Ni_{65}Nb_{35}$	500 to 550	
				$Ni_{80}Nb_{20}$	450 to 500	
Mo–Co	b.c.c.–h.c.p.	10	0	$Co_{65}Mo_{35}$	550 to 580	[6]
				$Co_{35}Mo_{65}$	610 to 630	
Mo–Ru		4	18	$Mo_{55}Ru_{45}$	500 to 550	[25]
Co–Au	h.c.p.–f.c.c.	14	25	$Au_{25}Co_{75}$	200	[3]
Ti–Au		1	38		400 to 430	[17]
				$Ti_{40}Au_{60}$	350 to 400	
Er–Ni		30	33	$Er_{65}Ni_{35}$	400 to 500	[6]
				$Er_{40}Ni_{60}$	400 to 500	
Hf–Ni		40	32	$Ni_{80}Hf_{20}$		[22]
				$Ni_{55}Hf_{45}$		
				$Ni_{20}Hf_{80}$		
Fe–W	b.c.c.–b.c.c.	11	6	$Fe_{70}W_{30}$	600	[21]
Ru–Zr	h.c.p.–h.c.p.	13	40	$Ru_{25}Zr_{75}$		[9, 28]
				$Ru_{75}Zr_{25}$		

r refers to the atomic radius, n refers to the electronegativity both taken from [44]. The larger r and n are used for references. T_{a-c} refers to the transition temperature from amorphous to crystalline states.

which is nearly a sufficient condition but not a necessary one. The rule states that an amorphous alloy will most likely be formed by ion mixing of metal layers in the system, if the two metals have different structures and the alloy composition is in the two-phase region of the phase diagram. The underlying mechanism of the rule was thought at that time to be the competition between two terminal metals resulting in a frustration of the crystallization process. By inspecting the equilibrium phase diagrams, one may find that two-phase regions can equally well occur in the binary systems, where the two metals are of the same structure. For example, as long as there exist intermetallic compounds in this type of system, two-phase regions do occur. Liu [9] has checked whether the rule also applies to this situation, by performing ion mixing experiments in the Ru–Zr system. Ru and Zr are both of h.c.p. structure, yet a compound RuZr divides the whole diagram into two portions, each featuring two-phase character. Two amorphous alloys, $Ru_{25}Zr_{75}$ and $Ru_{75}Zr_{25}$, were indeed formed by room temperature

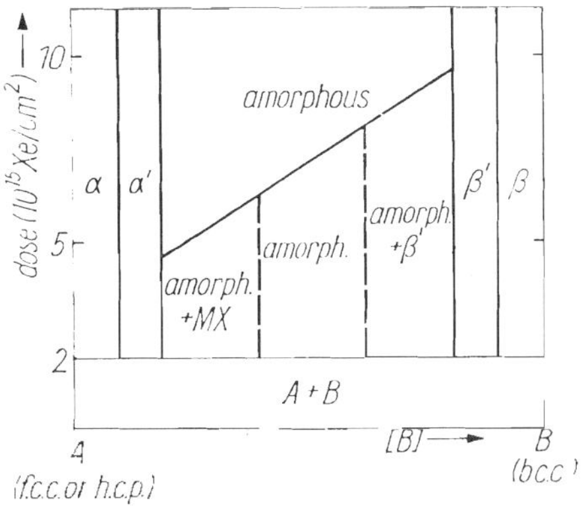

Fig. 5. Proposed ion-induced phase diagram, the corresponding phase diagram is shown in Fig. 4a. The sequence of events as a function of ion dose is shown. Extended (supersaturated) solid solutions α' and β' are obtained from both sides of the phase diagram. As the composition approaches the middle of the phase diagram from the A side, a mixture of amorphous phase and MX phase (h.c.p.) is formed at medium dose, while a mixture of an amorphous phase and β'-phase is obtained approaching from the B side. At high dose, a uniform amorphous phase is formed. In some cases, the amorphous phase may dissociate upon further ion irradiation (MX is a metastable electron compound with h.c.p. structure differing from h.c.p. A)

Taking the phase diagram of Fig. 4a as a representative phase diagram, the prediction of alloy phase formation can be summarized in the ion-induced phase diagram shown in Fig. 5. One sees that crystalline phases can only be formed on both sides near the terminal metals, while an amorphous alloy can be formed in a rather wide composition range.

We have shown in the previous discussions that nearly all the alloy phases obtained so far by ion mixing can be explained by the proposed model and confirm the empirical rules. However, a few special binary systems should be discussed again in detail, because the observations in these systems seemed to be the counter examples to the predictions, though most of them are actually not.

For the Ag–Co and Ag–Ni systems (see Table 3) ion mixing of multilayers resulted in two separate crystalline phases, while the first rule seems to expect the formation of amorphous alloys. The reason is probably the immiscibility of these systems even in the liquid state. Wang et al. have shown [39] that mixing could hardly be achieved in the Cu–W system, which has the same miscibility feature as these two systems. It is thus believed that though the BS spectra revealed the mixing of Ag–Co and Ag–Ni multilayers after ion irradiation, the real uniform mixing in a micro-scale has not been actually achieved, i.e. the necessary condition for forming a single-phase amorphous alloy has not been achieved. Instead, the compositions in the local areas probably fit to the corresponding two crystalline phases of simple structures, and these phases were formed through the rapid crystallization kinetics. The results in these systems are therefore not against the first rule for amorphous alloy formation. Alonso and Simozar [40] have proposed another interpretation for these systems, suggesting it was the large positive heat of formation that speaks against the amorphous phase formation by ion mixing. As the large positive heat of formation has been already related to the immiscibility in the equilibrium phase diagram, two ways of interpretation of course give the same answer.

For the Ag–Cu system, no amorphous phase has been observed for the alloy composition lying in the two-phase region, even if the ion mixing was performed at LN_2 temperature [3], while the first rule predicts that it is obtainable. It was reported recently that co-evaporation onto a cooled substrate resulted in the formation of Ag–Cu amorphous alloy, and the amorphons phase turned to the crystalline phase at a transition temperature around **100** °C [41]. The reason why ion mixing has not formed an amorphous phase is therefore connected with the effective temperature of the film being very close to or even higher than the T_T of the Ag–Cu amorphous alloy. This interpretation is also confirmed by the fact that $Au_{25}Co_{75}$ amorphous alloy with $T_T \approx$ $\approx$ **200** °C could only be formed by LN_2 ion mixing, hut not by RT ion mixing.

ion mixing. Also, the formation of a $Fe_{70}W_{30}$ amorphous phase reported earlier [21] confirms this idea. The structural difference rule has thus been extended, and it can be stated that an amorphous alloy is most likely to be formed in any two-phase region of the equilibrium phase diagram by ion mixing performed at suitably low temperature. Shortly, the extended rule can be called as two-phase competition rule, however, the two competing phases here are associated with the two adjacent phases, not necessarily the terminal ones. In Table 5 more than 20 amorphous alloys have been obtained supporting or consisting with the rule.

There are two points worthwhile mentioning.

(i) The rule includes the well-known deep eutectic criterion for forming metallic glasses by liquid melt quenching, and is more general than the criterion. The eutectic portion is only a special type of the two-phase region of the equilibrium phase diagram. Moreover, the rule applies to the eutectic portion, which is not restricted to "deep" eutectic ones. For example, liquid quenching has not succeeded in producing an amorphous Mo–Ru alloy at eutectic composition, as the melting point of the alloy is as high as 1900 °C [34], while room temperature ion mixing is able to make the alloy amorphous [25].

(ii) It is noticed that the transition temperatures of most of the amorphous alloys obtained by RT ion mixing are higher than 400 °C, while the $Au_{25}Co_{75}$ amorphous alloy having a $T_{a\text{-}c}$ of about 200 °C was only formed by LN_2 ion mixing, i.e. at −196 °C. This probably has to do with the effective temperature rise of the multilayered film caused by ion irradiation, e.g. a typical current density of 5 $\mu A/cm^2$ may cause a temperature rise of about 200 K. Consequently, those amorphous alloys having a $T_{a\text{-}c}$ considerably higher than 200 °C could be formed by RT ion mixing, while those amorphous alloys with $T_{a\text{-}c}$ lower than 200 °C are only obtainable by low-temperature ion mixing.

4.2 Alloy compositions in the vicinity of intermetallic compounds in the equilibrium phase diagram

The observation that only simple structures, i.e. one of the b.c.c., f.c.c., and h.c.p. structures, has been formed by multilayer ion mixing in the metal–metal systems mentioned in Section 3, implies that the kinetic conditions available for crystallization during the ion mixing process are restrictive, and perhaps are sufficient only for simple structures to crystallize. This leads one to consider the possibility that an amorphous phase might also be formed by ion mixing of multilayered samples with compositions at (or in the vicinity of) intermetallic compounds with complicated structure. In fact, [6] and [20] reported a few examples of amorphous alloys of this class, i.e. $Ni_{50}Mo_{50}$, $Ti_{50}Ni_{50}$, and $Fe_{55}Ti_{45}$. Moreover, the transition temperature of the $Ni_{50}Mo_{50}$ alloy from amorphous to crystalline state is the highest one (630 °C) among the ion-mixed amorphous alloys in the system (see data in Table 5), lending support to the idea that crystallization of the NiMo phase is more difficult than that of simple structures such as f.c.c. Ni or b.c.c. Mo. Later, Hung et al. [8], Liu [9], and Cheng et al. [28] have checked this idea by more ion mixing experiments, and showed more evidence in support of it. All these data are listed in Table 6 and we see indeed that some 20 amorphous alloys have been formed, and most of them are of complex structure (more than two atoms per unit cell). In Table 6, there are some crystalline phases formed by ion mixing, i.e., AlPd, AlNi, and Au–Al. It was argued by Hung et al. that AlPd and AlNi are of CsCl structure (two atoms per unit cell); ion mixing is therefore not able to make them amorphous. Nevertheless, there are more examples listed in Table 6 showing that CsCl structures could be amorphized by ion mixing. It is thus believed that in ion mixing in alloys containing Al, radiation-enhanced diffusion is probably

Table 6
Amorphous alloys formed by ion mixing with average compositions at/near equilibrium compounds

system	composition studied	nearby compound and structure	phase formed by RT IM	ref.
Ni–Mo	$Ni_{50}Mo_{50}$	NiMo δ-phase, orthorhombic	amorphous	[6]
Ti–Ni	$Ti_{50}Ni_{50}$	TiNi phase, CsCl cubic	amorphous	[6, 24, 27]
Fe–Ti	$Fe_{55}Ti_{45}$	FeTi phase, CsCl cubic	*77 K IM, amorphous	[20]
Al–Ni	in wide range	Al_3Ni phase, orthorhombic Al_3Ni_2 phase, hexagonal $AlNi_3$ phase, Cu_3Au (AlNi phase, CsCl cubic)	amorphous amorphous amorphous **crystal.)	[7, 15]
Al–Pd	in wide range	Al_3Pd phase, orthorhombic Al_3Pd_2 phase, hexagonal $AlPd_2$ phase, orthorhombic (AlPd phase, CsCl cubic)	amorphous amorphous amorphous **crystal.)	[7]
Al–Pt	in wide range	Al_2Pt phase, fluorite AlPt phase, cubic Al_3Pt_5 phase, orthorhombic $AlPt_3$ phase, tetragonal	amorphous amorphous amorphous amorphous	[7]
Ti–Au	$Ti_{75}Au_{25}$	Ti_3Au phase, β-W	amorphous	[9]
Ru–Zr	$Ru_{50}Zr_{50}$	RuZr phase, CsCl cubic	amorphous	[9]
Ti–Co	$Ti_{50}Co_{50}$	TiCo phase, cubic (b.c.)	amorphous	[8]
Al–Au	in wide range	Au_4Al phase, cubic (Au_2Al phase, cubic) (Al_2Au phase, cubic) Al_2Au phase, cubic	amorphous **crystal.) **crystal.) *4.2 K IM amorphous	[8] [14]
Ru–Ti	$Ru_{50}Ti_{50}$	RuTi phase, CsCl cubic	*77 K IM amorphous	[28]

Structure data were taken from [43] or [45]. Notes with * and ** are discussed in the context.

nvolved. In fact, the crystalline Al_2Au phase was obtained by RT ion mixing as reported by Hung et al., while Schmid and Ziemann [14] have succeeded in forming an Al_2Au amorphous phase by performing ion mixing at 4.2 K.

Experimental data offered thus far establishe that an amorphous phase is also possible to be formed by ion mixing, when the average composition of the multilayered film is the same as the equilibrium compound with complicated structure, though the precise definition of the complicated structure is needed to further clarify the issue. It appears that a second rule can be formulated phenomenologically: An amorphous phase is likely to be formed by ion mixing at suitably low temperature, when the composition is in a single-phase region of the phase diagram, and the phase has complicated structure (at present,, the complicated structure should at least be other than simple b.c.c., f.c.c., or h.c.p. structure).

It is of interest to point out that most of the intermetallic compounds are of complicated structures and typically have rather high melting points. To the author's knowledge neither liquid melt quenching can produce this type of amorphous alloys, nor can the pulsed laser beam or pulsed ion beam. For instance, ion mixing has easily produced $Ti_{75}Au_{25}$ amorphous alloy, while pulsed ion beam cannot make it amorphous. It is thus demonstrated that ion mixing is a powerful method in manufacturing new amorphous alloys, and this would certainly enhance the further connection between the ion beam method with some practical applications.

5. Phase Formation Mechanisms

5.1 General view orl ion mixing

Ion mixing is generally considered as a two-step process.

(i) A prompt process in which atomic collisions are initiated by the irradiating ions and result in mixing of the discrete layered film into a homogeneous mixture. The mixture is thought to consist of a random configuration of atoms containing lots of defects, and being in an excited state, because a certain amount of energy has been deposited into the multilayered film. The time period of this step is estimated to be about 10^{-12} s [35].

(ii) A relaxation process in which the excited mixture transits to a state of lower free energy. A rough estimation (thermalspike model) considering the spreading of the deposited energy to the surrounding matrix gives a time period of the order of 10^{-11} s [36]. It means that the effective cooling rate can be as high as 10^{14} K/s, if the temperature peak in the spike centre is assumed to be of the order of magnitude of 10^3 K.

The prompt process is usually treated by the theory of atomic collisions, and has been studied by computer simulation in recent years. However, no clear picture of the relaxation process on the atomic scale has been formulated so far. The emphasis here is to concern this process on the scale of "phase structure" of the outcome of ion mixing. In this sense, it is relevant to treat the relaxation process by considerations of thermodynamics of solids and kinetics of crystallization. It is commonly accepted that the structure of the ion-mixed alloy is formed during the relaxation process, but not in the prompt process, because the atoms are dynamically excited all the time during the prompt process. In principle, if the temperature and time conditions are sufficient for crystallization during relaxation, the random mixture transits to a crystal form, which either corresponds to the equilibrium phases expected by thermodynamics or to metastable phases. While those conditions are severely restricted, the random mixture is frozen in this atomic configuration and an amorphous phase is formed.

5.2 Simple model using free energy diagram

Using multilayered films in ion mixing to form the alloy phase, the average composition of the sample, hence the attained alloy composition can be designed intentionally in advance. Facing the equilibrium phase diagram being studied, one can find three possible situations of alloy composition located in three different phase regions in the diagram. Fig. 4a and b show a representative phase diagram and its corresponding free energy–composition plot (orfree energy diagram), respectively [37]. In the figures, three possible compositions are referred to by points 1, 2, and 3. Point 1 is in a single-phase region, and this phase is the solid solution with simple crystal structure, namely b.c.c., f.c.c., or h.c.p. Point 2 is in the so-called two-phase region, and the equilibrium state of this alloy is a two-phase mixture, each having its corresponding crystalline structure, i.e. α and y. Point 3 is again in a single-phase region, typically an intermetallic compound exists in a narrow composition range, and the compound is frequently of complicated structure. In the free energy diagram, points x, y, and z are

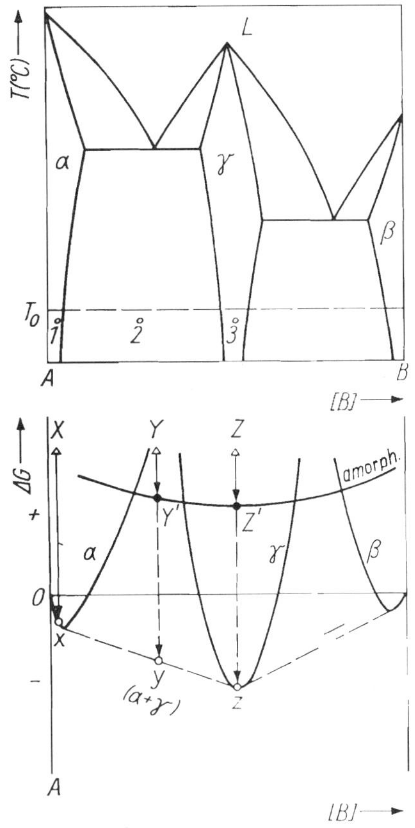

Fig. 4. a) Representative phase diagram and b) the corresponding free energy–composition diagram (△ excited state, ● amorphous state, o equilibrium state)

referred to the equilibrium states of the alloys having the compositions of 1, 2, and 3, respectively. Point y is lying on the common tangent line of the free energy curves of α- and y-phases, as the free energy of the random mixture obtained immediately after a prompt process is considerably higher than that of the equilibrium state. It is therefore reasonable to represent these excited states by points X, Y, and Z, though the exact values are not known and need not be known. Along the path toward equilibrium, metastable states may exist where atoms can be arrested. The free energy of the metastable states is of course higher than that of the equilibrium states and is assumed to be lower than that of the random mixtures. In Pig. 4b, curve amorph, refers to the amorphous states.

According to the thermodynamic law, the states of X, Y, and Z are unstable and would be driven toward equilibrium states. However, the transitions of X x, Y → y, and Z → z require their own necessary conditions quite differently. As mentioned in Section 2, in order to form a new alloy phase (frequently metastable), the typical ion mixing is performed at suitably low temperature, so that no significant atomic movement is able to take place during the relaxation process. In this case, the conditions for these transitions are limited. The formation of the alloy phases listed in Sections 3 and 4 can be interpreted by using Fig. 4a and b as follows:

(i) Transition Y → y requires first a chemical separation to adjust the composition into the fitting compositions of the equilibrium crystalline phases α and y, and then the crystallization of these phases is able to proceed and complete. The adjustment in composition requires large-scale atomic movement, e.g. through diffusion, and this type of atomic movement is probably suppressed resulting in the frustration of the formation of eauilibrium phases. while the transition Y → Y' (Y' is an amorphous phase) is polymorphic requiring no significant rearrangement of atoms, i.e. it is a diffusionless transition retaining the random configuration of atoms. Consequently, transition Y → Y' is favoured, i.e. the alloy with composition lying in the two-phase region is favourable to be amorphized by ion mixing. The formation of the amorphous alloys of the first class listed in Table **5** can be interpreted in this way.

(ii) For the alloy composition of 3, the transitions of the mixture Z to the equilibrium state z, and from Z to the amorphous state Z' are both polymorphic, i.e. both transitions require no composition change. However, if the y-phase has a complicated crystal structure, to crystallize this phase requires certainly stricter kinetic conditions than a simple structure phase. Under the condition of low-temperature ion mixing, these are probably not available. The crystallization of the y-phase is thus frustrated kinetically with the result that an amorphous alloy is formed instead. The amorphous alloys of the second class as listed in Table 6 can be explained in this way. We see that amorphous alloys of the second class are formed by kinetic frustration, while the amorphous alloys of the first class are formed by thermodynamic and kinetic frustration.

(iii) The transition X → x is also polymorphic, i.e. it is simply a crystallization process. Since the terminal solid solution of the a-phase (or on the opposite side, of the β-phase) always has a simple b.c.c., f.c.c., or h.c.p. crystal structure, and these structures have a rapid growth kinetics in crystallization, transition of X → x can be completed within the very short time period of 10^{-11} s available during relaxation, hence a single-phase solid solution is formed. This explains the formation of all the solid solutions listed in Table 3, except the Ag–Ni and Ag–Co phases. For those supersaturated solid solutions, the interpretation is the same, as no essential difference occurs in the sense of the polymorphic transition and the simplicity of the crystalline structure.

The formation of the metastable electron compounds listedin Table 4 can be explained as follows: First, the free energy curve of this MX phase should be similar to that of a compound, e.g., the y-phase, the transition from the random mixture to the MX state is therefore polymorphic. Second, the MX phase is of simple structure, i.e. an enlarged h.c.p. structure, therefore, the crystallization process can be completed during relaxation. Moreover, the MX phase seems likely to grow coherently from the lattice of the major metal, for Ti–Au, Co–Au, and Co–Mo phases, only the original h.c.p. structure is required to expand, while for Ni–Mo and Ni–Nb phases, apart from the expansion of the original unit cell, a slight shift of stacking order from ABCABC ... to ABAB ... is required. This type of structural coherency has also been observed in metal nitride formation by direct nitrogen implantation into metals, and the formation mechanisms have been attributed to the movement of dislocations [38].

5.3 Prediction of alloy phase formation using equilibrium phase diagram

From the experimental data and the proposed mechanisms discussed in the previous sections, some empirical rules have been formulated for predicting the alloy phase formation. In applying these rules, it is only required to inspect the location of the alloy composition being studied in the corresponding equilibrium phase diagram. It is a straightforward approach, because the equilibrium phase diagram is considered as a compass for studying alloy systems. Facing an equilibrium phase diagram, the phase formation of ion mixing of metal layers at suitably low temperature can now be predicted by the following rules:

(i) If the overall composition is in the two-phase region of the phase diagram, an amorphous alloy is most likely to be formed. This is the extended "structural difference rule".

(ii) If the overall composition is in or near the single-phase region of the phase diagram and the structure of this phase is not simple, an amorphous alloy is likely to be formed.

(iii) If the overall composition is in or near the single-phase region of the phase diagram and the structure of this phase is simple, a crystalline phase is to be formed.

Two notes should be added. First, as far as the alloy phase formation is concerned, it is assumed that uniform mixing throughout the film has been achieved by ion irradiation. Second, the phase region concerned here is the first available phase region below the liquid state, or the first state the random mixture can transit into during approaching equilibrium.

For the Au–Fe system (Fig. 6), an amorphous alloy is expected to be obtainable by the first rule in the two-phase region, yet Tsaur et al. [3] have not succeeded in obtaining it. Looking at the phase diagram in Fig. 6, one sees that a huge solid solution region exists over the two-phase region, and this single-phase region is the first state the random mixture reaches when going toward equilibrium during relaxation. That is why the alloy with composition of 60 at% Fe could not be amorphized by ion mixing, and an Au f.c.c. structure solid solution was formed instead. Moreover, as the solid solution region from both terminal metals can be extended by ion mixing, the composition range favouring amorphization would be narrower than it is in Fig. 6, hence it is difficult to form amorphous phases in this system. The same idea also applies to the Au–Ni system (Fig. 7), one sees again that there exists a continuous solid solution region in the whole composition range directly under the liquid state, though there is a two-phase region underneath. According to rule 3, ion mixing favours to form solid solutions in the full range of alloy compositions in this system.

The results of ion mixing in the Ru–Ti system [28] are perhaps the only exception from the above rules. Two multilayered films with alloy compositions of $Ru_{25}Ti_{75}$ and $Ru_{70}Ti_{30}$ both lying in two-phase regions, did not become amorphous by ion mixing at 77 and 300 K using a dose of 8×10^{15} Xe/cm^2, and two crystalline phases of b.c.c. and h.c.p., respectively, were formed instead. Those authors attributed these results to the substrate temperature of the films, and believed that the free energy of the crystalline phases at those temperatures was lower than that of the amorphous state. It would be interesting to see what would happen if the ion mixing extends to even higher doses and wider ranges of temperatures, as the author thinks that the dose of $8 \times$ X 10^{15} Xe/cm^2 was not enough to amorphize Ru-rich multilayered films. The important point from these results is that the calculation of the various metastable states, e.g., the free energy, is necessary for an ion mixing study.

From the above discussions the author believes that phase diagrams are indeed a good guidance for predicting the alloy phase formation. It is simple and straightforward in comparison with other proposed criteria, e.g., using polymorphic phase diagrams as suggested by Johnson et al. [10], and using a plot of the ratio of atomic radii versus heat of formation suggested by Alonso and Simozar [40], etc. However, the predic-

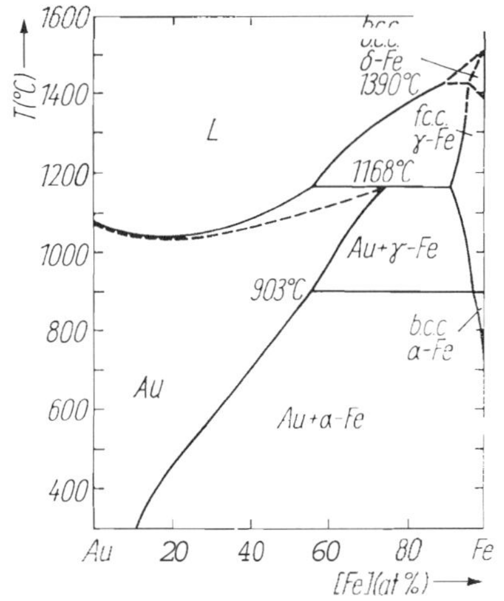

Fig. 6

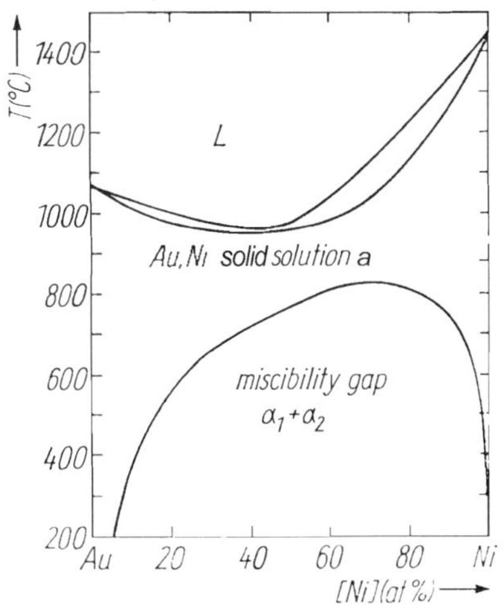

Fig. 7

Fig. 6. Phase diagram of the Au–Fe system

Fig. 7. Phase diagram of the Au–Ni system

tion using the phase diagram is excellent, because the equilibrium phase diagram contains most of the important materials characteristics, e.g., atomic, crystalographic, as well as thermodynamic parameters.

6. Some Phase Transformations Related to Ion Irradiation

6.1 Ion-induced crystal to amorphous and amorphous to crystal transitions

It was found in ion mixing studies that ion irradiation could cause both crystalline to amorphous, and amorphous to crystalline transitions in some cases. These observations are of interest, because they are new phenomena explored by ion beams and because the stability of the materials upon irradiation by energetic particles is an important aspect for the materials used in the radiation environment.

Table 7 shows some examples of crystalline to amorphous transitions. In this case, niultilayered films were first annealed to form the equilibrium phases expected by the phase diagram, and then irradiated by ions. One sees from Table 7 that twelve crystalline phases turned to amorphous states upon irradiation. Note that this type of transition is different from the formation of an amorphous phase by ion mixing of the as-deposited multilayered films, which contain the crystalline phases of the elemental metals. The amorphization process is thought to be similar to that discussed in Section **5**, i.e., the amorphous state is probably achieved by atomic collisions in the prompt step, but the crystallization of the equilibrium crystalline phases is frustrated during relaxation. Hung et al. [7] have reported some counter examples that the crystalline AlNi and AlPd crvstalline phases remained crvstalline upon RT ion irradiation. It seems likely that the amorphization is also achieved during the prompt process for these two phases, but the radiation enhanced diffusion acting during relaxation allows the crystallization process to be completed. The crystalline phase of Fe_7W_6 has a complicated structure and a rather high melting point. If amorphization had been achieved in the prompt process, the amorphous state would have remained after relaxation. Conversely, the crystalline form of Fe_7W_6 probably survived upon ion irradiation and only a slight perturbation was caused, which could be recovered afterwards.

Table 7

Transformations from crystalline to amorphous induced by ion irradiation

crystalline*)	irradiation by Xe ions	phase resulting	ref.
Ti_3Au	5×10^{15}, RT	amorphous	[9]
Ti_3Au + TiAu	5×10^{15}, RT	amorphous	[17]
Al_3Ni, Al_3Ni_2, $AlNi_3$	2×10^{14}, RT	all amorphous	[7]
Al_3Pd, Al_3Pd_2, $AlPd_2$	2×10^{14}, RT	all amorphous	[7]
Al_2Pt, AlPt, Al_3Pt_5, $AlPt_3$	2×10^{14}, RT	all amorphous	[7]

*) All these crystalline phases were formed by thermal annealing of the multilayered films with compositions fitting those of the equilibrium metallic compounds. Crystalline phases of Fe_7W_6, AlNi, and AlPd remained crystalline upon similar ion irradiation.

Table 8
Transformations of ion-mixed amorphous phase from amorphous to crystalline by ion irradiation

amorphous*)	irradiation by Xe ions	phase resulting	ref.
$Ti_{65}Au_{35}$	5 X 10^{15}, RT	cryst. Au + MX(h.c.p.)	[17]
$Ti_{40}Au_{60}$	1 × 10^{15}, RT	cryst. Au + (?) phase	[17]
$Co_{65}Mo_{35}$	1 X 10^{16}, RT	amorph. + MX(h.c.p.)	[41]
$Ni_{65}Mo_{35}$	1.3 X 10^{16}, RT	amorph. + MX(h.c.p.)	[6]
$Au_{70}Si_{30}$	2 X 10^{15}, RT	cryst. Au + MX(s.c.)	[42]

*) All these amorphous alloys were obtained by ion mixing of multilayered films with the compositions given.
An amorphous alloy of $Ni_{65}Nb_{35}$ remained amorphous upon Xe ion irradiation up to a dose of 1.2 X 10^{16} Xe/cm^2 at RT.

Table 8 shows another type of transition induced by ion irradiation. One sees that five amorphous alloys, including an Au–Si alloy, turned to the crystalline phase upon irradiation. This type of transition has been attributed to the ion deniixing effect first observed in the Au–Si system [42]. By means of ion demixing, two changes, i.e. composition and phase changes, take place upon ion irradiation, while in metal–metal systems, the composition change is not significant or even not visible in the BS spectra. The possible process of demixing is thought such that the ion-induced composition change leads the local compositions in some regions fitting those of the crystalline phases, and these phases crystallized during relaxation. Kung et al. [26] have reported that a $Ni_{65}Nb_{35}$ amorphous alloy remained unchanged upon Xe irradiation up to a dose of 1.2 × 10^{16} Xe/cm^2.

Those phases that change their state upon irradiation are called radiation-sensitive or radiation-soft materials, while those phases that remain unchanged are called radiation-hard ones. The observations listed here are limited and the understanding of ion-induced phase transformations certainly requires further studies to give more precise experimental evidence as well as some theoretical analysis.

6.2 Transition from crystal to amorphous upon aging

An unusual phase transformation, i.e. the crystalline MX to amorphous transition upon aging, was observed for two $Ni_{65}Mo_{35}$ multilayered films that had been irradiated to relatively low doses [9]. After irradiation, a MX phase of h.c.p. structure and an amorphous phase were formed as revealed by X-ray diffraction patterns (Read camera), but after storage at room temperature for about one month the X-ray diffraction pattern showed no crystalline diffraction lines and only the amorphous phase remained,

$$\text{(multilayers)}Ni_{65}Mo_{35} \xrightarrow{5 \times 10^{15}\ Xe/cm^2} MX(h.c.p.) + \text{amorph.} \xrightarrow{RT\ aging} \text{amorphous.}$$

From these observations (within the resolution of X-ray analysis), one concludes that the MX phase has turned to the amorphous state. In order to compare the free energy levels of-all the phases involved, Liu [9] performed post-annealing experiments with several ion-mixed Ni–Mo amorphous alloys. Table 9 shows the phase evolution of these alloys upon annealing. The important point is that the $Ni_{65}Mo_{35}$ and $Ni_{35}Mo_{65}$ alloys

Table 9

Phase transformation of Ni–Mo amorphous alloys upon thermal annealing

amorphous alloy	phase evolution with increasing temperature (T,)
$Ni_{65}Mo_{35}$	$\xrightarrow{<480\ °C}$ amorph. $\xrightarrow{500\ °C}$ amorph. + MX $\xrightarrow{higher}$ Ni + 8-phase
$Ni_{50}Mo_{50}$	$\xrightarrow{<600\ °C}$ amorph. $\xrightarrow{630\ °C}$ amorph. + 8-phase $\xrightarrow{higher}$ δ-phase
$Ni_{35}Mo_{65}$	$<580\ °C$ amorph. $\xrightarrow{600\ °C}$ amorph. + Mo $\xrightarrow{higher}$ Mo + &phase

Annealing time was **30** min at each temperature step.

first turned to intermediate states by precipitating extra Ni and Mo from the amorphous matrix (likely having the composition of $Ni_{50}Mo_{50}$). It led to a proposed scheniatical free energy diagram for the Ni–Mo system, including the free energy curves for MX and amorphous states (Fig. 8). Fig. 9 is a partially enlarged free energy diagram, by which the unexpected phase transition can be explained as follows. After irradiation, the film contains a range of composition, which can probably be represented in Fig. 9

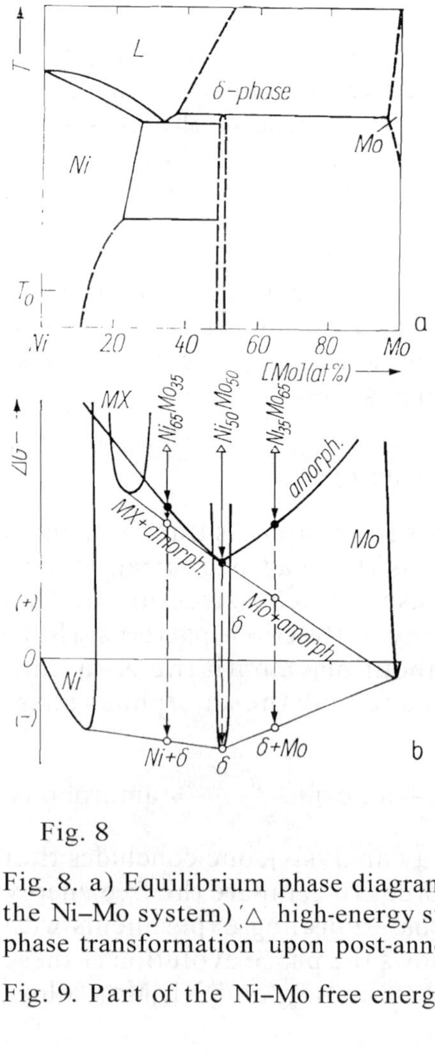

Fig. 8

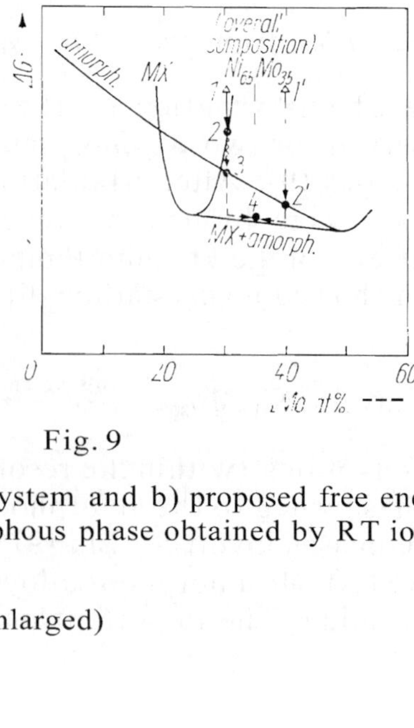

Fig. 9

Fig. 8. a) Equilibrium phase diagram of Ni–Mo system and b) proposed free energy diagram for the Ni–Mo system) (△ high-energy state, ● amorphous phase obtained by RT ion mixing, - - - - phase transformation upon post-annealing)

Fig. 9. Part of the Ni–Mo free energy diagram (enlarged)

by points 1 and 1'. After relaxation, two phases are present, i.e., MX and an amorphous phase (points 2 and 2'). As mentioned before, the MX phase has greater Ni content than the average one, the amorphous phase therefore should have more Mo in it. Then room temperature aging causes the MX phase to turn to the amorphous state of point 3. Thus the amorphous phase seen in the diffraction pattern after aging can probably be represented by points 2' and 3. It was established that high-temperature annealing at 480 to 500 °C dissociates the amorphous phases into a mixture (4) of MX and an amorphous phase again. The transition paths of the last phase transformation are not exactly known and therefore drawn by dashed lines in Fig. 9. One may argue that this interpretation is only a speculation, but as long as the free energy curves for MX and amorphous phases can intersect like those in Fig. 9 the above transition is possible. Moreover, a similar transition was also observed in the Ni–Nb system [9], it is thus believed that this type of phase transition is not peculiar to a few systems. Its understanding should certainly be improved by more experimental studies, e.g., tracing the transition by quantitative X-ray diffraction analysis, etc.

7. Concluding Remarks

(i) The structural character of the ion-mixed phase can now be predicted by the formulated rules with the aid of the equilibrium phase diagram.

(ii) Ion mixing is a unique method to manufacture new alloy thin films, especially a great variety of amorphous thin films, to meet the requirement of developing new materials with specific properties.

(iii) Ion mixing is a valuable means for studying some important topics in the field of physical metallurgy, e.g., the theory of the alloy phase and phase transformations, etc.

(iv) More studies are still required to promote the understanding of the ion-induced phenomena observed so far, e.g., calculation of the metastable states, crystallization kinetics of various phases, precise experiments, etc.

Acknowledgements

The author is grateful to his colleagues both in the Department of Engineering Physics, Tsinghua University, and at California Institute of Technology for their encouragement, without which this paper could hardly be written. The financial support to this project from the Administration of Tsinghua is also acknowledged.

Note

Some recent progress has been obtained in this group, which the author believes is of help to the understanding of the ion-induced amorphization. They are as follows:

(i) As mentioned in Section 5.3, no amorphous phase has been observed previously by ion mixing in the Ag–Cu system, however, according to the two-phase competition rule proposed by the author, an amorphous alloy should be obtainable in such an eutectic system. We have performed an ion mixing experiment at LN_2 with the Ag–Cu multilayered sample using 300 keV Xe ions, with the special care of keeping the ion current low (less than 1 $\mu A/cm^2$). After ion mixing, the sample was immediately examined by TEM, both SAD and bright field observation show the formation of the Ag–Cu amorphous alloy with the composition around 50–50.

(ii) As also mentioned in Section 5.3, no amorphous phase has been observed in Ag–Ni and Ag–Co systems by ion mixing. These results have been used as a strong support for Alonso's criterion, which predicts that no amorphous phase can be formed in a system having large positive heat of formation (greater than 10 kJ/mol). At the same time, these results are thus a strong challenge to the two-phase competition rule. To respond to this question, we have performed a similar ion mixing experiment for the Ag–Ni multilayered sample, and the Ag–Ni (around 50–50) amorphous alloy was formed indeed after an adequate dose ion mixing (greater than 10^{16} Xe/cm^2). It is believed that the large positive heat of formation does affect the mixing efficiency, yet does not strictly prohibit amorphization.

More experiments concerning this issue are now currently underway, and the results will be published in detail in forthcoming papers.

References

[1] See, for example, S. T. Picraux, Applications of Ion Beam to Materials, Ed. G. Carter, J. S. Colligon, and W. A. Grant, Inst. Phys., London **1975** (pp. **183** to **195**).

[2] See, for example, Ion Implantation Metallurgy, C. M. Preece and J. K. Hirvonen (Ed.), Metallurg. Soc. AIME, New York **1979**.

[3] B. Y. Tsaur, S. S. Lau, L. S. Hung, and J. W. Mayer, Nuclear Instrum. and Methods **1821183, 67 (1981)**.

[4] B. X. Liu, W. L. Johnson, M-A. Nicolet, and S. S. Lau, Appl. Phys. Letters **42, 45 (1983)**.

[5] S. S. Lau, B. X. Liu, and M-A. Nicolet, Nuclear Instrum. and Methods **2091210, 97 (1983)**.

[6] B. X. Liu, W. L. Johnson, M-A. Nicolet, and S. S. Lau, Nuclear Instrum. and Methods **2091210, 229 (1983)**.

[7] L. S. Hung, M. Nastasi, J. Gyulai, and J. W. Mayer, Appl. Phys. Letters **42, 672 (1983)**.

[8] L. S. Hung and J. W. Mayer, Nuclear Instrum. and Methods in Phys. Research B **7/8, 657 (1985)**.

[9] B. X. Liu, Nuclear Instrum. and Methods in Phys. Research B **7/8, 676 (1985)**.

[10] W. L. Johnson, Y. T. Cheng, M. Van Rossum, and M-A. Nicolet, Nuclear Instrum. and Methods in Phys. Research B **7/8, 547 (1985)**.

[11] J. W. Mayer, B. Y. Tsaur, S. S. Lau, and L. S. Hung, Nuclear Instrum. and Methods **1821183, 1 (1981)**.

[12] B. Y. Tsaur, S. S. Lau, and J. W. Mayer, Appl. Phys. Letters **36, 823 (1980)**.

[13] B. Y. Tsaur and J. W. Mayer, Appl. Phys. Letters **37, 389 (1980)**.

[14] A. Schmid and P. Ziemann, see [8].

[15] C. Jaouen, J. P. Riviere, A. Bellara, and J. Delafond, see [8].

[16] B. X. Liu and M-A. Nicolet, Thin Solid Films **101, 201 (1983)**.

[17] B. X. Liu, M-A. Nicolet, and S. S. Lau, phys. stat. sol. (a) **73, 183 (1982)**.

[18] W. Scholz, A. Leiber, and W. J. Standish, Nuclear Instrum. and Methods **209/210, 1019 (1983)**.

[19] B. Y. Tsaur, Thesis, California Institute of Technology, **1980**.

[20] J. Y. Feng, Thesis, Tsinghua University, Beijing (China) **1981**.

[21] G. Goltz, R. Fernandez, M-A. Nicolet, and D. K. Sadana, in: Metastable Materials Formation by Ion Implantation, MRS Symp. Proc., Vol. **7**, Ed. S. T. Picraux and W. J. Choyke, North-Holland Publ. Co., Amsterdam **1982** (p. **227**).

[22] M. Van Rossum, U. Shreter, W. L. Johnson, and M-A. Nicolet, Proc. MRS **1983**, Fall Meeting, Boston.

[23] B. X. Liu, unpublished data, Caltech. **1982**.

[24] R. S. Bhattacharya, P. P. Pronko, A. K. Rai, and A. W. McCormick, see [8].

[25] B. X. Liu, B. M. Clemens, R. Gaboriaud, W. L. Johnson, and M-A. Nicolet, Appl. Phys. Letters **42, 624 (1983)**.

[26] K. T-Y. Kung, B. X. Liu, and M-A. Nicolet, phys. stat. sol. (a) **77,355 (1983)**.

[27] R. Gaboriaud, C. Jaouen, and J. Delafond, Abstract Bocklet of **IBMIN-84** Conf., Cornell University (USA), July **1984**.

[28] Y-T. Cheng, W. L. Johnson, and M-A. Nicolet, Proc. MRS **1984**, Fall Meeting, Boston.

[29] S. Matteson and M-A. Nicolet, Annu. Rev. Mater. Sci. **13, 339 (1983)**.

[30] G. DEARNALEY, J. H. FREEMAN, R. S. NELSON, and J. STEPHEN, Ion Implantation, North-Holland Publ. Co., Amsterdam 1973
[31] P. D. TOWNSEND, J. C. KELLY, and N. E. W. HARTLEY, Ion Implantation, Sputtering and Their Applications, Academic Press 1976.
[32] H. JONES, in: The Theory of Brillouin Zones and Electronic States in Crystals, North-Holland Publ. Co., Amsterdam 1960 (p. 191).
[33] B. X. LIU, phys. stat. sol. (a) 75, K77 (1983).
[34] W. L. JOHNSON and A. R. WILLIAMS, Phys. Rev. B 20, 1640 (1979).
[35] S. MATTESON and M-A. NICOLET, see [21] (p. 3).
[36] M. W. THOMPSON, Defects and Radiation Damage in Metals, Chap. 4 and 5, Cambridge University Press, 1969 (p. 89).
[37] K. A. SWALIN, Thermodynamics of Solids, Wiley, New York 1962 (p. 191).
[38] E. MA, Thesis, Tsinghua University, Beijing (China) 1984.
[39] Z. L. WANG, J. F. M. WESTENDORP, S. DOORN, and F. W. SARIS, see [21] (p. 59).
[40] J. A. ALONSO and S. SIMOZAR, Solid State Commun. 48, 765 (1983).
[41] I. M. REDA, J. HAFNER, P. PONGRATZ, A. WAGENDRISTEL, H. BANGERT, and P. K. BHAT, phys. stat. sol. (a) *i2*, 313 (1982).
[42] B. X. LIU, L. WEILUNSKI, M-A. NICOLET, and S. S. LAU, see [21] (pp. 65 to 70).
[43] Powder Diffraction File, JCPDS (Joint Committee on Powder Diffraction Standards), Philadelphia (PA) 1971.
[44] Table of Periodic Properties of the Elements, Sargent-Welch Sci. Co., Skokie (Ill.) 1968.
[45] W. B. PEARSON, Handbook of Lattice Spacings and Structures of Metals, Vol. II, Chap. II, Wiley, New York 1967.

(Received March 11, 1985)

DIFFERENT BEHAVIOURS OF AMORPHIZATION INDUCED BY ION MIXING *

B.X. LIU, E. MA, J. LI and L.J. HUANG

Department of Engineering Physics, Tsinghua University, Beijing, China

Ion mixing of multiple metal layers was conducted at 77 K in five selected binary metal systems, i.e. the Ag–Cr, Co–Cu, Cu–Fe, Fe–Mo and Fe–Nd systems, which all have a nearly zero or positive heat of formation *(AH,,,)*. TEM examination showed a common microscopic feature of localized amorphization after high dose ion irradiation, i.e. the amorphous phase was frequently interspersed in a crystalline matrix. EDS analysis was therefore carried out to determine the actual compositions of the phases formed. It revealed that all local amorphous regions resided within rather narrow composition ranges. The narrow range found here for amorphization is probably the reason that amorphous alloy formation was difficult in these systems.

After comparing these observations with those reported earlier for the some 30 systems so far studied, it is found that the behaviour of ion mixing induced amorphization, and hence the binary metal systems, can be classified into two categories. The first category contains the readily amorphous phase forming systems and usually features very limited terminal solid solubilities along with large negative heat of formation. Typical examples are the Au–Ti, Ni–Mo, Ni–Nb and Ru–Zr systems. In these systems amorphization can be achieved over a wide composition range once a minimum dose is reached. For systems in the second category, amorphization is only allowed in a rather narrow composition range, as in the systems studied here. This is also the case when a system has a large solid solubility, even though its *AH,,* is rather negative, e.g. the Mo–Ru and Au–V systems. In such situations, the results of phase formation may be sensitive to the composition as well as to the ion irradiation dose. The possible mechanism responsible for the different behaviors of phase formation by ion mixing are also discussed.

1. Introduction

Since the early 70s, a new research area, namely alloy phase formation by ion mixing, has been in progress and growing rapidly. For the binary metal systems, a variety of alloys of thin film form, including supersaturated solid solutions, metastable electron compounds, equilibrium compounds, and especially a number of amorphous alloys, have been synthesized by this scheme in the past few years [1]. In the meantime, many investigators have focused their efforts on the phase formation mechanism [2–6], and they have succeeded in formulating several models for predicting the production of metallic glasses by ion mixing. B.X. Liu proposed a simple phenomenological model, using the equilibrium phase diagram with two empirical rules [1]. W.L. Johnson proposed constructing the polymorphic phase diagram and came up with some rules [5] similar to those formulated by Liu et al. Also, J.A. Alonso suggested a method to predict amorphization by calculating the heat of formation of the system [6]. Generally speaking, these models contain common intrinsic features and therefore frequently give the same prediction for many systems. For instance, many systems, that have wide two-phase regions, frequently also have large negative heats of formations. These models all predict that amorphization is possible by ion mixing in these systems. However, for some other systems, the predictions are different among the models. The discrepency was found in one of our previous projects dealing with the Ag–Cu and Ag–Ni systems [7], which showed that amorphization could still be induced by ion mixing in a system having a large positive heat of formation (+22 kJ/mol for the Ag–Ni system). In this case, the equilibrium phase diagram has a two-phase character over almost the whole composition range. Besides this, some interesting features of phase formation after ion irradiation were observed in these Ag-containing systems, which require further investigation.

The present work was undertaken for an extended and systematic study concerning the correlation between the heat of formation of the system and the phase formation behavior induced by ion mixing. Five systems were selected for this purpose, i.e. Ag–Cr, Co–Cu, Cu–Fe, Fe–Mo and Fe–Nd systems. All these systems have nearly zero or positive heat of formation.

2. Experimental procedure

Multilayered samples (frequently 4–6 layers) were prepared by vacuum deposition of two constituent metals alternatively onto the inert substrates of SiO_2 and/or cleaved NaCl for examination by transmission electron microscopy (TEM). The vacuum level was of

*Project supported in part by the Science Fund of the Chinese Academy of Sciences.

Nuclear Instruments and Methods B19/20, p.682-690 (1987).

the order of 10^{-7} Torr for the Fe–Mo multilayers, and was of the order of 10^{-6} Torr for all the other samples. The total thickness of the films was in the range of 50–80 nm, which matches the projected range, R,, plus the projected range straggling, ΔR_p, of the irradiation ions. 300 keV Xe^+ ions were chosen for ion mixing in this study. The desired composition for the multilayered films was realized by adjusting the relative thicknesses of the constituent metals, and was confirmed by Rutherford backscattering (RBS) analysis. As it was intended to form the metastable alloy phases by ion mixing, precautions were taken in this study to ensure that the effective temperature of the films was not high during ion irradiation. All the as-deposited films were irradiated at 77 K, i.e. the sample holders were always cooled by liquid nitrogen during ion mixing. The ion beam current density was confined to less than 1 $\mu A/cm^2$ to avoid over-heating. It was estimated that the effective temperature of the films being irradiated should be well below 273 K under these precautions. The vacuum in the target chamber was about 10^{-6} Torr. The phase identification was carried out by selected area diffraction (SAD) in the transmission electron microscope, and sometimes by our laboratory made Seemann-Bohlin X-ray diffraction of high sensitivity system, which is capable of providing a clear pattern from a 7 nm Au film within 30 min [8]. In addition, energy dispersive spectrum (EDS) analysis was employed to determine the actual compositions of the individual phases formed by ion mixing, instead of the average composition of the films as reported in most previous studies. This is of vital importance, especially if a phase-mixture was observed after ion irradiation. In this case, the nominal composition was no longer restricted to the individual phase composition. For some of the ion mixed amorphous alloys, the re-crystallization temperature from the amorphous state to crystalline state was determined by in situ annealing in the hot-stage of TEM. The rate of temperature increase during annealing was about 10 K/min.

3. Results and discussions

3.1. Sequence of phase formation

The features of the equilibrium phase diagrams and the heats of formation of the selected systems are given in table 1. The average compositions of all the multilayered films were chosen in the two-phase regions in the corresponding equilibrium phase diagrams. After a relatively low dose (5×10^{15}–1×10^{16} Xe^+/cm^2) of ion mixing, uniform mixing was not achieved in most cases, as is shown in the $Fe_{50}Mo_{50}$ sample results by the Rutherford backscattering spectra in fig. 1. This low mixing efficiency observed is consistent with that reported recently by Y.T. Cheng et al. [9]. Here the nearly zero or positive heat of formation acts as an unfavorable chemical driving force in the mixing process. Ion mixing was therefore conducted to doses greater than 1 X 10^{16} Xe+/cm^2. The results of phase formation by ion mixing were quite similar in all the systems studied here. Crystalline phases were formed after low dose ion irradiation, while high dose ion mixing resulted in a combination of amorphous and crystalline phases. It can be seen from table 1 that the metastable crystalline

Table 1
Phase formation by ion mixing in selected systems

System	Features of phase diagram	ΔH_{For} (kJ/mol)	Designed composition[a])	Phase formation 5 X 10^{15}	10^{16} (Xe/cm^2)
Ag–Cr	immiscible in solid and liquid	+40	$Ag_{80}Cr_{20}$	MX fcc[b])	amor. and fcc
Co–Cu	limited solid solubilities, pentectic	+10	$Co_{50}Cu_{50}$	MX fcc	amor. and fcc
Cu–Fe	limited solid solubilities, pentectic	+19	$Cu_{80}Fe_{20}$	MX fcc	amor. and fcc
Fe–Mo	medium solid solubilities, compounds	–3	$Fe_{50}Mo_{50}$	Fe-bcc Mo-bcc	amor. and bcc
Fe–Nd	limited solid solubilities, compounds	+1	$Fe_{68}Nd_{32}$	MX fcc	amor. and fcc

[a]) The compositions listed in the table are designed compositions of the multilayers, and were confirmed by RBS
[b]) MX stands for metastable crystalline phase.

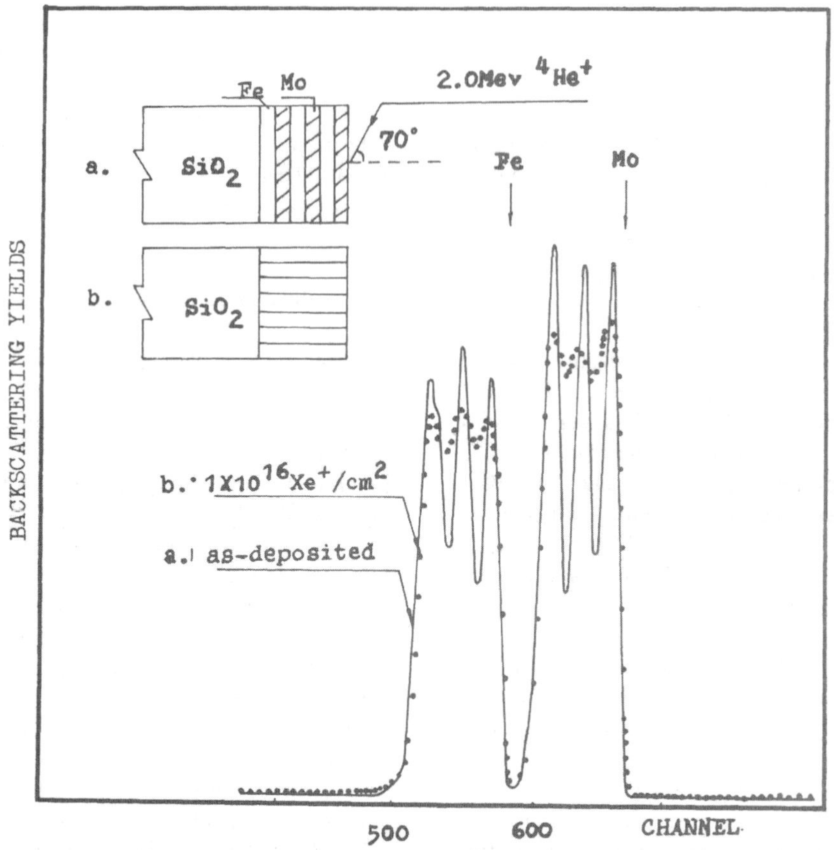

Fig. 1. 2.0 MeV $^4He^+$ backscattering spectra of $Fe_{50}Mo_{50}$ multilayered sample for a sample irradiated to a dose of 1×10^{16} Xe^+/cm^2.

phases (MX) formed in the Ag-Cr, Co-Cu and Fe-Nd systems were all of fcc structures. For the Cu-Fe system, few crystalline phases were formed after ion mixing, and the structures were all fcc with different planar spacings. The diffraction lines from the low dose mixed Fe-Mo samples were from two bcc structures, indicating the formation of Fe-based and Mo-based solid solutions with extended solubilities. The formation of an amorphous phase was confirmed by TEM examination, SAD and/or X-ray diffraction analysis. In these systems, the amorphous phase was frequently mixed with other crystalline phases. In other words, the samples were partially amorphized. We propose calling this phenomenon localized amorphization, and fig. 2 is a

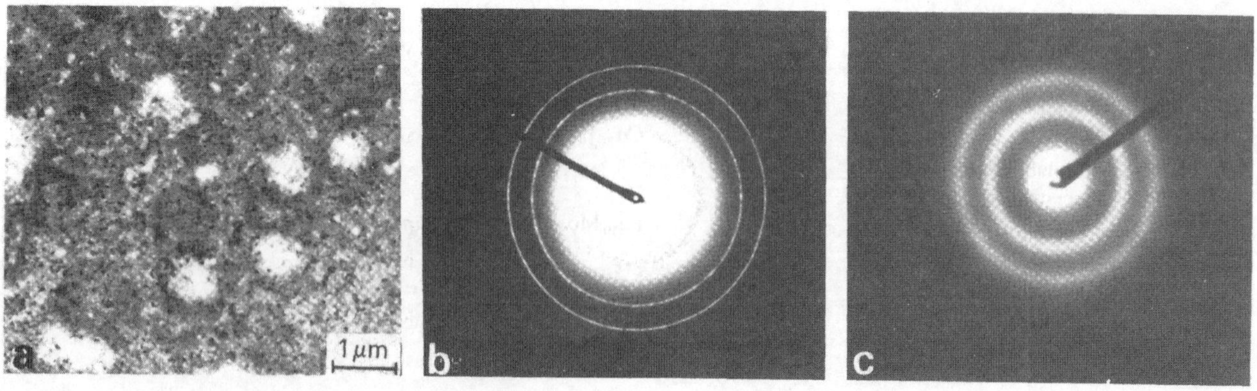

Fig. 2. Bright field image (a), SAD for the crystalline matrix (b), and SAD for the localized amorphous region (c) of the $Fe_{68}Nd_{32}$ multilayers after ion mixing to a dose of 1.5×10^{16} Xe^+/cm^2 at liquid nitrogen temperature.

typical example observed in an irradiated Fe–Nd film. The result of amorphization induced by ion mixing confirmed our prediction that the alloy composition lying in the two-phase region is favorable for the amorphous phase to form, even though the heat of formation of the system is more or less positive. In particular, the heats of formation of the Ag–Cr and Cu–Fe systems are +40 and +19 kJ/mol respectively, which according to Alonso's criterion are well beyond the border value of +10 kJ/mol allowed for an amorphous phase to form.

3.2. Microscopic features of Fe–Mo *metastable* phases

The localized amorphization was studied in detail in the Fe–Mo system with two adjacent alloy compositions of Fe,, Mo_{50} and $Fe_{40}Mo_{60}$. The multilayered samples were irradiated at 77 K to various doses. Fig. 3 shows two series of partial X-ray diffraction patterns, obtained by our Seemann-Bohlin attachment, to reveal the (110) lines of Fe and Mo. It can be seen from the patterns for the $Fe_{40}Mo_{60}$ films that the Fe and Mo lines move toward each other after 5×10^{15} Xe^+/cm^2 ion irradiation, and began to overlap at higher doses, indicating a tendency of transformation from equilibrium to metastable crystalline phase, and eventually to the amorphous phase. When the dose reached 1.5×10^{16} Xe^+/cm^2, the film became entirely amorphized, this was also confirmed by TEM analysis. Fig. 4 shows the bright field image and SAD photos of the $Fe_{40}Mo_{60}$ amorphous alloy so obtained. The last pattern of $Fe_{40}Mo_{60}$ film shows that the over-irradiation has caused the amorphous phase to dissociate, indicating the amorphization induced by ion irradiation is sensitive to the ion dose. This phenomenon can be attributed to the demixing effect [10]. For the $Fe_{50}Mo_{50}$ films, the X-ray diffraction patterns showed that the structure remained crystalline even after the highest dose irradiation performed in this study (2×10^{16} Xe^+/cm^2). With the increasing dose, two metastable crystalline phases gave rise to one prevailing Fe-riched phase.

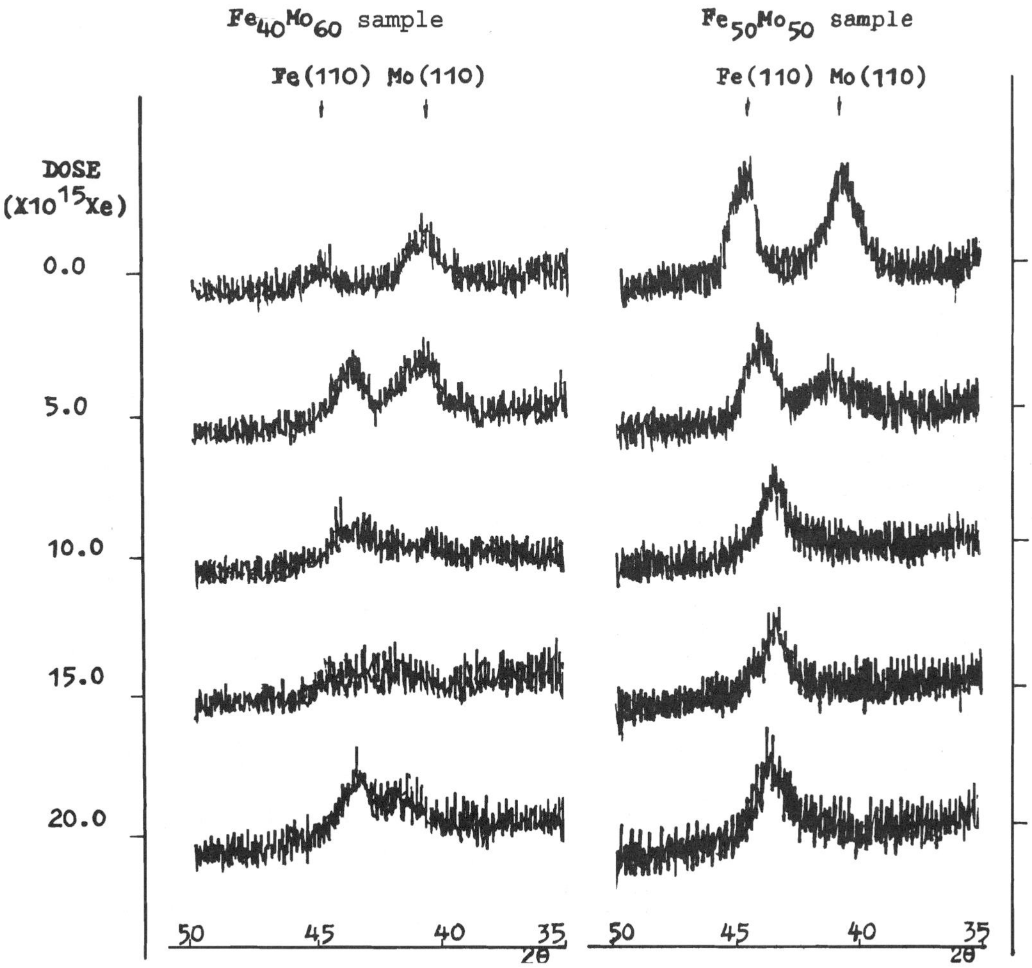

Fig. 3. The X-ray diffraction spectra (Seemann-Bohlin) of $Fe_{40}Mo_{60}$ and $Fe_{50}Mo_{50}$ samples upon irradiation.

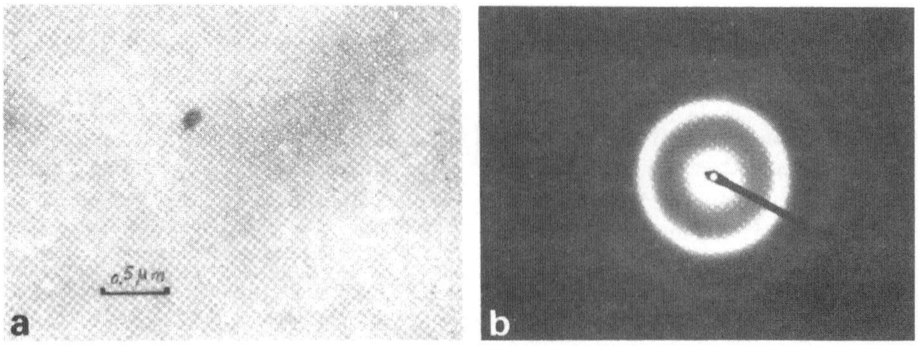

Fig. 4. Bright field image (a), and **SAD** photos for the $Fe_{40}Mo_{60}$ multilayered film after ion mixing to a dose of 1.5×10^{16} Xe^{+}/cm^{2} at liquid nitrogen temperature.

From these results, one sees that the phase formation behavior is quite sensitive to the alloy composition chosen, as only a **10** at.% difference was chosen for two samples. It is of interest that a careful TEM examination of the high dose irradiated $Fe_{50}Mo_{50}$ film revealed a few well amorphized local regions in the crystalline matrix. A typical morphological picture of this aspect and the corresponding SAD patterns are given in fig. **5.** In this situation, it is important to determine the actual compositions of the observed phases. EDS analysis was employed for this purpose, as the phase separation made it possible to do this with reasonable accuracy. The actual compositions of the amorphized regions and of the surrounding crystalline phases which formed simultaneously were determined by a series spot to spot EDS measurements. Results for $Fe_{50}Mo_{50}$, as well as for $Fe_{40}Mo_{60}$ samples whenever possible, are listed in table 2. It can be seen that the Mo concentration in the local amorphous regions in $Fe_{50}Mo_{50}$ films was about **70** at.%, whereas in the neighbouring crystalline phases, it was around **50** at.%, and that the Mo content in the entirely amorphized $Fe_{40}Mo_{60}$ alloy was determined to be around **60** at.%. The amorphous character of the local regions which have a very weak contrast appearance under TEM examination, was also confirmed by the fact that after heating up to **873** K, the amorphous phase transformed into the crystalline state. It can also be seen that the solid solubilities of Mo in Fe and vice versa can be extended by ion mixing up to 37 at.% Mo and **13** at.% Fe, respectively. Consequently, the favorable composition for ion mixing induced amorphization in the Fe–Mo system is likely to be limited within a rather narrow range around **60–70** at.% Mo. This is probably the reason that the amorphous alloy was difficult to obtain when the alloy composition was not within this regime. However, by determining the actual composition of the amorphous phase already formed in local regions, one is then able to select the appropriate composition and form uniform layers of the amorphous alloy in such systems.

The same analysis was also conducted for the Cu–Fe samples. The Fe content in the amorphous and surrounding crystalline phases were determined to be about **70** and **20** at.%, respectively. The re-crystallization temperature of the amorphous phase was about **673** K, as measured by in situ annealing in the TEM. These results showed again that the amorphization was sensitive to the alloy composition in the system studied here.

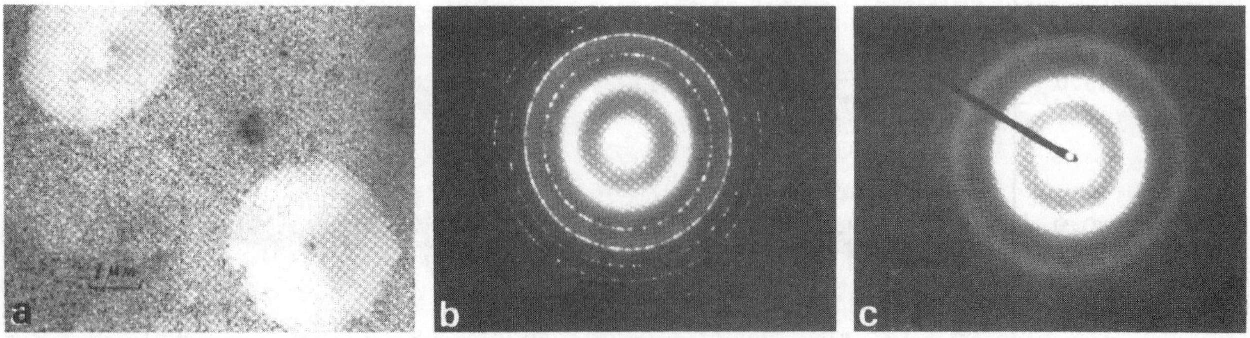

Fig. 5. Bright field image (a), **SAD** for crystalline matrix (b), and **SAD** for the localized amorphous region (c) of the $Fe_{50}Mo_{50}$ multilayers after ion mixing to a dose of 2×10^{16} Xe^{+}/cm^{2} at liquid nitrogen temperature.

Table 2
Phase evolution in ion mixed Fe–Mo samples and the actual compositions of the phases determined by energy dispersive spectrum

Dose (Xe^+/cm^2)	$Fe_{40}Mo_{46}$ samples	$Fe_{50}Mo_{50}$ samples
0	crystal Fe and Mo	crystal Fe and Mo
5×10^{15}	MX S.S 33 at.% Mo[a)] and crystal Mo	MX S.S. 20 at.% Mo and MX S.S. 13 at.% Fe
1×10^{16}	MX S.S. 33 at.% Mo amorphous $Fe_{40}Mo_{60}$ and trace of Mo	MX S.S. 33 at.% Mo and Mo-rich phase[c)]
1.5×10^{16}	amorphous $Fe_{40}Mo_{60}$	MX S.S. 33 at.% Mo and Mo-rich phase[c)]
2×10^{16}	MX S.S. 30 at.% Mo[b)] and Mo-rich phase, amorphous	MX S.S. 37 at.% Mo and amorphous Fe_{30} Mo,,

[a)] S.S. refers to solid solution, MX means metastable crystalline phase.
[b)] Only this composition was determined by X-ray diffraction data, by applying Vigard's law
"There should be a Mo-rich phase, but it was not detectable.

This type of ion mixing induced amorphization was also observed in an early studied system, i.e. the Mo–Ru system reported by Liu et al. [11]. Amorphous Mo–Ru alloy has only been formed at about 55 at.% Mo, and the amorphization induced by ion mixing was also sensitive to the irradiation dose. It is thus believed that this type of amorphization behaviour is common to a number of systems. It should be pointed out that the discussions so far of the sensitivity of amorphization to the alloy composition and irradiation dose are based only on the detected facts, i.e. the observations.

Regarding the mechanisms of how the composition variation and phase separation can occur, the main cause, we speculate, is due to irradiation induced up-hill mass transport. Take the Fe–Mo system as an example. It is likely that the most stable amorphous state, which corresponds to the free energy minimum in Fe–Mo system, is near the Mo-rich end around 60–70 at.% Mo. This energy minimum may serve as a trap for amorphization. As ion irradiation itself is a process inducing disorder and thus favoring amorphization, it may drive a biasing mass flow to accumulate the Mo content in some local regions, and when the composition reaches the right range, a catastrophic change in structure may occur. This issue certainly needs much more study to have a clear understanding.

3.3. *Metallic glass forming ability by ion mixing*

The above results demonstrate the possibility of producing metallic glasses by ion mixing in the presently studied systems, and reveal some interesting features of the amorphization behaviour. The amorphization behavior observed in these systems is quite different from that observed in some other systems, e.g. in the Au–Ti [2,3], Ni–Mo [2,3], Ni–Nb [12] and Ru–Zr [3] systems reported earlier by Liu et al. In these systems, several amorphous alloys of various compositions covering a relatively wide range have been formed by similar ion mixing experiments, and amorphization was frequently achieved within tolerant irradiation dose range. For example, four Ni–Nb amorphous alloys have been obtained by room temperature ion mixing in the composition range of 20–65 at.% Nb, and the $Ni_{55}Nb_{45}$ alloy was the most stable one upon heating. The dose range for amorphization was from 3×10^{15} to 1.7×10^{16} Xe^+/cm^2. These results indicate that amorphization in this type of system is insensitive to the irradiation dose. Since the structure characterization was mainly by the Read camera technique for the earlier studied systems, the microscopic features of those amorphous phases should be checked by the same TEM analysis used in the present study for an equal comparison. Two ion mixed Ni,, Mo,, amorphous films, one obtained in 1982 and the other formed recently, were examined carefully by TEM. It was found that they were both uniform amorphous phases within the resolution of the analysis method. All these results indicate that the amorphous alloy can readily be formed by ion mixing in these systems. The main reason is that the favorable composition range for ion mixing induced amorphization in such systems is relatively wide. This is why the phase formation is insensitive to the composition. This might also be one of the reasons why amorphization is insensitive to the irradiation dose. As ion irradiation can be considered to be a process inducing composition variation in the local regions, and if the variation was still within the favorable range of amorphization, the structure as a whole in the irradiated film would remain amorphous. The different behaviors of amorphization induced by ion mixing observed in two representative systems, Fe–Mo and Ni–Nb, are therefore attributed to the width of the favorable composition range for amorphization in the individual systems. According to the experimental results obtained in these two systems, and following the principle of constructing the free energy diagram [13], the schematic free energy diagrams for Fe–Mo and Nb–Ni systems were formulated and are shown in fig. 6. The phase evolution upon ion mixing in these systems are also illustrated in the figure, and this approach has also been used by others [14].

According to the amorphization behavior, the binary metal systems can be classified into two categories. Following the terminology employed in the field of metallic glass, we propose to name those systems of the first category the readily glass forming (RGF) systems (Ni–Nb system, etc.), while systems like those presently studied are named possible glass forming (PGF) systems. After re-examining the experimental results of ion mixing that have been so far reported for some 30 binary metal systems, it was found that there are 12 RGF and 11 PGF systems, respectively. Table 3 lists these systems as well as all other previously studied systems for completeness. For the Au–Ni, Mo–Nb and Ti–Zr systems, they all have the equilibrium phase diagrams of continuous solid solution type, having neither two-phase regions nor compounds. According to both Johnson's and our predictions, amorphous alloy can hardly be formed by ion mixing and this has been confirmed by the typical ion mixing experiments con-

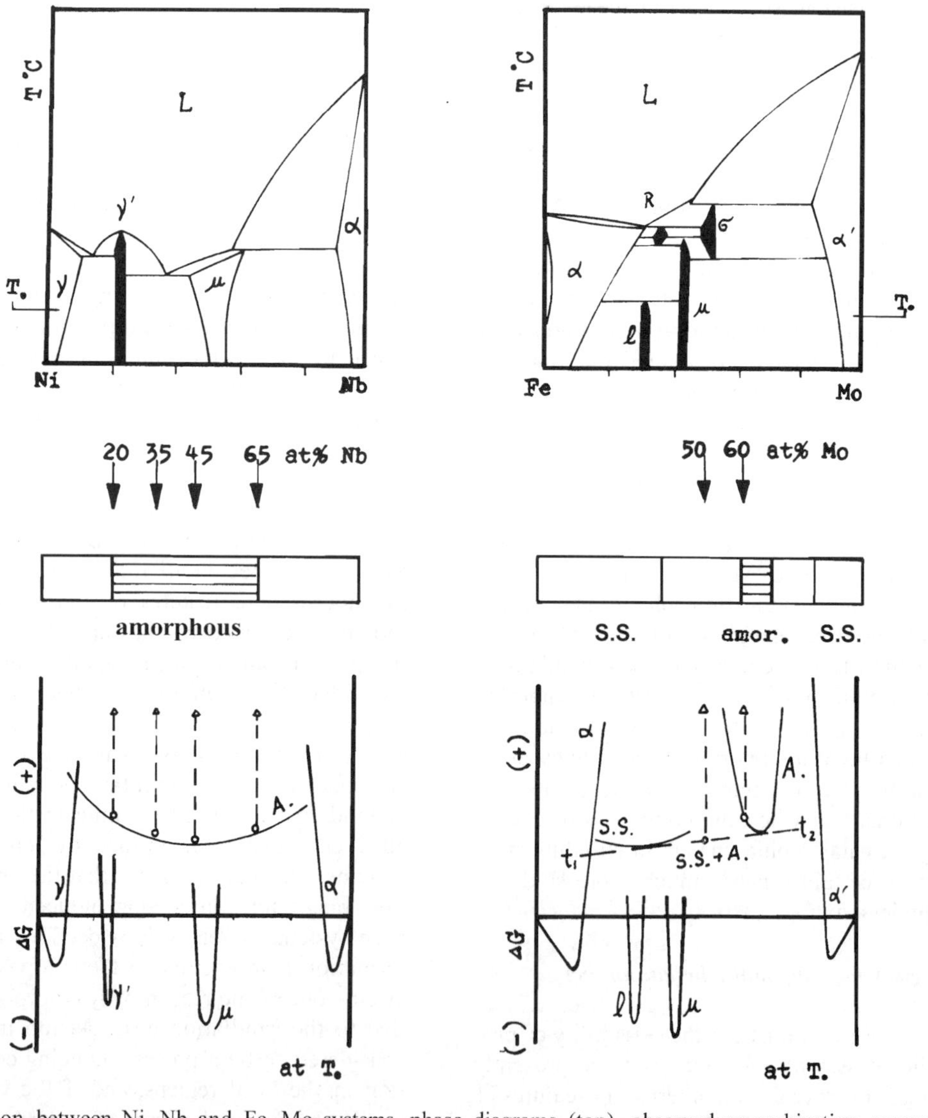

Fig. 6. Comparison between Ni–Nb and Fe–Mo systems, phase diagrams (top), observed amorphization ranges (middle), and hypothetical free energy diagrams (bottom). In the Fe–Mo system, a mixture was formed for the $Fe_{50}Mo_{50}$ sample, and entirely amorphous alloy was obtained for the $Fe_{40}Mo_{60}$ sample, however, it dissociated upon further irradiation (to the state on t_1-t_2).

Table 3
Glass forming ability of metal systems by ion mixing method

System	Amorphous phase formed	MPAR[a)] (%)	ΔH_{For} (kJ/mol)	Ref.
Readily glass forming systems				
Al–Au	several	84	−37	[18]
Al–Ni	several	80	−48	[4]
Al–Pd	several	82	−84	[4]
Al–Pt	several	90	−82	[4]
Au–Ti	3, 40–75 at.%Ti	72	−71	[2,3]
Co–Gd	4, 50–90 at.%Gd	90	−30	[19]
Co–Mo	2, 35–65 at.% Mo	76	− 7	[2]
Er–Ni	2, 35–60 at.% Ni	90	−48	[2]
Hf–Ni	3, 20–80 at.% Ni	90	−62	[20]
Mo–Ni	3, 35–65 at.% Ni	70	−11	[2,3]
Nb–Ni	4, 35–80 at.% Ni	86	−44	[12]
Ru–Zr	3, 25–75 at.%Zr	90	−86	[3]
Possible glass forming systems				
Ag–Cr	yes	100	+40	
Ag–Cu	yes	90	+ 3	[7]
Ag–Ni	yes	100	+22	[7]
Au–Co	1, around 75 at.% Co	74	+10	[16]
Au–V	1, around 60 at.% V	20	−29	[16]
Co–Cu	yes	83	+10	
Cu–Fe	yes	87	+19	
Fe–Mo	1, around 60–70 at.% Mo	62	− 3	
Fe–Nd	yes	90	+ 1	
Fe–W	1, around 70 at.% Fe	65	0	[21]
Mo–Ru	1, around 55 at.% Mo	30	−21	[11]
Hardly glass forming systems				
Au–Fe	no	17	+12	[16]
Au–Ni	no	0	+11	[16]
Mo–Nb	no	0	− 8	[22]
Ti–Zr	no	0	0	[22]
Systems to be classified when more data available				
Al–Co	yes	85	−42	[4]
Al–Nb	yes	77	−47	[2]
Co–Ti	yes	71	−42	[4]
Cu–Ta	yes	100	+ 3	[23]
Fe–Ti	yes	68	−25	[24]
Ni–Ti	yes	74	−51	[2]
Ru–Ti	yes	65	−64	[17]

[a)] MPAR refers to the maximum possible amorphization range

ducted so far. These systems can thus be named hardly glass forming (HGF) systems. The last seven systems are not classified at the moment, because the data available for these systems are limited, e.g. only one composition has been studied, however, they are at least PGF systems.

The next question is then what is the qualification to distinguish the binary metal systems in terms of their glass forming ability. To our present knowledge, at least two factors have to be considered. The first has to do with the equilibrium phase diagram. We propose defining a parameter MPAR, namely the maximum possible amorphization range expected by the equilibrium phase diagram. According to our model, MPAR equals 100% (as the whole composition range) minus the maximum terminal solid solubilities taken from the corresponding equilibrium phase diagram. The second parameter is the Miedema's heat of formation (AH„,) [15] first introduced into this research area by Alonso. These parameters were calculated for all listed systems and are included in table 3. One can easily find out that all the RGF systems have large MPAR and at the same time have rather negative AH„,, and that when either of these parameters goes the other way, i.e. is unfavored, the system is not an RGF system. Both the Au–V and Mo–Ru systems have large negative heats of formation, yet the small MPAR make them PGF systems. This is also the case for the Ag–Cr and Ag–Ni systems. These two systems both have large MPAR, however, the *AH,,,* of these systems are very positive. **An** extreme example is the Fe–Au system. The MPAR is only 17%, and could be even smaller as ion mixing could extend the terminal solid solubilities considerably. The AH_{For} of the system is also unfavored since it is positive. Tsaur has studied [16] this system by ion mixing for a wide composition range and failed to form any amorphous phase. Thus the Fe–Au system can be classified as an HGF system. The other three HGF systems all have zero MPAR. It is also of interest to mention the Ti–Ru system, which has the parameters of 65% of MPAR and −64 kJ/mol of *AH,,,*. This system could be an RGF system, while Y.T. Cheng et al. [17] reported that only an equatomic alloy composition led to the formation of an amorphous phase. In comparing the Ti–Ru to the Ru–Zr system, the terminal solid solubilities are considerably greater in the Ti–Ru system than in the Ru–Zr system. This is perhaps why the composition chosen to form an amorphous alloy was more or less critical in the Ti–Ru system than in the Ru–Zr system. It is concluded from the above discussions that a relatively large MPAR is an important condition for an RGF system, but it is not sufficient, unless the AH_{For} of the system is rather negative. The qualification of classification of the binary metal systems needs still more studies both experimentally and theoretically, i.e. whether or not there are other physical factors of importance in affecting the amorphization behavior. In addition, more quantitative studies of the proposed parameters are needed.

4. Concluding remarks

(i) The present study demonstrates the possibility of forming an amorphous alloy by ion mixing in the system having a two-phase region, even though the heat of formation is positive, for up to +40 kJ/mol.

(ii) This paper studied the issue of amorphization behavior, i.e. the readiness of glass forming by ion mixing. Two factors, namely MPAR and *AH,,,*, were found to be important in influencing the amorphization behavior.

(iii) The next step is to find out, by experiments and theoretical studies, the exact composition range favoring amorphous phase formation, as well as the underlying mechanisms.

The authors are indebted to Prof. M-A. Nicolet of the California Institute of Technology, USA for offering some multilayered samples, and to Dr. S.T. Picraux of Sandia National Laboratories for critical reading of the manuscript and many helpful suggestions. The authors also wish to thank K. Tao for help in X-ray diffraction analysis by the Seemann-Bohlin method, to Z.H. Yan for his assistance. Thanks also go to the TEM laboratory of Peking University for their efficient assistance. The financial support to this project from the Science Fund of the Chinese Academy of Sciences, as well as from the Administration of Tsinghua University, are gratefully acknowledged.

References

[1] B.X. Liu, Phys. Stat. Sol. 94A (1986) 11.
[2] B.X. Liu, W.L. Johnson, M-A. Nicolet and S.S. Lau, Nucl. Instr. and Meth. 209/210 (1983) 229.
[3] B.X. Liu, Nucl. Instr. and Meth. B7/8 (1985) 547.
[4] L.S. Hung, M. Nastasi, J. Gyulai and J.W. Mayer, Appl. Phys. Lett. 42 (1983) 672.
[5] W.L. Johnson, Y.T. Cheng, M. Van Rossum and M-A. Nicolet, Nucl. Instr. and Meth. B7/8 (1985) 657.
[6] J.A. Alonso and S. Simozar, Solid State Commun. 48 (1983) 765.
[7] B.X. Liu, L.J. Huang, J. Li and E. Ma, in: Thin Films- Interfaces and Phenomena, eds., R.J. Nemanich, P.S. Ho and S.S. Lau, MRS Symposia Proc. vol. 54 (North-Holland, Amsterdam, 1986) p. 217.
[8] K. Tao, Z.L. Dong, S.Y. Chen and B.G. Wang, ibid., p. 687.
[9] Y.T. Cheng, M. Van Rossum, W.L. Johnson and M-A. Nicolet, Appl. Phys. Lett. 45 (1984) 185.
[10] B.X. Liu, L. Wielunski, M-A. Nicolet and S.S. Lau, in: Metastable Materials Formation By Ion Implantation, eds., S.T. Picraux and W.J. Choyke, MRS Symposia Proc. vol. 7 (North-Holland, Amsterdam, 1982) p. 65.
[11] B.X. Liu, B.M. Clemens, R. Gaboriaud, W.L. Johnson and M-A. Nicolet, Appl. Phys. Lett. 42 (1983) 624.
[12] K.T-Y. Kung, B.X. Liu and M-A. Nicolet, Phys. Stat. Sol. 77A (1983) 355.
[13] U. Koster and P. Weiss, J. Non-Cryst. Solids 17 (1975) 359.
[14] A. Blatter and M. von Allmen, Phys. Rev. Lett. 54 (19) (1985) 2103.
[15] A.R. Miedema, Philips Technical Review 36 (8) (1976) 217.
[16] B.Y. Tsaur, S.S. Lau, L.S. Hung and J.W. Mayer, Nucl. Instr. and Meth. 182/183 (1981) 67.
[17] Y.T. Cheng, W.L. Johnson and M-A. Nicolet, presented at MRS Fall Meeting 1984, Boston (Nov. 26–30, 1984).
[18] A. Schmid and P. Ziemann, Nucl. Instr. and Meth. B7/8 (1985) 581.
[19] Z.H. Yan, B.X. Liu and H.D. Li, Phys. Stat. Sol. 94A (1986) 483.
[20] M. Van Rossum, U. Shreter, W.L. Johnson and M-A. Nicolet, in: Ion Implantation and Ion Beam Processing of Materials, eds., G.K. Hubler, O.W. Hill, C.R. Clayton and C.W. White (Elsevier, New York, 1983) p. 127.
[21] G. Goltz, R. Fernandez, M-A. Nicolet and D.K. Sadana, as in ref. [10], p. 227.
[22] B.X. Liu, unpublished data (1982).
[23] B.Y. Tsaur, Ph.D. Thesis, California Institute of Technology (1980).
[24] J.Y. Feng, Thesis, Tsinghua University (1981).

PHYSICAL REVIEW
LETTERS

VOLUME 59 | 17 AUGUST 1987 | NUMBER 7

Observations of Fractal Patterns Induced in Thin Solid Films by Ion Irradiation

B. X. Liu, L. J. Huang, K. Tao, C. H. Shang, and H.-D. Li
Department of Engineering Physics, Tsinghua University, Beijing, China
(Received 8 April 1987)

The formation of fractal patterns during an amorphous structural transition in Ni-Mo thin films after 200-keV xenon-ion irradiation is presented. The dimension of the ion-induced fractals is 1.72 ± 0.07. The fractal patterns, together with other microscopic features, are described and characterized. Our results are compared to the cluster-diffusion-limited-aggregation model. The growth habit is attributed to long-range correlation which occurs at a critical condition during the amorphous-crystal transition.

PACS numbers: 05.70.Jk, 05.70.Fh, 61.40.+b, 64.70.Pf

The current interest in fractal growth phenomena was stimulated by the diffusion-limited-aggregation (DLA) algorithm first introduced by Witten and Sander.[1] Although a variety of beautiful fractal patterns have been produced, the observations of fractal patterns from experiments are comparatively few, leading to numerous open questions concerning the essential factors which control pattern formation.[2] In this Letter, we address this issue by studying the growth of fractal patterns in ion-irradiated Ni-Mo alloy films.

In this study, ion-beam methods were employed to produce fractal patterns in thin solid films, as the methods have proved to be well suited for the study of metastable phase formation and transformation.[3,4] We present experimental observations of fractal patterns in Ni-Mo alloy films during amorphous-crystal phase transition induced by ion-beam irradiation. Possible correlations among fractal patterns, the influence of the amorphous structure, and the relationship to the critical behavior of the alloy are also discussed.

Ni-Mo multilayered films were prepared by the deposition of pure Ni and Mo alternately onto inert SiO_2 substrates in a vacuum system. The vacuum level during deposition was 5×10^{-7} Torr. The total thickness of the multilayers (about 40 nm) was designed to match the projectile range plus projectile-range straggling of the incident 200-keV xenon ions. The films consisted of three layers of Ni and two layers of Mo. The thickness of an individual layer was 7 to 10 nm. The relative thickness of the constituents was adjusted to obtain the desired alloy composition, being Ni rich for this study. The as-deposited films were then irradiated to various doses ranging from 1×10^{14} to 1×10^{16} Xe/cm^2. Irradiation was conducted at liquid-nitrogen temperature with an ion flux less than 1 μA/cm^2 to reduce the possible effects from irradiation-enhanced diffusion. The vacuum level during irradiation was better than 5×10^{-6} Torr.

The details of the experimentation can be found in our previous publications.[3,5] Rutherford backscattering, energy-dispersive spectra (EDS), x-ray diffraction, and transmission electron microscopy (TEM) were used to characterize the samples. After deposition, the overall alloy composition was determined by EDS to be $Ni_{55}Mo_{45}$.

Following doses exceeding 7×10^{14} Xe/cm^2, our Rutherford backscattering, TEM, and x-ray diffraction analysis revealed that the films were homogeneously mixed and amorphized. Lower doses induced only partial mixing, and the corresponding films are not discussed further. For doses around 7×10^{15} Xe/cm^2, a close TEM bright-field examination revealed that an atomic rearrangement took place resulting in rich microscopic features in the amorphous matrix, including islandlike structure (called cluster below), nickel-enriched precipitated phases, and fractal patterns. Two neighboring doses, i.e., 5×10^{15} and 1×10^{16} Xe/cm^2, resulted in a

Physical Review Letters 59, p.745-747 (1987).

homogeneous amorphous phase in both cases, indicating that doses around 7×10^{15} Xe/cm^2 correspond to a certain critical condition.

Figures 1 and 2 are typical examples of the ion-induced fractal patterns observed in the film irradiated to a dose of 7×10^{15} Xe/cm^2. The composition of these patterns was determined by EDS to be around $Ni_{50}Mo_{50}$, differing slightly from the average alloy composition of the films ($Ni_{55}Mo_{45}$). In Fig. 1, the bright-field TEM examination revealed that numerous compact clusters are distributed throughout the film, and one can also see that the fractal pattern is surrounded by a zone which is depleted in the islandlike clusters. The depletion zone was found by EDS to be molybdenum enriched. Moreover, whenever a cluster-depletion zone was present around the fractal pattern, the number density of small clusters reached its maximum at the edge of the depletion zone. By contrast, the depletion zone is not obvious in Fig. 2, and the clusters are seldom seen in the surroundings of the fractal pattern.

As the sizes of these patterns are 5–6 μm in radii, microbeam diffraction was employed to identify the structures of the observed fractal patterns. Every branch of the patterns contained several single crystals with various orientations, as the diffraction patterns changed when the analyzing beam moved from one spot to another. Diffraction patterns disappeared, however, after short exposure to the analyzing electron beam. This observation indicates that these crystals are extremely unstable.

All the ion-induced fractal patterns were quantitatively analyzed by an M-75 image-processing computer with a resolution of 512×512 pixels. The fractal dimensions were measured by our dividing the patterns into concentric disks with various radii R, and counting the occupied pixels. Occupation numbers scale as R^D, where D is the fractal dimension. Although D varied slightly from one to another, the dominant value was 1.72 ± 0.07. A remarkable characteristic is that all the patterns seem to be lopsided.

The ion-induced fractal patterns are noncentrosymmetric and have a large fractal dimension, 1.72 compared to 1.4 for the DLA model, indicating that the patterns are quite different from those produced by computer simulation based on the DLA model. The observed patterns look similar in some aspects to those stimulated by the cluster-diffusion-limited-aggregation (CDLA) model,[6] which is a generalization of single-particle DLA. For instance, both the measured fractal dimension and the depletion zone are consistent with the CDLA model. According to the CDLA model, growth begins by the occupation of a fraction of the available sites and the positioning of a seed at the origin. The occupied sites are visualized as particles that remain fixed, while the growing clusters undergo a random walk gathering up the fixed particles. Unfortunately, however, the driving force for cluster motion has not been identified, and so mapping the observed patterns onto the CDLA model is still questionable. The process of the formation of ion-induced fractal patterns in thin solid films seems likely to involve some stationary large clusters and the motion of small species. Besides, long-range correlation is prob-

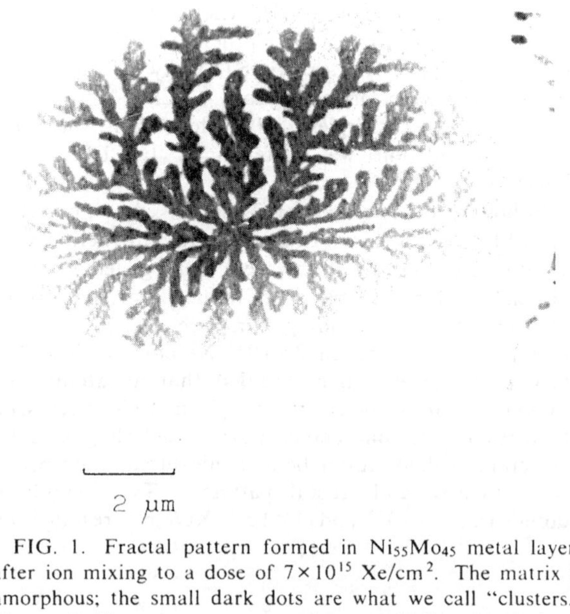

FIG. 1. Fractal pattern formed in $Ni_{55}Mo_{45}$ metal layers after ion mixing to a dose of 7×10^{15} Xe/cm^2. The matrix is amorphous; the small dark dots are what we call "clusters." The needlelike structures are precipitates of Ni-enriched phase.

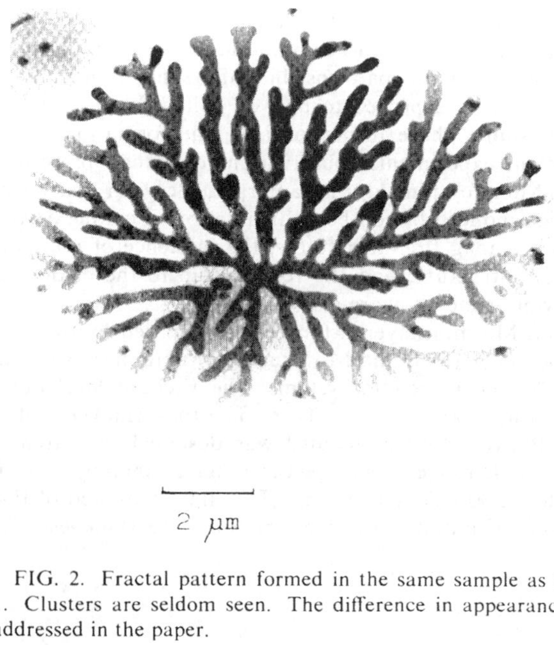

FIG. 2. Fractal pattern formed in the same sample as Fig 1. Clusters are seldom seen. The difference in appearance is addressed in the paper.

ably necessary for the formation of fractals in amorphous films. Overall, this issue needs still more studies both experimentally and theoretically.

As mentioned above, the fractal patterns were primarily composed of 1-μm single crystals, permitting composition analysis by EDS. The composition was around $Ni_{50}Mo_{50}$. This composition corresponds just to the δ phase in the Ni-Mo equilibrium phase diagram. The Ni-Mo δ phase, however, has a very complicated orthorhombic structure with 56 atoms in a unit cell forming a specific ordering configuration.[7] To crystallize such a sophisticated structure obviously requires higher temperatures and longer times than required for simple structures. Since these conditions are not met in our ion-irradiation experiments, these single crystals could not be the δ phase. The instability of the crystals under analyzing electron-beam irradiation also excludes the δ phase, since the δ phase is very stable. This conclusion is also supported by the fact that room-temperature ion mixing of $Ni_{50}Mo_{50}$ multilayers resulted in an amorphous phase, whereas the recrystallization temperature for the δ phase is over 600 °C.[8]

After exposure to the electron beam, the fractal patterns retained their shape, but the crystals transformed to the amorphous state as observed by high-resolution TEM. This structural change is similar to the observations by one of the authors[9] that a metastable crystalline Ni-Mo phase of hcp structure transformed into amorphous structure upon room-temperature aging.

It should be noted that the fractal patterns are frequently observed in an amorphous background. The amorphous structure therefore apparently plays an important role in the formation of the fractal patterns.

Ben-Jacob *et al.*[10] proposed that the dense branching morphology is generated in an amorphous annealing experiment. The reason why other kinds of patterns could not grow was thought to be due to the difference of the microscopic structures of the matrix. In our experiments, an amorphous matrix was also necessary for the fractal patterns to grow. This conclusion is based on the observations mentioned above as well as on the fact that at lower dose, when the films remained crystalline, nonfractal dendritic patterns were formed.[11] We therefore believe that the fractal patterns observed are due to a specific growth mode being excited in the isotropic amorphous matrix. The excitation idea was also proposed by Orbach[12] on the basis of his experimental results that fractal excitation could be achieved in an amorphous material.

As mentioned above, TEM examinations revealed that the amorphous films underwent an atomic rearrangement only under restricted conditions, namely after irradiation to the dose around 7×10^{15} Xe/cm^2, while in two other films irradiated to a little bit lower and higher doses, i.e., 5×10^{15} and 1×10^{16} Xe/cm^2, respectively, no fractal pattern but a homogeneous amorphous phase was observed. These indicate that the fractal patterns were formed at a critical condition during the amorphous structural phase transition. The amorphous phase transition, though not ideal, is a second-order phase transformation.[13] At such a transformation, long-range correlations are present and such correlations[14] would surely have a great influence on pattern formation. As Goldstein suggested in his approach to the relaxation behavior of the glass transition, these critical fluctuations would cause cluster motion.[15] In this study, TEM examination indeed revealed the islandlike clusters.

We conclude by stressing that our experiments show some correlations existing between the fractal patterns and the amorphous structural phase transformation. Our work also demonstrates the great potential of ion-beam methods for the investigation of pattern formation.

The authors thank Professor H. Q. Ye for the high-resolution examination, and Professor L. Chang for a critical reading of the manuscript. We thank the staffs of the TEM Laboratory of Beijing University and of the Analysis Center of Tsinghua University for their kind help. The fractal dimension was determined with help from the Image Center at Tsinghua University. Partial financial support from the International Atomic Energy Agency (Research Contract No. 4731/RB) is also acknowledged. This project was supported in part by the Science Fund of the Chinese Academy of Sciences.

[1] T. A. Witten and L. M. Sander, Phys. Rev. Lett. **47**, 1400 (1980), and Phys. Rev. B **27**, 5686 (1983).

[2] L. P. Kadanoff, Phys. Today **39**, No. 2, 6 (1986).

[3] B. X. Liu, Phys. Status Solidi (a) **94**, 11 (1986).

[4] D. A. Lilienfeld, L. S. Hung, and J. W. Mayer, Mater. Res. Soc. Bull. **12**, 31 (1987).

[5] B. X. Liu, E. Ma, J. Li, and L. J. Huang, Nucl. Instrum. Methods Phys. Res., Sect. B **19/20**, 682 (1987).

[6] R. F. Voss, J. Stat. Phys. **36**, 861 (1984).

[7] C. B. Shoemaker and D. P. Shoemaker, Acta Crystallogr. **16**, 997 (1963).

[8] B. X. Liu, W. L. Johnson, M.-A. Nicolet, and S. S. Lau, Nucl. Instrum. Methods **209/210**, 229 (1983).

[9] B. X. Liu, Nucl. Instrum. Methods Phys. Res., Sect. B **7/8**, 547 (1985).

[10] E. Ben-Jacob, G. Deutscher, P. Garik, N. G. Goldenfeld, and Y. Lareah, Phys. Rev. Lett. **57**, 1903 (1986).

[11] B. X. Liu, L. J. Huang, and C. H. Shang, Chin. Phys. Lett. **4**, 53 (1987).

[12] R. Orbach, J. Stat. Phys. **36**, 735 (1984).

[13] S. R. Elliott, *Physics of Amorphous Materials* (Longman, London, 1984).

[14] See, for example, R. Zallen, *The Physics of Amorphous Solids* (Wiley, New York, 1983).

[15] M. Goldstein, J. Chem. Phys. **51**, 3728 (1969).

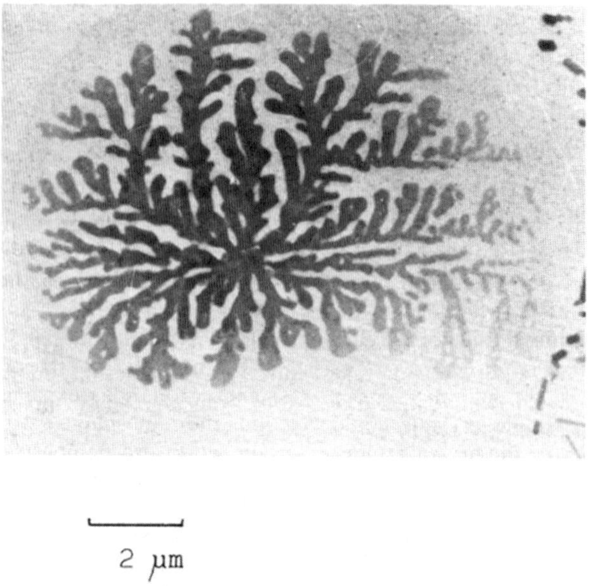

FIG. 1. Fractal pattern formed in $Ni_{55}Mo_{45}$ metal layers after ion mixing to a dose of 7×10^{15} Xe/cm^2. The matrix is amorphous; the small dark dots are what we call "clusters." The needlelike structures are precipitates of Ni-enriched phase.

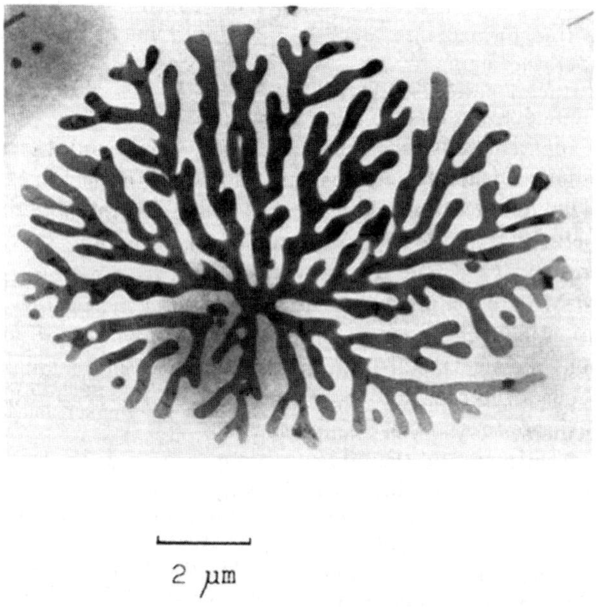

FIG. 2. Fractal pattern formed in the same sample as Fig. 1. Clusters are seldom seen. The difference in appearance is addressed in the paper.

Linear correlation of fractal dimension versus atomic magneton in magnetic-particle aggregation

B. X. Liu
Center of Condensed Matter and Radiation Physics, Chinese Center of Advanced Science and Technology (World Laboratory), Beijing, China
and Department of Materials Science and Engineering, Tsinghua University, Beijing, 100084, China

J. R. Ding
Department of Materials Science and Engineering, Tsinghua University, Beijing 100084, China
(Received 3 August 1989)

The fractal aggregation of magnetic particles on thin films was studied with Fe, Co, Cr, and Ni particles. It was revealed that the formation of the fractal aggregates was through a process of cluster diffusion-limited aggregation of magnetic particles. Our results clearly indicated a linear correlation between fractal dimension and the effective atomic magneton number of the aggregating particles. This finding reflects the important influence of magnetic interaction on the aggregation process and the resultant fractal structure. Besides, the fractal dimensions observed in this study are larger than those reported earlier by other authors.

Aggregation processes leading to fractal structures have been extensively studied.[1-4] Experiments[5,6] as well as computer simulations[7,8] have yielded deep understanding to the growth details of real aggregates. The diffusion-limited-aggregation (DLA) model[9,10] well described the aggregations of particles with no interaction among them. Recently, a few papers[11-14] reported the aggregations of particles with magnetic interaction among the particles. Experimental results and computer simulation[15] have exhibited some differences between aggregations with and without magnetic interaction. The observed trend was that the fractal dimension in the former case was smaller than that in the latter, and decreased when the magnetic interaction among the particles increased. However, no close relationship between fractal dimension and the magnetic interaction has been reported so far. Besides, the previous reported results were obtained under different conditions and thus are not comparable quantitatively. In order to investigate the possible correlation involved, we performed a systematic study of magnetic-particle aggregation by choosing four magnetic metals, i.e., iron, cobalt, chromium, and nickel, and by thin-film deposition under the same experimental conditions. These metals are known to have different effective atomic magneton numbers, which are believed to be a good measure of the magnetic interaction and listed in sequence from strong to weak (see Table I shown below).[16]

First, Fe, Co, Cr, and Ni thin films were prepared by evaporation of pure metals onto NaCl single-crystalline substrates in a vacuum system. The vacuum level before evaporation was better than 1×10^{16} Torr and was about 5×10^{-5} Torr during deposition. The evaporation was controlled at the low rate of 0.2–0.3 nm/sec, which was about one fourth of the deposition rate in the conventional techniques. The total thickness of the films was around 30–40 nm. The temperature of the NaCl substrates was below 100 °C during evaporation. After deposition, the films were taken out of the vacuum system and the substrates were dissolved by the deionized water. The metal films were collected on the Cu grids for transmission electron microscopy (TEM) examination (JEM-200CX or H-800). Energy-dispersive spectrum (EDS), selected-area diffraction (SAD), and x-ray photoelectron spectrum (XPS) were also employed to characterize the resultant microstructure.

TABLE I. The effective atomic magneton number m (in unit of the Bohr magneton μ_B) and the fractal dimension D_f.

Element	m (units of μ_B)	D_f
Fe	5.4	1.50
Co	4.8	1.52
Cr	3.7	1.58
Ni	3.2	1.59

Under the TEM bright-field examination, many fractal aggregates were observed on each thin film. Figure 1 is a typical image photo showing the distribution of fractal aggregates on a Cr thin film. The same features were also observed in three other metal films. Figures 2(a)–2(d) show the enlarged bright-field images of the aggregates observed on the surfaces of Fe, Co, Cr, and Ni films, respectively. Calculation results demonstrated that these aggregates kept the fractal geometry:

$$M \propto R^D \quad (R < \xi)\,, \tag{1}$$

where M is the mass of the aggregate within a circle of radius R, D is the fractal dimension, and ξ is the correlation length. The fractal dimensions were determined by the box-counting method and are listed in Table I. It can be seen that the aggregates of different metals are quite different. The aggregates of Fe and Co are rather open [see Figs. 2(a) and 2(b)], and have small mass dimensions ($D_f = 1.50 \pm 0.02$ for Fe aggregates and 1.52 ± 0.02 for Co aggregates, respectively). Whereas, those of Cr and Ni are relatively compact and have large mass dimensions ($D_f = 1.58 \pm 0.02$ for Cr aggregates and 1.59 ± 0.02 for

Physical Review B 40, p.7432-7434 (1989).

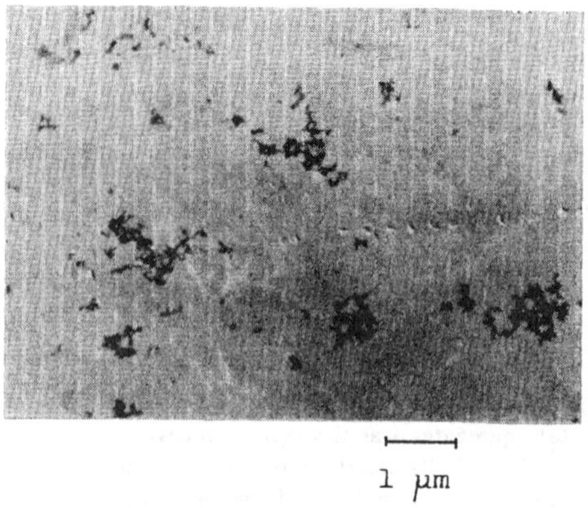

FIG. 1. The distribution of the fractal aggregates on the surface of Cr thin film. The same feature was also observed in the three other metal films studied.

Ni aggregates, respectively). Because individual aggregate observed in a sample was in a different stage of aggregation, it has a slightly different fractal dimension, e.g., $1.45 < D_f < 1.53$ for an Fe sample, etc. To reduce the experimental uncertainty, each mass dimension listed in Table I was an average over several similar fractal aggregates observed in the same film. To identify the chemical composition and structure of the particles that formed the fractals, various analysis methods were employed. By focusing at different areas of the films under TEM examination, SAD analysis revealed in all the studied films that both the fractal aggregates and the matrix were polycrystalline structures of the relative materials. Figure 3 shows a SAD pattern of the fractal aggregates on the surface of the Cr thin film, indicating a bcc structure of Cr metal. XPS and EDS analyses confirmed that the aggregates were pure Co, Cr, and Ni, respectively, on the relative metal films. While for the Fe case, it turned out that the matrix and the aggregates were both of iron oxide (Fe_2O_3), which were believed to have formed after the films were taken out of the vacuum system and kept in air.

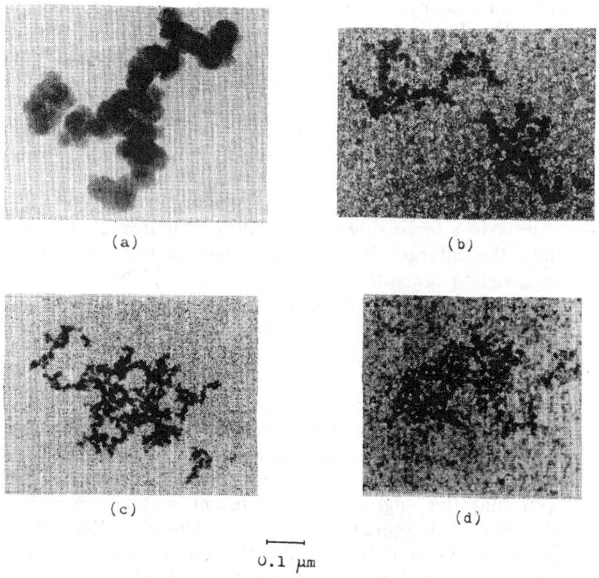

FIG. 2. The bright-field images of the fractal aggregates of magnetic particles observed on the surfaces of Fe, Co, Cr, and Ni thin films are shown in (a), (b), (c), and (d), respectively. The corresponding fractal dimensions are listed in Table I. The aggregates as well as the matrix are both polycrystalline structures. The difference of the grain size of the aggregates and the matrix created in the contrast under TEM bright-field examination. The aggregate in (a) is of Fe_2O_3, and are of pure Co, Cr, and Ni in (b), (c), and (d), respectively.

Concerning the fractal formation process, it was thought that after evaporation, those last deposited magnetic particles on surfaces were mobile and diffused to form the aggregates. From Fig. 2(a), one can see that a fractal aggregate consists of many small particles (the diameter of these particles is about 30 nm). It is also shown that [Figs. 2(a) and 2(b)] there are some clusters of particles which are not connected with the main aggregate. Therefore, we suppose that the fractal aggregates were the result of cluster diffusion-limited aggregation (CDLA) of magnetic particles on the surface of the metal films. Since the particles and the particle-formed clusters were both magnetic ones, the magnetic interaction among them certainly affected the aggregation process and resulted in a decreasing of the mass dimension being smaller than that expected by the CDLA model (1.72). The next question is why is the intrinsic parameter governing the magnetic interaction? In the CDLA process, there are big particles remaining stationary, and small particles being mobile and gathering all the particles to form a fractal pattern. Consequently, it is presumably the interaction among those mobile and aggregating particles that determines the final fractal structure. In this sense, taking the effective atomic magneton number of the metals is a good choice as an interaction measure. It should be pointed out that although the particle sizes seen in the figures are different from each other, the magnetic interactions that determine the fractal growth are not among those seen, but those small particles during the aggregation. Based

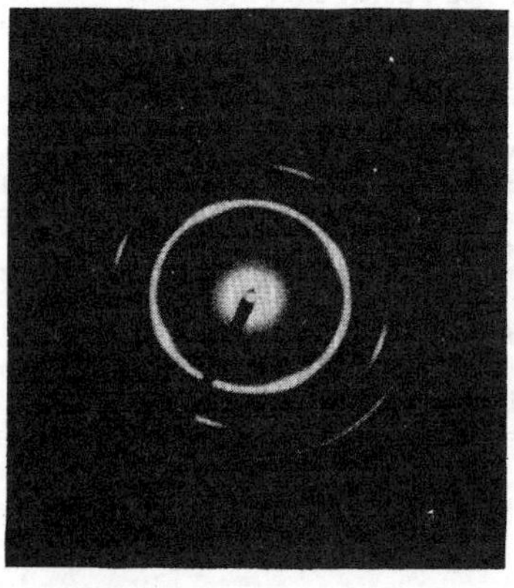

FIG. 3. The electron diffraction pattern of Cr aggregates. The polycrystalline structure is shown.

on this thought, a plot is constructed for the fractal dimensions versus the effective atomic magneton numbers listed in Table I for Co, Cr, and Ni metals. In Fig. 4, a linear relationship between them is indeed found within the experimental error. For the Fe case, we believe that during the aggregation process, the particles were Fe and that the observed Fe_2O_3 particles were the result of oxidation taking place later. The magnetic property of Fe instead of Fe_2O_3 is, therefore, an intrinsic parameter influencing the aggregation process. We therefore also put the Fe datum in the plot and it fitted the linearity very well. From Fig. 4, D_f can be expressed,

$$D_f = Km + C, \tag{2}$$

where D_f is the fractal dimension, m is the effective atomic magneton number, K and C are constants and were determined to be -0.041 and 1.72, respectively. Accordingly, when the magnetic interaction reduces to zero, i.e., $m=0$, D_f should be 1.72. This value is exactly the one expected by the CDLA model,[17] and also matches well with our previous results obtained in Ni-Mo alloy films ($D_f = 1.72 \pm 0.02$). In the Ni-Mo case, the observed fractal patterns were composed of NiMo metallic compounds, and the total magnetic moment of a NiMo molecule is just zero.[6] Therefore, all these results strongly support our finding of a linear correlation.

Obviously, our results are also in agreement with the reported trend that the mass dimension decreased when the magnetic interaction increased. Another interesting point is that the mass dimension observed in this study is larger than those reported by others. It is thought that the different processes of aggregation involved in the different experimental methods employed may be a crucial point to explain the difference.

In conclusion, the aggregations of magnetic particles, i.e., Fe, Co, Cr, and Ni particles, were observed on the surfaces of the respective and deposited thin films. A linear relationship between the fractal dimensions and the effective atomic magneton numbers was found. This linearity is supported by our previous observations in Ni-Mo alloy films and is consistent with the previous observations by others that fractal dimension decreased when the magnetic interaction increased. To explain this linear correlation, and the details of the growth process, many more studies—both theoretical and experimental—are needed.

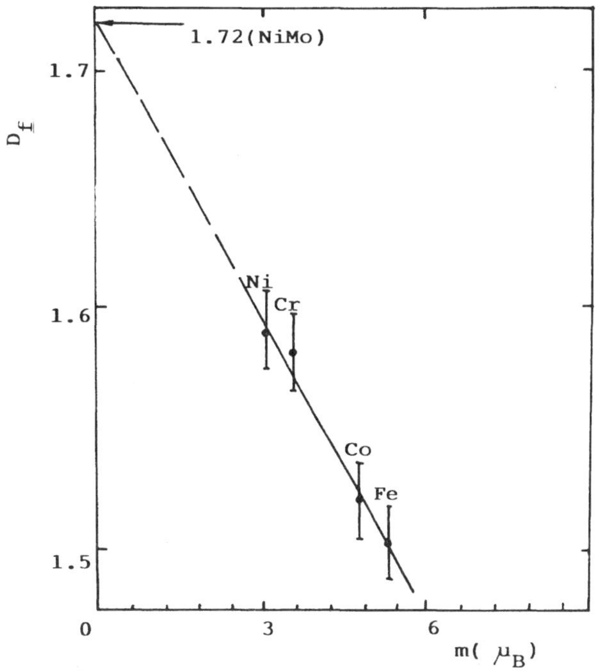

FIG. 4. The plot of the fractal dimensions D_f vs the effective atomic magneton numbers m. The fit line is $D_f = Km + C$, where K and C are -0.041 and 1.72, respectively.

The authors are grateful to the researchers of the TEM Laboratory of Beijing University and the Analysis Center of Tsinghua University for their kind help. Partial financial aid from the International Atomic Energy Agency (Contract No. 4731/R1/RB) is also acknowledged. This project was supported by the National Natural Science Foundation of China.

[1] *Kinetics of Aggregation and Gelation,* edited by F. Family and D. P. Landau (North-Holland, Amsterdam, 1984).
[2] *On Growth and Form,* edited by H. E. Stanely and N. Ostrowsky (Nijhoff, The Hague, 1985).
[3] *Fractal in Physics,* edited by L. Pietronero and E. Tosatti (North-Holland, Amsterdam, 1986).
[4] B. B. Mandelbrot, *The Fractal Geometry of Nature* (Freeman, San Francisco, 1982).
[5] J. H. Kaufmann, A. I. Nazzal, O. R. Melroy, and A. Kapitulnik, Phys. Rev. B **35**, 1881 (1987).
[6] B. X. Liu, L. J. Huang, K. Tao, C. H. Shang, and H-D. Li, Phys. Rev. Lett. **59**, 745 (1987).
[7] L. Niemeyer, L. Pietronero, and H. J. Weismann, Phys. Rev. Lett. **52**, 1033 (1984).
[8] B. Botet and R. Jullien, Phys. Rev. Lett. **55**, 1943 (1985).
[9] T. A. Witten and L. M. Sander, Phys. Rev. Lett. **47**, 1400 (1981).
[10] T. A. Witten and L. M. Sander, Phys. Rev. B **27**, 5686 (1983).
[11] G. A. Niklasson, A. Torebring, C. Larsson, C. G. Grangvist, and T. Farestam, Phys. Rev. Lett. **60**, 1735 (1988).
[12] G. Helgesen, A. T. Skjeltorp, P. M. Mors, R. Botet, and R. Jullien, Phys. Rev. Lett. **61**, 1736 (1988).
[13] S. G. Kim and J. R. Block, J. Appl. Phys. **60**, 509 (1985); J. Colloid Interface Sci. **116**, 431 (1987).
[14] L. J. Huang, B. X. Liu, J. R. Ding, and H-D. Li, Phys. Rev. B **40**, 858 (1989).
[15] P. M. Mors, R. Botet, and R. Jullien, J. Phys. A **20**, L975 (1987).
[16] *Magnetism of Metals and Alloys,* edited by M. Cyrot (North-Holland, Amsterdam, 1982).
[17] R. F. Voss, J. Stat. Phys. **36**, 861 (1984).

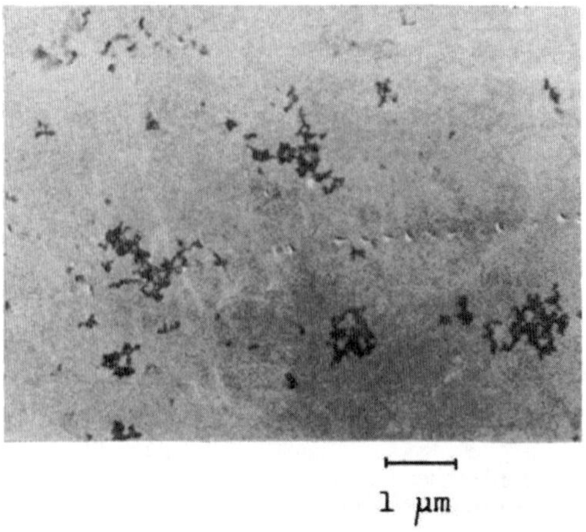

FIG. 1. The distribution of the fractal aggregates on the surface of Cr thin film. The same feature was also observed in the three other metal films studied.

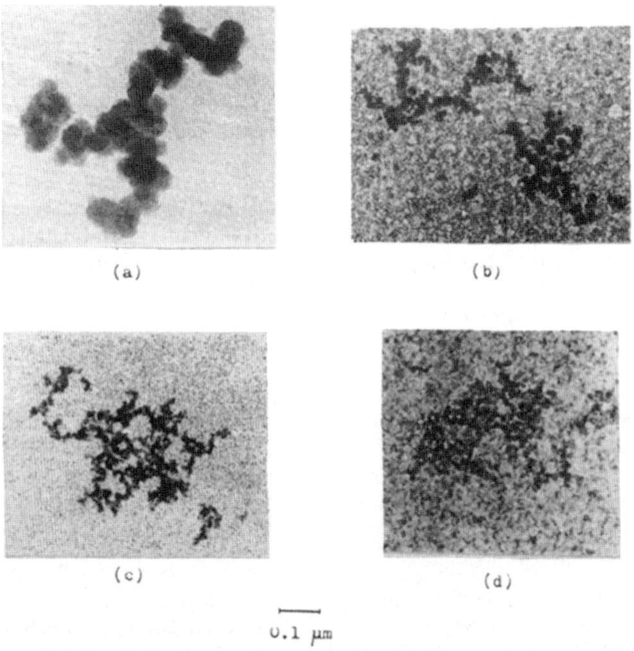

FIG. 2. The bright-field images of the fractal aggregates of magnetic particles observed on the surfaces of Fe, Co, Cr, and Ni thin films are shown in (a), (b), (c), and (d), respectively. The corresponding fractal dimensions are listed in Table I. The aggregates as well as the matrix are both polycrystalline structures. The difference of the grain size of the aggregates and the matrix created in the contrast under TEM bright-field examination. The aggregate in (a) is of Fe_2O_3, and are of pure Co, Cr, and Ni in (b), (c), and (d), respectively.

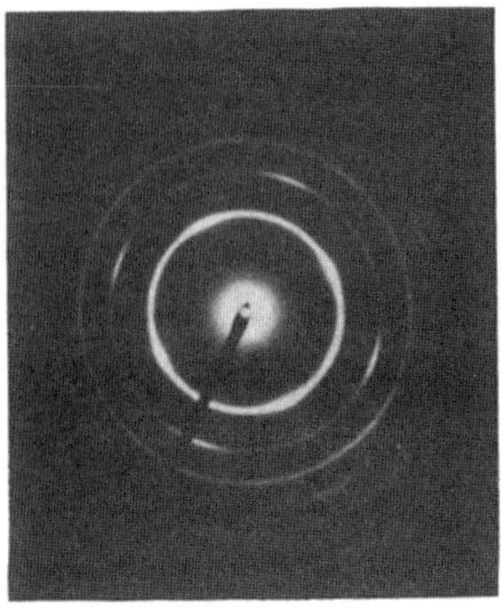

FIG. 3. The electron diffraction pattern of Cr aggregates. The polycrystalline structure is shown.

Review Article

phys. stat. sol. (a) **113, 11** (1989)

Subject classification: **61.80** and **64.60; 61.55;** S1.62

Center of Condensed Matter and Radiation Physics, CCAST, (World Laboratory) (a) and Department of Materials Science and Engineering, Tsinghua University (b), Beijing[1])

Thermodynamics and Growth Kinetical Consideration of Metal-Nitride Formation by Nitrogen Implantation[2])

By

B. X. Liu (a, b), X. Zhou (b), and H.-D. Li (b)

Contents

1. Introduction

Ion implantation has been found to be of significance for the development of novel materials although it was initially introduced as an alternative way of doping semiconductors [1]. By means of an ion beam technique the surface properties of materials can be modified via the variation of its composition and structure in the surface layers. For example, the resistance against wear and corrosion, optical, electrical, electrochemical properties and magnetic characteristics, etc., may be improved considerably. Furthermore, ion implantation has also been demonstrated to be an important way for the investigation on some interesting topics in the field of physical metallurgy, for instance, phase formation and transformation [2]. It has also been proved that ion implantation has the capability not only of producing a large number of metastable and amorphous alloys, but also of synthesizing various metal compounds in thin films [3 to 41]. It is well recognized that the kinetic condition available for structure transformation during implantation is very limited [7]. The duration that injected ions stop in the surface layer and are deposited into the matrix lattice in the form of precipitates is approximately 10^{-10} s [42]. Consequently, the phases produced by ion irradiation cannot be definitely predicted by the conventional principles of equilibrium thermodynamics in all cases.

Metal nitrides possess unique properties for application in many aspects, such as high melting points, great hardness, chemical stability, novel electrical and magnetic properties, etc. Direct nitrogen implantation into metals has been studied for nearly

[1]) Beijing **100084,** People's Republic of China.

[2]) Project supported by the National Natural Science Foundation of China.

Review Article, Phys. Stat. Sol. (a) 113, p.11-22 (1989).

two decades and great effort to reveal the formation mechanism of various metal nitrides has been made [12, 30, 43, 44]. Up-to-date results show that, under direct nitrogen implantation into metal films within a wide dose range, many metal nitrides possessing different types of crystal structure have been obtained [44]. Refractory metal nitrides, for instance, have high melting points (e.g. 3093 °C for TaN), and their formation usually requires high temperature (as high as 1100 to 1200 °C) treatment [45]. As a contrast, these nitrides have been obtained by direct nitrogen implantation at room temperature [9, 26, 311. This indicates that the situation of implantation is very different from that related to commonly used metallurgical techniques. Nevertheless, for some metal–nitrogen systems, the nitrides are more or less difficult to form or even not obtainable. There is also another category of nitrides with specific type of crystal structure, which could only form under rather restricted implantation conditions, and some of them appeared even tentatively and/or were very unstable.

The factors which were thought to influence the formation of metal nitrides by implantation were pointed out in earlier literature [8, 14, 15]. The previous examination showed that thermodynamic criteria are still valid in the process of ion implantation.

Concerning the factors determining the compound phases formed by oxygen or nitrogen implantation in metals, Kelly [44] gave sense to the mobility of implanted O or N ions at lower doses. The mobility is inferred from the diffusion lengths, $(Dt)^{1/2}$, which will be enhanced through ion irradiation. Generally, the mobility of O or N is high in most b.c.c. metals, in principle owing to the open lattices, contrasting that in f.c.c. or h.c.p. metals. Ge, Hf, Si, and Zr, on the contrary, have low O and N mobilities and would not be expected to yield new phases at low-dose implantation. When a saturated content of implanted ions was reached at high dose, the influence of mobility may be ignored [43].

Anttila et al. [46] studied the concentration profiles of nitrogen implantation of metals and proposed a sputtering scheme of nitride formation. The high sputtering yield of nitrogen ion bombardment will limit the maximum nitrogen concentration in the implanted metal layers and, therefore, has a basic restriction on the formation of metal nitrides. By means of the nuclear resonance broadening (NRB) methods, the nominal saturation concentration at maximum varied from 50 to 60 at% for most experimental cases. But for Cu, Ag, and Au, it was around 20 at%. In other words, no noble-metal nitride which has high N/M atomic ratio (M stands for metal) can be obtained due to the high sputtering yield. However, the average concentration of implanted nitrogen atoms may not be a critical factor determining the formation of nitrides. We have shown recently that the nitrogen content in an implanted layer after high-dose iniplantation may not be equal throughout the film due to the high density of defects produced by ion bombardment. In some regions the nitrogen concentration can deviate significantly from the average value of the film [47].

In a study of high-energy N_2^+ bombardment of several transition metals (Ti, Cr, Ni, Nb, Mo, and Ta), Belii et al. [9] used electron diffraction patterns to show that pure metal nitride phases were formed in all cases considered. The structural transformation (b.c.c. to f.c.c., f.c.c. to h.c.p., and h.c.p. to f.c.c.) in the process of nitride formation was related to the accumulation of radiation defects in the films [12]. This indicates that the mechanism of nitride formation in the environment of direct implantation is not completely the same as in conventional treatment.

Ma et al. [7] has proposed that in addition to the thermodynamic factor, the readiness of structural transformation may play a predominant part in many cases of the formation of individual nitrides. Only those nitrides which arc formed through a fast structural transition, e.g. martensitic shearing, could be achieved under the kinetic conditions of nitrogen implantation.

In this paper, based on summarizing the experimental results so far obtained, especially the observations in our systematic studies, we try to answer why and how a specific nitride may or map not be obtained by direct nitrogen implantation. Attentions were paid in particular to the Ti–N and noble-metal–N systems. For the Ti–N system, at very high implanting dose, we conduct a fine experiment to test what actually happens and focus on kinetic factors, especially the structural compatibility, which may play roles in the formation of titanium nitrides. Concerning noble metals. the nitrides are unfavoured both thermodynamically and kinetically because of the positive values of the heat of formation ($\Delta H_f > 0$) and the complexity of the crystal structures. We extended the dose of nitrogen implantation to even high levels in order to check if such nitrides can be formed and whether or not the sputtering argument is correct for the noble-metal nitride formation.

2. Experimental

The samples used in the investigations were in the form of either bulk or thin-film pure metals. For bulk specimens, the surface was polished carefully before ion implantation. The thin-film metals were prepared by depositing the pure metal element onto cleaved NaCl or SiO_2 substrates. The vacuum in the evaporation chamber was kept at a level better than 10^{-6} Torr. The thickness of the films was between 100 to 200 nm, which was designed to ensure the transmission of the analyzing electrons during TEM examination after implantation. Direct nitrogen implantation was performed at room temperature using nitrogen ions with an energy of several tens to hundred keV, e.g., 80 keV in our studies. The implanting dose rate was kept below 10 $\mu A/cm^2$ to prevent the samples from overheating and surface oxidizing. The sample holder in the target chamber was well cooled. The effective temperature rise of the samples resulting from beam heating was estimated to be around 100 °C and it was unable to intitiate the nitride formation thermally. In our tests we focused our sight especially on those films which were implanted to very high doses in order to see what would happen after saturation of implanted nitrogen concentration. In regard to Ti and noble metals, the implantation dose went up to a level as high as 2×10^{18} N/cm^2.

The phases produced in implanted samples were identified by transmission electron microscope (TEM) and electron spectroscopy for chemical analysis (ESCA). For bulk specimens, X-ray diffraction analysis was employed. The formation of nitrides was confirmed by indexing the diffraction lines in the SAD (selected area diffraction) pattern and compared with the data from PDP cards. With the aid of ESCA analysis, the atomic bonding between nitrogen and metal atoms can be revealed, from which one can also gain some insight into the nature of the nitride formation by implantation in metal films. The possible influence of surface contamination was avoided by argon ion sputtering before ESCA analysis.

Aging at room temperature was also performed in order to check the difference of the structures appearing in the implanted layers as-implanted and after aging, from which some thermodynamic rules could be revealed.

3. Two Categories of Metal Nitrides

The metal elements and their nitrides produced by nitrogen implantation so far reported are compiled in Table 1. We divided these nitrides into two categories. For the nitrides listed in the left column of Table 1, they are easy to obtain when the implanted nitrogen ions reach a certain value required by the stoichiometry of a particular nitride with increasing dosage. The corresponding ion doses usually fall into the range of (1 to 3) × 10^{17} N/cm^2, at which a considerable (20 to 50 at%) content of nitrogen in the film is predicted by the theory. Some metal–nitrogen systems, in which there are two or more nitrides existing in the equilibrium diagram, e.g., Cr–N, Mo–N, Nb–N, and Ta–N, were featured by step-like transition from nitride of low nitrogen content to high ones with rising N dose [9, 15, 27, 31].

Based on Miedima's model for the heat of formation in metal–nitrogen systems [48], ΔH_f (heat of formation) for the nitrides concerned are listed in Table 2. One can clearly see that AH, for those nitrides included in the left column of Table 1 are all negative and are therefore thermodynamically favourable to form. This indicated

Table 1
The nitrides in metal–nitrogen systems obtained by direct nitrogen implantation

metal	easy obtained nitride	hard obtained nitride	comment	ref.
Ag(f.c.c.)		AgN_3(orth.)		[4, 8]
Al(f.c.c.)	AlN(hex.)		no nitride obtained	[5, 6, 7, 9, 33, 36]
Au(f.c.c.)				[8, 9]
Co(f.c.c.)	Co_4N			[10]
	Co_3N(hex.)			[7, 11]
Cr(b.c.c.)	CrN(cubic)			[9, 10, 11]
	Cr_2N(hex.)			
Cu(f.c.c.)		CuN_3(tet.)		[8]
		Cu_xN		[38]
Fe(b.c.c.)	Fe_4N(cubic)			[10, 11, 12, 13, 39]
	$Fe_{2\text{ to }3}N$(hex.)			
	Fe_2N(orth.)			
Gd(h.c.p.)	GdN(NaCl)			[7, 31]
Ge(A4)	Ge_3N_4			[14]
Hf(h.c.p.)	HfN			[15]
Mn(cubic)	MnN_x		x is significantly greater than zero	[16]
Mo(b.c.c.)	MoN(hex.)			[9, 10, 12, 17, 18]
	Mo_2N(cubic)			
Nb(b.c.c.)	NbN(f.c.c.)			[9, 31]
	Nb_2N(hex.)			[31]
Ni(f.c.c.)	Ni_3N(hex.)			[10, 12, 19, 20]
Pb(f.c.c.)			no nitride	[21]
Re(h.c.p.)	$ReN_{0.43}$(cubic)			[22]
Si(A4)	Si_3N_4(hex.)			[21, 25]
Sn(A4)			no nitride	[21, 31]
Sb(rhom.)			no nitride	
Ta(b.c.c.)	Ta_2N(hex.)			[9, 25, 26, 27]
	TaN(hex.)			
Ti(h.c.p.)	TiN(NaCl)	Ti_2N(tet.)		[12, 28, 29, 30, 34, 40, 41]
V(b.c.c.)	VN(tet.)			[35]
	VN_x			[16]
W(b.c.c.)	WN(hex.)			[31]
	W_2N(cubic)			
Zn(h.c.p.)			no nitride	[16]
Zr(h.c.p.)	ZrN(NaCl)			[15, 32]

Table 2

The heat of formation (ΔH_f) for metal nitrides

nitride	ΔH_f (kJ/mol)	nitride	ΔH_f (kJ/mol)
&PIS,	+ 74	Mo_2N	− 38
AlN	− 52	NbN	−124
Co_4N	− 10	Nb_2N	− 92
Co_3N	− 12	Ni_3N	− 7
CrN	− 40	$ReN_{0.43}$	− 6
Cr_2N	− 38	Si_3N_4	− 26
CuN_3	+ 79	TaN	−118
Fe_4N	− 17	Ta_2N	− 88
Fe_2N	− 18	TiN	−155
GdN	−194	Ti_2N	−115
Ge_3N_4	− 28	VN	− 86
HfN	−121	WN	− 30
Mn_2N	− 52	W_2N	− 26
MoN	− 46	ZrN	−185

that it will reach the minimum level of free energy in the metal–nitrogen systems through nitride formation under N ion bombardment. The more negative the heat of formation for a nitride is, the greater is the driving force of its nucleation and growth and, as a result, this nitride is easily detected in the implanted layer. Such nitrides all belong to equilibrium nitrides in the equilibrium phase diagrams. This means that thermodynamic factors still prevail even in the non-equilibrium process of ion implantation. Physically the metals, such as Ti and Zr, have a strong tendency to attract the nitrogen atoms as nearest neighbours and to combine to nitrides because of the negative AH,. This nature holds true strongly even in the short duration of interaction during ion implantation [49]. Furthermore, as the implanted nitrogen is already in an atomic state, the change of the free energy during nitride formation is even more favourable than in the case of molecular N_2 interacting with metal. A nitride possessing a negative ΔH_f ($\Delta H_f < 0$) has a stronger tendency to be produced by monoatomic nitrogen ion implantation than by other techniques with molecular N_2.

In the right column of Table 1, those nitrides were compiled which had been obtained with difficulty. The appearance of these nitrides only occurred when extra energy or a rather restricted condition was provided. For those nitrides, except Ti_2N, the heats of formation of the nitrides are positive, indicating unfavourable conditions to form in terms of thermodynamics (see Table 2). Nevertheless, such nitrides with positive value of ΔH_f can even be formed under the condition of ion implantation. This demonstrated that direct ion implantation into the films is a powerful tool to produce the new phases which are hardly obtainable by other means [49]. The situation concerning the formation of this family of nitrides will be discussed later in this paper. For Ti_2N in the Ti–N system it was unusual and it will be investigated in detail also.

To determine whether a nitride could be formed by nitrogen implantation, one should consider not only thermodynamics but also kinetics. The negative value of ΔH_f ($\Delta H_f < 0$) for a nitride indicates its tendency to come into being. The more negative its AH,, the easier is its formation, provided that no kinetic barrier is existing. On a contrary, if a nitride has a positive ΔH_f (AH, > 0), its formation is also possible by implantation, as extra energy is deposited into the surface layer.

4. Geometrical Considerations

The metal nitride formation through implantation is not controlled only by thermodynamic factors. The geometrical and structural relationships should also be taken into account since the nitride phase is to be formed and grown right inside the metal matrix during ion implantation. This is similar to the precipitation process in a supersaturated solid solution [11].

Some of the structural relationships between the grown nitrides and the metal matrices can be revealed by properly grouping the observed results according to the crystal structures. The results are shown in Table 3. It may be pointed out that h.c.p. metals (Ti, Zr, and Gd) yield nitrides in which the metal atoms arrange themselves in an f.c.c. lattice and nitrogen atoms take octahedral interstices. Such a structure of nitrides has closer relations with the matrix. A little change of arrangement of metal atoms is needed and the nitrogen ions staying at interstices do not cause large expansions of the crystal lattice.

In a common sense. coherent growth can be achieved bv both diffusional and martensitic transformations. In the case of ion implantation where kinetic conditions are unique, the diffusionless martensitic transformation may play a role due to its cooperative and rapid kinetics. It should be noted that in most cases where nitrides are observed the structures of the nitrides are simple and a scheme of shears might be figured out to represent the change of the stacking order of the close-packed planes during transformation from h.c.p. to f.c.c. When a new phase forms according to this mechanism. it causes less lattice distortion and less atomic movement is needed. Such shearing may be easiest in the presence of interstitial nitrogen and transient environment of ion irradiation.

For the transformation of h.c.p. → f.c.c., for example, two possible ways of shearing which would eventually lead to the same change of stacking sequence from ABABAB... to ABCABC ... are shown in Fig. 1. Here $\boldsymbol{v}_1$ stands for a glide vector along a certain (1010) direction, and $\boldsymbol{v}_2$ along another (1010) direction. Fig. 1 a is the case of homogeneous shear where all the atoms move in the same direction and Fig. 1b is the case if the atoms in parallel (0002) planes are allowed to move in various (1010) directions.

Table **3**

Structures of metals and their nitrides produced by nitrogen implantation

metal	nitrides			
	M_4N	M_3N	M_2N	MN
Ti(h.c.p.)			Ti_2N(tet.)	TiN(NaCl)
Zr(h.c.p.)				ZrN(NaCl)
Gd(h.c.p.)				GdN(NaCl)
Co(h.c.p.)	Co_4N	Co_3N(hex.)		
Ni(f.c.c.)		Ni_3N(hex.)		
Al(f.c.c.)				AlN(hex.)
Nb(b.c.c.)			Nb_2N(hex.)	NbN(cubic)
Cr(b.c.c.)			Cr_2N(hex.)	CrN(cubic)
W(b.c.c.)			W_2N(f.c.c.)	WN(hex.)
Mo(b.c.c.)			Mo_2N(f.c.c.)	MoN(hex.)
V(b.c.c.)			V_2N(hex.)	VN(cubic)
Fe(b.c.c.)	Fe_4N(cubic)		Fe_2N(hex.)	

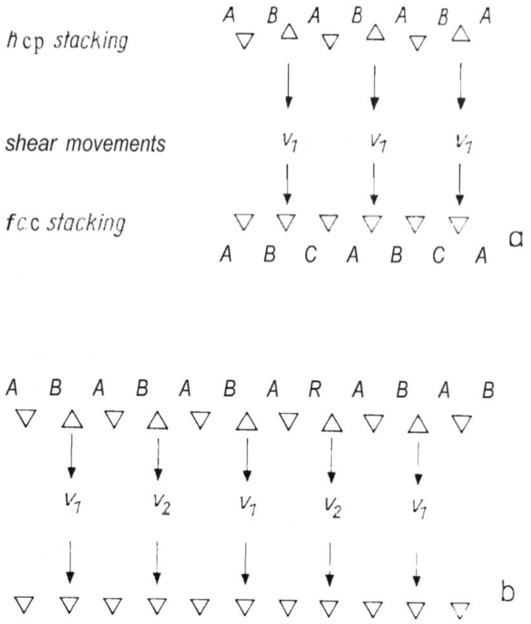

Fig. 1. Two possible ways of shearing for the stacking sequence changing in the h.c.p. → f.c.c. transition. V_1 stands for a glide vector along a specific $\langle 10\bar{1}0\rangle$ direction and V_2 is another $\langle 10\bar{1}0\rangle$ direction

The latter provides a diffusionless transformation without much change of shape and large shear strain [31] and will take place more possible in the phase formation in ion implantation. Furthermore, the filled interstitials will be convenient due to such a change of stacking order of the close-packed plane from h.c.p. to f.c.c. As for the b.c.c.–h.c.p. transition, a similar process involving shearing, though more complicated, may also be constructed based on the same principle.

However, the above discussion only serves to illustrate the point that both thermodynamic and structural factors should be taken into account and some kind of coherent growth, e.g. shear transformation, may be involved or even of advantage. When a nitride forms, it should be structurally compatible with the matrix as well as has the advantage of thermodynamic factors, e.g. negative ΔH_f. Martensitic shearing plays a role in the process of nitride formation. It must also be noted that the situation may not be described simply by the shearing mechanism if the implantation dose becomes very high and the structure of the film may be very distorted. This will be dealt with below.

The equilibrium nitrides which have not been observed or were not easily obtained including those listed in the right column of Table **1**, can be explained in terms of thermodynamic and/or structural factors. They are either thermodynamically unfavoured, or have complicated, delicate, or strictly ordered structures and involve large volume expansion during transformation. Besides, Ma et al. [31] have looked at this issue in another way. R_v was used as the molar volume expansion rate of a nitride when it is formed from the corresponding metal matrix. A large value of R_v inevitably inhibits the nitride formation and all the nitrides obtained have rather small R, values. $R_v <$ **1.3** may be regarded tentatively as equilibrium nitride by ion implantation, but not vice versa.

5. Fine Experiments on the Ti–N System

In the Ti–N system, there are two equilibrium nitrides, i.e. Ti_2N and TiN. As mentioned earlier, in most previous papers [44], only TiN was yielded after direct nitrogen implantation. Recently, Rauschenbach and Hochmuth [40] and Rauschenbach [41] claimed the appearance of a Ti_2N phase after very high fluence implantation. From Table 2 one can find that the ΔH_f values are **−155** kJ/mol for TiN and **−115** kJ/mol

Table 4
The titanium nitrides formed after N implantation (identified by SAD)

dose (N/cm^2)	phase detected	comment
5×10^{16}	—	no nitride
2×10^{17}	Ti + TiN	
1×10^{18}	TiN	Ti lines disappeared
2×10^{18}	TiN + Ti_2N	
5×10^{17}	Ti + TiN	as-implanted
	TiN + Ti_2N	aging for two months at RT

for Ti_2N. These negative ΔH_f indicate that both TiN and Ti_2N phases are thermodynamically favoured. At relatively low level of dosage, e.g. 2×10^{17} N/cm^2, sufficient nitrogen atoms have been deposited in the implanted layer and the thermodynamic condition was qualified for the formation of both TiN and Ti_2N. Starting from thermodynamic consideration, Ti_2N should be formed in the sample. But, in fact, it is not so in most reported experiment results. Therefore, in order to find what is behind such a phenomenon, we conducted a fine experiment for the Ti–N system [30]. The experimental observation showed that only the TiN phase is formed after 2×10^{17} N/cm^2 implantation. When the dose increased to 1×10^{18} N/cm^2, the whole film turned into the TiN phase. At 2×10^{18} N/cm^2, the Ti_2N phase appeared in the matrix, which was characterized by TEM and SAD examinations, see Table 4. These experimental results suggested that the phase transformation in the Ti–N system with increase of implanted nitrogen dose was in the sequence of Ti → TiN → Ti_2N. In order to check whether or not Ma's shearing model [31] works in the Ti–N system, a crystallographic analysis of the structural compatibility in the process of Ti nitride formation was performed.

During the formation of titanium nitride, TiN can be easily obtained through the change of the stacking sequence of titanium atoms from ABAB ... in the h.c.p. structure of the titanium matrix to ABCABC ... in the f.c.c. structure of TiN as discussed above. The nitrogen atoms take the octahedral interstitial sites in this course. Fig. 2 sketches the shearing steps in the transition TiN → Ti_2N. Each (111)plane of Ti atoms in the f.c.c. structure of TiN takes a shear of $\frac{1}{3}$ $[\bar{1}\bar{1}2]$ (see Fig. 2a). Then, another shear is performed by (121) plane sliding with a vector $\frac{1}{2}$ $[\bar{1}01]$ (see Fig. 2b). Such shearing may be achieved smoothly and the driving force for it is easily provided during nitrogen implantation.

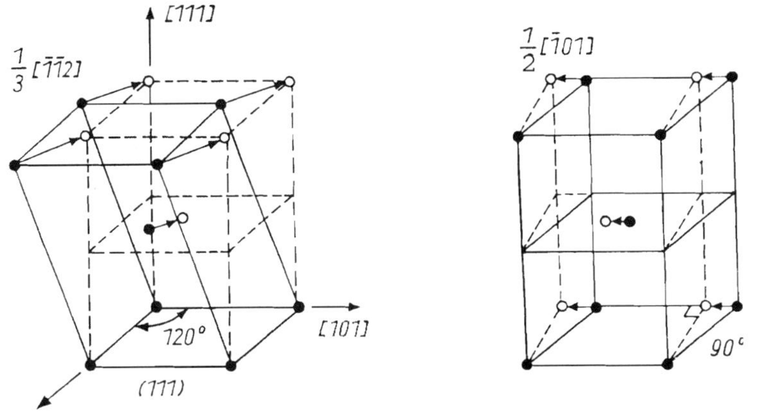

Fig. 2. TiN → Ti_2N transformation. The process can be executed in two steps. a) Each (111) plane in the f.c.c. structure takes a shear of $\frac{1}{6}$ $[\bar{1}\bar{1}2]$ and then, b) the (121)planes slide each other by a vector $\frac{1}{2}[\bar{1}01]$. ● Ti atoms before shearing and ○ after shearing

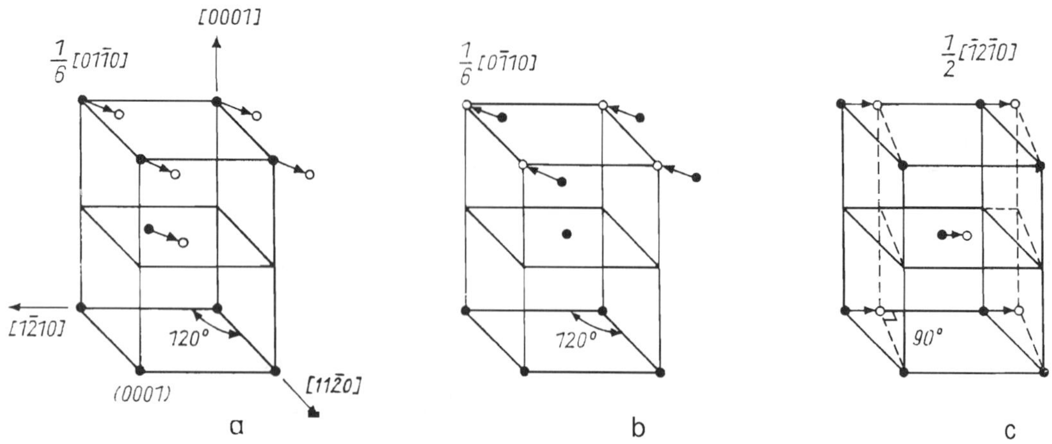

Pig. **3.** Ti → Ti_2N transformation. In **a)** and b), each neighbouring (0001) plane in the Ti h.c.p. structure slides in the opposite sense along $\frac{1}{6}$ [01$\bar{1}$0] and nitrogen atoms stay in distorted octahedral interstitials. In c), the (1010) plane undergoes a homogeneous shearing by $\frac{1}{2}[\bar{1}2\bar{1}0]$ ● Ti atoms before shearing and ○ after shearing

We also envisaged the transformation Ti → Ti_2N for comparison. This is shown in Fig. **3.** In the transition, three shearing steps would have to be involved. By such a way, the h.c.p. structure of titanium must suffer a shearing on a non-twinning plane and result in a large expansion along the [0001] direction. The unfavourable structural compatibility by this transition path made it hard to proceed. This is attributed to why the Ti_2N phase failed to appear right after 2×10^{17} N/cm^2 implantation. The fact that the formation of the Ti_2N phase was hindered due to the limited kinetic conditions was also supported by an aging test. One of the Ti samples, for instance, was surveyed immediately after implantation to a dose of 5×10^{17} N/cm^2. Only the TiN phase formed in the implanted layer (see Table 4). However, Ti_2N appeared in the same sample after it was aged at room temperature for about two months and checked again by TEM and SAD. Aging made the implanted layer approach to the equilibrium state and pursue local structural adjustments. This outcoming confirmed that the formation of the Ti_2N phase has much to do with the kinetics in the process of implantation and that the thermodynamic environment was qualified both for TiN and Ti_2N phases in a sample after 2 or 5×10^{17} N/cm^2 implantation. Inappropriate kinetic conditions caused Ti_2N not be obtained in an as-implanted sample. In this ease the kinetic factor played a predominant role controlling the formation of Ti_2N, and this may also be true in some other metal–nitrogen systems.

The Ti_2N appeared after the formation of TiN during the consecutive increase of the nitrogen dose to a very high level. These experimental observations also demonstrated that the average nitrogen concentration may not be a key factor determining the nitride formation. This will be discussed in detail in the case of noble-metal nitrides.

6. Formation of Noble-Metal Nitrides

Up to date, most published reports showed that no stable noble-metal nitride was observed by direct N implantation [7,9, 16]. Prabhawalkar et al. [38] claimed recently that a metastable copper nitride was observed by X-ray photoelectron spectroscopy (XPS). Examining the values of ΔH_f for noble-metal nitrides (see Table 2), all of these nitrides have positive ΔH_f. ΔH_f, for example, is +74 kJ/mol for AgN_3 and +79 kJ/mol for CuN_3. This means that the formation of noble-metal nitrides is thermodynamically unfavourable unless some extra energy is provided by some way. Anttila et al. [46] attributed the failure of the formation of noble-metal nitride to the high sputtering yield of nitrogen ion–noble metal couples, which prevented the average nitrogen con-

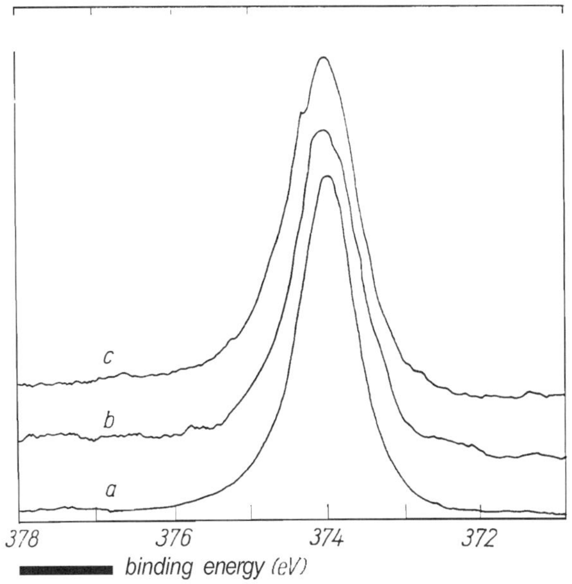

Fig. 4. Ag $3d_{3/2}$ (373.9 eV) ESCA spectra recorded for (a) unimplanted silver and implanted silver at doses of (b) 1 X 10^{18} and (c) 2 X × 10^{18} N/cm^2. When the dose went to a level as high as 2 X 10^{18} N/cm^2, a small shoulder (at 374.3 eV) appeared on the high-energy side of the silver $3d_{3/2}$ peak, indicating that a weak bonding was established among Ag and N atoms

centration in the implanted layer from reaching the value required for stoichiometry. The saturated maximum concentrations of N were about 18, 20, and 18at% in Cu, Ag, and Au films, respectively.

We have used 80 keV N^+ ions to implant Cu, Ag, and Au films to a dose as high as 2 × 10^{18} N/cm^2. Electron diffraction analysis revealed the formation of CuN_3 and AgN_3 phases in partial areas of the implanted Cu and Ag films [8]. The diffraction lines in SAD patterns were indexed and were in line with the data in the PDF cards. In order to confirm the formation of these nitrides, ESCA technique was employed to examine the change of the electron configuration. Fig. 4 shows the Ag $3d_{3/2}$ line (373.0 eV) in the ESCA spectra. After 2 × 10^{18} N/cm^2 implantation, a small shoulder was superimposed at 374.3 eV, indicating that a bonding was established between Ag and N atoms. This was in agreement with the result of SAD analysis. Because the shift of the shoulder from the silver matrix line was only 0.4 eV, the bonding between Ag and N atoms was very weak. This corresponded with the positive ΔH_f for silver nitride. The above experimental results proved that ion implantation is a very powerful method to form a compound which is thermodynamically unfavorable (having a positive AH,) and hard to obtain by other conventional techniques.

Tt is sure from our test that the maximum N concentration has been saturated by high-dose irradiation (2 × 10^{18} N/cm^2). The N/M ratios in AgN_3 or CuN_3 phase are higher than the saturated N content reported by Anttila et al. [46]. The formation of AgN_3 and CuN_3 nitrides and also Ti_2N as mentioned earlier after high-dose implantation proved that the content of nitrogen atoms in some local regions in the implanted layers may be considerably high or low. The average concentration in the implanted layers would not solely determine the new nitride formation. Sputtering arguments were found obviously not to work in the formation of noble-metal nitrides.

The problem remaining is that both AgN_3 and CuN_3 have an orthorhombic structure. In this case, the formation mechanism could not be explained by ordinary principles. After very high implantation, a large amount of extra energy deposited into the surface layer and the high density of defects enhanced the short-range adjustment of neighbouring noble-metal and N atoms to minimize the free energy in local areas. The transient environment at ion bombardment might make silver and copper nitrides seek crystal seeds to nucleate in some local regions where the nitrogen concentration was sufficient for the stoichiometric requirement. In the Ti–N system, on the contrary, a large amount of defects made the deposited nitrogen atoms to be removed and to accumulate to form bubbles [46] and the nitrogen content in some other part might fall down. Consequently, the transformation from TiN to Ti_2N could then proceed.

The failure of detecting any Au nitride under same implantation conditions suggested that the behaviour of gold upon N irradiation was not the same as that of Cu or Ag despite they are of one group in the Periodic Table. The electronic structure of Au may make it more difficult to form a nitride as compared with copper and silver [4].

It should be noted that the above discussion does not constitute a clear-cut line of demarcation or definite mechanism to explain the formation of noble-metal nitrides by direct nitrogen implantation. More deep-going studies are needed. Nevertheless, it serves to demonstrate that direct ion implantation is a new powerful technique to form metal nitrides in the near-surface region. Some nitrides which are difficult to form with conventional methods may be obtained under the peculiar conditions of ion irradiation. In the implanted layer, the average concentration of nitrogen may not stand for the local density of N atoms, and hence is not a key factor thought to hinder the formation of some particular nitrides.

7. Conclusions

1. Both thermodynamics and growth kinetics should be considered to understand the formation mechanism of metal nitride formation by nitrogen implantation.

2. The structural compatibility plays an important role in the process of metal atoms combining with implanted nitrogen ions to form a nitride. In some cases, such as Ti_2N in the Ti–N system, it is a predominant factor which determined whether the Ti_2N could be formed or not. These results also confirmed that the shearing model is a better guide to reveal the mechanism of nitride formation during direct nitrogen implantation.

3. The noble-metal nitrides, e.g. AgN_3 and CuN_3, in spite of their positive value of AH_n could be formed by direct nitrogen ion implantation, which probably provided the reaction energy to overcome this unfavourable thermodynamic factor. These evidences also showed that the high sputtering yield in the noble-metal case could not prevent the noble-metal nitrides from forming, as the local nitrogen content in the implanted layers could deviate from the average value determined by the sputtering yield.

4. Under the above-mentioned consideration and discussion, the nitrides so far obtained are classified into two categories. One is easily obtained, while the other is hard to form or even not accessible by conventional methods.

Acknowledgement

The financial aid from the International Atomic Energy Agency (Contract No. 4731/RB) is gratefully acknowledged.

References

[1] S. T. Picraux, Annu. Rev. Mater. Sci. **14, 335 (1984).**

[2] C. M. Preece and J. K. Hirvonen (Ed.), Ion Implantation Metallurgy, MS AIME, New York **1979.**

[3] P. V. Pavlov, Nuclear Instrum. and Methods **209/210, 791 (1983).**

[4] X. Zhou, H. D. Li, and B. X. Liu, J. Phys. C **21, L683 (1988).**

[5] O. Anciello, R. A. Baragiola, E. R. Salvatelli, and J. L. Spino, in: Ion Implantation in Semiconductors, Ed. F. Chernow, J. A. Borden, and D. K. Brice, Plenum Press, New York **1977** (p. **231**).

[6] I. M. Belii, F. F. Komarov, E. G. Openchuk, and S. Yu. Shiryaev, Soviet Phys. – Cryst. **24,** 233 (1979).

[7] E. MA, B. X. LIU, X. CHEN, and H. D. LI, Thin Solid Films 147, 49 (1987).
[8] X. ZHOU, H. D. LI, and B. X. LIU, IBMM'88, Tokyo, June 12 to 17, 1988; Nuclear Instrum. and Methods, to be published.
[9] I. M. BELII, F. F. KOMAROV, V. S. TISHKOV, and V. M. YANKOVSKII, phys. stat. sol. (a) 45, 343 (1978).
[10] P. V. PAVLOV, D. I. TETELBAUM, A. V. PAVLOV, and E. I. ZORIN, Soviet Phys. — Doklady 19, 399 (1975).
[11] H. D. LI, in: Thin Films, Proc. 1986 China–Japan Symp. Thin Films, Beijing, September 22 to 24, 1986, Japan. Soc. for the Promoting of Science, Tokyo 1986 (p. 77).
[12] V. N. BYKOV, V. A. TROYAN, G. G. ZDOROVTSEVA, and V. S. KHAJMOVICH, phys. stat. sol. (a) 32, 53 (1975).
[13] V. N. BYKOV, G. G. ZDOROVTSEVA, V. A. TROYAN, and V. S. KHAIMOVICH, Soviet Phys. — Cryst. 16, 699 (1972).
[14] G. BRAUER, H. MULLER, and G. KUHNER, J. less-common Metals 4, 533 (1962).
[15] R. G. DUCKWORTH and I. H. WILSON, Thin Solid Films 63, 289 (1979).
[16] G. M. LANCASTER and J. W. KABALAIS, J. phys. Chem. 83, 209 (1979).
[17] N. V. TROITSKAYA and Z. G. PINSKER, Soviet Phys. — Cryst. 4, 33 (1959).
[18] N. V. TROITSKAYA and Z. G. PINSKER, Soviet Phys. — Cryst. 6, 34 (1961).
[19] J. J. TRILLAT, L. TERTIAN, N. TERAO, and C. LECOMTE, Bull. Soc. Chim. Franc. 8, 804 (1957).
[20] J. J. TRILLAT, L. TERTIAN, and N. TERAO, C. R. Acad. Sci. (France) 243, 666 (1956).
[21] J. A. TAYLOR, G. M. LANCASTER, and J. W. RABALAIS, J. Electron Spectroscopy and related Phen. 13, 435 (1978).
[22] A. UL HAQ, Ph. D. Dissertation, Universität Karlsruhe, 1982.
[23] T. BAIRD, J. R. FRYER, and E. V. RIDDELL, Surface Sci. 28, 525 (1971).
[24] P. V. PAVLOV, Soviet Phys. — Doklady 23, 373 (1978).
[25] K. G. STEPHENS and I. H. WILSON, Thin Solid Films 50, 325 (1978).
[26] N. TERAO, Japan. J. appl. Phys. 10, 248 (1971).
[27] X. ZHOU, B. X. LIU, H. K. DONG, and H. D. LI, in: Internat. Symp. Application of Ion Beams Produced by Small Accelerators, Jinan (China), October 20 to 24, 1987; Vacuum, to be published.
[28] R. G. VARDIMAN and R. A. KANT, J. appl. Phys. 52, 690 (1982).
[29] H. T. LI, P. S. LIU, S. C. CHANG, H. C. LU, H. H. WANG, and K. TAO, Nuclear Instrum. and Methods 182/183, 915 (1981).
[30] X. ZHOU, H. K. DONG, H. D. LI, and B. X. LIU, J. appl. Phys. 63, 4942 (1988).
[31] E. MA, B. X. LIU, X. CHEN, and H. D. LI, Mater. Res. Soc. Symp. Proc. 54, 617 (1986).
[32] R. G. DUCKWORTH, Thin Solid Films 84, 307 (1981).
[33] S. OHIRA and M. LWAKI, Mater. Sci. Engng. 90, 143 (1987).
[34] P. ZHENG, J. C. PIVIN, and M. O. RUAULT, Europhys. Letters 8, 689 (1988).
[35] J. T. ELLIS, D. K. CHRISTEN, J. D. LEWIS, S. T. SEKULA, J. P. THOMPSON, and J. M. WILLIAMS, Nuclear Instrum. and Methods B 19/20, 167 (1987).
[36] S. OHIRA and M. IWAKI, Nuclear Instrum. and Methods B 19/20, 162 (1987).
[37] J. P. GAUTHIER, D. FLÈCHE, J. PIVOT, itnd J. A. ROGER, Vacuum 34, 1013 (1984).
[38] P. D. PRABHAWALKAR, D. C. KOTHARI, M. R. NAIR, and P. M. RAOLE, Nuclear Instrum. and Methods B 7/8, 147 (1985).
[39] V. M. DRAKO and G. A. GUMANSKIJ, Radiat. Eff. 66, 101 (1982).
[40] B. RAUSCHENBACH and K. HOCHMUTH, phys. stat. sol. (a) 94, 833 (1986).
[41] B. RAUSCHENBACH, J. Mater. Sci. 21, 395 (1986).
[42] W. L. JOHNSON, Y. T. CHENG, M. VAN ROSSUM, and M. A. NICOLET, Nuclear Instrum. and Methods B 7/8, 657 (1985).
[43] R. KELLY, Radiat. Eff. 64, 205 (1982).
[44] R. KELLY, J. Vacuum Sci. Technol. 21, 778 (1982).
[45] P. SCHWARZKOPF and R. KIEFFER, Refractory Hard Metals, Macmillan, New York 1963.
[46] A. ANTTILA, J. KEINONEN, M. UHRMACHER, and S. VAHVASELKA, J. appl. Phys. 57, 1423 (1985).
[47] M. I. GUSEVA and G. V. GORUEEVA, phys. stat. sol. (a) 95, 385 (1986).
[48] P. C. P. BOUTEN and A. R. MIEUEMA, J. less-common Metals 85, 217 (1979).
[49] P. WILKES, J. nuclear Mater. 83, 166 (1979).

(Received November 7, 1988)

Void swelling induced by 1 MeV electron irradiation in Ti- and Nb-modified 316 stainless steels

B.X. Liu [1,2], S.L. Lai [1], J.G. Sun [3], C.H. Shang [1] and D. Xu [1]

[1] *Department of Materials Science and Engineering, Tsinghua University, Beijing, 100084, China*
[2] *Centre of Condensed Matter and Radiation Physics, CCAST (World Lab.), Beijing, 100080, China*
[3] *HVEM Lab. of the General Research Institute of Nonferrous Metals, Beijing, 100088, China*

Received 13 November 1989; accepted 13 June 1990

Four 316 stainless steels, cold-worked and modified with minor elements of Ti and Nb, were irradiated by 1 MeV electrons in a HVEM at temperatures ranging from 823 to 883 K, up to 80 dpa. Void swelling, void densities and mean diameters were determined in each case. The experimental results show that swelling increases linearly with increasing of dose after an incubation period. Compared with the results obtained from solution-annealed 316 stainless steels, it is found that the influence of cold work on void swelling depends strongly on the modifying elements, and that Ti-modified 316 steels are superior to Nb-modified ones in swelling resistance.

1. Introduction

316 stainless steels modified with minor alloying elements, such as Ti, W, Nb, Zr etc, are very promising as structural materials for fast-neutron reactors [1]. In the last two decades, there have been many works reported in the literature concerning the study of radiation damage, especially the swelling behavior, and other properties of 316 steels [2–5]. However, it is still necessary to test newly modified 316 stainless steels for the long-term energy resource program. It is well known that electron beams from high voltage electron microscopes (HVEM) can be used to study the radiation damage of metals with several advantages, such as the ability to induce high damage rates without high densities of cascade occurring in the heavy ion irradiation cases and the in-situ observation of microstructural changes [6]. In this paper, we present the experimental results of the swelling behaviors of four 316 steels, which were differently cold-worked and modified by minor alloying elements, produced in China.

2. Experimental conditions

Table 1 shows the composition and the extent of cold work of the samples used in our experiments. After being annealed in a vacuum chamber at 1283 K, the 15 mm diameter steel rods were manufactured by cold-pulling. In this study, the rods were cut into 0.5 mm thick sheets using a line-saw, and polished mechanically to 50–70 pm in thickness. After that, 3 mm diameter

Table 1
Specification of Ti- and Nb-modified 316 stainless steels

Sample number	Extent of cold work	Composition (wt%)							
		C	Si	Mn	Cr	Ni	Mo	Ti	Nb
1164	10%	0.06	0.73	1.53	16.99	13.48	2.38	0.36	–
1165	20%	0.07	0.73	1.53	17.04	13.50	2.38	0.53	–
1166	20%	0.07	0.71	1.53	17.04	13.50	2.40	–	0.52
1167	10%	0.07	0.72	1.50	17.04	13.50	2.38	–	0.80

J. Nuclear Materials 175, p.129-134 (1990).

discs were punched from the sheets. Electropolishing was carried out at 276 K in a mixture of 95% acetic acid and 5% perchloric acid, and the polishing voltage was 30–35 V. No gas was injected after polishing. The samples were washed with alcohol and kept in it for use.

Irradiation was carried out in a HVEM of JEM-1000, using a beam of 1000 kV electrons with an intensity of $\sim 2.5\times10^{24}$ e/m^2 s at a central area and a total current of 0.17×10^{-6} A. This beam produced the displacements in steels at a rate of $\sim 8.0\times10^{-3}$ dpa/s, assuming a displacement threshold energy of 19 eV [7]. To coincide with this, the (110) crystalline direction was used for the irradiation. As the temperature is an important factor for swelling, particular care should be taken to obtain accurate control. In this experiment, the temperatures were measured with a Pt–Rh thermocouple which was equipped with the furnace in the HVEM. All the experiments were conducted at temperatures ranging from 823 to 883 K, because the previous studies have proved that 316 steels displayed the maximum swelling in this temperature region [8]. An increment of 30 K was added to all the measured temperatures as the result of the heating of the specimen by the 0.17 μA beam [9]. The thickness of the irradiated area was estimated to be 500 nm, which was enough to ensure that the results were similar to those of bulk materials [8]. The vacuum of the specimen chamber was maintained at $<2.0\times10^{-4}$ Pa.

The void parameters, i.e., void swelling, void density and mean diameter, were determined from micrographs. The volume of all the voids within a given area was summed and calculated by the following expression:

$$\frac{\Delta V}{V_0}=\frac{\Sigma nv}{MAh},\tag{1}$$

where Σnv is the total volume of voids in an area of A

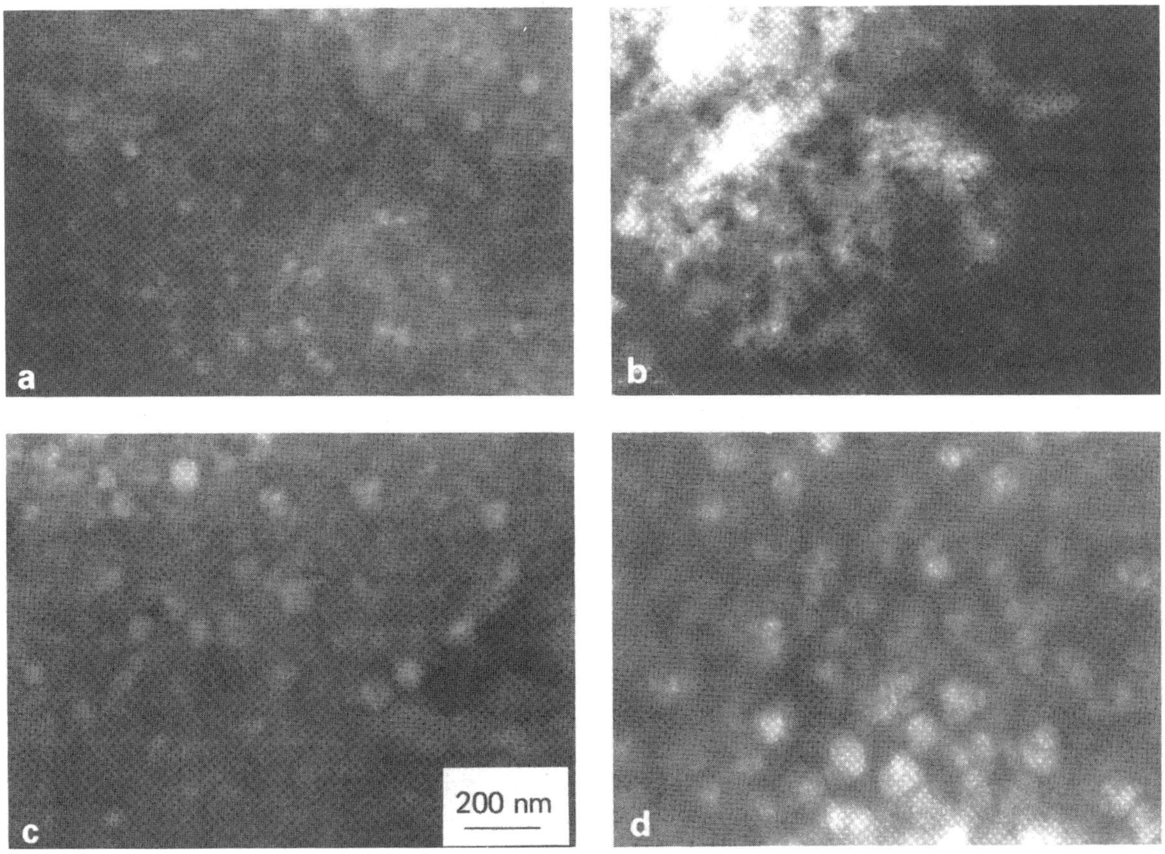

Fig. 1. Void structure formed during electron irradiation: (a) in the 1164 sample (0.36 wt% Ti) irradiated to 69 dpa at 868 K, and the swelling is 1.5%.(b) In the 1165 sample (0.53 wt%Ti) irradiated to 80 dpa at 863 K, no measurable voids appeared and the swelling is estimated to be less than 1%.(c) In the 1166 sample (0.52 wt% Nb) irradiated to 82 dpa at 823 K, and the swelling is 2.2%.(d) In the 1167 sample (0.80 wt% Nb) irradiated to 71 dpa and 883 K, and the swelling is 30%.

on a micrograph of magnification M, h is the void layer thickness, and $\Delta V/V_0$ is a measure of swelling. The void density is defined as

$$p = n/MAh, \tag{2}$$

while the mean diameter of the voids is:

$$d = \left(\frac{6}{\pi}\frac{1}{M^3}\frac{\Sigma nv}{n}\right)^{1/3}. \tag{3}$$

3. Results

Voids formed in four tested samples are shown in fig. 1, and the void parameters are listed in table 2. Based on these data, four curves have been plotted (figs. 2–5), among which fig. 2 and fig. 3 show swellings versus dose, and fig. 4 and fig. 5 show the void densities and the mean diameters of voids as a function of dose, respectively. The voids which appeared on micrograph films for 1165 steel were too small to allow the swelling to be calculated (see fig. 1(b)), even though the dose had been accumulated to the one corresponding to 80 dpa, indicating that this 316 steel has a high resistance to swelling upon irradiation. The other three curves show clearly that after an incubation period, the swelling increased linearly with increasing irradiation dose. Each steel had different incubation doses and swelling rates, which can be derived from empirical swelling equations given along with the figures. It can also be seen that swelling rate of the 1167 sample is one order larger in magnitude than those of 1164 and 1166, whereas the incubation doses of these three samples are of the same order, i.e., around 20 dpa. Obviously, 1165 sample had

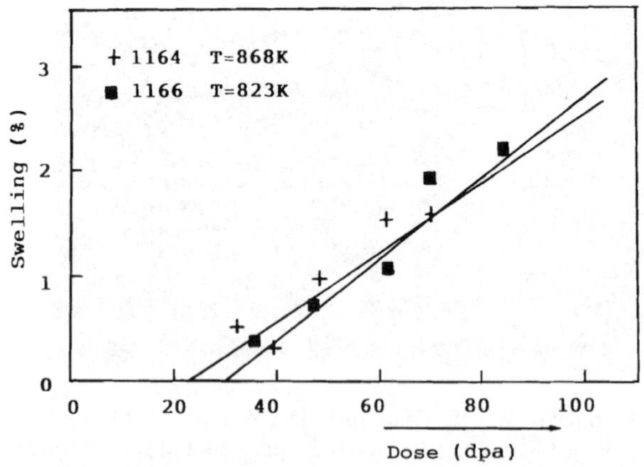

Fig. 2. Dose dependence of swelling in samples *1164* and *1166*, which can be expressed as $\Delta V/V_0 = 0.0374K - 0.7698$ and $\Delta V/V_0 = 0.0409K - 1.1856$ respectively (K refers to dose).

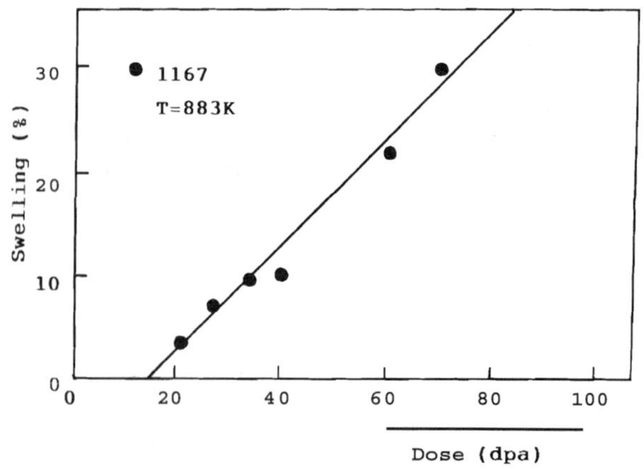

Fig. 3. Dose dependence of swelling in sample *1167*, which can be expressed as $\Delta V/V_0 = 0.517K - 8.479$ (K refers to dose).

the better anti-swelling property, while 1166 and 1164 stainless steels swelled 2–3% at a dose corresponding to 80 dpa. The 1167 sample swelled so much that this steel cannot be used in the reactors.

Fig. 4 shows that the number of voids in the 1167 sample decreased while those in the 1164 and 1166 samples increased. This means that voids more easily nucleated in the 1167 sample. These results of void density change indicate that the condition of Ti or a small amount of Nb delays the void nucleation. In other words, these elements can enhance the recombination

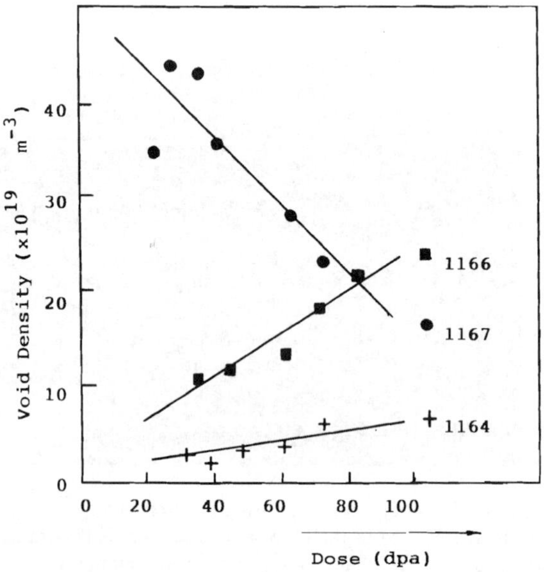

Fig. 4. Dose dependence of void density in cold-worked samples.

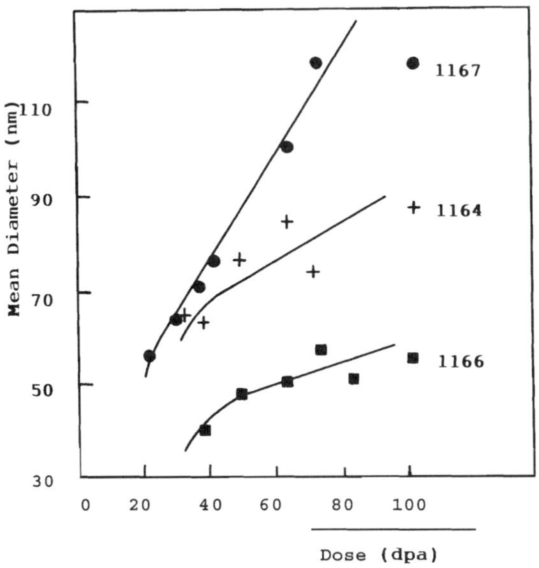

Fig. 5. Dose dependence of void mean diameters in cold-worked samples.

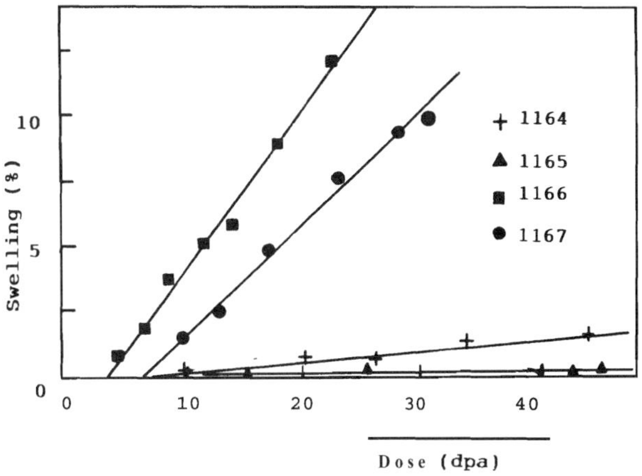

Fig. 6. Dose dependence of swelling in solution-annealed samples.

among point defects, or suppress the migration of point defects.

Fig. 5 shows the relations between the void mean diameters and the doses in which they do not show linearity. This suggests that at the first stage of swelling after the incubation period, the growth of voids was not at a constant rate.

4. Discussion

Figs. 6, 7 and 8 show three parameters of voids versus irradiation doses of solution-annealed stainless steels under electron irradiation [10]. The solution-an-

Table 2
Irradiation results of 316 stainless steels

No. 1164 (irradiated at 868 K)	Irradiation dose (dpa)	31.8	38.6	48.0	52.2	60.0	69.4
	Mean diameter of voids (nm)	64.8	63.5	76.9	88.3	83.0	74.4
	Density of voids ($\times 10^{19}/m^3$)	3.0	2.3	3.7	3.4	4.4	6.5
	Swelling $\Delta V/V$ (%)	0.46	0.33	0.95	1.3	1.5	1.5
No. 1166 (irradiated at 823 K)	Irradiation dose (dpa)	35.9	46.9	61.2	71.3	82.8	
	Mean diameter of voids (nm)	39.1	46.0	49.0	55.9	49.6	
	Density of voids ($\times 10^{20}/m^3$)	1.1	1.2	1.4	1.9	2.8	
	Swelling $\Delta V/V$ (%)	0.38	1.7	1.0	1.95	2.2	
No. 1167 (irradiated at 883 K)	Irradiation dose (dpa)	22.04	29.2	35.8	41.3	62.3	71.1
	Mean diameter of voids (nm)	56.5	63.8	71.0	75.9	102.7	118.4
	Density of voids ($\times 10^{20}/m^3$)	3.5	4.5	4.4	3.56	2.84	2.4
	Swelling $\Delta V/V$ (%)	3.8	7.0	9.8	10.1	22.1	29.9

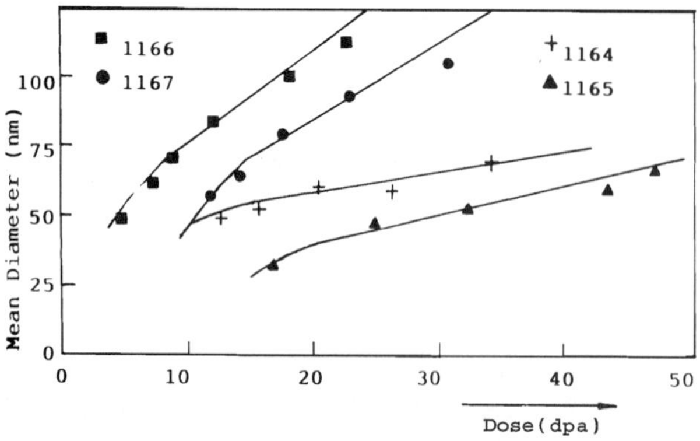

Fig. 7. Dose dependence of void mean diameter in solution-annealed samples.

nealed steels have the same composition as the cold-worked ones.

Comparison among them shows that void swellings increased at constant rates in both cold-worked and solution-annealed 316 stainless steels. However, for different treatment processes, the swelling rates of each sample varied. Cold work can improve the anti-swelling property of 1166 and 1167 steels more effectively. On the contrary, the two treating processes exert the same influence on the void swelling of Ti-modified samples, namely 1164 and 1165 steels, within the experimental error. Consequently, cold work has less influence on Ti-modified stainless steels than on Nb-modified ones.

From a comparison of the void densities and mean diameters after different treatments, cold-worked steels were seen to have smaller voids than those which were

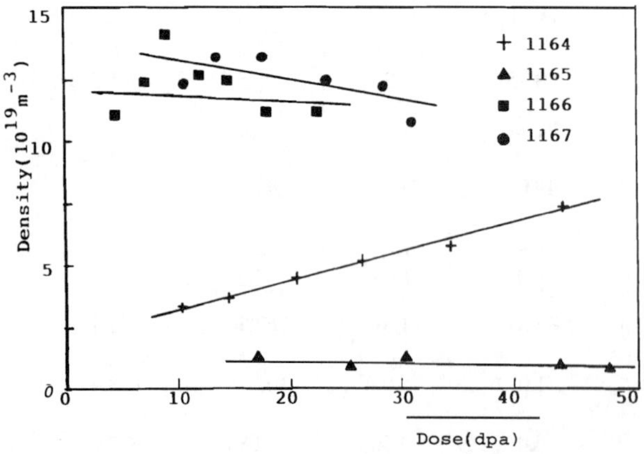

Fig. 8. Dose dependence of void density in solution-annealed samples.

solution-annealed. This influence also depends on the modifying elements. For Nb-modified 1166 steel, the cold work made the void densities increase with dose, whereas solid-solution annealing suppressed it. Different treatments can also strongly influence the void size.

From the experimental results and the above discussions, we can summarize that:

(i) The void swelling of four 316 steels increased linearly with irradiation dose after an incubation period of about 20 dpa. The linearity between void densities and irradiation doses is also shown.

(ii) After 80 dpa, no measurable voids appeared in 20% cold-worked steel with 0.53 wt% Ti and 0 wt% Nb, which means an excellent swelling resistant property, while 10% cold-worked steel containing 0.80 wt% Nb, 0 wt% Ti and 10%cw swelled considerably. The other two steels displayed good swelling properties, 2–3%, one of which was 10% cold-worked and contained 0.36 wt% Ti and 0 wt% Nb, and the other was 20% cold-worked and contained 0 wt% Ti and 0.52 wt% Nb.

(iii) Stainless steels modified with Ti had better swelling resistance properties than those of steels modified with Nb if the extent of cold work was the same. Compared with solution-annealing, cold work can suppress void swelling more efficiently.

Acknowledgements

We wish to thank the HVEM laboratory in the General Research Institute of Nonferrous Metals, especially Mr Z.Y. Zhao for his great help. This study is partly supported by the International Atomic Energy Agency (Contract No. 4731/R2/RB).

References

[1] D.R. Olander, Fundamental Aspects of Nuclear Reactor Fuel Elements (US ERDA Technical Information Center, Oak Ridge, 1976) Chapter 18.

[2] K. Shiraishi and Y. Katano, In-Situ Experiments With High Voltage Electron Microscopes, Ed. H. Fujita (Osaka University, 1985) p. 225.

[3] D.I.R. Norris and J.T. Buswell, J. Nucl. Mater. 59 (1976) 316.

[4] M.J. Markin, G.P. Walters and A.J.E. Foreman, J. Nucl. Mater. 95 (1980) 155.

[5] N. Igata, Y. Kohno and J. Nishimura, In-Situ Experiments With High Voltage Electron Microscopes, Ed. H. Fujita (Osaka University, 1985) p. 245.

[6] G.J.C. Carpenter and J.F. Watters, J. Nucl. Mater. 96 (1981) 213.
[7] M.J. Markin, S.N. Buckley and G.P. Walters, J. Nucl. Mater. 68 (1977) 161.
[8] J.J. Laider, F.A. Gamer and L.E. Thomas, Irradiation Damage in Metals 9–10 (1975) 194.
[9] M.J. Markin, UKAEA AERE Report R6957 (1971).
[10] J.G. Sun, unpublished.

Disclination loops in Ni–Mo amorphous alloy films induced by ion irradiation

B X Liu†, C H Shang and H D Li

Department of Materials Science and Engineering, Tsinghua University, Beijing 100084, People's Republic of China

Received 11 September 1990, in final form 19 March 1991

Abstract. Ni–Mo amorphous films were obtained by 200 keV xenon ion mixing at room temperature to dosages higher than 7×10^{14} ion cm^{-2}. It was found, for the first time, that when the irradiation dose went up to 7×10^{15} ion cm^{-2}, many odd lines appeared in the amorphous matrix. After excluding various possible explanations, we attribute the observed loops to line defects, i.e. disclinations in amorphous solids. Rich microstructures pertinent to disclination loops are described in detail. Scaling analysis showed that the observed disclinations shared a common fractal dimension in the small length scale. Moreover, approximation of gauge theory in the limit of elastic continuum media enables us to account for their anomalous properties successfully.

1. Introduction

Dislocations are a ubiquitous form of line defect in crystalline solids, controlling many of their mechanical properties [1]. The probable existence of similar defects in amorphous materials has been a long-standing argument which has aroused considerable interest among condensed matter physicists [2]. The topological study of amorphous structures in terms of SO(3) gauge theory [3] showed that dislocations of any kind are not structurally stable in amorphous elastic continua; instead it was proposed that an additional type of line defect, i.e. a rotational 2π disclination, exists as a single structurally stable constituent $Z_2\Pi_1(SO(3))$ in amorphous solids. The existence of disclinations allows one to speculate whether the liquid, crystalline, quasi-crystalline and amorphous states differ largely in the spatial organization and kinetics of such line defects [4]. To our knowledge, however, no direct evidence for such line defects in metallic glasses has ever been reported up until now, which makes this prospective approach remain a pedagogical discussion. Therefore, direct observation of disclination loops in amorphous states is of great importance from both the theoretical and experimental points of view. In this paper, we present, for the first time, strong evidence for the existence of such line defects, and discuss theoretically some items concerning the observed disclination loops. We hope our observations will stimulate increasing interest in this issue.

† Also at Centre of Condensed Matter and Radiation Physics CCAST (World Lab.), Beijing, China.

J. Physics: Condensed Matter 3, p.5769-5781 (1991).

2. Experimental procedure

Ni–Mo multilayered films were prepared by alternatively depositing three layers of Ni and two layers of Mo metals onto SiO_2 wafers with a glass-like surface in a high vacuum system. The vacuum level during deposition was 5×10^{-7} Torr. The overall composition and thickness of the deposited films were confirmed to be $Ni_{65}Mo_{35}$ and 42 nm, respectively, by Rutherford backscattering (RBS) measurement. Ion mixing was conducted at room temperature by using 200 keV scanning xenon ions to obtain high efficiency. More than ten doses were designed to cover the range from $1–100 \times 10^{14}$ ion cm^{-2}. The beam current density was maintained at less than 1 $\mu A\ cm^{-2}$ to minimize the beam heating. The vacuum level during irradiation was better than 1×10^{-6} Torr. The details of the experiment can be found in [5]. X-ray analysis was conducted in a D/max-IIIA diffractometer with an attachment for high sensitivity for thin film analysis. The samples were also checked by RBS measurements to unravel the configuration of the thin films, and to characterize the mixing efficiency induced by the ion irradiation. The resistive features of the solid films were measured by a standard four-point probe. For transmission electron microscopy (TEM, JEM-200CX and H-800, operated at 200 keV) examination, self-supported films were obtained by eroding the SiO_2 substrates in the HF acid, then cleaned in de-ionized water, and finally put onto the Cu grids. Selected area diffraction (SAD), *in situ* scanning electron microscopy (SEM), and energy dispersive spectroscopy (EDS) were also used to characterize the microstructure of the films.

3. Main results and contrast formulation

3.1. Formation of amorphous films

Figure 1 illustrates a set of backscattering spectra. As indicated in figure 1, the multilayered structures, i.e. three layers of Ni and two layers of Mo, were clearly shown in both the as-deposited samples and irradiated ones when the irradiation dose was lower than 7×10^{14} ion cm^{-2}. It can also be seen that the amplitude reflecting the structural oscillation decreased continuously with an increase in the ion fluence, and when the dosage reached 7×10^{14} ion cm^{-2}, all the zigzag vibration peaks were smeared out. These results clearly indicated that when the dosage was 7×10^{14} ion cm^{-2} and above, the Ni and Mo atoms were homogeneously mixed in the films. All the samples were also examined by x-ray diffraction to reveal the phase structures in the films. The diffraction results shown in figure 2 demonstrate that the dosage of 7×10^{14} ion cm^{-2} just corresponds to the dosage necessary to vitrify the films. When the irradiation dose was less than 7×10^{14} ion cm^{-2}, the two strongest diffraction peaks, i.e. Mo (110) and Ni (111), could be easily identified, indicating that the films were in a polycrystalline state. However, in other cases, as shown in figures 2(*d*)–(*e*), only widely spread halos could be recorded, which meant that the Ni–Mo alloys were uniformly vitrified as the irradiation dose equalled or exceeded 7×10^{14} ion cm^{-2}. The same amorphization procedure was also confirmed by the electron diffraction experiment by means of TEM. Four-point probe resistivity measurements again showed that the dose of 7×10^{14} ion cm^{-2} was the lowest one to saturate the sheet resistivity [6] at about 150 $\mu\Omega$ cm. Following the diffraction patterns shown in figures 2(*a*)–(*c*), it can be deduced that, with an increase in ion fluence, an increasing number of Ni atoms collided with the Mo lattice, and *vice versa*, which resulted in the two characteristic diffraction peaks moving toward each other and eventually overlapping. When a dose of 7×10^{14} ion cm^{-2} was reached, the two seriously distorted lattices, FCC and BCC, were intrinsically destabilized and transformed into a new atomic configuration, i.e. an amorphous structure. By now the essential point is that when the irradiation dosage was higher than or equal to 7×10^{14} ion cm^{-2}, the multilayered $Ni_{65}Mo_{35}$ alloy films were homogeneously mixed and uniformly vitrified.

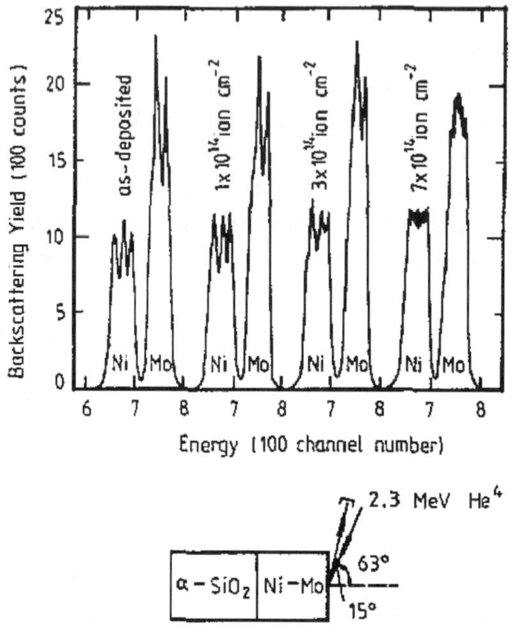

Figure 1. Backscattering spectra: as-deposited Ni–Mo films and samples irradiated to doses of 1, 3 and 7×10^{14} ion cm^{-2}, respectively.

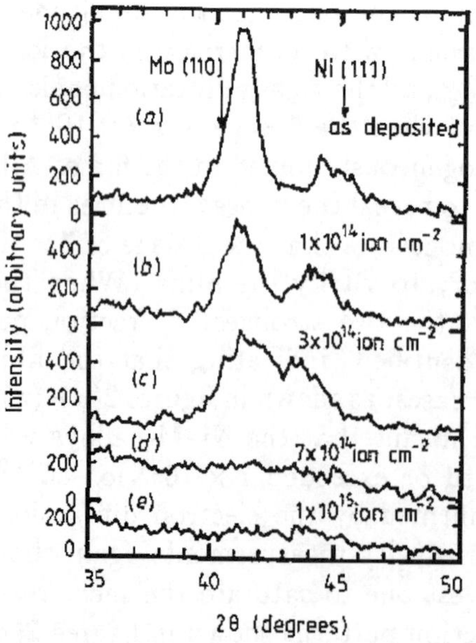

Figure 2. X-ray diffraction results: (*a*) as-deposited; (*b*) 1×10^{14} ion cm^{-2}; (*c*) 3×10^{14} ion cm^{-2}; (*d*) 7×10^{14} ion cm^{-2}; and (*e*) 1×10^{15} ion cm^{-2}.

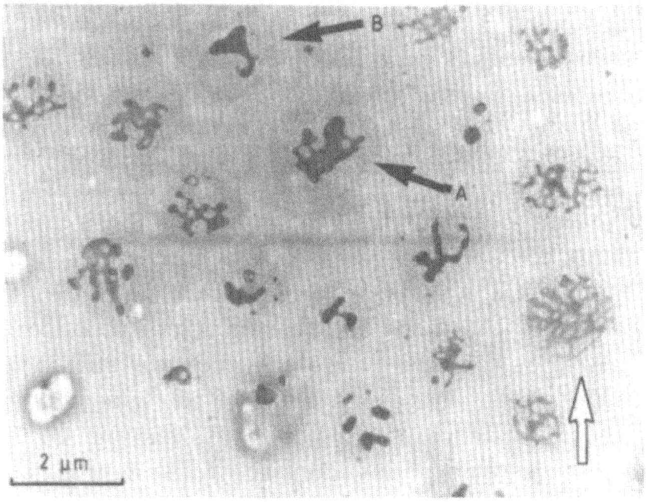

Figure 3. Disclinations formed in the $Ni_{65}Mo_{35}$ amorphous alloy films irradiated by xenon ions to a dosage of 7×10^{15} ion cm^{-2}. The dark appearance is the single crystalline metastable phase mediated by the interaction of the line defects.

3.2. Loops of odd lines and identification

A key idea of this study, which has not been carefully studied before, is to see what will happen to the as-vitrified structures if subjected to some additional doses of ion irradiation. As was expected, when the dose reached 7×10^{15} ion cm^{-2}, a remarkably odd morphology was observed, i.e. a large number of random loops of dark lines appeared in the amorphous matrix. Whereas two neighbouring doses, i.e. a lower dose of 5×10^{15} ion cm^{-2} and a higher one of 1×10^{16} ion cm^{-2}, both led to homogeneous amorphous phases. It is clearly seen in figure 3, a bright field image, that the randomly shaped loops seemed to be distributed homogeneously in the films. Each separate pattern consists of two sets of enclosed curves being differentiable everywhere. Many small hole-like patterns were surrounded by a large enclosed curve with an extremely random shape. The width of the dark lines was easily measured and ranged from 2 to 15 nm. The precipitates with a dark appearance in the space between these two enclosed curves, as noted by open arrows in figure 3, were identified to be the metastable phase described earlier by us [5]. All these patterns are located in a greyer basin than the surrounding matrix. The compositions of the dark precipitates, the grey basin, and the surrounding matrix were approximately $Ni_{50}Mo_{50}$, $Ni_{55}Mo_{45}$, and $NI_{65}Mi_{35}$, respectively, as determined by EDS measurement.

As shown in figure 3, the dark line contrast in different basins varied largely from one case to another. The loops with relative high and low contrasts are identified by full arrows A and B, respectively. Clearly, the dark lines marked B were hardly distinguishable. But the line contrast for a similar set of loops in a basin seemed to be uniform. By examining many different basins, it was found that each took on a different shape, and no specific symmetry could be attributed to the fat basins with random outlines. Figure 4 demonstrates a single set of loops at a higher magnification than that used in figure 3. The typical fringe morphology of amorphous structures can be readily identified in this bright field image, and no topological difference can be distinguished on either side of the dark lines. Electron diffraction analysis was conducted at three different areas marked A, B and C in figure 4. The corresponding diffraction patterns (DP) are shown in figures 5(*a*)–(*c*). Circle A in figure 4 concentrated on the dark precipitate and its DP in figure 5(a) was composed of sharp diffraction spots and a few diffuse halos from the amorphous matrix. This indicated that the dark precipitate was in a single crystalline state, and its dark contrast resulted from the diffraction deviation of the incident electron beam as it went through the crystalline precipitate. Circle C in figure 4 only enclosed the fringe regime away from the loops, and the corresponding DP in figure 5(c) consisted of several halos, indicating again the amorphous state of the uniform matrix. Finally, the diffraction pattern from the area including the segments of dark lines, as shown by circle B in figure 4, was also widely diffused halos (figure 5(a)) without any difference from that of the amorphous matrix. This fact demonstrated that no detectable small crystals decorated the dark lines. In other words the region including the dark lines was still in the amorphous state. For comparison, sharp diffraction rings from the invitrified films are shown in figure 5(d), indicating the coexistence of the polycrystalline Ni and Mo metals. It can be easily seen that the first amorphous halos shown in figures 5(a)–(c) are just located around the first two diffraction rings, Ni (111) and Mo (110), of the crystalline phases. From these diffraction results it can also be deduced that the contrast of the grey basins originated from differences in the atomic concentration and not from some kind of diffraction deviation.

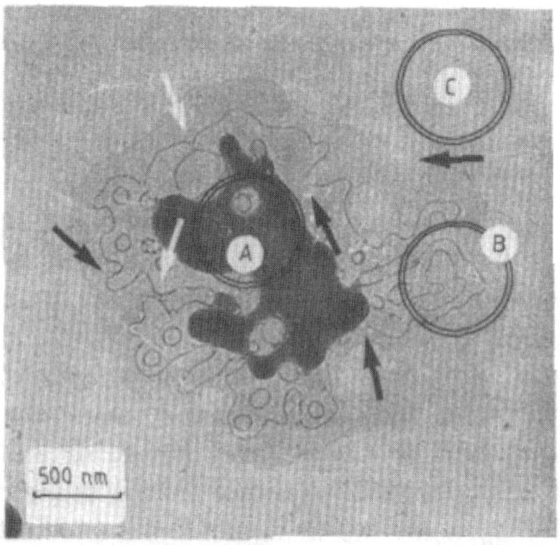

Figure 4. Bright field image of a set of magnified disclination loops. Full arrows indicating the fine voids. Open arrows specifying the tendency of self-reaction. Circles indicating the diffraction regions.

Scrutinizing figure 4 revealed another critical fact—that there were some fine white spots (about 25 nm in diameter) scattered in the amorphous matrix, and many of these were only located on the dark lines. As has been seen, the amorphous alloy films in this study were formed by the ion mixing technique. The dynamic collision process during energetic ion irradiation may generate a large number of defects [7] such as vacancies and aggregation of multi-vacancies will induce the formation of voids. In the area of the voids, the thicknesses of the films were thinned by the vacancy, and their (mass-depth) contrast in the bright field image would be white as in the case of crystalline solids. If a void was sufficiently small (say 30 nm in diameter), its fringe usually had a dark contrast due to the special diffraction geometry [7]. These inferences were in good agreement with our observations, and thus the fine spots appearing in the amorphous matrix were attributed to the small voids induced by ion irradiation. When the films

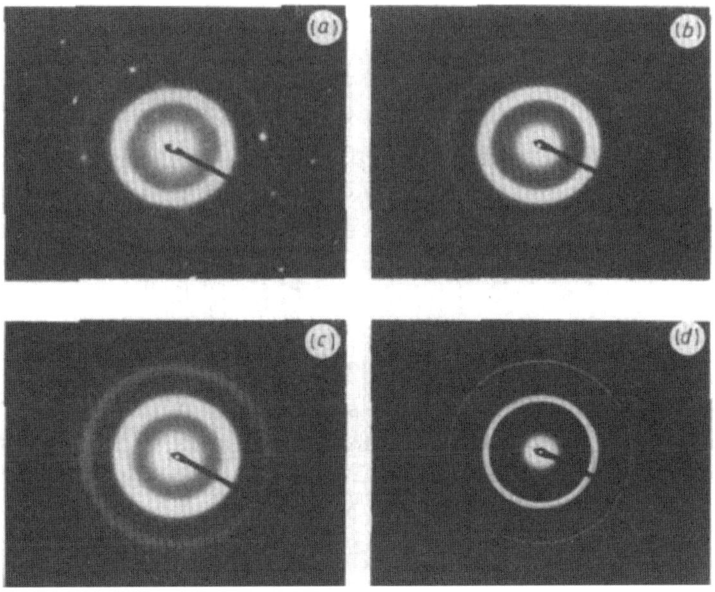

Figure 5. Electron diffraction patterns: (a)–(c) corresponding to the circled areas as shown in figure 4, indicating single crystals of the dark precipitate, and the amorphous structure of the matrix and the area including the disclination lines. (d) Polycrystalline rings before vitrification of the Ni–Mo films for comparison.

were irradiated to a higher dosage, e.g. 1.5×10^{16} ion cm^{-2}, the white voids became more evident. The density of the voids was also greatly increased, as shown in figure 6. The inset in figure 6 illustrates the diffraction pattern from the corresponding matrix. A few wide halos also indicated an amorphous state. In addition, a small diffuse ring was found within the first Ni–Mo amorphous halos in contrast with figures 5(a)–(c). The small ring was thought to result from the precipitation of over-saturated xenon atoms in the matrix. From this evidence, the dark loops cannot be the outline of voids in the ion mixed amorphous matrix. Moreover, a flat and extremely low contrast surface, as revealed by *in situ* SEM, showed that the dark lines were not from some kind of steps on the film surface either. From this, it can be deduced that the anomalous dark contrast loops were an intrinsic manifestation of the amorphous matrix.

Further TEM examination showed that as the sample was tilted with respect to the incident electron beam the relative contrast of loops in different basins changed in two different ways, i.e. some of them increased and others decreased, even disappeared. It was also observed that the line contrast became slightly more pronounced with a smaller objective aperture, and that a slight defocus seemed to widen and diffuse the dark lines. It is worthwhile pointing out that once a set of loops was visible its topological shape was invariant with the external conditions, and its contrast was almost uniform for the same set of loops. Dark field TEM examination revealed that the line loops in the bright field image turned into white line loops with the same geometry. We can therefore conclude that the interesting images resulted from the linear defects, i.e. disclination loops in the amorphous structures as predicted by Rivier *et al* [3].

To date, however, little is known about these defects, except that they are supposed to be established in the process of bond forming and breaking as atoms move [2]. As for the specific scheme of producing amorphous phases in our case, the dynamic collision

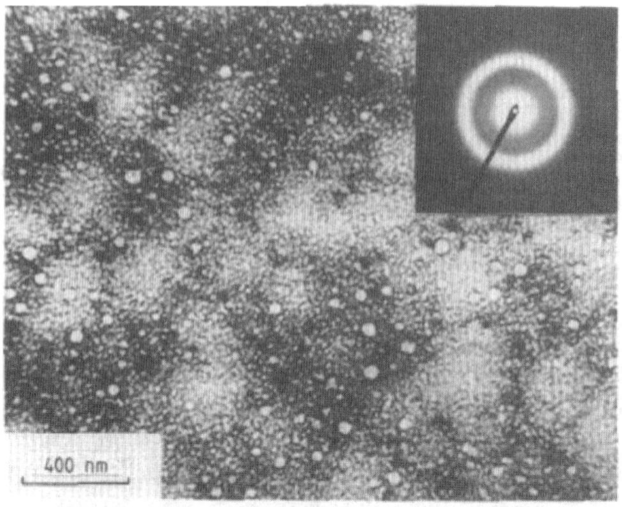

Figure 6. Voids in a TEM bright field image observed in the samples irradiated to 1.5×10^{16} ion cm^{-2}, the inset indicating the corresponding electron diffraction pattern.

process during energetic ion irradiation can stimulate the amorphous structures to a highly energetic intrinsic state, at which atoms and defects (mainly point defects) have a larger mobility, and hence are sufficiently able to perform such bond forming and breaking processes so as to rearrange themselves in a large scale. As is well known, disclination is a one-dimensional topological defect with a typical atomic distance. The visual width (2–15 nm) observed in the TEM bright field image was mainly caused by the surrounding stress field, and was of the same order as that of dislocations in crystals (3–10 nm). As a consequence, the line defect could be recorded by a TEM with a not extremely high resolution [10, 11]. Furthermore, because of the opposite effect of stress distortion of the amorphous networks, the visual position of the disclination would have a displacement (about the same order of its width) from its virtual location in the matrix. In most cases, therefore, a narrow white contrast band appears preferentially on one side of dark disclination lines, as can be seen by careful examination of figure 4. This notwithstanding, how the disclination lines were first initiated in the random networks of amorphous structures through the dynamic process and how the atoms arranged themselves locally around the linear defect certainly deserves further well-designed experimental investigation.

3.3. Contrast formation of disclination lines

First, considering a plane electron wave ($\boldsymbol{K}_i$) is incident normally on a film surface, the scattering amplitude in the observation direction $\boldsymbol{K}_f$ is given (in electron units) by [9] the summation of the amplitude from each atom i, having a position $\boldsymbol{r}$,

$$\Phi_s(\boldsymbol{K}) = \sum_i f_i \cdot e^{2\pi i \boldsymbol{K} \cdot \boldsymbol{r}} \tag{1}$$

where $\boldsymbol{K} = \boldsymbol{K}_f - \boldsymbol{K}_i$. For the elastic scattering, $|\boldsymbol{K}_f| = |\boldsymbol{K}_i|, |\boldsymbol{K}| = 2\pi \sin\theta/\lambda, 2\theta$ is the scattering angle. The scattered intensity is simply $\Phi_s(\boldsymbol{K})^* \Phi_s'(\boldsymbol{K})$. Expression (1) is known to be true for all materials whether crystalline or amorphous [9].

In the Column approximation [10], the scattered amplitude due to the atoms in the depth element $z \to z + dz$ per unit film area in the direction $\boldsymbol{K}_f$ can be expressed by

$$\mathrm{d}\phi_s(\boldsymbol{K}) = A\mathrm{e}^{2\pi\mathrm{i}\boldsymbol{K}\cdot\boldsymbol{r}}\,\mathrm{d}z \tag{2}$$

where the coefficient A may be relevant to the atomic scattering factor f_i and the number density of atoms ρ, which is reasonably supposed to be independent of the depth z. The existence of a defect will cause some distortion of its neighbouring area. The amplitude of the scattering electron wave by the depth element dz in a deformed area is described by

$$\mathrm{d}\phi_s^{\mathrm{d}}(\boldsymbol{K}) = A\mathrm{e}^{2\pi\mathrm{i}\boldsymbol{K}\cdot\boldsymbol{r}'}\,\mathrm{d}z \tag{3}$$

where $\boldsymbol{r}' = \boldsymbol{r} + \Delta\boldsymbol{r}$. The scattered vector $\boldsymbol{K}$ represents the diffraction geometry, and is assumed to be invariant under a defined direction of observation $\boldsymbol{K}_f$. In our nearly two-dimensional case, a disclination loop is assumed to be located entirely at a depth of y. The total scattered amplitude due to a disclination line can be written as

$$\phi_s^{\mathrm{d}} = AC\int_0^t \mathrm{e}^{\mathrm{i}(\alpha-\beta z/x)}\,\mathrm{d}z \tag{4}$$

where the distance parameter $\beta = -2\pi\boldsymbol{K}_z x$, $C = \exp[-2\pi\mathrm{i}(\boldsymbol{K}_x x + \boldsymbol{K}_y y)]$, and $|c|^2 = 1$. t is the film thickness. Clearly, it is the additional phase factor

$$\alpha = 2\pi\boldsymbol{K}\cdot\Delta\boldsymbol{r} \tag{5}$$

that leads to the contrast of the line defects. Accordingly, the contrast formalism of the disclination loops in amorphous films is analogous to that of dislocations in crystalline materials [11]. This is why the line contrast of the disclination was considerably affected by the incident geometry ($\boldsymbol{K}$). The contrast variation among sets of loops might be caused by different displacement ($\Delta\boldsymbol{r}$) of the line defect. Furthermore, if $\boldsymbol{K}\cdot\Delta\boldsymbol{r} = 0$, then $\alpha = 0$, the disclination becomes invisible, which is also qualitatively in accordance with our observations.

4. Self-consistent elucidation of disclination loops

In the previous sections, we have addressed the evidence for the appearance of disclination loops in Ni–Mo amorphous films, and accounted for their contrast features both experimentally and theoretically. However, many other distinguished features pertinent to the observed disclination remain unclear. For instance, why did the defect loops in the amorphous films manifest themselves as two sets of enclosed curves being differentiable almost everywhere, and why did a metastable crystal prefer to precipitate along the spacing between the two enclosed curves? In addition, what was responsible for the self-avoidance of the defect lines? And essentially, what made the defect line crumble randomly instead of being a single homogeneous circle-like loop. The following part is devoted to elucidating these intriguing questions.

4.1. Statics and dynamics of defect evolution

Provided that the uniformly mixed amorphous film is an elastic continuum media, *the differentiation of a defect line will be a direct consequence of spatial continuity.* Explicit argument of gauge theory indicates that only 2π-disclinations exist in amorphous structures [3, 8, 12]. This means that a local frame always rotates 2ϕ on going around a disclination, as illustrated in figure 7(*a*), where $\boldsymbol{T}(\boldsymbol{r})$ is a unit tangent vector at the position $\boldsymbol{r}$ on a defect line. Consequently, a disclination loop can be represented by a set of tangent vectors $\{\boldsymbol{T}(\boldsymbol{r})\}$. Furthermore, the interaction between two neighbouring defect elements in a plane can be approximately written as [2, 13]

$$f \propto \frac{\boldsymbol{T}(\boldsymbol{r}_1)\cdot\boldsymbol{T}(\boldsymbol{r}_2)}{|\boldsymbol{r}_1-\boldsymbol{r}_2|}. \tag{6}$$

This means that like pairs, i.e. $\boldsymbol{T}(\boldsymbol{r}_1) \parallel \boldsymbol{T}(\boldsymbol{r}_2)$, repel, and unlike pairs, $\boldsymbol{T}(\boldsymbol{r}_1) \parallel -\boldsymbol{T}(\boldsymbol{r}_2)$, attract. Equation (6) is the basis for the following discussion.

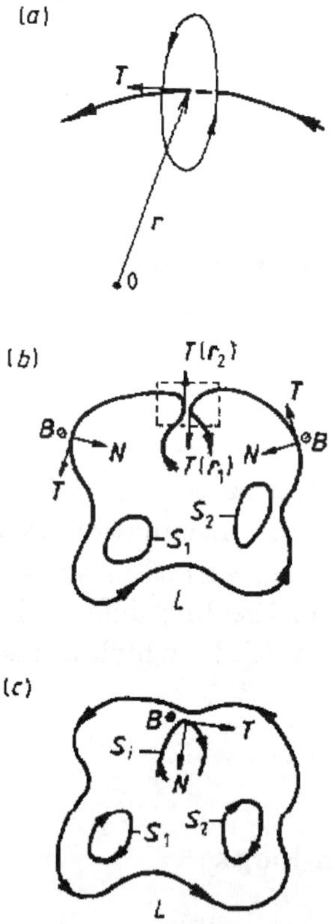

Figure 7. Illustrative defect lines: (*a*) tangent vector and local environment of a disclination line; (*b*) and (*c*) configuration of the defect loops before and after an attractive reaction takes place.

Furthermore, the observed differentiation or smoothness implies that the derivative, $\boldsymbol{T}'(\boldsymbol{r}) = |\boldsymbol{T}'(\boldsymbol{r})|\boldsymbol{N}(\boldsymbol{r})$, exists. $\boldsymbol{N}(\boldsymbol{r})$ is the unit normal at $\boldsymbol{r}$ satisfying $\boldsymbol{T}(\boldsymbol{r})\cdot\boldsymbol{N}(\boldsymbol{r}) = 0$. According to the classical theory of differential geometry [14], the corresponding unit subnormal is defined by $\boldsymbol{B}(\boldsymbol{r}) = \boldsymbol{T}(\boldsymbol{r}) \times \boldsymbol{N}(\boldsymbol{r})$. In our case of an approximately two-dimensional film, all defect loops were confined to being parallel to the film surface. The vector $\boldsymbol{B}(\boldsymbol{r})$ can only be directed out of or into the film plane, and the corresponding defect loops were denoted by L and S, respectively. We assume that each randomly shaped large loop is an L type, as shown in figure 7(b). Looking at the broken square in figure 7(b), the attractive force ($f < 0$) between $\boldsymbol{T}(\boldsymbol{r}_1)$ and $\boldsymbol{T}(\boldsymbol{r}_2)$ increases drastically as $\boldsymbol{r}_1$ approaches to $\boldsymbol{r}_2$. If $|\boldsymbol{r}_1 - \boldsymbol{r}_2| \to 0, f \to \infty$, then a reaction

$$\lim_{\boldsymbol{r}_1 \to \boldsymbol{r}_2} (\boldsymbol{T}(\boldsymbol{r}_1) + \boldsymbol{T}(\boldsymbol{r}_2)) = 0 \tag{7}$$

takes place, which results in the formation of an inner enclosed S-type curve and the self-avoidance of the defect loops, as illustrated in figure 7(c). The analogous procedure as shown in figure 7 can indeed be observed in the practical patterns, as specified in figure 4 by open arrows. Therefore, a developed linear defect always consists of two sets of loops, one L-type and many S-types ($S = \cup_i S_i$) ones in it (L). This inference is exactly in accordance with our observations.

In fact, considering the defect line in amorphous structures as a one-dimensional elastic manifold embedded in three- or two-dimensional space, the self-avoiding behaviour is therefore a straightforward result of a continuum theory of crumpled manifolds [15]. In our case, however, the self-avoidance was induced by the very attractive self-reaction (equation (7)) on contact, instead of a simple repulsion as studied earlier [15].

As previously stated, there were small amounts of fine voids dispersed in the amorphous matrix. The surrounding networks of these voids would be deformed relative to the previous cases and would thus introduce a local stress field. When the disclination lines approached the white voids, their two stress fields would interact with each other. The voids usually acted as unmovable objects and pinned the defect lines. Therefore, it was believed that the randomly located fine voids, their pinning effect and the linear tension along the defect lines were responsible for the irregular crumbling, and then the very self-reaction of disclination loops.

4.2. Defect mediated precipitation

The movement and the reaction of defect lines would eventually split a total amorphous film into two distinctly energetic regions. The regions between the two types of loop have been relaxed to a low energy state by the sweep of the defect lines. The total free energy E in these regions, where an attractive force dominates, is assumed to be $E < 0$. In contrast, the unscanned or unrelaxed areas both outside the L-type loops and inside the S-type loops are at a high energy state with a total energy $E > 0$, which corresponds to the repulsion field. While the free energy of the metastable and equilibrium crystalline phases in this system are represented by E_{m} and E_{c} ($E_{\mathrm{c}} < E_{\mathrm{m}} < 0$), respectively. In the attractive regions ($E < 0$), only if the free energy E, say E_i, $< E_{\mathrm{m}}$, can the metastable phase nucleate under the driving force $\Delta G = E_{\mathrm{m}} - E_i$. While $E > E_{\mathrm{m}}$, the metastable phase cannot nucleate even within the attractive areas with $E < 0$. Apparently, the equilibrium crystalline phase (E_{c}) is hard to nucleate in the relatively weak interaction field of linear defects. The excess energy (in heat form) during amorphous-to-crystalline phase transformation, i.e. the growth of metastable phases, will certainly enhance the precipitation process again. This is probably the reason why only the metastable phase precipitates in most cases in the spacing between the two enclosed curves, and sometimes goes beyond the spacing as shown in figure 3.

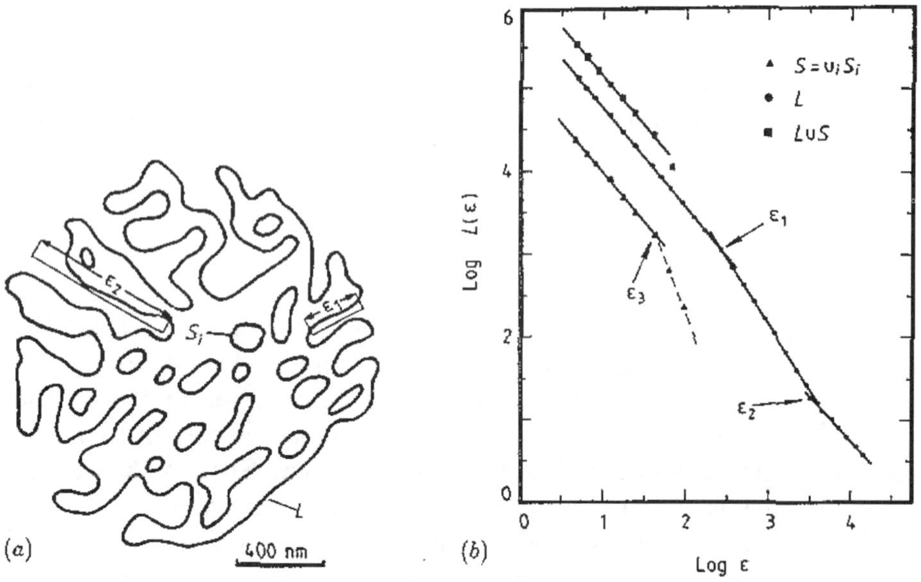

Figure 8. (a) An example of digitized disclination loops for fractal analysis. (b) Log–log plot of the maximum relative length $L(\epsilon)$ against the scale ϵ for the disclination shown in (a). The full circles indicating the results for the L-type loop, the triangles for the set of loop $S_i(S = \cup_i S_i$, and the squares for the whole disclination loop $(L \cup S)$.

5. Fractal nature of disclinations

It is well known that a fractal geometry has recently been developed as a powerful means of characterizing a variety of random systems [16]. The fractal structure of randomly shaped disclination loops is studied in terms of computer image processing. A set of disclination loops, one of which is shown in figure 8(a), was firstly extracted from a magnified electron micrograph, and then was digitized with a VAX image processor at 512 pixel × 512 pixel resolution. Any practical fractal structure will have a lower and an upper length scale cutoff. In the present case the width of disclination line, $\delta = 10$ nm, which corresponds to 2 pixel, is the lower cutoff ϵ_{min}. The upper cutoff is given by the linear dimension $\epsilon_{\max}$ of the L-type loop. Figure 8(b) shows the log–log plot of the relative length $L(\epsilon)$ in the scale of ϵ; the full circles indicate the results for the L-type loops in figure 8(a). Apparently, there are two crossovers at ϵ_1 and ϵ_2 in figure 8(b), which divide the whole experimental data into three regions. Each of them can be well fitted by a straight line. As for a fractal curve, the relative length satisfies

$$L(\epsilon) \propto \epsilon^{-D} \tag{8}$$

where D is called its fractal dimension. The relative perimeter $L(\epsilon)$ here is a maximum value obtained from more than ten reference points randomly taken on the disclination loop. The fractal dimension, as measured in the regions of $\epsilon_{\min} < \epsilon < \epsilon_1, \epsilon_1 < \epsilon < \epsilon_2$, and $\epsilon_2 < \epsilon < \epsilon_{\max}$ are 1.20, 1.44 and 1.16, respectively. The uncertainty in fractal dimensions, as estimated from the fit in figure 8(b), is about ±0.02. However, taking into account the error occurring in image processing and some other procedures, a more realistic error bar is at most ±0.06. Computer analysis showed that the lower crossover ϵ_1 measures the average depth of the disclination fjords, while the higher one ϵ_2 corresponds to their maximum depth, as indicated in figure 8(a).

In the region of the scale $\epsilon > \epsilon_2$, all fjords are smeared out, the fractal dimension of $D_3 = 1.16$ mostly revealed the outline of the L-type loop. It is in this sense that the disclination of the L-type loop seems to be a self-affine fractal [17], for which one must distinguish between local and global fractal dimensions. Whereas in our case, there are two local fractal dimensions D_1 and D_2. The fitting result of the S-type loop is also denoted in figure 8(b) by full triangles. The most striking thing is that in the scale range of $\epsilon_{min} < \epsilon < \epsilon_3$, the union set $S = \cup_i S_i$ of separate loops (S_i) is also self-similar with a fractal dimension D being exactly the same as that of the L-type loop in the low region of scale ϵ. Therefore, the total disclination, i.e. $L \cup S$, was also scale invariant with the same fractal dimension $D = 1.20$, as indicated in figure 8(b) by full squares. The same fact was found to be true for all digitized disclination loops (more than ten), which demonstrated the existence of a universal fractal dimension $D_f = 1.20 \pm 0.06$. This value, we believe, characterizes the underlying nature of the self-avoiding disclination loops, while the fractal dimension D_2 in the region of $\epsilon_1 < \epsilon < \epsilon_2$, varied from 1.20 to 1.80 for different cases. In the low limit of D_2, an L-type loop behaves like a statistically self-similar fractal curve in nearly the whole range of length scale.

The scaling structure of a random surface has been a subtle and fascinating subject for fractal study. Stanley *et al* [18] argued that the fractal dimension D_f of the total perimeter is higher than that of the external perimeter. In our case, however, they are all equal to each other in the low scale range. This, in fact, is quite reasonable in the sense that either the L-type loop or the S-type loop is an independent physical object, i.e. a line defect, in amorphous structures, instead of an external or internal surface of some other object if it existed. From the first part of this paper, we know that each Si loop had always been a segment of an L-type loop before the ith reaction occurred. The dominant differences between the two types of loops is the global direction of their subnormals, and there is no reason why this should affect their subtle scaling structures. If we visualize the relaxed area between the L- and S-type loops as an independent physical object such as a new phase, no meaningful scaling results could be found from the digitized pattern.

6. Conclusions

By irradiating the as-vitrified $Ni_{65}Mo_{35}$ films to a critical dose, many one-dimensional topological defects, i.e. disinclination loops, were formed in the amorphous matrix. The defect lines featured two types (L and S) of loop. It was found that point-like defects, i.e. randomly localized fine voids in our case, and the attractive self-reaction governed the evolution behaviour of the defect lines, and therefore induced the irregular geometrical shape. Metastable crystalline precipitation is direct evidence for the defect-mediated phase transition [19]. The scaling analysis of disclination loops reveals a universal fractal dimension $D_f = 1.20 \pm 0.06$, which well characterizes the subtle structures of the line defects in amorphous matter. A better understanding of the disclination loops remains a challenge for further theoretical consideration and computer simulation.

Acknowledgments

We are grateful to Dr J G Sun, Dr J Zhu, and Professor K H Kuo for helpful discussions. The staffs of the TEM Laboratories of Beijing University and the Analysis

Centre of Tsinghua University are also acknowledged for their assistance. This work was supported by the National Natural Science Foundation of China and the International Atomic Energy Agency (Research Contract No 4731/R3/RB).

References

[1] Priedel J 1979 *Disclination in Solids* vol 1, ed F R N Nabarro (Amsterdam: North-Holland) p 1

[2] Venkatarama G and Sahoo D 1985 *Contemp. Phys.* **26** 35; 1986 *Contemp. Phys.* **27** 1

[3] Rivier N 1979 *Philos. Mag.* A **40** 859
Rivier N and Duffy D M 1982 *J. Physique* **43** 293

[4] Sadoc J F and Rivier N 1987 *Philos. Mag.* B **55** 537
Bohsung J and Trebin H R 1987 *Phys. Rev. Lett.* **58** 1204

[5] Liu B X 1986 *Phys. Status Solidi* a **94** 11
Liu B X, Johnson W L, Nicolet M A and Lau S S 1983 *Nucl. Instrum. Methods* **209/210** 229

[6] Shang C H and Liu B X 1989 *Nucl. Instrum. Methods in Phys. Res.* B **37/38** 420

[7] Thompson M W 1969 *Defects and Radiation Damage in Metals* chs 4 and 5 (Cambridge: Cambridge University Press)

[8] Rivier N 1983 *Topological Disorder in Condensed Matter* ed F Yonezawa and T Ninomiya (Berlin: Springer) p 14

[9] Elliott S R 1983 *Physics of Amorphous Materials* (Harlow: Longman) p 53
Cowley J M 1975 *Diffraction Physics* (Amsterdam: North-Holland)

[10] Whelan M J 1970 *Modern Diffraction and Imaging Techniques in Material Science* ed S Amelinckx, R Gevers, G Remaut and J Van Landuyt (Amsterdam: North-Holland) p 62

[11] Hirsch P B, Howie A, Nicholson R B, Pashley D W and Whelan M J 1967 *Electron Microscopy of Thin Crystals* chs 13, 15, 18 (London: Butterworth)

[12] Duffy D M 1981 *PhD Thesis* Imperial College, University of London

[13] Chandrasekhar S and Ranganath G S 1986 *Adv. Phys.* **35** 5

[14] Hicks N J 1965 *Notes on Differential Geometry* (Princeton: D Van Nortrand)

[15] Kardar M and Nelson D R 1987 *Phys. Rev. Lett.* **58** 1289
Duplantier B 1987 *Phys. Rev. Lett.* **58** 2733

[16] Mandelbrot B B 1982 *The Fractal Geometry of Nature* (New York: Freeman)

[17] Feder J 1984 *Fractals* A **17** L373
Mandelbrot B B 1985 *Phys. Scr.* **32** 257

[18] Stanley H E 1986 *Fractals in Physics* ed L Pietronero and E Tosatti (Amsterdam: Elsevier) p 327
Bunde A, Herriman H J, Margolina A and Stanley H E 1985 *Phys. Rev. Lett.* **5** 653

[19] Nelson D R 1983 *Phase Transitions and Critical Phenomena* ed C Domb and J L Lebowitz (New York: Academic) pp 2–93

C54-$TiSi_2$ formed by direct high current Ti-ion implantation

D. H. Zhu, K. Tao, F. Pan, and B. X. Liu[a)]
Department of Materials Science and Engineering, Tsinghua University, Beijing 100084, China

(Received 24 August 1992; accepted for publication 16 February 1993)

We report, in this letter, the formation of $TiSi_2$ by direct Ti-ion implantation into silicon wafers using a metal vapor vacuum arc ion source. Implantation was conducted by 80 KeV Ti ions to a dose of $5\times10^{17}/cm^2$ with various ion current densities. When the ion current density exceeded 100 $\mu A/cm^2$, the equilibrium $TiSi_2$ of the C54 structure was uniquely formed. Additional evidence of the formation of C54-$TiSi_2$ was given by the resistivity measurements, i.e., the sheet resistivity was below 3.0 Ω/□. The formation mechanism is also discussed in terms of the beam heating effect during implantation.

Interest in the formation of metal silicides by solid-state reaction of thin metal films deposited on single-crystal silicon substrates upon thermal annealing[1] or ion beam mixing[2,3] is spurred by vital importance in microelectronic devices. Among the silicide-forming metals, titanium has special significance because its disilicide C54-$TiSi_2$, with the lowest resistivity among all metal silicides and good thermal properties, is an attractive alternative material to be used as the gate electrode and ohmic contact in the submicron silicon device technology.[4]

With the development of ion source, metal ions with high current density can now readily be extracted by means of a metal vapor vacuum arc (MEVVA) ion source invented in the mid 1980s.[5] Considering the heating effect caused by a high current ion beam, it can be inferred that the metal silicides would be formed directly by high current metal-ion implantation without postannealing or simultaneously heating the silicon wafers while implanting. In this letter, we report, for the first time, the formation of C54-$TiSi_2$ by direct high current Ti-ion implantation into single-crystal Si(111).

The silicon wafers used in this study were *p*-type Si(111) with 8–13 Ω cm. The wafers were cut into 1×1 cm^2 samples, cleaned by a standard chemical procedure, and then followed by dipping in a diluted HF solution. The samples were loaded on a steel-made sample holder without special cooling during implantation. The implantation was carried out in a MEVVA source implanter with an extract voltage of 40 kV (the energy of Ti^{+2} was therefore 80 keV), an ion dose of $5\times10^{17}/cm^2$, corresponding to 6% Ti^+, 82% Ti^{+2}, and 12% Ti^{+3}, respectively, and an ion-beam current density ranging from 25 to 125 $\mu A/cm^2$. Two sets of samples were implanted with either a tilt angle of 7° or 0°. The Rutherford backscattering spectroscopy (RBS) was employed to measure the composition of the implanted layers, and the phase structure was identified by a D/max-RB x-ray diffractometer. The four-point probe was used to measure the sheet resistivities.

As can be seen from Fig. 1(a), the result of x-ray diffraction shows that a $TiSi_2$ phase was formed in a tilted sample implanted by Ti ions with a current density of 125 $\mu A/cm^2$ to a dose of $5\times10^{17}/cm^2$. The measured interplanar spacings were in accord with those listed in the Joint Committee on Powder Diffraction Standards (JCPDS) card No. 33-1384. A similar result was also observed in the untilted sample and is shown in Fig. 1(b). The measured interplanar spacings of both tilted and untilted samples are listed in Table I together with those of $TiSi_2$ (C49 and C54), TiSi, and Ti_5Si_3. In Fig. 2, three RBS spectra are shown for tilted samples implanted by Ti ions to a dose of $5\times10^{17}/cm^2$, with varying current densities of 75, 100, and 125 $\mu A/cm^2$, respectively. The exact implanted titanium atoms in the silicon wafers were calculated from Fig. 2 and

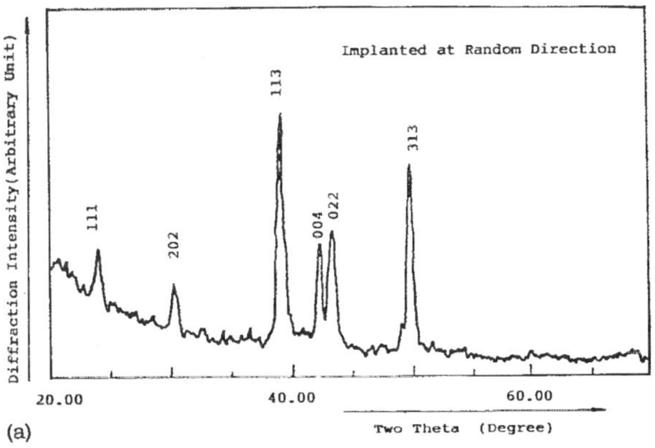

(a)

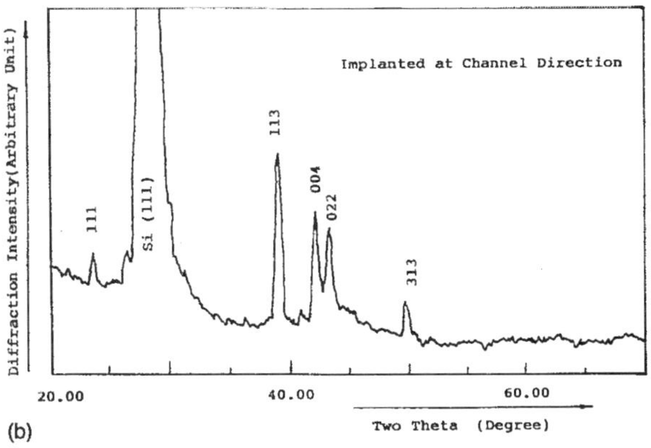

(b)

FIG. 1. X-ray diffraction patterns of (a) tilted and (b) untilted Si(111) samples implanted with Ti ions of 125 $\mu A/cm^2$ to a dose of 5×10^{17} cm^2.

[a)]Also at Center of Condensed Matter and Radiation Physics, CCAST (World Laboratory), Beijing 100080, China.

Applied Physics Letters 62(19), p.2356-2358 (1993).

TABLE I. Comparison of measured to listed interplanar spacings of titanium silicides for the samples implanted with 125 $\mu A/cm^2$.

Measured		Listed			
Tilted (nm)	Untilted (nm)	$TiSi_2$(C54)[a] (nm)	$TiSi_2$(C49)[b] (nm)	Ti_5Si_3[c] (nm)	TiSi[d] (nm)
0.3732	0.3732	0.3729(111)			
0.2960		0.2970(202)	0.284(130)	0.3015(111)	
0.2297	0.2301	0.2300(113)	0.229(060)	0.2388(012)	0.2335(102)
0.2135	0.2135	0.2136(004)	0.223(131)	0.2202(121)	0.2189(211)
0.2088	0.2089	0.2092(022)	0.219(150)	0.2149(030)	0.2000(301)
0.1828	0.1826	0.1831(313)	0.181(200)	0.1861(220)	0.1823(020)

[a]JCPDS 33-1384.
[b]JCPDS 10-225.
[c]JCPDS 29-1362.
[d]JCPDS 17-424.

they are 3.3×10^{17}, 4.6×10^{17}, and $4.4\times10^{17}/cm^2$, respectively. The difference between the nominal dose and the calculated ones is due to the sputtering effect, which, however, had not affected the formation of Ti silicide. In other words, the sputtering effect, in our case, is not that significant compared to the case of the traditional high dose implantation. The thickness of $TiSi_2$ formed in the tilted samples implanted with 100 and 125 $\mu A/cm^2$ were measured to be 120 and 80 nm, respectively. The change of sheet resistivity as a function of ion current density is listed in Table II and shown in Fig. 3. When the ion current density was 100 $\mu A/cm^2$, the sheet resistivities of both tilted and untilted samples were less than 3.0 Ω/□. The measured sheet resistivities of 3.0 and 2.4 Ω/□ for the two samples were converted to the resistivities of 36 and 20 $\mu\Omega$ cm, respectively.

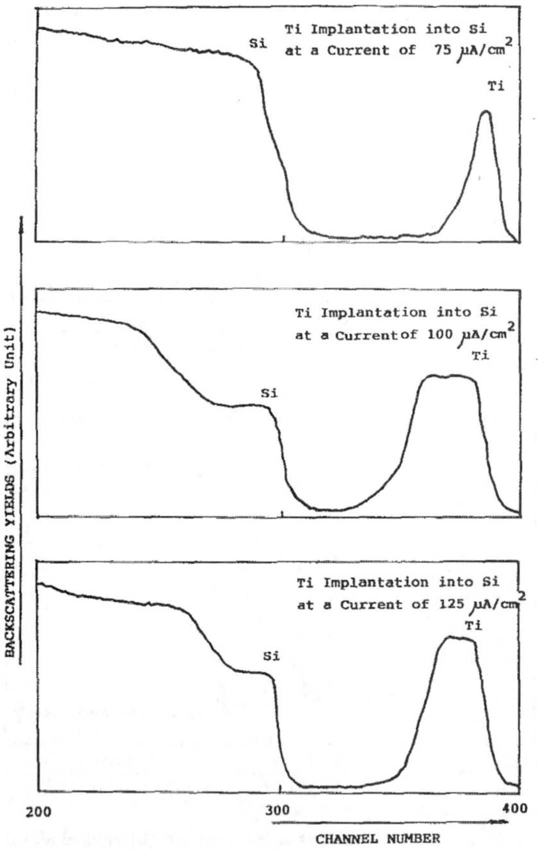

FIG. 2. RBS spectra of Si(111) tilted samples implanted to a dose of 5×10^{17} cm^2 with varying Ti-ion current density of 75, 100, 125 $\mu A/cm^2$, respectively.

The above x-ray diffraction results indicate that the formed $TiSi_2$ phase is certainly C54-$TiSi_2$ because of the obvious match between the measured interplanar spacings and those of C54-$TiSi_2$ listed in Table I. The resistivities of 36 and 20 $\mu\Omega$/cm are within the resistivity range of the equilibrium C54-$TiSi_2$ phase.[6] This also serves as evidence of the formation of C54-$TiSi_2$. An important factor responsible for the formation of C54-$TiSi_2$ by direct implantation with the MEVVA source is the beam heating effect. During the implantation, the temperature increase of the silicon wafers was evaluated according to Wittkower and Hirvonen's paper.[7] Under our experimental conditions, the temperatures of silicon wafers were calculated to be 280, 400, 480, 560, and 630 °C, corresponding to the ion current densities of 25, 50, 75, 100, 125 $\mu A/cm^2$, with total implantation times of 108, 54, 36, 27, and 22 min, respectively. Apparently, a thermal annealing process caused by beam heating took place simultaneously during implantation. It has been reported that $TiSi_2$(C49), TiSi, or Ti_5Si_3 were nucleated before the formation of $TiSi_2$(C54)[6,8–10] under solid-state reaction. However, in our case, no interplanar spacings detected by x-ray diffraction for implanted samples could be attributed to these phases, when ion current density was above 100 $\mu A/cm^2$. Nor could we observe

TABLE II. Change of sheet resistivity as a function of ion current density.

Current density ($\mu A/cm^2$)	Sheet resistivity (Ω/□)	
	Tilted	Untilted[a]
25	65±1	···
50	60±1	···
75	46±1	···
100	3.0±0.1	2.4±0.1
125	2.5±0.1	2.0±0.1

[a]··· stands for those experiments that have not been conducted.

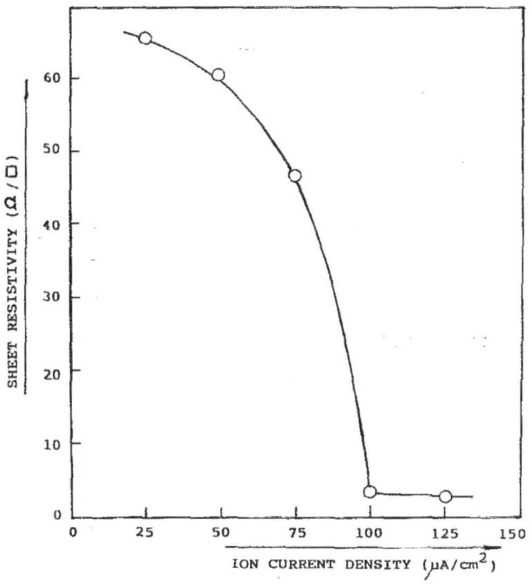

FIG. 3. Dependence of sheet resistivity as a function of ion current density on Si(111) tilted samples implanted with Ti ions to a dose of 5×10^{17} cm^2.

these phases in the samples implanted even with lower ion current density by using glancing angle incident x-ray diffraction. It is believed that the above-mentioned results have to do with the growth kinetic conditions. In principle, if the annealing time and temperature caused by the beam are long and high enough, all these phases, if formed, would turn to the equilibrium $TiSi_2$ phase (C54 structure) in a scheme of an unlimited supply of silicon. In our experimental arrangement, the silicon supply was unlimited and the effective annealing temperature and time were both favored for forming the equilibrium $TiSi_2$ phase when the ion current density exceeded 100 $\mu A/cm^2$, and the final resultant product was indeed a unique C54-$TiSi_2$. While for the samples implanted with lower ion current density, no visible x-ray diffraction lines of any silicide were observed, indicating that no titanium silicide, or at least no big enough grains of titanium silicide had been formed.

In conclusion, the equilibrium $TiSi_2$ of a C54 structure was formed directly after titanium-ion implantation with a MEVVA source, under the condition of an extract voltage of 40 kV, a dose of $5\times10^{17}/cm^2$, and an ion current density exceeding 100 $\mu A/cm^2$. The kinetic condition for growth of the C54-$TiSi_2$ phase was satisfied by these parameters, which provided adequate heat to activate and accomplish the phase-formation process. The formed C54-$TiSi_2$ phase showed low sheet resistivity, which was in the same range as reported in the literature yet prepared by other techniques.[11] It is believed that by varying implantation parameters, e.g., ion current density, dose, etc. to meet various growth kinetic requirements, the formation of other titanium silicides and other metal silicides by MEVVA implantation is possible. This topic is therefore now undertaken by this research group.

The research was supported by the National Natural Science Foundation of China. The authors gratefully acknowledge X. H. Zhang of Beijing Normal University for his kind help in implantation.

[1] S. P. Murarka, *Silicides for VLSI Application* (Academic, New York, 1983).
[2] K. L. Wang, F. Bacon, and R. F. Reihl, J. Vac. Sci. Technol. **16**, 130 (1979).
[3] F. M. d'Heurle, C. S. Peterson, and M. Y. Tsai, J. Appl. Phys. **51**, 5976 (1980).
[4] M. E. Alperin, T. C. Hollaway, R. A. Haken, C. D. Gosmeyer, R. V. Karnaugh, and W. A. Parmantie, IEEE Trans. Electron Devices **ED-32**, 41 (1985).
[5] I. G. Brown, J. E. Gavin, and R. A. MacGill, Appl. Phys. Lett. **47**, 358 (1985).
[6] R. Beyers and R. Sinclair, J. Appl. Phys. **57**, 5240 (1985).
[7] A. Wittkower and J. K. Hirvonen, Nucl. Instrum. Meth. Phys. Res. B **6**, 78 (1985).
[8] L. S. Hung, J. Gylai, and J. W. Mayer, J. Appl. Phys. **54**, 5076 (1983).
[9] L. J. M. M. Raaijmakers and K. B. Kim, J. Appl. Phys. **67**, 6255 (1990).
[10] M. H. Wang and L. J. Chen, Appl. Phys. Lett. **58**, 463 (1991).
[11] M. A. Nicolet and S. S. Lau, *Formation and Characterization of Transition Metal Silicides*, edited by N. G. Einspruch and G. B. Larabee (Academic, New York, 1983), Sec. II C, Tables VI, X, XI.

Anomalous alloying behavior induced by ion irradiation in a system with a large positive heat of mixing

Z. J. Zhang,* O. Jin, and B. X. Liu*
Department of Materials Science and Engineering, Tsinghua University, Beijing 100084, China
(Received 20 June 1994; revised manuscript received 3 October 1994)

Amorphization was achieved by room temperature 200-keV xenon ion mixing in two isolated composition ranges, i.e., $Y_{22}-Y_{27}$ and $Y_{72}-Y_{83}$, in the Y-Mo system, which has a positive heat of mixing exceeding +26 kJ/mol. In addition, three metastable crystalline (MX) phases, i.e., a Y-rich fcc (fcc-I), a Mo-rich hcp (hcp-I), and another fcc (fcc-II) phase, were observed at different irradiation stages. Kinetically, the fcc-I MX phase was formed through a single-step transition of hcp→fcc, while the hcp-I and fcc-II phases were formed sequentially via a two-step transition of bcc→hcp→fcc. To give further insight into the singularity of the amorphization behavior of the system and the MX phase formation, a Gibbs-free-energy diagram of the system was constructed by calculating the free energies of the amorphous phase, the solid solutions, three MX phases, and of the as-deposited Y-Mo multilayers, for which the interfacial free energies were added. The established diagram can explain well the irradiation-induced amorphization behavior and the MX phase formation in the Y-Mo system.

I. INTRODUCTION

Since the early 1980's, ion mixing (IM) has been employed as a powerful means for studying some important topics of physical metallurgy, e.g., the theory of alloy phase formation and transformation.[1] In the last decade, most research interests of IM have been focused on synthesizing amorphous alloys and studying the amorphization mechanism of the binary metal systems, especially of those with negative heats of mixing.[2-4] Using alternately deposited metals in an A and B multilayered arrangement, IM is capable of producing A_XB_{1-X} alloys without limitation of the desired alloy composition, as the relative thicknesses of A and B metals can be adjusted to obtain an arbitrary x from 0 to 1.[5] Up to date, some 70 systems have been investigated by IM of multilayers, and extensive data of the glass-forming ability (GFA) of binary metal systems have been obtained.[6] It was found that the GFA was greatly widened by IM and was continuous in composition for those systems with negative heats of mixing.[7] The amorphization behavior and GFA of systems with positive heats of mixing, however, have not yet been investigated thoroughly, and are still of interest. Recently, the formation of metastable crystalline (MX) phases has aroused enormous attention,[8] and considerable work has been carried out on the thermodynamic and kinetic aspects for a better understanding of the MX phase formation in binary metal systems mostly with negative heats of mixing.[9-11] Besides the quasicrystalline phases,[12-15] three types of MX phases have so far been observed in binary metal systems, i.e., (i) supersaturated solid solutions (SSSS);[16,17] (ii) a hexagonal phase in hcp-bcc or fcc-bcc pairs at the hcp-rich or fcc-rich side;[18-20] and (iii) a fcc phase formed in some bcc-based systems.[21] However, less attention concerning MX phase formation has been paid to systems with positive heats of mixing, leaving an open question to be further studied. The Y-Mo system, which has a positive heat of mixing exceeding +26 kJ/mol, was thus selected for this study to investigate the GFA and possible MX phase formation by IM.

Concerning the amorphization mechanism in binary metal systems, several empirical models have been proposed to predict the GFA from the crystalline structures and other static properties of the constituents and from the features of the equilibrium phase diagram,[22-24] though this problem has not been clarified on an atomic scale due to the complexity of the far-from-equilibrium nature of the IM process. Recently, a quantitative approach towards this issue has been proposed by Alonso, Gallego, and Lopez[25] on the basis of Miedema's model to calculate the free energies of the amorphous phase and the terminal solid solutions. By comparing their free-energy values, a measure of the GFA can be given under the condition of $\Delta G_a \leq \Delta G_s$, where ΔG_a and ΔG_s are the Gibbs free energies of the amorphous phase and the solid solutions, respectively.[26] This approach was quite good for the GFA in some systems. However, it cannot interpret the formation of the observed MX phases in some alloy systems,[27,28] and cannot interpret the amorphization in systems of positive heats of mixing either. Meanwhile, it has been argued that the calculation precision of the free energy is doubtful since Miedema's model and Alonso *et al.*'s method are still on a semiempirical basis. To give a precise estimation of the errors in such a calculation, however, seems quite difficult. An alternative ay to step forward was recently proposed by the authors: to conduct the steady-state thermal annealing of the as-deposited multilayers to confirm the relative energetic levels of the competing phases at certain composition points.[29] Since the as-deposited multilayers are in a highly energetic state due to the additional interfacial and surface free energies, they would relax down upon annealing to the available intermediate states of lower free

Physical Review B 51(13), p.8076-8085 (1995).

energies in the system.[30] The annealing results can thus be employed to confirm the relevance of the calculated diagram in its outline.

We report, in the present paper, the detailed experimental results of amorphization and MX phase formation induced by IM in the Y-Mo system. A thermodynamic interpretation of the singularity of the amorphization behavior and MX phase formation is given by constructing the free-energy diagram of the system on the basis of Miedema's model, with the special consideration of adding the free-energy curves of the MX phases obtained in this study and that of the as-deposited Y-Mo multilayers including the interfacial free energy. The growth kinetics of the MX phases are also discussed based on the far-from-equilibrium solid-state transition upon ion irradiation.

II. EXPERIMENTAL PROCEDURE

Multilayered Y-Mo films were prepared in an evaporation system with a vacuum level on the order of 10^{-7} Torr, by depositing pure yttrium (99.9% Y) and pure molybdenum (99.9% Mo) alternately onto newly cleaved NaCl single crystals as substrates. To reduce the possible oxidation of the constituent metals, Ti was evaporated first and deposited onto a spare SiO_2 substrate to adsorb some oxygen in the vacuum system before depositing the multilayered films. During deposition, the substrates were cooled by running water and the temperature increase of the substrates was estimated to be less than 200 °C. The total thickness of the Y-Mo films was designed to match the projected range plus the projected range straggling of the irradiation ions, i.e., about 500 Å for the 200-keV xenon ions. Seven layers were deposited for each sample. The composition of the films was controlled by adjusting the relative thickness of the two constituent metals and was later confirmed by energy-dispersive-spectrum (EDS) analysis with an error of less than 5%. The as-deposited Y-Mo multilayered films were immediately moved into and kept in a dry vacuum chamber to avoid contamination. The films were then irradiated by 200-keV xenon ions in an implanter with a vacuum level on the order of 10^{-6} Torr. The beam current density was controlled to be less than 0.5 $\mu A/cm^2$ to minimize beam heating effects, and the temperature increase of the substrates was estimated to be less than 100 °C. After irradiation, all the mixed films were removed from the substrates by deionized water and put on Cu or Mo grids for transmission electron microscopy (TEM) observation and selected-area diffraction (SAD) analysis to identify the structure. EDS was also employed to determine the real composition of the ion-mixed phases. Some as-deposited multilayered films were subjected to steady-state thermal annealing in a hot stage attached to the TEM, which had a vacuum level on the order of 10^{-7} Torr, to give an independent result of phase evolution for testing the validity of the calculated free-energy diagram.

III. RESULTS AND DISCUSSION

A. Amorphization induced by IM

Table I lists the phase changes in the Y-Mo system induced by room-temperature 200-keV xenon ion mixing as a function of irradiation doses. From the table, one sees that at the Y-rich side, Y_{83}-Mo_{17} films were amorphized at a dose of 1×10^{15} Xe^+/cm^2 and that the $Y_{72}Mo_{28}$ films were also amorphized at a dose of 3×10^{15} Xe^+/cm^2. Figures 1(a)–(d) show the bright-field images and the corresponding SAD patterns of the as-deposited and amorphized $Y_{72}Mo_{28}$ multilayered films. Meanwhile, at the Mo-rich side, $Y_{22}Mo_{78}$ and $Y_{27}Mo_{72}$ films were both amorphized at a dose of 1×10^{15} Xe^+/cm^2. Figures 2(a) and 2(b) show the SAD patterns of the as-deposited and amorphized $Y_{22}Mo_{78}$ multilayered films, respectively. In the other samples, i.e., $Y_{15}Mo_{85}$, $Y_{42}Mo_{58}$, and $Y_{65}Mo_{35}$ films, amorphization was not achieved at any irradiation doses, i.e., from 3×10^{14} to 7×10^{15} Xe^+/cm^2. These results suggest that amorphization can be achieved, yet in two isolated composition ranges in the Y-Mo system by IM.

B. Formation of the MX phases

The Y-rich $Y_{83}Mo_{17}$ films were amorphized at a dose of 1×10^{15} Xe^+/cm^2, and transformed into a fcc-I phase at a dose of 7×10^{15} Xe^+/cm^2. For the $Y_{72}Mo_{28}$ films, amorphization was achieved at a dose of 3×10^{15}

TABLE I. Phase changes in the Y-Mo multilayers induced by room-temperature 200-keV xenon ion mixing. (The dosages are in 10^{14} Xe^+/cm^2; "*A*" stands for amorphous phase; "bcc" is a Mo-rich solid solution; "hcp-I," "fcc-I," and "fcc-II" are three MX phases). The ion-induced phase formation in the $Y_{27}Mo_{73}$ multilayer was quite similar to that in the $Y_{22}Mo_{78}$ films and was thus not listed in the table.

Dosage	$Y_{15}Mo_{85}$	$Y_{22}Mo_{78}$	$Y_{42}Mo_{58}$	$Y_{65}Mo_{35}$	$Y_{72}Mo_{28}$	$Y_{83}Mo_{17}$
3	Y+Mo	Y+Mo	Y+Mo	Y+Mo	Y+Mo	Y+Mo
5	Y+Mo	Y+Mo	Y+Mo	Y+Mo	Y+Mo	Y+Mo
7	Y+Mo	Y+Mo	Y+Mo	Y+Mo	Y+Mo	Y+Mo
10	bcc	*A*	Y+Mo	Y+Mo	Y+Mo	*A*
30	hcp-I	hcp-I	Y+Mo	Y+Mo	*A*	*A*
50	hcp-I+fcc-II	hcp-I+fcc-II	Y+Mo	Y+Mo	*A*	*A*
70	fcc-II	fcc-II	Y+Mo	Y+Mo	fcc-I	fcc-I

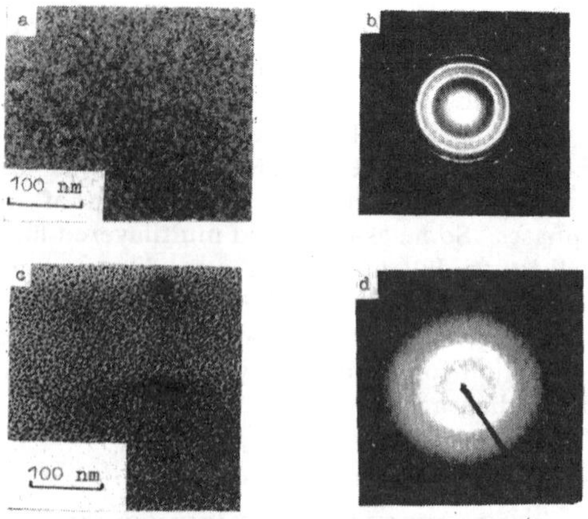

FIG. 1. (a) and (b) show a bright-field image and a corresponding SAD pattern of the as-deposited $Y_{72}Mo_{28}$ multilayers; (c) and (d) show a typical bright image and the corresponding SAD pattern of the amorphized multilayers at an irradiation dose of 3×10^{15} Xe^{+}/cm^{2} by room-temperature 200-keV xenon ion mixing.

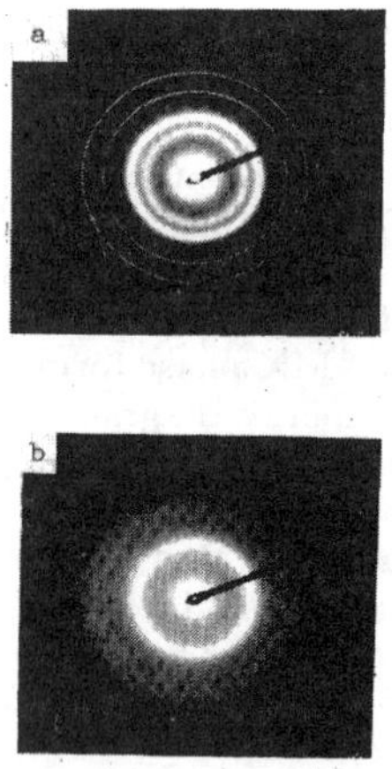

FIG. 2. (a) and (b) are the SAD patterns of the as-deposited $Y_{22}Mo_{78}$ multilayers and the corresponding amorphous phase formed by 200-keV room-temperature xenon ion mixing to a dose of 1×10^{15} Xe^{+}/cm^{2}.

Xe^{+}/cm^{2} [see Fig. 1(d)], and turned into a fcc-I phase at a higher dose of 7×10^{15} Xe^{+}/cm^{2}. Figures 3(a) and 3(b) show a typical bright-field image and the corresponding SAD pattern of the fcc-I phase, respectively. The lattice parameter of the fcc-I phase was determined to be $a=5.10$ Å. Table II lists the indexing results for the fcc-I phase. The formation of the fcc-I phase can therefore be viewed via an ion-induced transition of

$$Y_{72}Mo_{28}\xrightarrow[\text{RT}]{1\times10^{15}\ Xe^{+}/cm^{2}}\text{amorphous}\xrightarrow[\text{RT}]{7\times10^{15}\ Xe^{+}/cm^{2}}\text{fcc-I}\ . \tag{1}$$

At the Mo-rich side, when the $Y_{15}Mo_{85}$ films were irradiated to a dose of 1×10^{15} Xe^{+}/cm^{2}, the structure of the films was bcc, indicating the formulation of a Mo-rich solid solution. The films were changed into a hcp structure (hcp-I phase) at a dose of 3×10^{15} Xe^{+}/cm^{2}. The lattice parameters of the hcp-I phase were identified to be $a=2.89$ Å and $c=4.70$ Å. Table III lists the indexing results of the hcp-I phase. When the films were irradiated to a dose of 5×10^{15} Xe^{+}/cm^{2}, a mixture of the hcp-I and a new fcc-II phase was observed. When the films were irradiated to a dose of 7×10^{15} Xe^{+}/cm^{2}, a unique fcc-II phase was formed. Figures 4(a)–4(f) are a typical bright image and a corresponding SAD pattern of the as-deposited $Y_{15}Mo_{85}$ films, and the SAD patterns of the films at different irradiation stages. The lattice parameter of the fcc-II phase was determined to be $a=4.04$ Å. Table IV is the identification of the fcc-II phase. Similar results were also obtained in the $Y_{27}Mo_{73}$ and $Y_{22}Mo_{78}$ films at respective irradiation stages. These results can therefore be summarized as follows:

$$Y_{15}Mo_{85}\xrightarrow[\text{RT}]{1\times10^{15}\ Xe^{+}/cm^{2}}\text{bcc}\xrightarrow[\text{RT}]{3\times10^{15}\ Xe^{+}/cm^{2}}\text{hcp-I}\xrightarrow[\text{RT}]{7\times10^{15}\ Xe^{+}/cm^{2}}\text{fcc-II}\ . \tag{2}$$

TABLE II. Identification of the Y-rich fcc-I MX phase formed in the $Y_{83}Mo_{17}$ multilayers by 200-keV xenon ion mixing to a dose of 7×10^{15} Xe^{+}/cm^{2} at room temperature. $a=5.10$ Å.

$d_{\text{experimental}}$ (Å)	(hkl)	$d_{\text{calculation}}$ (Å)	$\lvert\Delta d\rvert$ (Å)	Intensity
2.93	111	2.94	0.01	strong
2.54	200	2.55	0.01	strong
1.81	220	1.80	0.01	strong
1.53	311	1.54	0.01	strong
1.45	222	1.47	0.02	medium
1.26	400	1.28	0.02	medium
1.17	331	1.17	0.00	medium
1.12	420	1.14	0.02	weak

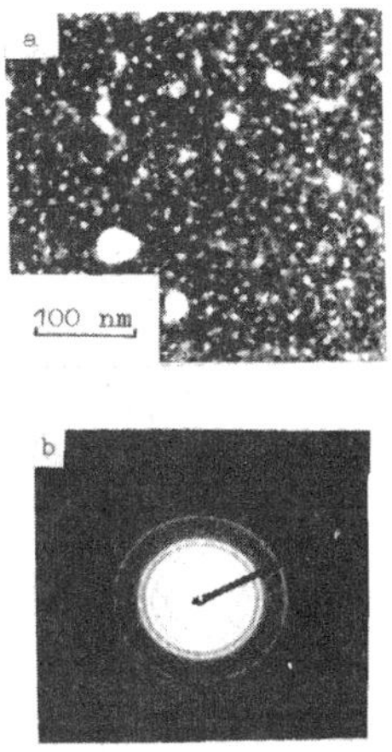

FIG. 3. (a) and (b) show a typical bright image and a corresponding SAD pattern of the Y-rich fcc-I MX phase formed in the $Y_{83}Mo_{17}$ multilayers by 200-keV xenon ion mixing to a dose of 7×10^{15} Xe^{+}/cm^{2} at room temperature.

Note that "bcc" is a Mo-rich solid solution.

It should be pointed out that the Y-rich fcc-I and Mo-rich hcp-I and fcc-II phases were metastable crystalline phases in the Y-Mo system since their diffraction lines could not be indexed to either those of the elemental metals or those of the possible Y, Mo, and (Y+Mo) oxides.

C. Thermodynamic interpretation

1. Survey of theory

Generally, the Gibbs free energy of a phase is calculated by $\Delta G=\Delta H\text{-}T\Delta S$, where ΔH and ΔS are the enthalpy and entropy terms, respectively. As a first approximation, the entropy term for a solid solution for an amorphous phase is simply taken as that of an ideal solid solution, i.e.,

$$\Delta S=-R[X_A\ln(X_A)+X_B\ln(X_B)]\ ,$$

in which R is the gas constant and X_A and X_A are atomic concentrations of A and B metals, respectively. According to Miedema, Chatel, and De Boer, the enthalpy change ΔH can be considered as a sum of three terms, i.e., $\Delta H=\Delta H^{c}+\Delta H^{e}+\Delta H^{s}$, corresponding to the chemical, elastic, and structural contributions. The chemical term ΔH^{c} is closely related to the electron redistribution generated at the boundary for the Wigner-Seitz unit cell when alloying, the elastic term ΔH^{e} is caused by the atomic size mismatch of the two constituent metals, while the structural term ΔH^{s} is deduced from the valence and crystal-structure changes.[31,32] These terms for the solid solutions, the amorphous phase, and the intermetallic compound can easily be calculated following

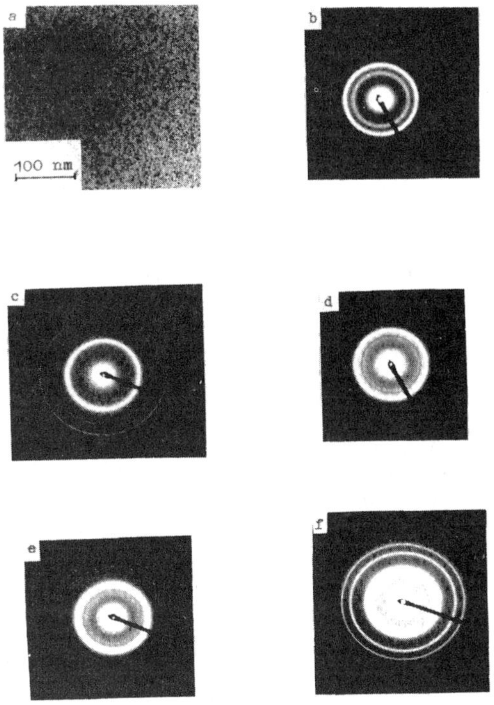

FIG. 4. (a),(b) Morphology and corresponding SAD pattern of the as-deposited $Y_{15}Mo_{85}$ multilayered films. (c)–(f) are the SAD patterns of the films at different irradiation stages upon 200-keV xenon ion mixing at room temperature: (c) a bcc solid solution formed at 1×10^{15} Xe^{+}/cm^{2}; (d) a hcp-I MX phase formed at 3×10^{15} Xe^{+}/cm^{2}; (e) a mixture of (hcp-I + fcc-II) formed at a dose of 5×10^{15} Xe^{+}/cm^{2}; and (f) a unique fcc-II MX phase formed at 7×10^{15} Xe^{+}/cm^{2}.

TABLE III. Indexing results of the Mo-rich hcp-I MX phase formed in the $Y_{15}Mo_{85}$ multilayers under 200-keV room-temperature xenon ion mixing to an irradiation dose of 3×10^{15} Xe^{+}/cm^{2}. $a=2.89$ Å, $c=4.70$ Å, and $c/a=1.63$.

$d_{\text{experimental}}$ (Å)	(hkl)	$d_{\text{calculation}}$ (Å)	$\lvert\Delta d\rvert$ (Å)	Intensity
2.52	100	2.50	0.02	medium
2.35	002	2.35	0.00	strong
2.22	101	2.21	0.01	strong
1.70	102	1.71	0.01	strong
1.44	110	1.45	0.01	strong
1.32	103	1.33	0.01	medium
1.23	112	1.23	0.00	medium
1.05	104	1.06	0.01	weak

the well-documented literature.[33] These terms for the MX phase, however, should be discussed in detail.

First, a MX phase is of an ordered structure, and the entropy term can be ignored since it only has a minor effect on the free-energy change just like that of an ordered equilibrium compound. The Gibbs-free-energy change of a MX phase is therefore

$$\Delta G_{MX}=\Delta H^{c}_{MX}+\Delta H^{s}_{MX}+\Delta H^{s}_{MX}\ , \tag{3}$$

where the three terms at the right side are chemical, elastic, and structural contributions of the MX phase, respectively. The chemical term ΔH^{c}_{MX} is accordingly calculated by

$$\Delta H^{c}_{MX}=\Delta H_{amp}X_A V_A^{2/3} f_{AB}\ , \tag{4}$$

where ΔH_{amp} is an amplitude and is a constant for a specific system, e.g., +16.5 kJ/mol cm^2 for the Y-Mo system. X_A and V_A are the atomic concentration and volume of atom A. f_{AB} is a function, namely, the extent of atom A surrounded by atom B. In the calculation of f_{AB}, a constant γ is used to describe the chemical short-range-order (CSRO) difference of the solid solutions, the amorphous phase, and the ordered compound. The values of γ are empirically taken as 0, 5, and 8 for the solid solution, the amorphous phase, and the compound, respectively.[34] As a MX phase is commonly considered as compoundlike, it is reasonable to assume that the CSRO in the MX phase is similar to that in an ordered compound. The value of γ is therefore taken as 8 for the MX phase.

Secondly, the elastic term of a MX phase is related to the lattice distortion caused by the size mismatch between the two constituent metals.[35] It is well known, however, that in an equilibrium compound the elastic energy can be neglected, since the lattice distortion caused by the atomic size mismatch of the two constituent metals can be relaxed down to a minimum by the ordered arrangement of the atoms. If a MX phase is formed near the eutectic point, where no corresponding equilibrium compound exists, the elastic term of the MX phase is negligible as the ordered arrangement of atoms in it can relax the lattice distortion to a minimum. Yet for a MX phase formed at a composition near an equilibrium compound, the elastic term of the MX phase cannot be neglected, as the structure and the atomic arrangement of the MX phase are different from that of the equilibrium compound and thus cannot relax the lattice distortion to a minimum. The elastic term for this MX phase is therefore

$$\Delta H^{e}_{MX}=X_A X_B[X_A\Delta H^{e}_{MX(B\text{ in }A)}+X_B\Delta H^{e}_{MX(A\text{ in }B)}]\ , \tag{5}$$

where $\Delta H^{e}_{MX(i\text{ in }j)}$, is the elastic contribution to the heat of solution of i in j in the MX phase, and can be calculated by the method proposed by de Boer, Miedema, and Boom.[36] It is worth mentioning that this formula can also be used to calculate the elastic term of the solid solution, but the values of the heat of solution $\Delta H_{(i\text{ in }j)}$ are different from those of $\Delta H^{e}_{MX(i\text{ in }j)}$. For the Y-Mo system, $\Delta H^{e}_{(Y\text{ in Mo})}$ and $\Delta H^{e}_{(Mo\text{ in }Y)}$ are +56 and + 131 kJ/mol, respectively.[37] The values of $\Delta H^{e}_{MX(i\text{ in }j)}$ for the fcc-I, hcp-I, and fcc-II phases were also calculated and listed in Table V for comparison.

Thirdly, the structure of a MX phase is different from the constituent metals, and thus the difference in structure has a contribution to the free-energy change. The structural contribution is then[7]

$$\Delta H^{s}_{MX}=E(Z)-X_A E(Z_A)-X_B E(Z_B)\ , \tag{6}$$

where $E(Z)$, $E(Z_A)$, and $E(Z_B)$ are the lattice stability of the MX phase and pure A and B metals, and Z, Z_A, and Z_B are the mean number of valence electrons of the MX phase and the number of valence electrons of pure metals A and B, respectively.[38] The dependence of the lattice stability on Z for paramagnetic and ferromagnetic transition metals has been calculated by Niessen *et al.*[39]

According to above discussion, the Gibbs-free-energy change of a MX phase can be classified into two types, (i) for a MX phase formed at a composition in the vicinity of an equilibrium compound,

$$\Delta G_{MX}=\Delta H^{c}_{MX}+\Delta H^{e}_{MX}+\Delta H^{s}_{MX}\ , \tag{7}$$

and (ii) for a MX phase formed at a composition near the eutectic point where no corresponding compound exists,

$$\Delta G_{MX}=\Delta H^{c}_{MX}+\Delta H^{s}_{MX}\ . \tag{8}$$

Accordingly, the Gibbs-free-energy changes of the Y-rich and Mo-rich solid solutions, the Y-Mo amorphous phases, and the fcc-I, hcp-I, and fcc-II MX phases were calculated. The values of the parameters used in the cal-

TABLE IV. Identification of the Mo-rich fcc-II MX phase formed in the $Y_{15}Mo_{85}$ multilayers upon room-temperature 200-keV xenon ion mixing to a dose of 7×10^{15} Xe^+/cm^2. a = 4.04 Å.

$d_{experimental}$ (Å)	(hkl)	$d_{calculation}$ (Å)	$\lvert\Delta d\rvert$ (Å)	Intensity
2.30	111	2.33	0.03	strong
2.01	200	2.02	0.01	strong
1.42	220	1.43	0.01	strong
1.24	311	1.22	0.02	strong
1.16	222	1.17	0.01	medium
1.02	400	1.01	0.01	medium
0.92	331	0.93	0.01	medium
0.89	420	0.90	0.01	weak

TABLE V. Values of the parameters used in calculating the free-energy diagram of the Y-Mo system and the free energy of the as-deposited Y-Mo multilayered films. (Note that "· · ·" means the data were not used, "films" stands for the as-deposited Y-Mo films, the unit of ΔH_{amp} is kJ/mol m^2, and the unit of $\Delta H_{(i\ \mathrm{in}\ j)}$ and $\Delta H^0_{(i\ \mathrm{in}\ j)}$ is kJ/mol.)

Parameter	Y	Mo	SS	A	fcc-I	hcp-I	fcc-II	Films
V (cm^3)	19.89	9.39	· · ·	· · ·	· · ·	· · ·	· · ·	· · ·
γ	· · ·	· · ·	0	5	8	8	8	· · ·
ΔH_{amp}	· · ·	· · ·	16.5	16.5	16.5	16.5	16.5	· · ·
$\Delta H^0_{(Y\ \mathrm{in}\ Mo)}$	· · ·	· · ·	56	· · ·	67	44	44	56
$\Delta H_{(Mo\ \mathrm{in}\ Y)}$	· · ·	· · ·	131	· · ·	172	127	127	131
γ^0 (mJ/m^2)	3000	1125	· · ·	· · ·	· · ·	· · ·	· · ·	· · ·
$\Delta H_{(Y\ \mathrm{in}\ Mo)}$	· · ·	· · ·	114	114	114	114	114	114
$\Delta H^0_{(Mo\ \mathrm{in}\ Y)}$	· · ·	· · ·	81	81	81	81	81	81
s_f (10^{5}m^2)	3.3	2.0	· · ·	· · ·	· · ·	· · ·	· · ·	· · ·

culation were listed in Table V. Figure 5 shows a calculated Gibbs-free-energy diagram of the Y-Mo system.

2. Steady-state thermal annealing results

Steady-state thermal annealing of some as-deposited multilayered films was conducted with increasing temperature. At the Y-rich side, the $Y_{72}Mo_{28}$ films were first amorphized after annealing at 250 °C for $1\frac{1}{2}$h, and then turned into the fcc-I phase when the temperature reached 350 °C and held for $\frac{1}{2}$ h. Further annealing at a higher temperature of 600 °C for 1 h caused the transformation from the fcc-I phase into a mixture of Y+Mo. Figures 6(a)–6(d) show the SAD patterns of the $Y_{72}Mo_{28}$ films at different annealing stages. In the Mo-rich $Y_{22}Mo_{78}$ multilayered films, a hcp-I phase was first formed when the films were annealed at a temperature of 500 °C for about an hour, and then the hcp-I phase changed into the fcc-II phase on annealing at a higher temperature of 600 °C for one more hour. The fcc-II phase is very stable upon further annealing up to 800 °C. Figures 7(a)–7(c) show the SAD patterns of the as-deposited $Y_{22}Mo_{78}$ films and the formed hcp-I and fcc-II phases, respectively. The annealing results of the Y-rich and Mo-rich films can be summarized as

$$Y_{72}Mo_{28}\frac{250\,^\circ\mathrm{C}}{90\ \mathrm{min}}>\mathrm{amorphous}\frac{350\,^\circ\mathrm{C}}{30\ \mathrm{min}}$$

$$>\mathrm{fcc\text{-}I}\frac{600\,^\circ\mathrm{C}}{60\ \mathrm{min}}>Y+Mo\ , \tag{9}$$

$$Y_{22}Mo_{78}\frac{500\,^\circ\mathrm{C}}{60\ \mathrm{min}}>\mathrm{hcp\text{-}I}\frac{600\,^\circ\mathrm{C}}{60\ \mathrm{min}}>\mathrm{fcc\text{-}II}\ . \tag{10}$$

From the phase appearance sequence upon steady-state thermal annealing just mentioned, it is obvious that the Y-rich fcc-I and Mo-rich hcp-I and fcc-II phases were indeed metastable phases in the Y-Mo system, and that the Y-rich fcc-I phase has lower free energy than the

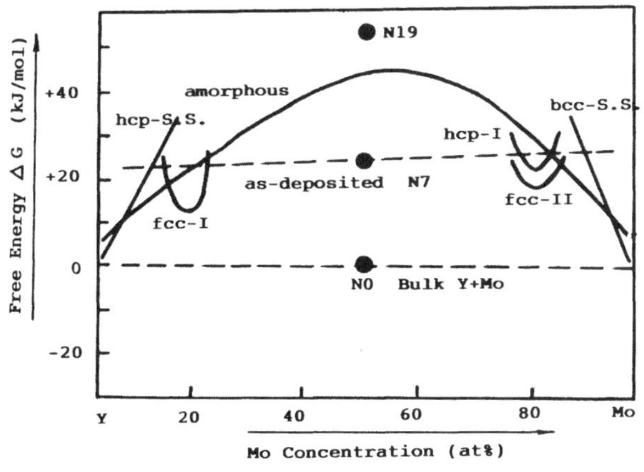

FIG. 5. A typical calculated Gibbs-free-energy diagram of the Y-Mo system. The dashed line shows the initial energetic levels of the as-deposited multilayers. N19 and N7 indicate samples with 19 and seven layers, respectively.

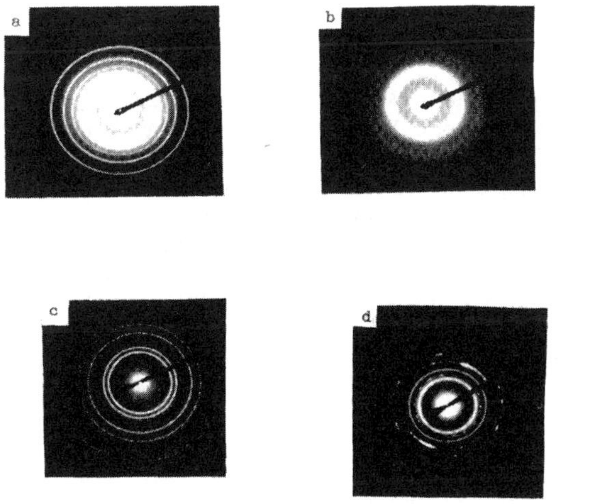

FIG. 6. SAD patterns of the $Y_{72}Mo_{28}$ multilayered films upon steady-state thermal annealing: (a) as deposited; (b) amorphized at 250 °C for 90 min; (c) the fcc-I MX phase formed after annealing at 350 °C for 30 min; and (d) the (Y+Mo) mixture reemerged when the temperature reached 600 °C and stayed for 60 min.

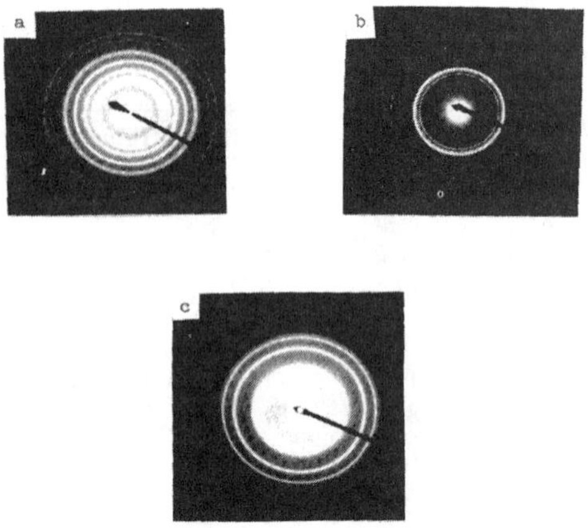

FIG. 7. SAD patterns of the $Y_{22}Mo_{78}$ multilayered films at different annealing stages: (a) as deposited; (b) the hcp-I MX phase formed after annealing at 500 °C for 60 min; and (c) the fcc-II MX phase formed after further annealing at 600 °C for 60 min.

corresponding amorphous phase, the Mo-rich fcc-II has lower free energy than the hcp-I one. These results are in agreement with the calculated free-energy diagram, and thus confirm the relevance of the calculated free-energy diagram in its outline.

3. *Interpretation to the GFA and MX phase formation*

a. The influence of the interfaces on the GFA. First, we focus on the GFA in the Y-Mo system. From Fig. 5, one may notice that the free-energy curves of the Y-rich, Mo-rich, and amorphous phases are convex in their shapes, and the amorphous phase has lower free energies than the two terminal solid solutions within a wide composition range, i.e., $Y_{12}-Y_{87}$. According to Alonso, Gallego, and Somozar,[20] the possible GFA of the Y-Mo system is $Y_{12}-Y_{87}$. Experimentally, however, the Y-Mo amorphous phase has so far been obtained in two isolated composition ranges, i.e., $Y_{22}-Y_{27}$ and $Y_{72}-Y_{83}$. It should be pointed out that at the compositions near the equiatomic stoichiometry, e.g., $Y_{45}Mo_{55}$ films, amorphization was not achieved, unlike in most of the previous results obtained in systems of negative heats of mixing.[40,41] From Fig. 5, it can be seen that both the solid solutions and the amorphous phases are thermodynamically unstable, as their free energies are much higher than that of a mixture of the two pure constituents.

It is well known that multilayered films consisting definitely of a certain number of interfaces can exist in a state of higher free energy than that of the corresponding bulk counterpart, as the interfaces can give a rise to an additional interfacial free energy.[42] The additional interfacial free energy, in some cases, may elevate the multilayers to a state of higher free energy than that of the amorphous state, and thus serves as a major driving force for the formation of some new phases.[43] According to Gerkema and Miedema[44] the interfacial free energy is

$$\Delta G_{[A]-[B],f}=S_f\times\gamma^{AB}\,, \tag{11}$$

where $\Delta G_{[A]-[B],f}$ is the interfacial free energy of a B atom on the A-atom layer, S_f is the surface area occupied by one mole of interfacial atoms, and γ^{AB} is a constant for a specific system and can be calculated by[44]

$$\gamma^{AB}=0.15(\gamma_A^0+\gamma_B^0)+\gamma_{AB}^{\text{chem}}\,, \tag{12}$$

where γ_A^0 and γ_B^0 are the surface energies of solid A and solid B, e.g., $\gamma_Y^0=+1125$ mJ/m^2, and $\gamma_{Mo}^0=+3000$ mJ/m^2. $\gamma_{AB}^{\text{chem}}$ is the chemical contribution concerning the reaction between A and B atoms. It is worth mentioning that the first part at the right side of Eq. (12) is the elastic term caused by mismatch of atomic sizes. According to Gerkema and Miedema $\gamma_{AB}^{\text{chem}}$ is a constant for a specific system and is given by $\gamma_{AB}^{\text{chem}}=\Delta H^0_{(A\text{ in }B)}/(c_0V_A^{2/3})$, where c_0 is a constant being 4.5×10^8, and $\Delta H^0_{(A\text{ in }B)}$ is a constant for a specific system, e.g., $\Delta H^0_{(\text{Y in Mo})}=+114$ kJ/mol and $\Delta H^0_{(\text{Mo in Y})}=+81$ kJ/mol for the Y-Mo system.

Figure 8 shows schematically the configuration of A-B multilayers. Suppose N_A and N_B are numbers of layers of metal A and B, $d_{A,i}$ and $d_{B,j}$ are the thicknesses of the ith layer of A and B, and $\Delta d_{A,i}$ and $\Delta d_{B,i}$ are the thicknesses of the ith interface of (A on B) and (B on A), respectively. Then the interfacial atoms are a fraction of total atoms,

$$\alpha=X_A\frac{\sum_i^{nA}\Delta d_{A,i}}{\sum_i^{N_A}d_{A,i}}+X_B\frac{\sum_i^{nB}\Delta d_{B,i}}{\sum_i^{N_B}d_{B,i}}\,. \tag{13}$$

In the formula, α is the fraction and n_A and n_B are the numbers of (A on B) interfaces and (B on A) interfaces, respectively. Obviously, n_A and n_B should match the relationship of $(n_A+n_B)+1=N_A+N_B$. For simplicity, the thicknesses of the interfaces, i.e., Δd_Y and Δd_{Mo}, were taken as a constant, being 5 Å in the calculation.[45] Formula (13) is then rewritten as $\alpha=\alpha_A=\alpha_B$, where

$$\alpha_A=X_A\frac{\sum_i^{nA}\Delta d_{A,i}}{\sum_i^{N_A}d_{A,i}}\quad\text{and}\quad\alpha_B=X_B\frac{\sum_i^{nB}\Delta d_{Bi}}{\sum_i^{N_B}d_{B,i}}\,. \tag{14}$$

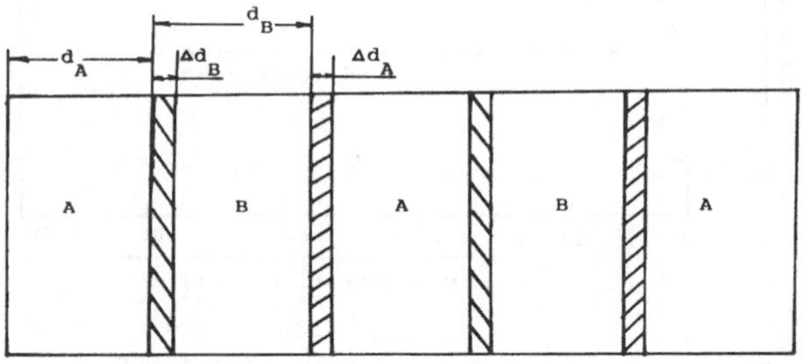

FIG. 8. Configuration of A and B component metals in an alternately deposited multilayered film. The thicknesses of the A and B layers and the (A on B) and (B on A) interfaces are shown schematically.

The interfacial free energies for the multilayers can then be calculated by

$$\Delta G_f = \alpha_A S_{fA} \gamma^{BA} + \alpha_B S_{fB} \gamma^{AB} , \quad (15)$$

where $S_{fY} = 3.3 \times 10^5$ m^2 and $S_{fMo} = 2.0 \times 10^5$ m^2, respectively.

The interfacial free energies for the as-deposited Y-Mo multilayered films were therefore calculated and the free-energy curve of the Y-Mo multilayers was added in Fig. 5 as a dashed line, representing the initial energy level of the as-deposited Y-Mo multilayers. Comparing with the free-energy curve of the amorphous phase, it is obvious that within the composition range of $Y_{21}-Y_{78}$ the amorphous alloy has higher free energy than the as-deposited films, suggesting that the amorphous phase is thermodynamically unfavored in the present case as there is no driving force responsible for amorphous phase formation in this composition range. Under the condition of $\Delta G_s \geq \Delta G_a \leq \Delta G_m$, where ΔG_m is the free energy of the multilayered films, the composition range favoring amorphization can be deduced from Fig. 5 to be $Y_{10}-Y_{21}$ and $Y_{78}-Y_{88}$, which agrees with the experimental ones, i.e., $Y_{22}-Y_{27}$, and $Y_{72}-Y_{83}$.

The next issue is the possibility of amorphization in the system at compositions around equiatomic stoichiometry by artificially adding extra interfaces into the Y-Mo multilayered films. To demonstrate the significant effect of the interfaces on amorphization behavior in a system with large positive heat of mixing like the Y-Mo system, two samples of $Y_{50}Mo_{50}$ multilayers with 19 layers (N19) and with seven layers (N7) were deposited and then annealed *in situ* in the hot stage attached to the TEM for comparison. It was found that the N19 sample was indeed amorphized after annealing at 350 °C for 2 h, and then transformed into a mixture of Y+Mo at a temperature of 650 °C. For the N7 multilayered films, the structure was a mixture of crystalline Y and Mo and remained unchanged up to a temperature as high as 800 °C. Figures 9(a)–(d) are a morphology and a corresponding SAD pattern of the as-deposited N19 multilayers and SAD patterns of the amorphous phase and Y+Mo mixture, respectively, after annealing. These results indicate that the amorphous phases, which are thermodynamically unstable in systems of positive heats of mixing, can be formed by thermal annealing of the multilayers, if the interfacial free energy is large enough, e.g., the N19 films. Accordingly, the initial energetic levels of the N19 and N7 multilayers were calculated, and were labeled by solid circles in Fig. 5. Obviously, it is the interfaces that elevated the multilayered films to a state of higher free energy than that of the bulk state, and in some cases elevated the state of the multilayered films to be higher than the amorphous one, as demonstrated by the N19 multilayered films. As a consequence, the excess free energy originating from the interfaces was responsible for the amorphous phase formation in the system by providing the thermodynamic driving force. In other words, the amorphous phase formation in the Y-Mo system with a rather positive heat of mixing was actually interface generated.

b. Thermodynamic interpretation of the MX phase formation. We now discuss the formation of the Y-rich fcc-I and Mo-rich hcp-I and fcc-II phases. It is clear from Fig. 5 that the three phases have lower free energies than that of the N7 films, and are therefore thermodynamically favored compared with the multilayered films. Besides, one can also see from the figure that the fcc-I phase has lower free energies at compositions around $Y_{80}Mo_{20}$ than both the Y-rich solid solution and the amorphous phase. For the Mo-rich hcp-I and fcc-II MX phases, the calculation illustrates that around $Y_{20}Mo_{80}$, the hcp-I and fcc-II phases are more stable than the Mo-rich solid solution and the amorphous phase, and the fcc-II phase is the most stable one among them, while hcp-I is the second most stable one. The possible emergence sequences of the related phases can thus be deduced from the calculated free-energy diagram as

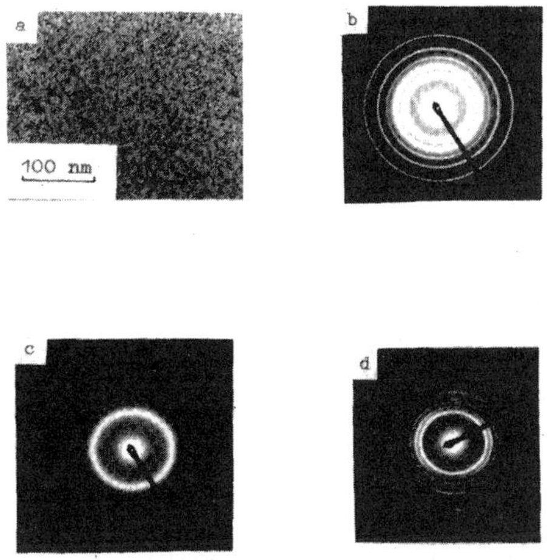

FIG. 9. (a) and (b) exhibit a typical morphology and a corresponding SAD pattern of the as-deposited N19 sample; (c) and (d) are the SAD patterns of the amorphized N19 sample at 350 °C, and the reemerged (Y+Mo) mixture at 650 °C, respectively.

$$Y_{80}Mo_{20} \rightarrow \text{amorphous} \rightarrow \text{fcc-I}$$

and

$$Y_{20}Mo_{80} \rightarrow \text{amorphous} \rightarrow \text{hcp-I} \rightarrow \text{fcc-II}$$

The deductions agree fairly well with the experimental results.

4. Structural compatibility between the MX phases and the matrix

The above calculations revealed the thermodynamic driving force for the formation of the fcc-I, hcp-I, and fcc-II phases. The next question is then how the three MX phases were formed under the restricted kinetic conditions available in IM. IM is generally recognized to be a two-step nonequilibrium process, i.e., first an atomic collision cascade and then a relaxation period lasting for only $10^{-10}-10^{-9}$ s, within which the structure of the newly formed phases was expected to grow. As a result, the alloy phase formed upon ion irradiation can only be of a simple crystalline structure or an amorphous structure, because such a short span of time prevents the nucleation and growth of a complicated structured phase as long-range diffusion is impossible.[46] Accordingly, only those fast and partitionless transition mechanisms can be executed. Since the phases synthesized by IM are through a solid-solid transition, the structural compatibility between the newly formed phase and the matrix frequently plays an important role in determining whether the new phase can grow or not.[47] The Y-rich fcc-I phase, in the present case, was formed from an amorphous matrix, which was believed to have been formed through a traditional nucleation and growth mechanism. The fcc-I phase, however, was still closely related with the matrix metal, i.e., Y, in some structural characteristics. As the atomic arrangement of the hcp and fcc structures is quite similar on the closely packed planes, i.e., $\{111\}_{fcc}$ and $\{0001\}_{hcp}$ planes, the transition of hcp→fcc can easily be realized by a sliding on the $\{0002\}_{hcp}$ plane along the $\langle 1\bar{1}00\rangle_{hcp}$ direction by a vector of $\frac{1}{3}\langle 1\bar{1}00\rangle_{hcp}$. From this sliding mechanism, the relationship between the two lattices can be deduced as $a_{fcc}=\sqrt{2}a_{hcp}$. Using the lattice parameter of the pure yttrium of $a_{hcp}=3.65$ Å, the lattice parameter of the fcc-I phase is calculated to be $a_{fcc}=5.16$ Å. Compared with the experimental value of 5.10 Å, the error is less than 2%.

Generally, direct transformation from a bcc to a fcc structure is somewhat difficult. A two-step transition, i.e., bcc→hcp→fcc,[48,49] however, can easily proceed under IM and was indeed observed in the Mo-rich $Y_{15}Mo_{85}$ films. From a crystallographic point of view, the first step of bcc→hcp can be fulfilled by a shearing which leads to a relationship of $a_{hcp}=(\sqrt{3/2})a_{bcc}$.[50] The second step of hcp→fcc, following the above discussion, can be realized by a sliding and results in $a_{fcc}=\sqrt{2}a_{hcp}$. The lattice-parameter relationship between the fcc and the bcc lattices is therefore deduced as $a_{fcc}=(\sqrt{6/2})a_{bcc}$. Using Vegard's law, the lattice parameter of a $Y_{15}Mo_{85}$ supersaturated solid solution is about 3.35 Å; the lattice parameter of the fcc-II phase is thus calculated to be 4.10 Å. Compared with the experimental value of 4.04 Å, the difference between them is less than 2%. For the hcp-I and fcc-II phases in other samples which were from an amorphous matrix, the formation was through a traditional nucleation and growth mechanisms.

IV. CONCLUDING REMARKS

(1) Amorphization was achieved in the Y-Mo system by 200-keV xenon ion mixing at room temperature within two isolated composition ranges, i.e., $Y_{22}-Y_{27}$ and $Y_{72}-Y_{83}$. In addition, three MX phases, i.e., Y-rich fcc-I and Mo-rich hcp-I and fcc-II, were formed.

(2) A Gibbs-free-energy diagram of the Y-Mo system was established by calculating the free-energy curves of the phases, especially including those of the three MX phases.

(3) Steady-state thermal annealing of the Y-Mo multilayered films with certain compositions was conducted. The annealing results revealed the relative energetic levels of the MX phases and in turn confirmed the relevance of the calculated free-energy diagram.

(4) The interfacial free energy of the as-deposited Y-Mo multilayers was calculated by using Gerkema and Miedema's model with varying number of interfaces. The calculated diagram together with the interface energies can give appropriate interpretation of the amorphization behavior and the GFA, and the formation of the three MX phases.

(5) The formation kinetics of the MX phases were considered to proceed via some solid-solid transition mechanisms and the lattice parameters so deduced agreed well with the experimental ones.

ACKNOWLEDGMENTS

The authors are grateful to the researchers in the TEM laboratory of the Peking University and the staff at the Analysis Center of Tsinghua University. Financial aid from the National Natural Science Foundation of China and from the Fundamental Research Foundation of Tsinghua University is acknowledged. The authors want to thank J. G. Sun and Z. Y. Zhao at the General Research Institute of Nonferrous Metals for their help in carrying out some experiments.

---

*Also at Center of Condensed Matter and Radiation Physics, CCAST (World Laboratory), Beijing 100080, China.

[1]G. Was, Prog. Surf. Sci. **32**, 211 (1989).

[2]L. S. Hung, M. Nastasi, J. Gyulai, and J. W. Mayer, Appl. Phys. Lett. **42**, 672 (1983).

[3]M. Nastasi, L. S. Hung, and J. W. Mayer, Appl. Phys. Lett. **43**, 831 (1983).

[4]J. L. Brimhall, H. E. Kissinger, and L. A. Charlot, in *Metastable Materials Formation by Ion Implantation,* edited by S. T. Picraux and W. J. Choyke, The MRS Symposia, Proceedings No. 7 (North-Holland, New York, 1982), p. 235.

[5]B. Y. Tsaur, S. S. Lau, and J. W. Mayer, Appl. Phys. Lett. **36**, 823 (1980).

[6]B. X. Liu, Vacuum **42**, 75 (1991).

[7]B. X. Liu, H. Y. Bai, Z. J. Zhang, and Q. L. Qiu, J. Alloys Compounds **196**, 37 (1993).

[8]H. U. Krebs, D. J. Webb, and A. F. Marshall, Phys. Rev. B **35**, 5393 (1987).

[9]D. G. Morris, Acta Metall. **31**, 1497 (1983).

[10]K. T.-Y. Kung, B. X. Liu, and M. A. Nicolet, Phys. Status Solidi A **77**, 355 (1983).

[11]B. X. Liu and M. A. Nicolet, Thin Solid Films **101**, 201 (1983).

[12]D. A. Lilienfeld, M. Nastasi, H. H. Johnson, D. G. Ast, and J. W. Mayer, Phys. Rev. Lett. **55**, 1587 (1985).

[13]D. A. Lilienfeld, M. Nastasi, H. H. Johnson, D. G. Ast, and J. W. Mayer, J. Mater. Res. **1**, 237 (1986).

[14]J. A. Knapp and D. M. Follstaedt, Phys. Rev. Lett. **55**, 1591 (1985).

[15]D. M. Follstaedt and J. A. Knapp, Phys. Rev. Lett. **56**, 1827 (1986).

[16]B. Y. Tsaur, S. S. Lau, L. S. Hung, and J. W. Mayer, Nucl. Instrum. Methods **182/183**, 67 (1981).
[17]Z. J. Zhang and B. X. Liu, J. Phys. Condens. Matter **6**, 9065 (1994).
[18]B. X. Liu, Phys. Status Solidi A **75**, K77 (1983).
[19]B. X. Liu, M. A. Nicolet, and S. S. Lau, Phys. Status Solidi A **73**, 183 (1983).
[20]J. A. Alonso, L. J. Gallego, and J. A. Somozar, Nuovo Cimento, **12**, 587 (1990).
[21]Z. J. Zhang and B. X. Liu, J. Appl. Phys. **76**, 3351 (1994).
[22]C. L. Chien, Phys. Rev. B **33**, 3243 (1986).
[23]K. Affolter, M. V. Allmen, H. P. Weber, and M. Witter, J. Non-Cryst. Solids **55**, 387 (1983).
[24]S. Simozar and J. A. Alonso, Phys. Status Solidi A **81**, 55 (1984).
[25]J. A. Alonso, L. J. Gallego, and J. M. Lopez, Philos. Mag. A **58**, 79 (1988).
[26]L. J. Gallego, J. A. Somozar, J. A. Alonso, and J. M. Lopez, Physica B **154**, 82 (1988).
[27]J. A. Alonso, L. J. Gallego, J. A. Somozar, and B. X. Liu, in *Thin films and Beam-Solid Interactions,* edited by L. Hung (Elsevier, Amsterdam, 1991), p. 197.
[28]L. J. Gallego, J. A. Somozar, H. M. Pernandez, and J. A. Alonso, in *Ordering and Disordering in Alloys,* edited by A. R. Yavari (Elsevier, London, 1992), p. 328.
[29]B. X. Liu and Z. J. Zhang, Phys Rev. B **49**, 12 519 (1994).
[30]R. B. Schwarz and J. B. Rubin, J. Alloys Compounds **194**, 189 (1993).
[31]A. R. Miedema, P. F. de Chatel, and F. R. De Boer, Physica B **100**, 1 (1980).
[32]A. K. Niessen and F. R. de Boer, J. Less-Common Met. **82**, 75 (1981).
[33]J. M. Lopez and J. A. Alonso, Z. Naturforsch. Teil A **40**, 1199 (1985).
[34]A. K. Niessen, F. R. de Boer, R. Boom, P. F. de Chatel, W. C. M. Matters, and A. R. Miedema (unpublished).
[35]R. Boom, F. R. de Boer, A. K. Niessen, and A. R. Miedema, Physica B **115**, 285 (1983).
[36]F. R. de Boer, A. R. Miedema, and R. Boom, Physica B **113**, 18 (1982).
[37]F. R. de Boer, R. Boom, W. C. M. Matters, A. R. Miedema, and A. K. Niessen, *Cohesion in Metals: Transition Metal Alloys* (North-Holland, Amsterdam, 1988), Chap. III.
[38]A. K. Niessen and A. R. Miedema, Ber. Bunsenges. Phys. Chem. **87**, 717 (1983).
[39]A. K. Niessen, A. R. Miedema, F. R. de Boer, and R. Boom, Physica B **151**, 401 (1988).
[40]B. X. Liu, Z. J. Zhang, and H. Y. Bai, J. Non-Cryst. Solids **156-158**, 603 (1993).
[41]Z. J. Zhang, H. Y. Bai, Q. L. Qiu, T. Yang, K. Tao, and B. X. Liu, J. Appl. Phys. **73**, 1702 (1993).
[42]C. Gente, M. Oehring, and R. Bormann, Phys. Rev. B **48**, 13 244 (1993).
[43]B. M. Clemens and T. C. Hufnagel, J. Alloys Compounds **194**, 221 (1993).
[44]J. Gerkema and A. R. Miedema, Surf. Sci. **124**, 351 (1981).
[45]F. Z. Cui, Y. D. Fan, Y. Wang, A. M. Vredenberg, H. J. G. Draaisma, and R. Xu, J. Appl. Phys. **68**, 701 (1990).
[46]M. W. Thompson, *Defects and Radiation Damage in Metals* (Cambridge University Press, Cambridge, England 1969), Chaps. 4 and 5.
[47]Z. J. Zhang and B. X. Liu, J. Phys. Condens. Matter **6**, 2647 (1994).
[48]Z. J. Zhang and B. X. Liu, J. Appl. Phys. **75**, 4948 (1994).
[49]B. X. Liu and Z. J. Zhang, J. Mater. Res. **9**, 3567 (1994).
[50]W. G. Burgers, Physica **1**, 561 (1934).

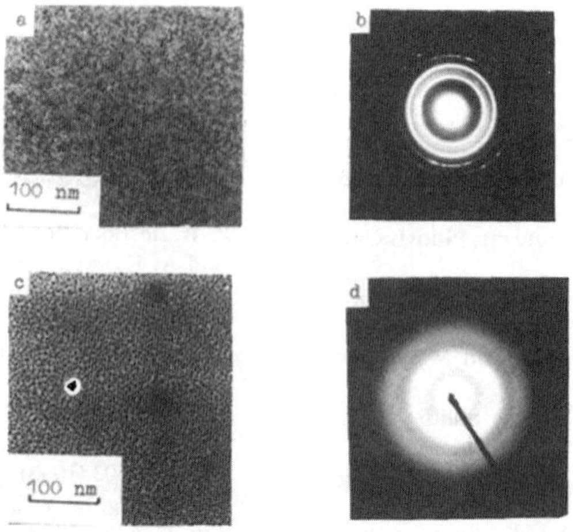

FIG. 1. (a) and (b) show a bright-field image and a corresponding SAD pattern of the as-deposited $Y_{72}Mo_{28}$ multilayers; (c) and (d) show a typical bright image and the corresponding SAD pattern of the amorphized multilayers at an irradiation dose of 3×10^{15} Xe^{+}/cm^{2} by room-temperature 200-keV xenon ion mixing.

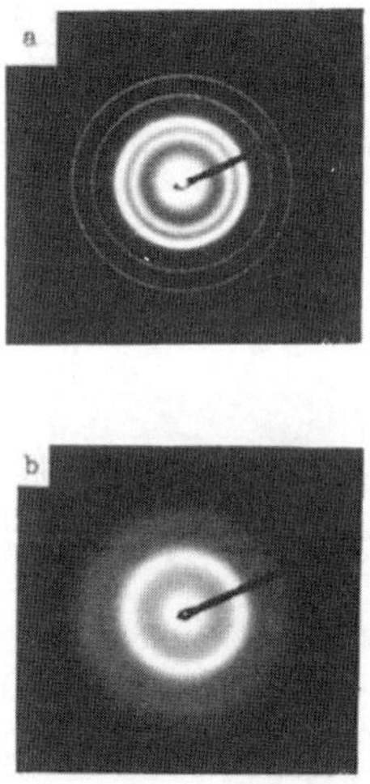

FIG. 2. (a) and (b) are the SAD patterns of the as-deposited $Y_{22}Mo_{78}$ multilayers and the corresponding amorphous phase formed by 200-keV room-temperature xenon ion mixing to a dose of 1×10^{15} Xe^{+}/cm^{2}.

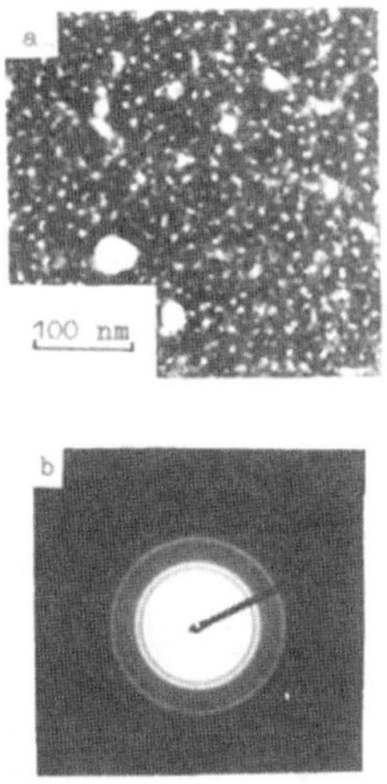

FIG. 3. (a) and (b) show a typical bright image and a corresponding SAD pattern of the Y-rich fcc-I MX phase formed in the $Y_{83}Mo_{17}$ multilayers by 200-keV xenon ion mixing to a dose of 7×10^{15} Xe^+/cm^2 at room temperature.

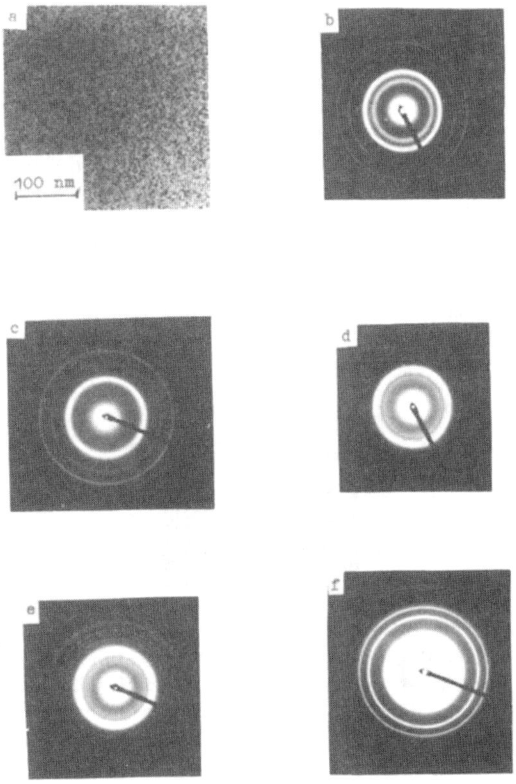

FIG. 4. (a),(b) Morphology and corresponding SAD pattern of the as-deposited $Y_{15}Mo_{85}$ multilayered films. (c)–(f) are the SAD patterns of the films at different irradiation stages upon 200-keV xenon ion mixing at room temperature: (c) a bcc solid solution formed at 1×10^{15} Xe^+/cm^2; (d) a hcp-I MX phase formed at 3×10^{15} Xe^+/cm^2; (e) a mixture of (hcp-I + fcc-II) formed at a dose of 5×10^{15} Xe^+/cm^2; and (f) a unique fcc-II MX phase formed at 7×10^{15} Xe^+/cm^2.

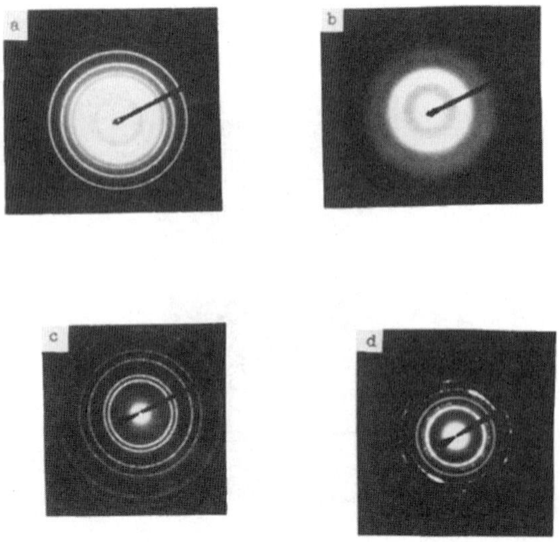

FIG. 6. SAD patterns of the $Y_{72}Mo_{28}$ multilayered films upon steady-state thermal annealing: (a) as deposited; (b) amorphized at 250 °C for 90 min; (c) the fcc-I MX phase formed after annealing at 350 °C for 30 min; and (d) the (Y+Mo) mixture reemerged when the temperature reached 600 °C and stayed for 60 min.

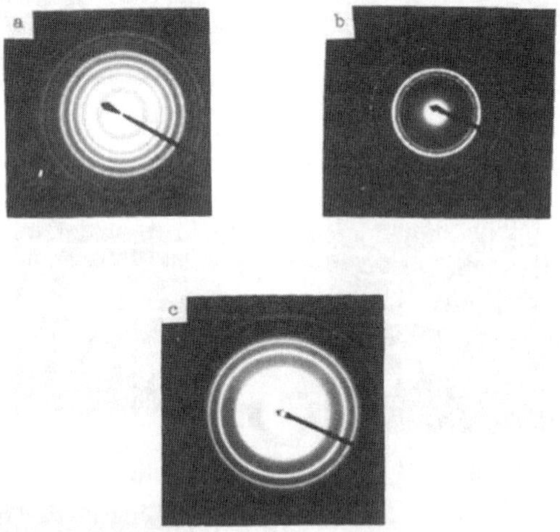

FIG. 7. SAD patterns of the $Y_{22}Mo_{78}$ multilayered films at different annealing stages: (a) as deposited; (b) the hcp-I MX phase formed after annealing at 500 °C for 60 min; and (c) the fcc-II MX phase formed after further annealing at 600 °C for 60 min.

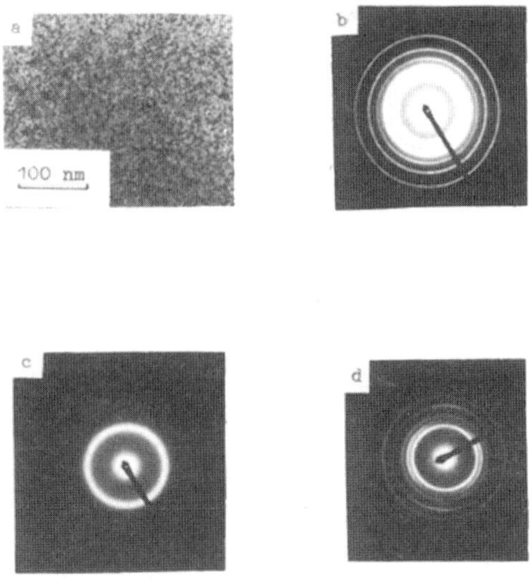

FIG. 9. (a) and (b) exhibit a typical morphology and a corresponding SAD pattern of the as-deposited N19 sample; (c) and (d) are the SAD patterns of the amorphized N19 sample at 350 °C, and the reemerged (Y+Mo) mixture at 650 °C, respectively.

Spontaneous vitrification in the Au–Ta system with a small size difference

F. Pan, Y. G. Chen, and B. X. Liu[a)]
Department of Materials Science and Engineering, Tsinghua University, Beijing 100084, China and Laboratory of Solid State Microstructure, Nanjing University, Nanjing 210008, China

(Received 3 April 1995; accepted for publication 27 May 1995)

Spontaneous vitrification was observed in the Au–Ta system, although the atomic size difference between Au and Ta is very small. It was found that among the various compositions studied, vitrification was only achieved at a composition of around $Au_{23}Ta_{77}$. Comparative data were obtained by ion mixing of Au–Ta multilayered films to support the spontaneous vitrification results. The amorphization mechanism was discussed in terms of competition between the amorphous phase against the nucleation and growth of the existing equilibrium compound, which explained the favorable composition range as well as the thermal stability of the obtained amorphous alloy. © *1995 American Institute of Physics.*

Amorphous alloys and metallic glasses are expected to have novel properties in many aspects, and various techniques have been developed to produce amorphous materials in the last three decades.[1–3] Since the pioneering work on spontaneous vitrification (SV) by Schwarz and Johnson[4] in 1983, solid-state interdiffusion has been employed to produce glassy alloys in some binary metal systems.[5–7.]

According to Schwarz and Johnson and other reports, spontaneous vitrification is expected to take place in metal systems having a large negative heat of formation and a large atomic size difference.[8] Here, the large negative heat of mixing provides the necessary thermodynamic driving force to transform the original crystalline components into amorphous alloys upon thermal annealing, while the size factor plays a kinetic role in preventing the growth of the possible competing crystalline phase against amorphization.

It has been found that amorphous alloys were formed by vapor deposition and ion mixing (IM) in some systems having atomic size ratios close to unity,[9,10] indicating the atomic size is not a decisive factor. It is therefore of interest to investigate the possibility of forming amorphous alloys by spontaneous vitrification, in those systems that have a small size difference.

The Au–Ta system was selected for this study because the atomic radius ratio and the volume ratio between Au and Ta were 1.008 and 0.936, respectively. Also, the Au–Ta system has a negative heat of mixing of -32 kJ/mol and its free energy diagram can be calculated by Miedema's model[11] as well as the method developed by Alonso reported in the literature.[12,13]

The Au/Ta multilayered samples were prepared by depositing alternatively pure tantalum (99.99%) and gold (99.99%) at rates of 0.1–0.2 nm/s onto an NaCl single-crystal substrate (with a freshly cleaved surface) in an e-gun evaporation system with a vacuum level on the order of 10^{-7} Torr. The total thickness of the films was about 40 nm. Each Au/Ta multilayer consisted of seven tantalum layers and seven gold layers, and the first layer on the substrate was tantalum. Five stoichiometries were chosen for this study; the average compositions of the multilayers were 23, 30, 40, 60, and 77 at. % of tantalum. The composition of the films was controlled by adjusting the relative layer thicknesses of constituent metals and was later confirmed by the energy dispersive spectrum (EDS) analysis within an experimental error of 5%. After deposition, the multilayers were subjected to thermal annealing in a hot stage of the transmission electron microscopy (TEM), of which the vacuum level was on the order of 10^{-7} Torr. The morphological and structural changes of the samples were observed and identified by bright field examination and selected area diffraction (SAD) analysis. The camera constant of the TEM SAD was calibrated by x-ray diffraction using the Au–Ta films.

Figure 1(a) is a typical SAD pattern of the as-deposited $Au_{23}Ta_{77}$ multilayers showing the crystalline structure of Au and Ta metals. When the $Au_{23}Ta_{77}$ multilayer was heated continuously at a rate of 5 K/min to 200 °C, partial amorphization was observed. After remaining at 200 °C for 30 min, the annealing temperature was further elevated to 350 °C and maintained for 30 min. The structure of the film became completely amorphous. Figures 1(b) and 1(c) exhibit two SAD patterns of the $Au_{23}Ta_{77}$ multilayers after annealing at 200 and 350 °C, respectively. When the temperature was raised to about 650 °C and maintained for 20 min, diffraction

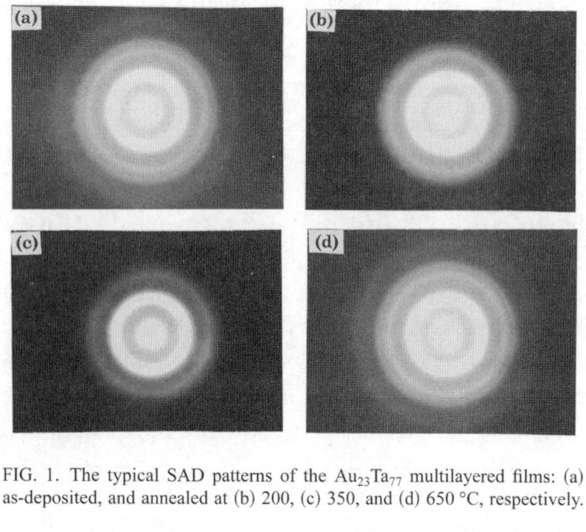

FIG. 1. The typical SAD patterns of the $Au_{23}Ta_{77}$ multilayered films: (a) as-deposited, and annealed at (b) 200, (c) 350, and (d) 650 °C, respectively.

[a)]Electronic mail: dmslbx@tsinghua.edu.cn

Applied Physics Letters 67(6), p.780-782 (1995).

TABLE I. Achievement of amorphous state in Au–Ta multilayers by thermal annealing and ion mixing.

Composition (at. % Ta)	23	30	40	60	77
Thermal annealing	No	No	No	No	Yes
Ion mixing	No	No	P[a]	Yes	Yes

[a]P=partially amorphized.

lines emerged again as shown in Fig. 1(d), indicating that the recrystallization temperature of the $Au_{23}Ta_{77}$ amorphous alloy was about 650 °C. The annealing experimental results revealed that, when the Ta concentration in the films was lower than 60 at. %, an amorphous phase did not form by a similar annealing process. These results suggest that the composition range favoring spontaneous vitrification in the Au–Ta system is relatively narrow and is located around the composition of $Au_{23}Ta_{77}$.

To have a better understanding of the glass-forming ability of the Au–Ta system, the structural phase transformation in the Ta–Au multilayers was studied by 190 keV xenon ion mixing at room temperature. Table I shows the amorphous alloy formation in the Au–Ta multilayers by thermal annealing and ion mixing. It can be seen that the composition range favoring amorphization by IM was larger than that by thermal annealing. The $Au_{23}Ta_{77}$ films were very easily completely amorphized by IM and the lowest dose for amorphization was about 3×10^{14} Xe^+/cm^2. The recrystallization temperature of the ion mixed $Au_{23}Ta_{77}$ amorphous alloy was determined to be about 650 °C, which was exactly the same as the one obtained by thermal annealing as mentioned above. This composition is therefore the best choice for forming the most stable amorphous alloy in the system. While for the $Au_{40}Ta_{60}$ films containing more Au than the above noted one, amorphization was achieved by IM at a dose of 1×10^{16} Xe^+/cm^2, yet not by SV. The recrystallization temperature of the ion mixed $Au_{40}Ta_{60}$ amorphous alloy was determined to be about 200 °C, implying that this amorphous alloy is very unstable, probably due to its larger Au concentration. In summary, the most favorable composition for amorphous alloy formation in the system was found to be around 77 at. % of Ta. At this composition, both IM and SV can cause the multilayers to become uniformly amorphous. When the composition was varied slightly to the Au side, i.e., $Au_{40}Ta_{60}$, the amorphous alloy was formed by IM, as IM is a nonequilibrium process and induced uniform mixing of Au and Ta in a disordered configuration. If the SV technique is employed to produce amorphous alloys, the annealing temperature should at least be lower than the recrystallization temperature of the expected amorphous phase, i.e., 200 °C. However, at such a low temperature, diffusion between the constituent metals was very difficult. In other words, the kinetic condition for forming the $Au_{40}Ta_{60}$ amorphous alloy by SV was not able to be achieved.

To interpret the above observations, a free-energy diagram of the Au–Ta system was constructed on the basis of the model of Niessen and Miedema[11–14] and the method proposed by Alonso *et al.*[15,16] Figures 2(a) and 2(b) are the equilibrium phase diagram[17] and the calculated free energy diagram of the Au–Ta system at 300 K. From the figures, one can see that the free energy curve of the amorphous phase is lower than that of the two terminal solid solutions within a narrow composition range of 56–80 at. % Ta. Simply taking this range as a measure of the glass-forming ability, the composition range favoring amorphization for the Au–Ta system is therefore from 56 to 80 at. % tantalum, which is in good agreement with both SV and IM experimental results. From the Au–Ta equilibrium phase diagram, one can also see that an equilibrium σ phase exists in the composition range of 75–78 at. % Ta below 600 °C, which corresponds to the most favorable composition for amorphization. Because the σ phase has a complicated structure, nucleation and growth require a relatively high temperature and extended time periods, which are not acceptable for either the IM or the SV process. Thus, the σ phase failed to be formed when compared with the corresponding amorphous alloy, which was obtained in both the IM and SV processes.

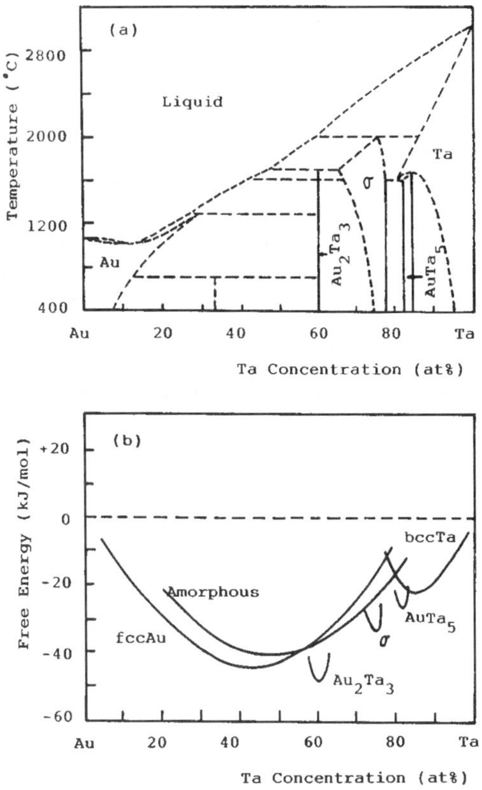

FIG. 2. (a) The equilibrium phase diagram (see Ref. 17) and (b) the calculated free energy diagram of the Au–Ta system.

In summary, we have shown that spontaneous vitrification can occur in a system with a small size difference, thus creating greater opportunity to produce metallic glass by SV, and that the existing equilibrium compound acting as a competing phase against amorphization should be considered in choosing the alloy composition for SV.

This work was supported in part by the National Natural Science Foundation of China and by the Administration of Tsinghua University. The authors are grateful to the researchers of the TEM Laboratory of Peking University and of the Analysis Center of Tsinghua University for their help.

[1] S. S. Lau, B. X. Liu, and M. A. Nicolet, Nucl. Instrum. Methods **209/210**, 97 (1983).
[2] B. X. Liu, Nucl. Instrum. Methods B **40/41**, 603 (1989).
[3] M. V. Allmen, in *Laser-Beam Interaction with Materials,* edited by J. Carl (Washington International Society for Optical Engineering, Washington, D.C., 1983), p. 140.
[4] R. B. Schwarz and W. L. Johnson, Phys. Rev. Lett. **51**, 415 (1983).
[5] *Solid State Amorphization Transformation: Proceedings of the Conference on Solid State Amorphizing Transformations,* Los Alamos, NM, August 10–13, 1987, edited by R. B. Schwarz and W. L. Johnson (Elsevier Sequoia S. A., Lausanne, Switzerland, 1988).
[6] B. M. Clemens and R. Sinclair, Mater. Res. Bull. **XV**, 19 (1990).
[7] B. X. Liu and Z. J. Zhang, Phys. Rev. B **49**, 12519 (1994).
[8] B. M. Clemens, Phys. Rev. B **33**, 7615 (1986).
[9] B. X. Liu, W. L. Johnson, M. A. Nicolet, and S. S. Lau, Appl. Phys. Lett. **42**, 45 (1983).
[10] G. J. Van der Kolk, A. R. Miedema, and A. K. Niessen, J. Less-Common Met. **145**, 1 (1988).
[11] A. R. Miedema, P. F. de Chatel, and F. R. de Boer, Physica B **100**, 1 (1980).
[12] A. K. Niessen, A. R. Miedema, F. R. de Boer, and R. Boom, Physica B **151**, 401 (1988).
[13] Z. J. Zhang, H. Y. Bai, Q. L. Qiu, T. Yang, K. Tao, and B. X. Liu, J. Appl. Phys. **73**, 1702 (1993).
[14] A. K. Niessen and A. R. Miedema, Ber. Bunsenges. Phys. Chem. **87**, 717 (1983).
[15] J. W. Alonso and S. Simozar, Solid State Commun. **46**, 765 (1983).
[16] J. A. Alonso, L. J. Gallego, and J. M. Lopez, Philos. Mag. A **58**, 79 (1988).
[17] H. Okamoto and T. B. Massalski, Bull. Alloy Phase Diagrams **6**, 319 (1985).

Review Article

phys. stat. sol. (a) **161, 3** (1997)
Subject classification: 64.75.+g; 61.43.Dq; 64.60.My; 68.55.Nq; S1; S4

Formation and Theoretical Modeling of Non-Equilibrium Alloy Phases by Ion Mixing

B.X. LIU[1]) and O. JIN

Department of Materials Science and Engineering, Tsinghua University, Beijing 100084, People's Republic of China

(Received March 22, 1996; in revised form February 10, 1997)

Contents

1. Survey of Ion Mixing and Alloy Phase Formation

Since the early sixties, ion beams from low energy accelerators have been used to modify materials properties, e.g. doping of semiconductors by ion implantation. About ten years

[1]) Corresponding author.

Review Article, Phys. Stat. Sol. (a) 161(1), p.3-33 (1997).

later, this technique was employed to deal with metals. It is now well established that ion implantation can form a number of new solid phases in surface layers of materials and thus the term "ion implantation metallurgy" [1,2] has been proposed. However, in this subject, direct implantation has sonie great disadvantages limiting its applications: e.g. the limitation of the maximuni obtainable coniposition of metallic alloy phases by sputtering effects and availability of a versatile metal ion source. Therefore, in this case, ion mixing was introduced in the early eighties and boomed up about a decade later. In contrast to direct implantation, the ion beam (typically an inert gas ion beam) is used here mainly to trigger atomic collisions for inducing intermixing between deposited material B and the matrix A, or both deposited A and B bilayer or multilayers on a substrate, and thus forming a uniform A–B alloy phase.

Over the past three decades, since the first glassy metallic alloy has been obtained by rapid quenching from the melt [3], extensive studies have been dedicated to synthesize new amorphous alloys, which are expected to feature unique properties in many aspects in comparison with their crystalline counterparts, and various techniques have been developed. To avoid crystallization, high cooling rates of 10^6 K/s or higher are needed [4 to 7]. After the splat quenching was developed in 1960 by Duwez et al. [3,8], cooling rates up to 10^7 K/s have been achieved. This resulted in expanding the number and types of glass forming materials to include a variety of compositions of metal–metalloid and metal–metal amorphous alloys [9]. Later, laser quenching has also been applied for producing amorphous alloys [10,11], as many intense laser sources have been available and can achieve a cooling rate of even 10^{12} K/s in the surface layer of the materials.

In the past 15 years, ion beam mixing of multilayers has been used extensively to study the formation of metastable alloy phases with either crystalline or amorphous structure, as its highest effective cooling rate, which will be further discussed in Section 2, can be as high as 10^{14} K/s and the experimental parameters are easy to control. So far, more than 90 binary metal–metal systems, according to published results, have been studied, which produced a great nuniber of metastable alloy phases including various amorphous and metastable crystalline (MX) alloys. Among these metastable alloys, many have not been obtained or are even not obtainable by traditional means like melt quenching. This has provided the materials scientist with a great opportunity to further study the glass forming ability (GFA) and the amorphization mechanism of the binary metal systems. To have an overview of the outcome of these studies, Table 1 lists these systems in alphabetical order of the chemical symbols of the constituent metals for convenience of searching.

In the last decade, researchers in this field have made great efforts to promote the understanding of the alloy phase formation mechanisms, and to predict glass forming ability (GFA) and glass forming range (GFR) of binary metal systems. Several empirical or phenomenological models have been proposed from the static properties of the components and the features of the equilibrium phase diagram. The structural difference rule proposed by Liu et al [64] established the predominant role of the crystalline structures of the two component metals in determining the possibility of the formation of amorphous alloys. In other words, an amorphous alloy would most likely be formed by ion mixing of multilayered samples when the two constituent metals are of different crystalline structures, regardless of their atomic size and electronegativity. A little later, Liu [65] further developed this rule into a phenomenological model for predicting GFA on the basis of two parameters: the maximum possible amorphization range (MPAR) which

Table 1
The studied binary metal–metal systems by ion mixing

No.	system	ΔH_f (kJ/mol)	MPAR (%)	metallic glass formed	ref.
1	Ag–Co	26	100	no	[12]
2	Ag–Cr	40	100	yes	[13]
3	Ag–Cu	3	90	yes	[14]
4	Ag–Fe	42	–	no	[15]
5	Ag–Ir	23	–	no	[16]
6	Ag–Mo	56	100	yes*	[17]
7	Ag–Nb	11	–	yes	[18]
8	Ag–Ni	22	100	yes	[14]
9	Ag–Os	42	–	no	[16]
10	Ag–Rh	14	–	no	[16]
11	Ag–Ru	35	100	no	[16]
12	Ag–Ta	23	–	yes*	[15]
13	Ag–V	25		yes*	[15]
14	Ag–W	65	–	no	[19]
15	Al–Au	−37	84	yes*	[20]
16	Al–Co	−42	85	yes	[21]
17	Al–Fe	−31	45	yes	[22]
18	Al–Mn	−43	60	yes	[23]
19	Al–Mo	−24	90	yes	[24]
20	Al–Nb	−44	77	yes	[25]
21	Al–Ni	−48	80	yes*	[26]
22	Al–Pd	−84	82	yes*	[26]
23	Al–Pt	−82	90	yes*	[26]
24	Al–Ta	− 5	88	yes*	[24]
25	Al–Ti	−67	80	yes	[27]
26	Al–Y	−69	100	yes	[28]
27	Al–Yb	–	95	yes	[29]
28	Au–Co	10	74	yes	[30]
29	Au–Cu	− 9	0	no	[31]
30	Au–Fe	12	17	no	[30]
31	Au–Ir	19	–	yes	[16]
32	An–Mo	5	–	yes*	[32]
33	Au–Ni	11	0	no	[30]
34	Au–Os	27	–	yes	[16]
35	Au–Rh	11	–	no	[16]
36	Au–Ru	23	100	yes	[24]
37	An–Ta	−49	55	yes	[33]
38	Au–Ti	−71	72	yes*	[34]
39	Au–V	−29	20	yes	[30]
40	Au–W	17	100	yes	[24]
41	Co–Cu	10	83	yes	[13]
42	Co–Gd	−30	90	yes*	[35]
43	Co–Hf	−51	95	yes*	[15]
44	Co–Mo	− 7	76	yes*	[25]
45	Co–Nb	−38	86	yes*	[36]
46	Co–Ta	−36	75	yes*	[37]
47	Co–Tb	−32	100	yes	[38]
48	Co–Ti	−42	71	yes	[21]
49	Co–Y	−31	100	yes	[28]
50	Co–Yb	−16	100	yes	[39]
51	Co–Zr	−59	95	yes*	[40]

Table 1 (continued)

No.	system	ΔH_f (kJ/mol)	MPAR (%)	metallic glass formed	ref.
52	Cr–Cu	20	100	no	[41]
53	Cu–Fe	19	87	yes	[42]
54	Cu–Ir	0	85	no	[16]
55	Cu–Nb	4	–	yes*	[15]
56	Cu–Os	21	100	no	[24]
57	Cu–Rh	– 4	0	no	[16]
58	Cu–Ta	3	100	yes	[43]
59	Cu–W	36	100	no	[24]
60	Cu–Y	–32	100	yes	[28]
61	Cu–Zr	43	95	yes	[28]
62	Er–Ni	–48	90	yes*	[25]
63	Fe–Gd	– 2	95	yes	[38]
64	Fe–Mo	– 3	65	yes*	[13]
65	Fe–Nb	–23	85	yes*	[44]
66	Fe–Nd	1	90	yes	[13]
67	Fe–Ta	–22	85	yes*	[45]
68	Fe–Tb	– 4	100	yes	[38]
69	Fe–Ti	–25	68	yes*	[46]
70	Fe–W	0	65	yes	[47]
71	Fe–Y	– 2	100	yes	[28]
72	Fe–Yb	12	100	no	[39]
73	Fe–Zr	–36	95	yes*	[40]
74	Hf–Nb	6	95	yes*	[48]
75	Hf–Ni	–62	90	yes*	[49]
76	Hf–Ta	4	75	yes*	[50]
77	Mo–Nb	– 8	0	no	[51]
78	Mo–Ni	–11	70	yes*	[25]
79	Mo–Ru	–21	30	yes	[52]
80	Mo–Y	35	–	yes*	[53]
81	Mo–Zr	– 9	95	yes*	[54]
82	Nb–Ni	–44	86	yes*	[55]
83	Nb–Zr	6	70	yes*	[56]
84	Ni–Ta	–44	65	yes*	[57]
85	Ni–Ti	–51	74	yes	[58]
86	Ni–Y	–44	100	yes	[28]
87	Ni–Yb	–29	90	yes	[39]
88	Ni–Zr	–72	95	yes*	[59]
89	Ru–Ti	–64	65	yes	[58]
90	Ru–Zr	– 6	90	yes*	[60]
91	Ta–Y	40	100	yes*	[61]
92	Ta–Zr	4	70	yes*	[62]
93	Ti–Y	22	100	yes	[28]
94	Ti–Zr	0	0	no	[51]
95	Y–Zr	14	100	yes*	[63]

– means data not available, * means amorphous phases have been obtained in several alloys.

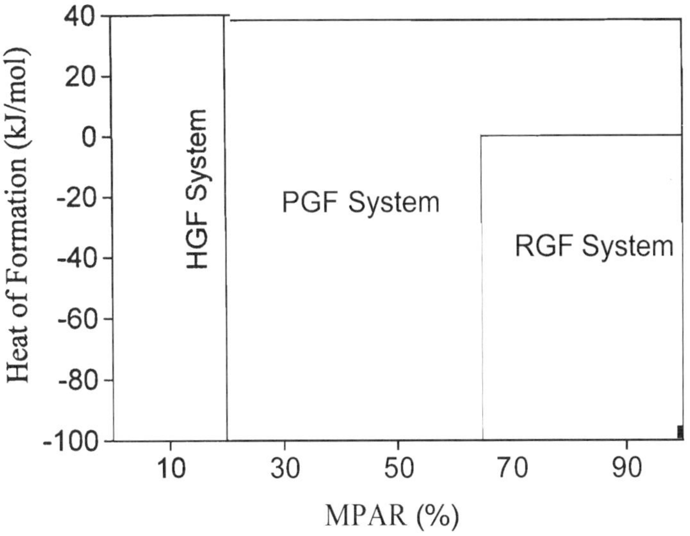

Fig. 1. According to the two parameters MPAR and heat of formation, binary metal systems are classified into three categories: readily, possibly and hardly glass forming systems (RGF, PGF and HGF, respectively)

is defined as 100% minus the maximum solid solubilities observed from the equilibrium phase diagram, and the heat of formation of the system. According to the combinations of these two parameters, binary metal systems are classified into three categories of readily, possibly and hardly glass forming systems, shown in Fig. 1. Alonso and Simozar [66] constructed a two-dimensional map to predict the glass forming ability upon ion beam mixing. The two coordinates of this map are the ratio of atomic radii r_A/r_B, and the heat of formation (ΔH_f) of an equiatomic compound, calculated by Miedema's model. This map is shown in Fig. 2. On summarizing the obtained experimental data. they separated the binary systems into amorphous and non-amorphous regions and predicted that no amorphous phase could be formed in those systems which have heats of formation exceeding +10 kJ/mol, such as the Pd–Re and Ag–Mo systems, etc. In 1990, Ossi [67] proposed an atomistic model to interpret the nucleation of amorphous or crystalline phases in several ion bombarded binary alloys and to separate glass forming from crystalline binary alloys. He suggested that it is the interatomic interactions which lead to the formation of amorphous or crystalline nuclei. This model was based on collision cascades and the related bombardment induced surface compositional changes, using

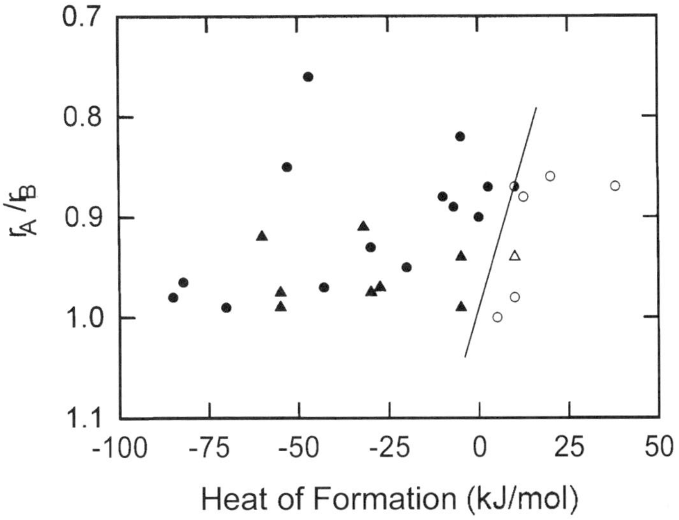

Fig. 2. Ratio of atomic radii versus heat of formation (○ metal–metal crystalline, ● metal–metal amorphous, △ metal–metalloid crystalline. ▲ metal–metalloid amorphous) (from [66])

two fundamental parameters, Φ^*, the work function of the constituent metals, and the electronic density at the boundary of the Wigner-Seitz cell.

Incidentally, in recent years, there were many reports dealing with another interesting topic concerning the influence caused by ion irradiation on the alloy phase stability and phase diagram. For this topic, the readers are referred to the published literature [68, 69].

2. Atomic Collision Process of Ion Mixing

Ion mixing is a process of atomic collisions and is commonly divided into two steps, i.e. the atomic collision cascade and the subsequent relaxation. After relaxation, the process can also be considered to last in a delayed step, which however, has no significant effect on the formed alloy phase structure. When an ion with an energy of E_1 impacts on the material surface and penetrates into depth, it collides with the atoms in the material. If an atom in the material receives an energy E_2 exceeding a threshold energy E_d, the atom will leave its own lattice site and a vacancy is created. This displaced atom is named knocked-out atom and it will, if E_2 is greater than E_d, trigger secondary collisions, then third ones, and so on and so forth. This sequence of collisions is named collision cascade. In describing atomic displacements and defect creation induced by irradiation in the materials, a parameter "dpa" is defined as the abbreviation of displacement per atom, which can be calculated through atomic collision theory,

$$\mathrm{dpa} = \frac{N_\mathrm{d}}{N_0} = \Phi\sigma_\mathrm{c} \int_{E_\mathrm{d}}^{E_2(\max)} \nu(E_2) \frac{\mathrm{d}\sigma}{\mathrm{d}E_2} \mathrm{d}E_2 \tag{1}$$

Here dpa is the displacement per atom; N_d and N_0 are the numbers of displaced atoms and total atoms, respectively; Φ is the ion flux, σ_c is the collision cross section; E_d and E_2 are the displacement threshold energy and the obtained energy of the knock-out atom, respectively; $\nu(E_2)$ is the number of displaced atoms created by the knock-out atom with an energy of E_2; $\mathrm{d}\sigma/\mathrm{d}E_2$ is the differential collision cross section at E_2.

The atomic collision cascade is responsible for the intermixing of the metals A and B deposited in multilayered form. As the energy of the ions is on the order of several 100 keV and the binding energy of the solids is of 5 to 10 eV, such atomic collision is certainly a far-from-equilibrium process. After receiving an adequate irradiation dose, the layered structure of the multilayered films is smeared out and metal A and B atoms mix uniformly and are in a highly disordered and energetic state. At the moment of termination of the cascade, the highly energetic mixture should somehow relax towards equilibrium governed by thermodynamics. However, whether the mixture can reach the equilibrium state depends on the temperature and time conditions available during the relaxation period. It is commonly recognized that the structure of the alloy phase is fixed in this step. Generally, the relaxation period is very short and the mixture cannot reach the equilibrium state in most cases. Instead, it frequently stops at some intermediate states, which correspond to either metastable crystalline or amorphous phases. In Section **3,** we calculate the free energy curves of the possible alloy phases on the basis of the thermodynamics of solids and newly developed methods to discuss the formation of alloy phases observed after relaxation of ion mixing. Viewing ion mixing in an alternative way of energy deposition by the irradiating ions into the multilayered films, a thermal spike concept was introduced on this issue. Suppose a target is irradiated by ions of an energy of 300 keV and a current density of 1 to 4 μA/cm^2 in a certain time period, a huge amount of energy would be deposited into the material surface within a very thin layer (corresponding to the range of the irradiating ions). An estimation showed that in a local region, e.g. using a cylinder geometry in the calculation, with a diameter of 50 Å diameter and a length of 1000 Å, the temperature could be as high as 10^3 to 10^4 K caused by ion beam heating and such high temperature region is referred to as thermal spike. At the same time, the surrounding material remains at ambient temperature, e.g. 300 K. According to thermal conduction calculations, the temperature relaxation time is approximately 10^{-10} to 10^{-9} s. and thus the effective cooling rate could be up to 10^{14} K/s. Therefore, the growth kinetics for the phase formation during such a short time is extremely restricted, which would certainly affect the structural characteristics of the phase to be formed.

On the other hand: the impinging ions. due to the energy loss by nuclear and electronic mechanisms, would eventually stop in the materials with a Gaussian depth distribution. which can be characterized by two parameters, i.e. the projected range *R,* and projected range straggling *AR,*. These parameters should be considered in multilayered film design and will be described in Section 4.1 in more detail.

3. Thermodynamics of Alloy Phase Formation

3.1 Miedema's theory and Alonso's method for alloy phases

Concerning phase formation and transition, the Gibbs free energy gives usually a criterion of the relative stabilities of the possible states in the systems. By comparing the Gibbs free energies of the competing phases, i.e. solid solutions, the amorphous and metastable crystalline (MX) phases, and the equilibrium compound, one can understand GFA and the observed phase evolution. In constructing a free energy diagram, the free energy curves of the alloy phases of interest can be calculated based on Miedema et al.'s model [70] and the method developed by Alonso et al.[71].

Generally, the Gibbs free energy of a phase is calculated by $AG = AH - T\,AS$, where AH and AS are the enthalpy and entropy of formation, respectively. The entropy usually plays only a secondary role in solid phase formation, and its expression can be taken. as a first approximation, as that of an ideal solid solution. i.e., $AS = -R(X_A \ln X_A + X_B \ln X_B)$, where R is the gas constant. and X_A and X_B are tlie atomic conceiitrations of metals A and B in the alloy, respectively. The enthalpy of formation, according to [72 to 74], of a substitutional solid solution of transition metals. can be considered as a sum of three contributions.

$$\Delta H = \Delta H^C + \Delta H^e + \Delta H^S\,, \tag{2}$$

where AH^C, AH^e and AH^S corresponded to chemical, elastic and structural contributions. respectively.

The chemical contribution, AH^C, which is due to the electron redistribution generated at the contact surface between dissimilar atomic cells. is described as follows [75]:

$$\Delta H^C = \Delta H_{amp} X_A V_A^{2/3} f_{AB}\,, \tag{3}$$

where V_A is the atomic volume of component A in the alloy, $AH_{,,,,}$ is an amplitude concerning the magnitude of the electron redistribution interaction and is constant for a specific metal system, f_{AB} is a function which accounts for the degree to which atoms of type A are surrounded by atoms of type B. ΔH_{amp} is given by [70]

$$\Delta H_{\mathrm{amp}}=\frac{V_{\mathrm{A}}^{2/3}}{(n_{\mathrm{WS}}^{-1/3})_{\mathrm{av}}}\left[-P(\Delta\varphi^{*})^{2}+Q(\Delta n_{\mathrm{WS}}^{1/3})^{2}\right], \tag{4}$$

where $(n_{\mathrm{WS}}^{-1/3})_{\mathrm{av}}$ is the mean value of the electron density at the boundary of the Wigner-Seitz cell as derived for the pure elements in the metallic state $(n_{\mathrm{WS}}^{-1/3})_{\mathrm{A}}$ and $(n_{\mathrm{WS}}^{-1/3})_{\mathrm{B}}$; $\Delta\varphi^{*}$ is the difference between $\varphi_{\mathrm{A}}^{*}$and φ_{B}^{*}, i.e. the work function of pure metallic elements A and B; P and Q are constants determined empirically. All the above values are obtainable from [70]. f_{AB} is given by [74]

$$f_{\mathrm{AB}}=X_{\mathrm{B}}^{\mathrm{S}}[1+\gamma(X_{\mathrm{A}}^{\mathrm{S}}X_{\mathrm{B}}^{\mathrm{S}})^{2}], \tag{5}$$

$$X_{\mathrm{B}}^{\mathrm{S}}=\frac{X_{\mathrm{B}}V_{\mathrm{B}}^{2/3}}{X_{\mathrm{A}}V_{\mathrm{A}}^{2/3}+X_{\mathrm{B}}V_{\mathrm{B}}^{2/3}}, \tag{6}$$

where y is an empirical constant which is used to describe the short-range order difference of solid solutions, amorphous phases, and ordered compounds, for which it is usually taken to be 0, 5, and 8, respectively.

The elastic contribution, AH^{e}, originates from atomic size mismatch and can be derived from the equation [76 to 79]

$$\Delta H^{\mathrm{e}}=X_{\mathrm{A}}X_{\mathrm{B}}[X_{\mathrm{A}}\,\Delta H_{(\mathrm{B\,in\,A})}^{\mathrm{e}}+X_{\mathrm{B}}\,\Delta H_{(\mathrm{A\,in\,B})}^{\mathrm{e}}], \tag{7}$$

where $\Delta H_{(\mathrm{i\,in\,j})}^{\mathrm{e}}$ is the elastic contribution to the heat of solution of i in j, which can be calculated by using the elastic constants of the constituent metals [80,81].

The structural contribution, ΔH^{S}, reflects the correlation between the number of valence (s+d) electrons and the crystal structure of transition metals. The expression for this term reads [80,81]

$$\Delta H^{\mathrm{S}}=E(Z)-X_{\mathrm{A}}E(Z_{\mathrm{A}})-X_{\mathrm{B}}E(Z_{\mathrm{B}}), \tag{8}$$

wliere $E(Z)$, $E(Z_{\mathrm{A}})$ and $E(Z_{\mathrm{B}})$ are the lattice stabilities [72,75] of the alloy phase and the pure A and B metals, and Z, Z_{A} and Z_{B} are the mean numbers of valence electrons of the alloy phase and of pure metals A and B, respectively. The dependence of the lattice stability on Z for paramagnetic transition metals in the three main crystallographic structures, i.e., b.c.c., f.c.c. and h.c.p., has been calculated by Niessen and Miedema [72]. Tlie corrections for systems including ferromagnetic metals have also been reported by these authors [75].

For the enthalpy of formation of the amorphous phase, both the elastic and the structural terms are absent. Following the suggestion by Niessen and Miedema, the enthalpy of the amorphous phase is given by [75]

$$\Delta H_{\mathrm{amorphous}}=\Delta H^{\mathrm{C}}+\alpha(X_{\mathrm{A}}T_{\mathrm{m,A}}+X_{\mathrm{B}}T_{\mathrm{m,B}}), \tag{9}$$

where α is an empirical constant equal to 3.5 J/mol K and $T_{\mathrm{m},i}$ is the melting point of the component i.

*3.2 Role of interfaces in phase forming ability in **multilayers***

It has recently been found that in the binary metal systems with positive heats of formation, the interfacial free energy in the multilayered films played an important role in

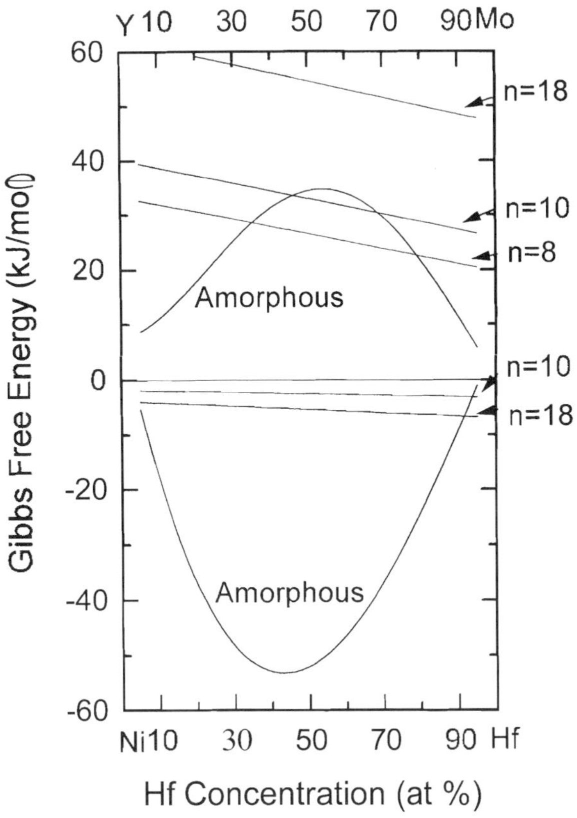

Fig. 3. Calculated free energy diagram of the Y–Mo and Ni–Hf systems, showing the different effects of interfacial free energy on positive and negative heat of formation systems. n stands for the number of interfaces in multilayers

amorphous and MX phase formation by ion mixing [17,18,48,50,53,61,82]. On the other hand, in the systems with negative heats of formation, the interfacial free energy has minor influence on the initial energetic state of the multilayers and its effect is therefore negligible. This can be illustrated by calculating the free energy curves of the amorphous phase and comparing them with tliose of multilayers in two representative systems, e.g. the Ni–Hf and Y–Mo systems with ΔH_f being **−63** and **+35** kJ/mol, respectively. Fig. 3 shows the results calculated for these systems. The details of the calculation of the interfacial free energy in the multilayers will be discussed in the next paragraph. From the figure, one sees that an increase of the number of layers or interfaces in multilayers changes significantly the initial energetic state of the films in the Y–Mo system, while in the Ni–Hf system the interface effect is minor.

The Gibbs free energy of the initial state of the A–B multilayered films was calculated by adding the interfacial free energy to the ground state of a mixture of A and B in bulk form. As pointed out by Turnbull [83], the interfacial energy between two solid phases can be split into physical and chemical contributions written as

$$\gamma_{SS}^{AB} = \gamma_{SS}^{geo} + \gamma_{SS}^{chem} . \tag{10}$$

For two solids of quite different lattice structure, the geometrical term γ_{SS}^{geo} stands for the energy of a large-angle grain boundary. It is estimated that the grain boundary enthalpy is about 30% of the surface energy at 0K [84] and the entropy contribution is neglected. Thus it is deduced

$$\gamma_{SS}^{AB} = 0.15(\gamma_A^{S,0} + \gamma_B^{S,0}) + \gamma_{SS}^{chem} , \tag{11}$$

where $\gamma_A^{S,0}$ and $\gamma_B^{S,0}$ are the surface energy of metals A and B, and γ_{SS}^{chem} is given by [85]

$$\gamma_{SS}^{chem} = \Delta H^0_{\mathrm{A\,in\,B}} / (C_0 V_A^{2/3}) , \tag{12}$$

where C_0 is a constant being 4.5 x 10^8, $\Delta H^0_{\mathrm{A\,in\,B}}$ is the heat of solution of metal A in metal B at infinite dilution [86]. According to Gerkema and Miedema [87], the interfa-

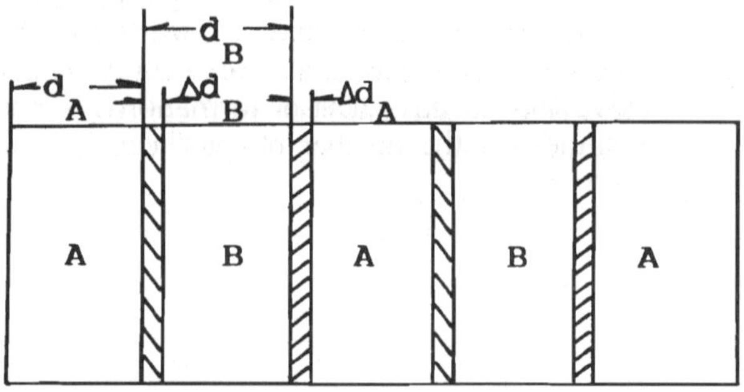

Fig. 4. Schematic configuration of A–B multilayers

cial free energy was calculated as follows:

$$\Delta G_{\text{mul}} = S_{\text{f}} \gamma_{\text{SS}}^{\text{AB}}, \tag{13}$$

where S_{f} is the surface area occupied by one mole of interfacial atoms.

Fig. 4 schematically shows the configuration of A–B multilayers. Suppose N_{A} and N_{B} are numbers of layers of metals A and B, $d_{\text{A},i}$ and $d_{\text{B},i}$ are the thicknesses of the i-th layers of metals A and B, respectively, n_{A} and n_{B} are numbers of interfaces (A on B) and (B on A), $\Delta d_{\text{A},i}$ and $\Delta d_{\text{B},i}$ are the thicknesses of the i-th interfaces (A on B) and (B on A), respectively. Obviously, the relationship $n_{\text{A}} + n_{\text{B}} + 1 = N_{\text{A}} + N_{\text{B}}$ always holds for these four parameters. The interfacial free energy for the multilayers can then be calculated by

$$\Delta G_{\text{mul}} = \alpha_{\text{A}} S_{\text{fA}} \gamma_{\text{BA}} + \alpha_{\text{B}} S_{\text{fB}} \gamma_{\text{AB}}, \tag{14}$$

where S_{fA} and S_{fB} are the surface areas occupied by one mole of atoms A and B, respectively, α_{A} and α_{B} are the fractions of interfacial atoms A and B versus the total number of atoms in the multilayered films, respectively, given by [53]

$$\alpha_{\text{A}} = X_{\text{A}} \frac{\sum_{i}^{n_{\text{A}}} \Delta d_{\text{A},i}}{\sum_{i}^{N_{\text{A}}} d_{\text{A},i}}, \qquad \alpha_{\text{B}} = X_{\text{B}} \frac{\sum_{j}^{n_{\text{B}}} \Delta d_{\text{B},j}}{\sum_{j}^{N_{\text{A}}} d_{\text{B},j}}, \tag{15}$$

where $\sum_{i}^{n_{\text{A}}} \Delta d_{\text{A},i} \Big/ \sum_{i}^{N_{\text{A}}} d_{\text{A},i}$ and $\sum_{3}^{n_{\text{B}}} \Delta d_{\text{B},j} \Big/ \sum_{j}^{N_{\text{B}}} d_{\text{B},j}$ are the fractions of interfacial A atoms versus total number of A and B atoms versus total number of B atoms, respectively. These terms multiplied by X_{A} and X_{B}, respectively, give the fractions of A and B interfacial atoms versus the total number of (A+B) atoms in the multilayers. According to published results of experimental studies of thin films [88] and for simplicity of calculation, the thickness of each interface was assumed to have the same value of 5 Å. It should be pointed out that in experimental studies one can always add extra interfaces in sample design to ensure a higher energetic state of the multilayers than that of the phase of interest, so that the effect of assuming this thickness in the calculation can be neglected.

3.3 Relevance of the constructed free energy diagram

The above calculations can give an estimate of the energetic states of the phases concerned. However, since the model of Miedema et al. [70] applied in the calculations is a

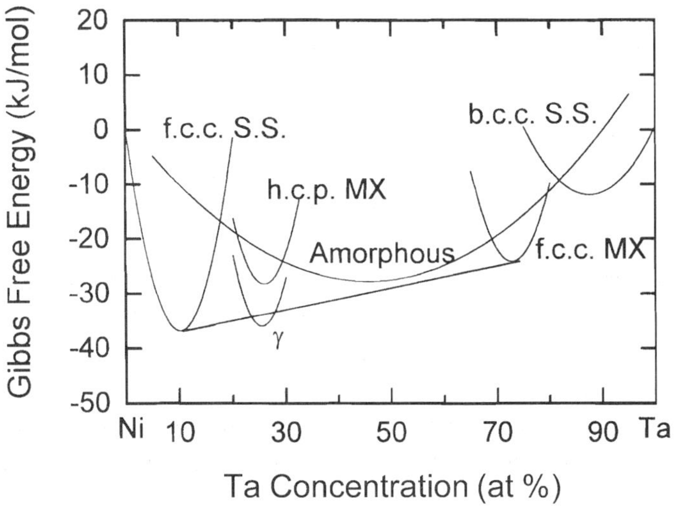

Fig. 5. Calculated free energy diagram of the Ni–Ta system

semi-empirical one, and ion mixing is a far-from-equilibrium process, one may argue that the precision of the calculation is doubtful, and thus it is not reliable to employ the calculated diagram to interpret the ion mixing results. To answer this question, a comparative experiment was suggested by the authors' group and carried out in some binary metal systems by in-situ thermal annealing in a transmission electron microscope (TEM) for as-deposited multilayers in order to observe the phase evolution sequence (see [89] as an example). So far, the tested results showed that the phase evolution sequence observed by thermal annealing was similar to that deduced from the calculated diagram, indicating the qualitative features are relevant.

Take the Ni–Ta system [57] as an example. Fig. 5 shows the calculated Gibbs free energy diagram of the system. In the diagram, besides the free energy curves of the solid solution and the amorphous phase, those of a Ni-rich h.c.p. MX phase and a Ta-rich f.c.c. MX phase were also calculated and included, because in the experiments these two MX phases were obtained by ion mixing of 200 keV xenon ions at room temperature. To testify the applicability of the calculated free energy diagram, some multilayered samples with specific compositions were selected and annealed in situ on the hot stage attached to the TEM to reveal the phase evolution sequence. The following equations show two examples of the phase evolution for alloy compositions of $Ni_{75}Ta_{25}$ and $Ni_{35}Ta_{65}$, respectively:

$$Ni_{75}Ta_{25} \xrightarrow{400\,^{\circ}C,\,60\,min} \text{amorphous} \xrightarrow{500\,^{\circ}C,\,30\,min} \text{h.c.p.} \xrightarrow{700\,^{\circ}C,\,20\,min} \text{f.c.c.} + Ni^{*}, \quad (16)$$

$$Ni_{35}Ta_{65} \xrightarrow{350\,^{\circ}C,\,30\,min} \text{f.c.c.} \xrightarrow{450\,^{\circ}C,\,60\,min} \text{amorphous} \xrightarrow{500\,^{\circ}C,\,30\,min} \text{f.c.c.} + Ni^{*}. \quad (17)$$

Here, “h.c.p.” and “f.c.c.” are the two MX phases, and "Ni*" is the Ni-rich solid solution.

In the $Ni_{75}Ta_{25}$ films, first the amorphous phase was observed after annealing at 400 °C for 1 h and then changed into the h.c.p. phase after annealing at 500 °C for 30 min. When the temperature was raised to 700 °C for 20 min, the h.c.p. MX phase transformed into a mixture of the Ni-rich solid solution and the Ta-rich f.c.c. MX phase. This phase appearance sequence upon steady state thermal annealing revealed that for the $Ni_{75}Ta_{25}$ alloy, the free energy of the amorphous phase should be higher than that of the Ni-rich h.c.p. MX phase and that of both these two phases should be higher than that of the mixture of Ni-rich solid solution and the Ta-rich f.c.c. phase. This matched quite well with what is deduced from the calculated free energy diagram, in which the energy of the mixture should be situated on the cotangent line of the two phases.

In the $Ni_{35}Ta_{65}$ films, first the f.c.c. MX phase was observed after annealing at **350** °C for **30** min and then turned amorphous at **450** °C. Further increase in temperature to **500** °C caused the transformation of the amorphous phase into a mixture of the f.c.c. MX phase plus the Ni-rich solid solution. This phase appearance sequence was also coherent with that suggested by the calculated diagram.

These annealing results confirmed the relevance of the free energy diagram calculated on the basis of Miedema's model and Alonso's method. The authors' group has performed similar annealing experiments for several other binary metal systems and the results were also in support of the calculations.

Although ion mixing, as a whole, is far from equilibrium, it is commonly divided into two steps, i.e. atomic collision cascade and relaxation period, as was stated in Section 2. The atomic collision cascade is initiated by high energy impinging ions in the materials surface layer and is essentially a non-equilibrium dynamic process, which resulted in a uniform mixture in a highly excited state. The secondary step, i.e. the relaxation period, then comes on stage during which the highly energized mixture should undergo a process towards equilibrium. In this sense, equilibrium thermodynamics should still govern the direction of the possible alloy phase formation. However, if the time and temperature conditions do not allow the mixture to go straightforward to the equilibrium state, it would instead stay on some intermediate states, resulting in the formation of either an amorphous or a metastable crystalline phase. It is therefore relevant to employ the calculated free energy diagram based on equilibrium thermodynamic methods to interpret and predict phase formation and transformation upon ion mixing.

4. Experimentation of Ion Mixing of Multilayered Films

4.1 Sample design and preparation

To design the multilayered sample, the total thickness should match the range of the irradiating ions. Inert gas ions, such as Xe, Kr, Ne, or Ar, are frequently chosen to be the irradiating ions. The advantages of employing inert gas ions are that no chemical impurity effect is involved, and that gas ion sources are always available for the common implanters. As heavy ions induce more efficient mixing than light ones when the other conditions are kept the same, Xe ions are therefore mostly used. The typical energy of the irradiating ions is several **100** keV.

It was found that uniform mixing could be well achieved, if the total thickness of the multilayered film was designed to be the projected range R_p plus the projected range straggling ΔR_p of the irradiating ions. R_p and ***AR,*** for elemental metals can be calculated easily by the LSS theory [90]. For an alloy target of A_xB_{100-x}, where refers to the atomic percentage of metal A, the projected range of the alloy can be calculated by the following equation [91]:

$$R_p(A_xB_{100-x}) = \frac{R_p(A)\,R_p(B)}{yR_p(B) + (100-x)\,R_p(A)}, \tag{18}$$

where y refers to the weight percentage of metal A in the alloy and can be obtained from x easily. The calculation of the projected range straggling ΔR_p for the alloys is rather complicated. However, considering the errors involved in the calculation itself, as well as in controlling the thickness during deposition, the above equation is good enough to estimate ΔR_p of the alloy, by substituting ΔR_p for R_p. The total thickness is divided into the thicknesses of metals A and B, according to the desired atomic ratio of the alloy being studied. The individual layers of each metal are always designed to be around 10 nm or less to obtain a good mixing efficiency. Clearly, ion mixing of multilayers designed in this way is capable of forming alloys with any required composition. The multilayered films are prepared in a vacuum system to deposit alternately the metals A and B onto an inert substrate supporting the film, e.g. SiO_2, Al_2O_3 or NaCl single crystals. The system is often a multi-crucible e-gun evaporation system with a vacuum level better than 10^{-5} Pa.

4.2 Ion mixing parameters

It was found experimentally that the dose required to homogenize a discrete layered film is in the range of 10^{14} to 10^{16} ions/cm^2 and varies from system to system. The ion beam current density should be controlled generally around 1 $\mu A/cm^2$, or at most up to 4 $\mu A/cm^2$ to avoid overheating of the multilayers during ion irradiation. In operating the implanter, the ion dose, which is measured by the electrical charge, is easy to adjust and control. Ion mixing thus offers a unique method for investigating the phase formation or transition processes step by step. For example, by irradiating the same multilayered samples with various doses, it is possible to examine the intermediate states of the phase formation or transformation, which can hardly be studied by other techniques.

Another important parameter in ion mixing is the temperature. As ion mixing often forms new metastable solid phases, ion irradiation was generally performed at low temperature, e.g. at room temperature or down to liquid nitrogen temperature. In the literature an example was reported concerning ion mixing at 4.2 K [20]. Nevertheless, the temperature mentioned for the experiments is often the nominal temperature measured at the sample holder instead of the effective temperature of the irradiated film. The effective temperature is an important parameter in the processes induced by ion irradiation, and it should be taken into account in comparison with two characteristic temperatures of the materials. One is the critical temperature T_c, below which the irradiation-enhanced diffusion effect is negligible. The other is the stable temperature of the newly formed phase, e.g., if one expects to form an amorphous alloy having a transition temperature T_{a-c} (from amorphous to crystalline), the effective temperature of the film during ion irradiation should of course be kept at a temperature far below T_{a-c}.

4.3 Characterization methods

1 to 2 MeV He ion Rutherford backscattering spectrometry (RBS) is frequently used to analyze the amount of mixing in the multilayered films. Fig. 6 and 7 show typical examples of Fe–Mo and Mo–Ru multilayers before and after ion mixing. In the Fe–Mo system, the two metals have quite different masses, while in the Mo–Ru system, the mass numbers of Mo(96) and Ru(101) are very close; resulting in the overlapping of their signals in the RBS spectra. However, by adjusting the tilt angle during the analysis to overlap the signal of the first Mo layer with that of the second Ru layer and so on, one is still able to see the initial discrete layer structure of the film, and the mixing effect by ion irradiation. In other cases, XPS, SIMS and Auger spectrometry are used to analyze the composition–depth profile of the mixed films.

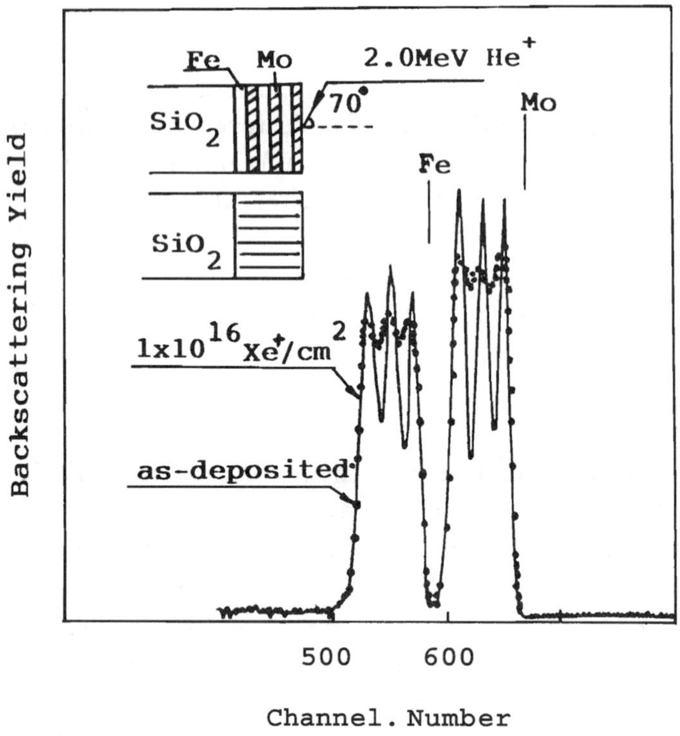

Fig. 6. Backscattering spectra of Fe–Mo multilayered films before (solid line) and after ion mixing (1×10^{16} Xe^+/cm^2 at RT)

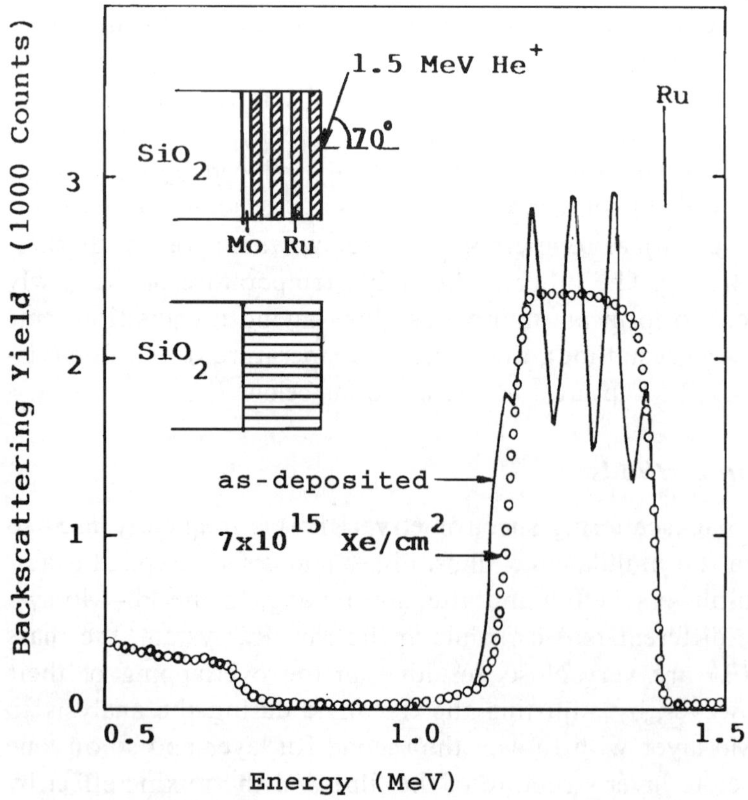

Fig. 7. Backscattering spectra of Mo–Ru multilagered films before (solid line) and after ion mixing (7×10^{15} Xe^+/cm^2 at RT)

The structure of the phase is identified mainly by X-ray diffraction and TEM. Four-point probe resistivity measurement is a supplemental method to give evidence of amorphous phase formation and transition to the crystalline state, because the resistivity of the amorphous alloys is often considerably greater than that of their crystalline counterpart.

5. Formation of Metastable Crystalline Phases

Ion beam mixing is an effective means of forming non-equilibrium or metastable alloy phases. With this method, metastable alloys which were previously not accessible can be readily produced and examined. Since the term "metastable" implies a phase with a free energy higher than that of the stable phase under the prevailing conditions of temperature and pressure, it is natural to look at thermodynamics for an explanation. Experimental results seem to indicate a strong role of thermodynamics in the tendency to form metastable phases. Intermetallic compounds with small ranges of solubility and complex crystal structures are prime candidates for transformation to a metastable phase [93]. Also, the change in the free energy of the solid due to ion induced defect build-up argues for a thermodynamic explanation [94]. However, not all transformations can be explained on a purely thermodynamic basis.

Hung and Mayer [95] provided a concise summary of the role of kinetics in metastable phase formation. They state that at low temperatures, ion mixing is similar to a quench process where the atom configurations are essentially determined during the relaxation period following the collision events. Because kinetics is restricted, the formation of complex crystalline structures is unlikely and ion mixing will usually result in solid solutions, simple cubic structures or amorphous structures. The structure of the metastable phase is, however, influenced by the equilibrium nature of the system. Those systems with many intermetallics will tend to form amorphous phases while those with no intermetallic compounds show a tendency to form solid solutions by ion mixing. At high temperature, the atomic mobility is significant and equilibrium phases will usually form.

Recently, based on substantial experimental results obtained by the authors' group, metastable crystalline phases formed by ion mixing in binary metal systems were suggested to be classified into five categories [96], that is, supersaturated solid solutions, the h.c.p.-I phases in h.c.p.- or f.c.c.-based alloys, and the newly observed f.c.c.-I phases in h.c.p.-based alloys, the h.c.p.-II and f.c.c.-II phases in b.c.c.-based alloys. Each category will be discussed in the following sections.

5.1 Solid solutions

Ion mixing of multilayered films can extend the solid solubility of binary metal alloys, and thus result in the formation of a number of supersaturated solid solutions always having the same simple crystalline structures as the major alloying metals. So far, it has been demonstrated that the solid solutions can be formed and extended to larger composition ranges not only in the systems with negative ΔH_f, but also in the systems with positive ΔH_f.

(i) Single-phase solid solutions were formed in the full composition range in the Au–Ni [30] system, which has a phase diagram of continuous solid solution type with miscibility gap in the solid state. The Ti–Zr and Mo–Nb [97] systems have similar diagrams, but no miscibility gap exists. These single-phase solid solutions were also formed by ion mixing for some arbitrarily chosen compositions, e.g. $Ti_{70}Zr_{30}$.

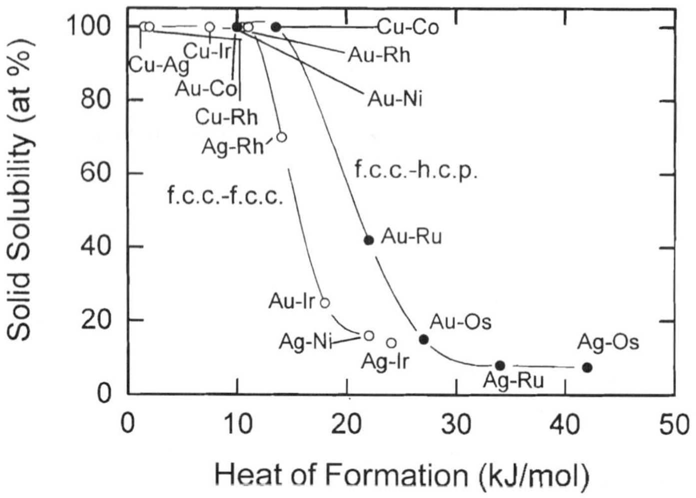

Fig. 8. Irradiation-induced solid solubilities for binary metal systems with positive heat of formation versus the heat of formation (from [16])

(ii) Single-phase solid solutions were formed in the full composition range in the simple eutectic systems Ag–Cu [98] and Au–Co [30], indicating that ion mixing is able to extend the solubility substantially in this type of phase diagram.

(iii) Two series of solid solutions with extended solubilities from both terminal metals were formed in Au–V [30], Au–Fe [30], and Fe–W [47] systems, in which intermetallic compounds divide the diagram into several sub-diagrams. That is the reason why solid solutions could not be formed throughout the full composition range.

All the above alloy phases were identified as solid solutions. Their lattice constants agreed quite well with those predicted by Vegard's law, and they were therefore substitutional solid solutions.

Tsaur and Mayer et al. have also investigated Ag–Ni [99] and Ag–Co [12] systems, in which the two metals are immiscible even in the liquid state, and hence alloys could not be formed by traditional liquid melt techniques. Ion mixing was capable of inducing mixing between the two metals and forming alloys, though the microstructure of the alloys was a two-phase mixture, each phase crystallizing in one of the structures of the metals. Recently, Peiner and Kopitzki [16] characterized ten binary metal systems with positive ΔH_f. In this study, multilayered samples of different overall compositions were bombarded at 77 K by 400 keV Kr^+ ions. For the systems Au–Ru, Cu–Ru, and Cu–Ir, whose components all have f.c.c. structures, a continuous series of single phase metastable f.c.c. solid solutions were produced by ion beam mixing. For the systems Au–Ir, Ag–Ir, and Ag–Rh, they obtained a continuous series of single phase solid solutions upon ion irradiation, and for the other systems an increased solid solubility of one component in the other was achieved. Fig. 8 [16] shows the largest solubility for each system versus ΔH_f to illustrate the influence of the magnitude of ΔH_f on the ion beam induced solid solubility. Note that the data points of the systems whose components have the same structures and of systems with components of different structure follow smooth curves. Both curves exhibit a rapid decrease from complete solubility to a solubility below 15 at% in a range of ΔH_f of about 12 kJ/mol. However, even at large values of ΔH_f, the solubility still has not disappeared. In all these systems, the lattice parameters of the solid solutions vary smoothly with composition and show small or moderate deviations from Vegard's law between the appropriate end-members.

5.2 H.c.p.-I and f.c.c.-I phases

A MX phase structurally similar to the h.c.p. structure has been formed by ion mixing in five binary (A–B) metal systems (Co–Au, Ti–Au, Co–Mo, Ni–Mo, and Ni–Nb) where A refers to the first entry in the alloy designation. The phases were formed in A-rich multilayered films with overall composition between 65 and 80 at%. The precise compositions of these phases are not known, as they were always mixed with other phases. E.g. in the Ni–Mo case, the MX phase was mixed with an amorphous phase.

These MX phases were named h.c.p.-I, since they have all about the same spacing (d_{cpp}) of the close packed planes, as shown in Table 2. Their formation was attributed to the valence electron effect. For a close packed hexagonal structure, the maximum number of electron states per atom, n, in the Jones' zone (including doubling for spin) can be calculated by the following equation [100]:

$$n = 2 - \frac{3}{4}\left(\frac{a}{c}\right)^2\left[1 - \frac{1}{4}\left(\frac{a}{c}\right)^2\right], \tag{19}$$

where a and c are the lattice constants of the h.c.p. structure. According to this calculation, the n values of these five phases are almost identical, i.e. n = 1.73 to 1.74, wliich is

Table 2

Structure data of the h.c.p.-I phase formed in five binary systems by ion mixing. These phases were considered as metastable electron compounds

system	MX phase lattice constants (A)	d_{cpp} (Å)	constituent metals lattice constants (Å)	d_{cpp} (Å)	ref.
Co–Au	h.c.p. a = 3.24 c = 5.21 c/a = 1.61	d_{002} = 2.60	Co h.c.p. a = 2.54 c = 4.07 c/a = 1.59	d_{002} = 2.023	[124]
			Au f.c.c. a = 4.08	d_{111} = 2.355	
Ti–Au	h.c.p. a = 3.27 c = 5.26 c/a = 1.61	d_{002} = 2.63	Ti h.c.p. a = 2.59 c = 4.69 c/a = 1.59	d_{002} = 2.34	[34]
			Au f.c.c. a = 4.08	d_{111} = 2.355	
Co–Mo	h.c.p. a = 3.27 c = 5.22 c/a = 1.60	d_{002} = 2.61	Co. h.c.p. a = 2.54 c = 4.07 c/a = 1.59	d_{002} = 2.023	[33]
			Mo b.c.c. a = 3.147	d_{110} = 2.225	
Ni–Mo	h.c.p. a = 3.25 c = 5.21 c/a = 1.60	d_{002} = 2.61	Ni f.c.c. a = 3.52	d_{111} = 2.034	[25]
			Mo b.c.c. a = 3.147	d_{110} = 2.225	
Ni–Nb	h.c.p. a = 3.28 c = 5.22 c/a = 1.59	d_{002} = 2.61	Ni f.c.c. a = 3.52	d_{111} = 2.034	[92]
			Nb b.c.c. a = 3.307	d_{110} = 2.33	

Table 3

F.c.c.-I MX phases formed in Co-, Y-, Zr-, and Hf-rich multilayered films by room temperature 200 keV xenon ion mixing

system and composition	mixing dose	lattice parameter (Å)
$Co_{94}Mo_6$ to $Co_{82}Mo_{18}$	3×10^{15} Xe^+/cm^2	3.55 to 3.60
$Co_{98}Ta_2$ to $Co_{80}Ta_{20}$	3×10^{15} Xe^+/cm^2	3.55 to 3.65
$Y_{73}Mo_{27}$ to $Y_{83}Mo_{17}$	7×10^{15} Xe^+/cm^2	5.10
$Y_{85}Ta_{15}$ to $Y_{75}Ta_{25}$	1×10^{15} Xe^+/cm^2	5.18
$Y_{90}Zr_{10}$ to $Y_{70}Zr_{30}$	5×10^{15} Xe^+/cm^2	4.96
$Y_{25}Zr_{75}$ to $Y_{85}Zr_{15}$	3×10^{15} Xe^+/cm^2	4.67
$Zr_{68}Nb_{32}$ to $Zr_{88}Nb_{12}$	7×10^{14} Xe^+/cm^2	4.80
$Hf_{75}Nb_{25}$ to $Hf_{90}Nb_{10}$	5×10^{14} Xe^+/cm^2	4.55

very close to the value of $7/4=1.75$, corresponding to the well-defined Hume-Rothery 7/4 electron compound. These phases can therefore be considered as metastable electron compounds [101].

Table 3 shows that MX phases of f.c.c. structure named f.c.c.-I have been formed in some h.c.p.-metal-rich multilayered films by ion mixing. From a crystallographic viewpoint, both the h.c.p. and f.c.c. structures are built by the stacking of close packed atomic planes differing only in stacking order. That is, the close packed plane of the f.c.c. structure, i.e. $(111)_{fcc}$, is quite similar in atomic arrangement to that of the h.c.p. structure, i.e., $(0002)_{hcp}$, and a sliding of atoms on the planes parallel to the $(0002)_{hcp}$ plane along $\langle 1\bar{1}00\rangle_{hcp}$ directions by a vector of $1/3\langle 1\bar{1}00\rangle_{hcp}$ can transform the h.c.p. structure into the f.c.c. structure, and its reverse procedure is the one transforming f.c.c. to h.c.p. Both slidings are fast phase transition mechanisms and can be executed in a short time available during the relaxation period of ion mixing. As described above, ion mixing starts with multilayered films of two crystalline metals as initial state, and the MX phase is the final state after ion mixing to a certain dose. The MX phases can therefore be considered to be formed through an ion irradiation induced phase transfromation by fast transition mechanisms. Take the f.c.c.-I phase formed in $Zr_{68}Nb_{32}$ multilayered films as an example, with increasing the ion dose, the original h.c.p. structure of Zr changed gradually due to the alloying of Nb atoms into Zr lattice and, at a certain dose, the h.c.p. structure transformed into a f..c.c. phase. A similar discussion is also true for the h.c.p.-I phases formed in the f.c.c. metal-based alloy films.

5.3 H.c.p.-II and f.c.c.-II phases based on b.c.c. metals

Table 4 shows that in some Nb-, Ta-, and Mo-rich multilayered films, two MX phases of h.c.p. and f.c.c. structures, respectively, were formed by ion mixing. The two MX phases were named h.c.p.-II and f.c.c.-II, respectively, in order to distinguish them from the MX phases mentioned in Section 5.2. These systems include the combinations of refractory metals with f.c.c.-structured metals Ni and Ag, h.c.p.-structured metals Co, Y, Zr, and Hf, or the b.c.c.-structured metal Fe. Some of the systems have negative ΔH_f, in which Fe, Co and Ni acted as constituents; some have positive ΔH_f, in which Ag, Y, Zr and Hf acted as constituents. The f.c.c. MX phases were formed in all these systems, while the h.c.p. MX phases were observed only in some cases.

Table 4
H.c.p.-II and f.c.c.-II MX phases formed in Nb-, Ta-, Mo-rich multilayered films by room temperature 200 keV xenon ion mixing

A–B	system and composition	h.c.p.-II	f.c.c.-II
f.c.c.–b.c.c.	$Ni_{23}Mo_{77}$	yes	yes
	$Ni_{20}Nb_{80}$	yes	yes
	$Ni_{35}Ta_{65}$	no	yes
	$Ni_{25}Ta_{75}$	no	yes
	$Ag_{24}Mo_{76}$	no	yes
	$Ag_{30}Mo_{70}$	no	yes
	$Ag_{25}Nb_{75}$	no	yes
	$Ag_{33}Nb_{67}$	no	yes
h.c.p.–b.c.c.	$Co_{20}Mo_{80}$	yes	yes
	$Co_{23}Nb_{77}$	yes	yes
	$Co_{30}Ta_{70}$	no	yes
	$Co_{25}Ta_{75}$	no	yes
	$Y_{15}Mo_{85}$	yes	yes
	$Y_{22}Mo_{78}$	yes	yes
	$Y_{27}Mo_{73}$	yes	yes
	$Y_{15}Ta_{85}$	yes	yes
	$Y_{25}Ta_{75}$	yes	yes
	$Zr_{7}Mo_{93}$	yes	yes
	$Zr_{19}Nb_{81}$	no	yes
	$Zr_{20}Ta_{80}$	no	yes
	$Zr_{26}Ta_{74}$	no	yes
	$Hf_{17}Nb_{83}$	no	yes
	$Hf_{30}Ta_{70}$	no	yes
b.c.c.–b.c.c.	$Fe_{24}Mo_{76}$	yes	yes
	$Fe_{20}Nb_{80}$	yes	yes
	$Fe_{20}Ta_{80}$	no	yes

It is more difficult to understand crystallographically the transformation from b.c.c. to f.c.c. structure. Some carefully performed experiments revealed that the h.c.p.-II phase was formed as an intermediate state of the formation of the f.c.c.-II phase. Thus a two-step transition of b.c.c. → h.c.p. → f.c.c. was proposed, a so-called reverse martensitic transformation. That is first to transform b.c.c. to h.c.p. through a shearing mechanism. During shearing, the $(111)_{bcc}$ acted as the habit plane, while $[\bar{1}1\bar{1}]_{bcc}$ (or $[110]_{hcp}$) acted as the shear axis [102]. Then the transformation of h.c.p. into f.c.c is easy to achieve by a sliding of atoms on the planes parallel to the $(0002)_{hcp}$ plane along $\langle 1\bar{1}00\rangle_{hcp}$ directions by a vector of $1/3\langle 1\bar{1}00\rangle_{hcp}$. Although the relaxation period of ion mixing is very limited, it is thought that it could meet the requirements of a shearing mechanism. The lattice parameters of h.c.p.-II and f.c.c.-II phases were deduced according to the two-step transition, which were in good agreement with the experimental results [103].

6. Formation of Amorphous Alloys

It is well known that aniorplious materials have in many respects unique properties, such as high strength, excellent corrosion resistance, good barrier properties against diffusion, etc. Since the first amorphous alloy was synthesized in a Au–Si system, a large number of researchers endeavored to develop new manufacturing techniques and to seek

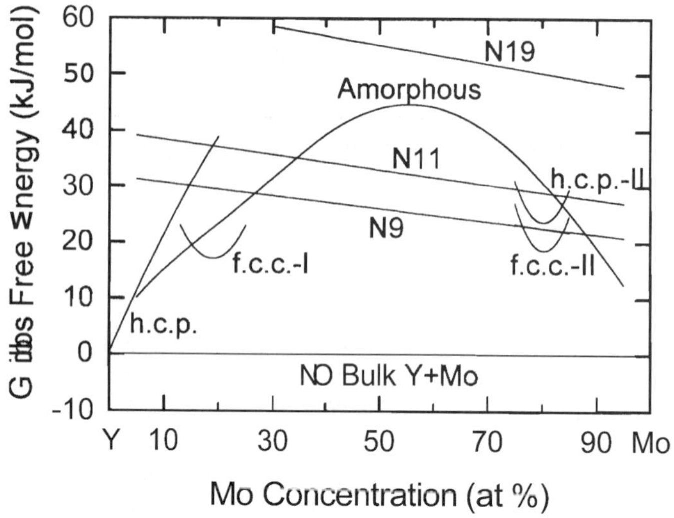

Fig. 9. Calculated free energy diagram of the Y–Mo system. *N* stands for the number of layers in multilayered films

the possibility of producing new amorphous materials, as well as to promote the understanding of the amorphization mechanism. In this field, ion mixing of multilayers has long been established as a valuable means because of its extremely high effective cooling rates. It is commonly accepted that amorphous alloys are relatively easy to form near deep eutectic compositions. In this case, there is no doubt that negative ΔH_f of the system studied should be a prerequisite. Negative ΔH_f usually makes it possible that the amorphous phases have lower free energy than a mixture of the two crystalline metals, and thus serves as a thermodynamic driving force for amorphization. Therefore, much effort has been exerted on such systems and a large number of amorphous alloys have been formed by ion mixing of multilayers. However, to form amorphous alloys in systems with positive ΔH_f seemed relatively difficult and some experiments failed. Therefore, it has been commonly recognized that the sign of ΔH_f has considerable effect on the amorphization behavior and even dooms the failure of amorphization in some systems with large positive ΔH_f. However, some amorphous alloys were indeed obtained, e.g. in Cu–Fe [42], Nb–Zr [56] systems, and the composition favoring amorphization was found to locate within narrow regions. These results stimulated a further study to re-examine the phase formation upon ion mixing in the positive ΔH_f systems. Recently, it was reported that a number of amorphous alloys have been obtained in some ten systems with positive ΔH_f ranging from nearly zero to +56 kJ/mol. An interesting feature of these systems was that the amorphous alloys were formed frequently in restricted composition regions close to the constituent metal ends instead of in the middle part of the phase diagrams. This is quite different from what is formed in the negative ΔH_f systems in which the alloys with compositions in the vicinity of equiatomic stoichiometry were usually the most favorable ones for amorphization. This difference drew attention towards the initial energetic state of multilayers, which could be increased by excess interfacial free energy in positive multilayer systems, with respect to that of a mixture of the constituent metals in bulk form. Fig. 9 shows a calculated free energy diagram of the Y–Mo system including free energy curves of the amorphous phase and the as-deposited multilayered films with different layers. It indicates that these two energy curves are very likely to intersect each other. This case makes the free energy of multilayers higher than that of the amorphous phase in the two discrete composition regions close to either constituent. On the other hand, in the intermediate composition region, the free energy of the amorphous phase is higher. Additionally, taking into account the competition with the formation of supersaturated solid solutions, the composition range thermodynamically favorable for amorphization becomes very narrow. Naturally, it can be deduced that amorphization could be achieved also at the equiatomic alloy compositions if adequate interfaces would be included in multilayers while keeping the total thickness unchanged (see Section 3.2). This indeed has been verified in some positive systems such as Y–Mo, Zr–Ta, Hf–Ta and will be presented in detail in the following section.

6.1 Glass forming ability of the negative heat of formation systems

So far, extensive ion mixing data have been accumulated for the systems with negative ΔH_f. Since 1983, when Liu et al. [64] proposed the structural difference rule, a lot of work concerning the GFA both experimentally and thermodynamically has made this issue rather simple, that is, one is capable of predicting GFA or even GFR approximately by inspecting the equilibrium phase diagram. Fig. 10 is a typical example of the equilibrium phase diagram of the Ni–Nb system with negative ΔH_f. The diagram is composed of terminal solid solution regions, intermetallic compound regions and two-phase regions. The two-phase regions commonly exist even if the two constituent metals have the same crystalline structures, as long as there exist intermetallic compounds. Substantial data confirmed that an amorphous alloy is most likely to be formed by ion mixing in these two-phase regions and thus the structural difference rule was extended to the two-phase competition rule. The two competing phases here refer to two adjacent phases, not necessarily the terminal ones. The easy formation of an amorphous alloy in the two-phase regions can be attributed to the competition of crystallization between the two crystalline phases, resultiiig in a frustration of nucleation and growth of either crystalline phase during the very limited relaxation period. Besides, it is also very probable to form amorphous alloys in (or in the vicinity of) intermetallic compounds with complicated structures, as the growth kinetic conditions during the ion mixing process only allow simple structured phases to crystallize.

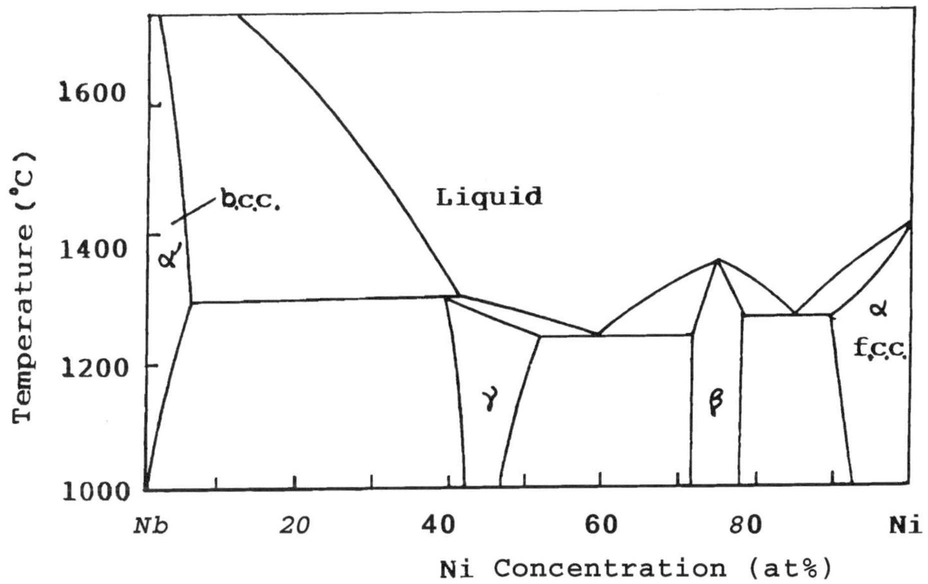

Fig. 10. Equilibrium phase diagram of the Ni–Nb system

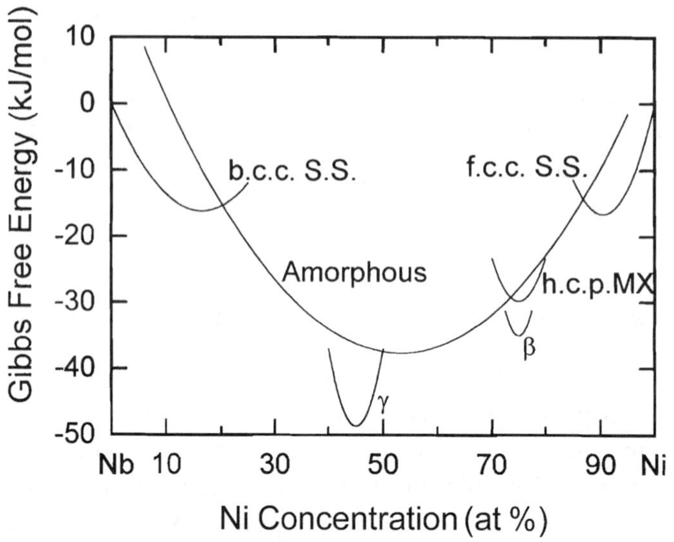

Fig. 11. Calculated free energy diagram of the Ni–Nb system

There are three points worth mentioning.

(i) The two-phase competition rule includes, and is more general than, the well-known deep eutectic criterion for forming metallic glasses by liquid melt quenching. The eutectic portion is only a special type of two-phase region of the equilibrium phase diagram. Moreover, the rule applies to the eutectic portion, yet is not restricted to "deep" eutectic ones. For example, liquid quenching has not succeeded in producing an amorphous Mo–Ru alloy at eutectic composition, as the melting point of the alloy is as high as 1900 °C [104], while room temperature (RT) ion mixing is able to make the alloy amorphous [105].

(ii) It is noticed that the transition temperatures of most of the amorphous alloys obtained by RT ion mixing are higher than 400 °C, while some amorphous alloys, e.g. $Au_{25}Co_{75}$, having a T_{a-c} about 200 °C could only be formed by ion mixing at liquid nitrogen (LN_2) temperature. This probably has to do with the effective temperature rise of the multilayered film caused by ion irradiation: a typical current density of 5 $\mu A/cm^2$ may cause a temperature rise of about 200 K. Consequently, those amorphous alloys having a T_{a-c} considerably higher than 200 °C could be formed by RT ion mixing, while

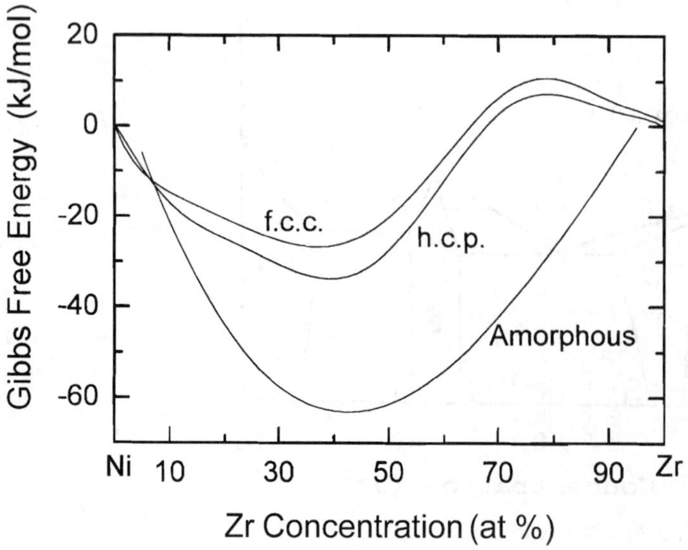

Fig. 12. Calculated free energy diagram of the Ni–Zr system

those amorphous alloys with T_{a-c} lower than 200 °C are only obtainable by low temperature ion mixing.

(iii) In most cases, amorphous alloys with compositions near the terminal solid solubilities cannot be formed because of the extension of the solid solubilities induced by ion mixing. Therefore, the GFR is usually smaller than MPAR.

In addition to judging GFA from equilibrium phase diagrams, a great effort has also been made to interpret phase evolution thermodynamically. According to the thermodynamic calculation, a free energy diagram typical for the systems with negative ΔH_f, is that of the Ni–Nb system shown in Fig. 11. One sees from the figure that the free energy curves of all the alloy phases are concave, including the amorphous phase, two ternzinal solid solution phases. equilibrium intermetallic compounds and MX phases. By comparing the free energy of the amorphous phase with that of other phases, it is possible to predict GFA and GFR. As the formation of intermetallic compounds is usually hindered kinetically, they need not be taken into account when discussing GFA even if they have lower free energy. Thus the amorphous phase is thermodynamically most favored to be formed near the equiatomic stoichiometry where its free energy curve reaches the nadir and is lower than those of two terminal solid solutions. The GFR was commoizly regarded as the conzposition range in which the free energy of the amorphous phase was below that of the solid solutions. One sees from Fig. 11 and 12 that according to the above definition. the GFR in Ni–Nb and Ni–Zr systems was from 20 to 85 at% Ni and from 10 to 90 at% Zr, respectively. The experimentally determined GFA of these systems matched well with the thermodynamic calculations, i.e. 20 to 85 at% Ni for the Ni–Nb system [55] and 10 to 80 at% Zr for the Ni–Zr system [59].

6.2 Glass forming ability of the positive heat of formation systems

Recently, some positive ΔH_f systems have been investigated by ion mixing of multilayered films and it was found that amorphization could be achieved in these systems even though the ΔH_f exceeded \$10 kJ/mol [17,53,61]. The composition range favoring amorphization was found to be discontinuous and amorphous alloys were rarely obtained near equiatomic compositions like in the negative ΔH_f systems. The amorphization behavior in the positive ΔH_f systems was attributed to the excess interfacial free energy stored in the as-deposited multilayered films.

In terms of thermodynamics, the driving force controlling alloy formation originates from the difference of the Gibbs free energy between the initial and final states. For the binary nzetal A–B system with a positive ΔH_f, as the free energy of the amorphous state was usually higher than that of a mixture of the crystalline metals A and B in bulk form, i.e.. the free energy curve of the amorphous phase was usually convex, amorphization was not obtainable through traditional techniques like liquid melt quenching. However, as the interfaces in multilayered films are generally regarded as transient layers of mixed A and B atoms, they increase the free energy of the films, making amorphization thermodynamically possible first in the composition regimes close to the constituent metal ends. By increasing the fraction of interfacial atoms, i.e. by including more interfaces in the films, it was possible to extend the amorphization compositions up to equiatonzic stoichiometry [96]. Accordingly, no nzatter how large the positive ΔH_f of a system was, it was possible to produce amorphous alloys by ion mixing of multilayers.

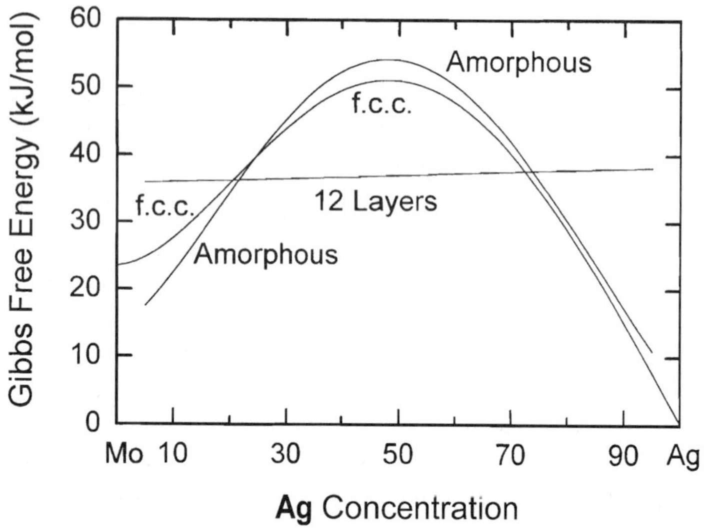

Fig. 13. Calculated free energy diagram of the Ag–hlo system

6.2.1 Amorphous alloys formed at restricted compositions

Fig. 13 shows a calculated free energy diagram of the Ag–Mo system [17] which has an extremely large equiatomic positive ΔH_f of +56 kJ/mol. The diagram includes the free energy curves of the amorphous phase and the as-deposited multilayered films containing twelve layers (or eleven interfaces), respectively. As observed from Fig. 13, the shape of the free energy curve of the amorphous phase is convex, typical of positive ΔH_f systems. The free energy curve for the multilayered films intersects that of the amorphous phase, dividing the diagram into three portions along the composition axis. In portion I and III, the free energy of multilayers is above that of the amorphous phase, suggesting that the alloys with compositions within those regions could be amorphized, while in portion II, i.e. the middle portion, the free energy of multilayers is lower than that of the amorphous phase, suggesting that the alloys with compositions in this region can hardly be amorphized. In ion mixing of the Ag–Mo system by 200 keV xenon ions at LN_2 temperature, amorphous alloys were obtained uniformly around 80 at% Mo and found to coexist with a Mo-based f.c.c. MX phase around 40 at% Mo. In some other systems like Nb–Zr [56], Y–Mo [53] and Y–Ta [61] with ΔH_f, the discontinuity of the composition range favoring amorphization was also observed. In fact, if one takes into account the competition between solid solubility and amorphization, it is obvious that the composition range where amorphization is favored may become so restricted, that it can easily be missed in experiments.

6.2.2 Amorphous alloys formed in broad composition ranges

As mentioned above, when increasing the fraction of interfacial atoms versus the total number of atoms in the multilayered films, the two isolated composition ranges favouring amorphization may become broader and approach the mid-composition. In the Zr–Ta and Hf–Ta systems, both with ΔH_f of +4 kJ/mol, the amorphous phase was obtained in very broad composition ranges excluding only compositions very close to the pure constituents which were suitable for the formation of solid solutions. As these two systems have only small positive ΔH_f, this has been achieved in multilayers including not more than ten layers. However, in the Y–Mo system, which has a positive ΔH_f of

Table 5
Prediction and experimental results of amorphous alloys formation in the Y–Mo multilayered films upon 200 keV xenon ion mixing at room temperature

layer number	9		11		19	
fraction *(a)*	8.1 at%		10.0 at%		18.1 at%	
composition	predicted	ion mixing	predicted	ion mixing	predicted	ion mixing
$Y_{80}Mo_{20}$	yea	yea	yes	yes	yes	yes
$Y_{60}Mo_{40}$	no	no	yes	yes	yes	yes
$Y_{50}Mo_{50}$	no	no	no	no	yes	yes
$Y_{40}Mo_{60}$	no	no	no	no	yes	yes
$Y_{20}Mo_{80}$	yes	yes	yes	yes	yes	yes

+35 kJ/mol, it was not so easy. Fig. 9 shows the calculated free energy diagram for the Y–Mo system, including the free energy curves of the amorphous phase and three multilayered films with different layer numbers of 9, 11 and 19, corresponding to interfacial atom fractions of 8.1, 10.0, and 18.1 at%, respectively. Table 5 lists the predicted composition ranges favoring amorphization for the three different cases. The Y–Mo multilayered films were prepared accordingly for the ion mixing investigation. The experimental results are in excellent agreement with the prediction and are also included in Table 5. These results suggested that through appropriate interface design, one is able to produce amorphous alloys in such positive ΔH_f systems even with a composition near the equiatomic stoichiometry, which has been considered to be the most difficult one to be amorphized.

7. Interface-Generated Solid State Vitrification in Immiscible Systems

From 1983 on [106], amorphous metallic alloys have been produced by solid-state reactions (SSR) between pairs of metals. Although most of the binary metallic systems that form amorphous alloys by the rapid quenching (RQ) method can also form amorphous alloys by the SSR method, the GFR of the two methods is sharply different. Unlike the GFR for the RQ method, the GFR for the SSR method is continuous in composition [29]. Recently, it has been found that amorphous alloys could be formed in many binary-metal systems by SSR in multilayers. Although it is easier to form amorphous alloys by ion mixing of multilayers, it is difficult to obtain thick amorphous films due to the limitation of the projected range of the irradiated ions. However, SSR is promising in this respect, because the multilayers can be deposited thick enough to meet any requirement as long as the spontaneous vitrification can take place between pairs of metals.

The observation of Schwarz and Johnson [106] that SSR of thin film multilayers of two different crystalline metals (La and Au) can lead to the formation of an amorphous alloy has significantly increased the interest in this amorphization process. From then on, it has been found that there exist a series of systems, mostly on the basis of one early transition metal, e.g. Zr, Hf, La, and one of the late transition metals, e.g. Cu, Co,

Table 6

Prediction and experimental results of amorphous alloy formation upon solid state reaction in the Y–Mo multilayered films. *a* is the fraction of the interfacial atoms (– stands for not checked conditions)

layer number	9		11		19	
fraction (*a*)	8.1 at%		10.0 at%		18.1at%	
composition	predicted	ion mixing	predicted	ion mixing	predicted	ion mixing
$Y_{80}Mo_{20}$	yes	yes	yes	yes	yes	–
$Y_{60}Mo_{40}$	no	no	yes	yes	yes	yes
$Y_{50}Mo_{50}$	no	no	no	no	yes	yes
$Y_{40}Mo_{60}$	no	no	no	no	yes	yes
$Y_{20}Mo_{80}$	yes	yes	yes	yes	yes	–

Ni, Fe, Au, in which the amorphous state is attainable via solid state reactions [107]. Johnson [108] listed 14 binary systems which had been found to exhibit glass formation and growth in thin film diffusion couples. Systems based on Zr and Hf have the advantage of a higher glass transition temperature and are less susceptible to oxidation than the La–Au system. This is why these systems have received most attention in various aspects in the past few years [109 to 120]. Additionally, the authors have found that in some other binary metal systems, amorphization could also be achieved by SSR. These include (Fe, Co, Ni)–(Nb, Mo, Ta) [44], Hf–Ta [50], Y–Mo [89], Au–Ta [121] and Cu–Ta [122] systems.

According to Schwarz and Johnson and other reports, spontaneous vitrification is expected to take place in metal systems featuring two characteristics [123]: 1. a rather negative heat of formation calculated by Miedema's model and 2. one metal diffusing anomalously fast in its partner, but not vice versa. It has been understood that the negative heat of formation results in a free energy of the amorphous phase that is lower than that of a mixture of two crystalline phases of the constituent metals, and thus provides the necessary thermodynamic driving force for the vitrification upon heating. Kinetically, the diffusional asymmetry, closely related to a large atomic size mismatch between the two constituent metals, prohibits the formation of intermetallic compounds as possible competing phases hindering amorphization. According to the above argument, spontaneous vitrificatioii is naturally regarded impossible in a system with positive ΔH_f. However, the authors recently found that spontaneous vitrification could also take place in the systems with positive ΔH_f, and in some cases, the positive ΔH_f could even be fairly large.

The Y–Mo multilayered films ($\Delta H_f = +35$ kJ/mol) including 9, 11 and 19 layers, were annealed in-situ in a hot stage attached to a TEM [89]. The experimental results are listed in Table 6. One sees that for the multilayered films with nine layers, it was found that only two multilayered films, i.e. $Y_{80}Mo_{20}$ and $Y_{20}Mo_{80}$, became amorphous after annealing at 250 °C for 1.5 h. With eleven layers, amorphization was achieved in the $Y_{80}Mo_{20}$, $Y_{60}Mo_{40}$ and $Y_{20}Mo_{80}$ multilayered films under similar annealing conditions. It was of importance that when there were 19 layers, $Y_{50}Mo_{50}$ the films transformed into the amorphous state after a 2 h anneal at 350 °C. The free energy of the

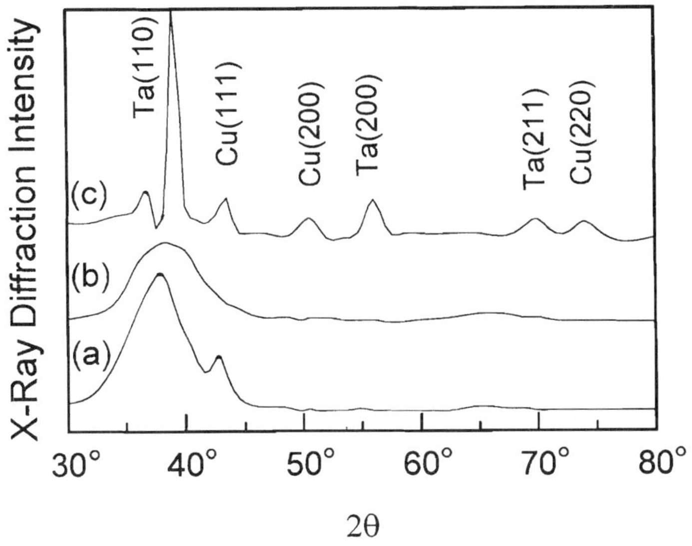

Fig. 14. X-ray diffraction patterns of [Ta(3.6 nm)/Cu(0.9 nm)]$_{170}$ multilayers. (a) As-deposited, (b) annealed at 450 °C, (c) recrystallized after annealing at 650 °C

amorphous state in such systems of rather large positive ΔH_f has the highest value around equiatomic stoichiometry and thus amorphization is most difficult to be obtained. Two other samples also with 19 layers, i.e. $Y_{40}Mo_{60}$ and $Y_{60}Mo_{40}$ multilayered films, were prepared and subjected to thermal annealing and they both transformed into the amorphous state after annealing at 400 °C for 2 h. These results strongly support the thermodynamic calculation results shown in Fig. 9.

In addition, amorphization was also achieved by SSR in the Hf–Ta [50] and Cu–Ta [122] systems with positive ΔH_f of +4 and +3 kJ/mol, respectively. Furthermore, Cu–Ta multilayered films with total thickness of 0.3 and 0.8 μm, respectively, were prepared and studied. The overall composition of the films was $Cu_{28}Ta_{72}$, which was previously confirmed to favor amorphization both by ion mixing and SSR in films around 40 nm thick. The thickness of individual layers was down to the nanometer scale and thus the films contained 67 and 170 Ta–Cu bilayers, respectively. As-deposited films were then annealed in an annealing furnace at 400 to 450 °C for 30 min and the microstructure changes were analyzed by X-ray diffraction. Fig. 14, curve a presents an X-ray diffraction pattern of the as-deposited [Ta(3.6 nm)/Cu(0.9 nm)]$_{170}$ film showing the presence of elemental Ta and Cu. The peaks were apparently broadened due to the small layer thicknesses. Fig. 14, curve b is the diffraction pattern of the sample after annealing at 450 °C. It exhibits a pattern typical of an amorphous alloy. Fig. 14, curve c shows the diffraction pattern of the same film after recrystallization at 650 °C, indicating the transformation back to Ta and Cu. The use of multilayers is apparently effective in forming relatively thick amorphous alloy films.

So far, most spontaneous vitrification has been observed in the binary systems in which the two constituent metals are very different in atomic size. Thus large atomic size mismatch was once believed necessary for the amorphization by SSR. To testify whether it is a decisive prerequisite, the Au–Ta system [121] was selected as the atomic radius ratio and the volume ratio between Au and Ta are nearly equal to unity, i.e. 1.008 and 0.936, respectively. Besides, the Au–Ta system has a negative heat of formation of −49 kJ/mol. When the $Au_{23}Ta_{77}$ multilayers were heated up continuously at a rate of 5 K/min to 200 °C, partial amorphization was observed. After staying at 200 °C for 30 min, the annealing temperature was further elevated to 350 °C and kept for

30 min. The structure of the film turned completely into amorphous state. When the temperature was raised to about 650 °C and kept for 20 min, diffraction lines emerged again, indicating the recrystallization of the $Au_{23}Ta_{77}$ amorphous alloy. The experimental results revealed that, when the Ta concentration in the films was lower than 60 at%, no amorphous phase was formed by a similar annealing process. These results suggested that the composition range favouring spontaneous vitrification in the Au–Ta system was relatively narrow and located around the composition of $Au_{23}Ta_{77}$.

8. Concluding Remarks

In the past 15 years, ion mixing of niultilayers has provided extensive data, which contributed significantly to the theory of alloy phases in the field of physical metallurgy, as ion mixing has so far formed a great number of new metastable crystalline and amorphous alloy phases, among which numerous alloys are not accessible by other techniques. Miedema's theory was employed for free energy calculation and steady-state thermal annealing results showed that the calculated energetic sequence of the phases was relevant, at least in its outline. Based on the calculation and by taking into account the interfacial free energy in the multilayers, a unified thermodynamic model was established for the metastable phase formation upon ion mixing in binary metal systems with both negative and positive heats of formation. Due to the restricted conditions in ion mixing for crystalline phases to grow, only simple structured phases can be obtained and the growth kinetics were revealed to be closely connected with the crystallographic characteristics of the newly formed phases and the matrix.

Acknowledgements The authors are grateful to many of their colleagues at Tsinghua University for their continuous contributions and encouragement in writing this review. Special thanks are given to Dr. Z.J. Zliang, Dr. F. Pan and Mr. Y.G. Chen. It should be mentioned as well the contributions made by many previous students who have ever worked in the authors' group during the past ten years. The financial support to this study by National Natural Science Foundation of China and the Administration of Tsinghua University are greatly appreciated.

References

[1] See, e. g., S.T. PICRAUX, in: Applications of Ion Beam to Materials, Ed. G. CARTER, J.S. COLLIGON, and W.A. GRANT, Inst. Phys., London 1975 (p. 183).
[2] See, e. g., C.M. PREECE and J.K. HIRVONEX (Ed.), Jon Implantation Metallurgy, MS AIME, New York 1979.
[3] P. DUWEZ, R.H. WILLENS, and W. KLEMENT, J. Appl. Phys. **31,** 1136 (1960).
[4] H.A. DAVIES, in: Amorphous Metallic Alloys, Ed. F.E. LUBORSKY, Butterworths, London 1983 (p.13).
[5] J. HAFNER, in: Metallic Glasses, Ed. H.-J. GUENTHERODT and H. BECK, Springer-Verlag, Berlin 1981 (p. 93).
[6] B.S. GIESSEN and S.H. WHANG, J. Phys. C **8,** 95 (1980).
[7] F. SOMMER, Z. Metallk. **72,** 219 (1981).
[8] W. KLEMENT, H. WILLENS, and P. DUWEZ, Nature **187,** 869 (1960).
[9] S. TAKAYAMA, J. Mater. Sci. **11,** 164 (1976).
[10] M.V. ALLMEN, in: Laser-Beam Interaction with Materials, Ed. J. CARL, Washington Internat.Soc. Optical Engineering, Washington D.C. 1983 (p. 140).
[11] C.J. LIN and F. SPAEPEN, in: Rapidly Solidified Metastable Materials, Ed. B.H. KEAR and B.C. GIESSEN, North-Holland Publ. Co., Amsterdam 1984.

[12] J.W. MAYER, B.Y. TSAUR, S.S. LAU, and L.S. HUNG, Nuclear Instrum. and Methods **182/183,** 1 (1981).
[13] B.X. LIU, E. MA, J. LI, and L.J. HUANG, in: Proc. 5th Internat. Conf. IBMM, 1986; Nuclear Instrum. and Methods B **19/20,** 682 (1987).
[14] B.X. LIU, L.J. HUANG, J. LI, and E. MA, in: Thin Films – Interfaces and Phenomena, MRS Symp. Proc., Vol. 54, Ed. R.J.NEMANICH, P.S. HO, and S.S. LAU, North-Holland Publ. Co., Amsterdam 1986 (p. 215).
[15] U.A. ANDERSEN, J. BÖTTIGER, and K. DYRBYE, Nuclear Instrum. and Methods B **51,** 125 (1990).
[16] E. PEINER and K. KOPITZKI, Nuclear. Instrum. and Methods B **34,** 173 (1988).
[17] O. JIN, Z.J. ZHANG, and B.X. LIU, Appl. Phys. Lett. **67,** 1524 (1995).
[18] O. JIN and B.X. LIU, Nuclear Instrum. and Methods B **114,** 56 (1996).
[19] W. HILLER, M. BUCHGEISTER, P. EITNER, K. KOPITZKI, V. LILIENTHAL, and E. PEINER, Mater. Sci. Engng. A **115,** 151 (1989).
[20] A. SCHMID and P. ZIEMANN, Nuclear Instrum. and Methods B **7/8,** 581 (1985).
[21] L.S. HUNG and J.W. MAYER, Nuclear Instrum. and Methods B **7/8,** 657 (1985).
[22] B. RAUSCHENBACH and K. HOHMUTH, Nuclear Instrum. and Methods B **23,** 323 (1987).
[23] J.A. KNAPP and D.M. FOLLSTAEDT, see [13]; Nuclear Instrum. and Methods B **19/20,** 611 (1987).
[24] J. MEISSNER, K. KOPITZKI, G. MERTLER, and E. PEINER, see [13]; Nuclear Instrum. and Methods B **19/20,** 669 (1987).
[25] B.X. LIU, W.L. JOHNSON, M.A. NICOLET, and S.S. LAU, Nuclear Instrum. and Methods **209/210,** 229 (1983).
[26] L.S. HUNG, M. NASTASI, J. GYULAI, and J.W. MAYER, Appl. Phys. Lett. **42,** 672 (1983).
[27] G.A. CHENG, Thesis, Tsinghua University, 1986.
[28] B.X. LIU, D.Z. CHE, Z.J. ZHANG, S.L. LAI, and J.R. DING, phys. stat. sol. (a) **128,** 345 (1991).
[29] J.R. DING, D.Z. CHE, H.B. ZHANG, K. TAO, and B.X. LIU, Appl. Phys. Lett. **60,** 944 (1992).
[30] B.Y. TSAUR, S.S. LAU, L.S. HUNG, and J.W. MAYER, Nuclear Instrum. and Methods **182/183,** 67 (1981).
[31] B. RAUSCHENBACH, Appl. Phys. A **40,** 47 (1986).
[32] F. PAN and B.X. LIU, J. Phys.: Condensed Matter **8,** 383 (1995).
[33] F. PAN, Y.G. CHEN, Z.J. ZHANG, and B.X. LIU, J. non-crystall. Solids **194,** 305 (1996).
[34] B.X. LIU, M.-A. NICOLET, and S.S. LAU, phys. stat. sol. (a) **73,** 183 (1982).
[35] Z.H. YAN, B.X. LIU, and H.D. LI, phys. stat. sol. (a) **94,** 483 (1986).
[36] Z.J. ZHANG and B.X. LIU, J. Phys.: Condensed Matter **6,** 2647 (1994).
[37] Z.J. ZHANG and B.X. LIU, J. Phys.: Condensed. Matter **6,** 9065 (1994).
[38] Z.H. YAN, B.X. LIU, and H.D. LI, see [13]; Nuclear Instrum. and Methods B **19/20,** 700 (1987).
[39] B.X. LIU, J.R. DING, H.B. ZHANG, and D.Z. CHE, phys. stat. sol. (a) **128.** 103 (1991).
[40] J. BØTTIGER, K. PAMPUS, and B. TORP, see [13]; Nuclear Instrum. and Methods B **19/20,** 696 (1987).
[41] S.M. SHIN, M.S. RAY, J.M. RIGSBEE, and J.E. GREENE, Appl. Phys. Lett. **43,** 249 (1983).
[42] L.J. HUANG and B.X. LIU, Nuclear Instrum. and Methods B **18,** 256 (1987).
[43] B.Y. TSAUR, Thesis, California Institute of Technology, 1980.
[44] Z.J. ZHANG, PhD Thesis, Tsinghua University (1995).
[45] Z.J. ZHANG, ibid.
[46] R. BRENIER, P. THEVENARD, T. CAPRA, A. PEREZ, M. TREILLEUX, L. ROMANA, J. DUPUY, and M. BRUNEL, see [13]; Nuclear Instrum. and Methods B **19/20,** 691 (1987).
[47] G. GOLTZ, R. FERNANDEZ, M.A. NICOLET, and D.K. SADANA, in: Metastable Materials Formation by Ion Implantation, MRS Symp. Proc., Vol. 7, Ed. S.T. PICRAUX and W.J. CHOYKE, North-Holland Publ. Co., Amsterdam 1982 (p. 227).
[48] O. JIN, Y. YE, and B.X. LIU, J. Phys.: Condensed Matter **7,** 7959 (1995).
[49] M. VAN ROSSUM, U. SHRETER, W.L. JOHNSON, and M.A. NICOLET, in: Proc. MRS Fall Meeting, Boston 1983.
[50] B.X. LIU, O. JIN, and Y. YE, J. Phys.: Condensed Matter **8,** L79 (1996).

[51] B.X. LIU, California Institute of Technology, 1982, unpublished.
[52] B.X. LIU, B.M. CLEMENS, R. GABORIAUD, W.L. JOHNSON, and M.A. NICOLET, Appl. Phys. Lett. 42, 624 (1983).
[53] Z.J. ZHANG, O. JIN, and B.X. LIU, Phys. Rev. B 51, 8076 (1995).
[54] 0. JIN and B.X. LIU, J. Phys.: Condensed Matter 7, 2667 (1995).
[55] Z.J. ZHANG, H.Y. BAI, Q.L. QIU, T. YANG, K. TAO, and B.X. LIU, J. Appl. Phys. 73, 1702 (1993).
[56] O. JIN and B.X. LIU, J. Phys.: Condensed Matter 6, L39 (1994).
[57] B.X. LIU and Z.J. ZHANG, Phys. Rev. B 49, 12519 (1994).
[58] Y.T. CHENG, W.L. JOHNSON, and M.A. NICOLET, in: Proc. MRS Fall Meeting, Boston 1984.
[59] J. BØTTIGER, K. DYRBYE, K. PAMPUS, and R. POULSEN, Phil. Mag. A59, 569 (1989).
[60] B.X. LIU, Nuclear Instrum. and Methods B **7/8**, 547 (1985).
[61] Z.J. ZHANG and B.X. LIU, Phys. Rev. B 51, 16475 (1995).
[62] O. JIN and B.X. LIU, J.non-crystall. Solids, in press.
[63] B.X. LIU, Z.J. ZHANG, and O. JIN, submitted to J. Mater. Res.
[64] B.X. LIU, W.L. JOHNSON, M-A. NICOLET, and S.S. LAU, Appl. Phys. Lett. 42, 45 (1983).
[65] B.X. LIU, Mater. Lett. 5, 322 (1987).
[66] J.A. ALONSO and S. SIMOZAR, Solid State Commun. 48, 765 (1983).
[67] P.M. OSSI, phys. stat. sol. (a) 119, 463 (1990).
[68] K.C. RUSSELL, Progr. Mater. Sci. 28, 229 (1984).
[69] G. MARTIN, F. SOISSON, and P. BELLON, J. Nuclear Mater. 205, 301 (1993).
[70] A.R. MIEDEMA, A.K. NIESSEN, F.R. DE BOER, R. BOOM, and W.C.M. MATTENS, Cohesion in Metals: Transition Metal Alloys, North-Holland Publ. Co., Amsterdam 1989.
[71] J.A. ALONSO, L.J. GALLEGO, and J.A. SIMOZAR, Nuovo Cimento 12, 587 (1990).
[72] A.K. NIESSEN and A.R. MIEDEMA, Ber. Bunsenges. Phys. Chem. 87, 717 (1983).
[73] J.M. LOPEZ and J.A. ALONSO, Z. Naturf. **40a**, 1199 (1985).
[74] A.W. WEEBER, J. Phys. F 17, 809 (1987).
[75] A.K. NIESSEN, A.R. MIEDEMA, F.R. DE BOER, and R. BOOM, Physica **151B**, 401 (1988).
[76] J.M. LOPEZ and J.A. ALONSO, phys. stat. sol. (a) 76, 675 (1983).
[77] J.M. LOPEZ and J.A. ALONSO, phys. stat. sol. (a) 85, 423 (1984).
[78] J. FRIEDEL, Adv. Phys. 3, 446 (1954).
[79] J.D. ESHELBY, Solid State Phys. 3, 79 (1956).
[80] J.M. LOPEZ and J.A. ALONSO, Z. Naturf. **40a**, 1199 (1985)
[81] P.I. LOEFF, A.W. WEEBER, and A.R. MIEDEMA, J. less-common Metals 140, 299 (1988).
[82] O. JIN, Z.J. ZHANG, and B.X. LIU, J. Appl. Phys. 78, 149 (1995).
[83] D. TURNBULL, in: Impurities and Imperfections, Amer. Soc. Met., Ohio 1955 (p. 121).
[84] L.E. MURR, in: Interfacial Phenomena in Metals and Alloys, Addison-Wesley, London 1975.
[85] A.R. MIEDEMA, Z. Metallk. 69, 455 (1978).
[86] A.R. MIEDEMA, Z. Metallk. 69, 287 (1978).
[87] J. GERKEMA and A.R. MIEDEMA, Surface Sci. 124, 351 (1981).
[88] F.Z. CUI, Y.D. FAN, Y. WANG, A.M. VREDENBERG, H.J.G. DRAAISMA, and R. XU, J. Appl. Phys. 68, 701 (1990).
[89] B.X. LIU and Z.J. ZHANG, J. Phys.: Condensed Matter 8, L165 (1996).
[90] G. DEARNALEY, J.H. FREEMAN, R.S. NELSON, and J. STEPHEN, Ion Implantation, North-Holland Publ. Co., Amsterdam 1973.
[91] P.D. TOWNSEND, J.C. KELLY, and N.E.W. Hartley, Ion Implantation, Sputtering and Their Applications, Academic Press, 1976.
[92] K.T-Y. KUNG, B.X. LIU, and M.-A. NICOLET, phys. stat. sol. (a) 77, 355 (1983).
[93] J.L. BRIMHALL, H.E. KISSINGER, and L.A. CHARLOT, Radiat. Eff. 77, 273 (1983).
[94] J.L. BRIMHALL and E.P. SIMONEN, Nuclear Instrum. and Methods. B 16, 187 (1986).
[95] L.S. HUNG, and J.W. MAYER, Nuclear Instrum. and Methods B **7/8**, 676 (1985).
[96] B.X. LIU, Z.J. ZHANG, O. JIN, and F. PAN, Nuclear. Instrum. and Methods B **106**, 17 (1995).
[97] B.X. LIU, unpublished data, Caltech., 1982.
[98] B.Y. TSAUR, S.S. LAU, and J.W. MAYER, Appl. Phys. Lett. 36, 823 (1980).
[99] B.Y. TSAUR and J.W. MAYER, Appl. Phys. Lett. 37, 389 (1980).
[100] H. JONES, in: The Theory of Brillouin Zones and Electronic States, in: Crystals, North-Holland Publ. Co., Amsterdam 1960 (p. 191).

[101] B.X. LIU, phys. stat. sol. (a) **75**,K77 (1983).
[102] B.X. LIU and Z.J. ZHANG, J. Mater. Res. **9**,357 (1994).
[103] Z.J. ZHANG and B.X. LIU, J. Appl. Phys. **75**,4948 (1994).
[104] W.L. JOHNSON and A.R. Williams, Phys. Rev. B **20**, 1640 (1979).
[105] B.X. LIU, B.M. CLEMENTS, R. GABORIAUD, W.L. JOHNSON, and M.-A. NICOLET, Appl. Phys. Lett. **42**,624 (1983).
[106] R.B. SCHWARZ and W.L. JOHNSON, Phys. Rev. Lett. **51**,415 (1983).
[107] K. SAMWER, Physics Rep. **161**,1 (1988).
[108] W.L. JOHNSON, Progr. Mater. Sci. **30**,81 (1986).
[109] M. ATZMON, J.D. VERHOEVEN, E.D. GIBSON, and W.L. JOHNSON, Appl. Phys. Lett. **45**, 1052 (1984).
[110] E.J. COTTS, W.J. MENG, and W.L. JOHNSON, Phys. Rev. Lett. **57**,2295 (1986).
[111] W.J. MENG, B. FULTZ, E. MA, and W.L. JOHNSON, Appl. Phys. Lett. **51**,661 (1987).
[112] W.J. MENG, C.W. NIEH, and W.L. JOHNSON, Appl. Phys. Lett. **51**,1693 (1987).
[113] H. SCHROEDER, K. SAMWER, and U. KOSTER, Phy. Rev. Lett. **54**,197 (1985).
[114] S.B. NEWCOMB and K.N. TU, Appl. Phys. Lett. **48**,1436 (1986).
[115] M. VAN ROSSUM, M-A. NICOLET, and W.L. JOHNSON, Phys. Rev. B. **29**,5498 (1984).
[116] B.E. WHITE, JR., M.E. PATT, and E.J. COTTS, Phys. Rev. B **42**,11017 (1990).
[117] A. PAESANO, JR., S.R. TEIXEIRA, and L. AMARAL, J. Appl. Phys. **70**,4870 (1991).
[118] W.S.L. BOYER and M. ATZMON, J. Alloys and Comp. **194**,213 (1993).
[119] E. MA and M. ATZMON, J. Alloys and Comp. **194**, 235 (1993).
[120] W. KIAUKA, W. KEUNE, T. SHINJO, and N. HOSOITO, J. Magnetism magnetic Mater. **93**, 494 (1991).
[121] F. PAN, Y.G. CHEN, and B.X. LIU, Appl. Phys. Lett. **67**,780 (1995).
[122] E. MA, J.-H. HE, P. J. SCHILLING, F. PAN, and B. X. LIU, Mater. Res. Soc. Symp. Proc. **398**,221 (1996)
[123] B.M. CLEMENS, Phys. Rev. B **33**,7615 (1986).
[124] B.X. LIU and M.-A. NICOLET, Thin Solid Films **101**,201 (1983).

Influence of interfacial texture and asymmetric growth in diffusion-limited amorphization in Ni-Zr multilayers upon medium-temperature annealing

W. S. Lai and B. X. Liu*

Department of Materials Science and Engineering, Tsinghua University, Beijing 100084, China and State Key Laboratory of Solid-State Microstructure Physics, Nanjing University, Nanjing 210093, China

(Received 18 July 1997; revised manuscript received 18 May 1998)

Molecular-dynamics simulation, based on an n-body potential, was performed to investigate the amorphization process in the Ni-Zr bilayer and multilayers upon annealing at medium temperatures of 373–873 K. Six sandwich models consisting of atomic planes with different orientations and one bilayer model with a preset disordered interfacial layer were constructed and simulated to reveal the effect of interfacial texture on and the kinetics of the growth of an amorphous layer, respectively, in detail. It was found that when the multilayers had semicoherent interfaces in those sandwich models consisting of Ni close-packed planes parallel to the interfaces, amorphization was frustrated even up to a temperature of 873 K, because of the large associated negative interfacial energies suppressing the interdiffusion at the interfaces. In all the other models constructed by non-close-packed planes of Ni, simulation results showed that amorphization could take place at a temperature down to 673 K and it was initiated through crossing-interface diffusion, diffusion-induced alloying and subsequent growth of the interfacial amorphous layer, resulting eventually in forming a uniform amorphous phase in the models. Concerning the kinetics, the growth of the amorphous layer was found to follow exactly a $t^{1/2}$ law, indicating that solid-state amorphization was indeed through a diffusion-limited reaction, and an asymmetric behavior was observed that the growing speeds towards Ni were greater than that directed to the Zr lattice. Besides, there was about a 1% volume expansion in the formed amorphous phase comparing to the original multilayers, which lent support to the excess free volume model proposed for the amorphous structure. [S0163-1829(98)08133-8]

I. INTRODUCTION

Solid-state amorphization by interdiffusion of two initial crystalline metals was observed in 1983 by Schwarz and Johnson in the Au-La system, which is characterized with a large negative heat of formation (ΔH_F) and a large difference in atomic size.[1] Since then, solid-state reaction to form amorphous alloy films has been studied by several groups in some other systems featuring characteristics similar to those of Au-La pairs.[2–7] It is commonly recognized that the ΔH_F and atomic size mismatch of a system are two important factors playing significant roles in the formation of amorphous alloys in the binary metal systems. As explicated by Schwarz and Johnson, a large size mismatch is related closely to the growth kinetics of an amorphous phase.[1] A large negative ΔH_F, as regarded by many researchers, usually lowers the free energy of the amorphous state below that of an equilibrium mixture of two crystalline phases of the constituent metals, and thus serves as a major thermodynamic driving force for amorphous alloy formation. However, recent experimental studies showed that solid-state vitrification was also observed in some binary metal systems with either a positive ΔH_F or a very small size mismatch.[8–10] It was reported that when the multilayers were designed to consist of a sufficient fraction of interfacial atoms, amorphous alloy films were formed in some positive ΔH_F systems simply by steady-state thermal annealing of the multilayers, and it was the excess interfacial free energy that drove the solid-state amorphization.[8,9]

At present, a clear understanding of solid-state amorphization at an atomic scale is still lacking for the negative ΔH_F systems and is an entirely open issue for the positive ΔH_F systems. In the case of negative ΔH_F systems, even in a same system, different interfacial textures between the two crystalline metals had a significant influence on the speed of, or even suppressed the solid-state amorphization.[3,11–15] For example, Clemens observed that solid-state amorphization took place upon annealing in the sputtering-deposited Ni/Ti multilayers with a large composition modulation wavelength (CMW) of 200 atomic planes per layer, yet it was frustrated by a small CMW less than 20 atomic planes per layer. Carefully performed x-ray-diffraction analysis led Clemens to claim that disordered interfacial regions were emerged in the multilayers with a large CMW, whereas coherent interfaces were formed in the multilayers with a small CMW.[3] Another representative example is from the extensively studied Ni-Zr system.[11–15] For instance, Meng prepared a Ni/Zr diffusion couple by depositing Ni on a recrystallized Zr foil with close-packed planes (001) parallel to the surface and observed no detectable reaction near the interface after annealing the diffusion couple at temperatures between 573 and 643 K for several hours.[7,15] It follows that the interfacial structures play an important role on solid-state amorphization, i.e., the close-packed planes may serve as a nucleation barrier or a kinetic barrier to amorphization which should be further investigated and it is one of the important objectives for the present study.

Molecular-dynamics (MD) simulation is known to be a unique method to model the solid-state reaction,[16–20] as it helps for a better understanding of the amorphization mecha-

Physical Review B 58(10), p.6063-6073 (1998).

nism at an atomic scale. For example, Massobrio, Pontikis, and Martin performed a MD study of the irradiation-induced crystal-to-amorphous transition of a crystalline $NiZr_2$ and found that chemical disorder was a major driving force for the transition.[18] One may conjecture that chemical disorder may also serve as a major driving force responsible for self-driven solid-state amorphizationlike interdiffusion of two pure metallic phases. In this respect, Weissmann, Ramírez, and Kiwi employed a specific pair potential, i.e., Lennard-Jones potential, to simulate a Zr-Co superlattice with an atomic size misfit of 22% upon annealing and claimed that all the Co atomic planes became disordered at 1100 K,[19] which was much higher than that observed in experiments. In addition, they did not observe any interdiffusion in the disordering process. Fernandes and Pontikis simulated a Ni-Zr superlattice with a many-body potential upon annealing at 1000 K and only observed some atomic diffusion via two surfaces perpendicular to the interface between the Ni and Zr lattices.[20] In short, the results from the above-mentioned simulations are not compatible with what have been observed in the experiments, i.e., solid-state vitrification took place at medium temperatures through interfacial interdiffusion.[2-5,11-15] In the present study, we chose the Ni-Zr system as a model system for MD simulation, as there are fruitful experimental data for comparison and a many-body potential has been developed[18] for the system. MD simulation was performed with the n-body potential for revealing the effect of interfacial texture on the amorphization behavior and the detailed kinetics of amorphization upon isothermal annealing at medium temperatures ranging from 373 to 873 K. We report, in this paper, the models set for the simulation, computational, and characterization methods and the simulation results together with some discussions.

II. MODELS FOR SIMULATION

A. Sandwich models

1. Models constructed with fcc-Ni and hcp-Zr

To study the effect of interfacial texture on the amorphization behavior, six Zr-Ni-Zr sandwich models with different crystalline orientations of the Ni and Zr lattices were constructed for simulation. The models were constructed by stacking Ni and Zr atomic planes along the z axis (and hereafter) and the orientations of the atomic planes were described by their Miller indices, e.g., [6 fcc (111) Ni] referred to a Ni lattice of fcc structure stacking by 6 (111) atomic planes, and [4 hcp (001) Zr] stood for a Zr lattice with a hcp structure stacking by 4 (001) atomic planes, etc. The interfaces between the two lattices were introduced as follows. When a Zr lattice and a Ni lattice approached each other along the z direction, an interface was created in the x-y plane and another interface was introduced by approaching another Zr lattice to the same Ni lattice from the other direction.

Six sandwich models were constructed by combining three types of Ni planes, i.e., (110), (100), and (111) in fcc structure, with two types of Zr planes, namely (100) and (001) of hcp structure and were abbreviated by the following symbols: [4 (100) Zr/8 (110) Ni/4 (100) Zr], [4 (100) Zr/6 (001) Ni/4 (100) Zr], [4 (100) Zr/6 (111) Ni/4 (100) Zr], [4 (001) Zr/8 (110) Ni/2 (001) Zr], [4 (001) Zr/6 (001) Ni/2 (001) Zr], and [4 (001) Zr/6 (111) Ni/2 (001) Zr]. To preserve the symmetry of the crystalline planes across the boundary, the orientations of above-mentioned atomic planes in the x-y planes were set as follows. The crystalline direction [100] of both hcp (100) and (001) planes were arranged to be parallel to the x axis. while the crystalline direction [−1 1 0] of both fcc (110) and (111) planes as well as [100] of fcc (001) plane were set to be pointing to the x direction. The other crystalline directions of these atomic planes pointing to the y direction were then determined by the above x-direction settings, i.e., [0 0 −1] for hcp (100), [120] for hcp (001), [001] for fcc (110), [−1 −1 2] for fcc (111), and [010] for fcc (001), respectively.

The sizes of the lattices, in the x-y plane, were chosen to have a mismatch at the Ni-Zr interface be as close as possible to an experimentally measured ratio of the lattice constants. It is known that the nearest-neighbor distances of Zr and Ni atoms are 3.18 and 2.49 Å in their single crystals, respectively, which makes approximately a ratio of 1.277. For example, in the sandwich model [4 (001) Zr/6 (111) Ni/2 (001) Zr], considering the manageable scale of the computation, the numbers of Ni and Zr atoms in their respective planes were selected to be $9\times9\times2=162$ for fcc Ni (111) plane and $7\times7\times2=98$ for hcp Zr (001) plane, corresponding to a ratio of $9/7=1.285$, which is quite close to a real situation. The size of the corresponding computational block in the z direction was obtained by varying the distances between Zr and Ni lattices to an optimized value corresponding to a minimum enthalpy for each model.

Concerning the boundary conditions, in the z direction, a periodic boundary condition was imposed, and two Zr lattices in the sandwich models were therefore adhered together to form a united lattice. While in the x-y plane, periodic boundary conditions using Ni lattice dimensions were adopted. Consequently, the computational block of a sandwich model was a representative unit of compositional modulated multilayers and simulation of such sandwich model was in fact to simulate the Ni-Zr multilayers, which were usually employed in experimental studies of solid-state reaction. It should be noted that the misfit caused by a difference between the dimensions of the Zr lattice and the periodic conditions along the x and y directions would result in, at most, a 1.4% decreasing of Zr density in the models. However, as pointed out by Mura *et al.* in their simulation of Ni-Zr multilayer upon loading, such a density reduction did not introduce spurious effects on the thermodynamic behavior up to a temperature $T\leqslant0.5T_m$ (T_m stands for the melting temperature).[21] Furthermore, Massobrio, Pontikis, and Martin reported that their potential included nonzero diagonal stress-tensor components of the order of 11.5 kbar, while fitting the potential to match exactly the experimental lattice parameters of $NiZr_2$, and that the potential was able to reproduce successfully both static and dynamic properties of $NiZr_2$, which were also in excellent agreement with the experimental data.[18] A brief estimation of the maximum stress caused by such a misfit in the Zr layer was conducted by the authors based on plane stress theory of elasticity, which gave

$$\sigma_x=\frac{E}{1-\mu^2}\left(\frac{\Delta y}{L_y}\mu+\frac{\Delta x}{L_x}\right)$$

and

$$\sigma_y = \frac{E}{1-\mu^2}\left(\frac{\Delta x}{L_x}\mu + \frac{\Delta y}{L_y}\right),$$

where E is a Young's modulus, μ refers to Poisson's ratio, L_x and L_y are the Zr lattice dimensions in the x and y directions, respectively, and Δx and Δy are the misfits between Zr lattice dimensions and the periodic conditions along the x and y directions, respectively. Referring to those elastic constants in the literature,[18] the maximum values of σ_x and σ_y were estimated to be of the same order of magnitude as the diagonal stress-tensor components in the potential. Moreover, the real stresses in the sandwich models for simulation should be much lower than the estimated ones, as the simulation models were obtained by relaxation of the as-set models at 300 K for 10 000 time steps to reach a state of reduced stress instead of the as-set models (this will be described in details later). We therefore believed that the influence of such existing stress in the Zr lattice would be very minor.

2. *Model constructed with fcc-Ni and fcc-Zr*

As the crystalline structures of fcc Zr and hcp Zr are quite similar in their atomic configurations and the energy difference between them is quite small, we conjectured that a similar amorphization behavior would emerge in the models built up by either Zr fcc or hcp lattice in combining with Ni fcc lattice. A sandwich model [4 fcc (001) Zr/6 fcc (001) Ni/2 fcc (001) Zr] was also simulated to confirm the similarity in amorphization behavior between [hcp Zr/fcc Ni/hcp Zr] and [fcc Zr/fcc Ni/fcc Zr] models.

B. Bilayer model

To study the detailed kinetics of amorphization process in the Ni-Zr system, a bilayer model of [12 Ni fcc (001)/12 Zr fcc (001)] was constructed and simulated for simplicity. The sizes of the lattices in the x-y plane were chosen according to the above-mentioned criterion and the numbers of Ni and Zr atoms in their respective planes were selected to be $9\times 9\times 2=162$ and $7\times 7\times 2=98$, respectively. In the x and y directions, periodic boundary conditions using Ni lattice dimensions were imposed. In the z direction, a free, instead of periodic, boundary condition was adopted to avoid the otherwise influence in growth kinetics of amorphization from having another interface in the model. Under such conditions, the atoms on both outmost planes in the z direction were free to move and an atom, if crossing the block, would be relocated onto the initial surface and set at zero energy. To avoid a possible drift of the block, an equal amount of the lost momentum was spread equally to all the atoms in the block. Such boundaries would not affect considerably the simulation results, as it would be seen later that the crystalline planes near the surface, except those next to the interface, remain almost unchanged upon annealing at a temperature up to 873 K.

To have the bilayer model with a starting configuration similar to the real situation like that reported by Clemens,[3] an initially disordered interlayer was first introduced by randomly exchanging an equal number of Ni and Zr atoms in the interlayer. To characterize quantitatively the amount of disorder created by exchanging atoms, the concept of long-range order (LRO) parameter originally proposed to describe the ordering in crystalline alloys[18] was employed in this study. The LRO parameter is defined as $\eta=(p-\gamma)/(1-\gamma)$, where p and γ are the probability of the presence of an A-type atom (A = Ni or Zr) on its own lattice site and the molar ratio of A atoms, respectively, both in the initial interlayer. Such disordered interlayer was preset in four atomic planes consisting of two Ni and Zr atomic planes next to each other. The amount of disorder in the interlayer was set to be $\eta=0$, corresponding to an exchange of 122 atoms in total. The bilayer model was employed in this study to reveal the detailed growth kinetics of the amorphous interlayer upon thermal annealing at medium temperatures.

III. COMPUTATION AND CHARACTERIZATION

A. Many-body potential and computation

A many-body potential for the Ni-Zr system derived from the second-moment approximation of the tight-binding scheme by Massobrio, Pontikis, and Martin[18] was employed in the simulation. The cohesion energy of an i_α atom of the α specimen is written as

$$E_{i_\alpha} = \sum_{\beta=1}^{2}\sum_{\substack{j_\beta=1\\ j_\beta\neq i_\alpha}}^{N_\beta} A_{\alpha\beta}\exp\left[-p_{\alpha\beta}\left(\frac{r_{i_\alpha j_\beta}}{d_{\alpha\beta}}-1\right)\right] - \sqrt{\sum_{\beta=1}^{2}\sum_{\substack{j_\beta=1\\ j_\beta\neq i_\alpha}}^{N_\beta} \xi_{\alpha\beta}^2\exp\left[-2q_{\alpha\beta}\left(\frac{r_{i_\alpha j_\beta}}{d_{\alpha\beta}}-1\right)\right]}, \tag{1}$$

where $r_{i_\alpha j_\beta}$ is the distance between i_α and j_β atoms, and $d_{\alpha\beta}$ is the nearest-neighbor distance in the crystal structure. The first pair potential term represents a repulsive Born-Mayer interaction, and the second attractive many-body term represents a second-moment approximation of a tight-binding band energy.[22] Such potential allows a quantitative simulation of most elastic properties of the metallic systems, such as Cauchy discrepancy[23] which, as is well known, cannot be simulated by any pair potential. The free parameters in Eq. (1) have been adjusted to reproduce cohesive energy and elastic constants of the $C16$ crystalline structure of $NiZr_2$. The potential, though involving only nearest-neighbor atomistic interactions, has been proved to result in some thermodynamic properties for pure metals, which are in good agreement with the experimental values up to a temperature around 0.65 melting point.[22] Besides, this potential has also been employed by other researchers to simulate the phase transformation by liquid melt quenching in the Ni-Zr system[24] and the growth of amorphous layer upon loading.[21] In short, this potential was believed to be appropriate, in a certain extent, for describing the interactions in the Ni-Zr system. In our case, since only the contributions from the nearest-neighbor atoms were taken into account in fitting the potential parameters,[18] the cutoff distances for interactions of the same atoms, i.e., Ni-Ni and Zr-Zr, were set to be at the middle of the first and second nearest-neighbor distances in the respective Ni and Zr single crystals. While the cutoff distance for the interactions of different atoms, i.e., Ni-Zr, was set to be 5.3 Å, suggested by Massobrio, Pontikis, and Martin in their simulation of amorphization in crystalline $NiZr_2$.[18]

Our simulation started by equilibrating the model at room temperature (300 K) for 10 000 MD steps to reach an equilibrium configuration as an initial state. From the initial state, the "computer experiments" of solid-state reaction were performed by first gradually raising the temperature of the model system through boosting the velocities of the atoms of the initial state in each time step at a rate of 4×10^{13} K/s, and then by isothermal annealing of the multilayers or bilayer as soon as the temperature of the system reached to the desired one within 373–873 K. As the velocities of the atoms would change during annealing, a time-to-time rescaling of the velocities to the assigned temperature was executed at every 100 time steps, if an average deviation from the assigned temperature was over 1 K. The simulation was carried out with Parrinello-Rahman molecular-dynamics scheme.[25] The equations of motion were solved using a fourth-order predictor-corrector algorithm of Gear with a time step $t=5\times10^{-15}$ s. The vectorize link cell method was adopted for neighbor counting to facilitate fast computation.[26]

B. Characterization methods

The most direct and convenient way to describe disordering process was simply to display graphically the distributions of atoms at different times onto a projected plane, e.g., x-z plane. To trail closely the detailed amorphization process of the models, two quantitative methods were implemented to calculate the degree of disorder, i.e., the evaluation of the planar structure factor and the pair-correlation function. The planar structure factor, namely the Fourier transformation of the density in each crystallographic plane parallel to x-y plane, is defined according to Phillpot, Yip, and Wolf as[27]

$$S(k,z)=\left\langle \frac{1}{N_z^2}\left|\sum_{j=1}^{N_z} \exp(ik\cdot r_j)\right|^2\right\rangle, \tag{2}$$

where z labels the crystal plane to which the point $\mathbf{r}_j$ belongs at initial configuration, and $\mathbf{k}$ is an arbitrary vector of the planar reciprocal lattice [in our case, $\mathbf{k}=(1,1)$ was used]. Accordingly, the planar structure factor $S=1$ refers to an entirely ordered crystal while $S=0$ is for a completely disordered state. The typical density profiles of each species along the z direction $\rho_\alpha(z)$ in the initial state of the model [4 (001) Zr/6 (001) Ni/2 (001) Zr] are illustrated in Fig. 1. The density profiles $\rho_\alpha(z)$ for the initial states of other simulating models exhibit the similar shapes as those in Fig. 1. The calculated $\rho_\alpha(z)$ allows us to define the position of a single atomic layer enabling one to evaluate the local (i.e., restricted to the single layer) thermodynamic and structural properties.[28] In practice, the atomic planes are defined as the original crystal planes and the planar structure factors can be used to indicate the degrees of disorder in the corresponding planes. The evaluation of the planar structure factor at each time step can indicate the change of the ordering of each atomic plane with increasing of time.

The pair-correlation function analysis was employed to identify the structure of the models, as this method is recognized to give convincing evidence for amorphous alloy formation. In our case, e.g., in the bilayer model, the structure of the local region grown from the interface was analyzed by pair-correlation function, in which the atoms sampled were those situated in the region of interest. To calculate the pair-correlation function $g(r)$, each atom in turn was imagined to be at the center of a series of concentric spheres. The atomic density is defined to be the number of atoms in each spherical shell divided by the volume of that shell, with a consideration of those periodic image atoms located outside the block. In our case, the results were obtained by averaging over all the atoms within 200 time steps. The $g(r)$ was then obtained by the following formula:

$$g(r)=\frac{\rho(r)}{\rho_0}, \tag{3}$$

where $\rho(r)$ denotes the atomic density at $r=|\mathbf{r}|$, $r=0$ defines the position of a reference atom, and ρ_0 is an average atomic density in the whole model.

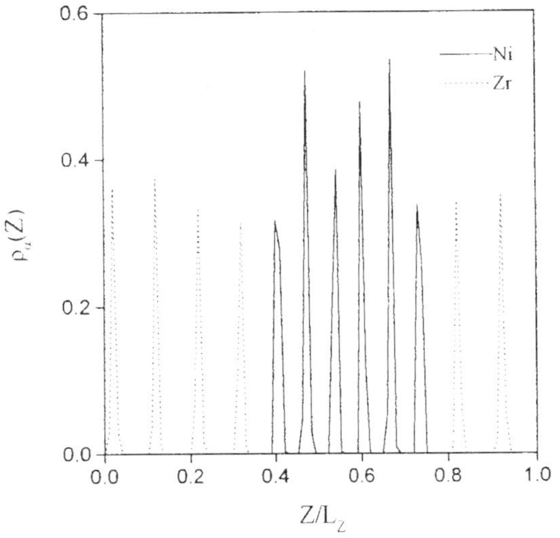

FIG. 1. The calculated density profiles $\rho_\alpha(z)$ of each species along the z direction at the initial state. $\rho_{Ni}(z)$ is represented by solid line and $\rho_{Zr}(z)$ by dotted line. Abscissa is expressed in the scaled coordinate and ordinate is in arbitrary unit.

IV. RESULTS AND DISCUSSION

A. Amorphization driven by diffusion

1. Amorphization in the multilayers constructed by hcp-Zr and fcc-Ni

We first discuss the simulation results obtained by 773 K isothermal annealing in a sandwich model constructed in a configuration of [4 (001) Zr/6 (001) Ni/2 (001) Zr]. The initial state before annealing is shown in Fig. 2 by a projection of the atomic positions on an x-z plane. One observes that the Ni and Zr crystalline lattices are sharply separated by two interfaces before any reaction taking place. Figures 3 and 4 display two snapshots of projection of the atomic positions on the x-z plane after annealing at 773 K for 17 925 and 30 000 time steps, respectively. The disordering process upon isothermal annealing can clearly be visualized in these

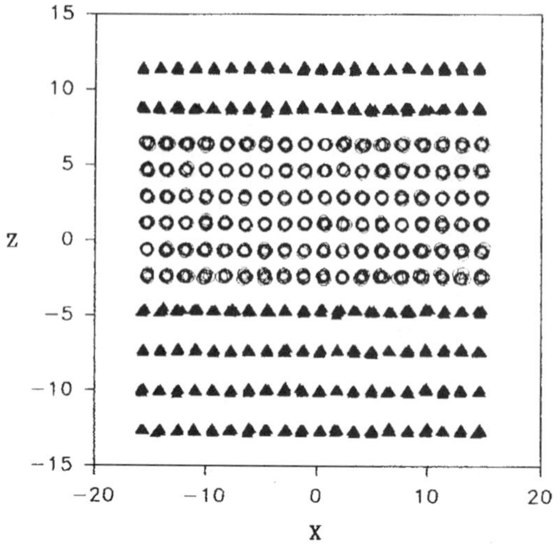

FIG. 2. Projection of the atomic positions on the x-z plane of the starting configuration for the sandwich model of [4 (001) Zr/6 (001) Ni/2 (001) Zr]. The Ni and Zr atoms are denoted by open circles and full triangles, respectively.

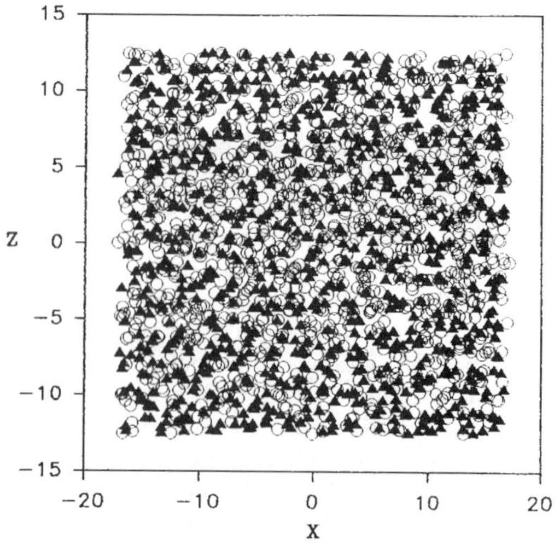

FIG. 4. A snapshot of projection of the atomic positions on the x-z plane after annealing the sandwich model at 773 K for 30 000 time steps. The Ni and Zr atoms are denoted by open circles and full triangles, respectively.

figures. One sees that the atomic planes next to the interfaces are first disordered while the other planes remain in crystalline structures as shown in Fig. 3 and that all the remaining crystalline planes gradually become disordered with increasing annealing time, resulting eventually in an amorphous configuration as evidenced by Fig. 4. A close look at Fig. 3 leads to an important finding that a certain number of Ni (Zr) atoms have diffused into the Zr (Ni) lattice, resulting in a significant alloying between the Ni and Zr layers next to the interfaces. Besides, the calculated density profiles, $\rho_\alpha(z)$, of each species along the z direction during annealing at various time steps also confirmed that mutual diffusion did take place and after 30 000 MD steps the density profiles $\rho_\alpha(z)$ for Ni and Zr were almost uniformly distributed along the z direction. To be precise, mutual diffusion was defined as the crossing-interface movement of either Ni or Zr atoms into their partner lattice. It is therefore concluded that prior to amorphization, mutual diffusion and alloying process between the Ni and Zr layers disrupt gradually the original crystalline structure of the atomic planes. In other words, solid-state reaction of the Ni-Zr multilayers upon thermal annealing proceeds in a sequence of diffusion, alloying and eventually amorphization, which, to authors' knowledge, has so far not been observed by previous MD simulations.

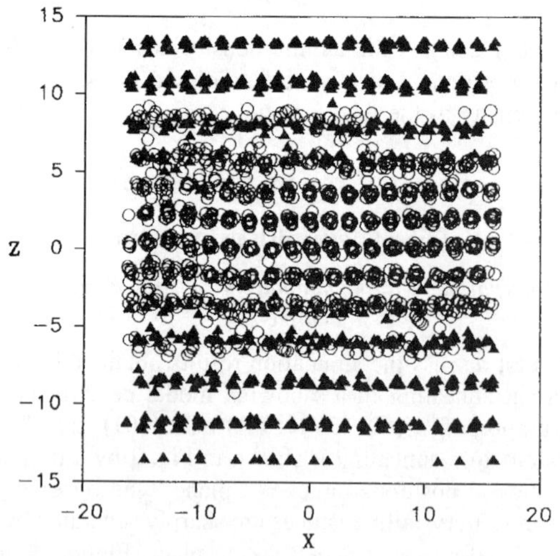

FIG. 3. A snapshot of projection of the atomic positions on the x-z plane after annealing the sandwich model at 773 K for 17 925 time steps. The Ni and Zr atoms are denoted by open circles and full triangles, respectively.

All the above peculiarities are corroborated by the structure factors $S(\mathbf{k})$, which are depicted in Fig. 5 for the initial state as well as another two states after isothermal annealing for two time steps. In the initial state, one interface is originally set between atomic planes 4 and 5 and the another one between planes 10 and 11. One sees that in the initial state all the atomic planes remain in crystalline structures as evidenced by their corresponding planar structure factors, $S(\mathbf{k})$,

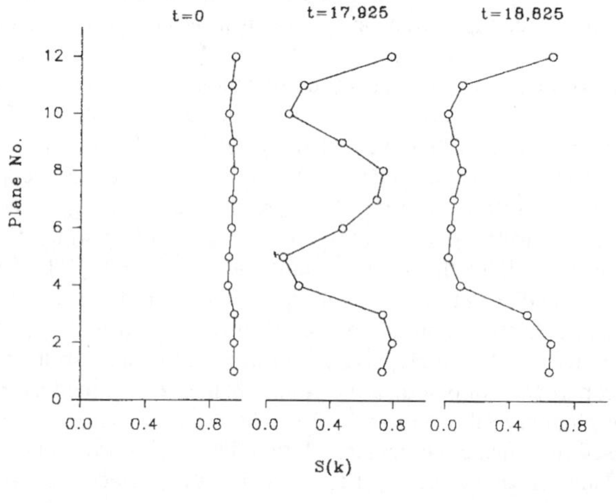

FIG. 5. The planar structure factors $S(\mathbf{k})$ for the starting state ($t=0$) and for the states after annealing at 773 K for 17 925 and 18 825 MD steps, respectively, for the sandwich model of [4 (001) Zr/6 (001) Ni/2 (001) Zr].

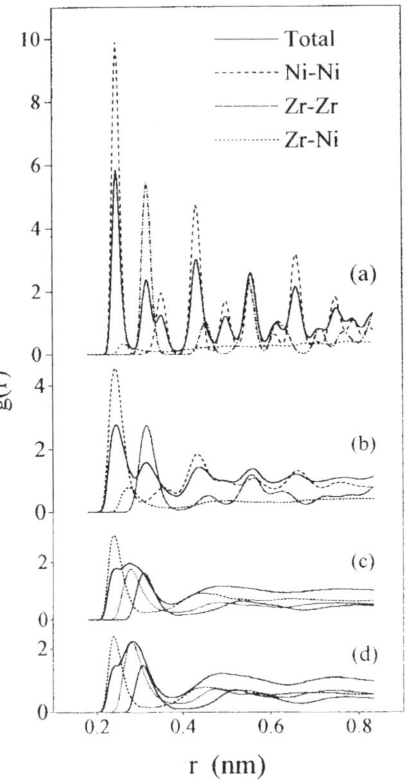

FIG. 6. Partial and total pair-correlation functions for the initial state (a) and another three states obtained by annealing at 773 K for (b) 17 925 time steps, (c) 22 000 time steps, and (d) 30 000 time steps, respectively.

being nearly one. This is also in support to that the misfit caused by the difference between the dimensions of Zr lattice and periodic conditions along the x and y directions did not deform the original Zr lattice considerably. After annealing at 773 K for 17 925 MD steps, one sees clearly from the figure that the atomic planes next to the interfaces, i.e., planes 4 and 5 and 10 and 11, become disordered and further running to 18 825 MD time steps results in a completely disordered state of all the Ni planes. Referring again to Figs. 3 and 5, it is concluded that the disordering of the atomic planes next to the interfaces is caused by diffusion and alloying.

To give firm evidence of the structural change taking place during annealing, four sets of partial and total pair-correlation functions for the simulating model calculated at various time steps are shown in Fig. 6. One observes that with increasing annealing time the strength of the Zr-Ni $g(r)$ first peak increases and those peaks of the total Ni-Ni, and Zr-Zr $g(r)s$ at long distances, gradually disappear and that after 22 000 time steps, the pair-correlation function curves feature apparently the shapes commonly known for the amorphous alloys. Incidentally, it was also found that after 21 430 time steps, all the Zr atomic planes became completely disordered as the corresponding planar structure factors $S(\mathbf{k})$ had approached zero. These results suggested that a crystal-to-amorphous transition was completed after approximately 22 000 steps running at 773 K. Further running for another 8000 time steps did not change the formed amorphous phase, as the pair-correlation function curves calculated at 30 000 steps feature the similar shapes as those for 22 000 steps. Besides, the above data also suggested that the extension of disordering was faster towards the Ni side than that directed to the Zr lattice, revealing an asymmetric growth of a Ni-Zr amorphous layer. The detailed kinetics of the asymmetric growth of an amorphous layer will be discussed later in the Ni-Zr bilayer model, in which there is no influence of having two interfaces.

To find out if the amorphization was initiated at interfaces, the pair-correlation functions for two interfacial layers each consisting of two atomic planes after annealing for 17 925 steps were also calculated and the resultant curves showed the similar shapes as those displayed in Fig. 6(d). To illustrate the changing of the atomic surroundings of the Ni and Zr atoms before and after annealing, the coordination numbers were calculated by taking the integral of $4\pi\rho_0 r^2 g(r)$ up to the first minimum, where ρ_0 was the number density of the model system. It was found that from the initial state to the annealed state shown in Fig. 6(d), the coordination numbers for Ni-Ni and Zr-Zr decreased from 10.67 to 4.73 and from 11 to 5.66, respectively, while those numbers for Ni-Zr and Zr-Ni increased from 0.98 to 6.58 and from 1.38 to 9.30, respectively. Apparently, the above results demonstrated that amorphization was initiated from the interfaces through diffusion and alloying and then the as-formed two amorphous interlayers grew to form a relatively uniform amorphous phase in the Zr-Ni-Zr sandwich.

It is worthwhile mentioning that a similar vitrification process was also observed in three other sandwich models, i.e., [4 (100) Zr/8 (110) Ni/4 (100) Zr], [4 (100) Zr/6 (001) Ni/4 (100) Zr], and [4 (001) Zr/8 (110) Ni/2 (001) Zr]. It was found that in these three sandwich models, vitrification could take place at a temperature of 773 K or lower. The correlation between the interfacial texture with the lowest temperature for driving solid-state amorphization will be discussed later.

2. Amorphization in the multilayers constructed by fcc-Zr and fcc-Ni

To find out if similar amorphization upon annealing would also take place in a sandwich model constructed by fcc-Ni and fcc-Zr, a Zr-Ni-Zr sandwich model of [4 fcc (001) Zr/6 fcc (001) Ni/2 fcc (001) Zr] was simulated at the temperatures ranging from 373 to 673 K. Figure 7 shows two sets of partial and total pair-correlation functions for the initial and another state after annealing at 573 K for 20 000 MD steps. One observes that the Zr-Ni first peak increases greatly from the initial to the annealed states and that the pair-correlation functions of the annealed state also feature the shapes commonly known for the amorphous alloys, suggesting annealing does result in the formation of amorphous phase in the Zr-Ni-Zr sandwich model. Moreover, it was found that the coordination numbers for Ni-Ni and Zr-Zr decreased from 10.67 to 5.29 and from 10.67 to 5.44, respectively, while those numbers for Ni-Zr and Zr-Ni increased from 0.78 to 5.87 and from 1.29 to 9.71, respectively. These results indicated that alloying did take place during solid-state reaction, which resulted eventually in the formation of an amorphous alloy. Comparing Fig. 6 with Fig. 7, one sees that in both [4 (001) Zr/6 (001) Ni/6 (001) Zr] and [4 fcc

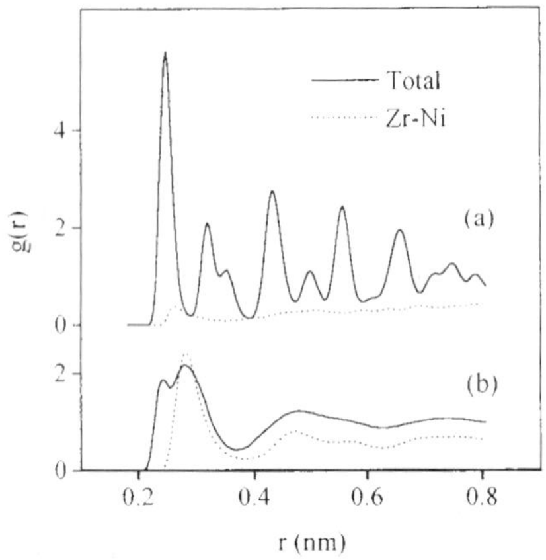

FIG. 7. Total and partial pair-correlation functions for the initial state (a) and another state obtained by annealing at 573 K for 20 000 MD steps (b) in the sandwich model of [4 fcc (001) Zr/6 fcc (001) Ni/2 fcc (001) Zr].

(001) Zr/6 fcc (001) Ni/6 fcc (001) Zr] sandwich models, the changes of the pair-correlation functions with increasing time are similar, suggesting a similar amorphization behavior in both models. Furthermore, amorphization was also initiated at the interfaces through diffusion and alloying.

Similar simulations at 373, 473, 535, and 673 K showed that vitrification in the sandwich model could take place at 535 and 673 K yet could not at and below 473 K, and that the speed of the vitrification process decreased with decreasing the annealing temperature. The variations of the enthalpy and volume of the sandwich model versus temperature were calculated and are displayed in Fig. 8. One sees that the slopes of both enthalpy and volume are discontinuous around 535 K which corresponds to a crystal-to-amorphous transition temperature. An abrupt volume increase at 535 K is due to a crystal-to-amorphous transition and the resultant amorphous phase possesses more excess free volume than that of its crystalline counterpart. To further confirm, the amorphous state obtained at 673 K was quenched down to room temperature and subsequently equilibrated. The corresponding enthalpy as well as the volume of the quenched state are also given in Fig. 8 with solid symbols. One observes that the enthalpy of the amorphous phase is lower than that of the original multilayers, while the volume of the amorphous phase has approximately 1% increase with respect to that of the original multilayers. The simulated result of 1% increase of free volume of the amorphous phase is in good agreement with a free volume model proposed for the amorphous structure predicting a volume increase of 1.0–2.5 % in respect to its crystalline counterpart[29] as well as with some experimental observations.[30]

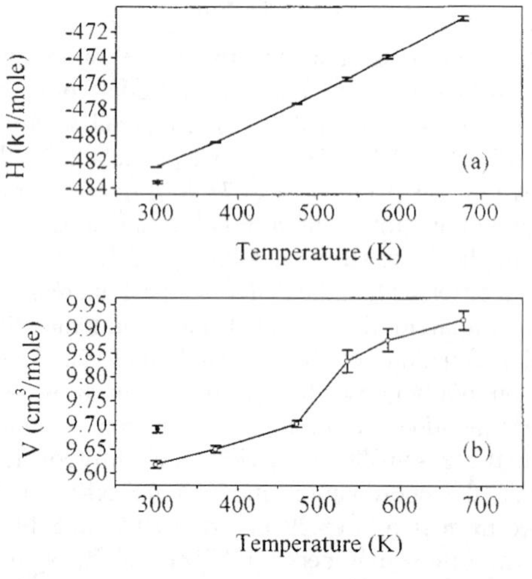

FIG. 8. Variations of the enthalpy and volume of the sandwich model versus temperature. Two datum points standing alone in the figure are for a quenched state, which was obtained by quenching and subsequently equilibrating of an amorphous phase obtained by 673 K annealing.

The above results confirmed the similarity of growing an amorphous layer in both sandwich models constructed by [hcp Zr/Ni/hcp Zr] and [fcc Zr/Ni/fcc Zr], and the similarity is ascribed to a very small energy difference between the Zr fcc and hcp structures. Besides, fcc Zr has been observed in experiments, e.g., in sputtered films.[31] All the above discussions suggested that the simulations using the models with Ni (fcc) combining with either Zr (hcp) or Zr (fcc) did reveal a similar amorphization behavior for the Ni-Zr system. It is therefore reasonable to construct a bilayer model, for simplicity, by fcc-Ni and fcc-Zr for a detailed study of the kinetics of solid-state amorphization in Sec. IV C.

B. Effect of interfacial texture

It was found that the sandwich models with different interfacial textures behaved differently in a solid-state reaction. For instance, in the sandwich model with close-packed planes of both Ni and Zr stacking along the z direction, no reaction was observed after annealing at 873 K for 40 000 steps, implying the interfaces were very stable, while in the sandwich model of [4 (100) Zr/8 (110) Ni/4 (100) Zr], intermixing of Ni and Zr atoms through interfaces took place even at 300 K, suggesting that the Zr (100)/Ni (110) interface was very unstable. To interpret the different behaviors, the interfacial energy, E^I, was calculated by

$$E^I=\frac{E^m-N_{\mathrm{Ni}}\cdot E_{\mathrm{Ni}}^{\mathrm{Coh}}-N_{\mathrm{Zr}}\cdot E_{\mathrm{Zr}}^{\mathrm{Coh}}}{\text{Interfacial area}}, \tag{4}$$

where E^m is the energy of the sandwich model after relaxation at 0 K, N_{Ni}, and N_{Zr} are the numbers of Ni and Zr atoms in the sandwich model, respectively, and $E_{\mathrm{Ni}}^{\mathrm{Coh}}$ and $E_{\mathrm{Zr}}^{\mathrm{Coh}}$ are the cohesion energies of Ni and Zr, respectively. Table I lists the calculated interfacial energies for various interfacial textures. One observes from the table that the interfacial energies in the sandwich models vary with different interfacial textures and that the interfaces in the sandwich model constructed by stacking the close-packed atomic planes has a lowest value, corresponding to a most stable interfacial state. Naturally, the stability of a specific interface is closely related to its interfacial energy and the lower the interfacial energy, the more stable the corresponding interface.

To further explicate the effect of interfacial texture on amorphization behavior, the sandwich models with different interfacial textures were subjected to isothermal anneal at various temperatures ranging from 373 to 873 K. It was

TABLE I. The interfacial energies, E^I, of various interfacial textures calculated at 0 K in the sandwich models constructed by hcp Zr and fcc Ni.

Interface	hcp(001)/ fcc(110)	hcp(001)/ fcc(001)	hcp(001)/ fcc(111)	hcp(100)/ fcc(110)	hcp(100)/ fcc(001)	hcp(100)/ fcc(111)
E^I (J/m^2)	0.055	−0.14	−0.46	(a)	0.034	−0.259

[a]Not calculated as the corresponding interface is unstable.

found that after annealing at 873 K for a time scale of 10^{-10} s, no any reaction was observed at the interfaces in a sandwich model of [4 (100) Zr/6 (111) Ni/4 (100) Zr], which had a large negative interfacial energy of -0.259 J/m^2, indicating the interfaces were very stable. This result was compatible with Meng's observation by high-resolution transmission electron microscopy that the interface between Ni (111) and Zr (101) remained sharp at an atomic scale after annealing at 573 K for 6 h.[15,7] In another sandwich model of [4 (001) Zr/6 (001) Ni/2 (001) Zr] with a less negative interfacial energy of -0.14 J/m^2, mutual diffusion took place and therefore solid-state amorphization was achieved after annealing at 773 K for 30 000 steps (please refer to Sec. IV A 1), yet it was suppressed at a temperature below 673 K. In other two sandwich models with positive interfacial energies as listed in Table I, interface reaction took place at a temperature as low as 673 K and a uniform amorphous phase was eventually formed.

The above results suggested that the close-packed planes have lower energies than those of the more open planes. Thermodynamically, the close-packed planes possessing lower energies provided a smaller driving force for forming amorphous alloy than that from the more open planes. However, such an interfacial energy difference did not lower the energetic level of the multilayers sufficiently to hinder solid-state reaction, because the Ni-Zr system has a large negative ΔH_F ($=-72$ kJ/mole for the equiatomic composition). The effect of the close-packed planes on suppressing solid-state amorphization is therefore believed to come from kinetics. In other words, the close-packed planes may serve as a nucleation barrier as well as kinetic barrier preventing atoms from diffusing into the partner lattices in the process of solid-state reaction. In a MD simulation for the Ni-Zr system performed by Mura *et al.*,[21] they first artificially introduced an amorphous interlayer, neglecting the nucleation details, in a Ni-Zr multilayer constructed by both Ni and Zr close-packed planes, and a subsequent annealing of the multilayer did not result in an extension of the amorphous interfacial layer. This suggested that the suppression of solid-state reaction was mainly from the kinetic barrier caused by the close-packed planes.

In summary, in the multilayers with semicoherent interfaces, an associated large negative E^I played an important role in suppressing the solid-state amorphization by kinetically blocking the mutual diffusion between the metal layers, whereas in the multilayers with some specific textures characterized by a positive E^I, solid-state amorphization through mutual diffusion at the interfaces could take place upon annealing at medium temperatures.

C. Asymmetric growth behavior

We now turn to a bilayer model to study the growth kinetics of the amorphous layer upon annealing. For convenience, the atomic planes stacking along the z direction in the bilayer model were recorded by 1–12 for Ni and 13 to 24 for Zr, respectively. The interface separating Ni and Zr crystalline lattices therefore lies between the atomic planes 12 and 13. The initial state in the bilayer model was obtained by exchanging a total number of 122 Ni and Zr atoms in an interlayer consisting of four atomic planes 11–14, and then equilibrating at 300 K for 5000 MD steps. It was found that after a 5000 steps run the bilayer model reached a somewhat equilibrium state and the planar structural factors for the atomic planes 11–14 were calculated to be of 0.18, 0, 0.05, and 0.25, respectively, indicating that the interlayer was in a disordered state, which was similar to that observed in the sputtering deposited Ni-Zr multilayers.[3] Furthermore, a total pair-correlation function calculation for the interlayer in the initial state resulted in a curve similar to that displayed in Fig. 7(b), indicating the interlayer was of amorphous structure. Starting from the initial state, the bilayer model was subjected to isothermal annealing at temperatures ranging from 623 to 873 K to trace the growth kinetics of the amorphous interlayer. The simulation results obtained at 773 K are discussed here as a representative example, as similar results were also obtained at 623, 673, and 873 K, respectively. Figure 9 shows the planar structure factors $S(\mathbf{k})$ for the initial state of the bilayer model and for another two states after running for 50 000 and 100 000 time steps, respectively. One observes that the interlayer of the initial state is disordered and gradually extends outwards with increasing annealing time, and that after 100 000 steps run the disordered interlayer extends to a total thickness corresponding to 11 atomic planes. Besides, the partial and total pair-correlation function calculations confirmed that these 11

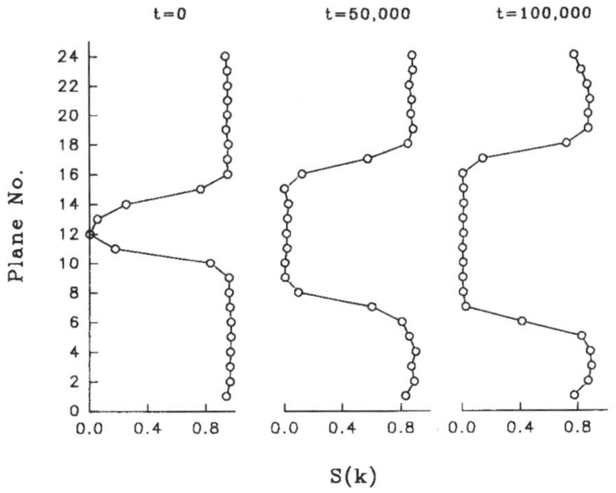

FIG. 9. The planar structure factors $S(\mathbf{k})$ for the starting state of the Ni-Zr bilayer model ($t=0$) and for the states after annealing at 773 K for 50 000 and 100 000 MD steps, respectively.

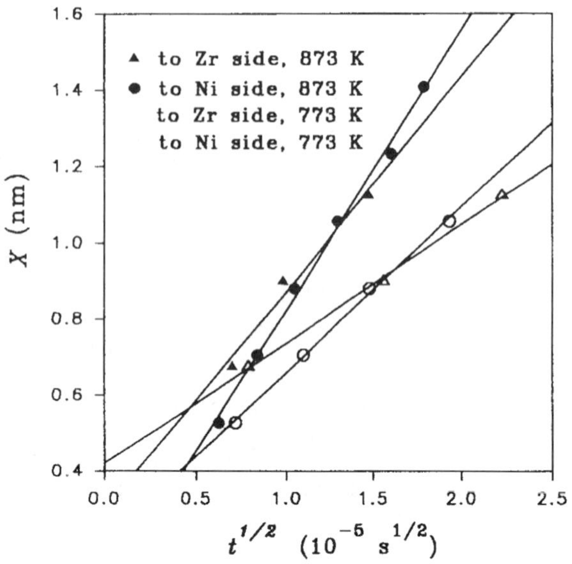

FIG. 10. The growing thicknesses (X) of the amorphous interlayer as a function of ($t^{1/2}$) in two opposite directions towards Ni and Zr lattices at 773 and 873 K, respectively.

atomic planes (7–17) were indeed of amorphous structure. The coordination numbers for a layer consisting of atomic planes 7–17 before and after annealing at 773 K for 100 000 steps were obtained by taking the integral of $4\pi r^2 \rho_0 g(r)$ up to the first minimum. It was found that the coordination numbers for Ni-Ni and Zr-Zr decreased from 9.51 to 6.16 and from 8.63 to 4.71, respectively, while those for Ni-Zr and Zr-Ni increased from 1.92 to 5.34 and from 4.45 to 10.89, respectively. Obviously, these changes in coordination numbers demonstrated that significant alloying between Ni and Zr atoms had taken place in this layer. One can draw another important result from Fig. 9 by a careful examination that outside this disordered layer, all the atomic planes remained almost unchanged, since no Ni (Zr) atoms as alloying elements have diffused into the Zr (Ni) lattice planes. The fact that the outside planes remained crystalline suggested that a free boundary condition in the z direction had no considerable effect on the simulation results. It was worthwhile mentioning that the total pair-correlation functions for the growing layer with increasing thickness at various running steps were also calculated and they all featured a similar shape with that of Fig. 7(b). It is therefore concluded that the growth of Ni-Zr amorphous phase upon solid-state reaction actually proceeds in a layer-by-layer mode through mutual diffusion and alloying prior to amorphization.

We now discuss the time dependence of the growth of the disordered interlayer. Figure 10 shows four curves for the thicknesses (X) of the growing amorphous interlayer as a function of time ($t^{1/2}$) in two opposite directions towards Ni and Zr lattices at 773 and 873 K, respectively. At a specific time, the corresponding thickness of the disordered layer was obtained by counting the atomic planes from the interface up to the outmost one with a planar structure factor $S<0.1$. One sees that four X-$t^{1/2}$ curves are all obviously linear, indicating that the growth of the amorphous interlayer follows exactly a diffusion governed $t^{1/2}$ law. One also notices that the slopes of the four curves are apparently different, suggesting the growing speeds are different. First, the slopes at 873 K are greater than those at 773 K, because the growing speeds at 873 K are naturally greater than those at 773 K for both Ni and Zr. Second, the slopes of Ni at both 773 and 873 K are greater than those of Zr at respective temperatures, suggesting a possible asymmetric growth of the disordered interlayer upon solid-state reaction in the Ni/Zr bilayer. Experimentally, the $t^{1/2}$ law for the growth of the amorphous layer has been observed in the Ni-Zr system,[3,5,13] yet it was obtained by fitting the data in a longer time than that in the MD simulation. Referring again to Ref. 12, Meng, Nieh, and Johnson performed the transmission electron microscopy observation of cross-sectional Ni-Zr samples and observed that after the amorphous NiZr interlayer reached a critical thickness, a NiZr intermetallic compound started to form at the amorphous-NiZr/Zr interface, suggesting that the growing speed of the disordered region towards Zr lattice was slower than that towards Ni side. Consequently, the above-described asymmetric growth behavior revealed by our MD simulation has also been observed in experiments.

D. Comparison with experiments

We now discuss the simulation results in comparison with the experimental observations. First, MD simulation showed clearly the crossing-interface atomic movement during solid-state reaction, thus giving a firm evidence that solid-state amorphization was governed by atomic diffusion. In experiments, a linear correlation was observed between the growing thickness of the amorphous layer and the $t^{1/2}$ over a long period, which suggested the growth of amorphous layer was also governed by diffusion.[3,4,5] Second, MD simulation showed that the interfacial texture had a significant influence on the speed of amorphization and that when the multilayers consisted of Ni close-packed planes, the interdiffusion was even suppressed by such semicoherent interfaces. Similarly in experiments, Meng, Nieh, and Johnson observed, by high-resolution transmission electron microscopy, that the interface between Ni (111) and Zr (101) remained atomically sharp after annealing at 573 K for 6 h.[15,7] Third, MD simulation revealed that the amorphous-NiZr/Ni interface moved faster to the Ni lattice than the amorphous-NiZr/Zr interface to the Zr side. Such asymmetric behavior has also been observed in the carefully performed experiments by Meng, i.e., an earlier frustration of amorphization was observed at Zr side.[12] Fourth, MD simulation demonstrated that solid-state amorphization did occur at relatively low temperatures down to 573 K, which is also in accordance with the experimentally observed reaction temperature range, i.e., 423–633 K.[3,12] To approach to a possible low-temperature limit for solid-state reaction in this system, MD simulation was also performed with a bilayer model at temperatures lower than 573 K and the results showed that at 473 K no any interdiffusion between Ni and Zr layers was observed after running up to 60 000 time steps. The low-temperature limit (about 535 K) suggested by simulation seems to be a little higher than that (423 K) observed in experiments.[3] Nonetheless, in the experiments, the polycrystalline Ni and Zr involved in the thin films usually contain some defects and grain boundaries, which would certainly enhance diffusion, thus resulting in a little lower limit temperature for reaction. Based on these comparisons, the simulation results of above-mentioned aspects are compatible with the experimental observations.

Concerning the comparison of the growth kinetics in a quantitative way, it may raise some questions. From Fig. 10, the chemical interdiffusion coefficients, denoted as $\tilde{\mathbf{D}}$, can be related to the slopes of those linear lines. According to the diffusion-limited growth formula $\Delta X=\sqrt{2\mathbf{a}\tilde{\mathbf{D}}\mathbf{t}}$, where ΔX was the amount of the growing amorphous layer and a was a numerical constant being near unity,[32–34] the chemical interdiffusion coefficients $\tilde{\mathbf{D}}_{\rm sim}$ were calculated to be 2.45×10^{-9} m^2/s and 8.45×10^{-9} m^2/s for 773 and 873 K, respectively. Whereas in experiments performed at temperatures lower than 773 K, Barbour *et al.* obtained a $\tilde{\mathbf{D}}_{\rm exp}$ at 523 K to be 1×10^{-21} m^2/s by Rutherford backscattering analysis and by using the similar formula in calculation.[35] In order to compare the data at the same temperatures, we deduced, according to the method and data reported by Hahn, Averback, and Rothman[36] that the values of $\tilde{\mathbf{D}}_{\rm exp}$ at 773 and 873 K would be 2.1×10^{-17} m^2/s and 1.2×10^{-16} m^2/s, respectively. Apparently, the $\tilde{\mathbf{D}}$ values obtained by MD simulation are nearly eight orders of magnitude higher than those deduced from experiments. A question is therefore raised why there is such a large difference in the diffusivities determined by simulation and experiments. To the authors' understanding, a most important factor is the time-scale difference involved in simulation and experiments. Precisely speaking, as the MD simulation lasts only for about 10^{-10} s, the diffusivities obtained by simulation are only for a very initial stage of the solid-state reaction. Whereas in experiments, the $t^{1/2}$ law governing the growth of the amorphous layer was obtained by averaging the data over a much longer time period than that dealt in the MD simulation and the diffusivities so obtained were therefore only for the respective time periods. It is noted that the X-$t^{1/2}$ linear lines in experiments did not start from the zero point. For example, Cheng and co-workers[37,38] obtained the $t^{1/2}$ growth behavior after the first 30 min of thermal annealing and this linear correlation cannot be extrapolated backward through this specific time of 30 min, which is obviously far beyond the total simulation time. Moreover, some experimental results even indicated that the average interdiffusion coefficients in a long time period were not exactly constants and would decrease as the reaction progressed.[39] For instance, van Rossum *et al.* observed, in a Ni-Hf sandwich, a considerable negative deviation from the $t^{1/2}$ law, indicating a decrease in diffusion coefficients or the growing speed at the time period closing to the completion of the solid-state reaction.[4] Taking experimental data for analysis,[7] if the linear lines representing $t^{1/2}$ law were extrapolated to $t=0$ (representing the state that reaction has not started yet), there would already be a certain thickness of the growing amorphous layer. In other words, the experimentally observed linear lines are only valid for the corresponding time period, but not allowed to extrapolate to the early stage of reaction. It follows naturally that the diffusivities as well as the growing speeds of the amorphous layer determined by experiments should not be compared with the simulation results, as the simulation reveals the reaction process at the initial stage.

We now discuss the relative diffusivities of the Ni and Zr in the NiZr amorphous matrix for both simulation and experiments. In principle, the diffusivity can be obtained by a calculation of a mean-square displacement in MD simulation and it was estimated to be 2×10^{-9} m^2/s for Ni and 8×10^{-10} m^2/s for Zr at 773 K, respectively. The diffusivity of Ni atoms in the amorphous matrix is therefore 2–3 times larger than that of Zr atoms, which is responsible for the revealed asymmetry in growth. Incidentally, the diffusivity obtained by MD simulation reported in the literature is in the same order of magnitude as those obtained by our simulation.[20] In the experiments using a thin tungsten (W) marker, Cheng and co-workers[37,38] found that the Ni atoms were the dominant moving species in the NiZr amorphous phase, as the "inert" W marker shifted to the Ni side during solid-state reaction and a tracer diffusivity of Ni was deduced to be greater, at least 20 times, than that of Zr. Besides, Hahn, Averback, and Rothman also employed Rutherford backscattering method to study the diffusion in the amorphous NiZr alloy and estimated that the tracer diffusivity of Ni was greater, at least 10 times, than that of Zr.[36] It should be noted that in Cheng's and Hahn's calculation, they both assumed that the Zr atoms did not move at all.[37,38,36] Such an assumption would bring in some errors. Besides, the limited resolution involved in the Rutherford backscattering measurement also contributed some errors. Comparing the experimentally obtained relative diffusivities of Ni and Zr with those deduced from MD simulation, the tendency is compatible, i.e., Ni diffuses faster than that of Zr in the NiZr amorphous matrix. For a quantitative comparison, however, the ratio of the diffusivities of Ni and Zr suggested by simulation is about 2–3, while it was calculated to be at least 10 or higher from experimental observations. The different situations for the simulation and experimental pursuing should be concerned in discussing this difference. As mentioned above, the diffusivities discussed in simulation and experiments are for two very different time periods, respectively, i.e., simulation is for the very initial stage of solid-state reaction, while the experiments are for a long period, excluding the first 30 min of the solid-state reaction. Certainly, the calculation in simulation may also contribute some errors in the resultant diffusivities, e.g., from the calculation procedure, from employing an empirical potential in the simulation, etc. To clearly understand this difference, it is necessary to perform further investigation.

V. CONCLUSIONS

(1) In the Ni-Zr multilayers consisting of Ni close-packed atomic planes parallel to the interfaces, amorphization was frustrated even up to 873 K, as an associated semicoherent interface having negative energy suppressed the crossing-interface diffusion. While in the multilayers with other interfacial textures possessing a positive interfacial energy, amorphization could proceed at a temperature down to 673 K.

(2) The amorphization process in the Ni-Zr bilayer model and sandwich models upon isothermal annealing was revealed to proceed as follows. Amorphization was first initiated at the interfaces through mutual diffusion and alloying, and then subsequent growth of the interfacial amorphous layer(s) in both Ni and Zr directions resulted in the formation of

a uniform amorphous phase. The expansion resulted from diffusing Ni and Zr atoms into the previously formed amorphous interlayer.

(3) The growth of the amorphous layer was found to follow exactly a $t^{1/2}$ law, indicating that solid-state amorphization was through a process of diffusion-limited reaction.

(4) An asymmetric behavior in the growth of an amorphous layer was observed that the growing speed towards the Ni side was faster than that directed to the Zr lattice.

ACKNOWLEDGMENTS

This study is supported by National Natural Science Foundation of China. Partial financial aid from the Tsinghua Administration is also gratefully acknowledged.

*Author to whom correspondence should be addressed; electronic address: dmslbx@tsinghua.edu.cn

[1] R. B. Schwarz and W. L. Johnson, Phys. Rev. Lett. **51**, 415 (1983).
[2] H. Schröder, K. Samwer, and U. Koster, Phys. Rev. Lett. **54**, 197 (1985).
[3] B. M. Clemens, Phys. Rev. B **33**, 7615 (1986).
[4] M. van Rossum, M.-A. Nicolet, and W. L. Johnson, Phys. Rev. B **29**, 5498 (1984).
[5] E. J. Cotts, W. J. Meng, and W. L. Johnson, Phys. Rev. Lett. **57**, 2295 (1986).
[6] W. L. Johnson, Prog. Mater. Sci. **30**, 81 (1986).
[7] K. Samwer, H. J. Fecht, and W. L. Johnson, in *Glassy Metals III: Amorphization Techniques, Catalysis, Electronic and Ionic structure*, edited by H. Beck and H. J. Güntherodt (Springer-Verlag, Berlin, 1995).
[8] Z. J. Zhang, O. Jin, and B. X. Liu, Phys. Rev. B **51**, 8076 (1995).
[9] Y. G. Chen and B. X. Liu, J. Non-Cryst. Solids **217**, 308 (1997).
[10] F. Pan, Y. G. Chen, and B. X. Liu, Appl. Phys. Lett. **67**, 780 (1995).
[11] W. J. Meng, B. Fultz, E. Ma, and W. L. Johnson, Appl. Phys. Lett. **51**, 661 (1987).
[12] W. J. Meng, C. W. Nieh, and W. L. Johnson, Appl. Phys. Lett. **51**, 1693 (1987).
[13] W. J. Meng, E. J. Cotts, and W. L. Johnson, in *Interfaces, Superlattices, and Thin Films*, edited by J. D. Dow and I. K. Schuller, MRS Symposia Proceedings No. 77 (Materials Research Society, Pittsburgh, 1987), p. 223.
[14] W. J. Meng, C. W. Nieh, E. Ma, B. Fultz, and W. L. Johnson, Mater. Sci. Eng. **97**, 87 (1988).
[15] W. J. Meng, Ph.D. thesis, California Institute of Technology, 1987.
[16] H. Hsieh and S. Yip, Phys. Rev. B **39**, 7476 (1989).
[17] J. Lu and J. A. Szpunar, J. Appl. Phys. **74**, 902 (1993).
[18] C. Massobrio, V. Pontikis, and G. Martin, Phys. Rev. B **41**, 10 486 (1990).
[19] M. Weissmann, R. Ramírez, and M. Kiwi, Phys. Rev. B **46**, 2577 (1992).
[20] M. G. Fernandes and V. Pontikis, Mater. Sci. Forum **207-209**, 173 (1996).
[21] P. Mura, P. Demontis, G. B. Suffritti, V. Rosato, and M. Vittori, Phys. Rev. B **50**, 2850 (1994).
[22] V. Rosato, M. Guillope, and B. Legrand, Philos. Mag. A **59**, 321 (1989).
[23] M. S. Daw, in *Proceedings of the International Workshop on Many-Atom Interactions in Solids*, edited by R. M. Nieminen, M. J. Puska, and M. J. Manninen (Springer-Verlag, Berlin, 1990), p. 48.
[24] T. Aihara, Jr., K. Aoki, and T. Masumoto, Scr. Metall. Mater. **28**, 1003 (1993).
[25] M. Parrinello and A. Rahman, Phys. Rev. Lett. **45**, 1196 (1980).
[26] M. W. Finnis, MOLDY6-A Molecular Dynamics Code for Simulation of Pure Metals, UKAEA Report AERE R13182 (1988).
[27] S. R. Phillpot, S. Yip, and D. Wolf, Comput. Phys. **3**, 20 (1989).
[28] V. Rosato, G. Ciccotti, and V. Pontikis, Phys. Rev. B **33**, 1860 (1986).
[29] A. van den Beukel and S. Radelaar, Acta Metall. **31**, 419 (1983).
[30] See, for example, Y. G. Chen and B. X. Liu, Appl. Phys. Lett. **68**, 3096 (1996).
[31] K. L. Chopra, M. R. Randlett, and R. H. Duff, Philos. Mag. A **16**, 261 (1967).
[32] U. Gösele and K. N. Tu, J. Appl. Phys. **53**, 3252 (1982).
[33] B. E. Deal and A. S. Grove, J. Appl. Phys. **36**, 3770 (1985).
[34] B. Dolgin, Ph.D. thesis, California Institute of Technology, 1984.
[35] J. C. Barbour, F. W. Saris, M. Nastasi, and J. W. Mayer, Phys. Rev. B **32**, 1363 (1985).
[36] H. Hahn, R. S. Averback, and S. J. Rothman, Phys. Rev. B **33**, 8825 (1986).
[37] Y.-T. Cheng, W. L. Johnson, and M-A. Nicolet, Appl. Phys. Lett. **47**, 800 (1986).
[38] Y.-T. Cheng, Ph.D. thesis, California Institute of Technology, 1987.
[39] D. Grosman and E. J. Cotts, Phys. Rev. B **48**, 5579 (1993).

INTERFACE-DRIVEN ALLOYING AND METALLIC GLASS FORMATION IN NANO-MULTILAYERS IN AN IMMISCIBLE Y–Nb SYSTEM

Y.G. CHEN[1,2] **and B.X. LIU**[1,2]†

[1]Department of Materials Science and Engineering, Tsinghua University, Beijing 100084, P.R. China and [2]State Key Laboratory of Physics of Solid State Microstructure, Nanjing University, Nanjing 210093, P.R. China

(Received 11 November 1997; accepted 14 September 1998)

Abstract—Several new amorphous alloys were obtained in an immiscible Y–Nb system by room temperature 190 keV xenon ion mixing of Y–Nb multilayered films, which were designed to include a sufficient fraction of interfacial atoms and thus possessed a high free energy comparable to that of the amorphous state. In addition, two metastable f.c.c. phases were formed in Y-rich and Nb-rich multilayered films, respectively. The growth kinetics of the f.c.c. phases and their effect on the composition range of amorphization are also discussed. To understand the observed unusual alloying behaviors, a Gibbs free-energy diagram was constructed based on Miedema's model. The diagram included the free-energy curves of all the involved phases as well as that of the Y–Nb multilayered films including the extra interfacial free energy and thus gave a qualitative and reasonable interpretation to the formation of metastable alloys upon ion mixing. Furthermore, some multilayered films with a sufficient fraction of interfacial atoms were subjected to steady-state thermal annealing, which also resulted in the formation of the Y–Nb amorphous phases, suggesting that alloying in this immiscible system was actually driven by the interfacial free energy.

1. INTRODUCTION

Metallic glasses (or amorphous alloys in some cases) behave quite differently in comparison to crystalline materials in many aspects and this behavior has been the subject of a considerable body of research in the past three decades. Since the first amorphous alloy was obtained by liquid melt quenching in 1960 [1], various techniques have been developed to produce a great number of new amorphous alloys. Beginning in the early 1980s, ion mixing (IM) of multilayers has been employed to study the glass-forming ability (GFA) of binary metal systems [2, 3]. It has been shown experimentally that IM is able to extend greatly the glass-forming range (GFR), as the effective quenching rate available in IM ($\approx 10^{13}$–10^{14} K/s) is likely to be the highest among the glass-producing techniques. Naturally, the total thickness of the multilayers in IM is limited by the penetrating range of the irradiating ions, e.g. for typically used 300 keV xenon ions, the total thickness is limited to below 100 nm for most of the transition metals. In 1983, Schwarz and Johnson reported for the first time that in the Au–La system with a large negative heat of formation (ΔH_f), amorphous alloys were obtained by solid-state reaction (SSR) [4]. SSR also begins with multilayers, yet has no film thickness limitation. Concerning the thermodynamic driving force for metallic glass formation, it is commonly recognized that for both IM and SSR, the sign of the ΔH_f calculated by Miedema's model [5] has significant influence on amorphization behavior as well as the alloying ability of the multilayers [6]. A large negative ΔH_f between the constituents is known to lower the free energy of the amorphous phase to a below that of an equilibrium mixture of two crystalline phases of the constituent metals, thus providing a driving force for solid-state amorphization. While dealing with the materials in a bulk form, thermodynamic calculation indicated that a positive ΔH_f was associated with an amorphous phase that had significantly higher free energy than that of an equilibrium state, leading to a situation unfavorable for amorphization [7]. Experimentally, however, beginning with a scheme of multilayers, IM and SSR have produced some new amorphous alloys in several positive ΔH_f systems [8–10]. It is known that the multilayered films definitely include a certain number of interfaces and an interface can generally be regarded as a transient layer of mixed constituent metals. Furthermore, it has been reported that the structure of the interfaces in some sputter-deposited multilayered films was detected by X-ray diffraction to be disordered and the thickness of the disordered layer was estimated to be several atomic planes [11]. It follows that the interfaces possess some excess free energy and would elevate the in-

†To whom all correspondence should be addressed.

Acta Materialia 47(4), p.1389-1397 (1999).

itial energetic state of the multilayered films to a higher level, making amorphization and alloying thermodynamically possible. The energetic state of the multilayers is therefore different from that of the corresponding bulk form. In practice, the multilayered films can be designed to include various fractions of interfacial atoms, thus changing the energetic sequence of the alloy phases of interest considerably. It is deduced that by increasing the fraction of interfacial atoms, i.e. by including more interfaces in the films, it is possible to form metallic glasses in a relatively broad composition range [12]. By taking into account the interfacial free energy in the multilayers, the authors' group has recently conducted some IM experiments in the Y–Mo [12] and Y–Ta [13] systems both featuring positive ΔH_f and succeeded in obtaining some new metallic glasses in these immiscible systems. To give further evidence in support of the interfacial free-energy concern, more experimental studies are still necessary. Moreover, it will be of interest to see if the interfacial free energy also plays an important role in SSR to form amorphous alloys in the positive ΔH_f systems. The Y–Nb ($\Delta H_f = +44$ kJ/mol) system was therefore selected for the present study to investigate the above-mentioned issues.

2. THERMODYNAMIC CONSIDERATIONS

2.1. Calculation of free energy for metastable crystalline and amorphous phases

Generally, the Gibbs free energy of a given phase is calculated by $\Delta G = \Delta H - T\Delta S$, where ΔH and ΔS are the enthalpy and entropy changes, respectively. The expression for the entropy change can be taken, as a first approximation, as that of an ideal solid solution, i.e.

$$\Delta S = -\mathrm{R}[x_A \ln(x_A) + x_B \ln(x_B)] \quad (1)$$

in which R is the gas constant and x_A and x_B are atomic concentrations of metals A and B, respectively. The expression for ΔH, which is a main concern of Miedema's model [5] and the related method [14], however, should be discussed in detail.

According to Miedema's model, the enthalpy change ΔH can be considered as a sum of three terms [15–17], i.e. $\Delta H = \Delta H^c + \Delta H^e + \Delta H^s$, corresponding to the chemical, elastic and structural contributions. The chemical term ΔH^c is related to the electron redistribution generated at the boundary of the Wigner–Seitz unit cell when alloying; the elastic term ΔH^e is caused by the atomic size mismatch of the two constituent metals; while the structural term ΔH^s is deduced from the valence and crystal structure changes.

The chemical term is given by

$$\Delta H^c = M x_A V_A^{2/3} f_{AB} \quad (2)$$

where M is an amplitude reflecting the magnitude of the electron redistribution interaction, V_A is the atomic volume of atom A, and f_{AB} is a function accounting for the degree to which atoms A are surrounded by atoms B.

The elastic term can be derived from the equation

$$\Delta H^e = x_A x_B (x_B L_{A\ in\ B} + x_A L_{B\ in\ A}) \quad (3)$$

where $L_{i\ in\ j}$ is the elastic contribution to the heat of solution i in j, which can be calculated from the elastic moduli of the two metals as indicated.

Finally, the structural contribution ΔH^s arises from the well-known correlation between the number of valence ($s + d$) electrons and the crystal structure of transition metals [14]. Structural effects in transition metal alloys are due to the formation of a common d-band during alloying, which is supported by the energy-band calculations [18]. The expression for ΔH^s is

$$\Delta H^s = E(\bar{Z}) - x_A E_A(Z_A) - x_B E_B(Z_B) \quad (4)$$

where $\bar{Z}$ is the average number of electrons per atom and E, E_A and E_B are the structural stabilities of the alloy, the pure component A and the pure component B, respectively.

Following the suggestion of Niessen *et al.*, the free-energy change of the formation of a metastable crystalline phase and an amorphous phase can be written as follows:

for a metastable crystalline phase,

$$\Delta G = \Delta H^c + \Delta H^e + \Delta H^s - T\Delta S \quad (5)$$

for an amorphous phase,

$$\Delta G_a = \Delta H_a^c + \alpha(x_A T_{m,A} + x_B T_{m,B}) - T\Delta S \quad (6)$$

where α is an empirical constant of 3.5 J/(mol·K) and $T_{m,i}$ is the melting point of the component metal i (i = A,B).

2.2. Calculation of interfacial free energy for the multilayered films

As pointed out by Turnbull [19], the interfacial energy between metals A and B can be split into physical and chemical contributions written as $\sigma_{AB} = \sigma_{geo} + \sigma_{chem}$. For metals A and B of quite different lattice structure, the physical term σ_{geo} stands for the energy of a large-angle grain boundary. It is estimated that the grain-boundary enthalpy is about 30% of the surface energy at 0 K [20] and the entropy contribution is neglected. Thus it is deduced

$$\sigma_{AB} = 0.15(\sigma_{A,0} + \sigma_{B,0}) + \sigma_{chem} \quad (7)$$

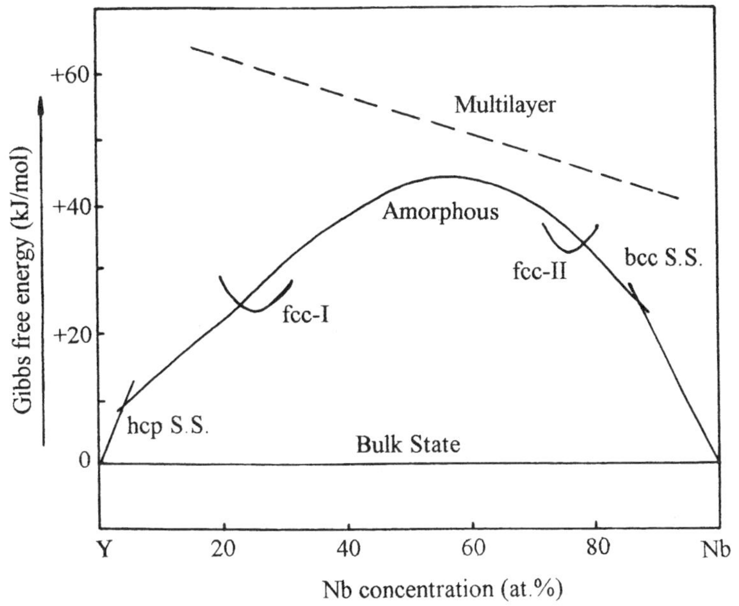

Fig. 1. A calculated free-energy diagram of the Y–Nb system. The dashed line shows the initial energetic level of the as-deposited Y–Nb multilayers with an interfacial atomic fraction of 17%.

where $\sigma_{A,0}$ and $\sigma_{B,0}$ are the surface energy of metals A and B, respectively. The chemical term σ_{chem} is given by [21] $\sigma_{chem} = L/\left(C_0 V_A^{2/3}\right)$, where C_0 is a constant being 4.5×10^8, and L is the heat of solution of metal A in metal B at infinite dilution [22]. According to Gerkema and Miedema [23] the interfacial free energy is calculated as follows

$$\Delta G_{mul} = S_f \times \sigma_{AB} \tag{8}$$

where S_f is the surface area occupied by one mole of interfacial atoms.

Suppose N_A and N_B are numbers of layers of metals A and B, $d_{A,i}$ and $d_{B,i}$ are the thicknesses of the ith layers of metals A and B, respectively; n_A and n_B are numbers of interfaces (A on B) and (B on A), $\Delta d_{A,i}$ and $\Delta d_{B,i}$ are the thicknesses of the ith interfaces (A on B) and (B on A), respectively. Obviously, the relationship of $n_A + n_B + 1 = N_A + N_B$ always holds for these four parameters. The interfacial free energy for the multilayers can then be expressed by

$$\Delta G_{mul} = I_{fA} S_{fA} \sigma_{BA} + I_{fB} S_{fB} \sigma_{AB} \tag{9}$$

where S_{fA} and S_{fB} are the surface areas occupied by one mole atoms A and B, respectively; I_{fA} and I_{fB} are the fractions of interfacial atoms A and B vs the total atoms in the multilayered films, respectively, given by

$$I_{fA} = x_A \frac{\sum_i^{n_A} \Delta d_{A,i}}{\sum_i^{N_A} d_{A,i}}, \quad I_{fB} = x_B \frac{\sum_j^{n_B} \Delta d_{B,j}}{\sum_j^{N_B} d_{B,j}} \tag{10}$$

Based on the above-mentioned model and methods [24, 25], the free-energy curves of the two terminal solid solutions, the amorphous phase, two non-equilibrium crystalline phases and the Y–Nb multilayered films containing 17% of interfacial atoms, were calculated and are exhibited in Fig. 1. The parameters used in the calculation are listed in Table 1, and the thickness of the interfacial layer was reasonably assumed to be 0.5 nm [11].

3. EXPERIMENTAL PROCEDURE

According to the calculated Gibbs free energy shown in Fig. 1, the Y–Nb multilayered films with a total thickness of 50 nm were designed to be 18 layers (noted as N18 hereafter) corresponding to a fraction of 17% of the interfacial atoms, and prepared by depositing pure yttrium and niobium

Table 1. Values of the parameters used in thermodynamic calculation for the Y–Nb system; "—" means the data were not used

Parameter	T_m (K)	M [kJ/(mol·cm^2)]	$V^{2/3}$ (cm^2)	γ	σ_0 (mJ/m^2)	$L_{Y\ in\ Nb}$ (kJ/mol)	$L_{Nb\ in\ Y}$ (kJ/mol)	S_f (10^5 m^2)
Y	1799	—	7.34	—	1125	—	—	3.3
Nb	2740	—	4.89	—	2700	—	—	2.2
Amorphous	—	20.00	—	5	—	+139	+102	—
Solid solution	—	20.00	—	0	—	+139	+102	—
As-deposited films	—	—	—	—	—	+139	+102	—

Table 2. Structural changes in Y–Nb-multilayered films upon room temperature 190 keV xenon ion mixing. (The mixing dose is in 10^{14} Xe^+/cm^2. "PA" and "A" indicate partial and complete amorphous phase, respectively; f.c.c.-I and f.c.c.-II are two non-equilibrium crystalline phases)

Dosage	$Y_{28}Nb_{72}$	$Y_{43}Nb_{57}$	$Y_{56}Nb_{44}$	$Y_{60}Nb_{40}$	$Y_{77}Nb_{23}$
As-deposited	Y + Nb	Y + Nb	Y + Nb	Y + Nb	Y + Nb
3	Y + Nb	Y + Nb	Y + Nb	Y + Nb	Y + Nb
5	Y + Nb	Y + Nb	Y + Nb	Y + Nb	A
10	Y + Nb	Y + Nb	Y + Nb	Y + Nb	A
30	f.c.c.-II	Y + Nb	Y + Nb	Y + Nb	A
50	f.c.c.-II	f.c.c.-II	PA	A	A + f.c.c.-I
70	f.c.c.-II	f.c.c.-II	A	A	f.c.c.-I

alternatively onto newly cleaved NaCl single crystals as substrates in an evaporation system with a vacuum level on the order of 10^{-5} Pa. The total thickness of the samples was designed to match the sum of the projected range and projected range straggling of 190 keV xenon ions, i.e. about 50 nm. During deposition, the composition of the samples was controlled by adjusting the relative thicknesses of the metal layers. The deposited films were then irradiated by 190 keV xenon ions at room temperature to doses ranging from 3×10^{14} to 7×10^{15} Xe^+/cm^2 in an implanter with a vacuum level on the order of 10^{-4} Pa. The xenon ion-beam current density was controlled to be less than 1 $\mu A/cm^2$ to minimize the beam-heating effect. Consecutive thermal annealing of the as-deposited samples was accomplished in the hot stage of a transmission electron microscope (TEM) or in a furnace to examine the structural phase evolution upon annealing. The samples were analyzed by TEM, selected area diffraction (SAD) and/or X-ray diffraction (XRD) to identify the microstructures emerging in the films. Meanwhile, wavelength dispersive spectrum (WDS) analysis was employed, because of its suitability for distinguishing Y and Nb, to determine the real composition of the resultant phases in the films within an experimental error of less than 5%.

4. RESULTS AND DISCUSSION

4.1. Metallic glasses formed by ion mixing

Table 2 lists the structural phase transition in the N18 Y–Nb multilayered films induced by 190 keV xenon ion mixing at room temperature with increasing ion irradiation doses. From the table, one sees clearly that amorphous alloys were only obtained in the three samples with Y-rich compositions, i.e. $Y_{77}Nb_{23}$, $Y_{60}Nb_{40}$ and $Y_{56}Nb_{44}$, but not in the two Nb-rich multilayered films. As a typical example, Figs 2(a) and (b) show, respectively, the sharp diffraction lines for the as-deposited films and halos from the ion-mixed $Y_{56}Nb_{44}$ amorphous alloy obtained after ion mixing to a dose of 7×10^{15} Xe^+/cm^2. The details of the IM results in this system can be found in our recent publication [26].

4.2. Metastable crystalline alloys formed by ion mixing

A unique new f.c.c.-I phase was observed in the $Y_{77}Nb_{23}$ films at a dose of 7×10^{15} Xe^+/cm^2.

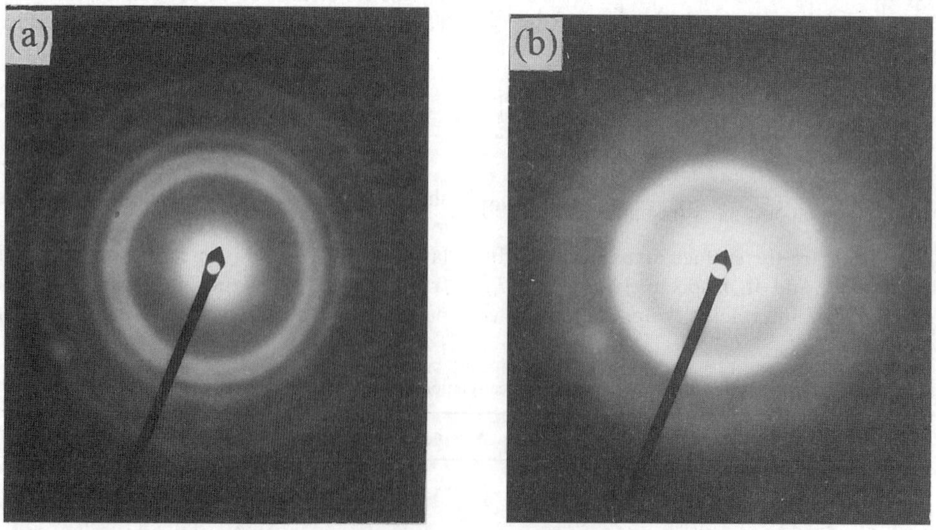

Fig. 2. SAD patterns of the $Y_{56}Nb_{44}$-multilayered films with 17 interfaces: (a) as-deposited; (b) amorphized at a dose of 7×10^{15} Xe^+/cm^2.

Table 3. Identification of the f.c.c.-I phase formed in the $Y_{77}Nb_{23}$-multilayered films by room temperature 190 keV ion mixing to a dose of 7×10^{15} Xe^+/cm^2; $a_{f.c.c.\text{-}I}=4.87$ Å

$d_{exp.}$ (Å)	(*hkl*)	$d_{cal.}$ (Å)	Intensity
2.81	111	2.82	strong
2.47	200	2.44	medium
1.74	220	1.72	strong
1.47	311	1.48	strong
1.41	222	1.40	strong
1.21	400	1.22	weak
1.12	331	1.12	weak
1.09	420	1.08	weak

Table 3 gives the indexing of the metastable f.c.c.-I phase with a lattice parameter of $a_{f.c.c.\text{-}I}=4.87$ Å. Figures 3(a)–(d) show SAD patterns of the as-deposited $Y_{77}Nb_{23}$ films and irradiated ones at different irradiation stages. Another new f.c.c.-II phase was observed in two Nb-enriched samples. In the $Y_{28}Nb_{72}$ and $Y_{43}Nb_{57}$ films, the f.c.c.-II phase was formed by ion mixing at the doses of 3×10^{15} Xe^+/cm^2 and 5×10^{15} Xe^+/cm^2, respectively. Figures 4(a)–(b) show the corresponding SAD patterns of the as-deposited films and the f.c.c.-II phase in the $Y_{43}Nb_{57}$ films. Table 4 gives the identification of the metastable f.c.c.-II phase. The lattice parameter of the new f.c.c.-II phase was determined to be $a_{f.c.c.\text{-}II}=4.10$ Å. After consulting the documented diffraction file, the ion-mixed Y-rich f.c.c.-I and Nb-rich f.c.c.-II phases were considered as metastable crystalline phases in this system, since their diffraction lines could neither be indexed to

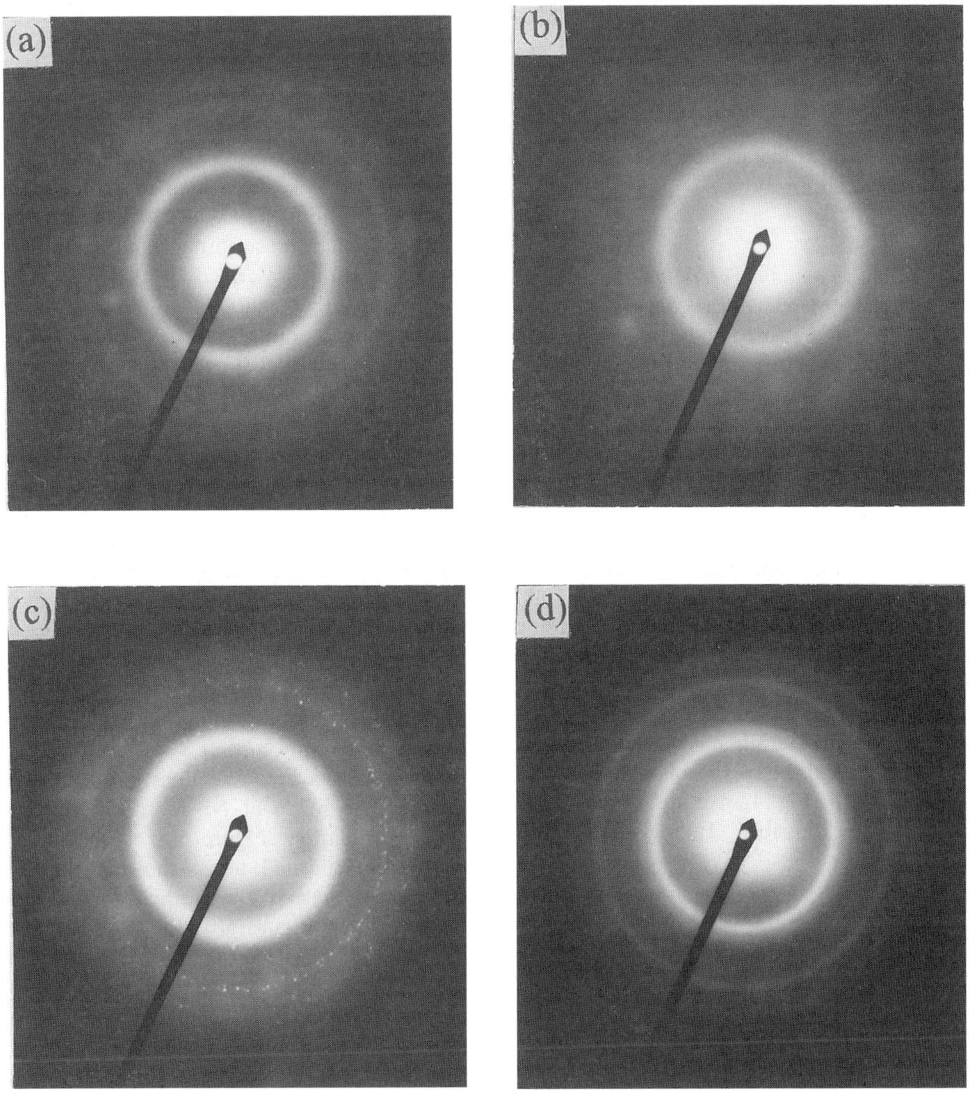

Fig. 3. SAD patterns of the $Y_{77}Nb_{23}$-multilayered films with 17 interfaces at different ion-mixing stages: (a) as-deposited; (b) amorphized at a dose of 5×10^{14} Xe^+/cm^2; (c) a mixture of amorphous and f.c.c.-I phase at a dose of 5×10^{15} Xe^+/cm^2; and (d) a unique f.c.c.-I phase formed at a dose of 7×10^{15} Xe^+/cm^2.

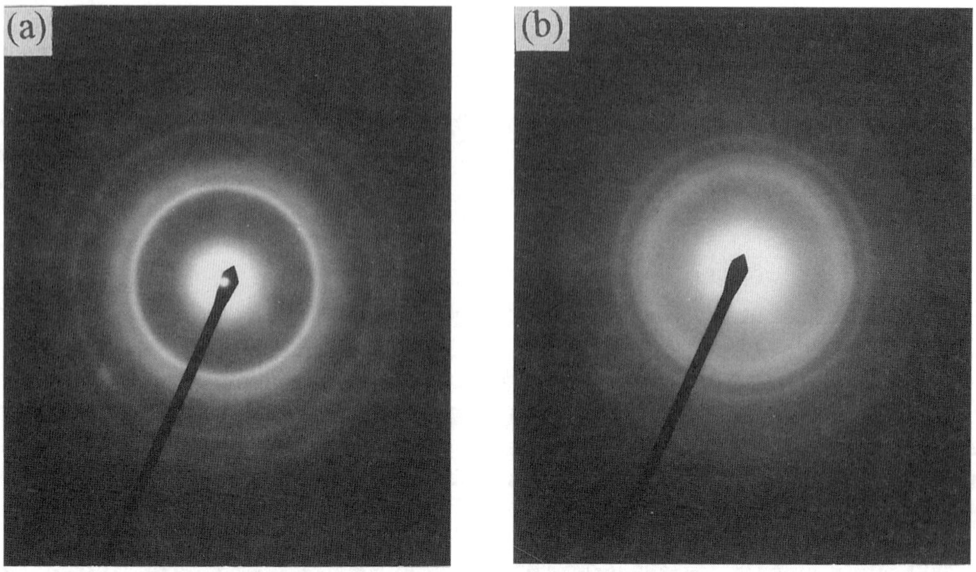

Fig. 4. SAD patterns of the $Y_{43}Nb_{57}$ films with 17 interfaces: (a) as-deposited; (b) f.c.c.-II phase formed at a dose of 5×10^{15} Xe^{+}/cm^{2}.

those of the elemental metals nor to those possible oxides of Y, Nb and (Y + Nb).

4.3. Discussion

4.3.1. Thermodynamic interpretation. The reaction between two elements can occur only if there is a thermodynamic driving force and a kinetic path for reaction to take place. In terms of thermodynamics, the driving force controlling the alloy formation originated from the difference of the Gibbs free energy between the initial and final states. From Fig. 1, one may observe that the free-energy curves of the amorphous, metastable crystalline phases and the solid solutions are well above that of the reference state of an equilibrium mixture of the two constituent metals considered in a bulk form, thus implying an unfavorable thermodynamic condition for alloying in this system. However, for multilayered films, the extra interfacial free energy does elevate the free energy of the films to a higher level than that of the two terminal solid solutions, the amorphous phase and the two metastable crystalline phases, as shown in Fig. 1, making amorphization thermodynamically possible. Taking the $Y_{77}Nb_{23}$ multilayered films as an example, the calculated energetic sequence from high to low is as-deposited state, amorphous state and then the f.c.c.-I phase, which is exactly in accordance with the experimental observations described by the SAD patterns in Fig. 3. For other multilayered films at those studied composition points, the calculated energetic sequences also match well with the experimental results. In other words, the calculated free-energy diagram can give a reasonable interpretation to amorphization as well as the metastable crystalline phase formation.

Table 4. Indexing results of the f.c.c.-II phase formed in the $Y_{43}Nb_{57}$-multilayered films by room temperature 190 keV ion mixing to a dose of 5×10^{15} Xe^{+}/cm^{2}; $a_{f.c.c.\text{-}II} = 4.10$ Å

$d_{exp.}$ (Å)	(*hkl*)	$d_{cal.}$ (Å)	Intensity
2.37	111	2.36	strong
2.05	200	2.05	strong
1.44	220	1.45	medium
1.21	311	1.23	weak
1.15	222	1.18	weak
1.01	400	1.03	weak
0.91	331	0.94	weak

To further verify the decisive role of the interfacial free energy in enhancing the alloying ability and even inducing amorphization in this positive ΔH_f system, solid-state reaction experiments were performed with relatively thick samples designed to include 17% of interfacial atoms, demonstrated by IM to be favorable for amorphization. Multilayered $Y_{72}Nb_{28}$ films with a total thickness of 350 nm were accordingly designed and prepared to have 121 layers. The first and top layers were intentionally made of Nb to reduce the possibility of contamination. Figure 5(a) is an XRD pattern of the as-deposited films, showing the crystalline structure of Y and Nb by their corresponding diffraction lines. Figure 5(b) shows that the $Y_{72}Nb_{28}$ multilayered films were amorphized after annealing at 300°C for 1.5 h as evidenced by the presence of a halo situated somewhere between the first diffraction lines of the crystalline Y and Nb metals. The location of the halo is the same as that observed for an amorphous phase by other glass-forming techniques, such as liquid melt quenching. Similar solid-state amorphization was reproduced in other, thinner N18 $Y_{60}Nb_{40}$ multilayered films,

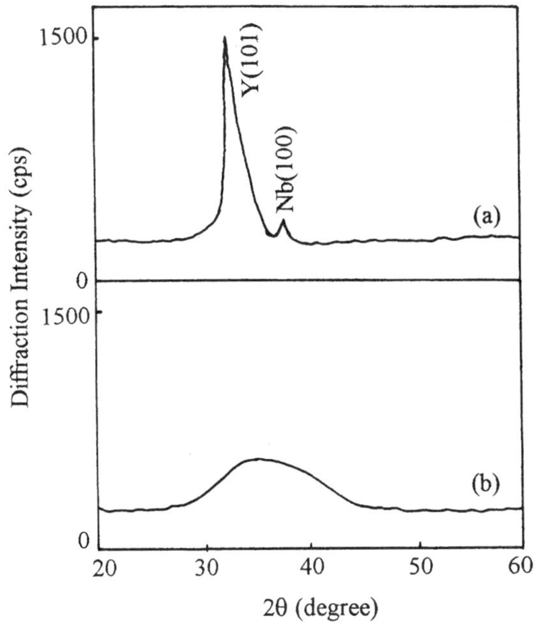

Fig. 5. X-ray diffraction patterns of the $Y_{72}Nb_{28}$-multilayered films with 121 layers and a total thickness of 350 nm before and after thermal annealing: (a) as-deposited; (b) amorphized at 300°C for 1.5 h.

i.e. amorphization was achieved in the films after thermal annealing at 350°C in the hot stage of the TEM for 1.5 h. After further annealing at 600°C for 1 h, the thermally formed $Y_{60}Nb_{40}$ amorphous phase recrystallized into an equilibrium mixture of (Y + Nb) crystalline metals. The evidence for crystal-to-amorphous and amorphous-to-crystal transitions upon thermal annealing in the $Y_{60}Nb_{40}$ multilayered films is shown by the SAD patterns in Figs 6(a)–(c). It is worthwhile noting that the sharp diffraction lines reflected from the crystalline Y and Nb metals in Fig. 6(c) are almost identical with those shown in Fig. 6(a), which indirectly supports the fact that the halo shown in Fig. 6(b) was reflected from the Y–Nb metallic glass.

These results indicate that, if the fraction (α) of the interfacial atoms is large enough for the multilayered films, metallic glasses can be formed in this positive ΔH_f system by either IM or SSR. Besides, the thermal annealing results from both thicker and thinner samples can serve as evidence confirming that the interfacial free energy provides a major driving force for amorphization and alloying. It is known that a favorable thermodynamic condition is a necessary one but not alone sufficient. In other words, one should also consider, at the same time, the growth kinetics to find out whether an amorphous phase can indeed be formed or not. In the present case, as there are some crystalline phases of simple structure, the competition between crystallization and amorphization would certainly affect the amorphous phase formation at some specific composition points. From Fig. 1, it is clear that the f.c.c.-I and f.c.c.-II phases have lower free energy than that of the multilayers within a certain composition range, i.e. the Y-rich f.c.c.-I and the Nb-rich f.c.c.-II phases have lower free energy than those of the corresponding solid solution and the amorphous phases, respectively. Consequently, the formation of f.c.c.-I and f.c.c.-II phases was favored and it hindered amorphization in this range. Recently, a similar SSR experiment was conducted by the authors in the Y–W system and some Y–W glasses were also obtained [27], indicating the above unusual alloying behavior is not peculiar to a few positive ΔH_f systems.

4.3.2. Growth kinetics of the metastable crystalline phases. The above calculations confirm that the excess free energy originating from the interfaces provide a major thermodynamic driving force for the formation of the f.c.c.-I and f.c.c.-II phases in the Y–Nb system. The next issue to discuss is the growth kinetics of the metastable crystalline phases formed by ion mixing. It is commonly known that IM is a far from equilibrium process consisting of two steps, i.e. the atomic collision cascade and a later step of relaxation lasting only $\approx 10^{-10}$–10^{-9} s [28]. The atomic collision is responsible for triggering intermixing between the metal layers, which results in a uniform mixture in a highly energetic state. During the second step, the atoms in the mixture should undergo relaxation, within which the structure of the anticipated alloy phase is to be formed. Within such a short span of time, long-range diffusion is apparently impossible and crystalline phases with complicated structures are hardly to be formed; instead, only simple structured phases can be obtained or the ion-mixed mixture remains in an amorphous state. In the present study, the metastable phases formed by IM are indeed either amorphous or simple-structured phases as described above.

The details of the growth kinetics of two metastable crystalline phases are thought to proceed as follows. From a structural point of view, the Y(h.c.p.)-rich f.c.c.-I phase was closely correlated to its major alloying metal Y(h.c.p.). As the atomic arrangement of the h.c.p. and f.c.c. structures is quite similar, i.e. they are built up by stacking the close-packed planes in the sequences of ABABAB... and ABCABCABC..., respectively, the transition of h.c.p. → f.c.c. can therefore be realized readily by a sliding on the $\{0002\}_{h.c.p.}$ plane along the $\langle 1\bar{1}00\rangle_{h.c.p.}$ direction by a vector of $1/3\langle 1\bar{1}00\rangle_{h.c.p.}$. Such sliding is a fast transition and can be completed during relaxation. According to this sliding mechanism, the relationship between the two lattices can be deduced as $a_{f.c.c.} = \sqrt{2}a_{h.c.p.}$. Using the lattice parameter of the yttrium-supersaturated solid solution of $a_{h.c.p.} = 3.51$ Å, the lattice parameter of the f.c.c.-I phase is calculated to be $a_{f.c.c.\text{-}I} = 4.96$ Å, which is in good agreement with the experimental value of 4.87 Å.

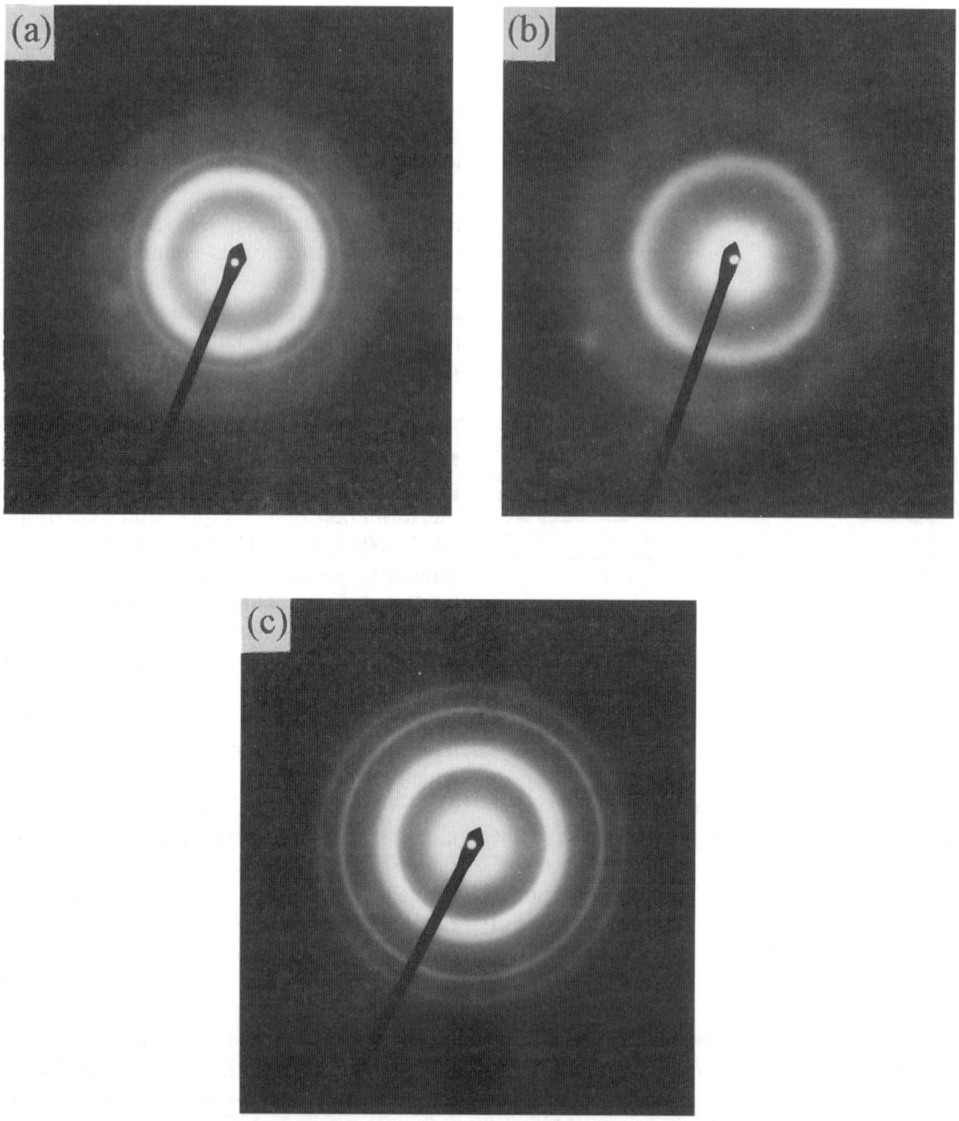

Fig. 6. SAD patterns of the $Y_{60}Nb_{40}$-multilayered films upon thermal annealing: (a) as-deposited; (b) amorphized at 350°C for 1.5 h; and (c) recrystallized at 600°C for 1 h.

The growth kinetics of the Nb(b.c.c.)-rich f.c.c.-II phase was not that straightforward, because to transform the b.c.c. structure directly into an f.c.c. one is a little difficult. Recently, the authors' group has proposed a two-step transition mechanism of b.c.c. → h.c.p. → f.c.c. [29], which can also be applied to the present case. That is first to transform b.c.c. to h.c.p. through a shearing mechanism. During shearing, the $(111)_{b.c.c.}$ acts as the habit plane, while $[\bar{1}1\bar{1}]_{b.c.c.}$ (or $[\bar{1}\bar{1}0]_{h.c.p.}$) acts as the shearing axis. Then the transformation of h.c.p. into f.c.c. is easy to achieve by a sliding of atoms on the planes parallel to the $(0002)_{h.c.p.}$ plane along $1\bar{1}00_{h.c.p.}$ directions by a vector of $1/31\bar{1}00_{h.c.p.}$. Both shearing and sliding are fast transition units and can be executed during relaxation. Accordingly, the relationship of the lattice parameters among the b.c.c., h.c.p. and f.c.c. structures can be figured out as follows. A transition of b.c.c. → h.c.p. can be fulfilled by a shearing, leading to a relationship of $a_{h.c.p.}=(\sqrt{3}/2)a_{b.c.c.}$, and another transition of h.c.p. → f.c.c. can be realized by a sliding and results in a relationship of $a_{f.c.c.}=\sqrt{2}a_{h.c.p.}$. The lattice parameter of the f.c.c. phase is therefore deduced to be $a_{f.c.c.}=(\sqrt{6}/2)a_{b.c.c.}$. Using Vegard's law, the lattice parameter of a $Y_{43}Nb_{57}$ supersaturated solid solution is about 3.45 Å. The lattice parameter of the f.c.c.-II phase is thus calculated to be 4.23 Å. Comparing with the experimental value of 4.10 Å, the difference between them is less than 5%.

5. CONCLUSIONS

In summary, by designing the multilayered films to include a sufficient fraction of interfacial atoms, both IM and SSR are capable of producing amorphous alloys in the immiscible Y–Nb system, and the thermodynamic driving force for amorphization or alloying comes mainly from the excess interfacial free energy. In addition, the results of SSR experiments can serve as indirect evidence confirming the relevance of the calculated free-energy diagram, at least in its outline, as the observed relative energetic levels of the involved phases upon annealing are in agreement with those deduced by the calculation. Further work in this area is still needed, e.g. to improve the accuracy of the calculation for the free energy of the phases as well as for the interface, to study atomic bonding preferences in the amorphous alloys obtained in the immiscible systems, closer examination of the microstructure to find out the difference, if any, between the glasses obtained in the systems with positive and negative ΔH_f, etc.

Acknowledgements—The authors are grateful to the National Natural Science Foundation of China and the Administration of Tsinghua University for financial aid to this study.

REFERENCES

1. Duwez, P., Williens, R.H. and Klement, W.J., *J. appl. Phys.*, 1960, **31**, 1136.
2. Johnson, W.L., *Prog. Mater. Sci.*, 1986, **30**, 81.
3. Liu, B.X., Johnson, W.L., Nicolet, M.-A. and Lau, S.S., *Appl. Phys. Lett.*, 1983, **42**, 45.
4. Schwarz, R.B. and Johnson, W.L., *Phys. Rev. Lett.*, 1983, **51**, 415.
5. de Boer, F.R., Boom, R.B., Matters, W.C.M., Miedema A.R. and Niessen, A.K., *Cohesion in Metals: Transion Metal Alloys*. North-Holland, Amsterdam, 1989.
6. Alonso, J.A. and Simozar, S., *Solid St. Commun.*, 1983, **46**, 765.
7. Clemens, B.M. and Hufnagel, T.C., *J. Alloys Compounds*, 1993, **194**, 221.
8. Huang, L.J. and Liu, B.X., *Appl. Phys. Lett.*, 1990, **57**, 1401.
9. Jin, O. and Liu, B.X., *J. Phys. Condens. Matter*, 1994, **6**, L39.
10. Meissener, J., Kopitzki, K., Mertler, G. and Peiner, E., *Nucl. Instrum. Methods*, 1987, **B19/20**, 669.
11. Clemens, B.M., *Phys. Rev.*, 1986, **B33**, 7615.
12. Zhang, Z.J., Jin, O. and Liu, B.X., *Phys. Rev.*, 1995, **B51**, 8076.
13. Zhang, Z.J. and Liu, B.X., *Phys. Rev.*, 1995, **B51**, 16475.
14. Alonso, J.A., Gallego, L.J. and Simozar, J.A., *Nuovo Cimento*, 1990, **D12**, 587.
15. Niessen, A.K. and Miedema, A.R., *Ber. Bunsenges. Phys. Chem.*, 1983, **87**, 717.
16. Lopez, J.M. and Alonso, J.A., *Z. Naturf.*, 1985, **A40**, 199.
17. Weeber, A.W., *J. Phys.*, 1987, **F17**, 809.
18. Niessen, A.K., Miedema, A.R., de Boer, F.R. and Boom, R., *Physica*, 1988, **B151**, 401.
19. Turnbull, D., *Impurities and Imperfections*. ASM, Metals Park, OH, 1955, p. 121.
20. Murr, L.E., *Interfacial Phenomena in Metals and Alloys*. Addision-Wesley, London, 1975.
21. Miedema, A.R., *Z. Metallk.*, 1978, **69**, 455.
22. Miedema, A.R., *Z. Metallk.*, 1978, **69**, 287.
23. Gerkema, J. and Miedema, A.R., *Surf. Sci.*, 1981, **124**, 351.
24. Alonso, J.A., Gallego, L.J. and Lopez, J.M., *Phil. Mag. A*, 1988, **58**, 79.
25. Liu, B.X. and Zhang, Z.J., *Phys. Rev.*, 1994, **B49**, 12519.
26. Chen, Y.G., Liu, B.X. and Zhang, Q., *J. Phys.: Condensed Matter*, 1997, **9**, 389.
27. Chen, Y.G. and Liu, B.X., *Appl. Phys.*, 1997, **A65**, 73.
28. Thompson, M.V., *Defects and Radiation Damage in Metals*, chaps. 4 and 5. Cambridge University Press, Cambridge, 1969.
29. Liu, B.X. and Zhang, Z.J., *J. Mater. Res.*, 1994, **9**, 357.

Glass-forming ability determined by the atomic interaction potential for the Ni-Mo system

Q. Zhang, W. S. Lai, and B. X. Liu*
Department of Materials Science and Engineering, Tsinghua University, Beijing 100084, China
and National Laboratory of Solid-State Microstructure Physics, Nanjing University, Nanjing 210093, China
(Received 4 November 1998)

Employing an *n*-body Ni-Mo potential, a molecular dynamics simulation is performed to study the crystal-to-amorphous transition of Ni- and Mo-rich solid solutions with increasing Mo and Ni content, respectively. It is found that the Ni- and Mo-rich supersaturated solid solutions become unstable and transform into amorphous states when the Mo and Ni contents are beyond the critical concentrations at 21 at. % of Mo and 25 at. % of Ni, respectively. The possible correlation of the calculated concentrations with the glass-forming ability of the Ni-Mo system is also discussed. [S0163-1829(99)15321-9]

Since the first Au-Si amorphous alloy was obtained in 1960 by liquid melt quenching (LMQ), a number of techniques have been developed to produce amorphous alloys (metallic glasses) and several empirical models have been proposed to predict the glass-forming ability (GFA) of the binary metal systems.[1–3] In practice, a quantitative measure of the GFA is of glass-forming composition range [referred to as the glass-forming range (GFR) hereafter], in which amorphous alloys can be obtained. Phenomenologically, the GFR seems to depend on the producing technique, as it has been observed that in a same system, the faster the cooling speed of the technique, the broader the GFR. Take the Ni-Nb system as an example; the GFR was within 40–70 at. % of Ni under LMQ, possessing a typical cooling speed of 10^{6-8} K/s, whereas it was considerably extended to a range from 20 to 85 at. % of Ni upon ion mixing (IM) of multiple metal layers,[4,5] indicating that a disordered state can exist in such a broad composition range. From a physical point of view, a binary metal system should have its own intrinsic GFA or GFR, as the existence of the atomic configurations in a disordered state is determined by its internal characteristics. Apparently, the intrinsic GFA or GFR should not be dependent on the employed glass-producing techniques, which only provide an external condition for growing an alloy phase in a specific atomic configuration. It is thus better to name an experimentally determined GFR as the nominal one, which is certainly always smaller than the intrinsic GFR of a system. Naturally, if a currently available technique with the greatest cooling speed is applied, the GFR determined by the technique is most likely the one closest to the intrinsic GFR. To the authors' knowledge, IM probably possesses the greatest cooling speed among the currently available techniques, as its effective cooling speed can be as high as on the order of 10^{14} K/s.[6] Consequently, the GFR revealed by IM may be the value closest to the intrinsic GFR. In fact, in many binary metal systems, the nominal GFR observed by IM extends almost over the whole composition range except the terminal regions favoring solid solutions with one of the simple fcc, bcc, and hcp structures. These lead Liu *et al.* to propose a parameter to predict a maximum possible GFR of a system, namely, the maximum possible amorphization range (MPAR), which is defined as 100% minus the maximum solid solubilities in two terminals observed from the corresponding equilibrium phase diagram.[7] According to the combinations of the MPAR and the heat of formation, the binary metal systems can be classified into three categories: readily, possibly, and hardly glass-forming ones. Although the model is an empirical and qualitative one, its prediction is in good agreement with most of the experimental results reported so far. In recent decades, numerous supersaturated solid solutions have been obtained by various techniques[8,9] and they make the corresponding solid solution lines towards the central portion in the equilibrium phase diagram. As a result, the above empirical model should be modified by taking into account the supersaturated solubilities of a system. A theoretical approach is therefore necessary to determine the maximum supersaturated solid solubilities of the two constituent metals of a system, from which an intrinsic GFR can therefore be obtained. In the present work, we employ molecular dynamics (MD) simulations to study the relative stability of solid solutions versus an amorphous state as a function of solute concentrations in the Ni-Mo system and to try to approach the maximum supersaturated solid solubilities in both Ni and Mo terminals. It will be shown later that spontaneous vitrification can take place in the supersaturated solid solutions when the compositions are beyond two critical values, respectively. Such spontaneous vitrification is similar to previous observations by simulation studies that amorphization can be initiated by introducing antisite defects in $NiZr_2$ intermetallic compounds,[10,11] in which the objectives were to study the chemical disorder, whereas in the present work a similar vitrification process results from changing the chemical composition of the solid solution and the main interest is in assessing the GFR of the Ni-Mo system.

The Ni-Mo system is selected for the present study, as an *n*-body potential has been constructed by the authors based on the framework proposed by Finnis and Sinclair and it reproduced some physical properties of the system. Furthermore, the potential has also been employed to simulate the solid-state interfacial reaction in the Ni-Mo system and the simulation clarified some detailed issues of solid-state amorphization, which were in good agreement with the experimental observations.[12] In the present work, we employ the potential to run a molecular dynamics simulation with the Parrinello-Rahman MD scheme[13] for studying the crystal-to-

Physical Review B 59(19), p.13521-13524 (1999).

amorphous transition of the solid solutions in the Ni-Mo system. In this scheme, the equations of motion are solved using a fourth-order predictor-corrector algorithm of Gear with a time step $t=5\times10^{-15}$ s.

The simulation model consists of $8\times8\times6\times4=1536$ atoms for fcc Ni crystalline and $9\times9\times8\times2=1296$ atoms for bcc Mo crystalline lattices, respectively. In both models, the [100], [010], and [001] crystalline directions are parallel to x, y, and z axes, respectively, and periodic boundary conditions are adopted in three directions. The solute atoms are added by randomly substituting a certain number of Mo (Ni) atoms into the Ni fcc (Mo bcc) lattice and the initial fcc Ni-rich (bcc Mo-rich) solid solution is thus obtained. Molecular dynamics simulations are performed for the solid solutions with gradually increasing the solute concentration to find out the critical compositions, at which crystalline lattices of the solid solutions become unstable and transform into disordered. After construction of the models, the simulation is then run at 27 °C for 5000–10 000 MD time steps to a relatively equilibrium state, at which all the related dynamic variables show no secular variation. It should be noted that the above defined equilibrium state is frequently metastable, as the simulation time is extremely short compared with that in real experiments for approaching an exact equilibrium state. The process of structural change in the Ni-Mo atomic model is monitored by two quantitative methods. The first one is the planar structure factor $S(k)$ for the individual atomic plane. According to the definition, $S=1$ refers to an entirely ordered crystal and $S=0$ stands for a completely disordered state. The second one is the pair-correlation function $g(r)$ for a block of materials, which is commonly recognized as a decisive parameter to identify an amorphous structure.

After running at 27 °C for 5000–10 000 MD time steps, Fig. 1 displays the total and partial pair-correlation functions $g(r)$ calculated for the Ni-rich fcc solid solutions consisting of Mo solute atoms up to 10, 17, 21, and 25 at. %, respectively. From the figure, one sees that the solid solutions with 10 and 17 at. % of Mo still retain fcc crystalline structure. While for the solid solution with 25 at. % of Mo, a crystal-to-amorphous transition apparently takes place, as evidenced by the shape of the $g(r)$ curves commonly observed for the amorphous alloys. The split of the second peak in the $g_{\text{Ni-Ni}}(r)$ can readily be seen, providing a solid confirmation of the resultant amorphous structure. For the case of 21 at. % of Mo, the shape of $g(r)$ curve is more or less ambiguous, indicating that the crystalline lattice of the solid solution starts to collapse at this composition. In addition, the calculation of the planar structure factors also provides evidence for the above structural changes in the model; i.e., $S(k)$ of the atomic planes are above 0.5 when x_{Mo} is below 21 at. % and decrease distinctly to less than 0.1 when x_{Mo} is 21 and 25 at. %, suggesting that 21 at. % of Mo is a critical solubility of the Ni-rich fcc supersaturated solid solution.

A similar simulation is also performed for Mo-rich bcc solid solutions with various compositions, and Fig. 2 shows the calculated total and partial pair-correlation functions $g(r)$ for the solid solutions at four compositions of 10, 25, 30, and 40 at. % of Ni. It can be seen that the peaks become gradually broadened and indistinguishable, corresponding to a disordering process, with increasing Ni concentration. When x_{Ni} is equal to or beyond 25 at. %, the $g(r)$ curves are in a typical shape, confirming that an amorphous structure is obtained. Comparatively, planar structure factors have not shown a distinct change, though they also decrease gradually as the Ni content increases.

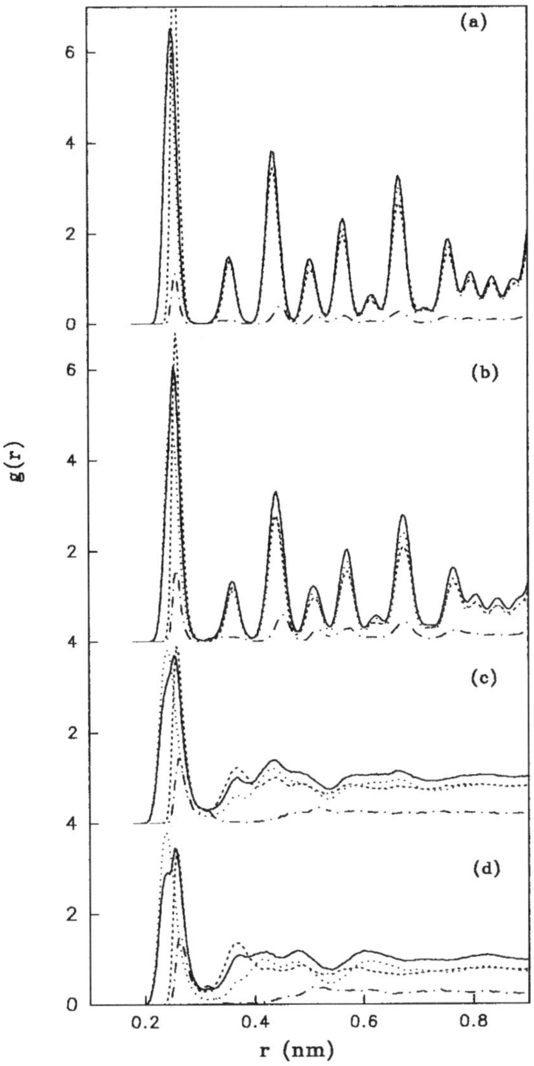

FIG. 1. Total and partial pair-correlation functions for the fcc Ni-rich solid solution after running at 27 °C for 5000–10 000 MD time steps. The compositions are at (a) 10 at. %, (b) 17 at. %, (c) 21 at. %, and (d) 25 at. % of Mo, respectively. The solid line is for the total $g(r)$, the short dashed line is for the Mo-Ni $g(r)$, the dotted line is for the Ni-Ni $g(r)$, and the dot-dashed line is for the Mo-Mo $g(r)$.

To obtain firm evidence of a crystal-to-amorphous transition taking place at the critical compositions determined above, the molar enthalpy and volume are calculated for the resultant Ni-Mo alloys from the initial fcc and bcc solid solutions. Figure 3 shows the changing of the molar enthalpy and volume versus alloy composition. From the Ni end, the enthalpy decreases, yet the volume increases, with increasing Mo content. At $x_{\text{Mo}}=21$ at. %, the slope of the enthalpy is discontinuous and there is a clear step increase in volume, indicating that a crystal-to-amorphous transition does take place. An abrupt increase in volume is from the formation of

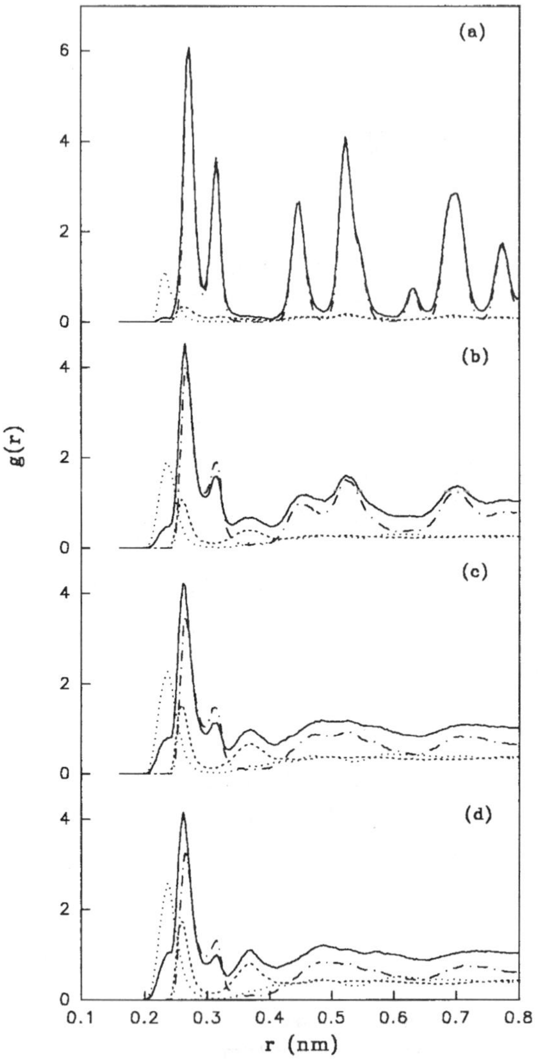

FIG. 2. Total and partial pair-correlation functions for the bcc Mo-rich solid solution after running at 27 °C for 5000–10 000 MD time steps. The compositions are at (a) 10 at.%, (b) 25 at.%, (c) 30 at.%, and (d) 40 at.% of Ni, respectively. The solid line is for the total $g(r)$; the short dashed line is for the Mo-Ni $g(r)$; the dotted line is for the Ni-Ni $g(r)$, and the dot-dashed line is for the Mo-Mo $g(r)$.

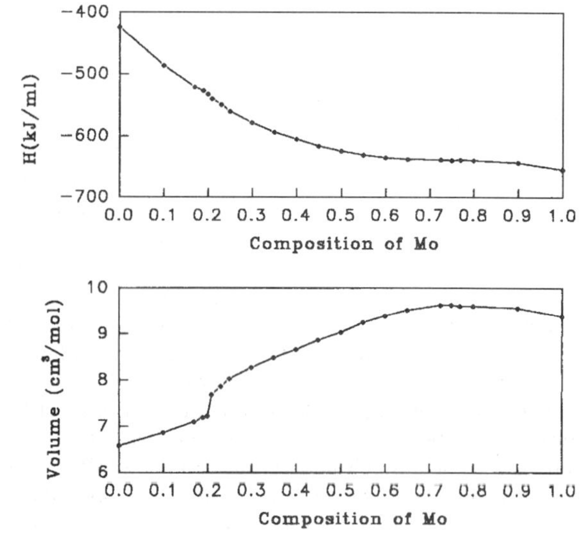

FIG. 3. Molar enthalpy and volume of the system at a relative equilibrium state vs compositions obtained after running at 27 °C for 5000–10 000 MD time steps from the Ni-rich fcc solid solution (0–50 at.% Mo) and Mo-rich bcc solid solution (50–100 at.% Mo).

a Ni-Mo amorphous phase, which is compatible with the theoretical prediction that an amorphous phase has a couple of percent excess free volume than its crystalline counterpart.[14] While at the Mo side, there is no distinct change in the molar enthalpy. Although the volume increase of the bcc Mo solid solutions with increasing Ni content is not abrupt, a kink does appear at $x_{Ni}=25$ at.%, which is the same as that found by a pair correlation function calculation. The volume expansion of the model is associated with a crystal-to-amorphous transition, resulting in the formation of a Mo-rich Ni-Mo amorphous phase. In summary, according to the above structural characterizations, the compositions for a crystal-to-amorphous transition to take place are deduced to be 21 at.% Mo and about 25 at.% Ni for the fcc Ni-rich and bcc Mo-rich solid solutions, respectively. It follows that in a central composition region between 21 and 75 at.% of Mo, the supersaturated solid solutions are unstable and will turn into an amorphous state. In other words, this composition range is favored for spontaneous vitrification and can therefore be considered to be very close to the glass-forming range of the Ni-Mo system, which can serve as guidance in choosing the alloy composition for producing metallic glasses. It should be noted that the glass-forming range is determined directly by the stability of the atomic configurations governed by the Ni-Mo potential and is therefore something intrinsic to the system, but not connected with any practically applied glass-producing technique.

It is of interest to compare the simulation results with the experimental observations. In fact, amorphization of the Ni-Mo multilayered samples has indeed been achieved upon solid-state reaction at medium temperatures and the amorphization range is at least extended from 25 to 75 at.% of Mo,[15] which is in excellent agreement with the simulated GFR of 21–75 at.% of Mo. Besides, ion beam mixing has also produced Ni-Mo amorphous alloys within the above GFR.[3] It will be interesting to perform some especially designed experiments to see whether either ion beam mixing or a solid-state reaction could produce Ni-Mo amorphous alloys extending in the whole region of the predicted GFR of the system.

In summary, based on an n-body Ni-Mo potential, MD simulations determine two critical terminal solubilities of the Ni-Mo system, beyond which both Ni- and Mo-rich solid solutions become unstable and a spontaneous glass transition takes place. The composition range bounded by the two critical values can therefore be considered as a good approximation of the intrinsic glass-forming range of the system, which is compatible with the experimental observations by solid-state reactions.

This project was supported by the National Natural Science Foundation of China.

*Author to whom correspondence should be addressed. Electronic address: dmslbx@tsinghua.edu.cn

[1] P. Duwez, R. H. Willens, and W. Klement, J. Appl. Phys. **31**, 1136 (1960).
[2] R. B. Schwarz and W. L. Johnson, Phys. Rev. Lett. **51**, 415 (1983).
[3] B. X. Liu, W. L. Johnson, M.-A. Nicolet, and S. S. Lau, Appl. Phys. Lett. **42**, 45 (1983).
[4] R. C. Ruhl, B. C. Giessen, M. Cohen, and N. J. Grant, Acta Metall. **15**, 1693 (1967).
[5] Z. J. Zhang, H. Y. Bai, Q. L. Qiu, T. Yang, K. Tao, and B. X. Liu, J. Appl. Phys. **73**, 1702 (1993).
[6] M. W. Thompson, *Defects and Radiation Damage in Metals* (Cambridge University Press, Cambridge, England, 1969), Chaps. 4 and 5.
[7] B. X. Liu, D. Z. Che, Z. J. Zhang, S. L. Lai, and J. R. Ding, Phys. Status Solidi A **128**, 345 (1991).
[8] B. X. Liu and O. Jin, Phys. Status Solidi A **161**, 3 (1997).
[9] R. Bormann and R. Busch, J. Non-Cryst. Solids **117-118**, 539 (1990).
[10] C. Massobrio, V. Pontikis, and G. Martin, Phys. Rev. B **41**, 10 486 (1990).
[11] R. Devanathan, N. Q. Lam, P. R. Okamoto, and M. Meshii, Phys. Rev. B **48**, 42 (1993).
[12] Q. Zhang, W. L. Lai, and B. X. Liu, Europhys. Lett. **43**, 416 (1998).
[13] M. Parrinello and A. Rahman, J. Appl. Phys. **52**, 7182 (1981).
[14] A. van den Beukel and S. Radelaar, Acta Metall. **31**, 419 (1983).
[15] Z. J. Zhang and B. X. Liu, J. Appl. Phys. **76**, 3351 (1994).

Metastable rhombohedral Fe phase formed in Fe/Sb multilayers and its magnetic properties

F. Pan, M. Zhang, M. Ding, and B. X. Liu
Department of Materials Science and Engineering, Tsinghua University, Beijing 100084, China

Y. M. Zhou and D. S. Wang
Laboratory for Surface Physics, Institute of Physics and Center for Condensed Matter Physics, Chinese Academy of Science, Beijing 100080, China

(Received 11 June 1998; revised manuscript received 21 September 1998)

Fe/Sb multilayer films with various Fe and Sb layer thicknesses were prepared by vapor deposition. A metastable rhombohedral Fe phase was formed in the Fe/Sb multilayered films, when the Fe layer thickness was of 1.7 nm and the Sb layer thickness was of 10 nm. In an opposite condition, a metastable bcc Sb phase was obtained, when the Fe layer was thicker than 4 nm and the Sb layer was thinner than 2.5 nm. Interestingly, the metastable rhombohedral Fe exhibited ferromagnetic behavior and its average magnetic moment was as high as $1.52\mu_B$. The magnetic behavior and electronic and magnetic structures of the rhombohedral Fe were calculated by the first-principles all-electron linearized augmented plane-wave method (LAPW) within the local spin-density functional approximation. The difference between the calculation of the Fe magnetic-moment amplitude $(3.32\mu_B)$ and the experimental determination $(1.52\mu_B)$ was discussed in terms of the presence of dead layers at the Fe/Sb interfaces. [S0163-1829(99)02017-2]

I. INTRODUCTION

In the last decade, magnetic multilayered films on a nanometer scale with artificial periodicity have attracted much attention because these films may feature some anomalous magnetic properties, such as changes in magnetization as the magnetic layer thickness is reduced, appearance in some cases of a uniaxial interfacial anisotropy, and giant magnetoresistance. These phenomena are probably correlated with the role of surface and interface states as dimensions become lower, e.g., the reduced coordination number and symmetry of atoms, formation of metastable phase, interface roughness accompanied by chemical disordering, etc.[1-4] In Fe-metal multilayers, some metastable Fe phases were obtained in some systems by various deposition methods, and these films behaved with different magnetic behavior. For example, Himpsel[5] and Macedo, Keune, and Ellerbrock[6] reported that fcc Fe grew epitaxially on Cu single crystals. In our recent study,[3] Fe grew also in fcc structure on polycrystalline Cu by electron-beam vapor deposition. In Fe/Pt, Fe/Pd, and Fe/Ti systems, fcc Fe was also observed by Croft *et al.*[7] and Zhang, Pan, and Liu[8,9] and it exhibited ferromagnetic behavior.[10] The hcp metastable Fe was formed in Fe/Ru superlattices with short periodicity by Maurer *et al.*[11] Besides, amorphous Fe was observed in Fe/Zr and Fe/Dy multilayers.[12-14] The observation of these metastable iron phases provides a way to explore the origin of the magnetization of the magnetic materials. With extensive data obtained for many multilayers systems, several models have been proposed for predicting the magnetization of the films.[1-2,15-20] The models generally rely on electron-spin density of the iron atom in an ideal magnetic-nonmagnetic interface or in the transitional structure sublayer (interface mixing). For example, based on an all-electron total-energy local spin-density approach, Freeman and co-workers[15-16] predicted that there would be a significant enhancement in two-dimensional magnetism at surfaces and interfaces in transition metals grown on noble metals. Tight-binding calculations of the magnetic surface, interface, and multilayers by Krompiewski and others[2,17] gave a similar prediction. Kübler's calculation revealed that both fcc and hcp bulk Fe phases should undergo a transition to a magnetic state at volume expansions of the order of 5%.[21-22] An alternative explanation for the magnetic modification in some Fe/metal films may be attributed to the so-called interface ''dead layer''[11,18-19] or ''active layer'' proposed by some researchers.[20] However, there is no good model to explain completely all the experimental results obtained in the Fe/metal films so far. Hence it is of interest to study further the magnetization of various metastable phases formed in Fe/metal films. The purpose of this paper is to get a metastable Fe phase to investigate the magnetic properties of this metastable phase. In Fe/Sb system, the atomic configurations in the (001) plane of rhombohedral Sb and in the (111) plane of bcc Fe are quite similar, and the atomic distances in the (001) Sb and (111) Fe were of 0.4307 and 0.4053 nm, respectively, i.e., a difference in their atomic distance is only 5.9%. It is possible to form a rhombohedral metastable Fe phase from a crystallographic point of view. Fe/Sb multilayers were therefore selected to get a rhombohedral metastable Fe phase. In this paper, we report a rhombohedral metastable Fe phase observed in the Fe/Sb multilayers prepared by electron-beam vapor deposition and its magnetic properties, the correlation between the magnetic properties and the microstructure emerged in the films, and we discuss the possible mechanisms responsible for the observations. Besides, the magnetic behaviors and electronic and magnetic structures of the rhombohedral Fe were also investigated by the first-principles all-electron linearized augmented plane-wave method (LAPW) in the local spin-density functional approximation.

Physical Review B 59(17), p.11458-11464 (1999).

II. EXPERIMENTAL PROCEDURE

The Fe/Sb multilayered films were prepared by depositing alternatively pure iron (99.99%) and antimony (99.9999%) at rates of 0.05–0.2 nm/s onto NaCl single-crystal chips with a freshly cleaved surface (for microstructure studies) and glass substrates 0.1 mm thick (for magnetic property measurement) in an electron-beam evaporation system at a vacuum level of 1×10^{-4} Pa. The first layer on the substrate was antimony. The thickness of the constituent metals (t_{Fe} and t_{Sb}) varied from 1–10 nm which was controlled by a quartz monitor in the evaporation system. The total thickness of the films was approximately 40 nm (for microstructure studies) and 120 nm (for magnetic property measurement), respectively. Samples were analyzed by transmission electron microscopy (TEM), selected area diffraction (SAD), and x-ray diffraction to identify the crystalline structure. Rutherford-backscattering spectroscopy (RBS) was employed to measure the thickness, periodicity, and chemical composition of the samples. The magnetic properties were measured with a vibrating-sample magnetometer (VSM), with a resolution of 5×10^{-6} emu, in a magnetic field of up to 10 kOe at room temperature. The size of the VSM samples was 4×6 mm. First, a hysteresis loop of the substrate together with the holder was measured and the saturation magnetization M_s was found to be about 1×10^{-4} emu, which was one to two orders of magnitude lower than that of the studied Fe/metal multilayered films. Then the hysteresis loops of the samples were measured and the magnetization of the substrate and holder were subtracted automatically by the computer. To reduce the experimental error, measurements were made on an assembly of five similar specimens. Consequently, the magnetic moment from the substrate and holder had a negligible effect on the measured values, and the precision of the measured magnetic moment of the films was estimated to be better than 1%. After measuring the magnetic properties, the films were dissolved in a 5 ml HNO_3 and the inductively coupled plasma atomic emission spectrum (ICP) was employed to determine the Fe content in the multilayered films. An average magnetic moment per Fe atom was then obtained using above data. The error involved in the ICP measurement was about 5% and the total error for the magnetic moment was therefore around 6%.

III. RESULTS AND DISCUSSION

A. Microstructure of the Fe/Sb multilayers

1. Determination of the periodicity

Low angle x-ray-diffraction and RBS results indicated that the composition, thickness, and periodicity of all the samples agreed with the nominal values. For instance, Fig. 1 shows a typical low angle x-ray-diffraction pattern of the $[Fe(4.0\,nm)/Sb(3.7\,nm)]_{20}$ (the subscript is the number of the Fe/Sb bilayers) multilayers. From this pattern, the third- and fourth-order diffraction peaks of the Fe/Sb multilayer can clearly be seen at 3.42 and 4.62°, respectively, which give a modulation periodicity of the multilayers to be 7.7 nm. Figure 2 shows a RBS spectrum of $[Fe(4.0\,nm)/Sb(10.0\,nm)]_{10}$ multilayers. The spectrum was obtained with 2.023 MeV He^+ ions and the laboratory backscattering angle was 165°. From the spectrum, one can see two peaks. The high channel

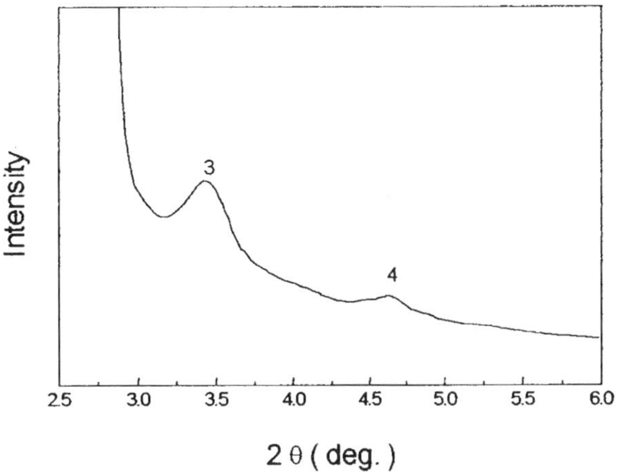

FIG. 1. The typical low angle x-ray-diffraction pattern of the $[Fe(4.0\,nm)/Sb(3.7\,nm)]_{20}$ multilayers.

one is from the Sb and the low channel is from the Fe. Although the detector used at these energies has insufficient energy resolution (about 10 nm) to resolve the individual layers, the Sb peak at its low-energy edge and the highest channel of the Fe signal can still be distinguished. By calculating the area and width of the Fe and Sb peaks, the total thickness is estimated to be about 140 nm, and the average thickness of each Fe and Sb layers agrees with the nominal deposited thickness. The same Fe/Sb periodicity of the Fe/Sb multilayers was also confirmed by the ICP measurement. In short, the characterization results confirmed that all the samples had a periodic structure along the normal to the films.

2. Microstructure analysis

The microstructure of the films was investigated by TEM SAD analysis. The experimental results revealed that the structure of Fe/Sb multilayers varied strongly with the variation of the layer thickness of the constituent metals. Figure 3 shows the SAD patterns of Fe/Sb multilayers with various Fe thicknesses, while the Sb layer thickness was kept at 10 nm. From Fig. 3(a), one can see that, when $t_{Fe}\leq1.7$ nm and $t_{Sb}=10$ nm, there is only one rhombohedral phase in the films,

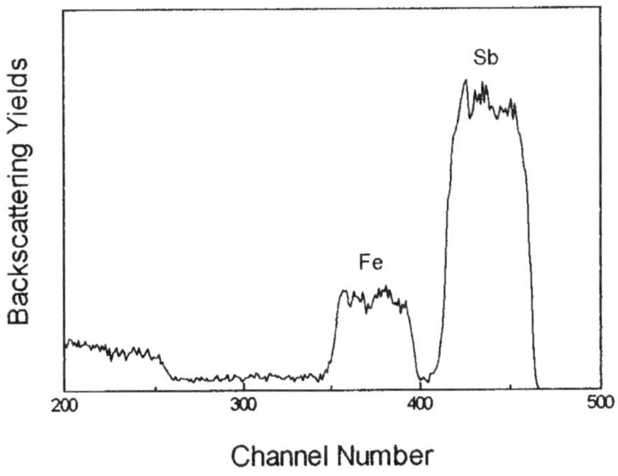

FIG. 2. The RBS spectrum of $[Fe(4.0\,nm)/Sb(10.0\,nm)]_{10}$ multilayers.

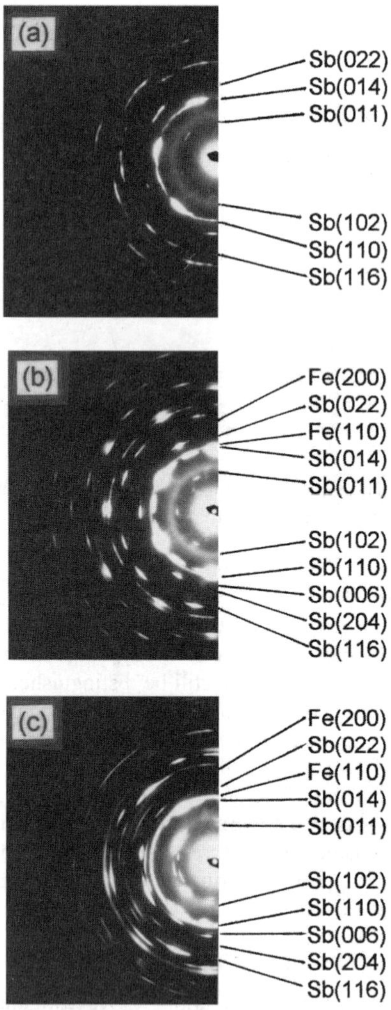

FIG. 3. The typical TEM SAD pattern of the Fe/Sb multilayers with various Fe thicknesses, while the Sb layer thickness was kept at 10 nm: (a) Fe(1.7 nm)/Sb(10.0 nm); (b) Fe(2.5 nm)/Sb(10 nm); (c) Fe(4.0 nm)/Sb(10.0 nm).

and its lattice parameters are determined to be $a=0.450\pm0.005$ nm and $\alpha=57.1°$ (i.e., $a=0.431\pm0.005$ nm and $c=1.127\pm0.005$ nm for hexagonal lattice), which are exactly the same of those of the pure Sb. When t_{Fe} reaches 2.5 nm, in addition to the diffraction lines from the rhombohedral phase, a bcc Fe (110) diffraction line emerges as shown in Fig. 3(b), indicating that the bcc Fe phase is formed in the films, i.e., the films consists of bcc Fe and rhombohedral Sb. From Fig. 3 it can also be found that when $t_{Sb}=10$ nm, the Sb grain size of the Fe/Sb films decreased with increasing t_{Fe}, which results in the diffraction lines in the SAD pattern having an increasing tendency from discontinuous to continuous. The average Sb grain size of the films was about 35, 20, and 2 μm when $t_{Fe}=1.7$, 2.5, and 4.0 nm, respectively, while the grain size of the bcc Fe was in a nanoscale, i.e., about 5–10 nm.

There are two possible mechanisms for the formation of only one rhombohedral phase in Fe/Sb multilayers, in which the Fe layers are thinner than 1.7 nm. First, the Fe atom might grow in a rhombohedral structure on polycrystalline rhombohedral Sb layers. Second, a rhombohedral solid solution might be formed at the Fe/Sb interfaces. According to the low angle x-ray-diffraction results, the films had a good periodic structure along the normal to the films. Besides, the lattice parameters of the observed rhombohedral phase is the same as that of pure Sb and the solubility of Fe in Sb is almost nil.[23] It could therefore be thought that, under our experimental conditions, the Fe atoms grew in a rhombohedral structure on thick Sb layer, which was similar to that some metastable Fe phases grew epitaxially in the Fe-base multilayers, e.g., a hcp Fe phase grew in Ru/Fe superlattice,[11] fcc Fe phases grew in Fe/Cu (Refs. 3 and 5) and Fe/Pt (Ref. 8) multilayers.

From a crystallographic point of view, the rhombohedral structure Fe phase formed on the thick Sb layer was also possible, because the atomic configurations in the (001) plane of rhombohedral Sb and in the (111) plane of bcc Fe are quite similar, and the atomic distances in the (001) Sb and (111) Fe were of 0.4307 and 0.4053 nm, respectively, i.e., a difference in their atomic distance is only 5.9%.

It should be noted that the structure discussed in this study was based on the analyses of results by TEM SAD, one can say that the experimental evidences of the rhombohedral structure Fe phase formed in the Fe/Sb multilayers are weak, because it is possible that the signal coming from the 1.7 nm Fe layer is too weak to be observable. Recalling our previous studies,[3,10] it can be found that, for Fe/Cu and Fe/Pd multilayers with the same total thickness of Fe/Sb ones, when the Fe layer thickness was 1.2 nm (lower than 1.7 nm), the diffraction lines from Fe phase can be clear observed by TEM SAD, i.e., if bcc Fe existed in the films, it would be detected by TEM SAD. These observations supported above argue that bcc Fe wasn't formed in the Fe/Sb multilayers, which provide an indirect evidence of the rhombohedral structure Fe phase formed in the Fe/Sb films. If the multilayers are characterized by extended x-ray-absorption fine structure or cross-section TEM investigations, detailed knowledge of the local structure could be obtained, this certainly deserves further study.

When t_{Fe} is thicker than 2.5 nm, the Fe atoms cannot grow in a rhombohedral structure because of the internal stress caused by a large mismatch between Fe and Sb, resulting in the formation of bcc Fe in the films. Figures 3(b) and 3(c) are the SAD patterns of Fe(2.5 nm)/Sb(10 nm) and Fe(4.0 nm)/Sb(10 nm) samples, respectively, showing the diffraction lines from the rhombohedral Sb and bcc Fe phases.

We also studied the possibility of growth of metastable bcc Sb on thick Fe layers in Fe/Sb multilayers. It turned out that when the Sb layer is thin and Fe layer is relatively thick, i.e., when $t_{Sb}=2.5$ nm and $t_{Fe}\geqslant4.0$ nm, there are only diffraction lines from a bcc phase appearing in the SAD patterns, and its lattice parameter is just the same of that of pure Fe (0.2866 nm). In other words, the metastable bcc Sb phase grew on thick Fe layer. For example, Fig. 4 is a SAD pattern of the Fe(8.0 nm)/Sb(2.5 nm) sample, showing only bcc diffraction lines. The grain size in the sample was about 10 nm, which is much smaller than that in the Fe/Sb films with $t_{Sb}=10.0$ nm.

Figure 5 shows the SAD patterns of the Fe/Sb multilayers with various Sb thicknesses, while the Fe layer thickness was

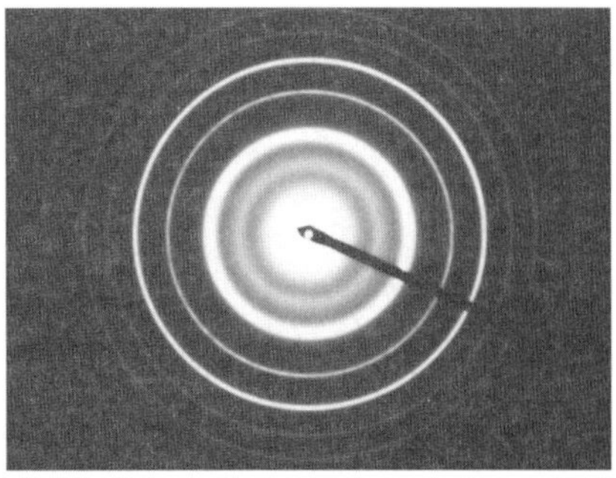

FIG. 4. The typical TEM SAD pattern of the Fe(8.0 nm)/Sb(2.5 nm) sample, showing only bcc diffraction lines.

kept at 2.5 nm. One can see that, though the films consisted of bcc Fe and the rhombohedral Sb phases, the Sb grain size of the samples increased obviously with increasing t_{Sb}, i.e., it was about 10 nm, 10 μm, and 20 μm for Fe(2.5 nm)/Sb(2.5 nm), Fe(2.5 nm)/Sb(6.0 nm), and Fe(2.5 nm)/Sb(10.0 nm) films, respectively, while the grain size of the bcc Fe was in a nanoscale, i.e., about 5–10 nm.

From Figs. 3, 4, and 5 it can also be found that, when $t_{Sb}>t_{Fe}$, the diffraction rings of the samples were discontinuous. These patterns indicated that texture structures were present in the films with some specific orientation relationships, yet the texture was not very distinct as diffraction rings still appeared. The textured decreased with increasing t_{Fe} and with decreasing t_{Sb}, respectively, and eventually the texture orientation disappeared. For example, there was no texture in the Fe(8.0 nm)/Sb(2.5 nm) films. The Sb grain size of the films can be changed from 50~10 nm for the Fe(8.0 nm)/Sb(2.5 nm) to 35 000 nm (i.e., 35 μm) for Fe(1.7 nm)/Sb(10.0 nm) films.

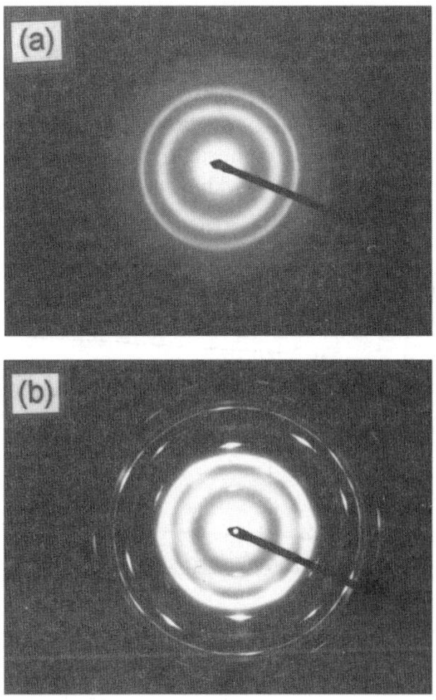

FIG. 5. The TEM SAD patterns of the Fe/Sb multilayers with various Sb thicknesses, while the Fe layer thickness was kept at 2.5 nm: (a) Fe(2.5 nm)/Sb(2.5 nm) and (b) Fe(2.5 nm)/Sb(6.0 nm).

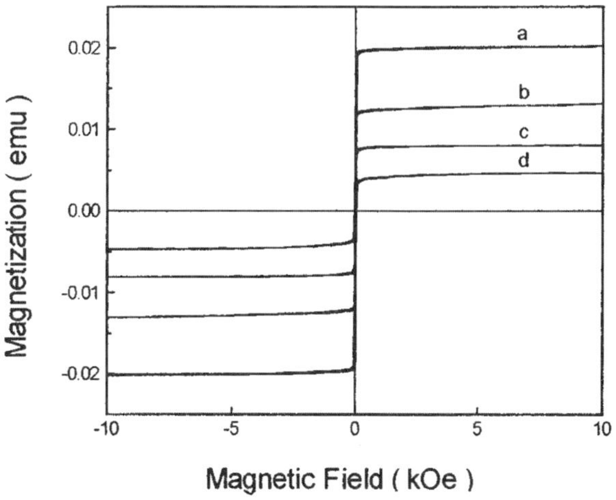

FIG. 6. The hysteresis loops of Fe/Sb multilayers in a magnetic field of up to 10 kOe parallel to the film plane: (a) Fe(6.0 nm)/Sb(2.5 nm); (b) Fe(4.0 nm)/Sb(2.5 nm); (c) Fe(4.0 nm)/Sb(6.0 nm); and (d) Fe(1.7 nm)/Sb(10.0 nm).

B. Magnetic properties of the films

To obtain a better understanding of the rhombohedral Fe phase formed in the Fe/Sb multilayers, the magnetic properties of the films were studied by VSM at room temperature. Figure 6 shows the hysteresis loops of the Fe/Sb multilayers in a magnetic field of up to 10 kOe parallel to the film plane. Table I shows the average magnetic moment per Fe atom in Fe/Sb multilayers. From Fig. 6 and Table I one can see that all the Fe/Sb multilayers, including the films with rhombohedral Fe, are ferromagnetic and have an in-plane easy axis of magnetization. The magnetic moment per Fe atom in Fe/Sb multilayers was about the same as in the bulk Fe when $t_{Fe}=8.0$ nm and $t_{Sb}=2.5$ nm, and it decreased with decreasing t_{Fe}. For Fe(1.7 nm)/Sb(10.0 nm) multilayers, the magnetic moment per Fe in the rhombohedral structure can still be as high as $1.52\mu_B$. In the previous works it was found that some solid solution (or amorphous phase) could be formed in the Fe/metal interface, and the solid solution exhibited paramagnetic behavior at room temperature.[12–14,24] Recalling the microstructural results of the films (Fig. 3), if the solid solution was formed in the Fe(1.7 nm)/Sb(10.0 nm) films, the sample would have very low magnetization. In our case, Fe(1.7 nm)/Sb(10.0 nm) films had higher magnetization, which suggested that the Fe layer did not grow in solid solution. In other words, the magnetic measurement provided

TABLE I. The average magnetic moment per Fe atom (μ_B) in Fe/Sb multilayers for various t_{Fe} and t_{Sb}.

		Thickness of Fe layer (t_{Fe} nm)				
		1.7	2.5	4.0	6.0	8.0
	1.4		1.658			
Thickness of Sb	2.5		1.728	1.796	1.651	2.190
layer	3.7		1.704			
(t_{Sb} nm)	6.0		1.683			
	10.0	1.520	1.806	1.767		

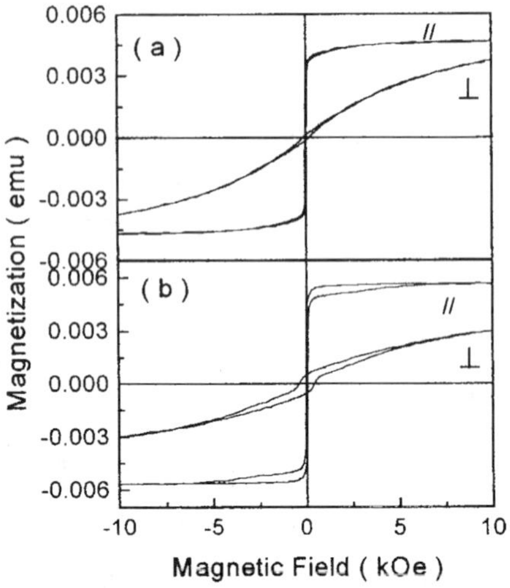

FIG. 7. The hysteresis loops of the Fe/Sb multilayers measured with the magnetic field parallel and perpendicular to the film plane for (a) Fe(1.7 nm)/Sb(10.0 nm) and (b) Fe(4.0 nm)/Sb(10.0 nm).

an indirect evidence for the formation of a metastable Fe phase in a rhombohedral structure and the new phase can behave ferromagnetically with a high magnetic moment.

Figure 7 shows two hysteresis loops of the Fe/Sb multilayers measured with the magnetic field parallel and perpendicular to the film plane. From the figure, the saturation field, for the perpendicular case, depended on the thickness of the Fe layer when $t_{Sb}=10\,nm$. Saturating the Fe(1.7 nm)/Sb(10.0 nm) multilayers was much easier than saturating the Fe(4.0 nm)/Sb(10.0 nm) ones. This revealed that as the t_{Fe} decreased, there was an increasing tendency for perpendicular magnetization in the Fe/Sb multilayers, which was similar to those observed in Fe/noble-metal multilayers.[3,10,25–26]

Concerning the effect of film structure on the magnetic properties of the Fe/Sb multilayers, as mentioned above, even though the grain size of Sb phase varied obviously with t_{Fe} and t_{Sb}, the grain size of bcc Fe was almost the same in all films, i.e., about 5–10 nm, which might mainly relate to the evaporation conditions of the samples, except the grain size of Fe phase was large in Fe(1.7 nm)/Sb(10 nm) multilayers owing to the epitaxial growth of the metastable rhombohedral Fe phase. Therefore, in our case, the grain size of films had a small effect on the magnetic properties of the films. From Table I, one can see that the magnetic moment of the Fe/Sb films varied with t_{Fe} and t_{Sb}, i.e., it decreased with decreasing t_{Fe}, which was probably related to the spin orientational configuration of the Fe atoms under the action of the Sb layer. According to the experimental results of a Mössbauer spectroscopy analysis by Maurer *et al.*,[11] a so-called interface "dead layer" existed in the multilayers, i.e., two interfacial layers bear no moment, similar results were also reported by Sato and others.[27–29] The relative thickness of dead layer (i.e., the thickness ratio of the nonmagnetic Fe layer to the magnetic Fe layer) increased with decreasing t_{Fe}, results in the above observed magnetic properties, i.e., the magnetic moment of the films with thin Fe layer was lower than that with thick Fe one.

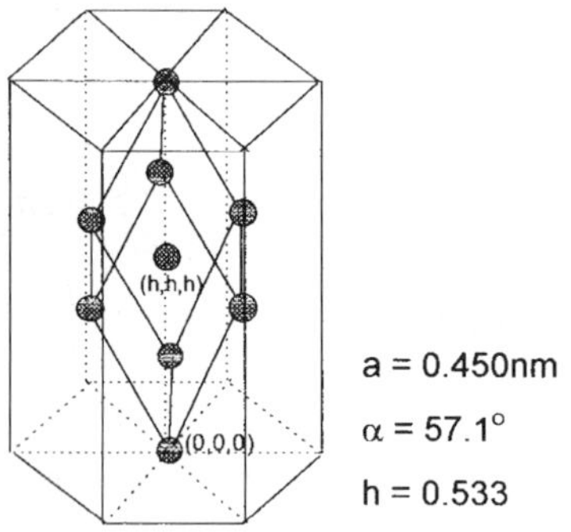

FIG. 8. The crystallographic lattice unit cell containing two atoms of the metastable rhombohedral Fe phase.

C. Simulation of the magnetic moment of the rhombohedral Fe phase

The rhombohedral Fe phase formed in Fe/Sb and its magnetic properties, to our knowledge, have not been reported previously. To interpret the observations and to probe the reason for the magnetic behaviors, the electronic and magnetic structure of the rhombohedral Fe was investigated by the first-principles all-electron linearized augmented plane-wave method (LAPW) (Refs. 19–21) in the local spin-density functional approximation. A crystallographic lattice unit cell which includes two atoms at (0, 0, 0) and (0.533, 0.533, 0.533) is used for convenience of programming (see Fig. 8). The lattice constant was selected from $a=0.405$ to 0.475 nm, while $\alpha=57.1°$. The basis size used in solving the eigenvalue problem was more than 50 LAPW's per atom and 4096 special k points in the first Brillouin zone of the rhombohedral unit cell were used to generate electron density. Core change density was computed self-consistently in a fully relativistic Dirac-Slater-type atomic structure program for every iteration and valence states are computed semirelativistically, i.e., the Dirac equation is solved including mass velocity and Darwin terms but without the spin-orbit coupling term. No shape approximations were made for the potential and charge density in the interstitial region, but the potential was assumed spherically symmetric inside the muffin-tin spheres.[19–21,30,31] The convergence measured by

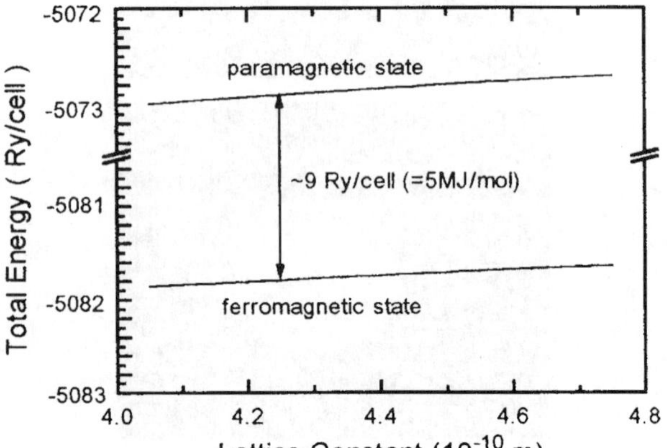

FIG. 9. The calculated total energy per atom of the rhombohedral Fe phase with various lattice constants.

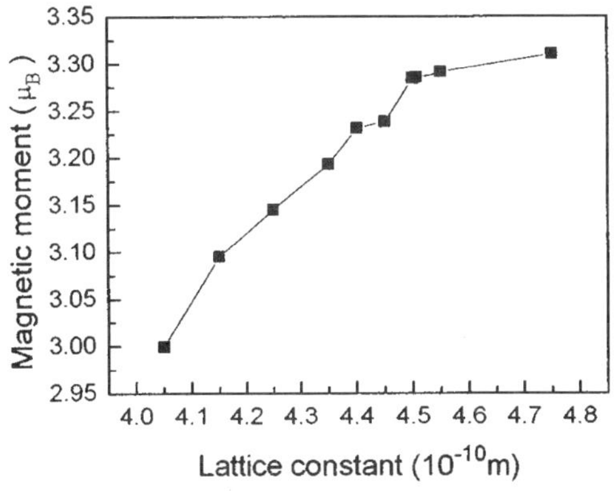

FIG. 10. The calculated magnetic moment per atom as a function of the lattice constant for the ferromagnetic (FM) state of the rhombohedral Fe phase.

the rms difference between input and output was better than 1 mRy for the sum of spin-up and spin-down potential (or 0.05 me/a.u.^{3} for charge density) and better than 0.02 mRy for their difference (or 0.005 me/a.u.^{3} for spin density).

Figure 9 shows the calculated total energy per atom of the rhombohedral Fe phase with various lattice constants. From this figure, one can see that all the calculated total energies of the ferromagnetic (FM) and the paramagnetic (PM) states increase with increasing lattice constant and that the calculated total energy of the FM state was about 9.0 Ry/cell (~5 MJ/mol) lower than that of PM state of rhombohedral Fe phase, suggesting the ground state of the rhombohedral Fe phase is the FM state.

Figure 10 gives the calculated magnetic moment per atom as a function of the lattice constant for the FM state of the rhombohedral Fe phase. The calculated magnetic moment per Fe atom in rhombohedral structure was about 3.23μ_B when the lattice constant was 0.450 nm (i.e., a=0.431 nm and c=1.127 nm for hexagonal lattice) and it decreased with decreasing lattice constant of the rhombohedral Fe phase.

It is noted that there is a difference in magnetic moment between the calculated and experimentally measured values. This is also related to the so-called ''die layer.'' In calculation of the magnetic moment of the rhombohedral Fe phase, the spin orientational configuration of the Fe atoms under the action of the Sb layer hadn't been taken into simulation of the magnetic moment. According to the experimental results of a Mössbauer spectroscopy analysis by Maurer *et al.*,[11] in hexagonal Fe/Ru superlattices with short periodicity, the internal Fe layer carry a moment of about 2μ_B, whereas the two interfacial layers bear no moment, i.e., the interface ''dead layer'' existed in the multilayers. In our case, according to the mean magnetic moment per Fe atom and the structural parameter of the Fe(1.7 nm)/Sb(10.0 nm) multilayers, the effective Fe layer was calculated as $1.7\times1.52/3.23=0.8$ nm, in which 3.23 was the calculated magnetic moment of bulk rhombohedral Fe phase by the first-principles all-electron linearized augmented plane-wave method (LAPW) (Refs. 19–21) in the local spin-density functional approximation. Therefore the thickness of the nonmagnetic Fe layer per interface in Fe(1.7 nm)/Sb(10.0 nm) was $1.7\times(1-1.52/3.23)/2=0.45$ nm, i.e., about two to three Fe monolayers, which agreed with the value in Fe/Ru films.[11] Hence, the above calculation can serve as a support to our experimental observations as well as the above discussed interpretation in a qualitative way.

IV. CONCLUSION

In summary, we have shown experimental evidence of a metastable rhombohedral Fe phase obtained in the Fe/Sb multilayers with $d_{Fe}\leq1.7$ nm and $d_{Sb}\geq10$ nm. The rhombohedral Fe metastable phase exhibits ferromagnetic behavior and its average magnetic moment in the Fe(1.7 nm)/Sb(10.0 nm) multilayers is 1.52μ_B. The magnetic behavior and electronic and magnetic structures of the rhombohedral Fe were calculated by the first-principle all-electron linearized augmented plane-wave method (LAPW) in the local spin-density functional approximation. The difference between the calculation of the Fe magnetic moment amplitude (3.23μ_B) and the experimental determination (1.52μ_B) was thought to relate with the dead layers probably formed at the Fe/Sb interfaces.

ACKNOWLEDGMENT

This work was supported in part by the National Natural Science Foundation of China and by the Administration of Tsinghua University.

[1] A. J. Freemam and R. Wu, J. Magn. Magn. Mater. **104–107**, 1 (1992).
[2] S. Krompiewski, U. Krauss, and U. Krey, J. Magn. Magn. Mater. **92**, L295 (1991).
[3] B. X. Liu and F. Pan, Phys. Rev. B **48**, 10 276 (1993).
[4] S. S. P. Parkin, Appl. Phys. Lett. **58**, 1473 (1991).
[5] F. J. Himpsel, Phys. Rev. Lett. **67**, 2363 (1991).
[6] W. A. A. Macedo, W. Keune, and E. D. Ellerbrock, J. Magn. Magn. Mater. **93**, 552 (1991).
[7] M. Croft, D. Sills, A. Sahiner, A. F. Jankowski, P. H. Ansari, E. Kemly, F. Lu, Y. Jeon, and T. Tsakalakos, Nanostruct. Mater. **9**, 1 (1997).
[8] M. Zhang, F. Pan, and B. X. Liu, J. Phys.: Condens. Matter **9**, 7623 (1997).
[9] M. Zhang, F. Pan, and B. X. Liu, J. Magn. Magn. Mater. **182**, 89 (1998).
[10] F. Pan, T. Yang, J. Zhang, and B. X. Liu, J. Phys.: Condens. Matter **5**, L507 (1993).
[11] M. Maurer, M. Piecuch, M. F. Raver, J. C. Ousset, J. P. Sánchez, C. Aaron, J. Dekoster, D. Raoux, A. De Andres, M. De Santis, A. Fontaine, F. Baudelet, J. L. Rouvière, and B. Dieny, J. Magn. Magn. Mater. **93**, 15 (1991).
[12] J. Landes, Ch. Sauer, B. Kabius, and W. Zinn, Phys. Rev. B **44**, 8342 (1991).
[13] S. Kraegermann, F. Stobiecki, T. Stobiecki, and K. Roell, J. Magn. Magn. Mater. **101**, 209 (1991).
[14] J. Dubowik, F. Stobiecki, H. Rohrmann, and K. Roll, J. Magn. Magn. Mater. **152**, 201 (1996).

[15] A. J. Freeman and C. L. Fu, J. Appl. Phys. **61**, 3356 (1987).
[16] C. L. Fu, A. J. Freeman, and T. Oguchi, Phys. Rev. Lett. **54**, 2700 (1985).
[17] J. Tersoff and L. M. Falicov, Phys. Rev. B **26**, 6186 (1982).
[18] C. S. Wang and A. J. Freeman, J. Magn. Magn. Mater. **15/18**, 869 (1980).
[19] R. H. Victora and L. M. Falicov, Phys. Rev. B **28**, 5232 (1983).
[20] R. Krishnan and M. Tessier, J. Appl. Phys. **67**, 5391 (1990).
[21] V. L. Moruzzi, P. M. Marcus, and J. Kübler, Phys. Rev. B **39**, 6957 (1989).
[22] J. Kübler, Solid State Commun. **72**, 631 (1989).
[23] Colin James Smithells, *Smithells Metals Reference Book*, 6th ed., edited by Eric A. Brandes (Butterworth, London, 1983), pp. 11–256.
[24] K. Yoden, N. Hosoito, K. Kawaguchi, K. Mibu, and T. Shinjo, Jpn. J. Appl. Phys., Part 1 **27**, 1680 (1988).
[25] H. J. G. Draaisma, W. J. M. de Jonger, and F. J. A. den Broeder, J. Magn. Magn. Mater. **66**, 351 (1987).
[26] C. J. Gutierrez, S. H. Mayer, and J. C. Walker, J. Magn. Magn. Mater. **80**, 299 (1989).
[27] N. Sato, J. Appl. Phys. **61**, 1979 (1987).
[28] F. Pan, Y. D. Fan, K. Tao, and B. X. Liu, Phys. Status Solidi A **153**, 481 (1996).
[29] D. D. Koelling and G. O. Arbman, J. Phys. F **5**, 2041 (1975).
[30] H. Krakauer, M. Posternak, and A. J. Freeman, Phys. Rev. B **19**, 1706 (1979).
[31] M. Posternak, H. Krakauer, A. J. Freeman, and D. D. Koelling, Phys. Rev. B **21**, 5601 (1980).

Prediction of solid-state amorphization in binary metal systems

C. Lin, G. W. Yang, and B. X. Liu*
Department of Materials Science and Engineering, Tsinghua University, Beijing 100084, China
(Received 3 May 1999; revised manuscript received 3 March 2000)

A criterion is proposed for predicting the possibility of solid-state amorphization in the binary metal systems based on thermodynamic and kinetic considerations. A thermodynamic factor ΔF is defined to be the Gibbs free-energy difference between the initial multilayered films and the resultant amorphous phase, while a kinetic factor κ is defined to correlate not only with the atomic volume ratio but also with the melting point difference of the constituent metals. It turns out that if κ of a system is greater than a critical value of 0.6 together with a negative ΔF, solid-state amorphization is likely to take place in the system. The prediction is relevantly compatible with the experimental observations in the previously studied systems featuring either positive or negative heat of mixing as well as various values of atomic size difference.

In 1983 Schwarz and Johnson observed the solid-state amorphization (SSA) in the Au-La multilayers and claimed that a large negative heat of mixing (ΔH_m) and a large size difference between the constituent metals are necessary for SSA.[1] Since then, SSA has been observed in some other systems with similar characteristics to those of the Au-La system, mostly combining one early transition metal, e.g., Zr, Hf, and another late transition metal, e.g., Cu, Ni, and Au. Meanwhile, Clemens[2] and Kwak *et al.*[3] have proposed to predict the possibility of SSA by using other parameters, which are basically similar to those employed by Schwarz and Johnson.[1] In the 1990s, however, SSA has been observed experimentally in some systems with neither a large negative ΔH_m (e.g., the Ni-Mo system[4]) nor a large size difference (e.g., the Au-Ta system[5]). Moreover, SSA has even been achieved in several systems with a positive ΔH_m, e.g., the Cu-Ta,[6] Cu-W,[7] and Y refractory metal systems,[8] etc., provided the initial multilayers included a sufficient fraction of interfacial atoms versus the total atoms and, in such cases, the individual layer was about 1.5–2.0 nm thick. The evidence of SSA in multilayers was from two consecutive structural changes identified by diffraction analysis. Firstly, upon medium-temperature (typically 300–400 °C) annealing, the sharp diffraction lines from the two crystalline metals changed into halo(s). Secondly, the halo(s) changed back to sharp diffraction lines upon further annealing at a little higher temperature (typically 450–500 °C).[4–8] Very recently, Kwon *et al.*[9] presented a direct evidence confirming that SSA did take place in the equilibrium immiscible Cu-Ta system by transmission electron microscopy examination of a cross-sectional Cu-Ta bilayer sample. It is thus established that SSA is possible to take place in the systems with a positive ΔH_m. To pursue further studying of SSA, a general criterion is necessary to be developed to predict the possibility of SSA in the binary metal systems with various characteristics.

In this Brief Report we propose to define two factors for predicting the possibility of SSA, i.e., a thermodynamic factor ΔF and a kinetic factor κ. The two necessary conditions for SSA to take place are (1) the formed amorphous phase must have a lower free energy than that of the initial multilayered films and (2) atoms of one metal diffuse very fast through the disordered interlayer to combine with the partner metal atoms, which diffuse very slowly. According to the previous studies, those binary metal systems exhibiting an anomalous fast diffusion in the amorphous phase also exhibit an anomalous fast diffusion in the parent crystalline metals. For example, in the Ni-Zr system, Ni atoms diffuse much faster in both amorphous Ni-Zr alloy and crystalline Zr metal than Zr atoms do. In other words, a larger diffusivity of one metal species in its partner metal than vice versa is favorable for SSA. In our approach, the thermodynamic factor ΔF is defined to be the Gibbs free-energy difference between the final amorphous phase and the initial multilayered films, in which the interfacial free energy is included in the calculation, while the kinetic factor κ is defined to describe the difference between the diffusivity of metal A in metal B and the self-diffusivity of metal B. It will be shown later that the kinetic factor κ is correlated not only with the atomic volume ratio but also the melting points of the constituent metals, which have a considerable effect on the interdiffusion between the metal layers.

We now calculate the thermodynamic factor ΔF based on the Miedema's model[10] and Alonso's calculation method.[11]

The Gibbs free energy of an amorphous phase can be calculated by

$$\Delta G^{\mathrm{amor}} = \Delta H^{\mathrm{amor}} - T\Delta S^{\mathrm{amor}}, \tag{1}$$

where ΔH^{amor} and ΔS^{amor} are the formation enthalpy and entropy of the amorphous phase, respectively. T is the annealing temperature and assumed to be 600 K. ΔH^{amor} is given by

$$\Delta H^{\mathrm{amor}} = \Delta H^{\mathrm{amor}}_{\mathrm{chemical}} + \alpha_0(C_A T_A + C_B T_B - T). \tag{2}$$

C_i ($i=A,B$) is the atomic concentration of metal A or B, α_0 is an empirical parameter being 3.5 J/mol K, and T_i ($i=A,B$) is the melting point of component i. The $\Delta H^{\mathrm{amor}}_{\mathrm{chemical}}$, resulting from the electron redistribution generated at the contacted surface between the dissimilar atomic cells, is expressed as

$$\Delta H^{\mathrm{amor}}_{\mathrm{chemical}} = C_A f^A_B \Delta H_{\mathrm{int}}, \tag{3}$$

Physical Review B 61(23), p.15649-15652 (2000)

where f_B^A is a function which accounts for the degree to which an atom A is surrounded by atom B, and is given by

$$f_B^A = C_B^S[1+\gamma(C_A^S C_B^S)^2],$$
$$C_B^S = \frac{C_B V_B^{2/3}}{C_A V_A^{2/3}+C_B V_B^{2/3}}, \quad C_A^S = \frac{C_A V_A^{2/3}}{C_A V_A^{2/3}+C_B V_B^{2/3}}, \tag{4}$$

where γ is an empirical constant for describing the short-range-order difference of the solid solution, amorphous phase, and ordered compound and is taken as 0, 5, and 8, respectively. V_A and V_B are the atomic volumes of the components A and B, respectively. ΔH_{int} is the microscopic interfacial energy at 0 K between the cells of dissimilar components A and B, and can be calculated by

$$\Delta H_{\text{int}} = \frac{V_A^{2/3}}{(n_{\text{WS}}^{-1/3})_{\text{av}}}[-P(\Delta\phi^*)^2+Q(\Delta n_{\text{WS}}^{1/3})^2], \tag{5}$$

where $(n_{\text{WS}})_{\text{av}}$ is the mean value of the electron density at the boundary of the Wigner-Seitz cell as derived for the pure elements in the metallic state. $\Delta\phi^*$ is the difference between ϕ_A^* and ϕ_B^* defined as the work functions of the pure metals A and B. P and Q are constants determined empirically to be $P=14.2$ kJ/[mol cm^2 V^2 (density unit)$^{1/3}$] and $Q=133.5$ kJ/[mol cm^2 (density unit)], respectively. The entropy of the amorphous phase is assumed as that of an ideal solid solution, namely,

$$\Delta S^{\text{amor}} = -R(C_A \ln C_A + C_B \ln C_B). \tag{6}$$

R is the gas constant. The values of V, n_{WS} and ϕ can be obtained in Ref. 10.

For a solid-state reaction beginning with multilayers, there are definitely a certain number of interfaces in the multilayers. The interfaces are, in fact, frequently transient layers with disordered structure, which has been directly observed by Kwon *et al.*[9] Such a disordered layer possesses an excess interfacial free energy, which should be included in the calculation of the initial energetic state of the multilayers.

The interfacial free energy consists of an enthalpy term from the solid phase at the interface, an entropy term from the amorphous phase at the interface, and a chemical term reflecting the interaction between the metal $[A]$ and amorphous $\{AB\}$,

$$\gamma_{[A]-\{AB\}} = \gamma_{[A]-\{AB\}}^{\text{enthalpy}} + \gamma_{[A]-\{AB\}}^{\text{entropy}} + \gamma_{[A]-\{AB\}}^{\text{chemical}} \tag{7}$$

in which

$$\gamma_{[A]-\{AB\}}^{\text{chemical}} = \frac{f_B^A \Delta H_{\text{int}}^{A\text{ in }B}}{C_0 V_A^{2/3}}, \quad \gamma_{[A]-\{AB\}}^{\text{enthalpy}} = \frac{\Delta H_A^{\text{fuse}}}{C_0 V_A^{2/3}},$$
$$\gamma_{[A]-\{AB\}}^{\text{entropy}} = \frac{2RT}{C_0 V_{AB}^{2/3}}, \tag{8}$$

where C_0 is a constant equal to 4.5×10^8, and γ_i^0 ($i=A$ or B) is the surface energy of A or B.

Figure 1(a) is a schematic figure for the multilayered structure with disordered interface, and the Gibbs free energy of the initial multilayers can be calculated by

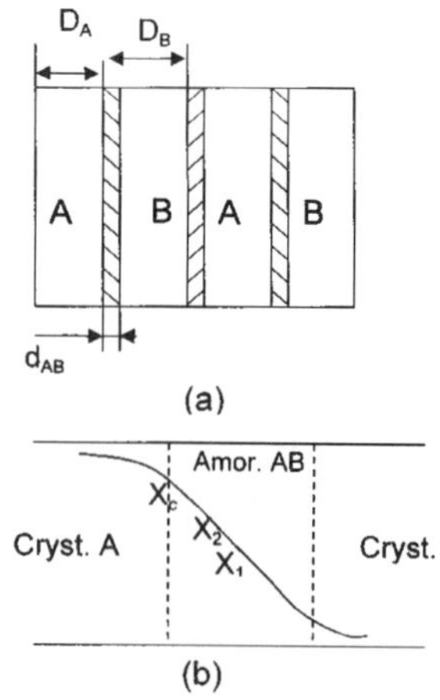

FIG. 1. (a) Configuration of the initial multilayered films with a disordered interlayer between the crystalline metals A and B and (b) a concentration profile of metal A in the disordered layer, showing the advance of the interface between the amorphous A-B and metal A accompanying by the increasing A concentration from x_1 to x_2 then to x_c.

$$G_i = 2\left(r_{[A]-\{AB\}} + r_{[B]-\{AB\}} + d_{AB}\frac{\Delta G_{\{AB\}}}{V_{\{AB\}}}\right). \tag{9}$$

From the above deduction, the thermodynamic factor ΔF can be expressed as

$$\Delta F = \frac{(D_A+D_B)\Delta G_{\{AB\}}}{V_{\{AB\}}} - 2\left(r_{[A]-\{AB\}} + r_{[B]-\{AB\}} + d_{AB}\frac{\Delta G_{\{AB\}}}{V_{\{AB\}}}\right). \tag{10}$$

It is important to note that upon solid-state reaction, the disordered layer would advance outwards directed to the crystalline metal layers A and B. Such advancing would consume some energy and would thus be terminated when the interface reaches a critical composition, beyond that the crystalline solid solution would be formed, resulting in the frustration of further growing of the disordered layer.

Figure 1(b) shows schematically the composition change of A across the interface in a binary metal system with positive ΔH_m. When the interface between the disordered and the crystalline layers advances, an accompanied composition change from $A_{x1}B_{1-x1}$ to $A_{x2}B_{1-x2}$ would take place and a corresponding interfacial free energy change can be calculated by

$$\Delta r_{[A]-\{AB\}} = r_{[A]-\{AB\}_2} - r_{[A]-\{AB\}_1}. \tag{11}$$

Substituting Eqs. (7) and (8) into Eq. (11) results in the following expression, in which only the difference between the chemical terms is left:

$$\Delta r_{[A]-\{AB\}} = \frac{[(f_B^A)_2-(f_B^A)_1]\Delta H_{\text{int}}^{A\text{ in }B}}{c_o V_A^{2/3}}, \tag{12}$$

where f_B^A can be calculated by Eq. (4). As f_B^A would decrease with increasing atomic concentration A, Δr is frequently

TABLE I. The parameters used in the calculation of the kinetic factor κ and thermodynamic factor ΔF for transition-metal–transition-metal and rare-earth–transition-metal systems, in which the SSA has been achieved, as well as the calculation results. (Note: The atomic concentration is $A_{50}B_{50}$; the thicknesses of a bilayer and disordered interfacial layer are 10 and 0.5 nm, respectively.)

	V_A^{eff}/V_B (cm^3)	ϕ_A^*/ϕ_B^* (V)	$(n_{\text{WS}}^{1/3})_A/(n_{\text{WS}}^{1/3})_B$ (density unit)$^{1/3}$	$\Delta H_A^{\text{fuse}}/\Delta H_B^{\text{fuse}}$ (kJ/mol)	T_A/T_B (K)	κ	ΔF (kJ/mol)	Ref.
Ni-Ti	6.15/10.8	5.2/3.8	1.75/1.52	17.6/20.9	1726/1943	0.68	−31	2
Ni-Zr	6.2/18.49	5.2/3.45	1.75/1.41	17.6/23	1726/2125	2.4	−38	14
Ni-Hf	5.81/13.6	5.2/3.6	1.75/1.45	17.6/25.1	1726/2500	1.55	−33	15
Ni-Nb	6.45/10.8	5.2/4.05	1.75/1.64	17.6/27.2	1726/2740	1.72	−23	8
Ni-Mo	6.6/9.4	5.2/4.65	1.75/1.77	17.6/27.6	1726/2890	1.84	−4	4
Co-Zr	5.75/14.1	5.1/3.45	1.75/1.41	15.2/23	1768/2125	1.02	−31	16
Cu-Zr	6.94/14.1	4.45/3.45	1.47/1.41	13/23	1358/2125	1.42	−16	17
Fe-Zr	6.16/6.16	4.93/3.45	1.77/1.41	14.9/23	1809/2125	0.94	−16	18
Au-Ta	10.33/10.9	5.15/4.05	1.57/1.63	12.7/31.4	1338/3287	2.7	−22	5
Cu-Er	6.2/18.49	4.45/3.22	1.47/1.23	13/17.2	1358/1795	2.4	−15	19
Ni-Er	4.19/18.49	5.2/3.22	1.75/1.23	17.6/17.2	1726/1795	2.45	−22	19
Ni-Ce	3.79/20.69	5.22/3.18	1.75/1.19	17.6/8.88	1726/1071	0.94	−42	20
Au-Y	7.63/19.95	5.15/3.2	1.57/1.21	12.7/17.2	1338/1799	2.34	−47	21
Au-La	7.24/22.53	5.15/3.17	1.57/1.18	12.7/10.1	1338/1193	0.97	−43	1

negative and it in turn serves as a driving force for the SSA. The thickness of the growing amorphous layer can be estimated by

$$\Delta d_{\{AB\}}=\frac{[(f_B^A)_1-(f_B^A)_2]\Delta H_{\text{int}}^{A\text{ in }B}V_{\{AB\}}}{\Delta G^{\text{amor}}c_o V_A^{2/3}}. \tag{13}$$

Based on the above discussion, the interfacial free energy can act as a driving force for SSA until the composition at the interface between the disordered and crystalline layers reaches a critical concentration. This is very compatible with the direct observation reported by Kwon *et al.*, i.e., the growing of the amorphous layer was terminated at a thickness around 4–5 nm.[9]

We now turn to deduce the kinetic factor κ. Concerning the fast diffusion of one metal into its partner, Bakker has found that the data given in the literature on fast metal-impurity diffusion can be rationalized as[12]

$$\ln\left(\frac{D_{A\text{ in }B}^A}{D_{\text{self}}^B}\right)_{T_B^{\text{fuse}}}=-\alpha\left(\frac{V_A^{\text{eff}}}{V_B}\right)+\beta, \tag{14}$$

where α and β are two constants for metal B, $D_{A\text{ in }B}^A$ and D_{self}^B are the impurity-diffusion and self-diffusion coefficients at the melting point of metal B, and V_A^{eff} is an effective volume of A in metal B with

$$V_A^{\text{eff}}=V_A-\Delta \overline{V}_{A\text{ in }B}^{o}, \tag{15}$$

where $\Delta \overline{V}_{A\text{ in }B}^0$ is the volume correction per mole A. If A atoms are fully surrounded by dissimilar B atoms, $\Delta \overline{V}_{A\text{ in }B}^0$ is given by

$$\Delta V_{A\text{ in }B}^0=P_V V_A^{2/3}(\Delta\phi^*)\left[\frac{(n_{\text{WS}}^A)^{-1}-(n_{\text{WS}}^B)^{-1}}{(n_{\text{WS}}^{-1/3})_{\text{av}}}\right], \tag{16}$$

where P_V is an empirical constant of 3 cm (density unit)$^{2/3}$ per volt. According to the general Arrhenius correlation

$$D=D_0\exp[-(Q/RT)], \tag{17}$$

where $Q=Q^0+pV$ and Q^0 is an activation energy at atmospheric pressure ($p\sim 0$), V is the activation volume, and D_0 is a preexponential parameter. Based on Eqs. (14)–(17), it can be deduced that

TABLE II. The parameters used in the calculation of the kinetic factor κ and thermodynamic factor ΔF for some binary metal systems with positive heat of mixing as well as the calculation results. (Note: The corresponding atomic concentrations are $Cu_{30}Ta_{70}$, $Cu_{60}W_{40}$, $Mo_{50}Y_{50}$, and $Nb_{30}Y_{70}$, respectively. The thickness of a bilayer is 5 nm.)

	V_A^{eff}/V_B (cm^3)	ϕ_A^*/ϕ_B^* (V)	$(n_{\text{WS}}^{1/3})_A/$ $(n_{\text{WS}}^{1/3})_B$ (density unit)$^{1/3}$	$\Delta H_A^{\text{fuse}}/$ ΔH_B^{fuse} (kJ/mol)	T_A/T_B (K)	$\gamma_{[A]}^0/\gamma_{[B]}^0$ (mJ/m^2)	κ	ΔF (kJ/mol)	Ref.
Cu-Ta	6.02/19.95	4.45/4.05	1.47/1.63	13/31.4	1358/3287	1825/3150	2.97	−13	6,9
Cu-W	6.92/9.55	4.45/4.80	1.47/1.81	13/35.3	1358/3653	1825/3675	3.06	−8	7
Mo-Y	7.19/19.95	4.65/3.2	1.77/1.21	27.6/17.2	2890/1799	3000/1125	0.83	−1.2	22
Nb-Y	9.65/19.95	4.05/3.2	1.64/1.21	27.2/17.2	2740/1799	2700/1125	0.79	−7.8	8

$$\left(\frac{D^A_{A\text{ in }B}}{D^B_{\text{eff}}}\right)_T = \exp\left[\beta - \alpha\frac{V_A^{\text{eff}}}{V_B} + (\gamma_A T_A - \gamma_B T_B)\left(\frac{1}{T_B} - \frac{1}{T}\right)\right], \tag{18}$$

where $\gamma_i = Q_i / RT_i$ $(i = A, B)$ is nearly a constant for a given crystal structure and bond type. The kinetic factor κ is defined to describe the diffusivity difference between metals A and B and can therefore be expressed by

$$\kappa = 1 - \frac{\alpha}{\beta}\frac{V_A^{\text{eff}}}{V_B} + \frac{\gamma_A T_A - \gamma_B T_B}{\beta}\left(\frac{1}{T_B} - \frac{1}{T}\right). \tag{19}$$

Based on the data summarized in the literature,[13] if metal B is a rare-earth metal, κ can approximately be calculated as

$$\kappa = 1 - \frac{3}{2}\frac{V_A^{\text{eff}}}{V_B} + (T_A - 2T_B)\left(\frac{1}{T_B} - \frac{1}{T}\right) \tag{20}$$

and for a system with two transition metals, κ can approximately be calculated as

$$\kappa = 1 - \frac{V_A^{\text{eff}}}{V_B} + (T_B - T_A)\left(\frac{1}{T} - \frac{1}{T_B}\right). \tag{21}$$

Apparently, the atomic volume and melting point are included in the kinetic factor κ and they would both play a role in influencing the SSA.

We now calculate ΔF and κ for those binary metal systems, in which the SSA has been observed. Table I lists the calculation results for the systems combining rare-earth and transition metals as well as two transition metals. Table II lists the calculation results of the systems with a positive ΔH_m. One sees clearly from the tables that for those systems where SSA has been achieved, the thermodynamic factor ΔF is negative together with a kinetic factor κ being greater than 0.6, which could be considered as a critical value.

The next question is what happens to a system with a positive ΔH_m together with a κ less than 0.6. Take the Fe-Cu system ($\Delta H_m = +13$ kJ/mol), as an example, when the individual layers of Fe and Cu in the multilayers are both designed to be 1.5 nm thick, the thermodynamic factor ΔF could be negative. However, the kinetic factor κ is calculated to be around 0.5. It is thus deduced that SSA hardly takes place in the Fe-Cu system, which is compatible with the fact that SSA has not been observed so far. Incidentally, an amorphous Fe-Cu phase was obtained by a room-temperature ion mixing of the Fe-Cu multilayers,[23] as ion mixing, a process of the far-from-equilibrium process, is capable of inducing intermixing between the equilibrium immiscible Fe and Cu metal layers, resulting in the amorphization of the multilayers regardless of the kinetic limitation emerged in the solid-state reaction.

It should be noted that the calculated interfacial free energy in this paper is for the case that the solid-solid interface is in a disordered state. If one deals with a coherent or semi-coherent interface, the calculation would be different. Under such condition, however, SSA hardly occured as shown by both experimental[24] and molecular-dynamics studies.[25]

In summary, by considering the interfacial free energy in the thermodynamic calculation as well as the effect of melting points and the atomic volume difference on interdiffusion, a criterion is proposed for predicting the possibility of solid-state amorphization in the binary metal systems and the prediction is in good agreement with the experimental observations so far reported.

Financial support from the Natural Science Foundation and the Ministry of Science and Technology of China are gratefully acknowledged.

*Author to whom correspondence should be addressed. FAX: 86-10-6277-1160. Electronic address: dmslbx@tsinghua.edu.cn

[1] R. B. Schwarz and W. L. Johnson, Phys. Rev. Lett. **51**, 415 (1983).
[2] B. M. Clemens, Phys. Rev. B **33**, 7616 (1986).
[3] J. S. Kwak, E. J. Chi, J. D. Choi, S. W. Park, H. K. Baik, M. G. So, and S. M. Lee, J. Appl. Phys. **78**, 983 (1995).
[4] Z. J. Zhang and B. X. Liu, J. Appl. Phys. **76**, 3351 (1994).
[5] F. Pan, Y. G. Chen, and B. X. Liu, Appl. Phys. Lett. **67**, 780 (1995).
[6] B. X. Liu, Z. J. Zhang, O. Jin, and F. Pan, in *Ion-Solid Interactions for Materials Modification and Processing*, edited by D. B. Poker, D. Ila, Y. T. Cheng, L. R. Harriott, and T. W. Sigmon, MRS Symposia Proceedings No. 396 (Materials Research Society, Pittsburgh, 1996), p. 71.
[7] Y. G. Chen and B. X. Liu, J. Phys. D **30**, 1729 (1997).
[8] Y. G. Chen and B. X. Liu, Acta. Mater. **33**, 167 (1997).
[9] K. W. Kwon, H. J. Lee, and R. Sinclair, Appl. Phys. Lett. **75**, 935 (1999).
[10] A. R. Miedema, A. K. Niessen, F. R. de Boer, R. Boom, and W. C. M. Matten, *Cohesion in Metals: Transition Metal Alloys* (North-Holland, Amsterdam, 1989).
[11] J. M. Lopez and J. A. Alonso, Phys. Status Solidi A **85**, 423 (1984).
[12] H. Bakker, J. Less-Common Met. **105**, 129 (1985).
[13] A. M. Brown and M. F. Ashby, Acta Metall. **28**, 1085 (1980).
[14] B. M. Clemens, W. L. Johnson, and R. B. Schwarz, J. Non-Cryst. Solids **61/62**, 817 (1984).
[15] M. Van. Rossum, M.-A. Nicolet, and W. L. Johnson, Phys. Rev. B **29**, 5498 (1984).
[16] H. Schrüer, K. Samwer, and U. Koster, Phys. Rev. Lett. **48**, 1437 (1986).
[17] M. Atzmon, J. D. Verhoven, E. D. Gibson, and W. L. Johnson, Appl. Phys. Lett. **45**, 1052 (1984).
[18] B. M. Clemens and M. J. Suchoski, Appl. Phys. Lett. **47**, 943 (1985).
[19] M. Atzmon, K. M. Unruh, and W. L. Johnson, J. Appl. Phys. **58**, 3865 (1985).
[20] C. Brouder, G. Krill, P. Guilmin, G. Marchal, E. Partype, A. Fontaine, and G. Tourillon, Phys. Rev. B **37**, 2433 (1988).
[21] R. B. Schwarz, K. L. Wong, W. L. Johnson, and B. M. Clemens, J. Non-Cryst. Solids **61/62**, 415 (1984).
[22] Y. G. Chen and B. X. Liu, Appl. Phys. Lett. **68**, 3096 (1996).
[23] G. W. Yang, W. S. Lai, C. Lin, and B. X. Liu, Appl. Phys. Lett. **74**, 3305 (1999).
[24] W. S. Lai and B. X. Liu, Phys. Rev. B **58**, 6063 (1998).
[25] W. J. Meng, Ph.D. thesis, California Institute of Technology, 1987.

Irradiation induced amorphization in metallic multilayers and calculation of glass-forming ability from atomistic potential in the binary metal systems

B.X. Liu*, W.S. Lai, Q. Zhang

Laboratory of Advanced Materials, Department of Materials Science and Engineering, Tsinghua University, Beijing 100084, China

Accepted 15 May 2000

Abstract

This review attempts to present first a brief summary of the up-to-date experimental studies on amorphization transition, which results in the formation of amorphous alloys or metallic glasses, by ion irradiation of multiple metal layers in the binary metal systems. Secondly, based on the framework of Miedema's theory, thermodynamic modeling of metallic glass formation is described with consideration of the significant role of interfacial free energy of the multilayers in amorphization. Thirdly, results of molecular dynamics simulations for some representative systems are presented to show the calculation of the intrinsic glass-forming ability from interatomic potential of the binary metal systems.

Keywords: Amorphous alloys; Ion irradiation; Metallic glass-forming ability; Thermodynamic modeling; Molecular-dynamics simulation

1. Introduction

In 1960, Duwez obtained the first metallic amorphous alloy, and named it metallic glass, by liquid melt quenching in the Au–Si system [1]. Because of their non-crystalline structure without any grain boundaries, the metallic glasses have frequently shown unique property in many aspects [2]. To obtain metallic glasses by liquid melt quenching, a cooling speed of 10^6 K/s is needed to avoid crystallization of any possible crystalline phase [3]. In recent decades, higher cooling speeds up to 10^{7-8} K/s have been achieved and helped in greatly enhancing the capability of producing new metallic glasses [4]. Besides, laser quenching of the melt has also been applied for producing amorphous alloys [5], as many intense laser sources have been available and can achieve a cooling speed as high as 10^{12} K/s [6]. In these techniques, metallic glasses are formed through a process of liquid-to-solid phase transformation. Based on the experimental data, the binary metal systems have been classified into two groups of glass-forming and non-glass-forming systems according to their glass-forming ability, which was defined to qualitatively distinguish the systems either able or unable to obtain the metallic glass upon liquid melt quenching. Meanwhile, ternary [7] and even quinary metal systems [8] have also been studied by liquid melt quenching technique to produce new metallic glasses.

* Corresponding author.

E-mail address: dmslbx@tsinghua.edu.cn (B.X. Liu)

Review Article, Materials Science and Engineering: Reports 29 (1-2), 1-48 (2000).

In the early 1980s, some new and powerful glass-producing techniques have been introduced, such as ion irradiation of multiple metal layers, or named ion beam mixing [9], solid-state reaction [10] and mechanical alloying [11]. In comparison to liquid melt quenching, the formation of metallic glasses by ion beam mixing is through a process of solid–solid phase transformation. Naturally, such a difference in phase transformation type would certainly result in significantly different behaviors in metallic glass formation. In fact, ion irradiation is capable of producing metallic glasses not only in those binary metal systems known as glass-forming ones, but also in some non-glass-forming systems defined based on liquid melt quenching data. For instance, some metallic glasses have been obtained by ion irradiation in some equilibrium immiscible systems [12]. Apparently, some basic concept and understanding concerning metallic glasses should be somewhat modified, e.g. the previously defined glass-forming/none-glass-forming systems, glass-forming ability or glass-forming composition range, etc.

In the 1970s, Miedema developed a semi-quantitative model, which is capable of calculating the thermodynamic properties of metals and alloys based on some intrinsic properties of the elements. The model has been employed to construct the Gibbs free energy diagram of the binary metal systems, including the calculated free energy curves of all the involved alloy phases as a function of alloy concentration. It turned out that the constructed free energy diagram could give relevant thermodynamic insight of the alloy phase formation and transformation [13]. Since the late 1980s, Miedema's theory has also been employed to develop relevant thermodynamic model for the formation of metastable alloy phases [14,15].

In the last decade, significant progress has been achieved in computational materials science [16]. Computation and/or simulation make it possible to approach a quantitative understanding of the alloy phase formation and transformation, as the computation deals with the mechanism down to an atomic scale or even into a depth of electronic structures of the solids. Very recently, it has been initiated to study the possibility of determining the glass-forming ability of a binary metal system directly from a realistic n-body potential of the system through molecular dynamics simulation [17].

The present review article is attempted to present a brief summary of the recent progress concerning the understanding of amorphization transition and the calculation of the glass-forming ability from atomic interaction potential. The discussion in the present article will be concentrating on the binary metal systems, of which fruitful experimental as well as important thermodynamic data have so far been accumulated.

1.1. Survey of metastable alloy phase formation by ion beam mixing

In the early 1980s, a scheme of ion beam mixing of multiple layers was introduced [18], in which the multilayered films consisted of both deposited materials A and B on an inert supporting substrate. By adjusting the relative thicknesses of the two materials, an A–B alloy can be formed with any desired composition. In ion beam mixing, an ion beam (typically an inert gas ion beam) is used mainly to trigger atomic collisions for inducing inter-mixing between the layers of materials A and B. After irradiation to an adequate ion dose, a uniform mixture of metals A and B can be achieved and a new A–B alloy phase is thus obtained. At the beginning, ion beam mixing of multilayered films has been employed mostly to study the possibility of synthesizing metal-silicides, which are known as important candidate materials to be applied in the electronic device and very large-scale integrated circuits (VLSI) technology [19]. A little later, ion beam mixing of multilayered films has also been employed to study the metastable alloy phase formation and transformation in the binary metal systems and significant progress has been achieved concerning the formation of metallic glasses [9].

1.2. Physical process of ion beam mixing

Ion beam mixing is a process of far-from-equilibrium and is commonly divided into three steps. The first step is of atomic collision cascade and the second step is of relaxation. After relaxation, the third step is a named delayed period. Generally, the third step has no considerable effect on the structure of the alloy phases formed by ion beam mixing. Concerning the detailed calculation of atomic collision and associated phenomena to be discussed in this section, the readers are referred to a very valuable and well-written monograph [20]. The first and second steps of ion beam mixing are therefore of importance in determining the structural characteristics of the alloy phases expected to be formed and they proceed like as follows. When an ion with an energy of E_1 impacts on the surface and penetrates into depth of the target material, it collides with the atoms in the material. If an atom in the material receives energy of E_2 exceeding a threshold value E_d, the atom will leave its own lattice site and a vacancy is left behind. This displaced atom is named primarily knocked-out atom and it will, if E_2 is still considerably greater than E_d, trigger secondary collisions, third ones, and so on and so forth. Such a series of atomic collisions is named atomic collision cascade, during which a large number of atoms are dynamically excited in motion.

The atomic collision cascade is responsible for the inter-mixing of the metals A and B in the multilayered films, as the atoms of metals A and B are excited by the impinging ions into motion and can migrate crossing the interfaces. Typically, the energy of the irradiating ions is in the order of several 100 keV to MeV, while the binding energy of the solids is of 5–10 eV, which is several magnitudes of order smaller than that of the irradiating ions. Consequently, the atomic collision emerging in the material is a dynamic process of far-from equilibrium. After receiving an adequate irradiation dose, the discrete layered structure of the multilayered films is smeared out and a uniform atomic mixture of A–B is thus obtained. The atomic mixture is highly disordered with higher energy than that of its corresponding equilibrium state. Apparently, the uniform mixing of metals A and B in ion beam mixing is induced by dynamic collision process together with the associated irradiation enhanced diffusion. In the second step of relaxation, the highly energetic mixture should somehow relax towards equilibrium. However, whether or not the mixture can reach an equilibrium state depends on the temperature and time conditions available during the relaxation period. It is commonly recognized that the structure of the newly formed alloy phase is fixed in the relaxation period, but not in the first step of atomic collision, during which a large number of atoms are in motion. According to the atomic collision theory, the relaxation period is very short and the mixture is not allowed to undergo directly to an equilibrium state in the most cases. Instead, it frequently resides at some intermediate states, which correspond to metastable crystalline, amorphous and some other alloy phases. An alternative way of examining the process of ion irradiation is to consider the energy deposition in the surface of the target material and a concept of thermal spike was introduced. Considering a cylinder with a diameter of 5 nm diameter and a length of 100 nm, an estimation showed that the temperature rise in the cylinder center could be as high as 10^3–10^4 K heated by the deposited energy. At the same time, the surrounding materials outside of the cylinder remain at ambient temperature (300 K). According to a thermal conduction calculation, for such a huge temperature rise to drop down and balance with the surroundings, the relaxation time is approximately 10^{-10}–10^{-9} s. The phenomenon that a temperature rise in the material goes up to 10^3–10^4 K and drops down to ambient temperature within very short time period is named thermal spike. From the above description of ion beam mixing process, the relaxation time period is very short, i.e. lasting only for 10^{-10}–10^{-9} s and an effective cooling speed available in ion beam mixing can therefore be deduced to be as high as 10^{13-14} K/s. Such a high cooling speed is probably the highest one among currently available techniques for producing metallic glasses or other metastable alloys. Meanwhile, such a short time of relaxation makes the kinetic condition for alloy phase formation to be extremely restricted and would certainly affect the structural characteristics of the alloy phase to be formed. In fact, during relaxation, only amorphous or simple structured crystalline alloy phases can be obtained.

Till now, some 100 binary metal–metal systems have been studied and a great number of amorphous and metastable crystalline alloys have been obtained, such as super-saturated solid solutions, electron compounds, etc. Among these metastable alloys, many have not been formed or are even not obtainable by other non-equilibrium techniques like liquid melt quenching, etc. Moreover, such fruitful information gained from ion beam mixing studies has also provided an opportunity to approach a better understanding of the glass-forming ability, the glass-forming composition range of the binary metal systems.

1.3. Empirical models for predicting metallic glass formation upon ion beam mixing

In the last two decades, researchers in the related fields have made great effort to promote the understanding concerning the mechanism of metastable alloy phase formation and to predict the glass-forming ability or glass-forming range of the binary metal systems. Several empirical or phenomenological models have been proposed from the static properties of the constituent metals and/or the features of the corresponding equilibrium phase diagram. The first rule, namely the structural difference rule, was proposed by Liu et al. [9], and it predicted that an amorphous alloy would most likely be formed in the binary metal systems with two constituent metals of different crystalline structures by ion beam mixing of multilayered films with an overall composition located in the mid of the two-phase region of the equilibrium phase diagram. Obviously, ion beam mixing should be executed under an appropriate condition, e.g. the films should be retained at a relatively low temperature, the ion beam current density should be relatively low to avoid otherwise the re-crystallization of the amorphous phase expected to be formed, etc. Moreover, further studies showed that when the overall composition of the multilayered films was located at or in the vicinity of those intermetallic compounds frequently with complicated crystalline structures, amorphous alloys could also be obtained by ion beam mixing, yet could not be produced by liquid melt quenching [21]. Also in the early 1980s, Alonso and Simozar [22] proposed to construct a two-dimensional map for predicting the glass-forming ability of the binary metal systems under ion beam mixing and a schematic map is with two parameters, i.e. the ratio of atomic radii of the metals A and B and the heat of formation (ΔH_f) of an equiatomic compound. By summarizing the obtained experimental data, they separated the binary metal systems into amorphous and non-amorphous regions and predicted that no amorphous phase could be formed in those systems with a ΔH_f exceeding +10 kJ/mol, e.g. in the Ag–Mo, Cu–Co and Pd–Re systems, etc. In the mid 1980s, however, there were some reports showing the possibility of forming metallic glasses in the systems, of which the ΔH_f was greater than +10 kJ/mol, though the underlying thermodynamics was not yet clarified at that moment [23]. These experimental observations showed that the ΔH_f of a system is not a decisive parameter, yet has some effect on the readiness and composition limitation in ion beam mixing induced amorphization. Taking into account the effect of ΔH_f, Liu et al. proposed a phenomenological model on the basis of two intrinsic parameters of the binary metal systems. The first parameter is defined as the maximum possible amorphization range (MPAR), which equals to 100% as the whole composition range minus the maximum solid solubilities observed from the equilibrium phase diagram as illustrated in Fig. 1. The second parameter is the ΔH_f of an equiatomic compound of the system. According to the semi-quantitative combinations of MPAR and ΔH_f, the binary metal systems are classified into three categories of readily, possibly and hardly glass-forming

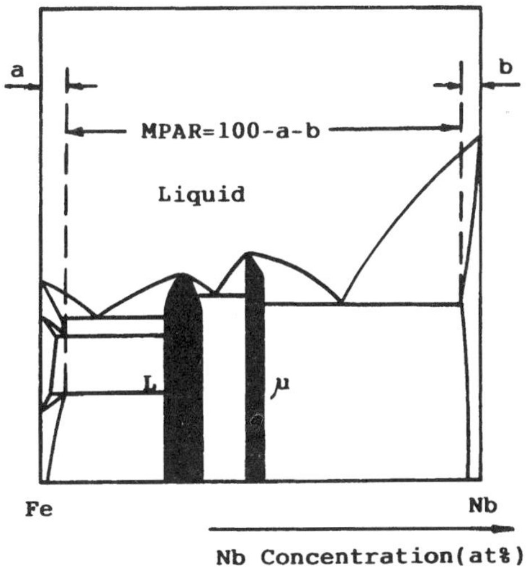

Fig. 1. A schematic diagram for the definition of the parameter MPAR (i.e. maximum possible amorphization range) of a binary metal system.

systems and the classification is in good agreement with the experimental observations [12,24]. Besides, in 1990, Ossi proposed an atomistic model to interpret the nucleation of amorphous or crystalline phases in several ion bombarded binary alloys and to separate the glass forming from crystalline binary alloys. The model was based on atomic collision cascades and the related bombardment induced surface compositional changes, using two parameters, i.e. the work function ϕ^* of the constituent metals and the electronic density at the boundary of the Wigner–Seitz cell [25].

2. Thermodynamics of alloy phase formation

As ion beam mixing is a process of far-from-equilibrium, the first question to be answered is when and how the equilibrium thermodynamics can be applied. As mentioned above, the first two steps of ion beam mixing are of importance in determining the structure of the alloy phase. In the first step of atomic collision cascade, a large number of atoms are excited to be in violent motion, during which the structure of the alloy phase can not be fixed. After receiving an adequate ion dose, the layered structure of the initial multilayers is smeared out, resulting in a uniform atomic A–B mixture in a highly energetic state. At the termination of the first step, the atomic mixture should somehow relax towards equilibrium. At this very moment, the equilibrium thermodynamics comes into play to govern the direction of relaxation as well as to indicate what kind of possible states for the atomic mixture to reside in. In this sense, equilibrium thermodynamics can be applied at the beginning of and during the relaxation to give insight to the formation of metastable alloy phases. In other words, though the ion beam mixing process, as a whole, is of far-from-equilibrium, the metastable alloy phase is formed in the second step of relaxation, during which the equilibrium thermodynamics is applicable and can give direction for the metastable alloy phase formation and transformation.

2.1. Miedema's theory and Alonso's method

Concerning the phase formation and transition, the Gibbs free energy usually gives a criterion of the relative stabilities of the possible states in the system under consideration. By comparing the

Gibbs free energies of the possible competing phases, i.e. solid solutions, amorphous, metastable crystalline phases, and the equilibrium compounds, one can understand the observed phase evolution and the glass-forming ability or glass-forming range of the system. In construction of a free energy diagram, the free energy curves of all the alloy phases of interest can be calculated based on Miedema's model and the method developed by Alonso et al. [26].

Generally, the Gibbs free energy of a phase is calculated by $\Delta G = \Delta H - T\Delta S$, where ΔH and ΔS are the enthalpy and entropy of formation, respectively. The entropy usually plays only a secondary role in solid phase formation. The expression for entropy can be taken, as a first approximation, as that of an ideal solid solution, i.e. $\Delta S = -R(X_A \ln X_A + X_B \ln X_B)$, where R is the gas constant, and X_A and X_B are the atomic concentrations of metals A and B in the alloy, respectively. According to Miedema et al., the enthalpy of formation of a substitutional solid solution of transition metals, can be considered as a sum of three contributions [27–29]

$$\Delta H = \Delta H^C + \Delta H^e + \Delta H^S \tag{2.1}$$

In the equation, ΔH^C, ΔH^e and ΔH^S are the chemical, elastic and structural contributions, respectively.

The chemical contribution, ΔH^C, which is due to the electron redistribution generated at the surface of contact between dissimilar atomic cells, is described by the following expression [30]:

$$\Delta H^C = X_A f_{AB} \Delta H_{amp} \tag{2.2}$$

where f_{AB} is a function which accounts for the degree to which atoms of type A are surrounded by atoms of type B. ΔH_{amp} is the amplitude concerning the magnitude of the electron redistribution interaction and is a constant for a specific binary metal system, which is given by [13]

$$\Delta H_{amp} = \frac{V_A^{2/3}}{(n_{WS}^{-1/3})_{av}}[-P(\Delta\phi^*)^2 + Q(\Delta n_{WS}^{1/3})^2] \tag{2.3}$$

where V_A is the atomic volume of component A in the alloy, $(n_{WS}^{-1/3})_{av}$ the mean value of the electron density at the boundary of the Wigner–Seitz cell as derived for the pure elements in the metallic state $(n_{WS}^{-1/3})_A$ and $(n_{WS}^{-1/3})_B$, $\Delta\phi^*$ the difference between ϕ_A^* and ϕ_B^*, i.e. the work function of pure metallic elements A and B, respectively, and P and Q are two constants, determined empirically. All the above values are obtainable from the documented reference [13]. f_{AB} is given by [29]

$$f_{AB} = X_B^S[1 + \gamma(X_A^S X_B^S)^2] \tag{2.4}$$

$$X_B^S = \frac{X_B V_B^{2/3}}{X_A V_A^{2/3} + X_B V_B^{2/3}} \tag{2.5}$$

In Eq. (2.4), γ is an empirical constant which is used to describe the short-range-order difference of solid solution, amorphous phase, and ordered compound, for which it is usually taken to be 0, 5, and 8, respectively.

The elastic contribution, ΔH^e, originates from atomic size mismatch and can be derived from the equation [31–34]

$$\Delta H^e = X_A X_B [X_A \Delta H^e_{(B\,in\,A)} + X_B \Delta H^e_{(A\,in\,B)}] \tag{2.6}$$

where $\Delta H^{e}_{(i\,\mathrm{in}\,j)}$ is the elastic contribution to the heat of solution of i in j, which can be calculated by using the elastic constants of the constituent metals [35,36].

The structural contribution, ΔH^{S}, reflects the correlation between the number of valence (s+d) electrons and the crystal structure of transition metals. The expression for this term reads [35,36]

$$\Delta H^{S} = E(Z) - X_{A}E(Z_{A}) - X_{B}E(Z_{B}) \tag{2.7}$$

where $E(Z)$, $E(Z_A)$ and $E(Z_B)$ are the lattice stability parameters [27,30] of the alloy phase and the pure A and B metals, and Z, Z_A and Z_B are the mean number of valence electrons of the alloy phase and the number of valence electrons of pure metals A and B, respectively. The dependence of the lattice stability on Z for paramagnetic transition metals in the three main crystallographic structures, i.e. bcc, fcc and hcp, has been calculated by Niessen and Miedema [27]. The corrections for systems including ferromagnetic metals have also been reported by Niessen et al. [30].

For the enthalpy of formation of the amorphous phase, both the elastic and the structural terms are absent. Following the suggestion by Niessen et al., the enthalpy of the amorphous phase is given by [30]

$$\Delta H_{\mathrm{amorphous}} = \Delta H^{C} + \alpha(X_{A}T_{m,A} + X_{B}T_{m,B}) \tag{2.8}$$

where α is an empirical constant equal to 3.5 J/mol K and $T_{m,i}$ is the melting point of the component i.

2.2. Role of interface in alloying behavior in the multilayers

It has recently been found that in the binary metal systems with positive heats of formation, the interfacial free energy in the multilayered films played an important role in amorphous and metastable crystalline phase formation by ion beam mixing. On the other hand, in the systems with negative heats of formation, the interfacial free energy has minor influence on the initial energetic state of the multilayers and its effect is therefore negligible. This can be illustrated by comparing the free energy curves of the amorphous phase with those of the multilayered films in two representative systems, e.g. the Ni–Hf and Y–Nb systems with ΔH_f being −63 and +35 kJ/mol, respectively. Fig. 2 shows the calculated results for the two systems. The details of the calculation of the interfacial free energy in the multilayers will be discussed in the next paragraph. One sees clearly from the figure that with increasing the number of layers or interfaces in the multilayers, the initial energetic state of the multilayers changes significantly in the Y–Nb system, whereas in the Ni–Hf system the effect of interface is indeed minor.

The Gibbs free energy of the initial state of the A–B multilayered films was calculated by adding the interfacial free energy to the ground state of a mixture of A and B in the bulk form, which is commonly considered as a reference state of G=0. As pointed out by Turnbull [37], the interfacial energy between two solid phases can be split into physical and chemical contributions, written as

$$\gamma_{SS}^{AB} = \gamma_{SS}^{geo} + \gamma_{SS}^{chem} \tag{2.9}$$

For two solids of quite different lattice structures, the geometrical term γ_{SS}^{geo} stands for the energy of a large angle grain boundary. It is estimated that the grain boundary enthalpy is about 30% of the surface energy at 0 K [38] and the entropy contribution is neglected. Thus, it is deduced that

$$\gamma_{SS}^{AB} = 0.15(\gamma_{A}^{S,0} + \gamma_{B}^{S,0}) + \gamma_{SS}^{chem} \tag{2.10}$$

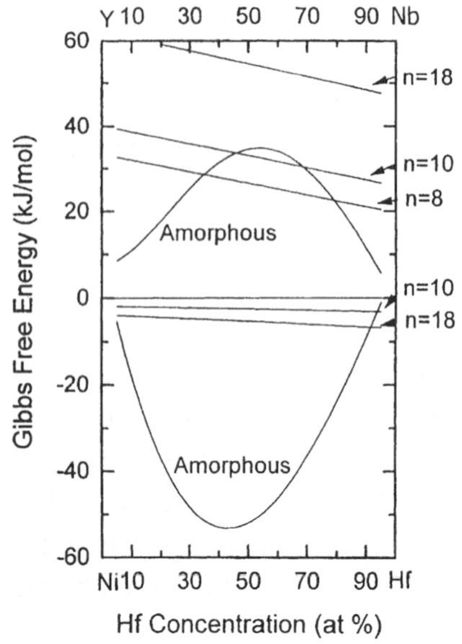

Fig. 2. Calculated free energy diagram of the Y–Nb and Ni–Hf systems, showing different effects of interfacial free energy on alloy phase formation in the positive and negative heat of formation systems. n stands for the number of interfaces in the multilayers.

where $\gamma_A^{S,0}$ and $\gamma_B^{S,0}$ are the surface energy of metals A and B, and γ_{SS}^{chem} is given by [39]

$$\gamma_{SS}^{chem} = \frac{\Delta H_{A\,in\,B}^0}{C_0 V_A^{2/3}} \tag{2.11}$$

where C_0 is a constant being 4.5×10^8. $\Delta H_{A\,in\,B}^0$ is the heat of solution of metal A in metal B at infinite dilution [40]. According to Gerkema and Miedema [41], the interfacial free energy can be calculated as follows:

$$\Delta G_{mul} = S_f \gamma_{SS}^{AB} \tag{2.12}$$

where S_f is the surface area occupied by 1 mol interfacial atoms.

Fig. 3 schematically shows the configuration of the A–B multilayered films. Suppose N_A and N_B are numbers of layers of metals A and B, $d_{A,i}$ and $d_{B,i}$ are the thicknesses of the ith layers of metals A and B, respectively, n_A and n_B are the numbers of the interfaces (A on B) and (B on A), $\Delta d_{A,i}$ and $\Delta d_{B,i}$ are the thicknesses of the ith interfaces (A on B) and (B on A), respectively. It is noted that the relationship of $n_A+n_B+1=N_A+N_B$ always holds for these four parameters. Accordingly, the interfacial free energy for the multilayered films can then be calculated by

$$\Delta G_{mul} = \alpha_A S_{fA} \gamma_{BA} + \alpha_B S_{fB} \gamma_{AB} \tag{2.13}$$

where S_{fA} and S_{fB} are the surface areas occupied by 1 mol of atoms A and B, respectively. α_A and α_B are the fractions of interfacial atoms A and B versus the total number of atoms in the multilayered films, respectively, and they are given by [15]

$$\alpha_A = X_A \frac{\sum_i^{n_A} \Delta d_{A,i}}{\sum_i^{N_A} d_{A,i}}, \qquad \alpha_B = X_B \frac{\sum_j^{n_B} \Delta d_{B,j}}{\sum_j^{N_A} d_{B,j}} \tag{2.14}$$

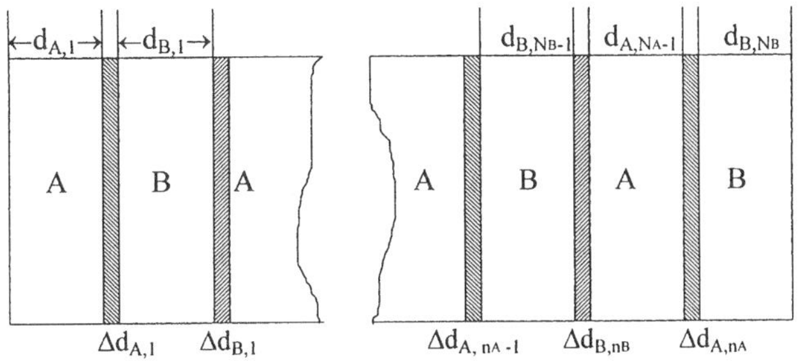

Fig. 3. Schematic configuration of the A–B multilayered films. N_A and N_B are numbers of layers of metals A and B, respectively, $d_{A,i}$ and $d_{B,i}$ are the thicknesses of the ith layers of metals A and B, respectively; n_A and n_B are the numbers of the interfaces (A on B) and (B on A), $\Delta d_{A,i}$ and $\Delta d_{B,i}$ are the thicknesses of the ith interfaces (A on B) and (B on A), respectively.

where $\sum_i^{n_A}\Delta d_{A,i}/\sum_i^{N_A} d_{A,i}$ and $\sum_j^{n_B}\Delta d_{B,j}/\sum_j^{N_A} d_{B,j}$ are the fractions of interfacial A atoms versus the total number of A atoms and B atoms versus the total number of B atoms, respectively. These terms multiplied by X_A and X_B, respectively, give the fractions of A and B interfacial atoms versus the total number of (A+B) atoms in the multilayers. According to some experimental results, e.g. Clemens has determined by X-ray diffraction that in the Ni–Ti multilayered films prepared by sputter deposition, an interfacial disordered layer could be several atomic layers thick [42], the thickness of each interface was reasonably assumed to be of 0.5 nm. Besides, for simplicity of calculation, the interfacial layers of A on B and B on A are assumed to be the same. It should be pointed that the above calculation is not precise, yet such a brief estimation can give guidance for multilayered sample design. In experiments, however, one can add some extra interfaces in sample design to ensure a higher initial energetic state of the multilayered films than that of the amorphous or other specific phase of interest. In other words, the above thickness assumption in calculation is not an essential point in studying the metastable alloy phase formation in the binary metal systems with a positive ΔH_f.

2.3. Relevance of the constructed free energy diagram

Since Miedema's model is still a semi-empirical one, its precision has been doubtful. To answer this question, a comparative experiment was suggested by authors' group and carried out in some binary metal systems to testify the validity of the constructed free energy diagram, by performing in situ thermal annealing of the as-deposited multilayered films in a hot-stage of the transmission electron microscope (TEM). It turned out that the observed phase evolution sequence in the multilayers upon thermal annealing was similar to that deduced from the calculation, confirming the relevance, at least in its outline, of the calculated free energy diagram.

Take the Ni–Ta system [14] as an example for the systems with negative ΔH_f. Fig. 4 shows the calculated Gibbs free energy diagram of the Ni–Ta system. In addition to the free energy curves of the solid solution and amorphous phase, the free energy curves of a Ni-rich metastable crystalline phase of hcp structure and a Ta-rich metastable crystalline phase with fcc structure were also calculated and are included in the figure. These two metastable crystalline phases were obtained by room temperature 200 keV xenon ion beam mixing. To testify the relevance of the calculated free energy diagram, two multilayered films with overall compositions of $Ni_{75}Ta_{25}$ and $Ni_{35}Ta_{65}$ were prepared and subjected to thermal annealing in the hot stage attached to the TEM and the results are as follows.

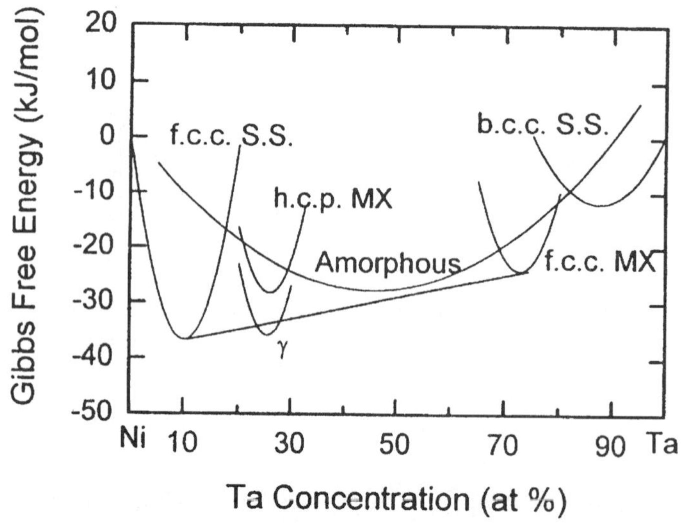

Fig. 4. Calculated Gibbs free energy diagram of the Ni–Ta system.

In the $Ni_{75}Ta_{25}$ films, amorphous phase was observed first after annealing at 400°C for 1 h and then changed into the hcp metastable crystalline phase after annealing at 500°C for 30 min. When the temperature was further raised up to 700°C and stayed for 20 min, the hcp metastable crystalline phase transformed into a mixture of Ni-rich solid solution and Ta-rich fcc metastable crystalline phase. The observed phase evolution can be summarized as follows:

$$Ni_{75}Ta_{25} \xrightarrow{400^\circ C, 60\,min} \text{amorphous} \xrightarrow{500^\circ C, 30\,min} \text{hcp} \xrightarrow{700^\circ C, 20\,min} \text{fcc} + Ni^*$$

In the equations, hcp and fcc stand for two metastable crystalline phases, and Ni^* is for the Ni-rich solid solution (the abbreviations are also for the next equation). Apparently, at the alloy composition of $Ni_{75}Ta_{25}$, the above sequence of phase appearance observed upon thermal annealing revealed that the free energy of the amorphous phase should be higher than that of the Ni-rich hcp metastable crystalline phase and that the free energy of both these two phases should be higher than that of the mixture of Ni-rich solid solution and the Ta-rich fcc metastable crystalline phase. Such sequence matches quite well with that deduced from the calculated free energy diagram, in which the free energy of the mixture should be situated on the cotangent line of the two phases.

In the $Ni_{35}Ta_{65}$ films, the fcc metastable crystalline phase was observed first after annealing at 350°C for 30 min and then it turned into amorphous at 450°C. Further increasing the annealing temperature to 500°C resulted in the transformation of the amorphous phase into a mixture of the fcc metastable crystalline phase plus the Ni-rich solid solution. The observed phase evolution can be expressed as follows.

$$Ni_{35}Ta_{65} \xrightarrow{350^\circ C, 30\,min} \text{fcc} \xrightarrow{450^\circ C, 60\,min} \text{amorphous} \xrightarrow{500^\circ C, 30\,min} \text{fcc} + Ni^*$$

Obviously, the observed sequence of phase evolution is also coherent with that suggested by the calculated free energy diagram.

Another example is for the Y–Zr system characterized by a positive $\Delta H_f = +14$ kJ/mol [43]. Fig. 5 shows the calculated Gibbs free energy diagram of the Y–Zr system. In addition to the free energy curves of amorphous phase and the two metastable crystalline phases of fcc and hcp structures, which were obtained in experiments, the initial energetic state of the Y–Zr multilayered

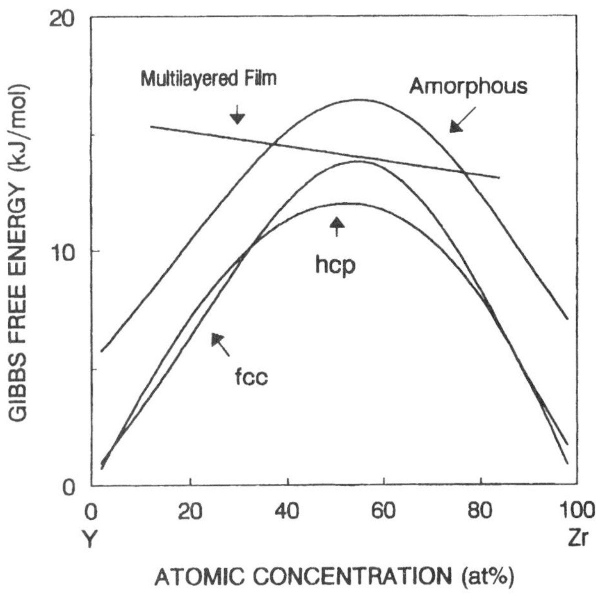

Fig. 5. Calculated Gibbs free energy diagram of the Y–Zr system.

films is also included. The total thickness of the multilayered films was 50 nm and the films consisted of nine layers. The estimation results showed that the fraction of the interfacial atoms versus the total number of the atoms in the films was about 10%. One sees from the figure that the free energy curve of the amorphous phase is convex in shape and is lower than that of the multilayered films in two separate regimes, i.e. Zr>72 at.% and Zr<37 at.%, suggesting the possibility of amorphous phase formation within two isolated composition ranges. However, there exists a fcc metastable crystalline phase with a lower free energy and would thus compete with amorphization. From the calculated free energy diagram, the phase evolution sequence within the two isolated composition ranges can be deduced as follows.

Take the Zr–Y multilayered films with the Zr concentration exceeding 72 at.% as an example, the phase evolution upon thermal annealing should be,

$$Y + \mathrm{Zr}\,(\text{multilayered films}) \rightarrow \text{amorphous} \rightarrow \text{fcc metastable crystalline phase}$$

In experiments, such sequence was indeed observed in the $Y_{25}Zr_{75}$ multilayered films. In fact, after annealing at a temperature between 150 and 200°C for 1 h, the polycrystalline Y and Zr reacted and transformed into an amorphous phase. Upon further annealing, the amorphous phase transformed into a uniform fcc metastable crystalline phase. Similar observations were also obtained for the Y-rich end.

In short, above thermal annealing experiments with some specifically designed multilayered films with appropriate alloy compositions confirmed the relevance of the free energy diagram calculated on the basis of Miedema's model and Alonso's method.

3. Experimentation of ion beam mixing

3.1. Sample design and preparation

In designing the metal–metal multilayered samples, three parameters should be considered, i.e. the total thickness of the films, the relative thicknesses of the two constituent metals, and the individual layer thickness in the films. The multilayered samples for SSR (solid-state reaction) have no limitation for the total thickness, which, however, should be designed to match with the range of the irradiating ions used in ion beam mixing experiments. The relative thicknesses of the two constituent metals depend on the desired composition of the alloy phase to be formed. The thickness of the individual layer should be reasonably thin to allow a good efficiency in interfacial reaction induced by either ion irradiation or thermal annealing. Especially, in studying the binary metal systems with positive ΔH_f, the design of layer thickness is based on how much interfacial free energy is needed to elevate the initial energetic state of the films to a specific level, e.g. to intersect with or even surpass that of the amorphous phase. In other words, the amount of the necessary interfacial free energy requires a certain number of interfaces and thus determines the individual layer thickness of the multilayered films.

In ion beam mixing experiments, inert gas ions, such as Xe, Kr, Ne, or Ar, are frequently employed to be the irradiating ions. The advantages of employing inert gas ions are that no chemical impurity effect is involved, and that gas ion sources are frequently available for the commercialized implanters. According to the atomic collision theory, heavy ions induce more efficient mixing than light ones when the other conditions are kept the same, Xe ions are therefore mostly employed to conduct ion beam mixing experiments. The typical energy of the irradiating ions is several 100 keV.

It was found that uniform mixing could be achieved well, if the total thickness of the multilayered film was designed to be the projected range R_p plus the projected range straggling ΔR_p of the irradiating ions. The R_p and ΔR_p for elemental metals can be calculated easily by the LSS theory and the data have been compiled in the table form for convenience of use [44]. For an alloy target of A_xB_{100-x}, where x refers to the atomic percentage of metal A in alloy A_xB_{100-x}, the projected range of the alloy can be calculated by the following equation [45]:

$$R_p(A_xB_{100-x}) = \frac{R_p(A)R_p(B)}{yR_p(B) + (100-x)R_p(A)} \tag{3.1}$$

In the equation, y refers to the weight percentage of metal A in the alloy A_xB_{100-x} and can be converted from x easily with the known density of the metals. The calculation of the projected range straggling ΔR_p for an alloy is rather complicated. However, considering the errors involved in the calculation itself, as well as in controlling the thickness during deposition, the above equation is also good enough to estimate the ΔR_p for an alloy by simply substituting ΔR_p for R_p in the equation. The accuracy of the above calculation concerning ΔR_p and R_p can be about 10%.

The relative thicknesses of the two constituent metals are determined by dividing the total thickness of the films according to the desired alloy composition.

The thickness of each individual metal layer is frequently designed to be around 5 nm or even thinner to achieve a good mixing efficiency upon ion beam mixing. In the case of studying the binary metal systems with positive ΔH_f, the number of interfaces should be determined first according to the consideration of the interfacial free energy as discussed in Section 2.2. In such a case, the individual layer thickness is around 2.0 nm.

The multilayered films are prepared in a vacuum system by depositing alternately the pure metals A and B onto an inert substrate supporting the films, e.g. SiO_2, Al_2O_3 or NaCl single crystals. The system is often a multi-crucible e-gun evaporation system with a vacuum level on the order of 10^{-5} Pa or even down to 10^{-7} Pa. During deposition, an in situ quartz oscillator is employed to monitor the thickness of the metal layers. The relative thicknesses of the metals are adjusted to attain the desired overall composition. After deposition, the real compositions can be measured and confirmed by energy dispersive spectrum (EDS).

3.2. Experimental parameters in ion beam mixing

It was found experimentally that the ion dose required to homogenize the discrete layered structure of the multilayered films is in the range of 10^{14}–10^{16} ions/cm^2, depending on the characteristics of the system. For instance, for the systems with positive ΔH_f, the mixing efficiency is low and therefore a little higher dose is required to induce uniform mixing and alloying. Since ion beam mixing is mostly to study the formation of metastable alloy phases, which are unstable at high temperature, the ion beam current density should be confined to be around 1 μA/cm^2 or even lower to avoid an otherwise over heating of the samples. In operating the implanter, the ion dose, which is measured by the electrical charge, is easy to adjust and control. Ion beam mixing thus offers a unique method for investigating the alloy phase formation or transition processes step-by-step. For example, by irradiating the same multilayered samples with various doses with fine intervals, it is possible to examine the intermediate states of the alloy phase formation or transformation.

Another important parameter in ion beam mixing is the temperature. Generally, ion irradiation should be conducted at relatively low temperature, e.g. at room temperature, liquid nitrogen temperature (77 K), or even down to liquid helium temperature (4.2 K). Nevertheless, the mentioned temperature in the experiments was often the nominal temperature measured at the sample holder instead of the effective temperature of the samples being irradiated. The effective temperature is an important parameter in the process induced by ion irradiation, and it should be taken into account in comparison with two characteristic temperatures of the materials. One is the critical temperature T_c, below which the irradiation-enhanced diffusion effect is negligible. Another one is the stable temperature of the newly formed phase. Apparently, if one expects to form an amorphous alloy having a transition temperature $T_{a\text{–}c}$ (a–c stands for transition from amorphous-to-crystalline and this temperature is named as re-crystallization temperature), the effective temperature of the sample during ion irradiation should of course be kept at a temperature far below $T_{a\text{–}c}$. For example, it has been reported in the early 1980s that ion beam mixing was not able to form amorphous alloy in the Ag–Cu system, though it has a typical eutectic phase diagram [19]. The failure of forming amorphous alloy was probably due to a relatively high effective temperature of the multilayered sample during ion beam mixing. The authors' group has studied the system again in the mid 1980s and succeeded in obtaining the $Ag_{50}Cu_{50}$ amorphous alloy by liquid nitrogen temperature ion beam mixing with a xenon ion current density of 1 μA/cm^2. Moreover, the re-crystallization temperature of the $Ag_{50}Cu_{50}$ amorphous alloy was determined to be about 120°C [23]. These results not only confirmed the possibility of forming amorphous alloy in the Ag–Cu system with a positive ΔH_f=+3 kJ/mol, but also demonstrated that an appropriate experimental condition is also of importance.

3.3. Characterization methods

Rutherford backscattering spectrometry (RBS) [46,47] is frequently employed to analyze the amount of mixing in the multilayered films with He ions of 1–2 MeV or higher energy. Fig. 6 shows a typical example of the Mo–Fe multilayers before and after ion beam mixing to a certain dose, respectively. In some cases, X-ray induced photon spectroscopy (XPS) and Auger spectrometry are used to analyze the composition depth profile of the multilayered films before and after ion irradiation at various stages.

EDS is employed not only to determine the real compositions of the as-deposited multilayered samples but also the resultant alloy phases obtained by ion beam mixing. X-ray diffraction (XRD) and selected area diffraction (SAD) using transmission electron microscopy (TEM) are frequently

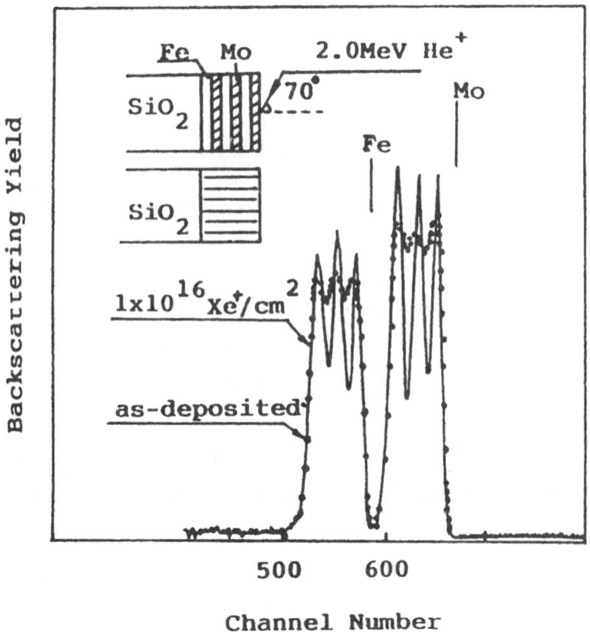

Fig. 6. Backscattering spectra of the Fe–Mo multilayered films before (solid line) and after ion mixing (1×10^{16} Xe^+/cm^2 at RT).

employed to identify the structure of the newly formed alloy phases in ion beam mixing or SSR. Four-point probe resistivity measurement is a supplemental method to give evidence of crystal-to-amorphous and vice versa, as the resistivity of the amorphous phase is often considerably greater than that of their crystalline counterpart.

4. Thermodynamic modeling of metallic glass formation by ion beam mixing

Ion beam mixing can usually produce metallic glasses in those binary metallic systems with negative ΔH_f, which makes the amorphous state to have a lower free energy than that of the initial energetic state of the multilayered films consisting of two crystalline metals and thus serves as a driving force for amorphization. On the contrary, if a system has a large positive ΔH_f, it is frequently essentially equilibrium immiscible. In such a case, the two constituent metals cannot even mix together to form an alloy melt and therefore liquid melt quenching is unable to obtain amorphous alloy in such systems. It has also been considered, for some time, to be difficult to produce metallic glasses by ion beam mixing in the systems with positive ΔH_f and some early experimental studies did fail in doing so [19]. Since the late 1980s, however, there have been some experimental results showing the possibility of forming metallic glasses in the systems featuring large positive ΔH_f and the alloy composition favoring amorphization was found to locate within a narrow composition region [24]. These results stimulated a further and systematic study to re-examine the possibility of metastable phase formation upon ion beam mixing in the positive ΔH_f systems. In fact, in the mid 1990s, ion beam mixing has produced a number of amorphous as well as metastable crystalline alloys in a number of systems with positive ΔH_f ranging from nearly zero to +56 kJ/mol [48,49]. These results seem to suggest that ΔH_f of a system is not a decisive parameter in determining whether the metallic glass can be formed or not, though it does affect the composition range favoring amorphization. Interestingly, in the systems with positive ΔH_f, metallic glass was frequently formed

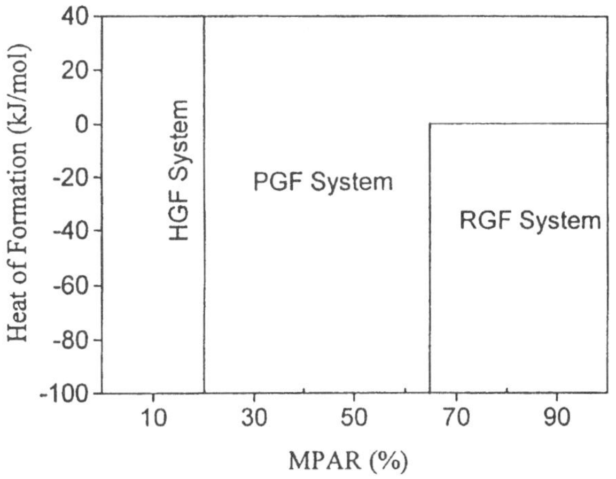

Fig. 7. According to the two defined parameters MPAR and heat of formation, the binary metal systems are classified into three categories: readily, possibly and hardly glass-forming systems (RGF, PGF and HGF, respectively).

in the restricted composition regions close to the constituent metals, but not in the central portion of the equilibrium phase diagram [49]. This phenomenon is sharply different from that observed in the systems with negative ΔH_f, in which the alloy composition in the vicinity of equiatomic stoichiometry is usually the most favored for amorphization, where the free energy of the amorphous phase reaches its minimum [50].

Concerning the glass-forming range of a binary metal system, the defined MPAR in the empirical model is believed to be an important parameter in predicting the glass-forming range and glass-forming ability of the system. Fig. 7 is a map using MPAR and ΔH_f as coordinates to approach a semi-quantitative classification of the binary metal systems in terms of their glass-forming range and glass-forming ability upon ion beam mixing. It can be clearly seen that MPAR>20% is a necessary condition for metallic glass formation upon ion beam mixing and the system is named as a possible glass-forming one. While for a system with MPAR<20%, the two-phase region is just too narrow and can even be diminished by the extension of the solid solubilities upon ion beam mixing. In such a case, metallic glass is hardly to be formed upon ion beam mixing. Extrapolating to an extreme value of MPAR=0%, the corresponding equilibrium phase diagram of the system is of continuous solid solution type with no two-phase region at all and the glass-forming range is therefore deduced to be zero. These systems are named as hardly glass-forming ones. Moreover, when the systems feature a MPAR>65% together with a negative ΔH_f, metallic glasses are readily to be formed in a broad composition range upon ion beam mixing and the systems are named as readily glass-forming ones, which of course belong to the group of the possible glass-forming systems [24]. The following discussion will show that the prediction of glass-forming range or glass-forming ability based on MPAR–ΔH_f model agrees reasonably well with the experimental results obtained so far and that by considering the excess interfacial free energy stored in the multilayered films, a unified thermodynamic model can be established for the metallic glass formation by ion beam mixing in the binary metal systems with either negative or positive ΔH_f.

4.1. *Glass-forming ability of the negative heat of formation systems*

Till now, extensive data have been accumulated by ion beam mixing experiments for the binary metal systems with negative ΔH_f. According to the MPAR–ΔH_f model, one is able to predict approximately the glass-forming range of a system by inspecting its equilibrium phase diagram. Take

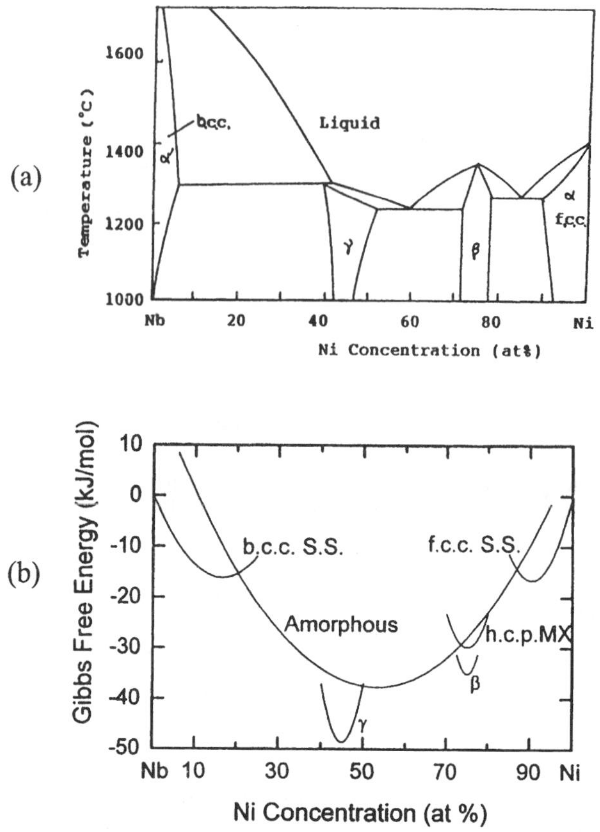

Fig. 8. (a) The equilibrium phase diagram of the Ni–Nb system; (b) calculated Gibbs free energy diagram of the Ni–Nb system.

the Ni–Nb system as a typical example, its $\Delta H_f = -45$ kJ/mol [13] and Fig. 8(a) exhibits its equilibrium phase diagram. In the phase diagram, the alloy composition range can be divided into three types, i.e. terminal solid solution, intermetallic compound and two-phase regions. As described above, an amorphous alloy is readily to be formed by ion beam mixing in the two-phase regions. The easy formation of metallic glasses in the two-phase regions can be attributed to the competition of crystallization between the two crystalline phases, resulting in a frustration of nucleation and growth of either crystalline phase during very restricted time period of relaxation in ion beam mixing. It has also been confirmed that it is possible to form metallic glasses by ion beam mixing of multilayered films with overall compositions located at (or in the vicinity of) the intermetallic compounds frequently with complicated structures, which are not allowed to grow during relaxation period in ion beam mixing. Thus, the two-phase regions in the phase diagram are connected each other and the composition range favoring amorphization is within a continuous region. Consequently, metallic glasses are possible to be formed by ion beam mixing in a continuous composition range, which is actually the total width of the two-phase regions, i.e. the defined MPAR as illustrated in Fig. 1. From the equilibrium phase diagram of the Ni–Nb system, the MPAR is from 5 to 90 at.% of Nb [13].

According to the thermodynamic calculation, a free energy diagram of the Ni–Nb system, as a typical example of the negative ΔH_f system, is shown in Fig. 8(b). One sees that the free energy curves of the amorphous phase, two terminal solid solutions and the equilibrium intermetallic compounds are concave. By comparing the free energy of the amorphous phase with those of crystalline phases, it is possible to predict glass-forming range. As the formation of intermetallic compounds is usually hindered kinetically, they need not to be taken into account when discussing glass-forming range, though they have even lower free energy than all other phases. Thus, the amorphous phase is thermodynamically most favored to be formed near the equiatomic stoichiometry where its free energy curve reaches the nadir and was lower than those of two terminal solid solutions. The glass-forming range was commonly regarded as the composition range in which the free energy of the amorphous phase was below that of the solid solutions. Consequently, the glass-forming range of the Ni–Nb system is from 15 to 80 at.% of Nb, which is reasonably a little narrower than the MPAR value. In the early 1990s, Zhang et al. have performed ion beam mixing experiment and determined that the glass-forming range was very close to 15–80 at.% of Nb, which is in excellent agreement with that from thermodynamic calculation [50]. It is worthwhile mentioning that there have been many ion beam mixing results showing the readiness of metallic glass formation in such binary metal systems featuring a negative ΔH_f, e.g. in the Ni–Zr system, the calculated glass-forming range is 10–90 at.% of Zr, and the ion beam mixing results showed the glass-forming range was around 10–80 at.% of Zr [51].

Considering the glass-forming range of the binary metal systems, there are two points worth mentioning:

1. In most cases, amorphous alloys can not be formed with the alloy compositions close to solid solidus, because ion beam mixing could extend the solid solubilities and form metastable crystalline phases, which are always with simple crystalline structure. As a result, the glass-forming range determined by ion beam mixing experiment is usually a little smaller than MPAR observed from the equilibrium phase diagram.
2. The prediction based on the parameter MPAR includes the well-known deep eutectic criterion for metallic glass formation upon liquid melt quenching, as eutectic portion is only a special type of two-phase region emerging in the equilibrium phase diagram. Moreover, ion beam mixing is able to produce metallic glasses in those systems, where the eutectic points are so high that liquid melt quenching was not able to obtain amorphous alloy. For example, liquid melt quenching has not succeeded in producing an amorphous Mo–Ru alloy at eutectic composition, because the eutectic point is as high as 1900°C, whereas room temperature (RT) xenon ion beam mixing was able to form an amorphous alloy with a composition around $Ru_{45}Mo_{55}$ [52].

4.2. Glass-forming ability of the positive heat of formation systems

For a binary metal system with a positive ΔH_f, the free energy curve of the amorphous phase is usually higher than that of an equilibrium mixture of crystalline metals A and B in the alternatively deposited multilayered films, leading to a situation unfavored for metallic glass formation. However, as the interfaces in the multilayered films are generally regarded as transient layers of mixed A and B atoms in a highly disordered configuration, the extra interfacial free energy plays an important role in alloy phase formation in the films. If an adequate fraction of interfacial atoms is included in the multilayered films, the free energy curve of the films can be elevated to intersect with that of the amorphous phase, resulting in the possibility of forming metallic glasses in some specific composition regions. Some examples of experimental results are given in the following discussion.

4.2.1. Metallic glasses formed within restricted composition ranges

Take the Ag–Mo system as a typical example, the system has a positive ΔH_f of +56 kJ/mol and is the second largest ΔH_f for the transition binary metal systems. The free energy curves of the amorphous phase and multilayered films designed to contain 12 layers (or 11 interfaces) are calculated and included in the free energy diagram shown in Fig. 9. One sees that the free energy

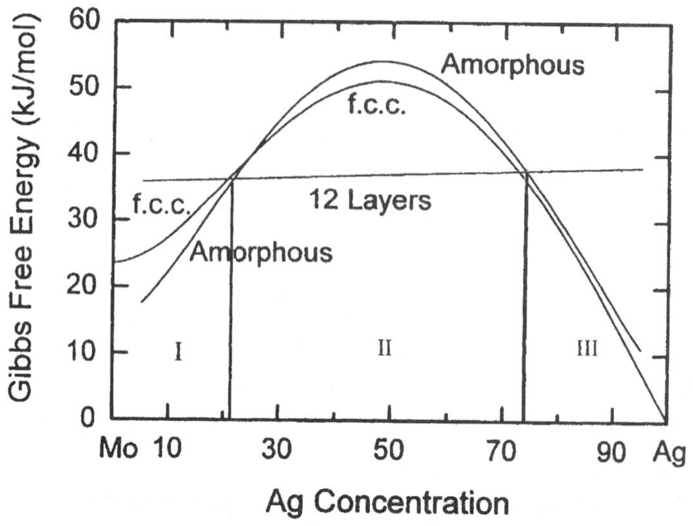

Fig. 9. Calculated Gibbs free energy diagram of the Ag–Mo system.

curve of the multilayered films intersects with that of the amorphous phase and thus the whole composition range is divided into three different regions. Obviously, in regions I and III, amorphous phase is possible to be formed, as its free energy is lower than that of the initial state of the films. While in region II, formation of metallic glass is hardly to be achieved, because the amorphous phase still has a higher free energy than the films. Ion beam mixing experiments were conducted with 200 keV xenon ions at liquid nitrogen temperature. It turned out that an amorphous alloy was indeed formed at the alloy composition near 80 at.% of Mo and that another amorphous phase was also formed together with a new Mo-based fcc metastable crystalline phase in the multilayered films with the alloy composition around 40 at.% of Mo [49]. Such compositional discontinuity in metallic glass formation in the positive ΔH_f systems has also been observed in some other systems, like the Nb–Zr [48], and Y–Ta [53] systems with positive ΔH_f of +6 and +40 kJ/mol, respectively. In fact, if one takes into account the competition between amorphization and the solid solutions with extended solubilities upon ion beam mixing, the composition region favoring metallic glass formation may become more restricted and can even be missed in the experiments. The extension of the solid solubility upon ion beam mixing will be discussed in details later in the next section.

4.2.2. Metallic glasses formed in broad composition range

As shown above, the location and width of the alloy composition regions favoring amorphization depend on the designed fraction of interfacial atoms in the multilayered films. One may then ask if further increasing the fraction of interfacial atoms can have the two separated composition regions favoring amorphization become broader and meet each other to unite into a continuous range. Take the Y–Mo system with a ΔH_f=+35 kJ/mol as an example, Fig. 10 shows the calculated free energy diagram of the system and it includes the free energy curve of the amorphous phase and three free energy curves for the multilayered films with various layer numbers of 9, 11 and 19 in a total fixed thickness of 45 nm, corresponding to the fractions of interfacial atoms of 8.1, 10.0 and 18.1 at.%, respectively. Table 1 lists the predicted composition ranges favoring amorphization for the three cases, respectively. The Y–Mo multilayered films were prepared accordingly for ion beam mixing experiments. It turned out that the ion beam mixing results were in excellent agreement with the prediction and are also included in Table 1 [15]. These results suggested that by appropriately designing the multilayered films, it is possible to form metallic glasses in such a

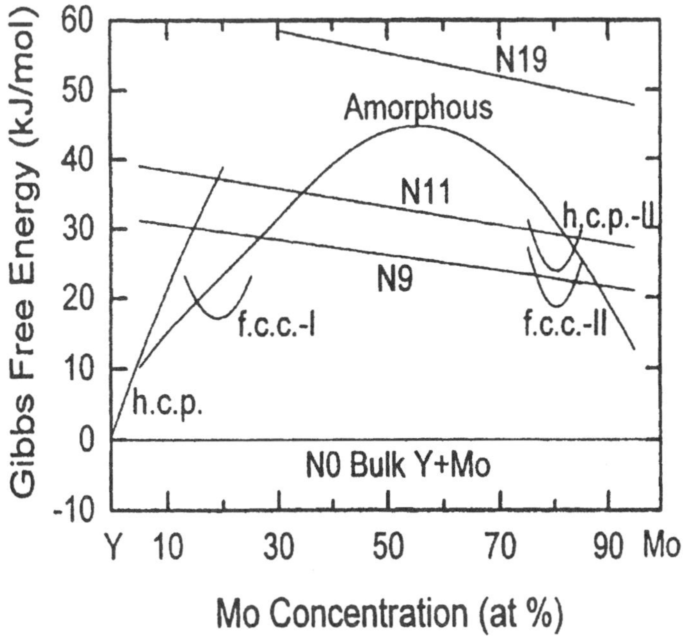

Fig. 10. Calculated Gibbs free energy diagram of the Y–Mo system. *N* stands for the number of layers in the Y–Mo multilayered films.

positive ΔH_f system even with an alloy composition near the equiatomic stoichiometry, where the amorphous phase frequently has the highest free energy. Obviously, even in the positive ΔH_f systems, the glass-forming range could be extended to a broad composition range close to the value of MPAR, when the multilayered films were properly designed to possess sufficient interfacial free energy.

To summarize the above discussion concerning the metallic glass formation upon ion beam mixing, Table 2 lists the ion beam mixing results obtained so far and the binary metal systems are listed in an alphabetical order for convenience of survey.

4.3. Nominal and intrinsic glass-forming ability

From both practical and theoretical points of view, prediction of glass-forming ability of the binary metal systems is of vital importance. The previously defined glass-forming ability was only to

Table 1
Prediction and experimental results of metallic glass formation in the Y–Mo multilayered films by 200 keV xenon ion beam mixing (IM) at room temperature

Layer number	Fraction, α (at.%)		Composition				
			$Y_{80}Mo_{20}$	$Y_{60}Mo_{40}$	$Y_{50}Mo_{50}$	$Y_{40}Mo_{60}$	$Y_{20}Mo_{80}$
9	8.1	Predicted	Yes	No	No	No	Yes
		IM Experiment	Yes	No	No	No	Yes
11	10.0	Predicted	Yes	Yes	No	No	Yes
		IM Experiment	Yes	Yes	No	No	Yes
19	18.1	Predicted	Yes	Yes	Yes	Yes	Yes
		IM Experiment	Yes	Yes	Yes	Yes	Yes

Table 2
Metallic glass formation in the binary metal systems by ion mixing of multiple metal layers

ΔH_f	System	Remarks
ΔH_f <0	Al–Au [55], Al–Co [56], Al–Fe [57], Al–Mn [58], Al–Mo [59], Al–Nb [60], Al–Ni [61], Al–Pd [61], Al–Pt [61], Al–Ta [59], Al–Ti [62], Al–Y [63], Al–Yb [64], Au–Ta [65], Au–Ti [66], Au–V [67], Co–Gd [68], Co–Hf [69], Co–Mo [60], Co–Nb [70], Co–Ta [71], Co–Tb [72], Co–Ti [56], Co–Y [63], Co–Yb [73]	Metallic glasses have been formed with various compositions
	Co–Zr [74], Cu–Y [63], Cu–Zr [63], Er–Ni [60], Fe–Gd [72], Fe–Mo [12], Fe–Nb [75], Fe–Ta [75], Fe–Tb [72], Fe–Ti [76], Fe–Y [63], Fe–Zr [74], Hf–Ni [77], Mo–Ni [60], Mo–Ru [52], Mo–Zr [78], Nb–Ni [50], Ni–Ta [14], Ni–Ti [79], Ni–Y [63], Ni–Yb [73], Ni–Zr [51], Ru–Ti [80], Ru–Zr [80]	In some systems, at least, one metallic glass has been formed within narrow composition range
ΔH_f <0	Au–Cu [81], Cu–Rh [82], Mo–Nb [83]	No glass has so far been formed
ΔH_f=0	Fe–W [84]	Metallic glasses have been formed
ΔH_f=0	Cu–Ir [82], Ti–Zr [83]	No glass has so far been formed
ΔH_f >0	Ag–Cr [12], Ag–Cu [23], Ag–Mo [49], Ag–Nb [85], Ag–Ni [23], Ag–Ta [69], Ag–V [69], Au–Co [86], Au–Ir [82], Au–Mo [87], Au–Os [82], Au–Ru [59]	Metallic glasses have been formed with various compositions
	Au–W [59], Co–Cu [12], Cu–Fe [88], Cu–Mo [89], Cu–Nb [69], Cu–Ta [18], Fe–Nd [72], Hf–Nb [90], Hf–Ta [91], Mo–Y [15], Nb–Ti [92], Nb–Zr [48], Ta–Ti [93], Ta–Y [53], Ta–Zr [94], Ti–Y [63], Y–Zr [95]	In some systems, at least, one metallic glass has been formed
ΔH_f >0	Ag–Co [96], Ag–Fe [69], Ag–Ir [82], Ag–Os [82], Ag–Rh [82], Ag–Ru [82], Ag–W [97], Au–Fe [98], Au–Ni [98], Au–Rh [82], Cr–Cu [99], Cu–Os [59], Cu–W [59], Fe–Yb [73]	No glass has so far been formed

classify the systems into two categories of glass-forming and non-glass-forming ones in a qualitative way and the classification was mostly based on the data from liquid melt quenching. As discussed above, however, by employing powerful means of ion beam mixing, many new metallic glasses have been obtained in those systems considered previously as non-glass-forming ones. Apparently, the definition or the physical meaning of glass-forming ability needs to be extended. Firstly, glass-forming ability of a system should reflect qualitatively whether metallic glass can be formed or not in the system. Furthermore, from a physical point of view, there exists an intrinsic glass-forming ability reflecting the capability of the system itself and it does not depend on the practically applied techniques. Secondly, it is also of necessity to have a quantitative measure for glass-forming ability that is able to compare the capabilities among the glass-forming systems. An experimentally determined glass-forming range, to authors' view, can be taken as a quantitative measure for glass-forming ability. Naturally, the larger the glass-forming range, the greater the glass-forming ability. It is true that if one employs a technique with a greater cooling speed, one may obtain glass in a broader composition range than that observed by a technique with a slower cooling speed. In this sense, an experimentally observed glass-forming range can only be considered as a nominal glass-forming ability [54]. Obviously, the greater the glass-forming range observed by a specific technique, the closer the glass-forming range to the intrinsic glass-forming ability. Consequently, to approach an intrinsic glass-forming ability of a system, one should look for a glass-producing technique with a cooling speed as high as possible. At present, ion beam mixing can be considered as the very technique capable of revealing the maximum glass-forming ability among the currently available glass-producing techniques.

The next question is how to correlate the nominal glass-forming range observed by ion beam mixing and the intrinsic glass-forming ability of the system. Based on ion beam mixing studies for the binary metal systems with either a negative or positive ΔH_f, the defined MPAR is a good approximation for predicting the composition range for metallic glass formation, which is also compatible with the above thermodynamic analysis. As ion beam mixing can frequently form some super-saturated solid solutions, which would actually reduce the total width of the two-phase regions. It is thus deduced that if one can determine the super-saturated solid solubilities of a specific system, the intrinsic glass-forming ability or glass-forming range can then be predicted by the modified MPAR, which equals 100% as the whole composition range minus the two super-saturated solid solubilities.

5. Free energy calculation of the metastable crystalline alloys

5.1. Structural classification of the metastable crystalline phases

It has been established that ion beam mixing is also an effective means to form new metastable crystalline phases, among which many could not be obtained by other techniques. Experimental results seem to indicate a strong role of thermodynamics in the tendency to form metastable phases. Besides, intermetallic compounds with small ranges of solubility and complex crystalline structures are also prime candidates for transformation to a metastable state [100]. Also, the change in the free energy of the solid due to the ion induced defect buildup argues for a thermodynamic explanation [101].

It has been argued that at low temperatures, ion beam mixing is similar to a quenching process where the atom configurations are essentially determined during the relaxation period following the atomic collision cascade [102]. Because the kinetics is restricted, the formation of complex crystalline structures is unlikely and ion beam mixing will usually result in the formation of solid solutions, other metastable crystalline phases with simple structures and amorphous phases. The structure of the metastable phase is, however, influenced by the equilibrium nature of the system. Those systems with intermetallic compounds will tend to form amorphous phases while those with no intermetallic compounds are favored to form solid solutions by ion beam mixing. At high temperature, atoms are mobile and equilibrium phases may be formed.

Based on substantial experimental results reported in the literature, the metastable crystalline phases formed by ion beam mixing of multilayered films in both negative and positive ΔH_f binary metal systems can be classified into five categories [103], that is, super-saturated solid solutions, the hcp-I phases in hcp- or fcc-based alloys, the fcc-I phases in hcp-based alloys, the hcp-II and fcc-II phases in bcc-based alloys.

5.1.1. Solid solutions

Ion bcam mixing of multilayered films can extend the solid solubility of the binary metal alloys, and thus resulted in the formation of a number of super-saturated solid solutions always having the same simple crystalline structures as the major alloying metals. In the following, we present some typical examples of the formation of solid solutions by ion beam mixing.

1. Single-phase solid solutions were formed in the full composition range in the Au–Ni [98] system, which has a phase diagram of continuous solid solution type with miscibility gap in the solid state. The Ti–Zr and Mo–Nb [83] systems have similar diagrams, but no miscibility gap exists. Also, these single-phase solid solutions were formed by ion beam mixing for some arbitrarily chosen compositions, e.g. $Ti_{70}Zr_{30}$.
2. Single-phase solid solutions were formed in the full composition range in the simple eutectic systems Ag–Cu [19] and Au–Co [98], indicating that ion beam mixing is able to extend the solubility substantially in this type of phase diagram.
3. Two series of solid solutions with extended solubilities from both terminal metals were formed in Au–V [98], Au–Fe [98], and Fe–W [84] systems, in which intermetallic compounds divide the diagram into several sub-diagrams. That is the reason why solid solutions could not be formed throughout the full composition range.

All above metastable crystalline phases were identified as solid solutions. Their lattice constants agreed quite well with those predicted by Vegard's law, and they were therefore substitutional solid solutions.

5.1.2. hcp-I and fcc-I phases

A structural similar metastable crystalline hcp phase has been formed by ion beam mixing in five binary A–B metal systems (i.e. the Co–Au, Ti–Au, Co–Mo, Ni–Mo, and Ni–Nb systems), where A refers to the first entry and B to another alloying metal in the alloy designation. These phases were formed in the A-rich multilayered films with overall composition designed to be 65–80 at.% of metal A and are named as hcp-I phase. The metastable crystalline hcp-I phases are likely enriched in metal A and have the composition close to a stoichiometry ratio of A_3B. The precise composition of the phases, however, is not known, as they always mixed with other phases, e.g. in the Ni–Mo case, the metastable crystalline Ni–Mo hcp-I phase was mixed with an amorphous phase. The structures of these phases are all hcp and their lattice sizes are quite similar. Table 3 lists the crystalline lattice parameters of the metastable crystalline hcp-I phases and of the constituent metals, as well as the spacing distance of the close-packed plane (d_{cpp}) in all mentioned structures. The parameter d_{cpp} was suggested to be a pertinent one in comparing the lattice size among various crystalline structures

Table 3
Structure data of the hcp-I metastable crystalline (MX) phases formed in five binary metal systems by ion mixing[a,b]

System	MX phase		Constituent metals		Reference
	Lattice constants (Å)	d_{cpp} (Å)	Lattice constants (Å)	d_{cpp} (Å)	
Co–Au	hcp a=3.24, c=5.21 c/a=1.61	d_{002}=2.60	Co hcp a=2.54, c=4.07 c/a=1.59 Au fcc a=4.08	d_{002}=2.023 d_{111}=2.355	[86]
Ti–Au	hcp a=3.27, c=5.26 c/a=1.61	d_{002}=2.63	Ti hcp a=2.59, c=4.69 c/a=1.59 Au fcc a=4.08	d_{002}=2.34 d_{111}=2.355	[66]
Co–Mo	hcp a=3.27, c=5.22 c/a=1.60	d_{002}=2.61	Co hcp a=2.54, c=4.07 c/a=1.59 Mo bcc a=3.147	d_{002}=2.023 d_{110}=2.225	[65]
Ni–Mo	hcp a=3.25, c=5.21 c/a=1.60	d_{002}=2.61	Ni fcc a=3.52 Mo bcc a=3.147	d_{111}=2.034 d_{110}=2.225	[60]
Ni–Nb	hcp a=3.28, c=5.22 c/a=1.59	d_{002}=2.61	Ni fcc a=3.52 Nb bcc a=3.307	d_{111}=2.034 d_{110}=2.33	[104]

[a] These phases were considered as metastable 7/4 electron compounds.
[b] d_{cpp} refers to the distance between the close-packed plane in the respective lattice.

[86]. According to the data given in Table 3, the lattice sizes of these phases are all considerably larger than those of A and B metals. As a result, any combinations (applying Vigard's law) of the d_{cpp} values of A and B metals cannot give the d_{cpp} value of the metastable crystalline phase, indicating that the metastable crystalline hcp-I phases are not substitutional solid solutions. These phases could not be interstitial solid solution either, because the difference in atomic sizes of the two constituent metals is too small. Interestingly, the formation of the metastable crystalline hcp-I phase can be correlated to the valence electron effect. It is known that for a close-packed hexagonal structure, the maximum number of electron states per atom, n, in the Jones' zone (including doubling for spin) can be calculated by the following equation [105]:

$$n = 2 - \frac{3}{4}\left(\frac{a}{c}\right)^2\left[1 - \frac{1}{4}\left(\frac{a}{c}\right)^2\right] \tag{5.1}$$

where a and c are the lattice constants of the hcp structure, respectively. Employing Eq. (5.1), the n values of these five phases are calculated to be almost identical, i.e. n=1.73–1.74, which is very close to the value of 7/4=1.75, corresponding to the well-defined Hume–Rothery 7/4 electron compound. These A_3B alloy phases can, therefore, be considered as metastable electron compounds [106].

Table 4 lists the formations of another type of metastable crystalline phases obtained in some hcp metal-rich multilayered films by ion beam mixing and are named as fcc-I phases. As both hcp and fcc structures are built up by the stacking of close-packed atomic planes differing only slightly in the stacking order. They can, therefore, easily transformed into each other, i.e. a sliding of atoms on

Table 4
fcc-I metastable crystalline phases formed in Co-, Y-, Zr-, and Hf-rich multilayered films by room temperature 200 keV xenon ion mixing

System and composition	Mixing dose (Xe^+/cm^2)	Lattice parameter (Å)
$Co_{94}Mo_6$–$Co_{82}Mo_{18}$	3×10^{15}	3.55–3.60
$Co_{98}Ta_2$–$Co_{80}Ta_{20}$	3×10^{15}	3.55–3.65
$Y_{73}Mo_{27}$–$Y_{83}Mo_{17}$	7×10^{15}	5.10
$Y_{85}Ta_{15}$–$Y_{75}Ta_{25}$	1×10^{15}	5.18
$Y_{25}Zr_{75}$–$Y_{85}Zr_{15}$	3×10^{15}	4.67
$Zr_{68}Nb_{32}$–$Zr_{88}Nb_{12}$	7×10^{14}	4.80
$Hf_{75}Nb_{25}$–$Hf_{90}Nb_{10}$	5×10^{14}	4.55

the planes parallel to the $(0\,0\,0\,2)_{hcp}$ plane along $\langle 1\,\bar{1}\,0\,0\rangle_{hcp}$ directions by a vector of $1/3\langle 1\,\bar{1}\,0\,0\rangle_{hcp}$ can transform the hcp structure into fcc, and its reverse procedure is the one transforming fcc to hcp [107].

5.1.3. hcp-II and fcc-II phases formed in bcc metal-based systems

In some Nb-, Ta-, and Mo-based systems, another two metastable crystalline phases, named hcp-II and fcc-II, respectively, were formed by ion beam mixing, and their compositions were around AB_3, in which B stands for the bcc metals. Table 5 lists the crystalline data for the hcp-II and fcc-II phases. One sees that some of the systems have negative ΔH_f, in which the refractory metals combine with Fe, Co and Ni metals and that some positive ΔH_f systems are the combinations of refractory metals with Ag, Y, Zr and Hf. Carefully performed experiments revealed that the hcp-II phase was observed as an intermediate state in the process of forming the fcc-II phase, i.e. the hcp-II phase formed prior to the formation of the fcc-II phase. A two-step phase transition of bcc → hcp → fcc was, therefore, proposed by authors' group and named as reverse martensitic

Table 5
hcp-II and fcc-II metastable crystalline phases formed in Nb-, Ta-, Mo-rich multilayered films by room temperature 200 keV xenon ion mixing

A–B	System and composition	hcp-II	fcc-II
fcc–bcc	$Ni_{23}Mo_{77}$	Yes	Yes
	$Ni_{20}Nb_{80}$	Yes	Yes
	$Ni_{35}Ta_{65}$	No	Yes
	$Ag_{30}Mo_{70}$	No	Yes
	$Ag_{33}Nb_{67}$	No	Yes
hcp–bcc	$Co_{20}Mo_{80}$	Yes	Yes
	$Co_{23}Nb_{77}$	Yes	Yes
	$Co_{30}Ta_{70}$	No	Yes
	$Y_{22}Mo_{78}$	Yes	Yes
	$Y_{25}Ta_{75}$	Yes	Yes
	Zr_7Mo_{93}	Yes	Yes
	$Zr_{19}Nb_{81}$	Yes	Yes
	$Zr_{20}Ta_{80}$	No	Yes
	$Hf_{17}Nb_{83}$	No	Yes
	$Hf_{30}Ta_{70}$	No	Yes
bcc–bcc	$Fe_{24}Mo_{76}$	Yes	Yes
	$Fe_{20}Nb_{80}$	Yes	Yes
	$Fe_{20}Ta_{80}$	No	Yes

transformation. Firstly, a shearing mechanism transformed the bcc to hcp. During shearing, the $(1\,1\,1)_{\text{bcc}}$ acted as the habit plane, while $[\bar{1}\,1\,\bar{1}]_{\text{bcc}}$ (or $[2\,\bar{1}\,\bar{1}\,0]_{\text{hcp}}$) acted as the shearing axis. Secondly, the transformation from hcp to fcc was easy to achieve by a sliding of the atoms on the planes parallel to the $(0\,0\,0\,2)_{\text{hcp}}$ plane along $\langle 1\,\bar{1}\,0\,0\rangle_{\text{hcp}}$ directions with a vector of $1/3\langle 1\,\bar{1}\,0\,0\rangle_{\text{hcp}}$. Although the relaxation period of ion beam mixing is very limited, it could still meet the requirement of a shearing as well as sliding mechanism. According to the proposed mechanism, the lattice parameters of the metastable crystalline hcp-II and fcc-II phases were deduced and they were in good agreement with the experimentally measured results [107,108].

5.2. Free energy calculation of the metastable crystalline phases

As mentioned above, ion beam mixing of multilayered films can form either amorphous or simple structured metastable crystalline phases and the growth of the metastable crystalline phases some times would hinder amorphization. It is, therefore, necessary to calculate the free energy of the metastable crystalline phase and to compare with that of the amorphous state. We will discuss later in Section 6 that the glass-forming ability of a binary metal system could be calculated through molecular dynamics simulation based on realistic interatomic potential of the system. While comparing the calculated glass-forming ability with experimental results, the possible metastable crystalline phase formation should also be considered.

A metastable crystalline phase is considered to be in an ordered structure, its entropy term can thus be neglected. The free energy of the metastable crystalline phase includes three terms and is therefore expressed by

$$\Delta G_{\text{MX}} = \Delta H^{\text{c}}_{\text{MX}} + \Delta H^{\text{e}}_{\text{MX}} + \Delta H^{\text{s}}_{\text{MX}} \tag{5.2}$$

The first term is the chemical contribution and is written as

$$\Delta H^{\text{c}}_{\text{MX}} = X_{\text{A}} f_{\text{AB}}\, \Delta H_{\text{amp}} \tag{5.3}$$

f_{AB} is a function to account for the degree to which atoms of metal A are surrounded by atoms of metal B, ΔH_{amp} is an amplitude concerning the magnitude of the electron redistribution interaction and is a constant for a specific binary metal system. In the calculation of f_{AB}, a constant γ is an empirical constant which is used to describe the short-range-order difference of solid solutions, amorphous phases, and ordered compounds, for which they are usually taken to be 0, 5 and 8, respectively. As a metastable crystalline phase is commonly considered as a compound-like phase, the value $\gamma=8$ is always taken.

The second term is of elastic contribution and can be derived from the equation

$$\Delta H^{\text{e}}_{\text{MX}} = X_{\text{A}} X_{\text{B}} \left[X_{\text{A}}\, \Delta H^{\text{e}}_{\text{MX(B in A)}} + X_{\text{B}}\, \Delta H^{\text{e}}_{\text{MX(A in B)}}\right] \tag{5.4}$$

where $\Delta H^{\text{e}}_{\text{MX}(i\,\text{in}\,j)}$ is the elastic contribution to the heat of solution of i in j, which can be calculated by using the elastic constants of the constituent metals.

The third term is structural contribution and written as

$$\Delta H^{\text{s}}_{\text{MX}} = E(Z) - X_{\text{A}} E(Z_{\text{A}}) - X_{\text{B}} E(Z_{\text{B}}) \tag{5.5}$$

where $E(Z)$, $E(Z_{\text{A}})$ and $E(Z_{\text{B}})$ are the structural stabilities of the alloy phase and the pure constituent metals A and B, and Z, Z_{A} and Z_{B} are the average numbers of the valence electrons of the alloy phase and of the pure constituent metals A and B, respectively.

In calculation, the metastable crystalline phases are classified into two different categories in terms of their alloy compositions. For a metastable crystalline phase formed at a composition in the vicinity of an intermetallic compound, the elastic term should be included as this term originates from the difference in structures between the metastable crystalline phase and intermetallic compound. This is for the case that the metastable crystalline phases were formed at a stoichiometry ratio of A_3B. Another situation is that the metastable crystalline phase was formed at the composition near the eutectic point, where no equilibrium compound exists. In this case, the metastable crystalline phase can be considered as in an ordered state, so as the elastic term can be relaxed to zero because of the ordering. This situation corresponds to the formation of the metastable crystalline phases with a composition of AB_3. In short, with the above assumption, the formula for calculation for the A_3B metastable crystalline phase is

$$\Delta G_{\mathrm{MX}} = \Delta G^{\mathrm{c}}_{\mathrm{MX}} + \Delta G^{\mathrm{e}}_{\mathrm{MX}} + \Delta G^{\mathrm{s}}_{\mathrm{MX}} \tag{5.6}$$

and for the AB_3 metastable crystalline phase is

$$\Delta G_{\mathrm{MX}} = \Delta G^{\mathrm{c}}_{\mathrm{MX}} + \Delta G^{\mathrm{s}}_{\mathrm{MX}} \tag{5.7}$$

Take the Ni–Mo system as an example, the free energy curves of the metastable crystalline phases formed in the Ni–Mo system were calculated according to the above equations and displayed in Fig. 11. Fig. 11(a) is the equilibrium phase diagram and Fig. 11(b) shows the constructed free energy diagram of the Ni–Mo system, in which the free energy curves of all the concerned phases are included. One sees that the free energy diagram is a little complicated because of involving some newly formed metastable crystalline phases. Before employing the calculated free energy diagram to interpret the metastable phase formation upon ion beam mixing, the relevance of the calculated results should first be confirmed. As mentioned in Section 2, an alternative way for checking the relevance of the calculation is to perform thermal annealing of the multilayered films at some specific compositions. Take two samples as examples and the phase appearance in the samples upon thermal annealing are as follows:

$$\mathrm{Ni_{75}Mo_{25}} \xrightarrow[30\,\mathrm{min}]{300^\circ\mathrm{C}} \mathrm{amorphous} \xrightarrow[60\,\mathrm{min}]{450^\circ\mathrm{C}} \mathrm{hcp\text{-}I} \xrightarrow[20\,\mathrm{min}]{650^\circ\mathrm{C}} \mathrm{Ni}^* + \mathrm{hcp\text{-}II} \xrightarrow[30\,\mathrm{min}]{800^\circ\mathrm{C}} \mathrm{Ni}^* + \mathrm{fcc}$$

$$\mathrm{Ni_{25}Mo_{75}} \xrightarrow[60\,\mathrm{min}]{350^\circ\mathrm{C}} \mathrm{amorphous} \xrightarrow[30\,\mathrm{min}]{500^\circ\mathrm{C}} \mathrm{hcp\text{-}II} \xrightarrow[30\,\mathrm{min}]{600^\circ\mathrm{C}} \mathrm{fcc}$$

Apparently, the phase evolution sequences emerged in these two multilayered films are in good agreement with that deduced from the calculated free energy diagram, thus confirming the applicability of Miedema's model in this respect [109]. Moreover, similar annealing experiments were also performed for several positive ΔH_{f} systems and the results were also in support of the calculation [110]. In short, Miedema's model is applicable for constructing the free energy diagram of the studied system and the calculated diagram can, therefore, be applied to give relevant thermodynamic insight to the metastable phase formation by ion beam mixing.

6. Calculation of glass-forming ability from interatomic potential

One of the important and fundamental issues in the field of Metallic Glasses is to establish theoretical model for predicting the glass-forming ability of the binary alloy systems [111,112]. As

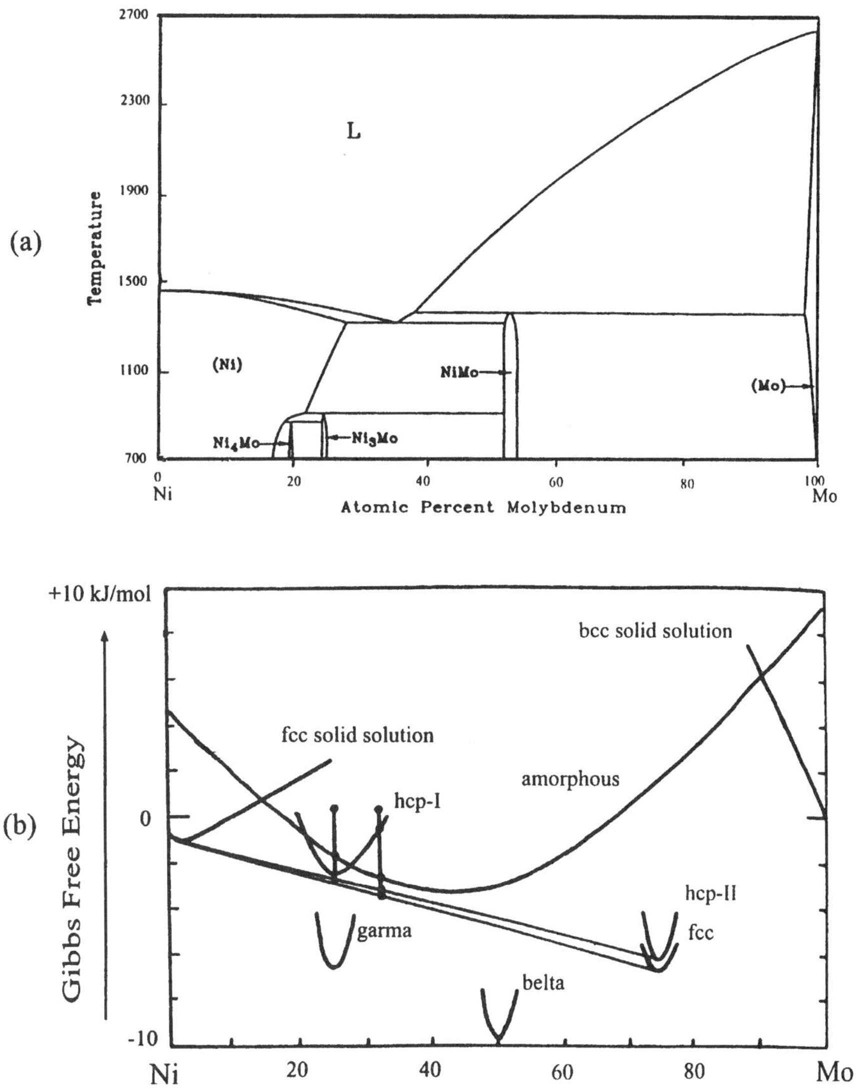

Fig. 11. (a) The equilibrium phase diagram of the Ni–Mo system; (b) calculated Gibbs free energy diagram of the Ni–Mo system.

described in Section 4, the glass-forming range, which is a quantitative measure of glass-forming ability of a system, determined by ion beam mixing could frequently extend over the entire composition range except the two terminal regions of solid solutions. The extraordinary capability of ion beam mixing in producing metallic glasses has led Liu et al. to propose an empirical parameter for predicting the possible glass-forming range of a system. The parameter was named as MPAR defined as 100% minus the two maximum terminal solid solubilities observed from the corresponding equilibrium phase diagram [63]. In Section 5, it has been shown that ion beam mixing could also extend the solid solubilities considerably beyond the equilibrium ones and the formed solid solutions are named super-saturated solid solutions. Consequently, the defined MPAR should be modified by taking into account of the extension of the solubility in predicting the glass-forming range of a system. In other words, prediction of glass-forming range becomes a question of determining the super-saturated solid solubilities of a binary metal system. From a physical point of view, the glass-forming range is determined by the relative stability of the solid solutions comparing to their amorphous counterparts and the relative structural stability of the crystalline versus amorphous phase is intrinsically determined by their corresponding atomic configurations, which are directly governed by the interatomic potential.

In this section, we will show that molecular dynamics simulation with a realistic interatomic potential of a binary metal system is capable of determining the super saturated solid solubilities, from which the glass-forming range of the system can thus be predicted.

6.1. Construction of n-body potentials for some Ni-based systems

To conduct molecular dynamics simulation in a binary metal system, a proven realistic potential of the system is necessary. In this respect, though the pair potential has been frequently used for molecular dynamics simulation [113,114], it has some drawbacks. Since 1980s, the problem has been solved through developing the so-called *n*-body models [115–117]. For example, Daw and Baskes proposed an approach named embedded-atom method, in which the interaction between two atoms was correlated not only to the interatomic distance but also to the local environment around the atom [115]. The basic idea of the embedded-atom method can be interpreted under the framework of density-functional theory, from which the energy required to place an impurity atom into a lattice is determined solely by the electron density at that particular site, without considering the origin of the electron density [116,118–120]. In the embedded-atom method, the total energy of an *n*-atom system is written as

$$E_{\mathrm{tot}} = \sum_i F_i(\rho_i) + \sum_{i>j} \varphi(r_{ij}), \tag{6.1}$$

In the equation, r_{ij} is the distance between atoms i and j, E_{tot} is the total energy, $\varphi(r_{ij})$ is the pair-wise interaction potential between atoms i and j, $F_i(\rho_i)$ is the embedding energy, ρ_i is the total electron density at atom i due to all other atoms.

$$\rho_i = \sum_{j(\neq i)} f(r_{ij}) \tag{6.2}$$

In the equation, $f(r_{ij})$ is the atom electron density for atom i contributed by atom j. In the original embedded-atom method model proposed by Daw and Baskes, the embedding energy F and repulsive item φ were given in the form of spline functions, i.e. in a numerical form [116], which would lead to some inconvenience in computation. For improvement, some researchers have constructed various embedded-atom method potential models [121–126]. For instance, Cai and Ye proposed an analytical embedded-atom method model, which has successfully been employed mainly for the fcc metals [126]. Accordingly, the embedding function was taken as a universal form suggested by Banerjea and Smith [127], which can be written as

$$F(\rho) = -F_0\left[1 - \ln\left(\frac{\rho}{\rho_e}\right)^n\right]\left(\frac{\rho}{\rho_e}\right)^n + F_1\left(\frac{\rho}{\rho_e}\right) \tag{6.3}$$

In the equation, $F_0 = E_c - E_v^f$, E_c and E_v^f are the cohesive energy and vacancy formation energy, respectively. Besides, ρ_e represents the host electron density at equilibrium and a linear term F_1 is added as an adjustable parameter. The atomic electron density $f(r)$ and pair potential $\varphi(r)$ are, respectively, defined as

$$f(r) = f_e \exp[-\chi(r - r_e)] \tag{6.4}$$

and

$$\varphi(r) = -\alpha\left[1+\beta\left(\frac{r}{r_{\rm a}-1}\right)\right]\exp\left[-\beta\left(\frac{r}{r_{\rm a}-1}\right)\right] \tag{6.5}$$

From the above equations, there are totally five potential parameters (χ, α, β, F_1 and r_a) for the atomic interaction. These potential parameters for a specific metal are determined by minimizing the square-root deviation between the calculated and experimental determined physical properties, such as the equilibrium lattice constant, cohesive energy, bulk modulus, elastic constants and vacancy formation energy, etc. In fitting, the cut-off distance is taken as $1.65a_0$ (a_0 is the lattice constant). Moreover, like other embedded-atom method potentials, the reproduced total energy of a system under Cai's model followed the universal equation of state formulated by Rose et al. [128]. The physical properties away from equilibrium were, therefore, already fitted and the potentials for pure metals can directly be applied to metallic alloys. To further testify the developed potential, some other physical properties should be reproduced, such as surface energy, formation energy and volume of defects, phonon dispersion curves and dynamic properties like melting point, thermal expansion coefficient, etc.

In addition, another two models of n-body potential have been proposed for the transition metals, i.e. the Finnis–Sinclair potential [117] and tight-binding potential [129]. The major difference between these two potentials with the embedded-atom method one is to do with the derivation and interpretation of ρ as well as embedding function F. The Finnis–Sinclair and tight-binding models are both based on the tight-binding theory of cohesion by assuming that the band energy is a sum of the occupied one-electron energies in a band, which is proportional to the square root of the second moment of its density of states (for transition metals, mainly the d-band density of the states) [130,131]. The density of the states can be expressed as a function of distance r_{ij}. The difference between the Finnis–Sinclair and tight-binding models is related to their specific function forms applied. According to Finnis and Sinclair, the total energy is written as

$$E_{\rm tot} = \sum_{i>j}\varphi(r_{ij}) - \sum_i\left[\sum_{j\neq i}A^2(r_{ij}-d)^2\right]^{1/2} \tag{6.6}$$

$$\varphi(r) = (r-c)^2\cdot(c_0+c_1r+c_2r^2) \tag{6.7}$$

where d and c are the cut-off distances for the cohesive and repulsive items, respectively [117]. Following this original formalism, some modified Finnis–Sinclair potentials were introduced, in which the F and φ functions were all in a polynomial form of distance [132–135]. The Finnis–Sinclair formalism has been employed to study the physical properties of some bcc and fcc metals as well as their alloys in a relatively satisfactory way [133].

The tight-binding or named as second-moment approximation of the tight-binding scheme, was firstly proposed by Tomanek et al. [129] and has been employed for a large number of transition metals and alloys [136,137]. In the tight-binding model, the cohesive and repulsive items of total energy are exponential functions of atomic distance. In a system with two types of metal α and β, the total energy is expressed by

$$E = \sum_i\left\{\sum_{j\neq i}A_{\alpha\beta}\exp\left[-p_{\alpha\beta}\left(\frac{r_{ij}}{d_{\alpha\beta}}-1\right)\right] - \sqrt{\sum_{j\neq i}\xi^2_{\alpha\beta}\exp\left[-2q_{\alpha\beta}\left(\frac{r_{ij}}{d_{\alpha\beta}}-1\right)\right]}\right\} \tag{6.8}$$

where r_{ij} is the distance between i and j atoms and $d_{\alpha\beta}$ is the nearest-neighbor distance in the crystal structure. The first pair potential term represents a repulsive Born–Mayer interaction and the second attractive many-body term does represent the second-moment approximation of a tight-binding band energy. Based on this scheme, many n-body potentials have been developed for a number of fcc and hcp transition metals. For the bcc metals, however, the second-moment approximation of the tight-binding scheme has been found to be inadequate in deriving those established physical features of the metallic bonding [137].

We now discuss the construction of n-body potentials for the Ni–Ti, Ni–Mo, Ni–Nb and Ni–Ta systems.

For the Ni–Ti system, we employed second-moment approximation of the tight-binding scheme to describe the Ni–Ti interatomic potential, as the scheme is suitable for the fcc and hcp transition metals and alloys [137]. As mentioned above, the total energy was given by Eq. (6.8). Accordingly, there were totally four adjustable parameters $A_{\alpha\beta}$, $p_{\alpha\beta}$, $\xi_{\alpha\beta}$ and $q_{\alpha\beta}$ for each constituent metals and alloy to be determined by fitting on their respective physical properties at 0 K. The parameters $A_{\alpha\beta}$, $p_{\alpha\beta}$, $\xi_{\alpha\beta}$ and $q_{\alpha\beta}$ were determined as follows: (i) for $\alpha=\beta$, a fit was performed on the cohesive energy, lattice parameters, elastic constants and the unrelaxed vacancy formation energy at 0 K of the pure elements Ni and Ti. The $d_{\alpha\alpha}$ was taken to be the nearest-neighbor distances of the pure elements Ni and Ti, respectively. (ii) For $\alpha\neq\beta$, the corresponding parameters were fitted on the cohesive energy and elastic constants of the B2 Ni–Ti phase at 0 K obtained from first principle calculations, i.e. the cohesive energy from the full-potential linear-muffin-tin-orbital calculation [138] and the elastic constants from the full-potential linearized augmented-plane-wave total-energy method [139]. The $d_{\alpha\beta}$ was taken to be the Ni–Ti nearest-neighbor distance in the B2 Ni–Ti phase. The cut-off radius r_c

Table 6
Values of cohesive energy E_c, nearest-neighbor distances d, elastic constants C_{ij}, and vacancy formation energy E_v^f, which are used for the fit of the potential (see text), and potential parameters $A_{\alpha\beta}$, $p_{\alpha\beta}$, $\xi_{\alpha\beta}$ and $q_{\alpha\beta}$ for Ni–Ni, Ti–Ti and Ni–Ti, where E_c, $A_{\alpha\beta}$, and $\xi_{\alpha\beta}$ are expressed in eV per atom, d in Å, C_{ij} in eV/Å^3, and E_v^f in eV

	Ni		Ti		Ni–Ti	
	This work	Experiment	This work	Experiment	This work	First principle calculated
E_c	4.44	4.44[a]	4.85	4.85[a]	5.02	5.02[b]
d	2.49[a]		2.95[a]		2.607[c]	
C_{11}	1.568	1.629[d]	1.103	1.0992[d]	1.279	1.112[e]
C_{12}	1.085	0.943[d]	0.549	0.5452[d]	0.846	0.921[e]
C_{13}			0.465	0.4263[d]		
C_{33}			1.187	1.1891[d]		
C_{44}	0.729	0.824[d]	0.193	0.3171[d]	0.297	0.306[e]
E_v^f	1.65	1.60[f]	1.56	1.55[g]		
A	0.104		0.153		0.3	
p	11.198		9.253		7.9	
ξ	1.591		1.879		2.48	
q	2.413		2.513		3.002	

[a] Reference [140].
[b] Reference [138].
[c] Reference [141].
[d] Reference [142].
[e] Reference [139].
[f] Reference [143].
[g] References [144,145].

for atomistic interaction was also treated as an adjustable parameter for an optimized fitting and was determined to be 0.42 nm. Table 6 lists the obtained potential parameters after optimization and a comparison between the physical quantities reproduced by the derived potential and those used initially for fitting. In addition, the cohesive energies and the lattice constants of some other Ni–Ti metastable and equilibrium crystalline phases pertaining to the 'unrelaxed' structures were also reproduced by the potential and the results were in good agreement with those from first principle calculations or experimental studies [146].

To further verify the potential, some other thermodynamic properties, e.g. enthalpy and volume, of the B2 Ni–Ti phase were also calculated by performing molecular dynamics simulation with the potential for a B2 Ni–Ti model consisting of $10\times10\times10$ unit cells (=2000 atoms) with periodic boundary conditions. Fig. 12 shows the variation of the enthalpy (*H*) and the volume (*V*) of B2 Ni–Ti versus temperature. One sees that an abrupt change for *H* and *V* appears at a same temperature regime and a melting point of the B2 Ni–Ti phase was thus estimated to be of 1612–1653 K. In addition, melting at T=1653 K was confirmed by a set of calculated pair-correlation functions showing liquid-like curves. Consequently, the computed melting point was in excellent agreement with the experimental one of 1583 K, as an overheating of a perfect crystal model was unavoidable and an overestimated value of ≈70 K is reasonable. Besides, the lattice stability of the B2 Ni–Ti phase as a function of composition was studied by randomly substituting Ni with Ti atoms or vice versa in the B2 crystal at the eutectic temperature (1391 K), which corresponded to the broadest composition range for the B2 phase in the equilibrium phase diagram. Fig. 13 gives the variation of molar enthalpy *H* and volume *V* as a function of composition. One sees that the abrupt changes of *H* and *V* take place at 46 and 60 at.% of Ni, respectively, suggesting that a spontaneous decay would take place at these two compositions. Naturally, the volume of the B2 phase would decrease with increasing Ni concentration, because the substitution of more Ni of small atomic radius for Ti of large radius into the ideal B2 crystal would certainly cause shrinkage of the lattice. An inverse

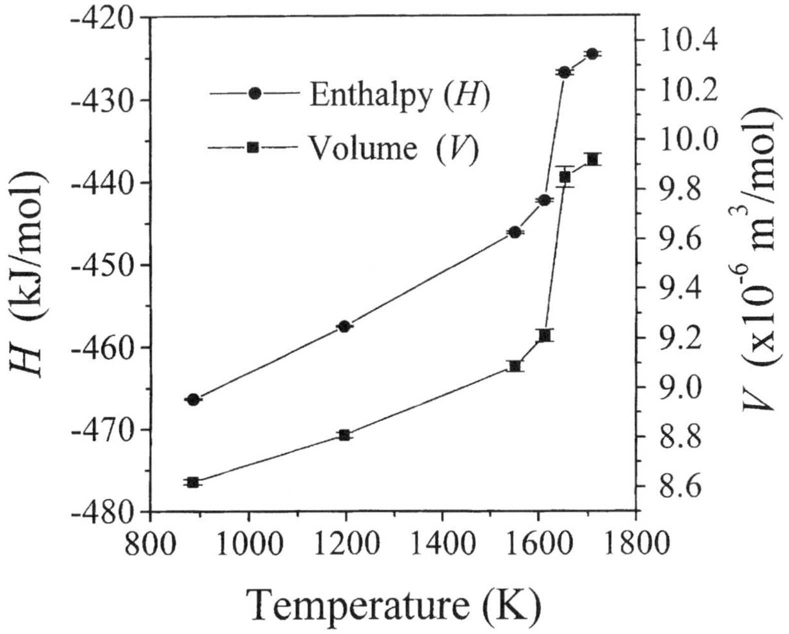

Fig. 12. Variation of the enthalpy *H* and the volume *V* as a function of temperature in the simulation model of B2 Ni–Ti crystal.

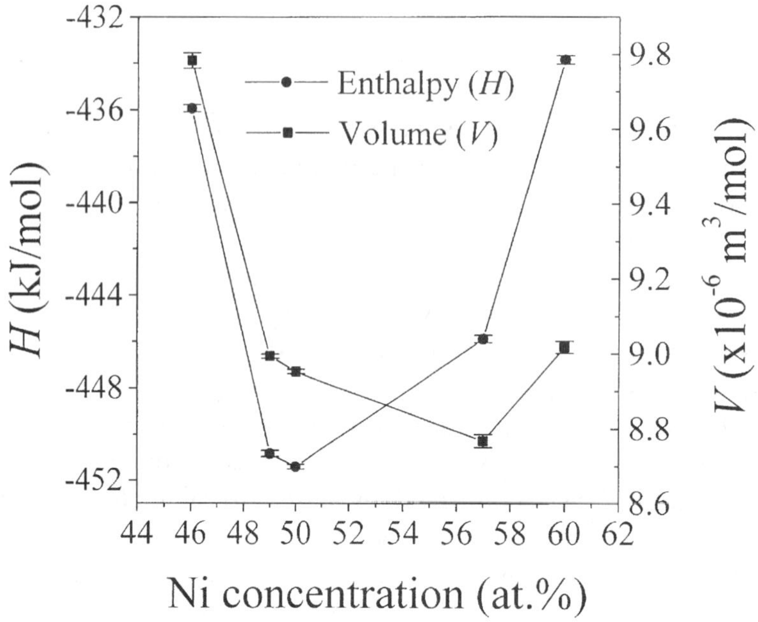

Fig. 13. Variation of the molar enthalpy H and the volume V as a function of alloy composition in the B2 Ni–Ti phase obtained after simulation performed at 1391 K for 20 000 molecular dynamics steps.

increase of V at the composition of 60 at.% of Ni was therefore believed to be due to the spontaneous vitrification of the crystal. Moreover, the vitrification of the B2 crystals with compositions at 46 and 60 at.% of Ni was also confirmed by the calculated pair-correlation functions showing the shapes known for amorphous alloys. In comparison, the lattices of the other three B2 phases with compositions at 49.5, 50, 57 at.% of Ni, respectively, were found to be stable within the simulation time (20 000 molecular dynamics steps). These results were in good agreement with that shown in the equilibrium phase diagram, i.e. in the composition range from 49.5 to 57 at.% Ni. In short, the derived Ni–Ti potential was of realistic one.

Because Mo is of bcc structure, the potential based on second-moment approximation of the tight-binding scheme is not suitable [137] and we therefore adopted the Finnis–Sinclair formalism to derive the n-body potential for the Ni–Mo system. In deriving the potential, a polynomial form up to r^6 was taken for the normal pair-wise energy $V(r)$, instead of a quartic one in Eq. (6.7), to obtain a better fitting results.

$$V(r) = \begin{cases} (r-c)^2(c_0 + c_1 r + c_2 r^2 + c_3 r^3 + c_4 r^4), & r \le c \\ 0, & r > c \end{cases} \tag{6.9}$$

The potential for Mo–Mo interaction was directly taken from that produced by Finnis and Sinclair [117]. Whereas the potential for Ni–Ni and cross-potential for Ni–Mo interactions were developed by using the same form as that of Mo–Mo potential for computational simplicity.

The Ni–Ni potential was determined by fitting the experimental data of cohesive energy, lattice constants, bulk modulus and shear elastic constants. In deriving the Ni–Mo potential, the calculated cohesive energies and lattice constants for some new metastable crystalline phases from linear-muffin-tin-orbital method [147,148] were employed, as the experimental data of the cohesive energies and elastic constants for three equilibrium Ni–Mo alloy phases, i.e. β(Ni_4Mo), γ(Ni_3Mo) and δ-phase, were not accessible. Table 7 lists the values used in fitting and a comparison of the cohesive energy and the lattice constants reproduced by the derived potential with either first

Table 7
A comparison of the physical properties derived from the constructed potential with those from the linear-muffin-tin-orbital (LMTO) calculations and experiments[a]

System	Structure	E_c		Lattice constant		
		LMTO[a]	This work	LMTO[a]	Experiment	This work
Ni_3Mo	$D0_{19}$	5.18[b]	5.18	2.614[b]	a=2.64[c]	2.637
	$D0_a$		5.40		c=4.448[d]	4.539
$NiMo_3$	$D0_{19}$	6.19	6.07	2.802	a=2.96[c]	2.815
	$L1_2$	6.21[b]	6.21	3.953[b]	a=4.22[c]	3.831
Ni_4Mo	$D1_a$		5.32		a=3.56[d]	3.64

[a] Reference [148].
[b] These data are the values used in fitting the potentials for Ni–Mo. Cohesive energy in eV per atom, lattice constant in Å. For $D0_{19}$, c/a=1.63; for $D0_a$, a/c=1.138, b/c=0.950; for $D1_a$, b/a=1.607.
[c] Reference [109].
[d] Reference [149].

principle calculations or experiments for the metastable crystalline as well as the equilibrium alloy phases. It is noted from Table 7 that the derived potential worked well in reflecting the stability of the alloy phases in the Ni–Mo system. Moreover, employing the potential, the bulk moduli of the Ni_3Mo ($D0_{19}$) and $NiMo_3$ ($L1_2$) phases were calculated to be 2.56 and 1.50, respectively, which were also compatible with those obtained by first principle calculations (2.5 for Ni_3Mo, and 2.4 for $NiMo_3$, respectively) [148]. In short, the constructed potential in the present form was of relevance for describing the atomic interactions for the Ni–Mo system. For convenience of use, all the potential parameters for the Ni–Mo system are listed in Table 8.

To develop the n-body potentials for the Ni–Nb and Ni–Ta systems, the analytic functions proposed firstly by Johnson and Oh for bcc metals and then extended by Cai et al. for fcc metals were adopted [122,126]. It was noted that in Johnson's bcc model and Cai's fcc model, the embedding functions $F(\rho)$ were actually quite similar, as they were both expressed by the Eq. (6.3) with a linear term F_1 treated as 0 and an adjustable parameter for bcc and fcc models, respectively. Since the embedding function $F(\rho)$ was universal and did not depend on the source of the host electron density, the electron density functions $f_{Ni}(r)$ and $f_{Nb}(r)$, the embedding energy functions $F_{Ni}(\rho)$ and $F_{Nb}(\rho)$ were assumed to be transferable from two mono-atomic systems to a binary metal system, so as the pair potential functions $\varphi_{Ni-Ni}(r)$ and $\varphi_{Nb-Nb}(r)$. In Eq. (6.4), the scaling factor f_e, which was taken as unit for pure metal system but could not be canceled in the binary metal system, was determined by the equation $f_e=E_c/\Omega$ (E_c is the cohesive energy and Ω is the atom volume) as pointed out by Johnson [125]. In Cai's original scheme, the cut-off distance was taken as $r_{cut}=1.65a_0$

Table 8
Parameters for the n-body potentials for Ni, Mo and Ni–Mo

	Ni–Ni	Mo–Mo[a]	Ni–Mo
A (eV)	1.042095	1.883457	1.144552
d (Å)	4.0	4.114825	5.25
c (Å)	3.72	3.25	4.05
c_0	2.1853329	43.4475218	49.418638
c_1	−0.6346408	−31.9332978	−60.373527
c_2	−0.4184836	6.0804249	27.366179
c_3	0.1364786	0.0	−5.388922
c_4	0.0	0.0	0.387794

[a] Reference [117].

Table 9
The potential parameters for Ni–Ni, Ni–Nb and Ni–Ta systems

	Ni–Ni		Ni–Nb	Ni–Ta
F_0 (eV)	2.97	c	3.8	3.8
χ (Å^{-1})	2.821497	c_0	51.68355	−40.85279
α (eV)	0.6080	c_1	−69.7978	57.15059
β	6.46	c_2	34.2912	−29.13327
F_1 (eV)	1.58	c_3	−7.189241	6.358747
r_a (Å)	2.1965	c_4	0.523113	−0.4990952
r_{cut} (Å)	3.9			

(a_0 is the equilibrium lattice constant), which was between the fifth- to sixth-neighbor. For the Ni–Nb and Ni–Ta systems, the r_{cut} of Ni was assumed to be between the second- to third-neighbor distances and was therefore compatible with that for Nb and Ta. The parameters in the Ni potential should, therefore, be refitted through an optimization procedure. The potential parameters for Nb–Nb and Ta–Ta interaction were adopted from Johnson's data [122], which are not listed here. The remaining functions that needed to be developed were the cross pair potential functions $\varphi_{Ni-Nb}(r)$ and $\varphi_{Ni-Ta}(r)$, which were assumed as Eq. (6.9) like that of the Ni–Mo potential. Because of the shortage of the experimental data for the equilibrium Ni–Nb and Ni–Ta alloy phases, some physical properties obtained from the linear-muffin-tin-orbital calculations for some metastable crystalline phases in the Ni–Nb and Ni–Ta systems [148,150] were employed in fitting the potential parameters. The fitting results are listed in Table 9. Similar to that done in the above mentioned Ni–Ti and Ni–Mo potentials, the obtained Ni–Nb and Ni–Ta potentials were also verified to be capable of reproducing some static and dynamic physical properties for some equilibrium as well as metastable crystalline phases in the Ni–Nb and Ni–Ta systems [151,152]. Besides, the Rose equation could also be reproduced by the derived potentials for these alloy phases.

6.2. *Simulation models and characterization methods*

To determine the maximum solid solubilities by molecular dynamics simulation, solid solution models were constructed for three major crystalline structures of fcc, bcc and hcp, i.e. the models consisted of 8×8×8×4=2048 atoms for fcc phase, 9×9×8×2=1296 atoms for bcc phase, and 10×6×6×4=1440 atoms for hcp phase, respectively. In fcc and bcc models, the [1 0 0], [0 1 0] and [0 0 1] atomic crystal directions were parallel to x, y and z-axis, respectively, and for hcp model, the [1 0 0], [0 0 1] and [1 2 0] crystalline directions were parallel to x, y and z-axes, respectively. In all three directions, periodic boundary conditions were adopted. The solute atoms were added by randomly substituting a certain number of metal B atoms into the metal A lattice. To avoid forming a cluster of solute atoms, the random substitution was performed in each unit cell of A lattice with a same probability and an initial state of A (B) solid solution for molecular dynamics simulation was thus obtained. molecular dynamics simulation was performed for the solid solution models with gradually increasing the solute concentration to find out the critical compositions, at which crystalline lattices of the solid solutions became unstable and transformed into a disordered state.

In molecular dynamics simulation, it is important to characterize the structure to be either crystalline or amorphous, or disordered. The pair-correlation function analysis was employed to identify the structure in simulation. To calculate the pair-correlation function $g(r)$, each atom in turn was imagined to be at the center of a series of concentric spheres. The atomic density was defined to be the number of atoms in each spherical shell divided by the volume of that shell, with a consideration of those periodic image atoms located outside the block. In simulation, the results were obtained by averaging over all the atoms within 200 time steps. The $g(r)$ can then be obtained by the following formula

$$g(r)=\frac{\rho(r)}{\rho_0} \tag{6.10}$$

where $\rho(r)$ denotes the atomic density at $r=|\boldsymbol{r}|$, $r=0$ defines the position of a reference atom, and ρ_0 is an average atomic density in the whole model. In addition, calculation of the enthalpy and volume of the system as a function of solute concentration will also give a firm evidence for crystalline-to-amorphous transition, as there is commonly a sudden change in the enthalpy and/or volume when crystalline-to-amorphous transition taking place at the critical solute concentration.

6.3. Glass-forming ability of some Ni-based systems

Employing molecular dynamics simulation with the proven realistic n-body potential, two critical concentrations of the terminal solid solutions could be determined, at which the supersaturated solid solutions were unstable and would turn into an amorphous state. As a result, the central region bounded by these two critical values, in which the amorphous state was more stable than solid solution, can therefore be considered as the glass-forming range of the binary metal system. Such a polymorphous glass-forming range is thus a property intrinsic to the system itself and not connected with any specific glass-producing technique, that may allow (partial) chemical partitioning and reduce the glass-forming range.

We now discuss the calculation results for some representative metal systems, i.e. the Ni–Mo, Ni–Ti, Ni–Zr and Ni–Ta systems.

For the Ni–Mo system, the compositions of fcc Ni-rich solid solutions were selected to be in the range of 0–50 at.% of Mo, and the compositions of the bcc Mo-rich solid solutions were 0–50 at.% of Ni. Each solid solution with a designed solute concentration was obtained by randomly substituting corresponding amount of Ni (Mo) with Mo (Ni) in the Ni fcc (Mo bcc) lattice. From the initial configuration, the model was then simulated at 300 K to reach a relatively equilibrium state. Fig. 14 displays the calculated total and partial pair-correlation function $g(r)$ for the Ni-rich fcc solid solutions with the solute concentrations of 10, 17, 21 and 25 at.% of Mo, one sees that the solid solutions with 10 and 17 at.% of Mo still remain fcc crystalline structure and that with increasing solute concentration, the peaks of $g(r)$ became broadened, implying the crystals become progressively disordered. Obviously, a crystalline-to-amorphous transition took place in the solid solution with 25 at.% Mo. While for the solid solution with 21 at.% of Mo, the shape of the calculated $g(r)$ was ambiguous, suggesting that structural transition has taken place yet not completed. On the Mo end, Fig. 15 shows the similar calculation results for the Mo bcc solid solutions with various solute concentrations of 10, 25, 30 and 40 at.% of Ni after annealing at 300 K. One sees that at the above $x_{Ni}=25\%$, the curves of $g(r)$ are of typical shape of amorphous structure, suggesting that $x_{Ni}=25\%$ is a critical value for crystalline-to-amorphous transition.

The molar enthalpy and volume as a function of composition were also calculated for the resultant Ni–Mo alloys. It was found that in the Ni-rich side, the enthalpy decreased and the volume increased with increasing of composition ratio of Mo and that at $x_{Mo}=21\%$, the slope of the enthalpy was discontinuous and there was a step increase in volume, corresponding to a crystalline-to-amorphous transition. The abrupt increase in volume was in consistent with a crystalline-to-amorphous transition accompanied by a volume expansion, as amorphous phase has an excess free

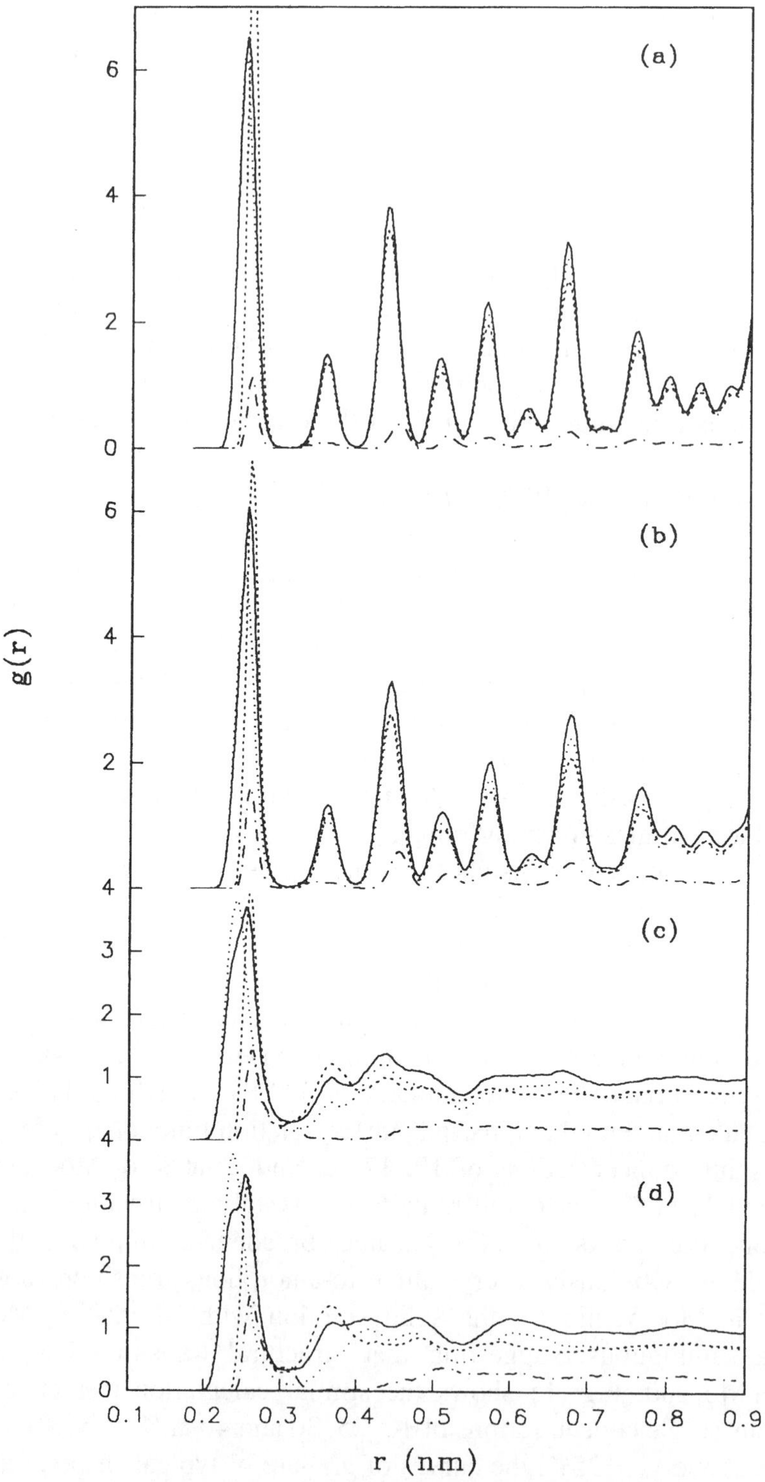

Fig. 14. Total and partial pair-correlation functions for the fcc Ni-rich solid solution after simulation performed at 300 K for 10,000 molecular-dynamics time steps. The compositions are at (a) 10 at.%, (b) 17 at.%, (c) 21 at.% and (d) 25 at.% of Mo, respectively. The solid line is for total $g(r)$; the short dashed line is for Mo–Ni $g(r)$; the dotted line is for Ni–Ni $g(r)$; and the dot-dashed line is for Mo–Mo $g(r)$, respectively.

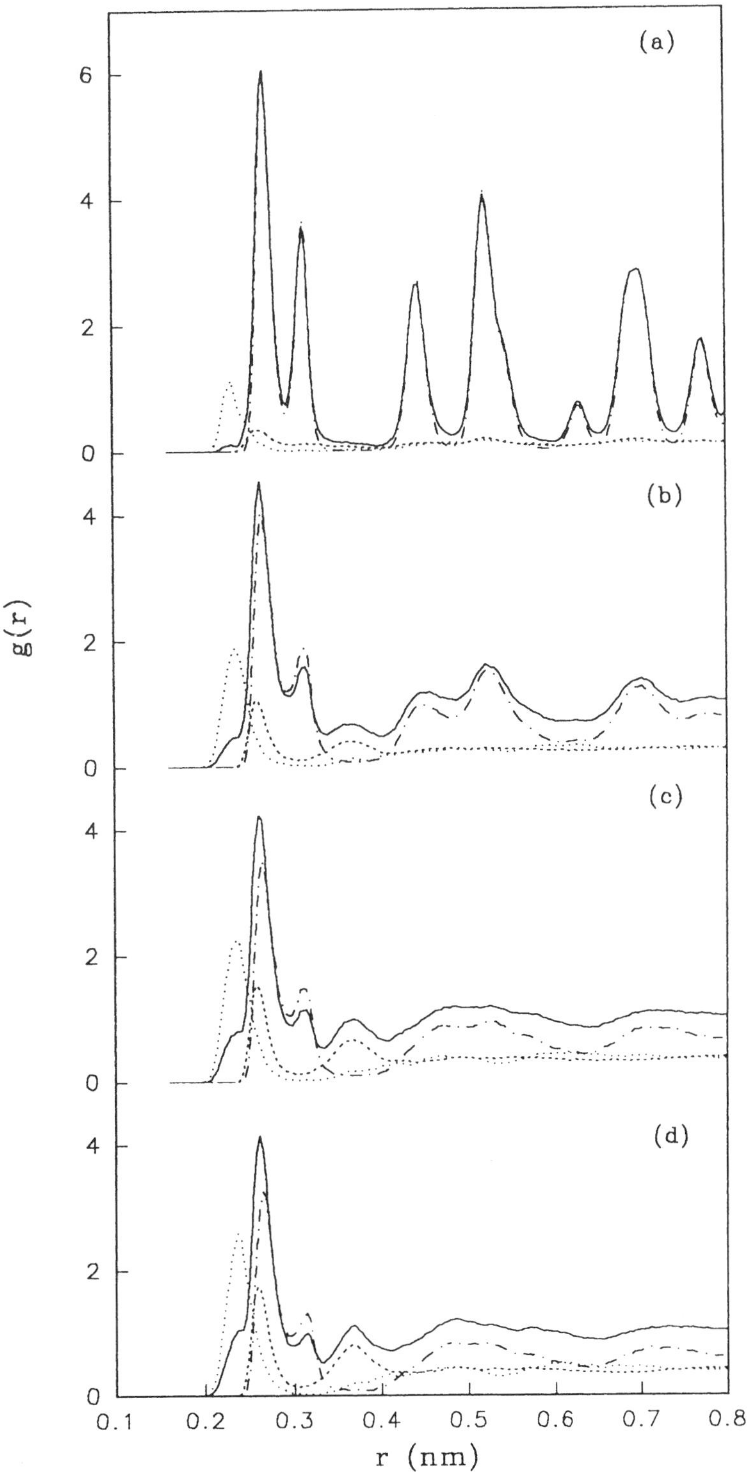

Fig. 15. Total and partial pair-correlation functions for the bcc Mo-rich solid solution after simulation performed at 300 K for 10 000 molecular-dynamics time steps. The compositions are at (a) 10 at.%, (b) 25 at.%, (c) 30 at.%, (d) 40 at.% of Ni, respectively. The solid line is for total $g(r)$; the short dashed line is for Mo–Ni $g(r)$; the dotted line is for Ni–Ni $g(r)$; and the dot-dashed line is for Mo–Mo $g(r)$, respectively.

volume in comparing with its crystalline counterpart [153,154]. It was also found that on the Mo-rich side, there was no distinct change in molar enthalpy and that with increasing of adding smaller atom Ni into Mo, the volume of bcc Mo crystal increased a little and then followed by a kink at x_{Ni}=25 at.%, which was also compatible with the pair correlation function calculation. According to Vegard's law, a volume expansion was not expected when Mo was replaced by smaller sized Ni and was therefore to be associated with a crystalline-to-amorphous transition, resulting in the formation of a Mo-rich Ni–Mo amorphous phase. In summary, the critical compositions for crystalline-to-amorphous transition were determined to be 21 at.% of Mo and 25 at.% of Ni for fcc Ni-rich and bcc Mo-rich solid solutions, respectively. In other words, the glass-forming range was determined to be within 21–75 at.% of Mo, in which crystalline solid solutions would be unstable and turn into an amorphous state.

Similar simulations were performed for the Ni–Ti system and Fig. 16 displays the calculated total and partial pair-correlation functions $g(r)$ for the Ni-rich fcc solid solutions consisting of Ti solute atoms up to 10, 38, and 50 at.%, respectively. One sees that the solid solution with 10 at.% of Ti still remains fcc crystalline structure, while for the solid solutions with 38 and 50 at.% of Ti, a crystalline-to-amorphous transition has apparently taken place. For the Ti-rich side, the crystalline-to-amorphous transition was observed when the Ni solute contents were greater than 15 at.%. Fig. 17 shows that in the Ti end, the enthalpy and volume both decrease with increasing of Ni content and that at x_{Ni}=15 at.% the slopes of enthalpy and volume are discontinuous with a clear kink in volume. While at the Ni side, there was a sudden drop in molar enthalpy at x_{Ti}=38 at.%. In addition, the volume change of the fcc Ni solid solutions with increasing of Ti content increased gradually and a kink appeared at x_{Ti}=38 at.%, which was the same determined by the pair correlation function calculation. The volume expansion of the Ni solid solution with increasing Ti content was caused by dissolving larger sized Ti atoms into the fcc Ni lattice and a sudden volume increase at x_{Ti}=38 at.% was associated with the formation of a Ni-rich Ni–Ti amorphous phase [153]. In short, the critical compositions for crystalline-to-amorphous transition were determined to be 15 at.% of Ni and 38 at.% of Ti for hcp Ti-rich and the fcc Ni-rich solid solutions, respectively.

For the Ni–Zr and Ni–Ta systems, their critical compositions for crystalline-to-amorphous transition were also determined by similar molecular dynamics simulations based on a second-moment approximation of the tight-binding scheme Ni–Zr potential derived by Massobrio et al. [155] and a newly developed Ni–Ta potential, respectively.

The maximum super-saturated solid solubilities determined for the above four systems are summarized in Table 10. It is of interest to compare the glass-forming range of the system by the simulated maximum solid solubility with the experimental observations.

For the Ni–Mo system, amorphization in the Ni–Mo mutilayers has been observed upon solid-state reaction and the composition range favoring amorphization was found to be 25–75% Mo [109], which is quite compatible with the intrinsic glass-forming range of 21–75 at.% of Mo determined by simulation.

For the Ni–Ti system, the nominal glass-forming range of the system determined by liquid melt quenching data was in a composition range of 30–40 at.% of Ni [156], which is apparently smaller than the intrinsic one revealed by molecular dynamics simulation. As mentioned above, ion beam mixing probably possesses the greatest cooling speed among the currently available glass-producing techniques, the glass-forming range determined by ion beam mixing may be most likely the one closest to the intrinsic glass-forming range. Ion beam mixing experiments were performed for the Ni–Ti multilayered samples with various overall compositions. It was found that the Ni-based solid solutions were obtained by ion beam mixing within a composition from 0 up to a maximum of 37 at.% of Ti and beyond this maximum a single amorphous phase was formed. These results

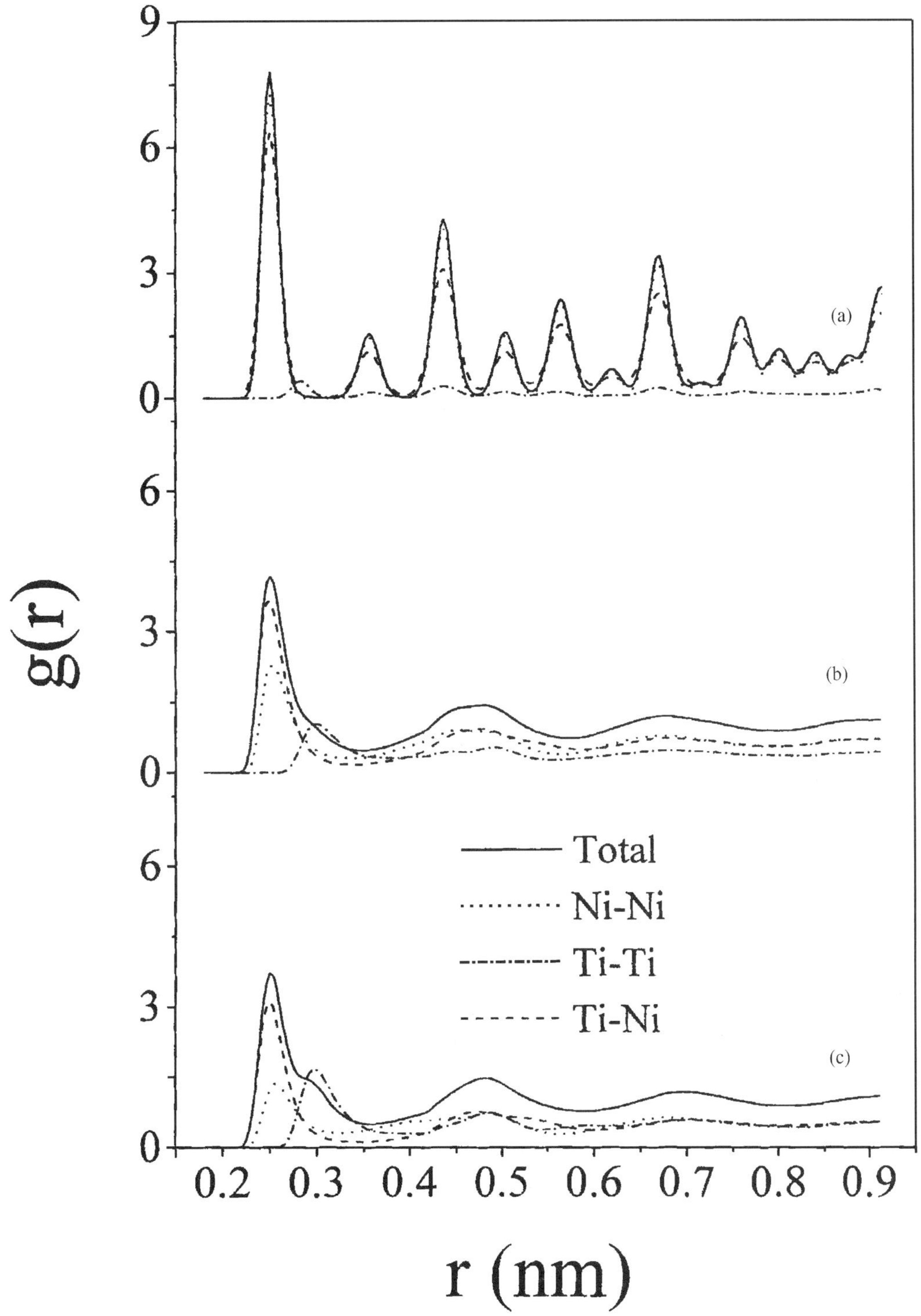

Fig. 16. Total and partial pair-correlation functions for the fcc Ni-rich solid solution after simulation performed at 300 K for 20 000 molecular-dynamics time steps. The compositions are at (a) 10 at.%, (b) 38 at.% and (c) 50 at.% of Ti, respectively. The solid line is for total $g(r)$; the dotted line is for Ni–Ni $g(r)$; the short dashed line is for Ti–Ni $g(r)$; and the dot-dashed line is for Ti–Ti $g(r)$, respectively.

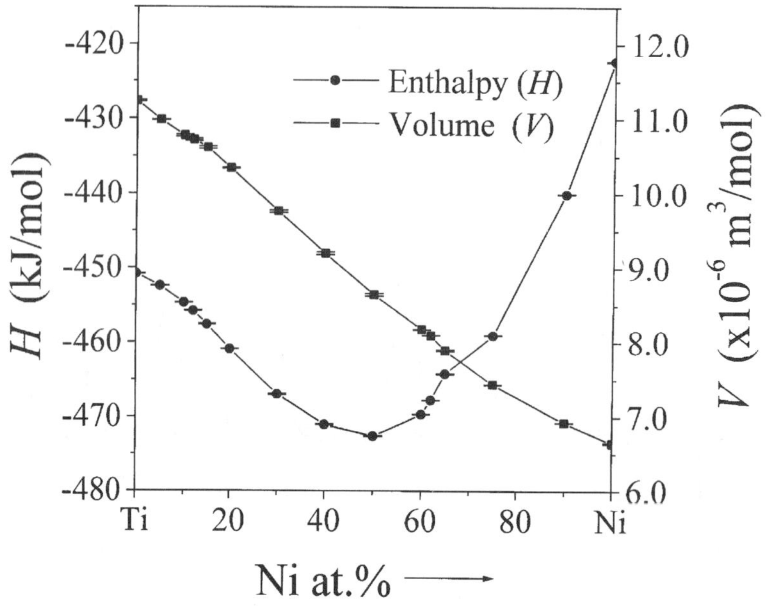

Fig. 17. The molar enthalpy and volume as a function of composition of the relatively equilibrium states obtained after simulation performed at 300 K for 20 000 molecular-dynamics time steps for the Ni-rich fcc solid solution (0–50% Ti) and Ti-rich hcp solid solution (50–100% Ti), respectively.

suggested that the maximum supersaturated solid solubility of Ti in Ni was less than 37 at.%. Apparently, the ion beam mixing experimental results were in good agreement with that from molecular dynamics simulation, as the error involved in experiments was about 3–5%.

For the Ni–Zr system, the calculated glass-forming range from molecular dynamics simulation is 14–75 at.% of Zr, which is compatible with that of 10–80 at.% of Zr determined from ion beam mixing experiments [51] within the experimental error around 3–5%.

6.4. Comparison of the glass-forming ability determined by simulation and other empirical criteria

During the past decades, several empirical criteria have been proposed to predict the glass-forming ability of the binary metal systems. It is, thus, of interest to compare the glass-forming ability calculated from the *n*-body potential with those predicted by the empirical criteria.

It is known that the elastic constants of a solid can provide valuable information about the crystalline-to-amorphous transition. In experiments, it has been observed that irradiation of some intermetallic compounds by high-energy particles was associated with a large decrease (about 50%) in the elastic constants and has been confirmed by molecular dynamics simulations [157–159]. Based on newly developed Ni–Ta potential with the approach proposed by Parrinello and Rahman [160–162], the elastic constants were calculated and Fig. 18 displays the tetragonal shear modulus

Table 10
The calculated critical compositions of the solid solutions, of which spontaneous vitrification can take place, in some Ni-based binary metal systems[a]

	Ti	Zr	Mo	Ta
Ni as solvent matrix	38	14	21	21
Ni as alloying solute	15	25	25	43

[a] Unit in at.%.

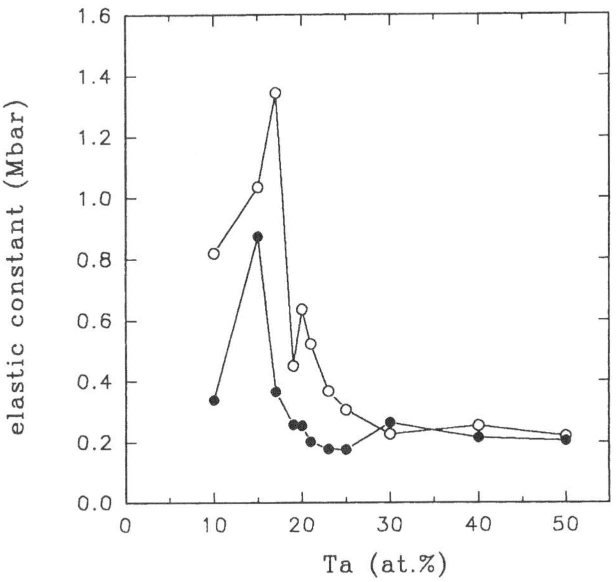

Fig. 18. Tetragonal shear modulus C' (filled circle) and rhombohedral C_{44} modulus (open circle) vs. composition of the fcc Ni (Ta) solid solutions after annealing at 27°C. The solid lines are drawn for a clear view.

$C'=(C_{11}-C_{12})/2$ as well as rhombohedral shear modulus C_{44} versus composition of the Ni (Ta) fcc solid solution after annealing at 300 K.

Since the fcc structure features the cubic symmetry, the following relation holds:

$$C_{11}=C_{22}=C_{33}, \qquad C_{12}=C_{23}=C_{13}, \qquad C_{44}=C_{55}=C_{66} \tag{6.11}$$

As a result, there were only three independent elastic constants. In calculation, there were some deviation among those supposed to be identical values, therefore the elastic constants C_{44} and C' were usually shown as the symmetry-averaged value and they are, respectively, defined as

$$C_{44}=\frac{C_{44}+C_{55}+C_{66}}{3} \tag{6.12}$$

$$C'=\frac{(C_{11}+C_{22}+C_{33})-(C_{12}+C_{23}+C_{13})}{6} \tag{6.13}$$

From the figure, one sees that both shear moduli of Ni fcc solid solution increase a little before a remarkable decrease. The initial increase of the shear moduli may be from the more rigid Ta atoms as solutes. The distinct magnitude of the moduli softening was found in the composition range of 17–19 at.% of Ta, which is very close, yet a little prior, to the critical value of 21 at.% of Ta determined by pair correlation function calculation. At 17 at.% of Ta, the tetragonal shear modulus dropped first about 58% from its value at 15 at.% of Ta. While the rhombohedral shear modulus decreased rapidly at 19 at.% of Ta with a dropping amount of 60%. It should be noted that the fcc crystalline state persisted up to 19 at.% of Ta at which shear modulus dropped abruptly. Further increasing of the Ta atom led to the completion of the crystalline-to-amorphous transition and the two shear elastic constants of the resultant amorphous alloy became identical, indicating an isotropic feature belong to the intrinsic characteristics of an amorphous solid. For the bcc Ta solid solution, the elastic constants decreased with increase of the solute atom Ni yet the declining of the modulus near the crystalline-to-amorphous transition was not as remarkable as that for Ni-based solid solution. The total amount in shear elastic constant declining upon crystalline-to-amorphous transition was about 50% of the initial value. In short, simulation results revealed a remarkable lattice softening accompanying with a crystalline-to-amorphous transition, which is compatible with that proposed by mechanical instability criterion.

It is well known that the generalized Lindemann melting criterion can also give a prediction of the glass-forming range [163]. We take the Ni–Mo system as a typical example to compare the glass-forming range derived from molecular dynamics simulation with that from Lindemann criterion. In the original Lindemann melting criterion [164], the lattice stability is correlated with melting, assuming that thermodynamic melting occurs when the root mean square of the thermal displacement of atoms divided by the nearest-neighbor spacing r_{nn}, $\langle \mu_{vib}^2 \rangle^{1/2}/r_m$, reaches a critical value, $\delta = \langle \mu_{cri}^2 \rangle^{1/2}/r_m$. The Lindemann criterion can be extended for the formation of glasses below the glass transition temperature, if the total mean-square atomic displacement is used, instead of using thermal component alone, i.e. to include both thermal and static components in the displacement. Such a generalized Lindemann melting criterion (GLMC) can be expressed formally by

$$\langle \mu_{tot}^2 \rangle = \langle \mu_{vib}^2 \rangle + \langle \mu_{sta}^2 \rangle = \langle \mu_{cri}^2 \rangle \tag{6.14}$$

where $\langle \mu_{cri}^2 \rangle$ is the critical mean square displacement for 'melting' (or amorphization) [163]. According to Okamoto et al. [163], the GLMC contains the basic spirits of the previous single-phase stability models, including the original Lindemann criterion as well as the Born elastic instability criterion [165] and Egami's model based on atomic size/volume effects [166], and is therefore a more appropriate criterion for interpreting the crystalline-to-amorphous transition as well as for determining the glass-forming range for a system. Based on the harmonic Debye model, the mean-square thermal displacement for a perfect monatomic crystal at a temperature T above the Debye temperature, θ_0, is given by [167]

$$\langle \mu_{vib}^2 \rangle = \frac{9\hbar^2 T}{Mk\theta_0^2} \tag{6.15}$$

where $\hbar$ is Plank's constant divided by 2π, k is the Boltzmann constant and M is the atomic mass. When T equals to the melting point T_m of the perfect crystal, the critical value $\langle \mu_{cri}^2 \rangle = \langle \mu_{vib}^2 \rangle$, can be obtained from the above equation. The $\langle \mu_{cri}^2 \rangle$ of Ni and Mo were thus calculated to be 6.339×10^{-4} nm^2 and 6.492×10^{-4} nm^2, respectively. For Mo, the value was very close to 6.786×10^{-4} nm^2, which was derived by Cho with a proposed atomistic model. While for Ni, the $\langle \mu_{cri}^2 \rangle$ calculated by Cho was 4.121×10^{-4} nm^2 and the experimental value was 2.377×10^{-4} nm^2, which are both smaller than that derived from Eq. (6.15) [168,169].

The critical concentrations or glass-forming range can be predicted based on the intersection of the T_0 line (the polymorphic melting curve) with the Kauzmann isentropic glass transition temperature curve, at which the entropy of super cooled liquid equals to that of the crystalline solid. In the following, an estimation of the T_0 line was made based on the GLMC. The generalized polymorphous (T_0) melting curve, representing a crystal-to-liquid or crystalline-to-amorphous transition, can be derived. For the detailed development, the readers are referred to [163]. Here, only the used equation is presented for calculating the polymorphous melting curve for the Ni_xMo_{1-x} alloy and it is expressed by

$$T_m^d(x) = \frac{\langle M(x)\rangle k\theta_d^2(x)}{9\hbar^2}\langle \mu_{cri}^2 \rangle = \frac{\langle M(x)\rangle k\theta_0^2(x)\langle \mu_{cri}^2 \rangle}{9\hbar^2}\left[1 - \frac{\langle \mu_{sta}^2 \rangle}{\langle \mu_{cri}^2 \rangle}\right] \tag{6.16}$$

where $\langle M(x)\rangle = xM_{Ni} + (1-x)M_{Mo}$ is an average atomic mass. θ_d and θ_0 are the Debye temperatures of the defective and perfect crystals, respectively. To estimate the Debye temperature of the Ni–Mo perfect solid solution $\theta_0(x)$, one may use the equation derived by Shirley, which is given by [170,171]

$$\langle M(x)\rangle\theta_0^2(x) = xM_A\theta_A^2 + (1-x)M_B\theta_B^2 + (\tau-1)(1-\alpha_1)x(1-x)(M_A\theta_A^2 + M_B\theta_B^2) \tag{6.17}$$

where θ_A and θ_B are the Debye temperatures of the A and B elemental solids, respectively. For Ni and Mo, θ_A and θ_B are 450 K [172]. τ is a dimensionless measure of the unlike nearest-neighbor atom force constant, and α_1 is the Cowley–Warren short-range order parameter for the first nearest-neighbor shell. For the Ni–Mo system, these parameters are not available for either Ni-based or Mo–based solid solution. In the literature, however, the Debye temperature of the bcc alloys has been calculated by the following approximation [171]

$$\theta(x) = \frac{1}{f}\left(\frac{1800T_m(x)}{M(x)a^2}\right)^{1/2} \tag{6.18}$$

where T_m is the melting point of the solid solution determined by the average of the liquidus and solidus temperatures, a is the lattice constant, f is a dimensionless constant and $M(x)$ is the average atomic weight. We, therefore, adopted such approximation for calculating the Debye temperature for Mo-based bcc solid solutions. In the calculation, f was derived from pure Mo to be 0.167 and a was assumed to be the lattice constant of pure Mo (3.1472 Å), which were reasonable at low solute concentration. As mentioned above, the $\langle \mu_{cri}^2\rangle$ of Mo was derived from Eq. (6.15) to be 6.492×10^{-4} nm^2. The only parameter left to be determined in Eq. (6.16) was the $\langle \mu_{sta}^2\rangle$, which was a function of the solute concentration in Mo bcc alloy. Shirley and Fisher derived a universal equation to calculate the $\langle \mu_{sta}^2\rangle$, for bcc binary alloys, the formula is

$$\langle \mu_{sta}^2\rangle = 2.846x(1-x)\gamma^2a^2(1+0.75\alpha_1+0.50\alpha_2-0.86\alpha_3+\cdots) \tag{6.19}$$

when the α_is are the Cowley–Warren short-range order parameters, a is the lattice constant, and γ is a measure of the composition dependence of the atomic size mismatch. As indicated by Shirley and Fisher, if the data are absent, $\gamma=1$ is the best estimate. For the perfect solid solution, α_is could be negligible, i.e. being 0. Therefore, the value of $\langle \mu_{sta}^2\rangle$ can be obtained through the above equation. $\langle \mu_{sta}^2\rangle$ is a linear function of $x(1-x)$, which is in agreement with the previous experiments [173]. The T_0-curve was then computed and the results are displayed in Fig. 19. By extrapolating down to 300 K, it is found that the minimum solute concentration for Mo lattice to decay is about 26 at.% of Ni, which is in good agreement with the simulated value of 25 at.% of Ni.

Such a calculation is not possible on the Ni side, as Eq. (6.18) no longer holds and Eq. (6.17) cannot be applied due to the lack of the necessary parameters either. A rough estimate of the T_0-curve is possible from the equilibrium phase diagram [174] through the mid-point between the solidus and liquidus of the Ni-rich solid solution. Thus, the critical value was estimated to be about 40 at.% of Mo, which was much larger than the simulated one being 21 at.% of Mo. However, such a simple T_0-curve extrapolation may be inadequate if there is a strong tendency to develop short-range ordering in Ni-rich amorphous alloy formed at low temperature. This tendency is likely while considering the fact that in the Ni–Mo equilibrium phase diagram, there exist two Ni-enriched intermetallic compounds, i.e. Ni_4Mo and Ni_3Mo [174]. Our molecular dynamics results seemed to suggest a steeply plunging T_0-curve at low temperatures. In summary, the above results indicate that the critical solute concentrations determined by molecular dynamics simulation for the crystalline lattices of the Ni- and Mo-based solid solutions to collapse are quite compatible with that estimated

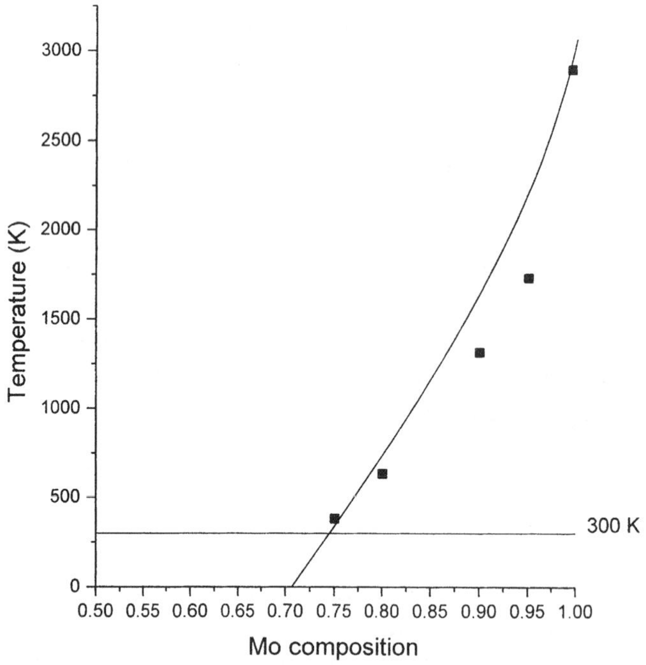

Fig. 19. T_0-curve for the Mo-rich bcc solid solution of the Ni–Mo system obtained by the generalized Lindemann melting criterion.

from T_0-curve consideration. From a physical point view, there should exist an intrinsic glass-forming range for a binary metal system. In the literature, the intrinsic glass-forming range has been considered from either a thermodynamic analysis or lattice instability criteria, which, to authors' view should be inherently incorporated with a realistic interatomic potential.

7. Concluding remarks

1. In ion beam mixing, the intermixing and alloying of the multilayers is mainly induced by dynamic atomic collision between different metal layers. This method is, therefore, capable of producing a great number of metallic glasses in a broad range of systems, including those featuring positive heats of formation or even essentially immiscible in equilibrium. It follows that the glass-forming range of a binary metal system determined by ion beam mixing is much broader than that known previously, and extends from the central composition to the maximum solid solubility of the two terminal solid solutions, thus approaching to an intrinsic glass-forming ability of the system.
2. As shown above, prediction of glass-forming range or glass-forming ability of a binary metal system becomes a question of determining the maximum solid solubility, which can be obtained directly from interatomic potentials through molecular dynamics simulation. For some representative Ni-based systems, their realistic n-body potentials were firstly developed. Applying the derived potentials, molecular dynamics simulation with solid solution models were performed and the maximum solid solubilities were obtained, from which the glass-forming range (glass-forming ability) of the systems were deduced to be located in a central composition range bounded by the two maximum solid solubilities. It turned out that the calculated glass-forming ability or glass-forming range is compatible with the experimental observations.

3. This review deals with the topics in the area of 'alloy phase formation and transformation', which is an important part in the field of 'physical metallurgy'. Experimental studies by ion beam mixing, thermodynamic consideration under the frame work of Miedema's model, and molecular dynamics simulations with proven realistic *n*-body potentials together helped in significantly promote the understanding of those studied topics from empirical correlation to thermodynamic interpretation as well as into a deeper insight at an atomic scale.

Acknowledgements

The authors are grateful to many colleagues and B.X. Liu's previous students for their direct valuable contributions and their encouragement or kind assistance in preparing this review paper. The continuous financial support from the National Natural Science Foundation of China through Grants no. 59231031, 19474030 and 59571011 as well as from the Administration of Tsinghua University is also acknowledged.

References

[1] W. Klement, R.H. Willens, P. Duwez, Nature 187 (1960) 869.
[2] A.L. Greer, Science 267 (1995) 1947.
[3] H.A. Davies, in: F.E. Luborsky (Ed.), Amorphous Metallic Alloys, Butterworths, London, 1983.
[4] J. Hafner, in: H.-J. Guentherodt, H. Beck (Eds.), Metallic Glasses, Springer, Berlin, 1981, p. 93.
[5] B.S. Giessen, S.H. Whang, J. Phys. C 8 (1980) 95.
[6] F. Sommer, Z. Metallkde. 72 (1981) 219.
[7] N. Nishiyama, A. Inoue, Acta Materialia 47 (1999) 1487.
[8] U. Geyer, S. Schneider, W.L. Johnson, Y. Qiu, T.A. Tombrello, Phys. Rev. Lett. 75 (1995) 2364.
[9] B.X. Liu, W.L. Johnson, M.-A. Nicolet, S.S. Lau, Appl. Phys. Lett. 42 (1983) 45.
[10] R.B. Schwarz, W.L. Johnson, Phys. Rev. Lett. 51 (1983) 415.
[11] C.C. Koch, et al., Appl. Phys. Lett. 43 (1983) 1017.
[12] B.X. Liu, E. Ma, J. Li, L.J. Huang, Nucl. Instrum. Methods Phys. Res. B 19/20 (1987) 682.
[13] F.R. deBoer, R. Boom, W.C.M. Mattens, A.R. Miedema, A.K. Niessen, Cohesion in Metals: Transition Metal Alloys, North-Holland, Amsterdam, 1989.
[14] B.X. Liu, Z.J. Zhang, Phys. Rev. B 49 (1994) 12519.
[15] Z.J. Zhang, O. Jin, B.X. Liu, Phys. Rev. B 51 (1995) 8076.
[16] M. Meyer, V. Pontikis (Eds.), Computer Simulation in Materials Science, Kluwer Academic Publishers, Dordrecht, 1991.
[17] Q. Zhang, W.S. Lai, B.X. Liu, Phys. Rev. B 59 (1999) 13521.
[18] B.Y. Tsaur, Ph.D. Thesis, California Institute of Technology, 1980.
[19] B.Y. Tsaur, S.S. Lau, J.W. Mayer, Appl. Phys. Lett. 36 (1980) 823.
[20] M.W. Thompson, Defects and Radiation Damage in Metals, Cambridge University Press, Cambridge, 1969 (Chapters 4–5).
[21] B.X. Liu, Phys. Stat. Sol. (a) 94 (1986) 11.
[22] J.A. Alonso, S. Simozar, Solid State Commun. 48 (1983) 765.
[23] B.X. Liu, L.J. Huang, J. Li, E. Ma, in: R.J. Nemanich, P.S. Ho, S.S. Lau (Eds.), Thin Films-Interfaces and Phenomena, Proceedings of the MRS Symposium, Vol. 54, North-Holland, Amsterdam, 1986, p. 215.
[24] B.X. Liu, Mater. Lett. 9 (1987) 322.
[25] P.M. Ossi, Phys. Stat. Sol. (a) 119 (1990) 463.
[26] J.A. Alonso, L.J. Gallego, J.A. Simozar, Nuovo Cimento 12 (1990) 587.
[27] A.K. Niessen, A.R. Miedema, Ber. Bunsenges. Phys. Chem. 87 (1983) 717.
[28] J.M. Lopez, J.A. Alonso, Z. Naturforsch. A 40 (1985) 1199.
[29] A.W. Weeber, J. Phys. F 17 (1987) 809.
[30] A.K. Niessen, A.R. Miedema, F.R. deBoer, R. Boom, Phys. B 151 (1988) 401.
[31] J.M. Lopez, J.A. Alonso, Phys. Stat. Sol. (a) 76 (1983) 675.
[32] J.M. Lopez, J.A. Alonso, Phys. Stat. Sol. (a) 85 (1984) 423.

[33] J. Friedel, Adv. Phys. 3 (1954) 446.
[34] J.D. Eshelby, Solid State Phys. 3 (1956) 79.
[35] J.M. Lopez, J.A. Alonso, Z. Naturforsch. 40a (1985) 1199.
[36] P.I. Loeff, A.W. Weeber, A.R. Miedema, J. Less-Common Metals 140 (1988) 299.
[37] D. Turbull, Impurities and Imperfections, American Society of Metals, OH, 1955, p. 121.
[38] L.E. Murr, Interfacial Phenomena in Metals and Alloys, Addison-Wesley, London, 1975.
[39] A.R. Miedema, Z. Metallkde. 69 (1978) 455.
[40] A.R. Miedema, Z. Metallkde. 69 (1978) 287.
[41] J. Gerkema, A.R. Miedema, Surf. Sci. 124 (1981) 351.
[42] B.M. Clemens, Phys. Rev. B 33 (1986) 7616.
[43] B.X. Liu, Z.J. Zhang, O. Jin, J. Alloys Compounds 270 (1998) 186.
[44] G. Dearnaley, J.H. Freeman, R.S. Nelson, J. Stephen, Ion Implantation, North-Holland, Amsterdam, 1973.
[45] P.D. Townsend, J.C. Kelly, N.E.W. Hartley, Ion Implantation, Sputtering and Their Applications, Academic Press, London, 1976.
[46] W.K. Chu, J.W. Mayer, M.-A. Nicolet, Backscattering Spectrometry, Academic Press, New York, 1978.
[47] J.R. Tesmer, M. Nastasi, Handbook of Modern Ion beam Materials Analysis, Materials Research Society, Pittsburgh, PA, USA, 1995.
[48] O. Jin, Z.J. Zhang, B.X. Liu, J. Appl. Phys. 77 (1995) 149.
[49] O. Jin, Z.J. Zhang, B.X. Liu, Appl. Phys. Lett. 67 (1995) 1524.
[50] Z.J. Zhang, H.Y. Bai, Q.L. Qiu, T. Yang, K. Tao, B.X. Liu, J. Appl. Phys. 73 (1993) 1702.
[51] J. Bøttiger, K. Dyrbye, K. Pampus, R. Poulsen, Philos. Mag. A 59 (1989) 569.
[52] B.X. Liu, B.M. Clemens, R. Gaboriaud, W.L. Johnson, M.-A. Nicolet, Appl. Phys. Lett. 42 (1983) 624.
[53] Z.J. Zhang, B.X. Liu, Phys. Rev. B 51 (1995) 16475.
[54] B.X. Liu, in: C. Surayanarayana (Ed.), Non-Equilibrium Processing of Materials, Pergamon Materials Series, Vol. 2, Elsevier, Amsterdam, 1999, Chapter 8, p. 197.
[55] A. Schmid, P. Ziemann, Nucl. Instrum. Methods Phys. Res. B 7/8 (1985) 581.
[56] L.S. Hung, J.W. Mayer, Nucl. Instrum. Methods Phys. Res. B 7/8 (1985) 657.
[57] B. Rauschenbach, K. Hohmuth, Nucl. Instrum. Methods Phys. Res. B 23 (1987) 323.
[58] J.A. Knapp, D.M. Follstaedt, Nucl. Instrum. Methods Phys. Res. B 19/20 (1987) 611.
[59] J. Meissner, K. Kopitzki, G. Mertler, E. Peiner, Nucl. Instrum. Methods Phys. Res. B 19/20 (1987) 669.
[60] B.X. Liu, W.L. Johnson, M.-A. Nicolet, S.S. Lau, Nucl. Instrum. Methods 209/210 (1983) 229.
[61] L.S. Hung, M. Nastasi, J. Gyulai, J.W. Mayer, Appl. Phys. Lett. 42 (1983) 672.
[62] G.A. Cheng, Thesis, Tsinghua University, 1986.
[63] B.X. Liu, D.Z. Che, Z.J. Zhang, S.L. Lai, J.R. Ding, Phys. Stat. Sol. (a) 128 (1991) 345.
[64] J.R. Ding, D.Z. Che, H.B. Zhang, K. Tao, B.X. Liu, Appl. Phys. Lett. 60 (1992) 944.
[65] F. Pan, Y.G. Chen, Z.J. Zhang, B.X. Liu, J. Non-Cryst. Solids 194 (1996) 305.
[66] B.X. Liu, M.-A. Nicolet, S.S. Lau, Phys. Stat. Sol. (a) 73 (1982) 183.
[67] B.Y. Tsaur, S.S. Lau, L.S. Hung, J.W. Mayer, Nucl. Instrum. Methods 182/183 (1981) 67.
[68] Z.H. Yan, B.X. Liu, H.D. Li, Phys. Stat. Sol. (a) 94 (1986) 483.
[69] U.A. Andersen, J. Bottiger, K. Dyrbye, Nucl. Instrum. Methods Phys. Res. B 51 (1990) 125.
[70] Z.J. Zhang, B.X. Liu, J. Phys.: Condensed Matter 6 (1994) 2647.
[71] Z.J. Zhang, B.X. Liu, J. Phys.: Condensed Matter 6 (1994) 9065.
[72] Z.H. Yan, B.X. Liu, H.D. Li, Nucl. Instrum. Methods Phys. Res. B 19/20 (1987) 700.
[73] B.X. Liu, J.R. Ding, H.B. Zhang, D.Z. Che, Phys. Stat. Sol. (a) 128 (1991) 103.
[74] J. BØttiger, K. Pampus, B. Torp, Nucl. Instrum. Methods Phys. Res. B 19/20 (1987) 696.
[75] Z.J. Zhang, Ph.D. Thesis, Tsinghua University, 1995.
[76] R. Brenier, P. Thevenard, T. Capra, A. Perez, M. Treilleux, L. Romana, J. Dupuy, M. Brunel, Nucl. Instrum. Methods Phys. Res. B 19/20 (1987) 691.
[77] M. van Rossum, U. Shreter, W.L. Johnson, M.A. Nicolet, Mater. Res. Soc. Symp. Proc. 27 (1984) 107.
[78] O. Jin, B.X. Liu, J. Phys.: Condensed Matter 7 (1995) 2667.
[79] Y.T. Cheng, W.L. Johnson, M.-A. Nicolet, Mater. Res. Soc. Symp. Proc. 37 (1985) 565.
[80] B.X. Liu, Nucl. Instrum. Methods Phys. Res. B 7/8 (1985) 547.
[81] B. Rauschenbach, Appl. Phys. A 40 (1986) 47.
[82] E. Peiner, K. Kopitzki, Nucl. Instrum. Methods Phys. Res. B 34 (1988) 173.
[83] B.X. Liu, California Institute of Technology, 1982, in press.
[84] G. Goltz, R. Fernandez, M.A. Nicolet, D.K. Sadana, Metstable materials formation by ion implantation, in: S.T. Picraux, W.J. Choyke (Eds.), Proceedings of the MRS Symposium, Vol. 7, North-Holland, Amsterdam, 1982, p. 227.
[85] O. Jin, B.X. Liu, Nucl. Instrum. Methods Phys. Res. B 114 (1996) 56.
[86] B.X. Liu, M.-A. Nicolet, Thin Solid Films 101 (1983) 201.
[87] F. Pan, B.X. Liu, J. Phys.: Condensed Matter 8 (1995) 383.
[88] L.J. Huang, B.X. Liu, Nucl. Instrum. Methods Phys. Res. B 18 (1987) 256.

[89] Y.G. Chen, B.X. Liu, J. Appl. Phys. 82 (1997) 3815.
[90] O. Jin, Y. Ye, B.X. Liu, J. Phys.: Condensed Matter 7 (1995) 7959.
[91] B.X. Liu, O. Jin, Y. Ye, J. Phys.: Condensed Matter 8 (1996) L79.
[92] Y.G. Chen, B.X. Liu, Mater. Sci. Eng. B 52 (1998) 1.
[93] Y.G. Chen, Q. Zhang, B.X. Liu, Nucl. Instrum. Methods Phys. Res. B 124 (1997) 523.
[94] O. Jin, B.X. Liu, J. Non-Cryst. Solids 211 (1997) 180.
[95] B.X. Liu, Z.J. Zhang, O. Jin, J. Alloys Compounds 270 (1998) 186.
[96] J.W. Mayer, B.Y. Tsaur, S.S. Lau, L.S. Hung, Nucl. Instrum. Methods 182/183 (1981) 1.
[97] W. Hiller, M. Buchgeister, P. Eitner, K. Kopitzki, V. Lilienthal, E. Peiner, Mater. Sci. Eng. A 115 (1989) 151.
[98] B.Y. Tsaur, S.S. Lau, L.S. Hung, J.W. Mayer, Nucl. Instrum. Methods 182/183 (1981) 67.
[99] S.M. Shin, M.S. Ray, J.M. Rigsbee, J.E. Greene, Appl. Phys. Lett. 43 (1983) 249.
[100] J.L. Brimhall, H.E. Kissinger, L.A. Charlot, Rad. Eff. 77 (1983) 273.
[101] J.L. Brimhall, E.P. Simonen, Nucl. Instrum. Methods Phys. Res. B 16 (1986) 187.
[102] L.S. Hung, J.W. Mayer, Nucl. Instrum. Methods Phys. Res. B 7/8 (1985) 676.
[103] B.X. Liu, Z.J. Zhang, O. Jin, F. Pan, Nucl. Instrum. Methods Phys. Res. B 106 (1995) 17.
[104] K.T.-Y. Kung, B.X. Liu, M.-A. Nicolet, Phys. Stat. Sol. (a) 77 (1983) 355.
[105] H. Jones, The Theory of Brillouin Zones and Electronic States in Crystals, North-Holland, Amsterdam, 1960, p. 191.
[106] B.X. Liu, Phys. Stat. Sol. (a) 75 (1983) K77.
[107] B.X. Liu, Z.J. Zhang, J. Mater. Res. 9 (1994) 357.
[108] Z.J. Zhang, B.X. Liu, J. Appl. Phys. 75 (1994) 4948.
[109] Z.J. Zhang, B.X. Liu, J. Appl. Phys. 76 (1994) 3351.
[110] Y.G. Chen, B.X. Liu, Appl. Phys. Lett. 68 (1996) 3096.
[111] R.C. Ruhl, B.C. Giessen, M. Cohen, N.J. Grant, Acta Metall. 15 (1967) 1693.
[112] S.J. Poon, W.L. Carter, Solid State Commun. 35 (1980) 249.
[113] J.K. Lee, Interatomic Potentials and Crystalline Defects, Metallic Society of AIME, New York, 1981.
[114] V. Vitek, Dislocations and Properties of Real Materials, The Institute of Metals, London, 1985.
[115] M.S. Daw, M.I. Baskes, Phys. Rev. Lett. 50 (1983) 1285.
[116] M.S. Daw, M.I. Baskes, Phys. Rev. B 29 (1984) 6443.
[117] M.W. Finnis, J.E. Sinclair, Philos. Mag. A 50 (1984) 45.
[118] P. Hohenberg, W. Kohn, Phys. Rev. B 13 (1964) 864.
[119] F. Ducastelle, Order and Phase Stability in Alloys, Elsevier, Amsterdam, 1991.
[120] H.L. Skriver, The LMTO Method, Springer, Berlin, Heidelberg, 1984.
[121] R.A. Johnson, Phys. Rev. B 37 (1988) 3924.
[122] R.A. Johnson, D.J. Oh, J. Mater. Res. 4 (1989) 1195.
[123] A.F. Voter, S.P. Chen, in: R.W. Siegal, J.R. Weetman, R. Sinclair (Eds.), Characterization of Defects in Materials, Proceedings of the MRS Symposia, Vol. 82, MRS, Pittsburgh, 1987, p. 175.
[124] R.A. Johnson, Phys. Rev. B 39 (1989) 12554.
[125] R.A. Johnson, Phys. Rev. B 41 (1990) 9717.
[126] J. Cai, Y.Y. Ye, Phys. Rev. B 54 (1996) 8398.
[127] A. Banerjea, J.R. Smith, Phys. Rev. B 37 (1988) 6632.
[128] J.H. Rose, J.R. Smith, F. Guinea, J. Ferrante, Phys. Rev. B 29 (1984) 2963.
[129] D. Tomanek, A.A. Aligia, C.A. Balseiro, Phys. Rev. B 32 (1985) 5051.
[130] F. Ducastelle, J. Phys. (Paris) 31 (1970) 1055.
[131] D. Tomanek, S. Mukherjee, K.H. Bennemann, Phys. Rev. B 28 (1983) 665.
[132] G.J. Ackland, G.I. Tichy, V. Vitek, M.W. Finnis, Philos. Mag. A 56 (1987) 735.
[133] M. Marchese, G. Jacucci, C.P. Flynn, Philos. Mag. Lett. 57 (1988) 25.
[134] G.J. Ackland, D.J. Bacon, A.F. Calder, T. Harry, Philos. Mag. A 75 (1997) 713.
[135] R. Rebonato, D.O. Welch, R.D. Hatcher, J.C. Bilello, Philos. Mag. A 55 (1987) 655.
[136] V. Rosato, M. Guillope, B. Legrand, Philos. Mag. A 59 (1989) 321.
[137] F. Cleri, V. Rosoto, Phys. Rev. B 48 (1993) 22.
[138] A. Pasturel, C. Colinet, D. Nguyen Manh, A.T. Paxton, M. van Schilfgaarde, Phys. Rev. B 52 (1995) 15176.
[139] G. Bihlmayer, R. Eibler, A. Neckel, Phys. Rev. B 50 (1994) 13113.
[140] C. Kittel, Introduction to Solid State Physics, Wiley/Interscience, New York, 1986.
[141] R. Hultgren, P.D. Desai, D.T. Hawkins, M. Gleiser, K.K. Kelly, Selected Values of Thermodynamic Properties of Binary Alloys, ASM, Metals Park, ASM, Ohio, 1973.
[142] G. Simmons, H. Wang, Single Crystal Elastic Constants and Calculated Aggregate Properties: A Handbook, MIT Press, Cambridge, Massachusetts, 1971.
[143] W. Wycisk, M. Feller-Knipmeier, J. Nucl. Mater. 69/70 (1978) 616.
[144] V.O. Shestopal, Fiz. Tverd. Tela (Leningrad) 7 (1966) 3461.
[145] V.O. Shestopal, Sov. Phys. Solid State 7 (1966) 2798.
[146] W.S. Lai, B.X. Liu, J. Phys.: Condensed Matter 12 (2000) L53.

[147] X.Y. Huang, J.S. Pan, Y.D. Fan, Phys. Rev. B 54 (1996) 16325.
[148] X.Y. Huang, Ph.D. Thesis, Department of Material Science and Engineering, Tsinghua University, Beijing, China, 1997.
[149] E.A. Brandes, G.B. Brook, Smithells Metals Reference Book, 7th Edition, Butterworths-Heinemann, Oxford, 1992.
[150] X.Y. Huang, J.S. Pan, Y.D. Fan, Solid State Commun. 104 (1997) 101.
[151] Q. Zhang, W.S. Lai, B.X. Liu, J. Non-Cryst. Solids 261 (2000) 137.
[152] Q. Zhang, W.S. Lai, B.X. Liu, Phys. Rev. B 61 (2000) 9345.
[153] A. van den Beukel, S. Radelaar, Acta Metall. 31 (1983) 419.
[154] D. Wolf, P.R. Okamoto, S. Yip, J.F. Lutsko, M. Kluge, J. Mater. Res. 5 (1990) 286.
[155] C. Massobrio, V. Pontikis, G. Martin, Phys. Rev. B 41 (1990) 10486.
[156] T. Fukunaga, W. Watanabe, K. Suzuki, J. Non-Cryst. Solids 61/62 (1984) 343.
[157] P.R. Okamoto, L.E. Rehn, J. Pearson, R. Bhadra, M. Grimsditch, J. Less-Common Metals 140 (1988) 231.
[158] H. Hsieh, S. Yip, Phys. Rev. Lett. 59 (1987) 2760.
[159] R. Devanathan, N.Q. Lam, P.R. Okamoto, M. Meshii, Phys. Rev. B 48 (1993) 42.
[160] M. Parrinello, A. Rahman, Phys. Rev. Lett. 45 (1980) 1196.
[161] M. Parrinello, A. Rahman, J. Appl. Phys. 52 (1981) 7172.
[162] M. Parrinello, A. Rahman, J. Chem. Phys. 76 (1982) 2662.
[163] P.R. Okamoto, N.Q. Lam, L.E. Rehn, Physics of crystal-to-glass transformations, Solid State Phys. 52 (1999) 1.
[164] F.A. Lindemann, Phys. Z. 11 (1910) 609.
[165] M. Born, J. Chem. Phys. 7 (1939) 591.
[166] T. Egami, Y. Waseda, J. Non-Cryst. Solids 64 (1984) 113.
[167] G. Grimvall, in: E.P. Wohlfarth (Ed.), Thermophysical Properties of Materials, Selected Topics in Solid State Physics, Vol. XVIII, North-Holland, Amsterdam, 1986.
[168] S.A. Cho, J. Phys. F: Met. Phys. 12 (1982) 1069.
[169] C.J. Mitra, D.A. O'Connor, J. Phys. C: Solid State Phys. 10 (1977) 3521.
[170] C.G. Shirley, Acta Crystallogr. A 31 (1975) 174.
[171] C.G. Sirley, R.M. Fisher, Philos. Mag. A 39 (1979) 91.
[172] American Institute of Physics Handbook, 3rd Edition, McGraw-Hill, New York, 1972.
[173] C.E. Krill III, J. Li, C. Ettl, C.M. Garland, C. Ettl, K. Samwer, W.B. Yelon, W.L. Johnson, J. Mater. Res. 10 (1995) 280.
[174] T.B. Massalski (Eds.), Binary Alloy Phase Diagram, 2nd Edition, ASM International, 1990.

Stability of a nonequilibrium phase in an immiscible Ag-Ni system studied by *ab initio* calculations and ion-beam-mixing experiment

J. B. Liu, Z. C. Li, and B. X. Liu*
Advanced Materials Laboratory, Department of Materials Science and Engineering, Tsinghua University, Beijing 100084, China and Laboratory of Solid State Microstructures, Nanjing University, Nanjing 210008, China

G. Kresse and J. Hafner
Institut für Materialphysik and Center for Computational Materials Science, Universität Wien, Sensengasse 8-12, A-1090 Wien, Austria

(Received 18 July 2000; revised manuscript received 17 October 2000; published 6 March 2001)

Employing the Vienna *ab initio* simulation package (VASP), a possible nonequilibrium intermediate state located near Ag_3Ni in the immiscible Ag-Ni system is predicted through calculating the total energy of six possible structures of A_3B type as a function of their lattice constants. The predicted state is confirmed by the fact that a metastable hcp Ag_3Ni phase was indeed obtained in the properly designed Ag-Ni multilayers upon 200 keV xenon ion irradiation at 77 K and its lattice constants determined by diffraction analysis were in good agreement with the calculated values.

DOI: 10.1103/PhysRevB.63.132204 PACS number(s): 61.43.Dq, 61.66.Dk, 71.20.Gj

I. INTRODUCTION

Nanostructures of successive Ag and Ni layers have attracted considerable attention as spin valve systems with giant magnetoresistances (GMR) and consequent technical potential.[1] Both as thin films and nanophases formed by mechanical milling, their structural characteristics have proven interesting from a much wider perspective for the remarkable departures from the equilibrium phase diagram. Central to an understanding of GMR in the granular systems is the relationship between the transport and structural properties of the possible alloying behaviors in the Ag-Ni system. In fact, curious new alloying effects have also been observed in monolayer structures with Ag and Ni components. These highly interesting behaviors trigger a strong motivation to investigate the possibility of synthesizing new metastable alloys in the Ag-Ni system by some nonequilibrium methods.

Since the pioneering work of Schwarz and Johnson, the scheme of solid-state reaction (SSR) of multilayers has been employed to synthesize amorphous alloy films.[2] In addition, another powerful method, namely, ion beam mixing (IBM) of multilayers, has also been introduced[3] and various nonequilibrium alloys have so far been obtained by IBM in about 100 binary metal systems.[4] It is noted that a number of similar nonequilibrium crystalline phases obtained by SSR and/or IBM have similar alloy compositions near A_3B, where A and B stand for the constituent metals A and B, respectively, and that these phases crystallize in similar structures (hcp or fcc), when the systems consist of both transition metals. Such a similar A_3B nonequilibrium crystalline phase raises a challenging issue for theoretical modeling or revealing the physical origin of its formation. In this respect, some researchers have studied the stability of the nonequilibrium phases in terms of thermodynamics. For instance, based on Miedema's semiempirical model, Alonso and Gallego attempted to calculate the free energy diagram for predicting the formation of nonequilibrium phases in the binary metal systems.[5] To obtain an understanding at a depth of electronic structure concerning the stability of the nonequilibrium phases in the immiscible systems, it is necessary to pursue first-principles calculation, which however, is still currently an open issue. In the present work, a first-principles calculation was performed to predict the possible metastable state of A_3B type in the Ag-Ni system, which is essentially equilibrium immiscible and has no any alloy phase over the whole composition range. In addition, specially designed IBM experiment was also conducted to confirm the existence of the predicted metastable state.

II. METHOD OF *ab initio* CALCULATION

It is known that there are about twenty possible different structures for the A_3B or AB_3 phases, i.e., $A15$, A_e, $D0_2$, $D0_3$, $D0_9$, $D0_{11}$, $D0_{18}$, $D0_{19}$, $D0_{20}$, $D0_{21}$, $D0_{22}$, $D0_{23}$, $D0_{24}$, $D0_a$, $D0_b$, $D0_c$, $D0_d$, $L1_2$, $L1_a$, and $L6_0$ structures. The choosing of the possible structures in our *ab initio* calculations was based on the following considerations. First, in the above twenty structures, some are very complicated, e.g., the $D0_2$, $D0_{21}$, and $L1_a$ structures composing more than 16 atoms per unit cell. For the $L1_a$ structure, it can also be considered as a complicated one, as it has 32 atoms per unit cell,[6,7] or 8 atoms per unit cell according to Pearson notation. Generally, a unit cell of an alloy phase containing more atoms frequently corresponds a larger size than the one composing less atoms, and therefore it probably requires a larger critical radius for nucleation and growth of the phase. It follows that the above mentioned phases of complicated structures require perhaps highly sufficient kinetic conditions to nucleate and grow, e.g., requiring relatively high temperature to enhancing the atomic mobility and long time enabling the atoms to organize themselves into an ordered configuration. The following fact may lend some support to this argument, i.e., ion irradiation of the $Ni_{50}Mo_{50}$ multiplayers resulted in the formation of a metastable hexagonal phase, instead of the most stable equilibrium δ phase,[8] which has an exact stoichiometry of $Ni_{50}Mo_{50}$. The hexagonal phase is certainly of simple structure with two atoms in a unit cell, while the δ phase has been characterized to be a very com-

Physical Review B 63(13), p.132204 (2001).

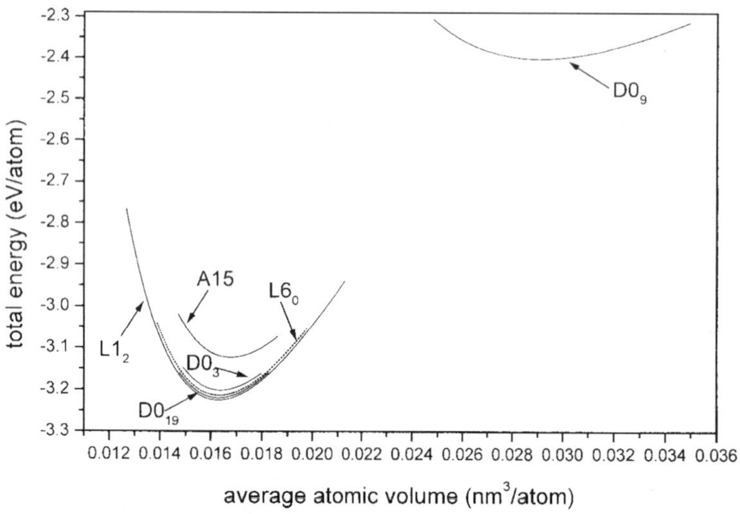

FIG. 1. The calculated total energy vs lattice constant for an Ag_3Ni metastable phase with different structures.

plicated and ordered orthorhombic structure with 56 atoms in a unit cell.[9] The structural complexity of the δ phase is believed to be the major factor that prevents its formation under an extremely restricted kinetic condition available in the ion irradiation process.[8] Secondly, the nonequilibrium crystalline phases obtained so far by SSR and/or IBM were usually of simple structures, such as hcp and fcc, but never of any possible complicated ones due to the restricted kinetic conditions. Consequently, the following six structures, i.e., $A15$, $D0_3$, $D0_9$, $D0_{19}$, $L6_0$, and $L1_2$, were calculated to find out if the respective nonequilibrium phases of A_3B type could also be relatively stable and to be formed by some nonequilibrium methods.

Our calculations are performed using the Vienna *ab initio* simulation program (VASP).[10,11] In the program the exchange and correlation items are described by the specially defined functions proposed by Perdew and Zunger,[12] in which the nonlocal corrections in the form of the generalized-gradient approximation (GGA) of Perdew and Wang[13] are added for improving the computation. The calculations are performed in a plane-wave basis, using fully nonlocal Vanderbilt-type ultrasoft pseudopotentials to describe the electron-ion interaction,[14] which allows the use of a moderate cutoff for the construction of the plane-wave basis for the transition metals. The integration in the Brillouin zone is done on special k points determined according to the Monckhorst-Pack scheme, which resulted in a mesh of 11 irreducible k points.

III. EXPERIMENTAL PROCEDURE

For IBM experiment, the multilayered samples were prepared by depositing alternately pure Ni and Ag onto the freshly cleaved NaCl single crystals in an *e*-gun evaporation system. The samples were designed to consist of eight bilayers with a total thickness of about 40 nm, which was to match the projected range plus the projected range straggling of 200 keV xenon ions employed in IBM experiment. The overall compositions of the samples were designed to be close to Ag_3Ni and were obtained by adjusting the relative thicknesses of the constituent metals. The vacuum level of the system was on the order of 10^{-11} Torr and during evaporation, it was better than 2×10^{-8} Torr. During evaporation, the sample holder was cooled by running water and a temperature rise of the samples was estimated to be below 200 °C. The thickness of each individual layer was monitored by an *in situ* quartz oscillator in the evaporation system. Energy dispersive spectrum (EDS) analysis with an experimental error of 3% was employed to confirm the overall compositions of the as-deposited samples as well as to determine the real compositions of the resultant alloy phase after IBM. The multilayered samples were then irradiated with 200 keV Xe ions to various doses ranging from 5 to 9 $\times10^{15}Xe^+/cm^2$ in an implanter with a vacuum level better than 5×10^{-6} Torr. During irradiation, the sample holder was cooled by liquid nitrogen (i.e., 77 K). The ion current density was confined to be less than 1 $\mu A/cm^2$ to minimize

TABLE I. The calculated equilibrium cohesive properties (lattice constant a and c/a, atomic volume V, cohesive energy E_{min}) of Ag_3Ni in the $D0_{19}$, $D0_3$, $L1_2$, $A15$, $D0_9$, and $L6_0$ structures.

	$D0_{19}$	$D0_3$	$L1_2$	$A15$	$D0_9$	$L6_0$
a (Å)	2.84	6.40	4.02	5.12	4.88	4.22
c/a	1.64					0.868
V (Å^3/atom)	16.267	16.384	16.241	16.777	29.054	16.308
E_{min} (eV/atom)	−3.2201	−3.2019	−3.2254	−3.1234	−2.4030	−3.2140

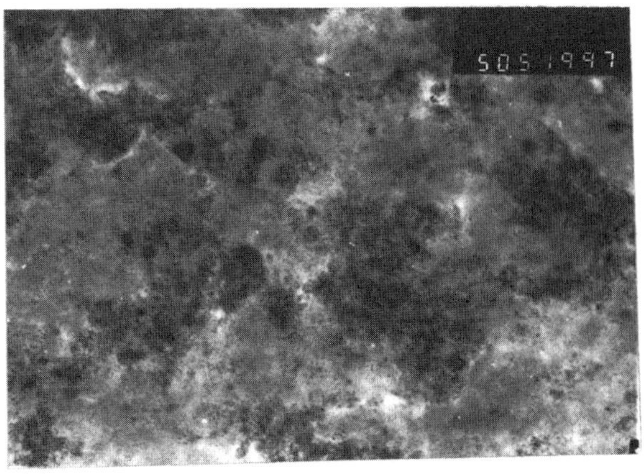

(a)

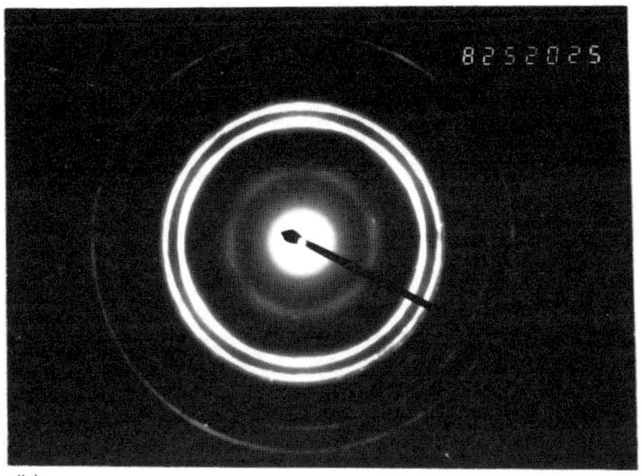

(b)

FIG. 2. A bright-field image and the corresponding selected area diffraction (SAD) of the multilayered films irradiated at 77 K by xenon ions to a dose of 5×10^{15} Xe^+/cm^2.

the beam heating effect. After irradiation, all the samples were removed from the NaCl substrates in deionized water and put on Mo grids for transmission electron microscopy (TEM) examination and selected area diffraction (SAD) analysis to identify the resultant structures.

IV. RESULTS AND DISCUSSION

A. *ab initio* calculation results

We first discuss the calculation results for the possible Ag_3Ni phase. The total energy was calculated as a function of the lattice constant(s) for six different structures, i.e., $D0_{19}$, $D0_3$, $L1_2$, $A15$, $D0_9$, and $L6_0$, respectively. The c/a ratios of the $D0_{19}$ and $L6_0$ structures were optimized. Figure 1 exhibits the six calculated curves showing the correlation of the total energy versus lattice constant(s). One sees from the figure that the increasing order of the relative structural stability for the possible Ag_3Ni phase is $D0_9$, $A15$, $D0_3$, $L6_0$, $D0_{19}$, and $L1_2$ and the six calculated structures can therefore be divided into two groups. In the first group, the differences of the minimum total energies of the $D0_3$, $L6_0$, $D0_{19}$, and $L1_2$ structures are very small, in which the $D0_{19}$ and $L1_2$ structures have the relatively lower minimum total energy than the $D0_3$ and $L6_0$ ones. Furthermore, though the $L1_2$ structure has a lower minimum energy than $D0_{19}$, a cohesive energy difference between the two structures was about 0.005 eV/atom, i.e., 0.16%. While in the second group, the $D0_9$ and $A15$ structures have evidently higher minimum total energies than the $D0_3$, $L6_0$, $D0_{19}$, and $L1_2$ structures, suggesting that the $A15$ and $D0_9$ structures are relatively unstable. These results indicated that the four structures in the first group are all energetically possible for the A_3B type in the Ag-Ni system. Moreover, the equilibrium cohesive properties for the above six structures were calculated for the Ag-Ni system and are listed in Table I. It can be seen that the difference of the atomic volume among the $D0_{19}$ and $L1_2$ structures is less than 0.2%, reflecting the well-known fact that the fcc and hcp structures are very much alike. Because of the similarity of the fcc and hcp structures in their atomic configurations, it is theoretically reasonable that the total energies of the fcc and hcp phases are very close. The calculated results seem to predict that either a fcc or hcp Ag_3Ni phase may be formed by some nonequilibrium methods under appropriate experimental conditions.

TABLE II. Indexing of the hcp phase formed in the $Ag_{75}Ni_{25}$ multilayed films induced by ion irradiation at a dose of 5×10^{15} Xe^+/cm^2.

D_{exp} (Å)	hkl	D_{cal} (Å)
2.54	100	2.56
1.48	110	1.48
1.30	200	1.28
1.12	104	1.12
0.96	210	0.97
0.85	300	0.85
0.79	205	0.78
0.76	303	0.76
0.73	220	0.74

B. Ion beam mixing experimental results

We now turn to discuss the structural change observed in the Ag-Ni multilayered samples upon 200 keV xenon IBM at 77 K. After irradiation to a dose of $5\times10^{15}Xe^+/cm^2$, a metastable crystalline phase was indeed formed, as evidenced by Fig. 2. Figures 2(a) and 2(b) show a bright-field image and a corresponding SAD pattern of the sample irradiated to the dose of $5\times10^{15}Xe^+/cm^2$, respectively. The newly formed metastable crystalline phase was identified to be of hcp structure. Table II lists the indexing results of the metastable hcp phase. The lattice parameters of the hcp phase were determined to be $a=2.96$ Å, $c=4.96$ Å, and $c/a=1.67$. The composition ratio of the hcp phase was determined by EDS analysis to be 75 at. % of Ag, i.e., the metastable hcp Ag-Ni phase is very close to the A_3B type. Note that the lattice constants from *ab initio* calculation are $a=2.84$ Å and $c=4.66$ Å, leading to a c/a ratio of 1.64. One sees that the experimental and calculated lattice constants of the formed hcp Ag_3Ni phase are quite compatible with an error around 4%. It should be noted that the above diffraction analysis only confirms an Ag_3Ni hcp structure, which is not exactly the ordered Ag_3Ni hcp structure required in VASP calculation, however, it confirms the existence of such a metastable state located near Ag_3Ni with a structure of hcp type in the equilibrium immiscible Ag-Ni system.

V. CONCLUDING REMARKS

In summary, employing the Vienna *ab initio* simulation package (VASP), the first principles calculation results are quite relevant in correctly predicting the existence of a non-equilibrium intermediate state in the Ag-Ni system and ion beam mixing did result in the formation of a metastable hcp Ag_3Ni alloy under appropriate conditions.

*Corresponding author. Email address: dmslbx@tsinghua.edu.cn

[1]D. J. Kubinski and H. Holloway, J. Appl. Phys. **77**, 782 (1995).
[2]R. B. Schwarz and W. L. Johnson, Phys. Rev. Lett. **51**, 415 (1983).
[3]B. X. Liu, W. L. Johnson, M.-A. Nicolet, and S. S. Lau, Appl. Phys. Lett. **42**, 45 (1983).
[4]B. X. Liu and O. Jin, Phys. Status Solidi A **161**, 3 (1997).
[5]A. R. Miedema, A. K. Niessen, F. R. de Boer, R. Boom, and W. C. M. Matterns, *Cohesion in Metals: Transition Metal Alloys* (North-Holland, Amsterdam, 1989).
[6]Y.-C. Tang, J. Appl. Crystallogr. **4**, 377 (1951).
[7]A. Schneider and U. Esch, Z. Elektrochem. **50**, 290 (1944).
[8]B. X. Liu, L. J. Huang, K. Tao, C. H. Shang, and H-D. Li, Phys. Rev. Lett. **59**, 745 (1987).
[9]C. B. Shoemaker and D. P. Shoemaker, J. Appl. Crystallogr. **16**, 997 (1963).
[10]G. Kresse and J. Hafner, Phys. Rev. B **47**, 558 (1993).
[11]G. Kresse and J. Furthmüller, Comput. Mater. Sci. **6**, 15 (1996); Phys. Rev. B **54**, 11 169 (1996).
[12]J. Perdew and A. Zunger, Phys. Rev. B **23**, 5048 (1981).
[13]J. P. Perdew and Y. Wang, Phys. Rev. B **45**, 13 244 (1992).
[14]D. Vanderbilt, Phys. Rev. B **41**, 7892 (1990).

Solid-state crystal-to-amorphous transition in metal–metal multilayers and its thermodynamic and atomistic modelling

B. X. LIU*, W. S. LAI and Z. J. ZHANG

Laboratory of advanced materials, Department of Materials Science and Engineering, Tsinghua University, Beijing 100084, PR China

[Received 31 May 2001; accepted 11 September 2001]

Abstract

In this review article, first a brief summary is presented concerning the formation of amorphous alloys (or metallic glasses) in binary metal systems by solid-state reaction of metallic multilayers. Secondly, under the framework of Miedema's model, thermodynamic modelling of crystal-to-amorphous transition is developed with special consideration of the excess interfacial free energy in metallic multilayers. Thirdly, the results of molecular dynamics simulations in some representative systems are presented, revealing the detailed kinetics of the crystal-to-amorphous transition on the atomic scale, such as the temperature/time dependence of interfacial reactions, the asymmetric growth of amorphous interlayers, and the nucleation and/or presence of growth barriers resulting from the interfacial texture. Fourthly, the critical solid solubilities of some representative systems are directly determined from the inter-atomic potentials through molecular dynamics simulations and then correlated with the metallic-glass-forming ability of the systems as well as their asymmetric growth during solid-state amorphization observed in experiments and/or simulations.

Contents

*To whom correspondence should be addressed. Fax: +86-10-6277-1160; e-mail: dmslbx@tsinghua.edu.cn

Review Article, Advances in Physics 50 (4), p.367-429 (2001).

1. Introduction

In 1960, Klement *et al.* obtained the first amorphous alloy (or metallic glass) by liquid melt quenching (LMQ) in the Au–Si system [1] and this newly discovered state of matter was later called the amorphous solid state [2]. Because of their non-crystalline structure with no grain boundaries, amorphous alloys frequently possess unique properties in many respects, e.g. superior corrosion resistance against acids, the presence of barrier functions preventing atomic diffusion, etc. [3]. Since the 1960s, LMQ has been widely employed to produce amorphous alloys in binary metal systems with different characteristics. In the beginning, available cooling speeds were of the order of $10^6\ K\ s^{-1}$ [4]. Later, cooling speeds increased up to $10^{7-8}\ K\ s^{-1}$ and even as high as $10^{12}\ K\ s^{-1}$ using intense lasers [5, 6, 7]. Evidently, in LMQ, metallic glasses are formed through a liquid-to-solid phase transition. Based on the experimental data, the glass-forming ability of binary metal systems was defined to distinguish qualitatively between systems from which it is either possible or not possible to obtain metallic glass by LMQ, and correspondingly the systems have been classified into two groups: glass-forming and non-glass-forming systems.

Since the early 1980s, two powerful schemes have been introduced for producing amorphous alloys as well as for studying some fundamental issues in the field of metallic glasses, i.e. solid-state reaction (SSR) and ion beam mixing (IBM), both beginning with metal–metal multilayers [8, 9]. It is commonly recognized that in SSR and IBM, metallic glasses are formed through a solid–solid phase transition that is sharply different from that involved in LMQ. Because of their powerful capability, SSR and IBM have so far produced a great number of non-equilibrium alloys with either an amorphous or a crystalline structure, not only in glass-forming systems but also in some non-glass-forming systems defined previously based on the experimental results from LMQ. For example, some new amorphous alloys have been obtained by SSR/IBM in some equilibrium immiscible systems in which LMQ is even unable to co-melt the constituent metals [10]. It follows naturally that some basic concepts and understanding concerning metallic glasses should be somewhat modified or further developed, e.g. the previously defined glass-forming and non-glass-forming systems, the glass-forming ability or glass-forming composition range of binary metal systems, etc.

In the mid-1970s, Miedema *et al.* developed a semi-quantitative model capable of calculating the thermodynamic properties of metals and alloys based on some intrinsic properties of the elements. Since then the model has been employed to construct Gibbs free energy diagrams for binary metal systems by calculating the free energy curves for all the alloy phases involved, and the diagram calculated can give relevant thermodynamic insight into alloy phase formation and transition [11]. Later, Miedema's model has also been employed for thermodynamic modelling of the formation of non-equilibrium alloys and the associated structural phase transition [12].

In the past 10 years, significant progress has been achieved in computational physics and materials science [13]. Computation and/or simulation make it possible to approach a quantitative understanding of alloy phase formation and transition on an atomic scale or even to a depth within the electronic structure of solids. For example, molecular dynamics (MD) simulation has been employed to study the detailed process of solid-state interfacial reactions, the kinetics of the crystal-to-amorphous transition and the associated property change in binary metal systems [14]. Moreover, applying proven realistic inter-atomic potentials, MD simulations were conducted to determine critical solid solubilities in some representative binary metal systems and the respective metallic-glass-forming abilities were hence deduced [15]. Very recently, some primary studies were reported concerning first principles calculations to predict possible non-equilibrium states in some binary metal systems, and the corresponding non-equilibrium alloy phases were indeed obtained by some non-equilibrium materials processing schemes [16].

Concerning the formation and theoretical modelling of non-equilibrium alloys by IBM, some review articles have been published in the literature [17] to which the reader is referred. The present review article is dedicated to discussing mainly progress to date concerning the crystal-to-amorphous transition in metallic multi-layers by solid-state interfacial reactions. First, a brief summary concerning the experimental observations of the crystal-to-amorphous transition in metallic multi-layers by SSR is presented. Secondly, under the framework of Miedema's theory, a thermodynamic and kinetic model is developed for predicting the possibility of solid-state amorphization and it can also give a relevant thermodynamic interpretation to metallic glass formation as well as the glass-forming range by SSR. Thirdly, atomistic modelling by molecular dynamics simulation is described to reveal the detailed growth kinetics of the amorphization transition on an atomic scale. Fourthly, the physical origin of the crystal-to-amorphous transition is clarified to be the crystalline lattice collapsing when solute atoms exceed the critical solid solubility, which can be determined directly from an inter-atomic potential of the system through MD simulation. It follows that the intrinsic glass-forming range (or ability) of a binary metal system is within the composition range bounded by the critical solid solubilities and it is a property governed by the internal characteristics of the system.

2. Survey of solid-state amorphization

In 1983, Schwarz and Johnson observed for the first time a phenomenon called solid-state amorphization (SSA) in Au–La multilayered films produced by medium temperature annealing and claimed that a large negative heat of formation (ΔH_f) and a large atomic size difference between the constituent metals of the binary metal system were necessary for SSA to take place [8]. The large negative ΔH_f makes an amorphous phase have a lower free energy than that of a mechanical mixture of two polycrystalline metals and thus serves as the thermodynamic driving force. Meanwhile, the large atomic size difference is responsible for asymmetric diffusion, i.e. atoms of one metal diffuse abnormally faster into its partner than vice versa, which in turn suppresses either nucleation or growth of the possible intermetallic compounds—frequently of complicated structure. Since then, SSA has been observed in some other binary metal systems having characteristics similar to those of the Au–La system. A little later, Clemens suggested two similar parameters to predict the possibility of SSA, i.e. a large negative ΔH_f and a small atomic volume ratio [18]. The small atomic volume ratio was thought to result in not only asymmetric diffusion but also the formation of a disordered interface, which could provide nucleation sites for growing an amorphous phase. Another model for predicting SSA was proposed by Kwak *et al.* and was based on a defined thermodynamic factor together with an effective driving force [19]. The thermodynamic factor was defined as the free energy difference between a resultant amorphous phase and the initial polycrystalline metals, while the effective driving force was a kinetic factor defined as the ratio of an effective radius of the interstitial site in the host matrix to that of the diffusing atom. In fact, the above models are based on similar or equivalent parameters and all predict that SSA can take place in binary metal systems having negative the ΔH_f.

In the last decade, however, SSA has also been observed in some binary metal systems having different characteristics from those of the Au–La system, e.g. in the Ni–Mo system with a small negative ΔH_f [20], in the immiscible Cu–Ta equilibrium system even with a positive ΔH_f [21], and in the Au–Ta system in which the two metals have almost identical atomic size [22]. In addition, SSA in the Ni–Mo system was also confirmed by MD simulation with a proven-to-be realistic Ni–Mo potential [23]. Moreover, SSA in positive ΔH_f systems was reproduced in several other systems, including Cu–Nb [24], Cu–W [25] and four Y-refractory metal systems [10, 26, 27, 28], provided the multilayered films were properly designed to include a sufficient fraction of interfacial atoms in the films, in which the individual layer thickness was about 2.0 nm. It should be noted that the claimed observations of SSA in multilayered films were based on two consecutive structural changes identified by means of diffraction analysis. First, after annealing at medium temperature (typically 300–400°C), the sharp diffraction lines (or rings) from the two crystalline metals in the as-deposited films changed into halo(s). Secondly, the halos changed back to sharp diffraction lines (or rings) upon further annealing at a slightly higher temperature (typically 450–500°C). If only the first structural change is addressed, one might attribute the halo(s) to an amorphous oxide. None the less, if such an argument were true, the amorphous oxide should have grown via additional oxidation upon further annealing and could never possibly transform back into crystalline metals. Very recently, SSA in the Cu–Ta system was directly observed by transmission electron microscopy examination using cross-sectional Cu–Ta bilayer samples [29]. For ease of presentation, table 1 lists

Table 1. Lists of binary metal–metal systems observed to exhibit solid-state amorphization upon SSR. The data of heat of formation ΔH_f are for equiatomic composition and cited from reference [11]. The atomic size difference is defined to be a ratio of the difference between atomic radii versus the larger atomic radius (r_1), i.e. $(r_1 - r_2)/r_1, r_1 > r_2$.

System	ΔH_f (kJ mol^{-1})	Atomic size difference (%)	Reference
Transition metal–rare-earth systems			
Au–La	−108	23.2	[8]
Cu–Er	—	27.3	[30]
Ni–Ce	−40	31.7	[31]
Ni–Er	−48	29.1	[30]
Simple-metal–transition-metal systems			
Al–Mn	−43	4.6	[32]
Al–Mo	−24	4.8	[33]
Al–Pt	−82	3.1	[34, 35]
Mg–Ni	−8	22.1	[36]
Sn–Co	−17	10.8	[37]
Transition-metal–transition-metal systems			
Au–Ta	−49	0.8	[22]
Au–Y	−110	20.0	[38]
Au–Zr	−112	9.3	[39]
Co–Zr	−60	21.2	[40]
Cu–Nb	+4	10.6	[24]
Cu–Ta	+3	9.4	[21, 29]
Cu–W	+33	6.8	[25]
Cu–Y	−32	29.1	[41]
Fe–Zr	−37	21.9	[42]
Hf–Ni	−63	20.3	[43]
Mo–Ni	−11	8.6	[20]
Mo–Y	+35	24.4	[10]
Nb–Ni	−45	12.8	[44]
Nb–Y	+44	20.7	[27]
Ni–Ta	−44	12.9	[12]
Ni–Ti	−52	14.0	[18]
Ni-Zr	−72	21.6	[45, 18]
Ta–Y	+40	21.8	[28]
W–Y	+35	24.0	[26]

the up-to-date observations of SSA in some 28 binary metal systems. Evidently, the development of a general criterion capable of predicting the possibility of SSA in binary metal systems with either positive or negative ΔH_f is needed. Meanwhile, another important question is raised concerning the kinetics, i.e. how can atoms of one metal diffuse into its partner in an equilibrium immiscible system. In this respect, there have been some experimental and simulation results showing the possibility of atomic diffusion through 'pinholes' or by a 'burrowing effect' in the immiscible Cu–Co [46] and Ag–Ni [47, 48] systems, respectively. These results seemed to suggest that atoms of one metal can embed into its partner lattice to a depth of several atomic layers, i.e. a couple of nanometres. Such results may give some hints for understanding the kinetic aspects of SSA taking place in systems with positive ΔH_f, however, the subject of kinetics is still an open question requiring much further investigation.

3. Experimentation on solid-state reactions

3.1. *Design and preparation of multilayered samples*

In designing the metal–metal multilayered samples, three geometrical parameters should be considered, i.e. the total thickness of the samples, the relative thicknesses of the two constituent metals, and the individual layer thicknesses.

The total thickness of the multilayered samples for solid-state reactions has no limitation. For convenience in laboratory studies, one can design the total thickness within the range 40–80 nm for ease of transmission electron microscopy (TEM) examination. For producing amorphous alloy films, the total thickness can be designed to fulfil the requirements of specific applications, e.g. up to a micron thick. The relative thicknesses of the two constituent metals in the films are determined by the desired overall composition. For instance, the relative thicknesses of metals A (L_A) and B (L_B) in a sample with a total thickness L and an overall composition A_xB_{1-x} can be calculated by $L_A V_B / L_B V_A = x/(1-x)$, where $L_A + L_B = L$, and V_A and V_B are the molar volumes of metals A and B, respectively. The individual layer thickness should be reasonably thin to allow good efficiency of solid-state interfacial reaction. In particular, for producing amorphous alloy films in binary metal systems with positive ΔH_f, the design of the layer thickness is based on how much interfacial free energy is needed to elevate the initial energetic state of the multilayered films to a specific level, i.e. to intersect with or even surpass that of an amorphous state in a specific composition range. In other words, the necessary amount of interfacial free energy requires multilayered samples to include a certain number of interfaces, thus determining the individual layer thickness. In practice, the thickness of each individual layer is frequently designed to be in the range 2–5 nm. The calculation of interfacial free energy will be discussed in detail in section 4.

Multilayered films are frequently prepared in electron-beam evaporation or sputtering deposition systems by alternately depositing the pure metals A and B onto an inert substrate, e.g. SiO_2, Al_2O_3 or NaCl single crystals. The system is usually equipped with an *in situ* quartz oscillator to monitor the thickness of the deposited metal layers. The vacuum level of the system is typically of the order 10^{-6}–10^{-8} Pa. After deposition, the real compositions of the samples are frequently measured by an energy dispersive X-ray spectrometer (EDS).

In SSR, thermal annealing of the as-deposited multilayered samples can either be conducted in a hot-stage attached to the TEM, i.e. *in situ* thermal annealing, or be conducted in a vacuum furnace. Two experimental parameters in SSR are annealing temperature and time. As SSR is frequently intended to induce an amorphization transition or the formation of non-equilibrium alloys, the annealing temperature should be relatively low and is gradually increased from room temperature up to 300–450°C, and the staying time at each annealing temperature is typically 0.5–1 hours. The relatively low annealing temperature and short annealing time are essential for the formation of amorphous or other non-equilibrium alloys by SSR, by frustrating the nucleation and growth of possible equilibrium compounds. In other words, it is the kinetic frustration that results in the formation of amorphous or other non-equilibrium alloys by SSR. After an amorphous phase is formed by SSR, further annealing is frequently conducted to determine the re-crystallization temperature of the amorphous phase formed, by gradually increasing the annealing temperature, e.g. with step increases of 50°C and a staying time of 0.5 hours.

3.2. *Characterization methods*

X-ray diffraction (XRD) and selected area diffraction (SAD) using an analysing electron beam in TEM are frequently employed to identify the structure of the alloys formed in the multilayered films by thermal annealing. Sometimes, cross-sectional TEM examination is employed to trace the interfacial reaction and alloy phase formation by SSR, if the cross-section samples could be prepared properly. EDS is employed to determine the real compositions of the as-deposited multilayered samples as well as the resultant alloy phases obtained by SSR. Rutherford backscattering spectrometry (RBS) [49, 50] is also a powerful analysis method and employed, in some cases, to trace the progress of the interfacial reaction in the multilayered films with typically 1–2 MeV He ions. In some cases, X-ray induced photon spectroscopy (XPS) and Auger spectrometry (AES) are used to analyse the composition depth profile of the multilayered films at various stages of SSR. Additionally, four-point probe resistivity measurement can be used to monitor the crystal-to-amorphous transition and vice versa, as the resistivity of an amorphous phase is often considerably greater than that of its crystalline counterpart.

4. Thermodynamics of alloy phase formation in multilayers

4.1. *Miedema's model and Alonso's method*

In the thermodynamics, the Gibbs free energy is usually used to evaluate the relative stability of alloy phases and to interpret the alloy phase formation and transition in a binary metal system. By comparing the Gibbs free energy of the possible competing alloy phases, e.g. the terminal solid solutions, the amorphous phase, the metastable crystalline (MX) phases and the equilibrium compounds, one can understand the sequence of structural phase evolution and the glass-forming ability (GFA) or the glass-forming composition range (GFR) of the system. This can be done by constructing a free energy diagram, which includes the free energy curves of all the alloy phases in the system calculated based on Miedema's model [11] and the method developed by Alonso *et al.* [51].

Generally, the Gibbs free energy of an alloy phase is calculated by

$$\Delta G = \Delta H - T\Delta S, \tag{4.1}$$

where T is the temperature, and ΔH and ΔS are the enthalpy and entropy of formation, respectively. The entropy of formation plays a secondary role in the free energy at low temperatures and, as a first approximation, can be expressed as that of an ideal solid solution:

$$\Delta S = -R(X_A \ln X_A + X_B \ln X_B). \tag{4.2}$$

Here, R is the gas constant, X_A and X_B are the atomic concentrations of the metals A and B in the alloy, respectively. According to Miedema's model, the enthalpy change of a substitutional solid solution of the transition metals is considered as a sum of three contributions [52–54]:

$$\Delta H = \Delta H^c + \Delta H^e + \Delta H^s \tag{4.3}$$

In the equation, ΔH^c, ΔH^e and ΔH^s are the chemical, elastic and structural contributions, respectively. The chemical contribution, ΔH^c, is due to an electron redistribution generated at the surface of contact between dissimilar atomic cells and is expressed by (see reference [55]):

$$\Delta H^{c} = X_{A} f_{AB} \Delta H_{amp}. \tag{4.4}$$

In equation (4.4), ΔH_{amp} is an amplitude concerning the magnitude of the electron redistribution interaction and is a constant for a specific binary metal system given by (see reference [11]):

$$\Delta H_{amp} = \frac{V_{A}^{2/3}}{(n_{WS}^{-1/3})_{av}} [-P(\Delta\phi^{*})^{2} + Q(\Delta n_{WS}^{1/3})^{2}]. \tag{4.5}$$

Here V_A is the atomic volume of the constituent metal A in the alloy; $(n_{WS}^{-1/3})_{av}$ is the mean value of the electron density at the boundary of the Wigner–Seitz cell derived from that of the pure elements in the metallic state, $(n_{WS}^{-1/3})_A$ and $(n_{WS}^{-1/3})_B$. $\Delta\phi^*$ is the difference between the work functions of metals A and B, i.e. ϕ_A^* and ϕ_B^*. P and Q are two empirical constants. The values of the above parameters can be obtained from the well-documented reference [11].

Another parameter in equation (4.4), i.e. f_{AB}, is a function accounting for the degree to which atoms of type A are surrounded by atoms of type B, and is given by (see reference [54]):

$$f_{AB} = X_{B}^{s}[1 + \gamma(X_{A}^{s} X_{B}^{s})^{2}] \tag{4.6}$$

$$X_{B}^{s} = \frac{X_{B} V_{B}^{2/3}}{X_{A} V_{A}^{2/3} + X_{B} V_{B}^{2/3}}. \tag{4.7}$$

In the equation (4.6), γ is an empirical constant describing the short range order of the solid solution, amorphous phase and ordered compound, and is taken to be 0, 5 and 8, respectively.

The elastic contribution, ΔH^{e}, originates from an atomic size mismatch of atoms A and B, and can be derived from the following equation (see references [56]–[59]):

$$\Delta H^{e} = x_{A} x_{B} [x_{A} \Delta H^{e}_{(B\ in\ A)} + x_{B} \Delta H^{e}_{(A\ in\ B)}]. \tag{4.8}$$

Here $\Delta H^{e}_{(i\ in\ j)}$ is an elastic contribution to the heat of solution of i in j and can be calculated by the elastic constants of the constituent metals [60, 61].

The structural contribution, ΔH^{s}, reflects the correlation between the number of valence (s + d) electrons and the crystal structure of the transition metals. The expression for the structural contribution reads (see references [60] and [61]):

$$\Delta H^{s} = E(Z) - X_{A} E(Z_{A}) - X_{B} E(Z_{B}). \tag{4.9}$$

In this equation, $E(Z)$, $E(Z_A)$ and $E(Z_B)$ are the lattice stability parameters [52, 54] of the alloy phase and the pure metals A and B, respectively. Z, Z_A and Z_B are the average numbers of valence electrons of the alloy phase and the pure metals A and B, respectively. The dependence of the lattice stability on Z for the paramagnetic transition metals of simple structures, i.e. bcc, fcc and hcp, has been calculated by the method proposed by Niessen and Miedema [52]. The corrected values for the lattice stability for the binary metal systems consisting of ferromagnetic metals can be found from the reference reported by Niessen *et al.* [55].

For an amorphous phase, both elastic and structural terms are absent in the enthalpy of formation. According to Niessen *et al.*, the enthalpy of the amorphous phase is therefore given by (see reference [55]):

$$\Delta H_{\text{amorphous}} = \Delta H^{\text{c}} + \alpha(X_{\text{A}} T_{\text{m,A}} + X_{\text{B}} T_{\text{m,B}}). \tag{4.10}$$

Here α is an empirical constant, being 3.5 J mol^{-1} K^{-1}. $T_{\text{m},i}$ is the melting point of component i.

It is known that in solid-state reaction (SSR), some metastable crystalline (MX) phases can also be formed in binary metal systems with either a negative or positive ΔH_{f}, and that the MX phases are frequently of a simple structure. In a binary metal system, the growth of an MX phase by SSR would compete with and therefore hinder the formation of an amorphous phase. It is therefore necessary to include the free energy curves of the possible MX phases in the free energy diagram and then compare with that of the amorphous state in predicting the GFA or GFR of the system. In SSR experiments, the MX phases obtained so far can be classified into five structural categories: (i) super-saturated solid solutions (SSSS)—SSSS phases always feature the same crystalline structures as that of the major alloying metals; the lattice constants of most of the SSSS phases, as determined by means of diffraction analysis, are frequently in good agreement with that predicted by Vegard's law, though their composition is normally beyond the respective equilibrium limits; these SSSS phases are therefore substitutional solid solutions; (ii) and (iii) the h.c.p.-I and f.c.c.-I MX phases—they were observed in fcc- and hcp-based alloy systems with an alloy composition around A_3B, where A is a constituent metal of fcc or hcp structure, respectively; (iv) and (v) h.c.p.-II and f.c.c.-II MX phases—they were formed in bcc-based alloy systems, e.g. in some Nb-, Ta-, and Mo-based alloy systems with an alloy composition around AB_3, where B is a refractory metal of bcc structure. Take the Ni–Mo system as an example, carefully performed experiments revealed a two-step phase transition mechanism of bcc→hcp→fcc for the formation of the h.c.p.-II and f.c.c.-II phases. The h.c.p.-II phase was formed through a bcc→hcp transition, while the f.c.c.-II phase was formed in an hcp→fcc transition. Accordingly, the lattice parameters of the h.c.p.-II and f.c.c.-II phases were deduced and were in agreement with the experimentally determined values [20].

We now discuss the free energy calculation of the MX phases. Since an MX phase is of an ordered structure with a negligible entropy term, its free energy includes only three terms:

$$\Delta G_{\text{MX}} = \Delta H^{\text{c}}_{\text{MX}} + \Delta H^{\text{e}}_{\text{MX}} + \Delta H^{\text{s}}_{\text{MX}}. \tag{4.11}$$

The chemical term $\Delta H^{\text{c}}_{\text{MX}}$ is written as

$$\Delta H^{\text{c}}_{\text{MX}} = X_{\text{A}} f_{\text{AB}} \Delta H_{\text{amp}}. \tag{4.12}$$

As an MX phase is commonly considered to be a compound-like phase, in calculating the parameter f_{AB} defined in the equation (4.6), γ is taken to be 8.

The second term $\Delta H^{\text{e}}_{\text{MX}}$ is an elastic contribution and can be derived from

$$\Delta H^{\text{e}}_{\text{MX}} = X_{\text{A}} X_{\text{B}} [X_{\text{A}} \Delta H^{\text{e}}_{\text{MX(B in A)}} + X_{\text{B}} \Delta H^{\text{e}}_{\text{MX(A in B)}}]. \tag{4.13}$$

Here $\Delta H^{\text{e}}_{\text{MX}(i \text{ in } j)}$ is an elastic contribution to the heat of solution of i in j, and is calculated with the elastic constants of the constituent metals.

The third term $\Delta H^{\text{s}}_{\text{MX}}$ is a structural contribution and can be written in a similar form to that shown by equation (4.9),

$$\Delta H^{\text{s}}_{\text{M}x} = E(Z) - X_{\text{A}} E(Z_{\text{A}}) - X_{\text{B}} E(Z_{\text{B}}). \tag{4.14}$$

All the notation is defined in the same way as for equation (4.9).

It has been proposed by the authors' group [12] that the MX phases can be classified into two different groups according to their alloy compositions. Firstly, for an MX phase formed at a composition in the vicinity of an intermetallic compound, the elastic term should be included, as this term originates from a structural difference between the MX phase and the intermetallic compound. This assumption is applied in calculating the free energy of the MX phases of A_3B type, which is expressed by

$$\Delta G_{MX} = \Delta G^{c}_{MX} + \Delta G^{e}_{MX} + \Delta G^{s}_{MX}. \tag{4.15}$$

Secondly, for an MX phase formed at a composition near a eutectic point, where no equilibrium compound exists, the MX phase can be considered as an ordered state, leading to an assumption that the ordering-induced elastic term could relax down to zero [62]. This assumption is applied in calculating the free energy of the MX phases of AB_3 type, which can be expressed by

$$\Delta G_{MX} = \Delta G^{c}_{MX} + \Delta G^{s}_{MX}. \tag{4.16}$$

It will be shown later that the calculation of the free energy of the MX phases of two different groups based on the above assumptions, respectively, are relevant.

4.2. *Role of interfaces in the alloying behaviour of multilayers*

Solid-state reaction (SSR) begins with metallic multilayered films, which certainly consist of a number of interfaces. An interface in the multilayered films is considered as a transient layer with a certain thickness and in a disordered state, which has been confirmed by experiments. For example, Clemens reported that in the Ni–Ti multilayered films prepared by sputtering deposition, the disordered interfacial layers were detected by X-ray diffraction analysis and that each interface consisted of several atomic layers [18]. Very recently, the disordered interfacial layer was directly observed by cross-sectional TEM examination of Cu–Ta bilayer samples [29]. Naturally, such an interfacial layer possesses excess free energy, which would play an important role in influencing alloying behaviour in multilayered films. Consequently, the Gibbs free energy of the initial state of multilayered films consisting of metals A and B can no longer be considered as a ground state of $G = 0$, corresponding to a mechanical mixture of the crystalline metals A and B in bulk form. Instead, it should be the sum of the excess interfacial free energy stored in the multilayered films and that of the ground state ($G = 0$), i.e. equalling the excess interfacial free energy.

For calculating the interfacial free energy, there are several proposed approaches in the literature with different approximations. In this section, we employ the method proposed by Turnbull [63] to make a brief estimation of the interfacial free energy to show the role of the interfacial free energy in influencing the alloying behavior as well as to guide the design of the multilatered films in SSR. According to Turnbull [63], the interfacial free energy between the two solid phases includes two terms, i.e. the physical (or geometrical) and the chemical contributions given by

$$\gamma^{AB}_{SS} = \gamma^{geo}_{SS} + \gamma^{chem}_{SS}. \tag{4.17}$$

For the two solid phases of different structure, the geometrical term γ^{geo}_{SS} stands for the energy of a large angle grain boundary and is always positive. It has been estimated that the grain boundary enthalpy is about 30% of the surface energy at 0 K [64] and the entropy contribution is neglected. Equation (4.17) then becomes

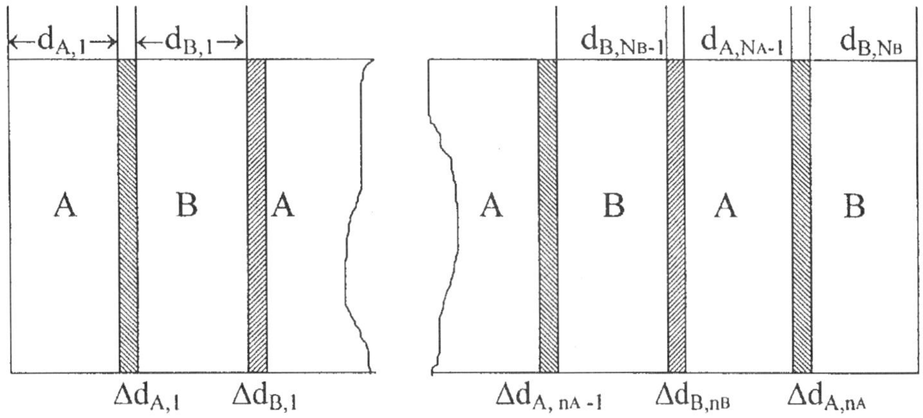

Figure 1. Schematic configuration of the A–B multilayered films. N_A and N_B are numbers of layers of metals A and B, respectively, $d_{A,i}$ and $d_{B,i}$ are the thicknesses of the ith layers of metals A and B, respectively; n_A and n_B are the numbers of the interfaces (A on B) and (B on A), $\Delta d_{A,i}$ and $\Delta d_{B,i}$ are the thicknesses of the ith interfaces (A on B) and (B on A), respectively.

$$\gamma_{SS}^{AB} = 0.15(\gamma_A^{s,0} + \gamma_B^{s,0}) + \gamma_{SS}^{chem}, \tag{4.18}$$

where $\gamma_A^{s,0}$ and $\gamma_B^{s,0}$ are the surface energies of the metals A and B at 0 K. The chemical contribution γ_{SS}^{chem} is given by (see reference [65]):

$$\gamma_{SS}^{chem} = \Delta H_{A\ in\ B}^0/(C_0 V_A^{2/3}), \tag{4.19}$$

where C_0 is a constant and takes the value 4.5×10^8; $\Delta H_{A\ in\ B}^0$ is the heat of solution of the metal A in metal B at infinite dilution [66]. Obviously, γ_{SS}^{chem} has the same sign as ΔH_f of the system and can be either positive or negative. Following Gerkema and Miedema [67], the free energy of one mole of interfacial atoms can be calculated by

$$\Delta G_{int} = S_f \times \gamma_{SS}^{AB} \tag{4.20}$$

Where S_f is the surface area occupied by one mole of interfacial atoms.

The amount of interfacial free energy in the multilayered films is certainly in positive proportion to the fraction of atoms involved in the interfaces. Figure 1 shows a schematic configuration of the multilayered films consisting of metals A and B for calculating the fraction of interfacial atoms versus the total number of atoms in the films. In the figure, N_A and N_B are the layer numbers of the metals A and B; $d_{A,i}$ and $d_{B,i}$ are the thicknesses of the ith layers of the metals A and B, respectively; n_A and n_B are the numbers of the interfaces (A on B) and (B on A), respectively; $\Delta d_{A,i}$ and $\Delta d_{B,i}$ are the thicknesses of the ith interfaces (A on B) and (B on A), respectively. It is noted that the relationship $(n_A + n_B + 1) = (N_A + N_B)$ always holds. Accordingly, the interfacial free energy of the multilayered films can then be calculated by

$$\Delta G_{mul} = \alpha_A \Delta G_{int,A} + \alpha_B \Delta_{int,B} \tag{4.21}$$

where $\Delta G_{int,\,i}$ is the free energy of a mole of interfacial i atoms calculated by equation (4.20), α_A and α_B are the fractions of the A and B atoms in the interfaces of the multilayered films, and are given by

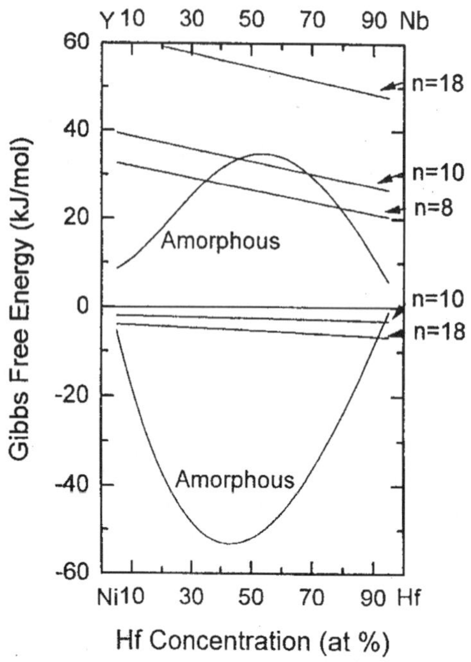

Figure 2. Calculated free energy diagram of the Nb–Y and Hi–Hf systems, showing different effects of interfacial free energy on alloy phase formation in the positive and negative heat of formation systems. *n* stands for the number of interfaces in the multilayers.

$$\alpha_{\mathrm{A}} = x_{\mathrm{A}} \frac{\sum_{i=1}^{n_{\mathrm{A}}} \Delta d_{\mathrm{A},i}}{\sum_{i=1}^{N_{\mathrm{A}}} d_{\mathrm{A,i}}}, \quad \alpha_{\mathrm{B}} = x_{\mathrm{B}} \frac{\sum_{i=1}^{n_{\mathrm{B}}} \Delta d_{\mathrm{B},i}}{\sum_{i=1}^{N_{\mathrm{B}}} d_{\mathrm{B,i}}}, \tag{4.22}$$

where $\sum_{i=1}^{n_{\mathrm{A}}} \Delta d_{\mathrm{A},i} / \sum_{i=1}^{N_{\mathrm{A}}} d_{\mathrm{A,i}}$ and $\sum_{i=1}^{n_{\mathrm{B}}} \Delta d_{\mathrm{B},i} / \sum_{i=1}^{N_{\mathrm{B}}} d_{\mathrm{B,i}}$ are the fractions of the interfacial atoms A and B versus the total numbers of atoms A and B, respectively.

For simplicity, the interfacial layers (A on B) and (B on A) are assumed to be the same. In calculation, the thickness of an interface, according to some experimental observations reported in the literature, is assumed to be within 0.4–0.6 nm. It should be pointed out that although the above calculation is a quick estimate, it could be used for designing multilayered samples. In experiments, one can add some extra interfaces to the samples to ensure their initial energetic state is higher than a desired level corresponding to an amorphous or other possible metastable phase.

We now show the effect of the interfacial free energy on the alloy behaviour in multilayered films for binary metal systems with ΔH_{f} having different signs. Take the Ni–Hf ($\Delta H_{\mathrm{f}} = -63\,\mathrm{kJ\,mol^{-1}}$) and Y–Nb ($\Delta H_{\mathrm{f}} = +35\,\mathrm{kJ\,mol^{-1}}$) systems as two representatives, the free energy curves for an amorphous phase and those for multilayered films consisting of different numbers of interfaces are calculated and shown in figure 2. For the Y–Nb system, one sees that the free energy curve of the amorphous phase is convex in shape and that, on increasing the number of interfaces, the initial energetic state of the multilayered films can be elevated significantly. In other words, the excess interfacial free energy stored in the multilayered films may serve as the driving force for reaction and alloying between the metal layers of A and B, whenever it is turned on by some activation means like thermal annealing in SSR. For the Ni–Hf system, which has a large negative ΔH_f, the free energy curve of the amorphous phase is deeply concave and is lower than that of the multilayered films. It follows that a negative ΔH_f itself may serve as the driving force for reaction and alloying between layers of metals A and B. In this case, the influence of the interfaces, as seen from figure 2, is negligible, as the chemical contribution is negative and the geometrical term is positive.

4.3. *Relevance of the calculated free energy confirmed by experiment and/or* ab initio *calculation*

Since Miedema's model is a semi-empirical one, the relevance of the calculated free energy diagram should be confirmed by some means before applying the calculated diagram to discuss the issues concerning non-equilibrium alloy phase formation and transition. In this respect, the authors' group has recently suggested performing thermal annealing experiments with the multilayered films designed with some specific compositions to examine if the sequence of structural phase evolution upon annealing is in accordance with that deduced from the calculated free energy diagram.

Taking the Ni–Mo system as an example, figure 3(*a*) is the Ni–Mo equilibrium phase diagram and figure 3(*b*) shows the constructed free energy diagram of the Ni–Mo system [20]. In the Ni–Mo system, three metastable crystalline (MX) phases have been obtained by ion beam mixing of the Ni–Mo multilayered films and they were Ni-rich h.c.p.-I, and Mo-rich h.c.p.-II and f.c.c.-II., respectively. The free energy curves for the MX phases were therefore calculated and are displayed in figure 3(*b*) together with those for the amorphous phase and the equilibrium compounds. For thermal annealing experiments, two multilayered films were prepared with the overall compositions $Ni_{75}Mo_{25}$ and $Ni_{25}Mo_{75}$, and the structural phase evolution sequence emerging in the films by thermal annealing are as follows:

$$Ni_{25}Mo_{75}\xrightarrow[60\,\mathrm{min}]{350^{\circ}\mathrm{C}}\text{amor.}\xrightarrow[30\,\mathrm{min}]{450^{\circ}\mathrm{C}}\text{h.c.p.-II}\xrightarrow[30\,\mathrm{min}]{600^{\circ}\mathrm{C}}\text{f.c.c.-II}$$

$$Ni_{75}Mo_{25}\xrightarrow[30\,\mathrm{min}]{300^{\circ}\mathrm{C}}\text{amor.}\xrightarrow[60\,\mathrm{min}]{450^{\circ}\mathrm{C}}\text{h.c.p.-I.}$$

Apparently, at the composition $Ni_{25}Mo_{75}$, the observed sequence of phases appearance upon thermal annealing suggested that the energetic sequence of the metastable phases from high to low should be the amorphous phase, the Mo-rich h.c.p.-II and then the Mo-rich f.c.c.-II phases, which matches very well with the calculation results shown in figure 3(*b*). It is also true for the composition of $Ni_{75}Mo_{25}$, as the observed sequence of phases appearance upon thermal annealing suggests that the free energy of the amorphous phase should be higher than that of the Ni-rich h.c.p.-I MX phase, which was in good agreement with that deduced from the calculated diagram. In short, the thermal annealing experiments strongly confirmed the relevance of the calculated free energy diagram for the Ni–Mo system.

Similar thermal annealing experiments have also been conducted, and similar results were obtained, for some other binary metal systems of negative ΔH_f as well as for some representative systems with positive ΔH_f [68, 69].

Additionally, the above thermal annealing results obtained from the Ni–Mo system also suggested that solid-state reaction (SSR) of the Ni–Mo multilayered

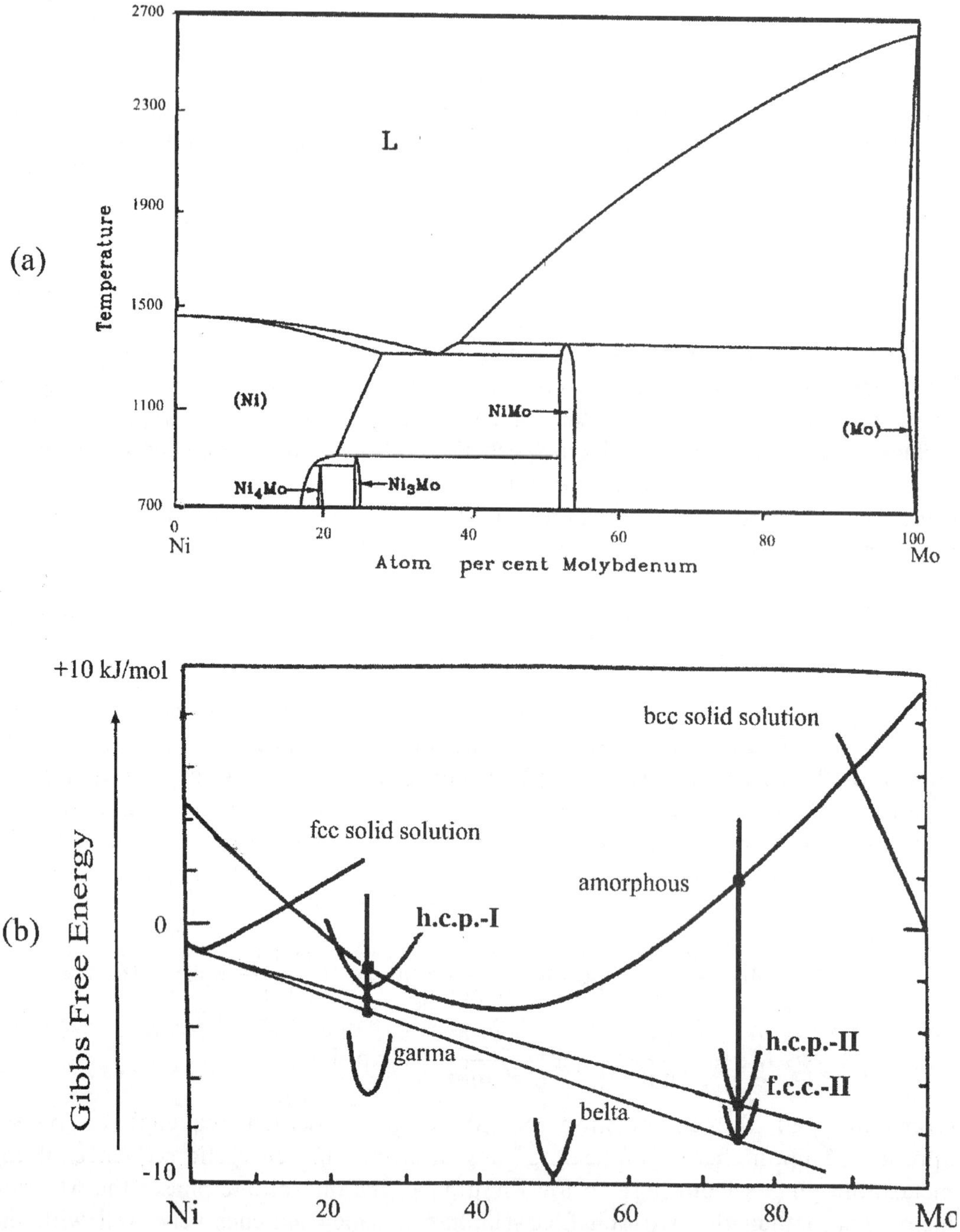

Figure 3. Equilibrium phase diagram of the Ni–Mo system (*a*) and calculated Gibbs free energy diagram of the Ni–Mo system (*b*).

films could produce Ni–Mo amorphous alloys, at least within an alloy composition range from 25 to 75 at.% Mo. It is of interest to note that such a composition range favouring metallic glass formation is quite broad in comparison with the fact that liquid melt quenching could only produce amorphous alloys within a narrow regime around the deep eutectic point(s). In the next section, the metallic glass-forming ability or glass-forming range will be further discussed for the binary metal systems characterized by either negative or positive ΔH_f.

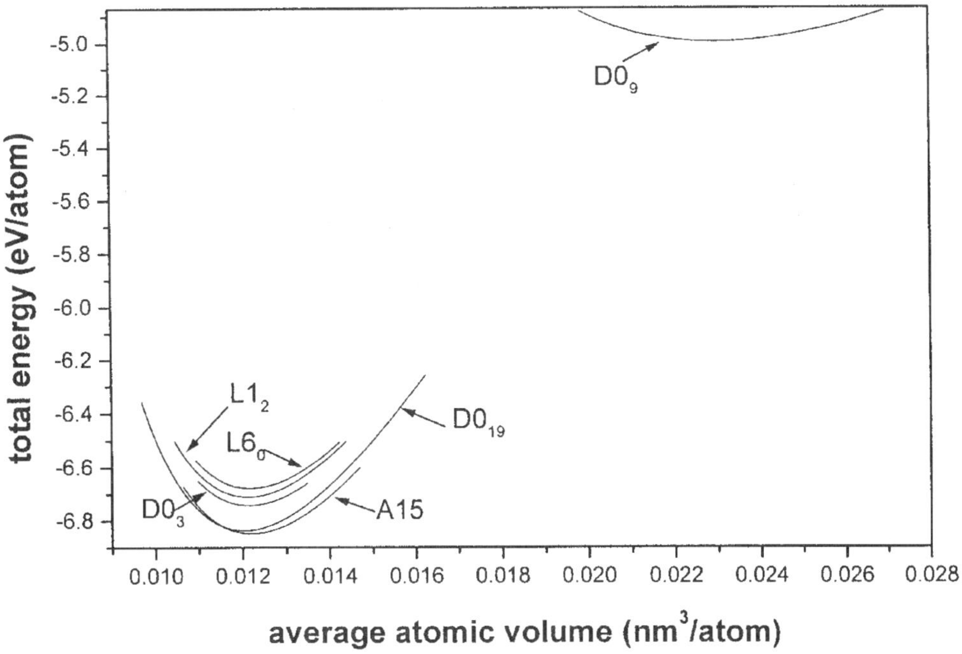

Figure 4. Calculated total energy versus lattice constant for an Ni_3Mo metastable phase with different possible structures.

Very recently, the authors' group has performed *ab initio* calculations for the MX phases of A_3B and AB_3 types in some representative binary metal systems using the Vienna *ab initio* simulation program (VASP) and the results also lend support to the relevance of the thermodynamic calculations. In the *ab initio* calculation, the exchange and correlation items were described by the specially defined functions proposed by Perdew and Zunger, in which the non-local corrections in the form of the generalized-gradient approximation of Perdew and Wang were added for an improved computation. The calculations were performed on a plane-wave basis, using fully non-local Vanderbilt–Kresse type ultrasoft pseudopotentials to describe the electron–ion interaction, which allowed the use of a moderate cutoff for the construction of the plane-wave basis for the transition metals. The integration in the Brillouin zone was done on special k points determined according to the Monckhorst–Pack scheme, which resulted in a mesh of 11 irreducible k points—enough for the calculation of simple structures [16, 70].

We now present the calculation results for the possible metastable state, corresponding to the Ni_3Mo phase, in the Ni–Mo system [71]. The total energies were calculated as a function of the lattice constant(s) for six relatively simple structures, i.e. $D0_{19}$, $D0_3$, $L1_2$, $A15$, $D0_9$ and $L6_0$, respectively. The c/a ratios of the $D0_{19}$ and $L6_0$ structures were optimized. Figure 4 exhibits the six calculated curves showing the correlation of the total energy versus the average atomic volume. One sees clearly from figure 4 that the increasing order of the relative structural stability for the possible Ni_3Mo phase is $D0_9$, $L6_0$, $L1_2$, $D0_3$, $D0_{19}$ and $A15$. It is evident that the $D0_9$, $L6_0$, $L1_2$ and $D0_3$ structures have higher minimum total energies than the $D0_{19}$ and $A15$ structures and are therefore unstable ones. Moreover, though the $A15$ structure has a lower minimum energy than $D0_{19}$, the cohesive energy difference between the two structures is very small, being about 0.012 eV per atom, i.e. only

Table 2. The calculated equilibrium cohesive properties (lattice constant a and c/a, atomic volume V, cohesive energy E_{min}) of Ni_3Mo in the *A15*, DO_{19}, DO_3, $L1_2$, $L6_0$ and DO_9 structures.

	A15	DO_{19}	DO_3	$L1_2$	$L6_0$	DO_9
a (Å)	4.60	2.58	5.80	3.65	3.84	4.51
C/a		1.62			0.86298	
V (Å^3 atom^{-1})	12.167	12.0469	12.1945	12.1568	12.2162	22.9335
E_{min} (eV atom^{-1})	−6.8474	−6.8359	−6.7419	−6.7101	−6.6781	−4.9954
E_f (eV atom^{-1})	−0.0783	−0.0668	0.0272	0.0590	0.0910	1.7737

about 0.17%, suggesting that both *A15* and DO_{19} structures are energetically possible for the A_3B type Ni–Mo system.

Additionally, the equilibrium cohesive properties of the above six structures in the Ni–Mo system were also calculated and are listed in table 2. It is commonly known that an energetic reference state at a specific alloy composition was refereed to a corresponding mechanical mixture of the constituent metals. The mechanical mixture of pure Ni and pure Mo with a chemical stoichiometry of 3:1 was therefore set as a reference state and its cohesion energy was calculated to be −6.7691 eV atom^{-1}. In the calculation, the formation energy of an alloy phase was defined to be the difference between the metastable and the reference states. Accordingly, the formation energies of the *A15* and DO_{19} structures were −0.0783 and −0.0668 eV atom^{-1}, respectively, which were lower than that of the reference state, suggesting that the metastable Ni_3Mo phase might be formed by SSR under an appropriate condition. In fact, the Ni_3Mo phase of h.c.p.-I structure was indeed obtained in $Ni_{72}Mo_{25}$ multilayers by thermal annealing, as mentioned above. Moreover, the lattice parameters of the h.c.p.-I phase were determined by SAD analysis to be $a_{hcp} = 2.64$ Å and $c_{hcp} = 4.28$ Å within an error of 4%. The composition ratio of the h.c.p.-I phase was determined by EDS analysis to be 74.6 at.% Ni, which was very close to the A_3B type [20]. In comparison, the lattice constant of the h.c.p.-I phase from *ab initio* calculation was $a_{hcp} = 2.58$ Å, which was in good agreement with the experimental value. Additionally, from the thermodynamic calculation the free energy of the h.c.p.-I phase was about 4 kJ mol^{-1} or 0.04 eV atom^{-1}, which was compatible with the *ab initio* calculation results that the free energy was around 7 kJ mol^{-1} or 0.07 eV atom^{-1}. Similar calculations were also performed for the case of $NiMo_3$ and the results also confirmed the corresponding MX phase observed in the experiments mentioned above.

Based on the above discussion, it is therefore concluded that the calculated free energy diagrams based on Miedema's model and Alonso's method are of relevance, at least, in their outlines.

5. Thermodynamic modelling of the amorphization transition in multilayers

5.1. *Definition and calculation of thermodynamic and kinetic factors*

We now describe a model proposed recently by the authors' group for predicting the possibility of solid-state amorphization (SSA) in binary metal systems with either negative or positive ΔH_f [72]. It is commonly recognized that two conditions have to be satisfied for an amorphous phase to be formed through a crystal-to-amorphous transition in solid-state reaction (SSR). Firstly, the amorphous phase formed should have a lower Gibbs free energy than the initial multilayered films. Secondly, a strong asymmetric diffusion of the system is necessary, i.e. atoms of one metal species diffuse very fast through the disordered interlayer and combine with the partner atoms, which diffuse slowly. As observed by many researchers, in those binary metal systems if a constituent metal exhibited anomalously fast diffusion in an amorphous alloy phase, it also exhibited abnormally fast diffusion in the parent crystalline metals. In other words, a large difference in diffusivity of the constituent metals would be favourable for SSA to take place. Accordingly, in thermodynamic modelling, two intrinsic parameters, i.e. a thermodynamic factor and a kinetic factor, were employed by the authors' group. The thermodynamic factor ΔF is defined to be the free energy difference between the final amorphous phase and the initial multilayers. Note that though the definition of ΔF is similar to that used by Kwak *et al.* [19], the calculation is quite different, i.e. the interfacial free energy for the multilayers is included in the authors' model. The kinetic factor κ is defined to reflect the difference in diffusivity of the constituent metals. It will be shown later that the kinetic factor is correlated not only with the atomic volume ratio but also with the melting points, which have considerable effect on the inter-diffusion between the metals; however, this has not been considered in previous models [8, 18, 19].

5.1.1. *Calculation of the thermodynamic factor*

The thermodynamic factor ΔF, which was defined as the difference between the Gibbs free energies of the final amorphous and the initial states in SSA, can be expressed by

$$\Delta F = \Delta G_{\text{amor}} - \Delta G_{\text{int}}. \tag{5.1}$$

The Gibbs free energy of the final state of an amorphous phase can be calculated by

$$\Delta G_{\text{amor}} = \Delta H_{\text{amor}} - T\Delta S_{\text{amor}}, \tag{5.2}$$

where ΔH_{amor} and ΔS_{amor} are the formation enthalpy and entropy of the amorphous phase, respectively, T is the annealing temperature and frequently assumed to be 600 K. Calculation, of ΔH_{amor} and ΔS_{amor} have been described in section 4 and the related equations are cited here again for convenience:

$$\Delta H_{\text{amor}} = \Delta H^{\text{c}} + \alpha(X_{\text{A}} T_{\text{m,A}} + X_{\text{B}} T_{\text{m,B}}) \tag{5.3}$$

$$\Delta S_{\text{amor}} = -R(X_{\text{A}} \ln X_{\text{A}} + X_{\text{B}} \ln X_{\text{B}}), \tag{5.4}$$

where R is the gas constant, and X_{A} and X_{B} are the atomic concentrations of the metals A and B in the alloy, respectively.

Calculation of the Gibbs free energy of the initial state is actually the calculation of the interfacial free energy stored in the as-deposited multilayered films. We employ here a more precise method for calculating the interfacial free energy than that used for the quick estimate described in section 4. Figure 5(*a*) shows schematically the real configuration of an interface in the multilayered films. Accordingly, the interfacial free energy consists of an enthalpy contribution from the solid phase at the interface, an entropy contribution from the amorphous phase at the interface and a chemical term reflecting the interaction between the metal [A] and amorphous {AB}.

$$\gamma_{[\text{A}]-\{\text{AB}\}} = \gamma^{\text{enthalpy}}_{[\text{A}]-\{\text{AB}\}} + \gamma^{\text{entropy}}_{[\text{A}]-\{\text{AB}\}} + \gamma^{\text{chemical}}_{[\text{A}]-\{\text{AB}\}} \tag{5.5}$$

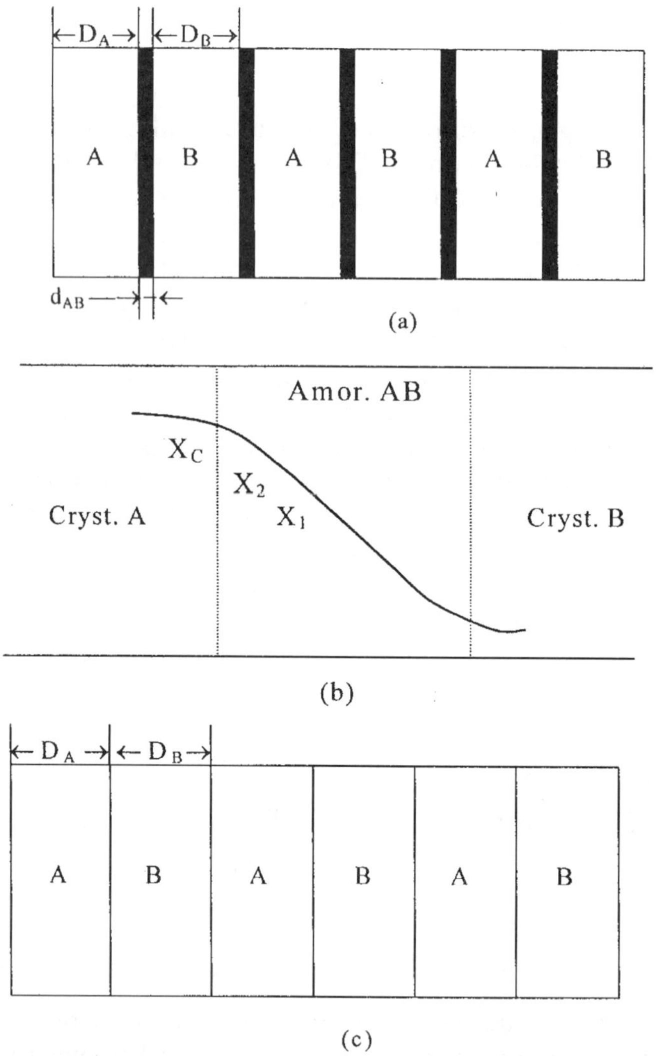

Figure 5. Configuration of A and B component metals in the multilayered states: (*a*) the multilayered films with a disordered interlayer between the crystalline metals; and (*b*) a schematic of the concentration changes of component A cross the disordered layer, showing the evolution of the interface accompanied by increasing A concentration in the interface from x_1 to x_2 then to x_C; (*c*) a schematic of the multilayered films with an incoherent interface used for calculating the maximum modulation wavelength for a binary metal system with positive heat of mixing.

and

$$\left.\begin{aligned} \gamma_{[A]-\{AB\}}^{\text{chemical}} &= \frac{f_{AB}\Delta H_{\text{amp}}}{C_0 V_A^{2/3}} \\ \gamma_{[A]-\{AB\}}^{\text{enthalpy}} &= \frac{\Delta H_A^{\text{fuse}}}{C_0 V_A^{2/3}} \\ \gamma_{[A]-\{AB\}}^{\text{entropy}} &= \frac{2RT}{C_0 V_{AB}^{2/3}}, \end{aligned}\right\} \tag{5.6}$$

where f_{AB} can be calculated by equations (4.6) and (4.7), accounting for the degree to which atoms of type A are surrounded by atoms of type B. ΔH_{amp} is the amplitude describing the magnitude of an electron redistribution interaction and can be calculated by equation (4.5). C_0 is a constant with value 4.5×10^8 and ΔH_A^{fuse} is the heat of fusion of metal A. The free energy of the initial state of the multilayered films can then be calculated by

$$\Delta G_{\text{ini}} = 2\left(r_{[A]-\{AB\}} + r_{[B]-\{AB\}} + d_{AB}\frac{\Delta G_{\{AB\}}}{V_{\{AB\}}}\right)\frac{V_{\{AB\}}}{(D_A + D_B)}. \tag{5.7}$$

Thus the thermodynamic factor is deduced to be

$$\Delta F = \Delta G_{\{AB\}} - 2\left(\gamma_{[A]-\{AB\}} + \gamma_{[B]-\{AB\}} + d_{AB}\frac{\Delta G_{\{AB\}}}{V_{\{AB\}}}\right)\frac{V_{\{AB\}}}{(D_A + D_B)}. \tag{5.8}$$

One notices from this equation that the thermodynamic factor is related to a parameter $D_A + D_B = \Lambda$, which is defined as the modulation wavelength, and the thickness of the disordered interlayer d_{AB}. Upon solid-state interfacial reaction, the interface between the disordered and crystalline layers advances towards the crystalline layers, thus resulting in an extension of the disordered interlayer as well as a reduction of the interfacial free energy. In other words, the growing of the amorphous interlayer was based on the cost of consuming the interfacial free energy. Figure 5(*b*) shows schematically the composition change of metal A across the interface during solid-state interfacial reaction in a binary metal system with a positive ΔH_f. When the interface between the disordered and crystalline layers advances accompanying a composition change from $A_{x_1}B_{1-x_1}$ to $A_{x_2}B_{1-x_2}$, the changing interfacial free energy can be calculated by

$$\Delta r_{[A]-\{AB\}} = r_{[A]-\{AB\}_2} - r_{[A]-\{AB\}_1}. \tag{5.9}$$

According to equations (5.5) and (5.6), only one item is left, i.e. the difference between the chemical terms expressed by

$$\Delta r_{[A]-\{AB\}} = \frac{[(f_{AB})_2 - (f_{AB})_1]\Delta H_{\text{amp}}}{C_0 V_A^{2/3}}. \tag{5.10}$$

As f_{AB} decreases with increasing concentration of A atoms, Δr is frequently negative and can thus serve as the driving force for the amorphization transition. The thickness change of the growing amorphous layer can accordingly be calculated by

$$\Delta d_{\{AB\}} = \frac{[(f_{AB})_1 - (f_{AB})_2]\Delta H_{\text{amp}} V_{\{AB\}}}{\Delta G^{\text{amor}} C_0 V_A^{2/3}}. \tag{5.11}$$

With the advance of the interface, the concentration of A atoms eventually approaches a critical value X_c, beyond which the crystalline solid solution is favoured and turns out to frustrate further growth of the amorphous layer. It is therefore concluded that the interfacial free energy can serve as the driving force for SSA until the composition of the interfacial layer between the disordered and crystalline layers reaches a critical concentration. The thickness limitation of the growing amorphous interlayer deduced from the calculation is in good agreement with the direct experimental observation reported by Kwon *et al.*, i.e., in the Cu–Ta bilayer sample, the growth of the amorphous Cu–Ta interlayer by thermal annealing is terminated at a thickness around 4–5 nm [29].

5.1.2. *Calculation of the maximum modulation wavelength*

According to the definition, the maximum modulation wavelength $\Lambda = D_A + D_B$ of a binary metal system corresponds to a value beyond which the thermodynamic factor cannot be negative in the system. In the calculation, an incoherent interface is considered because it had the highest interfacial free energy. Accordingly, the free energy of the incoherent interface can reasonably be calculated as the sum of the surface energies of the two constituent metals (see reference [11]):

$$\gamma_{[A]-[B]}^{\text{incoherent}} = \gamma_{[A]}^{0} + \gamma_{[B]}^{0}, \tag{5.12}$$

where γ_i^0 ($i = $ A or B) is the surface energy of A or B at 0 K. Figure 5(*c*) is a schematic configuration of A–B multilayered films with incoherent interfaces. The initial energetic state of a system with positive ΔH_f can be calculated by

$$\Delta G_{\text{ini}} = (\gamma_{[A]-[B]} + \gamma_{[B]-[A]})\frac{V_{\{AB\}}}{(D_A + D_B)}. \tag{5.13}$$

The final amorphous state can be calculated by

$$\Delta G_{\text{amor}} = \Delta G_{\{AB\}}, \tag{5.14}$$

where $V_{\{AB\}}$ is the volume of the amorphous phase formed, and $\Delta G_{\{AB\}}$ is the Gibbs free energy of the amorphous phase formed, which can be calculated by equation (5.2). For a system with positive ΔH_f, the free energy difference between the final amorphous and the initial states is then

$$\Delta F_{\max} = \Delta G_{\{AB\}} - (\gamma_{[A]-[B]} + \gamma_{[B]-[A]})\frac{V_{\{AB\}}}{\Lambda_{\max}}. \tag{5.15}$$

Assuming $X_A = X_B = 0.5$ and that ΔH^c has a small positive value, ΔF can be deduced to be approximately

$$\Delta F_{\max} = \tfrac{1}{2}\alpha_0(T_A + T_B)\frac{\Lambda_{\max}}{V_{\{AB\}}} - 2(r_{[A]}^0 + r_{[B]}^0). \tag{5.16}$$

Considering $V_{\{AB\}} \approx 0.5(V_A + V_B)$ and $\Delta F < 0$, the maximum modulation wavelength can be deduced to be

$$\Lambda_{\max} < \frac{0.57(r_{[A]}^0 + r_{[B]}^0)(V_A + V_B)}{T_A + T_B}. \tag{5.17}$$

Obviously, the maximum modulation wavelength is a parameter intrinsic to a binary metal system and has some correlation with the atomic volume as well as the melting points of the constituent metals.

5.1.3. *Calculation of the kinetic factor*

The kinetic factor κ is defined to reflect the difference in diffusivity of the constituent metals. Concerning the fast diffusion of one element into its partner, Bakker found that the data given in the literature on fast metal-impurity diffusion could be rationalized as [73]:

$$\ln\left(\frac{D_{\text{A in B}}^{\text{A}}}{D_{\text{self}}^{\text{B}}}\right)_{T_{\text{B}}^{\text{fuse}}} = -\alpha\left(\frac{V_{\text{A}}^{\text{eff}}}{V_{\text{B}}}\right) + \beta, \tag{5.18}$$

where α and β are two constants for the metal B, $D^{A}_{A\ in\ B}$ and D^{B}_{self} are the impurity-diffusion and self-diffusion coefficients at the melting point of the metal B, and V^{eff}_{A} is the effective volume of A in the matrix of the metal B with

$$V^{eff}_{A} = V_{A} - \Delta \bar{V}^{0}_{A\ in\ B}, \tag{5.19}$$

where $\Delta \bar{V}^{0}_{A\ in\ B}$ is the volume correction per mole of A, if A atoms are fully surrounded by the dissimilar B atoms, and is given by

$$\Delta V^{0}_{A\ in\ B} = P_{V} V^{2/3}_{A} (\Delta\phi^{*}) \left[\frac{(n^{A}_{WS})^{-1} - (n^{B}_{WS})^{-1}}{(n^{-1/3}_{WS})_{av}} \right], \tag{5.20}$$

where P_V is an empirical constant, being 3 cm (density unit)$^{2/3}$ per volt. According to the general Arrhenius relation

$$D = D_0 \exp\left[-\left(\frac{Q}{RT} \right) \right], \tag{5.21}$$

where $Q = Q^0 + pV$ and Q^0 is the activation energy at an atmospheric pressure ($p \sim 0$), V is the activation volume, R is the gas constant and D_0 is a pre-exponential factor. Based on equations (5.18)–(5.21), it is deduced that

$$\left(\frac{D^{A}_{A\ in\ B}}{D^{B}_{self}} \right)_{T} = \exp\left[\beta - \alpha \frac{V^{eff}_{A}}{V_{B}} + (\gamma_A T_A - \gamma_B T_B) \left(\frac{1}{T_B} - \frac{1}{T} \right) \right], \tag{5.22}$$

where $\gamma_i = Q_i / RT_i$ ($i = $ A, B) is nearly a constant for a given crystal structure and bond-type. To normalize the extent for a variety of binary metal systems, a kinetic factor κ is defined to reflect the difference in diffusivity of the constituent metals A and B:

$$\kappa = 1 - \frac{\alpha}{\beta} \frac{V^{eff}_{A}}{V_{B}} + \frac{\gamma_A T_A - \gamma_B Y_B}{\beta} \left(\frac{1}{T_B} - \frac{1}{T} \right). \tag{5.23}$$

Based on the data summarized in the literature [74], if B is a rare-earth metal, κ can be approximated by

$$\kappa = 1 - \frac{3}{2} \frac{V^{eff}_{A}}{V_{B}} + (T_A - 2T_B) \left(\frac{1}{T_B} - \frac{1}{T} \right). \tag{5.24}$$

If A and B are both transition metals, κ can be approximated by

$$\kappa = 1 - \frac{V^{eff}_{A}}{V_{B}} + (T_B - T_A) \left(\frac{1}{T} - \frac{1}{T_B} \right). \tag{5.25}$$

As discussed above, the greater the kinetic factor, the easier the situation for SSA to take place in a binary metal system. From equations (5.23), (5.24) and (5.25), it is obvious that not only the atomic volume but also the melting points of the constituent metals would play significant roles in influencing the possibility and the kinetic aspects of SSA.

5.2. *Prediction of solid-state amorphization*

We now present the results of calculating the thermodynamic factor ΔF and the kinetic facor κ for the binary metal systems in which solid-state reaction (SSR) has so far been studied. These systems consist of a rare earth and transition metals or two transition metals and the calculation results are listed in tables 3 and 4, respectively. In addition, table 5 lists the calculation results for binary metal systems

Table 3. The parameters used in the calculation of the kinetic factor κ of those rare earth-transition metal systems in which SSA has been achieved, and the calculation results (in the calculation, the atomic concentration is $A_{50}B_{50}$, the wavelength $(D_A + D_B)$ is 10 nm and the disordered interfacial layer is 0.5 nm thick.)

	V_A^{eff}/V_B (cm^3)	ϕ_A^*/ϕ_B^* (V)	$(n_{WS}^{1/3})_A/(n_{WS}^{1/3})_B$ (density unit)$^{1/3}$	$\Delta H_A^{fuse}/\Delta H_B^{fuse}$ (kJ mol^{-1})	T_A/T_B (K)	κ	ΔF (kJ mol^{-1})	Reference
Au–La	7.24/22.53	5.15/3.17	1.57/1.18	12.7/10.1	1338/1193	0.97	−43	[8]
Cu–Er	6.2/18.49	4.45/3.22	1.47/1.23	13/17.2	1358/1795	2.4	−15	[30]
Ni–Ce	3.79/20.69	5.22/3.18	1.75/1.19	17.6/8.88	1726/1071	0.94	−42	[31]
Ni–Er	4.19/18.49	5.2/3.22	1.75/1.23	17.6/17.2	1726/1795	2.45	−22	[30]

Table 4. The parameters used in the calculation for the kinetic factor κ of those transition metal-transition metal systems, in which SSA has been observed, and the calculation results (in the calculation, the atomic concentration is $A_{50}B_{50}$, the wavelength $(D_A + D_B)$ is 10 nm and the disordered interfacial layer is 0.5 nm thick).

	V_A^{eff}/V_B (cm^3)	ϕ_A^*/ϕ_B^* (V)	$(n_{WS}^{1/3})_A/(n_{WS}^{1/3})_B$ (density unit)$^{1/3}$	$\Delta H_A^{fuse}/\Delta H_B^{fuse}$ (kJ mol^{-1})	T_A/T_B (K)	κ	ΔF (kJ mol^{-1})	Reference
Au–Ta	10.33/10.9	5.15/4.05	1.57/1.63	12.7/31.4	1338/3287	2.7	−22	[22]
Au–Y	7.63/19.95	5.15/3.2	1.57/1.21	12.7/17.2	1338/1799	2.34	−47	[38]
Co–Zr	5.75/14.1	5.1/3.45	1.75/1.41	15.2/23	1768/2125	1.02	−31	[40]
Fe–Zr	6.16/6.16	4.93/3.45	1.77/1.41	14.9/23	1809/2125	0.94	−16	[42]
Hf–Ni	5.81/13.6	5.2/3.6	1.75/1.45	17.6/25.1	1726/2500	1.55	−33	[43]
Mo–Ni	6.6/9.4	5.2/4.65	1.75/1.77	17.6/27.6	1726/2890	1.84	−4	[20]
Nb–Ni	6.45/10.8	5.2/4.05	1.75/1.64	17.6/27.2	1726/2740	1.72	−23	[44]
Ni–Ti	6.15/10.8	5.2/3.8	1.75/1.52	17.6/20.9	1726/1943	0.68	−31	[18, 75]
Ni–Zr	6.2/18.49	5.2/3.45	1.75/1.41	17.6/23	1726/2125	2.4	−38	[45, 18]

Table 5. The parameters used in the calculation for the kinetic factor κ and thermodynamic driving force ΔF of binary metal systems with positive heat of mixing, and the calculation results (the wavelength $(D_A + D_B)$ is 5 nm and the atomic concentrations are $Cu_{30}Ta_{70}$, $Cu_{60}W_{40}$, $Mo_{50}Y_{50}$ and $Nb_{30}Y_{70}$, respectively).

	V_A^{eff}/V_B (cm^3)	ϕ_A^*/ϕ_B^* (V)	$(n_{WS}^{1/3})_A/(n_{WS}^{1/3})_B$ (density unit)$^{1/3}$	$\Delta H_A^{fuse}/\Delta H_B^{fuse}$ (kJ mol^{-1})	T_A/T_B (K)	$\gamma_{[A]}^0/\gamma_{[B]}^0$ (mJ m^{-2})	κ	ΔF (kJ mol^{-1})	Reference
Cu–Ta	6.02/10.9	4.45/4.05	1.47/1.63	13/31.4	1358/3287	1825/3150	2.97	−13	[21, 29]
Cu–W	6.92/9.55	4.45/4.80	1.47/1.81	13/35.3	1358/3653	1825/3675	3.06	−8	[25]
Mo–Y	7.19/19.95	4.65/3.2	1.77/1.21	27.6/17.2	2890/1799	3000/1125	0.93	−1.2	[10]
Nb–Y	9.65/19.95	4.05/3.2	1.64/1.21	27.2/17.2	2740/1799	2700/1125	0.79	−7.8	[27]

with positive ΔH_f. It can be deduced from the data listed in tables 3, 4 and 5 that when the kinetic factor κ is greater than a critical value around 0.6 together with a negative thermodynamic factor ΔF, SSA is likely to take place.

We now apply the defined thermodynamic and kinetic factors to discuss the situations for the Mo–Ni, Au–Ta and Cu–Ta systems, in which SSA has been predicted not to be favoured by the previously proposed criteria. Firstly, in the Mo–Ni system with the less negative ΔH_f of $-11\,kJ\,mol^{-1}$, the ΔF and κ factors were calculated for $Mo_{50}Ni_{50}$ multilayered films consisting of eight layers with a total thickness of 40 nm and they were $-4\,kJ\,mol^{-1}$ and 1.84, respectively, both favouring SSA to take place. Experimentally, thermal annealing of the $Mo_{50}Ni_{50}$ multilayered films at 400°C for 1.5 hours did result in SSA and the formation of an amorphous phase [20]. Secondly, the Au–Ta system has a large negative ΔH_f of $-49\,kJ\,mol^{-1}$, yet the two constituent metals have almost identical atomic sizes, i.e. 0.144 and 0.143 nm for Au and Ta, respectively. However, Au and Ta have a large difference in melting point, i.e. 1338 and 3287 K for Au and Ta, respectively. As a result, the calculation results show a negative ΔF of $-22\,kJ\,mol^{-1}$ together with a large κ of 2.7, suggesting that SSA is still favoured. Experimentally, it is shown that the $Au_{23}Ta_{77}$ multilayered films turn into an amorphous state upon annealing at 350°C for 0.5 hours [22]. Thirdly, although the Cu–Ta system has a small positive ΔH_f of $+3\,kJ\,mol^{-1}$, the parameters ΔF and κ for the properly designed $Cu_{30}Ta_{70}$ multilayered films were calculated to be $-9\,kJ\,mol^{-1}$ and 2.97, respectively. In experiments, SSA was indeed observed in $Cu_{28}Ta_{72}$ multilayered films upon annealing at about 400°C for 0.5 hours [21] as well as in the cross-sectional Cu–Ta bilayer samples reported recently [29].

The next question is to find out what would happen in systems with a positive ΔH_f and a small value of κ. We performed the calculation for the systems Fe–Cu and Co–Cu. When the modulation wavelengths were designed to be 4 nm, the initial free energy stored in the Fe–Cu and Co–Cu multilayered films could be higher than that of the amorphous phase, i.e. ΔF could be negative. However, the kinetic factors were calculated to be around 0.54 and 0.45 for the Fe–Cu and Co–Cu systems, respectively, suggesting SSA would probably not take place in either system. The predictions were compatible with the experimental observations reported so far [76]. Interestingly, however, an amorphous phase was obtained in Fe–Cu multilayered films upon room temperature xenon ion beam mixing (IBM) [77]. In IBM, ion irradiation can induce intermixing between the metal layers through a process of dynamic atomic collision, regardless of the restriction, which could not be overcome by only thermal activation as in the process of SSR described above.

Based on above discussion and calculation, it is predicted that a large value of the kinetic factor κ (for example, greater than a critical value around 0.6, based on currently available data) together with a negative ΔF is required for SSA to take place. It should be noted that the above calculation of the interfacial free energy was based on the assumption that the solid–solid interface is incoherent, or the interlayer is in a disordered state. It is known that in some cases, the solid–solid interface can be coherent or semi-coherent, for which the calculation of the interfacial free energy would be quite different. However, under such a situation SSA would hardly take place—as shown by both experimental studies [78] and molecular dynamics simulations [14] in some binary metal systems. Consequently, the above calculation and prediction would not cover such specific situations with coherent or semi-coherent interfaces.

5.3. *Metallic-glass-forming range upon solid-state reaction of multilayers*

As mentioned above, SSA has so far been observered in about 28 binary metal systems with either positive or negative ΔH_f by two experimental methods, i.e. thermal annealing of multilayered films and bilayer samples. Using a scheme of metal–metal multilayers, SSR is able to produce metallic glasses in thin-film form. In negative ΔH_f systems, the driving force comes from the ΔH_f itself. Generally speaking, the composition range favouring metallic glass formation can extend from the central portion, where the free energy of an amorphous state has its minimum, to a broad composition range close to the terminal solidus. While in positive ΔH_f systems, the driving force originates from excess interfacial free energy. The composition range favouring metallic glass formation depends on the amount of the interfacial free energy, which is related to the fraction of the interfacial atoms in the films. With increase of the fraction of the interfacial atoms, the glass-forming range (GFR) can extend from somewhere outside the two terminal solidi to the central portion. These were clearly illustrated in figure 2 for the Nb–Y system. By further increasing the fraction of interfacial atoms in multilayered films it is possible, for some binary metal systems with positive ΔH_f, to have the initial energetic state of the films surpass that of the amorphous phase in a broad composition range including the central portion, where the amorphous phase has its maximum free energy. Taking the Mo–Y system ($\Delta H_f = +35\,\mathrm{kJ\,mol^{-1}}$) as an example, the variation of the driving force as a function of the fraction of the interfacial atoms versus the total number of atom in the multilayered films is clearly illustrated in figure 6. In the figure, the calculated free energy diagram of the Mo–Y system includes a free energy curve for the amorphous phase and three free energy curves for three sets of multilayered films consisting of 9, 11 and 19 layers in a total fixed thickness of 42 nm, corresponding to fractions of interfacial atoms of 8.1, 10.0 and 18.1 at.%, respectively. Based on the calculated free energy diagram, composition ranges favouring metallic glass formation for three sets of multilayered films were predicted and are listed in table 6. SSR experiments were properly conducted with the designed Mo–Y multilayered films and the results were in excellent agreement with the predictions, which are also listed in table 6. It is worthwhile mentioning that the SSR results listed in table 6 include both 'Yes' and 'No', meaning that the corresponding SSR

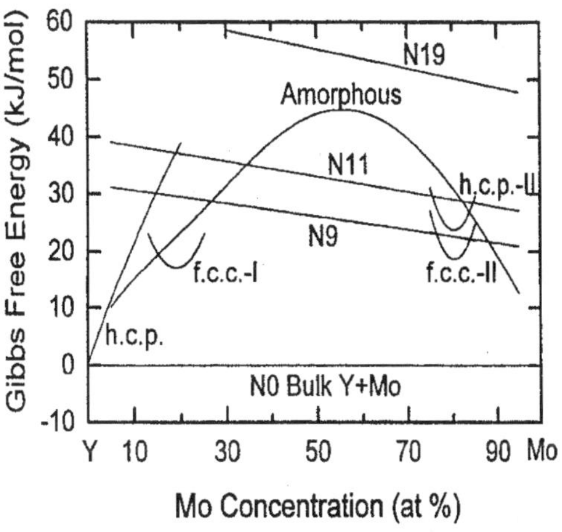

Figure 6. Calculated Gibbs free energy diagram for the Mo–Y system. *N* stands for the number of layers in the Mo–Y multilayered films.

Table 6. Prediction and experimental results of metallic glass formation in Y–Mo multilayered films upon solid-state reaction (SSR).

Layer number	Fraction, α (at.%)		Composition				
			$Y_{80}Mo_{20}$	$Y_{60}Mo_{40}$	$Y_{50}Mo_{50}$	$Y_{40}Mo_{60}$	$Y_{20}Mo_{80}$
19	18.1	Pridicted	Yes	Yes	Yes	Yes	Yes
		SSR Exper.	Yes	Yes	Yes	Yes	Yes
11	10.0	Pridicted	Yes	Yes	No	No	Yes
		SSR Exper.	Yes	Yes	No	No	Yes
9	8.1	Pridicted	Yes	No	No	No	Yes
		SSR Exper.	Yes	No	No	No	Yes

experiments were both performed. Apparently, the experimental results of 'Yes' and 'No' together firmly confirmed that in positive ΔH_f systems SSA was driven by the interfacial free energy and that the amorphization transition behaviour depended directly on the designed fraction of interfacial atoms as well as on the overall composition of the multilayered films. In other words, through properly designing the multilayered films, it is possible to produce metallic glasses within a broad composition range in binary metal systems with positive ΔH_f.

5.4. *Comparison of the amorphization transition in multilayers upon solid-state reaction and ion irradiation*

We now discuss the comparison of the amorphization transition in metal–metal multilayers upon solid-state reaction (SSR) and ion beam mixing (IBM) by choosing a representative system, i.e. the Y–Zr system characterized by a positive $\Delta H_f = +14\,\text{kJ mol}^{-1}$. The Y–Zr multilayers were designed to have a total thickness of 45 nm and consist of 9 layers or of 8 interfaces. The Gibbs free energy diagram for the Y–Zr system was accordingly calculated and is shown in figure 7. One sees clearly that in the central composition regime, the free energy of the amorphous phase is still higher than that of the initial state of the multilayered films with an overall composition of $Y_{50}Zr_{50}$, corresponding to the case of thermodynamic factor $\Delta F > 0$. Carefully performed thermal annealing experiments failed to observe an amorphization transition, and this is compatible with the prediction. In contrast, when $Y_{50}Zr_{50}$ multilayered films were subjected to 200 keV xenon IBM at room temperature to a dose of 5×10^{14} Xe cm^{-2}, an amorphization transition did take place and resulted in the formation of a uniform $Y_{50}Zr_{50}$ amorphous alloy [79]. Referring again to the free energy diagram in figure 7, one sees that there is a small energy gap between the amorphous phase and the initial energetic state of the $Y_{50}Zr_{50}$ multilayered films. This is why SSR could not drive an amorphization transition. However in IBM, which is a dynamic process far from equilibrium, some of the irradiation energy can elevate the energetic state of the multilayered films high enough to overcome such an energy gap. In other words, the amorphous $Y_{50}Zr_{50}$ alloy was formed by interface assisted IBM.

Another point worth mentioning is the comparison of the glass-forming ability (GFA) and glass-forming range (GFR) of a binary metal system by IBM and other

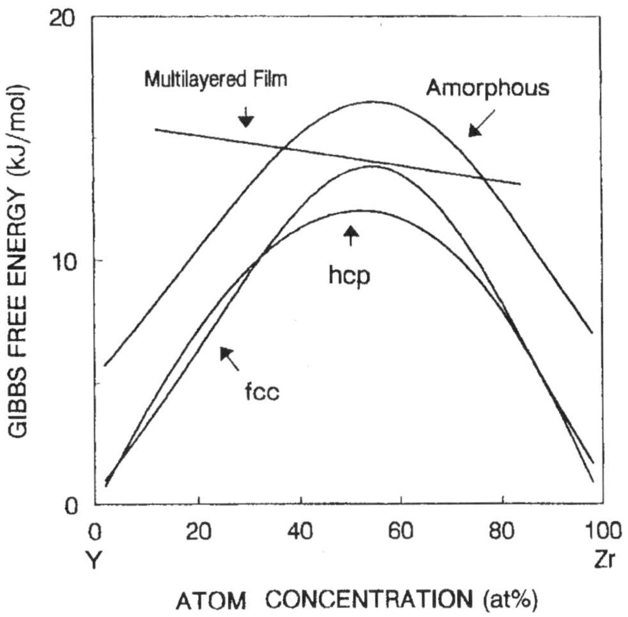

Figure 7. Calculated Gibbs free energy diagram (at 300 K) for the Y–Zr system.

metallic glass-producing techniques. Extensive experimental data showed that, in most of the systems studied so far, IBM was able to produce metallic glasses in a broad composition range, extending from the central portion towards close to the terminal solidus. Consequently, the GFR of the system could be approximately within the whole composition range minus the two maximum solid solubilities, and it is frequently broader than those revealed by other metallic glass-producing techniques [17].

6. Methods of molecular dynamics simulation

To study the issues of alloy phase formation and transition on an atomic scale, molecular dynamics (MD) and Monte Carlo (MC) simulations are two major methods that have been frequently employed so far. An advantage of the MD method over MC is that MD simulation gives information concerning the time dependence and the magnitude of fluctuations of position and momentum variables away from their equilibrium values, whereas MC simulation deals only with the position variables. In the present review, we present mainly the MD simulation results obtained in some representative binary metal systems concerning the atomistic mechanism of solid-state interfacial reaction as well as the calculation of the critical solid solubility and glass-forming range (GFR) of the respective systems. Concerning the methodology of simulations for condensed matter and materials physics, the reader is referred to those monographs, literature and conference proceedings [13, 80, 81].

To perform MD simulation in a binary metal system, a realistic potential for the system is necessary and should first be constructed. Previously, a pair potential has frequently been adopted. In the pair potential, the interaction between the two atoms is dependent on their positions without association with the surrounding atoms, leading to the following two distinct drawbacks not allowing for correctly simulating the reality. One is that it always overestimates the unrelaxed vacancy formation energy and the other is that it invariably reproduces a Cauchy pressure $(C_{12}-C_{44})/2$ to be zero, which does not apply to most of the metals. In the mid 1980s, a new scheme of many-body potentials was developed [75, 82, 83]. In that scheme, the total energy of a system is composed of a core–core repulsive term and an embedded energy. The former is a pair function of the atomic distance between atoms i and j, whereas the latter is a function of the host electronic density at atom i contributed by the surrounding atoms j. Consequently, the interaction of the two atoms depends not only on the atomic positions but also on the surrounding atoms, thus overcoming the above-mentioned drawbacks of the pair potential. Meanwhile, MD simulation with an n-body potential is still able to keep the capability of fast computation.

6.1. *Parrinello–Rahman's molecular dynamics scheme*

It is known that Anderson firstly proposed how the MD calculation could be modified to study a condensed matter system under a constant pressure by introducing the volume of the system as an additional dynamical variable [84]. Parrinello and Rahman then generalized Andersen's idea to develop a powerful scheme for studying the crystal structures and their relations to the pair potential [85, 86]. In this scheme, the edges of the MD cell $\vec{a}, \vec{b}$ and $\vec{c}$ are set to be time dependent. Let $\underline{h}$ be the matrix formed by $\{\vec{a}, \vec{b}, \vec{c}\}$; $\Omega = \det \underline{h} \equiv \vec{a} \cdot \vec{b} \times \vec{c}$ will then be the volume of the MD cell containing, say N particles, and it will vary with time. The position of particle i will be $\vec{r}_i = \xi_i \vec{a} + \eta_i \vec{b} + \zeta_i \vec{c} = \underline{h}\vec{s}_i$, where $\vec{s}_i$ has components (ξ_i, η_i, ζ_i) each going from 0 to 1. Using a dot and a prime to denote the time derivative and the transpose, respectively, the Lagrangian of the system containing N particles can be written as

$$L = \tfrac{1}{2}\sum_i^N m_i \dot{\vec{s}}_i' \underline{G} \dot{\vec{s}}_i - \sum_i^N \sum_{j>i}^N \varphi(r_{ij}) + \tfrac{1}{2} W \mathrm{Tr}\,(\underline{\dot{h}}'\underline{\dot{h}}) - p_{\mathrm{ext}}\Omega, \tag{6.1}$$

where $\underline{G} = \underline{h}'\underline{h}$, $r_{ij}^2 = (\vec{s}_i - \vec{s}_j)'\underline{G}(\vec{s}_i - \vec{s}_j)$, p_{ext} denotes the externally applied hydrostatic pressure, $\varphi(r)$ is the pair potential, and the kinetic term associated with time variation of $\underline{h}$ has a constant of proportionality W, which has the dimension of mass.

The Lagrangian equations of motion can easily be written as

$$\ddot{\vec{s}}_i = m_i^{-1} \sum_{j \neq i}^N \chi(r_{ij})(\vec{s}_i - \vec{s}_j) - \underline{G}^{-1}\underline{\dot{G}}\dot{\vec{s}}_i, \quad i = 1, 2, \ldots, N \tag{6.2}$$

$$\underline{\ddot{h}} = W^{-1}(\underline{\pi} - p_{\mathrm{ext}})\underline{\sigma}, \tag{6.3}$$

where

$$\chi(r) \equiv -\frac{1}{r}\frac{\mathrm{d}\varphi}{\mathrm{d}r}$$

the matrix $\underline{\sigma}$ has the elements

$$\sigma_{ij} \equiv \frac{\delta\Omega}{\delta h_{ij}}$$

the matrix $\underline{\pi}$ is given in dyadic tensor notation by

$$\Omega \overleftrightarrow{\pi} = \sum_i^N m_i \vec{v}_i \vec{v}_i + \sum_i^N \sum_{j>i}^N \chi(r_{ij})(\vec{r}_i - \vec{r}_j)(\vec{r}_i - \vec{r}_j), \tag{6.4}$$

where the vector $\vec{v}_i$ stands for $\underline{h}\dot{\vec{s}}_i$. Equations (6.2) and (6.3) govern the dynamics of a system consisting of N particles in a periodically repeating MD cell, which varies with time in both shape and volume. These equations of motion are solved numerically using a fourth-order predictor–corrector algorithm due to Gear with a time step $t = 5 \times 10^{-15}$ s.

6.2. *Formalisms for constructing n-body potentials*

It was mentioned above that to conduct MD simulation in a binary metal system a proved realistic potential describing the atomic interactions of the system is necessary. Previously, pair potentials have been widely used in computer simulations [87, 88], though they have some drawbacks. In the last fifteen years, various models for construction of many-body potentials have been developed [75, 82, 83]. For example, in 1983 Daw and Baskes proposed an approach called the embedded-atom method (EAM), in which the interaction between the two atoms was correlated not only to the inter-atomic distance but also to the local environment around the atom [82]. The basic idea of EAM can be interpreted under the framework of density-functional theory, from which the energy required to place an impurity atom into a lattice is determined solely by the electron density at that particular site without considering the origin of the electron density [83, 89–91]. In EAM, the total energy of an n-atom system is written as

$$E_{\text{tot}} = \sum_i F_i(\rho_i) + \sum_{i>j} \varphi(r_{ij}). \tag{6.5}$$

In this equation, r_{ij} is the distance between the atoms i and j, E_{tot} is the total energy, $\varphi(r_{ij})$ is the pair-wise interaction potential between atoms i and j, $F_i(\rho_i)$ is the embedded energy, and ρ_i is the total electron density at atom i due to all other atoms described by

$$\rho_i = \sum_{j(\neq i)} f(r_{ij}). \tag{6.6}$$

In this equation, $f(r_{ij})$ is an electron density for atom i contributed by atom j. In the original EAM model proposed by Daw and Baskes, the embedding energy F and repulsive item φ were given in the form of spline functions, i.e. in a numerical form [83]. Meanwile, some researchers have constructed various EAM potential models with some modifications [92–97]. For instance, Cai *et al.* proposed an analytical EAM model that has successfully been employed mainly for the fcc metals [97]. Accordingly, the embedding function was taken as the universal form suggested by Banerjea *et al.* [98], which can be written

$$F(\rho) = -F_0\left[1 - \ln\left(\frac{\rho}{\rho_e}\right)^n\right]\left(\frac{\rho}{\rho_e}\right)^n + F_1\left(\frac{\rho}{\rho_e}\right). \tag{6.7}$$

In this equation, $F_0 = E_c - E_v^f$, E_c and E_v^f are the cohesive energy and vacancy formation energy, respectively. Additionally, ρ_e represents the host electron density at equilibrium and a linear term F_1 is added to the original formula as an adjustable parameter. The atomic electron density $f(r)$ and pair potential $\varphi(r)$ are respectively defined as

$$f(r) = f_e \exp\left[-\chi(r - r_e)\right] \tag{6.8}$$

and

$$\varphi(r) = -\alpha[1 + \beta(r/r_a - 1)] \exp\left[-\beta(r/r_a - 1)\right]. \tag{6.9}$$

From the above equations, there are in total five potential parameters (χ, α, β, F_1 and r_a) for the atomic interaction. These potential parameters for a specific metal are determined by minimizing the square-root deviation between the calculated and experimentally determined physical properties, such as the equilibrium lattice constant, cohesive energy, bulk modulus, elastic constants and vacancy formation energy, etc. In fitting, the cut-off distance is taken as $1.65a_0$ (a_0 is the lattice constant). Moreover, like other EAM potentials, the reproduced total energy of a system under Cai's model follows a universal equation of state formulated by Rose *et al.* [99]. The physical properties away from equilibrium were therefore already fitted and the potentials for pure metals can be applied directly to the metallic alloys. Generally, to testify further the relevance of the potential developed, some other physical properties should be reproduced and compared with those from experimental results and/or theoretical calculations, such as surface energy, formation energy and volume of defects, phonon dispersion curves and some dynamic properties like melting point, thermal expansion coefficient, etc.

In addition to the EAM potential, another two kinds of n-body potentials have been proposed for the transition metals, i.e. the Finnis–Sinclair (FS) [75] and tight-binding (TB) potentials [100]. The major difference between these two potentials and EAM is to do with the derivation and interpretation of ρ as well as the embedding function F. The FS and TB models are both based on the tight-binding theory of cohesion by assuming that the band energy is the sum of the occupied one-electron energy in a band, which is proportional to the square root of the second moment of its density of states (for transition metals, mainly the d-band density of states) [101, 102]. The density of the states can be expressed as a function of distance r_{ij}. The difference between the FS and TB models is related to the specific function forms applied. According to Finnis and Sinclair, the total energy can be written as

$$E_{\text{tot}} = \sum_{i>j} \varphi(r_{ij}) - \sum_i \left[\sum_{j \neq i} A^2 (r_{ij} - d)^2 \right]^{1/2} \tag{6.10}$$

$$\varphi(r) = (r - c)^2 \cdot (c_0 + c_1 r + c_2 r^2), \tag{6.11}$$

where d and c are the cut-off distances for the cohesive and repulsive items, respectively [75]. Following the FS formalism, some modifications have been proposed to use a polynomial form of distance for the F and φ functions [103–106]. The FS potentials have been employed to study the physical properties of some bcc and fcc metals as well as their alloys in a relatively satisfactory way, though it still has some shortcomings, e.g. the derived thermal expansion parameters were much smaller than the realistic values [104].

The tight-binding or so-called second-moment approximation of the tight-binding scheme was proposed by Tomanek *et al.* [100] and has been employed for a large number of transition metals and alloys [107, 108]. In the tight-binding (TB) model, the cohesive and repulsive items of the total energy are exponential functions of the atomic distance. In an alloy system with two constituent metals α and β, the total energy is expressed by

$$E = \sum_i \left\{ \sum_{j \neq i} A_{\alpha\beta} \exp\left[-p_{\alpha\beta}\left(\frac{r_{ij}}{d_{\alpha\beta}} - 1 \right) \right] - \sqrt{\sum_{j \neq i} \xi_{\alpha\beta}^2 \exp\left[-2q_{\alpha\beta}\left(\frac{r_{ij}}{d_{\alpha\beta}} - 1 \right) \right]} \right\}, \tag{6.12}$$

where r_{ij} is the distance between atoms i and j and $d_{\alpha\beta}$ is the nearest-neighbour distance in the crystal structure. The first pair potential term represents a repulsive Born–Mayer interaction and the second many-body attractive term does represent the second-moment approximation of the tight-binding band energy. Accordingly, many n-body potentials have been developed for a number of fcc and hcp transition metals. For the bcc metals, however, the TB potential was found to be inadequate in deriving those established physical features of the metallic bonding.

6.3. *Simulation models and structural characterization methods*

In MD simulations, three categories of simulation model were constructed for studying the respective issues of interest, i.e. the sandwich model, bilayer model and solid-solution model. The details of construction of the models and the corresponding periodic conditions will be described in sections 7 and 8 when they are used to study the atomistic mechanisms of solid-state interfacial reaction.

To trace the atomic movement during solid-state interfacial reaction, the most direct and convenient way is to project the distributions of atoms onto a plane, e.g. the x–z plane, at various stages of interfacial reaction. In addition, to trail closely the detailed reaction process, three quantitative methods were implemented to calculate the degree of disordering, i.e. the density profile, the planar structure factor and the pair-correlation function.

In practice, the typical density profiles of each species along the z-direction $\rho_\alpha(z)$ were calculated during the interfacial reaction. The calculated $\rho_\alpha(z)$ allows one to define the position of a single atomic layer and enables the evaluation of the local (i.e. restricted to the single layer) thermodynamic, compositional and structural properties [109].

The planar structure factor, namely the Fourier transformation of the density in each crystallographic plane parallel to the x–y plane, was defined, according to Phillpot *et al.* [110], as

$$S(\mathbf{k}, z) = \left\langle \frac{1}{N_z^2} \left| \sum_{j=1}^{N_z} \exp(i\mathbf{k} \cdot \mathbf{r}_j) \right|^2 \right\rangle, \tag{6.13}$$

where z labels the crystal plane to which the point $\mathbf{r}_j$ belonged at the initial configuration, and $\mathbf{k}$ was an arbitary vector of the planar reciprocal lattice. In the following discussion, $\mathbf{k} = (2\pi/a)(1, 1)$ would be used and a is the lattice constant. Accordingly, $S = 1$ refers to an entirely ordered crystal, while $S = 0$ stands for a completely disordered state [110]. In practice, the atomic planes were defined as the original crystal planes and the planar structure factors were used to indicate the degrees of disordering in the corresponding atomic planes. The variation of the planar structure factor as a function of time therefore gave an indication of the ordering change in each atomic plane during the interfacial reaction.

The pair-correlation function analysis was employed to identify the structure of the models, as this method was recognized to give a convincing evidence for the formation of an amorphous alloy. For instance, in the bilayer model, the structure of a local region grown from the interface was analysed by sampling those atoms situated in the region of interest. To calculate the pair-correlation function $g(r)$, each atom in turn was imagined to be at the centre of a series of concentric spheres. The atomic density was defined to be the number of atoms in each spherical shell divided by the volume of that shell, taking into consideration those periodic image atoms located outside the block. In MD simulation, the results were obtained by averaging over all the atoms within 200 time steps. The $g(r)$ can then be obtained by the following formula:

$$g(r) = \frac{\rho(r)}{\rho_0}, \tag{6.14}$$

where $\rho(r)$ denotes the atomic density at $r = |\mathbf{r}|, r = 0$ defines the position of a reference atom, and ρ_0 is an average atomic density in the whole model.

In addition, in some cases, the coordination numbers were also calculated by taking the integral of $4\pi\rho_0 r^2 g(r)$ up to the first minimum. The calculated data helped in illustrating the changing atomic environment of the atoms before and after solid-state interfacial reaction.

7. Atomistic mechanism of solid-state interfacial reaction

In this section, the construction of *n*-body potentials of some representative binary metal systems, i.e. the Ni–Mo, Ni–Nb, Ni–Ta, Ni–Ti and Ni–Zr systems, is first described. Based on the derived potentials, MD simulations were performed with suitable simulation models to reveal the atomistic mechanism of solid-state interfacial reaction in the respective systems.

7.1. *Construction of n-body potentials for some Ni-based alloy systems*

7.1.1. *The Ni–Mo, Ni–Nb and Ni–Ta systems*

In construction of the *n*-body potentials for the Ni–Mo, Ni–Nb and Ni–Ta systems consisting of fcc Ni and bcc refractory metals (Mo, Nb and Ta), one should consider taking the appropriate and flexible potential forms suitable for both fcc and bcc structures.

For the Ni–Mo system, the Finnis–Sinclair formalism was employed to construct its potential and the function of the toal energy was given by equation (6.10). For computational flexibility to obtain a better fitting, the form of the normal pair-wise energy was modified by the authors' group [23] and is expressed by

$$\begin{aligned} V(r) &= (r-c)^2 \cdot (c_0 + c_1 r + c_2 r^2 + c_3 r^3 + c_4 r^4) \quad && r \leqslant c \\ &= 0 && r > c, \end{aligned} \tag{7.1}$$

where V(r) takes a polynomial form extending up to r^6, instead of the original quartic form [23]. The potential for the Mo–Mo interaction was taken from that derived by Finnis and Sinclair [75]. The potential for the Ni–Ni and the cross potential for the Ni–Mo interactions were developed by using the same form as that of the Mo–Mo potential for computational simplicity [23].

The Ni–Ni potential was determined by fitting the experimental data of the cohesive energy, lattice constants, bulk modulus and shear elastic constants. The interactions of φ and V were assumed not to extend further than the second shell of their neighbours, like those in deriving the Mo–Mo potential. The Ni–Ni potential so determined was able to reproduce some other physical properties, e.g. surface energy, vacancy formation energy and volume. The vacancy and surface energies were unrelaxed values and calculated by summing φ and V over the neighbours of those atoms within the ranges of the respective defects. It turned out that the reproduced physical properties were in a good and compromising agreement with the experimental values. For instance, the energy of the different surfaces was increased from the most stabilized close-packed (111) to (100) and then (110) planes, which was in agreement with that from the first principles calculation. Meanwhile, the reproduced surface energy for the (100), (110) and (111) planes were smaller than the experimental values, which has been common for an empirical potential [97].

In fitting the Ni–Mo potential, the cohesive energies and lattice constants of some metastable crystalline phases obtained from the first-principles calculations [111, 112] or experiments [113] were employed, as the respective data for three equilibrium Ni–Mo alloy phases, i.e. $\beta(Ni_4Mo)$, $\gamma(Ni_3Mo)$ and the δ-phase, were not accessible. Applying the derived poential, the reproduced cohesive energy and lattice constants were in good agreement with those either from first principles calculations or experiments not only for the metastable crystalline but also for the equilibrium alloy phases. The derived potential also correctly reflected the relative stability of the alloy phases in the Ni–Mo system. Moreover, employing the potential, the bulk moduli of the Ni_3Mo ($D0_{19}$) and $NiMo_3$ ($L1_2$) phases were calculated to be 2.56 and 1.50, respectively, which wee also compatible with those obtained by first principles calculation (2.5 for Ni_3Mo, and 2.4 for $NiMo_3$, respectively) [111]. In short, the constructed Ni–Mo potential was of relevance, and for convenience of use all the potential parameters are listed in table 7 [23].

For the Ni–Nb and Ni–Ta systems, we adopted the analytic functions developed recently by Cai for fcc metals [97] and those proposed by Johnson for the bcc metals [93]. In both models, the embedding functions $F(\rho)$ were quite similar. Recalling equation (6.7), there was a linear term F_1 for fcc metals and was an adjustable parameter. For bcc metals, F_1 equalled 0. It was thus convenient to combine the two models together for the Ni–Nb and Ni–Ta systems. Since the embedding function $F(\rho)$ was universal and did not depend on the source of the host electron density, the electron density functions $f_{Ni}(r)$ and $f_B(r)$ ($B=$ Nb or Ta), the embedding energy functions $F_{Ni}(\rho)$ and $F_B(\rho)$ were assumed to be transferable from two mono-atomic systems to the binary metal systems, and so the same as for the pair potential functions $\varphi_{Ni-Ni}(r)$ and $\varphi_{B-B}(r)$. The electron-density scaling factor f_e in equation (6.8) was determined by the equation $f_e = E_c/\Omega$ (E_c is the cohesive energy and Ω is the atom volume) [95]. For the Ni–Nb and Ni–Ta systems, the cut-off distance r_{cut}

Table 7. Parameters for the n-body potentials for Ni, Mo and Ni–Mo.

	Ni–Ni	Mo–Mo [75]	Ni–Mo
A (eV)	1.042 095	1.883 457	1.144 552
d (Å)	4.0	4.114 825	5.25
c (Å)	3.72	3.25	4.05
C_0	2.185 332 9	43.447 521 8	49.418 638
C_1	−0.634 640 8	−31.933 297 8	−60.373 527
C_2	−0.418 483 6	6.080 424 9	27.366 179
C_3	0.136 478 6	0.0	−5.388 922
C_4	0.0	0.0	0.387 794

Table 8. Potential parameters for the Ni–Nb and Ni–Ta systems.

	Ni–Ni		Nb–Nb	Ta–Ta [93]		Ni–Nb	Ni–Ta
n	0.5		0.787 1	0.642 16	c	3.8	3.8
F_0 (eV)	2.97		4.72	5.139	c_0	51.683 55	−40.852 79
f_e	0.408 12		0.415 43	0.449 11	c_1	−69.797 8	57.150 59
χ (Å^{-1})	2.821 497	η	6	6	c_2	34.291 2	−29.133 27
α (eV)	0.608 0	K_0 (eV)	−0.393 14	−0.435 31	c_3	−7.189 241	6.358 747
β	6.46	K_1 (eV)	−0.596 36	−1.064 84	c_4	0.523 113	−0.499 095 2
F_1 (eV)	1.58	K_2 (eV)	3.341 64	9.878 19			
r_a (Å)	2.196 5	K_3 (eV)	3.497 03	−10.612 19			
r_{cut}	3.9	k_a	47.357 14	16.744 9			

for Ni was assumed to be between the second- to third-neighbour distances and was therefore compatible with that for Nb and Ta. One sees from equations (6.8) and (6.9) in total five potential parameters (χ, α, β, F_1 and r_a) that should be fitted for the Ni–Ni interaction and were obtained through an optimization procedure. It was found that the derived Ni–Ni potential could reproduce the major intrinsic properties and the deduced equation of state was in good agreement with Rose *et al.* [99]. The fitting results are listed in table 8.

The potential parameters for the Nb–Nb and Ta–Ta interactions were adopted from those derived by Johnson [93]. In Johnson's analytic EAM model for the bcc metals, the cohesive part, i.e. the embedding energy, takes the same form as that expressed by equation (6.7) with $F_1 = 0$. The single atom electron density, $f(r)$, was assumed to have the form of a power term rather than an exponential form:

$$f(r) = f_e\left(\frac{r_e}{r}\right)^\eta, \tag{7.2}$$

where r_e is the first nearest neighbour distance in equilibrium and η is an adjustable parameter. The repulsive interaction, i.e. the so-called effective two-body potential, which requires $\mathrm{d}F/\mathrm{d}\rho|_e = 0$ and is satisfied by equation (6.7), is taken as a cubic equation:

$$\varphi(r) = \begin{cases} \phi(r) & r \geqslant r_e \\ \phi(r) + k_a[\phi(r) - \phi(r_e)]\left(\dfrac{r}{r_e} - 1\right)^2 & r < r_e, \end{cases} \tag{7.3}$$

where

$$\phi(r) = K_3\left(\frac{r}{r_e} - 1\right)^3 + K_2\left(\frac{r}{r_e} - 1\right)^2 + K_1\left(\frac{r}{r_e} - 1\right) + K_0$$

and K_3, K_2, K_1, K_0 and k_a are the potential parameters. The potential parameters for the Nb–Nb and Ta–Ta interactions are also listed in table 8.

The remaining functions, i.e. the cross pair potential functions $\varphi_{\mathrm{Ni-Nb}}(r)$ and $\varphi_{\mathrm{Ni-Ta}}(r)$, are assumed to take the form given by equation (7.1), which is used in deriving the Ni–Mo potential. Because of the shortage of experimental data for the equilibrium Ni–Nb and Ni–Ta alloy phases, the parameters in $\varphi_{\mathrm{Ni-Nb}}(r)$ and $\varphi_{\mathrm{Ni-Ta}}(r)$ are derived by using some physical properties obtained with linear muffin-tin orbital (LMTO) calculations for four Ni–Nb [114] and two Ni–Ta metastable crystalline phases [112], respectively. The fitting results are also listed in table 8.

To test the relevance further of the derived Ni–Nb potential, the lattice constants of the quilibrium β-Ni_3Nb phase are reproduced [115] and agreed well with the experimental values within an error of only 2% [116]. Moreover, one of the dynamic properties, i.e. the melting point of the βNi_3Nb phase is determined by MD simulation. From the calculated variations of the molar enthalpy and volume of the β-Ni_3Nb phase as a function of temperature, an abrupt change is observed at a temperature about 1750 K, which is in excellent agreement with the experimentally determined melting point of 1703 K [117]. Similarly, applying the derived Ni–Ta potential, some static and dynamic physical properties as well as the Rose equation can also be reproduced for some equilibrium and metastable crystalline phases of the Ni–Ta system [118].

Based on the above discussion, the derived n-body Ni–Nb and Ni–Ta potentials are of relevance and can be applied in MD simulation to study the issues of interest. For reference and convenience of use, all the potential parameters for the Ni–Nb and Ni–Ta systems are listed in table 8 [115, 118].

7.1.2. *The Ni–Ti system*

The Ni–Ti system consists of two transition metals of fcc and hcp structure and is therefore different from the above systems. In the literature, there has been an EAM Ni–Ti potential derived by Farkas *et al.*; however, this potential could not predict that the martensitic phase (B19′) was more stable than the B2 NiTi phase at low temperature. The problem was probably due to the fact that the cohesive energy of the B2 NiTi phase at high temperature was used in deriving the potential [119]. Moreover, applying the potential, MD simulation with the Ni–Ti multilayers was performed by the authors' group and it could not reproduce the experimentally observed solid-state amorphization (SSA) either.

To derive a realistic Ni–Ti potential, the second-moment approximation of tight binding (TB) theory was therefore employed [108]. In the scheme, the total energy of a system was given by equation (6.12). Accordingly, there were in total four adjustable parameters $A_{\alpha\beta}, p_{\alpha\beta}, \xi_{\alpha\beta}$ and $q_{\alpha\beta}$ to be determined. In the fitting procedure, the physical properties of the B2 NiTi phase of 0 K, instead of at high temperature, were used and they were obtained by first principles calculation, i.e. the cohesive energy from the full-potential linear-muffin-tin-orbital (FLMTO) calculation [120] and the elastic constants from the full-potential linearized augmented-plane-wave (FLAPW) total-energy methods [121]. Table 9 lists the parameters obtained for the (TB) Ni–Ti potential after optimization as well as a comparison between the physical quantities reproduced by the potential derived and those used initially for fitting [128]. It turns out that the constructed (TB) Ni–Ti potential can reproduce some physical properties of the system in good agreement with those obtained by first principles calculations or experimental studies. For instance, the derived (TB) Ni–Ti potential did predict that the martensitic phase (B19′) was more stable at 0 K than the B2 NiTi and $L1_0$ phases, as its cohesive energy was calculated to be 0.018 and 0.118 eV atom^{-1} greater than those of the B2 and $L1_0$ phases, respectively. In addition, based on the (TB) potential, the melting point of the B2 NiTi phase was estimated to be 1612–1653 K, which was also in good agreement with the experimental value of 1583 K. Moreover, the cohesive energy of the $D0_{24}Ni_3Ti$

Table 9. Values of cohesive energy E_c, nearest-neighbour distances d, elastic constants C_{ij}, and vacancy formation energy E_v^f, which are used for the fit of the potential (see text), and potential parameters $A_{\alpha\beta}, p_{\alpha\beta}, \xi_{\alpha\beta}$ and $q_{\alpha\beta}$ for Ni–Ni, Ti–Ti and Ni–Ti. E_c, $A_{\alpha\beta}$ and $\xi_{\alpha\beta}$ are expressed in eV atom^{-1}, d in Å, C_{ij} in eV Å^{-3} and E_v^f in eV.

	Ni		Ti		Ni–Ti	
	This work	Exp.	This work	Exp.	This work	FLMTO or FLAPW
E_c	4.44	4.44 [122]	4.85	4.85 [122]	5.02	5.02 [120]
d	2.49 [122]		2.95 [122]		2.607 [123]	
C_{11}	1.568	1.629 [124]	1.103	1.0992 [124]	1.279	1.112 [121]
C_{12}	1.085	0.943 [124]	0.549	0.5452 [124]	0.846	0.921 [121]
C_{13}			0.465	0.4263 [124]		
C_{33}			1.187	1.1891 [124]		
C_{44}	0.729	0.824 [124]	0.193	0.3171 [124]	0.297	0.306 [121]
E_v^f	1.65	1.60 [125]	1.56	1.55 [126, 127]		
A	0.104		0.153		0.3	
p	11.198		9.253		7.9	
ξ	1.591		1.879		2.48	
q	2.413		2.513		3.002	

phase at 0 K, which was not used in fitting, was reproduced to be 0.01 eV greater than that of $L1_2$ Ni_3Ti, suggesting a correct energetic sequence between the two phases [120]. It was therefore concluded that the newly derived (TB) Ni–Ti potential was of relevance in describing the atomic interactions for the Ni–Ti system.

In summary, the n-body potentials of the Ni–Mo, Ni–Nb, Ni–Ta and Ni–Ti systems were derived and testified to be of relevance by commonly employed methods. In the next few paragraphs as well as in section 8, the derived potentials will be aplied in MD simulations for studying solid-state interfacial reactions and other physical questions in the respective systems. It will be shown later that the simulation results are in good agreement with experimental observations. These results can also be considered to support the conclusion that the derived potentials are realistic.

7.2. *Solid-state reaction initiated by crossing-interface atomic diffusion*

We now turn to discuss the atomistic mechanism of solid-state interfacial reaction in some Ni-based alloy systems by MD simulations. To represent the real multilayered films used in experiments and study the effect of interfacial texture on solid-state interfacial reaction, sandwich models with different crystalline orientations of some specific metal lattices were constructed for simulation. Taking the Ni–Mo system as an example, simulation models were constructed by stacking the Ni and Mo atomic planes along the z-axis (and similar stacking of the atomic planes would also be used in the following simulation models) and the orientations of the atomic planes were indexed by their Miller indices, e.g. [6 (111) Ni] refers to an Ni lattice of fcc structure stacked by 6 (111) atomic planes, and [4 (001) Mo] stands for an Mo lattice with a bcc structure stacked by 4 (001) atomic planes, etc. Two interfaces between the Ni and Mo lattices were introduced as follows. When an Mo

Table 10. In the various sandwich models for simulation, the crystalline directions of the fcc (Ni), bcc (Mo, Nb, Ta) and hcp (Ti, Zr) atomic planes set parallel to the *x*-, *y*- and *z*-axes corresponding to various interfacial orientations.

	fcc (Ni)			bcc (Mo, Nb, Ta)			hcp (Ti, Zr)	
Axis	(110)	(001)	(111)	(111)	(001)	(110)	(100)	(001)
x	$[\bar{1}10]$	[100]	$[\bar{1}10]$	$[\bar{1}10]$	[100]	[001]	[100]	[100]
y	[001]	[010]	$[\bar{1}\bar{1}2]$	$[\bar{1}\bar{1}2]$	[010]	$[1\bar{1}0]$	$[00\bar{1}]$	[120]
z	[110]	[001]	[111]	[111]	[001]	[110]	[120]	[001]

lattice and an Ni lattice approach each other along the z-direction, an interface is created in the x–y plane and another interface is introduced by bringing another Mo lattice to the Ni lattice from the opposite direction.

For some Ni-based alloy systems, sandwich models were constructed by combining the low index atomic planes of fcc Ni with those of bcc metals (denoted by M1, M1=Mo, Nb, Ta) or hcp metals (denoted by M2, M2=Ti, Zr) parallel to the interfaces. The orientations of the atomic planes in the x–y plane were set to preserve the symmetry of the crystalline planes across the boundary. The first crystalline direction was arranged to be parallel to the x-direction, and the other crystalline direction of the atomic plane parallel to the y-direction was then determined by the x-direction setting. Table 10 lists the orientations of different atomic planes of fcc, bcc and hcp structures in models consisting of metals with different structures for simulation.

The sizes of the lattices in the x–y plane were chosen with two limitations. First, the mismatch at the interface should be as close as possible to the real ratio of their crystal lattices. Secondly, the numbers of atoms in the model should be within a manageable scale for computation. Taking a typical sandwich model [4 (001) Mo/8 (001) Ni/4 (001) Mo] as an example, the lattice parameters of Ni and Mo crystals are 0.3523 and 0.3147 nm, respectively, which makes a ratio of approximately 1.119. In simulation, the numbers of Mo and Ni atoms in their respective planes were selected to be $9 \times 9 = 81$ for the Mo (001) plane and $8 \times 8 \times 2 = 128$ for the Ni (001) plane, corresponding to a ratio of $9/8 = 1.125$, which is quite close to the real situation. The size of the corresponding computational block in the z-direction was obtained by varying the distances between the metal lattices to an optimized value corresponding to minimum enthalpy of the model.

A periodic condition was imposed in the z-direction and two outer lattices in sandwich models adhered together to form a united lattice, while in the x- and y-directions, the larger lattice dimension of the two constituent metals was adopted to set the periodic boundary conditions. Consequently, the computational block of a sandwich model was a representative unit of compositionally modulated multilayers and the simulation of such a sandwich model in fact represents the multilayers in a real experiment. It was estimated that a misfit caused by a difference between the dimensions of the two metal lattices and the periodic conditions along the x- and y-directions would result in decreasing the density of one metal in the model, but by no more than 2%. In this regard, Mura *et al.* have simulated Ni–Zr multilayers, which were subjected to a certain load, and shown that such a small density decrease does not affect the simulation results [129]. The authors' group has also conducted a brief estimation for a sandwich model [4 (001) Zr/6 (111) Ni/2 (001) Zr] with a 1.4% Zr density reduction, and determined the maximum stress, based on the plane stress theory of elasticity, to be on the same order of magnitude as the diagonal stress-tensor components in the Ni–Zr potential [130]. Moreover, the real stresses existing in the sandwich model should be much lower than the estimated values, as the initial state of the simulation-models was obtained after a relaxation of the as-set model at 300 K, typically for 10 000 time steps, to reach a state of reduced stress.

In some cases, a disordered layer was artifically introduced by exchanging an equal number of two metal atoms in the interfaces to surpass the necessary stage of nucleation at the interfaces for growing an amorphous interlayer and/or to study the effect of an interfacial disordered layer on the interfacial reaction. Following Highmore [131], it was thought that the initial reaction at the interface, within the limits of classical nucleation theory, was somehow related to the formation of a solid solution. To characterize quantitatively the amount of disordering created by exchanging the metal atoms, the concept of a long-range order (LRO) parameter proposed to describe the ordering in crystalline alloys was employed [130]. The LRO parameter was defined as $\eta = (p - \gamma)/(1 - \gamma)$, where p and γ were the probabilities of the presence of an A type atom on its own lattice site and the molar ratio of A atoms, respectively, both in the initial interlayer. Values $\eta = 0$ and 1 corresponded, respectively, to complete chemical disorder and an entirely ordered crystalline state. Some sandwich models with such disordered interfacial structures were studied and compared with those of the sharp interfaces to reveal the effect of interfacial structures on the solid-state interfacial reaction.

We first present the simulation results for an Ni–Ti sandwich model upon 723 K isothermal annealing. The model was constructed in a configuration of [4 (001) Ti/6 (001) Ni/2 (001) Ti]. The initial state is shown in figure 8 by a projection of the atomic positions on the x–z plane. One sees that though some disordering has already occurred in atomic plane No. 5 caused by a misfit at interfaces between the Ni and Ti crystals, all other atomic planes remain in a layered structure. The calculated planar structure factors for the atomic planes next to the interfaces (plane Nos 4–5 and 10–11) were greater than 0.5 and those for all other planes were greater than 0.8, confirming their original crystalline structure. One also sees that, with the exception of an Ni atom diffusing into Ti atomic plane No. 4, the Ni and Ti crystals are sharply separated by the two interfaces in the initial state. Figures 9 and 10 display two projections of the atomic positions on the x–z plane after annealing at 723 K for 50 000 and 70 000 time steps, respectively, showing the disordering process taking place in the Ni–Ti sandwich model. At 50 000 MD steps, all the Ti atomic planes became disordered, while the 4 Ni atomic planes (Nos 6–9) remained still in crystalline structures. Increasing annealing time to 70 000 MD steps, all the remaining Ni crystalline planes gradually became disordered, resulting eventually in an amorphous configuration of the whole model. Apparently, mutual atomic diffusion, defined as the crossing-interface migration of either Ni or Ti atoms into their partner lattice, did take place and resulted in a significant alloying between the Ni and Ti layers as well as an expansion of the disordered interlayer. In other words, solid-state interfacial reaction proceeeded in a sequence of diffusion, alloying and eventually amorphization. Referring to figure 9 again, one clearly sees that the disordered interlayers extend faster towards the Ti lattice than to the Ni side and this phenomenon is called asymmetric growth. The detailed kinetics will be discussed

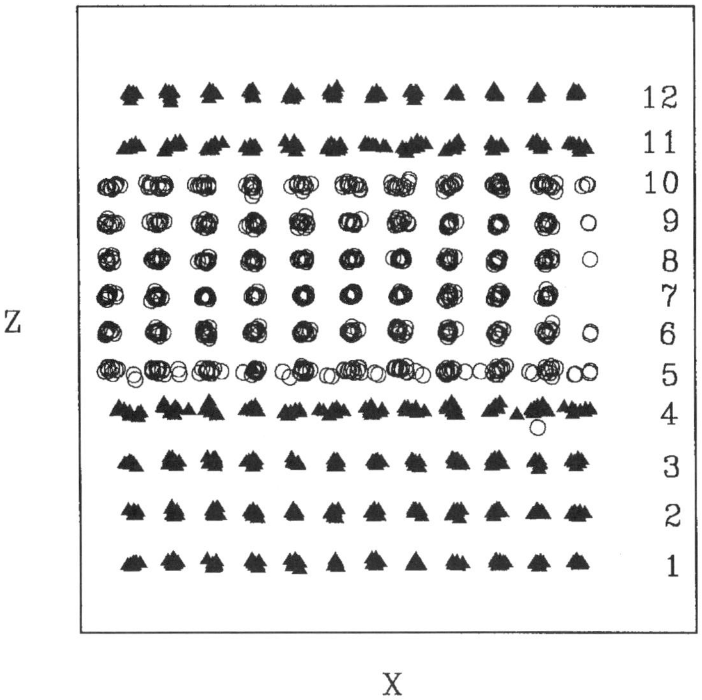

Figure 8. Projection of the atomic positions in the x–z plane for the starting configuration of a sandwich model [4 (001) Ti/6 (001) Ni/2 (001) Ti]. The open circles and filled triangles refer to the Ni and Ti atoms, respectively. The numbers of the atomic planes are indexed on the right-hand side.

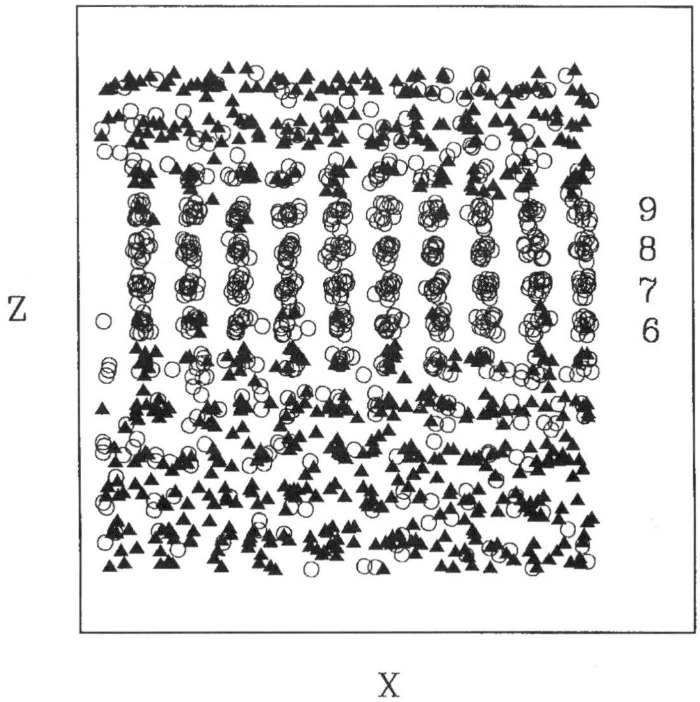

Figure 9. Projection of the atomic positions on the x–z plane for the sandwich model [4 (001) Ti/6 (001) Ni/2 (001) Ti] after annealing at 723 K for 50 000 MD time steps. The open circles and full triangles refer to the Ni and Ti atoms, respectively. The numbers of those atomic planes, which remain still in crystalline structure, are indexed on the right-hand side.

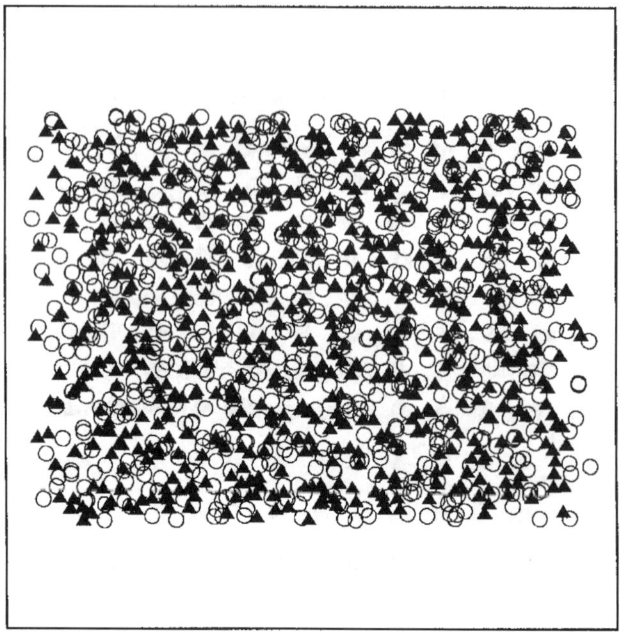

Figure 10. Projection of the atomic positions in the x–z plane for the sandwich model [4 (001) Ti/6 (001) Ni/2 (001) Ti] after annealing Ni-Ti at 723 K for 70 000 MD time steps. The open circles and filled triangles refer to the Ni and Ti atoms, respectively.

further in a quantitative way using bilayer model and the physical origin of the asymmetric growth will be discussed in section 8.

Three sets of partial and total pair-correlation functions for the Ni–Ti sandwich model were calculated at various time steps and are shown in figure 11. One observes that with increasing annealing time the strength of the Ti–Ni $g(r)$ first peak increases and those peaks of the total, Ni–Ni and Ti–Ti $g(r)$s gradually decrease and that the Ti–Ti and Ni–Ni peaks at long distances disappear after 50 000 and 70 000 time steps, respectively. These results suggest that after annealing at 723 K for 50 000 MD steps, the Ti crystal has transformed into an amorphous state, while some Ni still remains in the crystalline structure, resulting in the formation of a Ti-enriched Ni–Ti amorphous phase, as evidenced by figure 9. Further annealing for another 20 000 time steps, the Ti-enriched Ni–Ti amorphous phase consumed all the remaining Ni crystal to form a relatively uniform Ni–Ti amorphous phase, confirmed by the calculated pair-correlation function. Additionally, the structural evolution revealed by MD simulation was also reflected by the corresponding change of the molar enthalpy and volume of the model. Figure 12 shows that increasing the temperature from the initial state at 300 to 723 K causes both enthalpy and volume to increase and that during annealing at 723 K, the molar enthalpy and volume first gradually decrease, then suddenly drop at 60 000 steps, and remain nearly unchanged after reaching a plateau at 70 000 steps. From the above results, several conclusions can be drawn. First, the reaction emerges in the Ni–Ti multilayers initiated at the interfaces and the resultant disordered interlayers expand towards both the Ti and Ni lattices accompanied by a decrease of the enthalpy due to alloying between the Ti and Ni layers. Secondly, after 50 000 steps, the crystal-to-amorphous transition of the Ti

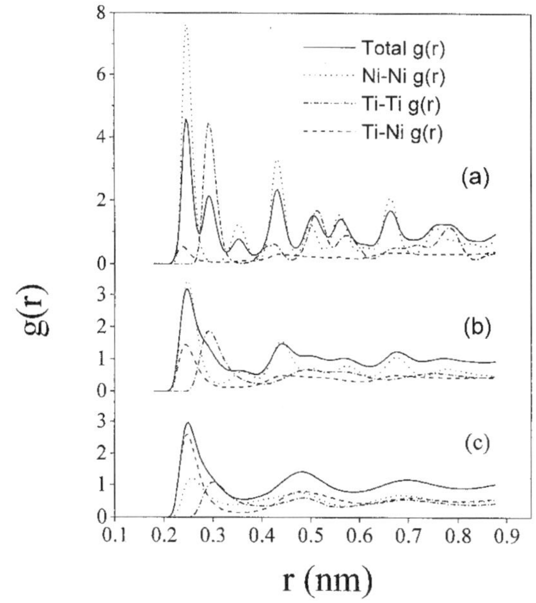

Figure 11. Partial and total pair correlation functions for the sandwich model [4 (001) Ti/6 (001) Ni/2 (001) Ti] at its initial state (*a*) and another two states obtained by annealing at 723 K for 50 000 MD time steps (*b*) and for 70 000 MD time steps (*c*), respectively.

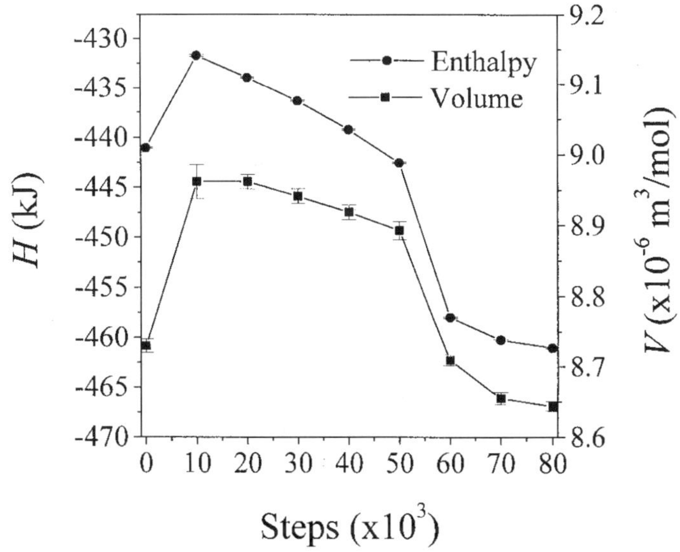

Figure 12. Upon isothermal annealing at 723 K, the variations of the molar enthalpy (H) and volume (V) of the sandwich model [4(001)Ti/6(001)Ni/2(001)Ti] versus time steps. The data are obtained by averaging between 1000 MD time steps starting from each step shown in the abscissa and those at 0 step are taken from the initial state at 300 K.

lattice is almost complete. Thirdly, the sudden drop and then remaining unchanged of the enthalpy at 60 000 and 70 000 steps could be attributed to the crystal-to-amorphous transition of the remaining Ni crystal and the completion of the solid-state amorphization (SSA), respectively. It is worthwhile noticing from figure 12 that after the completion of SSA, the enthalpy and volume at 723 K are even smaller than those of the initiate state at 300 K, suggesting that the reaction between the Ni and Ti crystals is exothermic and the amorphous Ni–Ti phase possesses a smaller volume than a mechanical mixture of the Ni and Ti crystallites in the as-deposited multilayers.

Further, to confirm that the amorphization process was initiated at the interfaces, the pair-correlation functions for the two disordered interfacial layers at various annealing stages were calculated and the resultant curves showed shapes similar to those known for the amorphous state. To illustrate the changing atomic surroundings of the Ni and Ti atoms before and after annealing, the coordination numbers were calculated by taking the integral of $4\pi\rho_0 r^2 g(r)$ up to the first minimum, where ρ_0 is the atomic density of the model. It was found that from the initial state shown in figure 11(*a*) to the annealed state shown in figure 11(*c*), the coordination numbers for Ni–Ni and Ti–Ti decreased from 10.67 to 5.42 and from 10.33 to 3.68, respectively, while those numbers for Ni–Ti and Ti–Ni increased from 1.02 to 6.69 and from 1.23 to 8.06, respectively. Evidently, these results also demonstrate that the process of SSA is indeed initiated from the interfaces through diffusion and alloying and the growth of the initially formed disordered interlayer eventually results in the formation of a relatively uniform amorphous phase in the Ti–Ni–Ti sandwich model.

Similar simulations were also conducted at 673 and 773 K and the results show that the annealing temperature has a strong influence on the amorphization speed in Ni–Ti multilayers, i.e. the higher the annealing temperature the faster the process of SSA. Incidentally, similar simulations were also performed for another sandwich model [4 (001) Ti/6 (001) Ni/2 (001) Ti] with a thin preset disordered interlayer consisting of one Ni and one Ti atomic planes next to an interface (i.e. planes 4–5) and a similar SSA process was also observed. It is thus concluded that in the sandwich model with configuration [4 (001) Ti/6 (001) Ni/2 (001) Ti], SSA was able to proceed with or without a preset disordered interlayer.

Similar MD simulations were also conducted for the Ni–Mo, Ni–Nb and Ni–Ta systems, based on the respective potentials derived by the authors' group as well as for the Ni–Zr system using the potential developed by Massobrio [130]. It turns out that the process of SSA proceeds in a way similar to that observed in the Ni–Ti system.

7.3. *Diffusion-limited and/or interface-limited growth of amorphous interlayers*

To study the detailed kinetics of solid-state interfacial reactions in a quantitative manner, bilayer models were employed in MD simulations. For a binary metal system consisting of metal A of fcc structure and metal B or either bcc or fcc structure, a typical bilayer model was constructed by sequentially stacking 12 fcc A (001) planes (Nos 1–12) and 12 bcc or fcc B (001) planes (Nos 13–34) along the *z*-direction. For convenience, the constructed model was abbreviated to [12 [001) A/12 (001) B]. The orientations of the atomic planes and the size of the lattices in the *x*-*y* plane were chosen to be like those in the sandwich models. In the *x*- and *y*-directions, periodic boundary conditions were imposed, while in the *z*-direction, a free boundary condition was adopted to avoid the influence on the growth kinetics of having another interface in the model. Under such conditions, the atoms on both outermost planes in the *z*-direction were free to move and an atom, if crossing the computation block, would be relocated onto the initial surface and set at zero energy. To avoid possible drifting of the block, an equal amount of the lost momentum was spread equally to all the atoms in the block. As the simulation results have shown that after annealing such a simulation model at a temperature up to 873 K for long time, the

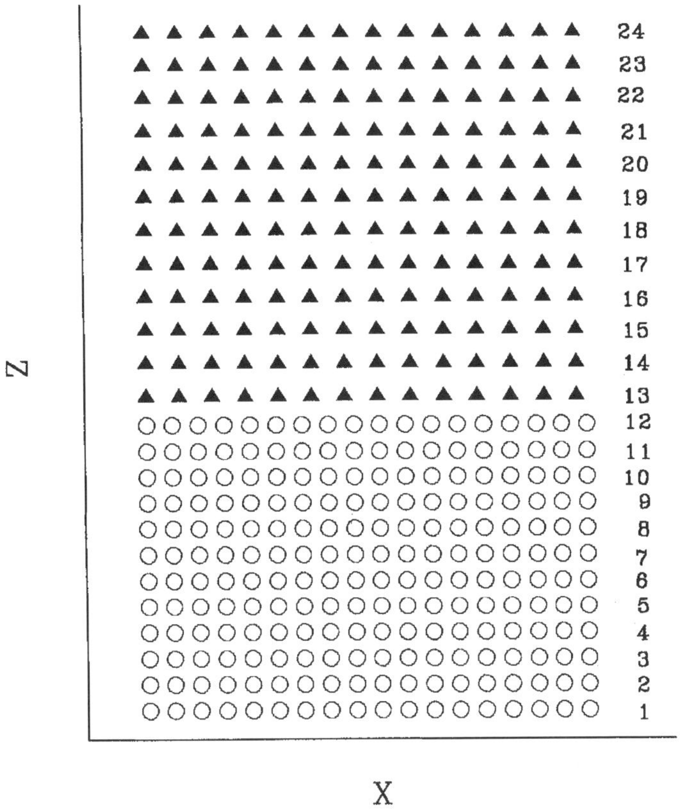

Figure 13. Projection of the atomic positions of a representative bilayer model on the x–z plane. The open circles and filled triangles refer to the Ni and M (M = Zr, Mo, Nb, Ta and Ti) atoms, respectively.

crystalline planes near the surface, except those next to the interface, remain almost unchanged, the above setting of the boundary conditions did not have considerable effect on the simulation results. Additionally, in some cases, a disordered interlayer was present in the bilayer models by randomly exchanging an equal number of A and B atoms in the atomic planes near the interface and the amount of disordering in the interlayer was set to be $\eta = 0$.

The growth kinetics of SSA was studied in detail by MD simulations with bilayer models in the Ni–Zr, Ni–Mo, Ni–Nb, Ni–Ta and Ni–Ti systems. For convenience, the atomic planes stacked along the z-direction in the bilayer model were recorded by Nos 1–12 for Ni and Nos 13–24 for M (M = Zr, Mo, Nb, Ta and Ti), respectively, as illustrated by figure 13. The interface separating the Ni and M crystalline lattices was therefore between the atomic planes 12 and 13.

We now discuss the simulation results obtained for the Ni–Zr system [14]. For an Ni–Zr bilayer model, a present disordered interlayer was introduced by exchanging a total number of 122 Ni and Zr atoms in an interlayer consisting of four atomic planes, Nos 11–14, as such a disordered interlayer has been observed in sputtering-deposited Ni–Zr multilayers [18]. The model was then equilibrated at 300 K for 5000 MD steps to reach an equilibrium state and the interlayer was indeed in a disordered state, as the planar structural factors for atomic planes 11–14 were calculated to be 0.18, 0, 0.05, and 0.25, respectively. In addition, a total pair-correlation function calculation for the interlayer in the initial state also confirmed

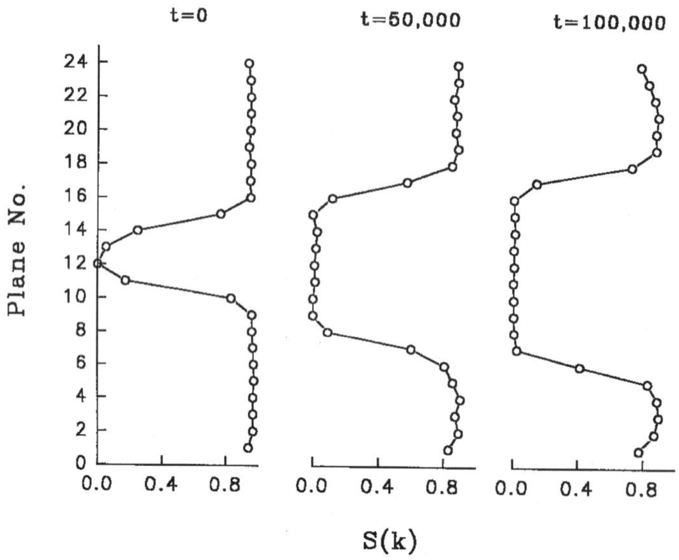

Figure 14. The planar structure factors $S(\mathrm{k})$ for the starting state of the Ni–Zr bilayer model ($t = 0$) and for another two states after annealing at 773 K for 50 000 and 100 000 MD time steps, respectively.

an amorphous structure. Starting from this initial state, the bilayer model was subjected to isothermal annealing at temperatures ranging from 623 to 873 K. The simulation results obtained at 773 K are discussed here as a typical example, as similar results were also obtained at 623, 673 and 873 K, respectively. Figure 14 shows the planar structure factors $S(\mathrm{k})$ for the initial state of the Ni–Zr bilayer model and another two annealed states after simulation up to 50 000 and 100 000 time steps, respectively. One observes that the interlayer in the initial state is disordered and it gradually extends outwards with increasing time, and that after 100 000 time steps the disordered interlayer extends to a total thickness corresponding to 11 atomic planes (Nos 7–17). The partial and total pair-correlation function calculations confirmed that these 11 atomic planes were indeed of amorphous structure. The coordination numbers in a layer consisting of atomic planes 7–17 before and after annealing at 773 K for 100 000 time steps were also calculated and the coordination numbers for Ni–Ni and Zr–Zr decreased from 9.51 to 6.16 and from 8.63 to 4.71, respectively, while the coordination numbers for Ni–Zr and Zr–Ni increased from 1.92 to 5.34 and from 4.45 to 10.89, respectively. These changes in coordination number demonstrate that significant alloying between the Ni and Zr metal does take place. One clearly sees from figure 14 that outside this disordered layer all the atomic planes remain almost unchanged, because no Ni (Zr) atom as alloying elements has didussed into the Zr(Ni) lattice planes. In addition, the total pair-correlation functions for the growing layer with increasing thickness at various time steps were also calculated and they also confirm the amorphous structure. It was therefore concluded that the growth of the Ni–Zr amorphous phase upon solid-state interfacial reaction proceeds in a layer-by-layer mode.

We now show the quantitative time dependence of the growth of the disordered interlayer in the Ni–Zr bilayer model. The thickness of the disordered interlayer at a specific time is calculated by counting the atomic planes from the interface up to the outermost one that had a planar structure factor $S < 0.1$. Additionally, the pair-correlation functions were calculated to confirm an amorphous structure. Figure 15

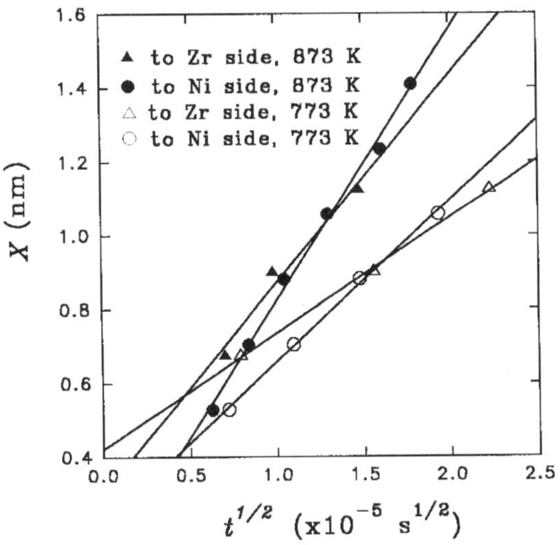

Figure 15. The growing thicknesses (X) of the amorphous interlayer as a function of ($t^{1/2}$) in two opposite directions towards the Ni and Zr lattices at 773 and 873 K, respectively.

exhibits four curves for the thickness (X) of the growing amorphous interlayer as a function of time ($t^{1/2}$) in two opposite directions towards the Ni and Zr lattices, respectively, upon interfacial reaction at 773 and 873 K. One sees that four calculated X–$t^{1/2}$ curves are all obviously linear, indicating that the growth of the amorphous interlayer follows exactly a diffusion-limited $t^{1/2}$ law. One also sees that the slopes of the four curves are different. First, the slopes at 873 K are greater than those obtained at 773 K, because the growth speeds at 873 K are naturally greater than the those at 773 K for both directions towards the Ni and Zr lattices. Secondly, the slopes of Ni at both 773 and 873 K are greater than those of Zr at the respective temperatures, showing an asymmetric growth behaviour, which was also observed in the Ni–Ti system described in section 7.2. Note that though the $t^{1/2}$ law for the growth of the amorphous layer has been experimentally observed in the Ni–Zr system [18, 78], it was obtained by fitting the data within a much longer time than in the MD simulation. While extrapolating the experimentally obtained linear line to $t = 0$, the thickness of the amorphous interlayer could not go to zero, suggesting that the empirical $t^{1/2}$ law was only valid for a long time period, yet not for the very initial stage. Interestingly, Meng *et al.* have performed a direct TEM examination of the Ni–Zr cross-section samples and observed that, after the amorphous NiZr interlayer grew to a critical thickness, an NiZr intermetallic compound started to form at the amorphous NiZr/Zr interface. Meng's experimental observation thus provided direct evidence that the growth speed of the disordered interlayer towards the Zr lattice was slower than that directed to the Ni side [132], which is compatible with the above simulation results. Note that the melting point of Zr (2125 K) is higher than that of Ni (1726 K).

We now show the temperature dependence of the growth of the amorphous interlayer revealed by MD simulations in the Ni–Zr bilayer model. The average speeds at the initial growing stage of the amorphous interlayer at various temperatures were obtained by determining the time interval for growing one atomic plane into both the Ni and Zr lattices. Figure 16 shows a linear correlation between the average growth speeds of the amorphous interlayer versus temperature in both directions towards the Ni and Zr lattices. By extrapolating the speeds to zero, the

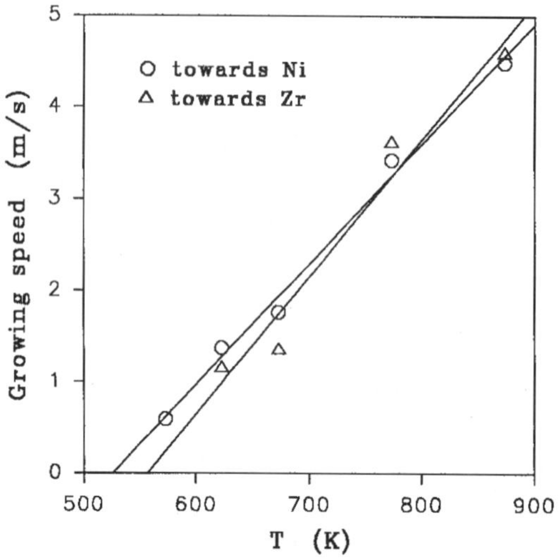

Figure 16. In the Ni/Zr bilayer, during the early growth stage, the average growing speeds of the amorphous interlayer as a function of temperature in two opposite directions towards Ni and Zr lattices, respectively.

lower temperature limits for growing the amorphous interlayer towards the Ni and Zr directions were determined to be 527 and 564 K, respectively, which are reasonably compatible with the onset temperatures observed in experiments [18, 132].

For the Ni–Mo system, similar MD simulations were conducted with an Ni–Mo bilayer model, in which a disordered interlayer was also preset by randomly exchanging an equal number of Ni and Mo atoms in one Ni and one Mo atomic plane next to each other (i.e. atomic planes 12 and 13). The model was pre-run at 300 K for equilibrating for 5000 MD time steps and then isothermally annealed at 573, 623, 773 and 873 K, respectively. Figure 17 shows two curves for the thickness (X) of the growing amorphous layer as a function of time ($t^{1/2}$) obtained at 873 K in two opposite directions towards the Ni and Mo lattices, respectively. It can be seen that the two X–$t^{1/2}$ curves are linear, indicating that the growth of the amorphous

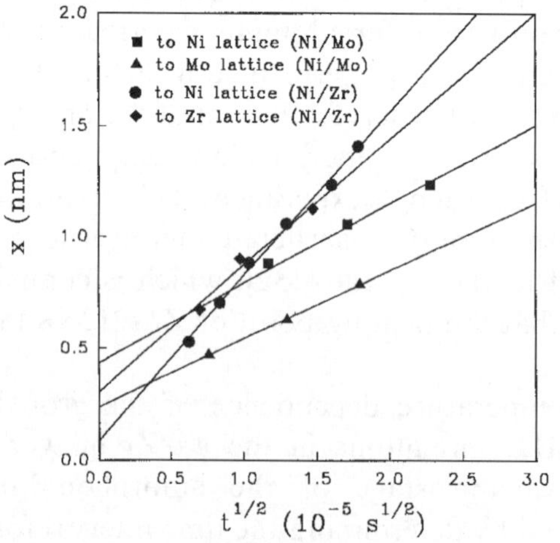

Figure 17. The growing thicknesses (X) of the amorphous interlayer as a function of ($t^{1/2}$) at 873 K towards the Ni and Mo lattices in the Ni/Mo bilayer and towards the Ni and Zr lattices in the Ni/Zr bilayer, respectively.

layer follows a $t^{1/2}$ law and that the slope for the Ni line is greater than that of the Mo line, showing an asymmetric growth behaviour in the Ni–Mo system. To compare the growth kinetics of SSA in the Ni–Mo and Ni–Zr systems, the two X–$t^{1/2}$ curves obtained for the Ni–Zr bilayer model after annealing at 873 K are added in figure 17. It is evident that the slopes of the two curves of the Ni–Zr system are greater than those observed for the Ni–Mo system [23]. Such a difference between the two systems can probably be correlated with their different characteristics. The Ni–Zr system has a large negative ΔH_f of $-72\ \mathrm{kJ\,mol^{-1}}$ and a large size mismatch of 22%, while the Ni–Mo system has a small negative ΔH_f of $-11\ \mathrm{kJ\,mol^{-1}}$ and a small size difference of 8.6%, which probably provides a relatively small driving force for SSA and results in a relatively slow speed of growth of the amorphous interlayer.

For the Ni–Nb and Ni–Ta systems, similar simulation results in the respective bilayer models with preset disordered interlayers were also obtained. In this cases, the growth speed of the amorphous interlayer was faster towards the Ni lattice than towards the refractory metals Nb or Ta, which have higher melting points than Ni [115, 118]. The simulation results obtained for the Ni–Zr, Ni–Mo, Ni–Nb and Ni–Ta systems seem to suggest that the growth speed of the amorphous interlayer was faster towards the metal (Ni) with the lower melting point than that directed to its partner metals (Zr, Mo, Nb and Ta) of higher melting temperature. However, in the next paragraph dealing with the Ni-Ti system, different behaviour will be shown in this regard and it will help to gain a better understanding concerning the kinetics of SSA.

For the Ni–Ti systems, MD simulations were performed based on the (TB) Ni–Ti potential derived by the authors' group [128] using two bilayer models with and without a preset disordered interlayer, respectively. The as-set bilayer models were relaxed first at room temperature (300 K) for equilbration and then subjected to thermal annealing at various temperatures ranging from 673 to 873 K. The simulation results show that, within the above annealing temperature range, the growth of an amorphous interlayer in both Ni–Ti bilayer models is also through a layer-by-layer mode.

Taking the Ni–Ti bilayer with no preset disordered interlayer as an example, figure 18 shows the changing planar structure factor $S(\mathrm{k})$ at the initial configuration and two annealed states obtained after annealing at 773 K for 10 000 and 140 000 MD steps, respectively. One sees that, at the initial state, all the atomic planes kept their crystalline structures and, upon annealing, disordering was initiated at the interface, and that after 140 000 time steps there were seven Ti atomic planes (Nos 13–19) but only three Ni atomic planes (Nos 10–12) transferred into a disordered state, showing the growth of the amorphous interlayer was faster towards the Ti lattice than towards the Ni side. Additionally, a layer-by-layer mode for the growth of the Ni–Ti amorphous phase was also confirmed by the calculated total and partial pair-correlation functions. To reveal the quantitative time dependence, figure 19 displays two calculated curves for the growing thickness (X) of the amorphous interlayer in the two directions towards the Ni and Ti lattices as a function of $t^{1/2}$. One sees that all the data points are on two linear X–$t^{1/2}$ lines, except the first two points towards the Ti lattice. An important finding here is that the growth towards the first three Ti atomic planes follows a linear X–t correlation, suggesting an interface-limited growth behaviour in the very early stage. Later, the growth follows a diffusion-limited $t^{1/2}$ law, which is the same observed in the above four Ni-based alloy systems. These results are displayed in an inset to figure 19. It appears that in the Ni–Ti system, at the beginning, an amorphous interlayer is

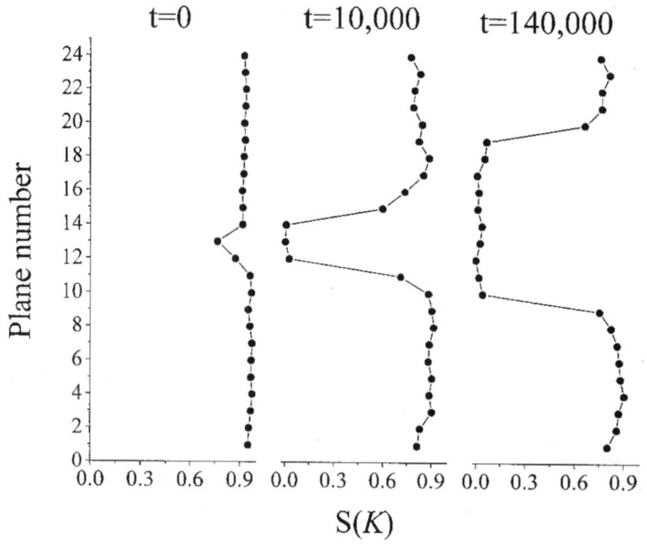

Figure 18. Change of the planar structure factors $S(\mathrm{k})$ of the Ni/Ti bilayer without a pre-disordered interlayer at the initial state ($t = 0$) and two annealed states obtained after annealing at 773 K for 10 000 and 140 000 MD time steps, respectively. The bilayer model consists of 12 Mi and 12 Ti atomic planes and they are numbered 1 to 12 for Ni and 13 to 24 for Ti, respectively.

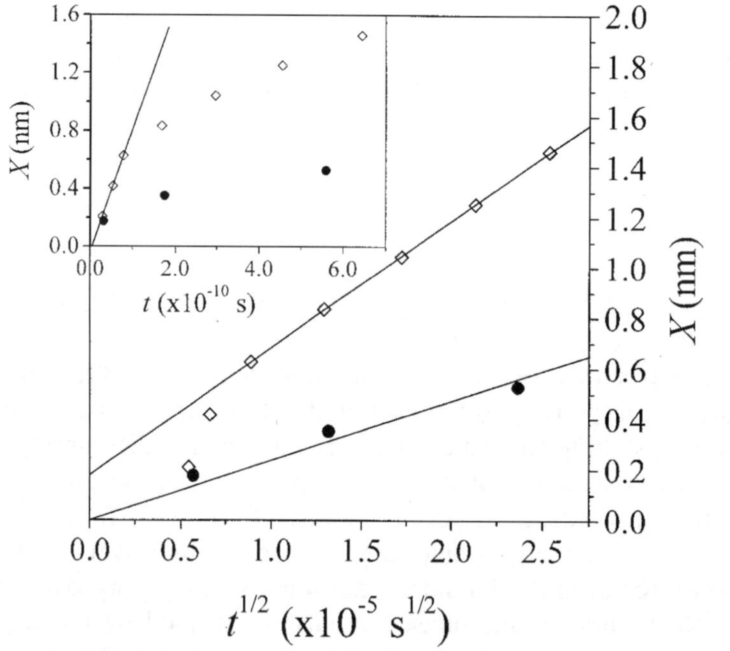

Figure 19. The growing thicknesses (X) of the amorphous interlayer as a function of $t^{1/2}$ or t (inset) in two opposite directions towards Ni (solid circle) and Ti (solid square) lattices at 773 K, respectively. The lines drawn are obtained from the best linear fit.

homogeneously nucleated at the interface and that, after growing to a thickness corresponding to 3–4 atomic planes, the growth changes from an interface-limited mode to a diffusion-limited mode. Figure 19 also shows that the slopes of the two X–$t^{1/2}$ lines are quite different and the slope directed to the Ti lattice is greater than that directed to the Ni side. Another important finding here is that though the Ti metal has a higher melting point (1933 K) than that of Ni (1726 K), the amorphous interlayer grows faster towards Ti than towards Ni, which is just the opposite from the observations in the Ni–Zr, Ni–Mo, Ni–Nb and Ni–Ta systems, where the amprphous interlayer grew faster towards the Ni lattice than towards the partner metals, which have higher melting points than that of Ni. It follows that the observed asymmetric growth during SSA cannot simply be correlated to the relative melting points of the constituent metals. Additionally, after checking the data in the literature, the asymmetric growth cannot simply be correlated to the relative diffusion coefficients either. From a physical point of view, the growth of the amorphous interlayer in solid-state interfacial reactions is the result of disordering of the crystalline lattices next to the amorphous interlayer, and disordering of a crystalline lattice is a result of the solute content exceeding the maximum allowable value that the lattice can accommodate. It is therefore deduced that a difference in the maximum (or critical) solid solubility of the constituent metals may be a relevant property to be correlated with the asymmetric growth, which will be further discussed and clarified in section 8.

7.4. *Nucleation and/or presence of growth barriers resulting from interfacial texture*

The texture of the interfacial structure was found to have a strong effect on solid-state interfacial reactions, which will be discussed here for some representative systems. The first system chosen is the Ni–Mo systems since a number of new phenomena in interfacial reactions and SSA have been observed in the system by MD simulation [23]. Six sandwich models were constructed by stacking the Mo (100) open plane and Mo (110) close-packed plane along the z-direction with Ni (110), (001) and (111), respectively. In the models, two interfaces were set between the atomic planes 4–5 and 12–13, respectively. To compare the relative stability of the models, the interfacial energy, E^{I}, of the sandwich models with various interfacial textures was calculated from

$$E^{\mathrm{I}} = \frac{E^{\mathrm{m}} - N_{\mathrm{Ni}} \cdot E_{\mathrm{Ni}}^{\mathrm{Coh}} - N_{\mathrm{Mo}} \cdot E_{\mathrm{Mo}}^{\mathrm{Coh}}}{\text{interfacial area}}, \tag{7.4}$$

where E^{m} is the energy of the sandwich model after relaxation at 0 K, N_{Ni} and N_{Mo} are the numbers of Ni and Mo atoms in the sandwich models, respectively, and $E_{\mathrm{Ni}}^{\mathrm{Coh}}$ and $E_{\mathrm{Mo}}^{\mathrm{Coh}}$ are the cohesive energies of the Ni and Mo lattices, respectively. Table 11 lists the calculated results for six different combinations of the interfaces. As the interfacial energy of the sandwich model [4 (110) Mo/9 (111) Ni/4 (110) Mo] constructed by both Ni and Mo close-packed atomic planes had the lowest value, it was defined as the reference state and set to zero.

We first discuss the simulation results from three sandwich models constructed with Mo (100) and Ni (110), (001) and (111) planes in the sequence low to high atomic density, respectively. The models were isothermally annealed at 723 K for various time steps. Only in the first model [6 (001) Mo/12 (110) Ni/4 (001) Mo] was SSA achieved—at 57 000 time steps. In the second model [4 (001) Mo/8 (001) Ni/4 (001) Mo], after running for 57 000 time steps, no mutual diffusion could be observed, because such a sharp interface entirely hindered the interfacial reaction and it actually served as a nucleation barrier against amorphization. In the third model [4 (100) Mo/6 (111) Ni/4 (100) Mo], no mutual diffusion was observed either after 57 000 time steps, which was expected because the interface (100) Mo/(111) Ni was more stable than that in the previous two models.

Table 11. The relative interfacial energies, ΔE^{I}, of various interfacial textures calculated at 0 K in the sandwich models constructed by bcc Mo and fcc Ni.

Interface	bcc(001)/ fcc(110)	bcc(001)/ fcc(001)	bcc(001)/ fcc(111)	bcc(110)/ fcc(110)	bcc(110)/ fcc(001)	bcc(110)/ fcc(111
ΔE^{I} (J m^{-2})	0.910	0.659	0.196	0.533	0.133	0.0

To start with a disordered interface similar to that observed in the experiments [18], a disordered interlayer was introduced into the second model [4 (001) Mo/8 (001) Ni/4 (001) Mo] by randomly exchanging four Ni and four Mo atoms in the two atomic planes 4 and 5, corresponding to an amount of disordering $\eta = 0.9$. Introducing the preset disordered interlayer did result in interfacial reaction in the model Figure 20 shows the calculated density profiles, $\rho_\alpha(n)$, of the model for the initial state and another three states after annealing at 723 K for 10 000, 20 000 and 40 000 time steps, respectively. In the initial state, the atomic planes remained in crystalline structures as the corresponding $S(\mathrm{k})$s were still greater than 0.9, except the four planes near the interfaces. At 10 000 time steps, the atomic planes 4 and 5 became disordered and some Ni (Mo) atoms have diffused into the

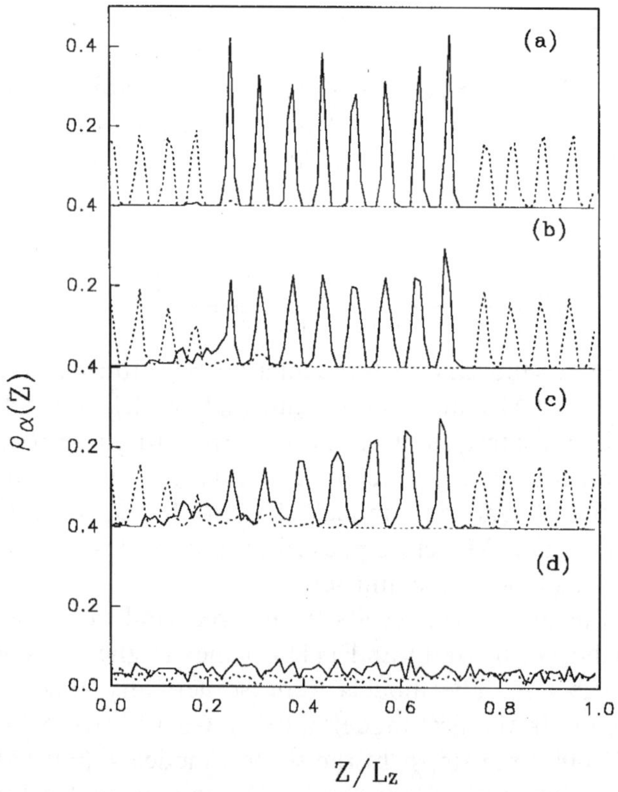

Figure 20. The calculated density profiles, $\rho_\alpha(z)$, of each species along the z-direction for the initial state and the states obtained by annealing at 773 K after 10 000, 20 000 and 40 000 MD time steps in the sandwich model [4 (001) Mo/8 (001) Ni/4 (001) Mo], respectively. The amount of initial disorder is set to be $\eta = 0.9$ in atomic planes 4–5. $\rho_{\mathrm{Ni}}(n)$ is represented by a solid line and $\rho_{\mathrm{Mo}}(n)$ by a dotted line, respectively. The ordinate is in arbitrary units.

partner Mo (Ni) lattice, whereas at another interface of the atomic planes 12–13, no mutual diffusion could be observed. Increasing up to 20 000 time steps, more mutual diffusion took place and resulted in disordering in several atomic planes next to the interface (between Nos 4 and 5) as well as in some other Ni planes. Upon further annealing up to 40 000 time steps, all the atomic planes became disordered. Additionally it is also true that introducing a preset disordered interlayer could facilitate the SSA process. For example, in the first model, SSA could be achieved at 57 000 time steps without a preset disordered interlayer, while SSA could be completed at 40 000 time steps if a chemical disordering of $\eta = 0.5$ was preset only in one of the interfaces. The above results indicated that a difference in the atomic density of the Ni planes was responsible for the different behaviours in interfacial reaction and that chemical disordering introduced into the interface(s) could either trigger or accelerate the process of interfacial reaction and SSA.

We now discuss the simulation results from another three sandwich-models constructed by stacking the close-packed plane (110) of the Mo lattice along the z-direction with three different Ni atomic planes, and the simulations were conducted at annealing temperatures ranging from 573 to 873 K. For the sandwich-model constructed with both Mo and Ni close-packed planes, i.e. [4 (110) Mo/9 (111) Ni/4 (110) Mo], although a disordered interlayer was introduced by setting $\eta = 0$ in the interfacial atomic planes 4 and 5, no diffusion could be observed after annealing at 873 K for 50 000 time steps. Under such conditions, both the Ni and Mo close-packed planes served as growth barriers against SSA, because the already preset disordered interlayer could not grow at all. In another sandwich model [4 (110) Mo/ 12 (110) Ni/4 (110) Mo] with two disordered interlayers (with $\eta = 0.5$) preset in the atomic planes 4–5 and 16–17, atomic diffusion was observed after annealing at 773 K for 30 000 time steps, resulting in amorphization in 14 atomic planes, as confirmed by the calculated pair correlation functions. Moreover, it was noted that the extension of the disordered interlayer towards the Mo lattice was completely suppressed, as six Mo atomic planes in the model remained in crystalline structure and did not change even up to 45 000 time steps. In the sandwich-model [4 (110) Mo/8 (001) Ni/4 (110) Mo] with preset disordered interlayers, upon similar isothermal annealing conditions all the Ni planes together with two Mo planes next to the repective interfaces became disordered, while the other Mo planes still remained in crystalline structure. It is of interest to note that in the latter two cases, though the disordered interlayer was already preset, the growth of the disordered interlayer was completely prevented by the Mo (110) close-packed plane, suggesting that the Mo (110) close-packed plane could serve as a growth barrier to the process of SSA.

According to the calculated energetic sequence of the interfaces listed in table 11, the lowest interfacial energy explains why interfacial reaction was completely frustrated in the model [4 (110) Mo/9 (111) Ni/4 (110) Mo], while the highest interfacial energy explains why SSA could take place spontaneously in the model [6 (001) Mo/12 (110) Ni/4 (001) Mo]. For the other four models, a preset disordered interlayer was necessary to drive the interfacial reaction and SSA. In such cases, the sharp interfaces in the initial states actually served as a nucleation barrier, because the nucleation of an amorphous phase could not initiate. In addition, in some cases the close-packed plane Mo (110) could also serve as a growth barrier. It is of interest to note that the model [4 (110) Mo/12 (110) Ni/4 (110) Mo] has a higher interfacial energy than that of [4 (001) Mo/6 (111) Ni/4 (001) Mo]. However, SSA did take place in the latter model, yet was suppressed in the former. The suppression of SSA in the model [4 (110) Mo/12 (110) Ni/4 (110) Mo] was therefore not from the thermodynamic factor, instead it was from a growth barrier preventing atomic diffusion crossing the Mo (110) close-packed plane. On the contrary, the close-packed plane Ni (111) behaved a little different from the close-packed plane Mo (110). For instance, in the model [4 (001) Mo/6 (111) Ni/4 (001) Mo] constructed from Ni (111) with Mo open planes, SSA could not only proceed but also carried on through all the multilayers, suggesting that the Ni (111) close-packed plane did not always prevent the amorphous layer from growing.

The second system is Ni–Ti, which has a large negative ΔH_f of $-52\,\text{kJ mol}^{-1}$ and an atomic size difference of 18%. MD simulations were performed for several Ni–Ti sandwich models with various textures in the interfaces [128] and the results were generally similar to those observed in the Ni–Mo system [23]. However, for a sandwich model constructed by both close-packed planes of Ni and Ti stacking along the z-direction, namely [4 (001) Ti/6 (111) Ni/2 (001) Ti], interesting results were obtained. First, if no disordered interlayer was present in the model, no interfacial reaction was observed after annealing at 873 K for 40 000 time steps, confirming that the coherent interfaces suppressed the interfacial reaction. Secondly, a disordered interlayer was preset into the model by introducing a chemical disorder $\eta = 0$ through randomly exchanging an equal amount of Ni with Ti atoms in one Ni and one Ti atomic planes next to an interface, i.e. in atomic planes No. 4–5. The model with preset disordered interlayer was equilibrated at 300 K for 10 000 time steps and then heated to 873 K for isothermally annealing. It turned out that during isothermal annealing the disordered interlayer could grow further towards both the Ni and Ti lattices and that after 40 000 time steps the whole model transferred into a relatively uniform amorphous state, suggesting that the close-packed planes in the Ni–Ti system did not serve as a growth barrier as in the Ni–Mo system. These results are in good agreement with the experimental observations reported very recently by Benedictus *et al.* of high-resolution TEM examination of Ni/Ti multilayers having both close-packed Ni (111) and Ti (001) parallel to the interface [133]. In general, the suppression of the solid-state interfacial reaction by the close-packed planes may arise from thermodynamics and/or kinetics. For the above sandwich model [4 (001) Ti/6 (111) Ni/2 (001) Ti], the numbers of Ni and Ti atoms were 936 and 660, respectively, and the Ni concentration was therefore about 58.6 at.%. Choosing a mechanical mixture of the Ni and Ti crystalline metals as a reference state, the energetic level of the sandwich was calculated to be $-6.3\,\text{kJ mol}^{-1}$, which was much higher than the calculated formation enthalpy to be of $-34.3\,\text{kJ mol}^{-1}$ for an amoprphous phase at an alloy composition of 58.6 at.% Ni, implying that SSA was thermodynamically favoured. Consequently, the effect of the close-packed planes on suppressing SSA in the Ni–Ti system was believed to be to do with the kinetics.

Summarizing the above MD simulation results, the effect of interfacial textures on solid-state interfacial reaction and SSA could be different in the binary metal systems. The systems studied above could accordingly be classified into two groups, and in each group the effect was similar. The first group consisted of the Ni–Mo [23], Ni–Nb [115] and Ni–Ta [118] systems, while the Ni–Zr [14] and Ni–Ti [128] systems belonged to the second group.

8. Physical origin of crystal-to-amorphous transition

One of the basic issues in the field of metallic glasses is to predict the glass-forming ability (GFA) or glass-forming range (GFR) of binary alloy systems [134, 135]. As mentioned in section 1, the originally defined GFA was only to classify the systems into two groups of glass-forming and non-glass-forming ones in a qualitative way based on the experimental results obtained from liquid melt quenching (LMQ). Employing the schemes of solid-state reaction (SSR) and/or ion beam mixing (IBM), which are both powerful glass-producing techniques, a great number of new metallic glasses were obtained in those systems, which have been considered as non-glass-forming ones. Apparently, the definition or the physical meaning of GFA needs to be extended and further clarified. First, the GFA of a system should reflect qualitatively whether metallic glass has the ability to be formed in the system or not. From a physical point of view, such an ability should be governed by some internal characteristics of the system. In other words, there should exist an intrinsic GFA for a system, reflecting the maximum capability of obtaining metallic glasses in the system, yet having no correlation with the glass-producing technique applied in practice. Secondly, it is also of necessity to have a quantitative measure for the GFA, with which the relative abilities among the glass-forming systems can be compared. In this regard, an experimentally determined GFR can be taken as a quantiative measure of GFA. In the authors' view, the experimentally determined GFR can only be considered as a nominal GFA, as it depends on the technique applied and is frequently smaller than the intrinsic GFA. Accordingly, to compare the GFA of two glass-forming systems, a greater GFR of a system also corresponds to a greater GFA than that of another, while for the same system, a greater GFR determined by a specific technique is closer to the intrinsic GFA of the system than that observed by other means. As described in section 5.4, IBM is one of the most powerful means for producing metallic glasses. Based on IBM results, Liu *et al.* have proposed predicting the possible GFR of a binary metal system by a simple parameter called the maximum possible amorphization range (MPAR). The parameter MPAR is defined to be the total width of the two-phase region(s) and can be obtained by 100%, as the whole composition range, minus the two maximum solid solubilities of the system. Meanwhile, it has also been shown that the solid solubilities of a system can be considerably extended beyond their equilibrium values by IBM. As a result, the GFR of the system would be reduced while taking into account of the super-saturated solid slubilities [17]. It follows naturally that the prediction of the GFR for a binary metal system becomes a scientific question of determining the maximum (or critical) solid solubilities of the system beyond which the solid solutions become unstable and would turn into an amorphous state. From a physical point of view, the relative stability of solid solutions versus their amorphous counterparts is determined by their respective atomic configurations, which is, in fact, directly governed by the inter-atomic potential of the system. It will be shown later that MD simulation with a proven realistic n-body potential is able to determine the two critical compositions of the system, beyond which the supersaturated solid solutions become unstable and decay spontaneously into an amorphous state. The central composition portion bounded by the two critical solid solubilities can therefore be considered as the GFR of the system. Such a polymorphous GFR is thus a property intrinsic to the system, yet has no connection with any practically applied glass-producing technique.

8.1. *Determination of critical solid solubility and glass-forming ability from inter-atomic potentials*

To determine the critical solid solubilities of some Ni-based alloy systems as representative ones through MD simulations, solid solution models (metal A) were constructed for three major crystalline structures of fcc, bcc and hcp, i.e. the models consisted of $8 \times 8 \times 8 \times 4 = 2048$ atoms for fcc, $9 \times 9 \times 8 \times 2 = 1296$ atoms for bcc, and $10 \times 6 \times 6 \times 4 = 1440$ atoms for hcp structures, respectively. In fcc and bcc models, the [100], [010] and [001] atomic crystal directions were parallel to the x-, y- and z-axes, respectively, and for hcp models, the [100], [001] and [120] crystalline directions were parallel to the x-, y- and z-axes, respectively. In all three directions, periodic boundary conditions were adaopted The solute atoms B were added into the solid solution of metal A by randomly substituting a certain number of atoms of metal B into the lattice of the metal A. To avoid forming clusters of the solute atoms, a random substitution was performed in each unit cell of the lattice of the metal A with the same probability and an initial state of A (B) solid solution for MD simulation was thus obtained. MD simulations were performed for the solid solution models while gradually increasing the solute concentration to find out the critical compositions at which the crystalline lattices of the solid solutions became unstable and collapse into a disordered state.

We now present the simulation results for the Ni–Ti, Ni–Mo, Ni–Zr and Ni–Ta systems, by MD simulations based on the respective n-body potentials described in section 7.

For the Ni–Ti system, the solid solution models were obtained by randomly substituting corresponding amount of Ni (Ti) with Ti (Ni) in the Ni fcc (Ti hcp) lattice. The compositions of fcc Nc-rich (hcp Ti-rich) solid solutions were selected to be in the range 0–50 at.% of Ti (0–50 at.% of Ni). From the initial configuration, the model was then run at 300 K until reaching relative equilibrium, at which all the dynamic parameters showed no secular variation. Figure 21 displays the total and partial pair-correlation functions $g(r)$ calculated for the Ni-rich fcc solid solutions consisting of Ti solute atoms up to 10, 38 and 50 at.%, respectively. From the figure, one sees that the solid solution with 10 at.% of Ti still remains in fcc crystalline structure, while for the solid solutions with 38 and 50 at.% Ti, a crystal-to-amorphous transition apparently takes place, as evidenced by the shape of the calculated $g(r)$ curves. Similar results were obtained for the Ti-rich hcp solid solution and figure 22 shows the calculated total and partial pair-correlation functions $g(r)$ for solute concentrations of 5, 15 and 40 at.% Ni, respectively. One sees that above $x_{Ni} = 15\%$ the calculated curves for $g(r)$ are of typical shape known for an amorphous structure, indicating that $x_{Ni} = 15\%$ is a critical value for the crystal-to-amorphous transition. To obtain firm evidence, the molar enthalpy and volume were calculated as a function of alloy composition and are displayed in figure 23. One sees that the enthalpy and volume of the Ti-rich hcp solid solutions both decrease with increasing Ni concentration and that at $x_{Ni} = 15$ at.% the slopes of both enthalpy and volume are discontinuous with a clear kink in volume change. For Ni-rich solid solutions, it was found that a sudden drop in molar enthalpy appeared at $x_{Ti} = 38$ at.% and the volume of the Ni-rich fcc solid solution increased gradually and a kink appeared also at $x_{Ti} = 38$ at.%, which was exactly the same as determined by the calculated pair correlation functions [136]. A volume expansion of the fcc Ni-rich solid solution with increasing Ti concentration was probably caused by dissolving some large sized Ti atoms into the fcc Ni lattice, and a sudden volume

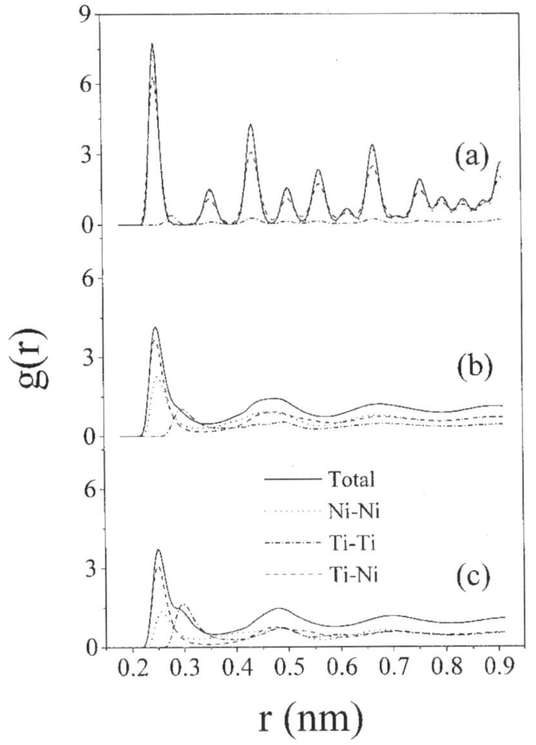

Figure 21. Total and partial pair-correlation functions for the fcc Ni-rich solid solution after running at 300 K for 20 000 MD time steps. The compositions are at (*a*) 10 at.%, (*b*) 38 at.% and (*c*) 50 at.% Ti, respectively. The solid line is for total $g(r)$; the dotted line is for Ni–Ni $g(r)$; the short dashed line is for Ti–Ni $g(r)$; and the dot–dashed line is for Ti–Ti $g(r)$, respectively.

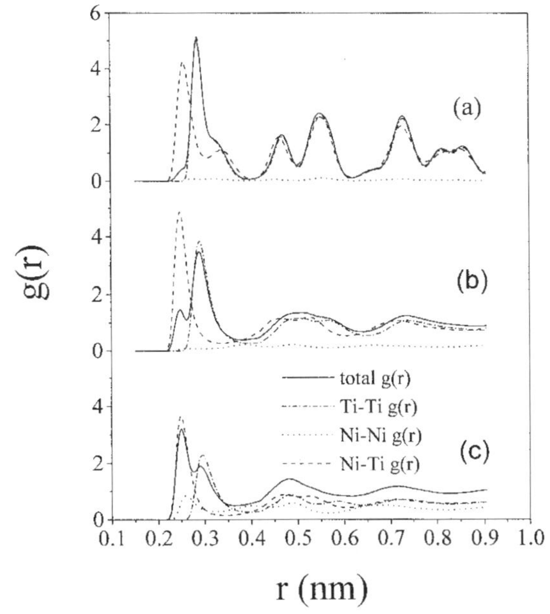

Figure 22. Total and partial pair-correlation functions for the hcp Ti-rich solid solution after simulations performed at 300 K for 20 000 MD time steps. The compositions are at (*a*) 5 at.%, (*b*) 15 at.% and (*c*) 40 at.% Ni, respectively. The solid line is for total $g(r)$; the dotted line is for Ni–Ni $g(r)$; the short dashed line is for Ti–Ni $g(r)$; and the dot–dashed line is for Ti–Ti $g(r)$.

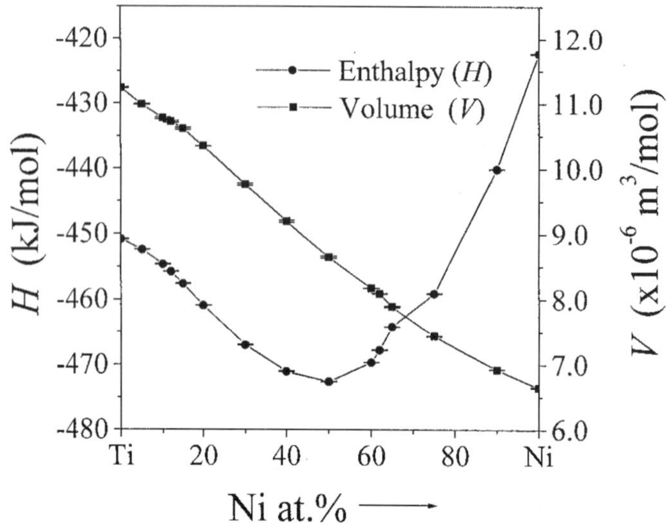

Figure 23. The molar enthalpy and volume as a function of composition of the almost equilibrium states obtained after simulation performed at 300 K for 20 000 MD time steps for the Ni-rich fcc solid solution (0–50% Ti) and Ti-rich hcp solid solution (50–100% Ti), respectively.

Table 12. The critical supersaturated solubilities and the glass forming ranges (GFR) of some Ni-based binary metal systems determined by their respective potentials through MD simulations using solid-solution models (units of alloy concentration are at.%).

		System			
		Ni–Ti	Ni–Zr	Ni–Mo	Ni–Ta
Solubility	Ni	38	14	21	21
	The other metal	15	25	25	43
GFR (Ni at.%)	Calc. value	15-62	25-86	25-79	43-79
	Exper. value	15-62	30-55 [18]	25-75 [20]	–

increase at $x_{Ti} = 38$ at.% was associated with the formation of an Ni-rich Ni–Ti amorphous phase, as an amorphous phase is predicted to have an excess free volume in comparison with its crystalline counterpart [137, 138]. In short, the critical compositions for the crystal-to-amorphous transition were determined to be 15 at.% Ni and 38 at.% Ti for hcp Ti-rich and fcc Ni-rich solid solutions, respectively, and the intrinsic GFR of the Ni–Ti system is therefore deduced to be within a composition range bounded by the two critical values, i.e. within 15–62 at.% Ni.

For the Ni–Mo, Ni–Zr and Ni–Ta systems, similar results were also obtained [23, 118, 136] and table 12 lists the calculated glass-forming ranges together with those observed from experiments, if available. For the Ni–Ti system, the authors' group performed a special 200 keV xenon IBM experiment using Ni–Ti multilayered films very recently and the results showed that at the Ni end the fcc Ni-rich solid solutions could be obtained up to an alloy composition of about 38 at.% Ti with an error of 5%. At the Ti end, an Ni–Ti amorphous alloy with composition 15 at.% Ni was obtained directly after alternately depositing Ni and Ti layers onto a newly cleaved

NaCl crystal in an ultra high vacuum. Incidentally, Ni–Ti metallic glasses have also been obtained by an LMQ technique in a composition range from 30 to 40 at.% Ni [139]. Obviously, all the experimental data matched quite well with that calculated from MD simulation based on the (TB) potential derived by the authors' group [128]. For the Ni–Mo system, amorphization in the Ni–Mo multilayers has been observed upon SSR and the composition range favouring amorphization could extend at least from 25 to 75 at.% Ni [20], which is quite compatible with the intrinsic GFR of 25–79 at.% Ni determined by MD simulation. For the Ni–Zr system, results from SSR experiments were in agreement with that calculated by MD simulation based on the potential developed by Massobrio [130]. In short, the experimentally observed GFRs in the above four systems all fell in the composition ranges determined by MD simulations and therefore were in good agreement with the simulation results.

8.2. *Solubility criterion for asymmetric growth in solid-state amorphization*

According to the MD simulation results, the expansion of an amorphous interlayer results from the disordering of the neighbouring crystalline metals through dissolving the partner metal atoms. Referring to the data listed in table 12, a faster amorphous interlayer growth speed towards metal A than directed to metal B can probably be correlated with the fact that the maximum or critical solid solubility of metal B in the lattice of metal A is lower than vice versa.

To verify the correlation between the solid solubility and asymmetric growth behaviour, a Ni/Ti bilayer model was simulated at 773 K to various time steps and the atomic density profiles along the z-direction were calculated and are displayed in figure 24. From the figure, one observes that the collapse of a crystalline plane is indeed caused when the solute concentration exceeds a critical value. It was also found that before Ti diffused into the Ni atomic plane 10, a large number of solute atoms (Ti) were accelerated towards the Ni/amorphous interface, raising the Ti concentration at the Ni/amorphous interface to more than that in the middle of the amorphous interlayer (see figure 24(*b*)). After the Ti atoms at the Ni/amorphous interface reached a certain number, they began to diffuse into the next Ni crystalline atomic plane (No. 10), while some Ni atoms in atomic plane 10 moved out and diffused into the amorphous matrix, resulting in the crystal-to-amorphous transition taking place in atomic plane 10, as shown in figure 24(*c*). By integrating the $\rho_\alpha(z)$ peak shown in figure 24 for each collapsing layer and the amorphous interlayer, respectively, the in-plane concentrations of the solute atoms C of the collapsing layers, and the average concentration of the amorphous interlayer $\bar{C}$ were obtained and are displayed in figure 25. One sees that the concentrations of the Ni solute atoms in the collapsing Ti layers are greater than 20 at.% and the Ti solute atoms in the collapsing Ni layers are greater than 30 at.% Ti. When a layer was sampled to consist of a collapsing Ni atomic plane together with a thin layer of same thickness in its neighbouring amorphous matrix, the solute concentration was calculated to be greater than 44 at.% Ti, as shown in figure 25 by the open squares. The estimated concentrations in the collapsing Ti and Ni atomic planes seem to be greater than those obtained by MD simulation. None the less, it is believed to be rational because first the estimated concentrations were greater than the critical ones determined by MD simulation and would certainly result in collapse of the crystalline atomic planes. Secondly, the limited concentration changes brought about by a Ti–Ni exchange would result in a greater solubility in the collapsing planes than the critical

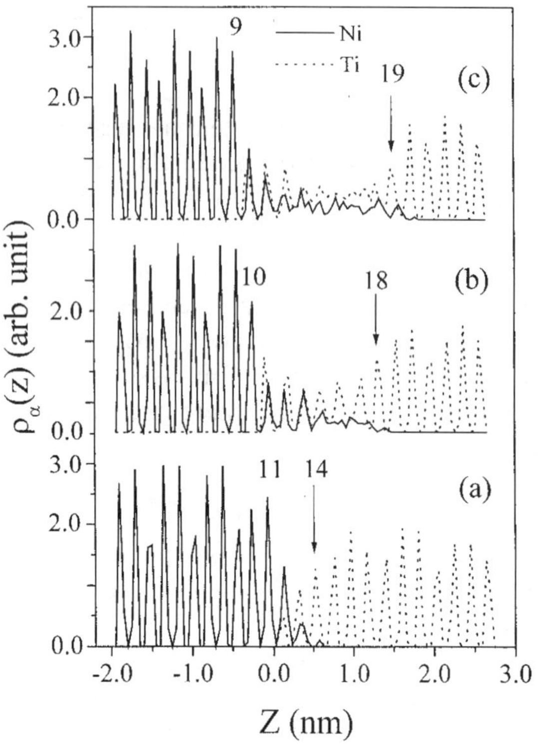

Figure 24. The atomic density profiles along the z-direction at various annealed states at 773 K obtained by averaging data between 50 time steps after simulation performed for 5840, 59 349 and 111 989 MD steps with the planar structure factor S(k)s of the atomic planes 12(a), 17(b) and 10(c) less than 0.1, respectively. The crystalline atomic planes next to the amorphous interlayer are denoted by their plane numbers.

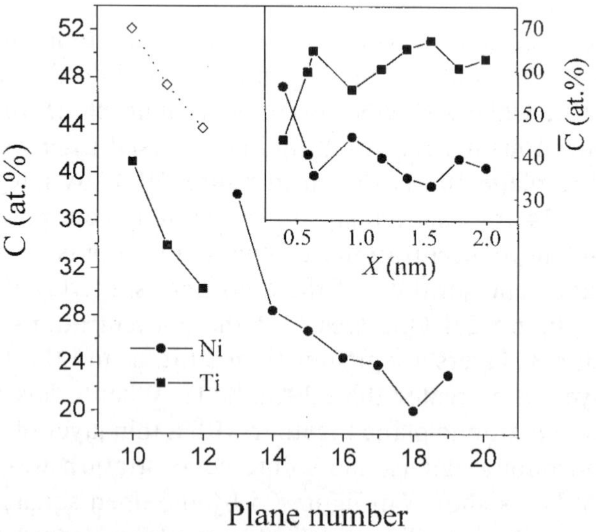

Figure 25. In-plane compositions of solute atoms C (solid symbols) versus atomic plane number obtained from figure 24 when the plane is collapsing. The hollow diamond symbols stand for the Ti compositions in a layer with a thickness of two Ni atomic planes consisting of a collapsing Ni atomic plane and its neighbouring amorphous matrix. The inset shows the corresponding average compositions of the amorphous interlayer versus its thickness.

values, because for exchanging one atom between the Ni and Ti planes, the concentration would change by 1.4 and 2% for Ni and Ti, respectively.

In short, the collapse of a crystalline atomic plane in a metal is caused by the dissolving solute atoms exceeding the maximum allowable solubility of the metal. A solubility criterion is therefore proposed and the criterion predicts that the amorphous interlayer will extend faster towards the metal with the lower critical solid solubility than vice versa. It is evident that the proposed solubility criterion is able to explain the asymmetric growth observed so far in the Ni-based systems listed in table 12 [14, 118, 140, 141]. Incidentally, the criterion can also explain a surprising obervation that emerged in the Ni–W multilayers upon 200 keV xenon IBM. In the IBM experiment, it was observed that when all the other parameters were basically the same, the W-enriched multilayered films underwent complete amorphization at a much lower dose than did the Ni-enriched multilayers [142]. Such an asymmetric amorphization behaviour is reasonably attributed to the fact that the equilibrium solid solubility of W is much smaller than that of Ni, though the melting point of W is much higher than that of Ni [143].

9. Conclusions

(1) In solid-state reaction of multilayers, negative heat of formation of a binary metal system itself serves as a major thermodynamic driving force for interfacial mixing and amorphization transition, resulting in the formation of metallic glass within a certain composition range of the system. However, in a system with positive heat of formation, the driving force originates from the excess interfacial free energy, which can be adjusted to broaden the metallic-glass-forming range of the system by appropriately designing the multilayers to include the necessary fraction of interfacial atoms.

(2) Based on the proven realistic n-body potentials of some binary metal systems, molecular dynamics simulations reveal some interesting phenomena in solid-state reaction, such as a possible linear time (t) dependence and/or an exact square root t law at a very early stage, an exponential temperature dependence, asymmetric growth of the amorphous interlayer towards the two constituent metals, and the possibility of interface texture playing a role in nucleation and/or growth barriers against the amorphization transition.

(3) The physical origin of the crystal-to-amorphous transition in metal–metal multilayers is attributed to collapse of the crystalline lattice when the solute concentration exceeds a critical solid solubility, which divides the alloy composition into different regions favouring a solid solution and a disordered state, respectively. The critical solid solubilities of a binary metal system can be directly determined by molecular dynamics simulation, based on a realistic n-body potential of the system. The metallic-glass-forming range of the system is therefore within such a composition range bounded by the two critical solid solubilities. Viewed in this light, a solubility criterion is proposed that predicts the amorphous interlayer will grow faster towards the metal having the lower solid solubility than its partner metal during solid-state amorphization.

(4) The issues discussed in this review article are important topics in the area known as 'Non-equilibrium alloy phase formation and transition' in the field of 'physical metallurgy' or, in a broad sense, 'condensed matter and materials physics'. By comprehensive studies with solid-state reaction experiments using metallic

mulilayers, thermodynamic modelling, atomistic modelling through molecular dynamics (MD) simulation based on realistic potentials and *ab initio* calculations, some progress has been achieved that promotes a better understanding of the underlying physics as well as the development of the respective theory in a quantitative manner.

Acknowledgements

The authors are grateful to the National Natural Science Foundation of China for continuous financial support over the past 20 years. Partial financial aid from the Ministry of Science and Technology (Grant No. G2000067207) and from the Administration of Tsinghua University is also acknowledged with great appreciation.

References

[1] Klement, W., Willens, R. H., and Duwez, P., 1960, *Nature*, **187,** 869–870.
[2] Zallen, Z., 1983, *The Physics of Amorphous Solid* (New York: Wiley-Interscience).
[3] Greer, A. L., 1995, *Science*, **267,** 1947–1953.
[4] Davies, H. A., 1983, in F. E. Luborsky (ed.), *Amorphous Metallic Alloys* (London: Butterworths).
[5] Hafner, J., 1981, in H.-J. Guentherodt and H. Beck (eds), *Metallic Glasses* (Berlin: Springer-Verlag), p. 93–98.
[6] Giessen, B. S., and Whang, S. H., 1980, *J. Metals*, **32**(80), 61–62.
[7] Sommer, F., 1981, *Z. Metallkde*, **72,** 219–229.
[8] Schwarz, R. B., and Johnson, W. L., 1983, *Phys. Rev. Lett.*, **51,** 415–418.
[9] Liu, B. X., Johnson, W. L., Nicolet, M.-A., and Lau, S. S., 1983, *Appl. Phys. Lett.*, **42,** 45–47.
[10] Chen, Y. G., and Liu, B. X., 1996, *Appl. Phys. Lett.*, **68,** 3096–3098.
[11] Deboer, F. R., Boom, R., Mattens, W. C. M., Miedema, A. R., and Niessen, A. K., 1989, *Cohesion in Metals: Transition Metal Alloys* (Amsterdam, The Netherlands: North-Holland Physics).
[12] Liu, B. X., and Zhang, Z. J., 1994, *Phys. Rev.* B, **49,** 12519–12527.
[13] Meyer, M., and Pontikis, V., (eds), 1991, *Computer Simulation in Materials Science* (Norwell, MA: Kluwer Academic).
[14] Lai, W. S., and Liu, B. X., 1998, *Phys. Rev.* B, **58,** 6063–6073.
[15] Zhang, Q., Lai, W. S., and Liu, B. X., 1999, *Phys. Rev.* B, **59,** 13521–13524.
[16] Liu, J. B., Yang, G. W., and Liu, B. X., 2000, *Phys. Rev.* B, **68,** 11277–11279.
[17] see for example, Liu, B. X., Lai, W. S., and Zhang, Q., 2000, *Materials Science and Engineering: Reports*, **29,** 1–48.
[18] Clemens, B. M., 1986, *Phys. Rev.* B, **33,** 7615–7624.
[19] Kwak, J. S., Chi, E. J., Choi, J. D., Park, S. W., Naik, H. K., So, M. G., and Lee, S. M., 1995, *J. appl. Phys.*, **78,** 983–987.
[20] Zhang, Z. J., and Liu, B. X., 1994, *J. appl. Phys.*, **76,** 3351–3356.
[21] Liu, B. X., Zhang, Z. J., Jin, O., and Pan, F., 1996, Role of interface in ion mixing or thermal annealing-induced amorphization in multilayers in some immiscible systems. *Materials Research Soc. Symp. Proc.*, **396,** 71–82.
[22] Pan, F., Chen, Y. G., and Liu, B. X., 1995, *Appl. Phys. Lett.*, **67,** 780–782.
[23] Zhang, Q., Lai, W. S., and Liu, B. X., 1998, *Phys. Rev.* B, **58,** 14020–14030.
[24] Pan, F., Ling, Z. F., Gao, K. Y., and Liu, B. X., 1996, Alloying in an immiscible Cu–Nb system upon solid-state reaction. *Materials Research Soc. Symp. Proc.*, **398,** 337–342.
[25] Chen, Y. G., and Liu, B. X., 1997, *J. Phys.* D: *appl. Phys.*, **30,** 1729–1733.
[26] Liu, B. X., and Chen, Y. G., 1998, *Thin solid Films*, **334,** 201–205.
[27] Chen, Y. G., and Liu, B. X., 1999, *Acta Materilia*, **47,** 1389–1397.
[28] Chen, Y. G., and Liu, B. X., 1997, *J. non-crystalline Solids*, **217,** 308–316.

[29] Kwon, K. W., Lee, H. J., and Sinclair, R., 1999, *Appl. Phys. Lett.*, **75,** 935–937.
[30] Atzmon, M., Unruh, K., and Johnson, W. L., 1985, *J. appl. Phys.*, **58,** 3865–3870.
[31] Brouder, C., Krill, G., Guilmin, P., Marchal, G., Partype, E., Fontaine, A., and Tourillon, G., 1988, *Phys. Rev.* B, **37,** 2433–2439.
[32] Firgerio, J. M., and Rivory, J., 1990, *J. Physique* C, **51,** 4163–4168.
[33] Ma, E., Nieh, C. W., Nicolet, M.-A., and Johnson, W. L., 1989, *J. Mater. Res.*, **4,** 1299–1302.
[34] Hung, L. S., Nastasi, M., Gyulai, J., and Mayer, J. W., 1983, *Appl. Phys. Lett.*, **42,** 672–674.
[35] Blainpain, B., Legresy, J. M., and Mayer, J. W., 1990, *J. Physique* C, **51,** 4131–4137.
[36] Ben Ameur, T., and Yavari, A. R., 1990, *J. Physique* C, **51,** 4219–4226.
[37] Guilmin, P., Guyot, P., and Marchal, G., 1985, *Phys. Lett.* A, **109,** 174–178.
[38] Schwarz, R. B., Wong, K. L., and Johnson, W. L., 1984, *J. non-cryst. Solids*, **61/62,** 129–134.
[39] Ding, F. R., Okamoto, P. R., and Rehn, L. E., 1989, *J. Mater. Res.*, **4,** 1444–1449.
[40] Schröder, H., Samwer, K., and Koster, U., 1985, *Phys. Rev. Lett.*, **54,** 197–200.
[41] Johnson, R. W., Ahn, C. C., and Ratner, E. R., 1989, *Phys. Rev.* B, **40,** 8139–8145.
[42] Clemens, B. M., and Suchoski, M. J., 1985, *Appl. Phys. Lett.*, **47,** 943–945.
[43] van Rossum, M., Nicolet, M.-A., and Johnson, W. L., 1984, *Phys. Rev.* B, **29,** 5498–5503.
[44] Yang, G. W., Lin, C., and Liu, B. X., 1999, *J. Mater. Res.*, **14,** 3027–3036.
[45] Clemens, B. M., Johnson, W. L., and Schwarz, R. B., 1984, *J. non-cryst. Solid*, **61/62,** 817–822.
[46] Li, H., and Tonner, B. P., 1990, *Surf. Sci.*, **237,** 141–152.
[47] Aufray, B., Giodano, H., Legrand, B., and Treglia, G., 1994, *Surf. Sci.*, **309,** 531–537.
[48] Roussel, J. M., Saul, A., Treglia, G., and Legrand, B., 1997, *Phys. Rev.* B, **55,** 10931–10937.
[49] Chu, W. K., Mayer, J. W., and Nicolet, M.-A., 1978, *Backscattering Spectrometry* (New York: Academic Press), Chap. 4.
[50] Tesmer, J. R., and Nastasi, M., 1995, *Handbook of Modern Ion Beam Materials Analysis* (Pittsburgh, PA: Materials Research Society), Chap. 4.
[51] Alonso, J. A., Gallego, L. J., and Simozar, J. A., 1990, *Nuovo Cimento*, **12,** 587–595.
[52] Niessen, A. K., and Miedema, A. R., 1983, *Ber. bunsenges. Phys. Chem.*, **87,** 717–725.
[53] Lopez, J. M., Alonso, J. A., and Gallego, L. J. 1987, *Phys Rev.* B, **37,** 3716–3722.
[54] Weeber, A. W., 1987, *J. Phys.* F, **17,** 809–813.
[55] Niessen, A. K., Miedema, A. R., Deboer, F. R., and Boom, R., 1988, *Physica* B, **151,** 401–432.
[56] Lopez, J. M., and Alonso, J. A., 1983, *Phys. Stat. sol.* (a), **76,** 675–682.
[57] Lopez, J. M., and Alonso, J. A., 1984, *Phys. Stat. sol.* (a), **85,** 423–428.
[58] Friedel, J., 1954, *Adv. Phys.*, **3,** 446–507.
[59] Eshelby, J. D., 1956, in D. Seitz and D. Turnbull (eds), *Solid State Physics*, Vol. 3 (New York: Academic Press), pp. 79–144.
[60] Lopez, J. M., and Alonso, J. A., 1985, *Z. Naturforsch.* A, **40,** 1199–1205.
[61] Loeff, P. I., Weeber, A. W., and Miedema, A. R., 1998, *J. less-common Metals*, **140,** 299–305.
[62] Jawson, M. A., and Wheeler, J. A., 1948, *Acta Crystallographia*, **1,** 216–224.
[63] Turnbull, D., 1955, in *Impurities and Imperfections, a seminar on impurities and imperfections held during the 36th National Metals Congress and Exhibition*, Chicago, IL, 30 October–5 November 1955 (Metals Park, OH: Amer. Soc. Met.), p. 121.
[64] Murr, L. E., 1975, in *Interfacial Phenomena in Metals and Alloys* (London: Addison-Wesley).
[65] Miedema, A. R., 1978, *Z. Metallkde.*, **69,** 455–461.
[66] Miedema, A. R., 1978, *Z. Metallkde.*, **69,** 287–292.
[67] Gerkema, J., and Miedema, A. R., 1981, *Surf. Sci.*, **124,** 351–371.
[68] Jin, O., Zhang, Z. J., and Liu, B. X., 1995, *J. appl. Phys.*, **77,** 149–154.

[69] Zhang, Z. J., and Liu, B. X., 1995, *Phys. Rev.* B, **51,** 16475–16478
[70] Liu, J. B., and Liu, B. X., 2001, *Phys. Rev.* B, **63,** 132204-(1-4).
[71] Liu, J. B., and Liu, B. X., 2001, *Phys. Rev.* B, submitted.
[72] Lin, C., Yang, G. W., and Liu, B. X., 2000, *Phys. Rev.* B, **61,** 15649–15652.
[73] Bakker, H., 1985, *J. less-common Met.*, **105,** 129–138.
[74] Brown, A. M., and Ashby, M. F., 1980, *Acta Metallurgica*, **28,** 1085–11012.
[75] Finnis, M. W., and Sinclair, J. E., 1984, *Phil. Mag.* A, **50,** 45–55.
[76] Li, Z. F., Lai, W. S., and Liu, B. X., 2000, *Appl. Phys. Lett.*, **77,** 3920–3922.
[77] Yang, G. W., Lai, W. S., Lin, C., and Liu, B. X., 1999, *Appl. Phys. Lett.*, **74,** 3305–3307.
[78] Meng, W. J., 1987, PhD thesis, Department of Applied Physics, California Institute of Technology.
[79] Liu, B. X., Zhang, Z. J., and Jin, O., 1998, *J. Alloys and Compounds*, **270,** 186–193.
[80] Ciccotti, G., Frenkel, D., and McDonald, I. R., 1987, in *Simulation of Liquids and Solids* (Amsterdam, The Netherlands: North-Holland).
[81] Alle, M. P., and Tildesley, D. J., 1987, in *Computer Simulation of Liquids* (Oxford, UK: Oxford University Press).
[82] Daw, M. S., and Baskes, M. I., 1983, *Phys. Rev. Lett.*, **50,** 1285–1288.
[83] Daw, M. S., and Baskes, M. I., 1984, *Phys. Rev.* B, **29,** 6443–6453.
[84] Andersen, H. C., 1980, *J. chem. Phys.*, **72,** 2384–2393.
[85] Parrinello, M., and Rahman, A., 1980, *Phys. Rev. Lett.*, **45,** 1196–1199.
[86] Parrinello, M., and Rahman, A., 1981, *J. appl. Phys.*, **52,** 7182–7190.
[87] Lee, J. K., 1981, in *Interatomic Potentials and Crystalline Defects* (New York: Metallurgy Society of the AIME).
[88] Vitek, V., 1985, *Dislocations and Properties of Real Materials* (London: The Institute of Metals).
[89] Hohenberg, P., and Kohn, W., 1964, *Phys. Rev.* B, **136,** 864–871.
[90] Duscastelle, F., 1991, *Order and Phase Stability in Alloys* (Amsterdam, The Netherlands: Elsevier Science).
[91] Skriver, H. L., 1984, *The LMTO Method* (Berlin: Springer-Verlag).
[92] Johnson, R. A., 1988, *Phys. Rev.* B, **37,** 3924–3931.
[93] Johnson, R. A., and Oh, D. J., 1989, *J. Mater. Res.*, **4,** 1195–1201.
[94] Voter, A. F., and Chen, S. P., 1987, Characterization of·defects in materials, in R. W. Siegal, J. R. Weetman and R. Sinclair (eds), *Materials Research Soc. Symp. Proc.*, **82,** 175–180.
[95] Johnson, R. A., 1989, *Phys. Rev.* B, **39,** 12554–12559.
[96] Johnson, R. A., 1990, *Phys. Rev.* B, **41,** 9717–9720.
[97] Cai, J., and Ye, Y. Y., 1996, *Phys. Rev.* B, **54,** 8398–8410.
[98] Banerjea, A., and Smith, J. R., 1988, *Phys. Rev.* B, **37,** 6632–6645.
[99] Rose, J. H., Smith, J. R., Guinea, F., and Ferrante, J., 1984, *Phys. Rev.* B, **29,** 2963–2969.
[100] Tomanek, D., Aligia, A. A., and Balseiro, C. A., 1985, *Phys. Rev.* B, **32,** 5051–5056.
[101] Ducastelle, F., and Cyrot-Lackmann, F., 1970, *J. Phys. Chem. Solids*, **31,** 1295–1306.
[102] Tomanek, D., Mukherjee, S., and Bennemann, K. H., 1983, *Phys. Rev.* B, **28,** 665–673.
[103] Ackland, G. J., Tichy, G. I., Vitek, V., and Finnis, M. W., 1987, *Phil. Mag.* A, **56,** 735–756.
[104] Marchese, M., Jacucci, G., and Flynn, C. P., 1988, *Phil. Mag. Lett.*, **57,** 25–30.
[105] Ackland, G. J., Bacon, D. J., Calder, A. F., and Harry, T., 1997, *Phil. Mag.* A, **75,** 713–732.
[106] Rebonato, R., Welch, D. O., Hatcher, R. D., and Bilello, J. C., 1987, *Phil. Mag.* A, **55,** 655–667.
[107] Rosato, V., Guillope, M., and Legrand, B., 1989, *Phil. Mag.* A, **59,** 321–336.
[108] Cleri, F., and Rosato, V., 1993, *Phys. Rev.* B, **48,** 22–33.
[109] Rosato, V., Ciccotti, G., and Pontikis, V., 1986, *Phys. Rev.* B, **33,** 1860–1870.
[110] Phillpot, S. R., Yip, S., and Wolf, D., 1989, *Comput. Phys.*, **3,** 20–31.

[111] HUANG, X. Y., PAN, J. S., and FAN, Y. D., 1996, *Phy. Rev.* B, **54,** 16325–16328.
[112] HUANG, X. Y., 1997, PhD thesis, Department of Materials Science and Engineering, Tsinghua University, Beijing, PR China.
[113] LIU, B. X., 1986, *Phys. Stat. sol.* (a), **94,** 11–34.
[114] HUANG, X. Y., PAN, J. S., and FAN, Y. D., 1997, *Solid State Commun.*, **104,** 101–105.
[115] ZHANG, Q., LAI, W. S., and LIU, B. X., 2000, *Europ. phys. J.* B, **16,** 223–231.
[116] *The Powder Diffraction Data*, Joint Committee of Powder Diffraction Standards (JCPDS), Swarthmore, PA, USA.
[117] BRANDES, E. A., and BROOK, G. B., 1992, *Smithells Metals Reference Book*, 7th edn (Oxford: Butterworth-Heinemann).
[118] ZHANG, Q., LAI, W. S., and LIU, B. X., 2000, *Phys. Rev.* B, **61,** 9345–9355.
[119] FARKAS, D., ROQUETA, D., VILLETTE, A., and TERNES, K., 1996, *Modelling Simul. mater. Sci. Eng.*, **4,** 359–369.
[120] PASTURAL, A., COLINET, C., NGUYEN MANH, D., PAXTON, A. T., and VAN SCHILFGAARDE, M., 1995, *Phys. Rev.* B, **52,** 15176–15190.
[121] BIHLMAYER, G., EIBLER, R., and NECHEL, A., 1994, *Phys. Rev.* B, **50,** 13113–13117.
[122] KITTEL, C., 1986, *Introduction to Solid State Physics* (New York: Wiley Interscience).
[123] HULTGREN, R., DESAI, P. D., HAWKINS, D. T., GLEISER, M., and KELLY, K. K., 1973, *Selected Values of Thermodynamic Properties of Binary Alloys* (Metals Park, OH: ASM).
[124] SIMMONS, G., and WANG, H., 1971, *Single Crystal Elastic Constants and Calculated Aggregate Properties: a Handbook* (Cambridge, MA: MIT Press).
[125] WYCISK, W., and FELLER-KNIPMEIER, M., 1978, *J. nucl. Mater.*, **69&70,** 616–619.
[126] SHESTOPAL, V. O., 1966, *Fiz. Tverd. Tela* (Leningrad), **7,** 3461–3465.
[127] SHESTOPAL, V. O., 1966, *Sov. Phys. solid State*, **7,** 2798–2802.
[128] LAI, W. S., ZHANG, Q., LIU, B. X., and MA, E., 2000, *J. phys. Soc. Jpn*, **9,** 2923–2937.
[129] MURA, P., DEMONTIS, P., SUFFRITTI, G. B., ROSATO, V., and VITTORI ANTISARI, M., 1994, *Phys. Rev.* B, **50,** 2850–2857.
[130] MASSOBRIO, C., PONTIKIS, V., and MARTIN, G., 1990, *Phys. Rev.* B, **41,** 10486–10497.
[131] HIGHMORE, R. J., 1990, *Phil. Mag.* B, **62,** 455–467.
[132] MENG, W. J., NIEH, C. W., and JOHNSON, W. L., 1987, *Appl. Phys. Lett.*, **51,** 1693–1695.
[133] BENEDICTUS, R., HAN, K., TRAEHOLT, C., BÖTTGER, A., and MITTEMEIJER, E. J., 1998, *Acta Mater.*, **46,** 5491–5508.
[134] RUHL, R. C., GIESSEN, B. C., COHEN, M., and GRANT, N. J., 1967, *Acta Metall.*, **15,** 1693–1702.
[135] POON, S. J., and CARTER, W. L., 1980, *Solid state Commun.*, **35,** 249–251.
[136] LAI, W. S., and LIU, B. X., 2001, *J. Mater. Res.*, **16,** 446–450.
[137] VAN DEN BEUKEL, A., and RADELAAR, S., 1983, *Acta Metall.*, **31,** 419–427.
[138] WOLF, D., OKAMOTO, P. R., YIP, S., LUTSKO, J. F., and KLUGE, M., 1990, *J. Mater. Res.*, **5,** 286–301.
[139] FUKUNAGA, T., WATANABE, W., and SUZUKI, K., 1984, *J. non-cryst. Solids*, **61&62,** 343–348.
[140] LAI, W. S., ZHANG, Q., LIU, B. X., and MA, E., 2001, *Phil. Mag. Lett.*, **81,** 45–53.
[141] ZHANG, Q., LAI, W. S., and LIU, B. X., 2000, *J. appl. Phys.*, **87,** 7696–7701.
[142] LI, Z. F., and LIU, B. X., 2001, *Jpn J. appl. Phys.*, submitted.
[143] KOZMA, L., and LABAR, L., 1981, *High Temperatures—High Pressures*, **13,** 521–527.

Metastable phase formation in an immiscible Cu-Ta system studied by ion-beam mixing, ab initio calculation, and molecular dynamics simulation

H.R. Gong [1], L.T. Kong [1], W.S. Lai [1], B.X. Liu [*,1]

Advanced Materials Laboratory, Department of Materials Science and Engineering, Tsinghua University, Beijing 100084, China

Received 6 January 2003; received in revised form 10 April 2003; accepted 10 April 2003

Abstract

Ion-beam mixing experiments show that amorphous phases are formed in the $Cu_{70}Ta_{30}$, $Cu_{65}Ta_{35}$, $Cu_{60}Ta_{40}$, and $Cu_{50}Ta_{50}$ multilayered samples, while a crystalline structure is retained in the $Cu_{75}Ta_{25}$ sample. These results suggest that the composition limit for forming an amorphous phase is around 30 at.% Ta, which confirms the same value of 30 at.% Ta predicted by recent atomistic modeling. For the metastable crystalline $Cu_{75}Ta_{25}$ phase, ab initio calculations identify its relatively stable structure to be $L1_2$ (fcc type) and determine some associated physical properties, which agree well with those derived from a proven realistic Cu-Ta potential through molecular dynamics simulations. Interestingly, an fcc $Cu_{75}Ta_{25}$ phase is indeed observed in ion-beam mixing experiments and its lattice constant determined by diffraction analysis matches well with those from theoretical calculations.

Keywords: Metastable phases; Ion-beam mixing; Ab-initio electron theory; Molecular dynamics; Copper alloys

1. Introduction

The interaction between the metals Cu and Ta has attracted much attention during the past decades, as copper has been used as an interconnection metal to replace aluminum in microelectronic circuits due to its unique properties, and tantalum has been used as a diffusion barrier in very large scale integrated circuits to prevent Cu atoms from diffusing into Si/SiO_2 [1–4]. It is known that the Cu-Ta system is an essentially immiscible one characterized with a positive heat of formation (ΔH_f) of +3 kJ/mol calculated by Miedema's model at an equi-stoichiometry and in its equilibrium phase diagram, there does not exist any Cu-Ta compound over the entire composition range [5]. Nonetheless, a lot of experiments have shown that various metastable Cu-Ta phases of either an amorphous or crystalline structure could be formed between Cu and Ta under some nonequilibrium conditions [6–11]. Apparently, the formation of any Cu-Ta meta-

* Corresponding author. Tel.: +86 106 2772 619; fax: +86 106 2771 160.

E-mail address: dmslbx@tsinghua.edu.cn (B.X. Liu).

[1] Also at Laboratory of Solid-State Microstructure, Nanjing University, Nanjing 210008, China

Acta Materialia 51(13), p.3885-3893(2003).

stable phase could bring about some effects to degrade the performance of Ta as a diffusion barrier as well as of Cu as an interconnection in the electronic devices. It is, therefore, of both practical and theoretical importance to have a thorough investigation of the Cu-Ta system concerning the metastable phase formation and to reveal the associated underlying physics for a deep understanding. Concerning the amorphous alloy formation, many experiments have been done for the Ta-rich region, e.g., $Cu_{30}Ta_{70}$ and other Ta-enriched amorphous alloys have been readily obtained by various means [9,11–13], while the Cu-rich region of the Cu-Ta system has less been studied experimentally and there are still some controversies. For instance, Kim et al., reported that the content of Ta should exceed 44 at.% for forming a Cu-rich Cu-Ta amorphous alloy [10], whereas Kwon et al., found that the lowest Ta content for amorphization was around 25 at.% [14].

In the past 20 years, ion-beam mixing (IBM) of metallic multilayers has been proven to be a powerful means to form various metastable phases in the binary metallic systems, as its effective cooling speed was estimated, based on a thermal spike model, to be as high as 10^{13-14} K/sec [15]. Another uniqueness of IBM is that the alloy composition could be readily varied to study the compositional dependence on the metastable phase formation, by simply adjusting the relative thicknesses of the constituent metallic layers. In the present study, IBM is employed to study the metastable phase formation in the Cu-Ta system with an emphasis on finding out the critical composition for the crystalline-to-amorphous transition in the Cu-rich side and to compare the experimental results with those determined by molecular dynamics (MD) simulations [16]. Another important issue of the present study is to conduct ab initio calculations and MD simulations for calculating the structural stability of the metastable crystalline Cu-Ta phases and the calculated results are compared with the experimental observations from IBM.

2. Experimental procedure and calculation methods

2.1. Experimental procedure of ion-beam mixing

It is known that the interfacial free energy stored in the multilayers is the major driving force for the formation of the metastable crystalline and amorphous phases in the binary metallic systems with positive heats of formation [17]. Consequently, the layer thicknesses of the multilayered films are specially designed to include enough interfacial free energy, which can elevate the initial energy state of the films to a specific level surpassing that of the desired alloy phase. In pursuing IBM with 200 keV xenon ions, the total thicknesses of the Cu-Ta multilayered films were calculated to be about 430 Å, matching the corresponding projected range plus projected range straggling for an efficient intermixing in the films. Based on Miedema's model [5] and Alonso's method [18], the free energies of the Cu-Ta multilayered films were intentionally designed to be higher than those of the corresponding amorphous phases. Accordingly, the Cu-Ta multilayered films were designed to consist of 8 bilayers and five alloy compositions, i.e., $Cu_{75}Ta_{25}$, $Cu_{70}Ta_{30}$, $Cu_{65}Ta_{35}$, $Cu_{60}Ta_{40}$, and $Cu_{50}Ta_{50}$, were selected for studying the composition dependence of the metastable phase formation.

The Cu-Ta multilayers were prepared by alternative deposition of Cu and Ta onto freshly cleaved NaCl single crystals in an e-gun evaporator with a vacuum level on the order of 10^{-8} Torr. The depositing rate was controlled at 0.5 Å/s and during deposition no special cooling was provided to the substrates. The real compositions of the films were confirmed by sequential x-ray fluorescence spectrometer (XRF–1700) within an error of less than 3%. The deposited films were then irradiated by 200 keV xenon ions at 77 K with various doses ranging from 5×10^{14} to 1×10^{16} Xe^+ cm^{-2}. The ion current density was confined to be 0.5 $\mu A \cdot cm^{-2}$ to avoid an otherwise overheating effect. For structural characterization, all the Cu-Ta multilayered films were removed from the NaCl substrates by de-ionized water and placed onto the Mo grids for transmission electron microscopy (TEM) examination and selected area diffraction (SAD) analysis.

2.2. Method of ab initio calculations

The well-established Vienna ab initio simulation package (VASP) is employed in the present study [19]. In the package, the calculations are conducted in a plane-wave basis, using fully nonlocal Vanderbilt-type ultrasoft pseudopotentials to describe the electron-ion interaction [20], which allows the use of a moderate cutoff for the construction of the plane-wave basis for the transition metals. The exchange and correlation items are described by the generalized-gradient approximation (GGA) of Perdew and Wang [21]. The integration in the Brillouin zone is done on special k points determined according to the Monkhorst-Pack scheme [22].

In studying the stability of the possible metastable crystalline Cu-Ta phase, we only select those simple crystalline structures for calculation, based on the following consideration and fact. For a complicated structure, its unit cell frequently contains more atoms and probably requires a relatively larger critical radius for nucleation and growth than a simple one. It follows that such a structure is hardly to be formed, because the kinetic conditions are usually restricted in those frequently applied nonequilibrium materials processing techniques. In fact, numerous experiments have shown that the metastable crystalline phases obtained so far in the binary metallic systems are of simple structures, such as fcc, bcc, and hcp structures, rather than complicated ones [15].

2.3. Scheme and models of molecular dynamics simulation

Molecular dynamics simulations are carried out with the Parrinello-Rahman constant pressure scheme and the equations of motion are solved using a fourth-order predictor-corrector algorithm of Gear with a time step of $t = 5 \times 10^{-15}$ s [23]. Naturally, it is necessary to have a proven realistic n-body potential to conduct MD simulations. In this respect, the construction of an n-body potential for the immiscible Cu-Ta system is a challenging task, as there does not exist any equilibrium Cu-Ta compound that could provide the necessary physical data for deriving the Cu-Ta cross potential. Very recently, a scheme was proposed by the present authors to adopt ab initio calculations for acquiring some physical properties of the metastable $L1_2$ $Cu_{75}Ta_{25}$ and B2 $Cu_{50}Ta_{50}$ phases and the obtained properties were then used in fitting the Cu-Ta potential [16]. The potential so derived was proven to be a realistic one and therefore is applied in the present study to conduct MD simulations.

Two different simulation models are employed, i.e., an $L1_2$ ordered structure model and an fcc solid solution model both consisting of $8 \times 8 \times 6 \times 4 = 1536$ atoms. In the models, the [100], [010], and [001] atomic crystal directions are parallel to the x, y, and z axes, respectively. Periodic boundary conditions are applied in three dimensions. Apparently, there are 12 (001) atomic planes along the z direction for the simulation models. To simulate the metastable Cu-Ta phases with various compositions, the initial fcc solid solution models are obtained by randomly substituting various amounts of Cu by Ta atoms. The models are then run at 300 K for adequate MD time steps to reach relatively stable states.

The processes of structural transitions in the models are monitored by pair-correlation function $g(r)$, planar structure factor S (**k**, z) and density profiles of each metal species along the z direction $\rho_\alpha(z)$. In addition, the distributions of atoms are displayed onto the projected x-y or y-z plane, which can provide a visualized atomic picture of the structural transition process.

3. Results and discussion

3.1. Amorphous phase formation

Table 1 lists the structural transitions in the Cu-Ta multilayered films induced by 200 keV xenon IBM at 77 K with increasing ion irradiation doses. From the Table, one sees clearly that amorphous alloys are obtained in the $Cu_{70}Ta_{30}$, $Cu_{65}Ta_{35}$, $Cu_{60}Ta_{40}$, and $Cu_{50}Ta_{50}$ multilayered samples. As typical examples, Fig. 1(a) and (b) show, respectively, the sharp diffraction lines of the as-deposited

Table 1
Structural changes of the Cu-Ta multilayered films upon 200 keV xeon-ion-beam mixing at 77 K. The mixing dosage is in the unit of 10^{14} $Xe^{+}cm^{-2}$; "Cu + Ta" represents a mixture of crystalline Cu and Ta; "PA" and "A" indicate a partial and complete amorphous phase, respectively; fcc-I is a metastable crystalline phase

Dosage	$Cu_{75}Ta_{25}$	$Cu_{70}Ta_{30}$	$Cu_{65}Ta_{35}$	$Cu_{60}Ta_{40}$	$Cu_{50}Ta_{50}$
As-deposited	Cu + Ta	Cu + Ta	Cu + Ta	Cu + Ta	Cu + Ta
5	Cu + Ta	Cu + Ta	Cu + Ta	Cu + Ta	PA
7	Cu + Ta	Cu + Ta	Cu + Ta	Cu + Ta	PA
9	Cu + Ta	Cu + Ta	Cu + Ta	Cu + Ta	PA
10	Cu + Ta	Cu + Ta	Cu + Ta	Cu + Ta	PA
30	Cu + Ta	Cu + Ta	Cu + Ta	Cu + Ta	PA
50	Cu + Ta	PA	Cu + Ta	PA	A
70	Cu + Ta	A	Cu + Ta	PA	A
90	fcc-I	PA	PA	PA	A
100	Cu + Ta	PA	A	A	A

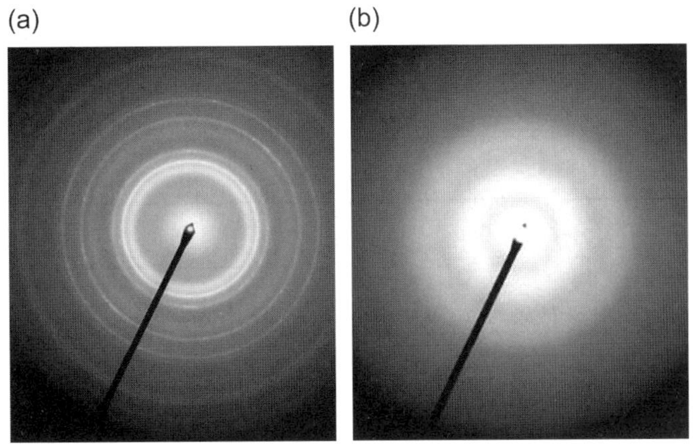

Fig. 1. SAD patterns of (a) the as-deposited state and (b) an amorphous alloy formed at a dose of 7×10^{15} $Xe^{+}cm^{-2}$ in the $Cu_{70}Ta_{30}$ multilayered films.

state and halos of an amorphous alloy formed at a dose of 7×10^{15} $Xe^{+}cm^{-2}$ in the $Cu_{70}Ta_{30}$ multilayered films. Fig. 2(a) and (b) exhibit the SAD patterns for the as-deposited $Cu_{50}Ta_{50}$ films and an amorphous alloy obtained at a dose of 5×10^{15} $Xe^{+}cm^{-2}$, respectively. Apparently, it can be deduced from Table 1 that 30 at.% Ta is the composition limit, beyond which the Cu-rich Cu-Ta solid solution would transform into an amorphous state.

MD simulations are performed for the solid solution models with various compositions, i.e., $Cu_{70}Ta_{30}$, $Cu_{65}Ta_{35}$, $Cu_{60}Ta_{40}$, and $Cu_{50}Ta_{50}$. It turned out that all the solid solutions become amorphous after annealing at 300 K for 0.5 ns. Taking the $Cu_{65}Ta_{35}$ model as a typical example, Fig. 3 exhibits the projections of the atomic positions on the *y-z* plane after annealing at 300 K for 0.5 ns and a uniform disordered structure can be observed vividly. In addition, the planar structure factors S (**k**, z) are calculated for the 12 atomic planes in the $Cu_{65}Ta_{35}$ model and the calculated values are reduced from about 1.0 of the initial state to almost 0 after annealing at 300 K for 0.5 ns, providing supplemental evidence that the $Cu_{65}Ta_{35}$ model has turned into a completely disordered structure. To give decisive confirmation of the resultant amorphous structure, the total and partial pair-correlation functions $g(r)$ of the five Cu-Ta solid solutions after annealing at 300 K for

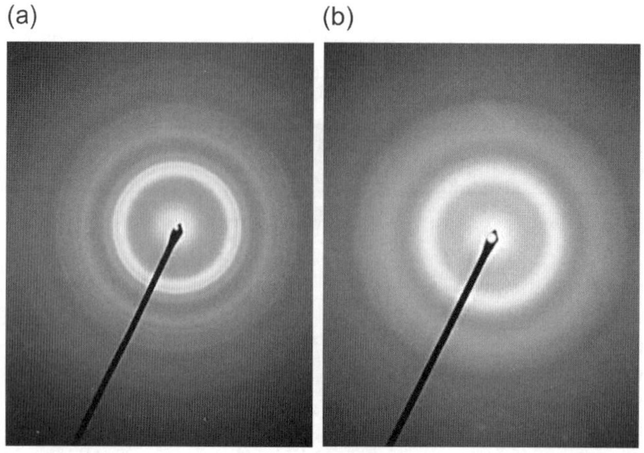

Fig. 2. SAD patterns of (a) the as-deposited state and (b) an amorphous alloy formed at a dose of 5×10^{15} $Xe^{+}cm^{-2}$ in the $Cu_{50}Ta_{50}$ multilayered films.

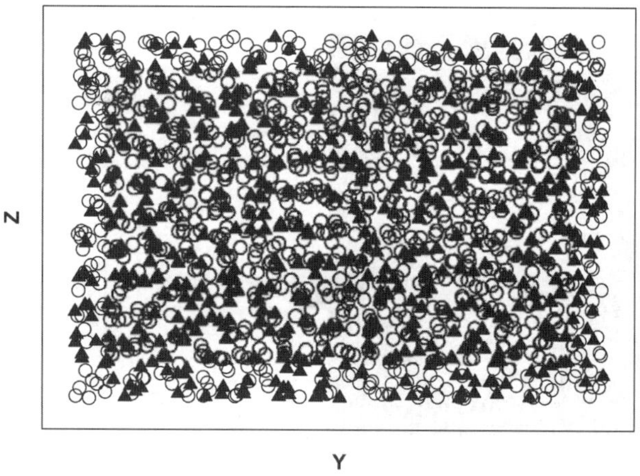

Fig. 3. The projections of atomic positions of the $Cu_{65}Ta_{35}$ solid solution after annealing at 300 K for 0.5 ns. Open circles: Cu. Filled triangles: Ta.

0.5 ns are calculated, respectively, and are shown in Fig. 4. One sees that the $Cu_{70}Ta_{30}$, $Cu_{65}Ta_{35}$, $Cu_{60}Ta_{40}$, and $Cu_{50}Ta_{50}$ solid solutions all become amorphous, whereas the $Cu_{75}Ta_{25}$ model retains an fcc structure after annealing. Consequently, the MD simulation results indicate that the critical composition for amorphous phase formation is around 30 at.% Ta for the Cu-rich solid solution [16], which is in excellent agreement with that suggested by the present IBM experiments. Incidentally, combining the present results and those reported in the literature [10], it can be concluded that amorphous alloys could be readily obtained in

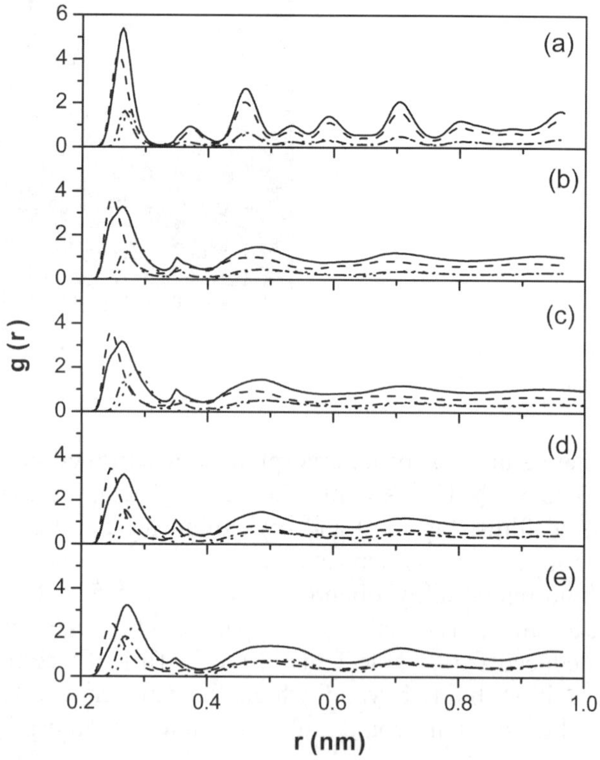

Fig. 4. Partial and total pair correlation functions of (a) $Cu_{75}Ta_{25}$, (b) $Cu_{70}Ta_{30}$, (c) $Cu_{65}Ta_{35}$, (d) $Cu_{60}Ta_{40}$, and (e) $Cu_{50}Ta_{50}$ fcc solid solutions after annealing at 300 K for 0.5 ns, respectively. The solid line is for the total $g(r)$, the dashed line is for Cu-Cu partial $g(r)$, the dotted line is for Ta-Ta partial $g(r)$, and the dash-dotted line is for Cu-Ta partial $g(r)$.

the immiscible Cu-Ta system within a composition range of 30–90 at.% Ta.

3.2. Stability of the metastable crystalline phases

Besides the amorphous phase formation, the metastable crystalline phases in the immiscible Cu-Ta system are also studied. We first present the calculated and experimental results of the metastable Cu-Ta phase at an alloy composition of $Cu_{75}Ta_{25}$. Ab initio calculations are performed to determine the total energies and lattice constants of the $Cu_{75}Ta_{25}$ phase with four possible simple structures, i.e., $D0_9$, A15, $L6_0$, and $L1_2$. Accordingly, the calculated results are shown in Fig. 5. It can be seen vividly from the Figure that the relatively stable structure of the $Cu_{75}Ta_{25}$ phase is $L1_2$, as it has lower minimum total energy than the other three possible structures. Consequently, ΔH_f of the $L1_2$ $Cu_{75}Ta_{25}$ phase is calculated to be 34.47 kJ/mol and its lattice constant is 3.82 Å.

Based on the proven realistic Cu-Ta potential, MD simulations are conducted and reveal that, for an alloy composition of $Cu_{75}Ta_{25}$, both the $L1_2$ ordered structure and fcc solid solution could retain their structures upon 300 K annealing. A typical example is given in Fig. 6 to exhibit the projections of the atomic positions on the *y-z* plane after annealing the $Cu_{75}Ta_{25}$ solid solution for 0.5 ns.

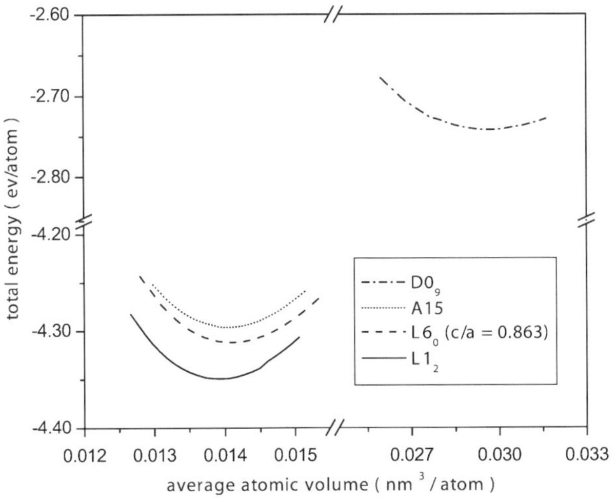

Fig. 5. The ab initio calculated total energy versus average atomic volume for the metastable $Cu_{75}Ta_{25}$ phase with different structures.

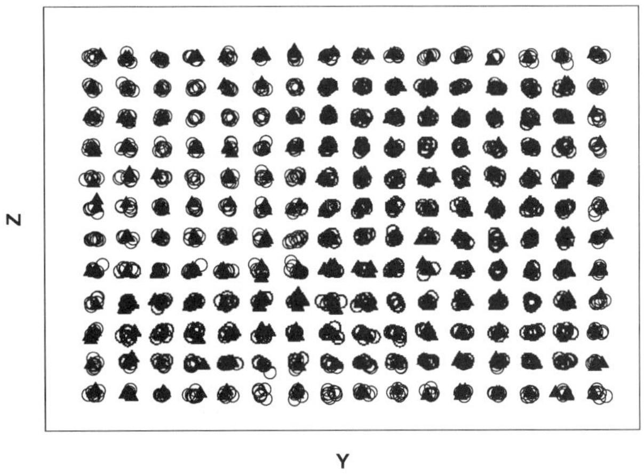

Fig. 6. The projections of atomic positions of the $Cu_{75}Ta_{25}$ solid solution after annealing at 300 K for 0.5 ns. Open circles: Cu. Filled triangles: Ta.

Obviously, the fcc lattice is still remained. In addition, the total and partial pair-correlation functions in Fig. 4 also confirm the crystalline structure of the fcc $Cu_{75}Ta_{25}$ solid solution after annealing. As a result of the MD simulations, the lattice constants of the $L1_2$ and fcc $Cu_{75}Ta_{25}$ phases are determined to be 3.84 and 3.83 Å, respectively, and their ΔH_f are calculated to be 34.75 and 28.99 kJ/mol, respectively.

For the $Cu_{75}Ta_{25}$ multilayered films, TEM examination reveals that a metastable fcc-I phase is indeed obtained after ion irradiation at a dose of 9×10^{15} Xe^+cm^{-2}. Fig. 7(a) is the SAD pattern of its as-deposited state and Fig. 7(b) is the diffraction lines of the sample upon an irradiation dose of 9×10^{15} Xe^+cm^{-2}, showing the formation of a metastable crystalline phase. Table 2 lists the indexing results of the newly formed phase, which is identified to be of an fcc structure and its lattice constant is 3.88 Å. Upon further irradiation, the fcc-I structure becomes unstable and at a dose of 1×10^{16} Xe^+cm^{-2} it transforms into an equilibrium mixture consisting of polycrystalline Cu and Ta. The above structural change of the $Cu_{75}Ta_{25}$ multilayered films upon IBM is summarized as follows:

$$Cu_{75}Ta_{25}\xrightarrow[\text{As-deposited}]{5\times10^{14}-7\times10^{15}Xe^+cm^{-2}}Cu$$

$$+\ Ta\xrightarrow{9\times10^{15}Xe^+cm^{-2}}\text{fcc-I}\xrightarrow{1\times10^{16}Xe^+cm_{-2}}Cu+Ta$$

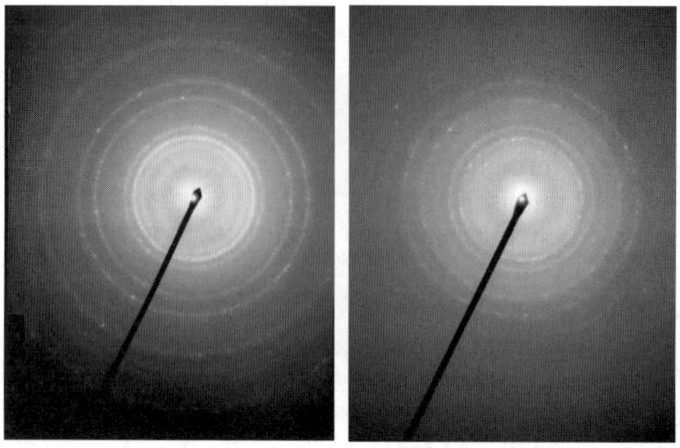

Fig. 7. SAD patterns of (a) the as-deposited state and (b) an fcc-I phase formed at a dose of 9×10^{15} $Xe^{+}cm^{-2}$ in the $Cu_{75}Ta_{25}$ multilayered films.

Table 2
Indexing of an fcc-I phase formed in the $Cu_{75}Ta_{25}$ multilayered films induced by ion-beam mixing at a dose of 9×10^{15} $Xe^{+}cm^{-2}$; a_{fcc-I} = 3.88 Å

$d_{exp.}$ (Å)	(hkl)	Intensity	$d_{cal.}$ (Å)
2.241	111	strong	2.240
1.933	200	strong	1.940
1.381	220	medium	1.372
1.181	311	strong	1.170
0.979	400	weak	0.970
0.903	331	weak	0.890

We now compare the above calculated and experimental data of the $Cu_{75}Ta_{25}$ phase, which are all listed in Table 3. It can be seen that the lattice constants derived from ab initio calculations, MD simulations, and IBM experiments agree fairly well with only a difference of 1.6% and their ΔH_f are also compatible with each other.

Incidentally, we have also studied the metastable $Cu_{25}Ta_{75}$ phase with an $L1_2$ structure. Some physical properties of the phase are obtained by ab initio calculations and derived from the Cu-Ta potential, respectively. The calculated results are all listed in Table 4. One sees that the total energies obtained from ab initio calculations and derived from the

Table 3
The structure, lattice constant a, and heat of formation ΔH_f of the metastable $Cu_{75}Ta_{25}$ phase derived from ab initio calculation, MD simulation, and IBM experiments, respectively

Method	Structure	a (Å)	ΔH_f (kJ/mol)
Ab initio	$L1_2$	3.82	34.47
MD	$L1_2$	3.84	34.75
MD	fcc solution	3.83	28.99
IBM	fcc	3.88	

Table 4
The comparison of the total energy E and lattice constant a of the metastable $Cu_{25}Ta_{75}$ phase derived from ab initio calculation and the Cu-Ta potential, respectively

	Structure	E (eV/atom)	a (Å)
Ab initio calculation	$L1_2$	−6.80	4.05
The Cu-Ta potential	$L1_2$	−6.71	4.14
Difference		1.3%	2.2%

Cu-Ta potential match well within a difference of 1.3% and their lattice constants are also consistent within an error of 2.2%. It is worthwhile mentioning that the listed properties of the $L1_2$ $Cu_{25}Ta_{75}$ phase from ab initio calculations were not used in deriving the Cu-Ta potential. Consequently, the above agreement revealed in the Table can also lend some support to the relevance of the previously constructed Cu-Ta potential.

4. Concluding remarks

Ion-beam mixing experiments have confirmed the verdict from atomistic modeling that 30 at.% Ta is the critical composition to form Cu-enriched amorphous phases in the equilibrium immiscible Cu-Ta system. We have also shown the feasibility of studying the metastable phase formation in the Cu-Ta system by combining ab initio calculations, molecular dynamics simulations, and ion-beam mixing experiments, as the respective outcomes are in good agreement with each other.

Acknowledgements

The authors are grateful to the financial support from the National Natural Science Foundation of China, The Ministry of Science and Technology of China (G20000672), as well as from Tsinghua University.

References

[1] Zielinski EM, Vinci RP, Bravman JC. Effects of barrier layer and annealing on abnormal grain growth in copper thin films. J Appl Phys 1994;76:4516–23.
[2] Kwon KW, Ryu C, Sinclair R, Wong SS. Evidence of heteroepitaxial growth of copper on beta-tantalum. Appl Phys Lett 1997;71:3069–71.
[3] Lee HJ, Kwon KW, Ryu C, Sinclair R. Thermal stability of a Cu/Ta multilayer: an intriguing interfacial reaction. Acta mater 1999;47:3965–75.
[4] Chen L, Magtoto N, Ekstrom B, Kelber J. Effect of surface impurities on the Cu/Ta interface. Thin Solid Films 2000;376:115–23.
[5] de Boer FR, Boom R, Mattens WCM, Miedema AR, Niessen AK. Cohesion in metals: Transition metal alloys. Amsterdam: North-Holland, 1989.
[6] Liu BX, Zhang ZJ, Jin O, Pan F. Role of interface in ion mixing of thermal annealing induced amorphization in multilayers in some immiscible systems. Mat Res Soc Symp Proc 1996;396:71–82.
[7] Cullis AG, Borders JA, Hirvonen JK, Poate JM. Metastable alloy layers produced by implantation of Ag^+ and Ta^+ ions into Cu crystals. Philos Mag B 1978;37:615–30.
[8] Nastasi M, Saris FW, Hung LS, Mayer JW. Stability of amorphous Cu/Ta and Cu/W alloys. J Appl Phys 1985;58:3052–8.
[9] Sakurai K, Yamada Y, Ito M, Lee CH, Fukunaga T, Mizutani U. Observation of solid-state amorphization in the immiscible system Cu-Ta. Appl Phys Lett 1990;57:2660–2.
[10] Kim JH, Yoshioka H, Habazaki H, Kawashima A, Asami K, Hashimoto K. Phases in sputter-deposited Cu-Ta alloys. Mater Sci and Eng 1992;A156:211–6.
[11] Zeng F, Ding M, Zhao B, Pan F. Amorphous alloy film formed in an immiscible Cu-Ta system by ion beam assisted deposition. Mater Lett 2002;53:40–3.
[12] Veltl G, Scholz B, Kunze H-D. Amorphization of Cu-Ta alloys by mechanical alloying. Mater Sci and Eng 1991;A134:1410–3.
[13] Mizutani U, Lee CH. Mechanical alloying in Cu-V and Cu-Ta systems characterized by positive heat of mixing (Overview). Mater Trans JIM 1995;36:210–7.
[14] Kwon KW, Lee HJ, Sinclair R. Solid-state amorphization at tetragonal-Ta/Cu interfaces. Appl Phys Lett 1999;75:935–7.
[15] Liu BX, Lai WS, Zhang Q. Irradiation induced amorphization in metallic multilayers and calculation of glass-forming ability from atomistic potential in the binary metal systems. Mater Sci & Eng R 2000;244:1–46.
[16] Gong HR, Kong LT, Lai WS, Liu BX. Atomistic modeling of solid-state amorphization in an immiscible Cu-Ta system. Phys Rev B 2002;66:104204(1–10).
[17] Liu BX, Lai WS, Zhang ZJ. Solid-state crystal-to-amorphous transition in metal-metal multilayers and its thermodynamic and atomistic modelling. Adv Phys 2001;50:367–429.

[18] Alonso JA, Simozar S. Prediction of amorphous alloy formation by ion beam mixing. Solid St Commun 1983;48:765–7.
[19] Kresse G, Hafner J. Ab initio molecular dynamics for liquid metals. Phys Rev B 1993;47:558–61.
[20] Vanderbilt D. Soft self-consistent pseudopotentials in a generalized eigenvalue formalism. Phys Rev B 1990;41:7892–995.
[21] Perdew J, Wang Y. Accurate and simple analytic representation of the electron-gas correlation energy. Phys Rev B 1992;45:13244–9.
[22] Monkhorst HJ, Pack JD. Special points for Brillouin-zone integrations. Phys Rev B 1976;13:5188–92.
[23] Parrinello M, Rahman A. Polymorphic transitions in single crystals: A new molecular dynamics method. J Appl Phys 1981;52:7182–90.

Correlation of magnetic moment versus spacing distance of metastable fcc structured iron

L. T. Kong and B. X. Liu[a)]
Advanced Materials Laboratory, Department of Materials Science and Engineering, Tsinghua University, 100084, China

(Received 2 September 2003; accepted 10 March 2004; published online 20 April 2004)

Based on the projector augmented-wave method, *ab initio* calculations confirm the ground state is of ferromagnetic bcc Fe and reveal a paramagnetic state for the hcp Fe. Interestingly, the calculations predict that there exist at least three distinct magnetic orderings for the metastable fcc structured Fe—a paramagnetic and low-spin and high-spin ferromagnetic states—within a lattice constant ranging from 0.34 to 0.38 nm, and that, upon increasing the atomic volume of Fe, the magnetic moment is enhanced and can even be greater than that of the equilibrium bcc Fe. [DOI: 10.1063/1.1738516]

The electronic and magnetic properties of metastable fcc Fe has been a subject of great interest for many years, because of both fundamental significance and practical application concerns.[1–9] Nonetheless, some issues concerning the magnetic states and electronic properties of fcc Fe still remain unclear. While isolated bulk fcc Fe is only stable above the Curie temperature, it can be stabilized at low temperatures either as coherent precipitates in supersaturated alloys[1,2] or thin films by epitaxial growth on fcc substrates.[3,4] The experimentally prepared fcc Fe frequently exhibited various magnetic properties, which attracted much attention for theoretical investigations.[5–9] At the beginning, local density approximation was employed to study the magnetic ordering of iron, yet it predicted a wrong ground state.[5] The generalized gradient approximation (GGA) was then developed and used in the first-principles calculations.[6–9] For instance, Asada *et al.* predicted a high-spin ferromagnetic (HS FM) state for fcc Fe by a linear muffin-tin orbital method in an atomic sphere approximation within the GGA.[6] A little later, some other methods were also developed within the GGA, such as the discrete variational method,[7] the linearized augmented plane-wave (LAPW) method,[8,9] and other plane-wave methods using ultrasoft pseudopotentials (USPPs).[10] Although a satisfactory agreement with all electron methods was found for most of the properties, a few discrepancies still remained while applying the USPP for spin-polarized calculations.[11] Recently, Blöchl further developed the USPP by combining the ideas from the pseudopotential and LAPW methods into a framework called the projector augmented-wave method (PAW).[12] The PAW was expected to have improved precision, especially in treating the transition metals.[13] We therefore employed the PAW method to carry out calculations to further clarify the structural as well as magnetic ordering of fcc Fe.

The calculations were performed using the Vienna *ab initio* simulation package VASP[14–16] based on the PAW pseudopotential.[12,13] The exchange and correlation effects were described by the functional due to Perdew and Zunger,[17] employing generalized gradient corrections proposed by Perdew *et al.*[18] Brillouin-zone integrations were performed using an $11\times11\times11$ Monkhorst–Pack[19] grid leading to 56 irreducible k points for both bcc and fcc structures, and a grid of $11\times11\times7$ corresponded to 64 irreducible k points for hcp Fe. A plane-wave cutoff energy of 334.9 eV was used. In addition, for all spin-polarized calculations, the Vosko–Wilk–Nusair interpolations were used for the correlation part of the exchange correlation functional.[20]

The energy–volume correlation of bcc Fe was first calculated and then fitted to the Murnaghan equation of states[21] to obtain its cohesive properties as well as to certify the validity of the present method. We find a FM ground state for the bcc Fe, and its lattice constant, magnetic moment, and bulk modulus are calculated to be 2.83 Å, 2.21 μ_B, and 1.76 Mbar, respectively, which are in good agreement with the experimental results of 2.87 Å,[22] 2.22 μ_B,[23] and 1.72 Mbar,[23] respectively. In the calculation, the paramagnetic (PM) bcc Fe is found to be energetically unfavored, as it has a 0.45 eV/atom higher energy than the FM phase. The fitted lattice constant and bulk modulus of the PM bcc Fe are 2.76 Å and 2.69 Mbar, respectively. Figure 1 shows the calculated correlations of the total energy and the corresponding magnetic moment against the lattice constant for the fcc Fe with different magnetic orderings. The fitted cohesive properties and the magnetic moments are listed in Table I. As can be seen, firstly, all the fcc phases of Fe has a higher minimum total energy than the FM bcc Fe, which matches well with the fact that the FM bcc phase is an equilibrium state at low temperatures. Secondly, the fcc Fe shows a rather complicated magnetic ordering, depending on its spacing distance.

From Fig. 1 it is seen that there exist at least three distinct magnetic states for the fcc Fe. When the lattice constant of fcc Fe lies below about $a=3.57$ Å, there coexist a paramagnetic and a low-spin ferromagnetic (LS-FM) states. The PM phase equilibrates at about $a=3.448$ Å, having a minimum total energy of -8.076 eV/atom, while the LS-FM one has its minimum total energy of -8.077 eV/atom at about $a=3.463$ Å. The magnetic moment of the LS-FM fcc Fe at its equilibrium atomic volume was calculated to be about 0.62 μ_B. When the lattice constant of the fcc Fe lies above

a)Electronic mail: dmslbx@tsinghua.edu.cn

Applied Physics Letters 84(18), p.3627-3629 (2004).

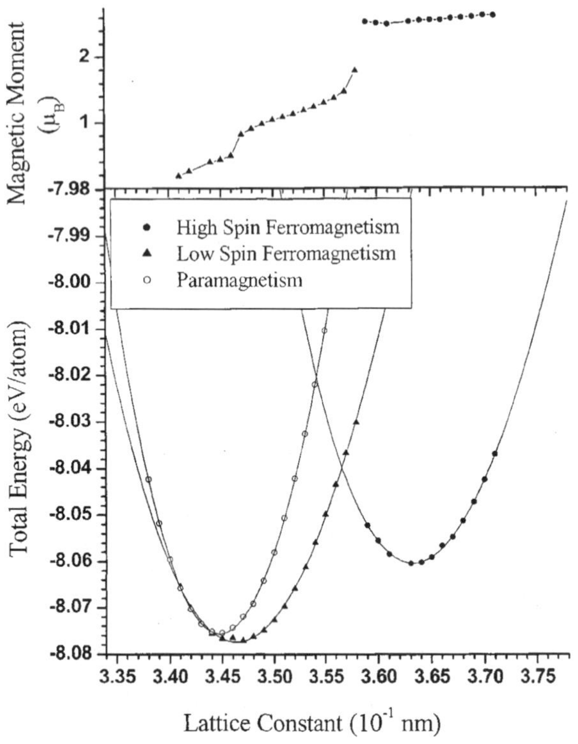

FIG. 1. Correlations of total energies (lower panel) and magnetic moments (upper panel) against the lattice constant of fcc iron obtained by *ab initio* calculations within the GGA.

3.57 Å, there appears a third magnetic state, which equilibrates at about a=3.632 Å and is denoted as a HS state of fcc Fe with a magnetic moment of about 2.54 μ_B. Careful examination of Fig. 1 shows that the LS state could actually be split into two substates. For $a \leqslant 3.460$ Å, the LS phase exhibits a rather small magnetic moment, which varies from 0.1 to 0.5 μ_B, and can be designated as LS1. At about a=3.460 Å, both the energy and magnetic moment have a jump. For $a>3.460$ Å, the magnetic moment of the LS phase varies from 0.8 to 1.8 μ_B; the phase is denoted as LS2. An interesting finding from Fig. 1 is that for each magnetic state (LS1, LS2, and HS), the magnetic moment of the Fe atom in the respective fcc structures seems to be enhanced, while the interatomic distance (or the spacing distance) expands. Such a trend was consistent with the experimental observations.[24] Incidentally, the present results for the fcc Fe are compatible with those obtained by other calculation methods.[8,9]

We now compare the calculation results with the retrievable experimental observations. As is clarified, the fcc Fe can only be stabilized as coherent precipitates in Cu or other matrixes, or by epitaxy onto suitable fcc substrates. Haneda *et al.*[4] obtained a nanosized fcc Fe particle by a technique based on the transversely excited atmospheric CO_2-laser-induced breakdown of $Fe(CO)_5$, and found that the fcc Fe particle was paramagnet down to a temperature of 1.8 K and stable over three years. This observation should lend some support to the predicted paramagnetic state of the fcc Fe by the present *ab initio* calculations. Del Bianco *et al.*[25] obtained an fcc Fe phase with a=3.51±0.05 Å, which lies in the spacing distance range of the LS2 state indicated by the present calculation. The magnetic moment of the obtained fcc Fe was lower than that of bulk Fe, which is also in agreement with the present prediction. Mitani *et al.*[24] prepared a series fcc-Fe/Cu(M)(001) (M=Au,Ni) superlattices, and found that the magnetic moment of Fe was increased up to 2.7 μ_B, when the interatomic distance was increased up to only 1% (i.e., a=3.65 Å), yet reduced to about 0 when the interatomic distance was decreased 1.8%. Apparently, the two different states fall in the presently calculated spacing distance ranges for the HS and LS2 states, respectively. Pan *et al.*[26] obtained two metastable fcc Fe phases and the lattice constants were 3.88±0.05 and 3.60 ±0.05 Å, respectively, lying in the spacing distance range of the HS state. The magnetic moments were measured to be about 2.35 and 3.27 μ_B, respectively, which agreed well with the present predictions. Interestingly, Macedo *et al.*[27] acquired a fcc Fe with the lattice constant of a=3.65 Å by epitaxial growth, and the magnetic moment was measured to be 2.5(1) μ_B, which matches well with the presently predicted value of 2.560 μ_B at a=3.65 Å. Moreover, a number of other experimental observations are also in support of the present calculations for fcc Fe.[28,29] To have a clear overview, a summary of the calculated magnetic moments of fcc Fe together with some experimental/theoretical data is displayed in Table II.

Similar calculations were also carried out for the metastable hcp Fe with a fully relaxation of the c/a ratio. Dissimilar to those observed by Panduani *et al.*[30] and Herper *et al.*,[8] we only obtained a paramagnetic state, which has a higher minimum total energy than the FM bcc Fe. The fitted lattice constants and bulk modulus of hcp Fe are 2.46 Å (c/a=1.58) and 2.88 Mbar, respectively, which are in good agreement with the experimental observations.[22]

In the present calculations, only the collinear spin configurations were considered. Among the various possible spin configurations, there could also exist the noncollinear spin configurations for fcc Fe. For example, Tsunoda has reported a spiral structure with a spiral vector of $q=2\pi/a$ (0.1,0,1) for fcc Fe.[2] Besides, by means of modified augmented spherical waves method, Knöpfle *et al.* have calculated the spiral magnetic properties of fcc Fe and found that the spiral structures could have lower total energies than the collinear ones.[31] Because of the complexity of the magnetic ordering, all the metastable fcc Fe, which correspond to those possible nonequilibrium states, are possible to be formed and appear under respectively suitable circumstances. As a result, the metastable fcc Fe could possess any or any combination of all its possible magnetic orderings, implying that whether a specific magnetic configuration could exist or not was not only determined by its relative stability, but also by its encountered circumstance. Generally speaking, the collinear magnetic states were frequently ob-

TABLE I. Calculated minimum total energy (E_{min}), heat of formation (ΔH), lattice constant (a), bulk modulus (B), and magnetic moment (M) of fcc iron with different magnetic ordering.

	E_{min} (eV/atom)	ΔH (eV/atom)	a (Å)	B (Mbar)	M (μ_B)
NM	−8.076	0.140	3.448	2.813	0
FM (LS)	−8.077	0.139	3.463	0.975	0.62
FM (HS)	−8.060	0.156	3.632	1.675	2.54

TABLE II. Calculated magnetic moment of fcc Fe with different magnetic ordering at various lattice constants together with some available experimental/theoretical data. a: lattice constant, in unit of Å; M: magnetic moment, in unit of μ_B/atom; expr.: experimental observations; theo: theoretical results.

	LS1				LS2			HS			
a	3.44	3.46	3.47	3.50	3.51	3.56	3.57	3.62	3.64	3.65	3.68
M	0.395	0.496	0.825	1.040	1.094	1.374	1.477	2.518	2.553	2.560	2.595
Expr. M					<2.2[a]			2.8[b]		2.5[c]	
Theo. M				1.02[d]				2.47[e]	2.57[d]		

[a]Reference 25.
[b]Reference 28.
[c]Reference 27.
[d]Reference 8.
[e]Reference 5.

served in experiments, although the spiral magnetic state might be energetically more favored. It is thus believed that it would make the *ab initio* results more significative if the spin spiral could also be considered in the present PAW calculations.

In summary, *ab initio* calculations based on PAW pseudopotentials correctly reproduced the ground state of Fe, which is ferromagnetic bcc Fe, and revealed a possible paramagnetic state for hcp Fe. For the metastable fcc Fe, the calculations predict that there exist at least three distinct magnetic orderings for the metastable fcc structured Fe—a paramagnetic, and low-spin and high-spin ferromagnetic states—within a lattice constant ranging from 0.34 to 0.38 nm, and that with increasing the atomic volume of Fe, the magnetic moment is enhanced and can even be greater than that of the equilibrium bcc Fe. Generally, the prediction is supported by the fact that all the predicted possible magnetic states have ever been observed in experiments.

The authors are grateful for the financial support from the National Natural Science Foundation of China, The Ministry of Science and Technology of China (G20000672), and the Administration of Tsinghua University.

[1]C. Berghout, Z. Metallkd. **52**, 179 (1961).
[2]Y. Tsunoda, J. Phys.: Condens. Matter **1**, 10427 (1989).
[3]W. Schwarzacher, W. Allison, R. F. Willis, J. Penfold, R. C. Ward, I. Jacob, and W. F. Egelhoff, Jr., Solid State Commun. **71**, 563 (1989).
[4]K. Haneda, Z. X. Zhou, A. H. Morrish, T. Majima, and T. Miyahara, Phys. Rev. B **46**, 13832 (1992).
[5]C. S. Wang, B. M. Klein, and H. Krakauer, Phys. Rev. Lett. **54**, 1852 (1985).
[6]T. Asada and K. Terakura, Phys. Rev. B **46**, 13599 (1992).
[7]J. A. Gomez and D. Guenzburger, J. Magn. Magn. Mater. **226–230**, 381 (2001).
[8]H. C. Herper, E. Hoffmann, and P. Entel, Phys. Rev. B **60**, 3839 (1999).
[9]Y. M. Zhou, S. C. Wu, and D. S. Wang, Solid State Commun. **111**, 101 (1999).
[10]D. Vanderbilt, Phys. Rev. B **41**, 7892 (1990).
[11]E. G. Moroni, G. Kresse, J. Hafner, and J. Furthmüller, Phys. Rev. B **56**, 15629 (1997).
[12]P. E. Blöchl, Phys. Rev. B **50**, 17953 (1994).
[13]G. Kresse and D. Joubert, Phys. Rev. B **59**, 1758 (1999).
[14]G. Kresse and J. Hafner, Phys. Rev. B **47**, 558 (1993).
[15]G. Kresse and J. Furthmüller, Comput. Mater. Sci. **6**, 15 (1996).
[16]G. Kresse and J. Furthmüller, Phys. Rev. B **54**, 11169 (1996).
[17]J. P. Perdew and A. Zunger, Phys. Rev. B **23**, 5048 (1981).
[18]J. P. Perdew, J. A. Chevary, S. H. Vosko, K. A. Jackson, M. R. Pederson, D. J. Singh, and C. Fiolhais, Phys. Rev. B **46**, 6671 (1992).
[19]H. J. Monkhorst and J. D. Pack, Phys. Rev. B **13**, 5188 (1976).
[20]S. H. Vosko, L. Wilk, and M. Nusair, Can. J. Phys. **58**, 1200 (1980).
[21]J. P. Poirier, *Introduction to the Physics of the Earth's Interior* (Cambridge University Press, Cambridge, 1991).
[22]X-Ray Powder JCPDS Diffraction Files 85.1410 and 34.0529.
[23]M. Acet, H. Zähres, E. F. Wassermann, and W. Pepperhoff, Phys. Rev. B **49**, 6012 (1994).
[24]S. Mitani, A. Kida, and M. Matsui, J. Magn. Magn. Mater. **126**, 76 (1993).
[25]L. Del Bianco, C. Ballesteros, J. M. Rojo, and A. Hernando, Phys. Rev. Lett. **81**, 4500 (1998).
[26]F. Pan and Z. S. Zhang, Physica B **293**, 237 (2001).
[27]W. A. A. Macedo, F. Sirotti, G. Panaccione, A. Schatz, W. Keune, W. N. Rodrigues, and G. Rossi, Phys. Rev. B **58**, 11534 (1998).
[28]D. Schmitz, C. Charton, A. Scholl, C. Carbone, and W. Eberhardt, Phys. Rev. B **59**, 4327 (1999).
[29]L. E. Bove, C. Petrillo, F. Sacchetti, and G. Mazzone, Phys. Rev. B **61**, 9457 (2000).
[30]C. Panduani and F. Franca, J. Magn. Magn. Mater. **145**, 147 (1995).
[31]K. Knöpfle, L. M. Sandratskii, and J. Kübler, Phys. Rev. B **62**, 5564 (2000).

Crystallographic and lattice point correlations of a new *hcp-to-fco* martensitic transformation observed in the Ni–Hf system

J.H. Li, H.B. Guo, B.X. Liu *,1

Advanced Materials Laboratory, Department of Materials Science and Engineering, Tsinghua University, Beijing 100084, China

Received 28 April 2004; received in revised form 11 October 2004; accepted 13 October 2004
Available online 13 November 2004

Abstract

A hexagonal close-packed to face-centered orthorhombic (*hcp-to-fco*) martensitic transformation in the Hf lattice upon dissolving Ni atoms is observed by molecular dynamics simulations based on a proven realistic Ni–Hf potential. It is proposed that the mechanism of the phase transformation takes place through four simultaneous actions, i.e. sliding, shearing, stretching and lattice constant adjusting, with a speed in an order of 100 m/s. Based on an analytical deduction, the crystallographic and lattice point correlations between the initial *hcp* and final *fco* structures are obtained, respectively, and the deduced correlations may also be of relevance for another two phase transformations: the hexagonal close-packed to body-centered tetragonal, and hexagonal close-packed to face-centered cubic martensitic phase transformations.

Keywords: Transition metals; Metastable phases; Martensitic phase transformation; Molecular dynamics; Phase transformation mechanism

In recent decades, some non-equilibrium materials processing techniques, e.g. ion beam mixing, solid-state interfacial reaction, and mechanical alloying, have been developed and employed to produce a great number of non-equilibrium (or metastable) alloys either in amorphous or in crystalline structures [1,2]. In producing metastable crystalline alloys, some interesting phase transformations have been observed. For example, Li et al. [3] synthesized a metastable face-centered cubic (*fcc*) alloy with a composition of approximately $Ru_{75}Ni_{25}$ by xenon ion beam mixing, and the metastable *fcc* alloy was formed through a hexagonal close-packed to face-centered cubic (*hcp-to-fcc*) phase transformation. Jin and Liu [4] observed a ploymorphic transformation in the hafnium thin films upon xenon ion irradiation, i.e. the equilibrium *hcp* lattice transformed into a metastable *fcc* structure. Nonetheless, the detailed phase transformation mechanism has so far not yet been clarified, especially at the atomic scale. Meanwhile, the first-principle calculations and molecular dynamics (MD) simulations have also been introduced to study the phase formation and transformation [5–9]. For example, employing the first-principle calculations, Alippi et al. [5] identified and analyzed the Bain paths of tetragonal state between two metastable tetragonal phases in vanadium, cobalt and copper, etc. Kulkova et al. [6] investigated the correlations between the electronic structure and the temperature of the martensitic transition in the NiMn(Ti) alloys. Based on the MD simulations, Kadau et al. [7] observed the face-centered cubic to body-centered cubic (*fcc-to-bcc*) martensitic phase transformation in the sintered Fe–Ni nanoparticles, initiating at the grain boundaries. In the present study, we investigate the phase transformation in the Ni–Hf system by MD

* Corresponding author. Tel.: +86 10 6277 2557; fax: +86 10 6277 1160.

E-mail address: dmslbx@tsinghua.edu.cn (B.X. Liu).

1 Also at: State Key Laboratory of Solid-State Microstructure, Nanjing University, Nanjing 210039, China.

Acta Materialia 53 (3), p.743-748 (2005).

simulations, using a proven realistic Ni–Hf potential derived recently by authors' group [10].

In the present study, the MD simulations are carried out with a Parrinello–Rahman constant-pressure scheme [11,12], which allows variations in the size and shape of the MD model with the dynamic equations. The motion equations are solved using a second-order four-value predictor-corrector algorithm developed by Gear with a time step $t = 5 \times 10^{-15}$ s [13]. The interactions between the atoms are described with an n-body potential under the framework of the second moment approximation of tight-binding (TB-SMA) scheme [14,15]. The solid solution models are employed [16,17] in the present simulations, i.e. an *hcp* Hf single-crystal model consisting of $10 \times 6 \times 6 \times 4 = 1440$ atoms is firstly constructed as the MD model. The axes A, B, and C of the MD model, corresponding to [1 0 0], [1 2 0], and [0 0 1] crystalline directions, are set to be parallel to the x, y, and z axes, respectively. Periodic boundary conditions are adopted in three directions. An assigned amount of Ni solute atoms are then randomly substituted into the *hcp* Hf lattice to form an *hcp* Hf-based solid solution. For the as-set solid solution model, the MD simulation is carried out at a constant temperature of 300 K and zero pressure for more than 50,000 MD time steps to reach a relatively stable state, at which all dynamic parameters show no secular variation. The density profiles $\rho_\alpha(z)$ of the atoms and the total pair-correlation functions $g(r)$ are calculated to characterize the structural change in the simulation model [18–20]. Besides, the projections of the atomic positions and the enthalpy change of the model are also presented to show the variation of the atomic configuration and the energetic evidence of the phase transformation. Further details of the construction of n-body potential, MD simulation and the characterization methods, can be found in some recent publications by the authors' group [16,17].

We now present the simulation results. It is found that when the concentration of the Ni solute atoms is less than 15 at.%, the *hcp* Hf lattice is preserved perfectly and that when the concentration of Ni reaches about 19 at.%, a new metastable crystalline phase is formed. The newly formed phase is identified to be a face-centered orthorhombic (*fco*) structure, and the lattice constants are determined to be $a' = 3.527$ Å, $b' = 4.892$ Å, and $c' = 4.913$ Å, respectively. These results suggest that an *hcp-to-fco* phase transformation has taken place in the *hcp* Hf lattice and it is responsible for the formation of the metastable $Hf_{81}Ni_{19}$ alloy of *fco* structure. Fig. 1 exhibits two projections of the atomic positions for the *hcp* Hf lattice before and after the *hcp-to-fco* phase transformation, respectively. It is noted that a unit cell of the newly formed *fco* phase is marked in Fig. 1(b) for attention. Fig. 2 presents the calculated total pair-correlation functions $g(r)$ to confirm the formation of the metastable $Hf_{81}Ni_{19}$ alloy of *fco* structure. In the following discussion, we concentrate on revealing the phase transformation mechanism for turning an *hcp* lattice into an *fco* structure.

Fig. 3 displays two calculated density profiles $\rho_\alpha(z)$ of the atoms along the Z directions for the *hcp* Hf lattice before and after the *hcp-to-fco* phase transformation, respectively. From Figs. 3 and 1, one sees that, firstly, the shape of the MD model has been changed and a shearing of $(1\ 2\ 0)_{hcp}$ plane along $[0\ 1\ 0]_{hcp}$ has taken place, and secondly, the layer structure of the newly formed *fco* phase is the same as the initial *hcp* phase. In fact, the layer structure is kept unchanged during the whole phase transformation. In order to reveal the detailed process involved in the *hcp-to-fco* phase transformation, more snapshots of the atoms on the 2nd, 3rd, 4th and 5th layers in the MD model are taken and shown in Fig. 4, in which a hexagonal unit cell is marked by the filled circles for attention. From Fig. 4,

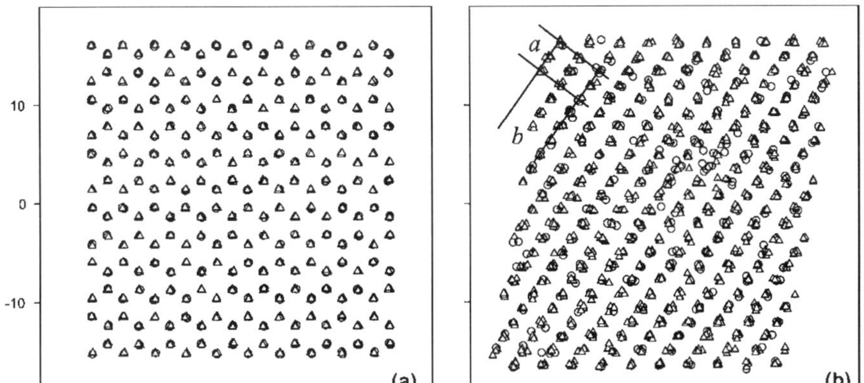

Fig. 1. Projections of the atomic positions on the x–y plane for the MD-model taken at simulation times of (a) 0.005 ns and (b) 0.25 ns, respectively, to show the *hcp-to-fco* phase transformation. Open circles and filled triangles stand for the Ni atoms and Hf atoms, respectively. The unit cell of the newly formed *fco* phase is marked in figure (b).

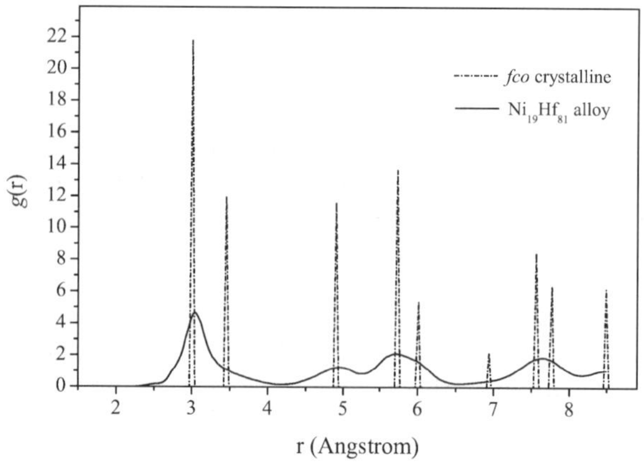

Fig. 2. Comparison between the total pair-correlation function $g(r)$ of the metastable $Hf_{81}Ni_{19}$ alloy upon the *hcp-to-fco* phase transformation with that of an ideal *fco* lattice with $a' = 3.527$ Å, $b' = 4.892$ Å and $c' = 4.913$ Å, respectively.

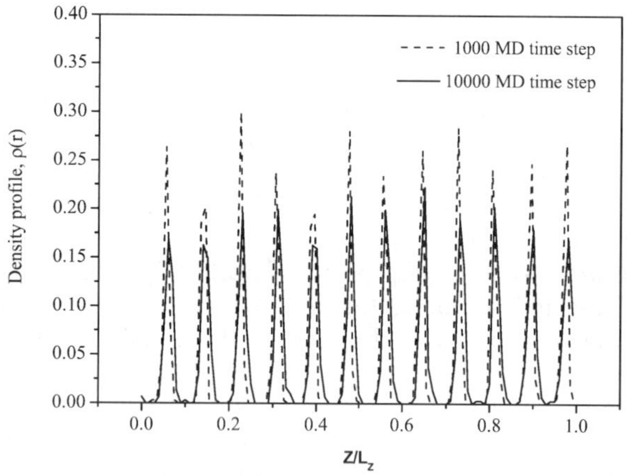

Fig. 3. The calculated density profiles $\rho_\alpha(z)$ of the atoms along Z directions before and after the *hcp-to-fco* phase transformation, i.e. at 1000 and 10,000 MD simulation time steps, respectively. The abscissa is expressed in the scaled coordinate and y-axis is in arbitrary unit.

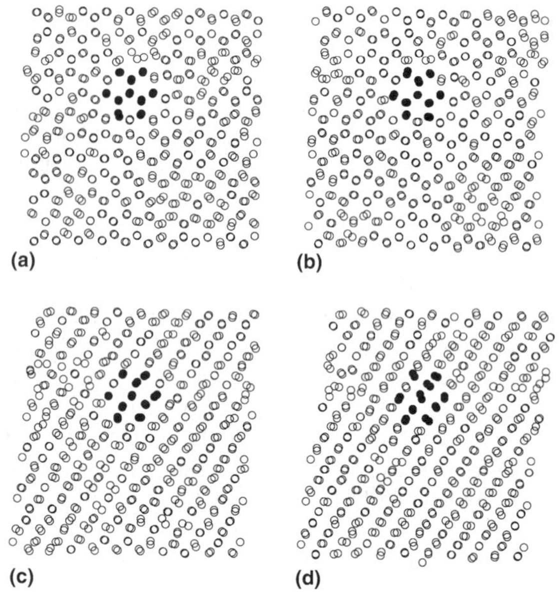

Fig. 4. Four projections of the atomic positions on the x–y plane of the atoms for the 3rd, 4th, 5th, and 6th layers in the MD-model upon the *hcp-to-fco* phase transformation. The projections are observed at the simulation times of (a) 0.0125 ns, (b) 0.02 ns, (c) 0.025 ns and (d) 0.04 ns, respectively. An *hcp* unit cell is marked in filled circles for attention.

one can vividly view the structural change process. It is obvious that the middle region in Fig. 4(a) is still preserved in the original *hcp* structure, whereas the structure of the right-bottom corner has been changed. Note that in Fig. 4(a), the marked hexagonal unit cell can clearly be recognized. In comparison, one can observe that in Fig. 4(b) and (c), the original hexagonal unit cell gradually becomes sort of askew. With increasing the simulation time, the hexagonal characteristics of the original unit cell disappeared completely, as shown in Fig. 4(d). Besides, one can clearly see from Fig. 4 that the area of the newly formed *fco* phase has been gradually enlarged with increasing simulation time. Moreover, by carefully examining the projections of the atomic positions exhibited in Fig. 4, one sees that the atoms inside the hexagonal unit cell change their positions, i.e. moving from $\left[\frac{1}{3}\,\frac{2}{3}\,0\right]_{hcp}$ to the vicinity of $\left[\frac{1}{2}\,\frac{1}{2}\,0\right]_{hcp}$, faster than other atoms of the unit cell, indicating that the $(0\,0\,2)_{hcp}$ atomic plane has experienced a relative sliding in addition to a uniform shearing. Fig. 5 presents the plots for the variations of the enthalpy, shape and size of the simulation model as a function of simulation time.

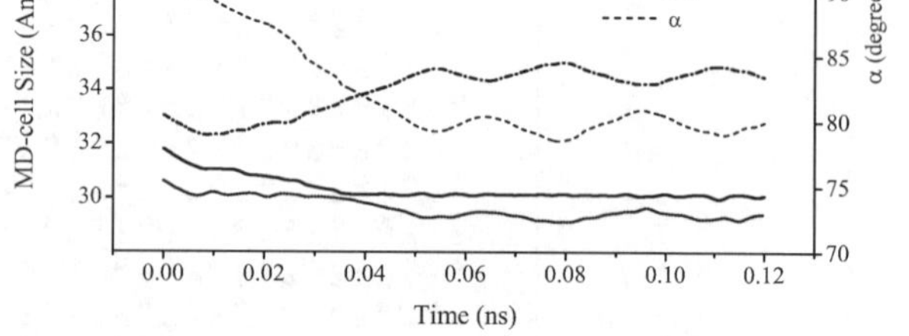

Fig. 5. Evolutions of the (a) enthalpy and (b) shape and size of the MD-model as a function of simulation time. For comparison, the enthalpy of an ideal *fco* phase with the same composition and the lattice constants of $a' = 3.527$ Å, $b' = 4.892$ Å and $c' = 4.913$ Å, respectively, is also plotted. Rx, Ry and Rz in figure (b) are three axes of the MD-model. α is the angle between the axes Rx and Ry. Fine arrow and bold arrow indicate the beginning and finishing times of the *hcp-to-fco* phase transformation.

From Fig. 5, one sees that there are another two actions that should be executed for the *hcp-to-fco* phase transformation. One is elongation along the $[1\,2\,0]_{hcp}$ axis of the model, and the other is the adjustment of the lattice constants in three principal crystalline axes of the *fco* lattice, thus leading to the formation of the final *fco* phase. Note that Fig. 4 together with Fig. 5 shows that the four actions described above take place almost simultaneously. In addition, Fig. 5 indicates that it takes about 0.035 ns to complete the *hcp-to-fco* phase transformation. Consequently, the speed of the *hcp-to-fco* phase transformation is thus estimated to be approximately 100 m/s, which is in the same order of the typical martensitic transformation. In short, based on above discussion, the *hcp-to-fco* phase transformation observed in the Ni–Hf system is executed in four simultaneous actions, i.e. (1) sliding $\frac{1}{6}[1\,\bar{1}\,0]_{hcp}$ of $(0\,0\,2)_{hcp}$ planes along $[1\,\bar{1}\,0]_{hcp}$ directions, (2) uniformly shearing θ on $(0\,1\,0)_{hcp}$ planes along $[0\,1\,0]_{hcp}$ directions, (3) stretching δ along $[1\,2\,0]_{hcp}$ direction, and (4) the lattice constant adjusting in three principal crystalline axes.

To further illustrate the phase transformation mechanism, Fig. 6 presents the geometrical correlation between the *hcp* and *fco* structures and the respective actions taking place for turning the *hcp* lattice into the *fco* structure. The lattice constants of the *hcp* lattice are denoted as a and c with $\beta = c/a$. The lattice constants of the *fco* phase are denoted as a', b' and c' with $\eta = b'/a'$ and $\chi = a'/a$. As shown in Fig. 6, the line DB and the line AC have changed into the line AC'' and line BD'' upon the *hcp-to-fco* phase transformation, respectively. Nonetheless, the geometrical correlations, i.e. AC perpendicular to BD and AC'' perpendicular to BD'', are unchanged before and after the phase transformation, indicating that the angular parameters θ and δ are not independent, yet are both related to the lattice constants of the *hcp* phase as well as the newly formed *fco* phase. Accordingly, after a step-by-step deduction, the correlation between the angular parameters θ and δ is obtained and can be expressed by

$$\begin{cases} \eta = \frac{BD''}{AC''} = \sqrt{\frac{(\sqrt{3}\tan\theta-3)^2+3(1+\delta)^2}{(\sqrt{3}\tan\theta+1)^2+3(1+\delta)^2}}, \\ \tan^2\theta - \frac{2}{3}\sqrt{3}\tan\theta + (1+\delta)^2 - 1 = 0, \end{cases} \tag{1}$$

where θ and δ are the angular parameters defined in Fig. 6. The lattice parameters a' and b' are for the *fco* phase and are marked in Figs. 1(b) and 6. In fact, the above equations describe the crystallographic constraint that governs the *hcp-to-fco* phase transformation. Generally speaking, the angular parameters θ and δ cannot be measured from the *fco* phase directly, however, they can be calculated from Eq. (1), whenever the lattice constants of the newly formed *fco* phase are available. Besides, the angles Φ, marked in Fig. 6, can be directly obtained from the *fco* lattice, and Ψ can be determined from the final shape of the resultant phase. Φ and Ψ can be used to check the values of θ and δ calculated from Eq. (1). According to the geometrical relationship, the correlation between the angles Φ and Ψ versus the other defined parameters of the newly formed *fco* phase is deduced and can be written as

$$\Phi = \angle C''AB = \arctan\frac{\sqrt{3}(1+\delta)}{1+\sqrt{3}\tan\theta} \tag{2}$$

and

$$\Psi = \arctan\frac{2\chi\cos\Phi - 1}{2\chi\sin\Phi}. \tag{3}$$

To test the validity of Eqs. (1)–(3), we substitute the lattice constants of the original *hcp* lattice, a_{hcp} = 3.178 Å and c_{hcp} = 5.10 Å, respectively, and the lattice constants of the newly formed *fco* phase, a' = 3.527 Å, b' = 4.892 Å, and c' = 4.913 Å, respectively, into the Eqs. (1)–(3), and obtain $\theta = 12°$, $\delta = 0.0956$, $\Phi = 54.2°$ and $\Psi = 9.4°$, respectively. Apparently, the calculated values are in good agreement with those measured from the newly formed *fco* phase, i.e. $\Phi = 56.5°$ and $\Psi = 9.432°$.

Furthermore, from the reference frame given in Fig. 6, the correlation of the lattice points between the initial and final states, i.e. the *hcp* and *fco* structures, can be determined uniquely. Let a lattice vector $[h\,k\,l]$ in the *fco* lattice correspond to a lattice vector $[H\,K\,L]$ in the *hcp* lattice. The following equations give the correlation between the components of each lattice vector for the initial and the final states.

$$\begin{pmatrix} h \\ k \\ l \end{pmatrix} = \begin{pmatrix} 1/2 & 1/2 & 0 \\ -1/2 & 1/2 & 0 \\ 0 & 0 & 1 \end{pmatrix} \begin{pmatrix} f(H) \\ g(H) \\ L \end{pmatrix}, \tag{4}$$

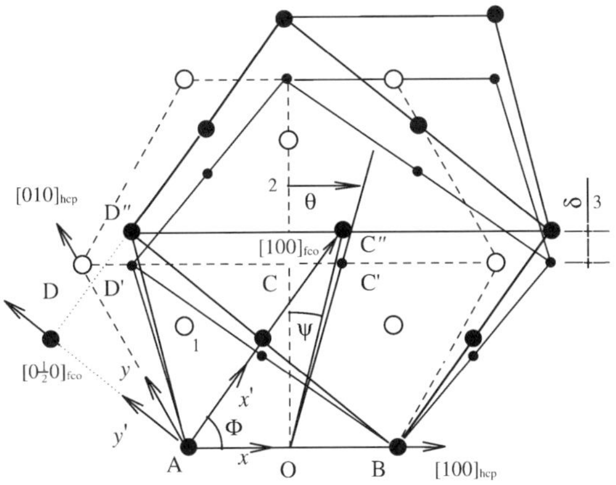

Fig. 6. Illustration of the geometric correlation in and the mechanism of the *hcp-to-fco* phase transformation. Open circles stand for the initial positions of atoms; gray dots stand for the transient positions of the atoms on the $(0\,0\,2)_{hcp}$ atomic plane after sliding; the small black dots stand for the transient positions of the atoms; and the filled circles stand for the final positions of atoms.

where $f(x)$ and $g(x)$ are two mathematics functions defined below to execute the sliding of $(0\ 0\ 2)_{hcp}$ plane.

$$f(x)=\begin{cases}x & \text{if } x=\text{int}(x),\\ x+1/6 & \text{if } x=\text{int}(x)+1/3,\end{cases} \tag{5}$$

$$g(x)=\begin{cases}x & \text{if } x=\text{int}(x),\\ x-1/6 & \text{if } x=\text{int}(x)+2/3.\end{cases} \tag{6}$$

We now discuss the signification and implication of the newly obtained results. First, for the case of the *hcp-to-fco* phase transformation, if it does execute through the mechanism proposed in the present study, then its crystallographic correlation and the lattice point correlation should satisfy the Eqs. (1)–(4) and vice versa. Second, if the lattice constants of the resultant phase are $a'=b'\neq c'$, then the newly formed phase could be named as the body-centered tetragonal (*bct*) structure. Accordingly, the transformation is named the *hcp-to-bct* transformation. Third, in the case of $a'=b'=c'$, the newly formed phase is therefore an *fcc* phase, and the transformation is named the *hcp-to-fcc* transformation. Concerning the angular relationship, in both the second and third cases, because of $a'=b'$, one obtains $\eta=1$, $\theta=30°$, $\delta=0.1547$ and $\Phi=45°$, and the phase transformations both execute through the proposed mechanism. Fourth, if there is no shearing during the phase transformation, i.e. $\theta=0$ and $\delta=0$, one obtains $\eta=1.732$ and $\Phi=60°$, which means that the phase transformation resultant is an *fco* phase ($c'\neq a'$ and $c'\neq b'$) or a *bct* phase ($c'=a'$ or $c'=b'$) and that the *bct* and *fco* phase could be formed without shearing under some specific circumstance, and the angular parameter Φ should be 60°. From the above discussion, it is suggested that the crystallographic and lattice point correlations obtained in present study are valid not only for the *hcp-to-fco* phase transformation observed in the Ni–Hf system, but also for some other phase transformations, e.g. *hcp-to-bct* and *hcp-to-fcc*, which could be considered to belong to a same family of phase transformation.

Based on above analysis and discussion, we propose to regard the observed *hcp-to-fco* phase transformation in the Hf–Ni system as a martensitic phase transformation. It is known that the martensitic phase and the martensitic phase transformation have extensively been studied in the past centuries, and a number of theories, such as Bain distortion and shearing mechanism, have been proposed to explain the phase transformation mechanism [9,21–23]. Nonetheless, most of previous literatures were related to some specific types of martensitic transformation, such as *fcc-to-bcc* (or *fcc-to-bct*), and *fcc-to-hcp* (or *bcc-to-hcp*, or *bct-to-hcp*) transformations [6–9,21–24]. To the authors' knowledge, the *hcp-to-fco* martensitic transformation is a new type of phase transformation. The present study has aimed to clarify its mechanism at the atomic scale via MD simulations. Undoubtedly, due to the limits of the MD simulation, e.g. the simulation time and the size of the simulation model, there is still much further work to be carried out concerning the martensitic phase transformation by both experimental investigations and theoretical modeling.

Acknowledgements

The authors are grateful to the financial support from the National Natural Science Foundation of China, the Ministry of Science and Technology of China (G20000672), and the Administration of Tsinghua University.

References

[1] Schwarz RB, Johnson WL. Formation of an amorphous alloy by solid-state reaction of the pure polycrystalline metals. Phys Rev Lett 1983;51:415–8.
[2] Liu BX, Zhang ZJ, Jin O, Pan F. Metastable alloys synthesized by ion mixing and thermodynamic and kinetic modelling. Nucl Instrum Meth B 1995;106:17–22.
[3] Li XY, Li ZF, Liu BX. Nonequilibrium *hcp* and *fcc* phases formed by ion mixing in an immiscible Ni–Ru system. J Alloy Compd 2002;334:167–72.
[4] Jin O, Liu BX. Hexagonal-closed-packed face-centered-cubic transformation in irradiated hafnium thin films. Mater Lett 1996;27:165–9.
[5] Alippi P, Marcus PM, Scheffler M. Strained tetragonal states and Bain paths in metals. Phys Rev Lett 1997;78:3892–5.
[6] Kulkova SE, Egorushkin VE. Electronic structure of NiMn(Ti) alloys and the influence of Ti on the temperature of the martensitic transitions. Mater Sci Eng A 1999;273:170–4.
[7] Kadau K, Entel P, Lomdahl PS. Molecular-dynamics study of martensitic transformations in sintered Fe–Ni Nanoparticles. Comput Phys Commun 2002;147:126–9.
[8] Fukuda T, Kakeshita T, Houjoh H, Shiraishi S, Saburi T. Electronic structure and stability of intermetallic compounds in the Ti–Ni system. Mater Sci Eng A 1999;273–275:166–9.
[9] Grujicic M, Dang P. Atomics-scale analysis of martensitic transformation in titanium alloyed with vanadium. Mater Sci Eng A 1996;205:153–76.
[10] Li JH, Kong LT, Liu BX. Structural transition and glass-forming ability of the Ni–Hf system studied by molecular dynamics simulation. J Mater Res 2004;19(12).
[11] Parrinello M, Rahman A. Polymorphic transitions in single crystals: a new molecular dynamics methods. J Appl Phys 1981;52:7182–90.
[12] Ciccotti, Hoover WG. Molecular-dynamics simulation of statistical-mechanical systems. North-Holland: ASI-NATO; 1986.
[13] Allen MP, Tildesley DJ. Computer simulation of liquids. UK: Oxford; 1987.
[14] Meyer M, Pontikis V. Computer simulation in materials science. Dordrecht: Dordrecht Academic; 1991.
[15] Cleri F, Rosato V. Tight-binding potentials for transition metals and alloys. Phys Rev B 1993;48:22–33.
[16] Lai WS, Liu BX. Lattice stability of some Ni–Ti alloy phases versus their chemical composition and disordering. J Phys: Condens Mater 2000;12:L53–60.

[17] Liu BX, Lai WS, Zhang ZJ. Solid-state crystal-to-amorphous transition in metal-metal multilayeres and its thermodynamic and atomistic modelling. Adv Phys 2001;50:367–429.
[18] Rosato V, Ciccotti G, Pontikis V. Molecular-dynamics study of surface premelting effects. Phys Rev B 1986;33:1860–70.
[19] Phillpot SR, Yip S, Wolf D. How do crystals melt?. Comput Phys 1989;3:20–31.
[20] Liebermann HH. Rapid solidified alloys: processes, structures, properties, applications. New York: Dekker; 1993.
[21] Morris EF, Meshii M, Wayman CM. Martensitic transformation. New York: Academic; 1978.
[22] Porter DA, Easterling KE. Phase transformations in metals and alloys. London: Chapman & Hall; 1992.
[23] Haasen P. Physical metallurgy. UK: Cambridge; 1996.
[24] Prem M, Krexner G, Blaschko O. Investigation of two martensitic phase transitions hcp-dhcp and dhcp-fcc in Co–0.85at.%Fe by neutron scattering. Mater Sci Eng A 1999;273:491–3.

Atomistic Modeling of Crystal-to-Amorphous Transition and Associated Kinetics in the Ni−Nb System by Molecular Dynamics Simulations

X. D. Dai, J. H. Li, and B. X. Liu*

Advanced Materials Laboratory, Department of Materials Science and Engineering, Tsinghua University, Beijing 100084, China, and State Key Lab of Solid-State Microstructure, Nanjing University, Nanjing 200093, China

Received: October 12, 2004; In Final Form: January 18, 2005

With the aid of ab initio calculations, an n-body potential of the Ni−Nb system is constructed under the Finnis−Sinclair formalism and the constructed potential is capable of not only reproducing some static physical properties but also revealing the atomistic mechanism of crystal-to-amorphous transition and associated kinetics. With application of the constructed potential, molecular dynamics simulations using the solid solution models reveal that the physical origin of crystal-to-amorphous transition is the crystalline lattice collapsing while the solute atoms are exceeding the critical solid solubilities, which are determined to be 19 atom % Ni and 13 atom % Nb for the Nb- and Ni-based solid solutions, respectively. It follows that an intrinsic glass-forming ability of the Ni−Nb system is within 19−87 atom % Ni, which matches well with that observed in ion beam mixing/solid-state reaction experiments. Simulations using the Nb/Ni/Nb (Ni/Nb/Ni) sandwich models indicate that the amorphous layer at the interfaces grows in a layer-by-layer mode and that, upon dissolving solute atoms, the Ni lattice approaches and exceeds its critical solid solubility faster than the Nb lattice, revealing an asymmetric behavior in growth kinetics. Moreover, an energy diagram is obtained by computing the energetic sequence of the Ni_xNb_{100-x} alloy in fcc, bcc, and amorphous structures, respectively, over the entire composition range, and the diagram could serve as a guide for predicting the metastable alloy formation in the Ni−Nb system.

I. Introduction

The first amorphous alloy (or metallic glass) was obtained in 1959 by P. Duwez et al. using liquid melt quenching (LMQ) to freeze an Au−Si alloy in its liquid state from the melt,[1] which, from a nature science point of view, was the discovery of a new state of matter, that is, the amorphous solid,[2] while, from a materials science point of view, was the birth of a new field of metallic glasses.[3] In the early 1980s, a powerful method, that is, ion beam mixing (IBM) of multiple metal layers, was developed, and numerous amorphous alloys have since been produced in a great number of binary metal systems to date. Because of its high capability, IBM is even able to produce metallic glasses in some equilibrium immiscible systems, in which LMQ is not able to co-melt the two constituent metals to form any alloy,[4,5] yet has so far not succeeded in obtaining amorphous alloys in some other systems, for example, the Ni−Ru system, which has a peritectic phase diagram at equilibrium.[6] A very basic issue has hereby been raised, that is, in which system and at what composition(s) an amorphous alloy could be obtained. In other words, one of the fundamental issues in the field is to clarify the physical origin of the crystal-to-amorphous transition as well as to predict the glass-forming ability/range (GFA/GFR) of a binary metal system.[7−11]

In the past decades, several empirical criteria and models, mainly based on the physical−chemical properties of a system or the constituent metals, have been proposed. Among them, the most successful one is the structural difference rule, which was based on considering the crystalline structure, atomic size, and electronegativity of the constituent metals, and its later extension by defining a single parameter, namely, the maximum possible amorphization range (MPAR) to predict the GFA/GFR of a system.[12−14] The physical meaning is that the MPAR corresponds to the total width of the two-phase region(s), in which amorphous alloy formation is favored, and accordingly, MPAR is equal to 100%, which represents the entire composition range, minus the two maximum terminal solid solubilities observed from the equilibrium phase diagram of the system. Although the prediction based on the empirical parameter MPAR has been quite successful, an obvious problem is that the maximum terminal solid solubilities are of equilibrium values, whereas the production of the amorphous alloys is certainly under a process of nonequilibrium or even far-from-equilibrium. Apparently, one should take into account the nonequilibrium solid solubilities to predict the GFA/GFR of a system. In fact, the present authors' group has recently revealed that the GFA/GFR of a system is indeed directly related to the two critical solid solubilities of the terminal supersaturated (i.e., nonequilibrium) solid solutions, which can directly be evaluated from a realistic interatomic potential of the system through molecular dynamics (MD) simulation.[15]

Also, in the early 1980s, another type of crystal-to-amorphous transition has been observed in the binary metal systems, that is, the first solid-state amorphization (SSA) taking place in the Au−La multilayered films reported by Schwarz and Johnson.[16] Since then, SSA has extensively been studied. For example, SSA has been observed not only in some systems having large negative heats of formation but also in some systems having small negative heats of formation, for example, in the Ni−Mo system or even in the equilibrium immiscible systems (e.g., the

* To whom correspondence should be addressed. E-mail: dmslbx@tsinghua.edu.cn.

J. of Physical Chemistry B 109 (10), p.4717-4725 (2005).

Cu−Ta system with a positive heat of formation).[17−19] In experimental studies, an interesting phenomenon, that is, an asymmetric growth of the amorphous interlayer during SSA, has been observed in the Zr−Ni and Zr−Co bilayered films.[20,21] For example, in a cross-sectional Co−Zr bilayer sample, the amorphous interlayer grew by consuming Co and Zr at two different speeds with an estimated ratio of ~2:1. In this respect, however, theoretical modeling concerning the detailed growth kinetics of SSA, especially at an atomic scale, needs much further investigation. In the present study, we dedicate ourselves to developing atomistic modeling for clarifying the underlying physics of crystal-to-amorphous transition and the associated asymmetric growth kinetics in a representative system, that is, the Ni−Nb system, by first deriving a realistic n-body Ni−Nb potential and then performing molecular dynamics (MD) simulation.

To our knowledge, there has been a published Ni−Nb potential based on the embedded-atom method (EAM),[22] which, however, was not able to reproduce the experimentally observed crystal-to-amorphous transition in the Ni−Nb multilayers.[23,24] Consequently, to develop atomistic modeling for the Ni−Nb system, we first reconstruct an n-body Ni−Nb potential based on the Finnis−Sinclair (FS) formalism[25] with the aid of ab initio calculations to acquire some physical properties for deriving the Ni−Nb cross-potential. Second, after proving the relevance of the derived Ni−Nb potential, MD simulations are performed using the solid solution models to reveal the physical mechanism of the crystal-to-amorphous transition as well as to determine the GFA/GFR of the Ni−Nb system. In performing the simulations, the main idea is to compare the relative stability of the solid solution versus its amorphous counterpart over the entire composition range, thus determining the two critical solid solubilities, at and beyond which the solid solutions become unstable and turn into the corresponding amorphous states. Third, MD simulations are also performed using the sandwich models to closely examine the interfacial reaction at the Ni/Nb interfaces for revealing the detailed kinetics of the resultant solid-state amorphization. Moreover, the correlation between the structure and formation energy of the possible metastable phases of different structures is examined through MD simulations for the Ni−Nb system over the entire composition range.

II. Construction of an n-Body Ni−Nb Potential

The formalism developed by Finnis and Sinclair,[25] that is, the FS formalism, is adopted in the present study as a computational framework to construct the n-body potential of the Ni−Nb system, since it has been proven to be capable of describing the interatomic interaction involved in the body-centered cubic (bcc) and face-centered cubic (fcc) metals and alloys in a relatively satisfactory way.[26−28] In the FS formalism, the total energy of a system is given by

$$U_{\text{tot}} = \frac{1}{2}\sum_{ij} V(r_{ij}) - \sum_{i}[\sum_{i\neq j} A^2\phi(r_{ij})]^{1/2} \tag{1}$$

The first term in eq 1 is a conventional central pair-potential summation, which is expressed by a hexad polynomial in the present study

$$V(r) = \begin{cases} (r-c)^2(c_0 + c_1 r + c_2 r^2 + c_3 r^3 + c_4 r^4), & r \le c \\ 0, & r > c \end{cases} \tag{2}$$

where c is a disposable parameter assumed to lie between the second and third neighbor atoms. c_0, c_1, c_2, c_3, and c_4 are the potential parameters to be fitted. The second term in eq 1 is the n-body term and takes a sum form over all atoms for a cohesive function as follows:

$$\phi(r) = \begin{cases} (r-d)^2, & r \le d \\ 0, & r > d \end{cases} \tag{3}$$

where d is also assumed to lie between the second and third neighbor atoms. Obviously, there is a total of eight potential parameters, that is, A, c, d, c_0, c_1, c_2, c_3, and c_4, to be fitted. For a perfect crystal, in which all the atoms are equivalent, the cohesive energy (E_c) is equal to the negative value of the energy per atom and can therefore be expressed as

$$E_c = A\sum_{i\neq 0}\sqrt{\phi(r_i)} - \frac{1}{2}\sum_{i\neq 0} V(r_i) \tag{4}$$

For a binary alloy, $A_xB_{(1-x)}$, one can obtain the cohesive energy (E_{AB}) by the following equation:

$$E_{AB} = -[xE_A + (1-x)E_B] \tag{5}$$

where E_A and E_B are the energies per atom A and B, respectively, in the $A_xB_{(1-x)}$ alloy.

The potential parameters for pure Ni and Nb are determined by fitting the experimental data of cohesive energy (E_c), lattice constant (a), elastic constants (C_{11}, C_{12}, and C_{44}), and the fitted potential parameters are listed in Table 1. The procedure of parametrization is similar to that described by Finnis and Sinclair.[25] The physical properties reproduced from the derived Ni and Nb potentials and the corresponding experimental data used in fitting are listed in Table 2. From Table 2, one can see that the derived Ni and Nb potentials work fairly well in reproducing some physical properties of the pure Ni and Nb, respectively.

As there are very few available experimental data related to the Ni−Nb compounds, it is a challenging task to fit the Ni−Nb cross-potential. In this respect, the first-principles calculation based on quantum mechanics is known to be a reliable way to acquire some physical properties of the alloy phases of

TABLE 1: Fitted Parameters of the n-Body Potentials for the Ni−Nb System

	Ni−Ni	Nb−Nb	Ni−Nb
A (eV·Å^{-1})	0.982 476 7	2.999 182	1.825 783
d (Å)	4.12	3.9	3.75
c (Å)	4.22	4.07	4.25
c_0 (eV·Å^{-2})	13.282 760	25.575 480	22.470 780
c_1 (eV·Å^{-3})	−17.085060	−26.842 730	−24.198 810
c_2 (eV·Å^{-4})	8.262 515	9.903 115	8.854 626
c_3 (eV·Å^{-5})	−1.770 480	−1.297 269	−1.098 587
c_4 (eV·Å^{-6})	0.141 390 2	0.014 288 83	0.0

TABLE 2: Comparison between Some Calculated Physical Properties Reproduced by the n-Body Potentials and the Experimental Values Used in Fitting the Potentials for Pure Ni and Nb (E_v^f Is the Unrelaxed Vacancy Formation Energy)

	Ni		Nb	
	experimental	calculated	experimental	calculated
E_c (eV)	4.44[a]	4.437	7.57[a]	7.572
a (Å)	3.52[a]	3.520	3.30[a]	3.300
C_{11} (Mbar)	2.45[b]	2.450	2.47[b]	2.470
C_{12} (Mbar)	1.40[b]	1.485	1.35[b]	1.347
C_{44} (Mbar)	1.25[b]	1.182	0.287[b]	0.2871
E_v^f (eV)	1.60[c]	1.624	2.75[d]	2.746

[a] Reference 29. [b] Reference 30. [c] Reference 31. [d] Reference 32.

TABLE 3: Comparison of the Cohesive Energy (E_c, eV) and Lattice Constant (a, Å) Derived from the Constructed Ni−Nb Potential versus Those from Experiments/ab Initio Calculation[a]

system	structure[b]	ab initio calculation		present study		experimental
Ni_3Nb	$L1_2$	$E_c = 5.361$	$a = 3.690$	$E_c = 5.230$	$a = 3.651$	
	$D0_{19}$	$E_c = 5.478$	$a = 2.625$	$E_c = 5.227$	$a = 2.603$	$a = 2.60^c$
					$c/a = 1.62$	$c/a = 1.62^c$
NiNb	B2	$E_c = 6.026$*	$a = 3.090$*	$E_c = 6.026$	$a = 3.090$	
$NiNb_3$	$L1_2$	$E_c = 6.692$*	$a = 4.050$*	$E_c = 6.698$	$a = 4.115$	$a = 4.11^d$
	$D0_{19}$	$E_c = 6.648$	$a = 2.875$	$E_c = 6.698$	$a = 2.911$	

[a] Note that, for the $D0_{19}$ structures, the values of c/a are optimized. For $D0_{19}$ Ni_3Nb, $c/a = 1.62$, and for $D0_{19}$ $NiNb_3$, $c/a = 1.63$. The data used in fitting are denoted by asterisks. [b] Reference 41. [c] Reference 42. [d] Reference 43.

TABLE 4: Calculated Lattice Constants (a) and Cohesive Energies (E_c) of Ni and Nb in Three Simple Structures (fcc, hcp, and bcc)

	Ni		Nb	
structure	a (Å)	E_c (eV)	a (Å)	E_c (eV)
fcc	3.520	4.437	4.218	7.247
hcp	2.488	4.436	2.983	7.247
bcc	2.788	4.357	3.300	7.572

interest.[33−35] In the present study, the first-principles calculations are carried out using the well-established Vienna ab initio simulation package (VASP).[36,37] In the calculation, plane-wave basis and fully nonlocal Vanderbilt-type ultrasoft pseudopotentials are employed.[38] The exchange and correlation items are described by the generalized-gradient approximation (GGA) proposed by Perdew and Wang.[39] The integration in the Brillouin zone is done in a mesh of 11 × 11 × 11 special k points determined according to the so-called Monkhorst−Pack scheme, as such an integration has proved to be sufficient for the computation of the simple structures.[40] The calculated results are listed in Table 3. With the calculated cohesive energies and lattice constants of the B2 NiNb and $L1_2$ $NiNb_3$ compounds, the cross-potential of Ni−Nb can be fitted, and the fitted parameters are also listed in Table 1.

To prove the relevance of the Ni and Nb potentials, we first reproduced the cohesive energies and lattice constants of the equilibrium structures and their metastable structures for pure Ni and Nb, respectively. The calculated results are listed in Table 4. From Table 4, one can clearly see that the cohesive energy of fcc Ni is greater than that of bcc Ni and that the cohesive energy of bcc Nb is greater than that of fcc Nb, reflecting well the fact that the equilibrium states of the pure Ni and Nb are fcc and bcc structures, respectively. In addition, we also compare the equation of state reproduced by the constructed potentials with Rose's equation, which is considered as a universal equation of state for metals,[44] and it turned out that they are in good agreement, as shown in Figure 1.

To test the Ni−Nb cross-potential, we employ the potential to reproduce the cohesive energies and the lattice constants of the Ni_3Nb, NiNb, and $NiNb_3$ metastable compounds, and the results are also listed in Table 3. In the table, the asterisks denote the values used in fitting the potential. One sees that the calculated properties from the constructed potential are in good agreement with those obtained from ab initio calculations. It is thus concluded that the newly constructed n-body Ni−Nb potential is of relevance in describing the atomic interactions in the Ni−Nb system.

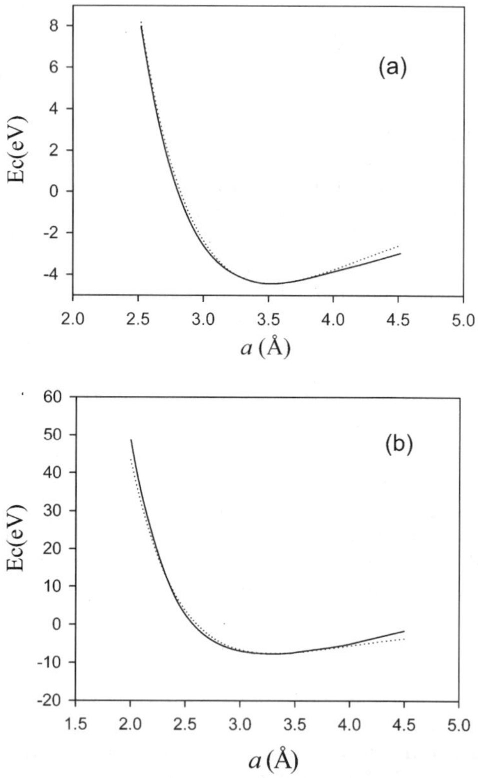

Figure 1. Equation of state reproduced from the constructed Ni−Nb potential (solid line) compared with Rose's equation (dotted line): (a) Ni; (b) Nb.

III. Simulation and Characterization Methods

A. Simulation Model (1): Solid Solution Models. On the basis of the constructed Ni−Nb potential, MD simulations are carried out at a constant temperature and at 0 Pa for the fcc Ni-based and bcc Nb-based solid solution models[15] with various solute concentrations, respectively. As the present study is mainly interested in the structural phase transition in the Ni−Nb system at room temperature, the constant temperature is set to be 300 K. The simulation models consist of 7 × 7 × 7 = 343 unit cells (1372 atoms) for the fcc Ni-based solid solution and 8 × 8 × 8 = 512 unit cells (1024 atoms) for the bcc Nb-based solid solution. For both solid solution models, the [100], [010], and [001] crystalline directions are parallel to the x, y, and z axes, respectively. Periodic boundary conditions are adopted in three axes. In setting the solid solution models, the solute atoms are added into the model by the random substitution of a desired number of solvent atoms to obtain the initial state of the solid solution models. In the present study, MD simulations are then carried out with the Parrinello−Rahman constant pressure scheme and the equations of motion are solved using the second-order four-value predictor−corrector algorithm of Gear with a time step of $t = 5 \times 10^{-15}$ s.[45−47] In the present study, MD simulations are conducted for 50 000−150 000 MD time steps to reach a relatively stable (i.e., metastable) state, at which all the related dynamic variables show no secular variation.

B. Simulation Model (2): Sandwich Models. To represent the multilayered samples frequently employed in IBM and solid-state reaction (SSR) experiments, we adopt a sandwich model with periodic boundary conditions in MD simulations. The sandwich model is constructed by stacking Ni(001) atomic planes and Nb(001) atomic planes along the z axis and parallel to the $x-y$ plane, and the orientations of the atomic planes were indexed by their Miller indices, for example, [6(111)Ni] refers to an Ni lattice of fcc structure stacked by six (111) atomic planes. The crystalline directions ⟨100⟩ of fcc Ni and ⟨100⟩ of bcc Nb are arranged to be parallel to the x and y axes with unit distances of 3.52 and 3.30 Å, respectively, leading to a size difference ratio of 1.067. Considering the number of the atoms in the simulation model to be within a manageable scale, the numbers of Ni and Nb unit cells in the $x-y$ plane are selected to be $11 \times 11 = 121$ and $12 \times 12 = 144$, respectively, resulting in a lattice difference ratio of $12/11 = 1.091$, which is reasonably close to the above-mentioned real situation. Periodic boundary conditions are also adopted in three axes. Obviously, such a setting would cause a misfit for the lattice dimension of Ni and result in a 2.2% density decrease of Ni in the simulation model. In this regard, Mura et al. have shown that such a small density decrease would only have a minor influence on the simulation results.[48]

In the present study, two sandwich models are constructed to simulate the solid-state interfacial reaction in the Ni−Nb system, that is, the [6(001)Nb/8(001)Ni/6(001)Nb] and [4(001)-Ni/8(001)Nb/4(001)Ni] models, which correspond to alloy concentrations of 52.84 and 62.69 atom % Ni, respectively. It will be shown later that the interfacial reactions taking place in the two sandwich models are essentially the same, regardless of whether the Ni or Nb layer is set as the interlayer.

C. Characterization Methods. The structural phase transition in the Ni−Nb solid solution and sandwich models is monitored by the pair-correlation function ($g(r)$), planar structure factor ($S(\mathbf{k,z})$), and density profiles of each species along the z direction ($\rho_\alpha(z)$). As one of the main criteria to determine an amorphous structure, $g(r)$ is commonly used to characterize the structure to be either crystalline or amorphous, or disordered. To calculate the pair-correlation function ($g(r)$), each atom was imagined to be at the center of a series of concentric spheres. The atomic density ($\rho(r)$) was defined to be the number of atoms in each spherical shell divided by the volume of that shell, with the consideration of those periodic images located outside the block. By averaging over all the atoms within 200 time steps, $g(r)$ can then be obtained by the following formula:

$$g(r) = \frac{\rho(r)}{\rho_0} \tag{6}$$

where $\rho(r)$ denotes the atomic density at $r = |\boldsymbol{r}|$ and $r = 0$ defines the position of a reference. ρ_0 is the average atomic density in the whole model. The planer structure factor ($S(\mathbf{k,z})$) is a Fourier transformation of the density in each crystallographic plane parallel to the $x-y$ plane and is defined by Phillpot et al. Accordingly, it can be expressed as[49]

$$S(\mathbf{k,z}) = \left\langle \frac{1}{N_z^2} \left| \sum_{j=1}^{N_z} \exp(i\mathbf{k}\cdot\boldsymbol{r}_j) \right|^2 \right\rangle \tag{7}$$

where $\mathbf{z}$ labels the crystal plane to which the point $\boldsymbol{r}_j$ belongs in the initial configuration and $\mathbf{k}$ is an arbitrary vector of the planar reciprocal lattice. In the present study, $\mathbf{k} = (1,1)$ is used. N_z is the number of layers perpendicular to the z axis, and the broken brackets mean that $S(\mathbf{k,z})$ is an average value obtained within some time steps in the MD simulation. Accordingly, the planar structure factor $S = 1$ refers to an entirely ordered crystal, while $S = 0$ is for a completely disordered state. The density profiles ($\rho_\alpha(z)$) of each species along the z direction are also calculated to define the position of a single atomic layer, indicating the local (i.e., restricted to the single layer) structural and compositional properties of the models.[50]

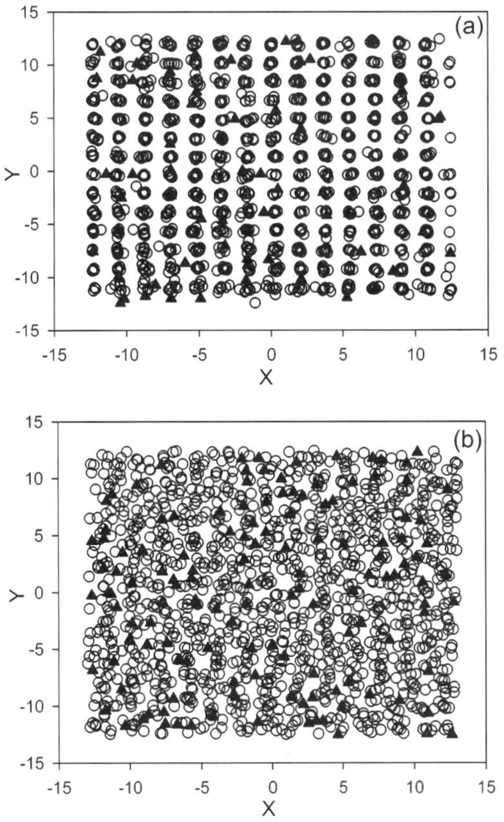

Figure 2. Projections of atomic positions for the (a) $Ni_{91}Nb_9$ and (b) $Ni_{87}Nb_{13}$ solid solutions after annealing at 300 K for 100 000 MD time steps. Open circles, Ni; filled triangles, Nb.

IV. Results and Discussion

A. Crystal-to-Amorphous Transition and the Intrinsic Glass-Forming Ability. We now present the simulation results for the fcc Ni-based solid solution models first. It has been estimated that the error of solid solubility determined by MD simulation is ~3−5 atom %;[10] therefore, we vary the solute concentration with an interval of 4 atom % to determine the critical solid solubility. Figure 2 displays the projections of atomic positions for the $Ni_{91}Nb_9$ and $Ni_{87}Nb_{13}$ fcc solid solutions after annealing at 300 K for 100 000 MD time steps, respectively. From Figure 2, one sees vividly that, for the solid solution with 9 atom % Nb, the fcc structure can be clearly visualized; that is, it still remains in its original fcc crystalline structure, while, for the solid solution with 13 atom % Nb, the lattice has apparently collapsed and turned into a disordered state; that is, a crystal-to-amorphous transition has obviously taken place. Figure 3 shows the corresponding density profiles ($\rho_\alpha(z)$) for the solid solutions with the alloy compositions $Ni_{91}Nb_9$, $Ni_{87}Nb_{13}$, and $Ni_{80}Nb_{20}$, respectively. It can be seen that, when the solute concentration is <13 atom % Nb, the atomic planes can clearly be distinguished from the density profiles; however, once

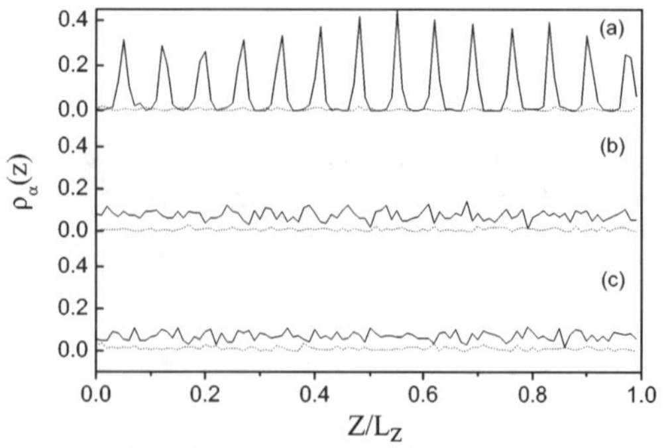

Figure 3. Calculated density profiles ($\rho_\alpha(z)$) of Ni and Nb atoms along the z direction in (a) $Ni_{91}Nb_9$, (b) $Ni_{87}Nb_{13}$, and (c) $Ni_{80}Nb_{20}$ solid solutions after annealing at 300 K for 100 000 MD time steps. $\rho_{Ni}(z)$ is represented by the solid line and $\rho_{Nb}(z)$ by the dotted line. The ordinate is in arbitrary units.

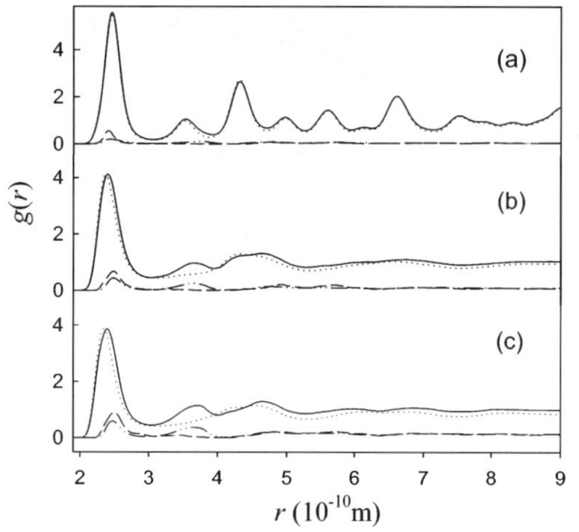

Figure 4. Total and partial pair-correlation functions for the fcc Ni-rich solid solutions after annealing at 300 K for 100 000 MD time steps. The compositions of the solid solutions are (a) 9 atom %, (b) 13 atom %, and (c) 20 atom % Nb. The solid line is for the total $g(r)$, the short-dashed line is for the Nb−Nb partial $g(r)$, the dotted line is for the Ni−Ni partial $g(r)$, and the dash−dot−dotted line is for the Ni−Nb partial $g(r)$.

the Nb concentration equals or exceeds 13 atom %, a relatively uniform distributed density profile appears. To have firm evidence, the total and partial pair-correlation functions ($g(r)$) for fcc Ni-based solid solutions are calculated and shown in Figure 4. In the figure, as the $g(r)$ curve of $Ni_{91}Nb_9$ remains apparent sharp peaks even at a large distance r, the $Ni_{91}Nb_9$ simulation model is still in a crystalline structure. Whereas for the $Ni_{87}Nb_{13}$ and $Ni_{80}Nb_{20}$ simulation models, the $g(r)$ curves become more or less smooth and the peaks, except for the first one, even disappear, indicating that a crystal-to-amorphous transition takes place when the Nb concentration equals or exceeds 13 atom % in the Ni-rich solid solutions. In fact, all the simulation models with Nb solute concentrations exceeding 13 atom % show obvious amorphous characteristics in their $\rho_\alpha(z)$ and $g(r)$ figures; therefore, only a typical model, $Ni_{80}Nb_{20}$, is given in the figures. It is noted that the calculated curves of the $Ni_{87}Nb_{13}$ and $Ni_{80}Nb_{20}$ simulation models are similar, as shown in Figures 3 and 4, respectively, implying that they have similar amorphous structures.

From the above results, it can be concluded that the critical solid solubility is 13 atom % Nb for the fcc Ni-based solid solutions. Note that the equilibrium solid solubility of Nb in Ni at low temperatures, for example, at 400 K, is ~2−3 atom %,[51]

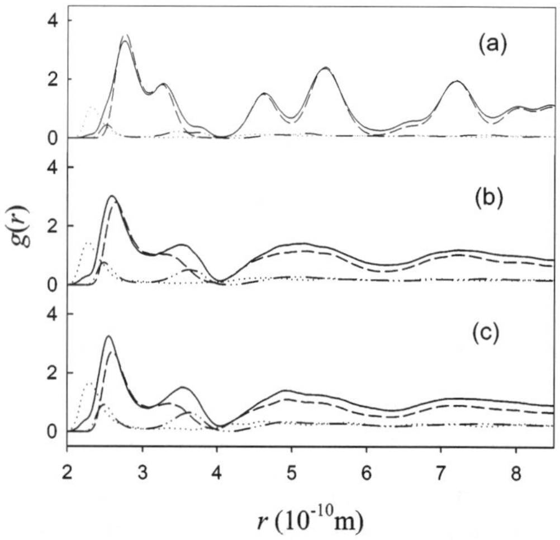

Figure 5. Total and partial pair-correlation functions for the fcc Nb-rich solid solutions after annealing at 300 K for 100 000 MD time steps. The compositions of the solid solutions are (a) 15 atom %, (b) 19 atom %, and (c) 25 atom % Ni. The solid line is for the total $g(r)$, the short-dashed line is for the Nb−Nb partial $g(r)$, the dotted line is for the Ni−Ni partial $g(r)$, and the dash−dot−dotted line is for the Nb−Ni partial $g(r)$.

indicating that, under nonequilibrium conditions, the solid solubility could be significantly extended. Apparently, the Ni-based solid solution containing 13 atom % Nb is therefore a supersaturated one. According to the thermodynamics of solids, the supersaturated Ni-based solid solution is in a metastable state and the higher the concentration of Nb is, the less stable the supersaturated solid solution is. Once the concentration of Nb exceeds the critical solid solubility, the solid solution would become unstable and turn into a disordered state, resulting in a crystal-to-amorphous transition. In other words, the physical origin of crystal-to-amorphous transition is the crystalline lattice collapsing while the solute atoms are exceeding the critical value. From an energetic point of view, when the concentration reaches or exceeds the critical solid solubility, the formation of an amorphous alloy is favored compared with the corresponding supersaturated solid solution of fcc structure.

Similarly, for the bcc Nb-based solid solution, the critical solid solubility is determined to be 19 atom % Ni, which is also considerably greater than the equilibrium value of around 5 atom % Ni in Nb.[51] Figure 5 displays the $g(r)$ curves for the Nb-rich bcc solid solutions with three different alloy compositions. Apparently, the $g(r)$ curves feature a bcc crystalline structure when the Ni concentration is <19 atom % Ni, whereas when the Ni concentration exceeds the critical solid solubility, the $g(r)$ curves are typical of an amorphous structure. We also calculated the atomic projections of the $x-z$ plane and the density profiles ($\rho_\alpha(z)$) of the Ni and Nb atoms along the z direction, and the calculated results all confirm that the supersaturated solid solution would collapse and turn into a disordered state when the concentration of Ni reaches or exceeds ~19 atom % Ni. It should be noted that, either in Figure 4 or in Figure 5, the height of the first peak changes slightly with increasing solute concentration, implying that the number of the first neighbor atoms in either the crystalline or amorphous state almost stays unchanged and that, in a short-range region, the amorphous state also features some ordering behavior.

From the above results, one can see that there are two critical solid solubilities: one is 13 atom % Nb for the fcc Ni-based solid solution, and the other is 19 atom % Ni for the bcc Nb-based solid solution. For the Ni−Nb system, an amorphous alloy

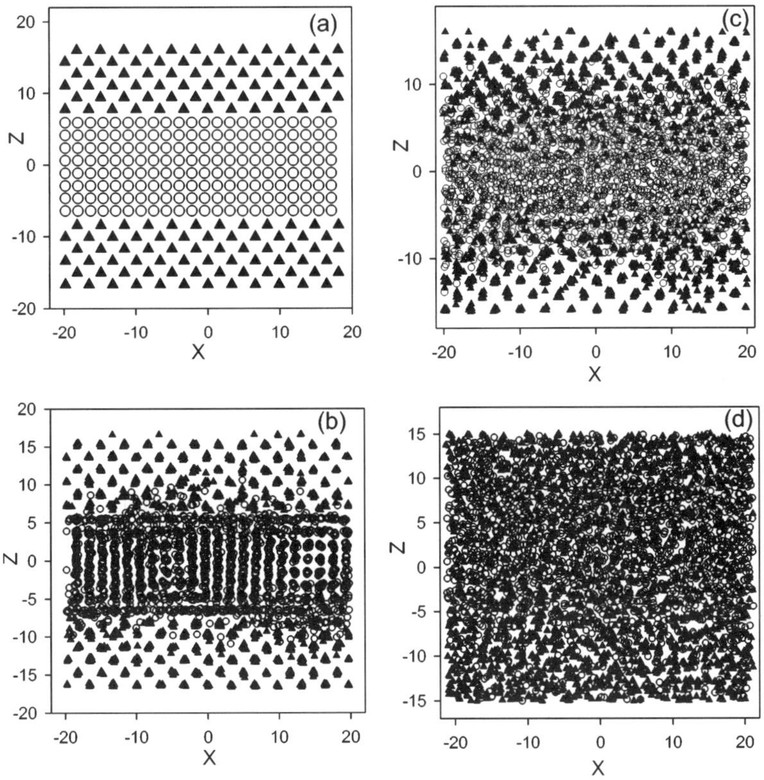

Figure 6. Projections of atomic positions on the $x-z$ plane of the [6(001)Nb/8(001)Ni/6(001)Nb] sandwich model upon isothermal annealing at 573 K for (a) 0 time steps, (b) 15 000 time steps, (c) 70 000 time steps, and (d) 300 000 time steps. Open circles, Ni; filled triangles, Nb.

would form when its composition falls into the composition range bounded by the two determined critical solid solubilities. It is therefore concluded that the glass-forming ability/range (GFA/GFR) of tthe Ni−Nb system is ~19−87 atom % Ni according to the present study. It is important to compare the above simulation results with other theoretical results as well as the experimental observations. For instance, by comparing the Gibbs free energies of the crystalline and amorphous phases of the Ni−Nb alloys, Gallego et al. have determined the GFR of the Ni−Nb system to be within 20−80 atom % Ni,[52] which falls in the GFR, that is, 19−87 atom % Ni, determined directly from the newly derived Ni−Nb potential through MD simulation. In IBM experiments conducted by Zhang et al.,[4] amorphous alloys were readily formed within a composition range of 20−85 atom % Ni, which also falls in the GFR determined by the present simulation. In short, the GFR determined from the interatomic potential through MD simulation matches well with other theoretical results as well as the experimental observations.

From a physical point of view, the GFR determined in the present study is directly calculated from the interatomic potential, which governs the atomic configurations, thus also governing the energetic states, of both solid solutions and the competing disordered states. The GFR thus determined can therefore be considered as an intrinsic property of a system and has nothing to do with any practically applied glass-producing technique. Comparatively, the experimentally measured GFR should then be considered as a nominal one, which depends on the specific glass-producing technique applied in practice. It is therefore deduced that the GFR measured in IBM experiments could be a little narrower than that determined by the potential. Clearly, one can see that the GFR determined in the present study is consistent with that obtained from IBM experiments, which, in turn, provides additional evidence for the relevance of the n-body potential constructed in the present study.

B. Asymmetric Growth Kinetics in Solid-State Interfacial Reaction. We now present the simulation results using the sandwich models for studying the growth kinetics of SSA in the Ni−Nb multilayers. Figure 6a shows the initial state of the sandwich model, in which the Ni and Nb crystalline lattices are sharply separated by two interfaces. The model is then isothermally annealed at 573 K. Parts b, c, and d of Figure 6 display three snapshots of the projections of the atomic positions on the $x-z$ plane after isothermal annealing for 15 000, 70 000, and 300 000 time steps, respectively. From Figure 6, one can find that the layers near the interface are disordered at 15 000 MD time steps and gradually extend outward with increasing time and that after 300 000 time steps, the disordered interlayers extend throughout the model, resulting in a uniform amorphous structure. By a close inspection of Figure 6, one can see that the Ni−Nb disordered region at the interfaces extends in a layer-by-layer mode. Figure 6c shows that all the Ni atomic planes have become disordered, while most of the Nb atomic planes still remain in crystalline structures. Figure 6b and c also indicates that the Ni lattice near the interlayer became disordered earlier than that of the Nb lattice next to the interlayer and that the extension/growth of the disordered region is faster toward the Ni lattice than that toward to the Nb side, exhibiting an asymmetric growth behavior of the amorphous interlayer during SSA taking place in the Ni−Nb system.

Figure 7 shows the changes of the density profiles ($\rho_\alpha(z)$) of each species along the z direction, perpendicular to the interface, upon isothermal annealing at 573 K with increasing time steps. One sees that mutual diffusion, which is defined as the migration of Ni and Nb atoms crossing the interface, does take place at

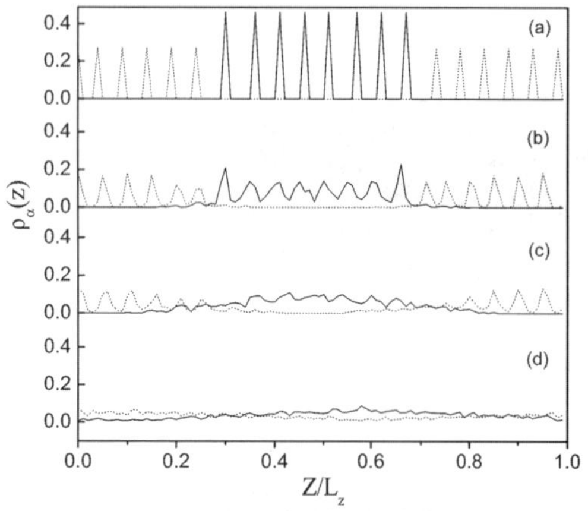

Figure 7. Calculated density profiles ($\rho_\alpha(z)$) of each species along the z direction, perpendicular to the interface, for (a) the initial state and the states obtained after annealing at 573 K for (b) 15 000, (c) 70 000, and (d) 300 000 time steps in the [6(001)Nb/8(001)Ni/6(001)-Nb] sandwich model. $\rho_{Ni}(z)$ is represented by the solid line and $\rho_{Nb}(z)$ by the dotted line. The ordinate is in arbitrary units.

573 K and that the amount of atomic diffusion increases with increasing simulation time, resulting eventually in the uniformly distributed density profiles ($\rho_\alpha(z)$) of both Ni and Nb along the z direction at 300 000 time steps. In Figure 7a and b, one can see that the $\rho_\alpha(z)$ of either Ni or Nb has obvious peaks, indicating that Ni and Nb are both in crystalline structures. However, in Figure 7c, one can see that the $\rho_\alpha(z)$ of Ni has become uniformly distributed, while that of Nb still retains obvious crystalline peaks after annealing at 573 K for 70 000 time steps, confirming the appearance of asymmetric growth during interfacial reaction in the Ni−Nb multilayers. Furthermore, the planar structure factors ($S(\mathbf{k},\mathbf{z})$) are calculated for the 20 atomic planes and they decrease from ~0.99 in the initial state to <0.1 after 300 000 time steps, confirming that the whole sandwich model has become completely disordered.

To further characterize the asymmetric growth during isothermal annealing, the partial and total pair-correlation functions for the Ni region (nos. 7−14 atomic planes) and the Nb region (nos. 1−6 atomic places) are calculated, respectively, after annealing at 573 K for 70 000 time steps, and they are shown in Figure 8. From the figure, one observes that, in the Ni region, the Ni−Ni $g(r)$ shows the shape commonly known for a typical amorphous phase, while, in the Nb region, the crystalline peaks of Nb−Nb $g(r)$ still remain, suggesting that the structure of Nb is more stable than that of Ni and the disordering speed of the Ni lattice is faster than that of the Nb lattice; that is, an asymmetric growth does take place during the process of SSA in the Ni−Nb multilayers. In addition, on the basis of the $S(\mathbf{k},\mathbf{z})$, $\rho_\alpha(z)$, and $g(r)$ calculated at various annealing times, the thicknesses (X) of the growing amorphous interlayer toward the Ni and Nb lattices, respectively, are monitored as a function of the annealing time (t), and the results are shown in Figure 9. From the figure, one sees that the disordering process toward Ni is obviously faster than that directed toward Nb, as the Ni fcc structure has become an amorphous state completely, while only two atomic planes of the Nb bcc structure have become disordered. To further examine the conclusion, we also perform MD simulations for another sandwich model of [4(001)Ni/8(001)Nb/4(001)Ni] upon isothermal annealing at 573 K, and similar results are obtained. As an example, Figure 9 also shows the correlations between the growth thicknesses (X) of the amorphous interlayer toward the Ni and Nb lattices, respectively, and annealing time (t) in the sandwich model. Apparently, the

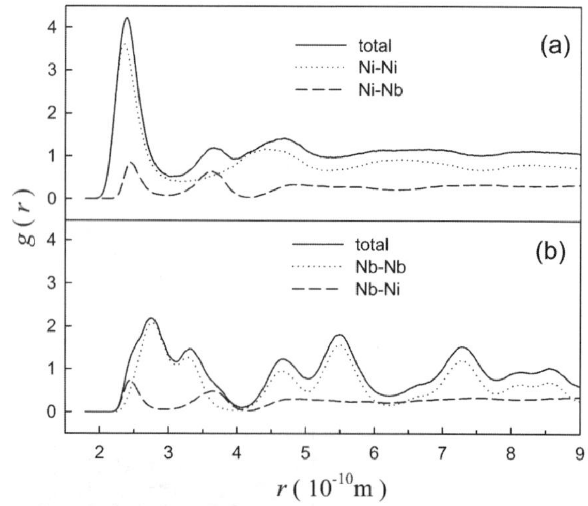

Figure 8. Total and partial pair-correlation functions for the (a) nos. 7−14 atomic planes and (b) nos. 1−6 atomic planes in the [6(001)-Nb/8(001)Ni/6(001)Nb] sandwich model upon isothermal annealing at 573 K for 70 000 MD time steps.

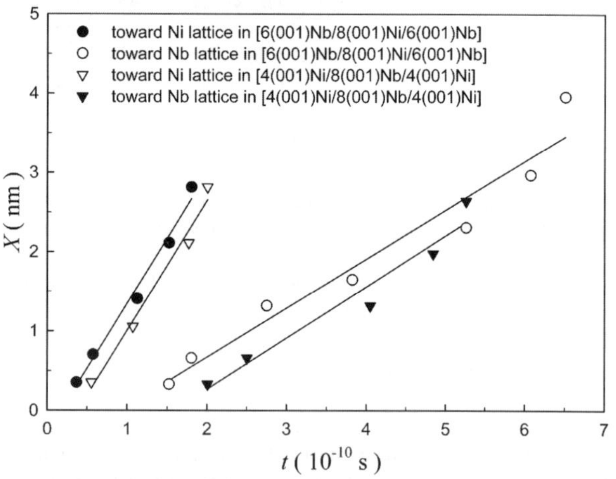

Figure 9. Growing thicknesses (X) of the amorphous interlayer as a function of annealing time (t) toward the Ni and Nb lattices, respectively, in the [6(001)Nb/8(001)Ni/6(001)Nb] and [4(001)Ni/8(001)Nb/4(001)Ni] sandwich models upon isothermal annealing at 573 K.

disordering process toward Ni is faster than that directed to Nb, indicating that asymmetric growth also took place in the model. Note that, in the first sandwich model, there are 12 Nb atomic layers, whereas, in the second sandwich model, there are 8 Nb atomic layers. Such a difference makes the second sandwich model become completely disordered in a shorter time than the first model does (see Figure 9). Nonetheless, similar asymmetric growth behaviors are revealed in both sandwich models, meaning that the simulation results are not affected by the stacking sequence of Ni and Nb in the sandwich models, that is, either by Ni/Nb/Ni or by Nb/Ni/Nb.

Experimentally, the asymmetric growth behavior of the amorphous interlayer has been observed in the Ni−Nb multilayers upon solid-state interfacial reaction.[23] Actually, the asymmetric growth kinetics can be well understood in terms of the physical origin of the crystal-to-amorphous transition revealed by the above MD simulations. We have determined that 19 atom % Ni solute atoms are necessary to destabilize and transform the Nb bcc solid solution into an amorphous state, whereas the critical concentration for the Ni solid solution is

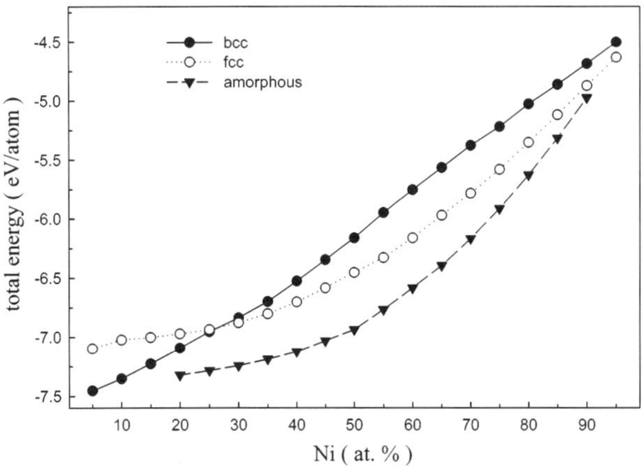

Figure 10. Calculated total energies of the Ni−Nb phases in different structures versus the Ni composition over the entire composition range. The values of the fcc and bcc Ni−Nb phases are obtained at 300 K from the fcc and bcc solid solution models, respectively. The values of the amorphous Ni−Nb phases in the ranges 19−50 and 50−87 Ni atom % are obtained from the bcc and fcc solid solution models, respectively, upon isothermal annealing at 300 K for 100 000 MD time steps.

~13 atom % Nb. Apparently, the critical composition of the fcc Ni is lower that that of the bcc Nb, which implies that the fcc Ni layers in the bilayer or the multilayer will approach and exceed the critical value faster than the Nb layer. Therefore, the Ni lattice is much easier to amorphize than the Nb lattice.

C. Structural Stability of the Metastable Ni−Nb Phases. On the basis of the constructed potential, the structural stability of the metastable Ni−Nb phases over the entire composition range can also be studied. Accordingly, we perform MD simulations to determine the energies of the fcc and bcc solid solutions, respectively, over the entire composition range as well as the energies of the amorphous phase in the above determined GFR of 19−87 atom % Ni. Consequently, an energy diagram for the metastable Ni_xNb_{100-x} phases is obtained and shown in Figure 10. In the figure, all the fcc and bcc solid solutions apparently have higher energies than their amorphous counterparts when $19 \leq x \leq 87$ and there appears to be a thermodynamic driving force for the formation of the amorphous alloys within this composition range. Obviously, the calculated energetic sequence comparing solid solutions and the amorphous phases is quite compatible with what was shown in determining the GFR by MD simulations using both fcc and bcc solid solution models. Besides, the fcc Ni_xNb_{100-x} phase has a lower energy than the bcc phase when $30 \leq x \leq 100$, while the bcc phase is more stable than the fcc phase when $0 \leq x \leq 25$. Interestingly, regarding the energetic sequence of the metastable Ni−Nb phases, there have been some experimental observations which are in good agreement with the above simulation results. For instance, the following structural evolution process has been observed in the $Ni_{48}Nb_{52}$ multilayered films upon thermal annealing:[23]

$$Ni_{48}Nb_{52} \xrightarrow[60\ min]{250\ °C} Ni + Nb \xrightarrow[60\ min]{350\ °C} A + Nb + fcc \xrightarrow[120\ min]{400\ °C} A + \text{trace of fcc} \quad (8)$$

where A is the amorphous state and fcc refers to a metastable phase with fcc structure. Apparently, the observed structural evolution process is quite compatible with the simulation results. Besides, in IBM experiments, the following structural evolution process has been observed in the $Ni_{70}Nb_{30}$ multilayered films:[4]

$$Ni_{70}Nb_{30} \xrightarrow{3 \times 10^{14}} hcp \xrightarrow{3 \times 10^{15}} A \quad (9)$$

It should be pointed out that fcc and hcp structures are similar close-packed structures and their energy difference is very little, which has been proved by thermodynamics calculation.[53] Consequently, the above structural evolution process is also compatible with the present simulation results. The good compatibility of these experimental observations with the present simulation results suggests that the calculated energy diagram from the Ni−Nb potential through MD simulations is of relevance, which in turn confirms the validation of the newly constructed Ni−Nb potential.

To compare the simulated results with those deduced from the calculations based on the thermodynamics of solids, we also calculate the heats of formation (ΔH_f) of the metastable Ni_xNb_{100-x} phases over the entire composition range. Figure 11 shows the calculated ΔH_f values versus the Ni concentration for the metastable fcc and bcc and amorphous Ni_xNb_{100-x} phases. From the figure, one sees clearly that the fcc structure is more likely to be formed than the bcc structure in a Ni concentration of $30 \leq x \leq 100$, while the bcc structure is energetically preferred within a composition range of $0 \leq x \leq 25$. Moreover, within the composition range $19 \leq x \leq 87$, an amorphous state has a lower ΔH_f value than its fcc or bcc counterpart. It is noted that the calculated heats of formation are also compatible with those derived from Miedema's theory;[54] that is, the minimum ΔH_f value appears somewhere near the equatomic stoichiometry and the ΔH_f value increases gradually while varying the alloy composition toward the two terminals. Especially, the present computational results indicate that a very negative heat of formation exists (i.e., minimum $\Delta H_f = -89.88$ kJ/mol) for the Ni−Nb amorphous state and such a large negative heat of formation is the major driving force for solid-state interfacial reaction as well as crystal-to-amorphous transition in the Ni−Nb system.

V. Conclusion

(1) With the important aid of ab initio calculations, an *n*-body potential is constructed for the Ni−Nb system based on the Finnis−Sinclair formalism. The constructed potential works fairly well in reproducing some physical properties obtained by experiments/ab initio calculations, and the equation of state derived from the potential is in good agreement with Rose's equation.

(2) On the basis of the constructed Ni−Nb potential, molecular dynamics simulations using solid solution models reveal that the physical origin of crystal-to-amorphous transition is the crystalline lattice collapsing while the solute atoms are exceeding the critical value and determine the glass-forming range of the Ni−Nb system to be within 19−87 atom % Ni, which is quite compatible with that observed by ion beam mixing experiments.

(3) On the basis of the constructed Ni−Nb potential, molecular dynamics simulations using sandwich models reveal an asymmetric growth behavior of the amorphous interlayer during solid-state amorphization; that is, the growing speed of the amorphous interlayer toward the Ni lattice is faster than that directed toward the Nb lattice, which is quite compatible with that observed in experiments.

(4) On the basis of the constructed Ni−Nb potential, molecular dynamics simulations are performed to calculate the energies of the alloy phases of interest, and the results show that, when $0 \leq x \leq 25$, the bcc Ni_xNb_{100-x} phase has a lower ΔH_f value and is more stable than the fcc phase and that, when

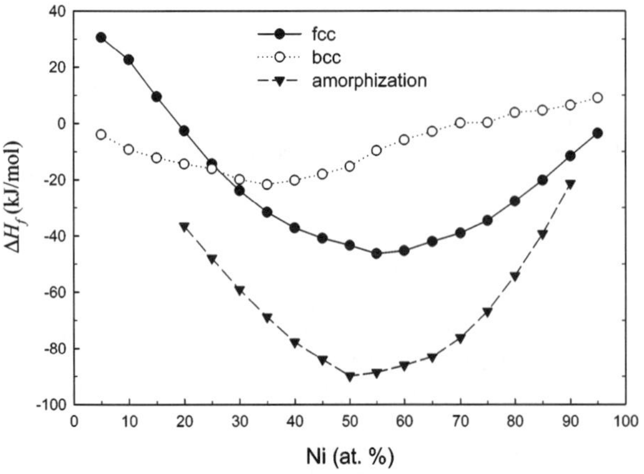

Figure 11. Calculated heats of formation (ΔH_f) of the metastable fcc and bcc and amorphous Ni−Nb phases, respectively, versus the Ni composition over the entire composition range. The values of the fcc and bcc Ni−Nb phases are obtained at 300 K from the fcc and bcc solid solution models, respectively. The values of the amorphous Ni−Nb phases in the ranges 19−50 and 50−87 Ni atom % are obtained from the bcc and fcc solid solution models, respectively, upon isothermal annealing at 300 K for 100 000 MD time steps.

$30 \le x \le 100$, the fcc Ni_xNb_{100-x} phase becomes energetically favored. In addition, all the fcc and bcc phases have higher energies than their amorphous counterparts in a composition range of $19 \le x \le 87$, which matches well with the GFR determined by molecular dynamics simulations using solid solution models.

Acknowledgment. The authors are grateful for the financial support from the National Natural Science Foundation of China, The Ministry of Science and Technology of China (G20000672), and Tsinghua University.

References and Notes

(1) Klement, W.; Willens, R. H.; Duwez, P. *Nature* **1960**, *187*, 869.
(2) Zallen, Z. *The Physics of Amorphous Solid*; Wiley-Interscience: New York, 1983.
(3) Greer, A. L. *Science* **1995**, *267*, 1947.
(4) Zhang, Z. J.; Bai, H. Y.; Qiu, Q. L.; Yang, T.; Tao, K.; Liu, B. X. *J. Appl. Phys.* **1993**, *73*, 1702.
(5) Liu, B. X.; Ou, J. *Phys. Status Solidi A* **1997**, *161*, 3.
(6) Li, J. H.; Guo, H. B.; Kong, L. T.; Liu, B. X. *Phys. Rev. B* **2005**, *71*, 014107.
(7) Alonso, J. A.; Simozar, S. *Solid State Commun.* **1983**, *48*, 765.
(8) Egami, T.; Waseda, Y. *J. Non-Cryst. Solids* **1984**, *64*, 113.
(9) Lopez, J. M.; Alonso, J. A.; Gallego, L. J. *Phys. Rev. B* **1987**, *36*, 3716.
(10) Lai, W. S.; Li, Q.; Lin, C.; Liu, B. X. *Phys. Status Solidi B* **2001**, *227*, 503.
(11) Lai, W. S.; Zhang, Q.; Liu, B. X. *Philos. Mag. Lett.* **2001**, *81*, 45.
(12) Liu, B. X. *Mater. Lett.* **1987**, *5*, 322.
(13) Gary, W. *Prog. Surf. Sci.* **1989**, *32*, 211.
(14) Ossi, P. M. *Phys. Status Solidi A* **1990**, *119*, 563.
(15) Liu, B. X.; Lai, W. S.; Zhang, Z. J. *Adv. Phys.* **2001**, *50*, 367.
(16) Schwarz, R. B.; Johnson, W. L. *Phys. Rev. Lett.* **1983**, *51*, 415.
(17) Zhang, Q.; Lai, W. S.; Liu, B. X. *Phys. Rev. B* **1998**, *58*, 14020.
(18) Kwon, K. W.; Lee, H. J.; Sinclair, R. *Appl. Phys. Lett.* **1999**, *75*, 935.
(19) Gong, H. R.; Kong, L. T.; Lai, W. S.; Liu, B. X. *Phys. Rev. B* **2002**, *66*, 104204.
(20) Meng, W. J.; Fultz, B.; Ma, E.; Johnson, W. L. *Appl. Phys. Lett.* **1987**, *51*, 661.
(21) Schröder, H.; Samwer, K.; Koster, U. *Phys. Rev. Lett.* **1985**, *54*, 197.
(22) Zhang, Q.; Lai, W. S.; Liu, B. X. *J. Non-Cryst. Solids* **2000**, *261*, 137.
(23) Yang, G. W.; Lin, C.; Liu, B. X. *Mater. Sci. Eng., B* **1999**, *65*, 139.
(24) Zhang, Q.; Lai, W. S.; Yang, G. W.; Liu, B. X. *J. Phys.: Condens. Matter* **2000**, *12*, 6991.
(25) Finnis, M. W.; Sinclair, J. E. *Philos. Mag. A* **1984**, *50*, 45.
(26) Yan, M.; Vitek, V.; Chen, S. P. *Acta Mater.* **1996**, *44*, 4351.
(27) Rebonato, R.; Welch, D. O. *Philos. Mag. A* **1989**, *60*, 649.
(28) Koleske, D. D.; Sibener, S. J. *Surf. Sci.* **1993**, *290*, 179.
(29) Kittel, C. *Introduction to Solid state Physics*, 7th ed.; John Wily & Sons: New York, 1996.
(30) Cohen, E. R.; Lide, D. R.; Trigg, G. L. *AIP Physics Desk Reference*, 3rd ed.; Springer: New York, 2003.
(31) Wycisk, W.; Feller-Knipmeier, M. *J. Nucl. Mater.* **1978**, *69−70*, 616.
(32) Maier, K.; Peo, M.; Saile, B.; Schaefer, H. E.; Seeger, A. *Philos. Mag. A* **1979**, *40*, 701.
(33) Luzzi, D. E.; Yan, M.; Šob, M.; Vitek, V. *Phys. Rev. Lett.* **1991**, *67*, 1894.
(34) Yan, M.; Šob, M.; Luzzi, D. E. Vitek, V.; Ackland, G. J.; Methfessel, M.; Rodriguez, C. O. *Phys. Rev. B* **1993**, *47*, 5571.
(35) Siegl, R.; Yan, M.; Vitek, V. *Modell. Simul. Mater. Sci. Eng.* **1997**, *5*, 105.
(36) Kresse, G.; Hafner, J. *Phys. Rev. B* **1993**, *47*, 558.
(37) Kresse, G.; Furthmuller, J. *Phys. Rev. B* **1996**, *54*, 11169.
(38) Vanderbilt, D. *Phys. Rev. B* **1990**, *41*, 7892.
(39) Perdew, J.; Wang, Y. *Phys. Rev. B* **1992**, *45*, 13244.
(40) Liu, J. B.; Liu, B. X. *Phys. Rev. B* **2001**, *63*, 132204.
(41) Brandes, E. A.; Brook, G. B. *Smithells Metals Reference Book*, 7th ed.; Butterworth-Heinemann: Oxford, U.K., 1992.
(42) Zhang, Z. J.; Huang, X. Y.; Zhang, Z. X. *Acta Mater.* **1998**, *46*, 4189.
(43) Zhang, Z. J.; Liu, B. X. *J. Appl. Phys.* **1994**, *75*, 4948.
(44) Rose, J. H.; Smith, J. R.; Guinea, F.; Ferrante, J. *Phys. Rev. B* **1984**, *29*, 2963.
(45) Parrinello, M.; Rahman, A. *J. Appl. Phys.* **1981**, *52*, 7182.
(46) Allen, M. P.; Tildesley, D. J. *Computer Simulation of Liquids*; Clarendon: Oxford, U.K., 1986.
(47) Ciccotti, G.; Hoover, W. G. *Molecular-Dynamics Simulation of Statistical-Mechanical Systems*; North-Holland: Amsterdam, The Netherlands, 1986.
(48) Mura, P.; Demontis, P.; Suffritti, G. B.; Rosato, V.; Vittori Antisari, M. *Phys. Rev. B* **1994**, *50*, 2850.
(49) Phillpot, S. R.; Yip, S.; Wolf, D. *Comput. Phys.* **1989**, *3*, 20.
(50) Rosato, V.; Ciccotti, G.; Pontikis, V. *Phys. Rev. B* **1986**, *33*, 1860.
(51) Okamoto, H.; Massalski, T. B. *J. Phase Equilib.* **1992**, *13*, 444.
(52) Gallego, L. J.; Somaza, J. A.; Alonso, J. A.; Lopez, J. M. *J. Phys. F: Met. Phys.* **1988**, *18*, 2149.
(53) Yang, G. W.; Lin, C.; Liu, J. B.; Liu, B. X. *J. Phys. D: Appl. Phys.* **1999**, *32*, 79.
(54) Boer, F. R.; Boom, R.; Mattens, W. C. M.; Miedema, A. R.; Niessen, A. K. *Cohesion in Metals-Transition Metal Alloys*; North-Holland: Amsterdam, The Netherlands, 1988.

Formation of Amorphous Alloys by Ion Beam Mixing and Its Multiscale Theoretical Modeling in the Equilibrium Immiscible Sc−W System

R. F. Zhang, Y. X. Shen, H. F. Yan, and B. X. Liu*

Advanced Materials Laboratory, Department of Materials Science and Engineering, Tsinghua University, Beijing 100084, China

Received: July 27, 2004; In Final Form: December 12, 2004

Unique amorphous alloys are synthesized at the compositions of 25 and 40 atom % of W by ion beam mixing in the equilibrium immiscible Sc−W system characterized by a positive heat of formation of +14 kJ/mol. In thermodynamic modeling, a Gibbs free energy diagram is constructed based on Miedema's theory, and the diagram predicts a glass-forming range of the Sc−W system to be within 12−58 atom % of W. To develop an atomistic model, ab initio calculations are first conducted to assist the construction of an *n*-body Sc−W potential under the embedded atom method. The proven realistic potential is applied in molecular dynamic simulations to study the crystal-to-amorphous transition in the Sc−W solid solutions, thus determining the glass-forming ability of the system to be within 15−50 atom % of W. Apparently, both theoretical predicted glass-forming ranges cover the experimentally measured one, showing an excellent agreement. We report, in this paper, the experimental results from ion beam mixing and the multiscale theoretical modeling concerning the amorphous alloy formation in the Sc−W system together with a brief discussion of the structural transition mechanism.

1. Introduction

In synthesizing new materials of high performance for various applications, a great effort has been paid, in recent decades, to the development of nonequilibrium materials processing techniques which are capable of producing new metastable alloys or fabricating artificial solid-state microstructures.[1] For instance, ion beam mixing (IBM) of multiple metal layers was introduced in the early 1980s and has since been employed to study the metastable alloy formation in the binary metal systems.[2] Up to now, a number of amorphous alloys (or metallic glasses) and metastable crystalline alloys have been obtained by IBM in the binary metal systems,[3] frequently featuring negative heats of formation (ΔH_f), defined in Miedema's theory and calculated at an equiatomic stoichiometry.[4,5] Recently, IBM has advanced significantly in two respects. First, to increase the interfacial free energy stored in the multilayered samples, the individual layer thickness was intentionally designed to be a couple of nanometers, differing considerably from a typical thickness of 5−8 nm in the previously conducted IBM. Second, much interest has been switched to the systems characterized by positive ΔH_f, among which, some are essentially immiscible at equilibrium. Under such circumstances, the interfacial free energy was significantly increased and played an important role in elevating the initial multilayered films to an energetic level higher than those of the possible metastable states existing in the system of interest.[6] Based on the design of interfacial free energy, the authors' group has recently succeeded in producing amorphous alloys in the equilibrium immiscible Au−W and Ag−W systems.[7,8] In the present study, the Sc−W system with a large positive heat of formation ($\Delta H_f = +14$ kJ/mol)[4] was selected to investigate the possibility of synthesizing nonequilibrium alloys by IBM as well as to reveal the detailed structural phase transition induced in the alternately deposited Sc−W multilayered samples by ion irradiation. Second, thermodynamic calculation based on Miedema's theory is conducted to interpret the amorphous alloy formation in terms of comparing the relative energetic levels of the competing phases in question. Third, with the aid of ab initio calculations, an *n*-body potential of the Sc−W system is constructed and molecular dynamic (MD) simulations are then performed for determining the glass-formation ability/range (GFA/GFR) of the system. A brief discussion is followed to compare the calculated results with the experimental observations from IBM.

* Corresponding author. E-mail: dmslbx@tsinghua.edu.cn.

2. Experimental Procedure and Theoretical Methods

2.1. Experimental Procedure of Ion-beam Mixing. Four sets of Sc−W multilayered samples with overall compositions of $Sc_{75}W_{25}$, $Sc_{60}W_{40}$, $Sc_{40}W_{60}$, and $Sc_{25}W_{75}$, respectively, were designed and prepared by alternately depositing thin Sc and W layers at a rate of 0.5 Å/s onto NaCl single crystals as substrates in an evaporator with a base vacuum of 10^{-9} Torr. During deposition, no special cooling was provided to the substrates and the temperature rise of the substrates was estimated to be below 473 K. The total thicknesses of $Sc_{75}W_{25}$, $Sc_{60}W_{40}$, $Sc_{40}W_{60}$, and $Sc_{25}W_{75}$ multilayered samples were designed to be 42, 42, 40, and 40 nm, respectively, to match the projected range plus the projected range straggling of 200 keV xenon ions used in the present study. The desired compositions of the samples were obtained by adjusting the relative layer thicknesses of constituent metals and were later confirmed by energy-dispersive spectra (EDS) and Rutherford backscattering spectra (RBS) with an experimental error of 5%. Accordingly, the $Sc_{75}W_{25}$, $Sc_{60}W_{40}$, $Sc_{40}W_{60}$, and $Sc_{25}W_{75}$ multilayered samples consisted of 9, 13, 18, and 15 layers, respectively, in which the minimum thicknesses of the individual layers in the samples were about 2.0, 2.1, 2.2, and 2.0 nm, respectively. After deposition, the Sc−W multilayered films were analyzed by RBS and Figure 1 shows the corresponding RBS spectra, from which

J. of Physical Chemistry B 109 (10), p.4391-4397 (2005).

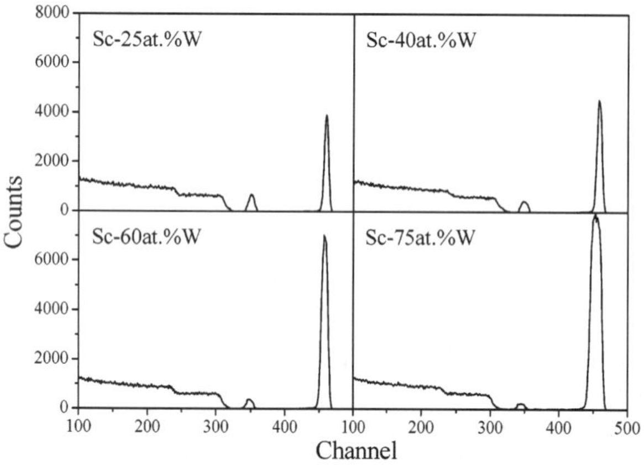

Figure 1. RBS spectra obtained for the as-deposited Sc−W multilayered samples.

the relative contents of Sc and W match approximately the designed overall compositions of the multilayered samples by SIMNI simulation.[9] The as-deposited multilayered samples were then irradiated by 200 keV xenon ions at room temperature in an implanter, which had a vacuum level on the order of 10^{-6} Torr, and the irradiation dose was in a range from 6×10^{14} to 9×10^{15} Xe^{+}/cm^{2}. The ion current density was controlled to be about 0.8−1 μAcm^{-2} to minimize the beam heating effect. Under the above precautions, the effective temperature of the Sc−W multilayered samples during irradiation was measured to be around 353 K. For structural characterization, all the Sc−W multilayered samples were removed from the substrates by deionized water and put onto the Cu grids and then analyzed by transmission electron microscopy (TEM) and selected area diffraction (SAD). Incidentally, it will be discussed later that SAD analysis provides some indirect evidence in confirming the layered structures of the as-deposited Sc−W multilayered films.

2.2. Thermodynamic Calculation. Generally, the Gibbs free energy of an alloy phase can be calculated by $\Delta G = \Delta H - T{\cdot}\Delta S$, where ΔH and ΔS are the enthalpy and entropy terms, respectively. As a first approximation, the entropy term for a concentrated solid solution (CSS) and amorphous phase is simply taken as that of an ideal solution, i.e., $\Delta S = -R[c_A \ln c_A + c_B \ln c_B]$, where R is the gas constant and c_A and c_B are the atomic concentrations of metals A and B, respectively.

According to Miedema's theory and Alonso's method,[4,10−12] the enthalpy change ΔH is the sum of three terms, namely $\Delta H = \Delta H^c + \Delta H^e + \Delta H^s$, corresponding to the chemical, elastic, and structural contributions, respectively.

The chemical term ΔH^c is closely related to the electron redistribution generated at the boundary for the Wigner−Seitz unit cell when alloying, and can be calculated by,

$$\Delta H^c = c_A c_B [c_B \Delta \bar{H}^{inter}_{AinB} + c_A \Delta \bar{H}^{inter}_{BinA}] \quad (1)$$

where $\Delta \bar{H}^{inter}_{AinB}$ and $\Delta \bar{H}^{inter}_{BinA}$ are the solution enthalpies of A solved in B and that of B solved in A, respectively, and all these values have been compiled by Niessen et al. [4,10]

In a similar way, the elastic term ΔH^e for a CSS is caused by the atomic size mismatch of the two constituent metals and can be expressed by taking the weighted average of the mismatch energies,[4,10]

$$\Delta H^e = c_A c_B [c_B \Delta \bar{H}^{elastic}_{AinB} + c_A \Delta \bar{H}^{elastic}_{BinA}] \quad (2)$$

where $\Delta \bar{H}^{elastic}_{AinB}$ and $\Delta \bar{H}^{elastic}_{BinA}$ are the partial elastic mismatch energies for A solved in B and B solved in A, respectively, and all these values can be found in some published books and/or comprehensive papers.[4,10]

The structural term ΔH^s is deduced from the lattice stability $E(Z)$ of the bcc, fcc, and hcp structures as a function of the number of valence electrons Z of the metal,[4,10]

$$\Delta H^s = E(Z) - c_A E(Z_B) - c_B E(Z_A) \quad (3)$$

where $E(Z)$, $E(Z_A)$, and $E(Z_B)$ are the lattice stability of the CSS and pure metals A and B, and Z, Z_A, and Z_B are the mean numbers of valence electrons of the CSS and the numbers of valence electrons of pure metals A and B, respectively. [4,10]

Comparing with the CSS, the structural and elastic terms for the formation enthalpy of an amorphous alloy are absent or significantly reduced, i.e., $\Delta H^e \approx 0$ and $\Delta H^s \approx 0$. There is, however, apart from the chemical term, another term contributing to the formation enthalpy of the amorphous alloy that reflects the relative disordering and therefore the formation enthalpy of the amorphous alloy can be expressed by, [4,10]

$$\Delta H^{amorphous} = \Delta H^c + \Delta H^{topological} \quad (4)$$

where the topological enthalpy $\Delta H^{topological}$ accounts for the difference between the crystalline and amorphous states, which can be calculated by, [4,10]

$$\Delta H^{topological} = 3.5{\cdot}(c_A T_{m,A} + c_B T_{m,B}) \quad (5)$$

where $T_{m,A}$ and $T_{m,B}$ are the melting temperatures of the metals A and B, respectively. Meanwhile, the chemical term of the amorphous alloy ΔH^c can be assumed to be equal to that of the CSS.

The Gibbs free energy of the initial state of the A−B multilayered samples should be calculated by adding the interfacial free energy to the ground state (i.e., the zero line) representing a mechanical mixture of A and B in the bulk form. According to Zhang et al.,[4,13−15] the excess interfacial free energy of the multilayered samples can be calculated by $\Delta G_{mul} = \alpha_A S_{fA} \gamma^{SS}_{BA} + \alpha_B S_{fB} \gamma^{SS}_{AB}$, where S_{fA} and S_{fB} are the surface areas occupied by one mole of atoms A and B, respectively, the parameters α_A and α_B are the fraction of interfacial atoms A and B versus the total number of atoms in the multilayered samples, and γ^{SS}_{AB} (or γ^{SS}_{BA}) is the interfacial free energy of 1 mol of atoms A (or B) solved in B (or A). These terms can easily be calculated following the well-documented literatures.[4,13−15]

2.3. Method of ab Initio Calculations. The first-principles calculation is based on the well-established Vienna ab initio simulation package (VASP).[16] In the package, the calculations are conducted in a plane-wave basis, using fully nonlocal Vanderbilt-type ultra-soft pseudopotentials to describe the electron−ion interaction,[17] which allows the use of a moderate cutoff for the construction of the plane-wave basis for the transition metals (241.62 eV in the present calculations). In the calculation, the exchange and correlation items are described by the generalized-gradient approximation (GGA) proposed by Perdew and Wang.[18] The integration in the Brillouin zone is done on special k points ($11 \times 11 \times 11$ Monkhorst−Pack grid leading to 56 irreducible k points in the present study) determined according to the Monkhorst−Pack scheme.[19]

In the present study, the cohesive energies and the lattice constants of two simple ordered structures, i.e., the $L1_2$ structure for the compositions of $Sc_{75}W_{25}$ and the B2 structure for the composition of $Sc_{50}W_{50}$, are calculated and later employed in deriving the n-body potential.

2.4. Method for Construction of *n*-Body Potential. In the present study, an n-body Sc−W potential is constructed under the framework of a well-known embedded atom method (EAM).[20] In the EAM, the total energy E_{tot}, which can be written as a unique function of the electron density ρ_i, is mainly the energy to embed the atom into the electron density of the neighboring atoms, and supplemented by a short-range doubly screened pair interaction, which accounts for the core−core repulsions.[21] Consequently, the total energy can be expressed by,

$$E_{\text{tot}} = \sum_i F_i(\rho_i) + \frac{1}{2}\sum_{i,j(i\neq j)} \phi_{ij}(r_{ij}) \tag{6}$$

where $F(\rho_i)$ is the energy required to embed atom i into the background electron density ρ_i, and $\rho_i = \sum_{j\neq i} f_j(r_{ij})$. $f_j(r_{ij})$ is the electron density at the site of atom i contributed by atom j. $\phi_{ij}(r_{ij})$ and r_{ij} are respectively the short-range pair potential and the separated distance between atom i and atom j. The electron density function is commonly taken as an exponentially decreasing function,[22] and at a first approximation, the atomic electron density $f(r)$ takes a function form of $f(r) = f_e \exp[-\chi(r/r_e - 1)]$ for both hcp and bcc metals, where f_e is a scaling factor determined by the cohesive energy E_c and the atomic volume Ω. r_e is an equilibrium nearest distance, and χ is an adjustable parameter to be fitted. The embedding function adopts a universal form suggested by Banerjea[22] and Cai.[23] Accordingly, the embedding function can be expressed by,

$$F(\rho_i) = -F_0\left[1 - \ln\left(\frac{\rho_i}{\rho_e}\right)^n\right]\left(\frac{\rho_i}{\rho_e}\right)^n + F_1\left(\frac{\rho_i}{\rho_e}\right) \tag{7}$$

where $F_0 = E_c - E_v^f$ and E_v^f is the vacancy formation energy. F_1 is an adjustable parameter for the hcp metal and it is set to be zero for the bcc metal. ρ_e is the host electron density at an equilibrium state. According to Banerjea and Smith,[22] a decreasing exponential curvature function combining with the universal embedding function could yield the model function of Rose et al.[24] Consequently, the function proposed by Cai and Ye[23] for the fcc metals is adopted and modified a little for the pair potential $\phi(r)$ of the hcp metals in the present study,

$$\phi_{hcp}(r) = -\alpha[1 + \beta(\{r/r_e\} - 1)]\exp[-\beta(\{r/r_e\} - 1)] \tag{8}$$

Meanwhile, the function proposed by Johnson and Oh[25] is used for the pair potential of the bcc metals in the present study,

$$\begin{aligned}\phi_{bcc}(r) = \Phi(r) &= k_0 + k_1(\{r/r_e\} - 1) + k_2(\{r/r_e\} - 1)^2 + k_3(\{r/r_e\} - 1)^3, \quad r_e \le r \le r_s \\ &= \Phi_a(r) = \Phi(r) + k_a[\Phi(r) - \Phi(r_e)](\{r/r_e\} - 1)^2, \quad r < r_e\end{aligned} \tag{9}$$

where r is the interatomic distance, r_e is an equilibrium first-neighbor distance, k_a is a constant in the form of $k_a = 4.5(1 + 4/(A_r - 0.1))$ depending on an anisotropy ratio A_r, and the cutoff distance (from r_s to r_c) is set to be between the second- and third-neighbor distances.[26]

The hcp−bcc cross potential takes a simplified form, which was recently proposed for the fcc−bcc metal systems by Gong et al.,[27] to combine the hcp−hcp and bcc−bcc potentials,

$$\phi_{hcp-bcc}(r) = A[\phi_{hcp}(r + B) + \phi_{bcc}(r + C)] \tag{10}$$

where A, B, and C are three potential parameters to be fitted.

2.5. Scheme of Molecular Dynamic Simulations. Based on the constructed EAM potential for the Sc−W system, MD simulation is carried out with the Parrinello−Rahman constant pressure scheme and the equations of motion are solved through a fourth-order predictor−corrector algorithm of Gear with a time step of $t = 5 \times 10^{-15}$ s.[28] In the present study, two kinds of simulation models are employed for the Sc−W system, i.e., for the Sc-rich side, an hcp solid solution model consisting of $10 \times 10 \times 6 \times 2 = 1200$ atoms, and for the W-rich side, a bcc solid solution model containing $9 \times 9 \times 8 \times 2 = 1296$ atoms, respectively. In the simulation models, the (100), (010), and (001) atomic crystal directions are parallel to the x, y, and z axes, respectively, and the periodic boundary conditions are adopted in three dimensions. To obtain a specific chemical stoichiometry for the Sc−W alloy, a desired number of Sc (W) atoms in the original hcp (bcc) lattice are randomly substituted by W (Sc) atoms. In the present study, MD simulation is conducted at room temperature (300 K) for adequate MD time steps (2 ns) until all the dynamic parameters show no secular variation.

3. Results and Discussion

3.1. Experimental Results. We now present the experimental results from IBM. Parts a and b of Figure 2 show the typical selected area diffraction (SAD) patterns of the as-deposited state and the irradiated state at a dose of 3×10^{15} Xe^+/cm^2, respectively, for the $Sc_{75}W_{25}$ multilayered samples. From Figure 2a, one can clearly see the sharp diffraction rings, which can be indexed to be from a polycrystalline hcp-Sc and a bcc-W, suggesting that in the as-deposited state, Sc and W were not mixed and most likely located in the separated Sc and W layers. When the $Sc_{75}W_{25}$ multilayered samples were subjected to 200 keV xenon ion irradiation at room temperature to doses lower than 5×10^{15} Xe^+/cm^2, the crystalline Sc and W remain, except some diffraction lines from bcc-W gradually widen as shown in Figure 2b. When the $Sc_{75}W_{25}$ multilayered samples were subjected to a further irradiation dose of 7×10^{15} Xe^+/cm^2, the widened diffraction lines disappeared gradually and transformed into some diffused halos as shown in Figure 2c, indicating that an amorphous phase was gradually formed. Finally, a unique amorphous phase was obtained at an irradiation dose of 9×10^{15} Xe^+/cm^2 and the corresponding SAD pattern is shown in Figure 2d. Comparing parts d and a of Figure 2, one can observe that the diffraction lines reflected from crystalline Sc and W have disappeared completely, and only the diffused halos are shown, indicating the formation of a unique amorphous phase. For the $Sc_{60}W_{40}$ multilayered samples, similar structural transition was also observed, as can be observed from the SAD patterns exhibited in parts a and b of Figure 3 for its as-deposited state and irradiated state at a dose of 9×10^{15} Xe^+/cm^2, respectively. From Figure 3b, it can be seen clearly that the initial crystalline Sc and W have transformed into an unique amorphous phase at an irradiation dose of 9×10^{15} Xe^+/cm^2 and the detailed structural phase transition is somehow similar to that appearing in the $Sc_{75}W_{25}$ samples.

For the W-rich side, Figure 4a exhibits a SAD pattern to show the structure of the as-deposited state of the $Sc_{40}W_{60}$ sample.

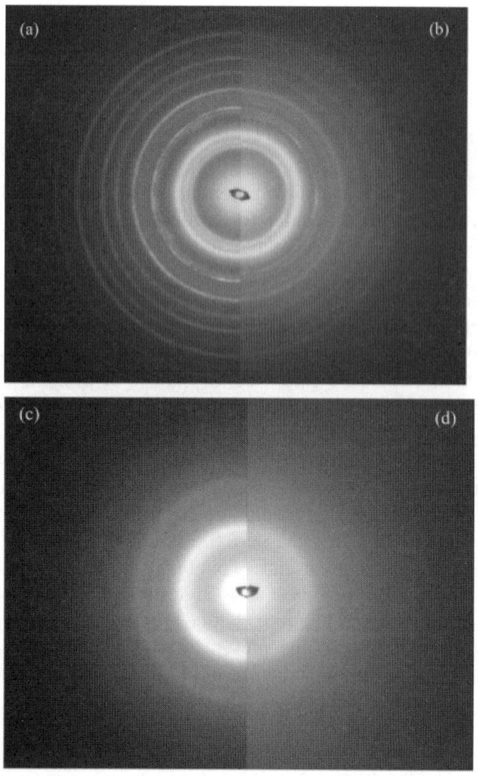

Figure 2. Selected area diffraction patterns for the $Sc_{75}W_{25}$ multilayered samples with 9 layers: (a) the as-deposited state, (b) the irradiated state at an irradiation dose of 3 × 10^{15} Xe^+/cm^2, (c) the irradiated state at an irradiation dose of 7 × 10^{15} Xe^+/cm^2, and (d) a unique amorphous phase formed at an irradiation dose of 9 × 10^{15} Xe^+/cm^2.

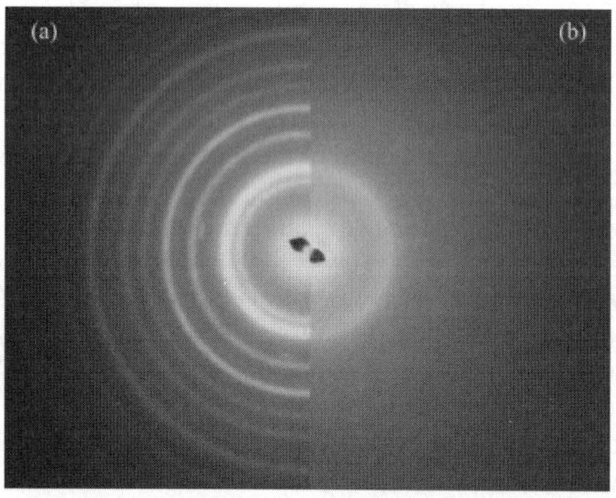

Figure 3. Selected area diffraction patterns for the $Sc_{60}W_{40}$ multilayered samples with 13 layers: (a) the as-deposited state and (b) an amorphous phase formed at an irradiation dose of 9 × 10^{15} Xe^+/cm^2.

From the pattern, one can clearly see that the W diffraction rings are sharp, while the diffraction lines of Sc are very weak, indicating that Sc was not well crystallized. When the samples were subjected to irradiation by 200 keV xenon ions, a metastable crystalline (MC) phase of bcc structure (lattice constant a = 3.39 ± 0.05 Å) was formed and remained unchanged up to an irradiation dose of 5 × 10^{15} Xe^+/cm^2. A typical SAD pattern of the MC bcc phase formed at an irradiation dose of 3 × 10^{15} Xe^+/cm^2 is exhibited in Figure 4b. These results mean that the MC bcc phase could be relatively stable upon irradiation as long as it was formed. Further increasing the irradiation dose from 5 × 10^{15} Xe^+/cm^2 to 9 × 10^{15} Xe^+/cm^2, a crystalline-to-amorphous transition occurred in the samples. Figure 4c exhibits a SAD pattern taken at an

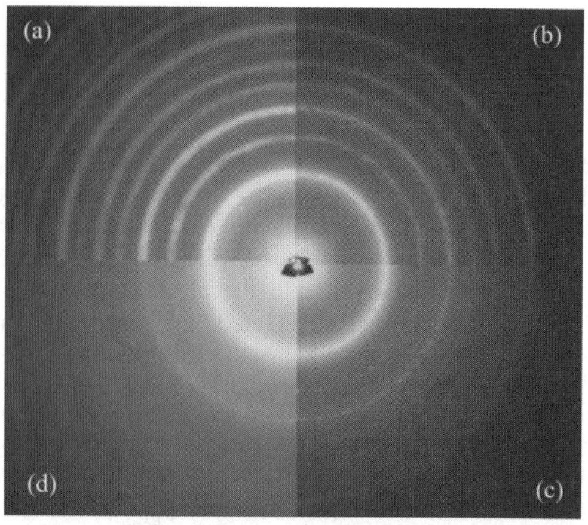

Figure 4. Selected area diffraction patterns for the $Sc_{40}W_{60}$ multilayered samples with 18 layers: (a) the as-deposited state, (b) the irradiated state at an irradiation dose of 5 × 10^{15} Xe^+/cm^2, (c) the irradiated state at an irradiation dose of 7 × 10^{15} Xe^+/cm^2, and (d) the irradiated state at an irradiation dose of 9 × 10^{15} Xe^+/cm^2.

TABLE 1: Structural Phase Evolution in the Sc−W Multilayered Samples upon IBM to Various Ion Doses[a]

alloy system	$Sc_{75}W_{25}$	$Sc_{60}W_{40}$	$Sc_{40}W_{60}$	$Sc_{25}W_{75}$
as-deposited	Sc + W	Sc + W	bcc	bcc
6 × 10^{14} Xe^+/cm^2	Sc + W	Sc + W	bcc	bcc
8 × 10^{14} Xe^+/cm^2	Sc + W	Sc + W	bcc	bcc
1 × 10^{15} Xe^+/cm^2	Sc + W	Sc + W	bcc	bcc
3 × 10^{15} Xe^+/cm^2	Sc + W	Sc + W	bcc	bcc
5 × 10^{15} Xe^+/cm^2	Sc + W	Sc + W	bcc	bcc
7 × 10^{15} Xe^+/cm^2	PA	PA	bcc	bcc
9 × 10^{15} Xe^+/cm^2	A	A	Bcc + PA	bcc

[a] bcc, bcc solid solution; A, completely amorphized; PA, partially amorphized.

irradiation dose of 7 × 10^{15} Xe^+/cm^2. It can be seen that the MC bcc phase has partially transformed into an amorphous phase, and finally at an irradiation dose of 9 × 10^{15} Xe^+/cm^2, most of the bcc phase has transformed into the amorphous phase, as only a few very weak diffraction rings reflected from a trace amount of crystalline W can still be visible in the SAD pattern shown in Figure 4d. Through a detailed analysis by EDS, the composition of the amorphous phase seen in the SAD pattern is estimated to be about 48 atom % of W. As for another composition, i.e., the $Sc_{25}W_{75}$ multilayered samples, only the bcc phase (a = 3.32 ± 0.05 Å) was found in the as-deposited state and it remained unchanged upon further irradiation from 6 × 10^{14} Xe^+/cm^2 to 9 × 10^{15} Xe^+/cm^2. Note that the lattice constants of the formed bcc phases in both $Sc_{40}W_{60}$ and $Sc_{25}W_{75}$ samples are a bit larger than that of the pure W (a = 3.16 Å), and the bcc phases can therefore be considered as a W-based bcc super-saturated solid solution (abbreviated as bcc-SSSS and hereafter).

To present the detailed structural phase transition in the four sets of Sc−W multilayered samples and furthermore to determine the GFR of the Sc−W system, the experimental results for the four sets of multilayered samples irradiated from 6 × 10^{14} Xe^+/cm^2 to 9 × 10^{15} Xe^+/cm^2 are listed in Table 1. From the table, one sees clearly that in the present study, the amorphous phase was obtained within the composition range of 25−48 atom % of W. Besides, the W-based bcc solid solution was formed within the composition range of 0−40 atom % of Sc.

3.2. Thermodynamic Calculation. Figure 5 is the Gibbs free-energy diagram of the Sc−W system constructed at room

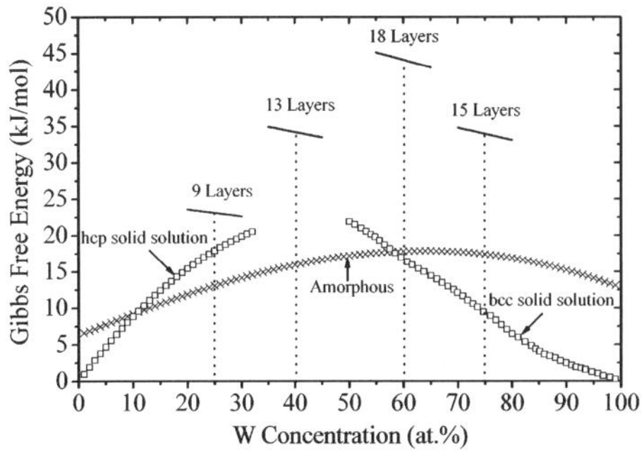

Figure 5. Constructed Gibbs free energy diagram of the Sc−W system based on Miedema's theory and Alonso's method.

TABLE 2: Fitted Parameters for the Sc−Sc, W−W, and Sc−W Potentials

Sc−Sc		W−W		Sc−W	
χ	6.417256	c	6.155980	A	1.10885
α (eV)	0.311282	k_0 (eV)	−0.547671		
β	1.226141	k_1 (eV)	−2.130315	B (Å)	0.69826
r_a (Å)	2.662559	k_2 (eV)	16.808946		
F_1 (eV)	0.712605	k_3 (eV)	−8.503413	C (Å)	0.30702
r_s (Å)	3.4	r_s (Å)	3.2		
r_c (Å)	4.4	r_c (Å)	4.4		
n	1.25	n	0.44		

temperature based on Miedema's theory. From the diagram, it is found that the free energy of the initial multilayered samples is higher than that of the corresponding solid solutions and amorphous phases, and that the free energy of the amorphous phases is lower than that of the corresponding solid solutions within the composition range of 12−58 atom % of W, which can therefore be simply taken as the glass-formation range of the Sc−W system according to thermodynamic calculations.

3.3. Construction of *n*-body Sc−W Potentials. In the construction of *n*-body potentials for the pure hcp metals, the present authors propose the following fitting approach, i.e., using the average bulk and shear moduli, instead of five independent linear elastic constants, together with the cohesive energy, vacancy formation energy, and equilibrium lattice constants to fit the potential parameters, and after fitting, five independent linear elastic constants are reproduced by the fitted potentials, thus confirming the relevance of the fitting as well as the parameters. It turns out that the proposed fitting approach is fairly effective.

For the Sc−W system, fitting the potential parameters is also challenging work, because there is no equilibrium compound and no physical property could be used for fitting the cross potential. In this regard, there have been some reports[29,30] showing that the first-principles calculations could be of significant help in acquiring some useful physical properties of the alloy phases necessary for deriving *n*-body potentials. Accordingly, applying the Vienna ab initio simulation package, the total energies and the lattice constants of the possible nonequilibrium $Sc_{75}W_{25}$ and $Sc_{50}W_{50}$ compounds with $L1_2$ and B2 structures, respectively, are first calculated and then used in deriving *n*-body potentials of the Sc−W system. Concerning the details of the calculations and the fitting procedure, the readers can refer to our recent publication. [31] After the fitting and optimization, the potential parameters are obtained and Table 2 lists the fitted parameters for the Sc−Sc, W−W, and Sc−W potentials, respectively. Table 3 lists the comparison between some physical properties reproduced by the constructed potentials and from experimental/ab initio calculated values used initially for fitting the potentials.[32−34] Evidently, the constructed

TABLE 3: Comparison between the Calculated and Experimental Values of the Cohesive Energy E_c (eV), Lattice Constant *a* (Å) and *c* (Å), Average Bulk Moduli *B* (Mbar), Average Shear Moduli *G* (Mbar), and Vacancy Formation Energy E_v^f (eV) of Sc and W Metals at Room Temperature[32−34]

		E_c (eV)	a (Å)	c (Å)	B (Mbar)	G (Mbar)	E_v^f (eV)
Sc	exptl	3.90	3.308	5.267	0.558*	Sc−W*	1.15
	this work	3.90	3.308	5.267	0.558	0.3067	1.15
W	exptl	8.66	3.165		1.599*	3.1029*	3.95
	this work	8.66	3.165		1.599	3.1029	3.95
$Sc_{75}W_{25}$	ab initio	4.9244	4.34				
($L1_2$)	fitted	4.9471	4.28				
$Sc_{50}W_{50}$	ab initio	5.8245	3.31				
(B2)	fitted	5.9148	3.39				

potentials of the Sc−W system work reasonably well in terms of reproducing some physical properties of the pure Sc and W as well as those of the possible nonequilibrium $Sc_{75}W_{25}$ and $Sc_{50}W_{50}$ compounds. In addition, the energy differences between the three major crystalline structures for pure metals Sc and W are also calculated by the constructed potentials to be $E_{bcc} - E_{hcp} = 0.01$ eV and $E_{fcc} - E_{hcp} = 0.0001$ eV for Sc, while $E_{fcc/hcp} - E_{bcc} = 0.03$ eV for W, which are in good agreement with the well-known facts that hcp is the most stable structure for Sc and bcc for W, respectively, and could therefore serve as additional evidence confirming the relevance of the newly constructed potentials.

3.4. Molecular Dynamic Simulations. Employing the constructed Sc−W potential, MD simulations are carried out by using the hcp and bcc solid solution models, respectively. It has been shown that the GFR of a binary metal system is the composition range bounded by the two terminal critical solid solubilities, below which the solid solution would retain its crystalline state, while beyond which the solid solution would transform into a disordered/amorphous state.[3] Accordingly, in the hcp solid solution model, the amount of W solute atoms is gradually increased until reaching a critical value, at and beyond which the solid solution becomes energetically unstable and collapses into a disordered state, thus determining the critical solid solubility of W in Sc. Similar simulations are also performed to determine the critical solid solubility of Sc in W. As a typical example to show the determination of the critical solid solubility, Figure 6 exhibits the projections of atomic positions of the $Sc_{90}W_{10}$ and $Sc_{80}W_{20}$ solid solution models after annealing at 300 K for 2 ns, respectively. It can be seen vividly that a uniform disordered structure is formed in the $Sc_{80}W_{20}$ solid solution model, while the $Sc_{90}W_{10}$ solid solution model still remains in an ordered state, indicating that the critical solid solubility to trigger crystal-to-amorphous transition is between 10 and 20 atom % of W. We further study the composition from 10 to 20 atom % of W in detail, and find that the critical solid solubility of the Sc−W system is 15 atom % of W in Sc. Besides, it is commonly recognized that the total pair correlation functions are considered as a decisive measure to confirm a disordered state. Figure 7 exhibits the calculated total pair correlation functions of the Sc-based hcp and W-based bcc solid solution models, respectively, upon annealing at 300 K for 2 ns. In Figure 7, the left five lines are for the hcp solid solution models and the right five lines are for the bcc solid solution models. One sees clearly that in the Sc-rich side, beyond 20 atom % of W, the hcp solid solutions have transformed into the amorphous states, and that in the W-rich side, the bcc solid solutions remain in the crystalline states, suggesting that amorphous alloys can readily be formed in the Sc-rich side, whereas in the W-rich side, amorphous alloy can hardly be

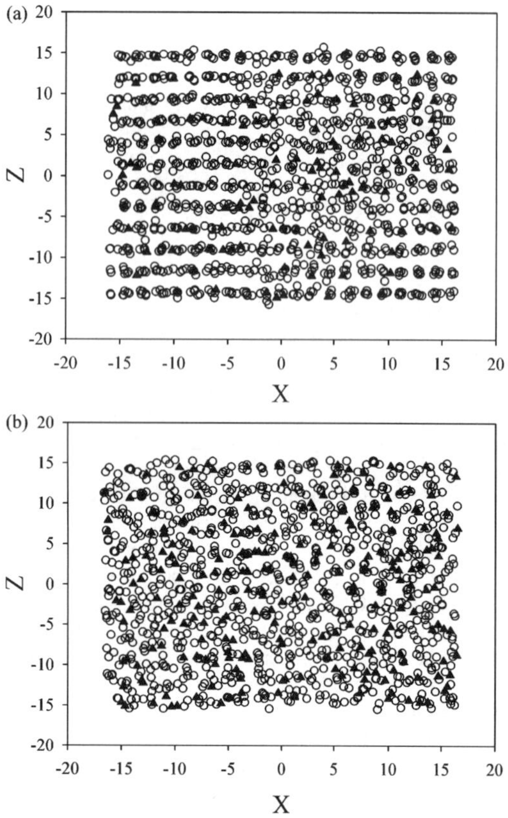

Figure 6. The projections of atomic positions of (a) $Sc_{90}W_{10}$ and (b) $Sc_{80}W_{20}$ solid solutions, respectively, after annealing at 300 K for 2 ns. Open circles: Sc. Filled triangles: W.

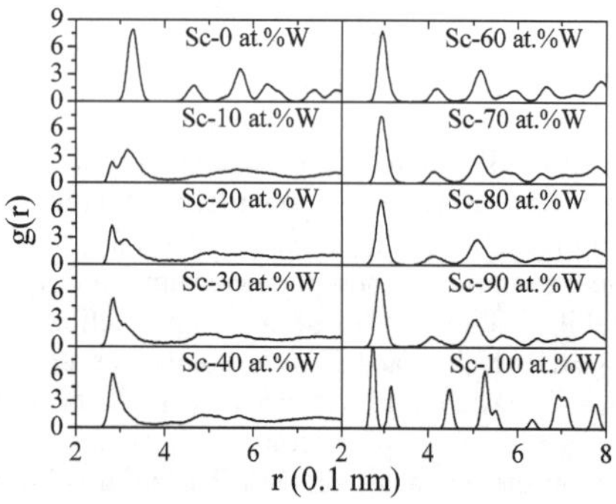

Figure 7. For the Sc−W system, the calculated total pair correlation functions of the solid solution models upon annealing at 300 K for 2 ns. (Note: the left five lines are for the hcp solid solution models and the right five lines are for the bcc solid solution models.)

obtained. Consequently, the GFR of the Sc−W system determined directly from the Sc−W potential through MD simulations is approximately within 15−50 atom % of W, which is in good agreement with the composition range of 25−48 atom % of W obtained from the present ion beam mixing experiments

3.5. Discussion. Comparing the calculated GFR by thermodynamic modeling described in section 3.2 and MD simulations described in section 3.4 with the experimentally determined GFR by ion beam mixing presented in section 3.1, one finds that the experimentally measured GFR of 25−48 atom % of W is a little narrower than the calculated GFR of 12−58 atom % of W and 15−50 atom % of W from thermodynamic calculation and molecular dynamic simulations, respectively, which is quite reasonable, because, in general, two GFRs deduced from theoretical modeling predict the maximum possible GFRs. Moreover, the experimentally measured GFR at low W concentration limit is at 25 atom % of W, which is higher than the theoretical values, i.e., 12 and 15 atom % of W, obtained in the present study. This is because in ion beam mixing experiments, only the alloy compositions of 25 atom % of W and higher were studied and the alloy compositions lower than 25 atom % of W may need to be examined further. Besides, the experimentally measured GFR at high W concentration limit is 48 atom % of W, which is found to be quite close to that from MD simulations and quite compatible with that from thermodynamic calculations.

We now turn to discuss the possible mechanism responsible for the formation of the amorphous alloys in the $Sc_{75}W_{25}$ and $Sc_{60}W_{40}$ multilayered samples. As described by the thermodynamic calculations, the Gibbs free energy of the amorphous phase is lower than that of the corresponding initial multilayered samples as shown in Figure 5, meaning that the amorphous phase is energetically favored and is indeed obtained by IBM. Kinetically, the detailed process of IBM can generally be divided into two steps, i.e., a first step of atomic collision cascade triggered by the impinging ions followed by a second step of relaxation.[35] In the present study, the atomic collision cascade was responsible for inducing the interfacial diffusion of Sc atoms into its partner W lattices and vice versa, resulting in a highly energetic Sc−W mixture. During the second step of relaxation, the time period is extremely short, lasting only for $10^{-10}-10^{-9}$ s, and the effective cooling speed available can be as high as 10^{13-14} deg K/s,[36] which allows only an extremely limited rearrangement of the atoms in the Sc−W mixture resulting from the atomic collision taking place in the first step of IBM. Under such a high effective cooling speed, the Sc−W mixture is not allowed to relax straightforward to its corresponding equilibrium state, yet to reside at one of the possible intermediate states. In addition, the very short time of relaxation prevents the nucleation and growth process of an alloy phase with a complicated structure, as long-range diffusion is impossible. Consequently, only an amorphous or simple structured crystalline alloy phase can be formed in the highly energetic Sc−W mixture. In the present study, two Sc−W amorphous alloys are formed by IBM. From the point of view of atomic mobility, the present MD simulations also reveal the physical mechanism of amorphous alloy formation vividly, i.e., when the W solute atoms in the Sc lattice reached the values beyond the maximal solid solubility (i.e., 15 atom % of W), the crystalline Sc lattice collapsed and turned into a disordered state, resulting in formation of the amorphous alloy, as evidenced by a typical example shown in Figure 6.

In addition, in the W-rich side, another metastable bcc-SSSS was also obtained and the formation mechanism of bcc-SSSS is discussed as follows. Around the composition of $Sc_{40}W_{60}$, as described by the thermodynamic calculations shown in Figure 5, prior to forming an amorphous phase, a bcc-SSSS may first be obtained because the bcc-SSSS phase has a slightly higher energy than that of the amorphous phase. However, the energy difference between the amorphous phase and the bcc-SSSS is quite small. Consequently, as shown in Figure 4d, a small amount of crystalline bcc phase still remained and coexisted with an amorphous phase at an irradiation dose of 9×10^{15} Xe^+/cm^2. From a kinetic point of view, during the first step of the atomic collision cascade, a lower dose irradiation (lower than 7×10^{15} Xe^+/cm^2) was mainly responsible for the formation of the crystalline bcc-SSSS phase, while a higher dose irradiation (up to 9 × 10^{15} Xe^+/cm^2) was responsible for damaging the previously formed bcc-SSSS phase, thus leading to a disordered state. Consequently, the kinetically preferred formation sequence is that the bcc-SSSS phase was formed first and then the bcc-SSSS was damaged and transformed into an amorphous state. During the second step of relaxation, the extremely short time was responsible for transforming the bcc-SSSS into the amorphous phase. The above interpretation can clearly be confirmed from Figure 4, parts a−d. When the W concentration in the samples is more than 65 atom % of W, with the increase of W content, the free energy of the bcc-SSSS decreases more rapidly than that of the amorphous phase, and the energy difference increases considerably. As a result, the bcc phase may dominant while competing with the amorphous phase and with further increasing W concentration, e.g., in the $Sc_{25}W_{75}$ multilayered sample, only the bcc-SSSS has been obtained.

Now we give some further physical interpretation from the point of view of empirical diffusion dynamics concerning the metastable phase formation exhibited in the Sc−W system. Nordlund et al.[37] have studied the IBM process across the Co/Cu and Ni/Cu interface by simulations and found that the difference in melting points of the constituent metals could lead to different re-crystallization rates, and the diffusion coefficient of the metal with a low melting point is higher than that of the metal with a high melting point during the relaxation period. According to the model proposed by Chang et al.,[38] the amount of atomic transport due to radiation-enhanced diffusion was determined by the magnitude of atomic radius, radiation damage density, and cohesive energy. Among these parameters, cohesive energy plays a dominant role in atomic transport, and atoms with small cohesive energy are more mobile than those with large cohesive energy. For the Sc−W binary system, the melting temperature of Sc (1814 K) is much lower than that of W (3695 K) and the cohesive energy of Sc (3.9 eV/atom) is much lower than that of W (8.66 eV/atom).[32] It is therefore deduced that the Sc atoms might be more mobile during IBM, and they could diffuse into the W layers more easily than the W atoms migrating into the Sc layers. Based on the above discussion, the multilayered samples with lower Sc content, W-based bcc solid solution is more likely to be formed than the amorphous phase, which is consistent with our experimental observations in the $Sc_{40}W_{60}$ and $Sc_{25}W_{75}$ multilayered samples upon IBM.

4. Concluding Remarks

(1) Based on properly designing and controlling the interfacial free energy in the Sc−W multilayered films, a unique amorphous phase and a metastable W-based bcc solid solution are formed in the Sc-rich side and W-rich side, respectively, by ion beam mixing in the equilibrium immiscible Sc−W system.

(2) Thermodynamic modeling, based on Miedema's theory, predicts the possibility of synthesizing amorphous alloys in the Sc−W system within a composition range of 12−58 atom % of W, which is in good agreement with the experimentally measured GFR.

(3) Atomistic modeling based on an ab initio derived Sc−W potential predicts the glass-forming range of the Sc−W system to be within a composition range of 15−50 atom % of W, which matches fairly well with the experimentally measured GFR.

Acknowledgment. The financial aid to the present study from the National Natural Science Foundation of China, The Ministry of Science and Technology (G20000627-07), and Tsinghua University is greatly acknowledged.

References and Notes

(1) Lu, Y. Q.; Zhu, Y. Y.; Chen, Y. F.; Zhu, S. N.; Ming, N. B.; Feng, Y. J. *Science* **1999**, *284*, 1822.

(2) Liu, B. X.; Johnson, W. L.; Nicolet, M. A.; Lau, S. S. *Appl. Phys. Lett.* **1983**, *42*, 45.

(3) Liu, B. X.; Lai, W. S.; Zhang, Q. *Mater. Sci., Eng. R* **2000**, *29*, 1.

(4) de Boer, F. R.; Boom, R.; Mattens, W. C. M.; Miedema, A. R.; Niessen, A. K. *Cohesion in Metals*: *Transition Metal Alloy*; North-Holland: Amsterdam, The Netherlands, 1989.

(5) Zhang, R. F.; Liu, B. X. *Appl. Phys. Lett.* **2002**, *81*, 1219.

(6) Li, Z. C.; Yu, D. P.; Liu, B. X. *Phys. Rev. B* **2002**, *65*, 245403.

(7) Zhang, R. F.; Liu, B. X. *J. Alloys Compd.* **2002**, *375*, 179.

(8) Zhang, R. F.; Liu, B. X. *J. Mater. Res.* **2003**, *18*, 1499.

(9) Ono, H.; Katsumata, T. *Appl. Phys. Lett.* **2001**, *78*, 1832.

(10) Bakker, H. *Enthalpies in Alloys*: *Miedema's Semi-Empirical Model*; Trans Tech: Zurich, Switzerland, 1998.

(11) Lopez, J. M.; Alonso, J. A. *Z. Naturforsch.* **1985**, *40a*, 1199.

(12) Alonso, J. A.; Gallego, L. J.; Simozar, J. A. *Nuovo Cimento* **1990**, *12*, 587.

(13) Miedema, A. R.; den Broeder, F. J. A. *Z. Metallkd.* **1979**, *70*, 14.

(14) Gerkema, J.; Miedema, A. R. *Surf. Sci.* **1983**, *124*, 351.

(15) Zhang, Z. J.; Liu, B. X. *Phys. Rev. B* **1995**, *51*, 8076.

(16) Kresse, G.; Hafner, J. *Phys. Rev. B* **1993**, *47*, 558.

(17) Vanderbilt, D. *Phys. Rev. B* **1990**, *41*, 7892.

(18) Perdew, J. P.; Wang, Y. *Phys Rev B* **1992**, *45*, 13244.

(19) Monkhorst, H. J.; Pack, J. D. *Phys. Rev. B* **1976**, *13*, 5188.

(20) Daw, M. S.; Baskes, M. I. *Phys. Rev. Lett.* **1983**, *50*, 1285.

(21) Foiles, S. M. *Phys. Rev. B* **1985**, *32*, 3409.

(22) Banerjea, A.; Smith, J. R. *Phys. Rev. B* **1988**, *37*, 6632.

(23) Cai, J.; Ye, Y. Y. *Phys. Rev. B* **1996**, *54*, 8398.

(24) Rose, J. H.; Smith, J. R.; Guinea, F.; Ferrante, J. *Phys. Rev. B* **1984**, *29*, 2963.

(25) Johnson, R. A.; Oh, D. J. *J. Mater. Res.* **1989**, *4*, 1195.

(26) Guellil, A. M.; Adams, J. B. *J. Mater. Res.* **1992**, *7*, 639.

(27) Gong, H. R.; Kong, L. T.; Lai, W. S.; Liu, B. X. *Phys. Rev. B* **2002**, *66*, 104204.

(28) Parrinello, M.; Rahman, A. *J. Appl. Phys.* **1981**, *52*, 7182.

(29) Luzzi, D. E.; Yan, M.; Sob, M.; Vitek, V. *Phys. Rev. Lett.* **1991**, *67*, 1894.

(30) Yan, M.; Sob, M.; Luzzi, D. E.; Vitek, V.; Ackland, G. J.; Methfessel, M.; Rodriguez, C. O. *Phys. Rev. B* **1993**, *47*, 5571.

(31) Zhang, R. F.; Kong, L. T.; Gong, H. R.; Liu, B. X. *J. Phys.: Condens. Matter* **2004**, *16*, 5251.

(32) Kittel, C. *Introduction to solid-state physics*, 6th ed.; Wiley: New York, 1986.

(33) Brandes, E. A.; Brook, G. B. *Smithells Metals Reference Book*, 7th ed.; Butterworth-Heinemann: Oxford, UK, 1992.

(34) Simmons, G.; Wang, H. *Single-Crystal Elastic Constants and Calculated Aggregate Properties: A Handbook*, 2nd ed.; MIT: Cambridge, MA, 1971.

(35) Liu, B. X.; Lai, W. S.; Zhang, Z. J. *Adv. Phys.* **2001**, *50*, 367.

(36) Thompson, M. W. *Defects and Radiation Damage in Metals*; Cambridge University Press: Cambridge, England, 1969.

(37) Nordlund, K.; Averback, R. S. *Phys. Rev. B* **1999**, *59*, 20.

(38) Chang, G. S.; Jung, S. M.; Song, J. H.; Kim, H. B.; Woo, J. J.; Byun, D. H. *Nucl. Instrum. Methods B* **1997**, *121*, 244.

Icositetrahedral and icosahedral atomic configurations observed in the Nb–Ag metallic glasses synthesized by ion beam mixing

K. P. Tai,[a] N. Gao, X. D. Dai, J. H. Li, W. S. Lai, and B. X. Liu[b]
Advanced Materials Laboratory, Department of Materials Science and Engineering, Tsinghua University, Beijing 100084, China

(Received 28 April 2006; accepted 3 July 2006; published online 31 August 2006)

Metallic glasses are obtained in an immiscible Nb–Ag system by ion beam mixing and an atomic configuration in the amorphous structure is discovered, i.e., an icositetrahedral ordering, which, together with an icosahedral ordering also observed in the Nb–Ag metallic glasses and in some previously reported systems, helps in formulating a structural spectrum of the amorphous solids. The experimental characterization and atomistic modeling with an *ab initio* derived Nb–Ag potential demonstrate the significance of *structural heredity*, i.e., the crystalline structures of the constituent metals play a decisive role in determining the atomic structure of the metallic glasses in the system. [DOI: 10.1063/1.2345041]

In 1960, Klement *et al.* obtained the first amorphous alloy, or metallic glass, by liquid melt quenching (LMQ) in the Au–Si system.[1] Since then, LMQ has been employed to produce amorphous alloys in the binary metal systems, which are miscible at equilibrium with negative heats of formation (ΔH_f), ensuring that the two constituent metals could be comelted. In the early 1980s, some new metallic glass-producing techniques have been introduced, e.g., ion beam mixing[2] (IBM) of multiple metal layers. It has been proven that IBM is capable of producing metallic glasses not only in those systems with negative ΔH_f but also in the immiscible systems at equilibrium with large positive ΔH_f. Due to the noncrystalline structure with no grain boundary, the metallic glasses have frequently shown some unique properties.[3] A long-standing basic issue has been to establish a relevant correlation between the structure and property, which requires first to explore an exact description of the disordered atomic structure of the amorphous solids. In the past decades, a number of structural models have been proposed for the metallic glasses, yet most of the proposals are mainly based on geometrical/topological considerations, such as dense random packing, efficient local packing, network packing, and fcc packing models.[4–6] Recently, there has been some attempt to characterize the atomic structure of the metallic glasses, e.g., Sheng *et al.* have studied the effect of the relative size of the constituent metals and claimed that the so-called icosahedral-type cluster was the predominate structural unit of the metallic glasses.[7] Note that in the study of Sheng *et al.*, all the systems are miscible and it is a question if their argument is also valid for the metallic glasses obtained in the immiscible systems. Up to now, the atomic structure of the metallic glasses formed in the positive ΔH_f systems has scarcely been studied. Much effort is therefore urgently needed to explore the description of the disordered atomic structure of the metallic glasses created between the immiscible atoms. Until then, it would be possible to formulate a general structural spectrum for the binary metallic glasses.

[a]Author to whom correspondence should be addressed; electronic mail: tkp04@mails.tsinghua.edu.cn
[b]Electronic mail: dmslbx@tsinghua.edu.cn

In the present study, we investigate the atomic structure of the metallic glasses in the Nb–Ag system ($\Delta H_f = +27$ kJ/mol) (Ref. 8) by ion beam mixing using 200 keV xenon ions. To match the irradiating ion range, the total thickness of the Nb–Ag multilayered films is calculated to be 45 nm by the TRIM program.[9] To include adequate interfacial free energies, the Nb–Ag multilayered films consist of 15, 17, 11, and 7 layers and their compositions are designed to be $Nb_{60}Ag_{40}$, $Nb_{70}Ag_{30}$, $Nb_{80}Ag_{20}$, and $Nb_{90}Ag_{10}$, respectively. The Nb–Ag multilayered films are prepared in a high vacuum evaporation system and then irradiated in an implanter to a dose range from 4×10^{14} to 5×10^{15} Xe^+/cm^2. During irradiation, the sample holder is cooled by liquid nitrogen. Various methods are used to characterize the structural transition and to determine the real compositions of the samples and resultant phases.

In the $Nb_{60}Ag_{40}$, $Nb_{70}Ag_{30}$, and $Nb_{80}Ag_{20}$ multilayered samples, after irradiation to a dose range of $4\times10^{14}-1\times10^{15}$ Xe^+/cm^2, crystalline diffraction lines from Nb and Ag remain, indicating an incomplete mixing. At a dose of 2×10^{15} Xe^+/cm^2, a bcc-Nb-based solid solution is obtained, as evidenced by the selected area diffraction (SAD) pattern in Fig. 1(a). Increasing the dose to 5×10^{15} Xe^+/cm^2, transmission electron microscopy examination exhibits a uniform gray matrix of a typical amorphous structure, which is confirmed by the halos observed in the SAD pattern in Fig. 1(b).

In the $Nb_{90}Ag_{10}$ multilayered sample, Fig. 1(c) shows a SAD pattern taken at a dose of 2×10^{15} Xe^+/cm^2. In the pattern, one sees two sets of diffraction rings, which can be indexed to be from two different-sized fcc phases, i.e., a Ag-rich fcc-I phase and a Nb-rich FCC-II phase, respectively. Increasing the dose to 3×10^{15} Xe^+/cm^2, SAD analysis shows that there appears a halo and a weak diffraction ring from the identified Nb-rich FCC-II phase. Further increasing the dose to 5×10^{15} Xe^+/cm^2, a unique amorphous phase is obtained, as evidenced by the SAD pattern in Fig. 1(d). Comparing the SAD patterns in Figs. 1(b) and 1(d), one sees that the radius of the halo in Fig. 1(d) for the $Nb_{90}Ag_{10}$ alloy is obviously smaller than that observed from Fig. 1(b) for the $Nb_{80}Ag_{20}$ alloy as well as for the $Nb_{60}Ag_{40}$ and $Nb_{70}Ag_{30}$ alloys. In addition, high-resolution electron micrograph and x-ray diffraction (XRD) examinations not only

Applied Physics Letters 89 (9), 094108 (2006).

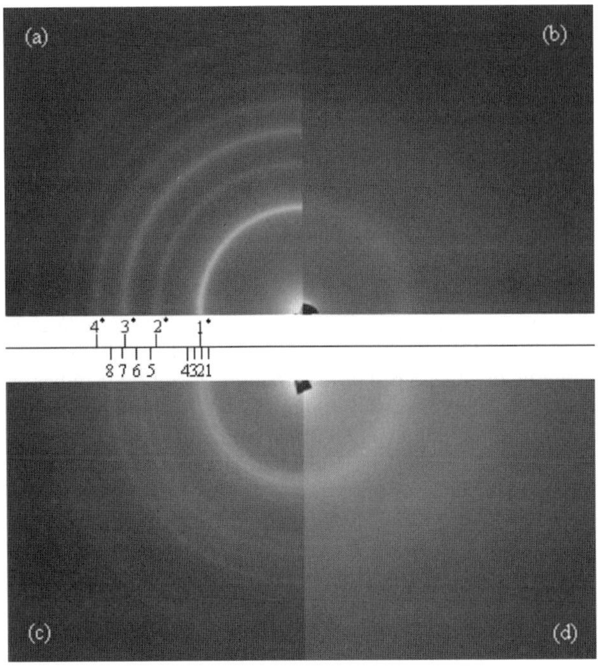

FIG. 1. SAD patterns of the Nb–Ag multilayered samples upon 200 keV xenon ion irradiation at 77 K. (a) The $Nb_{80}Ag_{20}$ sample at doses of 2×10^{15} Xe^+/cm^2 and (b) 5×10^{15} Xe^+/cm^2 and (c) the $Nb_{90}Ag_{10}$ sample at doses of 2×10^{15} Xe^+/cm^2 and (d) 5×10^{15} Xe^+/cm^2. Notes for the indexing: 1-fcc-II(111), 2-fcc-I(111), 3-fcc-II(200), 4-fcc-I(200), 5-fcc-II(220), 6-fcc-I(220), 7-fcc-II(311), 8-fcc-I(311), 1^*-bcc(110), 2^*-bcc(200), 3^*-bcc(211), and 4^*-bcc(220).

confirmed the formation of the Nb–Ag metallic glasses but also showed that the halo positions in XRD patterns (not shown) from the ion mixed $Nb_{60}Ag_{40}$, $Nb_{70}Ag_{30}$, and $Nb_{80}Ag_{20}$ metallic glasses are almost identical and locate at $2\theta\approx38°$, while the halo position of the $Nb_{90}Ag_{10}$ metallic glass obviously shifts and locates at $2\theta\approx36°$, suggesting that there could be different atomic structures in the Nb–Ag metallic glasses. In fact, the $Nb_{60}Ag_{40}$, $Nb_{70}Ag_{30}$, and $Nb_{80}Ag_{20}$ metallic glasses are formed from the bcc-Nb-based solid solutions, while the $Nb_{90}Ag_{10}$ metallic glass is formed from a fcc-Nb-based solid solution. In other words, the crystalline structure of the solvent metal Nb in the initial and/or intermediate states plays a decisive role in determining the atomic structure in the resultant metallic glasses, suggesting an important concept of *structural heredity*.

To reveal the atomic structure of the Nb–Ag metallic glasses, an n-body Nb–Ag potential is firstly derived, based on embedded atom method,[10,11] and then applied in molecular dynamics simulation under the Parrinello-Rahman scheme.[12] The potential parameters of Nb and Ag were taken from the reference,[13] and the parameters of the Nb–Ag cross potential were fitted to some physical properties obtained from *ab initio* calculations for some possible metastable $L1_2$-Ag_3Nb, $L1_2$-$AgNb_3$, $B1$-AgNb, and $B2$-AgNb compounds. Table I lists the fitted potential parameters of the Nb–Ag system. The simulation models are set as bcc-Nb-based solid solution (1024 atoms) for the $Nb_{60}Ag_{40}$, $Nb_{70}Ag_{30}$, and $Nb_{80}Ag_{20}$ alloys, and set as fcc-Nb-based solid solution (2048 atoms) for the $Nb_{90}Ag_{10}$ alloy, respectively. Periodic boundary conditions were applied in three directions.

TABLE I. Fitted parameters for the Ag–Ag, Nb–Nb, and Ag–Nb (EAM) potentials.

Ag–Ag[a]		Nb–Nb[a]		Ag–Nb	
χ	15.283 318	χ	10.403 652	A	0.757 214
α (ev)	0.223 098	k_0 (ev)	−0.393 145		
β	4.851 732	k_1 (ev)	−0.642 187	B(Å)	−0.167 791
r_a (Å)	2.566 213	k_2 (ev)	3.593 435		
F_1 (ev)	0.213 971	k_3 (ev)	3.787 160	C(Å)	−0.495 355
r_s (Å)	4.2	r_s (Å)	3.4		
r_c (Å)	4.62	r_c (Å)	4.4		
n	0.333 333	n	0.440 653		

[a]The fitted potential parameters are from Ref. 13.

After annealing at 300 K for 100 ps, the pair-correlation functions $g(r)$ are calculated for all simulated models. For the $Nb_{60}Ag_{40}$, $Nb_{70}Ag_{30}$, and $Nb_{80}Ag_{20}$ solid solution models, the $g(r)$ curves are similar and no discrete crystalline peak is observed, suggesting that the amorphous structures were formed and that the composition varying within 60–80 at. % of Nb has no considerable effect on amorphization. While comparing the $Nb_{80}Ag_{20}$ and $Nb_{90}Ag_{10}$ alloys, one sees from Fig. 2(a) that although both calculated $g(r)$ curves confirm the formation of the Nb–Ag amorphous phases, there appears significant difference between the curves, suggesting that there are distinct atomic configurations emerging in the respective metallic glasses. From the simulation results, the positions of the Nb and Ag atoms in the Nb–Ag metallic glasses can be derived to gain direct insight into their three-dimensional structure, as shown in Figs. 2(b) and 2(c), from which one sees some segregation of the similar atoms due to a repulsive interaction between the immiscible Nb and Ag atoms.[14]

To further characterize the atomic structure, a coordinate number (CN) is defined for a specific atom as the number of atoms in its first nearest neighboring shell.[15,16] Naturally, a

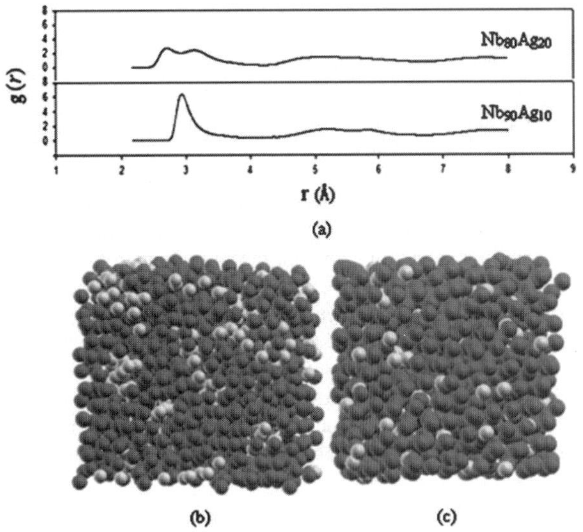

FIG. 2. (Color) Molecular dynamics simulated Nb–Ag alloys. (a) The calculated pair-correlation functions of the $Nb_{80}Ag_{20}$ (bcc) and $Nb_{90}Ag_{10}$ (fcc) solid solution models, respectively, after annealing at 300 K for 100 ps. Views of the atomic structure of (b) the $Nb_{80}Ag_{20}$ metallic glass and (c) the $Nb_{90}Ag_{10}$ metallic glasses. Note that the red and yellow balls represent the Nb and Ag atoms, respectively.

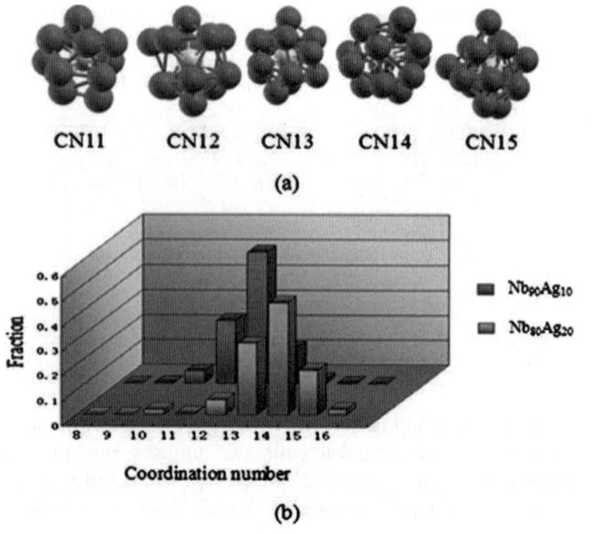

FIG. 3. (Color) Polyhedrons with various CNs and their distributions. (a) Five possible local structural packing units, i.e., five types of polyhedrons with CN=11, 12, 13, 14, and 15 in the Ng–Ag metallic glasses. Note that the red and yellow balls represent the Nb and Ag atoms, respectively. (b) The statistic distributions of the coordination number (CN) in the $Nb_{80}Ag_{20}$ and $Nb_{90}Ag_{10}$ metallic glasses, respectively.

specific atomic configuration (or ordering) corresponds to a specific CN, e.g., an icositetrahedral and an icosahedral atomic configurations correspond to CN=14 and 12,[7] respectively, as shown in Fig. 3(a). Topologically, a local packing unit could be defined as a polyhedron, which includes a specific atom together with its first nearest neighboring atoms. In reality, the polyhedrons may be distorted a little to fill the three-dimensional space of the metallic glass. In the present case, calculation results reveal that the Nb–Ag metallic glasses are filled with various local packing units, i.e., the polyhedrons with various CNs mostly to be 11, 12, 13, 14, and 15, respectively, and that the CN statistic distributions for the $Nb_{80}Ag_{20}$ and $Nb_{90}Ag_{10}$ metallic glasses are sharply different, as shown in Fig. 3(b). One sees that for the $Nb_{80}Ag_{20}$ metallic glass, which is transformed from a bcc-Nb-based solid solution, the dominant (about 45%) local packing unit is in an icositetrahedral atomic configuration with CN=14, or named icositetrahedron, whereas in the $Nb_{90}Ag_{10}$ metallic glass, which is transformed from a fcc-Nb-based solid solution, the dominant (52%) local packing unit is in an icosahedral atomic configuration with CN=12, or named icosahedron, showing the importance of structural heredity. From an atomic interaction point of view, the ground state of the Nb metal is in a bcc structure, in which one Nb atom has eight first and six second neighboring atoms, resulting in a total coordinate number of 14, if the two neighbors are squeezed into a mixed one. In IBM experiments, the predominant packing unit in the Nb–Ag metallic glasses formed from the bcc-Nb-based solid solution is indeed of icositetrahedral atomic configuration with CN=14. Similarly, if the Nb atoms are in a metastable state of fcc structure, the dominant packing unit in the corresponding resultant metallic glasses would be icosahedral atomic configuration with CN=12, which is indeed observed in IBM experiments too. Moreover, the above arguments are confirmed by atomistic modeling based on an *ab initio* derived Nb–Ag potential. In short, it is the intrinsic atomic interaction of the constituent metals that governs the atomic structures both in the crystalline and amorphous states. Incidentally, a first principles calculation showed that an energy difference between the Nb atoms in fcc and bcc structures is only 0.32 eV/at., which could explain why the Nb metal could be in either a bcc or fcc structure, resulting in either an icositetrahedral or icosahedral atomic configuration to be the corresponding dominant local packing unit in the respective Nb–Ag metallic glasses. Note that He *et al.* have reported that the structures of the metallic glasses were all characterized by an icosahedral short-range ordering, because the solvent metals were all of fcc structures.[15] It is deduced that if the two metals of a system are both fcc structures, the dominant atomic configuration of the metallic glasses formed in the system would be in an icosahedral ordering, which is just the case reported for the Ni–Ag system.[16]

In summary, we have found that in addition to the frequently observed icosahedral ordering, there is another important atomic configuration, i.e., the icositetrahedral ordering in the binary metallic glasses. We have proposed an important concept of structural heredity that the structure of the constituent metals plays a decisive role in determining the atomic structure of the resultant metallic glasses.

The financial supports from the National Natural Science Foundation and The Ministry of Science and Technology of China are acknowledged.

[1]W. Klement, R. H. Willens, and P. Duwez, Nature (London) **187**, 869 (1960).
[2]B. X. Liu, W. S. Lai, and Q. Zhang, Mater. Sci. Eng., R. **29**, 1 (2000).
[3]A. L. Greer, Science **267**, 1947 (1995).
[4]J. D. Bernal and J. Mason, Nature (London) **188**, 910 (1960).
[5]D. B. Miracle, W. S. Sanders, and O. N. Senkov, Philos. Mag. **83**, 2409 (2003).
[6]D. B. Miracle, Nature (London) **3**, 697 (2004).
[7]H. W. Sheng, W. K. Luo, F. M. Alamgir, J. M. Bai, and E. Ma, Nature (London) **439**, 419 (2006).
[8]F. R. de Boer, R. Boom, W. C. M. Mattens, A. R. Miedema, and A. K. Niessen, *Cohesion in Metals: Transition Metal Alloy* (North-Holland, Amsterdam, 1989).
[9]J. F. Ziegler and J. P. Biersack, *TRIM* (Pergamon, New York, 1992).
[10]R. A. Johnson and D. J. Oh, J. Mater. Res. **4**, 1195 (1989).
[11]A. M. Guellil and J. B. Adams, J. Mater. Res. **7**, 639 (1989).
[12]M. Parrinello and A. Rahman, Phys. Rev. Lett. **45**, 1196 (1980).
[13]R. F. Zhang, Ph.D. thesis, Tsinghua University, 2005.
[14]J. H. He, H. W. Sheng, P. J. Schilling, C.-L. Chien, and E. Ma, Phys. Rev. Lett. **86**, 2826 (2001).
[15]J. H. He and E. Ma, Phys. Rev. B **64**, 144206 (2001).
[16]W. K. Luo, H. W. Sheng, F. M. Alamgir, J. M. Bai, J. H. He, and E. Ma, Phys. Rev. Lett. **92**, 145502 (2004).

Nonequilibrium solid phases studied by thermodynamic calculation, molecular dynamics simulation, ab initio calculation and ion-beam manipulation in an immiscible Au–Co system at equilibrium

H.F. Yan, H.B. Guo, Y.X. Shen, J.H. Li, B.X. Liu *

Advanced Materials Laboratory, Department of Materials Science and Engineering, Tsinghua University, Beijing 100084, China

Received 12 January 2006; received in revised form 14 July 2006; accepted 18 July 2006
Available online 2 October 2006

Abstract

For an immiscible Au–Co system at equilibrium, a calculated Gibbs free energy diagram suggests that the composition range favoring metallic glass formation is approximately 22–83 at.% Co and that the nonequilibrium crystalline phases at both $Co_{75}Au_{25}$ and $Co_{25}Au_{75}$ prefer to be in a face-centred cubic (fcc) structure. Based on a proven realistic *n*-body Au–Co potential, molecular dynamics simulations predict that the metallic glass-forming range of the Au–Co system is 18–88 at.% Co. Employing the Vienna ab initio simulation package, the first principles calculations indicate that the $L1_2$ (fcc) and $D0_{19}$ (hexagonal close packed (hcp)) structures could relatively be stable for both nonequilibrium crystalline $AuCo_3$ and Au_3Co phases, whereas the B_h (hcp) structure could be stable for the AuCo phase. Interestingly, ion beam manipulation confirms that a uniform $Au_{42}Co_{58}$ amorphous phase is indeed obtained and that some nonequilibrium fcc-type and hcp-type Au–Co phases can also be formed, the lattice constants of which are in agreement with those derived from the ab initio calculations.

Keywords: Molecular dynamics; Ab initio calculation; Metastable phases; Ion-beam processing; Metallic glasses

1. Introduction

During the past decades, some nonequilibrium/far-from-equilibrium materials processing techniques, such as mechanical alloying [1–3], ion-beam mixing [4,5], vapor deposition [6,7], pulse laser deposition [8] and vapor quenching [9,10], have been developed and have proved to be very effective in producing a large number of nonequilibrium binary metallic alloys. Many alloys obtained from these processes have shown unique properties in a number of respects and have become potential for practical applications [1,6,7,11,12]. In particular, ion-beam mixing of multilayered films has been well recognized as a powerful means for producing nonequilibrium materials. This process is generally divided into two steps, i.e., the first step of the atomic collision triggered by impinging ions, followed by a second step of relaxation [5]. In the first step, the irradiating ions trigger a series of atomic collisions, known as the atomic collision cascade, which is responsible for the intermixing of the atoms in the multilayered films. After the atomic collision cascade, a short relaxation period, which lasts for 10^{-9}–10^{-10} s, allows only a limited atomic rearrangement, and only fast and partitionless transition mechanisms can take place within this extremely short time period. An alternative method, i.e. according to the so-called thermal spike model, offers an effective cooling speed in the relaxation period of ion-beam mixing estimated to be 10^{13}–10^{14} K/s [13,14], which enables the formation of various nonequilibrium solid phases. To date, a large number of nonequilibrium

* Corresponding author.
E-mail address: dmslbx@tsinghua.edu.cn (B.X. Liu).

Acta Materialia 54 (19), p.5293-5304 (2006).

solid phases and their formation mechanisms have been explored by ion-beam mixing not only in equilibrium miscible binary metal systems, but also in some immiscible systems at equilibrium [15,16]. In recent years, ion-beam mixing has been developed into a new system named ion-beam manipulation (IBM) [17,18], which is capable of producing various nonequilibrium solid phases in those immiscible systems characterized by large positive heats of formation [16]. There are two essential features involved in the IBM scheme. First, the metal–metal multilayered films were designed to have individual layer thicknesses of as little as a couple of nanometers, enabling the controllable interfacial free energy to elevate the initial multilayered films up to a desired highly energetic state. Second, ion irradiation was conducted to trigger interfacial mixing at low temperatures in order to minimize the repulsive interaction between the immiscible metals. Moreover, ion irradiation experiments have shown that the intervals between ion doses can be finely varied, thus enabling one to trace the details of the structural phase transition and to reveal some new intermediate states prior to forming the final nonequilibrium solid phase. Under such circumstances, IBM of nano-sized multilayered films is capable of synthesizing highly energetic nonequilibrium solid phases and artificial solid-state microstructures in the immiscible binary metal systems [17]. For instance, the authors' group has recently successfully obtained amorphous alloys by IBM in the immiscible Ag–W system, which has the largest positive $\Delta H_f = +65$ kJ/mol among the transition metal alloys [19,20].

Meanwhile, in recent years, demand has risen for theoretical studies to establish the calculation model for predicting the formation of the nonequilibrium solid phases as well as for explaining the mechanism of the structural phase transition in immiscible binary metal systems. A number of excellent research works have been published in the literature – Miedema's model and Alonso's method, for instance, have been proposed as a semi-empirical thermodynamic approach to explain or predict the formation of the nonequilibrium solid phases [19,21]. At an atomic level, molecular dynamics (MD) simulations have been performed not only to reveal the atomic rearrangement [22], but also to reveal the atomistic mechanism of the solid-state crystal-to-amorphous transition taking place in miscible and immiscible systems [23,24]. In recent years, first-principles calculations have been developed to gain a precise understanding at an electronic scale concerning metastability, i.e. the structural stability of the nonequilibrium solid phases, in binary metal systems [25,26].

In the present study, the Au–Co system with a positive heat of formation ($\Delta H_f = +11$ kJ/mol) was selected to investigate the structural stability of the possible nonequilibrium solid phases, as there are some issues concerning nonequilibrium solid phase formation that need to be clarified, both theoretically and experimentally, in such an equilibrium immiscible system. Although some researchers have combined theoretical calculations and IBM to investigate the stability of nonequilibrium solid phases in some immiscible systems in the past decade [14,15,22], some questions remain unanswered. Above all, although with the development of experimental methods, a number of new nonequilibrium solid phases with different structures have been obtained by IBM, a clear understanding has not yet been achieved. We therefore carried out a combination of semi-empirical thermodynamic calculations (at the macroscopic scale), MD simulations (at the atomic scale) and first-principles calculations (at the scale of electronic structure of solids), to predict the possible nonequilibrium solid phases in the Au–Co system. Experimentally, the powerful tool of IBM with a highly effective cooling speed is employed to form the predicted phases. The outline of the present work is as follows. First, thermodynamic calculations, based on Miedema's model and Alonso's method [19,21,27,28], are conducted to interpret the amorphous alloy formation by comparing the relative energetic levels of the competing phases in question. Second, the glass-forming range (GFR) is determined by MD simulations using the hexagonal close packed/face-centered cubic (hcp/fcc) solid solution model and the simulation results are compared with the thermodynamic calculations. Third, first-principles calculations are conducted to predict the other possible nonequilibrium Au_3Co, AuCo and $AuCo_3$ phases in the Au–Co system. Finally, IBM is performed under a far-from-equilibrium condition to confirm the GFR as well as some nonequilibrium solid phases predicted by theoretical calculations in the Au–Co system. We report, in this paper, the theoretical predictions and the experimental results of IBM. In addition, a brief discussion follows to compare the results from theoretical calculations and the experimental observations.

2. Calculation methods and experimental procedure

2.1. Thermodynamic calculation

Based on Miedema's model [19,27,28] and Alonso's method [21], the Gibbs free energy of a nonequilibrium phase can be calculated by $\Delta G = \Delta H - T \cdot \Delta S$, where ΔH and ΔS are the enthalpy and entropy terms, respectively. As a first approximation, the entropy term for a concentrated solid solution (CSS) and amorphous phase is simply taken as that of an ideal solution, i.e., $\Delta S = -R[C_A \ln C_A + C_B \ln C_B]$, where R is the gas constant and C_A and C_B are the atomic concentrations of metals A and B, respectively. The temperature, T, in this calculation is taken as 300 K.

The enthalpy change ΔH is the sum of three terms, i.e. $\Delta H_{MX} = \Delta H^c_{MX} + \Delta H^e_{MX} + \Delta H^s_{MX}$, corresponding to the chemical, elastic and structural contributions, respectively [19]. The chemical term ΔH^c_{MX} is accordingly calculated by $\Delta H^c_{MX} = \Delta H_{amp} V_A^{2/3} X_A f_{AB}$, where ΔH_{amp} is a constant amplitude for a specific system and can be obtained from the literature [19]. f_{AB} is a function accounting for the degree to which atoms of type A are surrounded by atoms of type B, and is given by [29]:

$$f_{AB} = X_B^S[1 + \gamma(X_A^S X_B^S)^2] \tag{1}$$

$$X_B^S = \frac{X_B V_B^{2/3}}{X_A V_A^{2/3} + X_B V_B^{2/3}} \tag{2}$$

In Eq. (1), γ is an empirical constant describing the chemical short-range order (CSRO) of the solid solution, the amorphous and the ordered compound, and is usually taken to be 0, 5 and 8, respectively.

For a nonequilibrium phase, the elastic energy is taken into account for the lattice distortion caused by atomic size mismatch of the two constituent metals. The elastic term is therefore expressed by

$$\Delta H^e_{MX} = X_A X_B \left[X_A \Delta H^e_{MX(B \text{ in } A)} + X_B \Delta H^e_{MX(A \text{ in } B)}\right], \tag{3}$$

where $\Delta H^e_{MX(i \text{ in } j)}$ is the elastic contribution to the heat of solution of the constituent i in j in the nonequilibrium phase, and can be calculated by the method proposed by de Boer [19]. For a nonequilibrium phase, the structural contribution to the free energy change is expressed by

$$\Delta H^s_{MX} = E(Z) - X_A E(Z_B) - X_B E(Z_A) \tag{4}$$

where $E(Z)$, $E(Z_A)$, $E(Z_B)$ are the lattice stabilities of the nonequilibrium phase and pure A and B metals, and Z, Z_A and Z_B are the average numbers of the valence electrons of the nonequilibrium phase and the numbers of valence electrons of pure metals A and B, respectively. The dependence of the lattice stability on Z for paramagnetic and ferromagnetic transition metals has been calculated and can be found in the literature [30].

The Gibbs free energy of the initial state of the Au–Co multilayered films should be calculated by adding the interfacial free energy to the ground state of a mixture of Au and Co in the bulk form. Generally, the interfacial free energy was in positive proportion to the fraction of the interfacial atoms versus the total atoms in the films and can therefore be controlled by adjusting the number of the interfaces, while keeping the total thickness of the multilayered film constant [16]. In the present calculation, the total thickness of the Au–Co multilayered films is designed to be 40 nm, consisting of 12 layers (6 bilayers), 10 layers (5 bilayers) and 8 layers (4 bilayers), respectively, in order to elevate the interfacial free energy of the Au–Co multilayered films up to the highly energetic states of the system. This enables one to obtain the corresponding nonequilibrium Au–Co phase in favor of the free energy concern.

2.2. *Scheme of the molecular dynamics simulation*

In the present study, an n-body Au–Co potential is constructed by using the second moment approximation of tight-binding (TB-SMA) method [31,32], which is suitable for the present case dealing with Co in hcp and Au in fcc structures, respectively. In the TB-SMA, the total energy E_{total} of N atoms is written as

$$E_{total} = \sum_i \left\{ \sum_{j \neq i} A_{\alpha\beta} \exp\left[-p_{\alpha\beta}\left(\frac{r_{ij}}{r_{\alpha\beta}} - 1\right)\right] - \sqrt{\sum_{j \neq i} \xi^2_{\alpha\beta} \exp\left[-2q_{\alpha\beta}\left(\frac{r_{ij}}{r_{\alpha\beta}} - 1\right)\right]} \right\} \tag{5}$$

where α and β denote the atom species, i.e., Co and Au in the present case; r_{ij} is a distance between the atoms numbered i and j; $d_{\alpha\beta}$ is the first neighbor distance; A, p, ζ and q are four adjustable parameters. Although the potential parameters of the pure metals Co and Au have been reported [33], they are refitted to a desired cutoff distance in the present study. The cutoff distances are 6.0 Å for Co and 6.5 Å for Au, respectively, which correspond to the ninth nearest distance in the hcp Co structure and the fifth nearest distance in the fcc Au, respectively. The detailed fitting procedure can be found in a recent publication [34]. The potential parameters for the Co–Au system used in the present MD simulations are listed in Table 1.

The MD simulation is carried out with a Parrinello–Rahman constant pressure scheme and the equations of motion are solved through a second-order four-value predictor–corrector Gear algorithm with a time step of $t = 5 \times 10^{-15}$ s [35]. In the present study, two kinds of simulation models are employed, i.e. an hcp solid solution model, which consists of $12 \times 7 \times 8 \times 2 = 1344$ atoms, and an fcc solid solution model, which contains $9 \times 9 \times 9 \times 4 = 2916$ atoms. In both simulation models, the [1 0 0], [0 1 0] and [0 0 1] atomic crystal directions are parallel to the x, y and z axes, respectively, and the periodic boundary conditions are adopted in the three dimensions. The solid solution models with desired chemical compositions are constructed through a process of randomly substituting the Co atoms by the Au atoms in the hcp model or substituting the Au atoms by the Co atoms in the fcc model. After setting, the models are annealed at 300 K for adequate MD time steps (typically for 2 ns) to reach a relatively stable state, at which all the dynamic parameters show no secular variation.

The pair-correlation function $g(r)$ and the projections of the atomic positions are the usual methods to determine the formation of an amorphous structure as well as to monitor the process of the structural phase transition in the models [36].

2.3. *First principles calculation*

The well-established Vienna ab initio simulation package (VASP) [37] is employed for the first principles calculation in the present study. The calculations are conducted

Table 1
Potential parameters for the Co–Au system

	A (eV)	ξ (eV)	p	q	r_0 (Å)	r_{cutoff} (Å)
Au–Au	0.2218	1.8874	9.9577	4.0136	2.885	6.5
Co–Co	0.1114	1.5453	10.9245	2.3667	2.494	6.0
Co–Au	0.1267	1.8811	8.8136	1.7016	2.776	6.5

on a plane-wave basis, using fully non-local Vanderbilt-type ultrasoft pseudopotentials to describe the electron–ion interaction [38]. This approach allows the use of a moderate cutoff for the construction of the plane-wave basis for the transition metals. The exchange and correlation items are described by the generalized-gradient approximation (GGA) proposed by Perdew and Wang [39]. The integration in the Brillouin zone is done on the special k points determined according to the Monkhorst–Pack scheme [40]. For the present calculations, the mesh of k points adopted is constitutive of 56 irreducible k points, which are sufficient for calculating the simple crystalline structures, and the cutoff energy for the plane-wave basis is 268.0 eV. In studying the stabilities of the possible nonequilibrium crystalline Au–Co phases, we only select those simple crystalline structures in the calculations, based on the following consideration and fact. For a complicated structure, the unit cell frequently contains more atoms and frequently requires a relatively larger critical radius for nucleation and growth than a simple one. It follows that such a complicated structure is hardly ever going to be formed, because the kinetic conditions are usually restricted in those frequently applied, nonequilibrium materials processing techniques. In fact, numerous experiments have shown that the nonequilibrium crystalline phases obtained so far in the binary metal systems are frequently of simple structures, such as fcc, body-centered cubic (bcc) and hcp, rather than complicated ones. Furthermore, the experimental observations of the simple structured nonequilibrium crystalline phases are also compatible with the far-from-equilibrium process of IBM, which is employed in the present study. It is commonly recognized that in IBM, either a simple crystalline structure or a disordered state, namely the amorphous phase, can be formed, because only fast and partitionless transition mechanisms can take place during an extremely short relaxation period lasting only for 10^{-10}–10^{-9} s, whereas the nucleation and growth of a complicated structured phase is frequently prohibited [13].

Accordingly, the first principles calculations are performed for 10 simple structured compounds, i.e., the A15, $D0_9$, $D0_{19}$, $L1_2$ and $L6_0$ for the chemical compositions of $Au_{75}Co_{25}$ and $Au_{25}Co_{75}$, respectively, and for another four simple structured compounds, i.e., the B1, B2, B3 and B_h for the chemical composition of $Au_{50}Co_{50}$.

2.4. Experimental procedure

In the present study, 200 keV Xe ions were used as irradiating ions in an IBM experiment. To match the projected range plus projected range straggling of the 200 keV Xe ions for an effective intermixing, the total thickness of the Au–Co multilayered samples was about 40 nm, according to the calculated ion range from the TRIM program [41]. Five Au–Co multilayered films with overall compositions of $Au_{25}Co_{75}$, $Au_{33}Co_{67}$, $Au_{50}Co_{50}$, $Au_{67}Co_{33}$ and $Au_{75}Co_{25}$ were designed and the Au–Co multilayered films consisted of totals of 12, 12, 12, 10, 8 layers, respectively. The desired overall compositions of the Au–Co multilayered films were obtained by adjusting the relative thicknesses of the individual Au and Co layers. The individual layer thicknesses of both Au and Co were accordingly calculated and each individual layer was designed to be greater than 2 nm (i.e. 20 Å) to ensure obtaining continuous deposited layers.

The designed Au–Co multilayered samples were prepared by alternately depositing pure Au and Co onto NaCl single crystals as substrates in an ultrahigh-vacuum (UHV) e-gun evaporation system with a background vacuum level of the order of 10^{-8} Torr. During deposition, the vacuum level was better than 3.0×10^{-6} Torr. The deposition rate for both Au and Co was controlled at 0.5 Å/s, and during deposition, the sample holders were always cooled by running water at about 10 °C. After deposition, the real compositions of the as-deposited multilayered films were confirmed to be $Au_{25}Co_{75}$, $Au_{42}Co_{58}$, $Au_{56}Co_{44}$, $Au_{72}Co_{28}$ and $Au_{79}Co_{21}$, respectively, by energy-dispersive spectrum (EDS) analysis with a measuring error of around 5%. Meanwhile, Rutherford backscattering spectrometry (RBS) was employed to confirm the multilayered configurations of the Au–Co samples using 3.9 MeV Li ions at a 150° scattering angle to measure the depth profile of the two constituent elements and simultaneously to determine the relative contents of both Au and Co. Fig. 1 shows the corresponding RBS spectra, which demonstrate that the Au–Co multilayered films indeed form a multilayered structure. Meanwhile, the relative thicknesses and contents of the individual Au and Co layers in the samples were simulated using the SIMNRA software [42]. The compositions of the samples were then respectively simulated to be consistent with that determined by EDS analysis. Table 2 lists the designed and the experimentally obtained values, respectively. From Table 2, the experimentally obtained total thicknesses and the thicknesses of individual Au and Co layers seem to be quite close the theoretical results. Moreover, Table 2 also lists the real compositions for the Au–Co multilayered samples determined by both EDS and RBS methods.

The as-deposited films were then subjected to 200 keV Xe ion irradiation to doses ranging from 5×10^{14} to 9×10^{15} Xe^+/cm^2 in an implanter with a base vacuum level of the order of 10^{-6} Torr. During irradiation, the sample holders were always cooled by liquid nitrogen and the ion current density was controlled to be less than 1 μA/cm² to avoid overheating. Under such precautions, the temperature of the Au–Co multilayered films was only a little higher than 77 K. For structural characterization, the Au–Co multilayered films were removed from the NaCl substrates by deionized water and placed onto the Cu grids for transmission electron microscope (TEM) observation and selected area diffraction (SAD) analysis to identify the structures in the as-deposited states as well as of those resultant Au–Co phases upon IBM. The examination was done at room temperature (around 300 K). The lattice

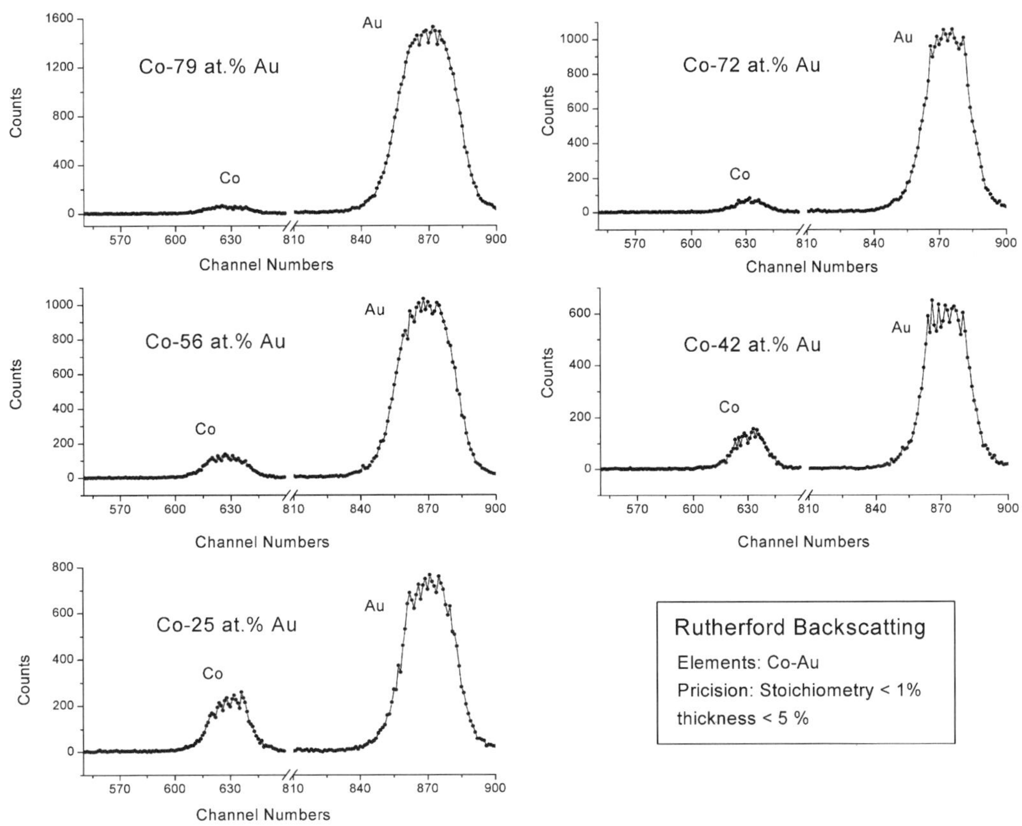

Fig. 1. Rutherford backscattering spectrometry (RBS) of the as-deposited multilayered Au–Co films.

Table 2
The total thicknesses derived from TRIM program and the designed relative thicknesses of the individual Au and Co layers in the five sets of the Au–Co multilayered samples

Designed samples		Calculated ion range (Å)	No. of bilayers (n)	Designed individual thickness (Å)		Obtained individual thickness (Å)		The obtained samples
				Au	Co	Au	Co	
1	$Au_{75}Co_{25}$	388	4	77	20	82	15	$Au_{79}Co_{21}$
2	$Au_{66}Co_{34}$	395	5	59	20	63	16	$Au_{72}Co_{28}$
3	$Au_{50}Co_{50}$	414	6	42	27	45	24	$Au_{56}Co_{44}$
4	$Au_{34}Co_{66}$	426	6	31	40	37	34	$Au_{42}Co_{58}$
5	$Au_{25}Co_{75}$	419	6	24	46	24	46	$Au_{25}Co_{75}$

constants of the resultant Au–Co crystalline phases were determined by the corresponding SAD patterns and their errors were around 5%.

3. Results and discussion

3.1. Gibbs free energy diagram to predict the nonequilibrium solid phases

A calculated Gibbs free energy diagram of the Au–Co system, shown in Fig. 2, includes the free energy curves of all the alloy phases in question as well as of the Au–Co multilayered films. From Fig. 2, one can see that the shape of the free energy curve of the amorphous phase is convex, as is usual for those observed in positive ΔH_f systems, and that the interfacial free energies (the straight lines) for the Au–Co multilayered films with 8, 10 and 12 layers, respectively are higher than those of both solid solution and amorphous phases. Moreover, one can see from the diagram that the free energy of the amorphous phase in the composition range of 22–83 at.% of Co is apparently lower than those of the corresponding solid solutions, and this composition range can therefore be considered as the maximum glass-formation range of the Au–Co system. In

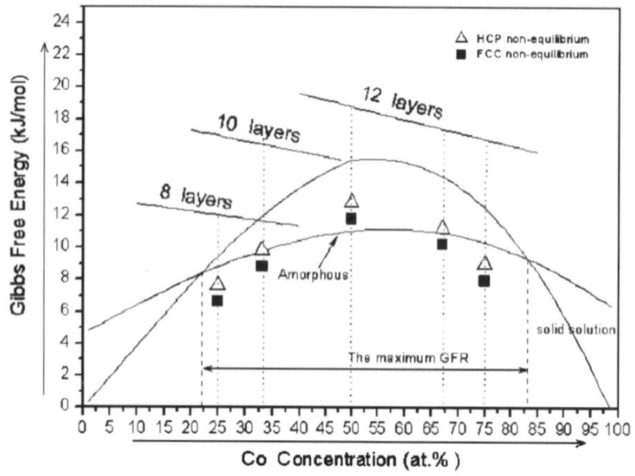

Fig. 2. A calculated Gibbs free energy diagram of the Au–Co system as a function of the atomic concentration. The straight lines stand for the interfacial energies of 8, 10 and 12 layers, respectively. The filled rectangles and open triangles stand for the fcc and hcp nonequilibrium phases respectively.

Fig. 2, the triangles and the filled squares represent the ordered hcp and fcc nonequilibrium phases with alloy compositions of Au_3Co, Au_2Co, AuCo, $AuCo_2$ and $AuCo_3$, respectively. In Fig. 2, the ordered phases have lower free energies than the solid solution and amorphous phases at compositions $AuCo_3$, Au_2Co, $AuCo_2$ and Au_3Co, respectively. While at the composition AuCo, the free energies of the ordered phases are lower than that of the solid solution but higher than that of the amorphous phase. In addition, the fcc ordered nonequilibrium phases have lower minimum values of free energy than the hcp phases, indicating that the formation of the fcc nonequilibrium phases are more energetically favored than the hcp ones.

3.2. Molecular dynamics simulations to predict the metallic glass-forming range

The metallic glass-forming range (GFR) of a binary metal system is of great importance for the determination of the glass-forming ability of the system. It is known as the composition range and is bounded by the two terminal critical values of solid solubility, below which the solid solution would retain its crystalline state, while beyond which the solid solution would transform into a disordered/amorphous state [16].

We first present the simulation results for the fcc Au-rich solid solution models. Fig. 3 shows the projections of the atomic positions for the $Co_{10}Au_{90}$, $Co_{17}Au_{83}$, $Co_{18}Au_{82}$ and $Co_{30}Au_{70}$ solid solution models after annealing at 300 K for 2 ns. It can clearly be seen from Fig. 3 that the ordered or crystalline states still remain in the $Co_{10}Au_{90}$ and $Co_{17}Au_{83}$ solid solution models, and that the uniform disordered structures have been formed in the $Co_{30}Au_{70}$ and $Co_{18}Au_{82}$ solid solution models. These results suggest that a crystal-to-amorphous phase transition has taken place at a critical composition around 18 at.% Co. To have firm evidence, the total and partial pair-correlation functions $g(r)$ for fcc Au-based solid solutions were calculated and are shown in Fig. 4. In Fig. 4, as the $g(r)$ curve of $Co_{17}Au_{83}$ shows a little more apparent sharp peak than that of $Co_{17}Au_{83}$, even at a large value of r, the $Co_{17}Au_{83}$ solid solution is considered to be still in its crystalline structure. However, for the $Co_{18}Au_{82}$ and $Co_{30}Au_{70}$ simulation models, the $g(r)$ curves become more or less smooth and the peaks, except for the first one, even disappear, indicating that a crystal-to-amorphous transition has taken place, when the Co concentration equals or exceeds 18 at.% in the Au-rich solid solutions.

Similarly, for the hcp Co-rich solid solution models, the critical solid solubility of Au in Co was determined to be 12 at.% Au (88 at.% Co). Fig. 5 shows the corresponding $g(r)$ curves for the $Co_{90}Au_{10}$, $Co_{89}Au_{11}$, $Co_{88}Au_{12}$ and $Co_{80}Au_{20}$ solid solution models after annealing at 300 K for 2 ns. Apparently, the $g(r)$ curves feature a crystalline structure when the Au concentration is lower than 12 at.% Au, whereas the $g(r)$ curves are typically of amorphous structures when the Au concentration exceeds 12 at.% Au.

Summarizing the detailed MD simulations, the GFR of the Au–Co system is determined to be 18–88 at.% Co (or 12–82 at.% Au), which is compatible with the 22–83 at.% Co predicted by thermodynamic calculations. In general, the GFR determined from MD simulations is considered to more precise than that from thermodynamic calculations. Moreover, the GFR is an intrinsic character of a binary metal system, as it is determined directly from the interatomic potential of the system.

3.3. First principles calculations to predict the nonequilibrium solid phases

The prediction of the possible nonequilibrium crystalline phases was performed with the first principles calculations for the correlations between the total energy and the average atomic volume of the phases. Fig. 6(a) shows the calculated correlation between the total energy and the average atomic volume for the possible nonequilibrium $Au_{75}Co_{25}$ phases. One can see that the total energies of the nonequilibrium $Au_{75}Co_{25}$ phases with $D0_{19}$ (hcp) and $L1_2$ (fcc) structures are lower than those of other structures, indicating that the $D0_{19}$ and $L1_2$ structures are relatively more stable than others. Similar calculations for the possible nonequilibrium $Au_{50}Co_{50}$ phases and $Au_{25}Co_{75}$ phases are, respectively, shown in Fig. 6(b) and (c). From Fig. 6(c), one sees clearly that the B_h (hexagonal-type) structure is the relatively stable structure for the $Au_{50}Co_{50}$ phase, and that the $L1_2$ and $D0_{19}$ structures are the relatively stable structures for the $Au_{25}Co_{75}$ phases. Table 3 lists the calculated lattice constants and cohesive energies of the possible nonequilibrium $Au_{75}Co_{25}$, $Au_{50}Co_{50}$ and $Au_{25}Co_{75}$ phases. From Table 3, the difference in cohesive energy between the $L1_2$ structure and $D0_{19}$ structure for the $Au_{75}Co_{25}$ as well as

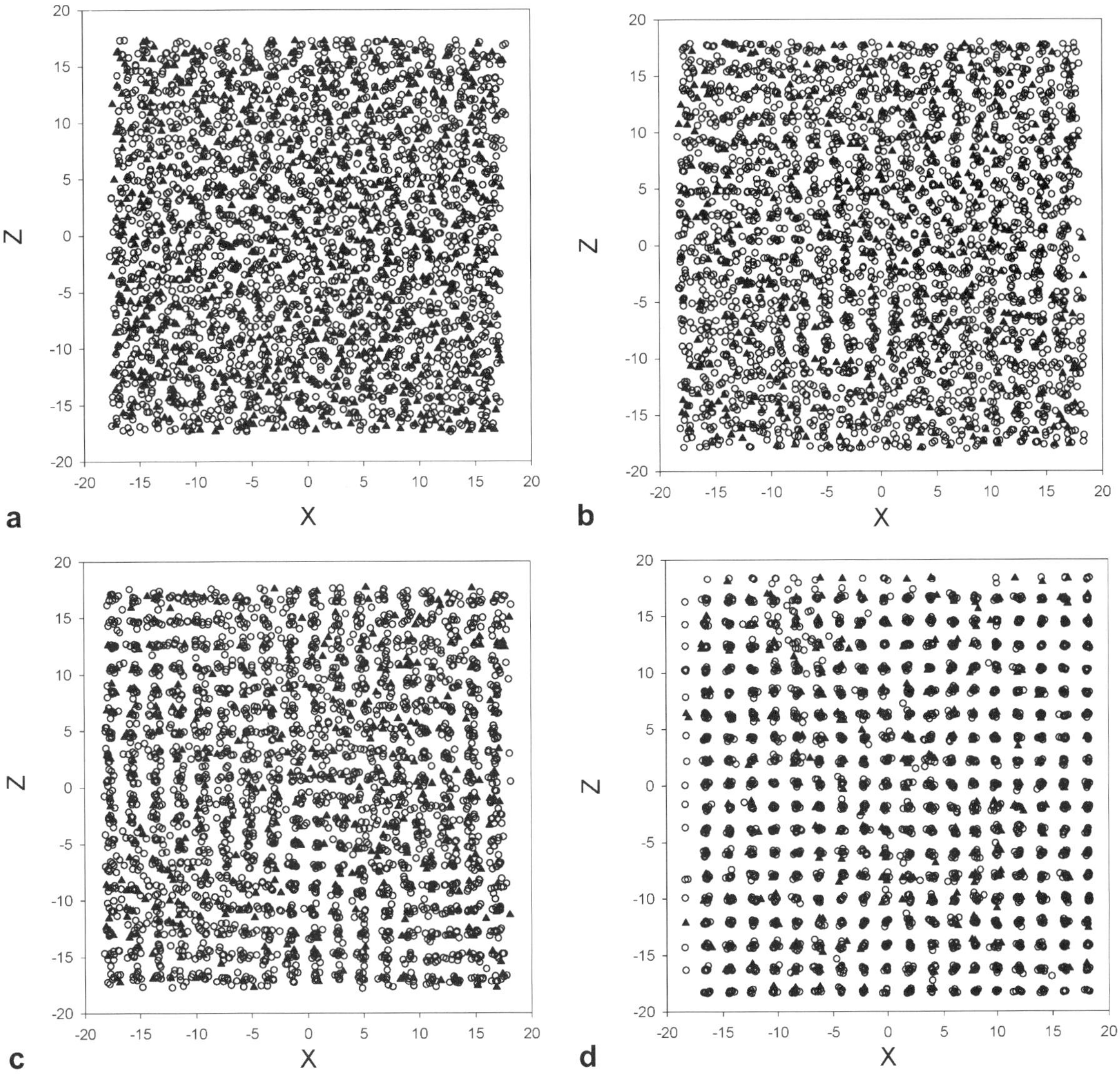

Fig. 3. The projections of atomic positions of: (a) $Co_{30}Au_{70}$, (b) $Co_{18}Au_{82}$, (c) $Co_{17}Au_{83}$ and (d) $Co_{10}Au_{90}$ solid solutions, respectively, after annealing at 300 K for 2 ns. Open circles: Au. Filled triangles: Co.

for the $Au_{25}Co_{75}$ phases is no more than 0.5%, suggesting that the formation of both the fcc and the hcp configurations are energetically favored.

3.4. Formation of nonequilibrium solid phases upon ion-beam manipulation

IBM in the five Au–Co multilayered samples with various overall compositions was carried out at 77 K (the sample holders were cooled with liquid nitrogen during ion irradiation) with 200 keV Xe ions. The observed structural phase transitions under various irradiation doses are listed in Table 4.

In the Au-rich region, i.e. in both $Au_{79}Co_{21}$ and $Au_{72}Co_{28}$ samples, at an irradiation dose of 5×10^{14} Xe^+/cm^2, a unique nonequilibrium fcc crystalline phase (marked as fcc-I in Table 4) was formed and remained unchanged upon further irradiation to a dose of 9×10^{15} Xe^+/cm^2. The composition of the formed fcc crystalline phase is around 72–79 at.%. The observed structural phase transition can be summarized as,

$$Au_{79}Co_{21}/Au_{72}Co_{28} \xrightarrow{5\times10^{14}Xe^+/cm^2} \text{fcc-I(Au-rich)}.$$

For the formed fcc-I phase in the $Au_{79}Co_{21}$ sample at the irradiation dose of 9×10^{14} Xe^+/cm^2 shown in Fig. 7(a), the lattice constant is determined to be 3.97 Å, which is compatible with the value of $a = 4.06$ Å for the $L1_2$ $Au_{75}Co_{25}$ phase predicted by the ab initio calculations. Recalling the above discussion, the ab initio calculations

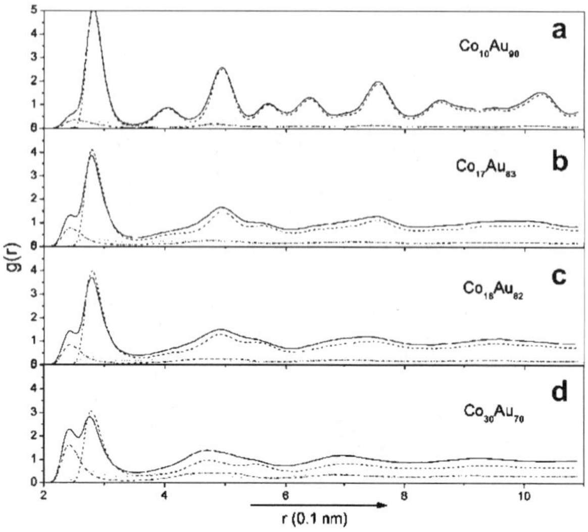

Fig. 4. The total and partial pair correlation functions of the fcc (a) $Co_{10}Au_{90}$, (b) $Co_{17}Au_{83}$, (c) $Co_{18}Au_{82}$ and (d) $Co_{30}Au_{70}$ solid solution models upon annealing at 300 K for 2 ns. The solid line is for the total $g(r)$, the dashed line is for the Au–Au partial $g(r)$, the dotted line is for the Co–Co partial $g(r)$, and the dash-dotted line is for the Au–Co partial $g(r)$.

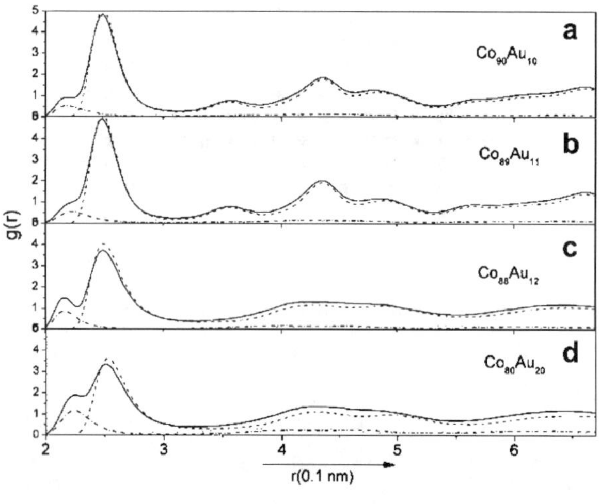

Fig. 5. The total and partial pair correlation functions of the hcp (a) $Co_{90}Au_{10}$, (b) $Co_{89}Au_{11}$, (c) $Co_{88}Au_{12}$ nd (d) $Co_{80}Au_{20}$ solid solution models upon annealing at 300 K for 2 ns. The solid line is for the total $g(r)$, the dashed line is for the Co–Co partial $g(r)$, the dotted line is for the Au–Au partial $g(r)$, and the dash-dotted line is for the Au–Co partial $g(r)$.

showed that both the $L1_2$ and $D0_{19}$ structures of the $Au_{75}Co_{25}$ alloys were energetically stable. In IBM experiments, the fcc-I phase with a similar composition ($Au_{79}Co_{21}/Au_{72}Co_{28}$) was indeed obtained, suggesting that formation of the $L1_2$ structure was favored, in agreement with the predictions of the ab initio calculations.

In the Co-rich region, in the $Au_{25}Co_{75}$ sample, a mixture of two crystalline phases was observed at an irradiation dose of 5×10^{14} Xe^+/cm^2, and remained unchanged even when the irradiation dose was increased to 9×10^{15} Xe^+/cm^2. The two crystalline phases can be observed from the SAD patterns shown in Fig. 7(b) and were identified to be both of fcc structures with distinctly different lattice constants of 3.97 and 3.68 Å, respectively. Note that one fcc phase has the same lattice constant (i.e. $a = 3.97$ Å) with the fcc-I phase observed in both $Au_{72}Co_{28}$ and $Au_{79}Co_{21}$ samples, suggesting that this fcc phase can be considered as the fcc-I phase. From the SAD pattern shown in Fig. 7(b), the lattice constant of the other fcc phase (denoted as fcc-II in Table 4) was determined to be 3.68 Å, which is very close to the value of $a = 3.71$ Å predicted by the ab initio calculations for the possible $L1_2$ $Au_{25}Co_{75}$ phase. In other words, the formation of the fcc-II phase was quite compatible with the prediction of the ab initio calculation. In summary, the structural phase transition in the $Au_{25}Co_{75}$ sample can be expressed by:

$$Au_{25}Co_{75}\xrightarrow{5\times10^{14}Xe^+/cm^2}\text{fcc-I(Au-rich)}+\text{fcc-II(Co-rich)}.$$

In the mid-composition region, the structural phase transition was relatively complicated. In the $Au_{56}Co_{44}$ sample, within an irradiation dose range of 5×10^{14} Xe^+/cm^2 to 1×10^{15} Xe^+/cm^2, a mixture of two nonequilibrium fcc phases and one hcp nonequilibrium phase was observed. Fig. 8(a) shows the SAD patterns taken for the mixture of the fcc-I, fcc-II and hcp-MX phases. The two nonequilibrium fcc phases were identified to have lattice constants of $a = 3.97$ Å and $a = 3.68$ Å, corresponding to the fcc-I phase and fcc-II phase, respectively, or the $L1_2$ $Au_{75}Co_{25}$ phase and the $L1_2$ $Au_{25}Co_{75}$ phase, respectively, while the hcp nonequilibrium phase (denoted as the hcp-MX phase in Table 4) was identified to have lattice constants of $a = 2.80$ Å and $c/a = 1.64$, which are very close to those values, i.e., $a = 2.85$ and $c/a = 1.64$, predicted from the ab initio calculations for the possible $D0_{19}$ $Au_{75}Co_{25}$ phase. When the irradiation dose was increased up to 4×10^{15} Xe^+/cm^2, the above-mentioned mixture turned into a uniform fcc structure (denoted as fcc** in Table 4) and remained unchanged upon further irradiation. Fig. 8(b) shows a SAD pattern taken for the fcc** phase. The fcc** phase was identified to have a lattice constant of $a = 3.92$ Å, which is a little smaller than that of the fcc-I phase, suggesting again that near the composition of $Au_{56}Co_{44}$, the fcc structured nonequilibrium phase was the most stable state due to its lowest free energy. The observed structural phase transition can be expressed by:

$$Au_{56}Co_{44}\xrightarrow{5\times10^{14}-1\times10^{15}Xe^+/cm^2}\text{fcc-I}+\text{fcc-II}+\text{hcp MX}\xrightarrow{4\times10^{15}Xe^+/cm^2}\text{fcc}^{**}$$

In the $Au_{42}Co_{58}$ sample, a mixture of an amorphous phase and an fcc phase was formed at an irradiation dose of 5×10^{14} Xe^+/cm^2. The fcc phase was identified to have a lattice constant of 3.96 Å, inferring fcc-I phase (where $a = 3.97$ Å). When the irradiation dose was increased to 9×10^{14} Xe^+/cm^2, a uniform amorphous phase was

Table 3
The calculated lattice constants (a and c/a), atomic volume V, and cohesive energy E_{min} of the (a) $Au_{75}Co_{25}$, (b) $Au_{50}Co_{50}$, and (c) $Au_{25}Co_{75}$ phases in the possible simple structures, respectively

	$D0_{19}$	A15	$L1_2$	$D0_9$	$L6_0$
(a) $Au_{75}Co_{25}$					
a (Å)	2.85	5.20	4.06	5.03	4.23
c/a	1.640				0.916
V (Å^3/atom)	18.890	17.576	16.731	31.727	17.377
E_{min} (eV/atom)	−3.9278*	−3.8026	−3.9126*	−2.9771	−3.8985
	B1	B2	B3	B_h	
(b) $Au_{50}Co_{50}$					
a (Å)	5.14	3.09	5.60	3.06	
c/a				1.259	
V (Å^3/atom)	16.975	14.752	21.952	17.973	
E_{min}(eV/atom)	−4.3965	−1.2022	−4.0112	−4.6249*	
	$D0_{19}$	A15	$L1_2$	$D0_9$	$L6_0$
(c) $Au_{25}Co_{75}$					
a (Å)	2.65	4.71	3.71	4.67	3.85
c/a	1.593				0.915
V (Å^3/atom)	14.760	13.061	12.766	25.424	13.056
E_{min}(eV/atom)	−5.9189*	−5.7787	−5.8799*	−4.1811	−5.8370

Note: The values with asterisks are for the structures with lowest cohesive energies.

Table 4
Structural phase transitions induced in the Au–Co multilayered films by 200 keV Xe ion irradiation at 77 K

Dosage (Xe$^+$/cm^2)	$Au_{79}Co_{21}$	$Au_{72}Co_{28}$	$Au_{56}Co_{44}$	$Au_{42}Co_{58}$	$Au_{25}Co_{75}$
5×10^{14}	fcc-I	fcc-I	fcc-I + fcc-II +hcp-MX	fcc-I + amorphous	fcc-I + fcc-II
9×10^{14}	fcc-I	fcc-I	fcc-I + fcc-II + hcp-MX	A#amorphous	fcc-I + fcc-II
1×10^{15}	fcc-I	fcc-I	fcc-I + fcc-II + hcp-MX	fcc*	fcc-I + fcc-II
4×10^{15}	fcc-I	fcc-I	fcc**	fcc*	fcc-I + fcc-II
7×10^{15}	fcc-I	fcc-I	fcc**	fcc*	fcc-I + fcc-II
9×10^{15}	fcc-I	fcc-I	fcc**	fcc*	fcc-I + fcc-II

fcc-I represents an Au-rich, nonequilibrium crystalline phase; fcc-II is a Co-rich, nonequilibrium crystalline phase; fcc* and fcc** represent the fcc nonequilibrium crystalline phase with smaller lattice constants. Amorphous represents an amorphous phase, and hcp-MX indicates the nonequilibrium hcp phase, respectively.

obtained which turned into a unique fcc structured phase (denoted fcc* phase in Table 4) upon additional irradiation to a dose of 1×10^{14} Xe$^+$/cm^2, i.e., after a total dose of 1×10^{15} Xe$^+$/cm^2. Fig. 9 shows the SAD patterns for the $Au_{42}Co_{58}$samples in as-deposited state and at various irradiation doses of 5×10^{14}, 9×10^{14} and 1×10^{15} Xe$^+$/cm^2. From the SAD patterns, the fcc* phase was determined to have a lattice constant of $a=3.90$ Å, which is slightly smaller than $a=3.97$ Å of the fcc-I phase. In short, the structural phase transition in the $Au_{42}Co_{58}$ sample can be expressed by:

$$Au_{42}Co_{58}\xrightarrow{5\times10^{14}Xe^+/cm^2}\text{fcc-I}+\text{Part Amorphous}$$
$$\xrightarrow{9\times10^{14}Xe^+/cm^2}\text{Amorphous}$$
$$\xrightarrow{1\times10^{15}Xe^+/cm^2}\text{fcc}^*.$$

The formation of the $Au_{42}Co_{58}$ amorphous phase confirmed that amorphous phase could be obtainable in the immiscible Au–Co system and the composition is indeed located within the predicted GFR by MD simulations as well as by thermodynamic calculation. Coincidently, Tsaur et al. have also reported [43] that an amorphous phase was formed by ion-beam mixing near the composition of $Au_{25}Co_{75}$, which was also located in the GFR determined by the present calculation. From a physical point of view, as the GFR of a system is directly calculated from the interatomic potential, which describes the atomic interactions, and thus also governs the energetic states of both solid solutions and the competing disordered states, the GFR determined is therefore an intrinsic property of the system. In comparison, the experimentally measured GFR was related to what specific nonequilibrium processing technique applied in practice and is, in general, frequently narrower than the intrinsic one. In the present case of the immiscible Au–Co system, two amorphous phases have been obtained with alloy compositions of $Au_{42}Co_{58}$ and $Au_{25}Co_{75}$, respectively, which are both located within the theoretically determined GFR, providing some support for the relevance of the derived n-body Au–Co potential as well as the corresponding MD simulations.

In addition, the observed fcc* and fcc** phases could be considered as supersaturated solid solutions, which were formed upon high-dose irradiation. Incidentally, the

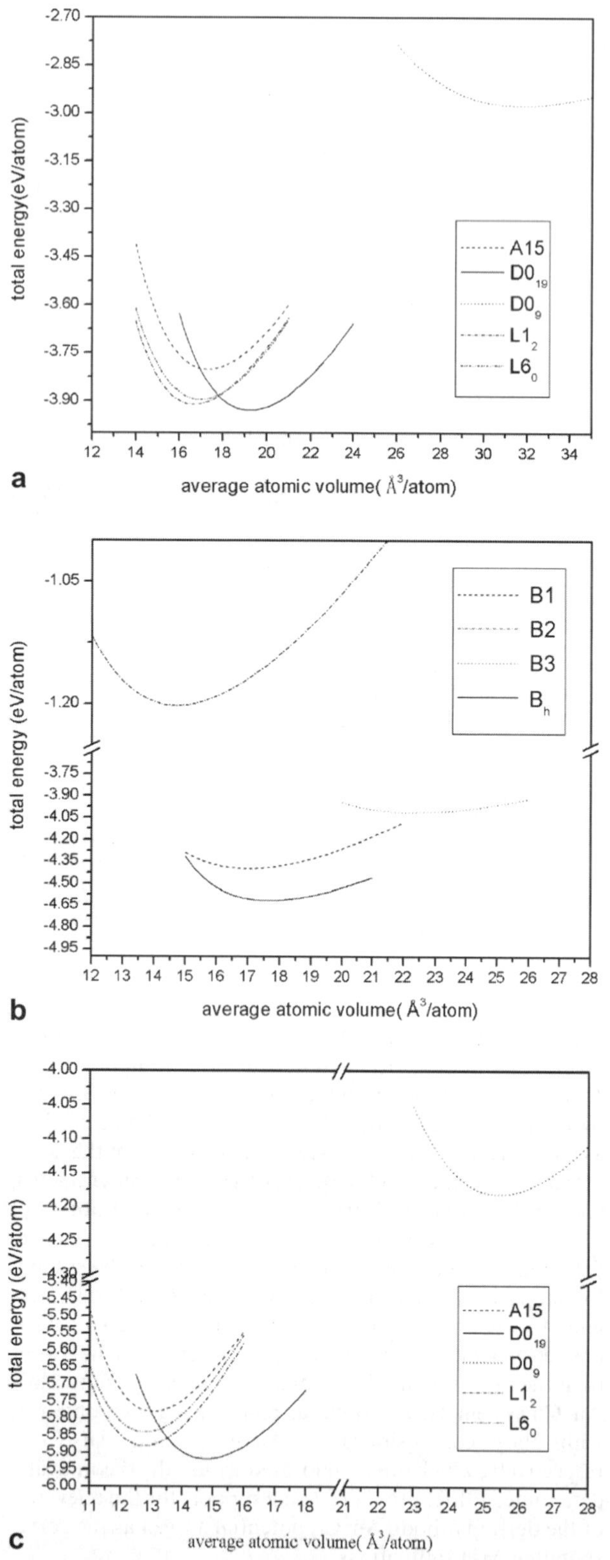

Fig. 6. The calculated total energy vs. the lattice constant for: (a) $Au_{75}Co_{25}$, (b) $Au_{50}Co_{50}$ and (c) $Au_{25}Co_{75}$ nonequilibrium phases with different structures.

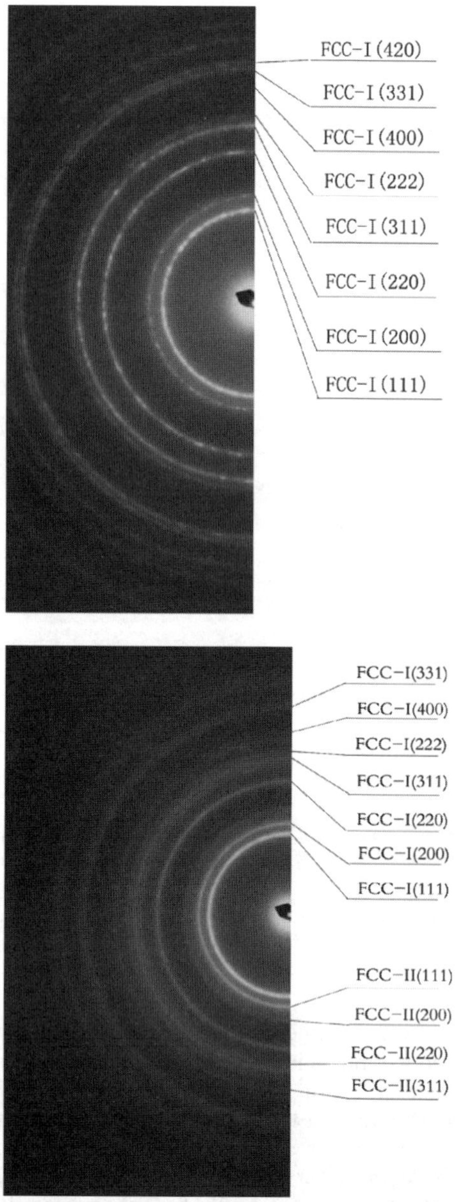

Fig. 7. Selected area diffraction (SAD) patterns of (a) the $Au_{79}Co_{21}$ multilayered films after irradiation to a dose of 9×10^{14} Xe^{+}/cm^{2} and (b) the $Au_{25}Co_{75}$ multilayered films after irradiation to a dose of 5×10^{14} Xe^{+}/cm^{2}.

formation of the supersaturated solid solutions has never been reported by aging Au–Co alloy films with Co concentrations greater than 38 at.% [44], which is consistent with the present IBM experiment. Recalling the calculated Gibbs free energy diagram in Fig. 2, the cohesive energies of both fcc* and fcc** solid solutions were higher than the corresponding amorphous phases, which explains why they were formed from the previously obtained amorphous phase upon further irradiation. Incidentally, such a structural transition sequence has also been observed by Tsaur et al.

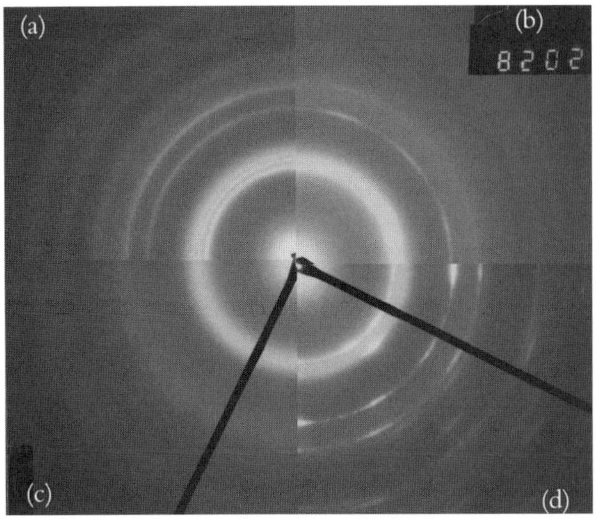

Fig. 8. Selected area diffraction (SAD) patterns for the $Au_{42}Co_{58}$ multilayered films (a) in the as-deposited state, (b) at the irradiation stage of 5×10^{14} Xe^{+}/cm^{2}, (c) at the irradiation stage of 9×10^{14} Xe^{+}/cm^{2} and (d) at the irradiation stage of 1×10^{15} Xe^{+}/cm^{2}, respectively.

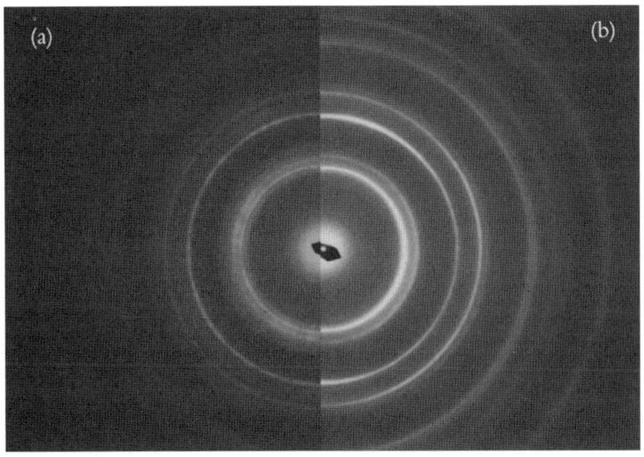

Fig. 9. Selected area diffraction (SAD) patterns for the $Au_{56}Co_{44}$ multilayered films after irradiation to the doses of (a) 9×10^{14} Xe^{+}/cm^{2} and (b) 4×10^{15} Xe^{+}/cm^{2}, respectively.

in their early study of the Au–Co system in which low-dose irradiation resulted in an amorphous phase, which turned into solid solution upon high-dose irradiation [43].

4. Concluding remarks

(1) Based on a realistic *n*-body Au–Co potential, MD simulations predict that the composition range favoring metallic glass formation is 18-88 at.% Co, which is the intrinsic GFR of the Au–Co system.
(2) The ab initio calculations predict that the nonequilibrium crystalline phases at $Co_{75}Au_{25}$ and $Co_{25}Au_{75}$ prefer to be in $L1_2$ (fcc) or $D0_{19}$ (hcp) structures.
(3) In IBM experiments, the $Au_{42}Co_{58}$ amorphous phase and some nonequilibrium crystalline phases of fcc-type or hcp-type structures were indeed obtained. The formation of the nonequilibrium phases and the related lattice parameters are, in general, in good agreement or compatible with the theoretical prediction/calculation.

Acknowledgements

The authors are grateful for the financial support from the National Natural Science Foundation of China, The Ministry of Science and Technology of China as well as from the Administration of Tsinghua University.

References

[1] Yavari AR, Desré PJ, Benameur T. Phys Rev Lett 1992;68:2235.
[2] Eckert J, Holzer JC, Krill CE, Johnson WL. J Appl Phys 1993;73:2794.
[3] Uenishi K, Kobayashi KF, Nasu S, Hatano H, Ishihara KN, Shingu PH. Z Metallkd 1992;83:132.
[4] Liu BX, Johnson WL, Nicolet MA, Lau SS. Appl Phys Lett 1983;42:45.
[5] Liu BX, Jin O. Phys State Sol A 1997;161:3.
[6] Chien CL, Liou SH, Kofalt D, Yu W, Egami T, McGuire TR. Phys Rev B 1986;33:3247.
[7] Liu BX, Pan F. Phys Rev B 1993;48:10276.
[8] Krebs HU. Int J Non-Equilibr Process (UK) 1997;10:3.
[9] Sumiyama K, Yoshitake Y, Nakamura Y. Acta Mater 1985;33:1785.
[10] Kneller EF. J Appl Phys 1964;35:2210.
[11] Ma E, Atzmon M, Pinkerton FE. J Appl Phys 1993;74:955.
[12] Crespo P, Hernando A, Garcia Escorial A. Phys Rev B 1994;49:13227.
[13] Thompson MW. In: Defects and radiation damage in metals. Cambridge: Cambridge University Press; 1969 [chapters 4 and 5].
[14] Bolse W. Mater Sci Eng A 1998;253:194.
[15] Wei LC, Averback RS. J Appl Phys 1997;81:2.
[16] Liu BX, Lai WS, Zhang Q. Mater Sci Eng R 2000;29:1.
[17] Li ZC, Yu DP, Liu BX. Phys Rev B 2002;65:245403.
[18] Li ZF, Zhang Q, Yu DP, Liu BX. Appl Phys Lett 1999;74:3305.
[19] De Boer FR, Boom R, Mattens MWC, Miedema AR, Niessen AK. In: Cohesion in metals: transition metal alloys. Amsterdam: North-Holland; 1989.
[20] Zhang RF, Liu BX. J Mater Res 2003;18:7.
[21] Alonso JA, Gallego LJ, Simozar JA. Nuovo Cimento 1990;12:587.
[22] Enrique RA, Nordlund K, Averback RS, Bellon P. J Appl Phys 2003;93:5.
[23] Zhang Q, Lai WS, Liu BX. Phys Rev B 1998;58:14020.
[24] Gong HR, Kong LT, Lai WS, Liu BX. Phys Rev B 2002;66:104204.
[25] Liu JB, Li ZC, Liu BX, Kresse G, Hafner J. Phys Rev B 2001;63:132204.
[26] Liu JB, Li ZF, Zhang JX, Liu BX, Kresse G, Hafner J. Phys Rev B 2001;64:054102.
[27] Gerkema J, Miedema AR. Surf Sci 1981;124:351.
[28] Zhang RF, Liu BX. Appl Phys Lett 2002;81:1219.
[29] Weeber AW. J Phys F 1987;17:809.
[30] Niessen AK, Miedema AR, de Boer FR, Boom R. Physica B 1988;151:401.
[31] Ducastelle F. In: Meyer M, Pontikis V, editors. Computer simulation in materials science. NATO ASI Series, Ser. E, Applied Physics, vol. 205. Dordrecht: Kluwer; 1991.
[32] Chadi DJ. Phys Rev B 1979;19:2074.
[33] Cleri F, Rosato V. Phys Rev B 1993;48:22.

[34] Guo HB, Liu BX. Phys Rev B 2004;70:19.
[35] Parrinello M, Rahman A. J Appl Phys 1981;52:7182.
[36] Waseda Y. In: The structure of non-crystalline materials: liquid and amorphous solids. New York (NY): McGraw-Hill; 1980.
[37] Kresse G, Hafner J. Phys Rev B 1993;47:558.
[38] Vanderbilt D. Phys Rev B 1990;41:7892.
[39] Perdew JP, Wang Y. Phys Rev B 1992;45:13244.
[40] Monkhorst HJ, Pack JD. Phys Rev B 1976;13:5188.
[41] Ziegler JF, Biersack JP, Littmark U. In: The stopping and range of ions in solids. New York (NY): Pergamon Press; 1985.
[42] Mayer M. SIMNRA User's Guide, Report IPP 9/113, Max-Planck-Institute fur Plasmaphysik, Garching, Germany, 1997.
[43] Tsaur BY, Lau SS, Mayer JW. Philos Mag B 1981;44:95.
[44] Hubin M, Garrault C, Monraye B. Thin Solid Films 1979;58: 353.

Atomistic mechanism of interfacial reaction and asymmetric growth kinetics in an immiscible Cu-Ru system at equilibrium

Xiang He, Su-Hui Liang, Jia-Hao Li, and Bai-Xin Liu*
Advanced Materials Laboratory, Department of Materials Science and Engineering, Tsinghua University, Beijing 100084, China
(Received 11 July 2006; revised manuscript received 18 October 2006; published 26 January 2007)

An n-body potential is first constructed for the immiscible Cu-Ru system at equilibrium with the aid of *ab initio* calculations for obtaining some physical properties necessary to fit the Cu-Ru cross-potential. Molecular dynamics simulations are then performed to pursue atomistic modeling of interfacial reaction between the Cu-Ru metal layers. Using the solid solution model, simulations reveal that the Cu-based and the Ru-based solid solutions collapse at their respective critical solid solubilities, i.e., 10 at. % of Ru and 20 at. % of Cu, thus determining an intrinsic glass-forming range of the system to be within 10–80 at. % Ru, which matches well with the observations in ion-beam mixing experiments. Using the Cu-Ru sandwich model, simulations clarify that the interfacial free energy is the major driving force for interfacial reaction, resulting in spontaneous solid-state amorphization and that when the interfacial free energy is completely consumed, the reaction terminates, thus determining a maximum amorphous interlayer to be 2.91 nm, which is in good agreement with that predicted from a recently proposed thermodynamic and kinetic model. Kinetically, simulations further reveal that the growth of the amorphous interlayer features an asymmetric behavior, i.e., the growth advances faster toward the Cu lattice than toward the Ru side, because the critical solid solubility of Ru in Cu (10 at. %) is smaller than that of Cu in Ru (20 at. %).

DOI: 10.1103/PhysRevB.75.045431　　PACS number(s): 68.55.−a, 05.70.Np, 31.15.Qg

I. INTRODUCTION

Copper has attracted much attention during past decades in the integrated circuits industry, as Cu has been used as an interconnection metal to replace aluminum in microelectronic circuits due to its favorable electrical conductivity and superior resistance to electromigration.[1] To prevent catastrophic contamination caused by Cu diffusing through interlayer dielectrics into silicon, diffusion barriers, such as tantalum and tantalum nitride (Ta/TaN), are currently used to protect the Cu interconnects.[2,3] As the trend of miniaturization continues in microelectronic fabrication, the current Ta/TaN diffusion barrier for Cu interconnects will encounter scaling difficulties at the 45 nm node. To maintain a low effective interconnect resistivity, an ultrathin diffusion barrier (about 5 nm) is needed to scale the next-generation integrated circuit technology for the 45 nm node.[4]

Ruthenium is an air-stable transition metal with a high melting point (2583 K) and is nearly twice as thermally and electrically conductive (7.6 $\mu\Omega$ cm) as Ta. More importantly, the Cu-Ru system is an essentially immiscible one characterized with a positive heat of formation (ΔH_f) of +10.44 kJ/mol calculated by Miedema's model.[5] Recently, there has been an increasing interest to utilize Ru as a Cu-plateable diffusion barrier.[6–8] Some researchers showed that the inherently favorable interfacial bonding manifested in the strong adhesion between the electroplated Cu and Ru substrate, even when annealing to over 870 K.[9] Obviously, the advent of solid-state amorphization would definitely degrade the performances of the electronic devices. Under such circumstances, theoretical modeling concerning the interfacial reaction between Cu and Ru is therefore of importance. On the other hand, the formation of any Cu-Ru metastable phase could bring about some effects to degrade the performance of Ru as a diffusion barrier, as well as of Cu as an interconnection in the electronic devices. It is therefore of both practical and theoretical importance to have a thorough investigation of the Cu-Ru system concerning the metastable phase formation, the interfacial stability, and the associated underlying physics for a deep understanding.

In synthesizing new nonequilibrium alloys, ion beam mixing (IBM) of multiple metal layers was introduced in early 1980s, and due to its very powerful capability, IBM has so far produced a variety of nonequilibrium alloys in numerous binary metal systems. Recently, IBM has been focused on studying the binary metal systems characterized by large positive ΔH_f, and the systems are essentially immiscible at equilibrium. To increase the interfacial free energy stored in the multilayered samples, the individual layer thickness was intentionally designed to be a couple of nanometers, differing considerably from the typical thickness of 5–8 nm in the previously conducted IBM. Accordingly, the interfacial free energy played an important role in elevating the initial multilayered films to an energetic level higher than those of the possible metastable states existing in the system of interest.[10]

In the present study, thermodynamic calculation is conducted, based on Miedema's model, to give macroscopic insight concerning the formation of the metastable phases by comparing the relative energetic levels of the competing phases in question. In atomistic modeling, with an aid of *ab initio* calculations for acquiring some physical data, a tight-binding potential of the Cu-Ru system is constructed and applied in molecular dynamic (MD) simulations to determine the glass-formation ability/range (GFA/GFR) of the system and to reveal the atomistic mechanism of interface stability and SSA of the Cu-Ru system. A brief discussion follows to compare the results of the theoretical modeling with the experimental observations.

Physical Review B 75 (4), 045431(2007).

II. CALCULATION METHODS AND EXPERIMENTAL PROCEDURE

A. Thermodynamic calculation

Generally, the Gibbs free energy of an alloy phase can be calculated by $\Delta G=\Delta H-T\cdot\Delta S$, where ΔH and ΔS are the enthalpy and entropy terms, respectively. As a first approximation, the entropy term for a concentrated solid solution (CSS) and amorphous phase is simply taken as that of an ideal solution, i.e., $\Delta S=-R[c_A\ln c_A+c_B\ln c_B]$, where R is the gas constant and c_A and c_B are the atomic concentrations of metals A and B, respectively.

According to Miedema's model and Alonso's method,[5,11–13] the enthalpy change ΔH is the sum of three terms, namely, $\Delta H=\Delta H^c+\Delta H^e+\Delta H^s$, corresponding to the chemical, elastic, and structural contributions, respectively. The chemical term ΔH^c is closely related to the electron redistribution generated at the boundary for the Wigner–Seitz unit cell when alloying, and can be calculated by

$$\Delta H^c = c_A c_B[c_B \Delta \bar{H}^{\text{inter}}_{AinB} + c_A \Delta \bar{H}^{\text{inter}}_{BinA}], \tag{1}$$

where $\Delta \bar{H}^{\text{inter}}_{AinB}$ and $\Delta \bar{H}^{\text{inter}}_{BinA}$ are the solution enthalpies of A solved in B and that of B solved in A, respectively, and all these values have been compiled by de Boer *et al.*[5] and Bakker.[11]

The elastic term ΔH^e for a CSS is caused by the atomic size mismatch of the two constituent metals and can be expressed by taking the weighted average of the mismatch energies[5,11]

$$\Delta H^e = c_A c_B[c_B \Delta \bar{H}^{elastic}_{AinB} + c_A \Delta \bar{H}^{elastic}_{BinA}] \tag{2}$$

where $\Delta \bar{H}^{elastic}_{AinB}$ and $\Delta \bar{H}^{elastic}_{BinA}$ are the partial elastic mismatch energies for A solved in B and B solved in A, respectively, and all these values can be found in some published books and/or comprehensive papers.[5,11]

The structure term ΔH^s is deduced from the lattice stability $E(Z)$ of the bcc, fcc, and hcp structures as a function of the number of valence electrons Z of the metal,[5,11]

$$\Delta H^s = E(Z) - c_A E(Z_B) - c_B E(Z_A), \tag{3}$$

where $E(Z)$, $E(Z_A)$, and $E(Z_B)$ are the lattice stability of the CSS and pure metals A and B, and Z, Z_A, and Z_B are the mean numbers of valence electrons of the CSS and the numbers of valence electrons of pure metals A and B, respectively.[5,11]

Comparing with the CSS, the structural and elastic terms for the formation enthalpy of an amorphous alloy are absent or significantly reduced, i.e., $\Delta H^e\approx 0$ and $\Delta H^s\approx 0$.[5,11] There is, however, apart from the chemical term, another term contributing to the formation enthalpy of the amorphous alloy that reflects the relative disordering and therefore the formation enthalpy of the amorphous alloy can be expressed by[5,11]

$$\Delta H^{amorphous} = \Delta H^c + \Delta H^{topological}, \tag{4}$$

where the topological enthalpy $\Delta H^{topological}$ accounts for the difference between the crystalline and amorphous states, which can be calculated by [5,11]

$$\Delta H^{topological} = 3.5(c_A T_{m,A} + c_B T_{m,B}), \tag{5}$$

where $T_{m,A}$ and $T_{m,B}$ are the melting temperatures of the metals A and B, respectively. Meanwhile, the chemical term of the amorphous alloy ΔH^c can be assumed to be equal to that of the CSS.

For a system with metals A and B, the Gibbs free energy of the initial state of the A-B multilayered samples should be calculated by adding the interfacial free energy to the ground state (i.e., the zero line) representing a mechanical mixture of A and B in the bulk form. According to Zhang *et al.*,[5,14–16] the excess interfacial free energy of the multilayered samples can be calculated by $\Delta G_{mul}=\alpha_A S_{fA}\gamma^{SS}_{BA}+\alpha_B S_{fB}\gamma^{SS}_{AB}$, where S_{fA} and S_{fB} are the surface areas occupied by one mole of atoms A and B, respectively; α_A and α_B are the fraction of the interfacial atoms A and B versus the total number of atoms in the A-B multilayered samples; and γ^{SS}_{AB} (or γ^{SS}_{BA}) are the interfacial free energy of one mole of atoms A (or B) solved in B (or A). These terms can easily be calculated following the well-documented literature.[5,14–16]

B. *Ab initio* calculation

Since we are dealing with the equilibrium immiscible Cu-Ru system, for which there are very few available experimental data related to the Cu-Ru compounds, it is a challenging task to fit the Cu-Ru cross potential. In this respect, the first-principle calculation based on quantum mechanics is known to be a reliable way to acquire some physical properties of some possible Cu-Ru compounds in question. In the calculations, we employed the Vienna *ab initio* simulation package VASP,[17–19] of which the PAW pseudopotentials have been constructed by considering the all-electrons effect. The exchange and correlation effects were described by the functional proposed by Perdew and Zunger,[20] employing the generalized gradient corrections.[21] Brillouin-zone integrations were performed using an $11\times 11\times 11$ Monkhorst–Pack[22] grid, leading to 56 irreducible k points. A plane-wave cutoff energy was set to be 341.6 eV. Besides, for all spin-polarized calculations, the Vosko–Wilk–Nusair interpolations were used for the correlation part of the exchange correlation functional.[23]

C. Construction of *n*-body Cu-Ru potential

The tight-binding potential, namely, the second-moment approximation of the tight-binding scheme (TB-SMA), is adopted to construct the *n*-body Cu-Ru potential, as the scheme has successfully been employed in a large number of fcc and/or hcp transition metals.[24–26] In the TB-SMA scheme, the repulsive portion is a Born–Mayer pairwise interaction and the attractive portion is a second-moment approximation of the tight-binding band energy. The cohesive and repulsive items of the total energy are exponential functions of the atomic distance as written below:

$$E_{total}=\sum_i\left\{\sum_{j\neq i}A_{\alpha\beta}\exp\left[-p_{\alpha\beta}\left(\frac{r_{ij}}{r_{\alpha\beta}}-1\right)\right]-\sqrt{\sum_{j\neq i}\xi_{\alpha\beta}^2\exp\left[-2q_{\alpha\beta}\left(\frac{r_{ij}}{r_{\alpha\beta}}-1\right)\right]}\right\}, \quad (6)$$

where α and β indicate the atomic species, r_{ij} is the distance between atoms i and j, and is calculated up to a distance r_{cutoff}, whereas $r_{\alpha\beta}$ is taken to be the nearest distance between atoms α and β in the crystal structure. $A_{\alpha\beta}$, $p_{\alpha\beta}$, $\xi_{\alpha\beta}$, and $q_{\alpha\beta}$ are adjustable potential parameters, which are generally determined by fitting to their respective physical properties. In the present study, these parameters are determined as follows: (i) For $\alpha=\beta$, the fitting procedures are performed on the cohesive energies, lattice constants, and elastic moduli at 0 K for the pure Cu and Ru metals. The parameters $r_{\alpha\alpha}$ and $r_{\beta\beta}$ are taken to be the nearest-neighbor distance, i.e., r_0, of the pure Cu and Ru metals, respectively. (ii) For $\alpha\neq\beta$, the corresponding parameters are fitted to the *ab initio* acquired lattice constants, cohesive energies elastic, and bulk moduli of the metastable $L1_2$ Cu_3Ru and $CuRu_3$ compounds.

D. Scheme of molecular dynamics simulation and simulations models

In the present study, MD simulation is carried out with Parrinello–Rahman constant pressure scheme and the equations of motion are solved using a fourth-order predictor-corrector algorithm of Gear with a time step $t=5\times10^{-15}$ s.[27,28] For a series of solid solutions with various compositions, the MD simulation is performed at 300 K and at zero pressure for 50 000–150 000 MD time steps to reach a relatively equilibrium (metastable) state, at which all the related dynamic variables show no secular variation. The process of structural change in the solid solution models is monitored by the pair-correlation functions $g(r)$.[29] Meanwhile, another indicator of structural change, namely, the planar structure factor $S(\mathbf{k},\mathbf{z})$, is also calculated to provide evidence of the structural change. Moreover, density profiles $\rho_\alpha(z)$ of each species along the z direction are also used to monitor the structural changes of interest.[30]

We use two types of simulation models in the present study, i.e., the solid solution model and the sandwich model.

In the first type, the simulation models are set to be the fcc and hcp solid solutions, respectively. The fcc solid solution models consist of $8\times8\times8\times4=2048$ atoms, and the hcp solid solution models consist of $10\times6\times6\times4=1440$ atoms, respectively. In both fcc and hcp models, the [100] and [001] crystalline directions are parallel to the x and z axes, respectively, and the crystalline directions along the y axis are [010] for fcc Cu and [120] for hcp Ru, respectively. The periodic boundary conditions are adopted in all three directions. In setting the solid solution models, the solute atoms are added by random substitution to a desired number of Ru (Cu) atoms into the Cu fcc (Ru hcp), obtaining the initial state of fcc Cu-rich (hcp Ru-rich) solid solution model.

In the second type to represent the real multilayered films used in experiments, the sandwich models are constructed by stacking, along the z axis, 10 fcc Cu (100) planes, 12 hcp Ru $(01\bar{1}0)$, and 10 fcc Cu (100) planes, which all parallel to the x-y plane. Two interfaces thus locate at no. 10-11 and no. 22-23 atomic planes. The crystalline direction [100] of fcc Cu and [2 -1 -1 0] of hcp Ru with the units distances of 3.615 and 2.704 Å, respectively, are arranged to be parallel to the x axis, leading to a size difference ratio of 1.337. Meanwhile, the crystalline direction [010] of fcc Cu and [0001] of hcp Ru with units distances of 3.615 and 4.282 Å, respectively, are arranged to parallel to the y axis, leading to a size difference ratio of 0.844. Considering the simulation to be under a manageable scale, the numbers of Cu and Ru atoms in the x-y plane are selected to be $10\times10\times2=200$ atoms and $13\times8\times3=312$ atoms, respectively, resulting in a lattice difference ratio of 1.337 in x axis and 0.844 in y axis, respectively, which are reasonably close to the above-mentioned real situation. The periodic conditions along the x and y directions are set by the larger lattice dimensions of the two lattices, and it has been proved that the influence of the resultant misfit could be neglected.[31,32] The periodic condition is also employed for the z direction and two Cu lattices in the model are therefore adhered together to form a united lattice. The numbers of Cu and Ru atoms in the sandwich model are 4000 and 1248, respectively. In practice, the interface between the two metals is frequently a thin transient layer, which has been proven in experiments to be a disordered state.[33] To have the sandwich model to include such a disordered layer, an equal number of Cu and Ru atoms are artificially exchanged in the interface. After exchanging the Cu and Ru atoms, the sandwich model is annealed at 300 K for 5×10^6 MD steps to reach a relatively stable state, at which all the related dynamic variables show no secular variation.

E. Ion beam mixing

In the present IBM experiment, three sets of Cu-Ru multilayered samples with overall compositions of $Cu_{25}Ru_{75}$, $Cu_{50}Ru_{50}$, $Cu_{75}Ru_{25}$, respectively, are designed, and 200 keV xenon ions are employed as the irradiating ions. According to the TRIM program,[34] the total thickness of the Cu-Ru multilayered films should be designed to be around 45 nm to match the range of the irradiating ions. The $Cu_{25}Ru_{75}$, $Cu_{50}Ru_{50}$, and $Cu_{75}Ru_{25}$ multilayered films consist of 9, 18 (and 12), and 13 layers [i.e., 8, 17 (and 11), and 12 interfaces], respectively, and the thickness of the individual metal layer is therefore in a range of 3–5 nm. The desired compositions of the films are obtained through adjusting the relative thicknesses of the individual Cu and Ru layers. Concerning the details of the calculation of the interfacial free energy and design of the multilayered films, the readers are referred to some previous publications from the authors' group.[35] The intrinsic energy difference of various states, i.e., between the initial Cu-Ru multilayered films and various metastable Cu-Ru phases, is the major thermodynamic driving force for the related structural phase transformation and ion irradiation is to trigger the intermixing between the Cu and Ru layers, resulting in forming the respective metastable Cu-Ru phases. The Cu-Ru multilayered samples are prepared by depositing alternatively pure Cu (99.9%) and Ru (99.9%) at a rate of 0.5 Å/s onto NaCl single crystals as substrates in an e-gun

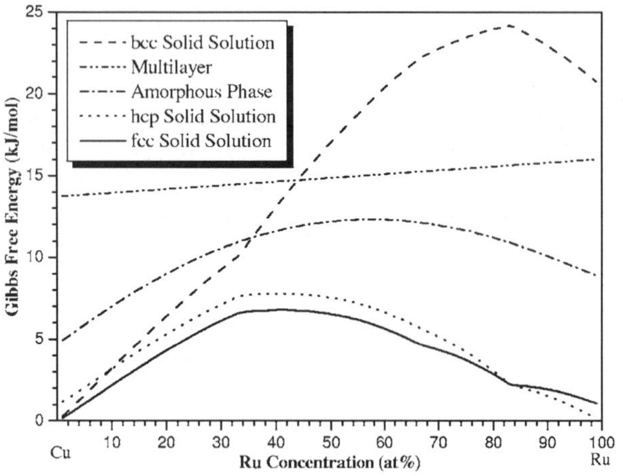

FIG. 1. The calculated Gibbs free energy diagram of the Cu-Ru system based on Miedema's theory and Alonso's method at the temperature of $T=300$ K.

evaporation system with a vacuum level of 10^{-6} Pa. The as-deposited Cu-Ru samples are then irradiated by xenon ions in an implanter with a vacuum level better than 5×10^{-4} Pa, and the irradiation dose is in a range from 4×10^{14} to 5×10^{15} Xe^{+}/cm^{2}. During xenon ion irradiation, the sample holder is cooled by liquid nitrogen (77 K) and the xenon ion current density is confined to be about 2 $\mu A/cm^{2}$ to minimize an otherwise heating effect. For structural characterization, all the Cu-Ru multilayered samples are removed from the substrates by deionized water and put onto the Cu grids for investigation by room temperature transmission electron microscopy (TEM) bright field examination and selected area diffraction (SAD) analysis to identify the structures in the films. Energy-dispersive spectroscopy (EDS) is also employed to determine the real compositions of the as-deposited films and the resultant alloy phases in the films. In the EDS analysis, the beam spot is about 0.3 μm, which could be considered the resolution of the measurement, and the measuring error in alloy composition is about 5%.

III. RESULTS AND DISCUSSION

A. Calculation of the Gibbs free energy diagram

We first construct a Gibbs free energy diagram of the Cu-Ru system at the temperature of 300 K by calculating the free energy curves of all the alloy phases in question by using the Miedema's model[14] and Alonso's method.[13] Figure 1 shows the calculated Gibbs free energy diagram, in which the energetic state of the Cu-Ru multilayered films containing 18 layers is also included to show the energetic sequence of the initial energetic state of the Cu-Ru multilayered films with the various possible metastable states/phases. From the diagram, one sees that the free energy curve of the amorphous phase is convex like in other systems with large positive ΔH_f. Besides, the initial energetic states of the multilayered films are higher than those of the corresponding solid solution and the amorphous phases over a broad composition range, which are therefore thermodynamically favored to be

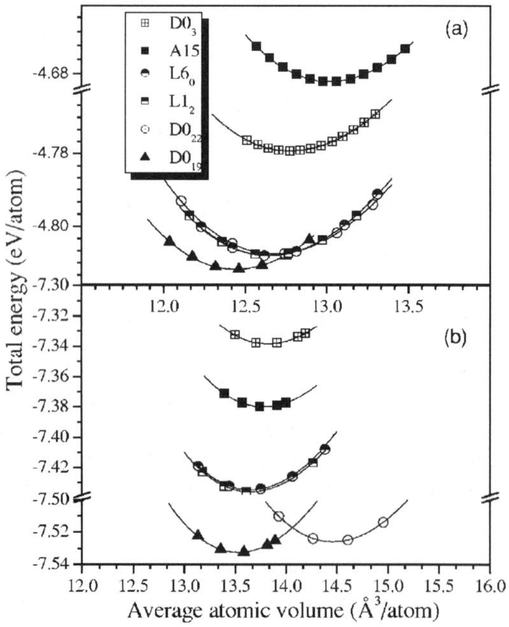

FIG. 2. Correlations of the total energies against the atomic volume of the Cu_3Ru (a) and $CuRu_3$ (b) alloys of some simple structures obtained by *ab initio* calculations.

formed. Moreover, within a composition range of 1–83 at. % of Ru, metastable fcc phase has the lowest free energy than other metastable states, which indicates metastable fcc phase is the most possible to be formed after iron irradiation. Interestingly, by IBM experiments, X. He *et al.* obtained fcc metastable phases in the $Cu_{50}Ru_{50}$ and $Cu_{25}Ru_{75}$ multilayered films, which remained in the fcc structure with increasing the irradiation dose.[36] It can be easily seen that the thermodynamic calculation and experimental results are quite compatible with each other.

B. *Ab initio* assisted deriving n-body Cu-Ru potential

We then present the results of *ab initio* calculations in acquiring the physical properties of a few possible Cu-Ru compounds. Figure 2(a) shows correlation of total energies against the lattice constant of $CuRu_3$ alloy obtained by *ab initio* calculations within the GGA. From Fig. 2(a), one sees that the A15 structure has the highest positive heat of formation, the $D0_3$ structure is in the second position, the $D0_{19}$, $D0_{22}$, L60, and $L1_2$ structures are almost in a same low energy level, and the $D0_{19}$ structure has the lowest heat of formation among the six studied structures. Interestingly, the relatively stable $L1_2$ structure predicted by above *ab initio* calculations has ever been observed in experiments, i.e., a metastable $Cu_{25}Ru_{75}$ alloy of fcc structure was obtained in thin films upon irradiation and its lattice constants were determined by diffraction analysis to be $a=3.65$ Å,[36] which was compatible with the calculated value of a=3.79 Å. The agreement between the *ab initio* calculation and experimental results, in this respect, could therefore be considered excellent. For the $Cu_{75}Ru_{25}$ alloy, similar results are obtained [Fig. 2(b)], and comparing the results, a metastable$Cu_{75}Ru_{25}$

TABLE I. Comparison of the physical properties of fcc Cu, hcp Ru, $L1_2$ Cu_3Ru, and $L1_2$ $CuRu_3$ obtained from *ab initio* calculation, fitted or reproduced from *n*-body potentials and the experimental observation (Refs. 37–39). Lattice constants *a* and *c* are expressed in nanometers. Elastic moduli C_{ij} are expressed in Mbar. Cohesive energies E_c, and formation E^f energies are expressed in electron volts.

		a	c	E_f	E_c	C_{11}	C_{12}	C_{13}	C_{33}	C_{44}
fcc Cu	Experimental	0.361			3.49	1.683	1.221			0.757
	Reproduced	0.361			3.58	1.690	1.218			0.756
hcp Ru	Experimental	0.270	0.428		6.74	5.626	1.878	1.682	6.242	1.806
	Reproduced	0.270	0.427		6.70	4.647	1.736	1.974	6.725	1.559
$L1_2$ Cu_3Ru	CASTEP	0.368		0.038		1.949	1.609			0.846
	Reproduced	0.378		0.038		1.876	1.701			0.914
$L1_2$ $CuRu_3$	CASTEP	0.370		0.096		3.331	2.018			0.836
	Reproduced	0.380		0.096		3.350	2.160			0.816

alloy of fcc structure was obtained in thin films upon irradiation and its lattice constants were determined by diffraction analysis to be $a=3.60$ Å, which was also compatible with the calculated value of $a=3.70$ Å.

Table I lists the calculated physical properties, such as the lattice constants, the formation energies, as well as the elastic moduli, of the $L1_2$ $Cu_{75}Ru_{25}$ and $L1_2$ $Cu_{25}Ru_{75}$ compounds, together with the experimental properties of fcc Cu and hcp Ru. One notices that the formation of the $L1_2$ $Cu_{75}Ru_{25}$ and $L1_2$ $Cu_{25}Ru_{75}$ compounds are both positive, indicating they are both unstable in an equilibrium state, which is in good agreement with the fact the Cu-Ru system is characterized by a positive ΔH_f of +10.44 kJ/mol atom. Using the data in the table and the procedure described above, the TB-SMA potential can be derived for the Cu-Ru system. The TB-SMA potential parameters for the Cu-Ru system are listed in Table II. In order to test its relevance, some physical properties of the Cu-Ru system are reproduced using the fitted potential. For convenience of comparison, the reproduced results are also listed in Table I.[37–39] From Table I, one can see obviously that the physical properties fitted or reproduced from the derived *n*-body potential agree with the *ab initio* calculations and/or the experimental results.

C. Crystal-to-amorphous transition in the Cu-Ru system

1. Glass forming range

We now present the simulation results for the hcp Ru-based solid solution models first. Figure 3 displays the projections of atomic positions for the Cu_5Ru_{95}, $Cu_{20}Ru_{80}$, and $Cu_{50}Ru_{50}$ hcp solid solutions upon annealing at 300 K for

TABLE II. Tight-binding potential parameters of the Cu-Ru system used in the present study. A and ξ are expressed in 10^{-19} J/at. %, and r_0 and r_{cutoff} are expressed in angstroms.

	p	q	A	ξ	r_0	r_{cutoff}
Cu-Cu	5.7662	1.2313	0.1411	1.727	2.78	5.0
Ru-Ru	19.1540	1.6631	0.078 58	3.1487	2.73	4.7
Cu-Ru	10.8624	6.6235	1.3863	6.4895	2.649	5.0

120 000 MD time steps, respectively. From the figure, one sees vividly that for the solid solution with 5 at. % of Cu, the hcp structure can be clearly visualized, i.e., it still remains in its original crystalline structure. While for the solid solution with solute Cu equal to or greater than 20 at. %, the projection of atomic position is obviously disordered, indicating that the crystal lattice has collapsed and turned into a disordered state, i.e., a crystal-to-amorphous transition has clearly taken place. Figure 4 shows the corresponding density profiles $\rho_\alpha(z)$ for the solid solutions with the alloy compositions of Cu_5Ru_{95}, $Cu_{20}Ru_{80}$, and $Cu_{50}Ru_{50}$, respectively. It can be seen that when the solute concentration is less than 20 at. %Cu, the atomic planes can clearly be distinguished from the density profiles; however, once the Cu concentration equals or exceeds 20 at. %, a relatively uniform distributed density profile appears. In order to have firm evidence, the total and partial pair-correlation functions $g(r)$ for hcp Ru-based solid solutions are calculated and shown in Fig. 5. In the figure, as the $g(r)$ curve of Cu_5Ru_{95} shows apparent sharp peaks even at a large distance r, the Cu_5Ru_{95} simulation model is considered to be still in a crystalline structure. In comparison, for the $Cu_{20}Ru_{80}$ simulation models, though the first peaks and the second peaks of the $g(r)$ curves are still clear, there are no discernible peaks beyond the third-nearest neighbors. In a classical works, R. Zallen has pointed that the short-range order of amorphous phase is characterized by the clear first- and second-nearest neighbor peaks in the radial distribution function (RDF) and discernible peaks in the RDF rarely occur beyond third-nearest neighbors.[40] Thus, based on Fig. 4 and Fig. 5, one can conclude that a crystal-to-amorphous transition takes place in the $Cu_{50}Ru_{50}$ and $Cu_{20}Ru_{80}$ simulation models. These results clearly indicate that in the Cu-Ru system, when the Cu concentration equals or exceeds 20 at. %, the hcp Ru-based solid solution becomes unstable and turns into an amorphous state.

From the above results, it can be concluded that the critical solid solubility is 20 at. % Cu for the hcp Ru-based solid solutions. Similarly, for the fcc Cu-based solid solution, the critical solid solubility is determined to be 10 at. % of Ru. Consequently, the two critical solid solubilities are determined to be 20 at. % of Cu for hcp Ru-based solid solution, and 10 at. % of Ru for the fcc Cu-based solid solution, re-

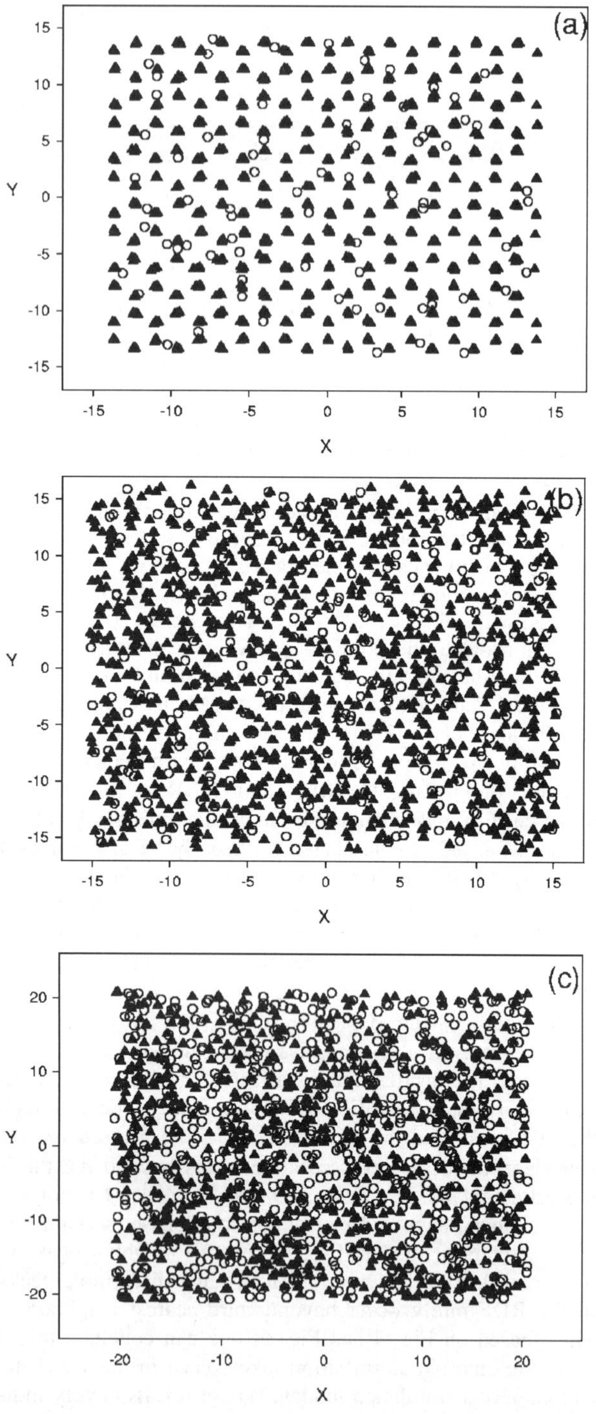

FIG. 3. The projections of atomic positions for the (a) Cu_5Ru_{95}, (b) $Cu_{20}Ru_{80}$, and (c) $Cu_{50}Ru_{50}$ hcp solid solutions after annealing at 300 K for 120 000 MD time steps, respectively. Open circles: Cu. Filled triangles: Ru.

spectively. It follows that an amorphous alloy would be formed, when its composition falls into the composition range bounded by the two determined critical solid solubilities and that the GFA/GFR of the Cu-Ru system is therefore within 10–80 at. % of Ru. More interestingly, an amorphous

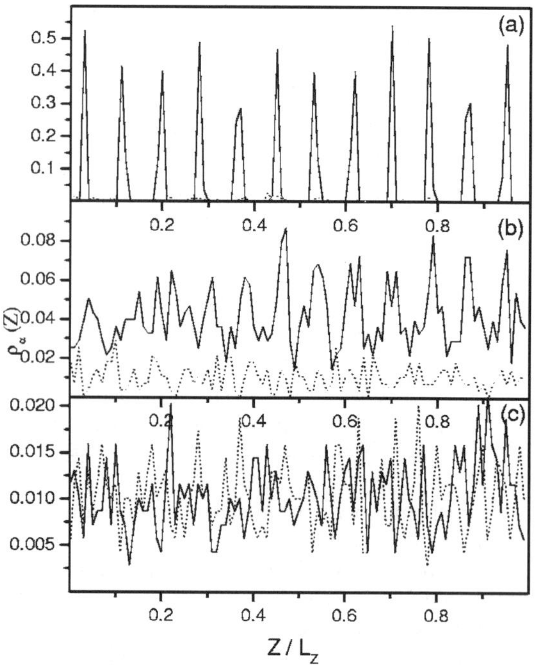

FIG. 4. The calculated density profiles $\rho_\alpha(z)$ of Cu and Ru atoms along the z direction in (a) Cu_5Ru_{95}, (b) $Cu_{20}Ru_{80}$, and (c) $Cu_{50}Ru_{50}$ hcp solid solutions after annealing at 300 K for 120 000 MD time steps, respectively. $\rho_{Ru}(z)$ is represented by the solid line and $\rho_{Cu}(z)$ by the dotted line. The ordinate is in arbitrary units.

phase was found at the composition of $Cu_{50}Ru_{50}$ by IBM experiment,[36] which is covered by the theoretically predicted result.

2. Interface stability

We finally present the detailed simulation results observed in the Cu-Ru sandwich model under the temperature of

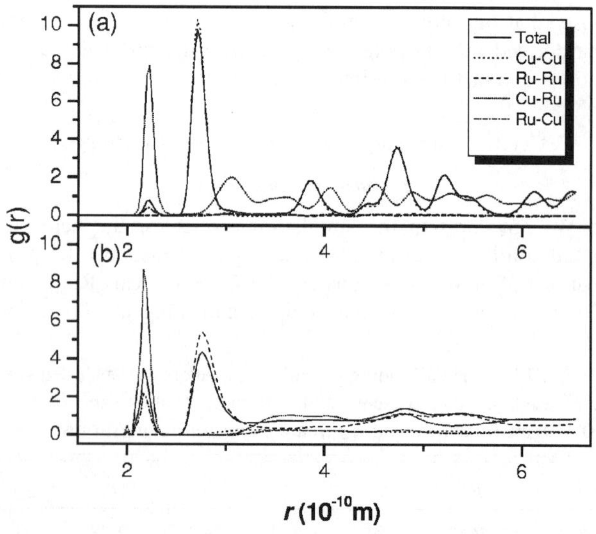

FIG. 5. Total pair-correlation functions $g(r)$ of (a) Cu_5Ru_{95} and (b) $Cu_{20}Ru_{80}$ hcp solid solutions after annealing at 300 K for 120 000 MD time steps, respectively.

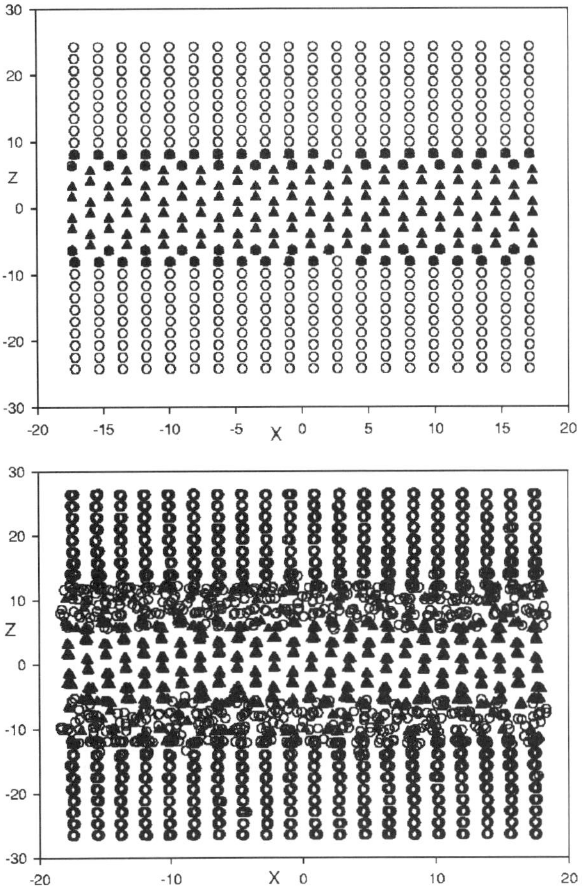

FIG. 6. The schemes of the Cu-Ru multilayers. (a) Configuration of the initial state with preset disordered interlayer between Cu and Ru. (b) The state after solid-state amorphization. The open circle symbols represent Cu and filled triangles represent Ru.

300 K. Figure 6 displays two projections of the atomic positions on the x-z plane of initial state and after isothermally annealing for 25 ns, respectively. The projections exhibit vividly the process of solid-state amorphization taking place in the Cu-Ru sandwich model. Figure 6(a) is the initial state of the sandwich model, in which some chemical disordering is present at the interface in order to simulate the real situation that in practice, a disordered interlayer could be formed at the Cu/Ru interface. After simulation of 0.05 ns, the majority of the atoms far from the interface in the sandwich model still retain their crystalline structure as in the initial state, whereas those atoms near the interface change into a disordered state, indicating that solid-state amorphization is taking place in the interface. With further increasing the simulation time to 25 ns, Fig. 6(b) shows that the amorphous interlayer does not increase further and remains in a stable thickness.

By carefully inspecting Fig. 6, one can see that the process of the solid-state amorphization features the following two characteristics. First, the growing speed of the amorphous interlayer gradually slows down and eventually approaches zero. Figure 7 shows the change of the Cu and Ru atomic density profiles, $\rho_\alpha(z)$, along the z direction, perpen-

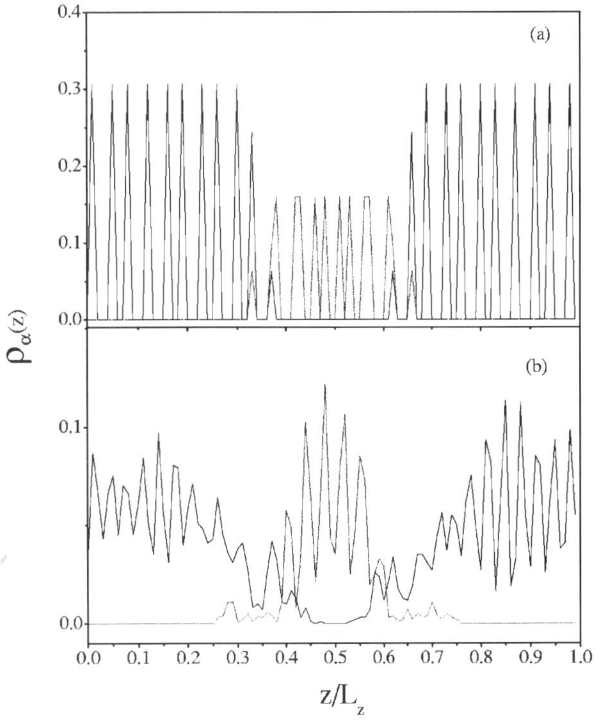

FIG. 7. The density profiles $\rho_\alpha(Z)$ of Cu (solid line) and Ru (dash line) along the z direction at the initial state (a) and the annealing states at 300 K for (b) 25 ns, respectively.

dicular to the interface with increasing MD simulation time steps. Figure 7(a) is the initial state of the sandwich model from which a perfect layered structure can be seen. After MD simulations up to 25 ns, Fig. 7(b) shows that some Ru (Cu) atoms near the interface diffuse into the partner Cu (Ru) lattice and thus result in interfacial amorphization. However, one can note that in the areas far away from the interface, the Cu and Ru lattices still reserve their respective crystalline structures, and the thickness of the amorphization area does not increase with increasing MD simulation time steps. Second, the observed solid-state amorphization in the Cu-Ru system features a so-called asymmetric-growth behavior, as one can see from Figs. 6 and 7 that the disordered interlayer extends faster toward the Cu lattice than toward the Ru direction.[33] As the cohesive energy of Ru is larger that of Cu, therefore one can consider that the Ru lattice is more stable than Cu lattice, i.e., Ru lattice is more difficult to turn into disordered state. It worth noting that the critical solid solubility of Ru in Cu (10 at. %) is smaller than that of Cu in Ru (20 at. %) according to above simulations, which fits well with the result obtained from the sandwich model.

We then make further discussion on the solid-state amorphization in the immiscible Cu-Ru multilayers from the thermodynamic as well as kinetic point of view. According to the model proposed by Lin *et al.*, two necessary conditions have to be satisfied for the solid-state amorphization to take place in a binary metal system.[41] First, the formed amorphous phase should have a lower Gibbs free energy than the initial energetic state of the multilayers, i.e., the thermodynamic factor ΔF, defined as that the energy difference between the

TABLE III. The thermodynamics parameters of Miedema's model and Alonso's method (Ref. 5) used in calculation for the thermodynamic factor ΔF and the kinetic factor κ of the Cu-Ru system.

	V (cm^3)	ϕ^* (V)	n_{ws} (density unit)	ΔH^{fuse} (kJ/mol)	T (K)	γ^0 (mJ/m^2)	κ	ΔF (kJ/mol)	Λ_{max} (nm)
Cu	7.11	4.45	3.18	13.00	1358	1825	1.65	−17	2.91
Ru	8.20	5.40	6.13	24.29	2523	3050			

amorphous phase and the multilayers should be negative. Second, the kinetic factor κ should be greater than 0.6 for a transition metal-metal system. According to the definitions, the thermodynamic factor ΔF and the kinetic factor κ can be respectively expressed by

$$\Delta F = \Delta G_{\{AB\}} - 2 \times \left(\gamma_{[A]-\{AB\}} + \gamma_{[B]-\{AB\}} + d_{AB}\frac{\Delta G_{\{AB\}}}{V_{\{AB\}}} \right) \frac{V_{\{AB\}}}{(D_A + D_B)} \quad (7)$$

$$\kappa = 1 - \frac{V_A^{eff}}{V_B} + (T_B - T_A)\left(\frac{1}{T} - \frac{1}{T_B}\right), \quad (8)$$

where $\Delta G_{\{AB\}}$ is the difference of Gibbs free energies between the amorphous state and the crystalline state of the A-B alloy (A and B stand for the constituent metals); $\gamma_{A\text{-}\{AB\}}$ and $\gamma_{B\text{-}\{AB\}}$ are the interfacial free energies of the A-$\{AB\}$ and B-$\{AB\}$ interface, respectively; D_A and D_B are the thicknesses of A and B layers, respectively; d_{AB} is the growing thickness of the amorphous interlayer; $V_{\{AB\}}$ is the mean value of the atom volumes of A and B; V_A^{eff} is effective volume of A in the matrix of the metal B; and T, T_A, and T_B are the annealing temperature and the melting points of metals A and B, respectively. Concerning the definitions and calculation of those variables, the readers are referred to the published literature.[41] From Eq. (7), by setting $F=0$, one can obtain the following equation to estimate the maximum thickness of the growing amorphous interlayer:

$$\Lambda_{max} = \frac{(\gamma_{[A]-[B]} + \gamma_{[B]-[A]})V_{\{AB\}}}{\Delta G_{\{AB\}}}. \quad (9)$$

Substituting the relevant quantities of the Cu-Ru system into the above equation, one can obtain that the thermodynamic factor ΔF, kinetic factor κ, and the maximum thickness of amorphous interlays of the Cu-Ru system are −17 kJ/mol, 1.65 and 2.91 nm, respectively. Table III lists the calculated results and the parameters used in the calculation. From Table III, one can clearly see that the thermodynamic factor ΔF is truly negative and kinetic factor κ is greater than 0.6, suggesting that the solid-state amorphization is possible to take place in the Cu-Ru system.

It is important to compare the theoretical calculation results with the experimental result. It has been shown by R. Chan *et al.* that the interfaces can be stable between Cu/Ru(20 nm)/Si after annealing at 720 K, and the Cu/Ru interface has very excellent adhesion ability.[42] Moreover, using Rutherford backscattering and high-resolution analytical electron microscopy, Arunagiri *et al.* showed that 5 nm Ru film can function as a directly plateable Cu diffusion barrier up to at least 573 K vacuum anneal.[43] It is worth noting that the MD simulations are performed at 300 K and under perfect interfacial conditions, while the real interfaces are always complex. The agreement between the MD simulation calculation and experimental results, in this respect, could therefore be considered excellent. The MD simulation calculations indicate that Ru thin film is a promising candidate as a directly plateable Cu diffusion barrier.

D. Ion beam mixing results

We now present the results of IBM experiment. The real compositions of the as-deposited Cu-Ru multilayered samples as well as the ion-mixed metastable phases in the samples are determined by EDS at various irradiation stages. In order to present the detailed structural transitions emerged in three sets of Cu-Ru multilayered samples and determined the GFR of the Cu-Ru system, we present all the experimental results for the Cu-Ru multilayered samples, which are irradiated to doses ranging from 4×10^{14} Xe^+/cm^2 to 5×10^{15} Xe^+/cm^2.

In the $Cu_{25}Ru_{75}$ multilayered sample, Fig. 8(a) a is a SAD

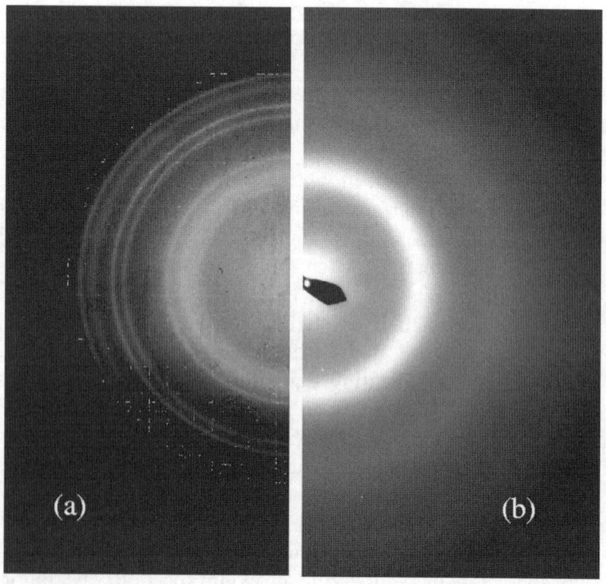

FIG. 8. Selected area diffraction (SAD) patterns for the $Cu_{25}Ru_{75}$ multilayered films of the as-deposited state (a) and amorphous state (b) after irradiation to a dose of 1×10^{15} Xe^+/cm^2.

pattern of the as-deposited $Cu_{25}Ru_{75}$ multilayered films. The sharp diffraction lines of polycrystalline Cu and Ru can clearly be observed. After 300 K ion irradiation to a small dose of $2\times10^{14}Xe^+/cm^2$, the diffraction lines of the polycrystalline Ru became weaker than those in the as-deposited state. With increasing the irradiation dose, the diffraction lines of the polycrystalline Ru showed a tendency to disappear, and at a dose of 1×10^{15} Xe^+/cm^2, an amorphous phase appeared clearly in the sight, as shown in Fig. 8(b). In the $Cu_{50}Ru_{50}$ multilayered sample, an amorphous phase was obtained after irradiation by 200 keV Xe ion at 300 K with a dose of $8\times10^{14}Xe^+/cm^2$.[36] Similarly, an amorphous phase was also obtained after irradiation by 200 keV Xe ion at 300 K with a dose of $5\times10^{14}Xe^+/cm^2$.

The IBM results show that amorphous alloys are indeed obtained in the three designed alloy compositions, suggesting that a composition range favoring amorphization is at least from 25 to 75 at. % Ru, which is quite compatible with that predicted by MD simulations, i.e. 10–80 at. % Ru.

Referring again to the MD simulation results, one finds that the above IBM results are in good agreement with the predictions. It is known that IBM is a process far-from-equilibrium and can generally be divided into two steps,[33] i.e., an atomic collision cascade triggered by impinging ions, followed by a relaxation. In the present study, the 200 keV xenon ions triggered the atomic collision cascade, which was responsible for inducing atomic mixing between the Cu and Ru layers in the as-deposited multilayered films. After receiving an adequate ion dose, the Cu and Ru atoms were uniformly mixed and the mixture was most likely in a highly energetic and disordered state. According to the atomic collision theory, the relaxation period is extremely short, which allows only a limited rearrangement of the atoms in the Cu-Ru mixture. Consequently, upon relaxation, the highly energetic and disordered Cu-Ru mixture could reside in one of the possible intermediate states of lower energy, e.g., amorphous state.

IV. CONCLUDING REMARKS

(1) An *n*-body potential is constructed for the immiscible Cu-Ru system at equilibrium with an aid of *ab initio* calculations for obtaining some physical properties necessary to fit the Cu-Ru cross-potential.

(2) Using the solid solution model, simulations reveal that the Cu-based and the Ru-based solid solutions collapse at their respective critical solid solubilities, i.e., 10 at. % Ru and 20 at. % Cu, thus determining an intrinsic glass-forming range of the system to be within 10–80 at. % Ru, which matches well with the observations in ion beam mixing experiment.

(3) Using the Cu-Ru sandwich model, simulations clarify that the interfacial free energy is the major driving force for interfacial reaction, resulting in spontaneous solid-state amorphization, and that when the interfacial free energy is completely consumed, the reaction terminates, thus determining a maximum amorphous interlayer to be 2.91 nm, which is in good agreement with that predicted by a recently proposed thermodynamic and kinetic model.

(4) Kinetically, simulations further reveal that the growth of the amorphous interlayer features an asymmetric behavior, i.e., the growth advances faster toward the Cu lattice than toward the Ru side, because the critical solid solubility of Ru in Cu (10 at. %) is smaller than that of Cu in Ru (20 at. %).

ACKNOWLEDGMENTS

The authors are grateful for financial support from the National Natural Science Foundation of China (50531040), the Ministry of Science and Technology of China (2006CB605201), and the Administration of Tsinghua University.

---

*Author to whom correspondence should be addressed.
Email address: dmslbx@tsinghua.edu.cn

[1] S. P. Murarka, I. V. Verner, and R. J. Gutmann, *Copper-Fundamental Mechanisms for Microelectronic Applications* (Wiley Interscience, New York, 2000).
[2] R. N. Hall and J. H. Racette, J. Appl. Phys. **35**, 379 (1964).
[3] P. K. Wu, G. R. Yang, and T. M. Lu, Appl. Phys. Lett. **65**, 508 (1994).
[4] International Technology Roadmap for Semiconductors, SEMATECH, Inc., Austin, TX (2001).
[5] F. R. de Boer, R. Boom, W. C. M. Mattens, A. R. Miedema, and A. K. Niessen, *Cohesion in Metals: Transition Metal Alloys* (North-Holland, Amsterdam, 1989).
[6] M. W. Lane, C. E. Murray, F. R. McFeely, P. M. Vereechen, and R. Rosenberg, Appl. Phys. Lett. **83**, 2330 (2003).
[7] D. Josell, D. Wheeler, C. Witt, and T. P. Moffat, Electrochem. Solid-State Lett. **6**, C143 (2003).
[8] Q. Wang, J. G. Ekerdt, D. Gay, Y. M. Sun, and J. M. White, Appl. Phys. Lett. **84**, 1380 (2004).
[9] Y. Zhang, L. Long, T. N. Arunagiri, O. Ojeda, S. Flores, O. Chyan, and R. M. Wallance, Electrochem. Solid-State Lett. **7**, C107 (2004).
[10] Z. C. Li, D. P. Yu, and B. X. Liu, Phys. Rev. B **65**, 245403 (2002).
[11] H. Bakker, *Enthalpies in Alloys: Miedema's Semi-Empirical Model* (Trans Tech, Zurich, 1998).
[12] J. M. Lopez and J. A. Alonso, Z. Naturforsch. A **40a**, 1199 (1985).
[13] J. A. Alonso, L. J. Gallego, and J. A. Simozar, Riv. Nuovo Cimento **12**, 587 (1990).
[14] A. R. Miedema and F. J. A. den Broeder, Z. Metallkd. **70**, 14 (1979).
[15] J. Gerkema and A. R. Miedema, Surf. Sci. **124**, 351 (1983).
[16] Z. J. Zhang, O. Jin, and B. X. Liu, Phys. Rev. B **51**, 8076 (1995).
[17] G. Kresse and J. Hafner, Phys. Rev. B **47**, 558 (1993).
[18] G. Kresse and J. Furthmüller, Comput. Mater. Sci. **6**, 15 (1996).

[19]G. Kresse and J. Furthmüller, Phys. Rev. B **54**, 11169 (1996).
[20]J. P. Perdew and A. Zunger, Phys. Rev. B **23**, 5048 (1981).
[21]J. P. Perdew, J. A. Chevary, S. H. Vosko, K. A. Jackson, M. R. Pederson, D. J. Singh, and C. Fiolhais, Phys. Rev. B **46**, 6671 (1992).
[22]J. Monkhorst and J. D. Pack, Phys. Rev. B **13**, 5188 (1976).
[23]H. Vosko, L. Wilk, and M. Nusair, Can. J. Phys. **58**, 1200 (1980).
[24]F. Ducastelle, in *Computer Simulation in Materials Science*, edited by M. Meyer and V. Pontikis, NATO Advanced Study Institute, Series E: Applied Physics (Kluwer, Dordrecht, 1991), Vol. 205.
[25]F. Cleri and V. Rosato, Phys. Rev. B **48**, 22 (1993).
[26]V. Rosato, M. Guillope, and B. Legrand, Philos. Mag. A **59**, 321 (1989).
[27]M. Parrinello and A. Rahman, J. Appl. Phys. **52**, 7182 (1981).
[28]G. Ciccotti and W. G. Hoover, *in Molecular-Dynamics Simulation of Statistical-Mechanical Systems*, ASI-NATO (North-Holland, Amsterdam, 1986).
[29]V. Rosato, G. Ciccotti, and V. Pontikis, Phys. Rev. B **33**, 1860 (1986).
[30]W. B. Pearson, *A Handbook of Lattice Spaces and Structures of Metals and Alloys* (Pergamon, London, 1958).
[31]C. Massobrio, V. Pontikis, and G. Matin, Phys. Rev. B **41**, 10486 (1990).
[32]P. Mura, P. Demontis, G. Suffritti, V. Rosato, and M. Antissari, Phys. Rev. B **50**, 2850 (1994).
[33]B. X. Liu, W. S. Lai, and Z. J. Zhang, Adv. Phys. **50**, 367 (2001).
[34]J. F. Ziegler and J. P. Biersack, *TRIM* (Pergamon Press, New York, 1992).
[35]Z. J. Zhang, O. Jin, and B. X. Liu, Phys. Rev. B **51**, 8076 (1995).
[36]X. He, X. Y. Li, and B. X. Liu, J. Phys. Soc. Jpn. **72**, 3032 (2003).
[37]W. B. Pearson, *A Handbook of Lattice Spaces and Structures of Metals and Alloys* (Pergamon, London, 1958).
[38]E. A. Brandes and G. B. Brook, *Smithells Metals Reference Book*, 7th ed. (Butterworth-Heinemann, Oxford, 1992).
[39]D. R. Lide, *Handbook of Lattice Spaces and Structures of Metals and Alloys* (CRC, New York, 2002).
[40]Richard Zallen, *The Physics of Amorphous Solids* (John Wiley & Sons, New York, 1983).
[41]C. Lin, G. W. Yang, and B. X. Liu, Phys. Rev. B **61**, 15649 (2000).
[42]R. Chan, T. N. Arunagiri, Y. Zhang, O. Chyan, R. M. Wallace, M. J. Kim, and T. Q. Hurd, Electrochem. Solid-State Lett. **7**, G154 (2004).
[43]T. N. Arunagiri, Y. Zhang, and O. Chyan, Appl. Phys. Lett. **86**, 083104 (2005).

Molecular statics calculation of the formation enthalpy for ternary metal systems based on the long-range empirical interatomic potentials

X. D. Dai, J. H. Li, and B. X. Liu[a)]
Department of Materials Science and Engineering, Tsinghua University, Beijing 100084, China

(Received 30 December 2006; accepted 20 February 2007; published online 27 March 2007)

A scheme is proposed in the present study to predict the formation enthalpy of the ternary metal system. Based on the long-range empirical potential model, the interatomic potentials are first constructed for the Cu–Ag–Au, Cu–Ag–Ni, Ag–Au–Ni, and Cu–Au–Ni systems, and then molecular statics calculations are performed to predict the formation enthalpies of the four systems. It is found that the predicted results by the present scheme match well with those obtained by experiments or *ab initio* calculations, exhibiting a more precise feature than Miedema's model.
 [DOI: 10.1063/1.2716361]

Formation enthalpy is a basic thermodynamic property and plays an important role in studying the fundamental issues in the field of physical metallurgy and materials science. Generally, systematically measuring the formation enthalpy for metal systems by experiments is unbearably time consuming and fund costing, so it is extremely important and significant to predict the formation enthalpy of metal systems through theoretical models. For the ternary metal system, the frequently used model is an empirical thermodynamic one, i.e., Miedema's model,[1,2] which could approximately predict the formation enthalpies of some ternary metal systems with the introduction of some empirical parameters and assumptions. At this aspect, *ab initio* calculations can provide the needed level of energy precision, nonetheless, they are currently limited to the study of matter systems consisting of only a few tens of atoms. By comparison, the calculation based on empirical interatomic potentials provides a practical compromise between efficiency and accuracy, since it could handle the matter systems involving a great number of atoms at an atomic scale. In the present study, we proposed a scheme to predict the formation enthalpy of ternary metal systems. In the proposed scheme, we first construct the interatomic potential for a ternary system, and then molecular statics (MS) calculation is performed based on the constructed potential to predict the formation enthalpy of the system. In the present study, the formation enthalpies of the Cu–Ag–Au, Cu–Ag–Ni, Ag–Au–Ni, and Cu–Au–Ni systems have been calculated, as there is extremely lack of experimental data in the four ternary systems.

To correctly predict the formation enthalpy through MS calculation, a relevant interatomic potential model is necessary. In the present study, we adopted the long-range empirical potential (LREP) model proposed by the authors.[3,4] Considering the interactions between the atoms, there should be six sets of potential parameters in a ternary *A-B-C* system, i.e., three sets to describe the interactions of pure *A-A*, *B-B*, and *C-C*, respectively, and the other three sets to describe the interactions of cross *A-B*, *A-C*, and *B-C*, respectively. Generally, the potential parameters for pure metals are determined by fitting to their cohesive energies, lattice constants, and elastic constants obtained by experiments. As for the cross potentials, as there is little available experimental data related to the alloys, *ab initio* calculations are carried out in the present study to obtain the necessary physical properties of alloys. The present *ab initio* calculations are conducted by using the Cambridge serial total energy package,[5] (CASTEP) and the computational setting is the same as that in previous work.[4] Through *ab initio* calculations, the lattice constants, cohesive energies, and elastic moduli of some hypothetic alloys are obtained and then applied in fitting the cross potentials.

In our previous paper, the pure potentials of Cu–Cu, Ag–Ag, Au–Au, and Ni–Ni have been constructed and the calculations based on these potentials proved that they can relevantly predict the properties of the metals at equilibrium state and nonequilibrium state, such as structural stabilities, equations of state, and phonon spectra.[4] The fitted parameters of the six cross potentials are listed in Table I. To validate the relevance of the constructed cross potentials, the lattice constants, cohesive energies, and elastic moduli of some hypothetical ternary alloys in the four ternary systems are calculated by the potentials, and the results are listed in Table II together with the results derived from *ab initio* calculations. One sees from the table that the reproduced results from the potentials are in excellent agreement with those derived from *ab initio* calculations. To further evaluate the relevance of the constructed potentials, we derived the equations of state from the potentials for some ternary alloys in the four systems and

TABLE I. Cross potential parameters for Ag–Au, Ag–Cu, Ag–Ni, Cu–Au, Cu–Ni, and Ni–Au. $m=4$, $n=6$, and r_{c1}, r_{c2}, and r_0 are expressed in Å. x_0, x_1, x_2, x_3, x_4, and α are expressed in eV Å^{-m}, eV Å^{-m-1}, 10^{-1} eV Å^{-m-2}, 10^{-2} eVÅ^{-m-3}, 10^{-3} eV Å^{m-4}, and 10^{-4} eV^2 Å^{-n}, respectively.

	Ag–Au	Ag–Cu	Ag–Ni	Cu–Au	Cu–Ni	Ni–Au
r_{c1}	6.0000	6.0000	6.0000	6.0000	6.0000	6.0000
r_{c2}	7.8000	7.5000	7.5000	7.8000	7.8000	7.8000
x_0	0.1650	0.2339	0.3179	0.2603	0.2198	0.4736
x_1	−0.1371	−0.2496	−0.3633	−0.2707	−0.2606	−0.5530
x_2	0.4531	1.0164	1.5472	1.0743	1.1369	2.3944
x_3	−0.7425	−1.8595	−2.9033	−1.9218	−2.1812	−4.5609
x_4	0.5245	1.2840	2.0415	1.3000	1.5822	3.2680
α	2.7511	2.0447	1.7026	1.9660	0.5872	1.3324
β	3.9898	2.9634	0.0370	3.3022	−1.1470	−1.7271
r_0	2.7367	2.6467	2.7566	2.6244	2.5494	2.7333

a)Author to whom correspondence should be addressed; electronic mail: dmslbx@tsinghua.edu.cn

Applied Physics Letters 90 (13), 131904(2007).

TABLE II. Lattice constants a (Å), cohesive energies E_c (eV), and bulk modulus B (Mbar) for some ternary alloys. For each alloy, the properties in the upper rows are from the LREP model and those in the lower rows are from *ab initio* calculations. The A_2BC alloys are in $L2_1$ structure and ABC alloys are in $C1_b$ structure.

Alloys	a	E_c	B	Alloys	a	E_c	B
Au_2CuAg	6.44	3.51	1.19	Cu_2NiAu	5.96	3.75	1.28
	6.41	3.50	1.26		5.96	3.77	1.53
Cu_2AgAu	6.23	3.44	1.26	Ni_2CuAu	5.99	3.98	1.53
	6.18	3.41	1.30		5.95	3.95	1.63
Ag_2CuAu	6.42	3.33	1.10	Au_2CuNi	6.19	3.79	1.43
	6.41	3.23	1.13		6.18	3.88	1.52
AgCuAu	6.13	3.11	0.73	CuNiAu	5.79	3.43	0.84
	6.15	3.03	0.81		5.74	3.60	1.19
Cu_2NiAg	5.93	3.39	1.25	Au_2AgNi	6.39	3.60	1.25
	5.93	3.46	1.39		6.39	3.68	1.41
Ni_2AgCu	5.93	3.60	1.38	Ni_2AgAu	6.18	3.80	1.50
	5.92	3.62	1.52		6.13	3.76	1.50
Ag_2CuNi	6.15	3.22	1.14	Ag_2NiAu	6.40	3.39	1.02
	6.14	3.28	1.27		6.38	3.39	1.15
AgCuNi	5.88	2.91	0.74	AgNiAu	6.12	3.18	0.62
	5.83	2.99	1.01		6.11	3.20	0.97

then compared them with those obtained from the Rose equation[6] in Fig. 1. One sees from Fig. 1 that the total energies and their derivatives derived from the potentials can keep smooth in the whole calculated range and match well with those derived from the Rose equation. Apparently, the constructed potentials are relevant in describing the atomic interaction of these ternary systems.

Based on the constructed potentials, MS calculations are carried out for the fcc solid solution models, which consist of $9\times9\times9=729$ unit cells (2916 atoms). In the fcc models, the [100], [010], and [001] crystalline directions are parallel to

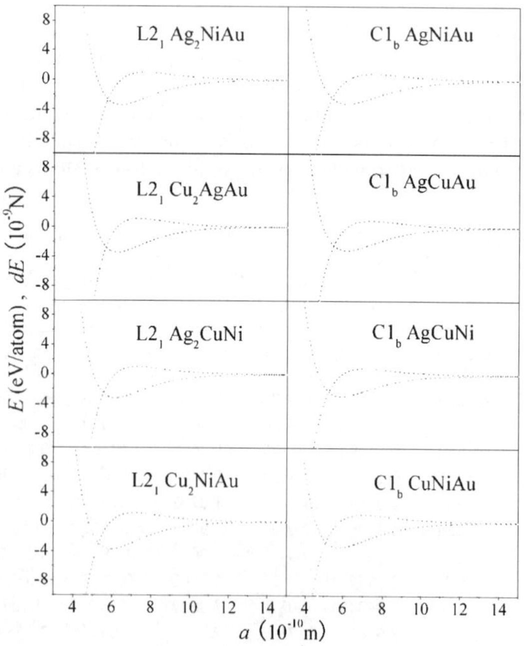

FIG. 1. Total energies E and their derivatives dE calculated from the LREP model (solid lines) and Rose equation (dotted lines), respectively, for some ternary alloys of Cu, Ag, Au, and Ni.

the x, y, and z axes, respectively, and in three directions, the periodic boundary conditions are imposed. In setting the solid solution models, the solute atoms are added into the model by randomly substituting a desired number of solvent atoms to obtain the initial state of the disordered solid solution models. After construction of the models, MS calculations are then carried out to optimize the solid solutions so as to find the minimum energies at different compositions. During energy optimization, the lattice constant is allowed to vary with a small interval (e.g., 0.001 Å), yet the model remains in fcc structure. In order to improve the computational efficiency, a cell-linked list method[7] is adopted in the present MS calculation. Assume that $E_{\min}$ is the minimum energy per atom of the $A_xB_yC_{1-x-y}$ alloy and E_A, E_B, and E_C are the experimental lattice energies of metals A, B, and C, respectively, the formation enthalpy ΔH for alloy $A_xB_yC_{1-x-y}$ can be expressed by

$$\Delta H = E_{\min} - [E_A x + E_B y + E_C(1-x-y)]. \qquad (2)$$

We now turn to discuss the calculated results of the Cu–Ag–Au, Cu–Ag–Ni, Ag–Au–Ni, and Cu–Au–Ni systems. Based on the formation enthalpies from MS calculations, the contours of the formation enthalpies for the four ternary systems are plotted in Fig. 2. One sees from the figure that in the four ternary systems, the formation enthalpies of Ag–Cu–Ni (from 0 to +26.1 kJ/mol) are positive at all compositions. As for the other three systems, the formation enthalpies are negative at some compositions and positive at other compositions, i.e., for the Cu–Ag–Au, Ag–Au–Ni, and Cu–Au–Ni systems, they are −11.4 ~ +11.4, −8.9 ~ +26.1, and −11.3 ~ +8.1 kJ/mol, respectively. Further inspecting the results in Fig. 2, one can find that the formation enthalpies of the ternary metal system are extremely affected by those of the constituent binary systems. Commonly, if the formation enthalpies of the three constituent binary systems are all positive (negative), those of the corresponding ternary system should also be positive (negative), such as the Cu–Ag–Ni system; if the formation enthalpies are positive in some constituent binary systems and negative in others, those of the ternary system would be positive at some compositions and negative at other compositions, such as the Cu–Ag–Au, Ag–Au–Ni, and Cu–Au–Ni systems.

It is interesting and important to compare the present results with those obtained by experiments and other theoretical models. Firstly, the present MS calculations reveal that the maximum positive or minimum negative formation enthalpies of the six binary systems, i.e., Ag–Cu, Ag–Au, Ag–Ni, Cu–Au, Cu–Ni, and Au–Ni systems, are +11.4, −8.9, +26.1, −11.3, +2.5, and +8.1 kJ/mol, respectively, which are quite consistent with the corresponding available experimental values or the results of *ab initio* calculations, i.e., +3.0, −4.6,+33.2, −11.4, +1.9, and +7.6 kJ/mol, respectively.[8,9] Note that although the formation enthalpy of the Cu–Ni system is calculated to be a positive value, the system is miscible at a normal temperature, e.g., 400 K. The reason may come from the small value of formation enthalpy, the small size difference, and the same structure between Cu and Ni. Secondly, we also compared the present results of the Cu–Ag–Au system with those obtained from experiments[10] and Zhang and Jesser's calculation based on Miedema's model[1] in Fig. 3. Although the experimental values are the mixing enthalpy in liquid state, one can still see from Fig. 3 that the agreement between the experimental values and the

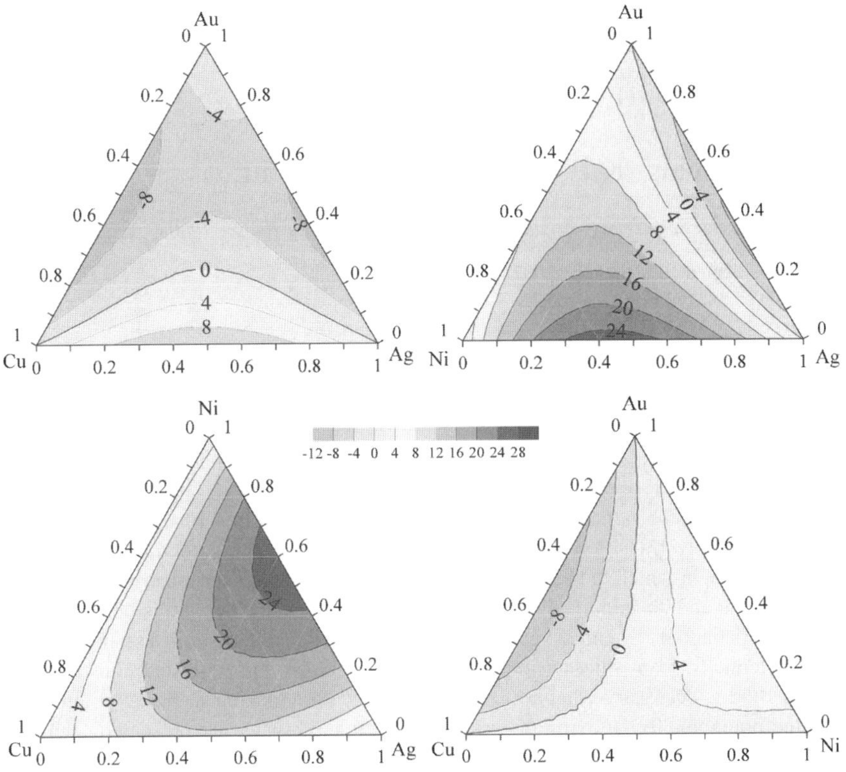

FIG. 2. (Color online) Formation enthalpies calculated from MS calculations for Cu–Ag–Au, Ag–Ni–Au, Cu–Ag–Ni, and Cu–Au–Ni systems.

present results is qualitatively good. Turning to inspect the results of Zhang and Jesser's calculation, one sees that the agreement between the calculated results and experimental values is bad. Apparently, the present scheme is more relevant than Miedema's model in predicting the formation enthalpy of the ternary metal system. For the other three ternary systems, there is no available experimental value; however, we found that the predicted formation enthalpies of the Ni_2AgCu, Ni_2CuAu, and Au_2AgNi alloys are +19.4, +4.0, and +7.3 kJ/mol, respectively, which are qualitatively consistent with the results derived from *ab initio* calculations for their $L2_1$ structure (+20.5, +9.3, and +7.2 kJ/mol, respectively), also reflecting the relevance of the present scheme.

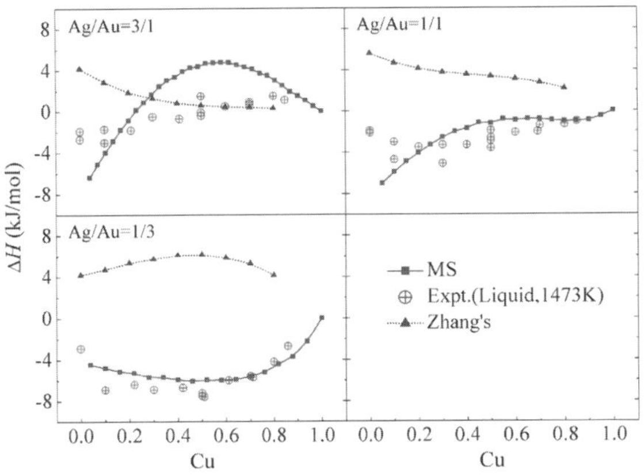

FIG. 3. Formation enthalpies from MS calculations and Zhang and Jesser's calculations (Ref. 1) together with the experimental mixing enthalpies (Ref. 10) for ternary CuAgAu alloys.

In summary, an efficient and relevant scheme has been proposed in the present study to predict the formation enthalpy of the ternary metal system. Note that the computational precision of the proposed scheme extremely depends on three key points, i.e., reasonably setting the solid solution, choosing an appropriate potential model, and fitting a relevant potential for the metal system. The proposed scheme can be applied not only in binary and ternary metal systems but also in more complex alloy systems.

The authors are grateful for the financial support from the National Natural Science Foundation of China (50531040), the Ministry of Science and Technology of China (2006CB605201), and the Administration of Tsinghua University.

[1] B. Zhang and W. A. Jesser, Physica B **315**, 123 (2002).
[2] Y. F. Ouyang, X. P. Zhong, Y. Du, Z. P. Jin, Y. H. He, and Z. H. Yuan, J. Alloys Compd. **416**, 148 (2006).
[3] X. D. Dai, J. H. Li, and Y. Kong, Phys. Rev. B **75**, 052102 (2007).
[4] X. D. Dai, Y. Kong, and J. H. Li, Phys. Rev. B **75**, 104101 (2007).
[5] M. D. Segall, P. L. Lindan, M. J. Probert, C. J. Pickard, P. J. Hasnip, S. J. Clark, and M. C. Payne, J. Phys.: Condens. Matter **14**, 2717 (2002).
[6] J. H. Rose, J. R. Smith, F. Guinea, and J. Ferrante, Phys. Rev. B **29**, 2963 (1984).
[7] M. P. Allen and D. J. Tildesley, *Computer Simulation of Liquids* (Oxford University Press, New York, 1990).
[8] R. Hultgren, P. D. Desal, D. T. Hawkins, M. Gleiser, and K. K. Kelley, *Selected Values of the Thermodynamic Properties of Binary Alloys* (American Society for Metals, Metals Park, OH, 1973).
[9] S. Takizawa, K. Terakura, and T. Mohri, Phys. Rev. B **39**, 5792 (1989).
[10] K. Fitzner and O. J. Kleppa, Metall. Trans. A **24**, 1827 (1993).

Interatomic potentials of the binary transition metal systems and some applications in materials physics

J.H. Li, X.D. Dai, S.H. Liang, K.P. Tai, Y. Kong, B.X. Liu*

Advanced Materials Laboratory, Department of Materials Science and Engineering, Tsinghua University, Beijing 100084, China

Accepted 10 September 2007
Available online 6 October 2007

editor: A.A. Maradudin

Abstract

The present article focuses on a discussion concerning the concept, method and detailed construction procedure of seven interatomic potentials currently available for *fcc*, *bcc* and *hcp* transition metals and their binary alloys. The potentials include the embedded atom method potential and its modified version, in which the cross-potential takes a three-parameter linear function, the second-moment approximation of tight-binding potential and its smoothed version, in which a truncation function is incorporated to improve the performance, the Finnis–Sinclair potential and its extended version, in which the atomic interaction is strengthened, and the recently proposed long-range empirical potential. Meanwhile, an important method, *i.e. ab initio* assisted construction of interatomic potentials, is introduced and the method is necessary whenever the physical data are lacking in fitting potentials. Moreover, applications of some twenty constructed potentials for studying materials science related issues are presented, such as the structural phase transitions, characteristics of metastable alloys, atomic structure of metallic glasses, and solid-state interfacial reaction/amorphization.

PACS: 34.20.C; 07.05.T; 61.43.D; 72.80.G

Keywords: Many-body interactions; Interatomic potentials; Molecular dynamics simulations; Binary transition metal systems

Contents

* Corresponding author. Tel.: +86 10 6277 2557; fax: +86 10 6277 1160.
E-mail address: dmslbx@tsinghua.edu.cn (B.X. Liu).

Review Article, Physics Reports 455 (1-3), p.1–134 (2008).
因篇幅较长，全文请见本书所附光盘.

Atomistic theory for predicting the binary metallic glass formation

J.H. Li, Y. Dai, Y.Y. Cui, B.X. Liu *

Advanced Materials Laboratory, Department of Materials Science and Engineering, Tsinghua University, Beijing 100084, China

A R T I C L E I N F O

Article history:
Available online xxx

Keywords:
Metallic glass
Glass-forming ability
Interatomic potential
Atomistic simulation

A B S T R A C T

In the present review article, firstly, the experimental observations of the binary metallic glass formation by various glass-producing techniques are briefly summarized. Secondly, a detailed discussion is presented concerning the concepts of the glass-forming ability and glass-forming range (GFA/GFR) of a binary metal system. Meanwhile, some of the proposed empirical criteria or rules for predicting the binary metallic glass formation are discussed and compared with the experimental observations. Thirdly, it is proposed to take the interatomic potential of a binary metal system as the starting base to develop an atomistic theory capable of predicting the binary metallic glass formation. Accordingly, eight binary metal systems are selected as representatives to cover the various structural combinations as well as various thermodynamic characteristics. The n-body potentials of eight representative systems are then constructed with the aid of *ab initio* calculations. Applying the constructed and proven realistic n-body potentials, a series of molecular dynamics simulations are carried out. In the simulations, solid solution models are employed to compare the relative stability of the solid solution versus its competing disordered counterpart (i.e. the amorphous or metallic glass phase) as a function of the solute concentration. Finally, based on the realistic interatomic potentials, molecular dynamics simulations not only reveal the physical origin of the binary metallic glass formation, but also quantitatively determine, for each system, an alloy composition range, within which the disordered state is energetically favored, thus leading to establish the atomistic theory capable of predicting the GFR, i.e. the quantitative GFA, of the binary metal systems.

Contents

* Corresponding author.
E-mail address: dmslbx@tsinghua.edu.cn (B.X. Liu).

Review Article: Materials Science and Engineering: Reports 70 (1-2), 1-28 (2011).

1. Introduction

In 1954, Buckel and Hilsch found that condensation of the metal vapors onto a cooled substrate could result in forming an amorphous alloy [1,2]. A few years later, Duwez et al. obtained the Au–Si metallic glass by using a technique named liquid melt quenching [3,4]. These pioneering works not only explored a new category of materials with a non-crystalline structure differing sharply from those widely used crystalline materials, such as steels, aluminum alloys, titanium alloys, but also discovered a new state of matter, in which the metal atoms are arranged in a disordered configuration [5–7]. Since the 1960s, liquid melt quenching has extensively been employed to produce a great number of metallic glasses in the binary metal systems [8–10]. In the early stage, metallic glasses obtained by liquid melt quenching were mostly thin films or foils. Since the late 1980s, researchers have found a number of multi-component metal systems (e.g. three to five metals), in which liquid melt quenching could readily produce the so-called bulk metallic glasses with a geometrical size of up to a magnitude of centimeter [11–15].

Based on the experimental data, the binary metal systems have once been classified into glass-forming and non-glass-forming systems depending on whether or not a metallic glass could be obtained in these systems upon liquid melt quenching. It is noted that in liquid melt quenching, the initial state is a liquid melt of the alloy and the liquid melt is rapidly quenched to result in freezing the liquid state, thus forming a metallic glass. Apparently, a prerequisite condition for forming the metallic glasses in a binary metal system by liquid melt quenching is that the two constituent metals of the system could be co-melted. It is known that the binary metal systems could be classified into two groups: equilibrium miscible systems frequently featuring negative heat of formation (ΔH_f) and equilibrium immiscible systems usually characterized by positive ΔH_f [16]. It follows that the equilibrium miscible systems could possibly be the glass-forming systems, whereas the equilibrium immiscible systems are obviously the non-glass-forming systems, because the two immiscible metals could even not be co-melted to form an alloy. In fact, the equilibrium immiscible binary metal systems have long been excluded from studying the metallic glass formation by liquid melt quenching.

In the early 1980s, some new powerful nonequilibrium material-processing techniques, such as ion beam mixing [17–19], solid-state amorphization [20,21] and mechanical alloying [22,23], were introduced to study the metallic glass formation. In these nonequilibrium material-processing techniques, the metallic glasses were formed under a far from equilibrium condition driven by some external force, such as ion irradiation in ion beam mixing [24]. It has been demonstrated that these nonequilibrium material-processing techniques are capable of producing metallic glasses not only in the equilibrium miscible, but also in the equilibrium immiscible binary metal systems [25–27]. Consequently, the fruitful experimental data so far obtained by these newly introduced techniques suggest that the previous understanding concerning the metallic glass formation of the binary metal systems based mainly on liquid melt quenching data needs to be reconsidered and clarified.

In the field of metallic glasses, one of the basic scientific issues is the so-called glass-forming ability (GFA), which relates to the ease or difficulty of the metallic glass formation. This issue has been discussed in the literature and in general approached in two ways [10,28–30]. Firstly, consideration is given to a specific alloy, i.e. the metallic glass formation is considered as the consequence of frustration of the crystallization due to the difficulties during freezing of liquids, or the consequence of possible enhanced stability of a liquid-like state down to low temperatures [29]. Secondly, consideration is given to a specific binary metal system, and in this situation, the glass-forming range (GFR) is employed to indicate whether or not and in which alloy composition range the metallic glasses could be obtained in the system by some materials producing techniques [30]. Martin and Bellon have proposed a phenomenological framework allowing for predicting the formation as well as the evolution path of some non-equilibrium materials as a function of the driving force conditions. However, due to the complexity of the metallic glass formation, these approaches are still rather qualitative and heuristic [24]. Moreover, the issue related to the GFA has still been one of the challenging topics and is far from adequately solved [29–32]. In the present work, we would focus our attention on the second meaning of the GFA, i.e. we would try to develop an atomistic theory that is capable of predicting not only whether the metallic glass could be formed or not, but also an quantitative alloy composition range energetically favored for metallic glass formation in a binary metal system, by using some glass-producing techniques.

In the present review article, firstly, the experimental observations of the binary metallic glass formation by various glass-producing techniques are briefly summarized. Secondly, based on the experimental results, an in-depth discussion is presented concerning the concepts of GFA/GFR. Meanwhile several empirical criteria or rules frequently cited in the literature to predict the binary metallic glass formation are discussed and compared to the experimental observations. Thirdly, a detailed description is presented concerning the development of an atomistic theory that is capable of predicting the binary metallic glass formation. Aiming to develop a theory valid in general, eight binary metal systems are selected as representatives to cover the various structural combinations as well as various thermodynamic characteristics ranging from a large negative to a large positive ΔH_f. The respective n-body potentials of the eight representative systems are constructed with the aid of *ab initio* calculations. The constructed and proven realistic n-body potentials are then applied in a series of molecular dynamics simulations. In the simulations, solid solution models are employed to compare the relative stability of the solid solution versus their competing disordered counterpart, as a function of the solute concentration. From the simulations, a unanimous verdict is achieved, i.e. starting with an n-body potential of a binary metal system, molecular dynamics simulations not only reveal the physical origin of the metallic glass formation, but also quantitatively determine, for each system, an alloy composition range, within which metallic glass formation is energetically favored, thus leading to develop the atomistic theory capable of predicting the GFR, i.e. the quantitative GFA, of the binary metal systems.

2. Experimental observations of the binary metallic glass formation

In the early stage, the metallic glasses were obtained by liquid melt quenching, or vapor quenching, etc. In liquid melt quenching, an alloy melt is first prepared and then rapidly quenched to freeze the alloy melt in its initial liquid state, thus forming an amorphous alloy, i.e. the metallic glass. The underlying physics of metallic glass formation upon liquid melt quenching is through a process of liquid-to-solid phase transformation. Over the past 50 years, the liquid melt quenching and other glass-producing techniques have extensively been developed and elaborated to produce a large number of metallic glasses. Since the 1980s, ion beam mixing of multiple metal layers [17–19], solid-state amorphization [20,21], and mechanical alloying [22,23] have also been employed to study the metallic glass formation in the binary metal systems. In contrast to the liquid melt quenching, the metallic glass formation upon these newly developed nonequilibrium techniques is through a process of solid-to-solid phase transformation. Due to their powerful capabilities, these nonequilibrium techniques have so far been employed to produce a great variety of metallic glasses not only in the equilibrium miscible, but also in the equilibrium immiscible binary metal systems [25–27].

In this section, we would discuss the formation of binary metallic glasses by liquid melt quenching, ion beam mixing, solid-state amorphization and mechanical alloying. The liquid melt quenching has been and currently is still an important glass-producing technique, and the latter three techniques have provided important data concerning the metallic glass formation, not only in the equilibrium miscible systems as supplemental data to those obtained by liquid melt quenching, but also in the equilibrium immiscible systems as newly obtained data, that were not known in the early years.

2.1. Binary metallic glass formation by liquid melt quenching

2.1.1. Glass transition

When a liquid melt is cooled, either crystallization occurs at the melting point T_m, or the liquid melt is supercooled at temperature below T_m, becoming more viscous with decreasing temperature and ultimately transforming into a *glass*. These behaviors can be identified by inspecting the volume-temperature or the energy-temperature curves, etc. The crystallization process is manifested by an abrupt change in both volume and energy at T_m, whereas the glass transition is characterized by a gradual change of slope. The temperature region, over which the change of slope occurs, is named as the glass transition temperature T_g, and may vary by as much as 10–20% depending on the cooling speed [6].

According to the definition for an order of a phase transition, a liquid-to-crystal transition, i.e. the traditional solidification, is a first-order phase transition, since the thermodynamic variables, e.g. the volume and energy, are discontinuous at the transition temperature T_m. In a glass transition, these thermodynamic variables are continuous, yet their derivatives with respect to temperature are discontinuous at the transition temperature T_g. It seems that the glass transition is a second-order phase transition. However, some experimental evidences show that the glass transition is not a simple second-order phase transition. To soundly interpret the complexity of the glass transition, some phenomenological models or concepts, such as the relaxation theory of liquid, mode coupling theory, free volume theory, have been proposed. For more details of the proposed theories, readers can be referred to the publications on this subject [5,6,33].

2.1.2. Summary of metallic glasses obtained by liquid melt quenching

To obtain the metallic glasses by liquid melt quenching, a cooling speed higher than 10^6 K/s is frequently needed to restrain crystallization of any possible crystalline phase. Perhaps the earliest method of liquid melt quenching was the gun technique devised by Duwez et al. In this technique, a molten alloy is atomized by expulsion from a shock tube and propelled against the surface of a substrate with a high thermal conductivity [3,4]. The major disadvantages of the gun technique are the discontinuous and porous nature of the obtained amorphous alloys. Consequently, the gun technique was soon superseded by a plethora of other melt quenching techniques, such as twin-roll quenching, melting spinning. The techniques developed later have received considerable attention, because these techniques demonstrated a great capability for producing continuous amorphous filaments, ribbons or sheets [9]. Another liquid melt quenching technique is the copper mold casting and it has so far been employed to produce a number of metallic glasses, including some bulk metallic glasses [10,34]. In recent years, a cooling speed up to as high as 10^7–10^8 K/s or even higher has been achieved and it has helped to greatly enhance the capability of producing a number of new metallic glasses [27].

Up-to-now, the list of the metallic glasses obtained by liquid melt quenching has ever been lengthening and there are found more than 100 binary metal systems, in which the metallic glasses have been obtained by this technique. The metallic glasses so far obtained could loosely be classified into four groups: (i) alloys of transition metals or noble metals with 15–25% metalloid; (ii) alloys of late transition metals with early transition metals; (iii) alloys with alkali or alkaline-earth metals; and (iv) alloys with rare earth metal or actinides. Table 1 lists alphabetically some representative binary metal systems and their GFRs.

One can easily see that only the alloys whose compositions are within or close to the eutectic trough or valleys or are on the low liquid-temperature plateaus in the equilibrium phase diagram of the system, tend to form metallic glasses upon liquid melt quenching. For example, in the Fe–Zr system, there are two eutectic points, i.e. the Fe-rich eutectic (~90 at% Fe) and Zr-rich eutectic (~76 at% Zr). By melting spinning technique, Buschow et al. and Altounian et al. have indeed obtained the Fe–Zr metallic glasses in the composition ranges of 87–91 at% Fe and of 57–82 at% Zr, respectively [70,107]. In fact, Turnbull was the first to propose a well-known deep eutectic criterion [141], predicting that the metallic glass formation should be easiest for the eutectic composition in a given binary metal system and that the deeper the eutectic point or the steeper the adjacent liquidus, the easier the formation of metallic glasses. For instance, the deep eutectic criterion predicts that the Pd–Si and Cu–Zr amorphous alloys and even bulk metallic glasses could be obtained, because there are two deep eutectic valleys in the Pd–Si equilibrium phase diagram and a deep eutectic basin in the Cu–Zr equilibrium phase diagram, respectively. Experimentally, the Pd–Si and Cu–Zr bulk metallic glasses have indeed been obtained by many research groups

Table 1
Glass-forming range (GFR, at% B) of the A–B binary metal systems obtained by liquid melt quenching.

System	GFR	References	System	GFR	References
Al–Ca	9–11, 55–85	[35–38]	Cu–Ti	25–65	[76–81]
Al–Ce	7–12	[39,40]	Cu–Zr	10–80	[71,75,79, 81–94]
Al–Dy	9–12	[41–43]	Fe–Gd	18–60	[95,96]
Al–Gd	8–12	[41–43]	Fe–Hf	8–10	[97]
Al–Ho	9–12	[41,42]	Fe–Nd	11–60	[98–101]
Al–La	7–14, 45–87	[40–42,44–51]	Fe–Pr	45–90	[102]
Al–Mn	15–25	[52]	Fe–Y	20–62	[103–106]
Al–Nd	8–14	[41,42,44,53]	Fe–Zr	9–13, 57–82	[70,107]
Al–Pr	9–11	[41,42]	Ge–Te	75–90	[108,109]
Al–Sm	8–16	[41–44,54–58]	Ge–Zr	81–88	[110,111]
Al–Tb	9–14	[41–43]	Hf–Ni	30–70	[75,112]
Al–Y	8–15	[39–42,59]	La–Ni	30–40	[46,113]
Al–Yb	9–13	[41,42]	Mg–Pd	10–35	[114–117]
Al–Ti	34–54	[60]	Mg–Y	15–16	[118]
Al–U	8–10	[61]	Mg–Zn	24–32	[119–122]
Al–Zr	45–53, 63–74	[62]	Nb–Ni	40–62.5	[123–129]
Be–Ti	59–63	[63,64]	Ni–Ta	30–50	[129–131]
Be–Zr	50–70	[64–67]	Ni–Zr	20–80	[82,132]
Co–Gd	62–71	[68]	Pd–Zr	65–70	[83,92, 133–136]
Co–Tb	45–65	[69]	Pt–Zr	70–80	[83,134, 137–139]
Co–Zr	42–80	[70]	Rh–Zr	66–80	[83]
Cu–Hf	30–70	[71–75]	Ti–Zr	15–22	[140]

[88,142]. Moreover, the same concept could also be applied to the ternary metal systems. Take the Cu–Zr–Ti system as an example, by adding the third metal Ti into the Cu–Zr alloy, the eutectic point becomes lower than that of the Cu–Zr system, so that the metallic glass with an alloy composition locating around the ternary eutectic point could easily be obtained [143–145]. It is further deduced that by adding the fourth and even fifth alloying elements into a metal system, the eutectic point could further be lowered and therefore the metallic glass formation could become much easier than that in the binary and ternary metal systems. Obviously, the deep eutectic criterion suggests that bulk metallic glasses are most likely to be obtained in the multi-component metal systems and in recent years, the criterion has indeed been shown to be a valuable guide in searching for the candidate metal systems to produce bulk metallic glasses.

2.2. Binary metallic glass formation by ion beam mixing

Ion beam mixing was introduced in 1980 to study the formation of metal-silicides between the metal and silicon layers by Tsaur et al. [146,147]. A little later it was employed to study the formation of nonequilibrium alloy phases with either a crystalline or amorphous structure [148,149]. In studying a A–B binary metal system by ion beam mixing, the A–B multilayered films with the desired overall composition A_xB_{1-x} (x = 0–1) are prepared by alternately depositing the A and B metals onto an inert substrate (e.g. NaCl, or SiO_2). In the as-deposited state, the A and B layers are frequently in their respective equilibrium polycrystalline structures. In ion beam mixing, the as-deposited A–B multilayered films are irradiated by inert gas ions (mostly by heavy ions, e.g. the xenon ions) of high energy (typically, 200–300 keV, or even higher) at ambient temperature (300 K) or at liquid nitrogen temperature (77 K) or even lower.

2.2.1. Physical process of ion beam mixing

In general, ion beam mixing proceeds in two consecutive steps, namely the atomic collision cascade and relaxation [150–154]. In the first step, the irradiating ions are decelerated by a series of elastic and inelastic collisions. The inelastic collision transfers the energy of the irradiating ions to the electrons and nuclei in the metal layers. In the elastic collision, the energy of the irradiating ions is transferred to the atoms, which are knocked out of their original lattice positions. The knocked out atoms are also highly energetic and able to generate a second generation of collisions, and so on so forth. This process is named as atomic collision cascade and it could trigger the intermixing of the metals A and B in the A–B multilayered films, as the atoms of metals A and B are excited by the irradiating ions and could migrate crossing the interfaces. After receiving an adequate irradiation dose, the discrete layered structure of the A–B multilayered films is smeared out and a uniform A–B atomic mixture is obtained. The A–B atomic mixture thus obtained is in a highly disordered state with much higher energy than that of its corresponding equilibrium state. Obviously, the atomic collision cascade is a process of far-from-equilibrium, as a large number of atoms are excited in violent motion in this step.

At the termination of the atomic collision cascade, the equilibrium thermodynamics comes into play to direct the highly disordered and energetic A–B atomic mixture to lower its energy towards equilibrium during the second step of relaxation. However, whether or not the A–B atomic mixture could go directly to its corresponding equilibrium state depends on the temperature and time conditions available during the relaxation step. It is commonly believed that the structure of the newly formed alloy phase by ion beam mixing is fixed in the relaxation step, but not in the first step of atomic collision cascade, during which a large number of atoms are in violent motion. According to the atomic collision theory [151,152,155], the duration of the relaxation step is extremely short and in the most cases, the A–B atomic mixture is not allowed to proceed straightforward to its equilibrium state. Instead, it frequently resides in one of the available or possible intermediate states that correspond to either metastable crystalline or amorphous phases.

To estimate the duration of the relaxation, we take an alternative way to examine the process of ion beam mixing, i.e. considering the energy deposition into the A–B multilayered films by the irradiating ions, giving rise to the thermal spike concept. This concept of the thermal spike was firstly introduced by Seitz and Koehler in 1956 and further elaborated by some well-known scientists, e.g. Averback et al. by conducting atomistic simulations [147] and Sigmund by theoretical consideration [154]. Considering a cylinder with a diameter of 5 nm and a length of 100 nm, a simple estimation shows that because the energy of the atoms transferred by the irradiating ions, the temperature at the cylinder center could be excited up to as high as 10^3–10^4 K [27,151]. At the same time, the materials surrounding the cylinder remain at ambient temperature. For such a huge temperature difference to equilibrate with the surroundings, it requires an extremely short time, approximately 10^{-10}–10^{-9} s. It is therefore deduced that an effective cooling speed available in ion beam mixing could be as high as 10^{13}–10^{14} K/s. Such a high cooling speed is probably the highest one among the currently available glass-producing techniques [27]. Naturally, such a short time of the relaxation not only severely restricts the kinetic condition for the alloy phase formation, but also affects the structural characteristics of the alloy phase to be formed. In fact, during the relaxation, either some limited atomic rearrangements take place, leading the atomic mixture to form a metastable crystalline phase frequently of simple structure, or the disordered state is still preserved, resulting in forming an amorphous phase, or metallic glass. In fact, extensive experimental results have shown that due to its far-from-equilibrium nature and the extremely restricted kinetic condition, the nonequilibrium alloys so far obtained by ion beam mixing are either amorphous alloys or simple structured crystalline alloys [148].

Table 2
Glass-forming range (GFR, at% B) of the A–B binary metal systems obtained by ion beam mixing.

System	ΔH_f	GFR	References	System	ΔH_f	GFR	References
Ag–Mo	Hf > 0	25–88	[157–159]	Fe–Zr	Hf < 0	10–27	[174]
Ag–Nb	Hf > 0	25–90	[159]	Hf–Ta	Hf > 0	26–90	[175]
Ag–Ta	Hf > 0	62–80	[160]	Mo–Ni	Hf < 0	35–65	[18]
Al–Mn	Hf < 0	12–21	[161]	Mo–Y	Hf > 0	22–78	[176]
Al–Pt	Hf < 0	33–75	[162]	Nb–Ni	Hf < 0	20–85	[177]
Al–Ti	Hf < 0	25–75	[163]	Nb–Zr	Hf > 0	8–88	[178,179]
Au–Mo	Hf > 0	75–85	[164]	Ni–Sc	Hf < 0	29–80	[180]
Co–Mo	Hf < 0	35–65	[18,165]	Ni–Ta	Hf < 0	25–75	[181]
Co–Nb	Hf < 0	20–77	[166]	Ni–Ti	Hf < 0	37.6–85	[182]
Co–Ta	Hf < 0	25–75	[167,168]	Ni–Zr	Hf < 0	30–65	[183]
Cu–Ru	Hf > 0	25–75	[169]	Rh–Ta	Hf < 0	43–65	[184]
Cu–Ta	Hf > 0	30–50	[170]	Sc–W	Hf > 0	25–40	[185]
Fe–Nb	Hf < 0	25–75	[171,172]	Ta–Zr	Hf > 0	31–80	[186]
Fe–Ta	Hf < 0	25–80	[171,173]	Y–Zr	Hf > 0	65–85	[187]

2.2.2. Summary of metallic glasses obtained by ion beam mixing

Due to its great capability, ion beam mixing has so far produced a great variety of amorphous alloys, or metallic glasses from some 100 binary metal systems, including a number of equilibrium immiscible binary metal systems. Clearly, the experimental results obtained by ion beam mixing indicate that the disorder state does exist in those equilibrium immiscible binary metal systems though, according to the liquid melt quenching study, they have previously been classified as non-glass forming systems. Meanwhile, researchers have endeavored to achieve a better understanding of the amorphous alloy formation upon ion beam mixing. For instance, Liu et al. have proposed a so-called structural difference rule [17], which states that an amorphous alloy would most likely be formed by ion beam mixing in a binary metal system, if the two metals are of different structures and the alloy composition is designed to reside in the middle of the two-phase region observed from its equilibrium phase diagram. It should be noted that the proposed rule is a sufficient condition but not a necessary one and that the ion beam mixing experiments should be properly executed [17,156]. To give an overview of ion beam mixing studies concerning the binary metallic glass formation, Table 2 alphabetically lists the binary metal systems that have so far been studied by ion beam mixing.

2.3. Binary metallic glass formation by solid-state amorphization

2.3.1. Summary of experimental observations of solid-state amorphization

In 1983, Schwarz and Johnson firstly reported that medium temperature thermal annealing of the Au–La multilayered films could result in the formation of an Au–La amorphous alloy and named the process as solid-state amorphization. They further argued that a large negative ΔH_f and a large size difference are favored conditions for solid-state amorphization to take place [20]. From the mid of 1990s, extensive experimental studies have been carried out and shown that solid-state amorphization could also take place in some binary metal systems having quite different characteristics from those of the Au–La system, for example, in the Ni–Mo system with a small negative $\Delta H_f = -7$ kJ/mol [188], in the equilibrium immiscible Cu–Ta system even with a positive $\Delta H_f = +3$ kJ/mol [189], and in the Au–Ta system with two metals having almost identical atomic sizes [190]. To give an overview, Table 3 lists the observations of solid-state amorphization in 28 binary metal systems [191].

2.3.2. Thermodynamics and kinetics of solid-state amorphization

At the beginning, Schwarz and Johnson attributed the solid-state amorphization observed in the Au–La system to the large negative ΔH_f and the large atomic size difference of the system. Since then, solid-state amorphization has been observed in some other binary metal systems with similar characteristics of the Au–La system [193,194,198]. Later, Clemens et al. proposed a similar model to predict the possibility of solid-state amorphization, suggesting that a large negative ΔH_f and a small atomic volume ratio would facilitate the solid-state amorphization [21]. The small atomic volume ratio not only results in an asymmetric diffusion, but also leads to the formation of a disordered interface that could provide some nucleation sites for the amorphous phase. Another model was proposed by Kwak et al. to predict the possibility of solid-state amorphization by considering the thermodynamic factor together with an effective driving force [215]. In this model, the thermodynamic factor was defined as the free energy difference between the resultant amorphous phase and the initial polycrystalline state. The effective driving force was defined as the ratio of the effective radius of the interstitial site in the host matrix to that of the diffusing atom. Apparently, all the above models are based on similar or equivalent parameters and all predict that solid-state amorphization could take place in the binary metal systems with negative ΔH_f.

However, the experimental studies conducted from the mid 1990s onward, have shown that solid-state amorphization could also take place in a binary metal system with a positive ΔH_f. Evidently, it is needed to develop a criterion capable of predicting the possibility of solid-state amorphization in the binary metal systems with either positive or negative ΔH_f. In this respect, Zhang et al. have attributed the solid-state amorphization taking place in a binary metal system with a positive ΔH_f to the interfacial free energy stored in the initial metal–metal multilayers, and showed that the amount of the interfacial free energy is in positive proportion to the number of the layers while the total thickness of the multilayers is fixed. It is therefore possible to synthesize the amorphous thin films in the equilibrium immiscible binary metal systems by properly designing the metal–metal multilayers [216].

Table 3
Metallic glasses obtained by solid-state-amorphization [186].

System	ΔH_f	Atomic size difference	References
Transition metal–rare-earth systems			
Au–La	−108	23.2	[20]
Cu–Er	–	27.3	[192]
Ni–Ce	−40	31.7	[193]
Ni–Er	−48	29.1	[192]
Simple-metal–transition-metal systems			
Al–Mn	−43	4.6	[194]
Al–Mo	−24	4.8	[195]
Al–Pt	−82	3.1	[162,196]
Mg–Ni	−8	22.1	[197]
Sn–Co	−17	10.8	[198]
Transition-metal–transition-metal systems			
Au–Ta	−49	0.8	[190]
Au–Y	−110	20	[199]
Au–Zr	−112	9.3	[200]
Co–Zr	−60	21.2	[201]
Cu–Nb	+4	10.6	[202]
Cu–Ta	+3	9.4	[170,203]
Cu–W	+33	6.8	[204]
Cu–Y	−32	29.1	[205]
Fe–Zr	−37	21.9	[206]
Hf–Ni	−63	20.3	[207,208]
Mo–Ni	−11	8.6	[188]
Mo–Y	+35	24.4	[209]
Nb–Ni	−45	12.8	[210]
Nb–Y	+44	20.7	[211]
Ni–Ta	−44	12.9	[181]
Ni–Ti	−52	14	[212]
Ni–Zr	−72	21.6	[21,212]
Ta–Y	+40	21.8	[213]
W–Y	+35	24	[214]

Moreover, Lin et al. have proposed a parameter, κ, to describe the differential diffusivity of a binary metal system, and found that a minimum value of κ, around 0.6, was required to ensure the solid-state amorphization to take place in the transition metal–metal multilayers [217]. For the detailed experimental observations and interpretation for solid-state amorphization taking place in the binary metal systems, the readers are referred to the author's review articles [26].

Concerning the kinetics of solid-state amorphization, some experimental results have shown that the growth of the amorphous interlayer in the metal–metal multilayers at medium temperature is an essentially diffusion-limited process [207, 218,219]. One can expect that the growing velocity of the amorphous interlayer falls like $t^{1/2}$. Meng et al. have proposed that when the growing velocity was less than a critical value, nucleation of the intermetallic compound would occur [220,221]. Highmore et al. have also developed a similar model and predicted that for the amorphous interlayer, there existed a critical thickness, beyond which nucleation and growth of the intermetallic compound would replace the further growth of the amorphous phase [222–225]. For the equilibrium immiscible system, in which there is no equilibrium compound, Liu et al. have argued that the extra interfacial energy stored in the metal–metal multilayers could serve as the major driving force for solid-state amorphization to take place, and that the amorphization process would be terminated when the extra interfacial energy was completely consumed with the growing of the amorphous interlayer [226].

2.4. Binary metallic glass formation by mechanical alloying

Mechanical milling is a process that is routinely used in powder metallurgy and mineral processing industries. It is traditionally used for blending powders or crushing rocks. White in 1979 and Koch et al. in 1983 have observed the formation of amorphous alloys in the Sn–Nb and Ni–Nb systems, respectively, by mechanical milling [22,227]. These observations raised the understanding of mechanical milling to a new level, i.e. it could be a material-processing to form alloys. Since then, the term mechanical alloying has been widely accepted and used. Stimulated by such a new understanding, many researchers have been attracted into the field of mechanical alloying, and an increasingly large number of publications have appeared to report the research results of mechanical alloying [228].

In mechanical alloying, an amorphous alloy is formed through a mechanical process, in which the initial metal powders are subjected to high-energy ball milling. The mechanical process not only creates interfaces with ultra-fine layered microstructure between the two crystalline metals, but also introduces high density of structural defects, such as vacancies, atomic site defects, dislocations [23]. The emergence of the interfaces and structural defects could cause a rapid increase of the free energy. When the free energy is elevated up to a higher level than that of the corresponding amorphous state and at the same time, the temperature is sufficiently high to facilitate the interdiffusion between the two metals, an amorphous alloy could be formed. Concerning the amorphization mechanism, Schwarz has argued that the formation of metallic glasses by mechanical alloying could be attributed to the interdiffusion-induced reaction between the two constituent metals and the underlying physics was therefore similar to that involved in the solid-state amorphization [8,20,191]. To have an overview, the metallic glasses so far obtained by mechanical alloying are summarized in Table 4. Comparing the data in Table 4 with those listed in Table 1, one can see that, in general, metallic glasses could be obtained by mechanical alloying in the broader composition ranges than that by liquid melt quenching. In addition, mechanical alloying has even been employed to produce metallic glasses in some equilibrium immiscible binary metal systems with positive ΔH_f, such as the Cu–Ta, Cu–V and Cu–W systems.

Table 4
Glass-forming range (GFR, at% B) of the A–B binary metal systems obtained by mechanical alloying.

System	GFR	Reference	System	GFR	Reference
Al–Fe	20–50	[229,230]	Fe–Nb	25–65	[248]
Al–Nb	15–75	[231,232]	Fe–W	30–60	[257]
Al–Ta	10–90	[233–235]	Fe–Zr	22–80	[247,250,255,258,259]
Al–Ti	25–90	[236–241]	Ge–Nb	70–88	[260]
Al–Zr	60–82.5	[242–244]	Mg–Ni	33–70	[261,262]
Co–Ti	15–20	[245]	Mn–Nb	40–65	[248]
Co–V	33–60	[246]	Mn–Zr	50–80	[247]
Co–Zr	8–73	[246,247]	Ni–Sn	20–40	[263]
Cr–Nb	30–68	[248]	Ni–Ta	20–90	[264,265]
Cu–Hf	10–80	[249,250]	Ni–Ti	28–90	[266,267]
Cu–Ta	20–50	[251,252]	Ni–V	40–65	[268]
Cu–Ti	10–90	[250,253]	Ni–Zr	15–83	[269–271]
Cu–W	30–60	[254]	Pd–Ti	42–85	[272]
Cu–Zr	40–60	[255,256]	Pd–Zr	40–55	[273]

One should bear in mind that some contamination could be introduced into the process of mechanical alloying. The contamination could substantially alter the constitution as well as the stability of the obtained amorphous alloys. In general, the presence of impurities frequently favors the amorphization [23]. In this regard, Yavari and co-workers have argued that when some specific gases [8,274,275], such as 5 at% oxygen or nitrogen, were dissolved in the metal powders during the process of mechanical alloying, there was no immiscibility left and the immiscibility-related positive ΔH_f (of the alloy in question) could become negative. For instance, it was reported that the Fe–Cr amorphous alloys were obtained only in the presence of oxygen [276]. A similar result was also observed in the Nb–Al system, in which an amorphous alloy could be obtained by milling the Nb_3Al powders in the presence of nitrogen gas, yet only a solid solution was formed while milling under a clean atmosphere [23]. In short, the process of mechanical alloying is somehow not adequately clean, and hence it should be very careful while using the related experimental data to discuss the amorphization mechanism, e.g. starting with two metal powders, the obtained amorphous alloys might contain some impurities and therefore they could no longer be considered as binary metal alloys.

3. Glass-forming ability of a binary metal system

3.1. Glass-forming ability and glass-forming range

The term of glass-forming ability (GFA) frequently relates to the ease or difficulty with which the metallic glasses are formed. As mentioned above, it has been approached generally in two different ways. Firstly, the consideration is given to a specific alloy, treating the glass formation as the consequence of a frustration of crystallization during freezing of the liquid melt [29]. This situation can be depicted as a competition between the crystallization temperature and the glass transition temperature. Secondly, the consideration is given to a specific metal system. This situation can be depicted as a competition between the crystalline and amorphous phases as a function of the alloy composition. For the second situation, the term glass-forming range (GFR) is frequently employed to indicate that in an exact alloy composition range, within which the metallic glass or amorphous alloy, is energetically favored to be formed [30]. One should note that not only there is a strong correlation, but also there is some subtle difference between the two situations. To be clarity, we propose to call the first and second meanings of the concept as the GFA of an *alloy* and the GFA of a *system*, respectively.

In practice, researchers frequently use some technical parameters to describe the GFA of an alloy or to compare the GFAs of two alloys. For example, when using the liquid melt quenching technique, the critical quenching speed or the maximum size of the attainable metallic glass is used to describe the GFA. The lower of the critical quenching speed or the larger of the obtained metallic glass, the greater the GFA of the alloy. However, the critical quenching speed is difficult to measure experimentally and also the maximum attainable size strongly depends on the applied glass-producing techniques [14]. Alternatively, a few simple parameters have been proposed based on the temperature or some other physical properties of the binary alloys. Among them, the most famous one is the reduced glass transition temperature T_{rg}, which is defined as the ratio of the glass transition temperature T_g and the liquidus temperature T_l of the alloy. This parameter was proposed firstly by Turnbull with the assumption that the nucleation frequency and growth of crystalline phase scaled inversely with the viscosity of the melt [28]. Later, the supercooled liquid region ΔT_{xg}, the temperature difference between the crystallization onset temperature T_x and the glass transition T_g, have been employed by Inoue et al. as a guidance to search for the better glass-forming alloys [132]. Though these parameters have commonly been used as the indicator for the GFA, one should bear in mind that they did show some contrasting trend for some alloys. For more details of this topic, the readers could refer to those published review articles [30,34,277,278].

Differing from the situation of a specific alloy, the GFA of a metal system is denoted by the GFR. The GFR not only shows whether or not metallic glasses could be obtained in a system, but also indicates the alloy composition range, within which metallic glasses could be formed by some glass-producing techniques. It follows that the wider the GFR, the greater the GFA of a metal system. If the GFR of a metal system is nil, no any metallic glass could be obtained in the system. One may note in the previous section that the GFA of a binary metal system may vary while using different glass-producing techniques. Take the Ni–Nb system as an example, liquid melt quenching could produce the metallic glasses in a composition range of 40–60 at% Nb [123–129], whereas ion beam mixing and mechanical alloying could produce the metallic glasses in the much broader ranges of 20–80 at% [177] and 20–85 at% Nb [248,279], respectively. Another example is the Ni–Mo system. Due to the high melting points of the constituent metals Ni and Mo, liquid melt quenching has not been able to obtain any metallic glass in the system so far, yet ion beam mixing and mechanical alloying techniques have produced the Ni–Mo metallic glasses in a broad composition range [18,188,280,281]. In this respect, to avoid confusion, the authors propose to name the experimentally observed GFA/GFR as the *nominal* GFA/GFR, since they are closely related to the applied glass-producing techniques.

From a physical point of view, a binary metal system should have an *intrinsic* GFA, which is governed or determined by the internal characteristics of the system itself, yet could have several nominal GFAs, which relate to the glass-producing techniques applied in practice. The intrinsic GFA reflects the maximum possible composition range energetically favored for the metallic glass formation. In principle, the intrinsic GFA of a binary metal system should be greater than any nominal GFA observed in experiment. In addition, if a specific glass-producing technique is more powerful than other glass-producing techniques, then the nominal GFA obtained by this technique could be greater than those obtained by other techniques, and moreover, could be closer to the intrinsic GFA of the system than those observed by other techniques. Incidentally, this argument is supported by those experimental results presented in Tables 1–4. For example, as ion beam mixing might be one of the most powerful glass-producing techniques among the available techniques and therefore the nominal GFA of a binary metal system observed from ion beam mixing could be closer to the intrinsic GFA of the system than those obtained by other glass-producing techniques. In this sense, ion beam mixing could be a unique scientific tool to obtain some valuable experimental data, which could greatly help in developing a relevant atomistic theory for predicting the binary metallic glass formation.

3.2. Empirical criteria and rules to predict the glass-forming ability

As summarized in the preceding section, a great variety of metallic glasses have been obtained in the past 50 years by various glass-producing techniques in over 100 equilibrium miscible and immiscible binary metal systems. Meanwhile, researchers have striven to achieve a clear understanding of the underlying physics for the binary metallic glass formation. To quantitatively predict the GFA, i.e. to estimate the GFR of a binary metal system, several empirical criteria or rules have been proposed, based on some specific properties or intrinsic characteristics of the system. For example, based on the equilibrium phase diagram of a binary metal system, Turnbull has proposed a well-known deep eutectic criterion to predict the metallic glass formation upon liquid melt quenching [141]. Egami and Waseda have proposed to predict the metallic glass formation by considering the atomic size difference of the constituent metals of a binary metal system [282]. Based on extensive ion beam mixing studies, Liu et al. have proposed a structural difference rule to predict the amorphous alloy formation by ion beam mixing [17] and further proposed that the total width of the two-phase region (or regions) observed from the equilibrium phase diagram could approximately be the GFR of a binary metal system [148]. In addition, thermodynamic approach, which considers the formation enthalpy and formation energy, has also been proposed to predict the binary metallic glass formation [283,284]. In this section, we would discuss some of the proposed criteria or rules as well as the comparison between the predictions with the experimental observations.

3.2.1. Deep eutectic criterion

Perhaps one of the most cited criteria concerning the metallic glass formation is the so-called deep eutectic criterion, which was proposed by Turnbull based on the equilibrium phase diagrams of the binary metal systems [141]. The criterion states that a metallic glass is likely to be formed by liquid melt quenching in the binary metal system that has a deep eutectic point (or several deep eutectic points) in its equilibrium phase diagram, and that the alloy with overall compositions locating in the vicinity of the eutectic point of the system is easy to be vitrified. In fact, the criterion highlights two essential points for the binary metallic glass formation. First, the eutectic composition is always located in a two-phase region of the corresponding equilibrium phase diagram and is therefore not good for crystallization for the two crystalline phases either of the constituent metals or of the intermetallic compounds. Second, a deep eutectic means a considerably low melting point, which ensures that the initial liquid melt could, during a rapid quenching, be maintained in an over-heating state for much longer time than in an under-cooling state. In fact, the criterion has successfully predicted a number of binary metal systems, in which metallic glasses have indeed been obtained by liquid melt quenching. Moreover, as mentioned previously, based on liquid melt quenching data, the binary metal systems have been classified into glass-forming and non-glass-forming systems. Accordingly, the glass-forming systems have their respective GFA or GFR, whereas for a non-glass-forming system, the GFA and GFR are both nil.

As shown in Tables 2 and 3, a great variety of metallic glasses have been obtained by ion beam mixing or solid-state amorphization, not only in those binary metal systems previously known as glass-forming systems, but also in many previously classified as the non-glass-forming systems based on liquid melt quenching data. In addition, a number of metallic glasses with overall compositions located away from the deep eutectic points have also been obtained by ion beam mixing or solid-state amorphization. Clearly, the deep eutectic criterion is inadequate, and further studies are necessary to develop a relevant theory or model capable of predicting the binary metallic glass formation for both equilibrium miscible and immiscible binary metal systems.

3.2.2. Size difference rule

In the classical theory of physical metallurgy, the well-known Hume–Rothery empirical rule has pointed out the importance of the atomic size, electro-negativity and crystalline structures of the constituent metals in influencing the structural feature of an alloy phase. For the metallic glass formation, Egami and Waseda have argued, by considering the atomic sizes, that due to the atomic size difference, the solute atoms would lead to an atomic level stress in the solvent lattice, and that once the solute concentration and atomic level stress achieve their respective critical points, the solvent lattice would become unstable and transform into an amorphous phase, resulting in forming a metallic glass [282]. For the A–B binary metal system, the critical concentrations $C^{\min}_{\mathrm{B\ in\ A}}$ and $C^{\min}_{\mathrm{A\ in\ B}}$ for metallic glass formation could be estimated by

$$C^{\min}_{\mathrm{A\ in\ B}} = \frac{0.1R_{\mathrm{A}}^3}{|R_{\mathrm{A}}^3 - R_{\mathrm{B}}^3|}, \tag{1a}$$

and

$$C^{\min}_{\mathrm{B\ in\ A}} = \frac{0.1R_B^3}{|R_B^3 - R_A^3|}, \tag{1b}$$

where R_{A} and R_{B} are the radius of atoms A and B, respectively. The two critical concentrations $C^{\min}_{\mathrm{B\ in\ A}}$ and $C^{\min}_{\mathrm{A\ in\ B}}$ would identify the GFR of the A–B binary metal system. It is noted that although the size difference rule is quite simple, it could predict a quantitative GFR for a binary metal system. Nonetheless, the prediction is not always reliable, probably because the atomic size difference of a binary metal system could only partially reflect the intrinsic characteristics of the system. A comparison of the predicted results and experimental observations for 60 binary metal systems shows that the relevance of the prediction is about 60%. For example, Table 5 shows the predicted and experimental GFRs for some representative binary metal systems.

It should be pointed out that for the size difference rule proposed by Egami and Waseda the critical concentrations is determined by the atomic level stress, in which only the substitutional solute atoms are considered. However, if the solute atom is much smaller than the solvent atom, then a substitutional occupancy is no longer the dominating factor. In this situation, the interstitial solute may play an important role related to the amorphous alloy formation. By considering the interstices occupancies of the solute atoms, Miracle and Senkov have proposed a topological model to predict the GFR of a binary metal system [288]. Miracle's model predicts that the specific radius ratios are preferred in the constitution of the metallic glasses, extending the previous model proposed to describe the topology influence on the metallic glass formation [289]. Miracle's model represents a simple idealization and gives a reasonable agreement with a number of experimental results. However, the main limitation of the model is that it does not take into account the chemical interaction between the atoms present in the alloy. In addition the volume change is also calculated by a linear superposition of the volume changes caused by the addition of each solute atom in a single component matrix. Furthermore, the model considers only the effects of topological factors on amorphization. Nonetheless, it is known that several other factors, such as heat of mixing and electron structure of atoms, are also correlated with the metallic glass formation. Moreover, the chemical interaction between the atoms influences the electronic structure, and hence the size of the constituent atoms is manifested through other features, such as the enthalpy of mixing. In other words, these factors would lead to a complex interdependence among other features known to influence the metallic glass formation in addition to the topology.

Table 5
Glass-forming range (GFR, at% B) of the A–B binary metal systems observed from experimental studies and predicted by the size difference rule.

System	Predicted	Experimental	References
Co–Hf	9.7–81.3	9–88	[112]
Co–Nb	22–64	20–77	[166]
Co–Zr	19–91	20–96	[285]
Cu–Ta	20–70	45–90	[285]
Cu–Zr	10–80	12–74	[285]
Fe–Gd	7.9–82.3	6–85	[286]
Fe–Zr	11.4–78.2	9–75	[287]
Ir–Ta	36–54	44–92	[285]
Mn–Zr	11–79	10–80	[285]
Ta–Zr	34–55	31–80	[186]
V–Zr	17–74	15–69	[285]

3.2.3. Structural difference rule

Based on a systematic ion beam mixing experiment, Liu et al. have demonstrated that for a binary metal system, the structures of the constituent metals play a decisive role in forming an amorphous alloy by ion beam mixing, whereas the effects of atomic size and electro-negativity are minor [17]. Liu et al. have therefore proposed a structural difference rule, stating that an amorphous alloy would most likely be formed in a binary metal system by ion beam mixing, when the two constituent metals are of different crystalline structures and the alloy composition is chosen to be in the middle of the two-phase region observed from the equilibrium phase diagram of the system. Actually, there are some similarities between the structural difference rule and deep eutectic criterion. First, according to the thermodynamics of solids [290], if two constituent metals are in different structures, they could not form an isomorphous phase diagram (i.e. continuous solid solution), implying that there should exist a two-phase region (or several two-phase regions) in the equilibrium phase diagram of the system. Second, an alloy composition located in the middle of a two-phase region is not favored for the crystallization of two crystalline phases either of constituent metals or intermetallic compounds, instead, is favored for the formation of an amorphous alloy.

In addition, further studies have shown that when the overall composition locates at or in the vicinity of the intermetallic compound, which frequently has a complicated structure and a high melting point, an amorphous alloy could also be formed by ion beam mixing, yet could hardly be obtained by liquid melt quenching. Based on above experimental results, Liu et al. have proposed an empirical model to estimate the GFA/GFR of a system by using a single parameter, i.e. MPAR, which is the abbreviation of the maximum possible amorphization range of the binary metal system. The physical meaning of the proposed MPAR of a binary metal system is that it represents the total width of the two-phase regions observed from the equilibrium phase diagram of the system. Accordingly, for a binary metal system, the MPAR is defined to equal to 100%, as the whole composition range, minus the two maximum terminal solid solubilities observed from the

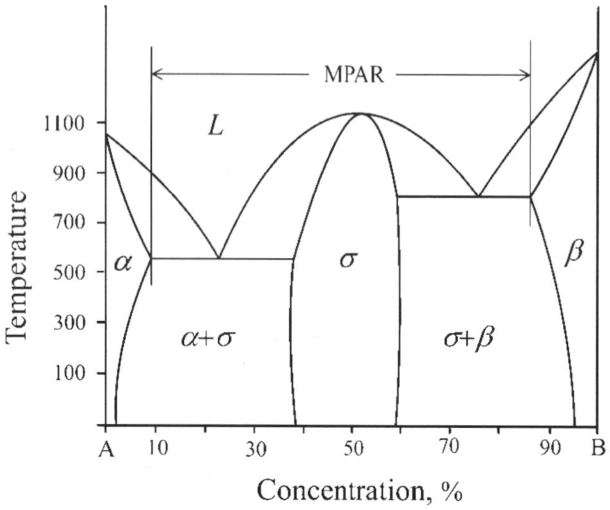

Fig. 1. Definition of the maximum possible amorphization range (MPAR).

corresponding equilibrium phase diagram, as shown in Fig. 1. By incorporating another thermodynamic parameter, i.e. the heat of formation, Liu and co-workers have proposed to classify the binary metal systems into three groups, i.e. the possibly, readily (also to be possibly) and hardly glass-forming systems, and the classification was well in agreement with the experimental observations [148,149,291]. Although the approach proposed by Liu et al. was based mostly on ion beam mixing studies, it could also serve as a guide for other glass-producing techniques to produce metallic glasses. In fact, for a binary metal system, as long as the metallic glasses have been obtained within an alloy composition range by ion beam mixing, it means that the alloy composition range is proven to be in favor for the corresponding disordered state to exist. It follows that when one uses other powerful glass-producing techniques, it is also possible to obtain the metallic glasses in this favored alloy composition range.

3.2.4. Thermodynamic approach

From a thermodynamic point of view, by comparing the Gibbs free energy of the competing alloy phases, e.g. the solid solution and the amorphous phase, the GFA/GFR of a binary metal system could be predicted. The Gibbs free energy could be calculated by using the Miedema-Alonso's model [16,277,283,292–295] or alternatively, by using the CALPHAD method [284,296,297]. When the free energies of the competing alloy phases are plotted against the alloy composition, one could determine the relative stabilities of the solid solution and amorphous phase. The GFR is just the alloy composition range, within which the amorphous phase is relatively more stable than its crystalline counterpart, i.e. the solid solution. Table 6 lists some examples of the GFRs of the binary metal systems predicted by the thermodynamic approach and those observed in experimental studies. Although Miedema-Alonso's model has been quite successful in predicting the GFRs for a number of binary metal systems, some discrepancies have been observed between the predictions and experimental observations. In this regard, Suryanaryana has argued that several factors could account for the observed discrepancies [23]. First, Miedema-Alonso's model still belongs to sort of empirical approach and the model is strictly valid only at low temperature. Second, in calculating the enthalpy, this model ignores the intermetallic compounds that possibly appear in the equilibrium phase diagram, instead it only takes into account of the terminal solid solution and amorphous phases. Incidentally, CALPHAD is considered to be superior in some cases, comparing to Miedema-Alonso's model, since CALPHAD is based on exact thermodynamic data, e.g. the equilibrium phase diagram of the system concerned. Nonetheless, the calculations are still inadequate due to some problems associated with insufficient experimental input, fitting errors, and invalid extrapolation to an under-cooling condition.

Table 6
Glass-forming range (GFR, at% B) of the A–B binary metal system calculated by the thermodynamic approach and observed from experimental studies.

	Experimental	Miedema	Calphad
Ti–Be	37–41%Be (LMQ) [63,64]		37–41%Be [298]
Co–Zr	42–80%Zr (LMQ) [70]		46–78%Zr [299]
Cu–Zr	10–80%Zr [71,75,79,81–94]	4–88%Zr [31]	26–72%Zr [299]
Ni–Zr	20–80%Zr (MA) [292]	17–76%Zr [292]	28–66%Zr [299]
Co–Nb	20–77%Nb (IBM) [166]	15–85%Nb [166]	15–74%Nb [248]
Ni–Ti	28–72% MA [267]; 28–90 SSA [266]	24–77 [292]	28–72%Ti [284]

One should bear in mind that these thermodynamic approaches ignore the defects, such as the vacancies and interstitial atoms, interfaces, composition inhomogeneity, and size-effect, implying that only the perfect structures are considered in calculating the free energies both in Miedema-Alonso and CALPHAD models. Although a quantitative evaluation of these effects is much complicated, with the aid of simple model together with some assumptions, Wolf has argued that upon ion irradiation, the true free energy of a system might be either increased or decreased depending on the specific situations, implying that irradiation could either overstabilize or destabilize a uniform solid solution. This argument corresponds to an increase or a decrease in solid solubility, respectively, observed in experiments [300]. Liu et al. have also found that for the equilibrium miscible systems, the extra interfaces could depress a little the free energy in the metal–metal multilayers, whereas for the equilibrium immiscible system, the extra interfaces could considerably boost the free energy. In the metal–metal multilayers of an equilibrium immiscible system, when the free energy of the metal–metal multilayers is elevated by the extra interfacial free energy to such a high level, the interfacial free energy could provide a sufficient driving force to have the solid-state amorphization to take place [26,301]. Besides, Martin and Bellon have also concluded that for a given producing process, several metastable configurations may exist and the respective stability of these competing structures could not be simply deduced from the "constraint free energy" arguments, that is, from the traditional free energy where the internal energy would be increased by the contribution of the stored defects. The energy stored in the defects does enter into the driving force for the phase formation. The noise level, which determines the most stable configuration, is not merely fixed by the temperature (as in the equilibrium situation), but also by the external driving force. For the detailed discussion, the readers can refer to the relevant review article [24].

4. Interatomic potential to predict the binary metallic glass formation

According to the discussion in the previous section, the GFA/GFR of a binary metal system is one of the important properties of the system and should therefore be determined by some intrinsic characteristics of the system. It is known that the interatomic potential of a binary metal system defines the atomic interactions among all of the atoms involved in the system, and therefore once the potential is known, many important properties and behaviors of the system could be computed or derived. It is therefore believed that for a binary metal system, the GFA could be determined from

Table 7
Representative binary metal systems selected for the present study.

A–B system	Structure	ΔH_f	Electronegative	Atomic radius	Potentials	References
Ni–Nb	bcc–fcc	−45	1.91–1.60	1.62–2.08	F–S	[302]
Ni–Mo	bcc–fcc	−11	1.91–2.16	1.62–2.01	F–S	[303–305]
Ag–Mo	bcc–fcc	+56	1.93–2.16	1.75–2.01	F–S	[158,306]
Cu–W	bcc–fcc	+33	1.90–2.36	1.57–2.02	EAM	[307]
Co–Nb	hcp–bcc	−37	1.88–1.60	1.67–2.08	EAM	[185,308]
Sc–W	hcp–bcc	+14	1.36–2.36	2.09–2.02	EAM	[185,308]
Ni–Hf	fcc–hcp	−63	1.91–1.30	1.62–2.16	TB-SMA	[309]
Cu–Ru	fcc–hcp	+10	1.90–2.2	1.57–1.89	TB-SMA	[310]

its interatomic potential through some appropriate computations and simulations.

As the process of producing the metallic glasses is always a far-from-equilibrium process and the related kinetic condition is extremely restricted, complicated structured phases could not nucleate and grow. It follows that the competing phase to metallic glass, or amorphous phase, is the terminal solid solution, which is frequently of simple structure, i.e. fcc, bcc or hcp. Consequently, the scientific issue related to predict the GFR of a binary metal system could be converted into an issue of comparing the relative stability of the solid solution versus its amorphous counterpart as a function of solute concentration, thus enabling to determine the two critical solid solubilities, beyond which the solid solutions become unstable and turn into the corresponding amorphous states (i.e. forming the metallic glass). Accordingly, the GFR, or the quantitative GFA of a binary metal system is thus deduced to be the alloy composition range bounded by the two determined critical solid solubilities, and within this alloy composition range, an amorphous state is energetically favored in comparison with its solid solution counterpart. Theoretically, in a binary metal system, the relative stability of the amorphous phase and the solid solution are both governed by the atomic interaction of the system and could hence be determined through appropriate computations or simulations.

In addition, extensive experimental studies, e.g. ion beam mixing experiments, have showed that for a binary metal system either equilibrium miscible or immiscible, the metallic glasses could be obtained in a broad alloy composition range, approximately equaling to the total width of the two-phase regions, i.e. extending from the central portion to near the edges of the two terminal solid solutions observed from the equilibrium phase diagram of the system. In other words, metallic glasses could be obtained in almost the entire alloy composition range, except in the regions that favor for the formation of solid solutions of simple structure. Consequently, the experimental observations suggested that the scientific issue of predicting the GFA/GFR of a binary metal system could be converted into an issue of determining the two critical solid solubilities, which split the entire alloy composition range into different regions, energetically favor for the formation of the solid solution and metallic glass.

The following route of computations and simulations is therefore designed to develop the atomistic theory capable of predicting the binary metallic glass formation. The first step is to construct the relevant interatomic potential of a binary metal system. The second step is to apply the constructed potential to carry out a series of molecular dynamics simulations. In the simulations, solid solution models are employed to compare the relative stability of the solid solution versus its disordered counterpart as a function of the solute concentration. In the following sections, we would discuss the detailed computations and simulations for developing the atomistic theory that is capable of predicting the binary metallic glass formation.

4.1. Selection of the representative binary metal systems

To develop an atomistic theory valid in general for predicting the binary metallic glass formation, eight representative binary metal systems are selected. They are the Ni–Nb [302], Ni–Mo [303–305], Ag–Mo [158,306], Cu–W [307], Co–Nb, Sc–W [185,308], Ni–Hf [309] and Cu–Ru [310] systems (listed in Table 7).

These systems are selected to cover the various structural combinations of the bcc, fcc and hcp structures, as well as various thermodynamic characteristics, ranging from a large negative to a large positive ΔH_f. For instance, for the Ni–Nb and Ni–Mo (fcc–bcc) systems, their ΔH_f are −44 and −11 kJ/mol [16], respectively, and each has three equilibrium compounds. For the Ag–Mo (fcc–bcc) system, its ΔH_f is very large positive (+56 kJ/mol) [16] and the Ag and Mo are almost insoluble in the solid state. The maximum solid solubilities are about 5.78 ppm Ag in bcc Mo and 0.15 at% Mo in fcc Ag, respectively. Moreover, even in the liquid state, Ag could only dissolve a few percent of Mo at 1400 K [311]. For the Ni–Hf (fcc–hcp) system, its ΔH_f is very large negative (−63 kJ/mol) [16] and there are seven Ni–Hf equilibrium compounds in the system. In addition, the atom-size differences and electro-negativity differences of the constituent metals of the selected systems randomly vary from system to system [312]. For instance, the atom-size difference is less than 3% in the Sc–W system, whereas around 25% in the Ni–Nb system. Similarly, for the selected systems, electronegativity differences also cover a wide range varying from 0.23 to 1.0 eV.

4.2. Construction of n-body potentials for the binary metal systems

In developing the atomistic theory capable of predicting the metallic glass formation in a binary metal system, the starting base is the interatomic potential of the system, and the key issue is to construct a realistic interatomic potential for the system. Since the 1980s, significant progress has been made in developing the n-body potentials and several schemes have been proposed to construct n-body potentials for the transition metal systems [313–317]. According to the detailed forms of the potential functions, the following three major n-body potentials are the most widely used currently: the embedded atom method (EAM) potentials [316,318], the second-moment approximation of tight-binding (TB-SMA) potentials [319–321], and the Finnis–Sinclair potentials [322–325]. For these n-body potentials, the energy of a metal system is expressed by the pair term and n-body term (i.e. the many-body term).

4.2.1. Ab initio assisted construction of n-body potentials

For an A–B binary metal system, there are three basic atomic interactions, i.e. A–A interaction, B–B interaction and A–B cross interaction. Thus three sets of potential parameters are to be fitted for the A–A, B–B and A–B interactions, i.e. $\{p,...\}_{A-A}$, $\{p,...\}_{B-B}$ and $\{p,...\}_{A-B}$, respectively. The parameters $\{p,...\}_{A-B}$ describes the cross interaction between dissimilar atoms A and B, and is often named as the cross potential.

The potential parameters are determined by fitting them to some physical properties of the system, such as the cohesive energies, lattice constants, bulk modules and elastic constants. These physical properties could be obtained in experiments or from theoretical calculations. In general, these physical properties of the constituent metals A and B and their compounds are used if available. However, because no any equilibrium compound exists in an equilibrium immiscible system, there is no any datum available to fit the cross potential, raising a problem in construction of the potential of the system. In addition, the problem could also be encountered even in some equilibrium miscible binary metal systems, in which some equilibrium compounds may exist, yet no adequate property data are available to fit the cross potential. To solve this problem, a unique method has been developed and the method is referred as *ab initio* assisted construction of n-body potential [315,317]. For a binary metal system, *ab initio* calculations are first conducted to acquire some important physical properties of some possible nonequilibrium (i.e. metastable) compounds in the system, such as the B2 and $L1_2$ structures [326,327]. The acquired properties are used to fit the cross potential of the system. Consequently, the n-body potentials thus constructed could be considered to bear some *ab initio* characteristics.

The *ab initio* calculations were conducted based on density functional theory [328], in the generalized gradient approximation (GGA), with projector augmented-wave (PAW) pseudo-potentials, as implemented in VASP [329–331]. For the GGA correlation energy, the Perdew-Wang parameterization (GGA-PW91) were employed [332]. Brillouin-zone integrations were performed using Monkhorst-Pack k-point meshes [333]. Depending on the structure, up to 518 k-points were used in the irreducible Brillouin zone. Total energies of each structure were optimized with respect to the volume, unit cell-external degree(s) of freedom (i.e. the unit-cell shape) and unit cell-internal degree(s) of freedom as permitted by the space-group symmetry of the crystal structure.

4.2.2. n-Body potentials constructed for the representative systems

With the aid of *ab initio* calculations, the authors' group has constructed the Finnis–Sinclair potentials for the Ni–Nb [302], Ni–Mo [303–305] and Ag–Mo systems [158,306], the EAM potentials for the Cu–W [307], Co–Nb and Sc–W systems [185,308], and the TB-SMA potentials for the Ni–Hf [309] and Cu–Ru systems [310], respectively. In the following, we would present in detail the construction of these n-body potentials and discuss their relevance.

4.2.2.1. Finnis–Sinclair potentials of the Ni–Nb, Ni–Mo and Ag–Mo systems. According to the formalism of the Finnis–Sinclair (F–S) potential [322], the total energy of a system is given by

$$E_{\text{tot}} = \sum_{j \neq i} V(r_{ij}) - \left[\sum_{j \neq i} A^2 \phi(r_{ij})\right]^{1/2}, \tag{2}$$

where the first term is a normal pair-wise energy consisting of a repulsive part, and the parameter A in the second term is a constant in positive value.

For the Ni–Nb system (fcc–bcc and $\Delta H_f < 0$), the following potential functions were used for the pair interaction term and the electron density term, respectively

$$V(r) = (r-c)^2(c_0 + c_1 r + c_2 r^2 + c_3 r^3 + c_4 r^4) \quad 0 < r < c, \tag{3a}$$

and

$$\phi(r) = (r-d)^2 + B(r-d)^3/d \quad 0 < r < d, \tag{3b}$$

Table 8

Finnis–Sinclair potential parameters of the Ni–Nb system.

	Ni–Ni	Nb–Nb	Ni–Nb
A (eV Å^{-1})	0.9824767	2.999182	1.825783
d (Å)	4.12	3.9	3.75
c (Å)	4.22	4.07	4.25
c_0 (eV Å^{-2})	13.28276	25.57548	22.47078
c_1 (eV Å^{-3})	17.08506	26.84273	24.19881
c_2 (eV Å^{-4})	8.262515	9.903115	8.854626
c_3 (eV Å^{-5})	1.77048	1.297269	1.098587
c_4 (eV Å^{-6})	0.1413902	0.01428883	0

where the cutoff radii c and d are two disposable parameters assumed to lie between the second- and third-neighbor atoms. There are totally 9 potential parameters, i.e. A, B, c, d, c_0, c_1, c_2, c_3 and c_4, to be fitted. Note that B, c_3 and c_4, which did not appear in original F–S formalism, were added to improve the flexibility of fitting.

As there are very few available experimental data related to the equilibrium Ni–Nb compounds, *ab initio* calculations were conducted to acquire the cohesive energies and lattice constants of possible B2 NiNb and $L1_2$ $NiNb_3$ metastable compounds, and then the calculated data were used to derive the Ni–Nb potential [302]. Table 8 lists the fitted parameters of the Ni–Nb potential. By employing the derived Ni–Nb potential, the cohesive energies and lattice constants of metastable $L1_2$ Ni_3Nb (not used in fitting), $NiNb_3$ and B2 NiNb compounds were reproduced and are listed in Table 9. The reproduced results are in good agreement with those obtained from *ab initio* calculations, showing that the constructed F–S Ni–Nb potential is of relevance in describing the atomic interactions in the Ni–Nb system.

Similarly, the parameters of the F–S Ni–Mo potential were obtained by fitting them to the corresponding experimental data of the cohesive energy, lattice constant, bulk modulus and shear elastic constants [303–305]. It could be proven that the constructed Ni–Mo potential could well reproduce some other physical properties, such as the surface energy, vacancy formation energy and vacancy formation volume. For example, the bulk modules of the metastable $D0_{19}$ Ni_3Mo and $L1_2$ $NiMo_3$ compounds were reproduced to be 2.56 and 1.50 Mbar, respectively, which were reasonably compatible with the *ab initio* calculated values of 2.5 and 2.4 Mbar, respectively. In summary, Table 10 lists all the fitted parameters for the F–S Ni–Mo potential.

For the Ag–Mo system, which is also of fcc–bcc system, yet it features a large positive ΔH_f, the F–S potential has also been constructed by the authors' group [158,306]. In the F–S potential, $V(r)$ was taken a polynomial form extending up to r^5, instead of a quadratic form in the original F–S formalism. In deriving the Ag–Mo cross potential, *ab initio* calculations were also carried out

Table 9

Comparison between the calculated physical properties reproduced by the *n*-body potentials and the experimental values used in fitting the potentials for pure Ni and Nb (E_v^f is the unrelaxed vacancy formation energy).

	Ni		Nb	
	Experimental	Calculated	Experimental	Calculated
E_c (eV)	4.44[a]	4.437	7.57[a]	7.572
a (Å)	3.52[a]	3.520	3.30[a]	3.300
C_{11} (Mbar)	2.45[b]	2.450	2.47[b]	2.470
C_{12} (Mbar)	1.40[b]	1.485	1.35[b]	1.347
C_{44} (Mbar)	1.25[b]	1.182	0.29[b]	0.287
E_v^f (eV)	1.60[c]	1.624	2.75[d]	2.746

[a] Ref. [334].
[b] Ref. [335].
[c] Ref. [336].
[d] Ref. [337].

Table 10
Finnis–Sinclair potential parameters of the Ni–Mo system.

	Ni-Ni	Mo-Mo[a]	Ni-Mo
A (eV Å^{-1})	1.042095	1.887117	1.144552
d (Å)	4.00	4.114825	5.25
c (Å)	3.72	3.25	4.05
c_0 (eV Å^{-2})	2.1853329	43.4475218	49.418638
c_1 (eV Å^{-3})	−0.6346408	−31.9332978	−60.377197
c_2 (eV Å^{-4})	−0.4184836	6.0804249	27.366179
c_3 (eV Å^{-5})	0.1364786	0.00	−5.388922
c_4 (eV Å^{-6})	0.00	0.00	0.387794
B (Å^{-1})	0.0	0.0	0.0

[a] Ref. [322].

to acquire the cohesive energies and lattice constants of the possible metastable L1$_2$ Ag$_3$Mo and B2 AgMo compounds, and the calculated data were then used to fit the Ag–Mo cross potential. Table 11 lists the data to compare the cohesive energies and lattice constants of the Ag–Mo phases reproduced from the constructed potential with those obtained from *ab initio* calculations. One sees from the table that the agreement is quite good, confirming that the constructed F–S Ag–Mo potential is relevant in describing the atomic interactions of the Ag–Mo system. Table 12 lists all the fitted parameters for the F–S Ag–Mo potential of the Ag–Mo system.

4.2.2.2. EAM potentials of the Cu–W, Sc–W and Co–Nb systems. Although the Cu–W system is similar to the Ag–Mo system, also consisting of fcc–bcc structures and featuring a positive ΔH_f, the authors' group has intentionally constructed an EAM potential for the Cu–W system [307]. The Cu–Cu and W–W potentials took the form proposed by Cai and Ye [338] and Johnson and Oh [339], with some modifications [340],

$$E_{tot} = \sum_i F_i(\rho_i) + \frac{1}{2}\sum_{i \neq j} \phi_{ij}(r_{ij}), \tag{4}$$

$$F(\rho) = -F_0\left[1 - \ln\left(\frac{\rho}{\rho_e}\right)^n\right]\left(\frac{\rho}{\rho_e}\right)^n + F_1\left(\frac{\rho}{\rho_e}\right), \tag{5}$$

$$\rho_i = \sum_{j \neq i} f(r_{ij}), \tag{6}$$

$$f(r) = f_e \exp\left[-\chi\left(\frac{r}{r_e} - 1\right)\right], \tag{7}$$

$$\phi_{Cu}(r) = -\alpha\left(1 + \beta\left(\frac{r}{r_a} - 1\right)\right)\exp\left(-\beta\left(\frac{r}{r_a} - 1\right)\right), \tag{8}$$

$$\phi_W(r) = \begin{cases} k_0 + k_1\left(\frac{r}{r_e} - 1\right) + k_2\left(\frac{r}{r_e} - 1\right)^2 + k_3\left(\frac{r}{r_e} - 1\right)^3 & r_e \le r \le r_s, \\ \phi_W(r) + k_a[(\phi_W(r) - \phi_W(r_e))]\left(\frac{r}{r_e} - 1\right)^2 & r \le r_e, \end{cases} \tag{9}$$

Table 11
Comparison of the cohesive Energy E_c (eV) and lattice constant a (Å) derived from the constructed Ag–Mo potential versus those from *ab initio* calculations.

System	Structure	*Ab initio* calculation		Present study	
		E_c	a	E_c	a
Ag$_3$Mo	L12	4.13	3.1166	4.13	3.1166
AgMo	B2	3.23	3.9161	3.23	3.9161
AgMo$_3$	L12	3.99	5.2072	3.99	5.4438

Table 12
Finnis–Sinclair potential parameters of the Ag–Mo system.

	Ag-Ag	Mo-Mo	Ag-Mo
A (eV Å^{-1})	0.325514	1.848648	0.625749
d (Å)	4.41	4.1472	4.2
c (Å)	4.76	3.2572	4.5
c_0 (eV Å^{-2})	10.6812	47.98066	44.40681
c_1 (eV Å^{-3})	12.04517	34.09924	45.49026
c_2 (eV Å^{-4})	5.203072	5.832293	15.60511
c_3 (eV Å^{-5})	1.013304	0.101749	1.793704
c_4 (eV Å^{-6})	0.0742308	0.0203934	0.00
B (Å^{-2})	1.293394	0.00	0.00

where E_{tot} is the total energy, $F(\rho)$ is the embedding energy, ρ_i is the total electron density at atom i due to all other atoms, $\phi(r_{ij})$is the pair potential between atoms i and j, and $f(r_{ij})$ is the electron density of atom i contributed by atom j. For simplicity, the function $f(r)$ of the W–W potential took the same form as that of the Cu–Cu potential. In Eq. (5), F_0, ρ_e, and n are constants. $F_0 = E_c - E_v^f$, where E_c and E_v^f are the cohesive energy and vacancy formation energy, respectively. The parameter ρ_e represents the host electron density at an equilibrium state for the Cu–Cu and W–W potentials. For bcc W, F_1 equals 0, whereas for fcc Cu, it is an adjustable parameter. In Eq. (5), r_e is the equilibrium first-neighbor distance, and f_e is a scaling factor determined by the relationship $f_e = E_c/\Omega$, where Ω is the atomic volume. In Eq. (9), k_a is the constant

$$k_a = 4.5\left[1 + \frac{4}{2C_{44}(C_{11} - C_{12}) - 0.1}\right]. \tag{10}$$

The cutoff function was adopted from the polynomial proposed by Guellil and Adams [341] and the cutoff distances were assumed to fall between the second and third neighbor distances for Cu–Cu and W–W. Clearly, there are five parameters (χ, α, β, r_a, F_1) to be fitted for the Cu–Cu potential and another five parameters (χ, k_0, k_1, k_2, k_3) to be fitted for the W–W potential.

For the Cu–W cross potential, a simple linear combination of the Cu–Cu and W–W potentials has been proposed by the author' group [340]:

$$\phi_{CuW}(r) = A[\phi_{Cu}(r + B) + \phi_W(r + C)], \tag{11}$$

where r is the distance between the Cu and W atoms. The quantities A, B, and C are three parameters to be fitted. Similarly, *ab initio* calculations were carried out to acquire the lattice constants and cohesive energies of some possible metastable Cu–W compounds. The cohesive energies of the L1$_2$ Cu$_3$W and B2 CuW compounds were determined to be 4.2478 and 5.4765 eV/atom and their lattice constants were determined to be 3.76 and 3.04 Å, respectively. These data were then used to fit the Cu–W cross potential. Table 13 lists the fitted parameters for the EAM Cu–W potential, which could be proven to be of relevance in describing the atomic interactions of the Cu–W system.

For the Co–Nb and Sc–W (hcp–bcc) systems, featuring a negative and a positive ΔH_f, respectively, the EAM potentials have

Table 13
EAM potential parameters of the Cu–W system.

Cu-Cu		W-W		Cu-W	
χ	11.134231	χ	6.18048	A	0.362635
a (eV)	0.725977	k_0 (eV)	−0.581958		
b	3.457434	k_1 (eV)	−2.17506	B (Å)	−0.22987
r_a (Å)	1.629356	k_2 (eV)	17.053662		
F_1 (eV)	0.676073	k_3 (eV)	−8.215108	C (Å)	0.094444
r_s (Å)	3.7	r_s (Å)	3.2		
r_c (Å)	4.4	r_c (Å)	4.4		
n	0.333333	n	0.440653		

Table 14
EAM potential parameters of the Co–Nb system.

Co–Co		Nb–Nb		Co–Nb	
χ	7.65919	χ	10.403652	A	1.6774
a (eV)	0.29156	k_0 (eV)	−0.393145		
b	3.34178	k_1 (eV)	−0.642187	B (Å)	−0.682548
r_a (Å)	2.49684	k_2 (eV)	3.593435		
F_1 (eV)	0.44719	k_3 (eV)	−3.78716	C (Å)	1.117879
r_s (Å)	3.6	r_s (Å)	3.4		
r_c (Å)	4.4	r_c (Å)	4.4		
n	0.82517	n	0.440653		

also been constructed [185,308]. Table 14 lists the fitted parameters for the EAM Co–Nb potential, which could work reasonably well in terms of reproducing some important physical properties of pure Co and Nb as well as of the metastable $L1_2$ Co_3Nb and B2 CoNb compounds. Moreover, the elastic constants of hcp Co and bcc Nb as well as the $L1_2$ Co_3Nb, and B2 CoNb compounds were also reproduced from the constructed Co–Nb potential and the reproduced results matched quite well with those observed from experiments and acquired from *ab initio* calculations. In addition, the energy differences between the three major crystalline structures for the metals Co and Nb were also reproduced from the constructed EAM Co–Nb potential. Apparently, the calculated results confirmed that the most stable structure of Nb was of bcc. To further test its relevance, the constructed EAM Co–Nb potential was employed to conduct molecular dynamics simulations to determine the melting points of pure Co and Nb metals. The melting points were determined to be 1910 and 2850 K for hcp Co and bcc Nb, respectively [308]. Interestingly, the experimentally obtained values were 1768 and 2741 K for Co and Nb, respectively, showing an excellent performance of the constructed EAM Co–Nb potential in describing the atomic interactions expediently even in the presence of inharmonic effects.

Similarly, for the Sc–W system, the EAM potential has also been constructed by the authors' group and Table 15 lists the fitted parameters for the Sc–W potential [308]. It turned that the constructed EAM Sc–W potential could reproduce some important physical properties of the pure Sc and W as well as those of the metastable $L1_2$ Sc_3W and B2 ScW compounds and the reproduced results were in agreement with those observed from experimental observations and from *ab initio* calculations.

4.2.2.3. TB-SMA potentials of the Ni–Hf and Cu–Ru systems. The Ni–Hf and Cu–Ru systems both consist of fcc–hcp structures yet featuring a negative and a positive ΔH_f, respectively. The scheme of second-moment approximation of the tight-binding (TB-SMA) potential is considered to be suitable for these systems. In the TB-SMA scheme, the repulsive portion is a Born–Mayer pair-wise interaction and the attractive portion is a second-moment approximation of the tight-binding band energy [320]. The total energy, consisting of the cohesive and repulsive items, could be computed by,

$$E_{tot} = \sum_{j\neq i} A_{\alpha\beta}\exp\left[-p_{\alpha\beta}\left(\frac{r_{ij}}{r_{\alpha\beta}}-1\right)\right] - \sqrt{\sum_{j\neq i}\xi^2_{\alpha\beta}\exp\left[-2q_{\alpha\beta}\left(\frac{r_{ij}}{r_{\alpha\beta}}-1\right)\right]}, \quad (12)$$

where α and β indicate the atomic species, r_{ij} is the distance between the atoms i and j and is calculated up to a distance r_{cutoff}. $r_{\alpha\beta}$ is the nearest distance between the atoms α and β in the crystalline structure and the quantities $A_{\alpha\beta}$, $p_{\alpha\beta}$, $\xi_{\alpha\beta}$ and $q_{\alpha\beta}$ are four adjustable potential parameters.

For the Ni–Hf system with a negative ΔH_f, a TB-SMA potential has been constructed by the authors' group and the four potential parameters were determined through the following procedure [309]. (i) For $\alpha = \beta$, the fitting procedures were performed with the cohesive energy, lattice constants, elastic constants, at 0 K both for the pure Ni and Hf metals. The parameters $r_{\alpha\alpha}$ and $r_{\beta\beta}$ were taken to be the nearest-neighbor distances of the pure Ni and Hf metals, respectively. For the Hf–Hf interaction, the approach proposed by Willaime and Massobrio [342] was employed, i.e. the atom volume was kept at a constant equaling to the experimental value, and at the same time, the c/a and cutoff distance r_{cutoff} were optimized during fitting. (ii) For, $\alpha \neq \beta$, the corresponding parameters were fitted to the cohesive energies and lattice constants of some Ni–Hf compounds. Among seven equilibrium Ni–Hf intermetallic compounds existing in the system [327,343], the physical properties of the $NiHf_2$, NiHf, Ni_2Hf and Ni_5Hf compounds were used to fit the Ni–Hf cross potential. The $r_{\alpha\beta}$, i.e. r_0, was taken to be 2.69 Å, i.e. the average value of the nearest atomic distance in the four compounds. The cutoff distance was taken to be 4.70 Å. Table 16 lists all the potential parameters for the TB-SMA Ni–Hf potential. It has been proven that the constructed potential could reproduce some important physical properties of the pure Ni and Hf metals as well as of four equilibrium Ni–Hf compounds. For example, the Ni–Hf potential reproduced cohesive energies confirmed that the fcc Ni and hcp Hf were the most stable ones comparing to their possible metastable structures, respectively. Besides, based on the constructed TB-SMA Ni–Hf potential, molecular dynamics simulations have also been carried out to determine the melting points of Ni, Hf, Ni_2Hf and $NiHf_2$. The determined melting points of the Ni, Hf, and $NiHf_2$ compounds were 1750, 2400, and 1850 K, respectively, matching well with the experimental melting points, 1726, 2500, and 1750 K, respectively [327]. Moreover, the lattice constants of the $NiHf_2$ compound determined from the simulations were 6.7742, 6.6694 and 5.0432 Å, respectively, matching well with the experimental measured values of 6.405, 6.405 and 5.252 Å, respectively. In short, the constructed TB-SMA Ni–Hf potential could be considered of relevance in describing the atomic interactions in the Ni–Hf system.

For the Cu–Ru system with a positive ΔH_f, *ab initio* calculations have been conducted and the calculated results showed that the metastable $L1_2$ Cu_3Ru and $CuRu_3$ compounds could possibly exist in the system and interestingly these metastable compounds have indeed been observed in ion beam mixing experiments. The *ab initio* calculated cohesive energies and lattice constants of these metastable compounds were used to fit the Cu–Ru cross potential.

Table 15
EAM potential parameters of the Sc–W system.

Sc–Sc		W–W		Sc–W	
χ	6.417256	χ	6.155980	A	1.10885
a (eV)	0.311282	k_0 (eV)	−0.547671		
b	1.226141	k_1 (eV)	−2.130315	B (Å)	0.69826
r_a (Å)	2.662559	k_2 (eV)	16.808946		
F_1 (eV)	0.712605	k_3 (eV)	−8.503413	C (Å)	0.30702
r_s (Å)	3.4	r_s (Å)	3.2		
r_c (Å)	4.4	r_c (Å)	4.4		
n	1.25	n	0.44		

Table 16
TB-SMA potential parameters of the Ni–Hf system.

	p	q	A	ξ	r_{cutoff}
Ni–Ni	11.6430	2.1331	0.0912	1.4763	4.65
Hf–Hf	10.557	1.961	0.1323	2.1516	5.200
Ni–Hf	10.9886	1.2829	0.1124	1.7766	4.70

Table 17
TB-SMA potential parameters of the Cu–Ru system.

	p	q	A	ξ	r_{cutoff}
Cu–Cu	5.7662	1.2313	0.1411	1.727	5.0
Ru–Ru	19.1540	1.6631	0.078	58	4.7
Cu–Ru	10.8624	6.6235	1.3863	1.7766	5.0

In summary, all the parameters of the TB-SMA Cu–Ru potential are listed in Table 17 [310]. It turned out that some of the important physical properties of the Cu–Ru system could be well reproduced by the constructed Cu–Ru potential, thus confirming the relevance of the Cu–Ru potential to be used in further computation and simulation.

4.3. Methods of molecular dynamics simulation and structural characterization

In this section, we would briefly describe the methods of molecular dynamics simulation and structural characterization. In the simulation, solid solution models were used to compare the relative stability of the crystalline solid solution versus the competing disordered counterpart, i.e. the amorphous phase. For the details of these computation and simulation methods, the readers are referred to some of the previous publications [344–346].

4.3.1. Solid solution simulation models

To investigate the relative stabilities of a solid solution versus its disordered counterpart (i.e. the amorphous phase), bcc, fcc and hcp structured solid solution models were first constructed. For the bcc and fcc solid solution models, the [1 0 0], [0 1 0] and [0 0 1] crystalline directions are parallel to the x, y and z axes, respectively. For the hcp solid solution model, the [1 0 .0], [1 2 .0] and [0 0 .1] crystalline directions are parallel to the x, y and z axes, respectively. For simplicity, the hcp solid solution model could be considered to be built of equivalent orthorhombic cells (see Fig. 2). Along the x, y and z directions, there are N_x, N_y and N_z conventional bcc, fcc and orthorhombic cells for the bcc, fcc and hcp solid solution models, respectively. The three edges of the simulation box are denoted by three column vectors $\vec{a}$, $\vec{b}$ and $\vec{c}$, respectively. The three column vectors form a matrix $h = (\vec{a}, \vec{b}, \vec{c})$, which describes the shape and volume $\Omega = |h|$ of the simulation box. The position vector of atom i in the simulation box is expressed by $\vec{r}_i = h\vec{s}_i$ and the column vector $\vec{s}_i = (\upsilon_i, \varsigma_i, \xi_i)^T$ denotes the scaled position, where superscript T stands for transpose. Three Cartesian components, $-0.5 < \upsilon_i, \varsigma_i, \xi_i \leq 0.5$, are coordinates of the atoms in the scaled space. In the simulations, for the bcc solid solution model, N_x, N_y and N_z were set to be 10 in the three directions, and there are $10 \times 10 \times 10 \times 2 = 2000$ atoms in the simulation box. For the fcc solid solution model, $N_x = 8$, $N_y = 8$ and $N_z = 8$, and there are $11 \times 7 \times 7 \times 4 = 2156$ atoms in the simulation box. For the hcp solid solution model, $N_x = 11$, $N_y = 7$ and $N_z = 7$, and there are $11 \times 7 \times 7 \times 4 = 2156$ atoms in the simulation box. In constructing the solid solution model, the solvent atoms were substituted randomly by a certain number of the solvent atoms to form a uniform solid solution with a desired solute concentration. The periodic boundary conditions were adopted in x-, y- and z-directions.

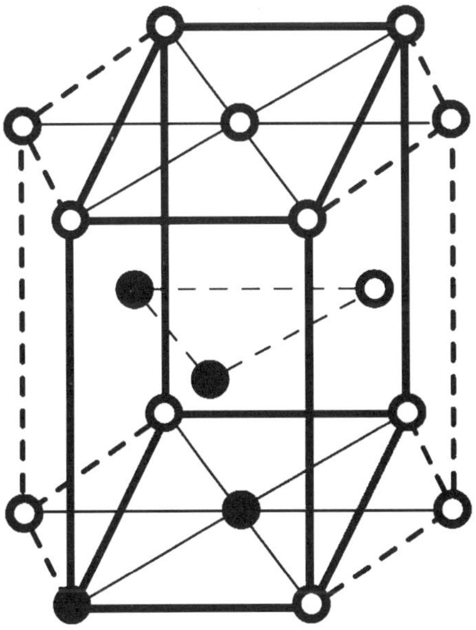

Fig. 2. The hcp solid solution model could also be considered being built of equivalent orthorhombic cells.

4.3.2. Parrinello and Rahman scheme for molecular dynamics simulation

Based on Anderson's work, Parrinello and Rahman developed a scheme to simulate a condensed matter system under constant pressure by introducing the volume and shape of the simulation box as the extended dynamical variables [347–349]. The scheme allows both the volume and shape of the simulation box to change or fluctuate depending on the imbalance between the external pressure and the internal instantaneous stress. In the Parrinello–Rahman scheme, the motion equations of the atoms and simulation box could be written as

$$\ddot{\vec{s}}_i = \frac{1}{m_i}\boldsymbol{h}^{-1}\vec{F}_i - \boldsymbol{G}^{-1}\dot{\boldsymbol{G}}\dot{\vec{s}}_i, \tag{13}$$

$$\ddot{\boldsymbol{h}} = \frac{\Omega}{W}(\Pi - p_{ext}\mathbf{I})\boldsymbol{h}^{-T}, \tag{14}$$

where $\vec{F}_i = -\nabla_i E_{potential}$ is the force acting on atom i due to the interatomic interaction and can be computed from local gradient of the potential energy. $G = h^T h$ is for the metric tensor of the simulation box, and $\Pi = (1/\Omega)\sum(m_i\dot{\vec{r}}_i \otimes \dot{\vec{r}}_i + F_i \otimes \vec{r}_i)$ is the internal stress tensor. W is the fictional mass of the extended system. p_{ext} is the applied external pressure and $\mathbf{I}$ is the unitary matrix. One dot and two dots above a variable denote the first- and second-derivatives with respect to time, respectively. The superscript $-T = -1 \times T$, where the superscripts -1 and T denote the inversion and transpose of a matrix or a tensor, respectively. The above motion equations of the atoms and simulation box were integrated using second-order-six-value predictor-corrector algorithm developed by Gear [344,350] with a time step of 5×10^{-15} s. The temperature of the system was regulated by directly scaling the velocities of the atoms to the corresponding value.

4.3.3. Structural characterization

Several methods were employed to characterize the structure and structural changing in the simulation models. The basic quantity was the structure factor $S(k)$, which is obtained by working in the reciprocal space [351,352]. To extract the topological characteristics of the structure, the planar structure factor could be computed by [353]

$$S_z(\vec{k}) = \left| \frac{1}{N_z}\sum_{j}^{N_z} \exp(\boldsymbol{i}\vec{k}_z \cdot \vec{r}_{z,j}) \right|^2, \tag{15}$$

where $\vec{k}_z = (2\pi/N_x,\ 2\pi/N_y)$, $\vec{r}_{z,l} = (\upsilon_l, \varsigma_l)$ and N_z is the number of the atoms in the atomic plane z. The structure factor $S_z(\vec{k})$ is defined here to reflect the amount of ordering of the atomic plan z. When the simulation model is a perfect crystalline structure, $S(\vec{k})$ and $S_z(\vec{k})$ should be 1 or very close to 1. In contrast, when their values decrease and approach to zero, it means that the simulation model turns into a disordered state.

The second method was the so-called pair-correlation function $g(r)$, i.e. the density autocorrelation in real space. This method is commonly recognized to provide a firm evidence for the formation of an amorphous or metallic glass phase. The pair-correlation function could be computed by [5]

$$g(r) = \frac{\Omega}{N^2}\sum_{i,j}^{N}\delta(r, r_{ij}), \tag{16}$$

where $\delta = 1$ for $r = r_{ij}$ and $\delta = 0$ for $r \neq r_{ij}$. r_{ij} is the distance between the atoms i and j, where r is the correlation length. For a crystalline structure, $g(r)$ exhibits a sequence of peaks that corresponding to the shells around an atom. For a liquid or disordered solid, $g(r)$ exhibits a few major peaks and oscillates with less pronounced peaks at long distance.

To give more evidence, the planar correlation functions were also be computed by

$$\rho_z(l) = \frac{1}{N}\sum_{i}^{N}\delta(l, \vec{r}_{i,x}). \tag{17}$$

This parameter could reflect the amount of ordering in the z-direction.

4.4. Prediction of the glass-forming ability of the binary metal systems

A series of molecular dynamics simulations, using solid solution models, were carried out for the eight selected representative binary metal systems. The simulation results all showed that a solid solution could keep its crystalline lattice, when the solute concentration was low, but the crystalline lattice of the solid solution would be severely distorted upon increasing the solute concentration, and that once the solute concentration exceeded a critical value, the crystalline lattice of the solid solution collapsed and turned into a disordered state. In the following, we would present the detailed simulation results, leading to develop the atomistic theory capable of predicting the binary metallic glass formation.

4.4.1. Simulation results of the eight representative systems

4.4.1.1. The Ni–Nb and Ni–Mo systems. For the Ni–Nb system, the constructed F–S Ni–Nb potential was applied to carry out a series of molecular dynamics simulations. In the simulations, both fcc Ni-based and bcc Nb-based solid solution models were used to study the relative stability of the crystalline solid solution versus its disordered counterpart (i.e. amorphous phase or metallic glass) as a function of solute concentration.

We first present the results of the molecular dynamics simulation for the Ni–Nb system [302]. To directly view the atomic configuration in the solid solution models upon 300 K annealing, Fig. 3 displays the projections of the atomic positions for the $Ni_{91}Nb_9$ and $Ni_{87}Nb_{13}$ fcc solid solution models after annealing at 300 K for adequate simulation times. One sees vividly that for the $Ni_{91}Nb_9$ solid solution model, the fcc structure can clearly be visualized, i.e. it still remains in its original fcc structure, and that for the $Ni_{87}Nb_{13}$ solid solution model, the crystalline lattice has collapsed and turned into a disordered state, i.e. a crystal-to-amorphous transition has taken place. Fig. 4 shows the corresponding density profiles for the $Ni_{91}Nb_9$, $Ni_{87}Nb_{13}$, and $Ni_{80}Nb_{20}$ fcc solid solution models. When the solute concentration is less than 13 at% Nb, the atomic planes can be clearly distinguished from the density profiles. However, once the Nb solute concentration exceeds 13 at%, a relatively uniformly distributed density profile appears. To have firm evidence, the total and partial pair-correlation functions for the $Ni_{91}Nb_9$, $Ni_{87}Nb_{13}$, and $Ni_{80}Nb_{20}$ fcc solid solution models were calculated and the calculated results are shown in Fig. 5. In the figure, one sees that the $g(r)$ curve of the $Ni_{91}Nb_9$ solid solution model remains sharp peaks even at a large distance r, showing that the $Ni_{91}Nb_9$ solid solution model is still in a crystalline structure. However, for the $Ni_{87}Nb_{13}$ and $Ni_{80}Nb_{20}$ simulation models, the $g(r)$ curves become more or less smoother and the peaks, except the first one, even disappear, indicating that a crystal-to-amorphous transition has taken place. In fact, all the simulation models with Nb solute concentrations exceeding 13 at% show obvious amorphous characteristics in their $g(r)$. It is noted that the calculated curves of the $Ni_{87}Nb_{13}$ and $Ni_{80}Nb_{20}$ solid solution models are similar, as shown in Fig. 5, implying that they have similar amorphous structures. From the above results, it can be concluded that for the fcc Ni-based solid solution, the critical solid solubility is 13 at% Nb, which is significantly greater than that observed from the Ni–Nb equilibrium phase diagram, e.g. the solid solubility of Nb in Ni at room temperature is about 2–3 at%. Consequently, the fcc Ni-based solid solution containing 13 at% Nb is a supersaturated one. From a thermodynamic point of view, the supersaturated Ni-based solid solution is in a metastable state and the higher the Nb concentration, the less stable the supersaturated solid solution. Once the Nb concentration exceeds the critical solid

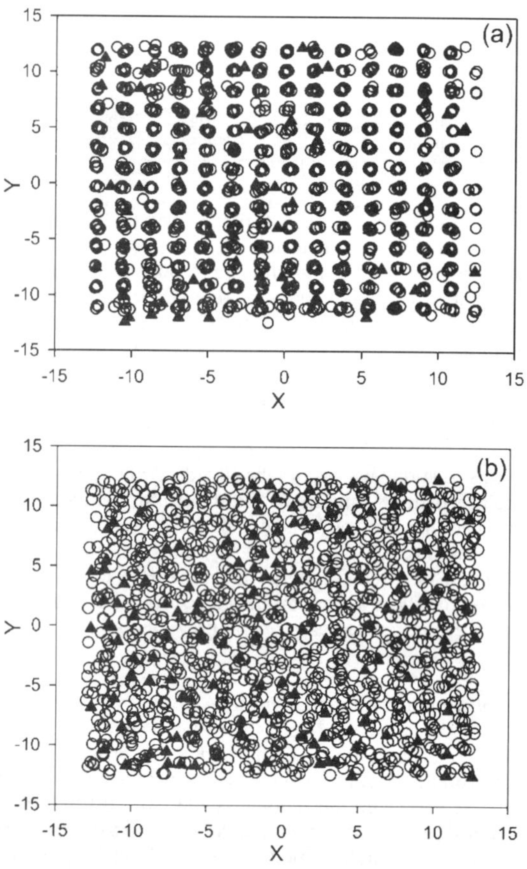

Fig. 3. Projections of the atomic positions of the $Ni_{91}Nb_9$ (a) and $Ni_{87}Nb_{13}$ (b) fcc solid solution models after annealing at 300 K for adequate simulation times.

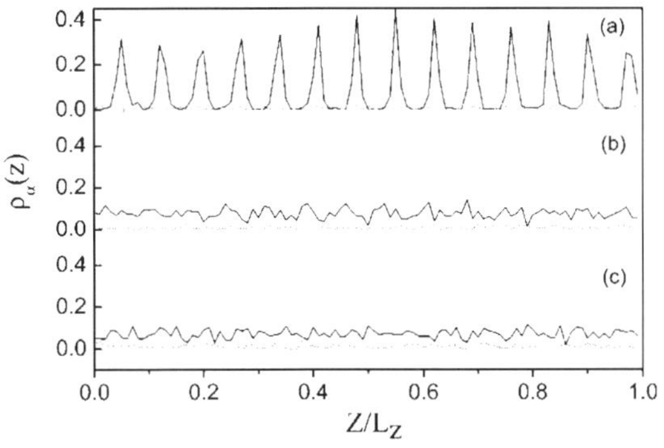

Fig. 4. Density profiles of the $Ni_{91}Nb_9$ (a), $Ni_{87}Nb_{13}$ (b), and $Ni_{80}Nb_{20}$ (c) fcc solid solution models after annealing at 300 K for adequate simulation times.

solubility, the solid solution would become unstable and turn into a disordered state, resulting in a crystal-to-amorphous transition.

Similarly, for the bcc Nb-based solid solution, Fig. 6 displays the $g(r)$ curves for the Nb-based bcc solid solutions with three different alloy compositions. Apparently, the $g(r)$ curves feature a bcc crystalline structure when the Ni concentration is less than 19 at% Ni, whereas when the Ni concentration exceeds the critical solid solubility, the $g(r)$ curves are typical of an amorphous structure. The critical solid solubility of bcc Nb-based solid solution was determined to be 19 at% Ni. Summarizing the above results, it is concluded that the GFR of the Ni–Nb system is 19–87 at% Ni (or 13–81 at% Nb). Interestingly, the predicted GFR is compatible with the prediction based on thermodynamic calculations. For instance, by comparing the Gibbs free energies of the crystalline and amorphous phases of the Ni–Nb alloys, Gallego et al. estimated that the GFR of the Ni–Nb system is 20–80 at% Ni [354], which is within the present prediction from the Ni–Nb potential.

We now discuss the simulation results for the Ni–Mo system [304,305]. Fig. 7 displays the calculated total and partial pair-correlation function $g(r)$ of the $Ni_{90}Mo_{10}$, $Ni_{83}Mo_{17}$, $NiMo_{21}$ and $Ni_{75}Mo_{25}$ fcc solid solution models upon 300 K annealing for adequate simulation times. One sees that the fcc Ni-based solid solution models with 10 and 17 at% Mo still remain in their crystalline structures and that, upon increasing the solute

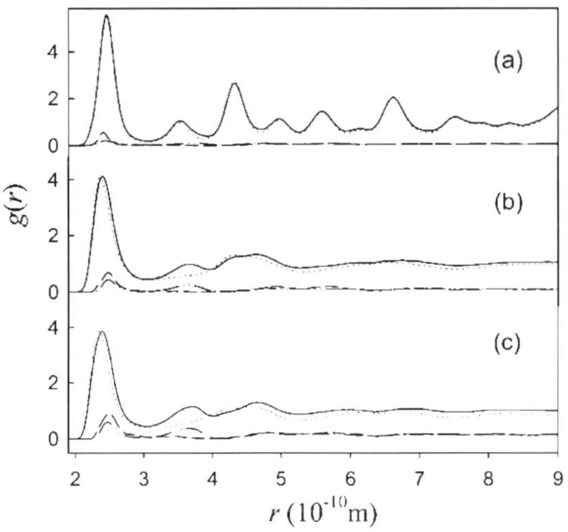

Fig. 5. Total and partial pair-correlation functions for the $Ni_{91}Nb_9$ (a), $Ni_{87}Nb_{13}$ (b) and $Ni_{80}Nb_{20}$ (c) fcc solid solution models after annealing at 300 K for adequate simulation times.

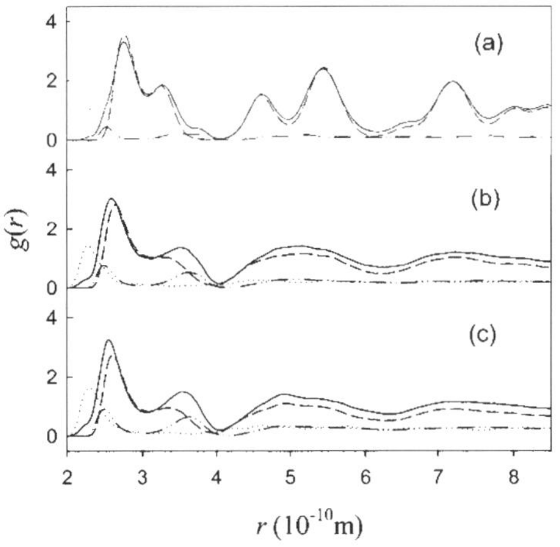

Fig. 6. Total and partial pair-correlation functions for the $Ni_{15}N_{85}$ (a), $Ni_{19}Nb_{81}$ (b), and $Ni_{25}Nb_{75}$ (c) bcc solid solution models after annealing at 300 K for adequate simulation times.

concentration, the peaks of $g(r)$ become broadened, implying the crystalline structure becomes progressively towards to the disordered state. For the fcc Ni-based solid solution model with 25 at% Mo, a crystal-to-amorphous transition has obviously taken place. It is of interest to note that for the fcc Ni-based solid solution model with 21 at% Mo, the shape of the calculated $g(r)$ is somewhat ambiguous, suggesting that a structural transition has taken place, yet probably not complete. Similarly, Fig. 8 shows their calculated total and partial pair-correlation function $g(r)$ of the $Ni_{10}Mo_{90}$, $Ni_{25}Mo_{75}$, $Ni_{30}Mo_{70}$ and $Ni_{40}Mo_{60}$ bcc solid solution models upon 300 K annealing for adequate simulation times. One sees that when the solute concentration exceeds 25 at% Ni, the $g(r)$ curves exhibit typical shape of an amorphous structure, suggesting that a critical solid solubility is 25 at% Ni for the crystal-to-amorphous transition to take place in the bcc Mo-based solid solution.

To obtain further evidence of the crystal-to-amorphous transition, the molar enthalpy and volume as a function of composition were also calculated and are shown in Fig. 9 [304,305]. These results reveal that on the Ni-rich side, the enthalpy decreases and the volume increases with increasing the Mo solute concentration and that, at the composition of 21 at% Mo, the enthalpy slope is discontinuous and also there is a step increase in the volume, indicating a crystal-to-amorphous transition has taken place. The abrupt increase in the volume is also in consistent with the fact that the crystal-to-amorphous transition is accompanied with a volume expansion, as the amorphous phase has an excess free volume in comparing with its crystalline counterpart. It is also found that with increasing of the solute concentration of Ni, which has a smaller atomic size than that of Mo, the volume of the bcc Mo-based solid solution increases a little at the concentration of 25 at% Ni, which is compatible with what is observed in the pair correlation function. In summary, the critical solid solubilities for crystal-to-amorphous transitions in the Ni–Mo system were determined to be 21 at% Mo for the fcc Ni-based solid solution and 25 at% Ni for the bcc Mo-based solid solution, respectively. In other words, the GFR of the Ni–Mo system is predicted to be 21–75 at% Mo (or alternatively 25–79 at% Ni), within which metallic glass formation is energetically favored [304,305].

4.4.1.2. The Ag–Mo and Cu–W systems. To support the above conclusion obtained from the two equilibrium miscible fcc–bcc systems, molecular dynamics simulations have also been carried out for another two equilibrium immiscible fcc–bcc systems, i.e. the Ag–Mo and Cu–W systems. As discussed in the above section,

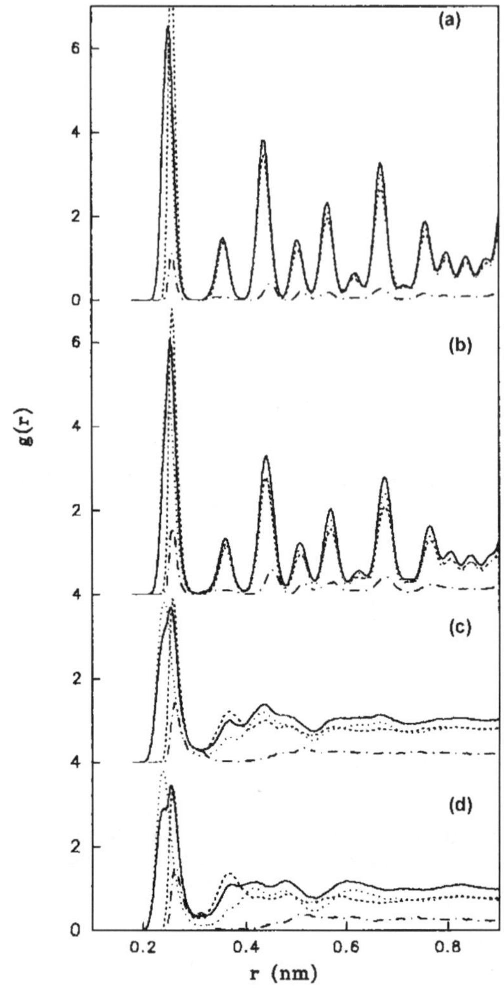

Fig. 7. Total and partial pair-correlation functions for the $Ni_{90}Mo_{10}$ (a), $Ni_{83}Mo_{17}$ (b), $NiMo_{21}$ (c), and $Ni_{75}Mo_{25}$ (d) fcc solid solution models after annealing at 300 K for adequate simulation times.

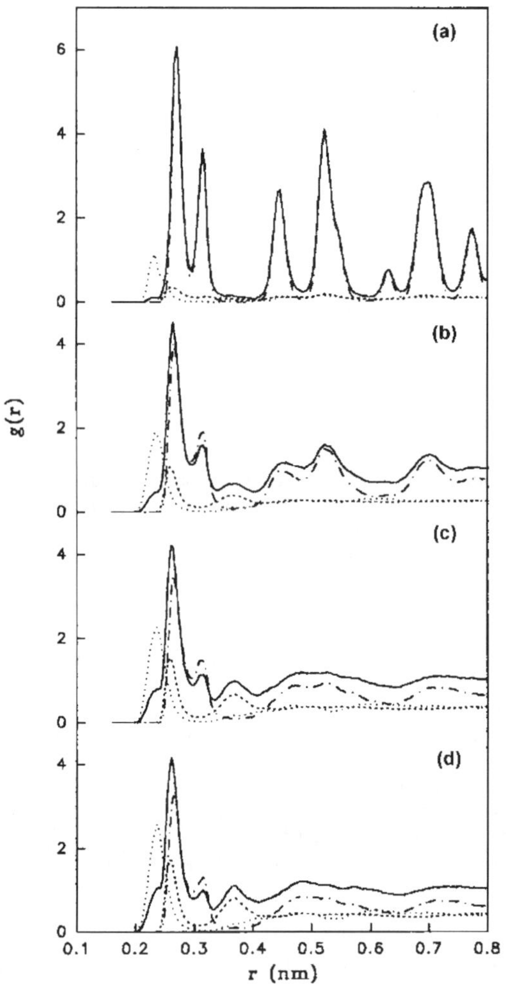

Fig. 8. Total and partial pair-correlation functions for $Ni_{10}Mo_{90}$ (a), $Ni_{25}Mo_{75}$ (b), $Ni_{30}Mo_{70}$ (c), and $Ni_{40}Mo_{60}$ (d) bcc solid solution models after annealing at 300 K for adequate simulation times.

the F–S Ag–Mo potential and the EAM Cu–W potential have been constructed, respectively. Incidentally, it was intentionally to use different potential formula for the Ag–Mo and Cu–W systems, to see if the potential formulism would affect the outcome drawn from the later performed molecular dynamics simulations.

We now present the simulation results for the Ag–Mo system [158]. Fig. 10 displays the projections of atomic positions for the $Ag_{95}Mo_5$, $Ag_{90}Mo_{10}$, and $Ag_{50}Mo_{50}$ fcc solid solution models upon annealing at 300 K for 120,000 time steps. One sees vividly that for the $Ag_{95}Mo_5$ solid solution model, the original fcc structure still remains and that, for the $Ag_{90}Mo_{10}$ and $Ag_{50}Mo_{50}$ solid solution models, the projections of atomic positions are obviously disordered, indicating that the crystalline lattices have collapsed and turned into their respective disordered states. Fig. 11 shows the corresponding density profiles $\rho_z(l)$ for the $Ag_{95}Mo_5$, $Ag_{90}Mo_{10}$, and $Ag_{50}Mo_{50}$ fcc solid solution models. It can be seen that, when the solute concentration is less than 10 at% Mo, the atomic planes can clearly be distinguished from the density profiles. However, once the Mo concentration equals to or exceeds 10 at%, a relatively uniformly distributed density profile appears. To have firm evidence, the total and partial pair correlation functions $g(r)$ for the fcc Ag-based solid solution models were calculated and are shown in Fig. 12. In this figure, because the $g(r)$ curve of the $Ag_{95}Mo_5$ solid solution model exhibits apparent sharp peaks even at a large distance r, the $Ag_{95}Mo_5$ solid solution is considered to still be in a crystalline structure. For the $Ag_{90}Mo_{10}$ and $Ag_{50}Mo_{50}$ solid solution models, the first and second peaks of the $g(r)$ curves are

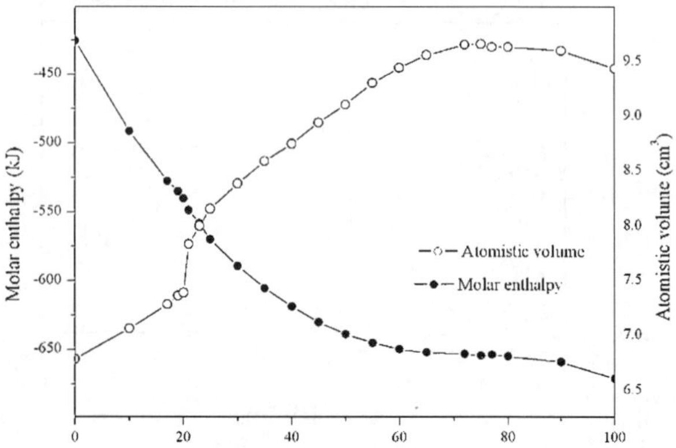

Fig. 9. Molar enthalpy and volume of the Ni–Mo alloys upon annealing at 300 K.

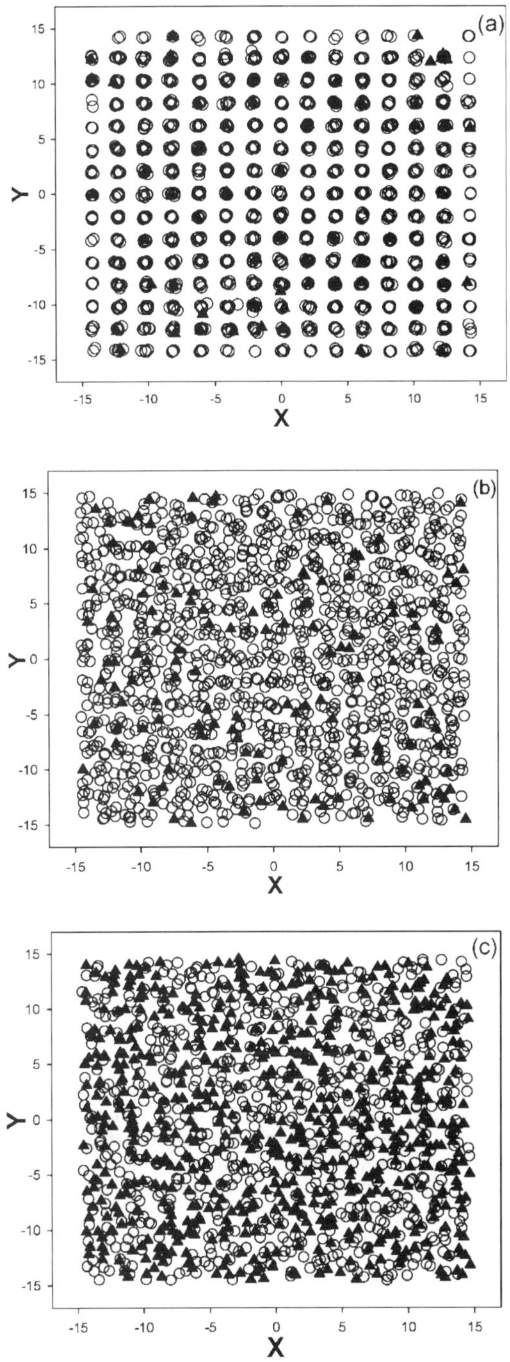

Fig. 10. Projections of atomic positions for the $Ag_{95}Mo_5$ (a), $Ag_{90}Mo_{10}$ (b), and $Ag_{50}Mo_{50}$ (c) fcc solid solution models upon annealing at 300 K for adequate simulation times.

still clear, but there are no discernible peaks beyond the third-nearest neighbors. Following Zallen's criterion [5], it is concluded that a crystal-amorphous transition has indeed taken place in both $Ag_{90}Mo_{10}$ and $Ag_{50}Mo_{50}$ solid solution models. These results suggest that, for the fcc Ag-based solid solution, the critical solid solubility is 10 at% Mo, beyond which, the solid solution prefers to transform into an amorphous state. Similar simulations and characterization have also been carried out for a number of bcc

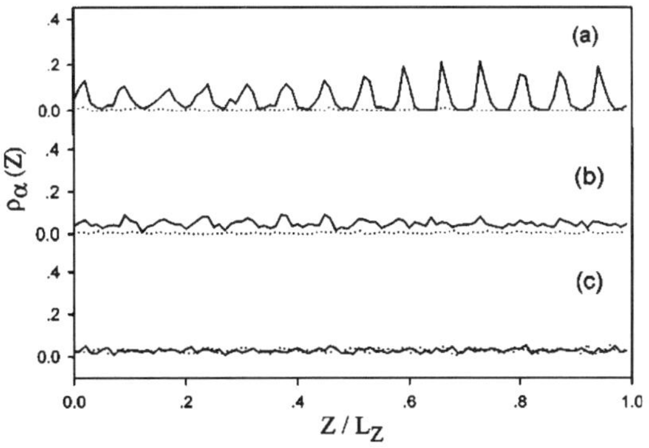

Fig. 11. Density profiles of the $Ag_{95}Mo_5$ (a), $Ag_{90}Mo_{10}$ (b), and $Ag_{50}Mo_{50}$ (c) fcc solid solution models after annealing at 300 K for adequate simulation times.

Mo-based solid solution models, and the critical solid solubility was determined to be 12 at% Ag. Consequently, the two critical solid solubilities of the Ag–Mo system were 10 at% Mo for the fcc Ag-based solid solution and 12 at% Ag for the bcc Mo-based solid solution, respectively, thus predicting the GFR of the Ag–Mo system to be 10–88 at% Mo (or alternatively 12–90 at% Ag).

Similarly, based on the constructed EAM Cu–W potential, molecular dynamics simulations have been performed for fcc Cu-base solid solution models and bcc W-based solid solution models, respectively [307]. Fig. 13 exhibits the projections of atomic positions for the $Cu_{35}W_{65}$ and $Cu_{30}W_{70}$ bcc solid solution models after annealing at 300 K for 0.5 ns. It can vividly be seen that a uniform disordered structure is formed in the $Cu_{35}W_{65}$ model, while the $Cu_{30}W_{70}$ model still remains in an ordered state, indicating that 35 at% Cu is the critical solid solubility to trigger a crystal-to- amorphous transition in the bcc W-based solid solution. In addition, the structural change has been monitored by the

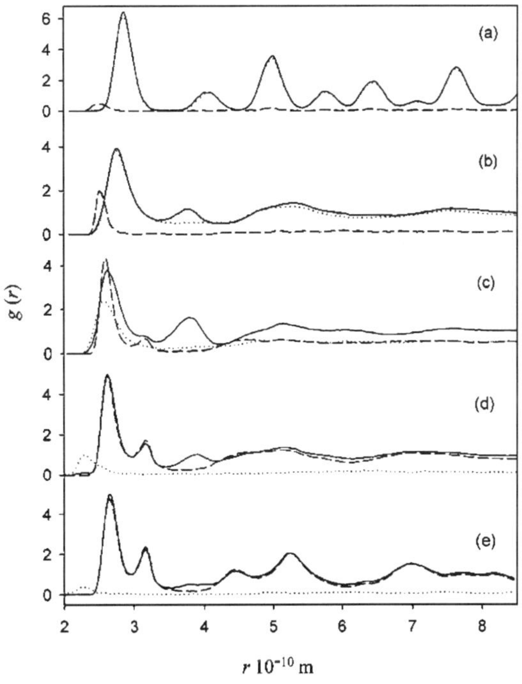

Fig. 12. Total and partial pair-correlation functions for the $Ag_{95}Mo_5$ (a), $Ag_{90}Mo_{10}$ (b), and $Ag_{50}Mo_{50}$ (c) fcc solid solution models and $Ag_{15}Mo_{85}$ (d) and $Ag_{10}Mo_{90}$ (e) bcc solid solution models after annealing at 300 K for adequate simulation times.

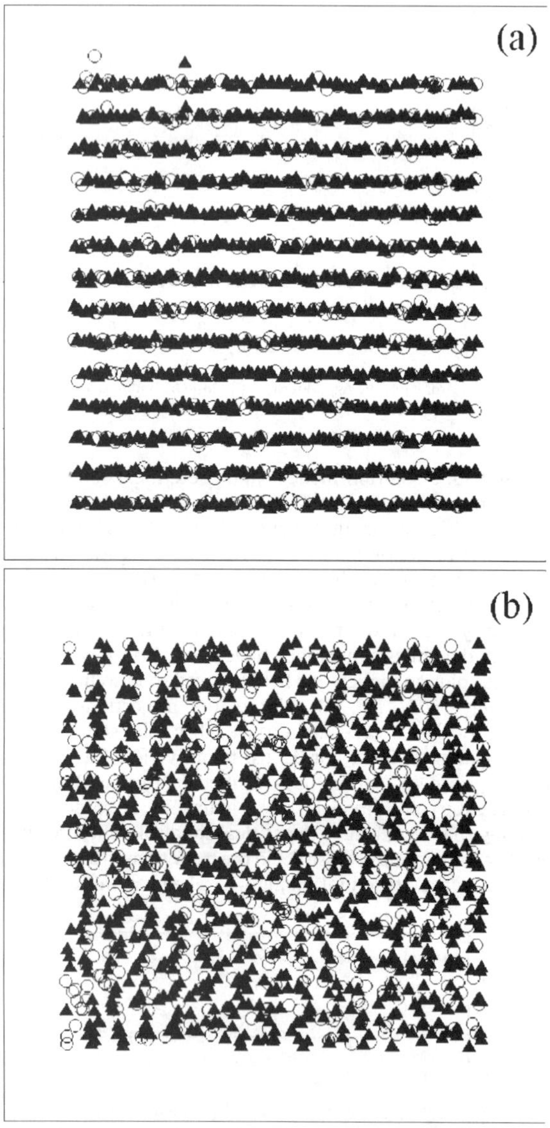

Fig. 13. Projections of atomic positions for the $Cu_{35}W_{65}$ (a) and $Cu_{30}W_{70}$ (b) bcc solid solution models after annealing at 300 K for adequate simulation times.

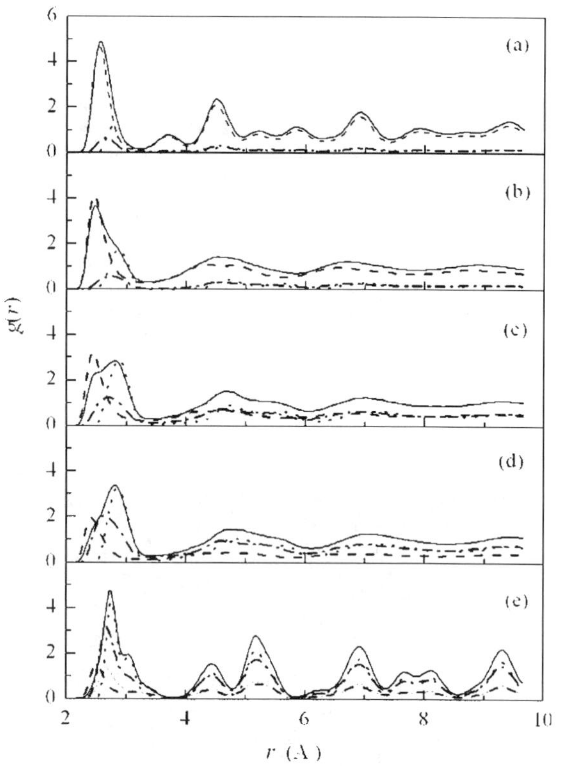

Fig. 14. Total and partial pair-correlation functions for the $Cu_{55}W_{15}$ (a), $Cu_{80}W_{20}$ (b), and $Cu_{50}W_{50}$ (c) fcc solid solution models and $Cu_{30}W_{70}$ (d) bcc solid solution model after annealing at 300 K for adequate simulation times.

partial and total pair correlation functions and the calculated results are shown in Fig. 14. The results indicate that, after annealing at 300 K for 0.5 ns, the $Cu_{85}W_{15}$ model remains in crystalline structure, whereas the $Cu_{80}W_{20}$, $Cu_{50}W_{50}$, and $Cu_{35}W_{65}$ models all become disordered, indicating that 20 at% W is the critical solid solubility of the fcc Cu-based solid solution. It follows that the GFR of the Cu–W system is predicted to be 20–65 at% W (or alternatively 35–80 at% Cu).

4.4.1.3. The Co–Nb and Sc–W systems. The simulation results presented above concerning the crystal-to-amorphous transition were obtained from the fcc–bcc binary metal systems with either negative (miscible) or positive (immiscible) ΔH_f. Here we present the simulation results for the hcp–bcc binary metal systems, i.e. the Co–Nb and Sc–W systems, featuring ΔH_f of −37 kJ/mol and +14 kJ/mol, respectively.

Based on the constructed EAM Co–Nb potential described above, molecular dynamics simulations have been carried out for the hcp Co-based solid solution models and bcc Nb-based solid solution models, respectively [185,308]. Fig. 15 shows the calculated total pair correlation functions $g(r)$ for the hcp Co-based and bcc Nb-based solid solution models upon annealing at 300 K for adequate time steps. One clearly sees that in the Co-rich side, beyond 20 at% Nb, the hcp solid solutions have transformed into the disordered states and that in the Nb-rich side, beyond 20 at% Co, the bcc solid solution models still remain in the crystalline states. Further simulations were carried out for the two composition ranges of 10–20 at% Nb and 10–20 at% Co, and the results determine the two critical solid solubilities for the Co–Nb system to be 18 at% Nb in hcp Co and 16 at% Co in bcc Nb, respectively. Consequently, the GFR of the Co–Nb system predicted directly from the EAM Co–Nb potential through MD simulations is within 18–84 at% Nb (or alternatively 16–82 at% Co). Interestingly, the prediction is supported by the experimental observations that the Co–Nb metallic glasses have been obtained in experiments within an alloy composition range from 20 to 80 at% Nb [166,355–357].

Similarly, for the Sc–W system, Fig. 16 shows the calculated total pair correlation functions of the hcp Sc-based and bcc W-based solid solution models, respectively, upon annealing at 300 K for 2 ns [185,308]. One clearly sees that, in the Sc-rich side, beyond 20 at% W, the hcp solid solution have transformed into the amorphous states, and that, in the W-rich side, the bcc solid solution models still remain in their crystalline states. These results suggest that metallic glasses could be formed in the Sc-rich side, yet could hardly be obtained in the W-rich side. Further simulations show that the GFR of the Sc–W system determined directly from the EAM Sc–W potential is approximately within 15–50 at% W (or alternatively 50–85 at% Sc). To check the predicted

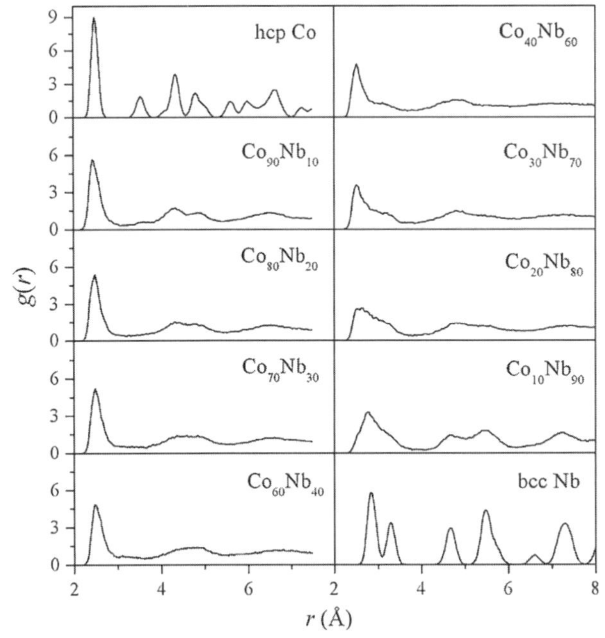

Fig. 15. Total pair correlation functions $g(r)$ for the hcp Co-based (left) and bcc Nb-based (right) solid solution models upon annealing at 300 K for adequate times.

GFR of the Sc–W system, the authors' group has performed ion beam mixing experiments and the results confirmed that amorphous alloys could be formed in a composition range around 25–48 at% W [185,308]. Table 18 lists the experimental results of ion beam mixing experiment, showing the formation of amorphous alloys within 25–48 at% W. Fig. 17 shows the selected area diffraction (SAD) patterns of the $Sc_{60}W_{40}$ multilayered sample in the as-deposited state and irradiated to an irradiation dose of 9×10^{15} Xe^+/cm^2. From Fig. 17, it can be seen that the initial

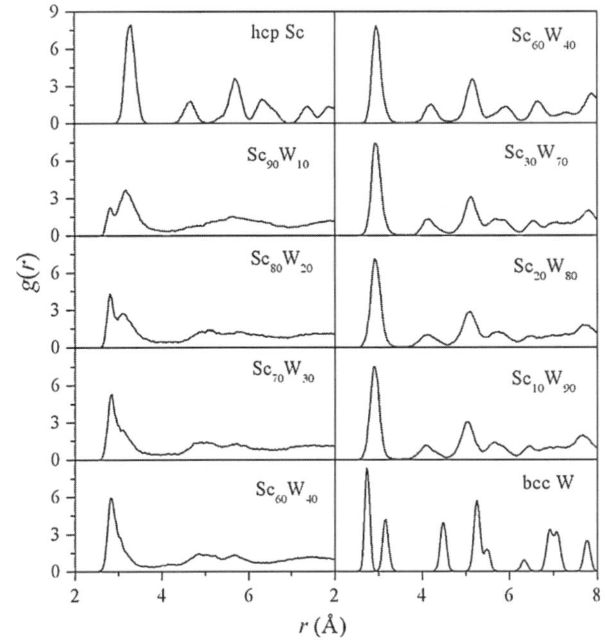

Fig. 16. Total pair correlation functions $g(r)$ for the hcp Sc-based (left) and bcc W-based (right) solid solution models upon annealing at 300 K for adequate times.

Table 18
Structural phase evolution in the Sc–W multilayers upon ion beam mixing.[a,b]

Multilayers	$Sc_{75}W_{25}$	$Sc_{60}W_{40}$	$Sc_{40}W_{60}$	$Sc_{25}W_{75}$
As-deposited	Sc + W	Sc + W	bcc	bcc
6	Sc + W	Sc + W	bcc	bcc
8	Sc + W	Sc + W	bcc	bcc
10	Sc + W	Sc + W	bcc	bcc
30	Sc + W	Sc + W	bcc	bcc
50	Sc + W	Sc + W	bcc	bcc
70	PA	PA	bcc	bcc
90	A	A	Bcc + PA	bcc

[a] The units of the dose in irradiation is 10^{14} Xe^+/cm^2.
[b] bcc, bcc solid solution; A, completely amorphized; PA, partially amorphized.

crystalline Sc and W have transformed into a unique amorphous phase. Apparently, the results from ion beam mixing studies are in support to the predicted GFR directly from the interatomic potential.

4.4.1.4. The Ni–Hf and Cu–Ru systems. To this point, the prediction of the GFRs directly from the respectively interatomic potentials has been discussed for the fcc–bcc and bcc–hcp binary metal systems in either equilibrium miscible or immiscible representative systems. For completeness, the fcc–hcp Ni–Hf and Cu–Ru binary metal systems have also been studied under the same concept and method. One notes that the Ni–Hf system is equilibrium miscible, while the Cu–Ru system is immiscible at equilibrium. In the above section, the TB-SMA Ni–Hf and Cu–Ru potentials were constructed and shown to be of relevance in describing the atomic interactions in these respective systems.

We now present the simulation results for the Ni–Hf system [309]. Fig. 18 displays the total and partial pair-correlation functions $g(r)$ calculated for the $Ni_{95}Hf_5$, $Ni_{90}Hf_{10}$, $Ni_{85}Hf_{15}$, $Ni_{82}Hf_{18}$ fcc solid solution models. From Fig. 18, one sees that the $Ni_{95}Hf_5$, $Ni_{90}Hf_{10}$ solid solution models still remain in the fcc crystalline structures. When the Hf solute concentration was increased up to 15 at%, some disordering began to develop in the crystalline lattice of the fcc Ni-based solid solution. Once the Hf solute concentration exceeded 18 at%, the crystalline lattice of the fcc Ni-based solid solution model collapsed completely, as evidenced by Fig. 18(d), in which the $g(r)$ curves are commonly observed for the amorphous alloys. Similarly, for the hcp Hf-based solid solution models, simulations showed that when the Ni concentration was increased up to about 25 at%, the crystal-to-amorphous transition took place. To obtain a thermodynamic image, the enthalpy of the fcc and hcp supersaturated solid

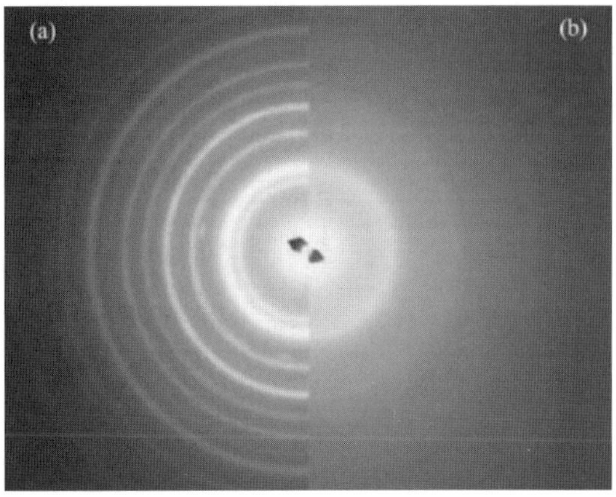

Fig. 17. SAD patterns of the $Sc_{60}W_{40}$ multilayered films: as-deposited (a) and after 200 keV xenon ion irradiation to a dose of 2×10^{15} Xe^+/cm^2 (b).

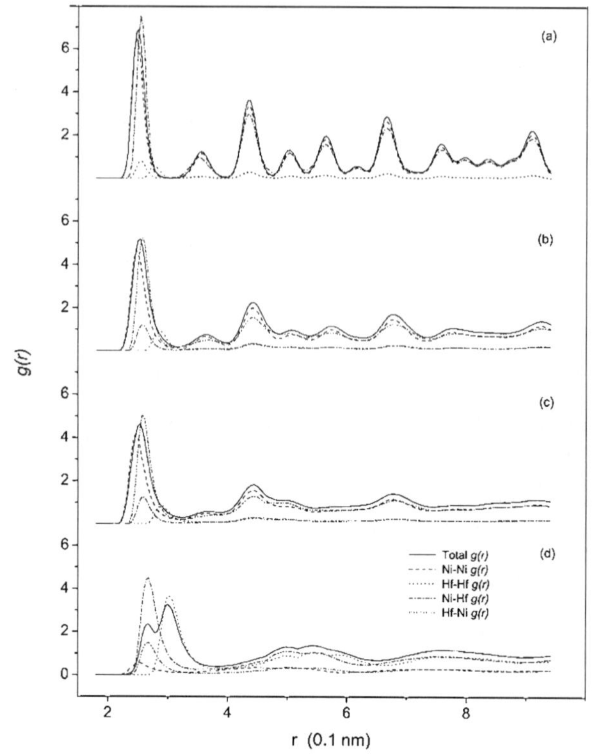

Fig. 18. Total and partial pair-correlation functions $g(r)$ calculated for the $Ni_{95}Hf_5$, $Ni_{90}Hf_{10}$, $Ni_{85}Hf_{15}$, $Ni_{82}Hf_{18}$ fcc solid solution models.

solution models have also been calculated and compared with those of the solid solutions based on those equilibrium intermetallic compounds. Fig. 19 shows the calculated molar enthalpy and atomic volume as a function of solute concentration in the super-saturated hcp ($\leq$50 at% Ni) and fcc ($\leq$50 at% of Hf) solid solutions as well as in the Ni_2Hf and $NiHf_2$ intermetallic compounds. One sees that the molar enthalpies of the intermetallic compounds are much lower than those of their amorphous counterparts, indicating that the intermetallic compounds are energetically more stable than the amorphous alloys. In addition, simulations show that the intermetallic compounds $NiHf_2$ and Ni_2Hf could have considerable solubility of either Ni or Hf, resulting in forming the respective solid solutions. More interestingly, for the $NiHf_2$ and Ni_2Hf super-saturated solid solutions, when the alloy compositions deviate to such an extent from their exact chemical stoichiometries, they behavior regress again to those of the fcc and hcp solid solutions, as showing in Fig. 19. One can see that there appear sudden changes in their respective molar enthalpy curves as well as in their atomic volume curves, indicating that the crystal-to-amorphous transitions have indeed taken place in the respective super-saturated solid solutions. From the above simulation results, it is predicted that the GFR of the Ni–Hf system is around 25–82 at% Ni (or alternatively 18–75 at% Hf).

Similarly, the GFR of the Cu–Ru system has also been determined from the constructed TB-SMA Cu–Ru potential through molecular dynamics simulations [310], and we present here some typical simulation results. Fig. 20 displays the projections of the atomic positions of the Cu_5Ru_{95}, $Cu_{20}Ru_{80}$, and $Cu_{50}Ru_{50}$ solid solution models upon 300 K annealing for an adequate simulation time. One sees vividly that for the Cu_5Ru_{95} solid solution, the hcp structure could clearly be visualized, i.e. it still remains in its original hcp structure. For the hcp solid solution models with Cu solute concentration of 20 at% or more, the projection of atomic position is obviously disordered, indicating that a crystal-to-amorphous transition has taken place. Fig. 21 shows the corresponding density profiles $\rho_z(l)$ for the Cu_5Ru_{95}, $Cu_{20}Ru_{80}$, and $Cu_{50}Ru_{50}$ solid solution models. It can be seen that when the Cu solute concentration is less than 20 at%, the atomic planes can clearly be distinguishable in the density profiles. However, once the Cu solute concentration exceeds 20 at%, a relatively uniformly distributed density profile appears. To have firm evidence, the total and partial pair-correlation functions $g(r)$ for the hcp Ru-based solid solution models were calculated and are shown in Fig. 22. In the figure, as the $g(r)$ curve of Cu_5Ru_{95} shows apparent sharp peaks even at a large distance r, the Cu_5Ru_{95} solid solution model is considered to be still in a crystalline structure. In comparison, for the $Cu_{20}Ru_{80}$ solid solution model, though the first and second peaks of the $g(r)$ curves are still clear, there is no discernible peak beyond the third-nearest neighbors. It is therefore concluded that a crystal-to-amorphous transition has taken place in both $Cu_{50}Ru_{50}$ and $Cu_{20}Ru_{80}$ solid solution models. In summary, for the Cu–Ru system, when the Cu concentration equals to or exceeds 20 at%, the hcp Ru-based solid solution would become unstable and turn into an amorphous state. Similarly, for the fcc Cu-based solid solution, the critical solid solubility is determined

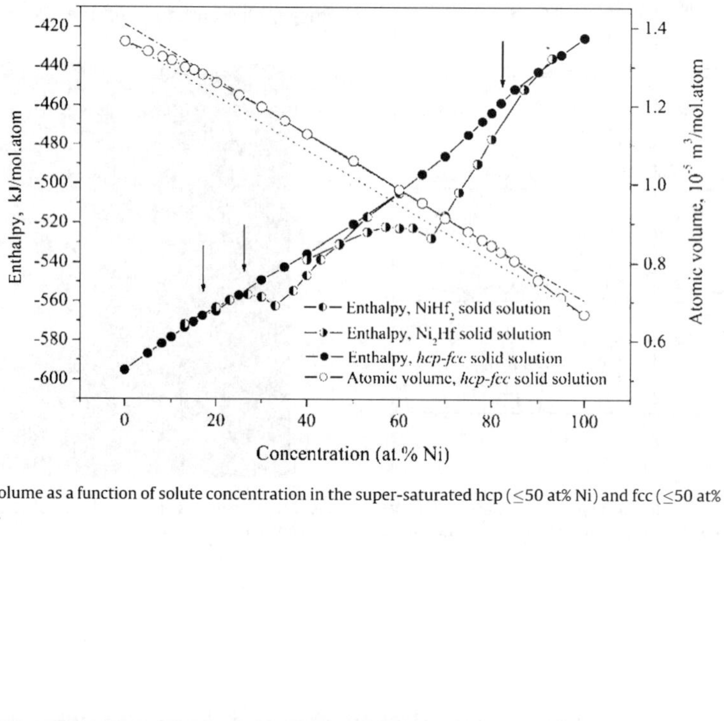

Fig. 19. Molar enthalpy and atomic volume as a function of solute concentration in the super-saturated hcp ($\leq$50 at% Ni) and fcc ($\leq$50 at% of Hf) solid solutions, and the Ni_2Hf and $NiHf_2$ intermetallic compounds.

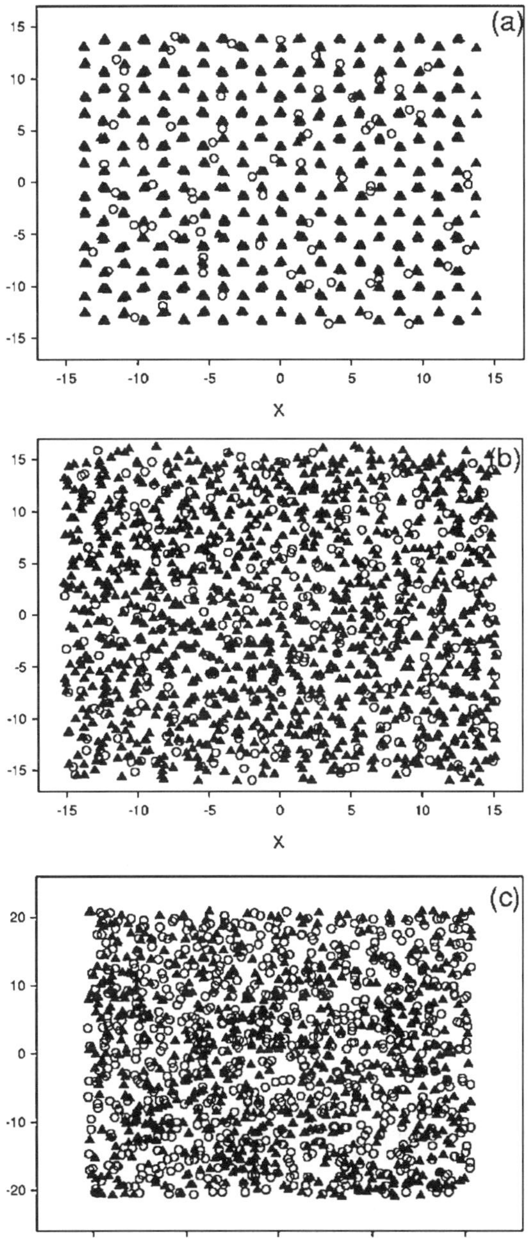

Fig. 20. Projections of the atomic positions of the Cu_5Ru_{95}, $Cu_{20}Ru_{80}$, and $Cu_{50}Ru_{50}$ solid solution models upon 300 K annealing for an adequate simulation time.

to be 10 at% Ru. It follows that the GFR of the Cu–Ru system is around 10–80 at% Ru (or alternatively 20–90 at% Cu), within which formation of metallic glasses is energetically favored.

4.4.2. Proposed atomistic theory for the binary metallic glass formation

In summary, the major objective is to develop an atomistic theory capable of predicting the metallic glass formation in a binary metal system, or to be precise, capable of predicting an alloy composition range of the system, within which metallic glass formation is energetically favored. The main idea is to take the interatomic potential of a binary metal system as the starting base,

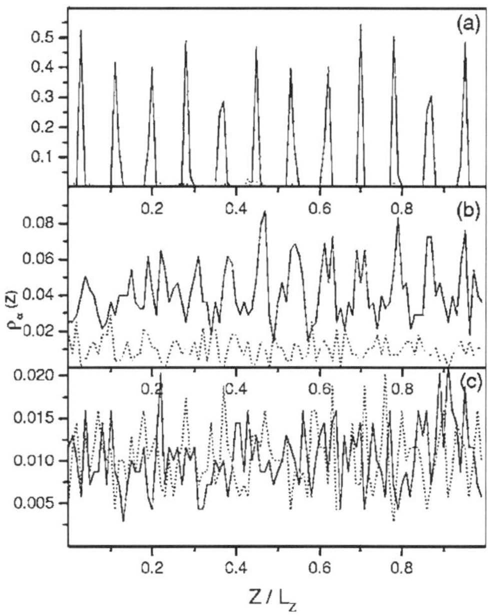

Fig. 21. Density profiles $\rho_z(l)$ for the Cu_5Ru_{95}, $Cu_{20}Ru_{80}$, and $Cu_{50}Ru_{50}$ solid solution models.

since the interatomic potential is believed to govern the major atomic interactions in the system.

To develop an atomistic theory valid in general, eight representative binary metal systems were selected: the Ni–Nb, Ni–Mo, Ag–Mo, Cu–W, Co–Nb, Sc–W, Ni–Hf and Cu–Ru systems. These systems cover the various structural combinations of the three major structures of fcc, bcc and hcp, as well as various thermodynamic characteristics featuring large negative to large positive ΔH_f. For the representative systems, their n-body potentials were constructed by using different potential formula and these potentials were shown to be of relevance in describing the atomic interactions in the respective systems. Applying the constructed n-body potentials, a series of molecular dynamics simulations were conducted for the eight representative binary metal systems and the solid solution models were used in the

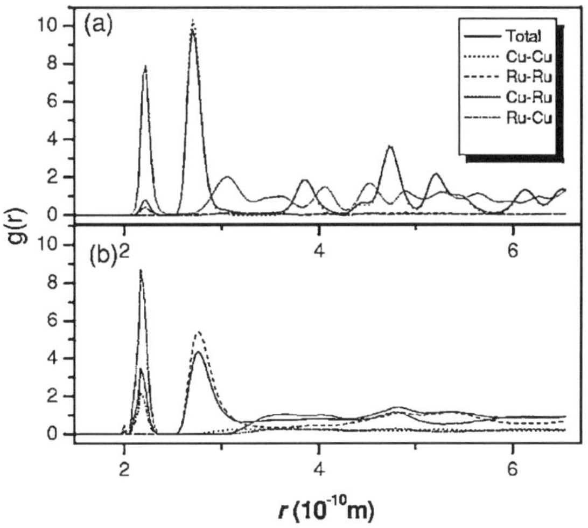

Fig. 22. Total and partial pair-correlation functions $g(r)$ for the hcp Ru-based solid solution models.

simulations to compare the relative stability of the crystalline solid solution versus its disordered counterpart (i.e. an amorphous or metallic glass phase), as a function of solute concentration. Interestingly, molecular dynamics simulations for the eight representative binary metal systems have given a unanimous verdict, leading to propose an atomistic theory capable of predicting the binary metallic glass formation as follows.

4.4.2.1. Physical origin of the binary metallic glass formation. As shown above, to a binary metal system, starting with its realistic n-body potential, molecular dynamics simulations, using solid solution models, reveal that when the solute concentration is less than the critical solid solubility, the crystalline solid solution is energetically favored comparing to the amorphous phase, and that whenever the solute concentration reaches and/or exceeds the critical solid solubility, the crystalline solid solution becomes unstable and collapses into the disordered state, giving rise to the formation of an amorphous phase, i.e. forming a metallic glass. In other words, the physical origin of the metallic glass formation, or of the crystal-to-amorphous transition, is the collapsing of the crystalline lattice, while the solute atoms are exceeding a critical value, i.e. the critical solid solubility. With such an understanding, if one is aim to produce an amorphous alloy, or metallic glass, in a specific binary metal system, one should design the alloy compositions away from the composition range, energetically favoring for forming the simple structured solid solution in the system.

4.4.2.2. Predicting the intrinsic glass-forming ability or glass-forming range. As shown above, to a binary metal system, based on its realistic n-body potential, molecular dynamics simulations, using solid solution models, determine two critical values for the two respective terminal solid solutions, i.e. the two critical solid solubilities of the system. The two determined critical solid solubilities locate an alloy composition range, within which metallic glass formation is energetically favored. It follows that the alloy composition range bounded by the two determined critical solid solubilities of the system is defined as the quantitative GFA, i.e. GFR of the system. Obviously, the GFA/GFR thus defined for a binary metal system could be named as intrinsic GFA/GFR of the system.

It is worthwhile mentioning again that the intrinsic GFR of a binary metal system is different from an experimentally obtained GFR by a specific glass-producing technique, and the experimentally measured GFR is named as the nominal GFR of the system. Moreover, the nominal GFR of a binary metal system is also different from the GFA/GFR under technical definition, as the nominal GFR is referred to an alloy composition range of the system, while the GFA frequently used in practice is described by some specific technical parameters, such as the cooling speed, size of the obtained metallic glasses.

To summarize the above molecular dynamics simulation results, Table 19 lists the GFAs/GFRs of the eight representative binary metal systems determined directly from their respective interatomic potentials through molecular dynamics simulations using solid solution models. For comparison, the GFAs/GFRs predicted by other proposed criteria or rules as well as obtained from experiments by various glass-producing techniques, if available, are also collected in Table 19.

4.4.2.3. Experimental observations in support to the proposed atomistic theory. Here we compare the GFRs of the eight representative binary metal systems predicted directly from their respective n-body potentials with the experimental results as well as with those predicted by other approaches.

For the Ni–Nb system, the GFR predicted from the constructed F-S Ni–Nb potential is 13–81 at% Nb. In comparison, based on

Table 19
Glass-forming ranges (GFRs, at% B) of the eight representative binary metal systems determined by their respective interatomic potentials and predicted by other proposed criteria or rules as well as measured in experiments.

A–B system	Present work	Thermodynamics	Size difference rule	Experiments
Ni–Nb	13–81	20–69 (Miedema)		37.5–60[a]
				15–80[b]
Ni–Mo	21–75			35–65[c]
				25–75[d]
Ag–Mo	10–88			25–88[e]
Cu–W	20–65			25–55[f]
Co–Nb	18–84	15–74 (Calphad)	22–64	20–77[g]
Sc–W	15–50	12–58 (Miedema)		25–40[h]
Ni–Hf	18–75	16–75 (Miedema)	10–81	30–70[i]
				20–75[j]
Cu–Ru	10–80			25–75[k]

[a] Liquid melt quenching [125,127,129].
[b] Ion beam mixing [177].
[c] Ion beam mixing [18,281].
[d] Solid state amorphization [188].
[e] Ion beam mixing [157–159].
[f] Vapor-deposition [358].
[g] Ion beam mixing [166].
[h] Ion beam mixing [185].
[i] Liquid melt quenching [75].
[j] Solid state amorphization [208].
[k] Ion beam mixing [169,310].

Miedema-Alonso's model, Zhang et al. have estimated that the composition range of 20–69 at% Nb was in favored for metallic glass formation. Experimentally, Skakov et al., Xia et al., and Hirota et al. have indeed produced the Ni–Nb metallic glasses in the composition range of 37.5–60 at% Nb by liquid melt quenching [125,127,129]. While using the scheme of ion beam mixing technique, Zhang et al. have obtained the Ni–Nb amorphous alloys in the composition range of 15–80 at% Nb [177]. Schanzer and Mehrer, and Petzoldt have produced the Ni–Nb amorphous alloys in the composition range of 20–80 at% Nb by mechanical alloying [248,279]. Obviously, the composition ranges of the Ni–Nb metallic glasses so far obtained in experiments by various glass-producing techniques all fall into the GFR predicted by the F-S Ni–Nb potential. Meanwhile, the GFR predicted by Miedema-Alonso's model is somehow too narrow to cover the experimental observations.

For the Ni–Mo system, ion beam mixing and solid-state amorphization studies showed that the metallic glasses could be obtained in the alloy composition ranges of 35–65 at% Mo and 25–75 at% Mo [18,281], respectively, which both fall into the GFR of 21–75 at% Mo predicted from the F-S Ni–Mo potential.

For the equilibrium immiscible Cu–W system, Gaffet et al. and Rizzo et al. have produced the Cu–W amorphous alloys in the alloy composition ranges of 30–60 at% and 25–55 at% W by mechanical alloying and vapor-deposition [254,358], respectively. Clearly, the experimentally obtained GFRs are both located within the predicted GFR of 20–65 at% W directly from the constructed EAM Cu–W potential. It is also true for the equilibrium immiscible Ag–Mo, Sc–W and Cu–Ru systems that the GFRs observed by ion beam mixing experiments were 25–88 at% Mo, 25–40 at% W and 25–75 at% Ru [157–159,169,185,310], respectively, and they all fall into the predicted GFRs of 10–88 at% Mo, 15–50 at% W and 10–80 at% Ru, respectively, from the constructed n-body potentials of the respective systems.

For the Co–Nb system, the GFRs observed in experiments were 20–77 at% Nb by ion beam mixing [166]. According to the size-difference rule proposed by Egami, the GFR of the Co–Nb system was estimated to be 22–64 at% Nb [282], and based on thermodynamic calculations, Schanzer and Mehrer predicted the GFR of the Co–Nb system to be 15–74 at% Nb [248]. Clearly, the two predictions are not satisfying, as they could not cover the experimental results. In comparison, the GFR of the Co–Nb system predicted from the constructed EAM Co–Nb potential is 18–84 at% Nb, showing a much better prediction than those from size difference rule and thermodynamic approach.

For the Ni–Hf system, Zhang, and Buschow and Beekmans have obtained the Ni–Hf metallic glasses in the composition range of 30–70 at% Hf by liquid melt quenching technique [75]. In solid state amorphization studying, Atzmon et al. have observed a broader favored composition range of 20–75 at% Hf than that observed from liquid melt quenching. The present atomistic theory predicts that the GFR of the Ni–Hf system is 17–75 at% Hf, which is also a good prediction to cover the experimental observations.

In addition to the eight representative systems just discussed above, similar results have been observed in some other binary metal systems. For instance, based on the constructed EAM Ag–Nb potential, molecular dynamics simulations predicted the GFR of the Ag–Nb system to be 20–90 at% Nb [359,360]. In ion beam mixing study, Tai et al. have found that the Ag–Nb amorphous alloys could be obtained in the alloy composition range of 25–90 at% Nb [359], which is in support to the prediction from the EAM Ag–Nb potential. Another example is the Ni–Ti system. The thermodynamic calculations suggested that the GFR of the system was 40–75 at% Ti [361]. In comparison, liquid melt quenching has produced the Ni–Ti metallic glasses in the composition rang of 40–70 at% Ti [70,75,82,83,107,362–364]. In this respect, based on the constructed TB-SMA Ni–Ti potential, simulations predicted that the GFR of the Ni–Ti system is 38–85 at% Ti [361], showing also an excellent prediction.

In short, the above discussion clearly demonstrate that prediction of the GFA/GFR of the binary metal systems from the proposed atomistic theory, i.e. the GFA/GFR predicted directly from the n-body potential of a binary metal system, is reasonable and in general, is superior than those previously proposed criteria or rules, in terms of matching with or covering the experimental observations.

5. Concluding remarks

(i) Summarizing the up-to-date experimental observations concerning the binary metallic glass formation by various glass-producing techniques, an important hint is that in a binary metal system, no matter miscible or immiscible at equilibrium, metallic glasses could probably be obtained in all the two-phase regions observed from the equilibrium phase diagram of the system. In other words, the favored alloy composition range for forming metallic glasses could extend from the central portion to near the edges of the two terminal solid solutions of the system.

(ii) Reviewing the frequently cited empirical criteria or rules proposed for predicting the binary metallic glass formation, it is understood that any proposal is based on a starting base, which is supposed to reflect the internal characteristics of a binary metal system. The authors' main idea is to start with the interatomic potential of a binary metal system as the very base and based on the potential, appropriate computations and simulations lead to develop an atomistic theory capable of predicting quantitatively an alloy composition range, within which metallic glass formation is energetically favored in the system.

(iii) To a binary metal system, as long as the metallic glasses have been obtained by a specific glass-producing technique, meaning that the disordered state does exist in the system. The above atomistic theory could reversely be applied to testify the relevance of the n-body potential being constructed for the system. For example, using the constructed potential to run molecular dynamics simulations using solid solution models, if the potential is relevant, the simulation model should collapse at those alloy compositions, where formation of metallic glasses was observed in experiment.

(iv) The same idea and computation/simulation methods have been applied to some ternary metal systems, such as the Ni–Hf–Ti and Ni–Nb–Ta systems [365,366], and similar results have been obtained, i.e. starting with an n-body potential of a ternary metal system, molecular dynamics simulations using solid solution models did quantitatively identify/locate a region in the alloy composition triangle, within which metallic glasses are energetically favored to be formed in the system.

(v) Naturally, the precision of the predicted quantitative glass-forming ability (GFA) or glass-forming range (GFR) from the interatomic potential of a metal system depends on the performance of the constructed potential. Currently, the n-body potentials for the transition metals and alloys are still constructed under some empirical potential formulae. Consequently, the prediction from a constructed potential for a binary or ternary metal system is therefore still an approximation. Nonetheless, the prediction is capable of locating an alloy composition range or region, for the binary or ternary metal systems, respectively, to guide the design of appropriate alloy compositions for producing the binary or ternary metallic glasses.

(vi) As the interatomic potential of a binary or ternary metal system governs the major atomic interactions in the system, it could also be applied to study some other scientific issues, e.g. the atomic structure of the metallic glasses and some other important physical or chemical properties of the system.

Acknowledgments

The authors are grateful for the financial support from the National Natural Science Foundation of China (50871058, 50971072), the Ministry of Science and Technology of China (2011CB606301), the Ministry of Education of China (2008000 30054) and the Administration of Tsinghua University. Thanks also go to Drs. W.S. Lai, Q. Zhang, J.B. Liu, L.T. Kong, H.R. Gong, R.F. Zhang, and X.D. Dai for their valuable contributions during their staying in the research group.

References

[1] W. Buckel, R. Hilsch, Zeitschrift fur Physik 138 (1954) 109–120.
[2] W. Buckel, Zeitschrift fur Physik 138 (1954) 136–150.
[3] W. Klement, R.H. Willens, P. Duwez, Nature 187 (1960) 869–870.
[4] P. Duwez, R.H. Willens, W. Klement, Journal of Applied Physics 31 (1960) 1136–1137.
[5] W. Zallen, The Physics of Amorphous Solids, John Wiley & Sons, New York, 1983
[6] S.R. Elliott, Physics of Amorphous Materials, Longman, London, 1984.
[7] A.L. Greer, Science 267 (1995) 1947–1953.
[8] H.J. Güntherodt, H. Beck, Glassy Metals, Springer-Verlag, New York, 1981.
[9] T.R. Anantharaman, Metallic Glasses: Production, Properties and Applications, Trans Tech Publications, Switzerland, 1984.
[10] F.E. Luborsky (Ed.), Amorphous Metallic Alloys, Butterworths, London, 1983.
[11] Y. Kawazoe, A.-P. Suzuki, J.-Z. Yu, T. Masumoto, Nonequilibrium Phase Diagrams of Ternary Amorphous Alloys, Springer-Verlag, Sendai, 1997.
[12] A. Inoue, Bulk Amorphous Alloys: Preparation and Fundamental Characteristics, Trans Tech Publications, Uetikon-Zuerich, Switzerland, 1998.
[13] W.H. Wang, C. Dong, C.H. Shek, Materials Science & Engineering R-Reports 44 (2004) 45-89.
[14] M. Miller, P. Liaw, Bulk Metallic Glasses: An Overview, Springer, Boston, 2007.
[15] P.K. Liaw, R.A. Buchanan, Bulk Metallic Glasses, the Minerals, Metals, and Materials Society, Warren dale, Pennsylvania, 2006.
[16] F.R. De Boer, R. Boom, A.R. Miedema, A.K. Niessen, Cohesion in Metals: Transition Metal Alloys, North-Holland, Amsterdam, 1989.
[17] B.X. Liu, W.L. Johnson, M.A. Nicolet, S.S. Lau, Applied Physics Letters 42 (1983) 45–47.
[18] B.X. Liu, W.L. Johnson, M.A. Nicolet, S.S. Lau, Nuclear Instruments & Methods in Physics Research 209 (1983) 229–234.

[19] B.X. Liu, B.M. Clemens, R. Gaboriaud, W.L. Johnson, M.A. Nicolet, Applied Physics Letters 42 (1983) 624–626.
[20] R.B. Schwarz, W.L. Johnson, Physical Review Letters 51 (1983) 415–418.
[21] B.M. Clemens, W.L. Johnson, R.B. Schwarz, Journal of Non-Crystalline Solids 61–62 (1984) 817–822.
[22] C.C. Koch, O.B. Cavin, C.G. Mckamey, J.O. Scarbrough, Applied Physics Letters 43 (1983) 1017–1019.
[23] C. Suryanarayana, Progress in Materials Science 46 (2001) 1–184.
[24] G. Martin, P. Bellon, Solid State Physics 50 (1996).
[25] Z.F. Li, B.X. Liu, Nuclear Instruments & Methods in Physics Research Section B 178 (2001) 224–228.
[26] B.X. Liu, W.S. Lai, Z.J. Zhang, Advances in Physics 50 (2001) 367–429.
[27] C. Suryanarayana, Non-equilibrium Processing of Materials, Pergamon, Oxford, 1999.
[28] D. Turnbull, Contemporary Physics 10 (1969) 473–488.
[29] T.B. Massalski, in: P. Hassen, R.I. Jaffee (Eds.), Amorphous Metals and Semiconductors: Proceeding of an International Workshop, Pergamon Press, Coronado, California, 1986.
[30] Z.P. Lu, H. Bei, C.T. Liu, Intermetallics 15 (2007) 618–624.
[31] J. Basu, B.S. Murty, S. Ranganathan, Journal of Alloys and Compounds 465 (2008) 163–172.
[32] B. Yang, Y. Du, Y. Liu, Transactions of Nonferrous Metals Society of China 2009 (2009).
[33] E. Donth, The Glass Transition: Relaxation Dynamics in Liquids and Disordered Materials, Springer, New York, 2001.
[34] W.L. Johnson, MRS Bulletin 24 (1999) 42–56.
[35] A. Inoue, N. Nishiyama, K. Hatakeyama, T. Masumoto, Materials Transactions JIM 35 (1994) 282–285.
[36] F.Q. Guo, S.J. Poon, G.J. Shiflet, Applied Physics Letters 84 (2004) 37–39.
[37] Z.T. Diao, Y. Yamada, T. Fukunaga, T. Matsuda, U. Mizutani, Materials Science and Engineering A 182 (1994) 1047–1050.
[38] W.A. Hines, P. Miller, A. Paoluzi, C.L. Tsai, B.C. Giessen, Journal of Applied Physics 53 (1982) 7789–7791.
[39] A. Inoue, K. Ohtera, A.P. Tsai, H. Kimura, T. Masumoto, Japanese Journal of Applied Physics Part 2-Letters 27 (1988) L1579–L1582.
[40] A. Inoue, K. Ohtera, T. Masumoto, Japanese Journal of Applied Physics Part 2-Letters 27 (1988) L736–L739.
[41] A. Inoue, Progress in Materials Science 43 (1998) 365–520.
[42] T.B. Massalski, Binary Alloy Phase Diagrams, American Society for Metals, Metals Park, OH, 1986.
[43] R. Bacewicz, J. Antonowicz, Scripta Materialia 54 (2006) 1187–1191.
[44] T. Zhang, ガラス遷移を示す金属 - 金属系アモルファス合金の生成と性質に関する研究, Doctor thesis, Tohoku University, Tokyo, 1990.
[45] A. Inoue, H. Yamaguchi, T. Zhang, T. Masumoto, Materials Transactions JIM 31 (1990) 104–109.
[46] A. Inoue, T. Zhang, T. Masumoto, Materials Transactions JIM 30 (1989) 965–972.
[47] A. Inoue, T. Masumoto, Materials Science and Engineering A 133 (1991) 6–9.
[48] A. Frenkel, E.A. Stern, A. Voronel, A. Rubshtein, Y. BenEzra, V. Fleurov, Physical Review B 54 (1996) 884–892.
[49] D.P. Yang, W.A. Hines, C.L. Tsai, B.C. Giessen, F.C. Lu, Journal of Applied Physics 69 (1991) 6225–6227.
[50] R. Delgado, H. Armbruster, D.G. Naugle, C.L. Tsai, W.L. Johnson, A. Williams, Physical Review B 34 (1986) 8288–8295.
[51] U. Schmidt, C. Eisenschmidt, F. Syrowatka, R. Bartusch, C.Y. Zahra, A.M. Zahra, Journal of Physics-Condensed Matter 15 (2003) 385–413.
[52] K. Fukamichi, T. Goto, Science Reports of the Research Institutes Tohoku University Series A 36 (1991) 143–158.
[53] A. Inoue, T. Ochiai, Y. Horio, T. Masumoto, Materials Science and Engineering A 179 (1994) 649–653.
[54] G. Wilde, H. Sieber, J.H. Perepezko, Scripta Materialia 40 (1999) 779–783.
[55] J.Q. Guo, K. Ohtera, K. Kita, J. Nagahora, N.S. Kazama, Materials Letters 24 (1995) 133–138.
[56] G. Wilde, H. Sieber, J.H. Perepezko, Journal of Non-Crystalline Solids 250 (1999) 621–625.
[57] J.C. Foley, D.R. Allen, J.H. Perepezko, Scripta Materialia 35 (1996) 655–660.
[58] L. Battezzati, M. Baricco, P. Schumacher, W.C. Shih, A.L. Greer, Materials Science and Engineering A 179 (1994) 600–604.
[59] I.A. Tomilin, A.A. Turchanin, S.A. Dogel, J. Latuch, T. Kulik, Metastable, Mechanically Alloyed and Nanocrystalline Materials, Pts 1 and 2 343–346 (2000) 37–42.
[60] E. Akiyama, H. Yoshioka, J.H. Kim, H. Habazaki, A. Kawashima, K. Asami, K. Hashimoto, Corrosion Science 34 (1993) 27–40.
[61] E. Fazakas, L.K. Varga, Reviews on Advanced Materials Science 18 (2008) 494–496.
[62] V.N. Gudzenko, A.F. Polesya, Fizika Metallov i Metallovedenie 39 (1975) 1313–1315.
[63] L.E. Tanner, Scripta Metallurgica 12 (1978) 703–708.
[64] L.E. Tanner, R. Ray, Acta Metallurgica 27 (1979) 1727–1747.
[65] L.E. Tanner, R. Ray, Scripta Metallurgica 11 (1977) 783–789.
[66] R. Hasegawa, L.E. Tanner, Journal of Applied Physics 49 (1978) 1196–1199.
[67] H. Riesemeier, K. Luders, H.C. Freyhardt, J. Reichelt, Journal of Non-Crystalline Solids 61–62 (1984) 991–996.
[68] C.L. Zhang, D.H. Wang, Z.D. Han, H.C. Xuan, B.X. Gu, Y.W. Du, Journal of Applied Physics 105 (2009) 013912–013915.
[69] N. Hassanain, A. Berrada, H. Lassri, R. Krishnan, Journal of Magnetism and Magnetic Materials 140 (1995) 337–338.
[70] K.H.J. Buschow, Journal of Physics F-Metal Physics 14 (1984) 593–607.
[71] A. Inoue, W. Zhang, Materials Transactions 45 (2004) 584–587.
[72] P. Jia, J. Xu, Journal of Materials Research 24 (2009) 96–106.
[73] S.T. Shan, L. Xia, D. Ding, Y.D. Dong, Chinese Physics Letters 23 (2006) 3101–3104.
[74] G. Duan, D.H. Xu, W.L. Johnson, Metallurgical and Materials Transactions A 36A (2005) 455–458.
[75] T. Zhang, A. Inoue, T. Masumoto, Materials Science and Engineering A 182 (1994) 1423–1426.
[76] K. Amiya, N. Nishiyama, A. Inoue, T. Masumoto, Materials Science and Engineering A 179 (1994) 692–696.
[77] H. Baxi, T.B. Massalski, Materials Science and Engineering 97 (1988) 291–296.
[78] T. Lin, J. Jiang, X.F. Bian, Y. Dong, Transactions of Nonferrous Metals Society of China 16 (2006) 604–606.
[79] H. Mizubayashi, M. Shibasaki, S. Murayama, Acta Materialia 47 (1999) 3331–3338.
[80] U. Koster, J. Meinhardt, A. Aronin, Y. Birol, Zeitschrift fur Metallkunde 86 (1995) 171–175.
[81] K. Brunelli, M. Dabala, R. Frattini, G. Sandona, I. Calliari, Journal of Alloys and Compounds 317 (2001) 595–602.
[82] Z. Altounian, J.O. Stromolsen, Physical Review B 27 (1983) 4149–4156.
[83] H.J. Eifert, B. Elschner, K.H.J. Buschow, Physical Review B 29 (1984) 2905–2911.
[84] D.H. Xu, B. Lohwongwatana, G. Duan, W.L. Johnson, C. Garland, Acta Materialia 52 (2004) 2621–2624.
[85] C.F. Li, L.M. Wang, A. Inoue, Journal of Non-Crystalline Solids 306 (2002) 175–181.
[86] M. Taniwaki, E. Hatta, M. Maeda, Materials Science and Engineering 99 (1988) 285–288.
[87] G.A. Almyras, C.E. Lekka, N. Mattern, G.A. Evangelakis, Scripta Materialia 62 (2010) 33–36.
[88] D. Wang, Y. Li, B.B. Sun, M.L. Sui, K. Lu, E. Ma, Applied Physics Letters 84 (2004) 4029–4031.
[89] W.H. Wang, J.J. Lewandowski, A.L. Greer, Journal of Materials Research 20 (2005) 2307–2313.
[90] W. Yang, F. Liu, H. Liu, H.F. Wang, Z. Chen, G.C. Yang, Journal of Alloys and Compounds 484 (2009) 702–707.
[91] K.H.J. Buschow, Journal of Applied Physics 52 (1981) 3319–3323.
[92] Y. Umakoshi, T. Nagase, T. Hosokawa, Materials Transactions 48 (2007) 1644–1650.
[93] N. Mattern, A. Schops, U. Kuhn, J. Acker, O. Khvostikova, J. Eckert, Journal of Non-Crystalline Solids 354 (2008) 1054–1060.
[94] K. Lad, M. Maaroof, K.G. Raval, A. Pratap, K.G. Raval, Progress in Crystal Growth and Characterization of Materials 45 (2002) 15–19.
[95] K. Yano, Journal of Magnetism and Magnetic Materials 208 (2000) 207–216.
[96] V. Petkov, K. Yano, E. Kita, Physica Status Solidi A 157 (1996) 365–372.
[97] D.H. Ryan, J.M.D. Coey, J.O. Stromolsen, Journal of Magnetism and Magnetic Materials 67 (1987) 148–154.
[98] M. Yamada, Y. Terashima, K. Tanaka, Materials Transactions JIM 34 (1993) 895–900.
[99] K. Siratori, K. Nagayama, H. Ino, N. Saito, Y. Nakagawa, IEEE Transactions on Magnetics 23 (1987) 2302–2304.
[100] K. Tanaka, M. Yamada, T. Okamoto, Y. Narita, H. Takaki, Materials Science and Engineering A 182 (1994) 932–936.
[101] J.J. Croat, Journal of Magnetism and Magnetic Materials 24 (1981) 125–131.
[102] J.J. Croat, Journal of Applied Physics 52 (1981) 2509–2511.
[103] B. Sahoo, V. Kuncser, W. Keune, J. Pieper, Hyperfine Interactions 165 (2005) 175–181.
[104] H. Tange, M. Ikeda, T. Ono, T. Kamimori, M. Goto, Journal of Magnetism and Magnetic Materials 140 (1995) 287–288.
[105] J.J. Croat, J.F. Herbst, Journal of Applied Physics 53 (1982) 2294–2296.
[106] H. Takano, S. Hikichi, S. Murayama, K. Hoshi, K. Yano, H. Yashiro, O. Osawa, N. Mori, Journal of Magnetism and Magnetic Materials 239 (2002) 518–520.
[107] Z. Altounian, C.A. Volkert, J.O. Stromolsen, Journal of Applied Physics 57 (1985) 1777–1782.
[108] I. Kaban, E. Dost, W. Hoyer, Journal of Alloys and Compounds 379 (2004) 166–170.
[109] J. Rocca, M. Erazu, M. Fontana, B. Arcondo, Journal of Non-Crystalline Solids 355 (2009) 2068–2073.
[110] A. Inoue, H.S. Chen, J.T. Krause, T. Masumoto, Journal of Non-Crystalline Solids 68 (1984) 63–73.
[111] A. Inoue, Y. Takahashi, N. Toyota, T. Fukase, T. Masumoto, Transactions of the Japan Institute of Metals 23 (1982) 693–702.
[112] K.H.J. Buschow, N.M. Beekmans, Journal of Applied Physics 50 (1979) 6348–6352.
[113] I. Yamamoto, J. Vanzytveld, H. Endo, Journal of Non-Crystalline Solids 156 (1993) 302–306.
[114] S. Nakano, S. Yamaura, A. Kitano, M. Sato, N. Umesaki, S. Uchinashi, H. Kimura, A. Inoue, Materials Transactions 46 (2005) 379–381.
[115] S. Nakano, S. Yamaura, S. Uchinashi, H. Kimura, A. Inoue, Sensors and Actuators B-Chemical 104 (2005) 75–79.
[116] S. Nakano, S.I. Yamaura, S. Uchinashi, H. Kimura, A. Inoue, Materials Transactions 45 (2004) 1367–1370.
[117] S. Yamaura, H. Kimura, A. Inoue, Materials Transactions 44 (2003) 1895–1898.
[118] H. Horikiri, A. Kato, A. Inoue, T. Masumoto, Materials Science and Engineering A 179 (1994) 702–706.
[119] R. Richter, D.V. Baxter, J.O. Stromolsen, Materials Science and Engineering 99 (1988) 183–186.

[120] A. Niikura, A.P. Tsai, N. Nishiyama, A. Inoue, T. Masumoto, Materials Science and Engineering A 182 (1994) 1387-1391.
[121] A. Calka, D.E. Polk, B.C. Giessen, H. Matyja, J.V. Sande, M. Madhava, Scripta Metallurgica 11 (1977) 65-70.
[122] P.G. Boswell, Materials Science and Engineering 34 (1978) 1-5.
[123] M. Leonhardt, W. Loser, H.G. Lindenkreuz, Acta Materialia 47 (1999) 2961-2968.
[124] Z.W. Zhu, H.F. Zhang, D.G. Pan, W.S. Sun, Z.Q. Hu, Advanced Engineering Materials 8 (2006) 953-957.
[125] Y.A. Skakov, N.P. Djakonova, N.V. Edneral, M.R. Koknaeva, V.K. Semina, Materials Science and Engineering A 133 (1991) 560-564.
[126] M. Lee, D. Bae, W. Kim, D. Kim, Materials Transactions 44 (2003) 2084-2087.
[127] L. Xia, W.H. Li, S.S. Fang, B.C. Wei, Y.D. Dong, Journal of Applied Physics 99 (2006) 026103-026105.
[128] M.H. Lee, W.T. Kim, D.H. Kim, Y.B. Kim, Materials Science and Engineering A 375-377 (2004) 336-340.
[129] A. Hirota, K. Ebidzuka, H. Habazaki, A. Kawashima, K. Asami, K. Hashimoto, in: C.R. Clayton, K. Hashimoto (Eds.), Proceedings of the Symposium on Corrosion, Electrochemistry and Catalysis of Metastable Metals and Intermetallics, The Electronchem. Soc., Pennington, 1993.
[130] H. Uhlig, L. Rohr, H.J. Guntherodt, P. Fischer, P. Lamparter, S. Steeb, Journal of Non-Crystalline Solids 156 (1993) 165-168.
[131] W. Zhang, K. Arai, C.L. Qin, F. Jia, A. Inoue, Materials Science and Engineering A 485 (2008) 690-694.
[132] A. Inoue, T. Zhang, T. Masumoto, Materials Transactions JIM 31 (1990) 177-183.
[133] L. Jastrow, U. Koster, M. Meuris, Materials Science and Engineering A 375-377 (2004) 440-443.
[134] J. Saida, T. Sanada, S. Sato, M. Imafuku, C.F. Li, A. Inoue, Zeitschrift fur Kristallographie 223 (2008) 726-730.
[135] R.C. Bowman, M.J. Rosker, W.L. Johnson, Journal of Non-Crystalline Solids 53 (1982) 105-122.
[136] L.E. Hazelton, W.L. Johnson, Journal of Non-Crystalline Solids 61-62 (1984) 667-672.
[137] M.H. Lee, X. Yang, M.J. Kramer, D.J. Sordelet, Philosophical Magazine 86 (2006) 443-449.
[138] J. Saida, M. Matsushita, A. Inoue, Materials Transactions 42 (2001) 1103-1108.
[139] D.J. Sordelet, R.T. Ott, M.Z. Li, S.Y. Wang, C.Z. Wang, M.F. Besser, A.C.Y. Liu, M.J. Kramer, Metallurgical and Materials Transactions A 39A (2008) 1908-1916.
[140] S.H. Whang, Scripta Metallurgica 18 (1984) 309-312.
[141] D. Turnbull, Journal de Physique 35 (1974), C4.1-C4.10.
[142] K.F. Yao, N. Chen, Science in China Series G 51 (2008) 414-420.
[143] C. Woychik, J. Dutkiewicz, T.B. Massalski, Journal of Metals 35 (1982) A66-A166.
[144] Q. Wang, J.B. Qiang, Y.M. Wang, J.H. Xia, C. Dong, Journal of Non-Crystalline Solids 353 (2007) 3425-3428.
[145] Q. Wang, J.B. Qiang, Y.M. Wang, J.H. Xia, Z. Lin, X.F. Zhang, C. Dong, Acta Physica Sinica 55 (2006) 378-385.
[146] B.Y. Tsaur, S.S. Lau, J.W. Mayer, Applied Physics Letters 36 (1980) 823-826.
[147] R.S. Averback, T.D. de la Rubia, Solid State Physics 51 (1998) 281-402.
[148] B.X. Liu, Physica Status Solidi A 94 (1986) 11-34.
[149] B.X. Liu, O. Jin, Physica Status Solidi A 161 (1997) 3-33.
[150] F. Seitz, J.S. Koehler, Solid State Physics 2 (1956) 305.
[151] M.W. Thompson, Defects and Radiation Damage in Metals, Cambridge University Press, Cambridge, 1969.
[152] K.C. Russell, Progress in Materials Science 28 (1984) 229-434.
[153] B.H. Bransden, Atomic Collision Theory, 2nd ed., Benjamin-Cummings Pub., London, 1983.
[154] P. Sigmund, Particle Penetration and Radiation Effects, Springer-Verlag, Berlin, Heidelberg, 2006.
[155] H.S.W. Massey, E.W. McDaniel, B. Bederson, Applied Atomic Collision Physics, Academic Press, New York, 1982-1984.
[156] B.X. Liu, Materials Letters 5 (1987) 322-327.
[157] O. Jin, Z.J. Zhang, B.X. Liu, Applied Physics Letters 67 (1995) 1524-1526.
[158] K.P. Tai, X.D. Dai, Y.X. Shen, B.X. Liu, Journal of Physical Chemistry B 110 (2006) 595-606.
[159] O. Jin, B.X. Liu, Nuclear Instruments & Methods in Physics Research Section B 114 (1996) 56-63.
[160] M. Zhao, X.D. Dai, Y.X. Shen, B.X. Liu, Journal of the Physical Society of Japan 77 (2008) 074601-074604.
[161] J.A. Knapp, D.M. Follstaedt, Nuclear Instruments & Methods in Physics Research Section B 19-22 (1987) 611-618.
[162] L.S. Hung, M. Nastasi, J. Gyulai, J.W. Mayer, Applied Physics Letters 42 (1983) 672-674.
[163] B.X. Liu, G.A. Cheng, Physica Status Solidi A 125 (1991) K93-K96.
[164] F. Pan, B.X. Liu, Journal of Physics-Condensed Matter 8 (1996) 383-388.
[165] C. Lin, G.W. Yang, B.X. Liu, Applied Physics A 70 (2000) 469-473.
[166] Z.J. Zhang, B.X. Liu, Journal of Physics-Condensed Matter 6 (1994) 2647-2658.
[167] Z.J. Zhang, B.X. Liu, Journal of Physics-Condensed Matter 6 (1994) 9065-9074.
[168] X. He, L.T. Kong, B.X. Liu, Journal of the Physical Society of Japan 74 (2005) 2501-2505.
[169] X. He, X.Y. Li, B.X. Liu, Journal of the Physical Society of Japan 72 (2003) 3032-3034.
[170] H.R. Gong, L.T. Kong, W.S. Lai, B.X. Liu, Acta Materialia 51 (2003) 3885-3893.
[171] C. Lin, G.W. Yang, B.X. Liu, Journal of Applied Physics 87 (2000) 2821-2824.
[172] K.P. Tai, Y. Dai, B.X. Liu, Journal of Applied Physics 104 (2008) 014914-014921.
[173] N. Ding, T.L. Wang, K.P. Tai, J.H. Li, X. He, Y. Dai, B.X. Liu, Journal of Alloys and Compounds 476 (2009) 253-256.
[174] K.V. Rao, N. Karpe, D.X. Chen, R. Goldfarb, J. Bottiger, K. Pampus, B. Torp, Journal of Applied Physics 61 (1987) 3249.
[175] B.X. Liu, O. Jin, Y. Ye, Journal of Physics-Condensed Matter 8 (1996) L79-L82.
[176] Z.J. Zhang, O. Jin, B.X. Liu, Physical Review B 51 (1995) 8076-8085.
[177] Z.J. Zhang, H.Y. Bai, Q.L. Qiu, T. Yang, K. Tao, B.X. Liu, Journal of Applied Physics 73 (1993) 1702-1710.
[178] O. Jin, Z.J. Zhang, B.X. Liu, Journal of Applied Physics 78 (1995) 149-154.
[179] T.L. Wang, S.H. Liang, J.H. Li, K.P. Tai, B.X. Liu, Journal of Physics D-Applied Physics 41 (2008) 095310-095316.
[180] L. Hu, Z.F. Li, W.S. Lai, B.X. Liu, Nuclear Instruments & Methods in Physics Research Section B 206 (2003) 127-131.
[181] B.X. Liu, Z.J. Zhang, Physical Review B 49 (1994) 12519-12527.
[182] W.S. Lai, Q. Li, C. Lin, B.X. Liu, Physica Status Solidi B 227 (2001) 503-514.
[183] L.J. Huang, J.R. Ding, H.D. Li, B.X. Liu, Journal of Applied Physics 63 (1988) 2879-2881.
[184] W.C. Wang, J.H. Li, Y. Dai, B.X. Liu, Scripta Materialia 59 (2008) 3-6.
[185] R.F. Zhang, Y.X. Shen, H.F. Yan, B.X. Liu, Journal of Physical Chemistry B 109 (2005) 4391-4397.
[186] O. Jin, B.X. Liu, Journal of Non-Crystalline Solids 211 (1997) 180-186.
[187] B.X. Liu, Z.J. Zhang, O. Jin, Journal of Alloys and Compounds 270 (1998) 186-193.
[188] Z.J. Zhang, B.X. Liu, Journal of Applied Physics 76 (1994) 3351-3356.
[189] B.X. Liu, Z.J. Zhang, O. Jin, F. Pan, Materials Research Society Symposium Proceedings 396 (1996) 71-82.
[190] F. Pan, Y.G. Chen, B.X. Liu, Applied Physics Letters 67 (1995) 780-782.
[191] G.P. Dinda, Nonequilibrium Processing of Amorphous and Nanostructured Materials, Doctor thesis, Universität des Saarlandes, Karlsruhe, 2006.
[192] M. Atzmon, K.M. Unruh, W.L. Johnson, Journal of Applied Physics 58 (1985) 3865-3870.
[193] C. Brouder, G. Krill, P. Guilmin, G. Marchal, E. Dartyge, A. Fontaine, G. Tourillon, Physical Review B 37 (1988) 2433-2439.
[194] J.M. Frigerio, J. Rivory, Journal de Physique 51 (1990) C4163-C4168.
[195] E. Ma, C.W. Nieh, M.A. Nicolet, W.L. Johnson, Journal of Materials Research 4 (1989) 1299-1302.
[196] B. Blanpain, J.M. Legresy, J.W. Mayer, Journal de Physique 51 (1990) C4131-C4137.
[197] T.B. Ameur, A.R. Yavari, Journal de Physique 51 (1990) C4219-C4226.
[198] P. Guilmin, P. Guyot, G. Marchal, Physics Letters A 109 (1985) 174-178.
[199] R.B. Schwarz, K.L. Wong, W.L. Johnson, B.M. Clemens, Journal of Non-Crystalline Solids 61-62 (1984) 129-134.
[200] F.R. Ding, P.R. Okamoto, L.E. Rehn, Journal of Materials Research 4 (1989) 1444-1449.
[201] H. Schroder, K. Samwer, U. Koster, Physical Review Letters 54 (1985) 197-200.
[202] H.R. Gong, B.X. Liu, Journal of Applied Physics 96 (2004) 3020-3022.
[203] K.W. Kwon, H.J. Lee, R. Sinclair, Applied Physics Letters 75 (1999) 935-937.
[204] Y.G. Chen, B.X. Liu, Journal of Physics D-Applied Physics 30 (1997) 1729-1733.
[205] R.W. Johnson, C.C. Ahn, E.R. Ratner, Physical Review B 40 (1989) 8139-8145.
[206] B.M. Clemens, M.J. Suchoski, Applied Physics Letters 47 (1985) 943-944.
[207] M. Vanrossum, M.A. Nicolet, W.L. Johnson, Physical Review B 29 (1984) 5498-5503.
[208] W.S.L. Boyer, M. Atzmon, Journal of Alloys and Compounds 194 (1993) 213-220.
[209] Y.G. Chen, B.X. Liu, Applied Physics Letters 68 (1996) 3096-3098.
[210] G.W. Yang, C. Lin, B.X. Liu, Materials Science and Engineering B 65 (1999) 139-143.
[211] Y.G. Chen, B.X. Liu, Acta Materialia 47 (1999) 1389-1397.
[212] B.M. Clemens, Physical Review B 33 (1986) 7615-7624.
[213] Y.G. Chen, B.X. Liu, Journal of Non-Crystalline Solids 217 (1997) 308-316.
[214] B.X. Liu, Y.G. Chen, Thin Solid Films 334 (1998) 201-205.
[215] J.S. Kwak, E.J. Chi, J.D. Choi, S.W. Park, H.K. Baik, M.G. So, S.M. Lee, Journal of Applied Physics 78 (1995) 983-987.
[216] Z.J. Zhang, B.X. Liu, Physical Review B 51 (1995) 16475-16478.
[217] C. Lin, G.W. Yang, B.X. Liu, Physical Review B 61 (2000) 15649-15652.
[218] K. Samwer, Physics Reports-Review Section of Physics Letters 161 (1988) 1-41.
[219] W. Dorner, H. Mehrer, Physical Review B 44 (1991) 101-114.
[220] W.J. Meng, C.W. Nieh, E. Ma, B. Fultz, W.L. Johnson, Materials Science and Engineering 97 (1988) 87-91.
[221] W.J. Meng, C.W. Nieh, W.L. Johnson, Applied Physics Letters 51 (1987) 1693-1695.
[222] R.J. Highmore, A.L. Greer, J.A. Leake, J.E. Evetts, Materials Letters 6 (1988) 401-405.
[223] R.J. Highmore, R.E. Somekh, J.E. Evetts, A.L. Greer, Journal of the Less-Common Metals 140 (1988) 353-360.
[224] R.J. Highmore, R.E. Somekh, A.L. Greer, J.E. Evetts, Materials Science and Engineering 97 (1988) 83-86.
[225] R.J. Highmore, J.E. Evetts, A.L. Greer, R.E. Somekh, Applied Physics Letters 50 (1987) 566-568.
[226] B.X. Liu, Z.C. Li, H.R. Gong, Surface & Coatings Technology 196 (2005).
[227] R.L. White, The Use of Mechanical Alloying in the Manufacture of Multifilamentary Superconductor Wire, Doctor thesis, Stanford University, 1979.
[228] D.L. Zhang, Progress in Materials Science 49 (2004) 537-560.
[229] B. Huang, K.N. Ishihara, P.H. Shingu, Materials Science and Engineering A 231 (1997) 72-79.
[230] Y.D. Dong, W.H. Wang, L. Liu, K.Q. Xiao, S.H. Tong, Y.Z. He, Materials Science and Engineering A 134 (1991) 867-871.
[231] Z. Peng, C. Suryanarayana, F.H. Froes, in: J.J. de Barbadillo, F.H. Froes, R. Schwarz (Eds.), Mechanical Alloying for Structural Applications, ASM International, Materials Park, Ohio, 1993.

[232] E. Hellstern, L. Schultz, R. Bormann, D. Lee, Applied Physics Letters 53 (1988) 1399–1401.
[233] M.S. Elesksndarany, F. Itoh, K. Aoki, K. Suzuki, Journal of Non-Crystalline Solids 117 (1990) 729–732.
[234] M.S. Eleskandarany, K. Aoki, K. Suzuki, Journal of Alloys and Compounds 186 (1992) 15–31.
[235] M.S. Eleskandarany, K. Aoki, K. Suzuki, Journal of Non-Crystalline Solids 150 (1992) 472–477.
[236] C. Suryanarayana, G.H. Chen, A. Frefer, F.H. Fores, Materials Science and Engineering A 158 (1992) 93–101.
[237] N. Burgio, W. Guo, S. Martelli, M. Magini, F. Padella, I. Soletta, in: J.J. de Barbadillo, F.H. Froes, R. Schwarz (Eds.), Mechanical Alloying for Structural Applications, ASM International, Materials Park, Ohio, 1993.
[238] W. Guo, A. Iasonna, M. Magini, S. Martelli, F. Padella, Journal of Materials Science 29 (1994) 2436–2444.
[239] M.S. El-Eskandarany, Journal of Alloys and Compounds 234 (1996) 67–82.
[240] L. Schultz, Materials Science and Engineering 97 (1988) 15–23.
[241] T. Itsukaichi, K. Masuyama, M. Umemoto, I. Okane, J.G. Cabanasmoreno, Journal of Materials Research 8 (1993) 1817–1828.
[242] E. Ma, M. Atzmon, Journal of Alloys and Compounds 194 (1993) 235–244.
[243] E. Ma, M. Atzmon, Physical Review Letters 67 (1991) 1126–1129.
[244] H.J. Fecht, G. Han, Z. Fu, W.L. Johnson, Journal of Applied Physics 67 (1990) 1744–1748.
[245] H. Kimura, F. Takada, W.N. Myung, Materials Science and Engineering 97 (1988) 125–128.
[246] J. Eckert, L. Schultz, K. Urban, Journal of the Less-Common Metals 166 (1990) 293–302.
[247] J. Eckert, L. Schultz, K. Urban, Journal of the Less-Common Metals 145 (1988) 283–291.
[248] M. Schanzer, H. Mehrer, Journal de Physique 51 (1990) C487–C493.
[249] J.R. Thompson, C. Politis, Y.C. Kim, Materials Science and Engineering 97 (1988) 31–34.
[250] W. Krauss, C. Politis, P. Weimar, Metal Powder Report 43 (1988) 231–238.
[251] G. Veltl, B. Scholz, H.D. Kunze, Metallurgica 45 (1991) 1131–1133.
[252] G. Veltl, B. Scholz, H.D. Kunze, Materials Science and Engineering A 134 (1991) 1410–1413.
[253] C. Politis, W.L. Johnson, Journal of Applied Physics 60 (1986) 1147–1151.
[254] E. Gaffet, C. Louison, M. Harmelin, F. Faudot, Materials Science and Engineering A 134 (1991) 1380–1384.
[255] E. Hellstern, L. Schultz, Applied Physics Letters 48 (1986) 124–126.
[256] J.S.C. Jang, C.C. Koch, Scripta Metallurgica 23 (1989) 1805–1810.
[257] X.S. Huang, T. Mashimo, Journal of Alloys and Compounds 296 (2000) 183–190.
[258] E. Hellstern, L. Schultz, Applied Physics Letters 49 (1986) 1163–1165.
[259] E. Hellstern, L. Schultz, Materials Science and Engineering 97 (1988) 39–42.
[260] Y.S. Cho, C.C. Koch, Materials Science and Engineering A 161 (1993) 65–73.
[261] S.J. Ji, J.C. Sun, X.L. Xu, Z.K. Hei, L. Yan, Rare Metal Materials and Engineering 27 (1998) 271–274.
[262] S.J. Ji, J.C. Sun, Z.W. Yu, Z.K. Hei, L. Yan, International Journal of Hydrogen Energy 24 (1999) 59–63.
[263] T.J. Tiainen, R.B. Schwarz, Journal of the Less-Common Metals 140 (1988) 99–112.
[264] P.Y. Lee, J.L. Yang, H.M. Lin, Journal of Materials Science 33 (1998) 235–239.
[265] P.Y. Lee, T.R. Chen, Journal of Materials Science Letters 13 (1994) 888–890.
[266] B.S. Murty, S. Ranganathan, M.M. Rao, Materials Science and Engineering A 149 (1992) 231–240.
[267] R.B. Schwarz, R.R. Petrich, C.K. Saw, Journal of Non-Crystalline Solids 76 (1985) 281–302.
[268] T. Fukunaga, Y. Homma, K. Suzuki, M. Misawa, Materials Science and Engineering A 134 (1991) 987–991.
[269] F. Petzoldt, B. Scholz, H.D. Kunze, Materials Science and Engineering 97 (1988) 25–29.
[270] J. Eckert, L. Schultz, E. Hellstern, K. Urban, Journal of Applied Physics 64 (1988) 3224–3228.
[271] P.Y. Lee, C.C. Koch, Journal of Materials Science 23 (1988) 2837–2845.
[272] J.R. Thompson, C. Politis, Europhysics Letters 3 (1987) 199–205.
[273] P.I. Loeff, F.H.M. Spit, H. Bakker, Journal of the Less-Common Metals 145 (1988) 271–275.
[274] A.R. Yavari, P.J. Desre, Materials Science and Engineering A 134 (1991) 1315–1322.
[275] A.R. Yavari, P.J. Desre, Physical Review Letters 65 (1990) 2571–2574.
[276] T. Koyano, T. Takizawa, T. Fukunaga, U. Mizutani, S. Kamizuru, E. Kita, A. Tasaki, Journal of Applied Physics 73 (1993) 429–433.
[277] J.A. Alonso, J.M. Lopez, Materials Letters 4 (1986) 316–319.
[278] A. Inoue, T. Zhang, T. Masumoto, Journal of Non-Crystalline Solids 156 (1993) 473–480.
[279] F. Petzoldt, Journal of the Less-Common Metals 140 (1988) 85–92.
[280] G. Cocco, S. Enzo, N.T. Barrett, K.J. Roberts, Physical Review B 45 (1992) 7066–7076.
[281] Z.C. Li, B.X. Liu, Chinese Physics Letters 16 (1999) 667–669.
[282] T. Egami, Y. Waseda, Journal of Non-Crystalline Solids 64 (1984) 113–134.
[283] A.W. Weeber, H. Bakker, Journal of Physics F-Metal Physics 18 (1988) 1359–1369.
[284] R. Bormann, F. Gartner, K. Zoltzer, Journal of the Less-Common Metals 145 (1988) 19–29.
[285] H. Hecht, G. Weigang, S. Eickert, U. Geyer, Zeitschrift fur Physik B-Condensed Matter 100 (1996) 47–51.
[286] P. Chaudhar, J.J. Cuomo, R.J. Gambino, Applied Physics Letters 22 (1973) 337–339.
[287] M. Nose, T. Masumoto, Science Reports of the Research Institutes Tohoku University Series A-Physics Chemistry and Metallurgy 28 (1980) 232–241.
[288] D.B. Miracle, O.N. Senkov, Materials Science and Engineering A 347 (2003) 50–58.
[289] Y.Q. Cheng, E. Ma, H.W. Sheng, Physical Review Letters 102 (2009) 245501.
[290] R.A. Swalin, Thermodynamics of Solids, John Wiley & Sons, Inc., New York, 1962
[291] P.M. Ossi, Physica Status Solidi A 119 (1990) 463–470.
[292] A.W. Weeber, H. Bakker, Physica B 153 (1988) 93–135.
[293] H. Bakker, Enthalpies in Alloys: Miedema's Semiempirical Model, Trans Tech, Zurich, 1998.
[294] J.A. Alonso, L.J. Gallego, J.A. Somoza, Nuovo Cimento Della Societa Italiana di Fisica D 12 (1990) 587–595.
[295] L.J. Gallego, J.A. Somoza, H.M. Fernandez, J.A. Alonso, Journal de Physique 51 (1990) C4111–C4117.
[296] M. Baricco, M. Palumbo, Advanced Engineering Materials 9 (2007) 454–467.
[297] R. Bormann, F. Gartner, P. Haasen, Zeitschrift fur Physikalische Chemie Neue Folge 157 (1988) 29–34.
[298] T. Tokunaga, H. Ohtani, M. Hasebe, Journal of Phase Equilibria and Diffusion 27 (2006) 83–91.
[299] N. Saunders, A.P. Miodownik, Journal of Materials Research 1 (1986) 38–46.
[300] W.G. Wolfer, Journal of Nuclear Materials 114 (1983) 292–304.
[301] J.H. Li, S.H. Liang, B.X. Liu, Journal of Physical Chemistry B 109 (2005) 16463–16468.
[302] X.D. Dai, J.H. Li, B.X. Liu, Journal of Physical Chemistry B 109 (2005) 4717–4725.
[303] Q. Zhang, W.S. Lai, B.X. Liu, Europhysics Letters 43 (1998) 416–421.
[304] Q. Zhang, Z.C. Li, C. Lin, B.X. Liu, E. Ma, Journal of Applied Physics 87 (2000) 4147–4152.
[305] Q. Zhang, W.S. Lai, B.X. Liu, Physical Review B 59 (1999) 13521–13524.
[306] X.D. Dai, H.R. Gong, B.X. Liu, Journal of the Physical Society of Japan 73 (2004) 1222–1227.
[307] H.R. Gong, L.T. Kong, W.S. Lai, B.X. Liu, Physical Review B 68 (2003) 144201–144207.
[308] R.F. Zhang, Y. Kong, B.X. Liu, Physical Review B 71 (2005) 214102–214109.
[309] J.H. Li, L.T. Kong, B.X. Liu, Journal of Materials Research 19 (2004) 3547–3555.
[310] X. He, S.H. Liang, J.H. Li, B.X. Liu, Physical Review B 75 (2007) 045431–045440.
[311] M.R. Baren, Journal of Phase Equilibria 11 (1990) 548–549.
[312] R.L. David, CRC Handbook of Chemistry and Physics: A Ready-reference Book of Chemical and Physical Data, CRC Press, Boca Raton, 2008.
[313] T.J. Raeker, A.E. Depristo, International Reviews in Physical Chemistry 10 (1991) 1–54.
[314] V. Heine, L.J. Robertston, M.C. Payne, Philosophical Transactions of the Royal Society of London Series A 334 (1991) 393–405.
[315] A.F. Voter, MRS Bulletin 21 (1996) 17–19.
[316] M.S. Daw, S.M. Foiles, M.I. Baskes, Materials Science Reports 9 (1993) 251–310.
[317] J.H. Li, X.D. Dai, S.H. Liang, K.P. Tai, Y. Kong, B.X. Liu, Physics Reports-Review Section of Physics Letters 455 (2008) 1–134.
[318] Y.R. Wu, W.Y. Hu, S.C. Han, Journal of Alloys and Compounds 420 (2006) 83–93.
[319] F. Ducastel, F. Cyrotlac, Journal of Physics and Chemistry of Solids 32 (1971) 285–301.
[320] F. Ducastel, F. Cyrotlac, Journal of Physics and Chemistry of Solids 31 (1970) 1295–1306.
[321] F. Cleri, V. Rosato, Physical Review B 48 (1993) 22–33.
[322] M.W. Finnis, J.E. Sinclair, Philosophical Magazine A 50 (1984) 45–55.
[323] A.P. Sutton, J. Chen, Philosophical Magazine Letters 61 (1990) 139–146.
[324] R. Rebonato, D.O. Welch, R.D. Hatcher, J.C. Bilello, Philosophical Magazine A 55 (1987) 655–667.
[325] G.J. Ackland, G. Tichy, V. Vitek, M.W. Finnis, Philosophical Magazine A 56 (1987) 735–756.
[326] W.B. Pearson, A Handbook of Lattice Spacing and Structure of Metals and Alloys, Pergamon Press, London, 1958.
[327] E.A. Brandes, G.B. Brook, Smithells Metals Reference Book, Butterworth-Heinemann, Oxford, 1992.
[328] W. Kohn, L.J. Sham, Physical Review 140 (1965) 1133.
[329] G. Kresse, D. Joubert, Physical Review B 59 (1999) 1758–1775.
[330] P.E. Blochl, Physical Review B 50 (1994) 17953–17979.
[331] G. Kresse, http://cms.mpi.univie.ac.at/vasp/vasp/vasp.html, 2003.
[332] J.P. Perdew, Y. Wang, Physical Review B 45 (1992) 13244–13249.
[333] H.J. Monkhorst, J.D. Pack, Physical Review B 13 (1976) 5188–5192.
[334] C. Kittel, Introduction to Solid state Physics, 7th ed., John Wily & Sons, New York, 1996.
[335] E.R. Cohen, D.R. Lide, G.L. Trigg, AIP Physics Desk Reference, 3rd ed., Springer, New York, 2003.
[336] W. Wycisk, M. Fellerkniepmeier, Journal of Nuclear Materials 69–67 (1978) 616–619.
[337] K. Maier, M. Peo, B. Saile, H.E. Schaefer, A. Seeger, Philosophical Magazine A 40 (1979) 701–728.
[338] J. Cai, Y.Y. Ye, Physical Review B 54 (1996) 8398–8410.
[339] R.A. Johnson, D.J. Oh, Journal of Materials Research 4 (1989) 1195–1201.
[340] H.R. Gong, L.T. Kong, W.S. Lai, B.X. Liu, Physical Review B 66 (2002) 104203–104204.
[341] A.M. Guellil, J.B. Adams, Journal of Materials Research 7 (1992) 639–652.
[342] F. Willaime, C. Massobrio, Physical Review B 43 (1991) 11653–11665.
[343] L. Bencze, K. Hilpert, Metallurgical and Materials Transactions A 27 (1996) 3576–3590.

[344] M.P. Allen, D.J. Tildesley, Computer Simulation of Liquids, Clarendon, Oxford, 1987.
[345] D.C. Rapaport, The Art of Molecular Dynamics Simulation, Cambridge University Press, New York, 2004.
[346] D. Frenkel, B. Simit, Understanding Molecular Simulation: from Algorithms to Applications, Academic Press, San Diego, 2002.
[347] H.C. Andersen, Journal of Chemical Physics 72 (1980) 2384–2393.
[348] M. Parrinello, A. Rahman, Journal of Applied Physics 52 (1981) 7182–7190.
[349] W.G. Hoover, Physical Review A 34 (1986) 2499–2500.
[350] G. Ciccotti, W.G. Hoover, Molecular-Dynamics Simulation of Statistical-Mechanical System, North-Holland, New York, 1985.
[351] J.P. Hansen, I.R. Mcdonald, Theory of Simple Liquids, Academic Press, London, 1976.
[352] A.M. Leshansky, J.F. Brady, Journal of Fluid Mechanics 527 (2005) 141–169.
[353] S.R. Phillpot, S. Yip, D. Wolf, Computers in Physics 3 (1989) 20–31.
[354] L.J. Gallego, J.A. Somoza, J.A. Alonso, J.M. Lopez, Journal of Physics F-Metal Physics 18 (1988) 2149–2157.
[355] J. Gfeller, A. Blatter, U. Kambli, M. Vonallmen, Helvetica Physica Acta 61 (1988) 154–1154.
[356] J. Gfeller, A. Blatter, U. Kambli, Journal of the Less-Common Metals 157 (1990) 223–231.
[357] A. Vandenbeukel, S. Radelaar, Acta Metallurgica 31 (1983) 419–427.
[358] H.F. Rizzo, T.B. Massalski, M. Nastasi, Metallurgical Transactions A 24 (1993) 1027–1037.
[359] K.P. Tai, N. Gao, X.D. Dai, J.H. Li, B.X. Liu, Journal of Applied Physics 101 (2007) 124905–124910.
[360] Q. Zhang, W.S. Lai, B.X. Liu, Physical Review B 61 (2000) 9345–9355.
[361] W.S. Lai, B.X. Liu, Journal of Materials Research 16 (2001) 446–450.
[362] Y. Yamada, Y. Itoh, U. Mizutani, Materials Science and Engineering 99 (1988) 289–293.
[363] Z. Altounian, G.H. Tu, J.O. Stromolsen, Journal of Applied Physics 54 (1983) 3111–3116.
[364] X.J. Liu, X.D. Hui, G.L. Chen, T. Liu, Physics Letters A 373 (2009) 2488–2493.
[365] X.D. Dai, J.H. Li, B.X. Liu, Scripta Materialia 57 (2007) 161–164.
[366] Y. Dai, J.H. Li, X.L. Che, B.X. Liu, Journal of Materials Research 24 (2009) 1815–1819.

Interatomic potential to calculate the driving force, optimized composition, and atomic structure of the Cu-Hf-Al metallic glasses

Y. Y. Cui, J. H. Li, Y. Dai, and B. X. Liu[a)]
Advanced Materials Laboratory, Department of Materials Science and Engineering, Tsinghua University, Beijing 100084, China

(Received 21 April 2011; accepted 14 June 2011; published online 7 July 2011)

An interatomic potential is proposed for the Cu-Hf-Al system and applied in molecular dynamics/statics simulations. Simulations predict a hexagonal composition region for the Cu-Hf-Al metallic glass formation. Kinetically, a local maximum driving force, defined by energy difference between the solid solution and disordered state, is predicted to be at $Cu_{48}Hf_{41}Al_{11}$, close to the experimentally measured optimized composition. Moreover, Voronoi tessellation analysis shows that though the icosahedron and icosidihedron are dominant configurations, the fractions of both icosihexahedron and icosioctahedron decrease with increasing Al content, correlating closely with the atomic radii and the heat of mixing of the component metals. © *2011 American Institute of Physics*. [doi:10.1063/1.3609861]

In recent years, the bulk metallic glasses (BMGs) have become a hot topic and there are a number of scientific issues remaining open for clarification, such as the formation mechanism and the atomic configurations of the metallic glasses.[1,2] Among the studied ternary metal systems, the Cu-Hf-Al system has attracted much attention.[1–3] For instance, Inoue and Zhang have studied the effect of Al addition on the glass-forming ability (GFA) of the Cu-Hf-Al metallic glasses.[1] Li *et al.* have studied the local structures and plasticity of the $Cu_{49}Hf_{42}Al_9$ metallic glass by reverse Monte Carlo method and density functional theory.[3] In both experimental and theoretical studies of the Cu-Hf-Al metallic glasses, one of the important issues is to develop a relevant model to predict a composition region in which the Cu-Hf-Al metallic glasses are energetically favored to be formed, and such a composition region can be defined as the glass forming region (GFR) or the glass forming ability (GFA) in a quantitative manner.[4,5] To the authors' view, it is a good choice to take the interatomic potential as starting base to determine the GFR of the system, because if a realistic interatomic potential is constructed, the interactions among all the atoms involved are known, and therefore, the GFR of the system can be determined through relevant computations or simulations.[5]

In this study, an interatomic potential was constructed for the Cu-Hf-Al system under a proposed formalism by the present authors' group, i.e., the smoothed and long-range second-moment-approximation of tight-binding (TB-SMA),[5,6] which can be written as follows:

$$E_i = \sum_{j\neq i}\phi(r_{ij}) - \sqrt{\sum_{j\neq i}\psi(r_{ij})}, \tag{1}$$

$$\phi(r_{ij}) = \begin{cases} A_1\exp[-p_1(\frac{r_{ij}}{r_0}-1)], & r_{ij}\le r_{m1}, \\ A_{1m}\exp[-p_{1m}(\frac{r_{ij}}{r_0}-1)](\frac{r_{c1}}{r_0}-\frac{r_{ij}}{r_0})^{n1}, & r_{m1}<r_{ij}\le r_{c1}, \end{cases} \tag{2}$$

$$\psi(r_{ij}) = \begin{cases} A_2\exp[-p_2(\frac{r_{ij}}{r_0}-1)], & r_{ij}\le r_{m2}, \\ A_{2m}\exp[-p_{2m}(\frac{r_{ij}}{r_0}-1)](\frac{r_{c2}}{r_0}-\frac{r_{ij}}{r_0})^{n2}, & r_{m2}<r_{ij}\le r_{c2}, \end{cases} \tag{3}$$

where E_i is the total potential energy of atom i, r_{ij} is the distance between atoms i and j of the system at equilibrium, r_{m1} and r_{m2} are the transition points of the pair and density items, r_{c1} and r_{c2} are the cutoff radii of the pair and density items; A_1, p_1, A_{1m}, p_{1m}, A_2, p_2, A_{2m}, and p_{2m} are the potential parameters. From Eqs. (2) and (3), one can see that the pair item and density item, as well as their high derivatives, can continuously and smoothly go to zero at the cutoff radii r_{c1} and r_{c2}, thus removing the jumps of energy and force and avoiding some non-physical behaviors in the simulations.[7] For the detailed process of fitting the potential parameters and the verification of the relevance of the Cu-Hf-Al potential, the readers can be referred to the Supplementary Data.[19]

Applied the constructed Cu-Hf-Al potential, a series of MD simulations were carried out using two types of solid solution models, i.e., the *fcc* and *hcp* solid solution models.[5] The *fcc* solid solution model consisted of $9\times9\times9\times4=2916$ atoms, and the *hcp* solid solution model consisted of $13\times8\times7\times4=2912$ atoms. In setting the solid solution models, the solute atoms were added by random substitution of a certain number of solvent atoms to obtain a desired concentration, and the periodic boundary conditions were adopted in three directions. The MD simulations were carried out with Parrinello-Rahman scheme at zero pressure and 300 K.[8,9] The motion equations were solved using a second-order four-value predictor corrector algorithm with a time step $t=5\times10^{-15}$ s.[11] The structural changes were monitored by the projection of atomic positions and the pair-correlation function $g(r)$.[5,7]

Inspecting the simulation results, the structures of the Cu-Hf-Al models exhibit three different states: a crystalline state, an ordered-disordered coexisting state, and an amorphous state. Taking three compositions, i.e., $Cu_{85}Hf_{10}Al_5$, $Cu_{80}Hf_{15}Al_5$, and $Cu_{70}Hf_{25}Al_5$, as examples, Figure 1 shows the pair-correlation function $g(r)$ and projections of atomic

a)Electronic mail: dmslbx@tsinghua.edu.cn.

Applied Physics Letters 99(1), 011911 (2011).

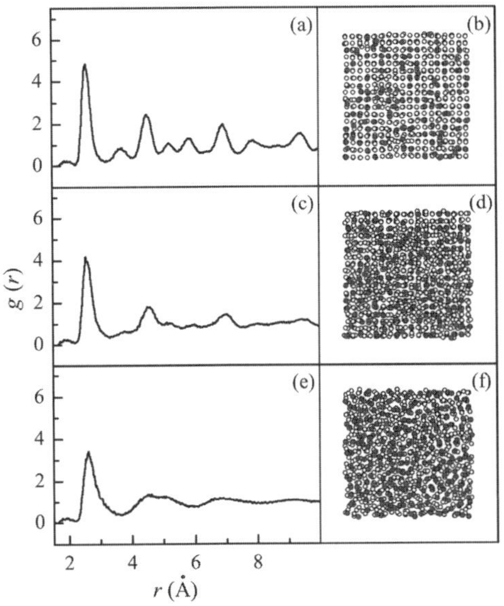

FIG. 1. (Color online) The projections of atomic positions and total pair-correlation functions $g(r)$ for (a, b) crystal state ($Cu_{85}Hf_{10}Al_5$), (c, d) transition state ($Cu_{80}Hf_{15}Al_5$), and (e, f) amorphous state ($Cu_{70}Hf_{25}Al_5$), respectively.

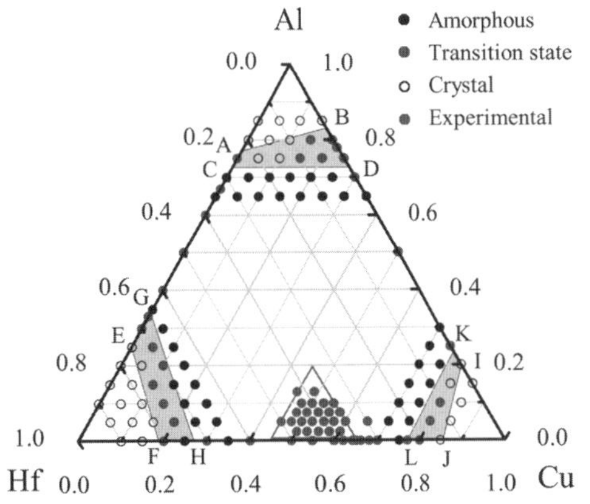

FIG. 2. (Color online) The glass forming composition diagram derived from MD simulations for the Cu-Hf-Al system.

positions for the three states. From the figure, one sees that the $g(r)$ curves of the $Cu_{85}Hf_{10}Al_5$ feature apparent crystalline peaks in Fig. 1(a), exhibiting a long-range ordered feature. For the $g(r)$ curves of the $Cu_{80}Hf_{15}Al_5$, some crystalline peaks have disappeared, whereas some others still remain in Fig. 1(c), exhibiting an ordered-disordered coexisting feature. For the $g(r)$ curves of the $Cu_{70}Hf_{25}Al_5$, the crystalline peaks beyond the second peak have all disappeared in Fig. 1(e), exhibiting a short-range ordered and long-range disordered feature. Further inspecting Fig. 1, one can see that the projections of the atomic positions of the $Cu_{85}Hf_{10}Al_5$ show a completely ordered state and those of the $Cu_{70}Hf_{25}Al_5$ show a completely disordered state. For the $Cu_{80}Hf_{15}Al_5$, the locally ordered regions coexist with locally disordered regions, exhibiting an ordered-disordered coexisting state.

According to the pair-correlation function $g(r)$ and projections of atomic positions, the Cu-Hf-Al composition triangle is spilt into seven regions by six critical solubility lines, and a metallic glass forming composition diagram is constructed in Fig. 2. One can see from Fig. 2, when an alloy composition locates on the AB, EF, or IJ lines and moving towards one of the three corners, the crystalline structure can remain stable. These regions were consequently classified as the crystalline regions. When the composition of the alloy moves from the CD, GH, and KL lines towards the central hexagonal region enclosed by CDKLHG, the crystalline structure becomes unstable and would collapse and turn into a disordered state. This hexagonal region was defined as the region favoring for metallic glass formation. Between the crystalline regions and the amorphous regions, there are ordered-disordered coexisting state regions, within which the initial solid solutions would transform into a state featuring with an ordered-disordered coexisting structure. To validate the metallic glass region in Fig. 2, experimental results were collected and marked by red solid circles,[1–3,10–14] which mostly fall within the hexagonal region, suggesting that the prediction by MD simulations is acceptable in determining the GFR/GFA of the Cu-Hf-Al system.

Further inspecting Fig. 2, one can find that the experimentally measured glass formation compositions densely gather in a small triangular area with the composition of $Cu_xHf_yAl_{100-x-y}$ ($x = 45 \sim 65$, $y = 35 \sim 55$).[1–3,10–14] The experimental results seem to suggest that the optimized composition of the Cu-Hf-Al metallic glass could be within this composition area; however, it would be rather time-consuming to experimentally determine the exact optimized composition point by point. From a thermodynamic point of view, the formation enthalpy difference between the Cu-Hf-Al amorphous phase and its crystalline solid solution counterpart could be considered as the driving force for metallic glass formation.[5] The energy difference can be written as $\Delta H^{am-s.s} = \Delta H^{am} - \Delta H^{s.s}$, where ΔH^{am} is the formation enthalpy of amorphous phase and $\Delta H^{s.s}$ is the formation enthalpy for solid solutions. The larger the formation enthalpy difference, the stronger the driving force for the metallic glass formation. In other words, the optimized metallic glass forming composition is defined as the one, at which the $\Delta H^{am-s.s}$ reaches its maximum value. ΔH^{am} has been calculated through the MD results in the previous section. For $\Delta H^{s.s}$, it could be calculated by an efficient and relevant scheme proposed by Dai *et al.* through molecular statics (MS) calculations.[15] The details of the calculations of the driving force can be referred to our recently published paper.[16]

The driving force of metallic glass formation for the compositions of $Cu_xHf_yAl_{100-x-y}$ ($x = 45 \sim 65$, $y = 35 \sim 55$) was plotted in Fig. 3. One sees that $\Delta H^{am-s.s}$ is negative over the whole calculated area, suggesting that ΔH^{am} is lower than $\Delta H^{s.s}$, meaning that the formation of metallic glasses is energetically favored within this area. Moreover, one can find that the compositions marked by red dots have lower $\Delta H^{am-s.s}$ than other calculated points, and the $Cu_{48}Hf_{41}Al_{11}$ composition marked by a black circle has the lowest $\Delta H^{am-s.s}$, suggesting that the locally optimized compositions for metallic glass formation can be pinpointed around $Cu_{48}Hf_{41}Al_{11}$. From a physical viewpoint, the predicted amorphous region and optimized composition are calculated

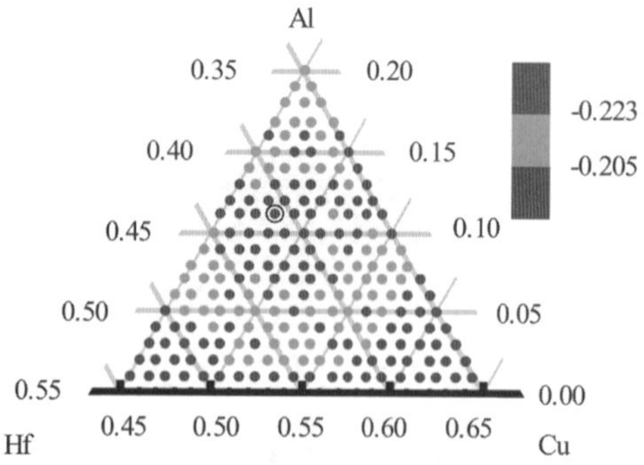

FIG. 3. (Color online) The glass formation driving force for the compositions of $Cu_xHf_yAl_{100-x-y}$ ($x=45\sim65$, $y=35\sim55$) calculated from MS simulations.

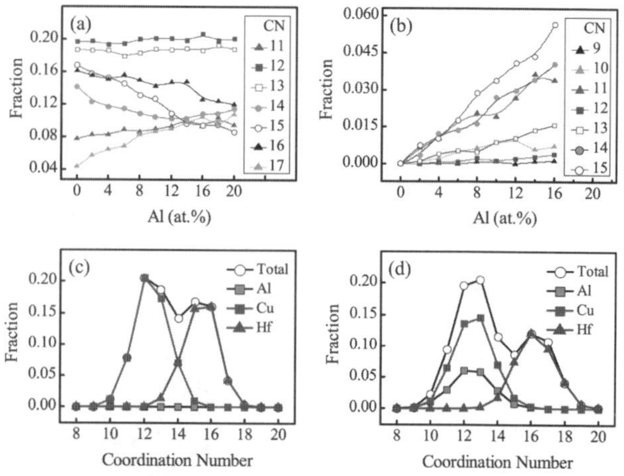

FIG. 4. (Color online) The correlations between the Al compositions and total fractions of CN (a), and the correlations between the Al compositions and the fractions of Al-centered CN (b), and the CN distribution of $Cu_{55}Hf_{45}$ (c), and $Cu_{45}Hf_{35}Al_{20}$ (d) metallic glasses.

from the realistic Cu-Hf-Al potential, which governs the atomic configurations, and thus in turn governs the energetic states of both solid solution and the amorphous phase. Generally speaking, the results from interatomic simulations are consistent with that from experiments.

In the following, the atomic configurations of the $Cu_{55-x/2}Hf_{45-x/2}Al_x$ ($x=0\sim20$) metallic glasses were analyzed by Voronoi tessellation method, which is often employed to characterize the local atomic structure of the metallic glasses.[7,17] It can clearly be seen from Fig. 4(a) that upon the Al addition, the amount of icosahedron (CN = 12) and icosidihedron (CN = 13) is almost unchanged, while the amount of icosihexahedron (CN = 15) and icosioctahedron (CN = 16) decreases. The observed correlation can be understood in terms of the atomic size difference and heat of mixing between Hf-Al, Hf-Cu, and Cu-Al, which is −37, −19, and −1 kJ/mol, respectively.[8] The large chemical affinity between Hf-Al determines that the Al atoms would prefer to locate around the Hf atoms, rather than near the Cu atoms. Meanwhile, the Goldschmidt atomic radii of Cu, Hf, and Al are 1.28 Å, 1.58 Å, and 1.43 Å, respectively.[18] As the atomic radius of Al is larger than that of Cu, the Al addition surrounding the Hf atoms would occupy larger room than Cu does, resulting in the decreasing of CN = 15 and 16 coordination polyhedra. The total and partial CN distributions in the $Cu_{45}Hf_{35}Al_{20}$ and $Cu_{55}Hf_{45}$ metallic glasses are shown in Figs. 4. It is clear that the icosahedron (CN = 12) and icosidihedron (CN = 13) are dominant in both metallic glasses, whereas the polyhedra with CN = 14, 15, and 16 are found in larger amounts in $Cu_{55}Hf_{45}$ than those in $Cu_{45}Hf_{35}Al_{20}$. Further inspecting the figure, one can see that the Cu atoms are mainly surrounded by icosahedron (CN = 12), whereas the dominating polyhedra of the Hf atoms are icosioctahedron (CN = 16). As Hf has larger atomic radii than Cu and Al, the predominant short-range local packing unit of Hf should have more coordination atoms than of Cu and Al, which is indeed observed in the Voronoi analysis.

In summary, based on a realistic Cu-Hf-Al interatomic potential, molecular dynamics simulations quantitatively determined a hexagonal composition region, within which the metallic glass formation is favored. The energy difference between the crystalline solid solution and its disordered counterpart is considered as the driving force for metallic glass formation, and molecular static calculations identified the local maximum driving force around the composition $Cu_{48}Hf_{41}Al_{11}$. In addition, Voronoi tessellation analysis identified that the icosahedron (CN = 12) and icosidihedron (CN = 13) were dominant atomic configurations in the Cu-Hf-Al metallic glasses, and the amount of icosihexahedron (CN = 15) and icosioctahedron (CN = 16) decreased with the increasing Al content.

The authors are grateful for the financial support from the National Natural Science Foundation of China (50871058 and 50971072), the Ministry of Science and Technology of China (2011CB606301), the Ministry of Education of China (200800030054), and the Administration of Tsinghua University.

[1]A. Inoue and W. Zhang, J. Mater. Res. **18**, 1435 (2003).
[2]P. Jia, H. Guo, Y. Li, J. Xu, and E. Ma, Scr. Mater. **54**, 2165 (2006).
[3]G. Q. Li, K. B. Borisenko, and D. J. H. Cockayne, J. Phys. Conf. Ser. **241**, 012066 (2010).
[4]H. B. Yu, W. H. Wang, and H. Y. Bai, Appl. Phys. Lett. **96**, 81902 (2010).
[5]J. H. Li, Y. Dai, Y. Y. Cui, and B. X. Liu, Mater. Sci. Eng. R. **72**, 1 (2011).
[6]J. H. Li, X. D. Dai, T. L. Wang, and B. X. Liu, J. Phys. Condens. Matter **19** 086228 (2007).
[7]D. Frenkel and B. Smit, *Understanding Molecular Simulation: From Algorithms to Applications*. (Academic, New York, 2002).
[8]M. Parrinello and A. Rahman, J. Appl. Phys. **52**, 7182 (1981).
[9]M. P. Allen and D. J. Tildesley, *Computer Simulation of Liquids*. (Clarendon, Oxford, 1981).
[10]P. Jia and J. Xu, J. Mater. Res. **24**, 96 (2009).
[11]J. Park, J. An, and H. Choi-Yim, J. Korean Phys. Soc. **56**, 666 (2010).
[12]E. Nagy, V. Ronto, J. Solyom, and A. Roosz, J. Phys. Conf. Ser. **144**,012034 (2009).
[13]H. Choi-Yim, J. Korean Phys. Soc. **54**, 200 (2009).
[14]M. S. El-Eskandarany, J. Alloy Compd. **284**, 295 (1999).
[15]X. D. Dai, J. H. Li, and B. X. Liu, Appl. Phys. Lett. **90**, 131904 (2007).
[16]Y. Y. Cui, J. H. Li, Y. Dai, and B. X. Liu, J. Phys. Chem. B **115**, 4703 (2011).
[17]S. Mechler, G. Schumacher, V. Koteski, H. Riesemeier, F. Scha Uml Fers, and H. E. Mahnke, Appl. Phys. Lett. **97**, 041913 (2010).
[18]C. Kittel, *Introduction to Solid State Physics* (Wiley, New York, 2002).
[19]See supplementary material at http://dx.doi.org/10.1063/1.3609861 for the potential parameters and the verification of the relevance of the Cu-Hf-Al potential.

First-principles molecular dynamics simulations to study the crystal-to-amorphous transition in the Mg–Zn system

Ye Dai, Jiahao Li, Baixin Liu*

Advanced Materials Laboratory, Department of Materials Science and Engineering, Tsinghua University, Beijing 100084, China

ARTICLE INFO

Article history:
Received 24 November 2011
Received in revised form
29 March 2012
Accepted 2 May 2012
Available online 28 May 2012

Keywords:
A. Intermetallics, miscellaneous
B. Glasses, metallic
E. Simulations, atomistic

ABSTRACT

First-principles molecular dynamics simulations are applied for the Mg–Zn system by using solid solution models with various solute concentrations. The simulations reveal that physical origin of metallic glass formation is the crystalline lattice collapsing while solute concentration exceeding critical solid solubility, thus determining 25 at.% of Zn and 31 at.% of Mg are two critical solid solubilities of the Mg–Zn system. The composition range between two critical solid solubilities, i.e. 25–69 at.% of Zn, is therefore defined/predicted to be the glass-forming range of the Mg–Zn system and is well supported by experimental observations.

It has been half a century, since the discovery of the disordered condensed matter state by Buckel and Hilsch [1,2] and P. Duwez et al. [3,4] in the 1950s. The discovery created a new field in physics, i.e. The Physics of Amorphous Solids [5] as well as a new field in materials science, i.e. the field of Amorphous Alloys, or Metallic Glasses, thus exploring a new category of materials. In these fields, there are still some basic scientific issues to be clarified and in general, these issues are related to three fundamental aspects, i.e. formation mechanism, structure, and property of the amorphous solids (alloys). Among them, the first priority issue is, in the present authors' view, to develop a relevant model/theory capable of predicting, for a binary metal system, an exact or approximate composition range, in which the amorphous alloys are favored to be formed. Such composition range has been defined as the (metallic) glass-forming range (GFR) [6], which reflects the quantitative glass-forming ability (GFA), of a binary metal system. In order to predict the quantitative glass-forming ability or to estimate the glass-forming range of a binary metal system, several empirical criteria/rules have been proposed. For example, Turnbull has proposed a well-known deep eutectic criterion based on the equilibrium phase diagram of the system to predict metallic glass formation upon liquid melt quenching [7]. Egami et al. have proposed a size difference rule to predict the metallic glass formation based on the atomic size difference of the constituent metals of the system [8]. A structural difference rule has been proposed by Liu et al. [9] to predict metallic glass formation based on the structural difference between the metal elements. Moreover, Liu et al. have further proposed to use the total width of the two-phase region observed from the equilibrium phase diagram of the system as the approximate glass-forming range of the system [10]. In addition, some criteria based on other thermodynamics properties, e.g. the formation enthalpy, the formation energy, etc, have been proposed to predict the binary metallic glass formation [11,12]. Obviously, each proposed criterion or rule [7–12] is developed from a starting base, which is supposed to be able to reflect the major interaction of a binary metal system thus governing the metallic glass formation in the system.

It was until the end of 1990s, the present authors' group has proposed to take the interatomic potential of a binary metal system as the starting base to develop an atomistic theory for the binary metallic glass formation [13,14]. On the one hand, the advantage of the proposal is that the interatomic potential could be better than taking other internal property as the starting base in reflecting the major interaction of a binary metal system and therefore capable of revealing the formation mechanism of the metallic glasses. On the other hand, because the used potentials were still empirical ones, the weak point is also to do with the potentials, which were derived by fitting the potential parameters to those experimental or theoretical calculated data. In the present work, the main idea is to conduct advanced first-principles molecular dynamics simulations to study the issue, i.e. to take density-functional theory as the starting base to develop a relevant theory capable of predicting the

* Corresponding author. Tel./fax: +86 010 6277 2619.
E-mail address: dmslbx@mail.tsinghua.edu.cn (B. Liu).

Intermetallics 29, p. 75-79 (2012).

binary metallic glass formation. Concerning the first-principles calculation, with the development of computer power and theoretical tools, it has been applied to a variety of problems in physics as well as in materials science. For instance, first-principles molecular dynamics simulations have provided profound insights into the structures and properties of the liquid metals [15–17]. The consistency between the simulations and experimental data lends strong support to further analysis of static and dynamic properties of the metallic alloy systems. In the present work, first-principles molecular dynamics simulations are applied to study a selected representative system, i.e. the Mg–Zn system. In recent years, the Mg–Zn alloys have attracted considerable attention because of their good biocompatibilities, biodegradation and mechanical properties [18–20]. Besides, Mg is the lightest metal available for industrial purposes and by alloying with zinc, its strength and surface properties could be significantly improved [18]. Moreover, amorphous Mg–Zn alloys have been obtained by using rapid quenching technique and shown superior corrosion resistance [19,20]. Theoretical computation has also shown interesting superconducting behavior of the amorphous $Mg_{70}Zn_{30}$ alloy [21]. Besides, the Mg–Zn system consists of relatively light metals, which would require reasonable computing time for the available servers.

In the present study, the simulation route is designed to take solid solutions as the simulation models to compare the relative stability of the crystalline solid solution versus the corresponding amorphous alloy as a function of solute concentration. The solid solution always has one of the three simplest crystalline structures of bcc, fcc and hcp and therefore it competes with the disordered state during the non-equilibrium materials processing. It is noted that in a binary metal system, there could possibly exist some intermetallic compounds, which frequently have complicated structures and that these compounds would not participate in competing with amorphous state due to the very restricted kinetic condition available during the non-equilibrium materials processing, though they are certainly more stable than the non-equilibrium amorphous phase. Moreover, extensive experimental data obtained so far, from traditional liquid melt quenching, ion beam mixing of far-from-equilibrium, solid-state-amorphization and mechanical alloying, etc. [22], have confirmed that for a binary metal system, either miscible or immiscible at equilibrium, metallic glasses could be obtained within a broad composition range extending from the central portion to about the edges of two terminal solid solutions. It suggested that the formation of metallic glasses is just a favored outcome in a competition between amorphous state and the corresponding crystalline solid solution.

We first construct the Mg- and Zn-based solid solution supercells with $4 \times 4 \times 4 = 64$ hexagonal (hcp) unit cells and each supercell consists of 128 atoms. For the hcp solid solution models, the $[2\bar{1}\bar{1}0]$, $[\bar{1}2\bar{1}0]$, and [0001] crystalline directions are parallel to the *x*, *y*, and *z* axes, respectively. Meanwhile, periodic boundary conditions are adopted in three respective axes. The desired solute atoms are added into the model by randomly substituting the solvent atoms. The solute concentration varies with an interval of 3.125 at.% near the critical composition points. The first-principles molecular dynamics simulations are implemented using the plane wave pseudopotential density-functional theory (DFT) code CASTEP [23,24]. The PW91 generalized gradient approximation (GGA) [25] with ultrasoft potentials [26] is used in the calculation, as supplied in the CASTEP library. The cutoff energy of the plane wave is 380 eV. The tolerance for accepting convergence of the total energy per atom is 10^{-6} eV/atom. The integration in the Brillouin zone is done in a mesh of $2 \times 2 \times 1$, special *k* points determined according to the Monkhorst Pack scheme [27]. The temperature control is implemented by the Nose–Hoover chain method proposed by Martyna et al. [28] and the thermostat relaxation time is 5×10^{-14} s. Pressure is controlled by the Parrinello–Rahman constant pressure scheme [29]. The forces are calculated from the ground state electronic configuration at each molecular dynamics step of 5×10^{-15} s. The molecular dynamics simulations are then conducted at 0 Pa. The simulation temperature is set to 300 K, which is much lower than the melting temperatures of the simulated alloy, to avoid the complex behavior of the alloy at its melting temperature or crystallization temperature. In order to reach a relatively stable (i.e. metastable) state, the longest molecular dynamics simulation time is 1000 molecular dynamics time steps for some solid solution models. As a compelling feature to identify an amorphous state, the pair-correlation functions are calculated at various simulation time steps to monitor the structural changes of the simulation models. The calculation of pair-correlation functions is performed as an averaging over permutations of the solute atoms.

The first-principles molecular dynamics simulations show that after equilibrating adequate molecular dynamics time steps at a given temperature, the simulation models generally exhibit two different states: a crystalline state and an amorphous state. Fig. 1 displays the projections of the atomic positions of the simulated Mg-rich Mg–Zn alloys. The positions of atoms in the last 100 time steps (after equilibrium) are averaged to eliminate the thermal vibration. As the atom positions in one step are strongly coupled with the atom positions in the last step, the averaged atom positions are chosen at an interval of 10 time steps. In Fig. 1, one can vividly see: (i) when the solute concentration of Zn is low, the Mg-based hcp solid solution lattice can keep its original crystalline state, (ii) when the solute concentration of Zn is increased up to about 18 at.% of Zn, the Mg-based hcp lattice begins to develop some disordering, and (iii) once the solute concentration of Zn exceeds 25 at.%, the Mg-based hcp lattice collapses completely and turns into a disordered state, resulting in forming an amorphous phase. Fig. 2 presents the corresponding calculated pair-correlation functions $g(r)$, as a compelling feature to identify an amorphous structure. Simulations show that Mg-based hcp lattice keep its crystalline state when the Zn concentration is in the range from 0 at.% to 22 at.%, the hcp lattice collapses completely when the Zn concentration is increased up to 25 at.%. It can be concluded that the critical solid solubility of Zn in Mg-rich solid solution is about 25 at.%. Similarly for the Zn-rich Mg–Zn alloys, Fig. 3 presents the projections of the atomic positions of the simulated Zn-rich solid solutions. Fig. 4 exhibits the corresponding calculated pair-correlation functions $g(r)$ to confirm the amorphous alloy formation. For the Zn-rich solid solutions, the results show: (i) when the solute concentration of the Mg atoms is less than 12.5 at.%, the Zn-based hcp lattice is preserved almost completely, (ii) when the solute concentration of Mg is increased up to about 19–28 at.%, the Zn-based hcp lattice begins to develop some disordering, and (iii) further increasing the solute concentration of Mg up about 31 at.%, the Zn-based hcp lattice transforms into an amorphous state. Consequently, the critical solid solubility of Mg in Zn-rich solid solution is about 31 at.%. The formation enthalpy (eV/atom) and volume per atom ($Å^3$/atom) are calculated as functions of alloy composition shown in Fig. 5. In the figure, with the increasing of the solute concentration, the formation enthalpy decreases and the lattice distortion becomes larger. While the free energy of the metallic glass is lower than that of the solid solution, the metallic glass is favored to be form. The difference between the solid solution and the amorphous alloy appears to be a thermodynamic driving force for the formation of the amorphous alloys within this composition range. From the above results, it is concluded that the underlying physics of the crystal-to-amorphous transition, i.e. the physical origin of solid-state-amorphization is the collapsing of the

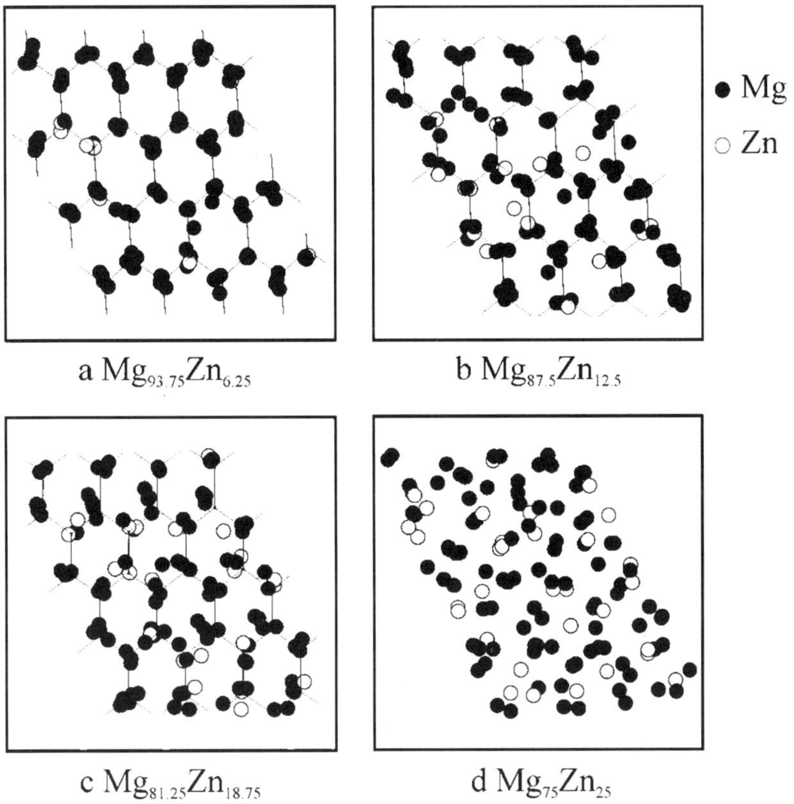

Fig. 1. The projections of the atomic positions of the simulated Mg-rich Mg–Zn alloys.

crystalline solid solution while the solute atoms exceeding the critical solid solubility of the Mg–Zn system.

According to the pair-correlation functions and projections of the atomic positions, the two respective critical solid solubilities of the Mg–Zn system are determined to be 25 at.% of Zn (75 at.% of Mg) and 31 at.% of Mg (69 at.% of Zn), and they thus divide the entire composition range of the system into three regions, i.e. a central region and two terminal regions. Consequently, when the composition falls into the central region bounded by the two critical solid solubilities, 31–75 at.% of Mg (i.e. 25–69 at.% of Zn), the corresponding amorphous alloy is favorable to form against its competing solid solution of simple crystalline structure. Whereas the composition falls into one of the terminal regions, i.e. outside the central region, either Mg-rich or Zn-rich crystalline solid solution is favorable to form against its competing amorphous alloy instead. The composition range between the two determined

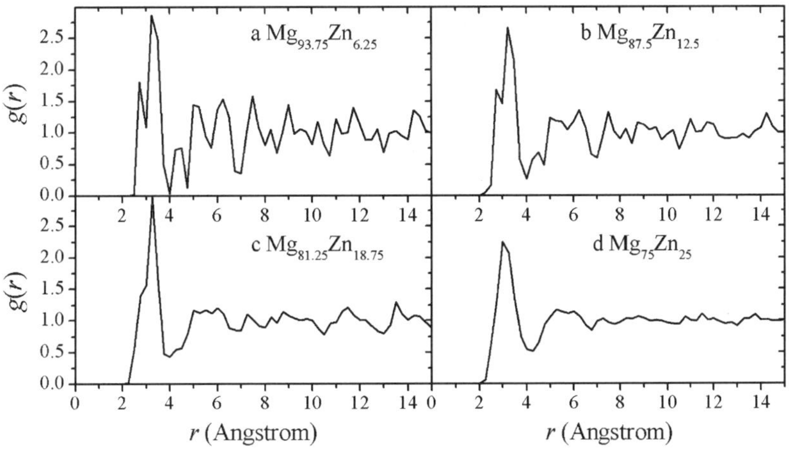

Fig. 2. The pair-correlation functions $g(r)$ of the simulated Mg-rich Mg–Zn alloys.

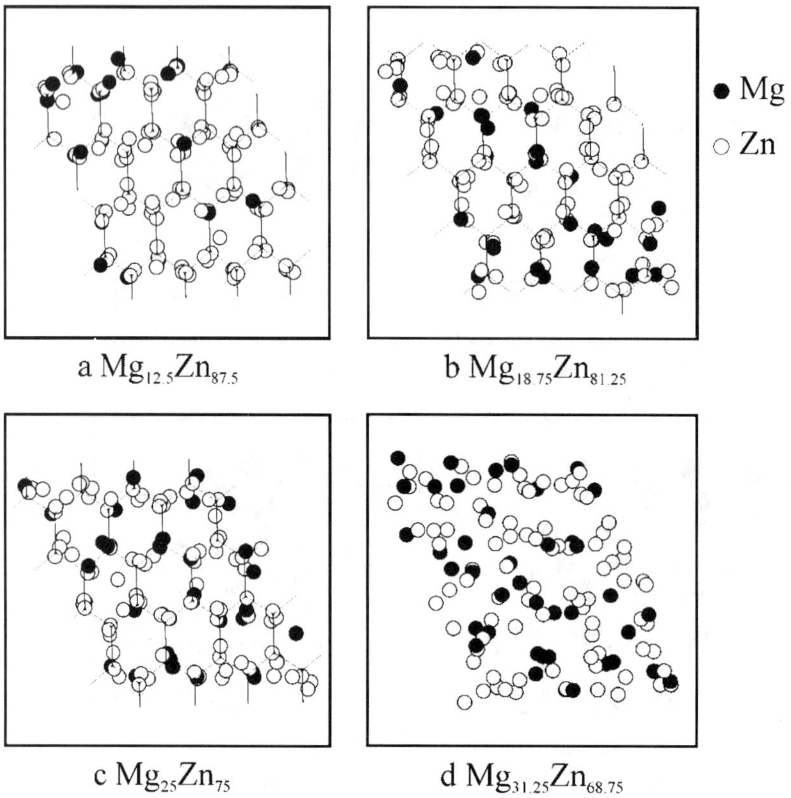

Fig. 3. The projections of the atomic positions of the simulated Zn-rich Mg–Zn alloys.

critical solid solubilities 31–75 at.% of Mg (i.e. 25–69 at.% of Zn) can thus be regarded as the intrinsic glass-forming range of the Mg–Zn system. Intrinsic GFR is a range in which the binary system could be amorphous, although it may not be achieved by a specific materials processing technique. It is worthwhile mentioning again that because the materials processing techniques for producing the metallic glasses are always non-equilibrium or even far-from-equilibrium ones, the complicated crystalline structured phases, such as intermetallic compounds, are not apt to nucleate and grow, due to the extremely restricted kinetic condition available in the processing. It follows that in the simulations, only the hcp solid solution should be considered as the competing phase versus the Mg–Zn metallic glass, whereas the complicated crystalline structured phases are not participating in such phase competing.

In order to validate the calculated glass-forming range of the Mg–Zn system, the experimental results are collected to compare with the calculated results. For instance, $Mg_{70}Zn_{30}$ and $Mg_{65}Zn_{35}$ metallic glasses have been obtained by Calka et al. [30–32] by

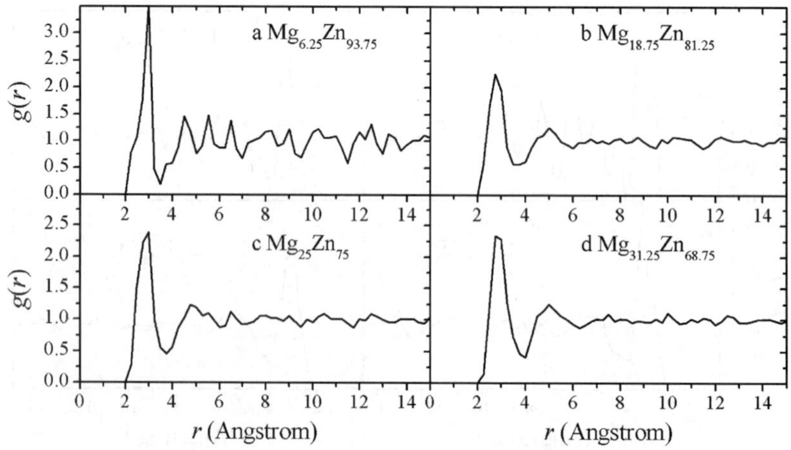

Fig. 4. The pair-correlation functions $g(r)$ of the simulated Zn-rich Mg–Zn alloys.

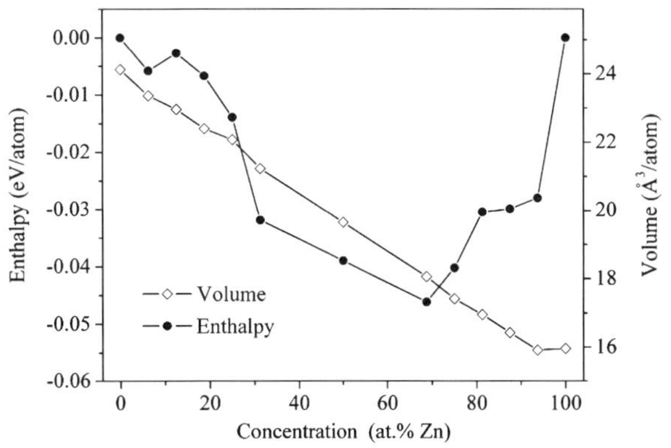

Fig. 5. The formation enthalpy (eV/atom) and volume per atom ($Å^3$/atom) vs. composition obtained after simulation.

mechanical alloying. Niikura et al. [19] have obtained the amorphous alloys with 60, 65, 70, 75 at.% Mg in rapidly solidified Mg–Zn alloys. Richter et al. [20,33] have reported the measured low-temperature magnetoresistance of high-purity $Mg_{70}Zn_{30}$ metallic glass. Apparently, the compositions of these Mg–Zn metallic glasses obtained in experiments are all located in the predicted glass-forming range in the present work. One can therefore conclude that the intrinsic glass-forming range determined from the first-principles molecular dynamics simulations is well supported by the experimental observations.

For the Mg-rich alloys, the most popular coordination number (CN) is 14 while the composition of Zn is less than 25 at.%. While the composition of Zn is increased up to 25 at.%, the fraction of atoms with CN = 15 is larger than the fraction of atoms with CN = 14. The average CN of Mg increases with increasing of the Zn composition. For the Zn-rich alloys, the most popular CN is 14 while the composition of Mg is about 6 at.% Mg. While the composition of Zn is increased up to about 31 at.%, the fraction of either CN = 12 or CN = 13 is larger than the fraction of CN = 14. The average CN of Zn decreases with increasing of Mg composition. As the Goldschmidt atomic radius of Mg (1.60 Å) is larger than that of Zn (1.39 Å), the average CN of Mg is larger than the average CN of Zn. For the same reason, the average CN of Mg atom increases with increasing Zn composition, while the average CN of Zn decreases.

In summary, for the Mg–Zn system, first-principles molecular dynamics simulations based on the density-functional theory not only reveal the physical origin of the solid-state-amorphization to be the collapsing of the crystalline solid solution while the solute atoms exceeding the critical solid solubility, but also predict the intrinsic glass-forming range to be within 31–75 at.% of Mg (i.e. 25–69 at.% of Zn) in the Mg–Zn system. The main concept in synthesizing metallic glasses is therefore to design the alloy composition beyond the critical solid solubility of the metal system concerned.

Acknowledgment

The authors are grateful for the financial support from the National Natural Science Foundation of China (50871058, 50971072), the Ministry of Science and Technology of China (2011CB606301), the Ministry of Education of China (200800030054) and the Administration of Tsinghua University.

References

[1] Buckel W, Hilsch R. Einfluss Der Kondensation Bei Tiefen Temperaturen Auf Den Elektrischen Widerstand Und Die Supraleitung Fur Verschiedene Metalle. Zeitschrift Fur Physik 1954;138:109.
[2] Buckel W. Elektronenbeugungs-Aufnahmen Von Dunnen Metallschichten Bei Tiefen Temperaturen. Zeitschrift Fur Physik 1954;138:136.
[3] Klement W, Willens RH, Duwez P. Non-crystalline structure in solidified gold–silicon alloys. Nature 1960;187:869.
[4] Duwez P, Willens RH, Klement W. Continuous series of metastable solid solutions in silver–copper alloys. J Appl Phys 1960;31:1136.
[5] Zallen W. The physics of amorphous solids. New York: John Wiley & Sons; 1983.
[6] Li JH, Dai XD, Liang SH, Tai KP, Kong Y, Liu BX. Interatomic potentials of the binary transition metal systems and some applications in materials physics. Phys Rep Rev Sec Phys Lett 2008;455:1.
[7] Turnbull D. Amorphous solid formation and interstitial solution behavior in metallic alloy systems. J Phys (Paris) 1974;35:C4.1.
[8] Egami T, Waseda Y. Atomic size effect on the formability of metallic glasses. J Non-Cryst Solids 1984;64:113.
[9] Liu BX, Johnson WL, Nicolet MA, Lau SS. Structural difference rule for amorphous alloy formation by ion mixing. Appl Phys Lett 1983;42:45.
[10] Liu BX. Ion mixing and metallic alloy phase formation. Phys Status Solidi A Appl Res 1986;94:11.
[11] Bormann R, Gartner F, Zoltzer K. Application of the calphad method for the prediction of amorphous phase formation. J Less Common Met 1988;145:19.
[12] Weeber AW, Bakker H. Extension of the glass-forming range of Ni–Zr by mechanical alloying. J Phys A Met Phys 1988;18:1359.
[13] Zhang Q, Lai WS, Liu BX. Glass-forming ability determined by the atomic interaction potential for the Ni–Mo system. Phys Rev B 1999;59:13521.
[14] Liu BX, Li JH, Lai WS. Interatomic potential to predict the binary metallic glass formation. J Mater Res 2010;25:976.
[15] Kresse G, Hafner J. Ab-Initio molecular-dynamics simulation of the liquid–metal amorphous-semiconductor transition in germanium. Phys Rev B 1994;49:14251.
[16] Zhu XF, Chen LF. Ab initio molecular-dynamics simulation of liquid As_xTe_{1-x} alloys. J Phys Condes Matter 2009;21:275602.
[17] Woodward C, Asta M, Trinkle DR, Lill J, Angioletti-Uberti S. Ab initio simulations of molten Ni alloys. J Appl Phys 2010;107:113522.
[18] Martinez OE, Archiopoli UC, Cesa Y, Mingolo N. Crystallization of glassy metal surfaces in Mg–Zn alloy determined by resonant photoacoustic detection. Appl Phys Mater Sci Process 2005;81:1667.
[19] Niikura A, Tsai AP, Nishiyama N, Inoue A, Masumoto T. Amorphous and quasi-crystalline phases in rapidly solidified Mg–Al–Zn alloys. Mater Sci Eng A Struct Mater Prop Microstruct Process 1994;182:1387.
[20] Richter R, Baxter DV, Stromolsen JO. Quantum Corrections to the conductivity in Mg-based metallic glasses. Phys Rev B 1988;38:10421.
[21] Vora AM. Pressure effects on Mg70Zn30 superconductor. Mod Phys Lett B 2009;23:1443.
[22] Li JH, Dai Y, Cui YY, Liu BX. Atomistic theory predicting binary metallic glass formation. Mater Sci Eng R Rep 2011;72:1.
[23] Segall MD, Lindan PJD, Probert MJ, Pickard CJ, Hasnip PJ, Clark SJ, et al. First-principles simulation: ideas, illustrations and the CASTEP code. J Phys Condes Matter 2002;14:2717.
[24] Clark SJ, Segall MD, Pickard CJ, Probert MJ, Refson K, Payne MC. First principles methods using CASTEP. Zeitschrift Fur Kristallographie 2005;220:567.
[25] Kresse G, Joubert D. From ultrasoft pseudopotentials to the projector augmented-wave method. Phys Rev B 1999;59:1758.
[26] Vanderbilt D. Soft self-consistent pseudopotentials in a generalized Eigenvalue formalism. Phys Rev B 1990;41:7892.
[27] Monkhorst HJ, Pack JD. Special points for Brillouin-zone integrations. Phys Rev B 1976;13:5188.
[28] Martyna GJ, Klein ML, Tuckerman M. Nose-Hoover chains – the canonical ensemble via continuous dynamics. J Chem Phys 1992;97:2635.
[29] Parrinello M, Rahman A. Polymorphic transitions in single-crystals – a new molecular-dynamics method. J Appl Phys 1981;52:7182.
[30] Calka A, Polk DE, Giessen BC, Matyja H, Sande JV, Madhava M. Transition-metal-free amorphous alloy-Mg.70zn.30. Scripta Metallurgica 1977;11:65.
[31] Calka A, Radlinski AP. Amorphization of Mg–Zn alloys by mechanical alloying. Mater Sci Eng A Struct Mater Prop Microstruct Process 1989;11:131.
[32] Calka A. The room-temperature stability of amorphous Mg–Zn alloys. J Phys F Met Phys 1986;16:1577.
[33] Richter R, Baxter DV, Stromolsen JO. Quantum corrections to the conductivity in $Mg_{70}Cu_{30-0}Au_0$, $Mg_{70}Cu_{30-1}Au_1$, $Mg_{70}Cu_{30-3}Au_3$, $Mg_{70}Cu_{30-9}Au_9$ and $Mg_{70}Zn_{30-0}Au_0$, $Mg_{70}Zn_{30-3}Au_3$. Mater Sci Eng 1988;99:183.

Atomic modeling to design favored compositions for the ternary Ni–Nb–Zr metallic glass formation

S.Y. Luo, J.H. Li, J.B. Liu, B.X. Liu *

Key Laboratory of Advanced Materials, School of Materials Science and Engineering, Tsinghua University, Beijing 100084, China

Received 26 April 2014; received in revised form 29 May 2014; accepted 2 June 2014
Available online 1 July 2014

Abstract

An interatomic potential is constructed for the Ni–Nb–Zr ternary metal system under the newly proposed long-range empirical formulism, which has been verified to be applicable for face-centered cubic, body-centered cubic and hexagonal close-packed transition metals and their alloys. Applying the constructed potential, Monte Carlo simulations were performed to study the alloy compositions favored for Ni–Nb–Zr metallic glass formation. Simulations reveal that the underlying physics of metallic glass formation is the collapse of the crystalline lattice when the solute concentration exceeds a critical value. An intrinsic glass formation region for the Ni–Nb–Zr system can then be predicted, reflecting the possible composition region energetically favored for metallic glass formation. Furthermore, an optimal composition sub-region was pinpointed within which the driving forces for the crystalline-to-amorphous transition are larger than those outside the sub-region. The Ni–Nb–Zr amorphous alloys with the optimal compositions are expected to be more stable or easier to be produced in practice. Moreover, Voronoi tessellation analysis reveals that the atomic structure of the Ni–Nb–Zr ternary metallic glass is obviously influenced by the alloy composition, the size difference and chemical interactions of constituent metals. Ni- (or Nb-centered) icosahedral clusters are inferred as the basic local structural feature in the Ni–Nb–Zr metallic glass.

Keywords: Ni–Nb–Zr metallic glasses; Interatomic potential; Glass-forming ability; Atomic structure; Monte Carlo simulation

1. Introduction

Since Duwez obtained the first metallic amorphous alloy (namely, metallic glass) by liquid melt quenching in the Au–Si system in 1959, numerous amorphous alloys have been produced in binary, ternary and multi-component metal systems [1,2]. In the 1980s, researchers found a number of ternary and multi-component metal systems in which liquid melt quenching could readily produce the so-called bulk metallic glasses (BMGs) with a geometrical size of the order of 1 cm [3,4]. From then on, the formation, structure and property investigations of BMGs have attracted increasing attention because of their fundamental scientific importance and engineering application potential [5–8]. The knowledge obtained from these studies was used to develop metallic alloys with increasingly higher glass-forming ability (GFA), which relates to the readiness or difficulty of the metallic glass formation, culminating in the synthesis of new and improved BMGs. In theoretical studies, one of the fundamental scientific issues in the field of metallic glass is to establish a reliable model to predict in which composition range or region the metallic glass can be produced in an alloy system by some specific glass-producing technique.

Several empirical criteria or rules have been proposed over the years to guide the development of metallic alloys with high GFA. For example, according to the corresponding equilibrium phase diagram, Turnbull [9] has proposed a well-known deep eutectic criterion to predict the metallic

* Corresponding author. Tel.: +86 10 62772557.
E-mail address: dmslbx@tsinghua.edu.cn (B.X. Liu).

Acta Materialia 76, p.482-492 (2014).

glass formation upon liquid melt quenching. Egami and Waseda [10] have predicted the metallic glass formation by considering the atomic size difference of the constituent metals of a binary metal system. Based on extensive ion beam mixing studies, Liu et al. have proposed a structural difference rule, predicting that amorphous alloys would most likely be formed in a binary metal system with two constituent metals of different crystalline structures [11]. Inoue [5] and Johnson [2] also framed the empirical rules to predict the element selection and composition range of glass-forming alloys. Although the above criteria or rules have been helpful as guidelines in producing amorphous alloys or metallic glasses in the past decades, they still belong to empirical approaches, and their predictions are unsatisfactory. For instance, the atomic sizes of Au and Ta are essentially identical; however, in this system, amorphization is still possible [12]. In contrast with the deep eutectic rule, the better glass formers in Zr–Cu binary alloy system such as $Zr_{35.5}Cu_{64.5}$ and $Zr_{50}Cu_{50}$ are off-eutectic [13]. Amorphous phases were synthesized by ion beam mixing in the Fe–Nb system with two body-centered cubic (bcc) structural metals, which does not conform to the structural difference rule [14]. Reviewing the frequently cited empirical criteria or rules proposed for predicting the metallic glass formation, it is understood that any proposal is based on some specific properties or characteristics of the system. Naturally, the starting base which does not fully reflect the internal characteristics of the metal system leads to the limitations of the criteria or rules. Therefore, in the authors' view, it is a good choice to take the interatomic potential as a starting base and conduct relevant atomistic simulations to study the alloy compositions favored for glass formation. From a physical point of view, the interatomic potential of a metal system describes the major interatomic interactions among all the atoms involved in the system, and specially governs the energetic states of all the alloy phases, of either crystalline or disordered structure. From a theoretical perspective, the GFA can be considered as the intrinsic characteristic of the alloy system, which should be governed by the interatomic interactions of the system. It would therefore be an appropriate choice to clarify the underlying physics of metallic glass formation of the system from its interatomic potential, because if a realistic interatomic potential of the system is constructed, the interactions among all the involved atoms can be deduced, and most of the physical behaviors, including the GFA as well as the atomic configurations of the system, can be derived though relevant computations and simulations [15,16].

Recently, the Ni–Nb–Zr ternary system, as a promising candidate for BMG, has been extensively studied with regard to its GFA and superior properties. For instance, Sakurai et al. searched the Ni–Nb–Zr system and found a new $Ni_{36}Nb_{39}Zr_{25}$ amorphous alloy, exhibiting high thermal stability, a high fracture stress of 1.3 GPa, a linear expansion coefficient of $8.3 \times 10^{-6}\,K^{-1}$, high oxidation resistance, good machinability and excellent anti-sticking properties, especially suitable to serve as optical glass device molding die materials [17]. Kimura et al. reported that the rapidly solidified Ni–Nb–Zr ribbons with a thickness of 20 μm were prepared by a single roller met-spinning technique and amorphous alloys were formed in the composition range of 20–75 at.% Ni, 0–60 at.% Nb and 0–80 at.% Zr [18]. Later, Zhu reported that BMGs were successfully prepared in a wide composition range of the Ni–Nb–Zr system and the maximum diameter of the as-cast glassy rods reached 3 mm by using the copper mold casting method [19]. To make best use of the Ni–Nb–Zr metallic glass, it is good practice to design the compositions favored for metallic glass formation, or at least provide estimates for such compositions to guide the experiments. Based on the empirical rules, the Ni–Nb–Zr ternary system should exhibit excellent GFA as a result of the large atomic size difference and strong negative interactions among constituent metals. In the present study, we aim to investigate the metallic glass formation of the Ni–Nb–Zr system at an atomic level, starting from its interatomic potential.

Concerning the previous work, we mainly focused on the binary or ternary transition metal systems containing at most two different structural metals, i.e. face-centered cubic (fcc)–bcc or fcc–hexagonal close-packed (hcp) [16]. In this study, an alloy system, consisting of three metals with different crystalline structures, namely the Ni–Nb–Zr system, was chosen for the first time. Initially, it was a challenging problem to construct a reliable interatomic potential for this specific ternary system. Several scientific issues are discussed in this paper: (i) a new long-range n-body potential was constructed for the Ni–Nb–Zr ternary system; (ii) Monte Carlo (MC) simulations were performed to predict not only the intrinsic glass formation region (GFR) of the Ni–Nb–Zr ternary system but also the optimal compositions with which the alloy would have a greater GFA; (iii) Voronoi tessellation analysis was employed to investigate the atomic-level structural evolutions associated with the metallic glass formation.

2. Method and model

2.1. Construction of Ni–Nb–Zr interatomic potential

It is well known that the interatomic potential plays a vitally important role in the atomic simulation, as whether the calculations and simulations can well reproduce the available experiment observations depends primarily on the interatomic potential. Consequently, great efforts have been made to develop realistic potentials. The most widely used ones are the embedded-atom method (EAM) potential [20], the Finnis–Sinclair (F–S) potential [21], the second-moment approximation of tight-binding (TB-SMA) potential [22] and their various modifications [23–26]. Although sharing some similar physical arguments, the EAM, F–S and TB-SMA potentials and their various modifications are all empirical approaches and hence have some limitations or drawbacks in the application. For example, it has been shown by rule of thumb that the EAM and F–S potentials are applicable to fcc and bcc metals, whereas the TB-SMA potential is suitable for fcc and hcp metals. In this case, it is a challenging problem to describe the interatomic interactions in a system consisting of both hcp and bcc metals.

Another problem is related to the cutoff radius. For an interatomic potential, the proper treatment at the cutoff radius, i.e. incorporating truncation functions, is needed. Otherwise, the energy and force described by the interatomic potential might jump when atoms go into or out of the cutoff radius, and a large number of these events can spoil the energy conservation, leading to unphysical behaviors in simulations. Besides, the atomic configurations in the first and second neighbors of fcc and hcp structures are very similar. As a result, the energy difference between them is considerably small and cannot be identified by the short-range potentials.

Recently, Dai et al. proposed a new long-range empirical potential (LREP), which has been shown capable of solving the inherent problems mentioned above [27–29]. The LREP can be expressed as

$$E_i = \frac{1}{2}\sum_{j\neq i}\phi(r_{ij}) - \sqrt{\sum_{j\neq i}\varphi(r_{ij})} \tag{1}$$

where E_i is the total potential energy of atom i, r_{ij} is the distance between atoms i and j of the system at equilibrium, $\phi(r_{ij})$ is the pair item and $\varphi(r_{ij})$ is the many-body part. They can be expressed as

$$\phi(r_{ij}) = (r_{ij} - r_{c1})^m\left(c_0 + c_1 r_{ij} + c_2 r_{ij}^2 + c_3 r_{ij}^3 + c_4 r_{ij}^4\right),\quad 0 < r_{ij} \leqslant r_{c1} \tag{2}$$

$$\varphi(r_{ij}) = \alpha^2(r_{ij} - r_{c2})^n,\quad 0 < r_{ij} \leqslant r_{c2} \tag{3}$$

Here, r_{c1} and r_{c2} are the cutoff radii for the pair item and many-body part, respectively. The exponents m and n are two integers and can be adjustable according to specific metals; α and c_i are the potential parameters to be fitted. The LREP has been proven to be relevant to identify the relative stabilities between stable and hypothetic structures of bcc, fcc or hcp metals. In particular, it can distinguish the energy difference between the fcc and hcp structures. Meanwhile, the total energy and force derived from the potential can keep continuous and smooth in the whole calculation range; thus, it can properly resolve the cutoff problem without a truncation function. Under the formalism of LREP, an interatomic n-body potential would be constructed for the Ni–Nb–Zr system.

Concerning the interactions between atoms, there should be six sets of potential parameters in the Ni–Nb–Zr ternary system: three sets for the interactions of pure metals Ni–Ni, Nb–Nb and Zr–Zr and the other three sets for the interactions of Ni–Nb, Ni–Zr and Nb–Zr. The latter three are commonly referred to as cross potentials, which describe the interactions of dissimilar atoms. Once the function form is known, the potential parameters need to be fitted. In general, the potential parameters are determined through the iterative optimization algorithm. Specifically, the potential parameters of pure metals are determined by fitting to the basic physical properties such as the cohesive energies, lattice constants, bulk moduli and elastic constants of pure metals, most of which are usually available [30]. The cross potentials are determined by fitting to the basic physical properties of the intermetallic compounds. As a common way to acquire some physical properties of the alloy phases, ab initio calculation is applied to acquire some properties of the compounds as a complement to experiments. In this study, ab initio calculations were carried out using the Cambridge serial total energy package (CASTEP) of Material Studio [31–33]. The geometry optimization was first performed to determine the lattice constants and total energies of the compounds at equilibrium, and then the elastic constants and bulk moduli were obtained. The cohesive energies of compounds were then easily derived from the total energies.

2.2. MC simulation

Since the process of producing metallic glasses is always non-equilibrium or even far from equilibrium, the related kinetic constraints are extremely restricted. For example, to obtain metallic glasses by liquid melt quenching, a cooling speed of 10^6 K s^{-1} is frequently required to avoid crystallization of any possible crystalline phase [6]. For another effective scheme, namely ion beam mixing, the cooling speed can be as high as 10^{14} K s^{-1} [34]. Summarizing the experimental observations from the commonly used glass producing techniques, i.e. liquid melt quenching, solid-state amorphization and ion beam mixing, it is found that the phases with complicated structures, e.g. intermetallic, can hardly nucleate or grow [16]. It follows that in such highly restricted kinetic conditions, the phase competing against metallic glass is the solid solution with simple structure. The experimental observations suggest that predicting the glass formation range of a metal system can be converted into an issue of determining the critical solid solubilities, which divide the entire alloy composition range into different parts that energetically favor the formation of solid solutions and metallic glasses, respectively. And the idea of phase competition has been supported by a large number of research results from both experimental and theoretical aspects [35–37]. Therefore, the issue related to the glass formation region of the Ni–Nb–Zr system is converted into an issue of comparing the relative stability of the solid solution with its amorphous (disordered) counterpart as a function of alloy composition, enabling one to determine the critical lines of solid solubility for the Ni–Nb–Zr system. Theoretically, the relative stabilities of the amorphous phases and solid solution are governed by the interatomic interaction of the system and can be derived from the interatomic potential through atomistic simulations.

Based on a realistic Ni–Nb–Zr n-body potential, MC simulations were carried out using the solid solution models over the entire composition triangle of the system.

We aim to systematically investigate the compositions favored for metallic glass formation of the system at room temperature, therefore MC simulations were performed at 300 K. Since the stable crystalline structures of Ni, Nb and Zr are fcc, bcc and hcp, respectively, three types of solid solution models, i.e. the fcc, bcc and hcp solid solution models, were constructed according to which type of atoms is dominant in the alloy composition. For fcc and bcc models, the [1 0 0], [0 1 0] and [0 0 1] crystalline directions are parallel to the x, y and z axes, respectively, while for the hcp model, the [1 0 0], [0 0 1] and [1 2 0] crystalline directions are parallel to the x, y and z axes, respectively. Periodic boundary conditions were adopted in the three directions. The fcc, bcc and hcp solid solution models consist of 4000 ($10 \times 10 \times 10 \times 4$) atoms, 3456 ($12 \times 12 \times 12 \times 4$) atoms and 3840 ($12 \times 10 \times 8 \times 4$) atoms, respectively. For the Ni–Nb–Zr ternary system, we varied x and y with a composition interval of 5% to construct the $Ni_xNb_yZr_{1-x-y}$ solid solution models over the entire composition triangle of the system. Since no lattice parameter was known for the $Ni_xNb_yZr_{1-x-y}$ solid solution, it was assumed that the initial lattice parameters at various compositions started out following Vegard's law. In setting the solid solution models, the solvent atoms were substituted randomly by a certain number of solute atoms to obtain a desired composition. The initial solid solutions were allowed to evolve at zero pressure and 300 K in MC simulation in the isothermal–isobaric ensemble.

In MC simulation, the edge vectors of the simulation box are $\vec{a}$, $\vec{b}$ and $\vec{c}$, which form the matrix $\boldsymbol{h} = (\vec{a}, \vec{b}, \vec{c})$ and describe the shape and volume $\Omega = |\boldsymbol{h}|$ of the simulation box. The position vector of atoms i in the simulation box is $\vec{r}_i = \boldsymbol{h}\vec{s}_i$ and the column $\vec{s}_i = (\upsilon_i, \varsigma_i, \xi_i)^T$ denotes the scaled position. $-0.5 < \upsilon_i, \varsigma_i, \xi_i \leqslant 0.5$ are three Cartesian components in scale space.

For the MC simulation in the isothermal–isobaric ensemble, there are two types of "moves": atom displacement and box deformation. For atom displacement, the simulation system can be treated as a canonical ensemble at constant NVT, i.e. the shape and volume of box are fixed. An atom i is chosen at random and given a uniform random displacement, $\Delta\vec{r}_i = (0.5 - \zeta_x, 0.5 - \zeta_y, 0.5 - \zeta_z) \times \delta^A$, to a new trial position. Here, ζ_x, ζ_y, ζ_z are three random uniformly distributing in the range of (0–1]. δ^A is the amplitude of this trial move. The trial move is accepted with a probability given by $\min(1, P^A_{move})$; here P^A_{move} is the ratio of the probabilities of the new and old state, which can be written as

$$P^A_{move} = \exp\left(-\frac{\Delta E}{k_B T}\right) \tag{4}$$

where $\Delta E = E^{trial} - E$ is the energy change resulting from the trial move of atom i, and k_B and T are Boltzmann constants and the temperature of the simulation system, respectively. For box deformation, the fractional coordinates of atoms in the box are fixed. The state of the simulation box is defined by the matrix $\boldsymbol{h}$, from which the trial state $\boldsymbol{h}^{\text{trial}}$ is generated by the following relations:

$$\boldsymbol{h}^{trial} = \boldsymbol{h} + \boldsymbol{h}\varepsilon^{trial} \tag{5}$$

$$\varepsilon^{trial} = \begin{pmatrix} 0.5-\zeta_{11} & 0.5-\zeta_{12} & 0.5-\zeta_{13} \\ 0.5-\zeta_{12} & 0.5-\zeta_{22} & 0.5-\zeta_{23} \\ 0.5-\zeta_{13} & 0.5-\zeta_{23} & 0.5-\zeta_{33} \end{pmatrix} \times \delta^B \tag{6}$$

where ε^{trial} is the trial strain tensor applied to the box, ζ_{ij} are random numbers uniformly distributing in the range of (0–1] and δ^B is the amplitude of this trial move. The trial move is accepted with a probability given by $\min(1, P^B_{move})$. Here, P^B_{move} is the ratio of the probabilities of the new and old states, which can be written as

$$P^B_{move} = \exp\left(-\frac{\Delta E + \Omega \mathrm{Tr}(\boldsymbol{\sigma} \cdot \boldsymbol{\varepsilon}^{trial}) - N\ln(\Omega^{trial}/\Omega)}{k_B T}\right) \tag{7}$$

where $\Delta E = E^{trial} - E$ is the energy change resulting from the trial move of the box, σ is the applied stress tensor and Ω^{trial} is the volume of the box in the trial state. When only hydrostatic pressure is applied, P^B_{move} can be computed by

$$P^B_{move} = \exp\left(-\frac{\Delta E + p_{\text{ext}}(\Omega^{trial} - \Omega) - N\ln(\Omega^{trial}/\Omega)}{k_B T}\right) \tag{8}$$

One can see from Eq. (6) that there are six independent elements in the strain tensor. In order to monitor the internal stress or pressure of the system, six strains are separately applied to the box in an MC step and therefore the internal stress can be synchronously computed by

$$\sigma_{\alpha\beta} = -\frac{1}{\Omega}\frac{\Delta E}{\varepsilon^{trial}_{\alpha\beta}} \tag{9}$$

For a system consisting of N atoms, there are a total of $N+6$ trial moves: N moves for atoms and six moves for the box. The $N+6$ trial moves are randomly chosen to be carried out in an MC step. In addition, if a move is rejected, the old state is recounted. The amplitudes of trial moves δ^{A} and δ^{B} are also adjusted so that the acceptance ratios of the trial moves are kept at ~50%.

After sufficient simulation time, the fully relaxed alloy reached a relatively stable state at which the related dynamic variables showed no secular variation. The structures of the alloys obtained in the MC simulation were collected and analyzed using the three-dimensional (3-D) atomic configurations, pair correlation function $g(r)$ and Voronoi tessellation analysis [38].

3. Results and discussions

3.1. Construction of Ni–Nb–Zr interatomic potential

For the Ni–Nb–Zr system, the n-body potentials expressed by Eqs. 1–3 have been constructed, and the fitted parameters are shown in Table 1. There should be six sets of potential parameters to describe the interactions of the Ni–Nb–Zr ternary system. For each set of potentials, there are 10 parameters to be fitted, i.e. $\{c_0, c_1, c_2, c_3, c_4, r_{c1}, r_{c2}, m, n, \alpha\}$. The interatomic potentials of three pure metals have been proven to be relevant to identify the relative stabilities between the stable and their hypothetic structures, and they could well describe the interactions among the involved atoms [29,39]. In the present work, the Ni–Nb, Ni–Zr and Nb–Zr cross potentials are determined by fitting to the basic physical properties of their intermetallic compounds. In the fitting process, compounds with different structures and different compositions are involved to ensure that the constructed potential can describe the interactions in the whole composition range and in different environments. Once the potential parameters are determined, the structures of these compounds are then optimized using the fitted potentials, i.e. fully relaxing the structure to their lowest energy states. The fully relaxed structures and corresponding physical properties, i.e. the lattice constants, cohesive energies and bulk moduli, are referred to as the reproduced physical properties. The reproduced physical properties of intermetallic compounds in the Ni–Nb, Ni–Zr and Nb–Zr binary systems are presented in Tables 2 and 3. For comparison, the results obtained by ab initio calculations are also listed in the tables. It can be seen that the physical properties reproduced from the interatomic potential match well with those obtained from ab initio calculations, which confirms that the constructed potentials could well derive the energies and structures of these compounds in the systems.

Another approach to evaluate the reliability of the constructed potential is to check whether the potential can describe the interatomic interaction of a system at non-equilibrium state, i.e. to derive the equation of state from the potential and then compare it with that obtained from other methods. The frequently used equation of state in this field is the Rose equation, which has been regarded to be universal for most categories of solids [40]. Fig. 1 plots the pair terms, many-body parts and the total energies as a function of the lattice constants calculated from the constructed potential, and the corresponding Rose equations for B2 NiNb, $L1_2$ Ni_3Nb, $L1_2$ $NiNb_3$, B2 NiZr, $L1_2$ Ni_3Zr, $L1_2$ $NiZr_3$, B2 NbZr, $L1_2$ Nb_3Zr and $L1_2$ $NbZr_3$. One can see from Fig. 1 that the pair terms, many-body parts and the total energies derived from the constructed potential can keep smooth in the whole calculation range. The calculated total energies also match well with the Rose equation. Meanwhile, there are no discontinuities in the energy curves of the compounds, which can avoid unphysical behavior in MC simulations. It follows that the constructed potentials can reasonably describe the interactions of the system, even if the system is far from the equilibrium state, thus providing additional evidence that the constructed potentials can be applied to the issues related to the structure and energy of the system. Consequently, the newly constructed n-body potentials under the formalism of LREP are competent for describing the interatomic interactions in the Ni–Nb–Zr ternary system, particularly consisting of fcc, bcc and hcp metals.

3.2. Glass formation region of the Ni–Nb–Zr system

GFA frequently refers to the easiness or difficulty of the metallic glass formation. Generally, there are two major understandings of this concept. Firstly, for a specific alloy, the glass formation is treated as the suppression of crystallization during the freezing of the liquid melt [41]. In practice, researchers frequently use some technical parameters to describe the GFA of a specific alloy, such as the cooling speed, the maximum size of the attainable metallic glass, etc. [42]. One can describe a material's GFA as being either inversely proportional to its critical cooling rate or proportional to its critical casting size [8]. Secondly, for a specific metal system, the glass formation can be depicted as a competition between the crystalline and amorphous phases as a function of the alloy composition [43]. In this situation, the glass-forming range/region (GFR) is often used to indicate the composition range/region within which the amorphous phase or metallic glass is energetically favored to form. It follows that the GFA of a metal system is quantitatively related to its GFR, i.e. the wider the GFR, the greater the GFA of a metal system. For clarity, we refer to the first and second understandings of the concept as the GFA of an alloy and the GFA of a system, respectively.

In the present study, we first focused on the GFA of the Ni–Nb–Zr ternary system, i.e. the GFR of the system. Starting with the constructed Ni–Nb–Zr n-body potential, the GFR of the system was determined by comparing the relative stabilities of the original solid solution vs. its

Table 1
Parameters of the constructed long-range n-body potential for the Ni–Nb–Zr system.

	Ni–Ni	Nb–Nb	Zr–Zr	Ni–Nb	Ni–Zr	Zr–Nb
m	4	4	4	4	4	4
n	6	8	4	4	5	4
r_{c1} (Å)	5.749526	4.851379	6.437549	5.25695	4.783337	7.040277
r_{c2} (Å)	7.171908	7.117045	7.222787	9.864774	7.385404	7.2984
c_0 (eV/Å^m)	0.294724	10.53168	0.788297	0.616469	0.633714	0.371087
c_1 (eV/Å^{m+1})	−0.35871	−14.4959	−0.84608	−0.65777	−0.82273	−0.39984
c_2 (eV/Å^{m+2})	0.163193	7.514826	0.341507	0.278365	0.485298	0.160857
c_3 (eV/Å^{m+3})	−0.03303	−1.72564	−0.0611	−0.05807	−0.14258	−0.02815
c_4 (eV/Å^{m+4})	0.002535	0.147777	0.004081	0.005397	0.016805	0.001819
α (eV/Å^n)	0.014612	0.011261	0.150093	0.04074	0.056287	−0.26622

Table 2
Lattice constants (a), cohesion energies (E_c), and bulk moduli (B_0) of B2 and $L1_2$ compounds reproduced from constructed LREP (first line) and the results from ab initio calculations (second line).

	NiNb	Ni_3Nb	$NiNb_3$	NiZr	Ni_3Zr	$NiZr_3$	NbZr	Nb_3Zr	$NbZr_3$
	B2	$L1_2$	$L1_2$	B2	$L1_2$	$L1_2$	B2	$L1_2$	$L1_2$
A (Å)	3.095	3.700	4.050	3.212	3.759	4.279	3.435	4.300	4.445
	3.105	3.830	3.977	3.162	3.770	4.297	3.432	4.337	4.445
E_c (eV)	6.047	5.376	6.707	3.774	5.342	5.803	6.803	6.957	6.447
	6.071	5.365	6.683	3.789	5.343	5.767	6.803	6.959	6.443
B_0 (Mbar)	2.166	1.898	1.765	1.422	1.697	1.071	1.258	1.430	1.066
	2.117	2.185	1.454	1.463	1.688	1.265	1.258	1.327	1.162

Table 3
Lattice constants (a), cohesion energies (E_c) and bulk moduli (B_0) of $D0_{19}$ compounds reproduced from constructed LREP (first line) and the results from ab initio calculations (second line).

	Ni_3Nb	$NiNb_3$	Ni_3Zr	$NiZr_3$	Nb_3Zr	$NbZr_3$
	D019	D019	D019	D019	D019	D019
A (Å)	5.250	5.750	5.297	5.960	5.850	6.255
	5.268	5.637	5.297	6.071	6.022	6.261
C (Å)	4.250	4.690	4.382	5.137	5.341	5.200
	4.232	4.613	4.382	5.006	5.269	5.274
E_c (eV)	5.478	6.648	5.345	5.764	6.971	6.440
	5.400	6.643	5.346	5.764	6.956	6.464
B_0 (Mbar)	1.905	2.570	1.049	1.696	1.415	1.091
	2.294	1.499	1.049	1.668	1.241	1.112

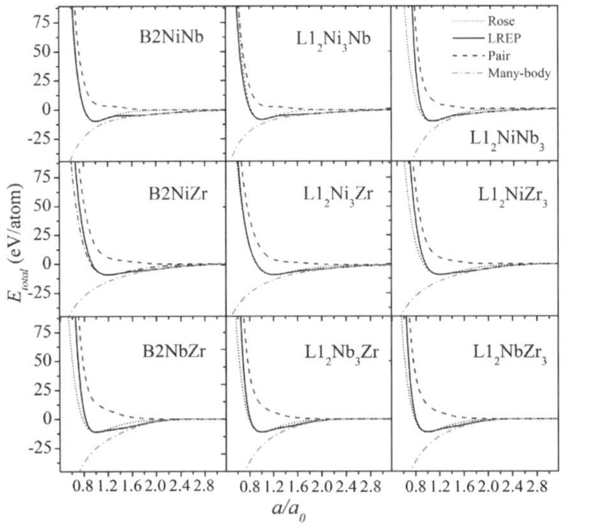

Fig. 1. The pair terms, many-body parts and the total energies as a function of the lattice constants calculated from the interatomic potential and the corresponding Rose equations for B2 NiNb, NiZr and NbZr; $L1_2$ Ni_3Nb, $NiNb_3$, Ni_3Zr, $NiZr_3$ Nb_3Zr and $NbZr_3$.

amorphous counterpart as a function of alloy composition over the entire composition triangle. The initial solid solution $Ni_xNb_yZr_{1-x-y}$ was evolved in MC simulation at 300 K for sufficient simulation time until all the related dynamics variables reached relative equilibrium. According to the 3-D atomic configurations and pair correlation functions $g(r)$, we classified all the $Ni_xNb_yZr_{1-x-y}$ alloys obtained in MC simulation after adequate evolution into three structure states: the crystalline state (CS), the transitional state (TS) and the amorphous state (AS), and then constructed the glass formation composition diagram of the Ni–Nb–Zr system at 300 K in Fig. 2. One can see from the figure that the Ni–Nb–Zr composition triangle is divided into four regions by three critical solubility lines AB, CD and EF. When an alloy composition locates beyond the lines moving towards one of the three corners, the Ni–Nb–Zr alloy tends to keep its crystalline structure, and these three corner regions are consequently classified as the crystalline regions. When an alloy composition falls into the central polygon region enclosed by the bold blue line, the crystalline solid solution becomes unstable and would completely collapse into the disordered state, giving rise to the formation of the amorphous phase, i.e. metallic glass. This region is therefore defined as the GFR of the Ni–Nb–Zr system. In other words, within the GFR, the amorphous phase is energetically favored to be formed compared with its crystalline counterpart. It is then concluded that the amorphous phase possesses higher stability than its competing crystalline counterpart within the GFR; thus the underlying physics of metallic glass formation is

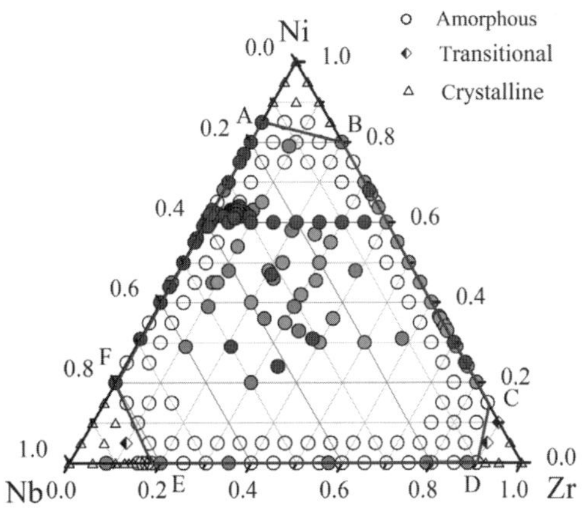

Fig. 2. Glass formation composition diagram derived from MC simulations at 300 K for the Ni–Nb–Zr system. Colored dots represent the experimental data obtained from different glass-producing techniques.

the spontaneous collapse of the crystalline lattice while the solute concentration exceeds a critical value.

It is of great interest and importance to compare the MC simulation results with the experimental observations. To validate the predicted GFR of the Ni–Nb–Zr system, experimental results obtained by various metallic glass-producing techniques [17–19,44–55] were collected and some were marked by colored dots, as shown in Fig. 2. The experimental data obtained from different glass-producing techniques are depicted in different colors. The red dots represent the compositions with which metallic glasses were fabricated by copper mold casting. The orange dots indicate glass forming compositions obtained from the melt-spinning technique, while the green ones represent some other methods, such as ion beam mixing, mechanical alloying and combinatorial arc plasma deposition. One can see from the figure that all of the experimental observations fall into the predicted GFR. Besides, there are also several other studies showing the glass-forming ranges of the Ni–Nb–Zr system. For instance, Sakurai et al. fabricated Ni–Nb–Zr thin films with 974 different compositions to search for new glass modeling die materials and 703 samples were confirmed to be single amorphous phases [17]. Kimura et al. reported that the rapidly solidified Ni–Nb–Zr amorphous alloys were formed in the composition range of 20–75 at.% Ni, 0–60 at.% Nb and 0–80 at.% Zr [18]. Zhu et al. discovered that bulk metallic glasses could be formed in a quite wide composition range of the Ni–Nb–Zr ternary system [19]. The above-mentioned composition ranges, which were not marked in Fig. 2, also locate in the predicted GFR of the Ni–Nb–Zr system. As a consequence, our predicted GFRs are well supported by the plentiful experimental data obtained by various glass-producing techniques, suggesting that the MC simulation results in the present study are indeed believable in determining the GFA of the Ni–Nb–Zr system. Thus it provides further evidence for the validity of the constructed Ni–Nb–Zr n-body potential under the formulism of LREP.

It is worthwhile mentioning that the GFR derived from the interatomic potential can be considered as the intrinsic characteristics of the system. The intrinsic GFR of a metal system reflects the possible composition range energetically favored for the metallic glass formation. However, the glass-forming compositions observed in experiments may not always be the same as the intrinsic GFR and also possibly vary with experiments, since the external factors and non-equilibrium effects, such as irradiation and mechanical alloying, can either stabilize or destabilize a uniform solid solution. For instance, if external factors, such as impurities, chemical and structural inhomogeneity, and even the producing process, increase the stability of the solid solutions, these factors would broaden the composition range within which the solid solutions could keep either stable or metastable, implying that the GFR observed under such conditions would become small. Therefore, the glass-forming compositions observed in experiments not only depend on the intrinsic characteristics of the system but also, to a large extent, are closely related to the applied glass-producing techniques and technical parameters, such as the cooling rate. In the process of metallic glass formation, the intrinsic characteristics of the system play a dominant role while the external conditions are subordinate factors, and hence the latter can be considered as a source of perturbation to the intrinsic characteristics of the system.

3.3. Optimization of compositions favored for metallic glass formation

Based on the constructed Ni–Nb–Zr n-body potential, the intrinsic GFR of the Ni–Nb–Zr system has been predicted. It follows that the Ni–Nb–Zr metallic glass can be obtained by some appropriate glass-producing techniques when its composition falls into this region. To further predict the GFA of a specific Ni–Nb–Zr alloy, i.e. to estimate which amorphous alloys in the GFR are more stable or attainable, the total energies of the $Ni_xNb_yZr_{1-x-y}$ solid solutions and real alloys were calculated, respectively, and the energy differences between the two states (crystalline and amorphous) were defined as the driving forces for crystalline-to-amorphous transition. The ideal solid solution was obtained by annealing the simulation model and optimizing its lattice constant and simultaneously keeping the crystal symmetry unchanged; while for the real Ni–Nb–Zr alloy, the initial solid solution was evolved and equilibrated at 300 K in MC simulations for sufficient simulation time.

After MC simulations and calculations, the contour map of the driving force for metallic glass formation was plotted in Fig. 3. One can see from the figure that the energy difference ΔE is negative over the whole GFR, suggesting that the energy of the amorphous phase is lower than that of the solid solution so that the formation of the amorphous phase, i.e. metallic glass is indeed energetically favored. Moreover, the larger the energy difference, the stronger the driving force for glass formation. It is

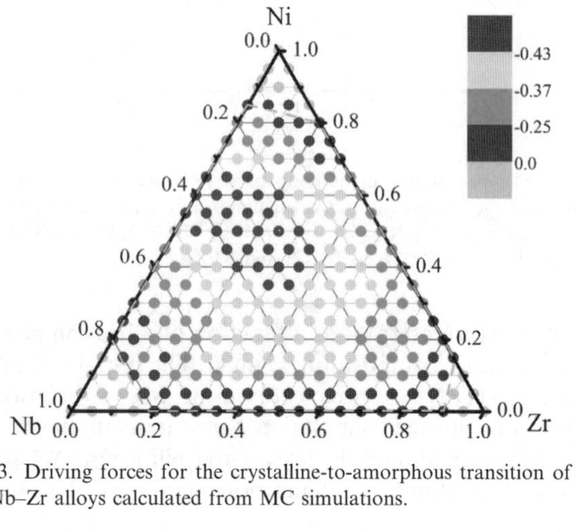

Fig. 3. Driving forces for the crystalline-to-amorphous transition of the Ni–Nb–Zr alloys calculated from MC simulations.

found that the small composition sub-region marked by red dots, as shown in Fig. 3, have a lower ΔE than other region, implying that there exists a stronger driving force for the Ni–Nb–Zr alloys to form metallic glasses. We define this composition sub-region as the optimal compositions for Ni–Nb–Zr metallic glass formation, within which the alloys have greater GFA than those alloys located outside the sub-region. Interestingly, the collected experimental data in Fig. 2 are mainly distributed in the optimal composition sub-region in Fig. 3. It follows that the Ni–Nb–Zr amorphous alloys with the optimal compositions are expected be more stable or attainable than other alloys in the system, thus providing basic guidelines to design appropriate alloy compositions for producing Ni–Nb–Zr metallic glasses. It turns out that the predictions derived from the constructed potential through atomistic simulations are well supported by the experimental observations reported so far in the literature. The relevance of the predicted intrinsic GFR and optimal compositions of the Ni–Nb–Zr system, as well as the validity of the constructed *n*-body potential have been further confirmed. It is therefore believed that the study of the crystalline-to-amorphous transition starting from a realistic interatomic potential of a ternary metal system is an appropriate scheme.

3.4. Atomic structures of Ni–Nb–Zr metallic glasses

It is well known that the formation and stability of condensed matters are closely related to their atomic structures. Therefore the atomic configurations of metallic alloys would have noticeable changes during the crystalline-to-amorphous transition. As shown in Fig. 2, the experimental observations are mostly located in the Ni–Nb-based compositions with minor Zr. Accordingly, the atomic structures and coordination polyhedra of $Ni_xNb_{90-x}Zr_{10}$ alloys obtained in MC simulation have been investigated. Fig. 4 shows the pair-correlation functions $g(r)$ of typical $Ni_xNb_{90-x}Zr_{10}$ alloys with various compositions. One can see that the $g(r)$ of $Nb_{90}Zr_{10}$ alloy shows apparent crystalline peaks, indicating that it still remains in the initial crystalline packing. With the addition of Ni content, the crystalline peaks beyond the second peak become less distinct, corresponding to the disturbance of the crystalline structure. When the concentration of Ni exceeds 10%, all the peaks except the first one gradually fade away, exhibiting a short-range order and long-range disorder feature. It suggests that the crystalline lattice completely collapses and turns into an amorphous state. We also observed that the first peak of $g(r)$ shifted to a smaller distance with the increasing of Ni content, implying the average interatomic distance of the $Ni_xNb_{90-x}Zr_{10}$ alloys decreased. This is due to the smaller radius of the Ni atom compared with that of the Nb atom [56].

In order to seek more detailed information about the local atomic configuration, the coordination polyhedra of the $Ni_xNb_{90-x}Zr_{10}$ alloys were analyzed by means of the

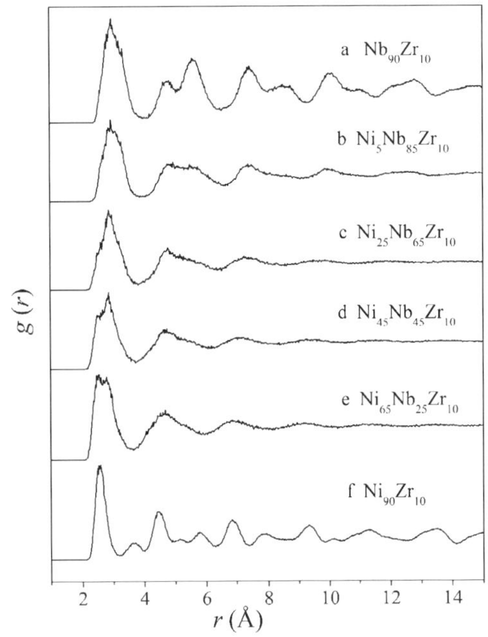

Fig. 4. Pair-correlation functions $g(r)$ of Ni–Nb–Zr alloys obtained from MC simulations.

Voronoi tessellation method [38]. The Voronoi polyhedra centered by Ni, Nb and Zr atoms were analyzed independently according to the numbers of Voronoi planes and their indices. The Voronoi index, $\langle n_3, n_4, n_5, n_6\rangle$, where n_i denotes the number of i-edged faces in Voronoi polyhedra, is used to designate the characteristics of the atomic cluster surrounding an atom. The most frequent coordination polyhedra for the simulated $Ni_xNb_{90-x}Zr_{10}$ alloys are presented in Fig. 5. It can be seen that for the crystalline $Nb_{90}Zr_{10}$ alloy, the absolutely dominant polyhedra are Nb-centered $\langle 0,6,0,8\rangle$ clusters, as shown in Fig. 5a, which is a typical crystalline arrangement [57]. As the crystalline-to-amorphous transition takes place, the types and distributions of coordination polyhedra of the alloys change dramatically. Specifically for the $Ni_5Zr_{10}Nb_{85}$ alloy, as seen in Fig. 5b, the population of $\langle 0,6,0,8\rangle$ obviously reduced, and there appear some other Nb-centered clusters indexed as $\langle 0,1,10,2\rangle$, $\langle 0,3,6,4\rangle$, $\langle 0,2,8,4\rangle$, $\langle 0,0,12,0\rangle$. The underlying origin of the changes concerning the topological features of the alloy is that the solvent and solute atoms alter their equilibrium positions to accommodate one another in order to relax the atomic-level stress resulting from the chemical interactions as well as the atomic size differences of the component atoms. Once the alloy composition is located in the GFR, i.e. forming metallic glass, the predominant polyhedra turn into $\langle 0,0,12,0\rangle$, $\langle 0,1,10,2\rangle$, $\langle 0,2,8,4\rangle$ and $\langle 0,3,6,4\rangle$. It can be seen from Fig. 5 that the population of $\langle 0,0,12,0\rangle$ gradually increases with the increasing of Ni content, and the $\langle 0,0,12,0\rangle$ clusters are mainly centered by Ni. It is well known that the $\langle 0,0,12,0\rangle$ cluster is regarded as the full icosahedron (FI)

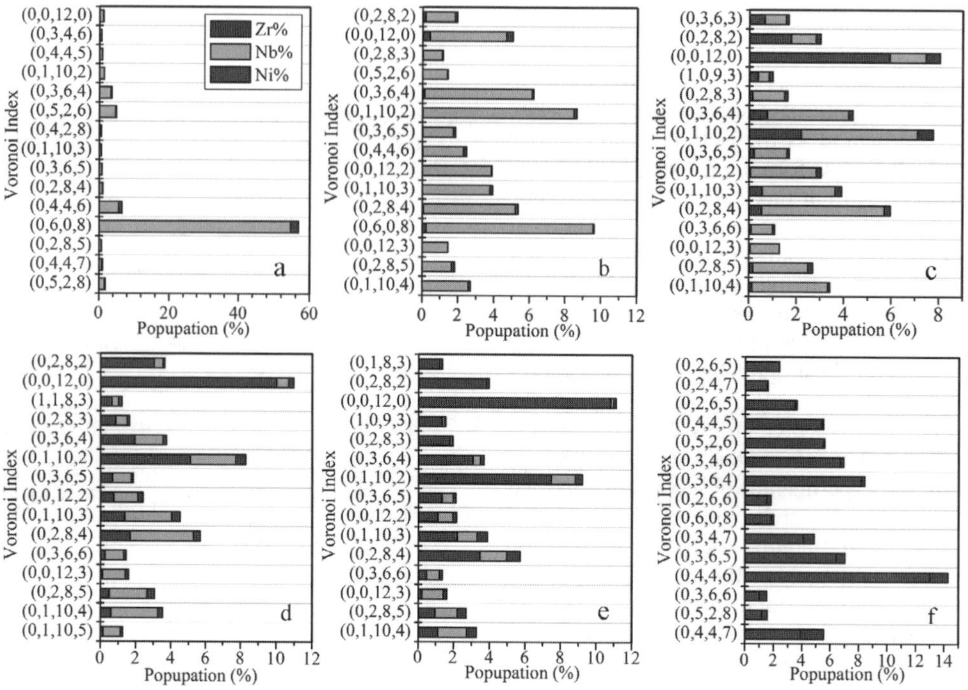

Fig. 5. Populations of the most frequent coordination polyhedra for the Ni–Nb–Zr alloys obtained from MC simulations: $Ni_{90}Zr_{10}$ (a), $Ni_5Nb_{85}Zr_{10}$ (b), $Ni_{25}Nb_{65}Zr_{10}$ (c), $Ni_{45}Nb_{45}Zr_{10}$ (d), $Ni_{65}Nb_{25}Zr_{10}$ (e) and $Ni_{90}Zr_{10}$ (f).

with complete five-fold symmetry and the number of FI would remarkably increase after the crystalline-to-amorphous transition. Cheng et al. has reported that the FI consisting of multiple species with different sizes and chemical properties as well as the complete five-fold environment would greatly enhance the transition barrier to crystals [58]. It follows that in the present study, proper increasing of Ni content could improve the GFA of Ni–Nb–Zr alloys. Additionally, it is of interest to compare the local atomic configuration around Ni and Nb atoms. Consider the $Ni_{45}Nb_{45}Zr_{10}$ alloy as an example, which contains equal amounts of Ni and Nb: the Voronoi polyhedron types around Ni and Nb atoms are quite different. One can see from Fig. 5d that the most favored coordination polyhedra around Ni indexed as $\langle 0,0,12,0\rangle$, $\langle 0,1,10,2\rangle$ and $\langle 0,2,8,2\rangle$. For the Nb-centered, the most prevalent Voronoi polyhedron types are $\langle 0,2,8,4\rangle$, $\langle 0,1,10,3\rangle$ and $\langle 0,1,10,4\rangle$. The Ni-centered clusters prefer a lower CN, 12–13, while the Nb-centered clusters prefer a higher CN, 14–15, due to the larger atomic size of Nb. It is then concluded that the atomic structure of the Ni–Nb–Zr ternary metallic glass is obviously influenced by the concentration of the component metals, and that the differences of the atomic radii also play a vital role in the atomic configuration of metallic glasses.

Combing through the distribution of Voronoi polyhedra in the $Ni_xNb_{90-x}Zr_{10}$ metallic glass, it is found that the most prevailing clusters are $\langle 0,0,12,0\rangle$, $\langle 0,1,10,2\rangle$, $\langle 0,2,8,4\rangle$, $\langle 0,1,10,3\rangle$, $\langle 0,3,6,4\rangle$ and $\langle 0,2,8,2\rangle$, in either Ni-rich or Nb-rich composition. Since the polyhedra of $\langle 0,1,10,2\rangle$, $\langle 0,2,8,4\rangle$, $\langle 0,1,10,3\rangle$, $\langle 0,3,6,4\rangle$ and $\langle 0,2,8,2\rangle$ can be considered as icosahedral-like (distorted or irregular icosahedra), it can be inferred that the icosahedral or icosahedral-like ordering (especially the FI with complete five-fold environment) should be the major local structural feature in the Ni–Nb–Zr metallic glass obtained in MC simulation. It is known that icosahedral or icosahedral-like polyhedra play an important role to stabilize the structure of metal–metal amorphous alloys [59]. Recently, Wu et al. analyzed the cluster energy for different kinds of local clusters and found that the $\langle 0,0,12,0\rangle$, $\langle 0,1,10,2\rangle$, $\langle 0,3,6,4\rangle$ and $\langle 0,2,8,2\rangle$ clusters have lower energies than other icosahedral clusters and the full icosahedron is the most stable structure in metallic glasses [60]. Oji et Al. proposed a possible structure model for the Ni–Nb–Zr glassy alloy, namely the distorted icosahedral clusters assembled in randomly packed manners [59]. Since the Goldschmidt radii of Ni, Nb and Zr atoms are 0.125 nm, 0.147 nm and 0.160 nm [56], respectively, the Ni–Nb–Zr ternary system is a typical system with small-, medium- and large-sized constituent elements. When forming metallic glasses, atoms with different sizes tend to coordinate in space and fill the vacant sites in the disordered structure in an efficient way, leading to an increase of the random packing density as well as the stability of ternary metallic glasses. Therefore, the atomic configurations of metallic alloys mostly depend on the alloy composition, the size difference and chemical interactions of constituent metals. Consequently, the results in other theoretical studies further confirm the feasibility and effectiveness of our simulations at an atomic-level starting from the newly proposed long-range n-body potential of the Ni–Nb–Zr system.

4. Concluding remarks

(1) A long-range empirical potential is firstly constructed for the Ni–Nb–Zr ternary system, particularly consisting of three constituent metals with different crystalline structures. The potentials are verified to be reliable and appropriate for describing the interatomic interactions in the system by well reproducing some basic physical properties of the system. The equation of state derived from the constructed potential is in good agreement with the Rose equation. Thus, the realistic Ni–Nb–Zr n-body potential can be reliably applied to the issues related to the energy and atomic structure of the system.

(2) Based on the constructed Ni–Nb–Zr n-body potential, MC simulations were carried out using the solid solution model to compare the relative stabilities of the crystalline solid solution vs. its disordered counterpart over the entire composition triangle of the system. Simulations not only reveal that the underlying physics of metallic glass formation is the spontaneous collapse of the crystalline lattice when the solute concentration exceeds a critical value, but also predict an intrinsic glass formation region of the Ni–Nb–Zr system, reflecting the possible composition range energetically favored for metallic glass formation. The predicted GFR is well supported by the plentiful experimental data obtained by various glass-producing techniques.

(3) Furthermore, the energy difference between the crystalline solid solution and the amorphous phase is proposed to be the driving force for the crystalline-to-amorphous transition. The optimal compositions with stronger driving forces for Ni–Nb–Zr metallic glass formation were then pinpointed, with which Ni–Nb–Zr amorphous alloys can be the more stable or easier to be produced in practice by specific glass-producing techniques. The predictions can serve as important guidance for designing favored alloy compositions to produce Ni–Nb–Zr metallic glasses.

(4) Concerning the structural changes during the crystalline-to-amorphous transition, atomic structures and coordination polyhedra of $Ni_xNb_{90-x}Zr_{10}$ alloys obtained in MC simulation have been investigated. It is revealed that the local atomic configurations of metallic alloys are mostly influenced by the alloy composition, the size difference and chemical interactions of constituent metals. Moreover, the icosahedral or icosahedral-like ordering is inferred as the major local structural feature in the Ni–Nb–Zr metallic glass, which leads to an increase of the random packing density as well as stability of ternary metallic glasses. Interestingly, the simulation results are well supported by the experimental observations and other theoretical studies, providing firm evidence for the relevance of the constructed interatomic potential as well as the atomistic approaches applied.

Acknowledgements

The authors are grateful for financial support from the National Natural Science Foundation of China (51131003), the Ministry of Science and Technology of China (973 Program 2011CB606301, 2012CB825700), and the Administration of Tsinghua University.

References

[1] Klement W, Willens R, Duwez P. Nature 1960;187:869.
[2] Johnson WL. MRS Bull 1999;24:42.
[3] Chen HS. Acta Metall 1974;22:1505.
[4] Inoue A, Zhang T, Masumoto T. Mater Trans. JIM 1989;30:965.
[5] Inoue A. Acta Mater 2000;48:279.
[6] Wang WH, Dong C, Shek CH. Mater Sci Eng R 2004;44:45.
[7] Miller M, Liaw PK. Bulk metallic glasses: an overview. Berlin: Springer; 2007.
[8] Schroers J. Phys Today 2013;66:32.
[9] Turnbull D. Contem Phys 1969;10:473.
[10] Egami T, Waseda Y. J Non Cryst Solids 1984;64:113.
[11] Liu BX, Johnson WL, Nicolet MA, Lau S. Appl Phys Lett 1983;42:45.
[12] Pan F, Chen YG, Liu BX. Appl Phys Lett 1995;67:780.
[13] Wang D, Li Y, Sun BB, Sui ML, Lu K, Ma E. Appl Phys Lett 2004;84:4029.
[14] Lin C, Yang GW, Liu BX. J Appl Phys 2000;87:2821.
[15] Li JH, Dai XD, Liang SH, Tai KP, Kong Y, Liu BX. Phys Rep 2008;455:1.
[16] Li JH, Dai Y, Cui YY, Liu BX. Mater Sci Eng R 2011;72:1.
[17] Sakurai J, Abe M, Ando M, Aono Y, Hata S. Precis Eng 2011;35:537.
[18] Kimura H, Inoue A, Yamaura S-I, Sasamori K, Nishida M, Shinpo Y, et al. Mater Trans 2003;44:1167.
[19] Zhu ZW, Zhang HF, Ding BZ, Hu ZQ. Mater Sci Eng A 2008;492:221.
[20] Baskes MI. Phys Rev Lett 1987;59:2666.
[21] Finnis MW, Sinclair JE. Philos Mag A 1984;50:45.
[22] Tomanek D, Aligia AA, Balseiro CA. Phys Rev B 1985;32:5051.
[23] Baskes MI. Phys Rev B 1992;46:2727.
[24] Cleri F, Rosato V. Phys Rev B 1993;48:22.
[25] Lee B-J, Baskes MI. Phys Rev B 2000;62:8564.
[26] Dai XD, Kong Y, Li JH, Liu BX. J Phys Condens Matter 2006;18:4527.
[27] Dai XD, Li JH, Kong Y. Phys Rev B 2007;75:052102.
[28] Dai XD, Kong Y, Li JH. Phys Rev B 2007;75:104101.
[29] Dai Y, Li JH, Liu BX. J Phys Condens Matter 2009;21:385402.
[30] Lide DR. CRC handbook of chemistry and physics. Boca Raton, FL: CRC Press; 2004.
[31] Segall MD, Lindan PJD, Probert MJ, Pickard CJ, Hasnip PJ, Clark SJ, et al. J Phys Condens Matter 2002;14:2717.
[32] Clark SJ, Segall MD, Pickard CJ, Hasnip PJ, Probert MJ, Refson K, et al. Z Kristallogr 2005;220:567.
[33] Perdew JP, Wang Y. Phys Rev B 1992;45:13244.
[34] Liu BX, Lai WS, Zhang Q. Mater Sci Eng R 2000;29:1.
[35] Sheng HW, Wilde G, Ma E. Acta Mater 2002;50:475.
[36] Basu J, Murty BS, Ranganathan S. J Alloys Compd 2008;465:163.
[37] He JH, Ma E. Phys Rev B 2001;64:144206.
[38] Cheng YQ, Ma E. Prog Mater Sci 2011;56:379.

[39] Dai Y, Li JH, Che XL, Liu BX. J Phys Chem B 2009;113:7282.
[40] Rose JH, Smith JR, Guinea F, Ferrante J. Phys Rev B 1984;29:2963.
[41] Lu ZP, Liu CT. Acta Mater 2002;50:3501.
[42] Lu ZP, Bei H, Liu CT. Intermetallics 2007;15:618.
[43] Li JH, Dai Y, Dai XD. Intermetallics 2012;31:292.
[44] Chang HJ, Park ES, Jung YS, Kim MK, Kim DH. J Alloys Compd 2007;434:156.
[45] Chen LY, Hu HT, Zhang GQ, Jiang JZ. J Alloys Compd 2007;443:109.
[46] Yamaura S-I, Nakata S, Kimura H, Inoue A. Mater Trans 2006;47:2991.
[47] Enayati MH, Schumacher P, Cantor B. J Mater Sci 2002;37:5255.
[48] Yuan L, Pang C, Wang YM, Wang Q, Qiang JB, Dong C. Intermetallics 2010;18:1800.
[49] Zhu ZW, Zhang HF, Sun WS, Hu ZQ. J Mater Res 2007;22:453.
[50] Li Y, Liang SH, Li N, Li JH, Liu BX. Mater Chem Phys 2013;141:960.
[51] Xia L, Li WH, Fang SS, Wei BC, Dong YD. J Appl Phys 2006;99:026103.
[52] Zhu Z, Zhang H, Pan D, Sun W, Hu Z. Adv Eng Mater 2006;8:953.
[53] Altounian Z, Guo-hua T, Strom-Olsen JO. J Appl Phys 1983;54:3111.
[54] Yamaura S-I, Sakurai M, Hasegawa M, Wakoh K, Shimpo Y, Nishida M, et al. Acta Mater 2005;53:3703.
[55] Paglieri SN, Pal NK, Dolan MD, Kim S-M, Chien W-M, Lamb J, et al. J Membr Sci 2011;378:42.
[56] Kittel C. Introduction to solid state physics. New York: Wiley; 1996.
[57] Wang SY, Kramer MJ, Xu M, Wu S, Hao SG, Sordelet DJ, et al. Phys Rev B 2009;79:144205.
[58] Cheng YQ, Ma E, Sheng HW. Phys Rev Lett 2009;102:245501.
[59] Oji H, Handa K, Ide J, Honma T, Yamaura S, Inoue A, et al. J Appl Phys 2009;105:113527.
[60] Wu SQ, Wang CZ, Hao SG, Zhu ZZ, Ho KM. Appl Phys Lett 2010;97:021901.

CrossMark
Cite this: DOI: 10.1039/c4cp02133a

Structural skeleton of preferentially interpenetrated clusters and correlation with shear localization in Mg–Cu–Ni ternary metallic glasses

Q. Wang, J. H. Li, J. B. Liu and B. X. Liu*

Received 16th May 2014,
Accepted 25th June 2014

DOI: 10.1039/c4cp02133a

www.rsc.org/pccp

Inherent hierarchical structure and its effect on shear localization were clarified for ternary Mg–Cu–Ni metallic glasses *via* molecular dynamics studies based on a newly constructed *n*-body potential for the system. Assisted by a proposed index to detect the medium-range correlation heterogeneity, it was found that the Cu/Ni-centered icosahedra and specific Mg-centered clusters exhibit a strong preference to interconnect, leading to the formation, over an extended scale, of a percolated network that serves as structural skeleton in the glassy matrix. In constituting the skeleton network, the clusters mainly integrate in an interpenetrating mode, while the noninterpenetrating linkages provide additional reinforcements, jointly consolidating the structural and energetic stability of the skeleton. Furthermore, by monitoring the structural evolution upon compressive deformation, it was revealed that the gradual collapse of the skeleton network is intimately correlated to the mechanical response of metallic glasses and acts as a structural signature of the initiation and propagation of shear bands.

1. Introduction

The atomic-level structure and structure–property relationship of metallic glasses (MGs) has long been a significant issue in the fields of materials science and solid-state physics.[1,2] The lack of long-range orders in MGs, unlike their crystalline counterparts, has made it challenging to give a proper description on their structures, which, in turn, hinders elucidating their formation and properties down to the atomic scale and imposes restrictions on their further application. In recent decades, it has been revealed that the distinct atomic sizes and multiple chemical interactions among various types of atoms in MGs do result in the formation of short-range order (SRO), which could be characterized by the local arrangement of the nearest-neighboring atoms.[3–10] However, how these local clusters interconnect to achieve efficient packing nearly as densely as the crystalline solids remains a mystery,[1] and much effort has been made to unravel this higher hierarchy of order, *i.e.*, medium-range order (MRO).[11–18] Nonetheless, owing to the complexity and diversity of internal interactions in various alloy systems,[19] the packing details in the MRO, which are indeed system dependent and composition dependent, are still matters of live debate. More significantly, the percolation of clusters eventually leads to the formation, over an extended scale, of a spatial network that fulfills the real space. Despite the fact that the formation of the spatial network stems from the existence of MRO, this network has its own characteristics, such as spatial connectivity and distribution and this scale is beyond the scope of the MRO in the narrow sense.[20] Up till now, many fundamental issues regarding the development of the spatial network and its influence on the macroscopic behavior of MGs still remain to be elucidated, although recently, some enlightening studies have been conducted.[20–23] For instance, in Cu–Zr MGs, it was revealed that the interpenetrating linkages of icosahedra exhibit strong correlation in space[20] and tend to aggregate and form string-like networks.[22] These studies indicate that the clusters in MGs exhibit heterogeneous spatial correlations, *i.e.*, some clusters, such as icosahedra in Cu–Zr MGs, which have a strong tendency to interconnect and thus could form densely packed networks that are distinguished from the remaining regions that are relatively loosely packed. Moreover, it was found that the icosahedra networks formed in Cu–Zr MGs are resistant to shear softening[20] and have high elastic rigidities.[23] Therefore, resolving the characteristics of the spatial network is crucial to provide an explicit picture of the hierarchical structure in MGs and more significantly, to further clarify the structure–property relationships.

Concerning the spatial network in MGs, most of the previous studies have focussed on the icosahedra network in Cu–Zr-based MGs.[20,22–24] However, despite the fact that icosahedra have been revealed to be the principal building blocks in a number of MGs, they are not necessarily the only characteristic structural motifs that exert influence on the properties of a specific glassy alloy. For example, Peng *et al.*[4] showed that some solvent Zr-centered

Key Laboratory of Advanced Materials (MOE), School of Materials Science and Engineering, Tsinghua University, Beijing 100084, China.
E-mail: dmslbx@tsinghua.edu.cn; Fax: +86 10 6277 1160; Tel: +86 10 6277 2557

Physical Chemistry and Chemical Physics 16, p.19590-601 (2014).

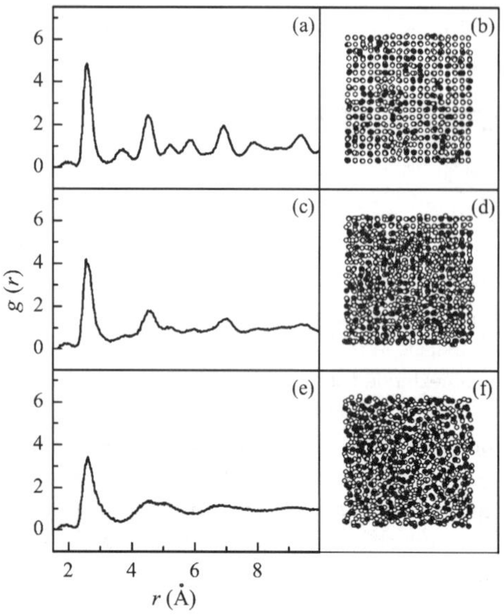

FIG. 1. (Color online) The projections of atomic positions and total pair-correlation functions $g(r)$ for (a, b) crystal state ($Cu_{85}Hf_{10}Al_5$), (c, d) transition state ($Cu_{80}Hf_{15}Al_5$), and (e, f) amorphous state ($Cu_{70}Hf_{25}Al_5$), respectively.

positions for the three states. From the figure, one sees that the $g(r)$ curves of the $Cu_{85}Hf_{10}Al_5$ feature apparent crystalline peaks in Fig. 1(a), exhibiting a long-range ordered feature. For the $g(r)$ curves of the $Cu_{80}Hf_{15}Al_5$, some crystalline peaks have disappeared, whereas some others still remain in Fig. 1(c), exhibiting an ordered-disordered coexisting feature. For the $g(r)$ curves of the $Cu_{70}Hf_{25}Al_5$, the crystalline peaks beyond the second peak have all disappeared in Fig. 1(e), exhibiting a short-range ordered and long-range disordered feature. Further inspecting Fig. 1, one can see that the projections of the atomic positions of the $Cu_{85}Hf_{10}Al_5$ show a completely ordered state and those of the $Cu_{70}Hf_{25}Al_5$ show a completely disordered state. For the $Cu_{80}Hf_{15}Al_5$, the locally ordered regions coexist with locally disordered regions, exhibiting an ordered-disordered coexisting state.

According to the pair-correlation function $g(r)$ and projections of atomic positions, the Cu-Hf-Al composition triangle is spilt into seven regions by six critical solubility lines, and a metallic glass forming composition diagram is constructed in Fig. 2. One can see from Fig. 2, when an alloy composition locates on the AB, EF, or IJ lines and moving towards one of the three corners, the crystalline structure can remain stable. These regions were consequently classified as the crystalline regions. When the composition of the alloy moves from the CD, GH, and KL lines towards the central hexagonal region enclosed by CDKLHG, the crystalline structure becomes unstable and would collapse and turn into a disordered state. This hexagonal region was defined as the region favoring for metallic glass formation. Between the crystalline regions and the amorphous regions, there are ordered-disordered coexisting state regions, within which the initial solid solutions would transform into a state featuring with an ordered-disordered coexisting structure. To validate the metallic glass region in Fig. 2, experimental results were collected and marked by red solid circles,[1–3,10–14] which

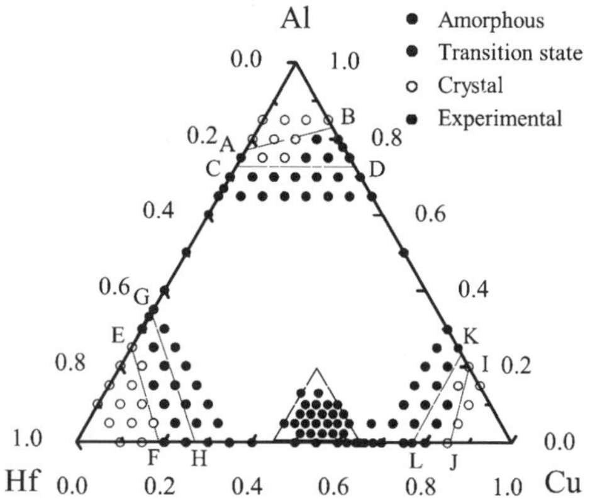

FIG. 2. (Color online) The glass forming composition diagram derived from MD simulations for the Cu-Hf-Al system.

mostly fall within the hexagonal region, suggesting that the prediction by MD simulations is acceptable in determining the GFR/GFA of the Cu-Hf-Al system.

Further inspecting Fig. 2, one can find that the experimentally measured glass formation compositions densely gather in a small triangular area with the composition of $Cu_xHf_yAl_{100-x-y}$ ($x=45\sim65$, $y=35\sim55$).[1–3,10–14] The experimental results seem to suggest that the optimized composition of the Cu-Hf-Al metallic glass could be within this composition area; however, it would be rather time-consuming to experimentally determine the exact optimized composition point by point. From a thermodynamic point of view, the formation enthalpy difference between the Cu-Hf-Al amorphous phase and its crystalline solid solution counterpart could be considered as the driving force for metallic glass formation.[5] The energy difference can be written as $\Delta H^{am-s.s}=\Delta H^{am}-\Delta H^{s.s}$, where ΔH^{am} is the formation enthalpy of amorphous phase and $\Delta H^{s.s}$ is the formation enthalpy for solid solutions. The larger the formation enthalpy difference, the stronger the driving force for the metallic glass formation. In other words, the optimized metallic glass forming composition is defined as the one, at which the $\Delta H^{am-s.s}$ reaches its maximum value. ΔH^{am} has been calculated through the MD results in the previous section. For $\Delta H^{s.s}$, it could be calculated by an efficient and relevant scheme proposed by Dai *et al.* through molecular statics (MS) calculations.[15] The details of the calculations of the driving force can be referred to our recently published paper.[16]

The driving force of metallic glass formation for the compositions of $Cu_xHf_yAl_{100-x-y}$ ($x=45\sim65$, $y=35\sim55$) was plotted in Fig. 3. One sees that $\Delta H^{am-s.s}$ is negative over the whole calculated area, suggesting that ΔH^{am} is lower than $\Delta H^{s.s}$, meaning that the formation of metallic glasses is energetically favored within this area. Moreover, one can find that the compositions marked by red dots have lower $\Delta H^{am-s.s}$ than other calculated points, and the $Cu_{48}Hf_{41}Al_{11}$ composition marked by a black circle has the lowest $\Delta H^{am-s.s}$, suggesting that the locally optimized compositions for metallic glass formation can be pinpointed around $Cu_{48}Hf_{41}Al_{11}$. From a physical viewpoint, the predicted amorphous region and optimized composition are calculated where E_i is the total potential energy of atom i, ϕ and ψ are here called the pair term and density term, respectively. r_{m1} and r_{m2} are the knots of the pair and density terms, and r_{c1} and r_{c2} are the cutoff radii for the pair and density terms, respectively. n_1 and n_2 are two indices, which should not be less than 3 and 5, respectively, so that there would be no discontinuity of the high derivatives of the interatomic potential. A_1, p_1, A_{1m}, p_{1m} and A_2, p_2, A_{2m}, p_{2m} are another eight potential parameters. From the form of the truncation functions expressed in eqn (2) and (3), one can clearly see that the pair and density terms as well as their high derivatives can continuously and smoothly approach zero at the cutoff radii r_{c1} and r_{c2}, respectively, thus removing the 'jumps' of total energy and some non-physical behavior in the simulations. In order to totally avoid the discontinuity of energy, pressure and force in the whole calculated range, the pair and density terms should be smoothed, and their first derivatives should be continuous at the transitional knots r_{m1} and r_{m1} when fitting the potential parameters.

For the Mg–Cu–Ni system, there should be six sets of potential parameters, *i.e.*, three sets for Cu–Cu, Mg–Mg and Ni–Ni, and three sets for Mg–Cu, Mg–Ni and Cu–Ni. The potential parameters of Cu–Cu, Mg–Mg and Ni–Ni were determined by fitting to the lattice constants, cohesive energies, elastic constants and bulk moduli of the Mg, Cu and Ni elements.[48–50] The Mg–Cu, Mg–Ni and Cu–Ni cross potentials were constructed by fitting to the physical properties, *i.e.*, the lattice constants, formation energies and bulk moduli of the stable or virtual intermetallic compounds within each of the binary systems, such as *cF*24-Cu_2Mg, *oF*48-$CuMg_2$ and so on. As there is not much available data for the related compounds, *ab initio* calculations using the Cambridge serial total energy package (CASTEP)[51,52] based on the density functional theory (DFT) were conducted by the present authors to derive the necessary physical properties of the compounds. During the *ab initio* calculations, the exchange–correlation energy functional was described by the well-established Perdew–Wang (PW91) version of the generalized gradient approximation (GGA),[53,54] and the ion–electron interactions were treated by the projector augmented wave (PAW) method[55] with $2p^6 3s^2$ valence electrons for Mg, $3d^{10} 4s^1$ for Cu, and $3d^8 4s^2$ for Ni, respectively. The cutoff energy was chosen to be 480.0 eV, and the Brillouin zone was sampled using the Monkhorst–Pack method[56] with nearly constant *k*-point densities for each calculation, roughly equivalent to a 12 × 12 × 12 mesh for a conventional fcc unit cell. These parameters have been tested to be sufficient for the convergence of calculation for the structures in this work.

Now we present the detailed fitting results of the Mg–Cu–Ni interatomic potential. The six sets of potential parameters are summarized in Table 1. Table 2 gives the fitted and experimental[48–50] lattice constants, cohesion energies, elastic constants and bulk moduli of the Mg, Cu, and Ni elements. Table 3 lists the lattice constants, formation energies and bulk moduli of the related compounds reproduced by the potential, in comparison with the corresponding *ab initio* derived results.

Table 1 Fitted parameters of the interatomic potential for the Mg–Cu–Ni system. A_1 and A_{1m} are expressed in eV, A_2 and A_{2m} are expressed in eV^2, r_{m1}, r_{c1}, r_{m2}, r_{c2} and r_0 are expressed in Å

	Mg	Cu	Ni	Mg–Cu	Mg–Ni	Cu–Ni
p_1	10.37307	9.625372	11.08757	7.831151	13.04967	9.787880
A_1	0.145780	0.315491	0.287580	0.257021	0.131361	0.287804
r_{m1}	3.522308	2.124148	1.976092	2.100661	2.961980	1.961680
n_1	4	4	4	4	4	4
p_{1m}	3.850843	2.860823	4.485833	3.867485	1.049777	3.348093
A_{1m}	0.538535	8.049825	8.372519	0.723304	6.578130	8.099770
r_{c1}	5.487015	3.634148	3.486092	5.005640	3.911276	3.528742
p_2	4.375061	4.903930	3.669412	3.735459	4.697471	4.820816
A_2	0.951887	3.854734	4.991288	2.685112	3.000155	4.215374
r_{m2}	2.588516	3.611361	2.803510	2.555986	3.271223	3.583014
n_2	5	5	5	5	5	5
p_{2m}	0.000378	0.000602	0.000695	0.000781	0.000653	0.000601
A_{2m}	1.130393	0.458708	0.671240	0.948748	1.091632	0.463089
r_{c2}	6.250000	6.215324	6.200000	6.409856	6.302914	6.200000
r_0	3.203567	2.553618	2.492155	2.878592	2.847861	2.522886

Table 2 Fitted and experimental properties[48–50] of the Mg, Cu, and Ni elements. Lattice constants *a* and *c* are expressed in Å, cohesive energies E_c in eV per atom, elastic constants C_{ij} and bulk moduli B_0 in Mbar

	hcp-Mg		fcc-Cu		fcc-Ni	
	Fitted	Exp.	Fitted	Exp.	Fitted	Exp.
a	3.209	3.209	3.611	3.615	3.524	3.517
c	5.235	5.211				
E_c	1.508	1.510	3.502	3.490	4.423	4.440
C_{11}	0.591	0.595	1.688	1.683	2.385	2.418
C_{12}	0.270	0.261	1.225	1.221	1.630	1.550
C_{13}	0.223	0.218				
C_{33}	0.642	0.616				
C_{44}	0.112	0.164	0.745	0.757	1.217	1.242
B_0	0.362	0.354	1.361	1.370	1.882	1.860

It can be seen from Tables 2 and 3 that the physical properties obtained by the potential match quite well with the experimental results or *ab initio* calculations. In the fitting process, the first derivative of the energy and the remnant stress of the fitted structures are very small, *i.e.*, less than 10^{-6} Mbar, indicating that the fitted structures are very close to their equilibrium states.

To further evaluate the relevance of the constructed potential for describing the atomic interactions under non-equilibrium conditions, the equation of state (EOS) was derived from the potential and then compared with the frequently used EOS in this field, *i.e.*, the Rose equation, which has been considered to be universal for all categories of solids.[57] Note that the EOSs have not been applied in the fitting process. The EOSs of hcp-Mg, fcc-Cu, fcc-Ni, B2-CuMg, B2-NiMg and B2-CuNi were derived from the potential and are exhibited in Fig. 1(a)–(f), respectively, together with the corresponding Rose equations. From Fig. 1, one can see that the total energies of these structures are smooth and continuous over the entire range without any 'jumps' or discontinuities, and the EOSs derived from the proposed potential agree well with the corresponding Rose equations, indicating that the constructed Mg–Cu–Ni potential could be applied to describe the atomic interactions of the system even far from the equilibrium state.

Table 3 Potential reproduced (first line) and *ab initio* derived properties (second line) of the Mg–Cu, Mg–Ni and Cu–Ni compounds. Lattice constants *a* and *c* are expressed in Å, cohesive energies E_c in eV per atom, and bulk moduli B_0 in Mbar

Compounds	Mg_2Cu	MgCu	$MgCu_2$	Mg_3Ni	MgNi	$MgNi_3$	$MgNi_3$	$CuNi_3$	CuNi	Cu_3Ni
Space group	*Fddd*	$Pm\bar{3}m$	$Fd\bar{3}m$	$F\bar{4}3m$	$Pm\bar{3}m$	$Pm\bar{3}m$	$F\bar{4}3m$	$Pm\bar{3}m$	$Pm\bar{3}m$	$Pm\bar{3}m$
a or *a*, *c* or *a*, *b*, *c*	9.156, 5.333, 18.55	3.194	7.118	6.673	3.120	3.724	5.930	3.557	2.778	3.547
	9.037, 5.304, 18.36	3.159	7.048	6.562	3.056	3.658	5.817	3.554	2.806	3.607
E_c	2.291	2.595	2.984	2.277	3.161	3.816	3.781	4.192	3.907	3.728
	2.292	2.594	2.984	2.277	3.161	3.819	3.782	4.191	3.980	3.727
B_0	0.497	0.532	0.806	0.609	1.078	1.506	1.424	1.716	1.514	1.539
	0.540	0.698	0.954	0.594	0.889	1.367	1.366	1.839	1.656	1.535

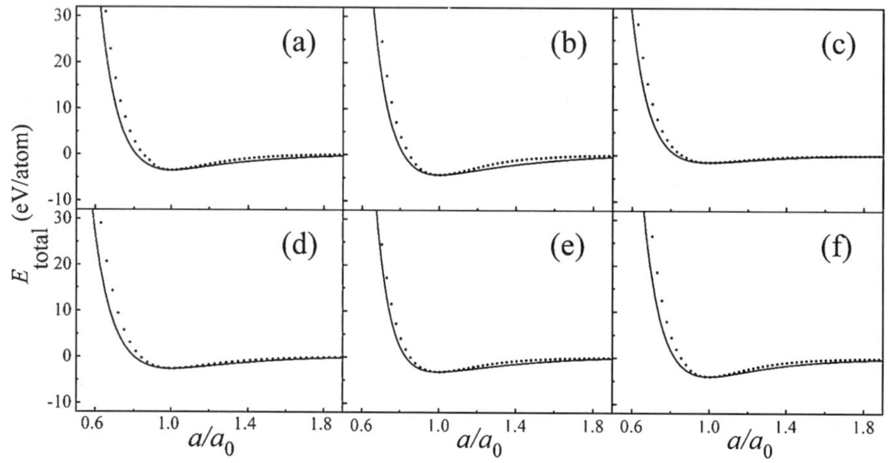

Fig. 1 Equations of state (EOSs) calculated from the constructed potential (solid lines) and Rose equation (dotted lines) for (a) fcc-Cu, (b) fcc-Ni, (c) hcp-Mg, (d) B2-CuMg, (e) B2-NiMg, and (f) B2-CuNi.

2.2. Preparation of metallic glasses

In the present study, the $Mg_{60}Cu_{17}Ni_{23}$ MG was selected as a principal model alloy. Recently, $Mg_{60}Cu_{17}Ni_{23}$ was found to be an optimized stoichiometry in the Mg–Cu–Ni system, at which the amorphization driving force, which is defined as the energy difference between the amorphous state *versus* that of the competing crystalline solid solution counterpart, reaches its maximum, suggesting that the $Mg_{60}Cu_{17}Ni_{23}$ MG could be quite obtainable and stable.[44] In addition, for discussion of the structure and its effect on the properties, another MG, *i.e.*, $Mg_{70}Cu_{13}Ni_{17}$, which deviates from the optimized stoichiometry and has a relatively lower amorphization driving force, was employed as a reference alloy.

Applying the constructed Mg–Cu–Ni potential, molecular dynamics (MD) simulations were then conducted to derive the unambiguous configurations of the two MGs, *i.e.*, $Mg_{60}Cu_{17}Ni_{23}$ and $Mg_{70}Cu_{13}Ni_{17}$. Simulations were performed on the three-dimensional cubic boxes with 23 328 atoms arranged in a volume of about 7.3 × 7.3 × 7.3 nm^3, with periodic boundary conditions (PBCs) applied in all three Cartesian dimensions. The Nose–Hoover barostat and thermostat were used to control the pressure and temperature, respectively. Under simulation, the systems were firstly heated from 300 K to 2300 K at a rate of 5×10^{10} K s^{-1} and then equilibrated at 2300 K for 1 ns, which was supposed to be long enough to equilibrate the melts. The melts were then quenched from 2300 K back to 300 K at the same rate of 5×10^{10} K s^{-1}, then equilibrated at 300 K for 1 ns, and the ultimate configurations of the $Mg_{60}Cu_{17}Ni_{23}$ and $Mg_{70}Cu_{13}Ni_{17}$ MGs were obtained.

The MD-derived three-dimensional configuration of $Mg_{60}Cu_{17}Ni_{23}$ is displayed in Fig. 2. To give a general structural description of $Mg_{60}Cu_{17}Ni_{23}$, the partial pair-correlation functions, $g_{ij}(r)$s (i, j = Mg, Cu, or Ni), were calculated and are shown in Fig. 2. The $g_{ij}(r)$s curves are characterized by a prominent first peak and a diffuse second peak that shows a tendency to split with a shoulder, demonstrating the amorphous character of the MG structures. To further quantitatively reveal the coordinating features of all six types of atom pairs, the position of the first peak, r_{ij}, was extracted from each $g_{ij}(r)$ and listed in Table 4. The corresponding nominal metallic and covalent bond distances which summate the metallic[58] and covalent[59] atomic radii for all the pairs are also exhibited in Table 4 for comparison. It can be seen from Table 4 that the bond lengths in $Mg_{60}Cu_{17}Ni_{23}$ are generally shorter than the nominal metallic bond distances. Similar results were also established in other studies, indicating that the bond lengths in the amorphous or liquid alloys are shorter than the arithmetic sum of the respective atomic radii.[7,13,43,60] This is correlated with the densification of atomic packing in the amorphous state and the negative mixing enthalpy between the specific constituent elements.

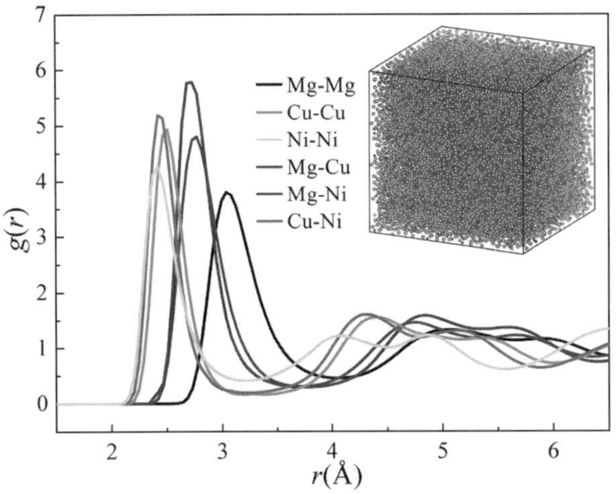

Fig. 2 Partial pair-correlation functions, $g_{ij}(r)$s, between the Mg, Cu, and Ni atom pairs for the $Mg_{60}Cu_{17}Ni_{23}$ MG. The inset displays the three-dimensional configuration of $Mg_{60}Cu_{17}Ni_{23}$ derived by MD simulations employing the constructed Mg-Cu-Ni *n*-body potential. The Mg, Cu, and Ni atoms are colored purple, orange and green, respectively.

Table 4 Positions of the first peak, r_{ij}, extracted from the partial pair-correlation functions, $g_{ij}(r)$s, between the Mg, Cu, and Ni atom pairs in $Mg_{60}Cu_{17}Ni_{23}$. These distances are compared with the corresponding metallic,[58] r_m, and covalent,[59] r_c, bond distances. All the distances are expressed in Å

	Mg–Mg	Mg–Cu	Mg–Ni	Cu–Cu	Cu–Ni	Ni–Ni
r_{ij}	3.08	2.76	2.71	2.50	2.45	2.41
r_m	3.20	2.88	2.84	2.56	2.52	2.48
r_c	2.82	2.73	2.65	2.64	2.56	2.48

2.3. Uniaxial compression test

The uniaxial compressive tests that are commonly used in laboratory experiments were employed in the present study to elucidate the influence of the spatial network on the mechanical properties of MGs, particularly the shear banding behavior. In order to investigate the inhomogeneous process of shear banding, considerably larger samples should be constructed to be able to accommodate the shear bands with typical widths of the order of 5–20 nm. In the present study, large slab samples of the $Mg_{60}Cu_{17}Ni_{23}$ and $Mg_{70}Cu_{13}Ni_{17}$ MGs with dimensions of about 51.2(*X*) × 25.6(*Y*) × 5.1(*Z*) nm^3 containing ~370 000 atoms were constructed by replication of a small box with ~7400 atoms. The samples were then annealed at 500 K for 1 ns and cooled to 50 K at a rate of 5×10^{10} K s^{-1} by MD simulations. During the compression tests, the *X* axis was the loading direction. The strain was applied homogenously throughout the sample at 50 K with a constant strain rate of 5×10^7 s^{-1}. PBCs were imposed in both the *X*- and *Z*-directions. Free surfaces were used in the *Y*-direction in order to allow shear offset to take place. The Nose–Hoover barostat and thermostat were applied to control the pressure and temperature, respectively. A low temperature of 50 K was applied to highlight the inhomogeneous deformation of the samples upon mechanical activation, as the computer quenched MG structure is more prone to thermal activations than real-world MGs which have experienced much more extended relaxation.[28,29]

3. Local atomic arrangements in the short-range

The local atomic arrangements, *i.e.*, short-range orders (SROs), in the model alloy $Mg_{60}Cu_{17}Ni_{23}$ were characterized as a preliminary step of structure characterization. The Voronoi tessellation method,[61] which is frequently applied to scrutinize the SROs in liquid and glassy structures, was employed. Specifically, a convex Voronoi polyhedron around the center atom is wrapped by the inner planes bisecting the lines connecting the central atom and all its neighboring atoms, and could be indexed as $\langle n_3, n_4, n_5, n_6, \ldots \rangle$, where n_i denotes the number of *i*-edged faces on the surface of this polyhedron. Each Voronoi polyhedron is embedded in a corresponding Voronoi cluster which is made up of the central atom connecting all its neighboring atoms. In this work, cell faces with less than 5% of the average face area were neglected to minimize the degeneracy problem and thermal vibration effects.[13,62]

Fig. 3(a)–(c) display the fractions of the prevalent Voronoi clusters centered with Cu, Ni, and Mg, respectively, in $Mg_{60}Cu_{17}Ni_{23}$. As exhibited in Fig. 3(a), the most populated clusters around Cu are revealed to be full icosahedra ⟨0,0,12,0⟩, followed by the slightly distorted ones such as ⟨0,2,8,2⟩ and ⟨0,3,6,4⟩. The latter sorts of clusters have 11–13 nearest-neighbors and a high percentage of five-fold coordinated vertices, making them similar to the full icosahedra and thus could be classified as icosahedra-like clusters.[15] Meanwhile, the four-fold and six-fold disclinations[63] in these icosahedra-like clusters also complement the five-fold symmetry to relieve the packing frustration.[2] Comparatively, among the Ni-centered Voronoi clusters, the population of full icosahedra ⟨0,0,12,0⟩ also ranks topmost and one can see from Fig. 3(a) and Fig. 3(b) that the fraction of Ni-centered icosahedra (~24.3%) is higher than that of the Cu-centered icosahedra (~16.1%), indicating a more centralized distribution of SROs around Ni. In contrast to the prevailing icosahedral or icosahedral-like packing around Cu and Ni, the SROs around Mg are more adaptable and diverse, of which the ⟨0,2,8,5⟩, ⟨0,2,8,4⟩ and ⟨0,1,10,4⟩ clusters with CNs of 14 and 15 are the most populated ones yet still cover relatively small fractions. Given their major concentration and larger atomic radii, the Mg atoms are supposed to serve as major neighbors for the Cu and Ni atoms and also act as 'glue' for the glassy structure in the Mg-rich MGs.[15,18] Thus it is plausible to expect that the Cu and Ni atoms could more readily develop the favored local environments at their preference, to be icosahedral packed in this case, while comparatively, the Mg atoms would experience more flexible local environments. Meanwhile, the larger atomic radii of the Mg atoms also permits more atoms to be accommodated in their nearest-neighboring shells and lead to larger CNs of 14–16.

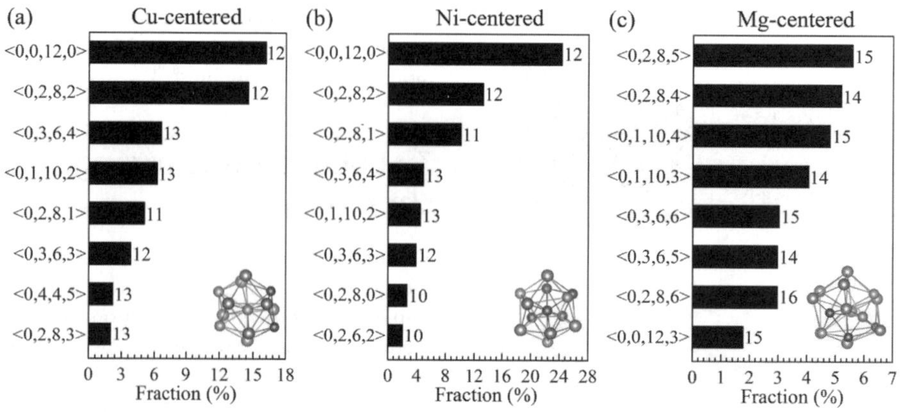

Fig. 3 Fractions of the most prevalent Voronoi clusters around (a) Cu, (b) Ni, and (c) Mg, respectively, in $Mg_{60}Cu_{17}Ni_{23}$. The insets exhibit typical configurations of the Cu-centered ⟨0,0,12,0⟩, Ni-centered ⟨0,0,12,0⟩ and Mg-centered ⟨0,2,8,5⟩ clusters, respectively. The Mg, Cu, and Ni atoms are colored in purple, orange and green, respectively.

4. Cluster correlation heterogeneity in the medium-range

Characterizing the SRO details alone and neglecting the heterogeneous correlations of various types of clusters that extend to medium-range and beyond is insufficient to account for the structure–property relationship of MGs. Moreover, the correlation heterogeneity among clusters in the medium-range is the direct cause of the contrast between the dense and loose regions in the global glassy structure. Therefore, it is crucial to develop an effective method capable of detecting the correlation heterogeneity of the enormous number of types of clusters in MGs.

Concerning this critical issue, Li *et al.*[22] proposed a nearest-neighboring correlation index $C_{ij} = \sqrt{p_{ij}/p_{ij}^{0} - 1}$ to evaluate the preference and avoidance of cluster type i and j being nearest-neighbors. By definition, C_{ij} is equal to C_{ji}, therefore it does not discriminate between the neighboring preference of the cluster type i towards type j *versus* conversely the neighboring preference of the cluster type j towards type i. In the present study, we have developed a new cluster correlation index (CCI), χ_{ij}, with a very straightforward physical meaning, to depict the neighboring preference of cluster type i towards type j,

$$\chi_{ij} = \frac{N_{ij}}{N_i x_j} - 1 \tag{4}$$

where N_{ij} is the number of neighboring pairs between cluster type i and j, N_i is the number of neighboring pairs that cluster type i participates in, and x_j is the nominal fraction of cluster type j. Here the clusters are considered to be neighbors only when they are connected in an interpenetrating mode, namely *via* TS linkages. Note that χ_{ij} is not necessarily equal to χ_{ij}, thereby enabling the respective neighboring preference to be distinguished and more structural information to be obtained. A positive χ_{ij} means that neighboring with cluster type *j* is favored for type i, a negative χ_{ij} denotes a repulsive-like interaction for type j around type i, and a $\chi_{ij} \sim 0$ indicates a random packing behavior.

Fig. 4 shows the matrix of χ_{ij} for the 9 types of most frequent Voronoi clusters in $Mg_{60}Cu_{17}Ni_{23}$. The horizontal grid displays the preference of one specific cluster type to be neighbored with all 9 types of clusters, while the vertical grid can overall reflect the neighboring popularity of the specific cluster type. One can see from Fig. 4 that the packing mode in $Mg_{60}Cu_{17}Ni_{23}$ deviates greatly from the random packing mode, exhibiting a large extent of heterogeneity in MRO. As exhibited in Fig. 4, the full icosahedra ⟨0,0,12,0⟩ centered with either Cu or Ni have a large positive χ_{ij} with each other, showing a strong tendency to interconnect and aggregate, thus forming chains and networks. This finding agrees with the previous studies on the icosahedra network in Cu–Zr MGs.[4,22] Moreover, interestingly, while the Cu/Ni-centered icosahedra exhibit no particular preference and even avoidance to interconnect with the other types of Cu- and Ni-centered clusters, they exhibit a relatively strong preference to be neighbored with the Mg-centered ⟨0,2,8,5⟩ and ⟨0,1,10,4⟩

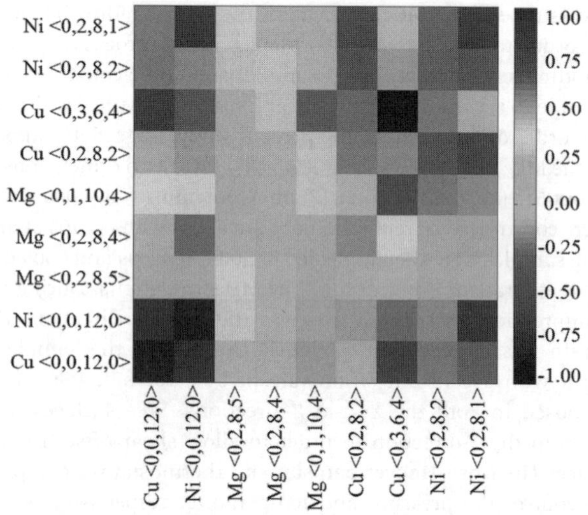

Fig. 4 Matrix of the newly proposed cluster correlation index (CCI) χ_{ij} for the 9 most frequent Voronoi clusters in $Mg_{60}Cu_{17}Ni_{23}$.

clusters. This indicates that the solvent Mg-centered clusters, especially the above pentagon-rich ones, indeed contribute largely to the connectivity enhancement of the solute-centered clusters,[4] and therefore, their roles should not be eliminated.

As stated above, in the previous studies of transition-metal-based MGs, such as the Cu–Zr MGs, icosahedra are often employed as the sole principal motifs in discussion of the glassy structure. From the CCI analysis, it is found that the structure of $Mg_{60}Cu_{17}Ni_{23}$ should not be simply pictured as being composed of interpenetrating icosahedra, and the roles of other clusters, especially that of the above Mg-centered clusters, should be taken into account as well. Accordingly, as the Cu/Ni-centered ⟨0,0,12,0⟩ and the Mg-centered ⟨0,2,8,5⟩, ⟨0,1,10,4⟩ clusters exhibit prominent preference to interconnect, they could be the effective participants of the dense network in $Mg_{60}Cu_{17}Ni_{23}$. The clustering trend of the small-sized solute-centered and large-sized solvent-centered clusters could also contribute to the efficient filling of space and the enhancement of structural stability.[18]

5. Structural skeleton in the extended scale

The percolated network formed among the preferentially interconnected clusters in $Mg_{60}Cu_{17}Ni_{23}$, *i.e.*, Cu/Ni-centered ⟨0,0,12,0⟩ and Mg-centered ⟨0,2,8,5⟩, ⟨0,1,10,4⟩ clusters, was analyzed in this section. In Fig. 5, the network of these clusters in $Mg_{60}Cu_{17}Ni_{23}$ is presented. Only the interpenetrating linkages, *i.e.*, the tetrahedra sharing (TS) linkages among the clusters are displayed. The isolated and dimerized clusters are not presented. One can see that the cross-linking degree of the network is very high. This network stretches in space and could serve as 'structural skeleton' in the glassy matrix. Here the network is termed as the structural skeleton in order to distinguish it from the relatively loose matrix that fills in the remaining space. The structural skeleton, interpenetrating in the real space, steps into the next level of structural hierarchy that exceeds beyond the medium-range in the narrow sense.

The above CCI analysis in Section 4 only considers the interpenetrating linkages, *i.e.*, the TS linkages, and one can see from Fig. 5 that these clusters are indeed well percolated in an interpenetrating mode, forming chains and patches. Furthermore, in addition to the interpenetrating linkages, there are also some other types of noninterpenetrating linkages that could contribute to the MRO and beyond, *i.e.*, the vertex (VS), edge (ES) and face (FS) linkages. It is thus of interest to explore the respective roles of these various types of linkages in forming the structural skeleton. By analyzing the configuration of the skeleton network in $Mg_{60}Cu_{17}Ni_{23}$, the respective fractions of the VS, ES, FS and TS linkages were calculated and are exhibited in Fig. 6. It can be seen from Fig. 6 that the TS linkages are the most frequent, despite the VS linkages also covering a large fraction. Considering that each TS linkage involves at least four common atoms and constrains the degree of freedom to the largest extent, the allocation of equal weight in the numeration would exaggerate the roles of other types of linkages, such as the VS linkage which requires only one common atom to form. Further analysis indicates that over 90% of the preferentially interconnected clusters in $Mg_{60}Cu_{17}Ni_{23}$ could be linked with other clusters merely in the TS way and only the remaining isolated clusters need the help of other types of cluster linkages to be attached to the skeleton, thus indicating that the TS

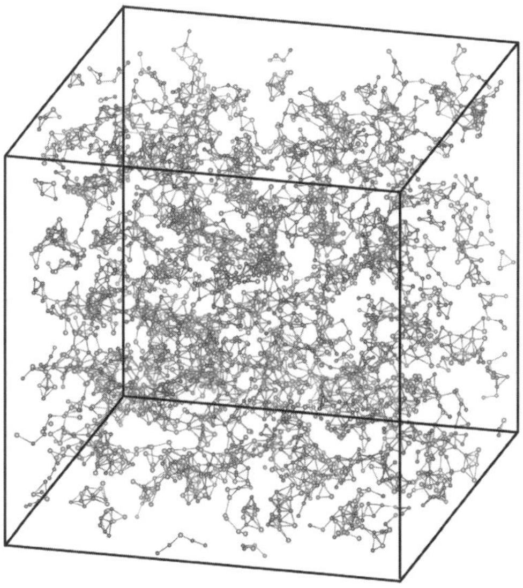

Fig. 5 The percolated network in $Mg_{60}Cu_{17}Ni_{23}$ formed through interpenetrating, *i.e.*, TS linkages (denoted by the solid bicolor lines) between the preferentially interconnected Cu-centered ⟨0,0,12,0⟩ (orange), Ni-centered ⟨0,0,12,0⟩ (green) and Mg-centered ⟨0,2,8,5⟩, ⟨0,1,10,4⟩ (purple) clusters. Only the central atoms of the clusters are plotted as points for a clear illustration. Isolated and dimerized clusters are eliminated from the presentation.

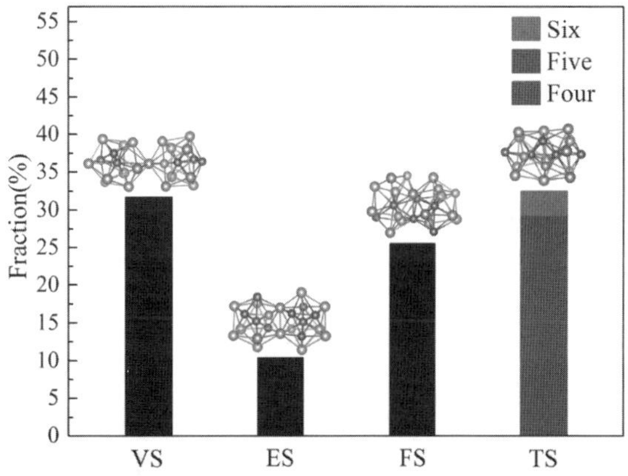

Fig. 6 Fractions of the four types of linkages for the preferentially interconnected Cu/Ni-centered ⟨0,0,12,0⟩ and Mg-centered ⟨0,2,8,5⟩, ⟨0,1,10,4⟩ clusters in $Mg_{60}Cu_{17}Ni_{23}$. VS (vertex sharing), ES (edge sharing), FS (face sharing), and TS (tetrahedra sharing) represent the four typical linking schemes. The TS scheme is further broken down into three categories depending on the number of common atoms between the clusters, *i.e.*, four, five and six. The insets are typical configurations of the four linkages extracted from the glassy structure. The Mg, Cu, and Ni atoms are colored in purple, orange and green, respectively.

linkages indeed play a dominating role in connecting these clusters. As the TS mode is revealed to be the most energetically favored[20] and structurally stable[23] of all the four types of cluster linkages, the major role of the TS linkages indicates the favorable energetic status and stable configuration of these clusters, which is a pre-requisite for the formation of the structural skeleton. Meanwhile, Fig. 6 also indicates that the sharing of five common neighbors, with a local five-fold symmetry, is dominant among the TS linked clusters. It could be inferred that the five-fold symmetry in the local sites would prepare the local environments to be strongly incompatible for crystalline-like four-fold or six-fold symmetry to occur, and thus facilitates the mutual connection between the pentagon-rich clusters. This finding indicates that spatial connection in the medium-range and beyond tends to be achieved by linking up favored motifs with polyhedral packing (triangulated faces and five-fold bonds), which appears to be a striking feature in many categories of MGs, and specifically, in this case, for the Mg–Cu–Ni MGs, the extension is realized *via* connection of the preferentially interconnected Cu/Ni-centered and Mg-centered Kasper-type clusters, rather than by sole connection of the icosahedra.[20,22]

Despite the fact that the VS, ES and FS linkages are not crucial for connection of these preferentially interconnected clusters, the interpenetrated network formed would undoubtedly be strengthened by these noninterpenetrating linkages. Even though most of the clusters are connected to other clusters and form densely packed patches, the fact that the five-fold symmetry is incompatible with long-range periodicity would inevitably result in 'occasional' discontinuity[20] among these patches, hindering the formation of a fully interconnected network that extends throughout the entire sample, and herein the noninterpenetrating linkages would come into play. These noninterpenetrating linkages build 'pinning' and 'bridging' connections among the discrete patches and contribute to the unification of the network.[25] Therefore, it could be revealed that in forming the structural skeleton, the clusters mainly integrate in an interpenetrating mode, while the noninterpenetrating linkages provide additional reinforcements, thereby jointly consolidating the structural and energetic stability of the skeleton. The relationship between the interpenetrating linkage, *i.e.*, the TS linkage, and the noninterpenetrating linkages, *i.e.*, the VS, ES and FS linkages is in some sense similar to the 'chemical bond' *versus* the 'intermolecular force' relationship for atoms, and just the atomic interactions turn into the cluster interactions, namely the TS linkage represents the strongest cluster interaction, while the VS, ES and FS linkages behave as relatively weaker interactions. The various cluster interactions function collectively to achieve the stabilized and efficient filling of space.

To give a complete picture of the hierarchical structure in the Mg–Cu–Ni MGs, the configurations in the short-range, medium-range, and further in the extended scale of the structural skeleton are illustrated in Fig. 7(a)–(c), respectively. The coordination mode in the short-range is exhibited by a typical Ni-centered ⟨0,0,12,0⟩ icosahedra in Fig. 7(a). The packing mode in the medium-range is exhibited by a nano-scale super-cluster formed by the neighboring clusters in Fig. 7(b). For the connection mode of the structural skeleton in the extended scale, a typical cross-linked patch containing 55 clusters is extracted from the $Mg_{60}Cu_{17}Ni_{23}$ MG and exhibited in Fig. 7(c). The four types of linkages, *i.e.*, VS, ES, FS and TS, between the clusters are all displayed in Fig. 7(c) to reveal how they are collectively hybridized together. It can be seen that the clusters in the

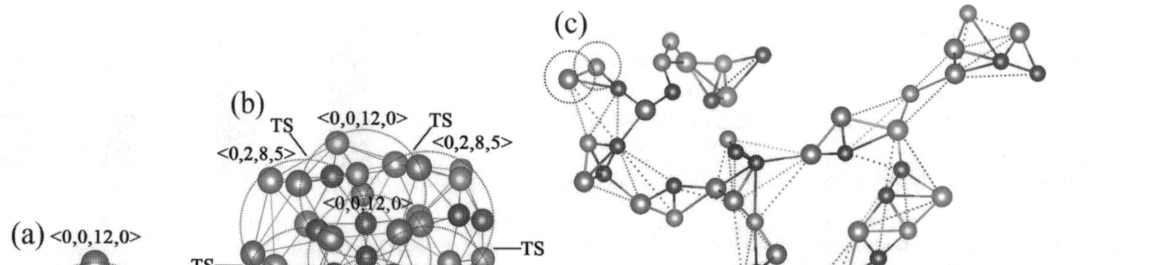

Fig. 7 Hierarchical configurations in $Mg_{60}Cu_{17}Ni_{23}$, *i.e.*, from SRO, MRO to the structural skeleton in the extended scale. (a) The coordination mode in the short-range is exhibited by a typical Ni-centered ⟨0,0,12,0⟩ icosahedra that designates the local environment. (b) The packing mode in the medium-range is exhibited by a super-cluster in the nanometer scale formed among the neighboring clusters. The Mg, Cu, and Ni atoms are colored purple, orange and green, respectively. (c) The connection mode of the structural skeleton in the extended scale is revealed by a cross-linked patch containing 55 clusters. These clusters are mainly extended in the interpenetrating mode, *i.e.*, TS linkage (denoted by the solid bicolor lines) and additionally strengthened by the VS, ES and FS linkages (denoted by the dotted lines with different colors and spacings). In (c), only the central atoms of the Cu-centered ⟨0,0,12,0⟩ (orange), Ni-centered ⟨0,0,12,0⟩ (green), and Mg-centered ⟨0,2,8,5⟩, ⟨0,1,10,4⟩ (purple) clusters are plotted as points for a clear demonstration, and the red dotted circles illustrate the hidden nearest-neighboring atoms around the central atoms.

presented patch are mainly chained by the TS linkages in an interpenetrating way, while the VS, ES, FS linkages contribute by reinforcing the skeleton network formed. The formation of the densely packed skeleton network that extends in the glassy matrix could exert a considerable effect on the macroscopic properties of the MGs.

6. Structural signature of shear localization

The mechanical properties of MGs are highly dependent on their internal structures. However, due to the wide span of time- and length-scales involved in the mechanical deformation,[32] it is rather difficult to establish the correlation between the macroscopic property and the microscopic structure of MGs. In the present study, large scale MD simulations were conducted to investigate the mechanical deformation of the Mg–Cu–Ni MGs and to further relate it to the internal structures. The $Mg_{60}Cu_{17}Ni_{23}$ was also employed as a principal model alloy. Moreover, as the MG structure is very sensitive to the alloy composition, another Mg-rich alloy, *i.e.*, $Mg_{70}Cu_{13}Ni_{17}$, was selected as a reference alloy,[44] as mentioned in Section 2.1, to examine the presence of structural skeletons in various Mg–Cu–Ni MGs and further explore their effect on the mechanical behavior.

The configuration of the $Mg_{70}Cu_{13}Ni_{17}$ MG was derived by liquid quenching using the MD simulation procedures introduced in Section 2.2. The skeleton network of the Cu/Ni-centered ⟨0,0,12,0⟩ and Mg-centered ⟨0,2,8,5⟩, ⟨0,1,10,4⟩ clusters in $Mg_{70}Cu_{13}Ni_{17}$ was then extracted and is exhibited in Fig. 8(a). Only the interpenetrating linkages, *i.e.*, the TS linkages between the clusters are displayed and the monomers and dimers are excluded from the diagram. Referring back to Fig. 6, one can see that the skeleton network in $Mg_{70}Cu_{13}Ni_{17}$ is less developed and interpenetrated than that in $Mg_{60}Cu_{17}Ni_{23}$. In order to quantitatively characterize the different degree of the skeleton networks in these two MGs, their respective connectivities were further analyzed in terms of bond number (N)[13] and the results are presented in Fig. 8(b). It can be seen that the population of the isolated clusters (N = 0) in $Mg_{70}Cu_{13}Ni_{17}$ is higher, while in $Mg_{60}Cu_{17}Ni_{23}$ not only have more clusters participated in the formation of the skeleton network but the cross-linking degree is also higher. This is because when the Mg content increases to 70%, the amount of ⟨0,0,12,0⟩ icosahedra experiences a severe decrease and gives away to the distorted ones such as ⟨0,2,8,2⟩ and ⟨0,2,8,1⟩ clusters, eventually leading to a lower degree of the skeleton network. Similar results have been reported by Ding *et al.*,[64] which indicated that when the effective size ratio changes, by adding another species with a large size, such as Y, or by changing the relative concentration in Mg-based MGs, the preferred motif changes and the icosahedra might no longer be the predominant building blocks.

In the present study, in order to demonstrate how the atomic structure, particularly the configuration of the skeleton network, impacts on the shear banding behavior and thus the macroscopic mechanical responses, we then simulated the uniaxial compressive deformation of the two model alloys $Mg_{60}Cu_{17}Ni_{23}$ and $Mg_{70}Cu_{13}Ni_{17}$. The simulation scheme of the compressive tests is introduced in Section 2.3.

The stress–strain (σ–ε) curves for $Mg_{60}Cu_{17}Ni_{23}$ and $Mg_{70}Cu_{13}Ni_{17}$ were derived and are contrasted in Fig. 9. In the initial elastic deformation stage for both MGs, stress increases linearly with strain, until reaching an elastic limit of ~4%. After that, the curves deviate from the initial linearity, signaling that the irreversible shear deformation zones (STZs) are emerging in the MGs. For $Mg_{60}Cu_{17}Ni_{23}$, the stress reaches its maximum (denoted as overshoot stress (σ_{over})) at a strain of ~6% and abruptly drops afterwards. This sudden drop is caused by the formation of shear bands. Subsequently, the stress enters into a more steady flow regime (denoted as flow stress (σ_{flow})) during which some serrations occur. This is caused by the propagation of shear bands. Once the shear bands start to propagate, the structural

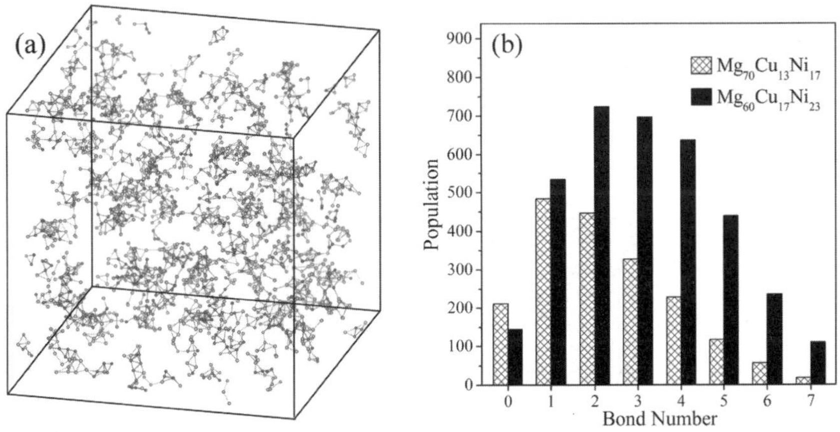

Fig. 8 (a) The skeleton network in $Mg_{70}Cu_{13}Ni_{17}$ formed through interpenetrating, *i.e.*, TS, linkages (denoted by the solid bicolor lines) between the Cu-centered ⟨0,0,12,0⟩ (orange), Ni-centered ⟨0,0,12,0⟩ (green) and Mg-centered ⟨0,2,8,5⟩, ⟨0,1,10,4⟩ (purple) clusters. Only the central atoms of the clusters are plotted as points, the isolated and dimerized clusters are not presented. (b) Distribution of the population of clusters with different bond numbers, *i.e.*, the number of interpenetrating linkages that the clusters are engaged in, in the skeleton networks of the $Mg_{60}Cu_{17}Ni_{23}$ and $Mg_{70}Cu_{13}Ni_{17}$ MGs.

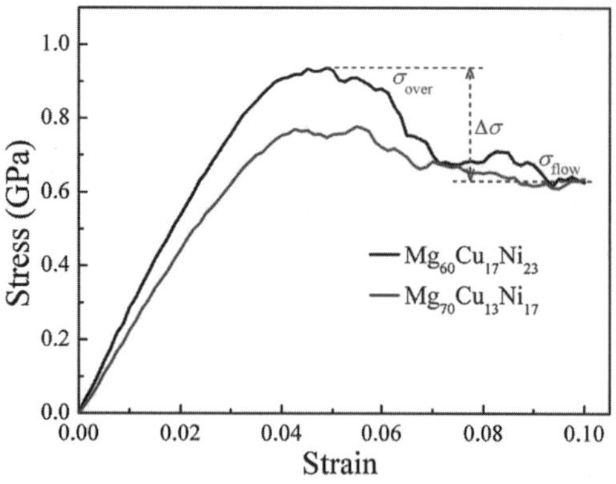

Fig. 9 Stress–strain (σ–ε) curves of $Mg_{60}Cu_{17}Ni_{23}$ and $Mg_{70}Cu_{13}Ni_{17}$ under uniaxial compressive tests. For $Mg_{60}Cu_{17}Ni_{23}$, the curve is characterized by an overshoot stress (σ_{over}) followed by a steady-state flow stress (σ_{flow}), which represents the intrinsic strength of the as-quenched state and the flow state, respectively, while the stress drop ($\Delta\sigma = \sigma_{over} - \sigma_{flow}$) reflects the strength contrast in the MG. For $Mg_{70}Cu_{13}Ni_{17}$, the curve is rather smooth and the deformation behavior is close to the homogeneous plastic response.

disordering becomes significant, resulting in softening in the deformed regions and entering into a steady-state flow.[65] The σ_{over} and σ_{flow} represent the intrinsic strength of the as-quenched state and the flow state, respectively, while the stress drop ($\Delta\sigma = \sigma_{over} - \sigma_{flow}$) reflects the strength contrast in the MG.[28] Comparatively, for $Mg_{70}Cu_{13}Ni_{17}$, the stress–strain curve is relatively smooth and the behavior is close to that of homogeneous plastic flow.

The distinct mechanical responses of these two alloys could be interpreted in terms of their different degree of skeleton networks. It is assumed that when constituting the skeleton network, the constituent atoms and clusters are relatively tightly nailed in the local structures, and thus their mobility would be dramatically restrained. Consequently, when the MG is subjected to mechanical loading, these 'locally frozen' motifs could avoid dramatic rearrangement and softening, thus elevating the deformation resistance and yielding a relatively high stress.[28,32] Therefore, the yield stress of $Mg_{60}Cu_{17}Ni_{23}$ is larger than that of $Mg_{70}Cu_{13}Ni_{17}$. On the other hand, the high degree of the compact skeleton network would inevitably suppress the presence of the relatively loose regions in the remaining space, and these regions, however, are revealed to be favored for the multiple nucleation of STZs.[30–32,66] Therefore, once the shear bands grow mature, the stress would experience an abrupt drop because of strain localization. This explains the stress drop of $Mg_{60}Cu_{17}Ni_{23}$ upon yielding. Comparatively, the lower degree of the skeleton network in $Mg_{70}Cu_{13}Ni_{17}$ could be responsible for its smaller stress drop and its more homogeneous deformation behavior. In the meantime, because of the large strength contrast between the compact and loose regions, the strain would be more likely to localize in the rejuvenated shear bands than to spread into unactivated regions, thus the MGs would be difficult to mediate large strains in the plastic deformation period.

To scrutinize the evolution of the skeleton networks during the deformation process, four typical deformation stages, *i.e.*, compressive strain $\varepsilon = 0.00$, 0.03, 0.06 and 0.09, were selected for $Mg_{60}Cu_{17}Ni_{23}$ and are exhibited in Fig. 10. In order to better visualize the structural evolution, only the skeleton network in a central slab with dimensions of $\sim 5.0 \times 5.0 \times 2.0\ nm^3$ was tracked and displayed. When $\varepsilon = 0.03$, as exhibited in Fig. 10(b), the skeleton network does not experience severe distortion from

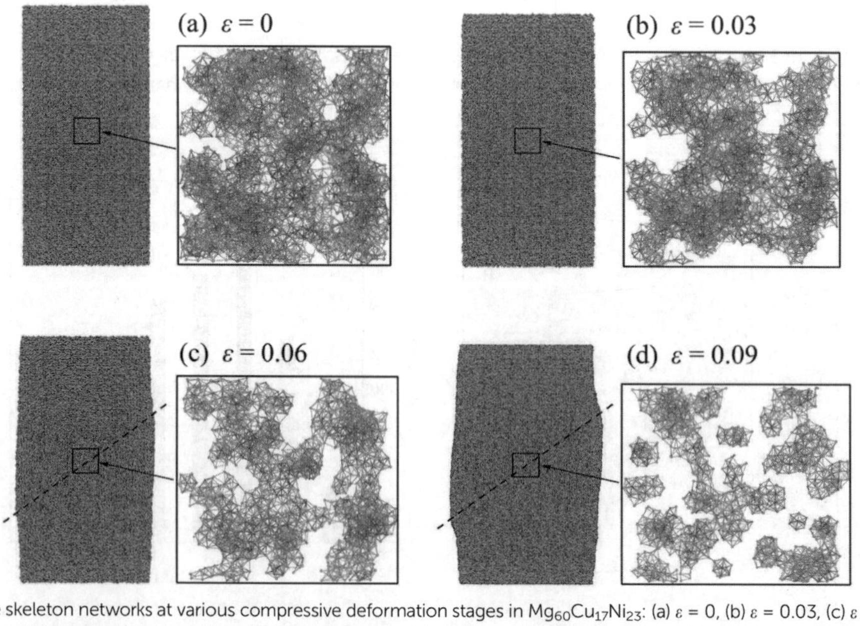

Fig. 10 Evolution of the skeleton networks at various compressive deformation stages in $Mg_{60}Cu_{17}Ni_{23}$: (a) $\varepsilon = 0$, (b) $\varepsilon = 0.03$, (c) $\varepsilon = 0.06$, and (d) $\varepsilon = 0.09$. The dashed lines in (c) and (d) denote the location that the shear band initiates and propagates. In order to give a clear demonstration, only the rearrangements of the skeleton networks in a central slab with dimensions of $\sim 5.0 \times 5.0 \times 2.0\ nm^3$ (denoted by the black squares in (a)–(d)) are tracked and displayed. The Mg, Cu, and Ni atoms are colored purple, orange and green, respectively.

the unstrained state exhibited in Fig. 10(a), indicating that at this stage the skeleton network could resist the compressive deformation in a rigid manner, thus the deformation resistance keeps increasing, as exhibited in the stress–strain curve in Fig. 9. When $\varepsilon = 0.06$, which is close to the onset of the abrupt stress drop in Fig. 9, the skeleton network starts to collapse, as exhibited in Fig. 10(c), thereby allowing the local inelastic deformation sites, *i.e.*, STZs, to percolate and form noticeable shear bands. The initiation of the shear band is also marked in the corresponding sample morphology in Fig. 10(c). Incorporating the evolution of the sample morphology and the skeleton network, as well as the mechanical responses, it can be seen that the deconstruction of the structural order, *i.e.*, SROs and more significantly, their connectivity in space, works almost concerted with the formation of shear bands, and the yielding of MG is the process of overcoming the interpenetrated rigidity developed in internal structure.[67] Afterwards, the skeleton network continues to fall apart, when $\varepsilon = 0.09$, the network has been destroyed into several discrete patches, as exhibited in Fig. 10(d), and the MG enters into the rejuvenated flow state. Therefore, it can be seen that the coverage and distribution of the skeleton network changes at the varying deformation stages, intimately correlating with the mechanical response, especially the initiation and propagation of shear bands in the MGs.

7. Concluding remarks

In summary, the atomic-level structure and its effect on the deformation behavior were investigated for Mg–Cu–Ni MGs by molecular dynamics simulations based on a newly constructed Mg–Cu–Ni interatomic potential. For the SROs, the Cu and Ni predominantly form icosahedral or icosahedral-like clusters, while the Mg atoms favor larger clusters and experience more flexible local environments. In order to characterize the MROs, a new cluster correlation index (CCI) is proposed to detect the correlation heterogeneity within the massive types of clusters, and the strong connection tendency between the Cu/Ni-centered icosahedra as well as some specific Mg-centered clusters is observed. In the extended scale, these preferentially interconnected clusters achieve their mutual percolation in space, leading to the formation of an energetically favored and structurally stabilized network that serves as the structural skeleton in the glassy matrix. In forming the structural skeleton, interpenetrating linkages, *i.e.*, TS linkages play a dominant role, while the network is additionally reinforced by VS, ES and FS sharing linkages, thereby jointly consolidating the energetic and structural stability of the skeleton. The skeleton network incorporates the hierarchical configurations in MGs, *i.e.*, the SROs, MROs as well as their spatial connectivity and steps into the extended scale of structural hierarchy. Furthermore, by monitoring the structural rearrangements during compressive deformation, it was revealed that the coverage and distribution of the skeleton network evolves at the varying deformation stages, and is closely correlated to the initiation and propagation of shear bands in MGs. The breakdown of the structural order, *i.e.*, SROs and more significantly, their spatial connectivity, behaves as a pre-requisite of yielding. These findings may promote the structural understanding of the deformation of MGs.

Acknowledgements

The authors are grateful for the financial support from the National Natural Science Foundation of China (51131003), the Ministry of Science and Technology of China (973 Program 2011CB606301, 2012CB825700), and the Administration of Tsinghua University.

References

1 A. R. Yavari, *Nature*, 2006, **439**, 405–406.
2 Y. Q. Cheng and E. Ma, *Prog. Mater. Sci.*, 2011, **56**, 379–473.
3 L. Q. Xing, T. C. Hufnagel, J. Eckert, W. Löser and L. Schultz, *Appl. Phys. Lett.*, 2000, **77**, 1970–1972.
4 H. L. Peng, M. Z. Li, W. H. Wang, C. Z. Wang and K. M. Ho, *Appl. Phys. Lett.*, 2010, **96**, 021901.
5 A. Hirata, L. J. Kang, T. Fujita, B. Klumov, K. Matsue, M. Kotani, A. R. Yavari and M. W. Chen, *Science*, 2013, **341**, 376–379.
6 A. Kartouzian, *Nanoscale Res. Lett.*, 2013, **8**, 1–4.
7 C. Fan, P. K. Liaw, T. W. Wilson, W. Dmowski, H. Choo, C. T. Liu, J. W. Richardson and T. Proffen, *Appl. Phys. Lett.*, 2006, **89**, 111905.
8 Z.-H. Jin, K. Lu, Y.-D. Gong and Z.-Q. Hu, *J. Chem. Phys.*, 1997, **106**, 8830–8840.
9 A. Pereira Goncalves, E. Branco Lopes, O. Rouleau and C. Godart, *J. Mater. Chem.*, 2010, **20**, 1516–1521.
10 J. Bednarcik, S. Michalik, V. Kolesar, U. Rutt and H. Franz, *Phys. Chem. Chem. Phys.*, 2013, **15**, 8470–8479.
11 A. Hirata, P. Guan, T. Fujita, Y. Hirotsu, A. Inoue, A. R. Yavari, T. Sakurai and M. Chen, *Nat. Mater.*, 2011, **10**, 28–33.
12 X. D. Wang, S. Yin, Q. P. Cao, J. Z. Jiang, H. Franz and Z. H. Jin, *Appl. Phys. Lett.*, 2008, **92**, 011902.
13 Y. Q. Cheng, E. Ma and H. W. Sheng, *Phys. Rev. Lett.*, 2009, **102**, 245501.
14 P. F. Guan, T. Fujita, A. Hirata, Y. H. Liu and M. W. Chen, *Phys. Rev. Lett.*, 2012, **108**, 175501.
15 H. W. Sheng, W. K. Luo, F. M. Alamgir, J. M. Bai and E. Ma, *Nature*, 2006, **439**, 419–425.
16 D. Ma, A. D. Stoica and X. L. Wang, *Nat. Mater.*, 2009, **8**, 30–34.
17 X. J. Liu, Y. Xu, X. Hui, Z. P. Lu, F. Li, G. L. Chen, J. Lu and C. T. Liu, *Phys. Rev. Lett.*, 2010, **105**, 155501.
18 D. B. Miracle, *Nat. Mater.*, 2004, **3**, 697–702.
19 J. H. Li, Y. Dai, Y. Y. Cui and B. X. Liu, *Mater. Sci. Eng., R*, 2011, **72**, 1–28.
20 M. Lee, C.-M. Lee, K.-R. Lee, E. Ma and J.-C. Lee, *Acta Mater.*, 2011, **59**, 159–170.
21 Y. Shi and M. L. Falk, *Scr. Mater.*, 2006, **54**, 381–386.
22 M. Li, C. Z. Wang, S. G. Hao, M. J. Kramer and K. M. Ho, *Phys. Rev. B: Condens. Matter Mater. Phys.*, 2009, **80**, 184201.
23 M. Wakeda and Y. Shibutani, *ActaMater.*, 2010, **58**, 3963–3969.

24 F. Delogu, *Acta Mater.*, 2011, **59**, 5961–5969.
25 R. Soklaski, Z. Nussinov, Z. Markow, K. F. Kelton and L. Yang, *Phys. Rev. B: Condens. Matter Mater. Phys.*, 2013, **87**, 184203.
26 A. Shavit and R. A. Riggleman, *Phys. Chem. Chem. Phys.*, 2014, **16**, 10301–10309.
27 Y. Y. Cui, T. L. Wang, J. H. Li, Y. Dai and B. X. Liu, *Phys. Chem. Chem. Phys.*, 2011, **13**, 4103–4108.
28 Y. Q. Cheng, A. J. Cao, H. W. Sheng and E. Ma, *Acta Mater.*, 2008, **56**, 5263–5275.
29 A. J. Cao, Y. Q. Cheng and E. Ma, *Acta Mater.*, 2009, **57**, 5146–5155.
30 Y. Shi and M. L. Falk, *Phys. Rev. B: Condens. Matter Mater. Phys.*, 2006, **73**, 214201.
31 M. L. Falk and J. S. Langer, *Phys. Rev. E: Stat. Phys., Plasmas, Fluids, Relat. Interdiscip. Top.*, 1998, **57**, 7192–7205.
32 Y. Shi and M. L. Falk, *Phys. Rev. Lett.*, 2005, **95**, 095502.
33 Y. Y. Cui, J. H. Li, Y. Dai and B. X. Liu, *Phys. Chem. Chem. Phys.*, 2012, **14**, 8290–8293.
34 H. R. Schober, *Phys. Chem. Chem. Phys.*, 2004, **6**, 3654–3658.
35 Y. Q. Cheng, E. Ma and H. W. Sheng, *Appl. Phys. Lett.*, 2008, **93**, 111913.
36 Q. Wang, J. H. Li, J. B. Liu and B. X. Liu, *J. Phys. Chem. B*, 2014, **118**, 4442–4449.
37 G. Yuan, K. Amiya and A. Inoue, *J. Non-Cryst. Solids*, 2005, **351**, 729–735.
38 H. Ma, E. Ma and J. Xu, *J. Mater. Res.*, 2003, **18**, 2288–2291.
39 E. S. Park and D. H. Kim, *J. Mater. Res.*, 2005, **20**, 1465–1469.
40 A. Inoue, A. Kato, T. Zhang, S. G. Kim and T. Masumoto, *Mater. Trans., JIM*, 1991, **32**, 609–616.
41 Y. Li, H. Jones and H. A. Davies, *Scr. Metall. Mater.*, 1992, **26**, 1371–1375.
42 Q. Zheng, H. Ma, E. Ma and J. Xu, *Scr. Mater.*, 2006, **55**, 541–544.
43 P. Jóvári, K. Saksl, N. Pryds, B. Lebech, N. P. Bailey, A. Mellergård, R. G. Delaplane and H. Franz, *Phys. Rev. B: Condens. Matter Mater. Phys.*, 2007, **76**, 054208.
44 Q. Wang, J. H. Li, Y. Y. Cui, J. B. Liu and B. X. Liu, *J. Appl. Phys.*, 2013, **114**, 153503.
45 J. H. Li, X. D. Dai, T. L. Wang and B. X. Liu, *J. Phys.: Condens. Matter*, 2007, **19**, 086228.
46 D. Frenkel and B. Smit, *Understanding molecular simulation: from algorithms to applications*, Academic press, New York, 2001.
47 V. Rosato, M. Guillope and B. Legrand, *Philos. Mag. A*, 1989, **59**, 321–336.
48 C. Kittel and P. McEuen, *Introduction to solid state physics*, Wiley, New York, 1996.
49 D. R. Lide and T. J. Bruno, *CRC Handbook of Chemistry and Physics*, CRC PressILlc, New York, 2012.
50 Y. Wang, S. Curtarolo, C. Jiang, R. Arroyave, T. Wang, G. Ceder, L. Q. Chen and Z. K. Liu, *Calphad*, 2004, **28**, 79–90.
51 M. D. Segall, J. D. L. Philip, M. J. Probert, C. J. Pickard, P. J. Hasnip, S. J. Clark and M. C. Payne, *J. Phys.: Condens. Matter*, 2002, **14**, 2717–2744.
52 S. J. Clark, M. D. Segall, C. J. Pickard, P. J. Hasnip, M. I. J. Probert, K. Refson and M. C. Payne, *Z. Kristallogr. - Cryst. Mater.*, 2005, **220**, 567–570.
53 J. P. Perdew, J. A. Chevary, S. H. Vosko, K. A. Jackson, M. R. Pederson, D. J. Singh and C. Fiolhais, *Phys. Rev. B: Condens. Matter Mater. Phys.*, 1992, **46**, 6671–6687.
54 J. P. Perdew, K. Burke and M. Ernzerhof, *Phys. Rev. Lett.*, 1996, **77**, 3865–3868.
55 P. E. Blöchl, *Phys. Rev. B: Condens. Matter Mater. Phys.*, 1994, **50**, 17953–17979.
56 H. J. Monkhorst and J. D. Pack, *Phys. Rev. B: Solid State*, 1976, **13**, 5188–5192.
57 J. H. Rose, J. R. Smith, F. Guinea and J. Ferrante, *Phys. Rev. B: Condens. Matter Mater. Phys.*, 1984, **29**, 2963–2969.
58 N. N. Greenwood and A. Earnshaw, *Chemistry of the Elements*, Butterworth-Heinemann Oxford, UK, 2nd edn, 1997.
59 B. Cordero, V. Gomez, A. E. Platero-Prats, M. Reves, J. Echeverria, E. Cremades, F. Barragan and S. Alvarez, *Dalton Trans.*, 2008, 2832–2838.
60 K. H. J. Buschow, *J. Phys. F: Met. Phys.*, 1984, **14**, 593–607.
61 J. L. Finney, *Proc. R. Soc. London, Ser. A*, 1970, **319**, 479–493.
62 J. Li, S. Zhao, Y. Dai, Y. Cui and B. Liu, *J. Appl. Phys.*, 2011, **109**, 113538.
63 D. R. Nelson, *Phys. Rev. B: Condens. Matter Mater. Phys.*, 1983, **28**, 5515–5535.
64 J. Ding, Y. Cheng and E. Ma, *Acta Mater.*, 2013, **61**, 3130–3140.
65 K.-W. Park, C.-M. Lee, M. Wakeda, Y. Shibutani, M. L. Falk and J.-C. Lee, *Acta Mater.*, 2008, **56**, 5440–5450.
66 J. Qiao, J.-M. Pelletier and R. Casalini, *J. Phys. Chem. B*, 2013, **117**, 13658–13666.
67 P. Guan, M. Chen and T. Egami, *Phys. Rev. Lett.*, 2010, **104**, 205701.

第四篇　培养的研究生名单

柳百新和李恒德教授联合培养的研究生名单

序号	姓名	毕业时间（年）及学位	毕业后工作情况
1	严志华	1986 MS	毕业后去中国科学院物理研究所学习并获博士学位
2	程国安	1987 MS	现任北京师范大学教授
3	黄立基	1988 PHD	论文曾获美国 MRS 研究生论文奖，毕业后在加拿大做博士后研究，现在美国做科技开发工作
4	马 恩	1989 PHD	清华-加州理工学院联合培养，毕业后在美国做博士后研究，现任 Johns Hopkins 大学教授
5	周 欣	1991 PHD	不详
6	尚昌和	1991 PHD	论文获 1992 年度吴健雄实验物理奖，毕业后在中国科学院物理研究所做博士后研究

柳百新培养的研究生名单

序号	姓名	毕业时间（年）及学位	毕业后工作情况
7	宋文杰	1989 MS	不详
8	赖守亮	1992 MS	毕业后去伊利诺依大学学习并获博士学位，现在美国做科技开发工作
9	朱慧娜	2000 MS	不详
10	王润顺	2002 MS	不详
11	胡 亮	2003 MS	毕业后去伊利诺依大学学习并获博士学位
12	丁菊仁	1991 PHD	毕业后在德国和美国做博士后研究，现任新科实业有限公司副总裁（香港）
13	潘 峰	1993 PHD	曾在美国做访问研究，现任清华大学材料学院教授
14	张政军	1995 PHD	毕业后在德国、日本和美国做博士后研究，现任清华大学材料学院教授
15	朱德华	1995 PHD	不详
16	金 瓯	1996 PHD	不详
17	陈益钢	1997 PHD	毕业后在德国和日本做博士后研究，现任上海大学材料学院教授
18	兰爱东	1998 PHD	毕业后在美国做博士后研究，现任太原理工大学副教授
19	赖文生	1998 PHD	曾在英国做访问研究，现任清华大学材料学院教授
20	杨 涛	1998 PHD	清华-东京大学联合培养，现在日本做科研工作
21	高坤元	1999 PHD	毕业后在德国做博士后研究，现任北京工业大学教授
22	林 川	2000 PHD	毕业后在日本做博士后研究，现在上海通用电气（中国）研究院工作
23	杨国伟	2000 PHD	毕业后在美国做博士后研究，现任中山大学教授
24	张 青	2000 PHD	毕业后在美国做博士后研究
25	马忠权	2001 PHD	毕业后在美国做博士后研究，现任上海大学教授
26	李兆峰	2002 PHD	毕业后在中国科学院半导体研究所做博士后研究
27	刘剑波	2002 PHD	毕业后在美国做博士后研究，现任清华大学材料学院助理研究员

续表

序号	姓名	毕业时间（年）及学位	毕业后工作情况
28	程向前	2003 PHD	不详
29	李正操	2003 PHD	毕业后在日本做博士后研究，现任清华大学材料学院副教授
30	龚浩然	2004 PHD	毕业后在美国做博士后研究，现任中南大学教授
31	孔令体	2005 PHD	毕业后在加拿大做博士后研究，现任上海交通大学副教授
32	张瑞丰	2005 PHD	毕业后在德国和美国做博士后研究，现任北京航空航天大学教授
33	李家好	2005 PHD	现任清华大学材料学院高级工程师
34	李新宇	2006 PHD	造币局科研所
35	郭海波	2006 PHD	毕业后在美国、加拿大和澳大利亚做博士后研究，现任上海大学材料学院副教授
36	孔　毅	2007 PHD	现任中南大学副教授
37	代晓东	2007 PHD	毕业后回部队工作
38	严华锋	2007 PHD	上海顿格电子贸易有限公司
39	何　翔	2007 PHD	广西南宁国家高新区纪检监察室主任（正处长级）
40	郇凯平	2009 PHD	毕业后在美国做博士后研究，现任中国科学院金属研究所研究员
41	梁苏会	2010 PHD	中核电
42	王文超	2010 PHD	北京通州街道书记
43	赵　满	2010 PHD	中船重工 714 所
44	王同乐	2011 PHD	德润特数字影像科技有限公司（北京）
45	赵世真	2012 PHD	北京保洁技术有限公司
46	戴　叶	2012 PHD	中国科学院上海应用物理研究所
47	崔苑苑	2013 PHD	现任上海大学材料学院讲师
48	丁　宁	2013 PHD	北京汽车股份有限公司
49	白　雪	2014 PHD	北京电子工程总体研究所

第五篇　主要获奖项目

GUOJIA ZIRAN KEXUE JIANG

为表彰在自然科学研究中做出的重要贡献，特颁发此证书，以资鼓励。

证 书

第六次(1993)国家自然科学奖

项目名称：　载能离子束与金属作用下合金相形成及分形生长现象的研究

主要研究者：　柳百新　黄立基　丁菊仁　尚昌和　(清华大学)

奖励等级：　二等

中华人民共和国
国家科学技术委员会主任　宋健
1994年1月

证书号：Z932181

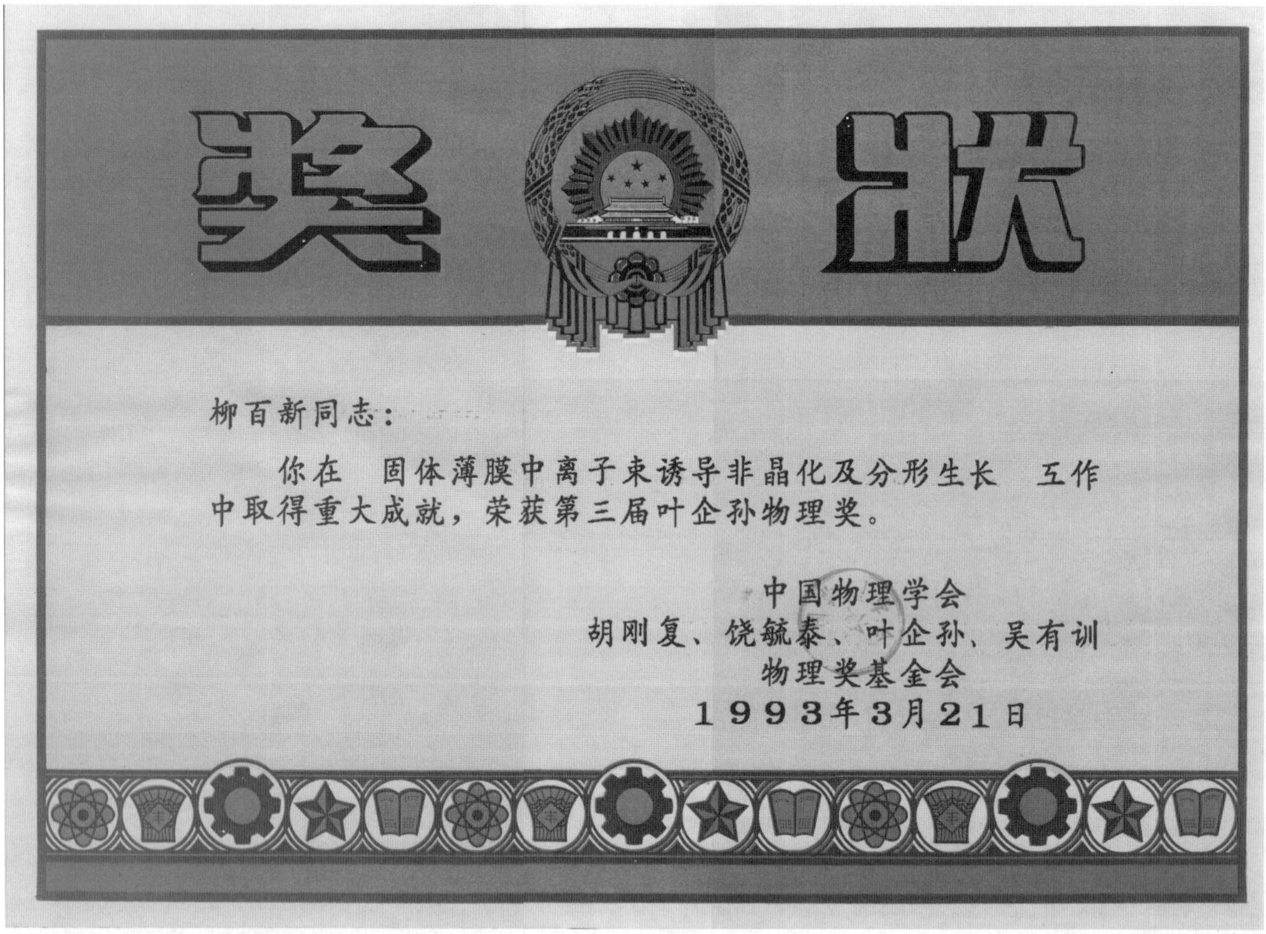

奖状

柳百新同志：

你在 固体薄膜中离子束诱导非晶化及分形生长 工作中取得重大成就，荣获第三届叶企孙物理奖。

中国物理学会

胡刚复、饶毓泰、叶企孙、吴有训

物理奖基金会

1993年3月21日

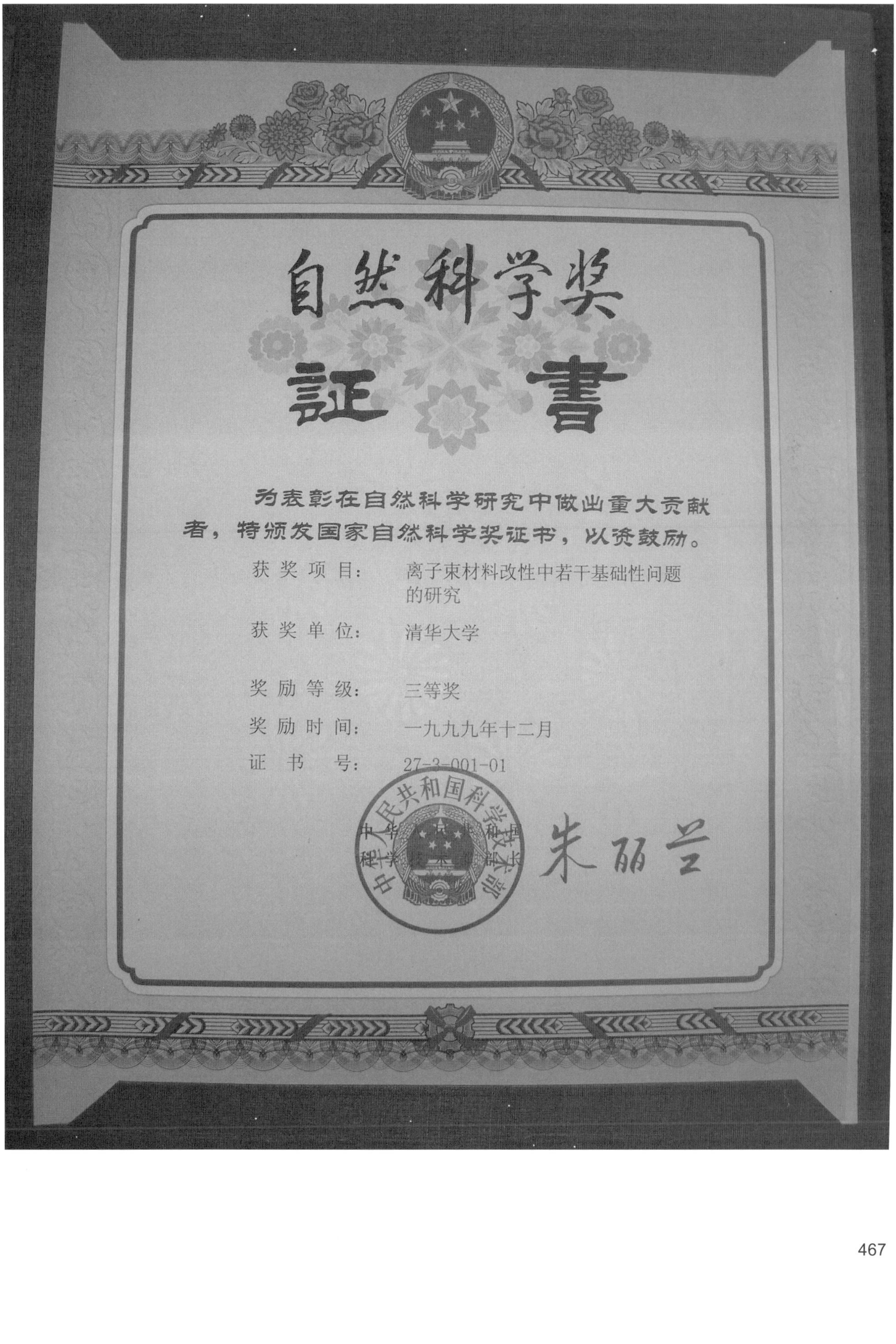
自然科学奖
証書
为表彰在自然科学研究中做出重大贡献者，特颁发国家自然科学奖证书，以资鼓励。
获奖项目：离子束材料改性中若干基础性问题的研究
获奖单位：清华大学
奖励等级：三等奖
奖励时间：一九九九年十二月
证书号：27-3-001-01
中华人民共和国科学技术部
中华人民共和国科学技术部部长
朱丽兰

第六篇　同学、同事和学生的回忆文章

散落的珍珠
——忆我和柳百新的童年生活点滴

文/邓柯

人老了，回忆近期的事，常常会“短路”……但是几十年前的经历却会异常清晰。每个人的“时光隧道”里，都有一台“过滤器”，它不停在筛选……最后能够沉淀下来的，总是一些干干净净的美好回忆，尤其是无邪的童年和不知忧愁滋味的少年时代。

我和柳百新曾经是小学和中学的同窗。

小学是上海协进女中的附小，解放后，学校没有了，学校的原址和校舍现在是上海市公安局的静安分局。他是1947年初，中途插班进校的学生，戴副眼镜，话不多，总是笑眯眯的，好像对任何事情都“胸有成竹”很自信的样子。

他的功课特别好，所有的主课和副课都被他轻轻松松一一搞定，而且均名列前茅，用现在的话来说：“×××是班上的骄傲或佼佼者。”

记得有一年我过生日，请他和几位同学来我家，他送给我很多张他手绘的“白描山水画”。很多年以后，我在从事美术工作时，才知道这些白描山水出于《芥子园画谱》，说明他很早就接触到中国画最基本的范本，而且还洋洋洒洒地付诸实践。

我的学习成绩比百新差很多，但是和他却能玩到一起。记得小学上课有十来分钟的课间活动，一二十名男生会涌到“乒乓球室”。

柳百新打乒乓球球技高一筹（邓柯作于2014年）

因为人多、时间短，于是有一种比赛法，叫“幺幺二大王”，连胜两把就是大王。大王要连输两把才让位。百新经常是坐在“霸主”的位置上。有些同学知道打不过百新，推推搡搡排到一块儿起哄而已，有的好不容易把球发了过去，也不知道百新回的球从哪边过来。尽管这样，大家还是玩得乐此不疲，这应该是今天最时髦的：“重在参与”“不计结果、享受过程”的雏形吧！后来，他好像不怎么打乒乓球了，改成进军篮球和足球，但是球好像粘在他的手上和脚下似的，同学们也就只能“望球兴叹”了。

我们的球队成员

前排：左一曹旭沧，右一张乃光；后排：左一邓柯，右一柳百新，右二朱铭璋（于 1954 年参加全国钢琴比赛，获第一名）

百新和我都爱看电影，那时候国产电影不多，内容好像都是给大人看的，我们爱看美国电影，常去的电影院都是离我们家较近的，如平安、美琪、大华等，有时也去国泰或大光明，如果口袋里刚好有家长给的零用钱，一定会在电影院里买一包“龙虾片”或“卜卜康”爆米花，边吃边看电影。

有些美国电影并不能全看懂，但是能知道好人、坏人。我们最爱看西部打斗片、滑稽片、卡通片。当年那些美国影星，如贾利·古柏、埃洛·弗林、劳莱、哈台、卓别林、英格丽·褒曼、桃乐赛·拉摩，狄斯耐的卡通……，我们都会似懂非懂。稍大一点儿就爱看劳伦斯·奥立佛、却尔斯·劳顿、费·雯丽等明星的片子了。

记得我们最高兴的事是和百新去踏“跑冰鞋”，从他家（南京西路、常德路口）或我家（南京西路、陕西北路口），经过陕西南路、淮海路、雁荡路，到普希金雕像下停住。然后，再换一条路线回到家里。20 世纪 40 年代末，马路上没有很多车，我们可以纵横驰骋，偶尔还来一个蹲下抱腿或转身后退。沿途吃两根美女牌棒冰，奢侈一点来两块紫雪糕。记得回到家里把“跑冰鞋”脱掉，两条腿好像轻得不得了，走起路来就像要飞起来的感觉，今天我写到这里，仍然感到是“妙不可言”！

踏“跑冰鞋”玩特技，路人侧目（邓柯作于 2014 年）

百新的家就在协进小学左侧的常德路上面对愚园路的春平坊一号（现在没有了，原址被拓宽成愚园路的延伸段），我常去他家玩，那是一幢典型的石库门三上三下的房子，他家住在二层楼上，窗明几净，家里有很多书，还有一箱箱的文库，典型的爱读书的家庭。

我对柳家姆妈印象很深，戴副眼镜，很儒雅的样子，对我们这些“小朋友”非常客气，小时候能得到大人的尊重这种感觉一辈子也忘不了。柳家伯伯好像不太常见到，但是我却在一本叫什么美术家名人大辞典里看到过：百新的父亲是柳荫——美术印刷雕刻大师（我从小喜欢美术，一沾有美术两个字的书总要去翻翻的）。

我与百新的两个哥哥接触不多，但是对他的姐姐——柳百敏却是印象很深，可能是姐姐特别疼爱弟弟，“爱屋及乌”，弟弟的同学也就沾光了，常常受到姐姐的款待，请我们吃“马宝山”或“戴康”的饼干等。记得她短发及耳，夏天爱穿跑鞋和裙服（不是裙子），应该是跑跳方便。当时我就想：伊真像阿拉学堂里的体操先生（她真像我们学校的体育老师），后来听说她确实是长年从事体育工作。

百新和他的二哥百成能分别当选为中国科学院和中国工程院院士，除了天资和自身努力以外，父母和家庭的影响也至关重要。

我和百新在小学里还有一位很要好的同学叫贝桐森，我们喜欢叫他阿贝。他们家的花园洋房在当时是很有名气的，前门开在南阳路，后门在北京西路，共有两栋互相连接的建筑组成，而且都有自动电梯。解放前，贝家对面是南阳公园，现在没有了，建成了高耸的南阳大楼。

因为他们家的房子大，房间多，我们可以无拘无束地疯玩。常常在一个大游戏厅里模仿刚刚看完的美国电影里西部牛仔在酒吧里用“左轮”双枪，打得昏天黑地或者像侠盗罗宾汉跳上跳下。最忘不了的是在他们家玩“官兵捉强盗”（捉迷藏），解放前他们家就有自动电梯，“强盗”常常躲进电梯里从一楼开到三楼或四楼，或者从楼上开到楼下，“官兵”是不容易抓到“强盗”的。

后来有些不灵了，只要“官兵”发现电梯自动往上走，“官兵”就疾步从楼梯往上跑，藏在电梯旁，还做持枪状，电梯门一打开，“强盗”探头探脑正要出来，“举起手来！”，“官兵”将“强盗”逮个正着。当然也有出洋相的时候，电梯门刚打开时，出来的是阿贝的姐姐或哥哥，大家就都乐了。贝桐森全家在 1949 年（上海解放前夕）迁往美国，很长一段时间没有联系，前些时候才恢复了书信联系。

1949 年，我和百新进入上海圣芳济中学（后改名时代中学），原校址是在福煦路（现在叫延安西路）的福煦坊里面（原校址现在好像是上海烟草公司的仓库）。进了中学，百新的功课更是出类拔萃，而我却恰恰相反。小学的算术，我手脚并用已经很吃力了。中学的代数、几何、化学，那些阿拉伯数字和各种符号，对我来讲简直是“天书”一样，颇有度日如年的无奈！

1951 年，我家里出现了一些大的“变故”，初二没有念完就辍学了。离开了学校和同窗好友，在我面前又展开了另一种新的生活。那时候的社会很宽容，我投师访友，自学美术，曾经画过比我的身高高出好几倍的电影海报，当过小越剧团的舞美设计，还给一些出版社画过幻灯片等等。

1954 年年底，天津人民美术出版社宽容地接纳了我，于是我成为出版社的一名助理美术编辑。工作多年后又转到天津画院工作，做我喜欢的创作。

20 世纪 60 年代，邓柯在天津画院的创作室，墙上悬挂的是当时的作品

因为工作需要，我常常去上海出差，组稿、访问画家。从另一位很要好的同学朱铭璋（当时他就读于上海音乐学院，几年前不幸去世了）那里，知道柳百新在清华大学读书，后来留校任教，这些都是我意料之中的事。但一直到“文化大革命”之后，我和百新才恢复了联系，他来天津找过我，那时我们已经是人到中年了。京津之间高铁通车后，百新也曾特意来我家看望，我们相聚时，每次谈到的总是离不开童年的纯真和少年的欢愉。

2011 年，柳百新专程从北京乘高铁来天津我家相聚

后来我移居澳大利亚。2014 年 11 月，百新从北京打越洋电话跟我说：“清华大学材料学院一起工作的学生和同事，正在为我明年八十生日编辑一本《论文集》。”他问我能否写一篇回忆童年生活的文章，而且他认为“这是他一生中非常值得回忆的美好时光”。

可不是吗？我们这代人风风雨雨、磕磕绊绊地几十年过来了。现在都老了，静下来了，安安静静地、干干净净地生活，静静地回忆那些干干净净的往事，最干净的莫过于童年、少年的纯真无邪。

澳大利亚从 11 月开始是夏季了，湛蓝的星空像水洗过一样，清风徐来朗月临窗。

谢谢百新给我这个机会，可以细细地去追寻人生中最最干净的往事，那些不经意的点点滴滴都能够使曾经世故、浑浊的心灵得到一次真正净化和洗礼。

谢谢你，百新！

祝我们和家庭都安安静静、干干净净、健健康康、快快乐乐地生活。

邓　柯

2014 年 12 月写于澳大利亚布里斯本

回忆童年的友情

文/曹旭沧

我和柳百新同学是在上海市协进女中附小四年级下学期认识的，那是1947年春节之后的事，到今天已经67个年头了。1949年夏天小学毕业后，同学们各怀梦想，追逐人生。我和柳百新一起进入了当时的圣芳济中学（后改名为时代中学），1952年初中毕业后，我进入上海航校学习，毕业后先后在北京和大西北的军工企业工作了20多年。改革开放后的1984年，我和夫人一起被调到杭州工作。

岁月飞逝，时事变迁，其间经历了“文化大革命”的十年，从1952年我和柳百新失去联系，到1990年在杭州重逢，计算起来相隔了有30多年。记得当时他为了参加863科研项目的答辩来到杭州，结束后他给我当时所在的无线电厂来了电话。于是30多年后，我们相聚了，追忆往事，觉得异常地亲近。后来，我携夫人到北京省亲，柳百新邀请我们到清华大学做客，陪同我们游览美丽的清华园。近年里柳百新和夫人几次来杭州出差或旅游，我们也一起在西湖边上以茶代酒，谈笑人生。逢年过节，电话问候，真是人生一大快事。

柳百新与曹旭沧合影

现在回忆起童年时的往事，仿若就在眼前。记得柳百新是因为搬家而转学到协进女中附小来学习的，他进校时是四年级下半学期的插班生，期末考试结束时，他就是全班的第一名，而且他到小学毕业一直是班上的第一名。五年级的时候，我和柳百新仍然在一个班，而且是同坐一条板凳。语文老师在教课后有时要我们背诵，许多同学背得不那么流畅，但是柳百新一口气背得出来。在班里他是一个突出的好学生，又能团结和帮助别的同学，他聪明有天赋，并且当上了班长，这也为他今后的人生打下了成功的基础。

他不仅在学习上是个模范，而且在运动场上也是个能手。在课余时间，我们一起打乒乓球，许多同学都打不过他。在篮球场上他投篮很准，也是一般同学比不上的。他平时对待同学总是笑嘻嘻、乐呵呵的，大家都感觉很亲近。我和他的家都住在上海静安区的常德路上，我家在南京路南，他家在路北，离得很近。记得我们放学后经常一起到一位周姓同学的私家花园（当时坐落在延安路上的周家花园）去玩耍和抓蟋蟀。有时我们一起骑自行车玩，或在小学隔壁的洋胡同里踢小足球。

今天回忆起来，总感觉到年少时建立起来的友情是纯真的、宝贵的。在幼小的心灵里我一直铭记到现在，愿我们的友谊永葆青春。

曹旭沧

2014 年 11 月 21 日

我的挚友柳百新

文/张乃光

柳百新是我在小学和中学的同窗，上大学我们不是在一所学校，他考入了清华大学的工程物理系；我是在上海交通大学。时间一晃就是几十年，但 65 年前的事情依然历历在目。我们就读的小学叫上海私立协进小学，坐落在现在的南京西路 1550 号常德路口，也就是在张爱玲故居的对面，张爱玲女士在 1934 年曾就读协进小学五年级，美中经贸促进会会长、美国太平洋规划设计中心董事长贝聿恺先生也曾在 1951 年就读上海私立协进小学。该校虽及不上当时的圣玛利亚（St. Maria）女中，但其教学质量和师资水平在当时的上海滩也算得上是上乘之列，校长黄轶如是一名女基督教徒，她对学生的各方面都有很高的要求，在学校纪律方面更是严格，学生见了她都非常害怕，只好老老实实、规规矩矩。1947 年初，柳百新进入该校成为四年级下学期的插班生，小小的个子，并没有什么与众不同的地方，只是小小年纪就带了一副几百度的眼镜。同学们对这位新来的伙伴并没有什么特别的感觉。可是到了期末大考后，情况就有了变化，原来一直考第一名的同学丢失了这个宝座，让柳百新坐上了第一名的位置，且保持五连冠直到 1949 年小学毕业。柳百新同学是一个很谦虚的人，并不因为自己功课好受到老师的青睐而感到高人一等，他和周围的同学都很融洽地打成一片，他在小学阶段就写得一手好字，我记得他的劳作（现在叫手工制作）也做得很好，而且他喜欢各种体育运动，用现在的话来说他是一个全面发展的学生。说来也奇怪，当时我们根本没有什么教学辅导材料，也不请什么家庭教师，就用学校规定的几本教科书，将小学的基础知识学到了手，我们没有感觉学习是很苦的事情，我记得柳百新在美术课有一件作品叫“读书乐”，可能就是他对求学的一个写照吧。柳百新在小学阶段在业务上已经初露锋芒，一是归结于他的天赋，二是归结于他善于学习和合理安排时间，做到各门功课都能融会贯通。这对于一个小学生来说是非常难能可贵的，也为他以后的成就打下了基础。

1949 年夏天我们小学毕业了。班上的男生多数选择了就读附近的私立圣芳济中学，当时上海刚解放，圣芳济中学还有一个英文名字叫 St. Francis Xavier’s College for Chinese，1874 年法国天主教耶稣会在上海法租界开办了圣芳济学院，是上海最早的外籍人士子弟学校，挂名是学院，其实是外国语小学，从 1884 年开始招收华人，但与洋人分开上课，是清一色的男子学校，但收费昂贵、条件苛刻，当时唯有宋子文、顾维钧（民国外交总长）那样家庭的人才能进入，直到 1935 年才开设国文课，也是上海最早的双语学校。1949 年该校位于延安中路 1157 弄内，圣芳济中学是一所门槛较高的学校，特别是英语要求很高，报了名还要考试并实行择优录取，为此学校专门办了暑期复习班，专为报考初中的学生进行复习迎考，柳百新和我都参加了暑期复习班，后来经过入学考试都顺利地进入了该校。因为该校是天主教会的学校，当时还有好多相公（英文叫 brother，洋人和中国的都有）担任学校的领导和执教。按照教会的传统相公都穿黑色长袍，脖子前面还有一块白色的胸牌。圣芳济中学的英语教学是特别见长的，这也是这所学校一贯的传统，另外在体育方面也是很有特色的，诸如排球、篮球、垒球等，当然在数理化方面也有颇高的水平。记得初一时学英语语法用的教科书就是《纳氏文法》（*Nasfield Grammar*），而且是原版的，厚厚的一本读起来得狠下一番工夫！当时柳百新同学的英文学得很好，我记得英文老师请他当“助教”，老师在教室里穿梭讲解，让柳百新站在讲台上用粉笔写下有关的内容，他的板书也令同学们折服。老师在讲授英文的时态（tense）时，让柳百新将各种时态写在黑板上作比较，至今我还有很深的印象。不管是数理化还是文史地，柳百新总是名列第一，他深得各位老师的喜欢和同学们的佩服。我想要告诉大家的是，柳百新绝对不是一个书呆子，他的学习方法很成功，也不是考试时抱佛脚、开夜车的人，他善于总结，能抓住重点，在考试前一天他经常会和我交流一下应该注意哪些内容，说穿了也就是猜猜老师会出什么考试题目。不瞒大家，80%的题目能猜对。这不能算是投机取巧而是科学的总结。柳百新的业务学习是拔尖的，在体育运动方面也是一个爱好者，他喜欢打篮球，打得也相当不错，虽然打球时戴了眼镜很不方便，眼镜也打碎了好几副，但他还是锲而不舍。另外他也喜欢打垒球（softball）。他在生活中是兴趣广泛的人，对古典音乐真是情有独钟，还爱玩桥牌，他的桥牌打得很好，虽然中学里还没有学过概率论，但是他的神机妙算真是令人叫绝，当然他桥牌打得好和他的惊人的记忆力也是分不开的。

柳百新、张乃光、赵汉钧三人合影

1955 年夏，张乃光与柳百新合影

1955 年六年的中学生活即将结束，这是长进知识的六年，也是从少年进入青年时期的六年，我们都特别感谢为我们付出辛勤劳动的各位老师，是他们为我们今后的发展打下了坚实的基础。柳百新对清华大学向往已久，可能是他二哥柳百成也就读于清华大学并留校执教的缘故，所以他填报的第一志愿就是清华大学，结果如愿以偿地被清华大学录取了，入学后因考试成绩优异被调入工程物理系。当时我们还有十多位同学被清华大学录取，这说明圣芳济中学的教学质量是不错的。顺便说一下，在 1952

年由于众所周知的原因，圣芳济中学改为公立学校，更名为上海时代中学，但是其优良的传统还是延续了好几年。值得庆幸的是，我等之辈都受到了良好的熏陶。

我们进入了大学之后，经常有书信来往，彼此交流大学里的新生活，每年有寒暑假两次见面的机会。1957年以后，我们就中断了书信往来，原因大家一定知道，这里就不必多叙了。虽然没有书信往来，可是我们的心是互相明白的，毕竟我们是儿时的朋友，大家是知根知底的，不在乎要在白纸上表白几句。大学毕业了柳百新在清华任教，我在上海交大任教。虽然业务上隔行如隔山不容易进行交流，但是我们的友谊和交情是没有任何阻隔的，还是一如既往、无话不谈。我们的关系犹如兄弟，见面时从来不用握手，因为我们的心是相通的。

20世纪80年代初，柳百新去了CalTech当访问学者，这是他业务上突飞猛进的时期，也是逢上了改革开放的好时机，他在学术上有了不小的成就、硕果累累，并被中国科学院选为院士，我们都为他感到高兴。2010年上海世博会期间柳百新和我在上海相逢，我感到他仍旧思路敏捷、非常健谈。他至今还承担着许多国家级的科研项目和研究生的培养。真是老骥伏枥，志在千里。在此我衷心祝愿我的挚友事业有成、身体健康，为培养接班人继续发光发热！

张乃光

退休教授，曾任上海交通大学管理学院、系统工程研究所副所长，

上海新加坡国际学校建校校长

写于2011年2月28日

金秋忆旧

文/赵汉钧

人逢佳节倍思亲，按我的理解不仅是至亲间的思念，还应包括青少年时代的同窗好友。那是人的一生中最纯真无邪、无忧无虑、活泼好动、学习向上，逐渐形成个人性格、爱好、理想的基础阶段。回想起来，自己与老师、同窗好友在一起相处的时间或许比与父母兄妹等亲人在一起的时间还要多。我们这一代人已步入老人（年过七旬）行列，50 余年前的小学、中学、大学同学无论在国内外，尚时有联系、互通信息、相互关心，实属弥足珍贵的情谊。今日恰逢新中国成立 60 周年大庆次日，又是中秋佳节前一天，晨接远在北京的中国科学院院士、清华大学材料科学与工程学院教授柳百新（他是我中学六年同窗挚友）来电晤谈之余，问询有无意向回忆记叙一些中学时代的情景趣事。这正合我意，我总觉得尽管 1955 年，高中毕业进入大学阶段，由于种种原因，有的迈入理想的院系就读深造，但也有不如预期甚至连入大学的门槛都进不去。但这些曲折不会改变青少年时代我们同窗学友之间的互相认知和理解，我觉得我们的中学时代（1949—1955 年）是相对稳定、和谐的年代，学习是一种享受，老师谆谆善诱、深入浅出，对学生严格要求。但不给学生过重负担，没有厚重的书包和到深夜才能完成的大量作业。很少有课余或假日请老师补习，为了取得考试好成绩而挤干学生课余时间的情形。下午 4 时准时放学以后，大部分同学仍在操场进行体育锻炼。打排球、篮球、垒球、踢足球等体育活动，这才是培养德、智、体人才的正确之道。下面我想回忆一些印象深刻的青少年时期的老师和校友。

小学六年无忧无虑地度过，1949 年 5 月上海解放，在崭新的景象中我们迈入中学学习生活。经父母推介进入 20 世纪上叶由法国天主教神父巴斯特创办的圣芳济中学，地处我家不远的福熙路（现延安中路）福熙坊内。校园不大，除运动场地（足、篮、排球场都有）外即是二层楼的教室、实验室及教员工作室，绿化欠佳。即便如此，却是解放前上海中学名校之一，由于私立性质，收费昂贵，不是一般家庭所能承担。圣芳济中学当时只收男生。与同样在上海著名的中西女中（现市三女中）正好相对，那时中西女中连教师均为女性。

1949 年入校以后，学校由私立圣芳济中学更名为上海市时代中学，但教员队伍基本未变。给我留下深刻印象的有以下几位老师。

童鉴清，资深英语教师，对学生要求严格，但心地善良。1995 年我们高中毕业后，他被调入北京外贸学院任英语副教授，继续培育英语人才，现已作古。

陆佩弦老师，记得在我们入校以后，他从美国留学回国到学校任物理老师，一天上早操课，他被校长介绍给全校师生，他身着白色纺绸长衫，戴金丝边眼镜，一派学者风度。授课井井有条，深入浅出，特能提升学生的学习精神。我们毕业后他被调入上海外国语大学任教授，今已作古。

吴厚成老师也是我们入校以后到校任职的体育老师。他中等身材，一口标准普通话，教学认真，为人和善。最值得一提的是，他为我校及上海市的排球运动水平的提升做出了很大贡献。培养出一批出色的排球运动员、教练员，我记得的有祝嘉铭、张祖恩（我们同届学友）、李宗墉、徐大用等。吴老师后来曾担任时代中学校长的职务。

沈浩明，化学老师，讲课十分生动，深入浅出，很受同学们欢迎。前两年在校庆纪念会上见到他，他记性很好，还能记得许多同学的名字。

下面记述我在时代中学的几位校友。

朱铭璋，高中六年同窗，从小课余学习钢琴，高中毕业考入上音钢琴系师从几位著名钢琴教授。遗憾天不随人愿，毕业前夕突患精神疾病，一直未能发挥他的才能。前几年已作古。

张乃光，与我同窗六载，是我中学阶段交往较多的同学之一，他学习勤奋，为人审慎。高中毕业时因病未参加高考。第二年被上海交通大学录取。毕业后留校任教，退休前已任教授，退休后曾在青浦由新加坡华侨投资兴办的国际小学任校长数年。

汪家起，六年同窗挚友。现今位于巨鹿路的上海人民美术出版社，曾是他家以前的住所。汪家起家境优越，但性格豪爽谦和、待人热诚、助人为乐，节假日常邀挚友去他家打乒乓球、台球或桥牌，他退休在家的父亲与好友会与我们年青学子对垒，不吝赐教。家起大约 1962 年去香港，后转赴美国佛州迈阿密进修法律，一直从事律师职业，在华人界颇有声望。改革开放以后，我们有了通信联系。1993 年，家起独生女汪俪婚嫁，他特地邀请我赴迈阿密参加婚礼。在获知我拿到签证后，又快递寄来往返机票。热情招待我在他家里住了一个月。

最后忆述中学六年同窗挚友柳百新。从 1949 年秋入学圣芳济中学开始相识相知且始终在一个班级上课，课余经常在一起参加各项文体娱乐活动，是我中学阶段联系较多的值得怀念的同学之一。他父母育有四子一女，各有所成，应是父母呕心沥血的成果。他大哥和大嫂早年参加革命，解放后在北京外国语大学工作，擅长西班牙文。他大姊是沪上著名运动员，曾得过市级冠军。他二哥柳百成是我们时代中学校友，1951 年毕业考入清华大学机械系，1955 年毕业后留校任教，后任清华大学教授，现为中国工程院院士。一门两院士。柳百新在我心目中其人如其名，学习方面，数、理、化、语文、外语、生物等均以高分名列前茅，我们班天资聪颖的“才童”不少，但他能年年第一名。课余及节假日和大家一样参加各项文体娱乐活动，而且不论排、篮、足、棒、羽毛球，田径项目均不甘落后。记得中学生百米的一般成绩十四秒多，他十三秒左右即能完成。他上课总在第一排（可能深度近视之故）认真听课，疑难之处在课堂上全解决了。我想说，他确实是我有幸在少年时期成为同窗挚友的一位天赋禀异、智慧超人的难得人才。他数十年刻苦学习与钻研，力争站上国际科学前沿，运用创新技术、研发新材料，为祖国现代化做出重大贡献，同时教书育人，把自己的科技学识、研究成果，与青年学子共享。期望青出于蓝而胜于蓝。因此，他屡次获国家级、教委和北京市的自然科学奖，叶企孙物理奖，等等。2001 年他当选为中国科学院院士，迈进中国最高科学殿堂是名至实归、水到渠成之为。时光如梭，百新年届七十有五（因病，小学辍学两年），比我年长两岁。

写到此，看官可能认为何人在此，说三道四，本人赵汉钧，学识浅陋，乏善可陈，1955 年时代中学毕业，高考后被统一分配到河北农学院（现河北农大）。记得有一次，百新、乃光与我三人一起在汾阳路和太原路交叉处的普希金铜像前留过合影，50 年后我们仨再到原地合影，当年倜傥青年已老态龙钟了！

遵百新嘱，恰逢新中国成立 60 周年大庆与中秋佳节巧合（仅差两天），随意记述陈年往事，疏漏难免，但均肺腑之言。

最后附上陈寅恪先生之名句与读者共勉

独立之精神
自由之思想

赵汉钧 草书
已丑年金秋
2009年10月2日—14日

1954年冬，柳百新与赵汉钧在中山公园合影

2004年，柳百新、张乃光、赵汉钧三人于普希金像前合影

2004年，柳百新、张乃光、赵汉钧三人合影

忆柳百新

文/何宇忠, 何宇信

20世纪50年代时，我们兄弟二人和柳百新在上海时代中学一起上中学，每日清晨步行去学校，半途必经百新家，百新也必下来和我们结伴同行，六年来来去去地成了好朋友，在学校里百新是个品学兼优的模范生，他与我们兄弟二人在课堂上友善地竞争，三人都常能名列前茅，为其他同学所羡慕，有空就课外一起打球，百新比我们更积极进步，学习社会主义，是个难能可贵的进步青年。

中学毕业后百新与宇忠去了清华大学，百新用功勤奋，凭他过人的才智，造就他今天的骄人成就，科技界世界闻名，作为清华大学教授、中国科学院院士，桃李满天下，为国为民，都做了伟大的贡献，人生至此，夫复何求。

我们兄弟二人在20世纪60年代去了美国，走了不同的人生过程，也少有成就。

今天我们与百新都届古稀之年，回首一望，不胜唏嘘，同学中很多人已作古。与百新在偶然的机会下重逢，又能把手言欢，仿如隔世，友情如旧。少年时的纯真友情是最可珍惜的，有那一天我们三人要回去上海延安路上走走，看是否还能捕捉当年结伴同行的影子。

宇 忠　宇 信 敬贺

2012年12月31日美国加州

柳百新与何宇忠、何宇信于美国西海岸的乔伊岬(Point Joe)合影

柳百新与何宇忠合影

柳百新与何宇信合影

良师益友，莫逆于心
——贺百新兄八十寿诞

文/李冠兴

百新兄高我一届，是比我年长的学长，20 世纪 50—60 年代我们同是清华大学工程物理系六年制的核材料专业的学生。由于课程非常重，不是同班的学友接触并不多。百新兄第一次给我留下深刻印象是在 1960 年，他顶替原来的授课老师给我们班上“固体物理”课。百新兄是 1961 年毕业的，所以他当时还没有毕业，也刚通过自学学习了“固体物理”，因此他给我们班上课属于“现买现卖”。虽然如此，但是课却上得不错，条理清晰，板书很好，得到了我们班同学们的认可。

1962 年大学毕业后，我留校攻读核材料物理专业研究生，师从现今的资深院士李恒德先生。百新兄早我一年毕业，已经留校当助教。当时全校的研究生都在学生宿舍三号楼住，我们核材料专业的研究生都集中住在一楼走廊北头的一个大房间内，最多住过 6 个人。其中作为青年教师的百新兄也有一个床位。百新兄和我都爱好乒乓球，常常下班后一起在工程物理系馆三层楼的一个大房间里打球，有时时间晚了，就一起到照澜院的一个小餐馆要碗馄饨和烧饼当晚餐，吃完后回去休息。

百新兄的生活习惯属于“百灵鸟”型，从不睡懒觉。我们在一个教研室共事约四年，直至 1966 年我离开学校，百新兄和我成为了挚友。真如《庄子·大宗师》中所述，“莫逆于心，遂相与为友”也。

改革开放后，百新兄先我一年去美国研修，1981—1982 年在美国加州理工学院当访问学者，真正取得突破是在 1982 年，他在系统的离子束混合实验研究的基础上，提出了预言非晶态合金形成的“结构差异规则”。记得他曾在与我的通信中，告诉我当时他与两位在此领域中的权威科学家详细地讨论了他的结果和提出的规则，得到两位科学家的肯定并评价为“perfect”。读了他的信，我非常理解他当时十分激动的心情，送上了我最衷心的祝贺！现在回想起来，这或许对百新兄而言，确实是具有里程碑意义的事件!

我在核工业系统工作多年，与已故的核材料界泰斗张沛霖院士（时任核工业部总师，因此大家习惯地称呼他为张总）不仅有工作上的联系，而且也受教于他良多，有一次向他提到百新兄的工作和发表的论文时，张总曾对我说：“你的这个同学了不得!”

李冠兴
中国工程院院士
2014 年 12 月 12 日

柳百新与李冠兴合影

亦师亦友亦兄长，风雨同舟一甲子

文/邱学良

柳先生，既是高我一届的学长，也是我的老师。我们之间的故事最早要追溯到1960年，我是1956年入学的，因为后来历次运动（诸如反右派、大跃进、反右倾等）的影响，打乱了教学秩序，我们班的有些基础课程没有能完整地学好，1960年上最后一门重要的固体物理课。当时的授课老师讲得很不好，同学们上课时就好像是听“天书”，根本就听不懂，几位同学就起来“造反”，向系主任写信要求换讲课的老师。当时的柳先生还没有毕业，教研组的领导临时让他来代替上课，真可以说是“临危受命”。记得当时讲台上的他温文尔雅，叙述详略得当，概念分析清晰，这位小“先生”一下子得到了我们班同学的认可，因此大家称呼他为柳先生。这是我和柳先生第一次比较直接的接触并留下很深刻的印象，而且对他这样地称呼一直延续至今。

1962年本科读完后，我留在核材料教研组做研究生，师从现为中国工程院的资深院士李恒德先生，与前一年留校做助教的柳先生在同一个教研组工作与学习，因此也有些交往。研究生毕业后，我被分配到坐落在远郊南口的清华大学核能技术设计研究院工作 (注：清华大学的师生们更愿意称该研究院为“200号”，因为该研究基地动工兴建的时候，其工程代号为200号)。

1966年“文化大革命”开始了，不久工军宣队就进校来领导一切。1969年军代表动员教工们去江西鲤鱼洲农场劳动改造，当时可能称为“接受再教育”。7月份，我跟柳先生同期被派到南昌市附近的鲤鱼洲农场劳动去了。我被安排在基建连，主要任务是搞运输；柳先生被安排在五连，主要任务是下田种水稻，秋收后他又被调到伙房去劳动。由于我们两个连的驻地离得比较近，所以平时能稍有接触。当时的知识分子在社会上被排在“臭老九”的地位，大家的感觉是前途一片渺茫，梦想都没了，何谈未来？可是，我偶然能有机会与柳先生聊天的时候，他还是相信我们学了这么多年的知识，将来有朝一日，应该还是会有用武之地的。

1969年下旬，中央批准了清华大学承担一项代号为820的重大工程，按当时200号技术领导人的说法是：要用一定量的核燃料发出电来，同时能再生产出新的核燃料。当时由军代表组成的校领导把这件事当作头等任务来落实。从各个系所调人来完成这项重大任务。因此，于1969年12月，我被调回200号工作。柳先生也因当时技术人才的需要被调到200号来工作。记得当时我们一起从南昌坐火车回北京，周末到的北京，星期一就上班搞起科研来了。从1970年起，到1976年10月份“四人帮”垮台（我们还一起亲眼见证了，江青在临垮台前到200号来，在生活区绕场一周接见群众的场面），我们一直在200号是“同一个战壕的战友”，勤勤恳恳地踏实工作，认认真真地完成各项实验任务。记得在这六年中，当时的技术领导人一共改变过两次大的工程方案。尽管我们做了许多与材料相关的科研，科研也是有些结果的，但大方案变了，许多结果也就没有用而被搁置起来了。回顾那段我们一起工作的经历，有几件事让我记忆犹新！

最初我们两人被分配在同一个研究小组，是具体干活的。这个组的任务是考验设计组选定的结构材料在液态金属铋中的腐蚀行为，按设计的需要，使用温度越高越好。

柳先生在科研中的表现，不但理论基础掌握的好，实践能力也非常强。在做静态腐蚀实验时，我设计和制备了能够在实验中提起样品的威尔森密封机构；实验中盛液态金属铋的坩埚是用石墨电极车成的，而这个坩埚就是柳先生在一台旧车床上车出来的。还有一个例子是，我们设计了实验用的管材试样，其内表面要求三花七的光洁度，但金工间的车工师傅认为管子的长度/内径比太大了，根本没法加工。金工间的技术负责人就找柳先生论理，并提出要退回设计。有意思的是，柳先生早已精心磨了一把高速钢的刀具，用那一台旧车床车出了符合要求的试样。因此，柳先生带了刀具到金工间做了示范，车工师傅们看了不得不服气。原来柳先生在大学三年级学过金工和实习课，所以能车出这样的试样来。

现在的博士生在做研究时，一般都建立在查证大量相关文献的基础上。但是在当时，查外文文献杂志很有可能被冠以“崇洋媚外”的“帽子”而受到批判，因此大家工作中都十分小心，承受着一定的心理压力。但柳先生有空的时候，还是到 200 号的图书馆里去看看书，并阅读一些新的文献。有一次他查阅了一本《金属手册》(*Metals Handbook*)，从中查到许多金属元素在不同温度的液态金属铋中的溶解度，但是其数值却是几个百分点（用%表示），而不是工程设计中希望的百万分之几(用 ppm 表示)。这些实验性的科学数据对当时的工程方案几乎是颠覆性的，印证了所选用的结构材料是不能胜任设计工况的。

改革开放后，柳先生回到清华大学工程物理系工作，我继续留在 200 号工作。1981—1982 年期间，柳先生到美国加州理工学院做访问学者。我到德国核研究中心研修一年，回来后一直从事高温气冷堆燃料组件的制备工作。虽然平时与柳先生不在一起，但工作之余常有联系。

2002 年以后，我很高兴有机会到柳先生的研究组里来工作了十年，我们一起筹建了离子注入和薄膜制备的实验室，使许多研究生能顺利地进行离子束与材料相互作用的实验研究。

人生弹指一挥间，我与柳先生相识转眼就快六十年了。我们已是共同经历过那么多的岁月、风雨同舟、情投意合的老朋友了。孟子言：人之相识，贵在相知，人之相知，贵在知心。如果说朋友是一笔财富，那么我们彼此对于对方来说都是一份无价之宝。

往事就像电影一样在眼前闪过，柳先生不仅是我值得信赖的朋友，更是一位非常值得我敬佩的兄长。他许多过人的特点深深地印在我的脑海中。一是他数十年如一日地勤奋工作，不屈不挠永攀科学高峰的意志。二是他对科学的高度敏感和超强的分析洞察能力，使他能一直站在学科的前沿，不断迎来新的发现。三是他教书育人，对研究生严格要求，从指导实验，到英文论文的修改，处处一丝不苟。四是他对科研经费使用的精打细算，结余的经费都用来改进设备。五是他的待人接物，总是真诚以对，交往中不忘关心大家的生活和健康。

朋友的谈笑声常在耳边，那温馨的友谊滋养在我们的心田。希望我们的友谊像高山流水源远流长，像青松顶风傲雪、郁郁葱葱。

谨以此文，写在柳先生 80 寿辰之际，衷心祝愿他健康幸福！

邱学良

2014 年 12 月 22 日于清华园

柳百新院士八十寿诞感言

文/周克崧

柳百新院士是我国杰出的材料科学家，长期致力于我国材料科学和教育事业。他在离子束与固体相互作用及材料改性、计算材料科学、薄膜和核材料等领域辛勤耕耘，硕果累累，例如他率先提出离子束混合形成二元非晶态合金的经验规则、热力学和原子尺度的模型，最早用离子束方法研究固体薄膜中的分形生长，等等。改革开放以来，他为我国材料科学事业赶超世界前沿、攀登科学巅峰做出了突出贡献。他热爱教育事业，重视学科建设和人才培养，为我国高等教育事业的发展也做出了重要的贡献。

左一为李冠兴，中间为周克崧，右一为柳百新

柳百新院士严谨治学，成就大师之道；为人师表，润育桃李天下。他长期关心我国材料表面工程领域的研究进展，尤其对我在本领域的工作给予了极大的关心和支持；他的渊博学识与循循指导，使我在几十年的现代表面工程技术研究实践中得以不断总结科研规律、提炼学术见解；他锐意创新的精神和严谨勤奋的作风，不断地激励我在学术科研道路上克服困难、砥砺前行。柳院士是我尊敬的良师

益友，他对我的关心、鼓励和支持，令我终身受益。

天道有常，春华秋实，值此柳院士八十寿诞之际，我衷心祝愿他福如东海、寿比南山、身体健康、万事如意！

周克崧
中国工程院院士、广州有色金属研究院（原）院长

How did the "structural difference rule" help shape my career?

文/Yang-Tse Cheng

The paper, "Structural difference rule for amorphous alloy formation by ion mixing" (Applied Physics Letters, 1983, (42): 45-47) is one of the most influential papers by Professor Bai-Xin Liu. It established "a sufficient condition that an amorphous binary alloy will be formed by ion mixing of multilayered samples when the two constituent metals are of different crystalline structure, regardless of their atomic sizes and electronegativity". In the past 30 years, Professor Liu and his group have persistently pushed forward the frontier of research in amorphous alloys through computational investigations and experimental discoveries. While his work has inspired several generations of students to pursue materials research, the "Structural Difference Rule" has had a long lasting influence on me.

I first met Professor Liu at Caltech in 1982 when he was working on the Structural Difference Rule and I was finishing my senior year there as an undergraduate student majoring in physics with a minor in mathematics. I did my first two years of undergraduate study in physics at Peking University before transferring to Caltech as a junior in 1980. I had the notion at the time that simple problems in science had been worked out and my generation was left with difficult problems that would require sophisticated and detailed knowledge in physical sciences and mathematics. I, therefore, took many hard classes and did some part-time research on testing detectors for high energy physics experiments. Although I did well in most of my classes and was accepted into PhD programs by several universities, I did not have a clear direction to pursue in graduate school. The world looked very complicated, daunting, and chaotic.

During a chance encounter, Professor Liu taught me some basics of amorphous metals and told me excitedly that he was on the verge of discovering "simple" rules for predicting amorphous phase formation. He then introduced me to his main collaborators, Professors W. L. Johnson and M.-A. Nicolet. Together, they showed me that good intuitions and novel ideas were paramount in scientific research. The "Structural Difference Rule" was the first of such examples I learned from them that helped form my own approach to research: "think simple, think different, and work hard". It has served me well.

In this happy occasion of his 80th birthday, I would like to thank Professor Liu for showing me the excitement of discovering rules of nature and the wonders of materials research.

Bai-Xin Liu and Yang-Tse Cheng both participated in MRS Fall Meeting

Biography: Y.T. Cheng is the Frank J. Derbyshire Professor of Materials Science in the Department of Chemical and Materials Engineering at the University of Kentucky. Prior to joining the faculty at Kentucky in the fall of 2008, he was a technical fellow and laboratory group manager for engineered surfaces and functional materials at the General Motors Research and Development Center in Warren, Michigan. He began his college education in physics at Peking University before transferring to the California Institute of Technology where he obtained his BS degree in physics with a minor in mathematics in 1982, and his MS and PhD degrees in applied physics in 1983 and 1987, respectively.

Dr. Cheng has authored or co-authored more than 140 publications and holds 47 US patents which cover topics such as ion-solid interactions and ion beam modification of materials; nano-indentation modeling and measurements of mechanical properties; growth, structure, and properties of nanostructured materials (e.g., amorphous materials, nano-composites, epitaxial single crystals, single crystal nanowires); microscopic shape memory and super-elastic effects; magnetorheological fluids; super-hydrophobic and super-hydrophilic surfaces; automotive applications of new materials and processes, including electrical contacts, high power-density engines and transmissions, environmentally friendly machining processes, hydrogen sensors, fuel cells, metal hydride batteries, and lithium ion batteries.

He is a Fellow of the American Physical Society and a Fellow of the Materials Research Society.

来自约翰·霍普金斯的贺信

文/马恩

JOHNS HOPKINS
UNIVERSITY

Department of Materials Science and Engineering
102 Maryland Hall / 3400 N. Charles Street
Baltimore MD 21218-2689
410-516-8145 / Fax 410-516-5293

I am delighted to learn that the School of Materials Science and Engineering is editing a book to compile selected works of Prof. Baixin Liu, on the occasion of his 80th birthday. It gives me much pleasure to compose this brief memory essay to accompany this commemorating book, as an opportunity to reflect on the years I had as a graduate student at Tsinghua with Prof. Liu in the 1980s, when I began my career in materials science.

Baixin and I go a long way back, 31 years back to be exact. We came together in 1983, and I was in the first group of graduate students he ever advised at Tsinghua. In this regard, I am also representing a number of other Tsinghua friends and classmates; they also worked with Prof. Liu in the labs and offices on the second floor of the Engineering Physics Building. Back then Baixin just came back to Tsinghua from his 2-year research sojourn at Caltech, starting his own group from scratch. So we witnessed the very beginning of his journey, i.e., the research career of Baixin at Tsinghua. And we were probably the authors who produced the first group of papers with him after his return to China.

The graduate student class I was in was special. We were from Class 77, the very first class that graduated at Tsinghua after the infamous 10-year long Cultural Revolution. Before us, from 1966 to 1976, for 10 years in a row, in China there was no higher education as we know it, and no graduate school either in its normal sense. Other than Fuzhai Cui (now a famous professor at Tsinghua), who was the first PhD student of Prof. H.D. Li back then and much more senior than us, I had no idea how graduate students would be like and what they would be doing. So we were in a clean slate from the get-go, and a fresh experiment on Tsinghua campus. The sense of mission pushed us forward to "make progress everyday", and everything we did seemed unprecedented.

I was lucky to have Prof. H.D. Li and Prof. Baixin Liu as my advisors. Baixin, being fresh back from Caltech, was probably the only one (or very few) in the department then who had just experienced how modern-day materials research was being conducted at a first-class graduate school. In Baixin, we saw a focused and hard-working scholar, highly-motivated to make a difference. His research-oriented approach and familiarity with the outside world helped us quickly reach the forefront of the field, in the area of ion beam modification of materials. His infectious ability to communicate effectively influenced us all, not only myself but also fellow students like Li-Ji Huang and Jian Li, who joined the group soon after me over the ensuing years. We became the first group of graduate students who wrote papers in English and got them published in international journals. This may be normal among today's students, but was a rare feat in China in the mid 1980s.

The student group back then was so small, and the advisors were so focused on their students, that the students/teachers were very close. For several years, day in and day out we practically shared all the times together in the labs and offices. We became personal friends as well. We invited Prof. Liu to students' badminton games and spent time with him in his recovery room when he was hospitalized. He routinely sat down to tell us his stories in California, sharing with us his thoughts about what needs to be done next. He even invited me to his home to watch TV (by the way, his colored TV was a rare commodity back then; for instance without it I would have missed the 35 National Day parade of 1984!). Baixin became an indispensable link in the chain of memory of our Tsinghua years.

Speaking of the influences he had on students, Baixin's personal experience showed me that the right next-move would be to spend time at a top school in the US. I followed his footsteps and went to Caltech in January1986 to work with Prof. Marc A. Nicolet, as a visiting graduate student. I came back to Tsinghua three years later in 1989. This was rare as well; in fact I was probably the first student at Tsinghua, to take on such a long international leave while pursuing PhD. Obviously, it was Baixin's vision and connection that made it happen.

I received a postdoc offer from MIT/IBM after my PhD defense. At that time, it was very hard to obtain permission to leave China. One must have a governmental affiliation to approve the "going abroad" to get passport, but I was graduating so Tsinghua was not prepared to be my "sponsor". I could not find another employer either: no one would want to go through the trouble since my intention was to leave China right away for a postdoc overseas. Yet, without such an affiliation there would be no passport, let alone the visa to the US. So I was stuck between a rock and a hard place. All that I could do was to petition the various offices of the Tsinghua authorities for many weeks, and repeatedly push for "at your next meeting, please discuss my case again, as an exception to your rules". Even today I still vividly remember Baixin standing outside the administration office leaning on the bicycle by his side, waiting to see how I did after I got a chance to plea for ~10 minutes to someone, such as a vice president or anyone who may have a say in the matter.

Over the past decades, I have visited Prof. Liu and Tsinghua from time to time, and have been amazed by his fast pace in publications, his passion to keep on pushing forward, and his ability to run/maintain his large group. Numerous students have come and gone, and Prof. Liu remains as diligent, healthy and influential as before. This is a life achievement very few people can reach at the age of 80.

Time flies. Thirty years ago in 1985, I obtained my MS degree at Tsinghua, working with Prof. Liu and Prof. Li.30 years have passed, and I have moved through a number of places, from Beijing to Baltimore. Prof. Liu is still within a few hundred yards from where we started, passionately and persistently laboring on his favorite subjects. We are now apart across the Pacific Ocean and may not have many opportunities to get together physically. But the fond memories are always there. And, believe it or not, 30 years later, I am still working on metastable materials today, ☺, albeit in different sub-areas.

En (Evan) Ma
Professor of Materials Science and Engineering
E-mail: ema@jhu.edu
2014-11-30

Brief biographical information:

E. Mais a professor of Materials Science and Engineering at Johns Hopkins University. He did his undergraduate studies at Tsinghua Univ. and graduate work at Tsinghua and Caltech, and was a postdoctoral fellow at MIT, Univ. of Michigan and UIUC. He was an assistant and associate professor at LSU before becoming a member of the JHU faculty in 1998. Prof. Ma has published ~285 papers (w/ ~15,500 citations and h index=66) and presented ~110 invited talks at international conferences. He is an elected Fellow of American Society for Metals, and also of American Physical Society. Since 2009, Dr. Ma has been an adjunct professor at Xi'an Jiaotong Univ. in China. His current research interests include amorphous metals, chalcogenidephase-change alloys for memory applications, nanostructured metals, dislocationsand twins in plastic deformation, in situ transmission electron microscopy, and elastic strain engineering of small-volume materials.

左一为金属所的徐坚教授，中间为柳百新，右一为马恩

栉风沐雨 80 载
——献给我的老师柳百新

文/王曦

春秋交替，岁月轮回！

我最尊敬的老师柳百新先生即将迎来 80 寿辰，在此，谨向柳先生献上最真诚的祝福，祝福他幸福安康，福寿绵长！

80 载的风雨沧桑。柳百新先生在从事长达几十年的材料科学研究中，孜孜不倦，努力进取，积极奉献于材料科学事业，做出了重大贡献，推动了我国材料科学的进步和发展。

一路耕耘，一路奉献；一路欢歌，一路辉煌。柳百新先生用他的行动演绎出老一辈科学家艰苦奋斗、刻苦攻关、团结协作、锲而不舍的精神，用他的人生轨迹诠释了老一辈科学家敢为天下先、勇攀科学高峰的风范。遥想在清华校园，柳先生言传身教，以大师的风范影响和带出了一大批优秀人才。柳先生对祖国的拳拳之心，对科学事业的执着追求，对学术研究的严谨作风，以及对人生乐观、豁达的态度，一直激励我们这些学生不懈地去实现更高的目标，去感受老一辈科学家的那种精神，使之化为无形的力量，将信念化为脚下的路，把憧憬变为手中的犁，以崭新的姿态、求新的思想、创新的行动，仰望新的晴空，去迎接更加美好的明天！

莫道桑榆晚，为霞尚满天。诚挚地祝愿柳百新先生青春焕发，再铸辉煌！

王曦

中国科学院院士、中国科学院上海微系统与信息技术研究所所长

2014 年 10 月

柳百新与王曦合影

出成果 育人才 展人生
——回忆分享与柳百新院士交往的快乐时光

文/朱慧珑

一、相识

算起来，我和柳百新先生相识至今已有二十六年。

柳百新先生是我国著名的材料科学家、教育家，中国科学院院士，执教清华大学五十余年。

第一次见到柳先生是在 1988 年。那年我在北京师范大学攻读博士学位，师从黄祖洽院士，做金属辐照损伤的理论物理研究。我完成了博士论文后，准备论文答辩，需请校外答辩委员会委员。从柳先生参与编译的一本专业书中得知他在材料领域很有造诣，于是我怀着试探的心情上门邀请他担任我的博士论文答辩委员会委员和论文评阅人。幸运的是，柳先生不仅欣然接受了我的邀请，还在百忙之中跟我讨论了一个半小时。当时我就对他的才思敏捷和平易近人印象深刻。从那以后，我还多次得到柳先生的指导和帮助。例如，我 1990 年能够获得赴美学习工作的机会，柳先生的介绍和推荐起到了关键作用。因他年长我二十余岁，于我亦师亦友，我们结为了忘年交。二十多年来，不论我过去回国探亲还是现在已回国长期工作，有机会我就会去拜访他，每次他和夫人倪先生都会热情地接待我这个晚辈。跟柳先生无拘无束的聊天是一种享受，他对新鲜事物和新兴科技总是保持着强烈的兴趣和敏锐的洞察力，多有独到的见解。柳先生到美国访问讲学时，也会拨冗来我家做客，我们还一起打乒乓球和郊游等。

二、贡献一流成果

“孜孜育人厚德载物，爱国求新自强不息”这两句话既包含了清华大学的百年校训，也是柳百新先生毕生追求的写照。柳先生祖籍江苏常州武进。身为一介寒儒的祖父离乡去上海发展，在中华书局谋得差事。从此柳家跟读书结下了不解之缘——父执辈多有知名文化人士和技术专家，其中姑姑和姑父创办了文化生活出版社，伯父生前任中国人民银行北京印钞厂的总工程师。柳百新先生 1935 年出生于上海，童年成长于战火纷飞、国家孱弱的年代，和同时代的老一辈科学家一样，童年的经历使他始终怀有强烈的报国之心和强国之梦。那时虽家境清寒，他父亲和母亲非常重视孩子们的教育，坚持让他们就读上海滩最好的教会小学和中学，为他们日后的成功打下了良好的基础。例如，教会学校系统和高水平的英语教学，使他打下了扎实的英语基础。他在跟我们聊天时在脑海中有时最先出现的是英语，所以时常夹杂着英语单词甚至整个的英文句子。

1955 年，柳百新先生受二哥柳百成院士的影响，也考入了当时二哥刚刚毕业并留校工作的清华大学机械制造系。入校后不久，他作为优选生转入当时新成立的“尖端”系——工程物理系。毕业后兄弟俩都在清华大学工作。共同的报国理想、良好的家庭教育、扎实的科研功底和国家的改革开放政策成就了后来的柳门传奇：柳百成和柳百新两院士是清华大学迄今唯一的“兄弟院士”。

柳百新先生不断地开辟新方向，长期坚持工作在科研第一线。在研究中特别重视并且善于理论和实验的相结合，勇于挑战和提出自己新的设想、实验方法和理论模型，因此成果既多又成系统。1981年初，凭借扎实的基础知识和突出的英语能力，他由国家教委选派到美国加州理工学院做访问学者。访问期间，加州理工学院所在研究组的教授交给他一项非常有挑战性的科研项目："用离子束方法制备出非晶态合金薄膜 "。他在仔细分析了前人二十余年的实验结果和关于非晶态形成理论的争论后，提出了他的科学假设，并用多层膜离子束混合在二元金属系统中形成非晶态合金的实验结果作出了坚实的论证，从而首次提出了非晶态合金形成的"结构差异规则"及相关的宏观模型，有关论文发表在《应用物理快讯》。1982 年回国后他带领学生进一步发展和完善了该模型。这项研究成果不仅多次应邀在国际会议上做特邀报告，还应邀撰写了综述文章，发表在 *Physica Status Solidi* 上，迄今还被大量引用。20 世纪 80 年代中期，他敏锐地注意到物理学界正在集中研究的分形现象，并力图将有关的概念应用于远离平衡态的材料研究中。他首创用离子束方法研究固体薄膜中的分形生长，并用分数维数来表征固体相变的行为。柳先生因在"固体薄膜中离子束诱导非晶化及分形生长"方面的突出贡献获得 1993 年中国物理学会的叶企孙物理奖。1998 年他由于"对离子束混合形成非晶合金的理解所做出的杰出贡献"，当选为美国物理学会的会士（Fellow）。

20 世纪 90 年代中期，柳先生带领他的研究组率先在国内开辟了"计算材料科学"这一新的交叉研究领域。在清华大学他们从编写相关模拟软件开始，一步步地建起了物理多尺度的计算与模拟平台，并开始从宏观和微观尺度上研究和解决金属材料中的科学问题。记得当时我正在从事分子动力学（molecular dynamics）方面的研究工作，为了了解前沿情况，他特意向我询问一些分子动力学模拟和第一性原理计算程序的情况，没过几年我吃惊地发现他们的研究已进入了国际前沿。例如，运用第一性原理他们计算了亚稳合金相的稳定性和磁学性能，发展和完善了第一性原理计算辅助构建多体势的方法，率先建立了能预言二元金属玻璃形成的原子尺度理论。2006 年，柳先生应邀为 *Physics Reports* 撰写了相关研究工作的综述文章，长达 134 页的综述文章竟占了该期刊的三期版面。

上述研究成果只是柳先生研究组所完成的成果举例。据我所知，他发表在国际著名杂志上的、基于他们自己研究成果的综述文章就有 7 篇之多。另外，他的成果还先后 5 次获得国家和教委的奖励，其中包括他以第一贡献者分别于 1993 年和 1999 年获得国家自然科学奖二等奖和三等奖各一次，获得过国家教委科学进步奖一等奖两次（1986 年和 1990 年）和国家教委自然科学奖二等奖一次（2013 年）。由于柳先生在材料基础科学领域的突出贡献，2001 年当选为中国科学院院士。这些成果和荣誉既反映了他们的工作在国内外的重要影响力，又能看出柳先生对研究工作的完美性和系统性的不懈追求，值得我们钦佩和认真学习。

柳先生在我眼里是一位典型的中国自己培养出来的极为杰出的学者，尽管有大约两年时间他在美国做过访问学者。他的研究工作绝大部分是在中国完成的，他经历过中国学者特有的"有幸"和"不幸"，这些起伏铸成了他的顽强精神和自尊个性，也造就了他事业的辉煌。

三、培育一流人才

柳先生十分重视育人，工作学习上对年轻人严格要求，日常生活上热心帮助。记得每当我在美国需要请他写推荐信时，他总会从繁忙的工作中抽时间及时地给予帮助。柳先生常深情地谈起他与学生的关系，"我们是师生，是合作者，更是朋友和忘年交"。我虽然不是他亲自带的学生，但在多年的交往中，能深切地体会到他把我们这些晚辈也是当作朋友看待。他强调博士研究生应该做国际一流的研究，热爱科学、勤奋工作、独立思考、勇于突破。他曾经总结自己二十余年的研究生指导经验，指出基础研究领域的研究生培养要围绕某个科学问题，学生从一开始就带着一个想法围绕该问题去调研、探索和论证。在指导学生完成一篇有论点、有实验、有论证的高质量学术论文的同时，要系统地培训学生去走完撰写一篇完整学术论文的全部过程，经过多次的循环往复，学生的学术水平就可得到不断地提升。正是得益于柳先生的先进教育理念，他培养出了一批又一批学生，其中许多学生取得了骄人的成绩。他的学生曾获吴健雄物理奖、全国百篇优秀博士论文奖，多名学生获得德国洪堡博士后奖学金、国家杰出青年基金、长江特聘教授和国家“千人计划”特聘专家等荣誉，还有多人在国内外著名大学担任教授。他本人也在 1995 年获得北京市优秀教师称号，1997 年因在“培养国际一流水平博士生的研究与实践”方面的杰出贡献获得北京市教学成果一等奖。

四、展现一流人生

严格地讲，一个人的生活质量跟他事业的成功与否并不一定有必然的联系，但当一个人热爱他所从事的事业时，事业的成功会给他带来无比的喜悦。柳先生就是一位热爱他的事业的人。当看到他滔滔不绝地聊起他的工作时，我们会感受到他对探究自然规律的热爱及所获成果的自豪，这也许就是人们常说的只可意会不可言传的幸福感。如何培养更多的像柳先生这样热爱科学的“纯”科学家是现在教育界遇到的一种挑战，我们可从柳先生的成才经历和生活态度中得到启示。所以我认为由中国科协等单位组织领导的“中国老科学家学术成长资料采集工程”是非常重要和及时的，它有利于总结在中国文化，尤其是新中国科技发展历史背景下，科学家的成长历程，利用、发展和改进我们的文化，使之为我国的创新发展和发展创新服务。

柳先生除了酷爱阅读专业书籍外，还有其他广泛的兴趣爱好。他爱好古典音乐，认为音乐艺术中贯穿的哲理和自然科学是相通的。他还特别喜欢体育，用自己的行动践行了“为祖国健康地工作五十年”这一清华体育精神。年轻时，他曾是中学全校运动会的跳高亚军、清华大学校羽毛球校队的队员、工程物理系排球队的主力。体育锻炼可以增强体质和磨炼毅力，这一点从柳先生的旺盛精力和勤奋精神上得到了体现。另外，他还有一种乐观向上的积极人生态度，这使他个人的，甚至他周围人的幸福指数提高许多。我有时会问，这与他爱好体育有无关联？我认为体育还有另外一种作用：人类社会活动的模拟器。因为人们在体育比赛前首先要做许多准备工作；在比赛中，要学习、遵守和运用比赛规则，要研究和运用比赛策略，要应对裁判公正和不公正的裁决，要面对友好或残酷的对抗，最后要学习如何面对胜利的喜悦或失败的沮丧；在比赛后还要总结经验等等。这些情况都是人们在工作和生活中经常遇到和需要处理的。所以，体育锻炼和比赛能使人更快地适应和面对社会。柳先生有时候也会谈到他所遇到过的一些不公正的对待和事情，但这并没有影响他的工作热情，他能始终保持着年轻的心态，蓬勃向上，带领着他的团队在科学的前沿辛勤和快乐地耕耘着。

我相信，作为新中国科技发展史中一位重要的参与者和见证人，柳先生会为他的贡献而感到无比的自豪，也会为自己所从事的事业能同时造福于社会和个人而感到由衷的欣慰。

2015 年是柳百新先生 80 寿辰，在此敬祝先生生日快乐、生活温馨和幸福!

1997 年冬，作者（左二）访问清华时与柳先生（右二）、马恩（左一）教授以及柳先生的学生赖文生（右一）博士生合影留念

在清华材料学院柳百新办公室，朱慧珑与柳先生二人合影

Huilong Zhu, Ph.D

(Institute of Microelectronics, Chinese Academy of Sciences Beijing 100029, PR China. Ph: 86-10-82995769 (w), E-mail: ZhuHuilong@ime.ac.cn)

Dr. Huilong Zhu is currently Chief Scientist of IC Advanced Process R&D Center, the Institute of Microelectronics of Chinese Academy of Sciences, PR China and is responsible for advanced CMOS technology research. As Program Chief Scientist of Chinese National Science & Technology Major Project 02, Dr. Zhu leads R&D program for 22nm-14nm CMOS technology in China.

Dr. Zhu obtained his B.S. in 1982 at the University of Science and Technology of China, Anhui, China, and his Ph.D in 1988 at the Beijing Normal University, Beijing, China, majoring both in physics. He has worked in USA at Argonne National Laboratory in 1990-1992, University of Illinois at Urbana-Champaign in 1992-1996, Digital Equipment Corporation in 1996-1998, Intel in 1998-2000, and IBM in 2000-2009. He joined the Institute of Microelectronics of Chinese Academy of Sciences in 2009 as a “Qianren (Thousand Talent) Plan” Researcher and National Expert.

Dr. Zhu was one of four IBM Corporate Leading Inventors in 2007 and the top of Master Inventors of IBM Semiconductor Research and Development Center in 2008. He is co-inventor and/or key contributor to several key technologies for CMOS performance enhancement such as Dual Stress Liner Technique, Stress Proximate Technique, and recessing gate to enhance channel stress of strained MOSFETs. As one of three outstanding contributors, Dr. Zhu received Outstanding Science and Technology Achievement Prize of Chinese Academy of Sciences in 2014.

Dr. Zhu has more than 260 issued US patents and published over 60 scientific and technical papers.

A tribute to the contributions of Professor Baixin Liu

文/ Julio A. Alonso

I first met Professor Baixin Liu when he visited the University of Valladolid in September 1989, and a picture of that visit is shown in Fig. 1. At that time I was already aware of the work of Professor Liu because of my interest on metallic glasses. In fact, in my first publication on metallic glasses (J. A. Alonso and S. Simozar, Solid State Communications 48, 765-767 (1983)), we cited the seminal paper of B. X. Liu, W. L. Johnson, M. A. Nicolet and S. S. Lau, Applied Physics Letters 42, 45-47 (1983), published a few months earlier. In that paper, which corresponds to work done by Professor Baixin Liu in CALTECH, he proposed a rule to predict the glass forming ability of metallic alloys. That rule states that an amorphous binary alloy will be formed by ion mixing of multi-layered samples when the two constituent metals are of different crystalline structure, regardless of their atomic sizes and electro-negativities. The *structural difference rule* was very useful at a time when predictions of the glass forming ability of alloys were still based on empirical rules. The structural difference rule also represented a novel way of thinking in the task of developing quantitative descriptions of the glass forming ability of alloys. This paper has received more than two hundred citations in the scientific literature, making that work a classic in the field of amorphous alloys. After checking the ISI web of knowledge I have discovered with great pleasure that my paper in Solid State Communications was one of the very first papers citing the work of Professor Liu, showing that I immediately recognized the relevance of the structural difference rule.

1989 年，柳百新与 Alonso 在 Valladolid 大学物理系馆前合影

Fig. 1 Professor Baixin Liu and J. A. Alonso at the entrance of the Physics Department, University of Valladolid, Spain, in September 1989.

During the visit of Professor Baixin Liu to Valladolid, we collaborated on the theoretical interpretation of some of his ion beam mixing experiments on Molybdenum-Nickel thin multilayers. I presented the results as an invited talk in Beijing, at the Chinese Materials Research Society International Conference in June 1990. That work was published in 1991 (On the formation of metastable alloys by ion mixing , J. A. Alonso, L. J. Gallego, J. A. Somoza and B. X. Liu, Thin Films and Beam-Solid Interactions. Edited by L. Huang. Elsevier, Amsterdam, pages 297-303 (1991)). That was my first visit to China, and after the Conference I spent a few unforgettable days as a visitor of Tsinghua University. My relation to the country was of the type "love at first sight", because of the beauties I discovered in China. The hospitality of Professor Baixin Liu and his coworkers at Tsinghua was splendid. The visits to the Forbidden City, Tiananmen Square, Summer Palace, Temple of Heaven, Great Wall, and other places in their company were a topic of lively conversations with my family and academic colleagues back home. All of them thought that I had been very fortunate visiting those famous places. A photograph taken at the International Departures Terminal of the Beijing Airport at the end of that visit is shown in Fig. 2.

2013 年, Alonso 与柳百新在清华大学的办公室合影

Fig. 2 Professor Baixin Liu and myself, at the International Departures Terminal of Beijing Airport, at the end on my visit to Beijing in June 1990.

Since that time I have been able to follow the work of Professor Baixin Liu, reading many of his articles on metallic glasses, and discussing topics of common interest during my visits to Tsinghua University. Some of his ideas have served of inspiration to my own work. Professor Liu is an experimentalist of high reputation. Even more, he is a dynamic scientist, open to explore new avenues. For this reason, in 1997, after realizing that the theoretical tools for interpreting glass formation in alloys, namely empirical rules and thermodynamic modelling, were useful but limited in predicting power, he initiated a new line of research consisting in the application of tools provided by computer simulation methods, like molecular dynamics, Monte Carlo and density functional methods. This new line complemented his experimental approach and resulted in robust papers where the experimental results are enriched by the theoretical methods of prediction and interpretation. First of all, he has developed interatomic potentials able to describe crystalline metallic alloys and amorphous alloys. The parameters of those potentials were fixed by fitting properties of metals and alloys to available experimental data; in the cases in which experimental data were not available, accurate density functional calculations were run to obtain reference data. In this way, Professor Baixin Liu has constructed interatomic potentials which are accurate and practical for the treatment of binary and multicomponent metallic alloys. In the course of those molecular dynamics simulations he made an important observation: for certain alloy compositions, the initial crystalline alloy experiences a phase transformation, that is, its atomistic structure changes to a new disordered phase, the amorphous alloy. In this way, by running molecular dynamics simulations for a number of different compositions of a given alloy system, it is possible to accurately predict the glass formation range, a prediction that provides a useful guide to experimentalists interested in preparing metallic glasses. I find this approach to the problem of predicting and interpreting the glass forming composition range highly original, and this has been recognized in the scientific literature by the abundant citations to Professor Liu's work.

Of high relevance are also the excellent reviews written by Professor Baixin Liu, which provide a comprehensive and knowledgeable presentation of the state of the art in the field of metallic glasses: Ion mixing and metallic alloy phase formation, Physica Status Solidi A 94, 11-34 (1986); Irradiation induced amorphization in metallic multilayers and calculation of glass-forming ability from atomistic potential in the binary metal systems, Materials Science and Engineering Reports, 29, 1-48 (2000); Solid-state crystal-to-amorphous transition in metal-metal multilayers and its thermodynamic and atomistic modelling, Advances in Physics, 50, 367-429 (2001); Interatomic potentials of the binary transition metal systems and some applications in materials physics, Physics Reports 455, 1-134 (2008).

The contribution of Professor Baixin Liu to chinese science has been substantial. He has maintained a continued research activity at Tsinghua University that has become a world reference in the field of metallic glasses. He has educated many young scientists who later have developed successful careers in science and education. This is enormously valuable, but I would like to stress also his humanistic side that I have been able to appreciate over many years, in particular his love for classical music. He has taken care of any detail during my visits to Tsinghua University, helping me in any way I could think. Scientific discussions with himself and his colleagues and students, visits to touristic attractions, conversations about the development of ours careers, splendid lunches were I received a good education on chinese food, conversations about our families, all this makes my relation with Professor Baixin Liu a lot more than just scientific, and I feel proud of being his friend.

Julio A. Alonso
Professor of Physics
University of Valladolid, Spain

学贯中西，儒雅人生
——贺柳百新先生八十华诞

文/魏炳波

时间过得真快，2015 年将迎来柳百新先生的八十华诞。但是，若非那一头银发标显了先生的年事，没人会相信他早已超越古稀。他作学术报告时语言仍然是那么犀利，分析科学问题时思维依然是那么敏锐，走起路来步履照样是那么稳健，甚至长年高度近视的眼睛经手术后居然视力大增。这一切让我们深信先生能够迈向期颐之年。当然，八旬的光辉里程碑也是值得认真庆贺的大事件。回顾多年来柳先生给予我学术指导和帮助的一幕幕情景，他的形象在我脑海中凝聚成了八个汉字：学贯中西，儒雅人生。

一、大师治学　中华情怀

柳先生是富有爱国主义精神的材料科学大师。

改革开放之初，柳先生积极倡导并率先实践了将载能离子束应用于金属材料表面改性和非晶化的研究，开拓了我国离子束作用下研究和制备非平衡金属材料的科学领域。20 世纪 90 年代中，他又敏感地意识到计算科学和信息技术的发展将对材料科学与工程产生巨大的推动作用，果断地将科学计算方法与实验分析技术并行发展，成为我国计算材料科学领域的奠基者之一。他的研究成果曾经两次荣获国家自然科学奖，这在众多材料科学工作者中是屈指可数的。

半个多世纪中，柳先生忠实地践行了中华民族厚德载物的古训。不论对朋友还是学界晚辈，他待人总是十分温和友善，从来不摆什么“大家风范”。很多年前的一个夏天，我第一次去拜访柳先生，向他求教正混合焓合金体系的相分离和非晶化等科学问题。对待我一个无名的后生晚辈，他竟然在办公室里提前准备了冷饮，并且让我先喝下消暑再讨论学术问题。然而，在坚持真理方面，他却变得刚性十足、严苛异常。大处，他对“文化大革命”中迫害过他的人可以不计前嫌，但是对学术界的不正之风却坚决抵制；小处，他不仅在学术讨论中待人平等、诲人不倦，而且不肯放过文稿中一个标点符号的错误。

大凡拥有欧美西洋风度者往往会有崇洋之嫌疑。柳先生的做事风格和生活情趣均有绅士风度，但是却坚守着一颗强大的中国心。他的人生哲学之一是：爱科学必须先爱国，爱国情怀是科研最大的动力。记得，第一次与他学术讨论时，他就严肃地告诫我：科学研究中决不可盲从跟踪外国学者，要有中国人的创新思想。去年，柳先生曾来西安参加一个学术会议。在迎接他的路上遇到严重交通堵塞，我随便发了几句牢骚表示嫌汽车太多了。不料，先生却说：“堵车固然不是好事。但是，汽车多说明我们国家富强了，是一件好事。想一想，你二十五年前在德国留学时买得起汽车吗？”先生的爱国之情溢于言表。

二、游戏英语　谐趣人生

柳先生是语言能力特强的乐观主义者。

对于我们大多数人来讲，英语只是科学技术或日常生活中的一种交流工具。在柳先生那里，英语简直可以说是他手中无形的魔方和桥牌。发表在 *Physics Reports*、*Advances in Physics* 和 *Materials Science and Engineering*: *Reports* 上的长篇综述论文仅展现了他精通英语的一个侧面，而他深厚的语言学造诣更多地显示在其他一些场景中。前几年，他应邀在全国材料研究会议期间，给研究人员做英文学术论文撰写的报告，和大家分享了他对英语中最简单和最常用到的“介词”的体会，并建议大家更多地用 of，而少用 on；还建议大家更多地用 concerning 这个词汇来代替 about，因为前者更雅。在和年轻学者交流时，他会问大家能记得多少个元素的英文。在和大家做文字游戏时会问大家：“柬埔寨的英文名字是什么？并告诉我们 Bangladesh 是孟加拉国，等等。因此，我常常猜想：若柳先生专攻英国语言学，他也可能成为一位语言学大师。

柳先生在科学研究中追求的是新益求新，生活中更是风趣幽默，热衷于体验各种新生事物。八年前，我刚学会开车五个月，买回新车两个月，多数朋友不敢坐我的车。恰逢先生来西安出差，于是开玩笑说：“您敢坐我的杀手车吗？”没想到他十分认真地说：“太好了，我就喜欢作做车和新手的新乘客。”两天后，他坚决谢绝由职业司机相送。我只好壮起胆子，小心翼翼地开车送他去机场。于是，他成了我学会开车后的第一位正式乘客。

三、热爱自然　创新摄影

柳先生是崇尚自然的锐意创新者。

我们的新校区位于秦岭北麓一公里的山脚下。柳先生前来进行学术交流的间隙时间里喜欢让我校的青年教师陪他进山采风摄影。山里没有多么豪华的旅游设施，多的是崎岖的山路和原生态的小溪流。但是，他竟然能够陶醉于这深山的大自然之中。有一次，他在山里看到峭壁上刻有一行大字：“一江清泉送北京”，高兴地像小孩一样欢呼：“看到我们在北京的饮水之源了！”更有趣的是，他坚持要求尝一尝这源头之水是否更甜美。恰好李金山教授是资深驴友，随身带有职业登山者配备的取水加热装置。李教授动作敏捷，在十五分钟内就地给柳先生沏出一壶泉水铁观音。饮罢，先生大声赞叹：“山涧泉茶味最美！”

我不懂摄影技术，但是发现柳先生是一位十分认真、洞察力敏锐的摄影内行里手。为了提高摄影水平，他不耻下问、随处学习。十年前，他来我实验室作学术报告并指导交流。对于所有展板上数以百计的图片，他都逐一过目浏览。最后，他停留在一张照片前：那是一条小鱼被悬浮在超声场中甩尾巴的瞬间特写。先生有点激动地说：“这是一位高水平摄影专家的佳作，不是你们这几位搞材料研究的青年人能拍摄出来的。快告诉我他是谁，希望有机会向人家请教。”第二天，我为他请来了此照片的拍摄者：西部著名摄影师、西北工业大学宣传部的郭友军先生。从此，他俩成为惺惺相惜的摄影知音朋友。为此，柳先生曾邀请郭老师和我到他家里去做客，并一起在清华园的全聚德餐厅品尝了正宗的北京烤鸭。

在历史长河中，八十年如白驹过隙。惭愧于自己脑钝笔拙，无以写出精美文字为柳先生庆贺。唯有学习先生不断创新之精神，继续历练二十载，待到先生期颐之年时，当弃拙达新再谢教诲之恩。

魏炳波
中国科学院院士、西北工业大学教授
2014 年 12 月 9 日

柳百新与魏炳波于机场合影

柳百新与魏炳波于西北工业大学合影

睿智勤奋的良师益友

文/潘峰

初识柳百新先生是1990年秋，当时已经工作五年的我萌生走进清华园进一步读书充实自己的念头，那时清华大学材料科学与工程系的机关还在现在六教附近的一所平房里。刚到系里，碰到的第一个老师就是柳先生，陪我来系里的李建保教授对我说，“你太有运气了，就跟着柳先生读博士吧。”就这样，我 1991 年 2 月开始在先生指导下开始了两年半的博士生生涯，并留校工作至今。二十多年来一直能在先生身边聆听教诲，可以说，我有幸是这个世界上受柳先生的教导最多的一个学生。

柳先生给我的印象是一个目标远大、非常睿智、勤奋、善于创新、会做科研、更会教书育人的良师益友。对柳先生睿智和善于创新的认识来自于我们第一次讨论博士生论文选题。我进入先生课题组时，柳先生在载能离子束与材料相互作用方面已取得了重大突破，提出了非晶态合金形成的“结构差异规则”，被同行简称为“柳氏规则”，成功预测并实现大量二元合金的非晶化；也开创了利用离子束诱导固体薄膜中分形生长的研究方向，早在 1987 年就在 *Physical Review Letters* 发表其重要成果。先生没有让我在上述方向做工作，继续巩固并扩大其成果，而是对我说：“你当了几年磁性材料厂长，我做了多年薄膜材料研究，发挥各自特长，那就给你两个关键词：薄膜和磁性，进行你博士论文研究吧。磁性薄膜应该是未来信息存储和处理的重要载体。”正是先生的睿智和对学科方向的高瞻远瞩，使我的论文工作如鱼得水，两年半时间里在贵金属磁性金属多层膜研究中取得快速进步，并在 *Physical Review B* 等刊物发表论文 10 余篇，也获得清华大学优秀博士生金奖和清华大学特等奖学金（当时每年全校五名，仅一名博士生），相关成果也因此获得 2000 年北京市科技进步奖二等奖。

先生目标远大、博学多识和专业造诣深厚成就了他的学术地位，他的远见卓识也体现在他在材料学科基础研究中对大方向的正确分析和把握，20 世纪 80 年代初赴美国加州理工学院研修后，开创了清华大学载能离子与材料相互作用的学科方向，并于 1993 年和 1999 年两次问鼎国家自然科学奖，并于 2001 年当选中国科学院院士。一定程度的“炒菜式”配方研究与物理学理性思考相结合是材料科学发展的理想模式。先生以其深厚的物理功底，自 20 世纪 80 年代以来，先后发展了二元合金系统、三元合金系统的非晶与亚稳合金相形成的热力学、动力学、原子尺度和第一性原理等多尺度计算研究方法，在物理学与材料科学之间建立起交互沟通的一条高速路，因此他穿梭于材料与物理学间的研究成果与日俱增，先生也因此应邀在材料科学顶尖刊物 *Materials Science and Engineering R: Reports* 和物理学顶级刊物 *Advanced in Physics* 上发表了有份量的综述论文介绍其系统性的研究进展。先生用计算材料科学的方法进行开创性的研究，与 2011 年 6 月 24 日美国总统奥巴马宣布的“材料基因组计划”的科学理念是一致的，充分体现出先生的高瞻远瞩。

也正是受先生的影响，我也学会了适时调整自己的研究兴趣与方向，2000 年在移动通信大发展的背景下，我联合中国科学院微电子研究所、中电集团第 26 所开始了声表面波滤波器材料与制备技术的研发，成功实现产业化，获得 2007 年度国家技术发明奖二等奖和 2009 年度国家科技进步奖二等奖。2005 年年底，自旋电子学与稀磁材料进入了人们的视野，我们又结合我们在声表面波滤波器研究中压电材料制备的优势，适时开展了稀磁、压电、阻变材料的研究，从而获得了 2012 年度国家自然科学奖二等奖。

勤奋、认真是先生让我们敬重的又一重要品格，现在大家对科学论文的看法由量向质转变，更关心的是论文影响力。早在 20 世纪 80 年代，偌大一个中国发表论文数在国际上仅排十几位，曾位于西班牙之后。为了鼓舞国内科技人员向国际科学前沿迈进，中国科技信息研究所每年公布国内学者在国际发表学术论文数的排行榜，柳先生曾以发表第一作者 SCI 论文而位居 1991 年排行榜首位，1997 年他的博士生陈益钢(现任上海大学教授)发表 SCI 收录学术论文位居全国第二名，这些都是先生勤奋最好的脚注。先生的勤奋、认真极有感染力，我仍清晰地记得在读博士期间，也就是 1992 年的春节，我在仔细分析所获得数据时发现了能证明多晶结构铁在铜层上外延的证据，这正是解释面心立方结构铁的磁学性能的重要证据。大年三十那天我非常兴奋地用电话向柳先生报告了这一发现，柳先生在电话中讨论后，让我尽快完成论文的撰写。正月初四一早我将已经写好的文章初稿送给先生审阅，原指望假期结束即可投稿，没想到先生当天下午就将已认真修改的稿子还给我，不仅对文章的结构、机理和结论严格把关，而且注重语言表达和文字推敲，并鼓励我尽快修改。我们从初四到初七的四天时间里三易其稿，并于初七下午通过邮局将稿件寄出，随后被德国固体物理杂志直接接收发表。现在计算机文字处理很方便，可当年每一次修改都需要用手动英文打字机打印，费时费力。为了论文良好的质量，先生甚至亲自帮我们把描绘在透明纸的曲线添加数字和标注。先生名下迄今已发表的论文将近 500 篇，每篇文章投稿前先生都要反复修改，这是先生的勤奋、认真、严谨和精益求精品格的诠释。先生的言传身教是我享用一生的财富。

柳百新与潘峰于材料学院实验室合影

柳先生更是一位了不起的长者，我们的良师益友，记得我一次跟中国真空学会前理事长庞世谨先生闲聊，庞先生突然问我：“潘老师，怎么做一个‘老人’？”当时我很认真地想了想，说：“老人好比大树，一种是大树底下好乘凉的大树，一种是大树底下不长草的大树，人和树是一样的，有些老人后面人才辈出，有些老人身后凄凉、人才凋零。”其实这也是我师从柳先生这么多年悟出来的，先生正是那棵好乘凉的参天大树。先生的包容、豁达、不拘一格培养人才，在先生的帮助下，他的学生在国内外都做出了重要成绩，有的已经当选为我们国家的院士，有多人在国内外大学任教授，有的成为国际大跨国公司的高级管理人员，有的成为国家机关的公务人员。留在清华的六个博士中，四人晋升为教授，两人获得国家杰出青年基金支持，张政军教授现在正担任材料学院首任院长。在柳先生的指导下，我们的学术团队健康成长，2008 年入选国家科技部新材料领域创新团队，2012 年入选教育部长江学者与创新团队发展计划，2013 年入选国家创新人才发展计划重点领域创新团队。

在先生身边耳濡目染到先生勇于创新的精神、严谨务实的作风、勤奋的工作态度，受益匪浅，先生是我永远敬重的老师。在柳先生八十华诞之际，衷心祝愿柳先生身体健康，长寿。

（注：潘峰，1993 年博士毕业，现任清华大学材料学院教授）

在柳先生组里读研究生的那些日子

文/张政军

前一阵子，收到潘峰师兄发来的邮件，提到明年是导师柳百新院士的 80 寿诞，心里感慨万分：柳先生明年就要 80 岁了！怎么一直感觉不到呢？细细想来，应该是柳先生一直勤奋的工作状态使我疏忽了岁月的流逝。他的办公室就在我的隔壁。经常，我早上来办公室的时候柳先生已经在工作了；经过他办公室门口时会看到他现在的学生坐在他的办公桌前，同他在讨论工作。这情景像极了 20 年前：在工物馆柳先生的办公室，我们也是坐在他的办公桌前，同他讨论科研中遇到的问题，聆听他的教诲。

时光过得好快，柳先生明年就 80 岁了。想到这，不禁回想起了 20 多年前在柳先生组里读研究生的那段岁月，回想起了柳先生那时对我们言传身教的点点滴滴。那段岁月，深深地刻在了我的脑海；柳先生的言传身教，深深地影响了我。

我 1991 年 9 月进入柳先生组里读硕士学位，1993 年 9 月开始提前攻读博士学位，1995 年 9 月毕业，获得博士学位。当时选择柳先生作为我的硕士学位导师，是受到了同宿舍好友程翔宇和斜对门宿舍好友车大志的影响。他们大三时就开始在柳先生组里做一些科研工作，也参加柳先生组里的组会讨论。两人经常对我说起对柳先生是如何如何地佩服——英文好、水平高、勤奋、对学生没架子、带的研究生都很牛，等等。这一切对我有极大的吸引力，因为我觉得读研究生就应该选择柳先生这样的导师。从 1991 年 3 月进入柳先生组里开始本科毕业论文工作，到 1995 年 9 月博士毕业这四年多的时间里，跟柳先生接触的多了，对柳先生有了更多的了解，也更加敬佩柳先生的为学、为人。

柳先生对学生的兴趣十分尊重，并鼓励和支持学生在感兴趣的方向上进行研究和探索。记得我本科毕业设计的主要内容是利用有色研究总院的高压电镜，对 316 不锈钢在 1 MeV 电子束辐照下缺陷的产生、运动、聚集、长大等进行原位观察，以理解作为快堆包壳材料的 316 不锈钢在快中子辐照下的损伤行为，为当时快堆包壳材料的研发与选材提供参考。这也成了我攻读硕士学位前期的主要研究内容。

我在完成这些工作的同时，读了一些关于离子束辐照和混合在薄膜内引起的相变与相形成等方面的一些文献，并产生了浓厚的兴趣，就大胆地向柳先生提出，能否也做些这方面的工作。我以为柳先生会劝我集中精力在辐照损伤研究上，没想到柳先生对我的想法给予了肯定和支持，并提出了许多建议。于是，在本科毕业设计期间，我又做了一些二元金属多层膜中离子束混合相变的实验研究工作。根据柳先生的建议，选择了 Ti-Y 体系，观察到由于离子束混合的溅射效应导致成分不均匀而发生的非晶化现象，确定了非晶化的成分范围。基于这些研究结果我和车大志在德国的学术期刊 *Physics Status Solidi*（*A*）上发表了一篇合作学术论文。随后，同赖守亮师兄合作的关于预注氦对 316 不锈钢在高能电子辐照下的肿胀行为的研究结果也发表在 *Physics Status Solidi* (*A*)上。这两篇论文的发表，激发了我对科学研究的兴趣，也坚定了我希望在柳先生组内攻读博士学位的决心。1993 年 9 月，在柳先生的支持下，我从硕士生转成了提前攻读博士学位的研究生。

在研究中，柳先生的学术思维极为活跃，在同他的讨论中经常会产生出新的想法。他非常支持我们去尝试新的想法，给出方向性的指导，并提出很多很好的建议。我记得在 1994 年年初，学术界还认为非晶化只能在生成热为负的体系中实现，而在生成热为正的体系中不能实现，因为缺乏驱动力。一次，在同柳先生进行讨论时，他说多层膜中由于界面的存在会提高多层膜体系的能量，在动力学上对生成热为负的二元体系的非晶化和亚稳晶相的形成是有利的，建议我在生成热为正的体系的研究中应该多关注界面的作用。这对我很有启发，想：对生成热为正的体系，如果增大多层膜中的界面能的贡献（增加界面的数量），是否可以采用离子束混合这种非平衡手段实现非晶化呢？这个想法当时有点怪异，但是得到了柳先生的大力支持，他和我进行了深入、仔细的讨论，确定了实验方案。在实验研究的基础上，1995 年我们报道了关于生成热为正的二元金属体系多层膜中的非晶化现象。同组的博士生金瓯也在 *Applied Physics Letters* 上报道了关于 Ag-Mo 多层膜中的非晶化现象。随后，组里开展了一系列关于生成热为正的体系的多层膜中离子束混合和固态退火的研究工作，探讨其中的非晶化现象和机制，并在 Miediema 生成热模型和界面能计算方法的的基础上，建立了生成热为正的二元金属多层膜中非晶化的热力学模型。采用非平衡手段，在生成热为正的二元体系中可以实现非晶化这一论断，后来也被国外的研究所证实。

柳先生给我的另一个深刻印象是他对研究工作的坚持和对研究工作的系统性、深入性的孜孜以求。记得 1992 年，柳先生让我跟从中国科学院物理研究所毕业后来清华做博士后研究的白海洋师姐一起，在 Miediema 生成热模型基础上，利用 Alonso 提出的关于非晶相、化合物、固溶体的自由能的计算方法，来构建二元合金体系亚稳相图的思路，由此成功地解释了 Ni-Mo 体系中的非晶化等现象。那个时候，在这些体系中还有许多亚稳晶相形成的报道。柳先生还建议进一步考虑亚稳晶相形成的热力学和动力学问题。因此我们将所观察到的亚稳合金相进行了分类，提出了计算它们的吉布斯自由能的方法，以及动力学机制，解释了这些亚稳晶相的形成。

实际上，从 1994 年开始，柳先生就考虑从原子、电子层次上深入理解亚稳晶相的形成和非晶化现象，招收了来自兰州大学、擅长理论计算与模拟的博士生赖文生开始这方面的工作。经过多年的坚持，借助于实验研究、热力学计算、分子动力学模拟、第一性原理计算等方法，柳先生研究组对于非晶化现象有了比较系统和深入的认识，发表了大量原创性的研究结果，并应邀在 *Materials Science and Engineering*: *Reports*、*Advances in Physics*、*Physics Reports* 等顶级材料科学和物理学国际期刊上发表了专论文章。时至今日，他还坚持对非晶化现象的研究，并不断在这个研究方向上取得突破。近年来，他的研究组在多元金属系统中的非晶化机理的研究中取得了进展，提出了预言金属玻璃形成能力的原子尺度理论，发表了多篇高水平的学术论文，引起了同行的广泛关注。

对于学生的未来发展，柳先生也给予很多关注和帮助。我记得 1992 年的时候，日本原子力研究所的 Naramoto 博士来组里访问，让我一起接待并陪 Naramoto 博士去长城参观。在交谈中，Naramoto 博士跟我提起说回日本后就帮我申请奖学金。我当时很坚定地告诉他，说希望跟柳先生读博士学位；如果将来有机会的话，愿意去他那儿做博士后研究。记得 1997 年我从德国转到 Naramoto 博士组里做博士后的时候，他还问我当时为什么不愿意去读博士。我告诉他，我很敬佩柳先生的为学和为人，希望从他那儿学到终生受益的东西。印象比较深的一件事情是，Naramoto 博士来访时，带了一瓶“乡音”威士忌酒给柳先生。柳先生知道我喜欢喝酒，就把酒给了我。那是一瓶很好的威士忌，里面加了不少的香料，香得有点过分了，以至于我们研究生班的几位同学一起在“大学生之家”的小饭馆里喝了它后，再接着喝啤酒时，大家都觉得啤酒是臭的。后来经常去日本，也喝过几次这个牌子的威士忌，只是再也没有喝出以前的那种感觉。在博士毕业前，我希望申请德国洪堡基金会的资助，去德国做博士后。柳先生帮我联系了奥格斯堡大学物理系的 Stritzker 教授，并写了非常肯定的推荐信。在申请日本原子力研究所和美国伦斯勒理工学院的博士后位置时，柳先生同样给予了鼎力支持。特别值得一提的是，在我申请加入清华大学材料系工作时，由于当时无法回国参加答辩，还是柳先生替我进行了答辩——这些是南策文院士后来告诉我的，这让我终生感动。

时光如同飞逝一般，转眼就过去了 20 多年，柳先生也要 80 岁了。想到这些，唏嘘不已，不禁庆幸自己居然能够成为柳先生的学生，也十分感激他指导和引导我选择了教师这个崇高的职业，并走上了我非常热爱的科学研究的道路。

（注：张政军，1995 年博士毕业，现任清华大学材料学院教授）

学高为师，身正为范
——祝贺柳百新先生八十华诞

文/陈益钢

在柳百新先生八十华诞之际，作为学生的我情不自禁地想起当年因为仰慕先生的学识和成就而进入先生的课题组学习的情景，以及多年来在先生的精心培育和关爱下从事研究的难忘历程。初次听到柳先生的大名，是源于聆听系里的一次专业讲座，如今已经记不得讲座的内容，印象里深刻的是先生的博学、严谨、简朴和轻松地探讨学问的风格，得知先生出生于江南，更有一种亲近感。所以，当年有直读博士生机会、选导师时就毫不犹豫地选择了柳先生，也幸得先生接纳。自从 1994 年成为柳先生的弟子近二十年以来，我无论是跟随先生在清华园求学，还是留学海外，直至近五年来任职上海大学，都一直感受着先生各方面的关怀，无论从事科学研究还是为人处事的方式方法，这些年先生都给了我极其深刻的影响。

柳先生是一位深受学界尊重的学者。他首次提出了离子束混合在二元金属系统中形成非晶态合金的经验规则和热力学模型，并用第一性原理计算论证了亚稳合金相的稳定性。提出金属多层膜中非晶化反应的判据，并用分子动力学方法揭示其原子运动机制。阐明了离子注入形成金属氮化物的规律。发展出强流金属离子注入制备金属硅化物的新技术。当年我跟随先生也主要从事其中某个方面的学习和研究工作。短短几年，先生的悉心指导为我从事科研工作打下了非常扎实的基础，至今受益匪浅。

先生的科研态度非常严谨和有计划性。记得那时候，我每周都会制订详细的实验计划，每周先生都会主动跟每个学生约好时间讨论上一周各自的实验结果。在如此细化的安排下，我们的日程总是排得满满的。记得跟着柳先生做研究的那几年，我几乎每周至少有 3~4 个晚上是赶实验到深夜，困了或者中间等待的时间就趴在实验室休息。每个周末，清华工物馆的走廊里几乎都是静悄悄的，但在我们简陋的研究室内，却总是有柳先生的学生在工作，其中也常常看到柳先生的身影。在那段时间里，柳先生经常放弃自己的休息时间，把年幼的孙子留给老伴倪老师照料，花费巨大的精力帮我一起探讨和分析各种实验数据，调整下一步的实验方案，逐字逐句地修改论文，更重要的是他告诉我们修改的理由。他对我们的要求非常严格，对实验数据绝对不允许存在“似是而非”“大概”“差不多”等说法。他一直告诉我，科学研究是容不得一丝一毫的作假和侥幸心理。在他的高标准严要求下，我只用了大约三年半的时间就提前完成了博士生阶段的学习。在这一阶段，我与课题组的老师和同学们分享了一些荣誉，例如 1996 年的国家教委科技进步奖三等奖；1997 年的第五届全国大学生“挑战杯”一等奖和年度 SCI 论文数全国排名第二（第一作者）；1998 年的北京市科技进步奖一等奖；1999 年国家自然科学奖三等奖。所有的这些荣誉，都是在柳先生手把手地教导下才取得的，尤其是他严谨的科学态度和精益求精的学者风范让我终生受益，如今的我不敢也不能忘记先生的教诲，坚持一丝不苟地按照先生当年的要求，传承给我现在的学生们。

柳先生又是非常善良和真诚地对待学生的生活方面的问题。先生在学术上对我们高标准严要求，但是在生活上却是很关心我们。经常会问我们食堂吃得如何？家里给的钱够用吗？春运了，回家的火车票买到了吗？每次开学去，先生都会问家里父母兄妹都好吗？最重要的是，先生在每个弟子毕业寻找出路之际，都会非常慎重地给出他的个人意见。更难得的是，他利用自己的人脉资源，亲历亲为地到外地或者联系国外的朋友安排弟子去适合他（她）的工作岗位。这在我所接触的大学者中是比较罕见的，可见先生对待学生真的是像对待自己的孩子一样，这让我一直钦佩，也让我一直感恩先生的所有付出。我提前一年半毕业，这在我们校史上也是不多见的，一般的导师都会尽量挽留学生多待在自己的课题组帮着带领低年级的学生们做课题，但是柳先生为了我的个人发展，主动提出帮我联系国外的朋友，我才得以在提前毕业后顺利地到德国从事洪堡博士后研究。这被身边不少的朋友所羡慕，我自己也深感荣幸。记得2000年适逢柳先生到法国开会，我从德国前去看望他时，他就为我今后的发展方向提出了很多建设性的意见，让我受益匪浅。先生一直希望我回到自己的国家来参与发展祖国的科学技术。如今，我回国工作已经有五个年头了。期间，柳先生多次带领他的科研团队到我所在的上海大学来指导工作和交流经验，我的师弟、师妹们也有多人到我们大学就职，他们谦逊、低调、务实、肯干、能干，在不同的岗位上将我们曾经的团队继续发扬光大。

陈益钢博士毕业与柳先生合影

在如今社会大环境浮夸的作风影响下，国内的科研风气也令人堪忧。但是柳先生以他一贯以来在自己的科学领域中所取得的建树和学术影响，坚持宣传求真、务实的科学态度和严谨的学风，仍然是我身边的一股清新的科研作风。我会遵循先生教导，鼓足勇气去倡导和保持“甘于清贫，甘于寂寞”的学风，坚决摒弃浮躁、虚夸的行为。

祝福柳先生和倪师母身体健康，幸福美满。

（注：陈益钢，1997年博士毕业，现任上海大学材料学院电子信息材料系教授）

师恩伴我前行

——记我的导师柳百新院士

文/赖文生

一、师生篇

清华大学是国内学术水平最高的大学之一，一直是我心中向往的求学圣地。在这里能师从柳百新教授，更是倍感荣幸！回想当年，至今仍历历在目。1984年我由江西龙南考入兰州大学，本科、硕士毕业后留校任教。留校两年后，我想进一步提高自己的学术水平，就有了再读博士的想法。于是我就写信联系一位当时已在清华读博的师弟，让他给我推荐一位学术水平高的清华博导。这样初识柳百新教授：学术水平很高，对学生既严格要求又和蔼可亲，跟柳先生读博可以学到真本领。我当即下定决心要跟柳先生读博，于是就立刻写信联系柳先生读博之事。过了不久，就收到柳先生的回信，他欢迎我报考他的博士生，并让我有时间到北京见一面。

1993年的冬天，我来到了北京，怀着一颗忐忑不安的心到工物馆去拜见柳先生。柳先生的办公室位于工物馆二层西北部252房间，252房是个大间，进了门是个过道，正对着的房子就是柳先生的实验室，实验室里面隔成两间，外间有10平方米左右，放了两张桌子，上面两台386电脑相对而放，是当时学生用来处理实验数据及写论文用的。里间，正是柳先生的办公室。办公室面积也约有10平方米，里面放了一张办公桌、几张椅子和几个书柜。我进到里间，就见到一位非常沉稳、儒雅，但很精神的中年学者，他戴副眼镜，微笑着招呼我坐下，正是柳百新教授本人。见面后柳先生的开朗豁达、平易近人，很快就让我的忐忑之心平静了下来。接着柳先生的侃侃而谈，更让我倍感亲切，相见恨晚应该就是这种感觉吧！我来时带了我在中文期刊及国际会议文集发表的几篇论文，柳先生看了一下论文，然后问我是否知道SCI论文？我告诉他，兰大很重视在国际3300种核心期刊上发表的论文，但我还没有发过此类论文。柳先生告诉我，他组里博士生的论文都是发表在这些期刊上的，其中在读的张政军已在国际物理权威期刊*Physical Review B*上发表了2篇论文。我听后心里感到柳先生组里学生的水平如此之高，是我望尘莫及的，于是更加希望能师从柳先生读博。通过交谈，在柳先生了解到我教“固体物理”及从事固体缺陷的计算机模拟研究工作后决定接受我。他当时告诉我说会给学校写信，争取让我免试进来读博，另一方面也让我准备复习博士生考试科目，做两手准备。他还告诉我，组里有个外校来的学生，在考英语时没考好，但他给学校写信，后来学校特批让这个学生进来跟柳先生读博。千里马常有，而伯乐不常有！柳先生在识人方面独具慧眼，果不其然，这位学生在柳先生指导下不仅英语过关了，而且科研工作做得非常出色，取得了丰硕成果！由于柳先生的学术水平很高，在清华享有声誉，最后学校批准了我免试入学读博，感激之情，难以言表！

1994年9月我便如愿地进到了柳先生的课题组读博，从此与柳先生结下了师生之缘！进入柳先生课题组读博后，我清晰记得，刚入学柳先生就找我谈话，让我了解了他先进的指导博士生的理念。他告诉我，读书方面你们是有能力的，上课认真听讲，把课程内容掌握就行了，有富余的精力要放到科研上，越早进入科研，工作就越主动，取得的科研成绩就会越多。师兄潘峰就是听从柳先生的教诲，用两年半时间就完成了博士论文，发表了十几篇SCI论文，给后来的学生树立了很好的榜样。我也很想按照先生的教诲行事，但实际上却没做到，原因是第一学年我除选修一些必修课外，还有助教工作。而助教工作内容对我来讲是全新的，所以花费了我大量的时间和精力。尽管如此，先生的教诲及师兄的榜样仍然鞭策着我要在科研上努力。所以第一学年我也抽出些时间对课题做了些调研。柳先生对我的课题安排是，能否与课题组的实验研究相结合，发挥自己的特长做些计算与模拟的工作？当时课题组主要从事金属多层膜的离子束混合及退火实验，研究材料中的固态相变规律，主要揭示非晶态合金或亚稳晶相形成的规律。我结合这些实验研究，做了相关的调研。第一学年我并没有实质性的工作进展，柳先生对我表现出相当的宽容，尽管他工作十分繁忙，但他还是抽出时间多次找我谈话，关心我的学习和生活，并与我讨论课题选择方面的问题。

在选定用分子动力学模拟研究固态非晶化反应为博士论文题目后，柳先生就为我争取到开展课题研究的物质条件。先是在材科教研组要到了一间小房间，是原来公用 X 光实验室里的一个洗照片用的暗室。房间较小，约 4 平方米，但很安静，我可以静下心来编写程序。1995 年柳先生又为我购置了一台 486 电脑，用于编程计算。半年后，课题组升级购置电脑，又为我优先置换了奔腾 586 电脑，以利我开展计算与模拟。在我读博的第二学年（1995.8—1996.7），我主要从事分子动力学模拟的编程工作。期间，柳先生经常找我谈话，关心我的进展情况，并讨论课题中出现的物理问题。通过这些讨论，指导了我的编程。柳先生对科研敏锐的判断和独到的见解给予了我科研的灵感，让我获益匪浅！

经过读博第二学年一年的编程工作，我的课题终于进入了令人鼓舞的新的阶段。当时为了加快计算，除了我专用的 586 电脑外，柳先生还让组里其他两台电脑在其他学生不用时也运行我的程序。1997 年我的研究终于有了可喜的结果，柳先生非常高兴，敦促我尽快把论文写出来。草稿出来后，柳先生马上在电脑上帮我修改。我坐在柳先生的旁边，柳先生一句一句整篇修改，不仅是修改英语语言，更是在修改中教会我如何更符合逻辑地撰写论文。一篇论文往往需要修改一周左右，期间还要反复修改多次。柳先生一丝不苟、严谨认真的工作态度由此可见一斑！作为学生的我，深受启迪并学会了如何写科技论文的真本领。我写的第一篇论文投到了 *Euro Physical Letter*，并很快就有了结果，于 1997 年 10 月在该期刊上正式发表。这是我在 SCI 上发表的第一篇论文，也是我人生的一次跨越：不自信的我从此开始变得有信心了，而且使我对科学研究有了更浓厚的兴趣。这一切都是在柳先生的帮助下实现的，刻骨铭心、永生难忘！

在发表论文过程中还有一件事让我记忆深刻，那就是柳先生与论文评审人的学术辩论。1997 年我重点研究了 Ni-Zr 多层膜的固态非晶化反应，对此做了深入的计算和分析，探讨了非晶化的机理、非晶相非对称生长及界面织构和温度对非晶化反应的影响等物理内容。柳先生鼓励我写一篇比较全面的论文投到 *Physical Review B* 上发表。评审人在第一轮评审中总体上还是肯定了我们的工作，但也提出了许多问题，如模拟的一些细节条件等。我们对这些问题作了一一答复，猜测修改稿寄回去后可能会被接收发表。但没想到在第二轮中，评审人又提出了一些问题，我们又一一作了答复。更没料到第三轮中，评审人又提出了更尖锐的问题：关于扩散系数的模拟结果如何与实验结果做比较。看到问题后，柳先生与我做了深入讨论，发现模拟的时间尺度(纳秒)与实验尺度（半小时）不同，因此模拟不能与实验做定量比较，模拟是非晶化反应的早期阶段，是对实验的补充，而其观察到的扩散控制非晶化过程，与后面较长时间的实验结果是一致的，从而揭示了非晶化过程是受扩散控制的。在与评审人的辩论中，我看到评审人不断提出新问题，且越来越尖锐，我对论文能否被接收深感忧虑。但柳先生在第三轮的回复信中，除正确答复问题之外，也表达了抗辩，即论文评审的程序应该是有序的，评审人有问题是合理的，应该一次性提出，而不应该不断提出新问题，使论文评审一直延续下去。编辑在看了我们第三次答复信后，随即做出决定，接收了我们的论文，发表出来一共有 11 页。通过这件事，我看到了柳先生作为中国学者的尊严与傲骨！在学术上，中国学者与外国学者一样平等，我们并不比人差，矮一头。柳先生据理力争、不卑不亢的态度获得国外同行的钦佩！这件事极大增强了我的自信心，对我今后的科研和工作产生了深远的影响。

1998 年在我们即将毕业时，先生和师母邀请杨涛、兰爱东、陈益钢和我一起到他家做客。共进午餐之后，先生和师母还为我们每人准备了不同的礼品（给我的是一条领带）。先生和师母祝贺我们拿到了博士学位，并鼓励我们要继续努力，追求更高的目标，将来做高级科学家。先生的关爱与期望给了我们巨大的鼓励和鞭策，促使我们要进一步努力去实现人生更高的目标。

四年以来，我们师生间从无浮华的赞美，也无世俗的客套，有的只是信任、尊重和爱戴！这种师生真情如陈年酒酿，愈久弥香！

二、同事篇

柳先生在 20 世纪 90 年代初就认识到计算材料学将会有很大的发展空间，将成为材料科学领域的一门新兴学科。1992 年创刊的 Elsevier 期刊 *Computational Materials Science* 和英国 IOP 期刊 *Modelling and Simulation in Materials Science and Engineering* 就是柳先生远见卓识的最好验证。1994 年我的加入使柳先生想尽早开展这方面工作的想法得以付诸实施。1997 年我的研究成果发表出来后，柳先生希望我毕业后留校工作，我欣然同意。1998 年柳先生以计算材料学是一门新兴学科、清华大学材料系需要相关科研人员为由，向系里打报告申请让我留校。我通过系里人才引进小组答辩后，便留校工作，从此由先生的学生转变为先生的同事。

1998 年 6 月留校后，我即担任了材 81 班新生班主任。柳先生非常关心我的成长，他告诉我当好大学教师，必须做好以下几件事：①获得经费资助是开展科研的必要条件，因此写好申请书，获得科研经费是非常重要的。②大学教师要提高业务水平，就要从事科研工作，带好研究生，发表高水平学术论文。③大学的根本任务是培养学生，因此讲好课是教师必备的技能。要做到这点，最好能做到教研相长。④大学教师要进行学术交流，参加学术会议，了解相关领域的研究前沿。先生的谆谆教诲，我始终铭记在心，并以此为镜不断要求和提升自己沿着这个方向奋力前行。

记得我留校后第一个新年就面临着写基金申请。先生建议我申请国家自然科学基金青年基金项目，为此他把以前的申请书提供给我，方便我参考。这是十分难得的！因为第一次写基金申请的我，看着基金申请书的各个栏目，一头雾水，无从下手，而柳先生的申请书如同雪中送炭，帮了我大忙。国家基金委靳达申处长曾经到清华作关于“如何申请基金”的报告，期间靳处长提到清华大学的柳百新教授基金申请书写得非常好，很标准，100%中标。当时听后，为先生的才华感到骄傲和自豪！更为作为他学生的自己感到荣幸！在后来的十几年里，柳先生基金申请一直保持了这个记录，是我国基金申请史上的一个传奇。也正是在参考了柳先生的申请书后，我完成了自己的基金申请书，更为幸运的是我的基金申请当年就获得批准！现今我还一直保留着柳先生当时给我的申请书，它同时作为一份厚爱被永远珍藏在我的记忆里！

柳先生在做科研、带研究生方面有着非常丰富的经验。早在我读研究生期间就已耳濡目染。工作后，柳先生仍细心传授我他带研究生的心得。柳先生带学生，希望学生与导师互动，这样学生可借助导师经验少走弯路，而学生及时把实验结果反馈，并与导师讨论和交流想法，可让导师了解学生的进展，及时给予指导。柳先生还时常召开组会，他先简要通报学生们的科研进展，然后与大家一起讨论科学问题。在组会上，柳先生会大力表扬科研做得好的学生，希望他们精益求精，百尺竿头更进一步；但先生很少会在组会上批评学生，对科研进展较慢的学生，柳先生会单独找他或她谈话，催促他们抓紧工作。先生以这种方式，不仅鼓励先进，而且又以委婉方式鞭策后进。先生非常重视总结科研成果，他嘱咐学生在做科研时要及时整理成果，并以撰写学术论文为牵引，让学生学会分析问题，总结论文的论点，完善论证过程和相关论据，再按规范格式及合理逻辑把论文写出来。学生写出论文初稿后，先生会及时让学生坐在他身边，然后在电脑上帮助学生逐字逐句地修改论文。正是先生这种勤奋认真、严谨治学的工作态度，使学生不仅提高了英文写作水平，而且掌握了做科研及论文写作的精髓！

在学术论文发表方面，柳先生是国内最先提倡发表 SCI 论文的学者之一。早在 20 世纪 80 年代末和 90 年代初，柳先生就在多种场合表达了做科研要发表 SCI 论文的观点。先生不仅这样说，而且身体力行，他获得了 1993 年国内以第一作者身份发表 SCI 论文数量第一名。在他的言传身教下，先生的弟子陈益钢获得了 1997 年国内以第一作者身份发表 SCI 论文数量第二名的殊荣。先生的真知灼见不仅使弟子受益，而且这种观点逐渐被国内其他学者所接受。目前，发表 SCI 论文已成为国内多数高校理工科博士生获得博士学位的要求。除了提倡发表 SCI 论文外，柳先生对发表高质量的 SCI 论文也非常重视。他经常跟我们讲，SCI 论文有三类：第一类是快报(Letters)，简要报道最新的科研成果。第二类是常规论文(Regular Articles)，详细报道具体的科研成果，这是多数人发表论文的形式。第三类是综述论文(Review Articles)，报道作者在某一领域的集成成果。第三类论文不是谁都能写的，而是由杂志社编辑约稿才能写的。一般作者须在该领域作出有份量的系统性成果，才会被期刊约稿。正是基于对 SCI 论文质量的深刻认识，柳先生经常系统深入地开展某个方面的科学研究，从而因成果累累被约稿而发表综述论文。他于 1986 年发表了第一篇 Review Article，后来的两篇 Review Article 我也参与了撰写，并分别发表于 2000 年材料类期刊影响因子排名第一的 *Materials Science and Engineering R-report* 和 2001 年物理类期刊影响因子排名第一的 *Advance in Physics* 期刊上。在先生的影响下，弟子潘峰教授和李家好博士近年里发表了多篇 Review Articles,所有这些成果都印证了先生在科研方面的高瞻远瞩以及影响力！先生的言传身教必定会让我们这些弟子们在科研这条道路上走得更稳、更高！

教学是大学教师的另一个非常重要的工作，也是培养学生的重要环节。因此，每位教师都应做到把书教好，而如何教好却大有玄机！我在读博士期间，选修了柳先生教授的“材料物理选题”课。记得柳先生当时上课时，给我们复印了离子束与材料作用方面的书，对书里内容，柳先生强调让我们自己去读，并出了一些题让我们做，而柳先生上课时则结合科研，介绍他的经验及相关领域的最新进展。由于我们都具备一定的自学能力，读书对我们而言不是难事，我们结合柳先生出的题，一边看书一边做题，很快就把相关的知识学懂了。然后在课堂上再听柳先生的科研经验及相关的前沿热点，让我们有耳目一新、融会贯通之感！由于我就在柳先生课题组里，他的课对我帮助更大，当时我还据此选定了博士生的论文课题：用分子动力学模拟研究固态非晶化反应。柳先生这种教研相长的观点深刻地影响着我！我在 2007 年开设的本科生“计算材料学”课里，也把自己的科研融入其中。在教学中我把原子作用势拟合的理论及我编写的程序教给学生，使他们学会了多体势的拟合，以及如何开展分子动力学模拟。我的教学方法受到学生的欢迎，在学生评教中，我得到了 8 个笑脸，获得的成绩比当年全校平均分高出了 5 分，正所谓名师出高徒！柳先生不仅在科研方面出色，教学方面更是卓尔不凡！

大学教师要从事科学研究，并了解前沿研究热点，进行学术交流就变得十分重要了。在这方面我得到了柳先生的大力帮助。记得我留校后不久，2000 年柳先生就带我去参加美国材料研究学会（MRS）举办的秋季国际材料大会。会议前柳先生和我都投了稿并获得了口头报告的资格。这是我第一次出国，一切对我而言都是全新的。临行前柳先生对出国访问的目的地、行程路线和住宿都事先做了非常周密的规划和安排。我们去美国，除了参加会议，还访问了四个单位，收获颇丰。一路上我和柳先生同吃同住，亲身经历了柳先生作为中国学者与人交往的自信、从容和真诚！

我们到达美国的第一站是访问位于 Ann Arbor 的密歇根大学（University of Michigan），这是应核能工程和放射科学系主任的邀请前去访问的，具体安排由王鲁敏教授接待我们，柳先生在系里做了学术报告：关于金属玻璃形成的原子尺度计算与模拟的结果。报告后，王鲁敏和系里另一位资深教授 Rodney C. Ewing 邀请我们一起喝咖啡，并进行了亲切交谈。晚上，系主任邀请我们一起进餐。

然后，我们到达波士顿，参加了 MRS 大会。对柳先生而言，作学术报告显得很轻松，把幻灯片往投影机上一放，就能流利地讲述其内容，出口成章。对我而言，却是件很头痛的事。我是第一次参加国际会议，并用英语作报告，心理充满紧张和焦虑。柳先生安慰我，并建议我把每张幻灯片要讲的内容写下来，然后在酒店的客房里反复练几遍。之后，柳先生当听众，让我试讲，并对讲得不太好之处提出建议。在柳先生的帮助下，我最后顺利在会上作了口头报告。

会后我们还应曾多年担任麻省理工学院（MIT）材料系主任的 Merton Flemings 教授邀请前去访问。Flemings 教授热情地款待我们，把我们安置在他和几位朋友合办的私人会所的客房住宿，周末他和夫人还邀请我们一起用晚餐。周一正式接待我们的是上一任材料系主任 Carl Thompson 教授，并安排我们到各个教授的研究组去交流，中午请我们一起在著名的海鲜餐馆用午餐。下午一点半报告正式开始，报告得到很高的评价。我心知能被邀请到世界一流名校 MIT 作学术报告，足见柳先生的学术水平之高。当时尤为让我感到惊讶的是，柳先生不仅英语水平高，作报告流畅自如，而且在与外国人一起用餐时谈笑风生，游刃有余。我被柳先生的渊博知识和学识所折服，这不是我能所及的，暗想唯有今后勤奋些，尽可能跟上柳先生的步伐。

我们接下来飞往华盛顿访问海军研究实验室（Navy Research Laboratory, NRL），柳先生在那里作了学术报告，我们住在 NRL 下属一个研究室主任 G. Hubler 教授家里。款待我们的教授是一位典型美国白人，他夫人是一位有色族裔的女士，他们非常热情地招待了我们。第二天，女主人还带我们去参观了她上班的地方——美国历史博物馆，并亲自给我们做讲解。给我留下深刻印象的是美国的博物馆都是免费对游人开放的。女主人曾来中国访问过，她对中国人民的热情和友善赞赏有加，并对中国的膏药情有独钟。临走时，女主人托我们回国后给她寄一些治疗颈椎的膏药。这次经历，我看到了中美人民之间的纯真友谊。最后，我们还顺访了柳先生的小学同学贝桐森先生工作的单位——美国国家标准与技术研究所(National Institute of Standard and Technology, NIST)。访问结束后，贝桐森先生在家里招待我们，并把柳先生的另一位同学汪家起先生从南方请过来一起相聚，并一起陪同我们参观了美国国家艺术博物馆，使我见证了友情的珍贵与恒久。之后，我们就从华盛顿飞回了北京，结束了此次美国之行。每次想起这段出国交流经历，总让我记忆犹新、感慨万千！柳先生学识之渊博、英语之流利和才华之横溢让我由衷钦佩！更让我感激的是，在柳先生的帮助下，我克服了内心紧张的情绪，实现了人生的一次超越，我对今后国际交流更有信心了。

2001 年，柳百新与赖文生博士于华盛顿艺术博物馆东廊合影

在我留校当教师成为先生的同事之后，写基金、带研究生、讲课以及国际交流这些作为当好大学教师的方方面面无不体现着先生的悉心指导以及无私帮助。的确，在我人生成长的过程中，无不渗透着恩师的心血和栽培！师恩如高山、师恩如流水，连绵不绝，永伴我前行！

三、朋友篇

在我读博士的时候，柳先生就反复给我说，我们之间有三重身份：师生、朋友、忘年之交。柳先生说，他比我们大约年长 30 岁，因此他与我们既是师生，也是朋友，更是忘年之交。因此，柳先生在与我们的交往中，既把我们当学生，也把我们当朋友。他经常与我们谈起他的一些往事（如“文革”期间在江西的劳动改造等），也和我们一起分享他的成功与喜悦（1993 年获得国家自然科学奖二等奖）及其间发生的故事。在我们眼里，柳先生既是德高望重的长辈，也是可以真心相交的朋友！遇到困难时我们也会向他倾诉或寻求他作为朋友的帮助。而先生对我们的关爱也是有目共睹的。记得我来清华读博不到一年时间，我的小孩就出生了。柳先生在鼓励我把心思放到做研究上的同时，在生活方面也非常关照我。他多次给我的小孩买了当时最好的雀巢奶粉，让我寄或带回家。在我博四不做助教的情况下，他还尽可能给我发补助，让我顺利完成学业。先生对我的爱护与照顾如戈壁中的涓涓细流、如冬日里的阳光时刻滋润并温暖着我！

在我留校工作的第一年，就遇上了实际困难。我的小孩由于疝气做了手术，手术后为了照顾得更好一些，我们决定把他及我的岳父岳母都接到北京，这样房子就成为我们急需解决的难题。当时我爱人还在中国科学院力学研究所读博，而我也留校工作不久，暂时还没有分到住房。那时还处于福利分房时期，学校会不定期地分批给教职工分房。记得，当时校房管处给了材料系（15 宿舍）一间房的分配权。这间房只是过渡房，即如果分给了教职工，而教职工在随后学校分房中分到了房，则此房要上交回学校，系里不再保留这间房的分配权。由于当时我的处境，就给系里写了申请，希望先借用此房以解燃眉之急。但由于当时系里留下的青年教师较多，大家都没房，所以把房分（或借）给谁？系里也很难办。当时系里主管分房的副主任提议，谁要这间房谁给系里交 8000 元，以示公平。我刚参加工作，没有积蓄，每月工资也就 800 多元，这笔钱对我而言也是一个大数目。当我把我的困难告诉柳先生后，柳先生二话不说，就替我交了这钱，解了我的燃眉之急。半年后（1999 年 7 月），学校给我分了三公寓的筒子楼改造房，我才把借的 15 宿舍房还给了系里，并把钱退返给柳先生。柳先生对我的慷慨和厚待让我感激涕零!

2001—2003 年我到英国利物浦大学工程系做博士后研究工作。尽管我在国外工作，仍时常与柳先生保持 email 联系。2002 年柳先生正好要到牛津参加国际会议，有机会到利物浦大学来顺访，柳先生就用 email 告诉我。我看过 email 后马上就着手订好了旅馆。柳先生如期而至，见到柳先生我非常高兴，也非常感谢柳先生能远道来看我。我所在组的 David Bacon 教授热情接待了柳先生，安排柳先生在系里作了学术报告，先生的精彩报告赢得在座师生的热烈掌声，尤其给予中国学生以巨大的鼓舞：中国学者一样可以做出出色的科研成果，赢得海内外学者的尊重！会后，Bacon 教授与柳先生和我一起共进午餐，并进行了亲切交谈。第二天，我们还一起参观了利物浦博物馆，了解了利物浦在英国作为港口城市的兴衰历史。期间我们从鸦片战争聊到了香港回归，并谈到中国的强大，必须靠国人的奋发努力。柳先生鼓励我要为国效力，我理解柳先生的深意是希望我能早日回国。先生不仅有着科学家放眼世界的胸襟，而且怀有一腔忧国忧民的爱国情结！先生常说：“科学是没有国界的，但科学家是有祖国的，科学家应该为自己的祖国做贡献。”先生这样讲，也是这么做的。先生中年时被公派到美国 Caltech 做访问学者，在那里做出非常出色的科研成果，两年后按时回国继续在清华任教，为国效力。正是因为先生的正直人品及出色的科研工作，于 1993 和 1999 年以第一作者两次获得国家自然科学奖，并于 1998 年当选为美国物理学会的会士(Fellow)。

柳先生也喜欢有机会带弟子们一同外出交流。2013 年上海大学准备成立材料高性能计算集成中心，并准备聘请柳先生出任该中心学术委员会主任。受上海大学罗宏杰校长的邀请，柳先生带着李家好、刘剑波和我一同前往上海大学交流。在这之前，我 3 月刚去南方出差，南方已呈现夏天的天气，穿衬衫就行。我回到北京，3 月 25 日就与柳先生一起飞往上海。因为我刚从南方出差回来，以为上海那里的气候也会较暖和，就没带冬天的衣服前往。没想到，刚到上海，就感受到了与北京 3 月一样寒冷的天气。我们一起出去时由于没穿冬天的衣服，我感到寒意逼人，不经意地打了一个寒战，柳先生见状，立刻把他的外套借给我穿，说他出来时多带了一些衣服。可见柳先生是多么的细致入微，对我的呵护让寒意尽散，带给我的都是温暖和感动！在交流期间，我们每个人都作了学术报告。在一个空闲的下午，柳先生以一个地道上海人的身份带我们去参观上海的市景。柳先生先带我们到繁华的商业街去购置著名的上海羊毛衫，我为自己和家人一共购买了三件，家人至今都赞不绝口！然后柳先生又帮我和剑波挑选了外套，我们都买了心仪的服装。接着，柳先生领我们去参观了他老家住地及他的中学旧址，并跟我们讲了他小时候一些故事及父母对他们的教育。他父亲是一位著名的雕刻师，家里并不富有，但对子女教育却十分重视。正是父母重教，子女争气，柳先生家出了两位院士。柳先生还领我们参观了上海西区的一些现代建筑。

2013 年 3 月上海静安寺前天桥上合影，从左至右为赖文生、柳百新、李家好

到了吃晚饭时，柳先生请我们在静安区的一家时尚餐馆用餐，还专门点了一道著名的长江鲥鱼。鲥鱼非常名贵，柳先生讲，他们小时候，父母只有在过年时才会买上巴掌大小的一块鲥鱼回家过年。当服务员给我们端上半条鲥鱼时，香气袭人，只见上面盖满酒糟，把酒糟拨至一边，即可食用。果不其然，鲥鱼肉质香嫩可口、回味无穷，是我吃过的少有美食之一。此行跟柳先生出来，让我们大开眼界、增长了见识！我们不仅与上海大学同行做了学术交流，而且观光了上海市容景观，了解了上海的历史变迁，也品尝了上海的美食。正是在柳先生这位朋友的引领下，一段难忘的旅程将永远留在我们的记忆!每当想起来，总有一种温馨和感动！

一路走来，柳先生始终是我敬重和爱戴的良师益友！先生在为人师表、严谨治学和与人相处方面都为我们这些学生树立了榜样！他的敬业精神和教育理念，深刻影响着他的学生们。先生一直教导我们要老老实实做人，实实在在做事，并通过他自己的一言一行潜移默化地感染着我们。我们一定会以先生为楷模，积极投身到中国的教育事业中去。在此对柳先生多年以来对我的厚爱和帮助，我想表达我一直未能通过言语说出的心声：衷心感谢恩师为学生所付出的一切！师恩茵茵，永生难忘！

值此柳先生八十寿诞之际，谨以此文向先生表达崇高的敬意！并祝柳先生和师母福如东海、寿比南山！

2014 年 11 月

（注：赖文生，博士，曾任兰州大学讲师、清华大学副教授，现为清华大学教授）

1998 年毕业季合影，从左至右为兰爱东、赖文生、柳百新、杨涛

越来越高大的身影
——记我的导师柳百新先生

文/蓝爱东

在回忆我攻读博士期间与我的导师中国科学院院士柳百新先生相处的点点滴滴时，我不由自主想起了自己在纽约帝国大厦下的经历。

那是在2000年一个阳光灿烂的秋日上午，我从麦迪逊广场花园的车站走出，平生第一次兴冲冲地走在纽约街头。在漫无目的的几个小时闲逛之后，我回头张望，突然发现，刚才吃中饭的麦当劳快餐店对面，就是赫赫有名的帝国大厦，蓝天白云间巍然矗立，于摩天大楼的丛林中鹤立鸡群。吃饭的时候，曾经端详过对面大楼的楼门，并无特异的感觉，又怎么能想到自己是在世界最有名的建筑下吞咽食物。那真是一个奇异的经历。

我对柳先生这样的学界巨人的认识过程与在纽约地标建筑下的经历何其相似。初识柳先生，由于自己学识浅陋，阅历寡鲜，浑不知柳先生为何许人也。只是后来随着自己专业视野拓宽，科研阅历加深，才开始体会和理解柳先生工作的非凡意义和他那特殊的巨大人格力量。事实上，我是离开柳先生身边多年以后，蓦然回首，才发现柳先生的身影的巨大，正如帝国大厦的恢宏。

1994年到1998年，我在清华大学进行博士阶段的学习，成为柳百新先生的学生。然而，事实求是说，我真正成为柳先生的学生应该是十年以后了。这主要是因为我那时的个人状态。我本科在国防科技大学应用物理专业学习。长沙潮湿的空气让我染上了风湿痛。一年四季，不间断的关节痛袭扰着我。因此，我本来脆弱敏感的性格上又加了一层阴郁的底色。有将近十几年的时间里整个人处于一种类似梦游的状态。那期间经历的人和事在记忆中都像蒙上了一层雾，模糊而遥远。直到2003年我34岁时，在美国新泽西的一间破旧公寓中坐困愁城。说不出的原因，让我从这种梦游状态中猛醒。自那时，在柳先生身边工作的情形变得一点点清晰起来。也就是从那时起，柳先生对我们的教诲在我心中开始产生了实实在在的共鸣。

1994年春天，在北京科技大学获得硕士学位后，我报考了柳先生的博士生。现在还依稀记得柳先生和陶琨先生主持的复试场面。多年过去，回答问题的细节现在已经模糊，只有先生和蔼可亲的询问依然历历在目。或许是这次的记忆深入我心，使得我日后自觉不自觉地仿效，自己成为老师后对学生的态度相当温和。

我的博士课题是当时国际科学前沿的研究热点纳米硅发光，以当时国内科研条件来说是极具挑战性的。刚开始时，柳先生安排白新德老师直接指导我。那时，柳先生的学生开始增多，柳先生只能采取排队处理的方式逐年开始重点指导。我是在博士第二年的下半段才开始接受柳先生的悉心指导。当时，柳先生的办公室在清华工物馆二层东面的尽头。那是一个不到15平方米的套间，外间摆放着两张老旧桌子，上面摆着一台386电脑和打印机。里面的房间就是柳先生的办公室。在不起眼的写字台上放着一部电话和一块玻璃板。玻璃板下整齐地放着柳先生为第一完成人的国家自然科学奖二等奖证书以及中国物理学会叶企孙物理奖的证书（我大概10年以后才完全明白这两张证书的份量）。有时我早晨8点来找柳先生，会发现师兄张政军博士已经在摇头晃脑地在计算机面前敲键盘写文章了，师弟陈益钢博士在桌子上动作麻利地准备样品。而柳先生已经在他的办公桌上工作将近一个小时了。陈益钢曾告诉我，柳先生每天五点钟起床工作。要是现在，我一定会羞愧自己的懒惰，但那时梦游的我没有什么感觉。其实，柳先生一直强调勤奋工作的重要性，他的口头禅是：Keep Working, Keep Thinking。柳先生传达的理念是，懒惰只能让我们的身体舒适，但绝不是现实生活的真谛。

由于我的研究课题不是柳先生的主攻方向非晶合金，在我攻读博士的前两年，我和柳先生近距离接触主要靠两周一次的组会。每隔两周的星期五下午，柳先生会让陈益钢买一些水果。当时所有的研究生，张政军、金瓯、杨涛、朱德华、陈益钢、赖文生、高坤元、林川和我在柳先生的办公室集合，吃着水果，开个两小时左右的会。有时，潘峰大师兄也会参加。会上，主要是柳先生在讲。柳先生的谈话内容是个人观察、科研经历、结果讨论、科学历史、研究动机和方法的奇妙混合物，从来没有乏味的说教。那时北京下午的阳光穿过窗棂在地上留下细碎的光影，小小的房间里回荡着柳先生温和悦耳的声音。我记忆中对柳先生的印象就是这样的时候刻画出来的。柳先生个子中等，肩有点内收，非常结实。已届花甲之年的他有一头标志性的花白浓发。透过厚厚的近视镜片，柳先生眼睛神采奕奕，经常闪烁出一种儿童才有的无畏纯真。面庞肤色偏白，高耸的鼻梁挺拔坚定，透露出发自内部的沉静。柳先生的微笑真诚，富有感染力。在清晰而自然的声音和语调中，柳先生和我们分享了他1981—1982年曾在美国加州理工学院访问研究的趣闻轶事，中学时就读于上海市圣芳济中学的收获，毕业后教授“固体物理”课时备课的辛劳等。从中让人体会到的是一个学者成长的经历，一段追求知识的成长史和一种生活历练下的执着。

柳先生那时说的最多的可能是加州理工学院活跃的学术氛围及学者们对基础研究的热情，以及柳先生在那里做出非晶领域重要发现时感受到的狂喜。我现在能毫不困难地接受到柳先生当时想传达给我们的信息。那就是要对科学有热爱，要乐在其中。这是从事基础科学研究最大的推动力。事实上，当时的中国正值下海潮初期，一切向钱看的思潮甚嚣尘上。时代变了，诱惑太多，很多人都无法静下心来做学问。柳先生在我们之中戮力营造从事基础研究所必须的踏踏实实、一心向学、勤奋工作的健康风气，用心良苦，难能可贵。小小的种子，开始世上所有的孕育。现在清华材料科学学科的兴盛，自然有柳先生的播种之功。

博士工作进入第二年，我的课题由于多方面的原因进展不利，我不禁开始怨天尤人。柳先生这时显示了他严师的本色。他毫不含糊地当面指出我努力程度的不足，事实证明那是我当时最需要的清醒剂。之后，我从深层梦游状态醒过来不少，工作的专注度显著提高。在柳先生的启发引导下，在博士工作的第二年，我在国内首先开展了离子束注入技术制备纳米级硅单晶的尝试，并系统地研究了离子注入在热生长的硅氧化层诱导生成的硅纳米晶尺寸与其光致发光特性之间的联系，最终以四篇第一作者 SCI 文章和一篇第二作者 SCI 文章的成绩在 1998 年获得清华大学工学博士学位。

毕业后我走南闯北。现在深切感到，作为柳先生的学生是多么的幸福。我博士期间的全部文章都是柳先生给一字一句给改出来的。事实上，我从没有看到有其他老师的学生能有这样的经历。只有我自己知道我的英文写作是从怎样的低点被柳先生一点一点带到我毕业的高度的。我的美国老板曾说过我的英文写作是他见过的外国人之中最好的。这全都是柳先生的功劳。

在逐字逐句的文章修改过程中，柳先生将他的科研思想和做学问的方法以春雨润物的耐心传授于我。记得有一次，在改文章的过程中，我和柳先生就其中一个论点有了不同的意见。年轻的我固执己见，根本看不到柳先生意见的妙处，竟然和柳先生争执起来，最终将一向优雅温和的柳先生给激怒而起身离去了。一旁的博士后赵新清赶紧指出我的问题，我也开始意识到自己的鲁莽和轻狂，暗自懊悔。正在我不知所措的时候，柳先生轻声步入房间，像一阵春风。他不动声色地在计算机前坐下，又开始用他惯用的食指敲键法开始输入。写完一句后，他转过头用温和的语调开始询问我的意见，满怀惭愧的我心神激荡，几乎要哭出来。那是我永远无法忘怀的一幕，柳先生又回来了！现在我生活经验渐长，更能体会柳先生当时的宽容大度，先生之风，山高水长。

如今博士毕业 16 年后，从中国科学院两年的博后，在美国游学八年，到而今在太原理工大学工作，一直在教育科研单位工作。其间遇到过很多优秀的人，也见过许多自命不凡的人。正如回首才看到气势恢宏的帝国大厦，如今我回首来时路，方能清晰地看到我的导师柳百新先生卓尔不群的杰出。在我心里，柳先生几乎可以说是自强不息、厚德载物清华精神的人格化身。

我个人生活和职业生涯有不少坎坷，思想和精神上经历过不少黑暗的时刻。但想到柳先生，总能给我力量。据我所知柳先生少时家庭并不富裕，壮年时下放到农场劳动，中年时也受到过不公正的对待，但从没看到过柳先生的退缩和犹疑。捋起袖子干活，不停地提升自己是柳先生的一贯作风，这也成为作为学生的我现在的行为准则。在美国八年，真切地体会到柳先生曾经工作过的加州理工学院的学术水平之高，条件之优越，也更钦佩柳先生当年能谢绝挽留，毅然回国的了不起。随着年龄增长，对中国历史的了解日深，开始理解和尊敬柳先生这一代人刚健朴素、深沉诚挚的爱国情感。像柳先生少年时曾经历过日本帝国主义对中国的侵略和国家经济落后、人民生活贫困的年代，对国家的感情自然和我们这些和平年代出生的人不同。柳先生常提爱国，那自是由衷而发，令人感佩。

1994—1998 年，从任何标准来看，这是我个人一生中极其重要的一段时间，因为那时，我有幸能在如此杰出的柳百新先生身边学习做学问的方法，学习做人做事的道理。毫无疑问，那将是一段我永志不忘的美好岁月。沧海横流，方显英雄本色，柳先生的身影将随时间的流逝愈发明晰高大。

谨以此文恭祝我敬爱的导师柳百新先生八十华诞！

（注：蓝爱东，1998 年博士毕业，现任太原理工大学副教授）

和柳百新先生的师生缘

文/杨涛

最早知道柳百新先生，还是在读本科时，看到学校的简讯报道材料系柳百新教授高水平论文发表位居全国前列。在基础科研领域，论文自然是评价学术水平的第一标准。那时候材料系还没有学部委员（院士）。和外校的学生谈论起自己的专业的水平实力时，虽然有清华这个大牌子，还是每每觉得底气不足。所以看到本专业原来有这么厉害的教授，很受鼓舞。也暗自想，如果以后能投入这位教授名下搞科研，那就好了。说实话，至今我美梦成真的事也没几件。还好，这个愿望实现了。1992 年毕业设计时，进入了柳先生的课题组，开始结下和先生二十多年的师生缘。

进课题组之前，虽然已经念了十多年的书，也一直憧憬科学研究，但实际上对科研基本上一无所知。得遇明师，那也是幸运之至。柳先生虽然是很有名望的教授，但也很关心我们这些初进实验室的本科生。当时实验室有潘峰师兄、张政军师兄，都是柳先生的得意弟子。他们科研能力很强，带我们这些本科生师弟绰绰有余。但柳先生还是亲自过问我们的毕业论文课题，还抽时间就和我们聊天。潜移默化之中，让我们对科学研究有了初步了解。

本科毕业之后，上了直博，正式拜入柳先生门下。柳先生对学生的要求，自然是很严格的。这也符合严谨的科学精神。但柳先生严格却不严厉，我从没有见到先生训过学生。先生总是身体力行，循循善诱，让学生掌握正确的思维方式和研究方法，以及养成持之以恒的科研精神。先生不但指导学生提高科研能力，还尽可能帮助学生提供积累科研资历的机会，比如鼓励学生写论文，总结自己的研究成果。

在柳先生门下两年后，我得到了去东京大学留学的机会。能得到这个机会，一则是柳先生大力推荐，另外也是因为在柳先生门下，已经有一些科研成果，相对于校内其他候选人还是比较有竞争力。这次留学对我以后的人生道路影响很大，使我有机会扩大眼界，到领先于世界的科研环境中继续研究工作。但也因为出去留学了，没机会继续接受柳先生的熏陶，不能不说也是一件憾事。去年我换工作从日本到美国时，得到了丁菊仁师兄、张政军师兄以及尚昌和师兄的帮助，饮水思源，这也是因为我们都曾是柳先生的学生这个缘。

除了在科研上，柳先生在生活上也对我们这些学生关怀备至。记得上研究生后，柳先生知道我们没有洗衣机，就把自己家的一台洗衣机送给了我们。当时学生宿舍生活条件不怎么样，特别是冬天洗衣服是一件非常痛苦的事。柳先生给我们的洗衣机解决了我们很大的问题。另外，柳先生带我们去吃比萨饼的情景也还历历在目。那时候，比萨饼在北京也还是比较少见的。

柳先生那一代人，因为“文革”的影响，被耽误了很多年。直到 20 世纪 80 年代初才有机会真正开始科研。但凭借自己的才能以及不懈的坚持和努力，取得了极大的成就，成为了名副其实的国际知名学者和科学院院士。光阴似箭，转眼我自己也已经到了柳百新先生初次出国做研究的年龄。惭愧的是，虽然碰上了好的时代和机遇，毕业后这十几年来却没有什么建树。虽然也写了一些过得去的论文，申请了些专利，但却缺乏在某一领域的深耕。自我反省，应该还是缺乏了柳先生那样的韧性和坚持的精神。我现在虽然已离开了基础研究，投入到工业界进行产品技术的研究开发，但柳先生的那种坚持不懈的科研精神，将会一直成为我工作上的鼓舞和动力。

1992 年，工物馆柳先生办公室

1998 年，工物馆柳先生办公室

2008 年，名古屋

（注：杨涛，1998 年博士毕业，现任职于希捷 Seagate Technology Cor 公司）

回忆与柳先生在清华园的时光

文/高坤元

时光如梭，一晃离开清华园已有十五年的光阴。如今的我，也在大学里从事挚爱的科研工作。而我做科研的态度、方法，与学生的交流方式，仔细想想竟有许多与十五年前柳先生教我的方式如出一辙。事实上，是先生将彼时懵懂的我带入科学的殿堂。很快，柳先生将迎来他的八十寿辰，在这样的时刻，作为弟子的我细细回想与柳先生在清华园的时光，和柳先生对我的培育，深深感觉一切都蕴藏在平常言传身教的点滴之中。

回想当年很期待的一件事就是我们的组会。组会差不多每两周开一次。组会令人期待的一个原因是每次会有水果瓜子什么的，另外的原因当然是内容。一般在组会上，除了讨论正在进行课题中的问题，就是柳先生讲述一些科研相关的事儿。记得一次他讲述在早期做分形研究的时候，一直比较偏理论，材料方面没有相关的实验支持。一次在分析极薄膜的生长形态的时候，看上去非常地无规律。柳先生也一直在思考，晚上他突然联想到分形指数，马上打电话给师兄，让他画出不同时间分形指数的曲线，果然结果非常漂亮，规律清晰。这是分形这样很数学的概念与材料的生长具有如此美妙的关联，给了我很深的印象。这只是柳先生讲的一个小故事，但这么多年来我时常会回想起来。在我面对实验数据迷茫的时候，在我反复研究终于获得一些精彩结果的时候，在发现又有新的理论发展的时候，这个故事总是浮现在我的脑海中。还有一次，柳先生这样评价，他说每个人博士阶段的研究工作都要有一个 excitement，如果有两个就更加棒了。只有有了 excitement 的工作才能获得他的同意毕业。这种评价在我之后的科研生涯中反复自问，我的工作有 excitement 吗？每每发现回答是 Yes，心中就会无比快乐起来。正是来自柳先生这样一件件小事上的言传身教，使得我们成长起来。

迄今我还常常和我的学生提起的是柳先生给我改的第一篇英文论文。记得当年，我大量阅读文献，努力做实验，认真分析，精心写作，当我把自己的第一篇文章交给柳先生的时候，心里满是期待，也很惶恐。当天下午，柳先生就来找我，我坐在一边，看着柳先生一边阅读，一边告诉我什么地方不清楚，应该怎么表述，一边快速地将相应段落改好。差不多一个下午，柳先生帮我改完整篇文章，最后写好题目和摘要，告诉我可以去试着投 JAP（*Journal of Applied Physics*）。面对几乎被柳先生重写的论文，那天晚上我辗转难眠，一方面目瞪口呆，痛恨自己的英语水平如此有限，一方面学习了很多科学论文的写作过程中自己不太把握的措辞，心中很不平静。后来那篇文章被 JAP 顺利接收，极大地鼓舞了我，之后我反复阅读理解我和柳先生的版本，自己感觉到了差别，受益良多，也更加努力地学习英语，阅读文献。在第二篇以及更多后面的文章，我都再没有花柳先生那么长的时间修改。今天的我也花很多的时间给学生修改他们的第一篇论文，并且常常提起柳先生给我改的那篇文章。希望我的学生也能像当年的我一样受益多多。

柳先生还是非常儒雅的人，在清华从师四年，我从未听先生说话速度加快，口气不佳，更不要说大发雷霆了。学生如果有问题是怎么办？别人的情况我不大清楚，对于我，总要体会一下才知道柳先生在批评我了。记得当年我总是很努力工作直到完成一篇文章，之后的那两周就会觉得很累，不免有些懒散，去实验室也不是很积极。每当这种时候，柳先生就开始和我讨论他在国外的时候实验条件有多么好，水平比我们高，然后语重心长地对我说："小高啊，你看我们实验条件比不上国外，我们没有别的办法，只有努力、努力，更加努力才行啊。"这时我才意识到那几天我迟到了，于是赶紧收心，重新投入到紧张的工作中去。现在我也是高校教师，我自己其实很容易着急，学生懒散的时候不免生气。但是每每想发脾气就想起先生春风化雨的育人态度，也就缓下语气。

还有让我记忆深刻的是在校时与国外学者的交流和国际会议的参加。20世纪90年代，中国的科研经费还捉襟见肘，通常学生们很难有机会参加国际会议或与国外学者交流。但在我们组里，柳先生常常会邀请国外著名学者访问，除了他与这些学者深入交流，我们学生也常常要求用英语汇报自己的工作。这对于我们绝对是个挑战，同时也很锻炼人。柳先生还鼓励我们和国外学者直接交流，为此我们要不仅准备好自己的报告，还要去阅读对方的文章，思考可讨论的问题。当然在讲不清楚时，柳先生会帮忙。这也给我们的勇敢提供了有力的支持。经过了这些锻炼，一次柳先生有事，没法参加中日薄膜双边会议，让我与师妹去参加。刚开始，主办方的老师看见只有我们两个小姑娘很是担心，轮到我们作报告时特意从另一个会议室赶过来听。当听我作报告到一半时，脸上露出放心的微笑。之后还特意表扬了我们的工作和英语表达。这都归功于柳先生平常对我们的培养和锻炼。而且，这也为我博士毕业后到国外大学工作顺利交流奠定了基础。

在清华大学与柳先生学习的四年是我难忘的时光。这不仅因为清华大学的校园曾是皇家的园林，这里有二校门、工字厅、水木清华、近春园、大礼堂、清华学堂等等所在，美轮美奂！更大的原因是来自柳先生。大学的本质来自大师，柳先生给我和我的师兄弟姐妹们带来的岂止是仅仅拿到博士证书！和柳先生在清华园的学习使我的人生从此真正踏上科研之路！

祝柳先生健康长寿，事事顺心，福禄吉祥！

（注：高坤元，1999年博士毕业，现任北京工业大学教授）

我的老师柳先生

文/杨国伟

此生注定与清华有缘，因为我的三个导师都来自于清华。我本科在郑州大学读物理学，毕业论文是在刘宏亚教授指导下研究广义相对论中的坐标变换对称性，刘老师20世纪70年代毕业于清华机械系，后来成为周培源先生的第一个博士，他生性有些木讷却有哲人气质。后来我到合肥工业大学读应用物理硕士学位，在导师毛友德教授实验室开展金刚石薄膜生长研究，毛老师20世纪60年代毕业于清华电真空专业，他待人极为厚道并且学识渊博。我的博士学位是在清华材料系读的，也就是在那个时候，结识了一位对我个人学术发展有重要影响的老师，我的博士导师柳百新先生。

去清华读博士前，我一直从事化学气相沉积金刚石薄膜的实验和理论研究，论文多发表于国内中文刊物，但是总期待着能够驰骋于国际学术舞台与同行共享自己的研究成果，所以诚惶诚恐地去清华叩柳先生办公室希望求教于门下。我清楚地记得在清华园工物馆一个宁静而狭小的房间里，柳先生在亲切而耐心地询问了我的情况后，热情地鼓励我来清华读博士，并且充满自信地告诉会在清华得到我学术上所期待的。这第一次的见面开启了我在清华的求学之路。另外，我去清华还有一个原因就是喜欢它校训中“厚德载物”四个字，做人应该先“厚德”然后才能“载物”。

柳先生既是一位饱浸中国传统文化的儒雅之士，又是一位深谙西方现代科学的著名科学家，他谦谦待人，在清华园被人尊称为“先生”，淡泊名利，数十年献身于科学研究，硕果累累。在清华读书时，材料系的师生只称呼两个教授为“先生”，一个是德高望重的李恒德院士，而另一个就是柳百新教授。当时颇为不解，因为清华园里的院士比比皆是，但是人们大多也只是称呼他们为“某老师”，而柳先生那个时候还不是院士却被称为“先生”已数年了。后来慢慢地就体会到了其中端倪，因为柳先生数十年来勤勉致学，脚踏实地地践行了“天行健，君子以自强不息；地势坤，君子以厚德载物”的古训。

做柳先生的学生时，有许多不经意的“小事”却能让我受益终生。柳先生的研究组有一个传统，那就是每一位研究生在读期间都会有很多的机会就相关的科学问题与柳先生单独地“面对面交流”，学生们不仅可以在谈话中毫无顾忌地阐述与先生不尽相同的学术观点，更多的是能从先生那里汲取到更有深度的科学洞察力和积极向上的科学研究态度，从而使得自己的学术层次和学术品位得到很大的提升。柳先生是一位很好的倾听者，会静静而完整地听完学生的讲述，不会在中间打断你的；同时，他又是一位犀利的批评者，会一针见血地指出你研究中的真正科学问题是什么。所以，在很多次的“面对面”讨论中，我学会了如何去发现实验数据背后的深刻物理，还学会了如何去欣赏和评价“好”的科学研究。柳先生办公室的摆设有点“怪”，与很多教授的办公室不大一样，偌大的大班台上几乎空空如也，大班椅也不怎么坐，而旁边靠墙的一个小书桌上则放着电脑并堆着一些文献，桌前有两把小靠背椅，柳先生在办公室的绝大部分时间就是在这个小书桌前，对着电脑上的实验数据和学生“面对面”地讨论学术问题。有一次在讨论完问题后，柳先生告诉我：让他最高兴的事就是知道学生们研究上又取得了新进展。后来在媒体上看到李政道先生在谈起他指导研究生的“窍门”之一就是一定要与学生“面对面交流”时，心中油然而生对柳先生“为师之道”的钦佩。

这让我想起刚从美国回来时去江南一所大学访问遇到的一件趣事。某教授领我参观完他的“高端大气上档次”的实验室后路过一个教室模样的房间，里面黑压压的坐着二三十人，每人一个小小的隔板位和一台电脑，我以为是学生在上计算机课，不料这位教授却豪迈地告诉我：里面全是他的研究生！“这么多学生怎么指导呀？”我本能地问了一句。他似乎很享受地说：一个也是养，一群也是带嘛。如果这样的话，也许有的学生几年都不会有与导师“面对面交流”的机会。真不知道这是导师的悲哀还是学生的悲哀。不禁感慨自己能够去清华成为柳先生的学生是一件多么幸运的事呀。

现在，我也指导研究生，除了假期、上课和出差以外，每天上午九点整都会在我的办公室里与学生“面对面交流”，讨论学生们的研究进展和问题，日复一日，年复一年，不知窗外桑田沧海。我的电脑也放在一个靠墙的小书桌上，每当学生们的研究有突破时，我都会在这个小书桌前与他们一起分享成功的快乐。有一次央视记者来做访问，她进我办公室的第一句话就是：杨教授的办公桌是我见过的最干净的办公桌了！可不是嘛，学校给我配的大班台上空无一物、一尘不染。我很喜欢英国诗人兰德的一句诗：我和谁都不争，和谁争我都不屑。不知怎么，每当我读到这句诗时就会想起柳先生。

（注：杨国伟，2000年博士毕业，现任中山大学物理科学与工程技术学院教授）

贺恩师柳百新先生八十大寿
——记先生二三事

文/刘剑波

我的恩师柳百新先生，是一位治学严谨的学者，是一位和蔼可亲的长者，是弟子们的良师益友。

我认识先生，从在先生门下攻读博士学位，到游学美国，三年前又回到母校任教，再次进入先生的研究组，到现在近十七个年头。

还在本科低年级的时候，就对先生大名如雷贯耳，知道先生做了很多高水平的学术工作，发表很多 SCI 论文，在清华校内独树一帜。初次见到先生，是 1996 年做专业课实验的时候，远远地看到先生从门口走过。只记得先生的头发花白，微微驼背，背影高大。那时候并没有和先生有交流，其实算不得初识吧。

时间到了 1997 年秋，我在清华大学的学习，进入了第五个秋天。在那年的秋天，我面临着一次关键的人生抉择。是加入找工作大军，还是对美国大学教授进行电邮轰炸，抑或选择本校推荐直读研究生，这是摆在我们全班同学面前的几个选择。有人说，漫漫人生路，有无数的选择，但紧要处只有几步，不同的选择，可能会决定我们不同的人生道路。考虑再三，觉得留在本校攻读博士学位，对我是一个很好的选择。在选择博士生导师的时候，我想何不试试一直慕名的柳先生呢。于是我冒昧地闯进了柳先生的办公室。很不巧，柳先生那天身体不适，不在办公室。好心的张师姐给柳先生家里打电话，讲明情况，于是我第一次得以在先生家里见到了柳先生。

那时先生还住在西南小区，是老式的单元房，面积不大，陈设朴实，这是我对先生家的第一印象。我和先生对面而坐，心里忐忑不安，毕竟这是一次关系到我未来人生的紧要关口啊！先生容貌清瘦，头发花白，戴着厚厚的近视眼镜，典型的中国高级知识分子的形象。先生很和蔼，说话速度不快，声音也不大，但是很清晰。先生先随口问了我几句，了解下情况，不经意间，平复了我紧张的心情。然后问我，为什么要读研究生。我愣了一下，回答说，我对科研感兴趣，想在先生这里做出点工作来。先生显得很高兴，说清华的学生，都是全国各地来的优秀生，高中成绩一般都很好，但是高中和本科的成绩好坏，并不能说明什么，进入研究生阶段，所有的成绩都要归零。本科注重学习，研究生阶段除了学习知识，更重要的是 Do research，某种意义上讲，研究生特别是博士生，更多的是要创造知识。先生的话让我印象深刻，多年以后，当我也成为一名教师，在指导我的研究生的时候，我也是这么跟我的学生开宗明义地说明本科和研究生阶段的不同的。先生说最重要的就是要有做出好工作的意愿，正所谓聪明出于勤奋，天才在于积累，勤能补拙。

先生的话总是既浅显又富有哲理。于是，在 1997 年的秋天，我成为了先生众多弟子中的一员。先生在指导学生的时候，有着其独特的一套哲学。他总是循循善诱，对弟子的工作，一般以鼓励为主，非常注意保护学生的工作积极性，对弟子极具包容性。记得我从 1998 年 9 月正式开始在先生的指导下攻读博士学位，我的研究方向选定为第一性原理计算研究合金亚稳相的结构。这对于我们研究组，算是一个全新的研究方向。记得当时组里购买了 SGI Octane 工作站和 VASP 第一性原理计算程序。当时的我，对于 UNIX/LINUX 系统一无所知，VASP 程序也是以源代码的方式发行的，所以摆在我面前的第一道难题就是掌握 UINIX 系统的操作和编译出 VASP 程序的可执行文件。我花了三个月的时间掌握的 UNIX 系统的基本操作，并成功编译出 VASP 程序，期间柳先生多次过问，并给予鼓励。接下来我又花了大约半年的时间自己学习 VASP 程序的使用。那时候国内做材料计算与模拟的人远不如现在这么多，有关学习 VASP 的资料也很少，应该说我们组是国内较早就开展材料计算与模拟的课题组之一，而我选择的研究方向，对于我们组来说也是一次新的尝试，没有师兄师姐们的现成经验供我参考。所以，在刚开始做第一性原理计算的时候，我身上的压力还是比较大的。跟我同一届进入课题组的兆峰，做实验已经取得了相当多的成果，文章都已经发表了一篇了，而我还处于学习 VASP 程序的阶段。那时候的我，内心其实是相当焦虑的。柳先生多次鼓励我，并和我讨论课题的进展，在研究中给了很多有用的建议。可以说如果没有先生的不断鼓励和帮助，我不知道我能不能够坚持下来。终于在我博士二年级的时候，工作小有进展，这时候，先生鼓励我写一篇小短文，把那阶段的工作成果，做一个小结。

记得我花费了数个白天与黑夜的奋战，写出来的初稿，柳先生很快就看完并给出了反馈意见。这是先生的工作特点。先生工作作风从不拖沓，什么事情都是走在别人前面。学生的文章，先生一般一天就会处理完毕。回想起来，我的第一篇文章初稿，写得实在是很差，不像学术论文，倒像是实验报告了。先生并没有说什么批评的话，他指导我对文章的结构做了调整。当我完成第二稿之后，自己也感觉论文像样多了。先生和我一起坐在电脑前面修改文章，这是先生的工作方式之一。他喜欢坐在电脑前和学生一起修改文章，边修改边讲解为什么这么修改，为什么句子这么写会更好。这样的工作方式，保证了师生之间能够实时无障碍地交流。窃以为，这其实是先生工作高效多产的秘诀之一。终于，经过多次 Referee 的评审，我的第一篇论文在数次投稿与修改之后，于 2000 年的夏天被 *Physical Review B* 杂志接收发表。至今，我还记得柳先生告诉我这个消息的时候脸上的笑容，还记得听到这个消息后，我心中那种如释重负的感觉。

柳先生对弟子的学习、工作和生活总是很关心。在我博士四年级的时候，我决定争取去美国做博士后研究。我联系到了 PSU 的 Prof. Chen 和 UIUC 的 Prof. Johnson，先生给我写了推荐信。虽然我没有看到推荐信的原文，但我猜想先生的推荐信起到了关键性的作用。最终这两位教授，都同意接收我去做博士后研究。先生又毫无保留地把他对 PSU 和 UIUC 这两所学校的印象，以及他多年来和国外教授交流的经验，传授给我。最终我选择到 UIUC 去做博士后。

记得我毕业后，经过漫长的等待和烦琐的程序，终于在 2003 年 2 月拿到了去美国工作的 H1b 签证。为了送别我即将去美国做博士后研究，在 2 月中旬的一个晚上，柳先生和师母倪老师邀请我、我太太和我父母一起聚餐。晚餐间先生说到，他和弟子之间有三重关系，既是师生关系，也是朋友关系，并说他把学生也看成是自己的子女一样。一席话，让我全家人都很感动，心里暖洋洋的。是的，先生对我的关怀无微不至。那天晚上，先生给我讲了很多在美国生活和学习的经验。他询问了我的航班，告诉我在 Detroit 机场如何入关，如何倒航班。如果没有先生的经验之谈，估计在第一次踏上美国的国土时，我会更加手忙脚乱吧。

多年以后，我选择再次回到清华，回到材料系工作。柳先生又为我工作的事情，前后奔走。我真的很幸运，能够再次回到先生的身边，加入他的研究团队工作。感激之情无以言表，可以说没有柳先生的帮助和关怀，就没有我的今天。

谨以此短文，祝贺柳先生八十大寿！

（注：刘剑波，2002 年博士毕业，现任清华大学材料学院讲师）

先生言传身教 促我学术成长

文/李正操

1998年初秋，打算推研的我在工物馆了解材料方向研究生导师的情况。在走廊的宣传栏里，一张柳先生指导研究生的照片吸引了我，同时在研究生获得国外学术奖励一栏，我注意到“柳百新”老师同时是多位获奖者的导师——这是我第一次留意到柳先生的名字。巧得很，一字班的学姐张青恰好从走廊经过，看到了我，问：“小操，你在这儿做什么呢？”我告诉学姐，我打算找一位材料方向的导师，我要读研究生。她便介绍我去见柳先生。当时柳先生的办公室空间小，条件简陋，没有空调，只有一台落地扇。我忐忑地说明来意，没想到柳先生待我非常亲切，鼓励我尝试申请到他组里读直博。

获得直博资格后，我很早就开始进实验室了。柳先生专注科研，工作勤奋，每天不到八点就已经到办公室了。偶尔不忙时，他会向我讲起自己早年求学的经历，让我觉得现在这么好的学习机会和条件真的是来之不易。他还常忆起改革开放后出国做访问学者和参加国际学术会议的故事，让我深受教育。

在读博期间，我参与过几位外宾的接待工作，其中西班牙的 Alonso 和美国的 Perepezko 先生给我留下的印象最深。Alonso 这个名字我以前在论文中见到过，发展出基于 Miedema 模型的半定量热力学计算方法，我们当时称 Miedema 模型和 Alonso 方法。而 Perepezko 是美国工程院的院士，大名鼎鼎的学者。回想起来，当年跟他们的近距离接触对我后来走上从教之路也起到了一定的激励作用。

柳先生积极参加国际学术交流活动。早在1981年，他就因做访问学者期间工作出色而在美国材料研究学会（Materials Research Society）的秋季会议上做过口头报告，回国后柳先生在科研上不断创新，多次带学生参会并获得好评。离子束材料改性（Ion Beam Modification of Materials）国际会议，每两年一次，在美洲、欧洲、亚洲等几大洲轮流举行，柳先生曾在法国、意大利、美国、荷兰、澳大利亚等不同国家出席，并做大会报告或特邀报告。国际快冷和亚稳态材料大会（Rapid Quenching）系列会议都曾有他的身影，他还先后十多次到访日本等国家进行学术交流。每次参加完国际会议后，柳先生都给我们讲会上的所见所闻所获，总结该如何准备国际会议的报告，如何回答同行提出的问题，等等。

参加国际交流活动，英语表达直接影响到学术报告水平和沟通效果。因为口语交流与单纯撰写英文文章有很大的不同。文章写作有很多文献可以参考学习，细细推敲，但在参加国际学术会议时，需要面对面的交流，面对听众的提问，需要短时间内回应和作答。我自知英语基础一般，刚开始参加国际会议心里总有些底气不足。但正是柳先生的言传身教让我日后敢于参与国际交流活动，并在会上大胆地展示自己的学术成果，这给我后来从事学术研究工作带来了重要的影响。

我至今仍清晰地记得，最初参加两次中国材料研究学会的会议时，柳先生每次都让我们提前准备好 PPT，并帮助我们修改，柳先生还会告诉我们听众可能会提到的问题，并提示我们应该如何应答。我两次参加会议，都遵循柳先生的指导做了比较充分的准备，因此两次都赢得了中国材料研究学会颁发的优秀论文奖。同时，让我印象特别深刻的是，2002年在中国材料研究学会学术交流大会上，柳先生应邀作大会报告，他讲得非常流利，主线也格外清晰，赢得了全场听众的热烈掌声。同年，中国科协在深圳大学组织召开首届全国优秀博士生论坛，柳先生也非常支持并鼓励我前去参与交流。这三次会议虽然都是国内会议，但柳先生都非常重视，并让我认真准备，通过这三次会议，我增长了学识，增强了信心，开阔了视野，积累了经验，可谓是收获颇丰。

2003 年博士毕业时，我得益于柳先生的言传身教，申请到了东京大学一个助理教授的岗位。日方还专门派了一位老师到北京面试。我当时很紧张，毕竟这是我第一次被国外单位面试，柳先生给我讲了好多东京大学核学科方面的背景情况，并提醒我应该如何准备面试。这个时候我知道了东京大学核学科的几位前辈，比如 Hashiguchi、Ishino 先生等学术大家。有了充分的准备，我在面试中有了较好的发挥，最终顺利获得了这个助理教授的岗位。

2003 年至 2006 年在东京大学的那段时间，我在量子工程与系统科学系工作，主要从事核材料辐照损伤方面的工作。我时常与柳先生联系，了解到柳先生带着师弟们去欧洲等地参加国际学术会议，这让青年学子很早就有了国际学术交流的经历，这些宝贵经历无疑对他们日后的成长和发展是非常有帮助的。我还记得 2004 年，柳先生带领孔令体和龚浩然两位师弟一起到意大利参加计算材料科学的国际会议，使他们有很大收获。孔令体毕业后到加拿大做博士后，后来回到上海交通大学工作，现在在上海交通大学材料学院任教。龚浩然毕业后去美国做博士后研究，回国后在中南大学任教。他们在工作中也十分重视国际学术交流，这应该就是一种传承吧。

2006 年，我回到母校清华大学，继续在核材料领域开展学术研究工作。我仍然坚持参加领域内的一些重要学术会议，最初经常是作一些口头报告，甚至个别时候是墙报展示。后来随着工作的深入，一些学术成果受到了国际同行的关注，开始作更多的邀请报告和大会报告。2013 年 5 月参加了在法国召开的第 17 届国际反应堆压力容器材料辐照脆化机制研讨会，大会主席在开幕式上宣布我成为国际辐照损伤机制委员会（IGRDM）的第一位中国成员，这时候获得博士学位已经将近十年的时间，正是这十年的坚持和柳先生教给我的“国际学术交流要不卑不亢”让我能够在国际学术交往中取得了这样的成绩。

2012 年，柳先生受聘担任中广核国际顾问委员会委员， 2012 年和 2013 年我连续两次作为陪同人员和柳先生一起去参加了顾问委员会的会议，这两次会议上的“旁听”，也让我更多地了解到国际核电厂材料和部件老化的情况。在第二次顾问委员会上，有一天讨论到反应堆压力容器的脆化问题，这时候负责解答该问题的是一位国外专家，他做了简单的回应，并提到如果希望了解更多，可以寻求国际辐照损伤机制委员会（IGRDM）的帮助。当时在场的顾问委员会主席、美国工程院院士 Dr. Roger Staehle 也说目前国际顾问委员会的委员中还没有人在国际辐照损伤机制委员会中。这时候在会场“旁听”的我举手请求发言，我说我有幸参加了 IGRDM，目前是 IGRDM 的成员。记得当时 Dr. Staehle 很激动，连忙拿着纸笔过来记下我的名字和联系方式，并在随后的茶歇中专门找我聊了一会儿，希望我能在反应堆压力容器辐照脆化方面的咨询工作中发挥更大作用。这次会后，柳先生及时地了解到反应堆压力容器脆化问题在国际顾问委员会的工作中的重要性，让我准备了一份简历，并向中广核国际顾问委员会推荐我成为一名委员。经柳先生的推荐，Staehle 主席征询了顾问委员会全体委员的意见后，中广核正式邀请我加入到国际顾问委员会中参加工作。

十六年来，我从柳先生的殷殷教诲中感悟了很多，博士毕业后我也走上了高校教师这个神圣的岗位。在我指导研究生的这些年，我也积极鼓励和支持学生参加国内外学术交流活动，希望把这种重视学术交流的精神传承下去，我也相信，这种精神一定会使更多的青年学子像我一样受益，走在学术研究的前端。

（注：李正操，2003 年博士毕业，现任清华大学材料学院教授）

难忘师恩情

文/龚浩然

时光飞逝，转眼间，博士毕业已过十年。回想在清华读博的日子里与柳先生相处的点点滴滴，仍然历历在目，仿佛昨日；恩师柳先生的谆谆指导和殷切教诲，恰似余音犹在，仍绕耳旁。

记得第一次见到柳先生，是在2000年的冬天。那时候，我在湖南株洲的一家公司上班，萌发了继续读博的想法。趁着在北京学习的一个机会，我拨通了柳先生的电话，于是柳先生热情地约我在他的办公室见面。柳先生给我的第一印象是一位思维敏捷、精神矍铄的老人，满头银发，厚重的眼镜片里发射出睿智的光芒。那天，他详细询问了我的个人情况，对我工作多年还想求学的想法给与了充分的肯定。柳先生还带我参观了课题组的实验室，并叫了对面办公室的程向前师兄过来一起聊天。愉快难忘的见面给我留下了深刻的印象，也使我下定决心要报考柳先生的博士。进入课题组后我才慢慢发现，将几位弟子喊到自己的办公室“聊天”，在看似随便的聊天讨论中产生许多灵感和idea，是柳先生的一大工作风格。

2001年读博初期，柳先生安排我做的第一个课题是Cu-Ta多体势的建立。在此之前，我们课题组已经毕业的赖文生师兄和张青师姐等在多体势的建立和分子动力学模拟方面已做了大量的杰出工作，他们的工作主要集中在生成热为负的二元系统。至于生成热为正的系统，课题组当时还没有建立相关的多体势，而Cu-Ta系统正是一个生成热为正的二元系统。在孔令体师兄的大力帮助下，在赖文生师兄和张青师姐工作的基础上，我慢慢掌握了Cu-Cu和Ta-Ta势的建立。然而Cu-Ta交叉势的建立，却遇到了极大的困难：我发现文献中已有的几种交叉势形式对于Cu-Ta来说拟合的效果都很不好。在反复尝试、不断失败的几个月中，我感觉很挫败和沮丧。当时，柳先生没有丝毫的批评和指责，反而经常安慰、启发和激励。后来，我在文献中某种交叉势的基础上，经过修改和数学变换，提出了一种新的交叉势函数形式，获得了较好的Cu-Ta交叉势拟合效果。不过，对于这样的大胆尝试，我心里是忐忑不安的，担心得不到同行的认可。正是柳先生的大力肯定和鼓励，使我才有信心将这个新的Cu-Ta交叉势和相应的分子动力学模拟结果，写成论文，从而在*Physical Review B*发表了第一篇文章。

柳先生对科研工作非常热爱，也非常勤奋。记得他会将一些重点论文改动十遍以上，并且会叫学生坐在他的电脑旁一起修改论文，这样的修改模式真的使我受益颇多。我晚上发给他的论文，会发现他经常第二天早上就改好返回给我了。柳先生的勤奋，也在不知不觉地影响和感染着我。记得我那时会每天较早到实验室，经常晚上和周末也会在实验室，柳先生打电话或者来实验室，就知道我常在办公室，他因而笑称我为“常委”。 我想，正是柳先生的言传身教，激发了我对科研的兴趣和勤奋，柳先生应是常委中的常委。

2004年博士毕业后，我去了美国做博士后，后来回到中南大学当了一名老师。这么多年来，柳先生的勤奋、对科研的热爱和执着，以及正面表扬和肯定学生，一直成为我学习和效仿的榜样。

（注：龚浩然，2004年博士毕业，现任中南大学教授）

五载师生情，一世不了缘
——贺恩师柳先生八十华诞

文/孔令体

不经意间，日历已悄然地行将翻到2015年。2015年于我来讲有点不平凡：博士毕业十年，离开恩师柳先生也已十年。巧合的是，2015年也恰逢恩师八十华诞。忆及十余年前的求学经历，往事历历在目；虽然距离千里之遥，先生的教诲亦似在耳畔萦绕。古人云，“一日为师，终生为父”，在先生门下短短五年的博士生涯，却是一生最宝贵的回忆。

初入师门，即为柳先生的勤奋所折服。2000年春，我进入柳先生的课题组开始本科毕业设计的工作。彼时先生已是六十有五，放在常人，也许早就退休在家颐养天年了。但先生却是每日五点多即起床开始工作，一两个小时后洗漱吃饭，再在八点前赶到办公室。中午回家就餐、小憩，下午两点之前又会准时出现在办公室里。下午六点下班回家之后，先生也时常会在家继续工作。作为一个初出茅庐的本科生，当时着实有点不理解：先生极其聪慧，知识渊博，成果丰硕自然不在话下，还如此拼搏，所为者何？跟先生处久了，才慢慢揭开了谜底。先生跟我们讲，他们这一代人在“文革”期间，错失了人生极为宝贵的青春岁月。国门打开之后，看到中国与西方的巨大差距，终于能够一展抱负的他们，充盈着“报效祖国”的责任感和使命感，期望能够通过自己的不懈努力，尽力缩小这一差距。先生的勤奋，竟是有着“爱国爱科学”的巨大动力源。在先生的感召下，我也日渐勤奋起来；毕竟，我不像先生那样聪明睿智，如果再不勤奋，又如何能够期望在学术的道路上取得令先生、自己满意的成绩呢？

在其后的求学过程中，更是逐渐感受到了柳先生治学的严谨。毕业设计结束之际，终于完成了毕业论文的撰写。虽不敢说完美，内心还是有点小小的自负，觉得自己写得还是不错的。提交给先生两天之后，拿到了从摘要到结论乃至致谢数不过来的修改意见。怀着忐忑之心作了修改后，再次提交给先生，又反馈回来不少修改意见。三次之后，先生终于说了句：现在基本可以了。进入研究生课题后，每一篇学术论文的写作，又必然会重复上面的故事。每次修改的时候，先生经常是让我们与他一起坐在计算机前，一方面是为了随时与我们讨论，确认一些实验和计算结果的细节，另一方面更是为了教导我们如何去理顺思路、弄清逻辑以及规划好论文的结构，并顺便教会我们一些英文词汇和语句的正确用法。至今还记得先生有一次为了给我讲解 for、of 和 on 等介词的用法，举了许多例子让我来体会它们的区别。对于每一篇论文，尽管经历了数轮的修改，在正式投稿之前，先生还是会通读全文，修改掉阅读起来不够顺畅的语句，力求完美。我们也时常会看到，先生凌晨五点多钟对论文进行修改的痕迹。在先生的言传身教下，我们也逐渐体会到了“严谨治学”的真谛，并在我们自己的工作中不断地去践行。

先生虽年长于我们，追求“新知”之心却一点也不亚于我们。对于新知识、新事物、新技术，先生总是保有一颗好奇之心。先生告诉我们，他20世纪80年代在加州理工学院访学的时候，下很大的工夫学习自己独立操作两台加速器等实验设备和分析仪器。在我进组的时候，计算机和网络还刚刚开始普及。在我刚刚开始学习电子邮件使用方法的时候，柳先生已经是这方面的高手了。先生还让剑波师兄架设起了课题组的 ftp 站点，便于实验室同学之间数据文件的传输、交流和保存。在那个年代，论文的投稿也还以航空邮件寄送为主。在一些杂志社推出了在线投稿的方式之后，先生就积极地鼓励我们去“尝尝螃蟹”。手机兴起之后，先生还在“古稀之年”学会了收发短信。我想，也许就是这种“活到老学到老”的求知之心，使得先生能够在学术上不断地去开拓新的研究方向吧。先生是在改革开放以后进入到离子束材料改性这个交叉领域的。20 世纪 80 年代初，先生在加州理工学院访问研究期间，又进入到非晶态材料的领域，他设计并完成了一个系统性的离子束混合实验，提出了有名的、能预言二元非晶态合金形成的“结构差异规则”。回国后，他一直把远离平衡态的离子束混合作为一种科学方法，来研究非晶态合金（即金属玻璃）的形成原理、结构、性能以及它们之间的相关性。但从 90 年代中期开始，先生就领着赖文生师兄和张青师姐开辟了以物理多尺度的科学计算为研究手段的新方向。迄今为止，先生已培养了近十位从事计算材料学研究的博士，并发表了许多有份量的论文，包括数篇与计算方法相关的综述性论文。先生的这颗年轻的心，也在潜移默化中影响着我们，让我们在各自的学术道路上不断去开拓前行。

先生治学，也很看重“平等”思想。在工作中，他时常跟我们讲，在学术面前，不管是研究生还是知名学者，大家都是“among equal”的。先生经常告诫我们不要迷信权威、迷信书本，鼓励我们要勇于挑战、勇于开拓、勇于创新；但是挑战也不能是盲目的，而是基于科学认识和科学态度的思想交锋。先生常跟我们讲的一个例子，就是关于非晶态合金学形成的一种学术观点，认为只有在具有较大负生成热的系统中才能够获得非晶态合金。他和张政军师兄一起经过分析后认为，在多层膜的实验研究中，有可能通过增加界面能的方法，在正生成热的系统中制备出非晶态合金，并给出了相应的热力学解释。先生注意到我在这方面还不够“open”，有时在思想上还过于“拘谨”，除了在国外教授来访时特意安排与这些知名教授进行面对面的沟通外，还带着我和浩然师弟一起到意大利去参加有关计算和模拟的国际会议来进一步开拓眼界。在先生的鞭策之下，毕业之后，我也选择了留学之路。也是秉承先生“为国尽力”的思想，在完成博士后工作之后，我来到了上海交通大学工作；目前除了教学科研之外，还负责学院的国际化办学工作，时常与国外名校、名师进行沟通、协商和协作。

掐指算来，离开先生的课题组，已整十年。“十年光阴简直似水流连”，时常总会怀念在先生身边学习的时光。虽年近八十，先生仍然奋斗在教学科研一线，作为后辈的我们，除了敬佩先生，祈求先生健康平安，唯有在工作岗位上，更加勤奋、严谨、求真、开拓，力求为国家为科学多做一点贡献，才能回馈先生对我们的培育之恩。

（注：孔令体，2005 年博士毕业，现任上海交通大学材料学院副教授）

师恩无私深似海
——记我的恩师柳百新院士

文/张瑞丰

“八年游子心，落定北京城”，这是我的志向也是恩师柳百新院士的殷切希望和谆谆教导。八年多的德国科研生涯和美国求学之路，恩师那种“志当存高远”的教诲时刻铭记于心，激发我的求学奋进和炙热的归国情怀。时光转瞬，恩师已近八旬，眉宇间增添了更多的岁月痕迹。每次回国，必将驻足于母校清华大学看望恩师。恩师那些发自肺腑的叮嘱和期待每次都使我百感惆怅。恩师“春雨润物、明德育才”的大师风范和淡泊名利的高风亮节无时不在触动着、感染着、净化着我的心灵。

11 月的北京秋高气爽，褪去了夏日的烦躁，每日秋叶的飘落均给我带来无尽的凉意。在这个静谧的时光，我摒弃了繁杂的事务让自己的心沉静下来，眺望窗外，感受着皎洁的月色，让思绪也在这样安静的时节轻舞飞扬，以此来记录下十余年来的求学、求新和归国之路，表达我对恩师的知遇之恩、教诲之情。

一、一次邂逅注定与恩师的师生情缘

2000 年夏，那是一个风景如画的季节，阳光明媚，百花绚烂，燕舞莺啼。那时的我，为求学之路踏上了进京联系导师的漫漫长路。面对中国最高学府清华大学而言，昔日里自信的我，在向往中增添了些许焦虑。我的恩师柳百新院士，当时已经是材料领域和物理领域享有崇高声望的学者，治学严谨、德高望重。冒昧来到清华大学，心中百感交集。徘徊于逸夫技术科技楼内，可能是上天的安排，我邂逅了恩师，并为他的学者风范和人格魅力所折服，为恩师的热情和虚怀若谷所触动。恩师没有使用华丽的词语向我介绍他已经取得的成绩，相反，他以朴实无华的事实和实例为我打开了心扉。恩师首先向我介绍了研究组的情况和研究方向等，并亲自带我参观了实验室。那天，恩师跟我聊了很多，聊他所带领的团队，聊学术能力培养及个人综合素质提升，聊学生的就业情况，聊科学研究的国际前沿和国家的需求等等。他完全是一位亲切和蔼的长者，谆谆教导，循循善诱。虽然是第一次见面，我却已经被恩师的高风亮节的人格魅力所深深吸引了，原有的一丝拘谨与紧张荡然无存，反而觉得心里特别轻松。从恩师办公室出来的那一刻，我就在心里暗暗下定决心，一定争取成为恩师的学生，进入恩师的团队。

二、恩师点燃了我科学研究的热情

2001 年秋季学期，我顺利来到清华大学攻读博士学位，开始沐浴恩师的博大和宽广。通过近距离接触，我逐渐体悟到恩师那种学术大师身上的优良素养：第一，精湛的学术造诣。一个高水平的导师，不仅具有渊博的知识，而且具有足够广阔的视野。第二，严谨的治学态度。良好的治学态度，是一个科学工作者必备的基本素质。第三，高尚的人格魅力。好的导师，不仅需要指导学生如何为学，而且需要教导学生如何为人。第四，敏锐的洞察力。学术上来不得半点虚假，只有具有敏锐的洞察力才能指导出优秀的学生，所谓“强将手下无弱兵”。恩师体现出的这些优秀素养将我牢牢地绑在了科研这条艰辛的征途上，为我点燃了对科学研究的热情。在科研过程中，“与学生坦诚交流，教之，友之，信之”

这是我感受到的恩师育人之道。恩师非常注重和学生的交流，他把学生当成朋友，愿意倾听每个学生心中的声音。针对学生的不同情况，恩师精心栽培，因材施教；针对学生的烦恼，恩师以友代之，助其排忧解难；针对学生的科学研究探索，恩师总是给予最大的信任和鼓励。记得博士的第一年，尚处于学习实验设备阶段的我，读到一篇文献，发现报道的实验数据与经典的Miedema模型的计算结果存在系统的偏差。出于好奇，我大胆地向恩师汇报了这一发现。恩师不仅没有怀疑我提出的看法，反而与我展开了深入的讨论，并鼓励我挖掘出偏差的根源。也正是这一坦诚的交流，我了解到了恩师渊博的知识和敏锐的洞察力。以此为契机，入学第一年，我便完成了博士期间第一篇论文的撰写。

恩师在我的科研之路上，播下了颗颗科研的火种，点燃了我科研的热情，为我铺下了层层台阶，铺平了我科研前进的道路，为我打开了前进的灯塔，照亮了我追求的目标。恩师赋予了我知识，启迪了我的智慧，赋予了我探索创新的精神，他是我尊敬爱戴和铭记终生的伯乐。

三、高瞻远瞩的科学信仰为我的远渡重洋的求学之路埋下坚定的基石

“立志、成才、报国”是一种高瞻远瞩的科学信仰。恩师对于我们的教育不仅仅体现在我们的学业，更体现在他对学生将来的关心和志向的引导。相信所有恩师的学生，都还记得他在美国访问研究期间那些热情洋溢的故事；相信所有恩师的学生，都还记得他无微不至的关怀。博士毕业对于每个学生来说都是一个新的起点。恩师并没有因为学生的离去而弃之，相反，恩师以最真挚的情怀引导学生选择就业或进一步出国深造。恩师的学生中大多具有国外研究经历，这与恩师的科学信仰是息息相关的。“走出去，才能了解的更多，学的更多，才能更好地为国服务。闭门造车和自我欣赏已经不再适应时代发展的需求。”为此，恩师以最大的努力，鼓励和支持学生走出国门学习发达国家的先进科学技术。在此高瞻远瞩的科学信仰指引下，我在恩师的支持帮助下成功申请到了著名的德国“洪堡基金”和具有相当影响力的美国洛斯阿拉莫斯国家实验室“院长奖博士后研究基金”。这些成绩的取得都是与恩师的支持和帮助息息相关。

四、朴素的师生情谊和爱国情怀使我坚定地走上归国服务的道路

离开恩师远渡重洋并没有隔断我与恩师那种朴素的师生情谊，相反使我更加体悟到恩师那种深深的爱国情怀。十余年来与恩师的交往，我一直深深感受着恩师的言传身教。身处异乡的我每每回忆起恩师那些娓娓道来的科研往事，就像品味陈年的老酒，格外津津有味。恩师在国家最需要的时候并没有选择留在国外，相反，他将一腔热血奉献于国内的教育科研事业。恩师归国后，潜心科研、辛勤耕耘无不体现着恩师那种深深的爱国情怀。我的归国旅程也并非一帆风顺，如果没有恩师的支持和鼓励，归国报效祖国的宏远志向还不知如何实现。结束德国的求学生涯之时，恩师在第一时间向我提出“回国报效祖国”的建议。语重心长的话语使我彻底打消了留在德国的念头，放弃了来之不易的德国永久居留权。当得知我有可能去美国国家实验室做研究时，恩师又鼓励我尽力争取：“美国的科研经历对于你将来回国发展会更有帮助”，这句朴素的话语为我的美国求学之路和科研的提升无疑提出了更高的要求。在美国四年多的时光，我了解到美国科技的进步与发展，掌握了世界上多项先进计算材料科学技术，比如大尺度非平衡分子动力学模拟技术、材料基因组解析技术等。在此阶段，恩师时刻没有忘记鼓励我探索科学的制高点的决心和回国服务的初衷。无论思想上还是行动上，恩师在我的归国之路上助我一步一步走向最终目标。如今我的归国是我与恩师朴素的师生情谊和深深爱国情怀的

必然结果。

如今，已经归国的我更加体悟到：恩师就像滋润我心田的春雨；像黑夜中的一盏明灯，给我光明；像严冬里的万道阳光，给我温暖。恩师的“明德育人，风范及远”的为师之道和独特的人格魅力是我们这些弟子们从恩师身上体悟到的崇高精神。如今恩师的弟子“桃李遍天下”，作为后继者们，我们将牢记“泽流及远，千里思源”的古训，继恩师的脚印，追求科学的制高点，饱含报国深情，投身祖国的繁荣事业。

（注：张瑞丰，2005 年博士毕业，现任北京航空航天大学材料学院教授）

兹兹师恩，悠悠情深
——祝柳百新院士八十华诞有感

文/李家好

2015年欣逢先生八十华诞，应师兄潘峰教授提议，就“弟子们眼中的柳先生”撰文志贺，遂成此文。兹兹，念念不忘，源自《尚书　大禹谟》：“帝念哉！念兹在兹，释兹在兹。名言兹在兹，允出兹在兹，惟帝念功。”

大学，非大楼之谓也，乃大师之谓也，此说即缘起清华大学。清华园内云集了众多名师大家，柳百新院士就是其中的一员。我2002年进入清华大学材料系攻读博士学位，从那时起就一直跟随柳先生从事科学研究工作。先生为了我本人的工作，可以说是苦心孤诣、呕心沥血，终于在万千纷扰中营造出一片田地，让我能够在这方净土中耕耘收获，领略科学探索的魅力，享受清华园中的酸甜苦辣。每每回顾起这十多年的经历，先生的言谈举止和人格魅力总能让我油然而生一种高山仰止的心情，尤其是先生的护犊深情更让我难以忘怀。

我依然记得第一次见到先生的情景。先生对我讲，做科研先做人，要勤奋、踏实、严谨。写文章一定要“有话则长、无话则短”，做到“文如其人、言为心声”。虽然是科学论文，但仍然要让读者从字里行间体会到作者的人文品格。先生不仅自己这样做，还教导我们也要这样做。我和其他弟子一样，刚开始写不好，甚至可以说根本就不会写科学论文，先生就不厌其烦地、手把手地帮我逐字逐句地修改论文。为了一个句子一个短语，反复斟酌推敲。一篇论文来回修改十几次，有时候甚至多达二十多次。看到被先生修改得红色满篇的论文，我心底总有五味杂陈的感觉。一是心存愧疚，深感由于自己的能力不足，让先生花费了这么多的辛劳。但当看到一块“朽木”经先生之手，被精雕细琢成一款精美的艺术品时，心底也不由地荡漾起一丝兴奋来。而此时先生已忘掉了疲劳，心情愉悦地与弟子们一起把玩欣赏这件千锤百炼打造出来的“宝贝”。在先生的指导下，我和其他弟子一样工作能力逐步提高。我们也能感觉到，先生看到弟子哪怕一丁点进步都非常欣慰。在弟子的眼中先生就是“俯首甘为孺子牛”的典型代表。

先生常对弟子说：由于个人经历和文化传统等因素，中国学者往往有些保守心理。某件事情还没有做，就开始在意别人的看法或非议，担心失败了怎么办。2007年，先生提议让我负责与其他同学一起准备一篇综述性论文，一方面是要把过去研究组所做的工作系统地整理一下，另一方面也是为了与同行分享研究成果以及由此积累的研究经验。研究组在先生带领下前前后后做了大量的工作，而先生让我来做这份工作，我不仅担心自己能否完成这么重要的工作，也顾虑由我来做这件事是否合适。针对我的犹豫不前，先生耐心地做我的思想工作，消除了我的顾虑。先生鼓励我要大胆尝试：“尝试的后果或者成功或者失败，而不尝试永远不会成功。”在先生的鼓励、指导与帮助下，我和代晓东等合作者经过大半年的努力，终于在2007年完成了这篇论文。该论文后来发表在*Physics Reports*这本物理学领域的著名期刊上，这也是当时由中国大陆本土学者在该期刊所发表的为数不多的论文之一。由此我体会到，所谓的“失败是成功之母”就是，做工作要勇于尝试、不要怕失败，“不断总结在失败中的经验和教训，就一定能走上成功之路”。

先生经常教育弟子，“科学面前人人平等”。任何一项科学发现都不是一蹴而就的，都要经过严格验证和反复考验。无论是对自己的还是对别人的研究成果，都要敢于怀疑、严谨求证。对经过考验、证明是正确的结果要敢于坚持。做科学研究一定要实事求是、坚持真理。研究组基于十多年的工作，提出了“预言金属玻璃形成的原子尺度理论”。该理论刚提出的时候，一些人不太了解，甚至一些著名学者也经常就此与我们“交流”。遇到这种情况，研究组的一些成员心中就没底了，开始怀疑我们的工作是否真的存在什么问题。为此，先生带领我们反复核查过去的工作，仔细检查出现这种情况的原因。后来发现，该理论的核心部分没问题，只是部分表述容易产生误解。因此先生提出在吸取同行建议的基础上，改进部分文字上的表达。这样，原子尺度理论终于得到同行的认可。以原子尺度理论为核心的研究成果获得了2013年度教育部优秀成果自然科学类二等奖。这件事使我明白，做科研就要有坚定的信念和执着的精神。

先生对弟子们不仅要“扶上马”，还要“送一程”。除了精心指导弟子们在校期间的研究工作外，先生也非常关心我们毕业后的工作问题和事业发展。比如我知道的孔令体和郭海波师兄以及崔苑苑师妹等的工作，在先生的关注下都走上了“康庄大道”。与已毕业的其他弟子们相比，可以说我在这方面的体会尤其深切。2006年1月博士毕业时，留校工作进展不顺。后经先生多方奔波，学校决定让我先以校内博士后的身份留在材料系，协助先生开展教学与科研工作。到了2008年，博士后出站留校工作还是不顺。两年两次的折磨让我备受打击，我的心情低落到极致，有种万念俱灰的苦闷。这件事也让先生心里非常难受，但他还是帮我分析利益得失，劝我从大局出发、抓主要矛盾。要我做到“不畏浮云遮望眼，留得青山有柴烧”。先生苦口婆心地劝解，让我渐渐恢复了精神，重新燃起对未来的信心。更让我感动的是，先生还千辛万苦地东奔西走、上下协调，尽量为我的工作争取一个好的结果。经过先生的不懈努力，清华大学最终允许我留在先生身边继续工作。这件事让我深深体会到，世界上最宽广的是大海，比大海还要宽广的是先生对弟子们的悠悠恩情。

回顾这十多年来，我有时候也曾经气馁过、迷茫过，但非常幸运的是，先生一直在我身边。每当我遇到困难的时候，先生就言传身教、苦口婆心地开导我、激励我，催我自新，鼓起我战胜困难的勇气。在工作中也曾被误解过、非议过，但当我想到先生对我的辛苦付出，我就本着“有则改之、无则加勉”的态度反躬自省，以“人不知而不愠不亦君子乎”来告诫自己——“躲进系馆成一统，任凭风雨雷电声”。先生对弟子的恩情让我不敢懈怠,我只能更加努力地工作。一直谨记先生的告诫，“做科学研究既要只争朝夕，又不能急于求成”。像先生教导的那样，每个时间段都要有计划，要不断地学习、努力工作，用新的知识和成绩来丰富完善自己——“日知其所亡，以就懿德”。在先生领导的研究组里，我体会到了“学而时习之”的乐趣，也经常与同学和同行等分享经验教训与收获的喜悦。在先生的呵护下，我得以做些自己喜爱的事情，我倍感欣喜。也衷心感谢先生给我创造的这个小环境。

“有先生在我们身边，真好！”在跟随先生的日子里，我见识过暴雨，领略过彩虹，欣赏到阳光明媚春风拂面的美景，也经历过荆棘遍地沟壑起伏的考验。无论是耕耘的辛苦，还是丰收的喜悦，都极大地丰富了我的人生体验。这经历让我体会到生活的多彩，也更懂得了人生的意义。可以说，先生是我人生经历的见证人。没有先生，就没有我在清华的一切。在我的眼中，先生就是我前进的动力、指路的明灯、攀登科学高峰的引路人。

（注：李家好，2005年博士毕业，现任清华大学材料学院高级工程师）

师恩绵长
——写于导师柳先生八十寿诞

文/郭海波

我第一次见到柳先生是在2000年。那时我本科四年级，需要选择毕业设计的指导老师，而且我有读研的想法，也需要选择导师。在柳先生的办公室里，我和另外一位同学一起聆听柳先生介绍研究方向，门外还有往来的学生等候询问毕业设计和选导师的事情。我当时对研究课题还有些模糊，但对柳先生的平易近人和自信从容特别向往。这似乎是一次普通而简短的面谈，但对我来说，却是人生选择中一个关键的时刻。后来再经过一两次交流，我就决定在柳先生的研究组做本科生毕业设计，继而攻读博士学位。

从2001年到2006年的5年博士生期间，柳先生的言传身教给我留下了无法磨灭的印象。我记得一次柳先生问我们博士学位的意义，我除了“博士学位是最高学位”之外，再也想不出其他。当时柳先生很耐心地告诉我，攻读博士学位对一个人而言是很重要的一个经历，柳先生大约讲了两层意思，第一层意思是，在做博士论文时，首先需要通过阅读文献了解拟研究方向的发展现状，并在此基础上做出有创新性的研究成果，而且本人做的工作还需要有相当的份量，这才能算完成一篇博士论文。第二层意思是，通过博士论文的锻炼，将使人具备独立从事科学研究的能力去承担科研项目，如果假以时日，有可能带领一个团队一起去完成重要的科研项目。这也是柳先生判断博士研究生能否毕业的标准，比起学校里制定的研究生学位的要求指标（比如发表多少篇学术论文等），这样的标准虽然不易量化，但更反映博士学位的实质，而且柳先生研究组的学生都是早早达到了学校的指标。我现在也在上海大学做了硕士生导师，在指导学生时也在思考柳先生的话语，学习柳先生的指导方式。

我在博士生期间一开始科研不太顺利。我的研究方向是材料计算与模拟，但在学习和使用计算材料学的专业软件时屡屡受挫，经常遇到因为设置错误而返工的情况。和我一起来课题组的研究生已有论文发表，而我还迟迟不见研究成果，对着一些杂乱的数据和图表苦苦思索。我那时注意到柳先生只是非常平常地询问我的进展，还安慰我说科学研究从来都不是一帆风顺的。我后来才意识到，柳先生在刻意地不施加压力，并且缓解我的焦虑，给我时间来学习和体会。柳先生常常鼓励我遇到困难时要在研究组内多多讨论、交流、合作。我就把问题跟大家说出来，之后得到了非常积极的回应和帮助，有时候甚至是激烈的争论，极大地开阔了我的研究思路和视角，使我从中收益良多。就这样，大约一年后，我科研上有了进展，慢慢地有论文发表出来。现在回想起来，我一开始没有意识到自己遇到的困难是因为我闭门造车引起的。自己去查阅文献、说明书，哪里有解决不了的问题呢？但是，一个人的理解毕竟有限，特别是当思路堵塞时，会对所见所闻选择性地接受而无视其他。查阅文献和说明书或许可以解决绝大部分的问题，但在很多情况下不是最有效率的方法。与兴趣、经验相近的同行交流，可以开阔思路，消除一些想当然的谬误。柳先生在恰当时机的点拨，让我在实践中充分领会了这一点。

柳先生是我见过的最勤奋而且最耐心的人。研究组里的论文每一篇在投寄出去之前都要由柳先生反复修改。直到现在我想起柳先生，最先浮现在我眼前的影像还是我并排坐在柳先生的旁边，看柳先生在电脑上逐字逐句地修改我地论文草稿时的情景。可想而知的是，在我初次接触用英语写作科技论文时，写出来的论文满篇都是语法错误、逻辑不通和中文习惯。我现在也会为别人修改文章，也体会到了修改论文所需要的耐心和细致。柳先生的英语非常好，也非常乐于和我们分享，经常跟我说起他在遣词造句时的考虑，这对训练我的科技英语写作是很有帮助的。这样经过一两篇文章之后，我就可以自己写出结构完整、基本通顺的文章来，虽然还要经过几轮的修改润色才能投寄出去，但对我来说是飞跃性质的进阶。

柳先生的研究组就像一个大家庭，我经常感受到来自这个大家庭的温暖。我记得博士研究生二年级寒假前的一天，柳先生讲起他最近看到的一条新闻里，一个家境贫寒的学生没有路费回家过年。柳先生询问了我们回家的车费，为我们每个人补贴了往返路费。秋季流感发作之前，柳先生考虑到研究组里有容易感染的研究生，督促我们打了流感疫苗，担心我们怕花钱不去打疫苗，还为我们支付了费用。

柳先生不仅在科研上是我的导师，在为人处事上也给了我很多启发，为我树立了生动鲜明的榜样。柳先生非常喜欢跟我们交谈，当然交谈的内容并不局限于科研。柳先生注重实干，说踏踏实实把科研和学生培养做好了，其他的事情都是自然而然的了。碰巧我家乡的一个亲戚在职务晋升上想要通过关系走捷径，得到一个长辈的告诫也是“踏实做业务，职务是水到渠成的事情”。尽管我那时还从未经历过复杂的人际关系，但已经能感觉到智者的哲学是相通的。受柳先生的影响，我也抱定这样的观点，即学校里同事之间的关系越简单越好，重视别人在学术上对自己的评价，但不要为之所累。与一些干扰性的人际关系相比，埋头苦干、专心科研是更重要的事情。我后来才意识到，柳先生和我们的交谈也是一种教育方式，不是那种说教式的，而是隐藏在他所讲述的经历和故事中。只可惜我性格内向，没有经常主动去找柳先生交流，没有更多聆听柳先生的教诲。

我在2006年博士毕业，柳先生对我的影响并没有随着我的毕业而结束，而是一直伴随着我，给我指引和鼓励。我在毕业后去了美国和澳大利亚做博士后研究，直到2012年回国，期间一直和柳先生保持着联系，向柳先生汇报我的状况和进展。我每当面临比较重大的选择时，都想征询柳先生的意见。在第一期博士后研究工作完结后，我有两个工作选择，一是在美国一个大学里做高性能计算的管理和相关的研究工作，二是到澳大利亚继续从事科研工作。柳先生了解情况之后，鼓励我继续科研工作，不要偏离原来的人生规划。从澳大利亚回来时，我又面临选择，受到柳先生的指引和鼓励，来到上海大学任教。

一步步走来，我把柳先生当作我人生的导师和指引的智者。我虽然愚鲁，但愿意听从智者的教诲。师恩绵长，无法言谢，值柳先生八十大寿之际，祝愿柳先生健康平安快乐，再为国家和社会培养输送科技栋梁之材。

（注：郭海波，2006年博士毕业，现任上海大学材料学院副教授）

我心目中的柳先生

文/孔毅

喜闻柳先生八十寿诞，祝先生身体健康，福如东海，寿比南山！

十年有余，仍然清晰记得和柳先生的第一次见面。那是2002年10月22日上午，中国材料研讨会，一个很大的礼堂，柳先生神采飞扬地作着大会特邀报告。我因联系报考博士研究生事宜，之前就和柳先生有过几次邮件来往。等柳先生回到自己的位置上，我怀着忐忑的心冒昧上前自我介绍。因是第一次见面，柳先生刚开始不知道我是谁，还是非常和蔼地和我交谈。这是我作为湖南大学一名普通的硕士研究生，与2001年就当选为中国科学院院士的柳先生的第一次见面。柳先生那平易近人的态度，与刚才作大会特邀报告时的神采飞扬相比，让我更加向往要跟随柳先生学习。

2003年我如愿考入清华大学材料系，加入了柳先生课题组就读博士研究生，到2007年毕业，得到了柳先生四年的精心指点。入学的时候，柳先生已近古稀，本应是含饴弄孙、颐养天年的年纪，而先生除了外出开会，在每个工作日的上下午，都会步行按时来办公室上班。他对科学研究的热爱，对工作的认真负责，都让我由衷的敬佩。

柳先生的课题组，大致分成实验和计算两个方向。组里有两个学生的办公室，基本按研究方向分的。虽然我们学生不全坐在一起，但柳先生组里气氛一直很融洽，让我能够很快融入到清华的学校生活和新的科研课题之中。这离不开师兄们的关心和帮助，更离不开柳先生的言传身教和对学生的关心。而柳先生的善于言传身教，给我的印象最深。特别是柳先生帮我修改我的第一篇英文论文时的情景，我至今还历历在目。

当时进入柳先生课题组后，在师兄之前工作的基础上，结合我先前所掌握的计算方法，很快有了些有意思的结果。我和师兄一起拿给柳先生看。先生看后很是高兴，积极和我们讨论分析技术结果的物理意义，指导我们如何改进和完善之前的计算方案，不知不觉就到了中午吃饭时间。柳先生看看表，幽默地说：我们精神上是很满足，不过肚子还是要填饱，今天我们就吃一回工作餐。于是就带着师兄和我，走到清华南门外的一家上海菜馆。吃着地道的本帮菜，先生一边继续刚才的讨论，一边也会不时地点评下他上海老家那边地道本帮菜的味道，以及讲讲他做学生时候的故事。做了课题有了有价值的结果就可以写论文。之前读硕士的时候，我虽然读了许多的英文文献，但在硕士研究生阶段发表的几篇论文都是用中文写的。第一次将自己的结果写成英文论文。由于没有经验，虽然经师兄们的修改后，还是有很多问题。柳先生拿到我的初稿后，并不是我原先想象的那样，打印出来用笔在纸上修改，再返回纸质的修改稿给我。因为毕竟快70岁了，我本以为柳先生不熟悉电脑操作。结果柳先生直接把我叫到了他办公室电脑前，让我搬了个凳子坐在旁边，他直接在电脑前操作。柳先生从标题开始，一句一句地念出来。柳先生说，英文写作也是有语感的，如果念的通顺就下一句，遇到语感不对的句子，就要停下来修改。不时，柳先生也会问我这样改怎么样，会不会改变原意等。就这样，我的第一篇英文论文，就是先生这样一句一句地读，一个术语一个术语地斟酌下，改了好多遍，最后投到美国的《应用物理快报》，一个字没改就发表了。后来我又陆续写了五篇英文论文，柳先生都是这样把我叫到他电脑旁边，帮我一字一句地琢磨修改好的。柳先生对英语写作的精通让我相当佩服，同时他的指导也为我熟练运用英文及日后的留学打下了良好的基础。先生指导学生时的耐心和循循善诱的工作方式也一直影响着我现在的工作秉性。

在科研上，柳先生也很开明，善于发现我们的兴趣所在，并加以引导。一直以来我对物理、计算机编程和材料都很感兴趣。而我在柳先生课题组时的研究方向，正是将凝聚态物理理论，通过计算机编制程序，应用到材料研究中来，满足了我的兴趣。因此，在就读博士研究生四年期间，一边向师兄们请教，一边自己摸索，学习和运用了许多的计算软件和计算方法，感觉是过得很充实很投入的一段时光。虽然我的研究方向偏向理论计算，在柳先生的支持下，我还在清华材料系的中心实验室做了两年半的实验室助理，负责协助管理和操作 X 射线衍射仪和扫描电镜等设备，补上了一直缺乏的材料测试实验动手能力。没有柳先生的开明与对学生的真正关心，这些都是难以做到的。

在清华的时光过得很快，转眼就面临毕业与就业的问题。在柳先生课题组这三年多时间里，在柳先生的精心指导，课题组内师兄弟妹们的帮助下，我发表了一些论文。接下来在国内几个高校，都顺利获得了工作面试机会，并最终在湖南省长沙市的中南大学粉末冶金国家重点实验室，以引进人才的资格加入中南大学。这对于一个从没出过国的国内应届毕业博士来说是个有难度却是很重要的机会。这样难得的机会，与柳先生在我找工作时的大力推荐分不开，更与柳先生热心科研的言传身教所激励我们投入科研工作而取得些许成绩分不开。

愉快的时光总是匆匆，转眼毕业答辩。离校手续办完，最后与柳先生话别时，柳先生鼓励我要坚持严谨的科学态度，在工作上保持热忱，希冀我在工作上取得成绩，最后并送了我一条领带。此后，每次出去和国内外同行交流，收拾行李时，不管有没有佩戴的机会，我都会将柳先生赠送的这条领带放进行李箱中。至今它已随我漂洋过海，去过了几大洲，参加过许多次国际会议。我虽然从柳先生课题组毕业已经七八年了，但柳先生的教诲和关怀，就像这条领带一样，一直陪伴我，成为我工作和生活的指针。感谢恩师！

（注：孔毅，2007 年博士毕业，现任中南大学副教授）

记师从柳百新先生的那些年

文/何翔

转眼间，离开柳先生的研究组已经六年了。这六年里，我虽然工作忙，也难得有回北京的机会，而且每次都来去匆匆，但是只要到北京，我都会回到清华，向柳先生汇报一下近况，看看研究组的师弟师妹们又取得了哪些新的进展，听听柳先生的教诲。每当此时，我都会回忆起在清华师从柳先生的那些年。

一、三种关系

初“识”柳先生是在 2001 年 12 月，这个“识”是指我开始认识和从别人的只言片语中了解柳先生。记得那天下午，我在逸夫技术科学楼上完课，经过二楼大厅时，看到一张字非常大的红色海报，上面写着“狂贺百新当选院士”，这是我第一次听说柳先生。从同学口中听到，说柳先生是我们系新当选的院士，学术很厉害，更是桃李满天下，现在给我们上课的好几个教授都是他的学生。我当时听了后的感觉除了崇拜就是崇拜，自己那时的成绩在全年级里并不是拔尖的，心里还真的没敢奢望能当柳先生的学生，想不到的是，自己一年后竟然真的有缘做了柳先生的学生。

再“识”柳先生是在 2002 年 9 月，这次才是我真正意义上在柳先生脑子里“挂上号”。那会还是大四上学期，清华本科的学生如果成绩符合条件，可以免试推荐研究生，如果要直博，就要求排名必须在年级前一半。材料系的学生本科毕业后通常有 1/3 会申请出国留学，不巧的是，那年是 911 事件之后西方国家收紧留学生招收和签证政策的第一年，不少原本计划出国留学的同学都准备放弃，以退为进，先免试读硕士，然后再申请出国。虽然我当时 TOEFL 和 GRE 都准备好了，但是内心里确实也对出国没有那么向往，当时我成绩排名在年级前 1/3，符合推荐直博的条件，也不想像很多同学那样用读硕士来过渡几年再出国。于是就想认真思考一下自己到底想要做些什么，如何规划自己将来的事业。当时我在材料系学生科协工作，就找了同在科协工作的 8 字班师兄严华锋，向他取取经。具体说了哪些我也记不太清了，就是记着他现在是柳百新院士的直博生，柳先生学术水平很高，拿过国家自然科学奖二等奖，研究组氛围也很好，柳先生对学生都是一个一个亲自指导，只要肯用功，绝对能写出高水平的论文，毕业更是不在话下等等。后来我又了解了整个系里的情况，心里认为既然要留下来读博士，就一定要跟最好的老师，真正学到本领。在系里的老师中，柳先生对我产生的影响最深，经过几天的考虑，我决定去找柳先生，看他愿不愿意收我这个学生。于是在严师兄的引荐下，我约好柳先生去“推销”自己。站在办公室门口，我反复梳理着每个可能的关于专业知识的提问，想象着各种可能遇到的情况，甚至都想到了如果柳先生拒绝了，我该说些什么。硬着头皮敲门进去以后，我看见柳先生正坐在电脑前，认真地看着文稿，虽然他头发已经花白，但是精神矍铄，一副厚厚的眼镜后面遮不住那双炯炯有神的眼睛。柳先生让我坐在旁边的沙发上，他好像看出来我有点紧张，看了看我的简历问：“你也是上海人啊？”

“我父亲是，他们是支援大西北全家迁到陕西的，我是陕西人。”我回答道。

“也是半个老乡啊，会说上海话吗？”

“我已经不会了，只是能听懂一些。”

那天聊了很多，其中关于科研，柳先生说："我和学生之间是三种关系：我们是师生，是合作者，更是朋友，是忘年交，到我们研究组需要很刻苦努力，要在前人工作的基础上创造性地开展科学研究，这样才能取得更大的成绩。"

我坚定地表态："我希望能有机会跟您学习，努力工作，做好科研。"

我记得整个谈话过程就是长辈在和晚辈谈心，谈的非常愉快，事先准备好的台词一个也没用上，真没想到一个大院士竟然这样平易近人，跟一个本科生的交流都是那么平等。就是这次谈话，让我对在柳先生的研究组工作充满期待，给了我坚定的信心。我坚信在柳先生这样的好导师的指导下，自己一定能够取得优异的成绩。推研时同学之间竞争的压力和对不确定未来的茫然全部一扫而空，那天是我最激动、最兴奋的一天，因为我可能很快就能成为柳先生的学生了！

二、并行工作

经过推研报名、面试、公示，我就开始进到实验室工作了，是在技科楼 2335 办公室。当时实验室里有严华锋、李新宇、张瑞丰、程向前等。我的第一个师傅就是李新宇。第一个任务就是做好本科的毕业设计。我首先选择的是互不固溶的 Cu-Ru 系统，因为在集成电路工业中有研究者尝试将 Ru 用作 Cu 的扩散阻挡层材料，对 Cu-Ru 系统的亚稳合金相的研究可以指导实际生产和应用，提高产品性能。好在有李新宇师兄的帮助，大概一个多月，我们就已经完成了离子束混合实验，拿到了实验结果，可是对结果的进一步分析却总是没有头绪，我只是把各种现象罗列出来，却解释不了原因。于是我又开始看文献资料，研究进度就慢慢落了下来。柳先生有一个习惯，每天早上会很早来实验室，看到哪个学生在房间里，就会把他叫到办公室里聊聊研究进展，看看有什么问题。开始我是有点怕的，怕自己工作进展慢、怕自己回答不上柳先生的问题，被柳先生批评。有一天恰好就我自己在办公室，柳先生走进来说："何翔，到我办公室坐坐，我们聊聊。"跟着柳先生进到办公室，我又坐在那张沙发上，有点忐忑，心里很没底。

"最近实验结果出来了吧，怎么样？"柳先生问道。

"出来了，我已经整理成一个表格了。"

"对照热力学计算结果了吗？"

"对照了，主要是觉得结果还很单薄。"我回答道。

可以看出来，柳先生对于进展还是不满意的。"你要运用多种手段，我们实验室那么多资源，不仅能通过实验研究，还有第一性原理计算和分子动力学模拟啊，要学会综合分析，可以多向其他师兄学习，一起合作。"

他很婉转地批评了我："做研究工作一定是要并行开展，在大学里面的时间是有限的，如果是串行的模式，等着一个完成再来下一个，能够做的研究就太少了；如果并行开展，手上一边做实验，同时又有研究的系统在服务器上计算，有之前做的系统的实验结果分析，又有文章在手上写，就能最大限度地利用好时间，提高工作效率。"

根据柳先生的建议，我调整自己的工作思路，开始"并行模式"。一边整理现有的结果，把实验结果写成一篇文章，一边向李家好师兄学习，请他指导我通过分子动力学模拟和实验结果进行对照。大四毕业设计前，我先投了一篇关于实验结果分析的文章，后来发表在 *Journal of the Physical Society of Japan* 上，然后在梁苏会师妹的帮助下，我又通过第一性原理计算和分子动力学模拟丰富了研究成果，

在 *Physical Review B* 上又发了一篇文章，这篇文章已被引用 16 次。同时我开始接触计算材料学，向我的第二个师傅孔令体师兄学习第一性原理计算，第一个计算任务是亚稳态的 Bcc 和 Hcp 结构的 Ni 的磁性。后来发表在 *Journal of Applied Physics* 上，被引用 20 次。

有了这些研究手段的支持，我的工作越来越顺利，后来又研究了 Co-Ta，Fe-Ru 以及 Ni-Ru 系统，在博士研究期间取得了丰富的研究成果。后来我总结出来一个经验，一定要多找柳先生交流，每次跟柳先生的讨论，都会让我受益匪浅，柳先生思维敏捷、逻辑清晰，有时候真的是很难跟上他的节奏，但是一旦你理解了他的想法，你会有一种豁然开朗的感觉。我从以前怕被柳先生叫到办公室，变成后来只要有新的想法就主动约柳先生去讨论，甚至有跟柳先生讨论少了自己会吃亏的感觉。正是在柳先生的指导下，我做到了每年发表一篇文章，截至毕业时，已发表 6 篇文章，有 3 篇影响因子在 3 以上，这样的成果在其他研究组也是不多见的。

三、工作助理

为了锻炼学生们，柳先生设置了几个助理岗位，分别负责镀膜机、注入机、服务器等大型实验设备和实验室日常工作管理。大家在助理岗位上得到了很好的锻炼，特别是对自己负责的设备基本上成了半个专家，要想镀膜就找新宇，要注入就找华锋和文超，大家配合的非常好，兄弟姐妹们的感情也变得非常深。由于原来负责实验室日常工作的孔令体师兄要毕业了，2005 年开始我慢慢接手帮助柳先生处理一些实验室事务，也相当于是秘书的工作。这个岗位是很锻炼人的。不仅要配合师兄们团结好组里的兄弟姐妹们，搞好“精神文明建设”，还要协助柳先生当好管家，维持好实验室的正常运行，做好“物质文明建设”。要及时了解各项经费的使用情况，分门别类，做好统筹。哪些要中期，哪些要结题，结余资金如何使用。在这期间我的大局观得到了很大的锻炼，文字水平也有了很大提高，特别是在申请课题、资金、奖励中，我一遍遍读柳先生修改过的申请书，认真体会为什么柳先生要这样改，为什么要加这些内容。记得有一次，一份基金申请书柳先生改过 6 次还不满意，在临提交前的那天早上，柳先生又打电话过来，让我修改其中的一个词语。柳先生那种严谨认真的态度和极高的文字整理能力对我产生了非常深刻的影响。工作期间，我还需要跟学校相关部门以及方方面面的人打交道，维护好跟他们的关系，保证按照要求完成各项任务，这段经历对我提高人际交往能力，增强协调能力起到了重要作用。正是这段时间柳先生对我的锻炼，为我后来成为省级领导的秘书奠定了基础。

四、爱国敬业

柳先生经常教育我们要爱国奉献，他自己也正是用行动去践行着这一信念。他当时作为访问学者到了美国，在完成工作任务后，面对优越的生活条件和先进的实验条件，面对着一流大学的邀请，他毅然决定回到清华，继续在他热爱的科研事业上辛勤耕耘，用心培养着一批批优秀的晚辈学子。他那高尚的情操是非常值得我们学习的。针对一些年轻人去了美国后，拿了美国绿卡，宣誓效忠美利坚合众国，几年后看到国内的条件慢慢变好了，对人才更重视了，给的待遇优厚了，他们又以海外华人的身份回来。柳先生对一个为了个人利益连国籍都可以放弃的人，他的价值观是有问题的。我记得他谈到了从事科学研究所必备的精神时，很严肃地指出两点“一是爱国，这是最基本的；二是对科学，对高科技的热爱，这是你从事科研最大的驱动力”。

柳先生是非常勤奋和敬业的。他每天很早就会来到实验室，处理邮件，修改论文，找学生讨论研究成果。我们的每篇论文柳先生都是要亲自改的，从文章大纲、结构、内容到具体的一个一个单词，一篇文章往往要往返五六次。这点也是其他研究组的老师难以做到的。柳先生雷厉风行，改的文章要求不过夜，今天晚上传给他，明早肯定已经改好了。于是我养成了一个习惯，写出来的文章放到服务器后，第二天起床第一件事就是看看柳先生是不是提出了修改意见，然后早早赶到实验室去跟柳先生当面讨论，有时候仔细一看文件都是柳先生五六点改出来的。只要没有特殊情况，他都会到办公室来指导学生们，这是非常难得的。很多别的组的同学都羡慕地说："你有这样一个好导师真是太幸福了。"柳先生非常敬业，没有其他职务，不像很多老师在外有很多兼职，他全身心地投入到科研事业里，投入到我们这些学生身上，正是因为他这样的倾心付出，我们研究组才取得了这样好的成绩，培养出了在各行各业表现出色的兄弟姐妹们。

五、时尚达人

不要以为柳先生年纪大，跟不上潮流，柳先生会让人出乎意料的。他对于时尚甚至比很多年轻人知道的都多。他是个"发烧友"，家里的音响和功放还是他当年在美国做访问学者的时候用节省下来的生活费购买。电脑、服务器这些基本工具柳先生是不需要人教的，在苹果的 Facetime 功能没有发明出来的时候，柳先生已经用 Skype 打视频电话了。对单反相机他也是行家里手，只要出差，都会用相机记录下生活的点点滴滴，他和倪老师拍了不少非常经典的照片，还专门出了一个相册集。柳先生用手机不只是打打电话那么简单，只要屏幕的字足够大，发短信，听音乐都不在话下。2013 年年底柳先生做了白内障手术之后，视力有很大提高，看东西也清楚了不少。我惊奇地发现，柳先生也开始用苹果手机了。也许正是因为柳先生永远对事物保持着好奇心和求知欲，才让他永远走在科技发展的前面，对高科技的热爱也是柳先生从事科研工作的重要驱动力。

六、胜似亲人

柳先生把每一个学生都当作自己的孩子一样。不仅在科研上悉心指导，在生活上对我们更是关心的无微不至。每到冬天，不少兄弟姐妹容易感冒发烧，柳先生就会提出自掏腰包让我们打流感预防针。他会亲自为每一个毕业的弟子挑选一个礼物，2007 年年底我毕业的时候，柳先生送给我一条领带，我往往在比较重要的场合才会戴。我父亲 2006 年过年期间去世了，柳先生知道后不停安慰我，担心家里没人照顾，反复提出要帮我租个房子，把母亲接过来一起生活。我怕给柳先生添麻烦就谢绝了。到了 2008 年年初，家里地震非常严重，房子也开裂了，家人都搬到了外面，住进了防震棚，柳先生十分担心我家里的情况，又提出要我把母亲接到北京来，他帮我安排住下来。在柳先生的一再坚持下，我还是把母亲接到北京，住到了亲戚家里。柳先生让我们这些在北京求学的孩子们感受到了家的温暖，在柳先生带领下的研究组里就像一个大家庭一样，有时举行聚会和聚餐，大家围坐一起、畅所欲言。直到现在，我还会时不时地想起那时的情景，多希望还能够回到那个时候。

柳先生常说"铁打的营盘流水的兵"，虽然我们这些学生换了一批又一批，但是不变的还是柳先生在科研的道路上孜孜不倦地探索，在教书育人的岗位上勤勤恳恳地工作。我们这些兄弟姐妹们虽然奔赴大江南北，各行各业，但是都永远不会忘记柳先生，永远感激柳先生。跟柳先生在一起的那些美好的日子，我们将永远珍藏在心里。

（注：何翔，2007 年博士毕业，现任广西南宁国家高新区纪检监察室主任）

跟随授业恩师“闻道”十载的珍贵点滴

文/郃凯平

近日我非常高兴地获悉，柳先生的弟子们为了 2015 年庆祝先生的八十寿辰，正在编辑一部先生 30 年来发表的论文集，并将由科学出版社出版，其中将收录弟子们在先生的研究组里学习和工作的感受与体会，而我将有机会为这部文集“出一份力”，心情很激动，很激动！刚过而立之年的我，跟随恩师已经整整十年了，这段时间是我人生中非常重要的阶段。我不善文笔，愿将与先生相处的珍贵点滴真实感受记录，与众人分享难忘师恩……

一、初识

我的思绪被倒回了 2004 年的夏天。我有幸进入清华大学材料科学与工程系跟随柳先生攻读博士研究生。当年结识先生的场景至今犹新。先生给我的第一印象是一位满头银发、衣着朴实、风度翩翩、和蔼可亲、精力十分充沛的“老人”。这是我人生第一次聆听先生的“传道、授业、解惑”。先生花了一下午的时间，耐心地给我讲解了本研究组的科研方向、最新科研进展和取得的精彩科研成就。随后，先生引领我参观了课题组的实验室和计算机房。给我印象很深的是，先生走路的节奏很快，当时我几乎是一路小跑才跟上先生的步伐，这很让我吃惊，即使是在我这个精力旺盛的年纪也是不及的。虽然限于我当时的知识背景和接受能力，我并不能完全领会先生传授的知识(我当时的直观感受就是科研工作太神奇了！)，但的的确确为我启蒙和引导对科学研究的执迷，并最终影响我选择科研作为自己的终生职业，如今回想，先生是何等的用心，令人钦佩！

二、“闻道”

记得刚刚加入先生的科研组时，虽然自己利用暑假的时间补充了一些相关背景知识，但仍然感觉有些“手忙脚乱”，跟不上组里的“科研节奏”。入学后的一天下午，先生约我到办公室长谈。回想起来，这次谈话是先生在为我的科研规划打下牢固的根基！这次谈话给我印象很深。先生笑容可掬，并没有马上谈及科研工作，而是首先详细询问了我的生活状况，是否适应北京的生活，是否有需要帮助的地方，我心里顿时感觉暖暖的。先生的为人和学识都是十分令人钦佩的。先生要求弟子们要做爱国、爱科学的科研工作者。先生常说“科学面前人人平等”“研发展是硬道理”“要讨论科研工作，欢迎随时可以来我办公室，不用预约”，鼓励发挥学生的科研主动性，最大限度地挖掘学生们的潜能。“一个学生科研工作做得好，往往会同时进行三件事：其一，开展目前手上的研究工作；其二，整理已有研究成果撰写论文；其三，调研文献规划下一步的研究工作。”这其实也是现在我向我的学生讲授的话，每当重复这些话时我就会想起当年聆听先生教诲的场景……，我想这就是一种传承吧！先生几乎每天都很早就来到办公室，兢兢业业指导每一位学生的研究工作。先生的科研思路非常清晰和敏捷，每每有新的研究结果去和先生讨论，先生都会神采奕奕地引导我发掘出深层次的科学知识。每次和先生的讨论，都会使我感到非常兴奋，有时也会因跟不上先生活跃的思路而感到压力，在获得知识的同时更获得了研究科学问题的方法，使我受益终生。先生对于科学方向的把握和研究结果的归纳与升华，不断鼓舞着我在不平坦的科研探索道路上“勇敢”前行。如今参加工作后，自己要在科研道路上独立闯荡，每每遇到棘手的难题时，我都在想，可不可以和先生请教一下？但由于我身处异地，不在先生身边工作，拿起电话后我又不情愿地放下，生怕打扰了先生的工作和休息。这些年和先生的感情一直很深，先生更愿意将我这样年纪的弟子看作是自己的孩子一样去关爱，先生在我的心中也更像是一位慈父。

2006年的夏天，先生原本计划要带李家好师兄和我一起前往意大利参加“国际离子束材料改性大会”。清楚地记得临行前，先生到医院做身体常规检查，但结果出来后需要住院做一个外科手术。听到这一消息后，全组的学生们心情都很沉重。当时先生已年过七旬，我们非常非常为先生的身体担忧。在先生住院期间，我和几位师兄弟主动负担起照顾先生的职责，共同度过了那段难忘的时刻。与先生朝夕相处的这段日子里，先生身体行动不便需要卧床休息，弟子们都竭尽所能照顾好先生的起居和饮食，尽一份做弟子的孝心。虽然病患在身，先生的精神状态却一直很好，从先生的眼中我看到的是一颗无比坚强的心。在医护人员、家人和弟子们的悉心照顾之下，先生的身体很快恢复了健康，并重返工作岗位，精力与过去比也没有多大差别。先生在我的心中是一位献身于科研事业的强者，更是一位生活中的强者，先生用自己的言行育化着一代又一代的弟子，一切的一切都是无法用言语表达的。

三、毕业和工作

2009年的夏天我顺利毕业于清华大学材料系，获得博士学位，此时我跟随先生学习已满五年，但依然觉得时间太短。所谓读万卷书，还须行万里路。毕业后，我选择了到美国继续从事博士后研究工作。先生也鼓励我到外面锻炼一下，开阔眼界，增长见识。先生叮嘱我，科学虽无国界，“但一定要做爱国的科学家”，此话意味深长。出国前，我心中实在有些忐忑，一方面始终放心不下先生的身体，嘱托师弟师妹们照顾好先生；另一方面，自己即将进入一个新的工作环境，离开先生的指导，不知自己能否面对新的挑战。在美国的工作生活非常紧张，难有机会回国探望先生，也只是每逢佳节和先生通电话问安，汇报自己的工作进展。“是凯平啊？！”在大洋彼岸的那端电话中传来先生那熟悉的声音，这口吻更像是年迈的父亲在关切询问远在他乡的游子，“是的先生，是我，我是凯平”，每次还未等我开口向先生问好，先生总是先向我嘘寒问暖，嘱咐我多多注意身体，掌握科研节奏，在外不容易，照顾好自己……眼泪润湿了我的眼角，“好的，先生，您也多多保重身体……”即便是身在海外，我的一举一动，也都在牵动着先生的心。2014年，我在美国工作已将近第五个年头，科研成绩虽算不上十分出色，但也有可圈可点的亮点。此时作为八零后的我面临着在美国继续发展还是回国创业的抉择。由于在自己研究领域做出了一项有新意的成果，我应邀获得了美国普林斯顿大学中的一个较为理想的科研岗位。站在人生的又一个十字路口，何去何从？经过几次与先生通话，听取先生的意见，“回国发展是对的，建立自己的事业，为国出力”。身在国外，科研工作做得再出色也只是在为他人服务，对，下定决心回国发展，做一位爱国的科研工作者！

过去的十年，是我从青年到成年的十年，是打基础的十年，是人生最关键的十年，是我追随先生“闻道”成长的十年。我人生的轨迹离不开先生的引导，我事业上的每一步进展都离不开先生的“雕琢”。如今先生已桃李天下，在我的心中，先生不仅是一位杰出的科学家、教育家，更是一位慈父。先生的言行永远是我学习的榜样！

祝愿柳先生健康长寿，工作顺利，万事如意！

弟子 凯平 敬上

（注：郃凯平，2009年博士毕业，现任中国科学院金属研究所研究员）

回忆和柳先生共同的日子
——写在恩师八十寿辰之际

文/梁苏会

我还记得第一次与柳先生交流是在2004年的夏天，即将升入本科大四的我，惴惴地敲开贴有“柳百新教授”门牌的办公室，向柳先生表达推研时能加入课题组的愿望。当时的柳先生头发已经花白，却有着年轻人一般的笑容和热情，他极富感染力地向我介绍课题组的研究工作：镀膜、非晶、结构差异规则……作为一名本科生，我需要集中百分之二百的注意力才能记住这些学术名词，才能跟得上柳先生流利的英文。最后，我获赠了一本柳先生发表在 *Advances in Physics* 上的论文 *Solid-state crystal-to-amorphous transition in metal-metal multilayers and its thermodynamic and atomistic modelling*，也正是这本论文，引领我进入了博士的研究领域。就是这样一本B5大小、没有封面装帧的小册子，后来不知被我翻阅了多少次，如今页面已经泛黄，边角已经卷曲。

随后，柳先生带我到课题组博士生的办公室，也就是后来像家一样的逸夫技术科学楼2302。路上，柳先生对我说：“小梁，目前课题组你有十个师兄，我们课题组的上一个女生，是2001年博士毕业的。”正是如此悬殊的比例，让我获得了不少优待，比如指派给我靠窗且面积最大的办公桌，比如外出就餐时和柳先生、倪老师同乘一车，比如师兄们的帮助和照顾……后来，课题组里的女生渐渐多了起来，每当我向师妹们介绍我当初进组时清一色全是师兄时，她们都艳羡不已。

2004年9月，我顺利完成了大四上学期的推研考核，成为柳先生课题组的预备成员；2005年上半年，我正式加入柳先生课题组，完成我的本科生毕业设计工作。初入课题组的我对自己要求很严格，每天早上八点第一个离开寝室，可是每次气喘吁吁骑车赶到逸夫楼，柳先生都已经在办公室了，或是在阅读文献，或是在和师兄讨论问题，或是在电脑前聚精会神修改论文。我向师兄感叹柳先生来得好早，师兄让我去课题组FTP上看看，那里赫然显示着一篇论文的修改时间是当天早上的六点多，也就是说，来到办公室之前，柳先生已经在家开始工作了。言传身教，润物无声，勤勉，是柳先生教会我的第一课。

读博士五年的时间，无论是刻苦程度还是学术成果，我都和“学霸”级的同门师兄弟相距甚远，但是柳先生对我的悉心教导和耐心付出仍会让我一生铭记。还记得清晨伴着轻轻的交响乐和淡淡的咖啡香，与柳先生一起坐在电脑前字斟句酌修改论文摘要，重视提炼成果和科学的表达，体现了柳先生“授人以渔”的育人方式。还记得柳先生偶在万圣书园读到《原子弹秘史》后与我们兴致盎然的分享，我慕名也买了这本书，至今还有时从家中的书架上拿出来翻一翻，感受学术大家投身科研事业的情怀。还记得毕业前夕柳先生亲自选购了一个很职业的手提包送给我，步入职场前恩师的殷殷关怀让我倍感温暖。

最难忘的是2007年，作为一名三年级直博生，正是陆续发表研究成果、面临中期考核的关键阶段，而作为一名北京奥运会的骨干志愿者，各项培训筹备工作也在紧锣密鼓地开展，有时活动一多，我的科研工作未免受到影响。现在回想起来，对每一个学生都万分负责任的柳先生一定早就察觉到了我状态不佳，只是在找寻合适的机会点醒我，而我却乐此不疲浑然不觉。直到有一天，研工部的老师紧急给我打电话约我到办公室，问我是不是社会工作太多耽误了科研学习，我才意识到事情的严重性。柳先生在一次小组会上严肃提出了社会工作影响博士生正常学习科研的问题。自知理亏，没有借口，我只有一个选择，就是用更多的时间和更专注的精力，迎头赶上。回忆起 2007 年、2008 年两年，真是迄今为止最忙碌、最充实，也最拼命的两年，柳先生没有严厉的批评、死板的说教，却用一种更为“迂回”的方式，让我自感压力、心悦诚服。也正是因为柳先生的及时“点醒”，在北京奥运会开幕前，我的论文发表达到了博士毕业要求，科研工作也有了新的进展，而这些为我安心志愿服务北京奥运会、残奥会提供了强大的心理支持。北京奥运会后，激情和荣誉归于平淡，我平静从容地走过最后一段博士生生涯，写论文、求职、毕业……柳先生传授给我的，不只是学术思想，不只是科研方法，更是百折不弯的毅力，更是战胜困难的的拼劲儿！还记得奖学金答辩会上，一位老师问我：“这么多的社会工作是不是耽误科研？”我可以自信地回答：“我有信心，挤时间抽时间也不耽误科研进度！”记得一次学术会议上，柳先生高兴地向陈旭老师（清华党委书记）展示自己新发表的综述论文，指着合作作者名单说：“看，梁苏会是我的学生！”记得一次韩景阳老师（清华党委副书记）来课题组看望柳先生，柳先生不忘带她来到我们博士生的办公室说：“你不知道吧，梁苏会是我的博士生！”几个片段中，柳先生这种小小的赞赏的流露，成为我回忆中最最温暖的部分。

转眼毕业五年，虽然同在清华园中，和柳先生的交流却只有寥寥几次，柳先生却能如数家珍般说起每一位师兄师弟和师妹的近况。我们像一只只羽翼渐丰的雏燕，最终飞离了温暖的巢，而柳先生一直在我们身后默默守望。值此柳先生八十寿辰之际，学生能做的，也只是寥寥数笔，回忆和柳先生共同的日子，表达心中的感恩与祝福。水木清华，春风化雨，恭贺恩师柳百新先生八十寿辰，身体康健，桃李满园。

（注：梁苏会，2010 年博士毕业，现为清华大学中国工程科技发展战略研究院博士后）

柳先生与我的三层关系

文/王同乐

今天是教师节，回望二十余年的求学路，很多教师都给予了我无法替代的帮助，他们的帮助让我得以顺利完成自己的学业，帮我得以完成自身的成长，我需要深深地感谢。在我的恩师之中，最需要感谢的是我的博士生导师柳百新院士，大家都称他为柳先生。柳先生悉心指导了我六年，不仅帮助我完成了学业，更帮助我成功地从学校走向社会，他的学识、态度和精神将会影响我一生。在清华读本科时偶尔到系馆做实验时看到教师介绍，尤以柳先生最引我注目，而这一点很多见过他的人都有共识，他的面貌和身形让人一看就是一个很绅士睿智的大科学家。然而，他的院士身份也让我感觉离自己有些遥远。

2005 年秋季推研的时候，在我的辅导员陈雷的建议下，我决定鼓起勇气报名柳先生的博士生。而后在何翔师兄的推荐下，一次课间休息时间我在系馆见到了柳先生。那时柳先生已满头白发年届七十，但精神矍铄，思维敏捷。我很紧张地简单介绍了一下自己的情况，他听了之后只提了一个问题，那就是将来在这里需要发不少的 SCI 论文，需要努力，然后就很和蔼地说快去上课吧，不要耽误了下一节课，让我倍感亲切。之后的六年，就是柳先生给我不断指导和帮助的六年。六年的经历，可以用柳先生经常和我们讲的三层关系概括，那就是“我们是师生关系，我们是合作伙伴，我们是忘年交”。

推研之后，在没有课的时候我就到实验室去了解博士阶段将要学习和进行的工作。柳先生不仅安排师兄师姐带领和指导我慢慢加深对实验室和博士工作的理解，还更亲自指导。他精心挑选了自己发表的代表性论文和综述让我认真阅读，而后更是多次就论文的内容对我讲解。刚开始看英文论文，很多地方没有看懂，他就拿着论文从头到尾跟我讲解每个部分，不仅讲解这些论文的主题思想和结构，更讲解论文中用到的常见语法和特殊句型、词语；不仅讲解论文本身，更讲解论文的成型过程，从设计实验、进行实验、分析结果到撰写论文都详细地讲解；不仅讲解一篇论文，更讲解不同论文的区别和联系，那时候他常常能讲整整一个上午。

在柳先生的悉心指导下我很快对实验室的研究方向有了基本的了解。他跟我说，做实验是科研的基础，做计算模拟是新研究的发展方向，无论将来做什么研究，起步时应该都学习一些，于是就安排我跟两个师兄分别学习不同的内容，而这也为我完成博士论文打下了很好的基础。同时，他给我制订了一个小的科研计划，说应该先准备明年春天的本科毕业论文，如果有好的结果还可以早点撰写成论文，这样就可以抓住机会走在别人的前面。正是柳先生的这个指导，让我认识到早做准备早为人先是十分重要的。这一指导也是十分明显的，在随后的本科毕业论文时，别人开题时我可以做类似中期的汇报，别人做中期汇报时我可以汇报出基本的结果，获得了评委老师的一致好评。而这也一直影响到我的博士阶段，较早地发表了第一篇论文，较早地完成开题、中期考核和达到毕业要求，显著地减轻了博士毕业论文的压力。在工作时，早做准备早点起步仍然给了我很大的启示。

在我设计好实验计划后，每一步都要向柳先生汇报，而他也每周都会关注进度。实验上的问题，实验结果的分析，计算模拟的结果，他都要详细了解。有一次当我把整理好的实验结果给他看时，他直接就看出其中的问题，问我要了电镜照片对着灯光观察，然后发现了照片中不太明显的环说，你再仔细看看这个样品和与之对比的样品。在我再次去做实验观察后，果然发现了一套明显的衍射环，而这之前并未被我发觉，得到了十分有新意的结果。这让我领悟到柳先生对科研的敏锐、认真和严谨。他的思维十分敏捷，常常能从普通的结果中发现不常之处，也很快从不同的结果中总结出规律，令我十分钦佩，也十分值得我学习。

柳先生不仅对实验过程严谨，对结果也是严格要求的。撰写第一篇论文时，他刚从一次大病中恢复，就指导帮助我整理实验结果，指导我进行论文结构的安排和撰写。那是我的第一篇论文，他从头到尾帮我检查，提出建议，然后我再修改，如此多次反复。到修改得差不多的时候，还同我一起在电脑旁逐段逐句地进行检查。他的英语非常好，因此还帮我修改语法错误和采用更精彩的词汇。在他的悉心指导下很快我的第一篇论文就发表了，而那时其他同学还都在上博士生课程。在各种开题中期答辩等演讲之前，他还对每一张幻灯片都进行严格的指导。这不仅仅是对我，对实验室的其他同学也是如此指导。先生虽然七十多岁，但仍孜孜不倦，不仅每天都到办公室工作，到实验室同我们交流，晚上还经常给我们修改论文。通常他上午找我们面谈交流，下午和晚上修改论文资料。有的时候很晚仍给我们打电话讨论论文，很早就给我们发邮件让我们分析实验、修改论文。记得有一位小师妹在写第一篇论文时，想法很多而没有很好的论文结构和思路，那时候每天白天她修改论文，柳先生晚上看完后给出修改建议，如果差距比较大就次日上午当面讨论，这样每天修改持续了一月有余，论文得以顺利发表。柳先生对科研的认真态度，对学生的耐心指导是最美好的师生关系。当然，柳先生与我的师生关系不仅仅体现在他对科研和对学生负责上，更体现在他传递给我的精神。那时候，他时常跟我们谈话，讲他对国家的热爱，讲他年轻时候的留学经历，讲他在科研道路上遇到的困难和奋斗的历程，讲他对各种事情的看法，不仅教我们为学，更教我们为人。

柳先生称我们为合作伙伴，其实是一种十分谦虚的方式，因为无论在为人、科研还是生活方面，他都给予我很多的指导，很多地方是我们需要学习的。然而，在实际中，很多时候柳先生不以师长的身份而高居在上。在科研上，他十分尊重学生的意见，同学生们讨论实验方案和结果，鼓励我们提出自己的想法而与我们探讨；在撰写论文时他同我们共同构思结构、修改内容，而仅以合作作者的方式出现在论文列表中；他安排学生管理实验设备，而给我们发放勤工俭学补助。在博士生期间，主要的工作是做好科研工作，但仍有课程学习、考试和生活上的各种琐事，虽然柳先生总说实验和论文要抓紧，但在遇到要上课和准备考试或者生活上有紧急事情时，他则鼓励我们先解决好紧急的事情，然后再将全身心投入到实验论文工作上。柳先生十分尊重学生们的意愿，有的时候因为不方便需要某个学生帮助他办一点事情，他总是十分客气地说“柳先生想请你帮我……”，而没有任何长辈的口气。这种相处方式使得我们都愿意和他交流，而减小我们之间的年龄和师生的隔阂，逐渐形成更亲密的关系。这不仅仅是“忘年交”的关系，我更觉得有更进一步的亲人关系。

柳先生与我爷爷的年纪相近，加之平常对我们都十分亲切，让我感觉更像是亲人关系。柳先生十分关心学生们的生活，经常将节日收到的水果礼物等带到实验室让大家分享。还每学期组织几次聚餐，同我们一起吃饭聊天，就像家长带着一群孩子吃饭一样。为了适应新环境，搞好科研工作，柳先生不鼓励低年级博士生参加社会工作。然而，在我博士一年级的时候，柳先生知道我的家庭比较困难，就即刻安排我参与实验室设备管理的勤工俭学，给我发放补助，同时在科研工作上更积极地监督我，帮助我同时适应两方面的压力。暑假期间，当他来实验室工作时，看到我没有回家，就执意给我发放补助，要求我回家探望父母。在系里，无论是本科还是博士开题中期答辩，柳先生都会亲自参加，给予我们鼓励。柳先生不摆面子，我们邀请他照毕业照他都欣然答应，留下美好的回忆。毕业的时候，他会给每个毕业生送上一份礼物，留作纪念。他送给我一条自己亲自挑选的意大利领带说，“柳先生亲自选了这条领带，希望你将来戴上它的时候能够想起我。”毕业之后，每逢重要场合，我都会选择这条领带，牢记先生曾给予的教诲和帮助，我想这条领带正是我们之间美好关系的见证。

先生给我的教导、帮助和树立的榜样，将让我受益终身，十分感谢。一晃毕业 3 年，到与柳先生初次见面已整整 9 年，柳先生已年近八旬。最近见面，柳先生依然精神矍铄、思维敏捷。祝愿先生与师母身体健康长寿，生活幸福美满！

（注：王同乐，2011 年博士毕业，现于德润特数字影像科技有限公司工作）

日记里的柳先生

文/崔苑苑

我有一本厚厚的日记，记录了在清华园的日子，里面有个出现最多的词——“柳先生”。

2009.7.28

今天我的第一篇文章被接收了，当我看到编辑通知 E-mail 时，高兴得差点欢呼起来。“小崔，祝贺你！”听着柳先生的祝贺，我的心里既欢喜又惭愧。柳先生总是和我们说作为一名博士生，手里要有三件事情同时在做，一项实验在进行，一篇文章在撰写，一篇文章在审稿。而我由于自己的懈怠，第一篇文章从数据整理到最终发表，花了大半年的时间。其实我知道这只是一篇很小的文章，柳先生却为我前前后后修改了不下三次，从文章的框架结构到摘要里的每一个字，都凝聚着柳先生的心血。谢谢柳先生，总是鼓励我的每一次进步。

2011.6.15

我的文章被 APL 接收了！

其实在一个星期前，这篇文章是被 APL 拒稿的。当我逐条阅读审稿意见后，我发现审稿人犯了一个错误，审稿人没有看清文中一幅图的坐标数值，将一个小区域的计算模拟结果，认为是整个合金系统的全区域的结果，按照审稿人这样的理解，我的工作自然是不对的。

我叹了口气，把审稿结果告诉了柳先生，柳先生听完后笑着说：“看来审稿人也粗心啦。没关系，我们给编辑写封信吧，解释一下，看看是不是请对方重新审稿啊。”我却打了退堂鼓：“柳先生，算了吧，我投到其他期刊试试”，我低下头继续说：“APL 的编辑和审稿人都是应用物理方面的专家，我只一个研究生，要我指出他们的失误，是不是……”。听完我的话，柳先生收起脸上的笑容，语重心长地告诉我：“小崔，你要记住一句话，科学面前人人平等，不能因为对方是大专家，你是学生，就自我贬低，这是不对的。”柳先生停顿了一会儿，似乎在等我想明白，然后他接着说：“小崔，我们诚恳地向对方说明原因，尊重研究事实，也是对自己研究工作负责呀。”在那一瞬间，我真的明白了，我抬起头说：“柳先生，我明白了！”柳先生的脸上露出了欣慰的笑容。

在后来的几天里，我鼓起勇气给 APL 的编辑写了一封邮件。在邮件发出之前，柳先生多次为我修改邮件的措辞，让邮件读起来既诚恳又坚定。6 月 14 号早上，我把这封邮件发给了 APL 的编辑，没想到一天之后就收到回复！编辑和审稿人在邮件中对自己的失误表达了歉意，对我们工作给出了很高的评价，直接接收发表了。看着编辑的邮件，我满心喜悦，耳边又响起柳先生的教诲“科学面前，人人平等”。

2011.7.23

“本台最新消息，今天 20 点 30 分左右，北京南站开往福州站的 D301 次动车组列车运行至永嘉站至温州南站间双屿路段，与前行的 D3115 次动车组列车发生追尾事故，后车四节车厢从高架桥上坠下。事故目前造成数十人死亡，百余人受伤……”我惊呆了，因为我刚把一张火车票放进行李包，车票上写着“2011 年 7 月 24 日，D301 次，北京—福州”，这是我暑假回家的车票。

电话响了，传来柳先生急切的声音："小崔，你在哪里？还在学校吗？"

我："柳先生，我在学校的。"

柳先生的声音立刻放松下来："那就好，那就好。我刚看到新闻，说动车追尾了。我心里咯噔一下，我知道你也是坐这趟车的，赶紧给你打电话。"

我："柳先生，我的车票是明天的，万幸，没有买今天的。"

柳先生："小崔，这样吧，你坐飞机回家吧，这样安全些，机票的事让秘书小牛帮你办理。"

在柳先生的关心下，我退掉火车票改乘飞机回到了久违的家。刚进家门，手机铃就响了，亲切而熟悉的声音传来："小崔，你平安到家了吧？""是，平安到家！"我激动地回答，接着眼眶就湿润了……这就是我的导师，可亲可敬的柳先生，时刻心系学生的柳先生。

2012.3.25

一年一度的学院课题组羽毛球赛拉开序幕了，各个课题组展开了激烈的角逐。我们课题组自然不能示弱，所以早早就组建了参赛的队伍。在赛场上，师弟出色的扣杀球为我们争夺了不少比分，师妹严密的防守技术多次让局势化险为夷，最终我们课题组齐心协力地捧回了二等奖。当柳先生看到我们红艳艳的大奖状时，满脸的欣喜，他动容地回忆起自己初入清华园时，在忙碌的课程学习外，还是清华大学羽毛球队的队员，在赛场上挥汗如雨的日子，他收获了强健的体魄和豁达的胸怀，最后柳先生笑眯眯地说"哎呀，可惜现在倪老师不让我打球了，要不然就和你们一起挥拍子去"，引得我们哈哈大笑。

2013.5.22

今天是我博士论文答辩的日子，一切都进行得很顺利，当答辩进入尾声时，我满含深情地说到"衷心感谢我的导师柳百新院士多年的悉心培养，在这些年中，柳先生教我做科研，教我为人处世的道理，更教我热爱科学，热爱我们的国家。在我遇到困难举步不前的时候，柳先生给予了我最大的帮助，我……"说到这里，我哽咽了，然后深深地鞠躬，台下一片掌声。在泪光中，我看到柳先生面带微笑，轻轻颔首。

五年的时光如白驹过隙，细细想来却历历在目，每次外出开会，柳先生总会打电话提醒我们带好证件，安全出行；每次看到柳先生在清晨五六点发来的邮件，总会惭愧于自己的懒散和懈怠；每次和柳先生讨论问题，总会带回画满思路的稿纸和崭新的启发。柳先生书桌上的台历年年翻页，那支木质笔筒依然如故，我想，它们都记得这些，都记得我是多么幸运，能成为柳先生的学生。桃李不言，唯愿先生永远幸福安康！

（注：崔苑苑，2013 年博士毕业，现任上海大学材料科学与工程学院讲师）

问道五载，受用一生

文/李楠

聆听先生的指导教诲已经五年有余。先生虽已年过古稀，但其对科研的热情执着让我由衷景仰；先生虽已学至泰斗，但其对工作的严谨认真让我由衷敬佩；先生虽已位极院士，但其对学生的无微不至让我由衷感谢。求学先生这五年，感触最多的是幸运，幸运能够在先生门下徜徉于科海；收获最多的是恩情，感谢先生无私的爱；影响最大的是为人，熏陶于先生为人处事的无愧于心。

初见先生是 2009 年 8 月 5 日。我怀着对先生的敬仰和紧张的心情，来到先生办公室门前。时值假期，楼中无人，但先生的房门已开，灯光已明。办公室幽雅整齐，先生戴着眼镜，端坐在电脑面前，认真查看并回复每封邮件。当时就感叹先生在如此年岁还能熟练地使用最新电脑系统，竟然还能迅速地在键盘上输入。后来才得知，先生早在 2000 年左右就开始接触计算机，而自己在三年后才开始懵懂地了解和使用。

先生招呼我在办公桌前坐下，开始和我交谈。他和蔼地看着我，言语间充满关爱和慈祥，让我紧张的心情得到缓解。交谈中，先生向我介绍了课题组的研究方向和大致的研究流程，流利的英语表达让我大吃一惊，同时也羞愧于自己英语水平尚需提高。后来才得知，先生是第一批出国留学的研究者之一，在出国前英语水平就出类拔萃，更在国外大学科研工作中得到了十足的修炼。也正是在先生严格的要求下，我们才开始尝试写作英文学术论文，才开始不断提高自己的英文表达，才能与世界的研究者们顺利交流。

当得知我喜爱从事实验研究时，先生很高兴，立刻站起来，带着我从三楼的办公室去到一楼的实验室。先生健步如飞，我跟随在先生之后，吃惊于先生如此矫健的步伐。更让我吃惊的是，介绍完一楼的实验室后，先生又带着我从步行梯到四楼的实验室，其上楼的速度让我这青壮小伙也要紧赶慢赶才跟得上。后来才知道，先生酷爱羽毛球，求学于清华园时曾是学校羽毛球队的一员，健硕的体质从那时就锻炼起来了。时至今日，先生也超额完成了清华学子“为祖国健康工作五十年”的誓言。

进入先生课题组后，在先生和大师兄的指导下，通过广泛调研文献和结合课题组研究方向，我选定了实验方案并顺利完成了第一个实验成果的发表。此后，先生要求我转到计算模拟方向，从事计算研究。而此时，我对系统的实验研究产生了浓厚的兴趣。先生知晓我的想法后，没有强迫我从事计算研究，而是很认可我按照自己的想法去从事实验研究，并在实验室原材料、实验经费等方面毫无保留地支持我。后来先生告诉我，他需要各位研究生按照课题组研究项目所需进行研究，但也支持学生按照自己的想法从事有兴趣的方向。正是先生开放包容的胸怀，才使我们的各种奇思妙想有了发芽的土壤。

先生对我们要求严格，多次要求我们以学期为时间单位，开展一项科学研究，发表一篇学术论文。先生指导我们要在学期初开始设计实验方案，在学期中完成预定实验，在学期末整理好数据、撰写和投递论文，并着手规划下一学期的实验方案。开展这种项目模式的科研，大家都能在论文发表的喜悦中有信心继续冲刺新的科研难题，并潜移默化地锻炼了项目管理和时间把控的能力。后来才了解，先生在自己求学时就亲身验证了这种工作模式的有效性，并在此后的几十年教育生涯中如此培养了数十名优秀的师兄师姐。

先生常与我们分享他的故事，印象最深的是他会在截止时间前尽早完成任务。先生常说，在申请各项基金时，他总是第一个提交申请材料的。因为每年基金申请的时间基本固定，按照各个节点提前完成准备工作，既可以有充足的时间更好地完成材料，也可避免因遗忘导致错过申请的遗憾。先生常会在作报告前很长一段时间就准备好报告材料，也从未给我们布置非常紧急的任务。不把任务拖延到最后一刻，先生如此，拖延症也未有再侵蚀我们的身体。

对科研，我偶尔会懈怠，偶尔会因为其他琐碎小事而耽搁。先生常教育我科研要投入，并告诉我他在国外访问的两年成果丰硕盖因为大年三十还坚持做实验。先生虽已不在一线从事科研，但也坚持每天到办公室浏览学术动态，为我们的科研答疑解惑，也坚持带着浑浊的视线为我们修改论文。先生始终保持着充沛的精神，在科海中带领我们前行，“一万个小时”和“三百篇文献”是我们扬帆远航前必需的体能储备。

科海多风暴，在我遇到科研难题而丧失信心之际，先生会及时安慰鼓励。攻读博士第三年，虽投入满腔热情，付出艰辛努力，也尚未有一篇文章发表，更闻师姐第三年收获最为丰厚，垂头丧气之情难掩。先生鼓励我，相信自己的成果有价值，终究能够获得认可，尚缺的仅是时间。最终所有的成果如先生所言，有了最好的归宿。对自己的坚定，对未来的乐观，先生给了我科研之外的财富。

先生能够乐意并能很快地学习和接纳新事物，具有国际化的视野，具有健硕的身体，关心并支持学生的创造性，教会我们合理规划、不拖延、不懈怠，乐观积极，坚定自我。跟随先生五载，其在科研中倾注的时间和精力，在培养学生中倾注的心血和热情，在生活中的积极乐观和坚定，我都有幸能亲身感悟。伴随先生的孜孜教诲，带着先生给我的精神食粮，不论大海荒漠，都能扬帆策马。

（注：李楠，现为柳先生研究组 2010 级在校研究生，即将于 2015 年毕业）

先生之风，山高水长
——记我心目中的恩师柳百新院士

文/罗诗瑶

范仲淹在《严先生祠堂记》中有一句话：云山苍苍，江水泱泱，先生之风，山高水长。先生是一个传承数千年的敬语。对恩师柳百新院士，可以有老师、导师、教授等诸多称谓，但终不及“先生”二字来得亲切和大气。道一声“先生”，有高山仰止、景行行止，有言传身教、立世修身，有大师风范、人格风骨——这就是我心目中的恩师柳百新院士。

一、初次见面平易近人的大师

第一次见柳先生是 2009 年 9 月。当时，我还是一名大四的学生，由于大学前三年取得的课业成绩，让我有幸获得免试推荐攻读研究生的机会。我事先了解了柳先生的研究方向，主要是离子束与固体的作用及材料改性、离子束与固体的作用及材料改性、计算材料科学，对柳先生所做的很多开创性的工作以及发表的学术论文深表敬佩，再加上自己对这一领域的兴趣使然，让我对拜投到柳先生门下继续深造产生了迫切的期望。抱着试一试的想法，我给柳先生写了一封邮件，介绍了自己的学习成绩和个人情况，但心中始终有些忐忑，觉得柳先生身为院士，事务繁忙，不一定会看我的邮件。没想到，第二天我就收到了柳先生的回复，邀请我到他的办公室面谈。

怀着激动而又紧张的心情，我走进柳先生的院士办公室。没有想象的望而生畏、不苟言笑，取而代之的是平易近人、和蔼可亲。见面后先生问我是哪里人，我说来自河北石家庄，柳先生马上叫来秘书，“小牛，你的老乡要来我们组读博士了。”几句寒暄，让我紧张的情绪放松下来，认真聆听这位材料学大师介绍自己的研究工作和教学理念。办公室一面墙上挂着柳先生的获奖证书，叶企孙物理奖、国家自然科学奖二等奖、国家教委科技进步奖一等奖、北京市科技成果奖一等奖……一张张证书，默默向我诉说着柳先生在材料科学领域所取得的一系列重要建树，以及对国家和社会作出的重要贡献。看到柳先生带领学生们取得的科研成果、发表的学术论文，我深受震撼，也非常敬佩柳先生的教学理念，为学生提供很好的研究平台，任其施展才能。

短暂的会面，更加坚定了我申请到柳先生门下读博的决心。在我的青春岁月中，能够聆听先生教诲，真正潜下心来，学些东西、做些研究、有所创新，很有意义，倍感荣幸！

二、谆谆教导学术路上的引领者

经过申请、面试等环节，我如愿成为先生的一名弟子，跟随柳先生学习、做科学研究。

柳先生对学生有独特的培养模式：博士入学第一年要上必修课程，边上课边开始科研探索，知行合一，而不是上完课才投入科研；一学期一个 research unit，学期末要对本学期研究工作有总结和阶段性成果；博士生资格考试时，不仅要求学位课程优秀，而且在科研上，对于自己的课题，必须有充分的文献调研，了解国内外研究进展，更要通过一定的研究探索取得初步的成果。

博士入学的第一学期，当我和同学们忙着适应新环境，学习必修课程的同时，柳先生已经开始指导我们进行科研探索。先生详细讲解了课题组取得的研究成果和最新研究方向，当时课题组已在若干二元合金系统中利用离子束混合技术，制备出了金属玻璃及亚稳合金，柳先生又率先提出要尝试在三元合金系统中开展相关研究，并鼓励我选取一个三元系统进行研究。

通过查阅、研读文献，向柳先生请教，我选取了一个三元合金系统 Cu-Hf-Nb。最初我的关注点放在了合金的完全非晶化，即得到金属玻璃，但由于该三元系统中 Cu-Nb，Hf-Nb 的生成热为正，从热力学上讲非晶化的“阻力”较大，在我选取的七个成分点中，只有两个成分制备出了均一的非晶相，其余都是部分非晶化，得到非晶相和晶相的混合物。面对这样的实验结果，我第一感觉就是失败了。

记得那是一个周日的下午，我正在办公室为“不理想”的实验结果而忧虑，柳先生走进办公室，和我一起研讨。柳先生说：“我们做一个实验，不能提前设定实验结果，而且实验结果并没有好坏之分，关键是要对实验结果进行合理分析和科学解释，搞清楚其中蕴含的科学问题和科学含义，最终构建科学“故事”。比如，你现在的实验结果，并不一定得到非晶才是好结果，我们在多个成分下制备出了非晶+晶相的复合物，据我所知，均一的非晶相弹塑性较差，而非晶基复合物，引起了很多研究者的关注，你可以查查相关文献。”

与柳先生的求教和讨论，使我茅塞顿开，为什么不换一个角度思考问题。我查阅了大量文献，非晶基晶相复合物确实在弹性性能方面表现优异。经过与先生多次讨论，我对实验结果有了更加深入的认识，并在先生的指导下开始写第一篇学术文章，先生帮我明晰思路、修改文章、润色语言，一步步教我怎么构思和撰写一篇学术论文。这篇文章寒假期间投出，春节后开学不久就被美国物理学会的 *Journal of Applied Physics* 接收发表，这对我是一个很大的鼓励。多数同年级的同学们还在为新课题一头雾水时，我已经在柳先生的指导下发表了第一篇论文。和柳先生一起工作，总能感受到先生的思维活跃、讲求高效、雷厉风行、意识超前、目光长远，这种 professor Liu’s working style 一直影响着我，激励着我，提升着我。

在先生的指导下，我的求学、研究之路不断向前，通过离子束混合技术制备非晶及亚稳相的实验，使我更好地理解了金属玻璃形成的非平衡过程。由于实验上每次选取的成分点比较有限，为了更好地研究非晶形成的相关问题，我的研究重点转移到计算模拟上，即通过构建原子间相互作用势，利用原子尺度的模拟研究三元合金系统中金属玻璃形成及结构等问题。我先后选取了包含两种不同结构金属的三元系统 Cu-Zr-Hf，Ni-Nb-Ag，构建其原子间相互作用势，研究非晶形成范围、非晶化驱动力、非晶结构等问题，发表了三篇学术论文。

总结之前研究组的工作，我们已经构建了若干三元系统的原子间相互作用势，研究系统的非晶化等问题，但包含有三种不同结构金属的三元系统还未有研究。经与柳先生商量，我选取了 Ni-Nb-Zr 三元合金系统尝试研究，这三种金属代表了三种不同的结构，而且据文献记载前人没有做过这类系统的研究，这件工作与之前的相比是更靠前沿的，同时颇具挑战性。由于已有的势函数形式具有一定的局限性，例如，EAM 势，FS 势较好地适用于 fcc 和 bcc 金属单质及其合金系统，TB-SMA 势，能较好地描述 fcc 和 hcp 的金属单质及其合金系统的原子相互作用。

对于包含三种不同结构(fcc-bcc-hcp)的 Ni-Nb-Zr 系统，势函数的构建就是一个新的课题。刚开始，势函数的构建不是很顺利，很长时间没有进展，柳先生没有严厉地催促我、向我要结果，而是耐心地和我一起分析讨论，想办法改进、攻克难关，最终我们成功地采用本研究组提出的势函数形式，构建出该三元系统较好的原子互作用多体势，并应用多体势通过模拟得到了该系统的玻璃形成范围和非晶化驱动力。

我写了一篇学术论文初稿，柳先生看完觉得文章平平，没有充分挖掘出实验结果中的科学含义。随后，先生多次和我一起研讨，一起坐在电脑前逐字逐句修改文章，指导我应该怎样设计论文思路、讲述科学故事，并将研究组近年来的精髓思想与我现有实验结果相结合，极大地提升了文章高度。先生曾在美国做访问学者，多年出国访学、作报告，英语水平很高。他总能将我们文章中语言生涩、表达不到位的地方，经过润色、改写变得更为流畅、地道、精彩。这篇文章在高水平国际期刊 *ActaMaterialia* 上成功发表，我感到欣喜万分、倍受鼓舞。

非常感谢柳先生的悉心教导和培养，一步步地指导我怎样做科学研究，由简入深，循循善诱。有了实验结果之后，更重要的是提炼出科学含义，撰写好科学文章，讲述好科学故事，这也是一名博士生所必须具备的能力。

三、良师益友　莘莘学子的百科全书

柳先生学识深广、阅历丰富，犹如学生们的一部百科全书。柳先生经常在工作之余，给我们讲述他的早年趣事，声情并茂、娓娓道来，这是和柳先生一起工作的另一大乐趣。每当此时，我的思绪就跟随先生走到了世界各地。仿佛看到了先生在美国加州理工实验室勤奋工作的情景；仿佛体验到先生放弃春节休假，冲进实验室看到实验成功后的兴奋与激动；仿佛置身其中，和先生一起在各地大学、研究所传播自己的学术成果，深入浅出，激扬文字……在这些故事中，我深切感受到柳先生对学术的热爱与执着。因为热爱，所以执着，因为执着，所以勤勉，这种榜样的力量将会一直激励着我们勤奋工作、努力探索。

工作之外，柳先生也是个热爱生活、兴趣广泛的人。科研之余，先生经常和大家一起谈论体育赛事，美职篮、斯诺克、网球、羽毛球等等，他都能讲出竞赛规则、明星选手、近期赛事。通过与学生交流，增进师生感情，拉近与学生的距离，缓解大家的工作压力。作为良师益友，柳先生就像一部百科全书，让学生们从中不断汲取营养，一直激励大家前行。

现在已是金秋十月，正是收获季节。跟随柳先生一起工作学习四年，四年来，我收获的不仅是如何做科学研究和撰写学术论文，更重要的是柳先生对祖国的赤诚、对事业的执着、对生活的热爱，这样一种人生态度，将一直影响我、激励我，勇往前行！

最后，我想用“治学数茎白发，桃李一片青山”，这两个质朴的短句，来概括我心目中柳先生的情怀、事业和成就。

（注：罗诗瑶，现为柳先生研究组 2010 级在校研究生，即将于 2015 年毕业）

师恩如山

——记与恩师柳先生相处四载岁月

文/李洋

时间如白驹过隙，一晃已在柳先生组里学习了将近四年。回首与恩师柳先生相处的日子，不禁感慨道师恩厚重如山，无以为报。

还记得第一次见柳先生是在一个明亮的上午，在2325办公室，我见到了久闻大名的柳先生。在本科期间我有幸聆听过三位柳先生弟子（潘老师、赖老师和李老师）讲解的课程，不禁对柳先生培育出如此多优秀的老师感到由衷的敬佩。柳先生和蔼地向我介绍了课题组的相关情况。虽然柳先生头发已经花白了，但是精神矍铄、言语健谈，思维敏捷丝毫不逊年轻人，让我不禁感叹柳先生身体真好，充满了活力。交谈期间柳先生丝毫没有院士的架子，对我很亲切，让我受宠若惊。一番交谈下来不仅了解了课题组的研究方向，更是聆听了一次大师的讲座，经受了一番精神洗礼，受益匪浅。与柳先生的一番谈话让我坚定了在其课题组读博的信念，对未来的研究生生涯充满了信心。

进入课题组后，柳先生对我悉心培养。在实验上，安排我向博士五年级的王同乐大师兄学习操作电子束真空镀膜的设备，培养我的动手实验能力。从镀膜到离子注入，再到电镜观察的每一步，柳先生都十分关注。在其指导下，我的实验能力显著提高。实验结果出来之后，柳先生建议我总结归纳形成科学论文。在论文写作过程中，柳先生也不辞辛苦，逐句修改手稿，给我讲解怎样安排论文结构逻辑成文，如何进行论证，增强说服力。第一次论文历经反复修改，最终发表为SCI论文。第一篇SCI论文对于我来说不仅是一项成就，更凝聚了柳先生的心血。

完成一个系统的实验工作后，柳先生还希望我能将计算与实验相结合，进行相应的模拟。柳先生对我的期望，让我倍受鼓舞，全身心地投入到计算模拟中。在模拟过程中，柳先生要求所有的模拟结果必须与实验进行对比，应不断调整参数提高模拟的准确性，模拟与实际的偏差应评估其影响。柳先生严谨求实的工作态度给我留下了深刻印象，使我体会到对待科学问题应有的严谨和实事求是的态度。做计算期间，柳先生多次关心我的进展情况，经常与我讨论结果。从选系统到势的拟合，以及相应的分子动力学模拟，柳先生都全程指导，让我少走了很多弯路，快速的上手进行模拟计算。同时我也逐步了解到做学问应有的素质。柳先生引领我走上了学术之路。在与柳先生学术探讨期间，有些时候没有跟上柳先生的思路，没有细细体会柳先生的言语，与柳先生的看法意见有一些相左的地方。事后每每想起此事，不禁扼腕而叹，没有思虑恩师的深意，而对其有所误解，心理颇有懊悔。柳先生对我期望很高，可惜我资质驽钝，有时候没领悟其想法。在学术上虽略有收获，但是还没有达到柳先生的期望。在以后的学习中还应抓紧时间，继续努力。

除了在学术上的关怀，恩师对我在生活上也很关心。每回放假回来，柳先生就像一个和蔼慈祥的长辈，对我们嘘寒问暖。课题组氛围融洽，其乐融融，形成了一个和谐的大家庭。受柳先生器重，我有幸担任院士助理一职，承担一些实验室服务器的维护工作。服务器状态的好坏直接影响到计算模拟的效率。为了更有效地监督服务器运行状态，每天查看服务器机房温度以及节点运行情况。根据服务器的负载状况，调节空调运行状态，使机房温度在合理的范围内，保证服务器的正常运行。

在担任助理期间，我有幸于2013年年底，在恩师做白内障手术期间在医院相陪，聆听柳先生的教诲。柳先生在手术期间不忘实验室的同学们，还要求我们汇报工作，督促我们继续工作，争取早出成果。我们都深受感动，决心努力工作，不负柳先生的嘱托。在医院陪伴柳先生的日子里，常与柳先生聊天，听其忆往昔峥嵘岁月。柳先生于20世纪80年代初，在加州理工学院做访问学者。在两年的时间里，发了十几篇SCI论文，都是高质量的论文。柳先生在学术交流中，经常在国际大会上作特邀报告，获得了国际同行的高度评价。一股敬佩之情油然而生。柳先生中年时期受“文革”影响，有将近10年的时间与科研无缘，后来又重新回到了学校走上科研岗位。柳先生很珍惜这来之不易的科研机会，全身心地投入到学术研究中，硕果累累。柳先生常告诫我们年轻时身体好，要好好利用，认真科研。从柳先生身上感受到的一种时不我待的紧迫感一直激励着我努力科研，奋发向上。听着柳先生的逸闻趣事，我不禁感叹恩师阅历之广泛，经验之丰富。柳先生不仅在学术上，在为人处世等方面也有很多值得我学习的地方。柳先生在我心中的形象日益高大巍峨。恩师除了学术上成果斐然，他英语也特别好，口语非常流利。20世纪80年代初，柳先生尚未走出过国门，就帮助微电子所在引进大型离子束注入机时，担任技术和经费谈判的英文翻译。

柳先生虽然年事已高，但科研的热情丝毫不减，无论寒暑，无畏风雪，几乎每天都来实验室办公。柳先生以身作则，坚持科研的作风让我深受鼓舞。每当科研遇到瓶颈，心情烦躁时，想到柳先生数十年如一日的坚持科研，心理就一阵惭愧，重新调整状态，继续科研。

柳先生的大师风范不禁让人“高山仰止、景行行止”。作为弟子“虽不能至、然心向往之”。柳先生的高尚品格、勤奋作风、为学为人等方面都值得我一辈子去学习。柳先生就像我人生中的灯塔，驱散了黑暗，指引着光明的前途。一日为师，终生为师，我必努力科研，不负师恩。

值柳先生八十大寿之际，谨以此文恭贺柳先生福如东海、寿比南山、身体健康、万事顺心！

弟子李洋敬上

2014年 9月8日

（注：李洋，现为柳先生研究组2011级在校研究生）

春风化雨，德艺双馨
——记我的导师柳百新

文/王琦

能够来到清华园，能够遇到柳先生这样的导师，我是幸运的。

一、初结师生缘

有幸与柳先生结下师生缘，是源于研究生推免阶段。还记得那是大三结束的暑假，我怀着忐忑不安的心情，把简历、成绩单等资料用邮件发给了柳先生，希望能够投到柳先生门下。当时，我本以为会几天之后才能收到柳先生的回复，没想到，二十分钟左右，我居然就接到了柳先生的电话，让我感到非常受宠若惊。在与柳先生的交谈中，柳先生和蔼可亲的风度以及大气的学者风范更是让我非常钦佩，当时我在心里就默默做出决定，跟定柳先生了，一定要成为柳先生的学生。在之后的推免材料提交和面试等诸多环节，柳先生也都及时地予以我帮助，最终我也如愿以偿地成为了柳先生的学生。

二、科研上的领路人

等到真正进到柳先生的组里，我更是愈发深刻地领略到柳先生的深厚的学术造诣。作为一位国内外知名的院士，柳先生已经获得奖项和荣誉无数，但是柳先生仍从未停止过对学术的追求，仰之弥高，钻之弥坚，带领我们勇攀一个个科研高峰。“古之学者必有师，师者，所以传道授业解惑也。”记得我刚进组的时候，师兄师姐就告诉我，科研遇到瓶颈的时候，一定要找柳先生讨论，柳先生总会给我们指明一条前进的路。现在，我已经从一个刚进组的师妹，成长为一个四年级的师姐，在这个过程中，这些话已经被无数次地印证。柳先生有极其敏锐的学术洞察力，常常能够一针见血地指出问题的核心所在。很多时候，当我无所适从地、带着苦恼已久的问题走入柳先生的办公室，经过柳先生的一番分析和点拨，总会有种拨开云雾见月明的轻松感，然后信心满满地开展下一步的工作。柳先生也经常会产生很多新的想法，并及时地跟我们分享和讨论，其中很多想法被证明是非常切实可行的金玉良言。同时，柳先生严谨的治学态度也让我受益匪浅，比如撰写文章的时候，大到行文架构，小到遣词用句，柳先生都会反复斟酌。我想我永远也忘不了，几次我都搬一个凳子，坐在柳先生身边，看柳先生耐心细致地帮我改文章。这温暖的场景已经深深地烙印在了我的脑海中，时常激励我不断努力。柳先生不仅用他深厚的学术造诣，为我们树立了科研道路上的奋斗目标，更重要的是，柳先生还把他数十载的宝贵科研经验，毫无保留地传授给我们，让我们走得更快，走得更好。

三、从不拖延的 working style

讲到科研，就不能不提到柳先生的“working style”（工作模式）。柳先生的工作模式是把工作都做在前面，从不拖延。柳先生常常说，既然一件事情你迟早要做，为什么不早点完成，这样还能从容地开展后面的工作。所以，柳先生的基金申请书和要求上交的各种报告总是系里第一个提交的，柳先生的会议 ppt 总是提前几个月就准备好，柳先生帮我们改文章总能在一天之内给出回复……多少次，每当我早上八点左右慢悠悠地刷开邮箱，看到柳先生在五六点给我回复的邮件，我心里总会充满着感动；

每当我自己的文章都没顾得上好好修改，柳先生就已经帮我润色了三四遍的时候，我心里又会自责地感到汗颜。一个七旬的老者尚能如此孜孜不倦地致力于科研，我们这些青年学生如何能够心思倦怠，徘徊不前？！每每想到这里，我都会深深地被柳先生这些老一辈科研工作者的敬业和忘我的精神所感动，我想，这种科研精神和工作模式，值得我用一生去体会和学习。

四、学高为师

柳先生的学识之广博，总是让我仰止。柳先生不仅在非平衡材料的实验和计算方面是集大成者，而且对材料的其他领域，甚至是物理、化学、生物等其他学科也是如数家珍。在柳先生那儿，总是有听不完的故事，无论是各个学科的重大进展，还是科研过程中的奇闻轶事，柳先生都是信手拈来，让我们受教良多。柳先生也会经常分享他在清华求学以及在 Caltech 做访问研究等阶段的有趣的经历，比如钻研俄文书籍、刻苦学习四大力学；周末在 Caltech 做一整天的实验，并最终提出非晶态合金形成的结构差异规则等等。柳先生的故事，是那么地生动和立体，随便拿出一小段都让我有一种与君一席话胜读十年书的感觉。我想，只有像柳先生这种经历过这么多风风雨雨、大风大浪的长者，才会让每个经历和体会都值得我们去解读和学习。

五、身正为范

柳先生还是一个极有原则的学者。还记得博一的暑假，我跟柳先生一起去青岛参加离子束改性的国际会议，柳先生当时是受邀作第一个大会特邀报告，而我的报告排在同一个时段的最后一个，大约是上午十一点左右。与此同时，为了庆祝会议在青岛的成功召开，青岛市的领导还在当天中午安排了一个宴会，倾情邀请柳先生等知名学者参与。但是，柳先生在精彩地完成大会特邀报告之后，却选择了谢绝参加会，继续留在会场直至听完我的报告。那是我第一次参加国际会议，而且还要完成口头报告，我的心里不免有些担心，但当我看到柳先生一直留在会场，我真的非常非常感动，也在心里暗暗地鼓了一把劲，一定要把报告讲好。最终，我也圆满地完成了口头报告。后来在午餐期间，柳先生对我说，我们是来做国际学术交流的，这是我们此行的主要目的，任何其他事情都是次要的。是的，这就是柳先生作为一个知名学者的原则。这次经历使我真的深深地为柳先生的人格魅力所折服。同时，在系里和学校里的诸多事务上，柳先生也时刻秉持公正严明、不偏不倚的原则，在同仁间也赢得了极好的口碑。

六、师生情谊，细水长流

柳先生对学生的关怀，亦是如春风般温暖。柳先生非常注重培养学生的综合素质，从提出问题到摸索方法到解决问题，他都会给予我们足够大的发挥空间，不约束，不拘囿。在讨论问题的时候，柳先生总会耐心启发，循循善诱，给学生足够的鼓励和信任。同时，柳先生还给我们创造了非常良好的科研环境，不给我们分配科研之外的琐事杂事，让我们可以全身心地投入科研。在生活上，柳先生更是如同一位慈爱的长辈，细致入微地关怀着我们。还记得我在去广东进行博士生实践之前，柳先生就给我介绍了很多广东的情况，消除了我对这个陌生城市的生疏感。我初到广东，略微有些水土不服，柳先生也打电话来询问我的情况，嘱咐我要尽快适应南方的饮食和气候，同时也要时刻注意安全。每次跟柳先生到外地参加会议，从确定出行日期、出行方式，到预定车票、房间，柳先生总是会事无巨细地把一切安排妥当，让我们没有任何后顾之忧。柳先生对学生的关心和爱护，就像是家人的温暖一样，时常让我们感动不已。我们课题组也像是一个温暖的大家庭，在这里，我们挥洒拼搏的汗水，感受家庭的温暖，收获成功的喜悦和感动。

七、兴趣广泛，知识渊博

同时，柳先生的兴趣非常广泛，文学、音乐和体育等方面都造诣颇深。还记得，有一次柳先生讲到《简爱》，还用流利的英文声情并茂地还原了其中几处的经典场景，让我非常惊叹。有时，走进柳先生的办公室，会有悠扬的古典音乐传来，柳先生还会把音乐创作的来源或表达的深刻内涵向我们介绍，让我们一同徜徉在音乐优美的意境中。柳先生羽毛球打得非常好，同时对其他运动，像篮球、网球、斯诺克等等，也都非常熟悉，常常还会给我们讲解计分的规则，扩展我们的知识面。每次跟柳先生交谈，都会有新的收获。

八、结语

经师易遇，人师难求。转眼间，研究生生活不知不觉已经走过了三个年头。当我回望来时的路，我真的感到非常庆幸，庆幸能够进入清华园，庆幸能够做柳先生的学生。言传身教，师恩似海，柳先生不仅用他深厚的学术造诣，引领着我们走向学术的圣殿，还用他非凡的人格魅力和言行风范，让我们领悟做人的真谛。此刻，我想再多的赞美之词也显苍白，海纳百川，有容乃大，桃李不言，下自成蹊。有导师如斯，何其幸乎！

（注：王琦，现为柳先生研究组 2011 级在校研究生）

我读柳先生

文/牛晓彦

2007年年底，我回河北石家庄老家过年。刚进家门，还没顾得上跟爹妈撒娇，手机响了，是谁呢？“喂，请问是牛晓彦吗？”我回答：“是啊!”“我是清华大学的柳百新，我收到你的简历，感觉蛮好的，如果愿意的话，下学期开学过来上班吧!”然后还告诉了我确切的时间及办公室。这是我第一次听到柳先生的声音。那声音听上去至少比他的真实年龄要年轻二十岁，好似三四十岁的年富力强的人，透着生命的蓬勃，透着爽快的个性，透着生活的热情——这就是柳先生留给我的第一印象，可谓“不见其人，先闻其声”。

2008年2月开学前夕，我走进了位于逸夫技术科学楼的这间办公室。岁月如梭，转眼已成7年多以前的事了。当时跨进清华大学校门的时候，心情是激动中稍有忐忑的。我激动，因为我对这片校园、这块土地的敬畏，我对那“自强不息，厚德载物”两句校训的热爱；我忐忑，因为我从没有见过院士是什么样的。要知道中国十几亿人才有一千多个如此成就斐然的学者啊！怀着这样复杂的心情，我上了逸夫技术科学楼东侧的台阶。“当当当”敲门，进去一看，他早坐在那里等我啦。

一头银发，是博学和岁月的见证。眼睛里透着随和，面容里露着和善。耳垂特大，中国人老讲“耳朵大有福”，当真是福大名大之人！他很爱笑，笑起来声音跟天真的孩童一样“哏哏”的。说话亲切，言语生动。个子不高，身体灵活，走起路来像年轻人一样矫健——我心里一块石头落了地。从小胆小，最怕遇见脾气古怪或一脸严肃之人，幸而这两样跟他都不沾边儿！人常说：“越是大人物，越是和蔼可亲；越是半瓶子的人，越不可一世。”真是有道理。

2008年刚来时，柳先生研究组里的博士生都直呼我“小牛”，现如今我成了名副其实的“小牛姐”了。我虽不是柳先生的学生，但我比一般的直博生待在组里的时间都要更长些。耳濡目染，多年来从工作态度和习惯到处事风格等等，我都受益良多。

追忆六年时光，从陌生到熟悉，从熟悉到深深的理解。在清华园，我喜欢默默地用眼睛和耳朵去读人读事，去总结自己的感受和观点。

我读柳先生，读出了六个“多”：时间多、荣誉多、童心多、朋友多、操心多、“故事”多。有“多”当然有“少”，他身上还有三个“少”：少“知足”、少批评、少端架子。

第一，时间多。有人会说我“说胡话”，上点年纪的人好多都感叹时间少，不够用呢！我要讲柳先生时间多，因为他从小养成的习惯，早上五点多钟就起床。每天起来就开始工作，收发邮件，看新闻，给学生改论文。别人还在睡梦中时，他早已工作了将近两个小时啦！七点半左右当许多人匆匆忙忙睡眼惺忪地往办公室赶的时候，他却悠闲地迎着朝阳身轻气爽地走进系里。年轻老师都还没到，有的学生喜欢睡懒觉来得更晚，柳先生对这一现象百思不得其解。除了早起外，柳先生喜欢万事赶在前面，决不拖拖拉拉。系办公室的工作人员，常感慨：如果人人都像柳先生一样按时或提前上交有关的文件材料，办什么事都这么利索，不用催，我们的工作就好做多啦！还有一点，他时间观念超强，与人约好了见面，宁愿早到了先在那里等一小会儿，也决不迟到让别人等。天天早起、遇事往前赶、从来不迟到，这三点加起来算一下，他的有效时间和生命不是要比其他人更加富裕了吗？

第二，荣誉多。请看办公室的墙上挂着的荣誉证书：1993年的国家自然科学奖二等奖，1999年的国家自然科学奖三等奖，北京市科技进步奖一等奖，第三届叶企孙物理奖，等等。柜子里还有一排排……这些奖，很多人即使一生得一个，也是相当了不起了，但他却集众多奖项于一身。荣誉是对他成就的认可，奖状是对他勤奋和智慧的肯定。面对荣誉，他是自豪的。但他经常讲："重要的是我做了什么！"他更看重的是科研，是那一篇篇证明研究成果的沉甸甸的论文和学生们的学有所成。

第三，童心多。"真正成功的人，是那些历经岁月沧桑却依然保持一颗童心的人。"柳先生是这话的印证人。他童心未泯，笑起来宛若可爱的孩童。他喜欢孩子，经常讲起他唯一的外孙成长的故事，也常常提到邻居家可爱的的三胞胎男孩大宝、二宝和小宝。他以一颗真纯的心对人对事，而从无损害他人之心。他以童真的执着追求自己应该得到的。在这个竞争激烈的国家一等学府里，他以他独特的风格让朋友，也让对手折服。

第四，朋友多。儿时的伙伴，无论学习的成绩，也不论其家世如何，都与他关系融洽。不光是同行里国内外知名学者、教授，还有很多各行各业的人。给他看过病的医生，帮他订飞机票的先生，他朋友的朋友，都是他的朋友。这些朋友当中，还有许多让我想都想不到的人。校复印室的小孩子们，提起他来都知道。有一次，我去中国科学院帮他递材料，一个年轻人，听说我是帮柳先生做事，就笑脸相迎很是热情。主管的人不在，他主动帮我去找。还当着满屋的人讲："清华的柳先生，我知道，他喜欢看电影……"我忍不住笑一笑。原来在象牙塔外的四角天空，这么多的人知道清华有个柳先生，他们喜欢他，喜欢替他办事。他在他们心目中是有情趣的，是善解人意的，是可敬的长者，也是很亲近的朋友。

第五，操心多。柳先生是个爱操心的人，他善于照顾身边每个人的心思。与女士在一起，他绝对的绅士风度。朋友住院，他都要问候；朋友远道归来，他及时送上祝贺；亲人来京，他送上深深关怀；晚辈考大学，他也要忙前忙后给以鼓励。他总不忘在别人临行前送上亲切的叮咛，他总不忘在别人求助时送上及时的关怀，他总不忘在别人需要的时候送上及时的问候。就连我哥家生了女儿，我去医院探望，他都会及时打来电话贺喜。他就是这样一个人，为事业操持一生，对朋友关爱一生。

第六，"故事"多。七十多年人生见闻，本身就是一部丰富的历史。柳先生是个"故事篓子"。他喜欢讲故事，他的故事内容太广泛了。儿时成长的校园、以前的老电影、经典的音乐、体坛的风云、流行的电视剧、曾经的老照片、海外学术会议的见闻等，他都可以讲得趣味横生。他的记忆力特别好，他能准确地讲出几十年前看过的老电影的人物姓名及详细故事情节；他形象表达能力也特别好，能把专业的材料科学方面的知识讲得通俗易懂，让门外汉听着一点都不觉得生硬。工作累了，叫上我这个"小朋友"来讲讲故事，权当休息。讲的人津津乐道，听的人兴趣盎然，也真算一番其乐融融的有趣景象。

以上说了他"多"的一面，当然，他也不是什么都多，他身上也有很多"少"的一面。我总结为三"少"：少"知足"、少批评、少摆谱。

一少"知足"。生命不止，奋斗不息。年过七十，天天早起。家事、校事、朋友事、国家事，事事有追求。科研上总想再上一层楼，学术上要争当先进。他就是不服老，他就是天天精神十足，谈笑风生。他喜欢看到丰收的硕果，他喜欢把论文变成铅字，他喜欢学生们各有成就，他喜欢把研究成果以开放的胸怀讲给同行听，他喜欢这种成就感。所以不懈追求，永不知足。只要能干，他就愿意干下去，无怨无悔。

二少批评。我跟随他多年，知道他从不爱批评人。即使个别学生做的不对了，他也很委婉地指出，以致可能有些学生都觉得他不够威严。有一次，他跟我讲："我不愿直接批评学生，我这个年纪，又是院士，一旦直接说了，就显得比较重了，让学生有负担，影响他们的情绪和工作。"我深知他这个特点，所以偶尔做错了事，或没把事做到最好，就很自责，暗暗发誓下次一定做好。

三少摆谱。柳先生极反感某些人自以为是的样子，一旦成了"龙"就高人一等，不把普通人看在眼里。他不端架子，曾经对学生们说："大家既是我的学生，也是我们一块儿搞科研的合作者，更是忘年交的朋友关系。"在日常生活中，无论是对维修中心的师傅，还是看门的大叔，还是问路的陌生人，他也都平等相待，以诚示人。当然，柳先生也不是绝对的不摆谱儿，对当今社会有些公司或单位喜欢拿院士做招牌的行为，他会说一声："柳先生是院士啊！怎么能随便出动呢？"瞧，他端架子的时候，也让人从心底折服。

今天就写到这儿吧！如果真的要写他的话，想写的太多了。几十万字的小说也说不完他的故事。暂总结六"多"三"少"，告一段落，如有妄下断言之处，希望他能海涵。

值柳先生八十华诞之际，谨以此文衷心祝愿他健康长寿，万事如意！

（注：牛晓彦，2008年2月至今任柳先生研究组秘书工作）